The pioneer missionaries of the Church in the Northwest were the truest of apostles, men fashioned upon the divine Model Himself, full worthy to have walked through Palestine and Greece with the Peters and the Pauls, men whom we can never sufficiently know and love.

Archbishop Ireland

The Catholic Church
IN THE
DIOCESE OF ST. PAUL

from earliest origin to centennial achievement

A FACTUAL NARRATIVE BY

James Michael Reardon, P.A.

OF THE ARCHDIOCESE OF ST. PAUL

1952

PUBLISHED BY THE NORTH CENTRAL PUBLISHING COMPANY

ST. PAUL, MINNESOTA

GRATEFULLY DEDICATED

TO THE MEMORY OF

Most Reverend John Ireland, D. D.

FIRST ARCHBISHOP OF ST. PAUL

WHO ORDAINED ME

UNDER WHOM I SERVED

FOR MORE THAN TWENTY YEARS

FOREWORD

The author of the present work has brought to his task a rich experience of sixty years arising from his associations with the people in this area in his capacity as ecclesiastical student, teacher on the faculty of St. Paul Seminary, Superior of the St. Paul Diocesan Missionary Band, Editor-in-Chief of the St. Paul Catholic Bulletin and pastor, first in St. Paul where he built St. Mary's Church and School, and later in Minneapolis where he brought to completion the Basilica of St. Mary with its sacristy and pastoral residence.

To be such an important contributor to making the history of the Diocese of St. Paul for more than half the century of its existence indicates his qualifications for setting forth in an adequate manner the record of the achievements in which he played a prominent role.

He has chosen for the fundamental guiding principle in his work the admonition of Pope Leo XIII in his famous letter, SAEPENUMERO CONSIDERANTES, written August 18, 1883, "the first law of history is never to dare say anything false; then never dare not to say the truth; in writing let there never be a suspicion either of favor or animosity".

In view of the studied efforts of the priests, bishops and people of the Diocese either to conceal or destroy all evidence of their participation in the events of the past century with the result that data for a historian is very meagre a full measure of credit must be given to the author for his discovery of the illuminating facts herein presented. His three years of toil in widespread research have produced a treasure for which we and future generations owe him a debt of gratitude.

✠John Gregory Murray,
ARCHBISHOP OF ST. PAUL

March 25, 1952

ix

PREFACE

This history was compiled in the scant leisure of a busy parochial life that left little time for serious study and less for scholarly research. It was undertaken at the urgent request of the Most Reverend Archbishop of St. Paul as a contribution to the celebration of the one hundredth anniversary of the erection of the Diocese on July 19, 1850.

It makes no claim to being a definitive history of the Catholic Church in Minnesota. It is nothing more than an attempt to tell, in chronological sequence, the story of its origin and development and thus make available to the future historian facts and figures, events and dates, names and records of personages hidden in musty tomes and scattered documents, in books and periodicals that may be lost in the course of time as many have been lost in the past.

It is not offered as the work of a trained historian nor skilled biographer for the writer lays no claim to such talent.

Many of the pioneer missionaries, before they passed away, regretted that they had not kept diaries of their activities; but they were too busy doing the work of God to make a note of it. They were doers of the word, not writers thereof. Their successors, busy about many things, made little, if any, effort to learn the story of their inheritance or gather and treasure historical data that would now be invaluable. As a result, diocesan, parochial and institutional archives are meager in content or practically non-existent.

In the compilation of this volume the writer followed the example of the late Dr. Guilday who "emphasized the importance of the biographical approach to the study of American Church history", by making the five bishops of the Diocese of St. Paul the central figures in the narrative. Their achievements constitute its glory. They determined its traditions; they moulded its course; they personalized its accomplishments. They were the leaders whom clergy and laity deemed it an honor to follow, whose programs and projects they labored to execute. They made the Diocese what it is and what it stands for before the country and the world. It is their lengthening shadows, the projection of their personalities. In its history they live again and have an assured niche in the temple of those who have wrought great things for the Church in America. The clergy and the laity revered them as guides, monitors and exemplars, and they, in turn, relied with a confidence not misplaced upon these auxiliaries to carry out their plans.

Since this history was compiled for the ordinary reader, uninterested in archival material and primary source, its pages are free of footnotes; but a comparatively restricted number of references is given at the end of the text for the benefit of those who may desire to know or check the principal sources from which this factual narrative is drawn.

It was impracticable for the writer to go beyond the limits of the diocese in search of historical data to supplement or amplify what local archives had to offer. A few friends were kind enough to allow the use of source material in their possession and for that he thanks them.

He, likewise, acknowledges his indebtedness to the Most Reverend John Gregory Murray, S.T.D., Archbishop of St. Paul, to the Right Reverend James H. Moynihan, Pastor of the Church of the Incarnation, Minneapolis, and to the Reverend William Busch of the St. Paul Seminary faculty for a critical and scholarly reading of the manuscript and many valuable suggestions incorporated in the text. His thanks are also tendered to his sister, Miss Agnes M. Reardon, who typed the manuscript, and to the North Central Publishing Company for its efficiency, accuracy and technical aid in the press work.

Feast of the Annunciation, 1952.

JAMES MICHAEL REARDON

CONTENTS

I

THE FIRST WHITE MEN IN MINNESOTA 3

II

FROM QUEBEC TO ST. PAUL 13

III

PIONEER CHAPELS OF THE NORTHWEST 27

IV

FATHER GALTIER: PROTO-PASTOR OF MINNESOTA 39

V

FATHER RAVOUX: LONE SENTINEL OF ROME 51

VI

ST. PAUL AND ITS FIRST BISHOP 61

VII

THE WIDOWED DIOCESE AND ITS ADMINISTRATOR . . . 123

VIII

LIFE AND TIMES OF BISHOP GRACE 137

IX

THE FIRST ARCHBISHOP OF ST. PAUL 213

X

THE DOWLING DECADE 437

XI

TWENTY YEARS OF PROGRESS 507

XII

PARISH CHRONICLES 581

XIII

DIOCESAN INSTITUTIONS 653

XIV

APPENDIX 679

XV

REFERENCES 691

XVI

INDEX 708

ILLUSTRATIONS

THE KENSINGTON RUNE STONE 5

SANCTUARY OF THE BASILICA, QUEBEC 12

SANCTUARY, ST. PAUL CATHEDRAL 12

CHAPEL OF FORT BEAUHARNOIS, 1727 26

LOG CHAPEL OF ST. PAUL, 1841 26

CHAPEL OF THE ASSUMPTION, PEMBINA, 1848 26

REVEREND LUCIEN GALTIER 38

RIGHT REVEREND AUGUSTINE RAVOUX 50

RIGHT REVEREND JOSEPH CRETIN 60

CHAPEL OF ST. PAUL, WITH ADDITION, 1847 122

THIRD CATHEDRAL OF ST. PAUL, 1858 126

MOST REVEREND THOMAS LANGDON GRACE 136

MOST REVEREND JOHN IRELAND 212

MOST REVEREND AUSTIN DOWLING 436

MOST REVEREND JOHN GREGORY MURRAY 506

THE CATHOLIC CHURCH
IN THE
DIOCESE OF ST. PAUL

THE FIRST WHITE MEN IN MINNESOTA

F OR MORE THAN four thousand years of recorded history the Western World was unknown to civilized men. For centuries prior to its discovery the only voice that broke the silence of its vast solitudes was that of the savage whose remote ancestors probably came from the interior of Asia in a migration across Behring Strait and the Aleutian Islands to what is now Alaska and thence spread over the continent.

From these oriental forbears were descended the two thousand scattered groupings of Indians with distinctive tribal names found in North America when it was discovered by Columbus. At that time what is now the State of Minnesota was the home and hunting-ground of several tribes of these redmen who roamed its prairies and primeval forests or paddled their canoes on its myriad lakes or along its mighty rivers centuries, it may be, before St. Brendan and his companions reached the Atlantic seaboard or Ericson's dragon-prowed ships touched the shore of Vinland. As a sequence to this Viking visit the first white men found their way into the very heart of Minnesota and inscribed the record of their journey on the Kensington Rune Stone.

Nearly six centuries ago a group of Swedes and Norwegians made a journey west from Vinland and camped beside a lake on what is now Minnesota soil. The written record of that amazing voyage, unique in the annals of travel, tells the story of the heroic and tragic wanderings of this group of Catholic explorers from the distant fiords of Scandinavia who, in their hour of peril, invoked the aid of the Mother of God in the first prayer of which we have any extant account in the Western World.

This record[1] came to light on November 8, 1898, when a Swedish farmer, Olof Ohman, living about three miles northeast of Kensington in Douglas County, unearthed a stone with peculiar markings on it as he was clearing a wooded knoll for cultivation, a knoll which rises to a height of about fifty feet above a sedgy marsh which surrounds what, probably, was an island a century or more ago. That inscribed stone, known as the Kensington Rune Stone, but more fittingly described as the Minnesota Rune Stone, is believed to be the oldest native historical document on the continent, if not in the Western Hemisphere, and gives our state a place in the sun peculiarly its own. The inscription on it is written in what is known as runic characters not uncommon in Scandinavian countries in the Middle Ages.

If it be genuine, and the consensus of competent scholarly opinion points in that direction, it proves beyond reasonable doubt that Christ was in Minnesota more than a century before Columbus, that representatives of the Catholic Church, one of whom may have been a priest, were in the state in Pre-Columbian days, and that the first prayer of record on the continent was borne heavenward from the shore of one of its ten thousand lakes.

The Rune Stone and Its Inscription

Before detailing the circumstances under which the stone was discovered and the efforts made to decipher its message we append .a translation[2] of the inscription:

Eight Goths (Swedes) and twenty-two Norwegians upon a journey of discovery from Vinland westward. We had a camp by two skerries (rocks in the water) one day's journey from this stone. We were out fishing one day. When we returned home we found ten men red with blood and dead. A V M (Ave Maria or Ave Virgo Maria) save us from evil.
We have ten men by the sea to look after our vessel, fourteen days' journey from this island. Year 1362.

The Rune Stone is rectangular in shape, approximately 30 by 16 by 6 inches in size, and weighs over two hundred pounds. It is roughly beveled at one end and, when found, was lying on its inscribed face covered with six inches of soil, and held as in a vise by the roots of a poplar tree, about ten inches in diameter, flattened against its top and two sides. An examination of the tree led experts to believe that it was not less than fifty years old, and, therefore, it must have taken root at a time when no white man lived within a hundred miles of the locality where the stone was found, and when there was no railroad within four hundred miles of the place.[3] In other words, the stone was cradled in the soil at least a generation before the tide of immigration bore the modern Scandinavian into that part of the state.

The stone, evidently rifted from a graywacke boulder common in the locality, is as durable as granite. The inscription consists of nine lines on the smooth surface and three on one edge evidently chiseled to receive them. The lines are evenly spaced, the letters uniform and about an inch in height; the words, sixty-two in number, are separated from one another by double dots, making it one of the longest runic

The Kensington Rune Stone

inscriptions in existence — 206 runes, 3 Latin capitals and 12 numerals. The letters, carved with a sharp instrument, are clear-cut and distinct in outline; the edges and angles are acute and show no apparent alteration from weathering. It is a simple obituary record of ten men, telling who they and their companions were, whence they came, the provision made for their return, and the circumstances surrounding their tragic death. It omits all unimportant details such as the name of the leader of the group, of the king who authorized the expedition, and makes no mention of the fact that Indians had killed the men, though that is implied in the statement that they were "red with blood and dead", evidently scalped. The survivors took refuge on an island in Pelican Lake where they carved their tragic story on enduring granite "amid the ominous silence of a savage wilderness."

A True Historical Record

For a time after its discovery the Rune Stone was exhibited in Kensington, then sent to Minneapolis for examination by Professor O. J. Breda of the department of Scandinavian literature of the University of Minnesota, who, although unable to decipher the numerals and certain words, felt no hesitation in declaring it "a transparent fake" and "not genuine".[4] This apparently scientific opinion silenced all who were interested in the stone and nothing further was heard about it for a decade of years. It was returned to the owner in March, 1899, and for eight years served as a doorstep for his granary, fortunately with the inscribed face downward. In 1907 Hjalmar R. Holand of Ephraim, Wisconsin, a graduate of the University of Wisconsin, well versed in Scandinavian history and literature, obtained possession of it and after years of study and comparison with Scandinavian documents of the fourteenth century, during which he took it to twenty-three universities in Europe for study by experts, declared the inscription genuine and thus brought the Rune Stone and its message into the forum for public discussion. It would take too long to summarize the facts and reasoning that led him to that conclusion, but he presented a formidable array of evidence for its genuineness.[5] Suffice to say that the verdict was concurred in by the committee appointed by the Minnesota Historical Society to study the question from every angle and who, after two years of patient investigation and consultation and "after carefully considering all the opposing arguments", declared the inscription to be a "true historical record".[6] The committee consisted of Reverend E. C. Mitchell, (Chairman) antiquarian; N. H. Winchell, geologist and state archaeologist; Reverend F. J. Schaefer, ecclesiastical historian; O. D. Wheeler, attorney; Warren Upham, geologist and secretary of the society. Two of these the writer knew personally and can vouch for their scholarship and unimpeachable integrity. The others were prominent in the community and competent in their professions. All were recognized scholars, capable of judging the value and force of linguistic arguments and weighing judicially the evidence adduced. In their investigation they had the help of American and European experts in runology and Scandinavian literature. One of the members of the committee, Dr. Upham, the eminent glacial geologist, wrote in 1910: "The conclusion is inevitable that the inscription must have been carved many hundred years ago". Professor Winchell, in a statement issued for publication in the Journal of American History, says, "I am convinced from the geological conditions and the physical changes which the region has experienced, probably during the last 500 years, that the stone contains a genuine record of a Scandinavian exploration into Minnesota and must be accepted as such for the date named".[7]

However, not all Scandinavian scholars are in agreement regarding the authenticity of the text. Those who assert that the inscription is not genuine base their contention for the most part on the linguistic difficulties it exhibits.[8] But, admitting the fact that there are such difficulties, it would seem that they are not so insurmountable as to cast serious doubts on the genuineness of the Rune Stone and the reliability of its message. The Smithsonian Institution, Washington, D. C., which had the custody of the stone in 1948, issued no opinion[9] as to its genuineness because no member of its staff was thoroughly versed in runic inscriptions, medieval Scandinavian literature and history; nor would it place an official guarantee of genuineness on the stone in the present state of the evidence.

However, a press release from the Smithsonian on March 12, 1948, says that the authenticity of the Rune Stone "now is widely accepted by archaeologists . . . even if it cannot be indisputably authenticated, the confirmatory evidence that the stone constitutes a genuine record is so strong that this relic is regarded by the Smithsonian archaeologists as one of the most significant historical objects ever found in the New World . . . one bit of evidence after another that has come to light indicates that the relic is genuine", but they reserve judgment on its authenticity. As late as September 23, 1951, the Institution took "no position with regard to its authenticity".[10]

A Recent Critical Study

But this does not militate against the fact that all the internal evidence appears to be in favor of its authenticity; and so far nothing has been adduced to contradict its contents. On the contrary, a comparatively recent detailed study of the language of the inscription made by S. N. Hagan and published in Speculum, a Journal of Mediaeval

Studies, for July, 1950, leads to the conclusion that "belief in its genuineness is now growing".

Mr. Hagan who was born about sixty miles south of Kensington offers a scholarly analysis of the inscription from the linguistic standpoint. He gives a translation of it which differs from the one already given only by the substitution of "sheds" for "skerries" and "tortured" for "dead".[11] He maintains that the sheds were birch bark cabins abandoned by the Dakota Indians when they moved to another locality. Probably some of them returned to the old camping ground and finding "strange-looking trespassers" in possession "tortured" them by scalping, as was their custom.

He asserts that "the Kensington alphabet is a synthesis of old un-simplified runes, later dotted runes, and a number of Latin letters, some of them more or less modified in order to make them fit, after a fashion, into runic surroundings". This gives the alphabet the appearance of "having been improvised from memory", and goes to show that the inscriber who used these signs "could not have been a professional runic scribe before he left his homeland", as Holand has suggested. He agrees with Holand that it is "a genuine record of a Scandinavian expedition into the very heart of North America in 1362",[12] and believes that "a future generation of scholars . . .will find the inscription as genuine" as other accepted runes; and will regard it "as an important Scandinavian and American historical document and as a deeply moving human document".

Hence there would seem to be little, if any, reason to doubt the genuineness of the incription which declares that Catholic explorers were in Minnesota centuries before colonists came to furrow its prairies, three hundred years after Leif Ericson landed on our eastern shore, and one hundred and thirty years before the Admiral of the Santa Maria reported the discovery of land beyond the western horizon of the then known world.

In their hour of danger these Catholic adventurers sought help from heaven by appealing to the Blessed Virgin Mary to save them from evil in an invocation characteristic of Norsemen prior to the Reformation, and evidenced by the carving of her initials on the epitaph of their murdered comrades. In these far-off days Sweden and Norway were as Catholic as all other christian nations and cultivated filial devotion to the Mother of God. Every word of this prayer "bears witness to the fact that it was uttered and recorded by a man who lived in the fourteenth century, not in the nineteenth". It is found literally in an ancient folklore poem[13] harking back to the time of the Black Plague. The last two lines of the first stanza serve as a refrain throughout the ballad.

"Help us God and Virgin Mary,
Save us all from evil".

This Catholic prayer chipped out on a Minnesota stone was the proto-type of many others uttered by voyageur and missionary in subsequent years as they ventured into the unexplored region of the upper Missis-sippi. These Norsemen, whose subsequent history is unknown, left the earliest Catholic footprints on what is now Minnesota soil.

If the Rune Stone were a forgery of modern times would the Swedish or Norwegian perpetrator of the hoax have added a petition to the Blessed Virgin in whose intercession he did not believe? The "A V M, save us from evil" is distinctively Catholic — the first part of the Hail Mary and the last part of the Our Father. The salutation so impressed Archbishop Ireland that he regarded it as strong evidence of the fact that it was written in the Middle Ages, and "could not have been written by a modern forger".[14] On the supposition that the stone is not genuine it is an anachronism that would hardly be introduced by an imposter; nor would he take pains to describe the location of the camp with reference to the stone and the distant sea; nor mention the "skerries" in a near-by lake; nor designate as an "island" the place where the stone was found, for it had not been an island for more than a hundred years at least.

On this point the late Father Betten, S. J., of the department of history of Marquette University, Milwaukee, says:

The spot in which the stone rested when discovered is called an island in the inscription. It is not an island now . . . This one word (island) makes the assertion that the stone and its inscription is a fraud untenable.

He adds:

The Kensington Stone is the oldest document of American history written on the new continent itself, by white men. It is the only runic inscription found in America and it belongs to a period almost devoid of runic literature . . . whatever linguistic difficulties remain unsolved cannot interfere with the genuineness of the Kensington Stone and the reliability of its message.[15]

It is quite generally admitted that the well documented account of the pertinent facts as assembled by the Norwegian Society of Minneapolis, by the Minnesota Historical Society, and by Holand, cannot be shaken. This has been very troublesome to those who believe the inscription to be a forgery.

An Unsolved Mystery

If the stone were planted to fool succeeding generations the author of the inscription must have been an expert archaeologist, geologist, linguist and historian, who made his way into the Minnesota wilderness a century ago, and of whose existence there is no record. If we accept the Rune Stone as genuine we are confronted with the astounding fact that the Hail Mary was said in Minnesota nearly six hundred years ago by a lost colony of Vikings whose visit conferred baptism on the state by the shedding of Catholic blood.

Whence came these Norsemen to the heart of the continent? It is a historical fact that, in the eleventh century and afterwards, their for-bears made frequent visits to the eastern shore of North America which they named Vinland. In 1354 Magnus "King of Norway, Sweden and Skaane" authorized[16] Paul Knutson, a distinguished knight, to fit out an expedition to go to the rescue of Norsemen in Greenland threatened with extinction by the Eskimos. He sailed from Bergen the following year and, probably, made his headquarters in Vinland whence some of his followers may have journeyed as far inland as Minnesota by way of the St. Lawrence, Ottawa and Mattawa rivers, Lakes Huron and Superior; but it is more probable that they sailed northward through the Gulf of St. Lawrence, along the bleak coast of Labrador, turned westward into Hudson Bay, berthed their ship at the mouth of the Nelson river, leaving it in charge of ten men, while the other thirty paddled their canoes down the Nelson river, through Lake Winnipeg, and the Red River of the North to the rapids near Fergus Falls, Min-nesota, and thence traveled inland by way of streams, lakes and portages to the place where they came in contact with the Indians.

The inscription on the Rune Stone says nothing about the length of time spent on the journey of about one thousand miles from the sea where they left their ship to Kensington. "The fourteen-days' journey from this island" was, undoubtedly, their estimate of the time required for the return journey during which they would be rowing with the current of the Red River, not against it. It is possible that they under-estimated it.

It will remain an unsolved mystery whether or not these explorers returned to the waiting ship, perished in the attempt to navigate the intervening waters, or were delayed so long that the "ten men by the sea" thought it useless to await their coming any longer and sailed for home leaving them to their fate. Professor Winchell was the first to suggest that these twenty wanderers may have been taken captive by the Mandan Indians or received with genuine hospitality and incor-porated into the tribe by marriage.

After a critical and scholarly examination of the text, Professor Hagen declares,

> This inscription should be a perfect joy to the linguist because it is such a delightfully honest and unsophisticated record of its author's own speech. A forger would have tried to imitate a language other than

his own. It is clear that this author tried to imitate no language but his own. In branding this beautiful inscription as a forgery scholars have thrown away not only an important historical document but also a faithful record of mediaeval Scandinavian speech. It is fortunately of considerable length, and this has made it possible to test its authenticity at a very considerable number of points.[17]

With the foregoing preluding prayer to the Mother of God from the stricken hearts of these Catholic Norsemen in pre-historic Minnesota we enter the realm of ascertainable fact and verifiable history.

Sanctuary
The Basilica
Quebec, Canada

Sanctuary
St. Paul Cathedral
St. Paul, Minn.

Chapter II

FROM QUEBEC TO ST. PAUL

1492–1950

I T MAY NOT BE uninteresting to recall that, after the discovery of the Western World by Columbus in 1492, efforts were made by the Kings of Spain and of France to explore the new land for the purpose of colonizing and developing it and bringing the message of the gospel to the aboriginal inhabitants and early settlers.

The new land beyond the unchartered Atlantic, known as the West Indies, belonged to Spain by right of discovery by a Genoese navigator sailing under the Spanish flag, and its rulers exercised at least nominal sway over it. Their claim was ratified by the Bull of Pope Alexander VI, issued May 4, 1493,[1] by which he also conferred upon the Spanish sovereigns the title of "Catholic". What is now Minnesota was then iucluded in the domain of their Catholic Majesties, Ferdinand and Isabella.

With the beginning of French exploration in the sixteenth century Minnesota became part of the realm of their Most Christian Majesties, the Kings of France.

The King of Spain authorized Hernando de Soto to head an expedition of several hundred men, a dozen priests, secular and religious, sailing from the homeland on April 6, 1538, for the Indies to instruct "the natives of that province in our holy Catholic faith".[2] The only one of the priests known to posterity is Father John de Gallegos. The expedition finally landed in Tampa Bay, Florida, on May 25, 1539, to conquer the New World. In its journey to the West it was attacked by hostile Indians in the battle of Mauvila (Mobile) in October, 1540, and seventy Spaniards were killed and De Soto and many officers wounded. Their supplies and the requisites for celebrating Mass were destroyed by fire. Nevertheless the remnant pushed its way northward towards the interior, finally crossing the Mississippi near the present city of Memphis. They spent the winter of 1541-2 in what is now northwestern Arkansas, and in the spring retraced their steps to the great river where death

13

ended the leader's career on June 20, 1542. His body ultimately found a resting-place in the murky waters of the river he had discovered. With the possible exception of Alvarez de Pineda who, in 1520, is said to have named the lower Mississippi the River of the Holy Ghost, De Soto was the first European to see the Father of Waters, but he made no conquest and there is no record that any of the accompanying priests survived long enough to celebrate Mass or utter a prayer beside its waters. Spain made no further attempt to trace the river to its source.

The Founding of Quebec

An expedition sent out by the King of France and led by Jacques Cartier of Saint Malo, discovered and named the St. Lawrence river in 1535, and thus paved the way for the exploration and colonization of the territory along its banks and the evangelization of the redmen, its only inhabitants.

With the founding of Quebec by Samuel de Champlain on July 3, 1608, the roots of the Catholic faith were planted in the New World under the aegis of France. Champlain was a fervent Catholic and wished to spread the blessings of religion among the aboriginal savages of the country. He it was who established the first colony on the rocky promontory that guards the St. Lawrence waterway, and initiated the fur trade with the Indians and the work of christianizing them. At his request Denis Jamay (Superior), John d'Olbeau and Joseph le Caron — three Recollect Fathers — and a lay brother, Pacificus du Plessis, came from France to Quebec on March 25, 1615,[3] to minister to the pioneer settlers, and preach the gospel to the Algonquins and Hurons, numbering upwards of a hundred thousand on the St. Lawrence and Ottawa rivers and in the Niagara peninsula. Other Recollects came to their assistance and for ten years labored with heroic dedication, but with little fruit, among the colonists and savages. One of them, Father Nicholas Viel, who arrived in Canada in 1623 and was sent westward to the Huron country as a missionary, was hurled to death in the Ottawa river by an apostate Indian. He was the first to die in New France for the cause of Christ. "For ten years did these grey friars practice the rites of the church in the Canadian woods, all the way from the fishing and trading outposts of Tadoussac to the western lake of the Nipissings. Barefooted, save for heavy wooden sandals, coarsely clad in gown and hood, enduring in a rigorous climate, to which they were unused, all manner of hardships by flood and field, they were earnestly devoted to their laborious calling in a time when elsewhere the air of New France was noisy with the strife of self-seeking traders and politicians. Yet somehow their mission seemed without important result".[4] But the task was too great for one community and the Recollects asked the Jesuits to join them in the work, and Father Charles Lalemant, John de Brébeuf and Enemond Masse, landed in Quebec on June 19, 1625, to continue the work and widen its scope to include all the roving hordes of Indians from Quebec to Lake Huron.

In the meantime the development of the nascent colony was hampered by changes in the administration at home and the efforts of the missionaries thwarted by the "Company of the Hundred Associates". As a result, in July, 1629, Champlain was forced to surrender to the English fleet under Captain Kirk who took Quebec, compelled the Jesuits and Recollects to return to France, and left the Catholics without priest or altar until 1632, when the colony was restored to France by the Treaty of Saint-Germain-en-Laye.

With the landing at Quebec on July 15, 1632, of Fathers Paul le Jeune and Anne de Noue, with a lay brother, the Jesuits resumed the task of christianizing the aborigines, and the Huron mission became one of the glories of the Church in the New World by the fervent faith and heroic virtue of the neophytes, one of whom, Kateri Tekakwitha, awaits the cachet of canonization before her statue will occupy a niche in our sanctuaries. The hatred and fury of the Iroquois drove the Hurons westward and the missionaries followed them. In 1641 Fathers Jogues and Raymbaut were the first white men to pass through Sault Ste. Marie and stand on the shore of Lake Superior whence they could turn their gaze to the land of the Ojibways in the upper valley of the Mississippi. Here, as Shea writes, "the two Jesuits planted the Cross of Christianity, looking still further west, and forming plans for the conversion of the Dakotas, of whom they had heard by their Algonquin name, Nadouessis".[5] With the exception of Father Joseph de la Roche Daillon, a Recollect, they were the first priests from Canada to penetrate into the present territory of the United States. The Jesuits continued their missionary work among the Hurons. Jogues and his companions were taken prisoners by the warlike Iroquois and were among the eight sons of Ignatius, six priests and two lay brothers, who fertilized the soil of New France with martyr blood during the decade prior to 1650.

Explorers and Missionaries

The French were pioneers in making discoveries in the region of the Great Lakes and in the country westward to the Mississippi. Explorers and missionaries penetrated into the heart of this vast continent and the possessions of France soon included not only the whole of Canada but all the country south of the St. Lawrence extending from the Atlantic seaboard to the Rocky mountains. The eastern part bordering on the St. Lawrence and the Great Lakes was known as New France, while the lands of the west, drained and fertilized by the Mississippi, were named Louisiana in honor of the French King by La Salle, the explorer of the lower Mississippi.

These natural waterways became the classic trails of trader, coureur de bois, and missionary, each in the pursuit of his vocation. The hardy voyageurs sought adventure and new outposts of trade with the Indian, bartering the baubles of civilization for the products of the chase; the men of God sought souls to save without thought of self or earthly recompense. Then, too, there burned in the hearts of the adventurous voyageurs the hope of reaching the western sea at the end of the rainbow, of discovering a new waterway to the shores of Cathay. The Indians spoke of a great river to the west which many interpreted to mean a great ocean, and efforts were made to reach it. Among the leaders in this enterprise was Sieur Nicollet who came to Green Bay in 1634 and descended the Fox and the Wisconsin rivers for some distance, lured by the hope of reaching the South Sea as it was called, but ultimately he returned to Quebec without achieving his goal. He was drowned at Sillery, Quebec, October 29, 1642. In October, 1661, Father René Ménard began a mission among the Chippewas on the southern shore of Lake Superior, not far from the village of L'Anse. He was alone in the heart of the continent, his nearest priestly neighbor a thousand miles away. He spent a winter of extreme hardship among the Ottawas, and lost his life on an errand of mercy the next summer.[6] In 1665 he was succeeded by Father Claude Allouez who, some years later, with Fathers Claude Dablon, Gabriel Druillettes, Louis Andre, Jacques Marquette, Sieur Louis Joliet and Daumont de Saint-Lusson as agent of Talon, Intendant of New France, attended a council convoked by Nicholas Perrot, one of the oldest and most daring of French voyageurs, in the name af Marquis Denonville, Governor of New France, and met the representatives of fourteen Indian tribes at Sault Ste. Marie in May, 1671. Following this council, on June 14, the vast empire of France in the New World was formally taken possession of by solemn proclamation of Saint-Lusson at a historic ceremony in the Jesuit mission. The proclamation set forth the extent of his vast empire comprising, as it did,

> Lakes Huron and Superior, and all the countries, lakes, rivers and territories, contiguous and adjacent thereunto as were discovered, or to be discovered, bounded on the one side by the northern and western seas and on the other side by the south seas.

On that occasion a large cross was blessed and erected, the Fleur-de-lis was unfurled, an official record drawn up, duly signed, and affixed to a cedar post bearing a copper plate on which was engraved the royal arms of France. Father Allouez made a lengthy address extolling the power and authority of France, and Saint-Lusson, sword in hand, declared the country with its lakes and rivers the property of the

King of France and the natives his vassals bound to obey his laws and follow his customs. In this formal manner did France assert her claim to all the land from sea to sea, including the Mississippi valley, as a theater of future exploration, colonization and evangelization.

On May 17, 1673, Father Marquette and Louis Joliet set out from St. Ignace mission in the hope of reaching the great river about which they had heard from the Indians. They skirted along the north shore of Lake Michigan into Green Bay, paddled down the Fox river and portaged to the Wisconsin which empties into the Mississippi at Prairie du Chien. On June 17, 1673, they set eyes upon the great and mysterious Father of Waters. They sailed down its broad expanse in their bark canoes as far as the confluence of the Arkansas, the first white men to explore this portion of the mighty river and to almost demonstrate with certainty that it flowed south into the Gulf of Mexico and not west into the Pacific Ocean. "Fear of hostile Indians and the enmity of the Spaniards prompted them to turn their canoes northward." On the return voyage they guided their frail barks into the Illinois river and finally arrived at the Mission of St. Francis Xavier, at the head of Green Bay, in July, having traveled twenty-seven hundred miles.[7]

They were not the first to explore the upper part of the Mississippi. As early as the middle of the seventeenth century attempts were made to find a water-route across the continent to the shores of China. The Great Lakes and their connections offered a natural and inviting avenue for entering this unknown land. They formed the first stage of a journey which, it was fondly hoped, would ultimately lead to the western ocean. Along this classic highway voyageurs and traders paddled their canoes and by portage and stream reached the Mississippi and the present State of Minnesota.

Groseilliers and Radisson

Early in the year 1655, Groseilliers and Radisson, brothers-in-law, left Three Rivers north of Quebec and by way of the St. Lawrence, Ottawa and Mattawa rivers, Lake Nipissing, French river, Georgian Bay and Green Bay, the Fox and the Wisconsin rivers reached the Mississippi up which they directed their course. They passed through Lake Pepin and established their headquarters on what was then, or afterwards, known as Isle Pelée, Bald Island, now Prairie Island, in the Mississippi a few miles below the present town of Hastings.[8] They reached their destination in May and encountered Huron refugees driven by the Iroquois from their homeland in the vicinity of Georgian Bay. They were the first men to penetrate beyond the Great Lakes, further than white men had ever ventured before, the first to set foot on what was destined to be the State of Minnesota.

Groseilliers and Radisson remained on Prairie Island for more than a year and during that time built a chapel in which they imparted religious instructions to adults and children, held prayer meetings and administered the Sacrament of Baptism to the dying,[9] especially to children, whenever feasible. In other words, they performed the duties of lay missionaries and apostles, the first to engage in Catholic Action in Minnesota.

The records make no mention of a priest as a member of the party and, consequently, we infer that the Holy Sacrifice of the Mass was not offered during their residence on the island. This primitive chapel was the first religious edifice to cast its beneficent shadow on the soil of Minnesota, the pioneer in a series of log chapels which, in later years, yielded to more pretentious structures until they reached the zenith of architectural splendor and magnificence in the granite Cathedral of St. Paul which overlooks the city from its commanding eminence on the brow of St. Anthony Hill.

Groseilliers and Radisson were anxious to return to Quebec with their cargo of beaver pelts but the refugees besought them to remain because, otherwise, there would be no one to baptize their children. This appeal bore fruit for a time but eventually the date of departure was decided on and towards the end of June, 1656, fifty canoes laden with peltries, each manned by ten stalwart men, sailed away from the island and arrived in Quebec about the end of August. The leaders went into retirement for a time but the lure of adventure would not permit them to remain inactive indefinitely. With a flotilla of Indian canoes Groseilliers and Radisson set out from Three Rivers in August, 1659, and, following the usual trail, entered Lake Superior, the first Frenchmen to navigate this largest of American lakes. They established headquarters at Chequamegon Bay whence, in the following January, they departed for a rendezvous with the Indians near Knife Lake, about fifteen miles southeast of Mille Lacs in Kanabec County, Minnesota, and later on visited the Prairie Sioux villages in the southwestern part of the state to conclude treaties of peace with the Crees and Sioux for the promotion of trade. Some months afterwards they met the Crees in the vicinity of Two Harbors, east of Duluth, and finally returned to Quebec in the summer of 1660. In all their travels they did what lay apostles could do, as opportunity offered, to aid the Indians spiritually and insure the salvation of dying infants.

They were the first white explorers to repeat the Hail Mary of the Norsemen in Minnesota, the first to confer any of the sacraments. The narrative of Radisson implying that they had baptized the dying children of Huron refugees on Prairie Island is confirmed and supplemented by the Jesuit Relations for 1655-56, stating that "three hundred little children" had been regenerated by them during the first trip to the west. Furthermore, the Relations declare that in a subsequent voyage they baptized "two hundred little children of the Algonkin nation". According to these historical records, therefore, Groseilliers and Radisson were the first to exercise the ministry of lay Catholics in Minnesota.

Father Hennepin

Groseilliers and Radisson were trail-blazers. In their wake others came to the western plains. A quarter of a century later, in 1679-80, Daniel Graysolon, Sieur Du Lhut, following the usual route from the east to the Mississippi and turning northward, reached the western end of Lake Superior and traversed the Mille Lacs region and the country around the Twin Cities of the future. In the course of his wanderings he encountered the Franciscan Recollect, Father Louis Hennepin, shortly after the latter discovered and named the Falls of St. Anthony, now within the corporate limits of the City of Minneapolis, and rescued him and his companions, Anthony Augelle and Michael Accault, from the hands of the Sioux who had taken them captive in the early part of the year 1680.

Father Hennepin was born at Ath[10] in the Belgian Province of Hainaut, the sixth child of Gaspard Hennepin and Robertine Leleup, and baptized in the church of St. Julian on April 7, 1640. He joined the Recollect branch of the Franciscan Order and came to Quebec in September, 1675, with Robert Cavelier, Sieur de la Salle, the newly appointed Governor of Frontenac, an important outpost in New France, now the site of the city of Kingston, Ontario. He accompanied La Salle on his trip to the West from Niagara over the Great Lakes in the Griffin to Michili-mackinac, now St. Ignace, thence along the western shore of Lake Michigan to the Illinois river, where La Salle built Fort Crevecoeur, near the present city of Peoria. When La Salle found it necessary to return to the East he left the fort in command of his lieutenant, Henry de Tonty, and authorized Father Hennepin, Anthony Augelle and Michael Accault to continue the journey westward and explore the Mississippi "and not to lose the opportunity of preaching the gospel to the nations that dwelt above, and who had never yet heard it spoken of".

On February 29, 1680, they set out in a birch bark canoe down the Illinois to the Mississippi, into which they entered on March 6, turned northward, and were taken prisoners in Lake Pepin by the Assati Sioux under Chief Cloud Man, on April 12,[11] and brought up the river to Kaposia, an Indian village about fifteen miles below the site of the city of St. Paul, and thence overland through what is now the Twin Cities area to the Sioux encampment on the shore of Mille Lacs, where they lived for a time the wretched life of white men among barbarians. The

Indians robbed Father Hennepin of his vestments, and the want of wine deprived him of the honor of saying the first Mass in Minnesota. They would not touch his chalice as they considered it the abode of a shining spirit. He did not say Mass until he arrived at the Jesuit Mission at Green Bay, nine months later. During his sojourn in the locality — set aside as "Father Hennepin State Memorial Wayside Park", near the village of Isle, by the State Legislature in April, 1941 — he preached the gospel under difficulties to his captors, and baptized at least one dying child whom he named Antoinette[12] in honor of her sponsor, Anthony Augelle, and thus gave Minnesota its first saint of which we have any record. According to the historian Shea, Father Hennepin was "the first (priest) to announce the gospel in the land of the Dakotas". He went with the Sioux on their annual buffalo hunt down the St. Francis, now the Rum river, and once more reached the Mississippi on whose placid waters he canoed to the falls which he saw for the first time on July 4, 1680, and to which he gave the name of his patron, St. Anthony of Padua.

> The fall is thirty or forty feet high, and the river is narrower there than elsewhere. There is an island in the middle of the fall, and the two banks of the river are no longer skirted by mountains . . . but the ground on both sides is covered with open woods . . . oaks and other hard woods planted far apart, which grow only on poor soil.[13]

He was permitted to go down the river as far as the Wisconsin in search of supplies to be sent by La Salle, but returned empty-handed. He and his companions were finally rescued from the Sioux by Du Lhut, as already stated, and some months later he returned to France.

When his former commander, La Salle, descended the Mississippi to its mouth he was accompanied by the Recollect Father Zenobius Membre, Henry de Tonty and others. He named it the river of the Immaculate Conception. On reaching the estuary he and his companions sang the Vexilla Regis and the Te Deum and, on April 9, 1682, set up a cross to commemorate the achievement while he took possession of the newly-discovered country in the name of his sovereign in whose honor he called it Louisiana. The discovery of the mouth of this great river was the glorious climax of a life of tragic drama. He made an attempt to colonize the new territory but the expedition met with disaster and he with a violent death, at the hands of his own men.

The act of taking possession of the territory bordering the Mississippi was "a great and important event, as the starting-point of the French possession of Louisiana", out of the northern part of which was carved the Territory of Minnesota on March 3, 1849.

La Salle's title to be considered the first to trace the Mississippi to its mouth was challenged by Father Hennepin in his "New Discovery" published in Utrecht in 1697, wherein he declared that he and his companions, Augelle and Accault, had reached the Gulf of Mexico in 1680 and set up a cross to commemorate the event. When he returned to France after his captivity in the West he published his "Description of Louisiana" in Paris in 1683 wherein he gave an account of his explorations in the New World, narrated the story of his contacts with and life among the Indians and described the cataract he discovered and named beside whose leaping waters a great metropolis was to rise with its worldwide marts of commerce and its magnificent sanctuaries of Catholic faith. In this book he not only made no mention of exploring the lower Mississippi, but stated that he did not go down the river below the confluence of the Illinois.

> We had some design of proceeding down to the mouth of the river Colbert (Mississippi) . . . but these tribes that seized us gave us no time to sail up and down this river.[14]

In the "New Discovery" he accounts for this omission by saying that he did not wish to rob La Salle, his commander, of the honor of having been the first to follow the river to the gulf.

> I have concealed (this discovery) to the present, so as not to mortify the Sieur de le Salle who wished to have alone all the glory and all the most secret knowledge of this discovery.[15]

It is difficult, to say the least, to fit the alleged journey into the itinerary described in his first book which is generally accepted as a statement of fact.

It is on the strength of the Utrecht publication that Father Hennepin has been accused of misrepresentation, if not of actual prevarication, to enhance his own reputation by detracting from the glory of La Salle. Many years ago a detailed study and scrutiny of this volume were made by the late John Gilmary Shea who declared that

> it is evident, whatever we may think of the remainder of the book, that the ten pages containing the so-called voyage to the lower Mississippi, were an interpolation in the volume after it had issued from the press.

In this way Shea tried to save the reputation of Father Hennepin as a trustworthy historian. The question is still debatable. Many years ago the writer asked Canon Paul Halflants of Brussels to suggest to a student of Louvain University that he make this mooted point the subject of his doctoral thesis but nothing was done about it.

Father Hennepin was the first white man to visit the site of Minneapolis whose main arterial thoroughfare is named after him as well as the county of which it is the chief city. He was the pioneer standard-bearer of the christian faith in a region theretofore untrodden by the footsteps of civilization.

On May 8, 1689, less than a decade after his departure another formal assertion of sovereignty was made in behalf of France by Nicholas Perrot at Green Bay, in presence of Father Marest, S.J., and others, laying claim to

> the Country of the Nadouesions, on the border of the river Saint Croix, and to the mouth of the river Saint Peter . . . and farther up to the interior to the northeast of the Mississippi . . . to take possession for and in the name of the King, of the countries and rivers inhabited by the said tribes, and of which they are the proprietors. The present act done in our presence and signed with our hand and subscribed of the 8th day of May, 1689.[16]

This included the State of Minnesota.

It was the same Perrot who in 1683 established a small trading post, Fort Perrot, on the western shore of Lake Pepin, near the present town of Wabasha, and two years later Fort Antoine on the opposite shore, near Pepin, Wisconsin. With him was Father Marest, S.J. who spent some time among the Sioux Indians between 1689 and 1700. In 1695 Pierre Charles Le Sueur, a contemporary of Perrot, erected a fort on Prairie Island; and five years afterwards Fort l'Huillier on the Blue Earth river three miles from its junction with the Mississippi.[17] He thought the green earth abounding in that locality contained crude copper, some of which he shipped to France. The Dakota word, Mahkah-to, meaning blue or green earth, is preserved in Mankato, the county seat of Blue Earth County.

Heralds of Christianity

With the explorers or in their wake came the heralds of Christianity to sow the seeds of divine truth in savage breasts, to bend the stubborn wills of haughty chiefs to the sweet yoke of the gospel. The Recollects and Jesuits were the first in the field. In the beginning they received faculties from the Holy See and then from the Archbishop of Rouen who claimed jurisidiction over New France. In 1647 he appointed Father Jerome Lalemant, Superior of the Canadian Missions, his Vicar General. Shortly afterwards the Holy See erected the territory into a Vicariate Apostolic under the direction of Francis de Montmorency Laval who was preconized Titular Bishop of Petraea in May, 1658, and, over the protest of the Archbishop of Rouen, consecrated on December 8[18] of that year. With a few priests to aid him in his work he arrived in his residential see on June 16, 1659, and was graciously received by missionaries and people. He undertook a visitation of the Vicariate and projected new missions in the distant west, including Louisiana which became part of his extensive diocese after 1682.

Before the vanguard of civilization reached the lands of the west diocesan and regular priests vied with one another to bring the teachings of christianity and the blessings of civilization to the Indian tribes who roamed this immense area. They were under the direction of the Bishops of Quebec who appointed Vicars General to supervise and regularize their efforts. In so doing these prelates exercised ordinary jurisdiction for, according to the Bull of erection, issued in 1674, "the See of Quebec comprehended all the possessions of France in North America . . . all New France from the Atlantic to the plains of the far west, the valley of the Mississippi and Louisiana, a territory much larger than Europe".[19] The Recollects claimed the entire region as their special field and petitioned the Holy See to establish vicariates which was actually done. But Bishop St. Vallier, the successor of Bishop Laval, protested on the score that Louisiana formed part of his diocese by right of discovery and evangelization and should not be dismembered without his knowledge and consent. The Propaganda revoked its action, the Recollects soon withdrew and the Jesuits were left in possession.

The Bishops of Quebec watched with great solicitude over the missions in this remote part of the vicariate. When the priests of the Seminary of Quebec, affiliated with the Foreign Mission Society of Paris, felt it incumbent on them to have a share in preaching the gospel to the Indians of these far-off regions, they petitioned Bishop St. Vallier to authorize them to establish a missionary outpost in the valley of the Mississippi.

By Letters Patent of May first, 1698, he

> granted to the Superior and Directors of the Seminary of the Foreign Missions of Quebec ample power to establish themselves and to found missions among all the nations which are on both sides of the Mississippi River as well as all the length of this river and on all the rivers which flow into it.[20]

Later on he commissioned three priests—Fathers Francis Jolliet de Montigny (Superior and Vicar General), Anthony Davion and John Francis Buisson de St. Cosme—to undertake the work and in May, 1699, they founded the Holy Family Mission[21] among the Tamaroa Indians at what was to be the Cahokia of later days on the east bank of the river opposite the limestone bluffs on which the future City of St. Louis was to rise. Cahokia was the first permanent settlement in the Mississippi valley and celebrated the two hundred and fiftieth anniversary of its existence in 1949. It was situated to the south of the country of the Illinois Indians where the Jesuits were well established but they claimed it as a dependency of their territory. They were exploring the possibility of establishing a new mission there when the Foreign Mission priests entered the field. The Jesuits regarded the newcomers as intruders and asked the Bishop of Quebec for exclusive rights in the territory, which he refused. As a result strained relations existed between the seminary priests and the Jesuits for some time. In 1700 the Indians abandoned their villages on the Illinois and found a new home, Kaskaskia, at the mouth of the Des Peres River within the limits of the present St. Louis, two or three leagues below Cahokia on the west bank of the river. This gave rise to the question of jurisdictional rights in the locality; but the controversy was amicably settled in the course of time. After sixty years of struggle the seminary priests abandoned the work as a protest against the shabby treatment meted out to them and the Jesuits by the French government.

Our Diocesan Lineage

At one time, therefore, this immense inland empire was included in the far-flung diocese over which the early Bishops of Quebec exercised jurisdiction. The present State of Minnesota was part of it and was affiliated by spiritual ties to the primatial see of the continent until 1783 when, after the Treaty of Paris, the Diocese of Quebec was restricted to the Dominion of Canada, and all of North America, except the Spanish west, became a British possession. The Catholic Church came under the spiritual jurisdiction of the Vicar Apostolic of England until the appointment of the Reverend John Carroll as Prefect Apostolic in 1784. Six years later, on August 15, he was consecrated Bishop of Baltimore by the Right Reverend Charles Walmesley, Senior Vicar Apostolic of England, in the chapel of Lulworth Castle. He was the first bishop of the United States and had the whole country for his diocese. To relieve him of part of his administrative burdens the Diocese of New Orleans was founded in 1793[22] and placed in charge of Spanish bishops till 1809 when it once more reverted to Bishop Carroll who appointed Father Dubourg Vicar General to administer its affairs. In 1815 Father Dubourg was consecrated bishop of the diocese. In the meantime the Diocese of Bardstown (now Louisville) was erected in 1808 and included not only Kentucky and Tennessee but the whole of the Northwest Territory lying between the Ohio and the Great Lakes and comprising a small part of the future Minnesota between the Mississippi and the St. Croix rivers. The rest of the State was in the Diocese of New Orleans until 1826 when the Diocese of St. Louis was formed out of the northern portion of the Louisiana Territory. From it the Diocese of Dubuque was carved in 1837 with a territory bounded by the State of Missouri on the South, Canada on the North, the Mississippi on the East and the Missouri on the West. The upper part of the area, from the State of Iowa to the Canadian boundary and from the Mississippi and St. Croix to the Missouri, became the Diocese of St. Paul on July 19, 1850, the segment between the Mississippi and the St. Croix being taken from the Diocese of Milwaukee erected in 1843.

This dual origin of the Diocese of St. Paul connotes a twofold line of descent from the See of Baltimore—the one through Dubuque, St. Louis and New Orleans, the other through Milwaukee, Detroit, Cincinnati and Bardstown—a noble lineage running back to Bishop Laval, thus linking the St. Lawrence with the Mississippi and Quebec with St. Paul.

It goes without saying that the venturesome explorers who opened up to colonization the interior of the American continent, from which these and many other dioceses were fashioned, as well as the pioneer missionaries who accompanied them or followed in their footsteps, were for the most part sons of France or in the service of the French kings. They were Catholics, all of them, and to their daring and self-sacrifice for God and country go the honor and glory of a conquest for faith and fatherland without parallel in the annals of missionary endeavor.

Chapel of St. Michael the Archangel Fort Beauharnois, near Frontenac where Mass was said for the first time in Minnesota on November 4, 1727

Chapel of St. Paul 1841

Chapel of the Assumption Pembina, 1848

Chapter III

PIONEER CHAPELS OF THE NORTHWEST
1655–1841

Fort Beauharnois

THE hope of discovering a river-route to the Pacific Ocean was almost an obsession with the early French explorers. Nicollet tried to find it and failed. Groseilliers and Radisson were lured by this will-o-the-wisp further west than any other white man had penetrated. They, too, failed as all were destined to fail for the very obvious reason that there is no such waterway. Nevertheless attempts continued to be made by the undaunted French traders. Du Lhut suggested the erection of forts in the country of the Sioux in furtherance of the project to reach the western sea. Several routes were proposed and the Duke of Orleans, Regent of France from 1715 to 1723, was importuned to authorize an expedition to bear the Fleur-de-lis across the continent to the Orient.

In 1720 Father Charlevoix, the historian of New France, who was collecting information for the discovery of the Western Sea, made similar recommendations after a trip from Quebec to New Orleans; but it was not until 1726 that King Louis XV authorized Governor Beauharnois of New France to fit out an expedition in charge of a commanding officer and two Jesuit missionaries to establish a trading post in the upper Mississippi valley. On June 6 of that year the Governor entered into a contract with the Company of the Sioux which, in return for exclusive trading rights among the Indians, agreed to erect a stockade with a chapel and houses for the commanding officer and the missionaries, supply everything necessary for the enterprise while the contract lasted, and not do anything to obstruct the work of christianizing the savages.

René Bouchard, Sieur de la Perrière, was placed in command and the Jesuit Fathers Michael Guignas and Nicholas de Gonner accompanied him.[1] They left Montreal on June 16, 1727, and reached the western shore of Lake Pepin, opposite Maiden Rock in Wisconsin, on

27

September 4, where they built a fort, one hundred feet square, enclosed by four rows of wooden posts, twelve feet high, with two bastions. Within the stockade three log buildings, 30, 38 and 25 feet long and 16 feet wide, served as a chapel and residences for the commandant and the missionaries. It was named Fort Beauharnois in honor of the Governor and the chapel was dedicated to St. Michael the Archangel, the patron of Father Guignas and of the Governor. The savages assembled around the post to the number of one hundred and fifty in ninety huts; but there is no evidence that a school was connected with the mission.

This was the second chapel built in Minnesota, almost three quarters of a century after the log structure erected on Prairie Island by Groseilliers and Radisson. On its primitive altar was celebrated the first Mass said in Minnesota. There is a record that on November 4, 1727, the feast of St. Charles, patron of Governor Beauharnois, the Holy Sacrifice was offered up for him, and a display of fireworks held in his honor to the great consternation of the Indians who were terrified at the sight of the stars falling from heaven as they thought.

The fort was inundated the following spring and had to be evacuated. Father de Gonner returned to the East in 1728 and the hostile attitude of the Sioux caused many of the shareholders of the Company to withdraw their support.

In October, 1728, Father Guignas and eleven Frenchmen departed for Canada, were taken prisoners by the Indians and held in captivity for five months during which they were often in danger of being burned at the stake, but were finally liberated and continued their journey to Canada in 1730. Efforts were made to restore the fort and in 1732 it was transferred to higher ground with Godefroy de Linctot in command and Father Guignas as resident chaplain. The fort collected and shipped tens of thousands of beaver pelts annually until 1735 to the home market and the Company prospered. St. Pierre succeeded Linctot as commandant in 1735; but hostility between the Sioux and the Foxes finally led to the abandonment of the fort on May 30, 1737. It was reoccupied in 1750 at the urgent request of the Marquis de la Jonquière, Governor of New France, but was finally evacuated five years later.

As far as can be ascertained it is probable that the second fort was built on the high plateau on which Villa Maria Academy, near Frontenac, now stands. The school, in charge of the Ursuline Sisters, was dedicated by Archbishop Ireland on September 8, 1891, when the convent chapel was placed under the protection of St. Michael the Archangel, thus linking it with the pioneer chapel in which the first Mass was celebrated in this state.

The Goodhue County Historical Society arranged and successfully carried into effect an appropriate celebration at Frontenac on September 17, 1927, for the 200th. anniversary of the building of Fort Beauharnois on the shore of Lake Pepin. The central feature of the program was the unveiling of a bronze tablet bearing the inscription:

"Near this spot Fort Beauharnois was erected by the French in September, 1727. Here also stood the Mission of St. Michael the Archangel, the first Christian Chapel in the present boundaries of Minnesota".

Fort St. Charles

Fort Beauharnois was one of several outposts established by the French in their efforts to reach the Pacific. A contemporary was Fort St. Charles on the most northerly point in Minnesota, in the Lake of the Woods, beyond the international boundary.[2] It was built in 1732 by Pierre Gaultier de Varennes, Sieur de la Verendrye, who had obtained from Governor Beauharnois a monopoly of the fur trade in the country he proposed to explore, and the backing of some of the leading merchants of Montreal in outfitting an expedition. With his three sons, a nephew, fifty soldiers and voyageurs he set out for the West in 1731 and at Michilimakinac secured the services of Father Charles Mesaiger, S.J., as missionary. Verendrye and some of his men passed the winter at Kaministikwia while the others pushed on to Rainy River, built Fort Pierre and began to trade with the Indians.

In June, 1732, Verendrye and his group arrived at Fort Pierre and, after a rest, continued their journey into the Lake of the Woods where they erected Fort St. Charles, named in honor of the Governor and Father Mesaiger, on the southern shore of Northwest Angle Inlet. It was the usual type, one hundred feet long and sixty wide, with four bastions, and contained a chapel, houses for the commandant and the missionary, a powder magazine, a warehouse and an observation tower.

In the spring of 1733 Father Mesaiger, being ill, accompanied Verendrye's nephew, La Jemmeraye, to Montreal. A year later Verendrye had to make the trip to reassure his partners and equip a new expedition with which he returned to the West in 1735, bringing with him as missionary young Father Jean Aulneau, S. J. They reached their destination on September 6. The non-arrival of expected supplies caused a great scarcity of food for the garrison during the winter and made it necessary to send a convoy to Machilimakinac on June 5, 1736, in charge of Verendrye's eldest son, John Baptist. Father Aulneau begged to go along as he wished to consult a priest. With them went nineteen Frenchmen. Less than twenty miles from the Fort they were surprised while in camp by a band of Sioux and all were massacred and scalped. The details are not known with certainty. When the news of the massacre reached the Fort, Verendrye sent a detachment to bury the bodies of the nineteen Frenchmen on the island and bring those of his son and Father Aulneau and the heads of the others to the Fort where they were interred beneath the chapel. Since then the island has been known as Massacre Island.

In the course of time all traces of the Fort and chapel disappeared and the very location was veiled in uncertainty. As early as 1890[3] the Jesuits of St. Joseph's College, St. Boniface, Manitoba, visited Massacre Island and erected a cross in memory of Father Aulneau. In the summer of 1902 Archbishop Langevin of St. Boniface headed an expedition which, after visiting Massacre Island, entered the Northwest Angle Inlet and, on its northern shore, found traces of a fort which they concluded was Fort St. Charles. They erected a memorial cross with the inscription in French: "Fort St. Charles, erected in 1732, visited in 1902". In 1905 the Archbishop made another trip to Massacre Island and built a chapel dedicated to the Queen of Martyrs. During these years the conviction was growing that they had not located the real Fort St. Charles. In 1908 they visited the Northwest Angle Inlet again and explored the southern shore and to their great joy their persistence was rewarded by the finding of the original Fort and the chapel the outlines of which they were able to trace from the charred remains of the palisades. Beneath the chapel they found the bones of those buried in 1736—the headless skeletons of Father Aulneau and young Verendrye, and the skulls of their nineteen companions together with other objects— all of which were reverently transferred to St. Boniface and sacredly preserved in the college museum. They changed the inscription on the cross to read: "Fort St. Charles, founded in 1732, discovered in 1908". The Jesuit college was completely destroyed by fire in 1921 and only the charred bones of the massacred Frenchmen remain. They are preserved in the museum in the crypt of the Cathedral of St. Boniface. The site of the Fort is now on Magnussen Island separated from the mainland by a narrow, shallow channel.

For a time even the Jesuits knew very little about Father Aulneau.[4] A providential occurrence in the little town of La Vendee in France gave them the information they sought. In Advent of the year 1889, priests of the Society of Jesus were giving a mission in that town which was attended by a descendent of the Aulneau family who informed them that a number of letters written by Father Aulneau or about him was in his possession. He allowed the letters to be copied and they were first published in the Canadian Messenger and afterwards in book form by Reverend Arthur E. Jones, S. J., in Montreal in 1893. From these we learn that Jean Pierre Aulneau de la Touche was born of a noble family at Moutier, in La Vendee, France, on April 21, 1705, and joined the Society of Jesus at the age of fifteen. Of his three brothers, one became likewise a Jesuit, and one a Sulpician; and a sister joined a religious community. On May 29, 1734, he sailed from La Rochelle, France, for Canada on the king's vessel, the "Ruby", and landed at Quebec on August 12. Owing to the filthy and crowded condition of the vessel an epidemic broke out among the passengers, and young Aulneau labored among the sick to alleviate their bodily sufferings and to bring peace to their souls. He was stricken with the dread disease after landing, and twice was at the point of death. However he recovered and in the spring of 1735 was ordained and appointed to the distant mission of Fort St. Charles to replace Father Mesaiger. We know what happened after he reached that post.

But how account for the fact that the site of Fort St. Charles is in Minnesota and yet beyond the 49th degree of latitude? After the Revolutionary War the American treaty-makers wanted to include the sources of the Mississippi within Minnesota, and its northern boundary line was run from Rainy River to the northwestern part of the Lake of the Woods and thence directly south to the international boundary west of the lake. This dividing line remained even after it was discovered that the sources of the Mississippi were much further south. The site of Fort St. Charles is, therefore, on Magnussen Island off the most northerly point of Beltrami County and cannot be reached from Minnesota except by sailing across the lake or crossing the international boundary directly into Manitoba to which it is attached. It is now part of the Diocese of Crookston, and a church in memory of Father Aulneau is been erected at Warroad, the town nearest the site of Fort St. Charles.

The writer recalls very distinctly having heard Archbishop Ireland assert on more than one occasion that the United States Government had promised him to set aside forty acres, including the site of the ancient fort, as a memorial park and public reservation.

This is borne out by an article in the St. Paul Dispatch for July 3, 1909; "The United States Government will within a reasonable time set aside the land on which the site of old Fort St. Charles was discovered last year, for a reservation and monument . . . The Federal Government will set off a tract of some forty acres, including the ancient site, as a reservation park, and private initiative will see to it that a chapel is built where the fort stood, as a memorial of the early days and of the brave men who lay buried there for many years . . . Assurances have been made to Archbishop Ireland that that will be done". No definite steps seem to have been taken to carry out the project.

On March 19, 1914, the Oblate Fathers of Manitoba bought the site of the ancient fort[5]—Lots 2 to 6, Section 24, Township 168, Range 34 of Lake of the Woods County, Minnesota, comprising 157 acres—from Martin P. Magnussen and transferred it to the Oblates of Mary Immaculate in Duluth on February 19, 1928, who defaulted in the payment of taxes and it reverted to the state. Then a Mrs. Loiselle of Minneapolis acquired possession of it as tax delinquent land and she, too, let it go by default. In 1943 the County Board of Lake of the Woods County transferred the site of the Old Fort, together with about nine thousand acres of surrounding land, to the State of Minnesota, a transfer declared legal by the Attorney General of the State in 1947.

Subsequent to that date various persons, among them officers of the State Council of the Fourth Degree, Knights of Columbus, became interested in having the site of Fort St. Charles set apart as a historic monument, and an application was made to the Board of County Commissioners for cancellation of the certificate of forfeiture on the ground that these lots, having been used for religious purposes, were exempt from taxation. A hearing was instituted before Mr. Howard Spaeth, Commissioner of Taxation for the State of Minnesota, and the attorneys for the Knights were able to prove to his satisfaction that at least part of the premises in question was used for religious services from time to time. As a result, lots 3 and 4, comprising about thirty-six acres, surrounding the site of the old Fort, reverted to the Oblate Fathers of Duluth who, in the course of time, conveyed them to the Diocese of Crookston. The Knights then proceeded with their plan to mark the site of the St. Charles chapel with a massive granite altar for outdoor religious services and granite markers at the corners of the original fort.

The memorial altar, weighing three thousand pounds, was manufactured in St. Cloud, shipped to Warroad, transported by barge to Magnussen Island and erected in the latter part of June, 1951, by the Knights of Columbus on the site of the original chapel cleared by them. The altar was dedicated[6] by Bishop Schenk of Crookston on July 5 who said Mass on it in presence of fifteen priests, the State Master and a dozen members of the Fourth Degree in regalia and 115 men and women who had been transported across the Lake of the Woods in a flotilla of boats to the dock leading to the site erected by Mrs. Francis Cole of Penasse. The Knights formed a guard of honor while Mass was being said and at the end of the sacred rite, A. L. Grabenstetter of St. Paul, chairman of the project committee, introduced Bishop Schenk, George F. Parkos of New Prague, Master of the Fourth Degree for Minnesota, and Dr. Paul LaFleche of Winnipeg, Master of the Fourth Degree for Manitoba, who delivered brief addresses, and Father Shanahan of the parish of Warroad in which the site is located who thanked all for the honor of their presence and their interest in the project. During the program a deed to the property was delivered to Bishop Schenk, thus restoring this historic shrine to the Catholic Church.

The Bishop of Crookston has given permission for the erection of a memorial church in honor of Father Aulneau, Minnesota's forgotten martyr, at Warroad, within the parochial boundaries of which is the site of this ancient fort where Mass was said as early as 1732.

The Pembina Chapels

The pioneer missionaries thus briefly referred to inaugurated in Minnesota, under the aegis of New France, a Catholic religious movement among the Indians which, if carried to its logical conclusion, would have enriched them with the knowledge of the True Faith and the blessings of civilization. Its death knell was sounded when French sovereignty in North America ended, and Canada became an English colony in 1763. When the sceptre passed from the hand of France to that of England with it passed away the rights and privileges the Church had previously enjoyed; and the glorious missionary movement in behalf of the Indians of the New World came to an abrupt close. Had France continued to dominate the American continent Catholic missionaries would have garnered an abundant harvest from the good seed sown by their apostolic forbears.

Parkman in "The Jesuits in North America", page 447, admits that, had France been able to retain her power in North America, Catholic missionaries would have effected the civilization of the savages.

Their habits of agriculture would have been developed and their instincts of mutual slaughter repressed. The swift decline of the Indian population would have been arrested, and it would have been made, through the fur trade, a source of prosperity to New France.

But, in spite of the changes brought about by the Treaty of Paris, the work of the "blackrobe" remained a hallowed memory among the aborigines of field and forest, who did not forget the salutary teachings of the devoted priests of this early missionary epoch. When the work was resumed in later years it produced a worthwhile harvest, for some of the seed had fallen "upon good ground and being sprung up yielded fruit a hundred-fold".

A new era of evangelization dawned for the nomadic tribes of the Northwest when the vanguard of immigration that began its trek towards the western skyline in the early years of the nineteenth century was borne northward on the breast of the Father of Waters. Colonists came in ever-increasing numbers to contend with the aborigines for the possession of their huntlands—the feeding-grounds of the lumbering buffalo and the virgin prairies that billowed to the horizon from the banks of the Mississippi and the Red River of the North. With them came the zealous missionary to evangelize the redmen of the plains and minister to the white settlers on the farms and in the timbered areas. Almost overnight hamlet and village expanded into town and city as the advancing tide of colonization flowed into the fertile valleys and spread across the wind-swept plains. "The germ of the Church was there, the children of the Old World, the fathers of the New". The Church soon took cognizance of the increase in Catholic population. Parish bourgeoned into diocese and diocese into province, as the seed sown in the dark loam of virginal earth produced the biblical increase. Missionaries yielded to pastors and bishops came with apostolic mandate to rule the Church of God.

It is interesting to note that the first Mass celebrated in the nineteenth century in what is now the Ecclesiastical Province of St. Paul, comprising Minnesota and the two Dakotas, was offered up in St. Francis Xavier chapel in Pembina, now in North Dakota, by Father Severe Joseph Nicolas Dumoulin in September, 1818.[7] With Father Joseph Norbert Provencher, destined to become the first Vicar Apostolic of Western Canada, he left Montreal on May 19 of that year and, after a brief sojourn in the Red River Valley, came to Pembina to organize a mission for the Catholic settlers who had gone thither from Lord Selkirk's colony in the vicinity of Fort Douglas, now St. Boniface, as well as for the half-breeds and Chippewa Indians who lived in the neighborhood. The mission consisted of a log chapel, 60 by 40 feet, under the protection of St. Francis Xavier, a residence, 40 by 27 feet, a store 24 by 18 feet, and a small school taught by William Edge, a catechist, who had accompanied the two priests from the East. The spiritual harvest was very satisfactory. A strenuous campaign against the evils to which Indian and half-breeds were exposed was inaugurated. Chief among these were the old tribal marriage customs which tolerated polygamy and divorce, and drunkenness, the curse of frontier life.

In January, 1819, Father Provencher visited Pembina to examine into the condition of the new parish and found everything in excellent order. There were sixty pupils in the school. In four months Father Dumoulin had baptized fifty-two persons, rehabilitated a large number of marriages, and grouped around the site of the chapel about three hundred souls. Pembina was a growing mission. On May 25, 1821, as many as 313 baptisms, 53 marriages and 31 funerals were to its credit.[8] For a time, in fact, it was more important than St. Boniface where Father Provencher had established his headquarters.

Except for occasional visits from Father Provencher, Father Dumoulin was the only priest in a territory where now nine bishops and nearly sixteen hundred priests minister to the needs of a thriving church. When it was finally determined that Pembina was in the United States and not a British possession, it was abandoned by Father Dumoulin who returned to Montreal in July, 1823, leaving a record of 800 baptisms of children and adults, 120 marriages celebrated or validated, 48 burials and 150 first communions, with a large number preparing for baptism or communion. Many Protestants had abjured their errors, a school had been maintained where several children had made progress in their studies, and the Indians had turned to the faith of Christ.

For twenty-five years no pastor came to take his place and make the mission a center of renewed Catholic life and activity. There were, it is true, sporadic visits from Father Destroismaison before he returned to Quebec, Fathers Harper, Boucher and others but it remained for Father Belcourt to restore the once flourishing Catholic life of the community, as its second resident pastor.

Father George Anthony Belcourt, born near Three Rivers in the Province of Quebec, on April 22, 1803, and ordained in Nicolet Seminary on March 10, 1827, came to St. Boniface in 1831 and spent seventeen years on the missions in the Red River valley before moving to Pembina in June, 1848, to revive interest in the Church and her teaching among the dusky children of the plains.[9] He built a chapel, dedicated to the Assumption of the Blessed Virgin, a school for the spiritual and educational training of the neophytes and founded a religious community of native, half-breed young women, known as the Sisters of the Propagation of the Faith, who, because they were familiar with the language and customs of the Indians, were well qualified to conduct a school in English, French and Indian. The community was not very numerous, perhaps never more than seven, and ceased to exist when Father Belcourt left the mission in 1859. A few years after settling in Pembina, in 1853, Father Belcourt opened another mission at St. Joseph, later Walhalla, now Leroy, about thirty miles West and took up his residence there, ministering to a congregation of about fifteen hundred souls while retaining charge of Pembina under the direction of his assistant, Father Lacombe. There he built a log chapel under the patronage of St. Joseph, a presbytery, a school and a flour mill, the first in North Dakota, and from that as a center traveled throughout the state and in a special way evangelized the Turtle Mountain region and erected on Butte St. Paul, the highest point in the vicinity, the saving symbol of our holy faith. The late Bishop Shanley of Fargo calls him "North Dakota's greatest pioneer priest". In his pastoral work he had such well known assistants as Father Lacombe, already mentioned, afterwards the famous Oblate "blackrobe" among the Indians of Western Canada; Reverend John Fayolle, second pastor of the original frame church of St. Anthony in Minneapolis; and Reverend Joseph Goiffon whose experience in a blizzard in November, 1860, is a thrilling episode in the annals of the Church in the Northwest.

Grand Portage Chapels

The Grand Portage Mission, on the shore of Lake Superior near the mouth of the Pigeon River in the extreme northeastern tip of Minnesota, was founded[10] in 1838 by the Reverend Francis Xavier Pierz, a Slovenian missionary among the Ottawa Indians of Michigan. In anticipation of his coming, about which a rumor had reached them, the Indians built a temporary chapel of cedar bark and deerskin under the direction of Mrs. Pierre Cotté, the wife of the resident fur-trader, which was dedicated by Father Pierz on July 25, 1838, and placed under the patronage of St. Peter. He opened a school for old and young in which were enrolled thirty-one adults—nineteen Indian and twelve French—and forty-four children of whom thirty-nine were Indians and five French. In less than a year he administered sixty-four baptisms. He visioned Grand Portage as a permanent mission center with subsidiary stations, but it was not to be, though it flourished for several years under the care of the Jesuits. In obedience to the wish of his superior, Bishop Resé of Detroit, he took charge of Arbre Croche, now Harbor Springs, Michigan, in 1840; but revisited Grand Portage in the spring of 1842 and built a birch chapel near the mouth of the Pigeon River, about one mile from Lake Superior and four from Grand Portage, where he opened a school attended by forty-five pupils, and began a permanent church which was never completed. On October 15 he was recalled to his home mission at Arbre Croche.

In August, 1844, Bishop Henni of Milwaukee was petitioned by the Indians of Grand Portage to send a resident missionary to say Mass for them, to administer the sacraments, baptize the children and bury the dead, but he was obliged to refuse their request because he had no priest qualified for the place.

In July, 1846, Father Otto Skolla, pastor of La Pointe on what is now Madeline Island in Lake Superior, came to Grand Portage,[11] said Mass for the people, gave holy communion to twenty persons, and baptized a few children in a chapel of bark and branches, 60 by 12 feet in size, which also served as his dwelling during his stay. At that time the congregation comprised about eighty adult Indians who lived in small huts and subsisted on fish, potatoes and rice. He also visited Pigeon River mission where the chapel begun by Father Pierz was still without a roof.

When Father Pierz revisited the locality for a brief period prior to August 16, 1847, he found the Indians keeping up their religious practices despite the absence of a priest. Twice on Sundays and holydays they assembled for prayer and singing.

The third chapel[12] of logs was erected in Grand Portage about four hundred feet south of the local cemetery and east of the stockade close to the shore line. It was replaced in 1865 on a different site by the present substantial church of logs joined by wooden dowels and known as the Church of the Holy Rosary. It is attended by Reverend Lawrence Schmidt, O.S.B., pastor of the Church of St. John the Baptist, Grand Marais.

The first missionary to set foot on Grand Portage was Father Charles Mesaiger, S.J., in 1731, on his way to the Lake of the Woods with La Verendrye, the founder of Fort St. Charles in northern Minnesota. Four years later his successor, Father Jean Aulneau, followed in his footsteps Father Frederick Baraga, a missionary among the Indians of Michigan, spent a few hours there in 1837 and baptized eight children, according to the records of Holy Family Church, Bayfield, Wisconsin. He came again as Vicar Apostolic of Upper Michigan in 1856 and on July 20 confirmed fifty-three persons, the largest class in the history of the mission. This occurred during the pastorate of Reverend Dominic du Ranquet, S.J., who came to Grand Portage in 1851 and for approximately eighteen years traversed the surrounding country by canoe in summer and dogsled and snowshoes in winter, ministering to the Indians and whites along the north shore. It was under his supervision that the present church was built.

REV. LUCIEN GALTIER
First Pastor in the Diocese
1840-1844

Chapter IV

FATHER GALTIER: PROTO-PASTOR OF MINNESOTA

1840–1844

THE Holy Sacrifice of the Mass was offered up for the first time in what is now the Archdiocese of St. Paul by the Right Reverend Mathias Loras, first Bishop of Dubuque, Iowa, towards the end of June, 1839, after he and the Reverend Anthony Pelamourgues had sailed up the Mississippi in the "Virginia" to St. Peter's, (now Mendota) following his installation in the frontier diocese which then included the whole of Minnesota. It was his second visitation after taking formal possession of the new see.

In a letter to his sister, dated July 26, 1839, the Bishop wrote:

I have just returned from St. Peter's, where I made my second mission or episcopal visitation. Though it lasted only a month, it has been crowned with success. I left Dubuque on the 23rd. of June, on board a large and magnificent steam vessel, and was accompanied by the Abbe Pelamourgues and a young man, who served as an interpreter with the Sioux. After a successful voyage of some days along the Mississippi and the beautiful Lake Pepin, we reached St. Peter's. This fort built at the confluence of a river of the same name, and the Mississippi, is advantageously situated; the soil is very fertile and the mountains around of no considerable elevation. Our arrival was a cause of great joy to the Catholics, who had never before seen a Priest or Bishop in these remote regions; they manifested a great desire to assist at divine worship, and to approach the sacraments of the Church. The wife of our host, who had already received some religious instruction, was baptized and confirmed; she subsequently received the sacrament of Matrimony and made her first communion. The Catholics of St. Peter's amount to one hundred and eighty-five, fifty-six of whom we baptized, administered confirmation to eight, communion to thirty-three adults, and gave the nuptial blessing to four couples.

Arrangements have been made for the construction of a church next summer, and a clergyman is to be sent, when he is able to speak French (which is the language of the majority), English and the Sioux.[1]

In another letter he writes:

On Thursday, the sixty-third anniversary of the independence of the United States, I was at the altar, offering my prayers to heaven in favor of my adopted country.

For the first time, in the future Diocese of St. Paul, the Fourth of July, was observed by the offering of the Holy Sacrifice of the Mass.

The Catholics whom Bishop Loras found in the vicinity of Fort Snelling were "traders who had settled around St. Peter's, farmers on the reservation and traders and coureurs de bois from scattered parts of the Northwest".

With the promise to send a priest to St. Peter's, Bishop Loras took the first step towards organizing the Church in Minnesota. Prior to his visit the Catholics among the traders and the soldiers in the garrison had been without priestly ministration. The coming of a resident pastor to the locality would inaugurate a new era of spiritual life for the faithful.

Bishop Loras and his companion remained two weeks at St. Peter's and gave the Catholics an opportunity to fulfil their religious duties and the well-disposed non-Catholics to learn something about the history, doctrines and practices of the Church.

On the return journey he and Father Pelamourgues visited the Indian villages along the banks of the river where they were well received and their instructions listened to with interest and respect. To enable them to do this they purchased a canoe hollowed out of a single log and paddled by a young savage familiar with the redmen, their customs and language. In one of the villages the Bishop was presented with "a long pipe, made of flat wood, painted all over, and ornamented with ribbons, feathers, hair dyed red, and curious hieroglyphics". In Lake Pepin a violent storm delayed their progress but at length they arrived safely at Dog's Meadow (Prairie du Chien), a French village of about a thousand inhabitants without church or priest. They remained eleven days celebrating Mass, hearing confessions and preaching. Twenty-five catechumens were baptized, twenty marriages blessed, fifty-two persons confirmed, eighty-five given Holy Communion and the cornerstone of a church, 100 by 50 feet, blessed and laid in place. Father Pelamourgues was put in charge of the parish.

The apostolic bishop was pleased with the result of the "excursion"— 76 (81?) persons baptized, 60 adults confirmed, 24 marriages blessed, 119 holy communions distributed. In addition arrangements were made for the construction of two churches and for the removal to St. Peter's next year of a hundred Catholic families from the Red River that "they may have the blessing of religion within their reach". In this way did Bishop Loras prepare the field for the arrival of the first resident pastor in the Minnesota of the future.

First Pastor in Minnesota

For that post he chose the Reverend Lucien Galtier, a native of the Department of Ardesches, France, born in 1811, who with the Bishop and others arrived in New York from Havre in the autumn of 1838 and spent a year at Mount St. Mary's Seminary, Emmitsburg, Maryland, to complete his studies for the priesthood and learn English. He was ordained[2] in St. Raphael's Cathedral, Dubuque, with the Reverends Augustine Ravoux and Jacques Causse on January 5, 1840, and assigned to parish duty in the Cathedral. Less than four months afterwards, on April 26, to be exact, he was missioned to St. Peter's in the northern part of the diocese and, with little time for preparation, boarded the first steam boat of the season on its way from St. Louis to Fort Snelling, for there was then no St. Paul and only a single log shanty occupied by Edward Phelan, a discharged soldier, on the site of the future metropolis.

In the first glow of priestly fervor and apostolic zeal Father Galtier turned his face to the North eager to begin his career as a missionary. For that he had left kindred and fatherland and sacrificed the comforts of parochial life in the country of his birth. Had he remained in France, his talents and his virtues would probably have marked him for high honors, but he preferred the rugged lot and privation of pioneer life to the power and fame for which petty men strive. He was "a slim young priest recently from France. He looked better fitted to serve in the quiet of a monastery, for his was the face of a scholar and saint".[3]

It was his first journey into the wilderness and he must have admired the bold and picturesque scenery of the upper Mississippi as seen through the eyes of a visitor a decade of years later.

> The scenery is exceedingly bold and picturesque . . . In some places the rocks rise perpendicularly from the river to a height of two or three hundred feet and assume at times the wildest and most fantastic forms. Frequently a column shoots up far above the cliffs like a watch tower, and often—for long spaces—the rocks appear like castle ruins—the outlines of battlements plainly designated as if they had been erected by the hand of man.[4]

Another writer described the bluffs below Lake Pepin as "rising three and four hundred feet above the river, their grim summits broken by intervening chasms and rounded into forms of every conceivable outline, and affording a scene of rare grandeur and magnificence".

In due time the steamer came to a halt at Fort Snelling Landing and Father Galtier stepped for the first time on Minnesota soil. He was well pleased with the prospect. The country derived from the banks of the Mississippi a varied, but grand aspect; lofty mountains of the most picturesque forms; at one time covered with verdure, at another lifting their steep summits to the height of four or five hundred feet and presenting to the sight only their bare sides.[5] The Fort occupied a high triangular promonotory at the junction of the Mississippi and the St. Peter (now the Minnesota) river. There were a few houses on the St. Peter's side and only two on the Fort side, in the midst of a dense wilderness where souls were few and opportunities for suffering, privation and hardship all the most heroic missionary could desire. For a month he lodged at the home of Scott Campbell, the Indian interpreter, who lived on the Snelling side of the river but outside the enclosure of the Fort. Mrs. Campbell was a Catholic who, with her husband and seven children, had offered hospitality to Bishop Loras and Father Pelamourgues the previous year. Scott Campbell was a half-breed from Prairie du Chien, "a man of great worth and efficiency, a true friend of the Americans".

At the end of a month Father Galtier procured a place for himself, part of which he used as a chapel, and with his own hands built a primitive altar for the celebration of the Holy Sacrifice. His parish consisted of six families—Campbell, Bruce, Resike, Quinn, Papin and Resh, together with a number of Catholic soldiers—on the Fort Snelling side; and five families—Faribault, Turpin, (2), Martin, Lord and a few single men employed by the Fur Company—on the other side of the river.[6] Besides these there were several families in the vicinity of St. Croix Lake whom he visited from time to time.

During the following year he was prostrated for nearly two months in the military hospital with a severe attack of bilious fever and ague, and Divine Providence sent him a visitor in the person of the Right Reverend Charles Joseph Forbin-Janson, Bishop of Nancy in France, who was returning from a visit to Canada through the Northwest. The Bishop, hearing of the illness of the local priest as he alighted from the boat, called on him, heard his confession, consoled and comforted him before resuming his journey. He was the second bishop to visit Minnesota. Perhaps it was what he saw in the mission area through which he traveled that prompted him, on his return to France, to found the Association of the Holy Childhood in 1843, to inculcate interest in mission work among children. Another episcopal visitor to Fort Snelling was Bishop Provencher of St. Boniface, on his way to Quebec in 1843, via the Red River route and St. Paul.

Thirty-three years afterwards Father Galtier, in a letter requested by Bishop Grace, gave an account of his coming to St. Peter's and the founding of the log chapel of St. Paul. It was written from Prairie du Chien, Wisconsin, on January 14, 1864. It tells of his arrival at St. Peter's, the reception accorded him, the difficulties under which he labored with the nearest priest three hundred miles away and gives a lengthy narrative of the circumstances which made it necessary for him to found a new parish at some distance from his headquarters. He writes:

A painful circumstance commenced to better my state by procuring to me a change and a new station. Some families who had come from the Red River settlement in the British possessions, on account of the flood there and the loss of their crops the previous year, 1837-1838, had located themselves all along the right side of the Mississippi and opposite Fort Snelling, but, unfortunately, some soldiers, who now and then crossed the Mississippi and returned intoxicated, sometimes remaining out a day or two or more without reporting to their quarters and answering their call, procured much annoyance to the commanding officer. In consequence a deputy marshall (A.B.) of Prairie du Chien was sent forth: he with the help of some few soldiers went on, and one after another unroofed the poor cottages extending about five miles in length, thus rendering the inmates homeless and forcing them to make up for new homes.

The Log Chapel of St. Paul

Father Galtier felt it incumbent on him to follow these dispossessed parishioners with the ministrations of religion, and finally decided to build a chapel for their convenience in the new locality in which they had settled. Three sites were available—one several miles down the river at Point Leclair, in the vicinity of Pig's Eye sand bar, was liable to inundation and, therefore, unsuitable for the purpose; another on what is now Dayton's Bluff, was inaccessible from the river because of its elevation and the absence of facilities for a boat landing; the third was a bluff overlooking the river and nearer Fort Snelling, where two farmers, Vital Guerin and Benjamin Gervais, occupying contiguous claims, offered to donate sufficient ground for a church, garden and graveyard. He accepted their offer. No finer site could have been chosen. It was one hundred feet above the river, accessible from both ends as it sloped gently to the level of the river, forming landing-places for passengers and freight about a mile apart. Trees were cut down and logs roughly hewn on or near the site and willing hands helped to build the chapel, 18 by 20 feet in size, which was dedicated to St. Paul.

> On the first day of November 1841, I blessed the new basilica smaller, indeed, than that of St. Paul at Rome, extra muros, but in this as well as in the other good hearts could expand without limits. This church remained thus dedicated to St. Paul and I expressed the wish to call the place by no other name. . . . St. Paul as applied to a town or city was well appropriated, this monosyllable is short, sounds good, it is understood by all christian denominations. Hence when an attempt was made to change it, I opposed the vain project—even by writing from Prairie du Chien.

Soon steamboats began to stop at the new settlement on their way up and down the river and the place became known as St. Paul's Landing, which gradually supplanted the name, Pig's Eye, foisted on the locality, but never current among the French colonists.

More interesting details are given about the log chapel by Isaac Labissonière, the survivor of the eight men who erected it, whose father,

Joseph, superintended the building operations on Bench Street, for years the principal thoroughfare of the town.

Isaac was born in Pembina on July 7, 1823, and died in St. Paul on June 20, 1910. He was, therefore, eighteen years old when the log chapel was built. The ground selected for the site of the chapel, he stated in an interview in 1907,

> was thinly covered with groves of red oak and white oak. Where the Cathedral stands (Sixth and St. Peter Streets) was then a tamarack swamp. The logs for the chapel were cut on the spot, and the tamarack swamp in the rear was made to contribute rafters and roofpieces . . . the logs, rough and undressed, prepared merely by the axe, were made secure by wooden pins. The roof was made of steeply slanting bark-covered slabs, donated by a mill-owner in Stillwater . . . carried to St. Paul by a steamboat, the captain accepting in payment a few days' service of one of the men. These slabs were landed at Jackson Street, and drawn up the hill by hand with ropes. The slabs were likewise put to good use in the construction of the floor and the benches.
>
> The chapel, as I remember it, was about twenty-five feet long, eighteen feet wide, and ten feet high. It had a single window on each side and it faced the river. It was completed in a few days, and could not have represented an expenditure in labor value of more than $65.[7]

Nowhere does Father Galtier or his successor, Father Ravoux, give the exact dimensions of the original log chapel. It is believed to have been about 18 by 20 feet in size with a ten foot ceiling, one window of a single sash in each side, and a wooden cross over the door in front. Archbishop Ireland who, as a boy coming to St. Paul in 1852, saw the original log chapel says it "was of rough, unhewn logs and the roof was covered with bark-sided slabs. It was 27 by 20 feet in size. . . . In 1847 Father Ravoux added eighteen feet to the log chapel, built it of square logs with large windows and shingled roof".[8] W. G. Leduc in "Minnesota Year Book for 1851" says it was 18 feet square.

The addition put to it by Father Ravoux in 1847 was about the same size as the original building as shown on a map subsequently published by him, though he may have been mistaken as the map was not prepared until 1902 and the details may have become dimmed by the interval of over sixty years. In his "Reminiscences and Memoirs" he says the enlarged church was "about forty-five feet long and eighteen wide".[9] Probably the addition was a little smaller than the original log chapel for it served as a sacristy after the arrival of Bishop Cretin and was used by him as a seminary for the instruction of the young levites who came with him from France after his consecration. At any rate it was the first house of worship within the limits of the present City of St. Paul and was destined to be the first Cathedral of the diocese erected on July 19, 1850. It was visited at regular intervals by Father Galtier as long as he remained at St. Peter's. On June 5, 1842, Bishop Loras confirmed a few persons within its hallowed sanctuary.

A portion of the land on the east of the block on which it stood was set apart as a cemetery in which two persons were buried before the chapel was dedicated—Cécile Labissonière, on August 22, and Marie Pepin on September first. According to the records in the Cathedral archives made by Father Galtier up to 1843 and by Father Ravoux in the following years, ten persons were interred within its sacred enclosure between November 8, 1841, and February 6, 1846.[10] Few, if any, were buried there after 1849 because another cemetery was opened that year.

Father Galtier's opposition to the "vain project" of changing the name of St. Paul, derived from the original log chapel, was uncompromising to the end of his life as shown by the following affidavit:

> I, the undersigned, Catholic priest of Prairie du Chien, Wisconsin, heretofore employed in the Catholic missions of St. Peter's of Mendota (now in Minnesota) and neighborhood, as far as St. Croix of Wisconsin, do certify to whom it may belong, that in the year of our Lord 1841, a lot or parcel of ground, being on the premises and forming the limits of the previous farm of Mr. Vital (Guerin) and Benjamin Gervais and on the south bank of the Mississippi river, was given me simply by Mr. Vital (Guerin) and Benjamin Gervais, for a Catholic church or chapel, and a small graveyard, without any reserve to all or condition whatever for the future.
>
> And moreover that conformably to the donors' desire a log church was there constructed and blessed, in the year 1841 and on the first day of November, under the title of St. Paul: this being the very origin or nucleus of the present City of St. Paul Minnesota Territory.
>
> In faith whereof I have written this present affidavit in Prairie du Chien on the 19th of June A. D. 1856, and signed it
>
> L. Galtier
Pre.
>
> State of Wisconsin,⎱
Crawford County ⎰
>
> I hereby certify that the above affidavit or certificate was sworn to in due form of law, before me on this 19th day of June A. D. 1856.
>
> Ira W. Brunson
County Judge
Crawford County, Wis.

Mendota Chapels

After the migrants from the Selkirk Colony had been driven down the Mississippi, Father Galtier left his first residence in the vicinity of the Fort and moved across the river to St. Peter's where Mr. Faribault offered him a small dwelling, 13 by 26 feet, with a top-heavy roof covered with bark and earth, which he set aside for a chapel with the exception of a small bedroom in a corner. To the new mission in St. Paul he added two others—St. Croix Settlement and Willow river (now, Hudson)—and visited them regularly.

Father Galtier was sent to minister to the whites (including the half-breeds) and not to the Indians who were the special charge of Father

Ravoux. In the summer of 1842 he made a missionary tour of his territory during which he visited a colony of forty men working in the saw mills on the Chippewa river in Wisconsin who were very pleased to see a priest who could instruct them in their christian duties and prepare them for the reception of the sacraments. During his absence Father Ravoux had charge of St. Peter's and narrowly escaped death one night when a supporting beam broke over his head and the roof threatened to come tumbling down on him.[11] When Father Galtier heard of the accident which left him homeless and without a chapel he hurried back to the parish, secured lumber from Chippewa Falls and erected a combination church and residence which he blessed on October 2, 1842. It was destined to serve the needs of the congregation for a decade of years. Its little bell, the first in Minnesota, was blessed on October 29.

The Catholic Almanac for 1844, which gives the statistics for 1843, the last year of Father Galtier's residence in Minnesota, furnishes the following information about the number of Catholics in St. Peter's and vicinity under his pastoral care:

> St. Peter's, in Iowa, with a chapel and a house for the priest, at the confluence of the river of the same name and the Mississippi, at 8 miles from St. Anthony Falls, served by Lucien Galtier. It has but 130 Catholics and these include the Catholic persons of Fort Snelling and those of Lake Pepin which is 111 miles lower down than St. Peter on the banks of the Mississippi river, and who cannot be visited because of their great distance.
> St. Paul, a new place and which increases every year, in Wisconsin, 7 miles from St. Peter's, with a provisional chapel, is visited from St. Peter's. It embraces 454 Catholic souls (at least) and includes those at Little Crow, the falls and the entry of Ste. Croix, and the Catholics employed in the environs of the Chippewa River.

During his missionary career at St. Peter's Father Galtier not only taught the half-breeds the doctrines and practices of the Church but trained them to sing the praises of God in canticles translated from the French into Sioux. According to Father Ravoux, he was "a good singer. His voice was clear, sweet, noble, rich and strong. The half-breeds, his pupils, could sing well the French canticles, and their voices were no less harmonious when they were singing them in the Sioux language".[12]

During the years of his pastorate in St. Peter's Father Galtier baptized 137 persons, according to the registers in the Cathedral archives—40 in 1840; 35 in 1841 and in 1842; and 27 in 1843. "His flock was small but, dispersed as they were, themselves strangers to material comfort, it required no small degree of courage and self-denial in a clergyman to labor among them".

Father Galtier Transferred

Father Galtier terminated his ministry at St. Peter's on May 25, 1844, "leaving to better hands", as he wrote to Bishop Loras, "the yet barren

fields of my first mission; neither without regret nor without friends"
He was placed in charge of Keokuk, Iowa, by Bishop Loras where he
built a log church for the seventy-four Catholics of the parish, and,
during the short time he remained there, baptized six children, blessed
two marriages and validated a third, gave Holy Communion to fifteen
persons, made one convert, had two boys for catechism, and received
nothing from the people for his support.[13] He was much worse off than
at St. Peter's of which he seems to have grown tired. His experiences on
the mission probably embittered him and made him somewhat cen-
sorious. After his transfer to Keokuk he criticized Bishop Loras and
caused the latter anxiety, if not pain, by threatening to leave his post
without permission unless his reiterated requests to join the diocese of
Milwaukee were complied with at once. In one of his letters to the
Bishop he refers to the continuous privations and sufferings he endured
at St. Peter's.

The hardships of missionary life must have changed him from what
he was in the early days of his ministry when he was described as "a
man of remarkable personality and power; he had the face of a Caesar
and the heart of a Madonna; in him strength and tenderness, culture and
simplicity met and mingled in the making of a noble character". A priest
with "the heart of a Madonna" does not write to his superior as he did to
Bishop Loras. Did he not know that Bishop Loras was enduring, and
without recrimination, the rugged lot and privation of pioneer life and, in
addition, the importunities of a disgruntled priest? In 1845 Bishop Loras
yielded to his persistent demands and gave him the necessary permission
to enter the Diocese of Milwaukee.

In 1845 Father Galtier returned to France with the intention of spending the remainder of his days in the land of his forefathers. But he was
not satisfied. The longing for the missionary life of a priest on the
missions in America became irresistible and he returned to the Diocese
of Milwaukee and in 1847 was appointed pastor of St. Gabriel's Church,
Prairie du Chien, by Bishop Henni where he remained till his death on
February 21, 1866.

Honors came to him in his new diocese. He was appointed one of the
Vicars General in 1858; and his name was third on the roster of priests
proposed for the vacant Diocese of St. Paul by the ten bishops of the
Provincial Synod of St. Louis on September 12, 1858.[14] Three years prior
thereto Prairie du Chien was chosen as the seat of a new diocese by
the Fathers of the First Provincial Council of St. Louis, but the recommendation did not receive the approval of the Holy See.[15]

No Fitting Memorial.

In 1853 and again in 1865 Father Galtier visited St. Paul and saw how
the city, whose birth he had witnessed, whose cradle he had rocked, had

developed during the intervening years, surpassing his most sanguine visions of its future. Did he experience regret that he had not retained citizenship in it by remaining at his first post of duty? He loved the city and its people and was always interested in its progress. But St. Paul did not remember him in any more substantial or public manner than by naming an obscure street after him in 1876 and a public school. Even today no fitting monument to its founder graces any public square or park of the city. All that marks the site of the pioneer chapel that gave the metropolis its name is a rough granite boulder on Kellogg Boulevard with two inset bronze plates bearing a likeness of this pioneer priest and a brief inscription attesting the fact that it designates approximately the location of the first house for divine worship in St. Paul built by the loving hands of impoverished pioneers under his direction in 1841— an insignificant and inconspicuous monument for a noble priest whom Church and City should delight to honor. When will a fitting memorial, perhaps in the form of a heroic statue, be erected in front of the majestic Cathedral overlooking the site of the rude chapel from which Archdiocese and metropolis derive their name?

Who more worthy of honor than this priest who has been described as a man

> of great decision of character, with a rather strong cast of countenance, large mouth and overshadowing eyebrows. His head sat upon his shoulders like a military chieftian, and he was well chosen to mould and control a heterogeneous mass of men whose lives had been spent exclusively upon the frontier. He was a well proportioned man, with a fixed determination to accomplish what he undertook, and he succeeded . . . an honest, self-sacrificing priest.[16]

What became of the primitive chapel he erected in St. Paul? One account says it was dismantled in 1856, the logs and other pieces marked and numbered, and taken to the site of the present St. Joseph's Academy, then a cemetery, to be erected and preserved for future generations.[17] But just at that time preparations were underway to transfer the bodies of the dead to Calvary cemetery on November 2 of that year, and it is said that the workmen engaged in disinterring them, knowing not what they did, used the logs to kindle a fire to warm themselves, and thus the most precious relic of pioneer days went up in smoke. From the charred remains of one of the logs two gavels were fashioned but they, too, have disappeared with many another souvenir of a historic past. And yet the Northwestern Chronicle for August 9, 1889, says the logs "are still preserved in one of the buildings connected with St. Joseph's Academy".

Archbishop Ireland, preaching in the Cathedral on Sunday evening, November 1, 1891, the golden jubilee of the dedication of the log chapel, said, "Some time after the Bishop moved to Sixth Street, the original chapel was taken down to prevent its falling down, the addition was given a modern siding and was used as a convent chapel until 1864 when it was demolished".[18] In his "Memoir of Rev. Lucien Galtier" published in the Minnesota Historical Society Collections, volume 111, part 2, St. Paul, 1874, he says the log chapel "was taken down some years ago; the logs are secure and it is the intention to have them put together, as they formerly were and thus have the old church preserved". The truth of the matter seems to be that no one knows just when the chapel was dismantled or what became of the logs.

His Tomb in Prairie du Chien

In his last will and testament Father Galtier bequeathed a brick house and several lots to the Bishop of Milwaukee for school purposes; his library to the seminary; his vestments to the parish, with the exception of two chasubles, one of gold cloth, and a silver chalice to his nephew and namesake, Reverend Lucien Galtier; and the residue of the estate to his two brothers, his sister and his housekeeper.

His mortal remains lie buried near the western front of St. Gabriel's Church in Prairie du Chien. The grave is marked by a horizontal block of marble, seven feet long, three feet wide and two and a half feet high, and on its surface is sculptured the outline of a cross within which is this inscription:

Very Reverend Lucien Galtier, Born in France Dec. 17, 1812; Died at Prairie du Chien, Wisconsin, Feb. 21, 1866. Pray for a sinner. Requiescat in Pace.

In his "Memoir of Rev. Lucien Galtier: The First Catholic Priest of St. Paul" read before the members of the Minnesota Historical Society in 1874, Father Ireland thus closes his eulogy:

In 1848 he returned to France, intending to spend there the remainder of his life. He had been strongly pressed to take charge of the French congregation of the Cathedral of St. Louis, but refused. After some time spent in Europe, he again longed for the missionary life of an American priest, and again crossed the Atlantic. On his return he was placed at Prairie du Chien, where he remained until his death, Feb. 21st, 1866.
He loved our city and our state dearly; nothing in his old age used to afford him more pleasure than to meet with persons from St. Paul, and to enquire of them how our city was progressing.

There is some question about the date of his return from Europe. Reverend F. Bonduel, pastor of St. Gabriel's parish, Prairie du Chien, in a letter to Senator Jones of Iowa, on October 1, 1846, said, inter alia, "The Rev. Father Galtier, whose return from France is daily expected, is to take charge of the parish". The Catholic Almanac for 1848 lists him as pastor (in 1847). The Reverend John F. Kempker of Dubuque in an article sent to Archbishop Ireland, now in the Archives of the Catholic Bulletin, says Father Galtier was pastor of Prairie du Chien from 1847 to 1866.

RT. REV. AUGUSTINE RAVOUX
Second Pastor in the Diocese
1844-1906

Chapter V

FATHER RAVOUX: LONE SENTINEL OF ROME
1841-1851

W HEN Father Galtier was transferred from St. Peter's to Keokuk in 1844, his place was taken by his classmate and friend, Reverend Augustine Ravoux, a missionary among the nomadic Sioux of Minnesota. No one was better equipped by training and experience for the position. As a result of four years of unremitting labor among the Indians Father Ravoux was no stranger to hardship and privation but rather inured to them. Nevertheless it was with genuine regret, and only in obedience to the voice of authority, that he severed his official connection with the redmen, though he made several journeys into their territory in subsequent years. As a matter of fact he thought the appointment to St. Peter's only a temporary one, but Bishop Loras had no one else to send and Father Ravoux remained the lone sentinel of Rome in the locality until 1851.

The Reverend Augustine Ravoux was born January 11, 1815, at Langeac,[1] in Auvergne, France, not far from Puy where he spent three years in the Petit Seminary and four in the Grand Seminary before he was promoted to the subdiaconate, following in the footsteps of an elder brother, his godfather, and a priest who died about 1850. The visit of Mathias Loras to the seminary, after his consecration as Bishop of Dubuque, and his talk to the student body turned the thoughts of young Ravoux to America as a mission field. He decided to follow the inspiration and accompanied the Bishop and other clerics on the return trip to New York where they arrived on October 10, 1838, after a stormy passage of forty-five days. He and three other subdeacons were sent to St. Mary's Seminary, Emmitsburg, Maryland, to complete their theological studies and acquire a knowledge of the English language. He was ordained in St. Raphael's Cathedral, Dubuque, on January 5, 1840, with Lucien Galtier and Jacques Causse.

A few days after ordination Father Ravoux was sent to Prairie du

Chien where he exercised the ministry as the first regular pastor of St. Gabriel's parish. His first baptism, that of an Indian woman, Marie Louise, aged 35, was in March, 1840, and his last in September, 1841, that of John Lawless. When he was transferred to the northern part of the diocese of Dubuque (now Minnesota) to found a mission among the Sioux, he spent a few days with Father Galtier, already well established in his sparsely-settled but extensive parish, before beginning the work of converting the Indians at Traverse des Sioux (near St. Peter) where, as the guest of Mr. Provençal, a trader among them for forty-five years, he preached through an interpreter and baptized ten persons before Christmas. He applied himself to the study of the Sioux language with such diligence and success that in a few years he became proficient in it. He visited Little Rock (near Fort Ridgley) on the Minnesota river where he remained about four weeks and then went to Lac qui Parle, instructing and baptizing as occasion offered. So successful were his missionary efforts that they caused marked uneasiness and concern among the Protestant missionaries who noted "the diminution in our Sabbath assemblies" wherever he appeared. Therefore, the Reverend Thomas Williamson admonished Samuel Pond on August 3, 1842, to "caution any whom you may employ and all our members who may go there (to Lac Travers) to keep aloof from the priest and have nothing to do with him".

Of his missionary zeal and success Bishop Loras writes:

Without any other support than Providence, without any other means of conversion than a burning zeal, he has wrought in the space of six months a happy revolution among the Sioux. From the time of his arrival he has been occupied, night and day, in the study of their language, and he has made such rapid progress, that he has already been able to translate our principal prayers, to compose some canticles, to draw up a small catechism, and to collect the first elements of an Indian grammar. When he instructs the savages, he speaks to them with so much fire, whilst showing them a large copper crucifix which he carries on his breast, that he makes the strongest impression on them.[2]

A fellow-missionary paid the following tribute to him:

It would not be easy to describe the virtues of this Missionary, in whom a perfect contempt of the world, charity the most ardent, humility, modesty, patience, the spirit of prayer and penance render him dear and precious in the sight of the Lord. Always joyous and content in the direst poverty and affliction, he busied himself in learning the language of the Sioux, amongst whom he had fixed his abode; he translated the prayers and the Catechism into that dialect and taught the truths of the gospel to the Indians.[3]

Father Ravoux spent the summer of 1842 at St. Peter's during the absence of Father Galtier on a missionary tour among the Catholics of Lake Pepin and the Chippewa river and one night narrowly escaped severe injury, if not death, when the heavy roof of the chapel, behind which was his little bedroom, crashed down on him.

Among the Nomadic Sioux

While in Mendota he paid a visit to Little Crow's village at Kaposia (near South St. Paul) where a battle had taken place between the Sioux and the Chippewa and ministered to the wounded through an interpreter. He gave much time and thought to the completion of the text of his Catechism of Christian Doctrine in the Sioux language and availed himself of the presence of expert interpreters to adapt it to the capacity of the redmen.

He decided to open a permanent mission at Little Prairie (now, Chaska) where J. B. Faribault had his trading post for the Sioux, and ultimately built a log chapel, 15 by 30 feet, at a cost of about $250.00. Three years after leaving Chaska he wrote Bishop Loras that the chapel was in danger of being burned by the Indians if not removed to another place. Father Ravoux requested the Bishop to allow him to take it to St. Paul but the Bishop refused as St. Paul was in the Diocese of Milwaukee. There was need of a chapel at Wabasha and the Bishop allowed the Catholics in the locality to dismantle the building and float it down the Minnesota and the Mississippi to Wabasha where it was re-erected. Its subsequent history is unknown.[4]

In a letter to Bishop Loras, dated January 3, 1844, he complained about the time he had to give to manual labor—four months helping to build a house—instead "of studying Sioux and visiting the sick". He needed a horse to visit the Indians in outlying districts, a wagon to transport supplies to the mission, vestments and altar linens for Mass, a silver receptacle for the Holy Oils, a breviary, crosses and medals and personal effects. Only fifteen or twenty Indians are under instructions; in a month he baptized only four adults and two children and blessed two marriages. A month later he informed the Bishop that "the progress of religion among the Indians is not very consoling . . . Conversions are rare". Drink is an obstacle and the bad example of some christians. Some Indians hear the word of God with attention and respect; the fear of ridicule and of poison, threatened by the Medicine Chiefs, keep many from openly favoring Christianity. He has no difficulty with the language. "I know enough of the Sioux tongue to explain the truths of Christianity to the savages and to hear confessions". Then, too, "Calumny attacks us with force". We are here to enrich ourselves and to exact from the Indians pay for the instruction we give them. Despite reports that may have come to the Bishop there is no enmity between him and Father Godfert.

Father Ravoux endured the greatest hardships while he lived at Little Prairie ministering to the Sioux. He had not even the most meager comforts of civilized life. He lived in an unheated house; said Mass in a chapel where the wine froze in the chalice; lacked blankets and other coverings for his bed which he shared with the catechist. He had no servant to cultivate the garden, to look after his horse, to enable him to retain the respect of the savages who disdained him for doing menial work. He did his own cooking. He wore "scandalous pantaloons" because there was no one to repair his old clothes: rarely did he have bread to eat.[5]

To add to his tribulations he was given an assistant in the person of Reverend Antoine Godfert, ordained in Dubuque on September 11, 1842, an imprudent, obstinate young missionary who sorely tried his patience before he was recalled by the Bishop.

Father Galtier visited them on one occasion and wrote Bishop Loras: Their furniture is pitiable; they have only one chair, half-broken, which fell to them by charity; a single table knife, one coffee cup, 2 spoons, 2 napkins, the rest in proportion to their poverty. In spite of these discomforts and because of his sufferings Father Ravoux had all the merit that a holy priest can desire in his ministry.

While stationed in Little Prairie Father Ravoux wrote a catechism, a prayer book and a series of instructions in Sioux and had them published in book form on Father Cretin's printing press at Prairie du Chien in 1843. It took two weeks to make the trip to Dubuque on account of the floating ice in the river. After visiting Bishop Loras he went to Prairie du Chien to supervise the publication of his book entitled: "Wakantanka Ti Ki Chanku" (The Path to the House of God). The original manuscript of this catechism and hymn-book is in the museum of the Catholic Historical Society of St. Paul. It was donated by Brother Murelian who in the middle nineties found it, together with hundreds of loose sheets, in the attic of the old building alongside the St. Paul Cathedral.[6] In addition to this precious document the museum has three reprints of the Catechism presented by Father Jerome Hunt, O.S.B., veteran missionary among the Sioux at Fort Totten, North Dakota. Father Ravoux' work in Little Prairie bore fruit when, in the early months of 1844, he baptized twenty-three Indians and half-breeds. In a register of baptisms and marriages, owned by the Catholic Historical Society of St. Paul, he records 43 baptisms and 7 marriages between October 10, 1841, and December 21, 1843, 53 baptisms and 4 marriages in 1844, and 6 baptisms in 1845. The prospects for the future of the mission were very encouraging when, in the spring of that year, he was sent to St. Peter's to take Father Galtier's place temporarily, as he thought, but in reality for good.

In his new field of labor he had under his charge not only Mendota but St. Paul, Lake Pepin, St. Croix and St. Anthony where he began the construction of a church in 1849, making periodic trips of inspection up the Mississippi in a canoe. It is not improbable that he said Mass from time to time in these localities before chapels were available.

In a letter to Bishop Loras on January 5, 1847, he relates with evident pleasure that

> At midnight Mass the chapel at St. Peter, which is 20 by 40, was crowded and in a room from which the altar can be seen there were about 20 persons. There were several good singers who sang hymns for an hour and a half before Mass. For four hours the chapel was filled. During the holiday season about 30 persons received the sacraments. The Catholic soldiers gave me $75. Several families made a subscription of forty dollars, though I had not asked for anything. Several drunkards have signed the temperance pledge.[7]

Missionary Trips

During these years, in addition to ministering to his scattered flock, he made a number of missionary trips to bring the benefits of religion to Catholic settlers and pagan Indians in widely separated localities. Two of his most extensive journeys took him as far west as the Missouri river in South Dakota. On August 8, 1845,[8] accompanied by a guide, he set out for Vermillion on its eastern bank via Traverse des Sioux, Little Rock, Sleepy Eye and Pipestone and on the way saw thousands of buffalo grazing on the lush grass of the prairie. His sleep under the stars was often broken by the barking of prairie dogs, or wolves, following the herds. At Vermillion he instructed the four or five Catholic families living there and baptized five children. A memorial tablet erected, on July 4, 1939, by the Catholic Order of Foresters of Aberdeen near Sand Lake, seven and a half miles north of Columbia, in Brown County, says that "In 1845 near this spot in a Cuthead Indian village Father Alexandra (sic) Ravoux celebrated the first Mass of record in South Dakota"—a statement that can scarcely be upheld in view of the fact that Father De Smet, S. J., was in the state as early as 1839.

On the return journey from the west he had several formal repasts with the Sioux but ate sparingly of the dog meat provided as a delicacy in his honor, and arrived home, by way of Des Moines and Mankato, without mishap.

Two years later, in July, 1847,[9] he set out to visit Fort Pierre on the west bank of the Missouri where a number of Catholic families resided. On the way he waded through swamps, crossed timberless, rolling prairies and nearly famished from drought. Towards the end of the month he reached his destination, Fort Pierre, the principal trading-post of the American Fur Company in the Northwest, where he married one couple, instructed the Catholics, baptized thirteen of their children, and fifty-five from Sioux families at the request of their parents. The baptismal register already referred to contains the names of 89 persons baptized in Fort Pierre and vicinity, 1 at Traverse des Sioux, 2 at Lac-qui-parle and 2 at Council Bluffs. Two or three years previously Father De Smet, the famous Jesuit missionary, had visited the locality and baptized several children and they had not forgotten his teaching. Father Ravoux took occasion to preach to the Brules and the Blackfeet Sioux in the vicinity and was heard with great attention and evidence of respect for the Word of God. At the Grand Bend of the Missouri he baptized eighteen children and an eighty year old Indian. Chief Four Bears would have him remain among them as a missionary but his time was limited and he took advantage of a steamboat to St. Louis for a visit with Archbishop Kenrick whence he returned by steamer to Mendota after an absence of two and a half months. As a result of this visit, he wrote Bishop Loras on September 21, 1847, suggesting the establishment of a mission among the Gros Ventres Indians of the Missouri river who did not speak Sioux but live in villages nearly all the year and cultivate the soil.

But his work among the Indians was only incidental. Had his superior so willed he would have preferred to spend the rest of his days among them, making himself as far as possible one of them that he might the more fruitfully inculcate the principles of Christianity. He recognized their good qualities but did not shut his eyes to the defects of their character. As pagans they lived according to the natural law because they knew no better. He maintained that in many ways they were not inferior to the whites. They loved their children and mourned their dead with loud expressions of grief. They tortured themselves to curry favor with their gods; and showed excessive cruelty in dealing with their enemies. When the truths of the gospel were presented to them they reacted as palefaces do. Some accepted its doctrine and code of morals while others elected to follow their own inclinations. They believed in a Great Spirit whom they invoked but they worshipped a large number of deities and offered them sacrifices and prayers for success in war and in the chase, for health and protection from evil. They feared the power of the spirits and propitiated them by offerings and sacrifices on stone altars. They believed in a future life and brought to the grave food for the departed one.

In 1847 Father Ravoux published a booklet of six lectures in Dubuque in which he charged the Reverend Dr. Williamson, a missionary at Little Crow (Kaposia, now South St. Paul) with using his knowledge of medicine as an excuse for visiting Catholic families and distributing a pamphlet written in French attacking the Catholic Church. In this brochure he refuted the false statements of Dr. Williamson and followed it up by warning the faithful against him at Mass on Sundays in St. Paul and

Mendota, thus effectively silencing him and saving the faithful from danger to their faith.

Addition to Log Chapel

For several years after the departure of Father Galtier, Father Ravoux alternated on Sundays between Mendota and St. Paul, preaching in French and English. For half that time he was two consecutive Sundays in Mendota and the third in St. Paul, but as the latter continued to outstrip the former in population and importance he found it necessary to say Mass every second Sunday in each place. In 1847 he built an addition to the original Saint Paul chapel to accommodate the increasing congregation, many of whom came from Little Canada, Stillwater, St. Anthony and other places, so that the faithful in St. Paul and vicinity outnumbered those at Mendota and Fort Snelling and needed more frequent opportunities for the practice of their faith. He appealed to the Bishop of Milwaukee, in whose diocese St. Paul actually was, to send a priest to minister to the faithful, but without avail.[10] He wanted one who would reside permanently in St. Paul. In his letter to Father Ravoux on January 31, 1850, Bishop Henni forgave him for the "kind lecture" he had read him, and expressed the hope that before long a new diocese would be erected in the Territory of Minnesota, organized on March 3, 1849, and that St. Paul would be the episcopal see. This was good news for Father Ravoux who was alone for six years in his ministrations to the congregation made up of Catholics scattered along the Minnesota as far as Traverse des Sioux, up and down the Mississippi valley, and near St. Croix Falls—French, English, Sioux and Chippewa. He rejoiced, therefore, when he learned that his friend, Father Cretin, Vicar General of the Diocese of Dubuque, had been nominated first Bishop of St. Paul and strongly urged him to accept the appointment. The establishment of this frontier diocese marked the inauguration of a new era in the history of the Church in the Northwest and brought relief to the Bishops of Milwaukee and Dubuque from whose immense territories the new diocese was carved.

The change was to mean added responsibilities for Father Ravoux. The energy and foresight which had crowned with success his ministry among the Sioux and at St. Peter's would be more necessary to the new regime. The nascent Diocese of St. Paul would owe much to the practical mind and prophetic vision of this pioneer priest. He took counsel of the future and made provision for the temporal as well as the spiritual needs of the coming years. In the development of the diocese about to be organized Father Ravoux was to play an important role and live to see his plans and hopes realized beyond his most sanguine dreams. He was to leave an indelible impress on the history of the Church in Minnesota and earn an enduring niche in the temple of her founders.

Father Ravoux urged Bishop-elect Cretin to come to St. Paul at once and buy property for a new cathedral site telling him that entire blocks in a suitable location were getting scarce and more costly every day. When the Bishop-elect did not come before his departure for France to be consecrated Father Ravoux bought from Vital Guerin for $900.00, twenty-two lots bounded by Wabasha, St. Peter, Sixth and Seventh Streets. It was one of the choicest locations in the city, even as it is today, a most fortunate transaction for the nascent church and a source of revenue for the diocese. When Bishop Cretin arrived in St. Paul in 1851 he paid for the property and received the deeds. The property is still owned by the diocese but occupied by revenue-producing buildings.

It was the privilege of Father Ravoux to meet the Bishop on his arrival and escort him from the Landing at the foot of Jackson Street to the Cathedral, the enlarged log chapel, and the episcopal palace an even more primitive log shanty, about eighteen feet square and a story and a half high. The Bishop was not surprised at this evidence of the poverty of the Cathedral and of the new diocese for he had been informed of everything. He was accustomed to pioneer conditions, to poverty and hardship, and he made himself at home in his new surroundings.

First Stone Church

After the installation of Bishop Cretin Father Ravoux, appointed Vicar General on July 5, 1851, returned to his pastoral duties among the half-breeds of St. Peter's who constituted the majority of his congregation of about four hundred souls.[11] In 1853 he replaced the log chapel built by Father Galtier in 1842 with a stone church, 75 by 35 feet in size, with a small tower, on a more commanding site at a cost of $4,425.80, all of which was paid before 1856. This is the present church of Mendota with the exception of the larger tower and loftier spire which replaced the original and which was blown down in a recent windstorm. It is the oldest stone church in Minnesota. He remained in the parish as pastor till February, 1857.

During these years whenever the Bishop wanted to consult his Vicar General he summoned him by hanging a flag from the casement of his window which could be seen from St. Peter's as there were no sky-scrapers to intercept the view.[12]

In 1853 Father Ravoux was sent to Europe to place John Ireland and Thomas O'Gorman in the preparatory seminary of Meximieux and to secure recruits for the missionary work of the diocese.[13] On the return journey he left Le Havre for Southampton on May 24, 1854, with seven seminarians—Anatole Oster, Louis E. Caillet, Claude Robert, George

Keller, Valentine Sommereisen, Felix Tissot, and Francis Hurth. In England each one was given a dictionary and an English grammar. They left Southampton on May 26 on the steamer "Herman" and landed in New York on June 7. On the journey west they spent Sunday in Buffalo, assisted at Mass in the Church of St. Louis, and reached Galena on June 15, the feast of Corpus Christi. After a brief visit to Dubuque to receive the blessing of Bishop Loras they came to St. Paul where they were heartily welcomed by Bishop Cretin.

RT. REV. JOSEPH CRETIN, D. D.
First Bishop of St. Paul
1851–1857

Chapter VI

ST. PAUL AND ITS FIRST BISHOP
RT. REV. JOSEPH CRETIN, D. D.

1799–1857

T HE State of Minnesota has had a unique history. At one time, with the rest of the continent, it was part of the overseas dominion of their Catholic Majesties, Ferdinand and Isabella of Spain, by right of discovery confirmed by a decree of Pope Alexander VI issued on May 4, 1493. Subsequently it was included in New France, that vast unexplored area in Central North America over which their Christian Majesties, the Kings of France, exercised imperial sway after the historic ceremony at Sault Ste. Marie in 1671. In the seventeenth and eighteenth centuries it was part of the Louisiana Territory of 900,000 square miles ceded by France to the United States on April 30, 1803, for $15,000,000 or less than three cents an acre. On April 6, 1682, La Salle, the first to trace the Mississippi to its mouth, took possession of the lands drained and watered by it, south of the Illinois river, in the name of his sovereign, Louis XIV, in whose honor he called it Louisiana. But France did not limit her claim to this lower region but embraced within it all the territory between the Gulf of Mexico and the British boundary, the Mississippi and the Rockies, an area as large as Europe, out of which was formed, in whole or part, fourteen states of the union, among them Minnesota.

Minnesota occupies the most northerly section of what was Louisiana and part of the territory ceded to the United States by Great Britain in 1818. A glance at the map shows that it is nearly bisected by the Mississippi river and a line drawn due north from its headwaters to the western shore of the Lake of the Woods. It was under the flag of France from 1671 to 1763[1] when France ceded to England the whole of Canada and all the territory east of the Mississippi, and to Spain, in 1762, all to the west of the river. From that time each half of Minnesota was under a different flag until the United States became an independent nation on September 3, 1783. Even after it came under the Stars and Stripes the area of Minnesota was parcelled out among different Territories until the whole was included in Michigan Territory from 1834 to 1836 and in Wisconsin Territory from 1836 to 1838. Once more it was bisected and the western portion became part of Iowa Territory from 1836 to 1846 when, after three years of unorganized existence, it was united to the eastern half taken from Wisconsin to form the Territory of Minnesota on March 3, 1849. The new Territory, therefore, embraced all the lands lying between Iowa and the Canadian boundary and west of Wisconsin to the Missouri and White Earth rivers in the Dakotas, an area of about 166,000 square miles. This immense territory, of which the part between the Mississippi and St. Croix rivers had been ceded to the United States in 1837 by the Sioux and Chippewa Indians and opened to white settlers, became the Diocese of St. Paul on July 19, 1850, with the Right Reverend Joseph Cretin, Vicar General of Dubuque, as first Bishop of St. Paul, its capital city.

The ecclesiastical history of the Diocese of St. Paul is as varied and unique as the civil history of the state. More than two centuries before it was organized into a separate diocese it was under the spiritual jurisdiction of the Archbishop of Rouen and then of the Bishops of Quebec. After the Louisiana purchase it belonged successively in whole or in part to the dioceses of Baltimore, New Orleans, St. Louis, Bardstown, Milwaukee and Dubuque. When erected into a diocese St. Paul was assigned to the Archdiocese of St. Louis as suffragan until February 12, 1875, when it was transferred to the Archdiocese of Milwaukee. It became a Metropolitan See in its own right on May 4, 1888.

The Frontier Village

The choice of St. Paul, the Territorial capital, as an episcopal see was fraught with far-reaching consequences for the Northwest. The need of a new ecclesiastical jurisdiction in the northern part of the diocese of Dubuque was apparent for some time before any official action was taken to establish it. Pembina in the north, a much older settlement, was a rival of St. Paul and in some ways more important, and the possibility of its becoming the see-city of a new diocese was considered; but it did not materialize probably because it was too inaccessible, too far removed from civilization and too near the Diocese of St. Boniface only sixty miles distant across the border. St. Paul was chosen by the Fathers of the Seventh Provincial Council held in Baltimore in May, 1849.[2] An announcement of their action reached the Northwest on January 9 of the next year when the Minnesota Pioneer made known to its readers that the Catholic Church was "about to found a diocese in Minnesota with the seat of the Bishop at St. Paul". There was no intimation that the Council had proposed the name of the first occupant of the see. It was not until November 21 that it was announced, on the authority of the Dubuque Express, that Joseph Cretin, Vicar General of the Diocese of Dubuque, had been appointed Bishop of St. Paul.

The frontier village of St. Paul was the logical place for a bishop even though it was almost unheard-of when the Territory of Minnesota was formed on March 3, 1849. A decade before that time it was not even a name on the map. If any one thought about it, it was regarded as the western suburb of Pig's Eye, a settlement further down the river named after its founder and first citizen, Pierre Parrant, who had a peculiar cast of eye that suggested the sobriquet and eventually the name of the locality which, however, never became current among the French colonists. After Father Galtier dedicated the log chapel to the Apostle of the Gentiles on the bluff overlooking the river, Pig's Eye hid its diminished head and the star of St. Paul rose above the horizon.

The origin of the future city was most humble. It was born and baptized on November 1, 1841. The primitive log chapel blessed on that day by Father Galtier was its most important and, with one exception, its only building, a landmark on Bench Street facing the river. There was one thing in its favor. It had a picturesque and commanding site overlooking the Mississippi from the east, even though it had not a dollar's worth of taxable property. It had a future visualized by few, if any. In 1843 it had three or four log houses and twelve white people. In 1846 it was one of the "points" on the upper Mississippi where steamboats stopped to discharge freight. The first frame house in the village was owned by Louis Robert. It stood on Bench Street, at the corner of Robert. It was destroyed by fire but rebuilt in 1847. In 1846 there were ten families and a white population of fifty. When St. Paul became the capital of the Territory it had a population of fewer than nine hundred,[3] mostly French Canadians and half-breeds, housed in scattered log shanties with tamarack roofs or in more pretentious frame dwellings. There was not a brick or stone building in the place. It had three hotels, several churches and a number of saloons. It had just acquired its first newspaper, the Minnesota Pioneer, and had one mail a week by team from Prairie du Chien. In a word, St. Paul in 1849 was not unlike the small country village of today with narrow, winding, unpaved, unlighted streets, unpainted, if not delapidated houses, and a few stores catering to the farming population.

Bench Street was the principal thoroughfare. According to the Minnesota Pioneer (1850)

the people in St. Paul seem to express a general wish that no building should be erected on the margin of the bluff, on the south side of Bench street. That street, when built up, as it soon will be with good buildings, from one extreme to the other of the town, will be unsurpassed for beauty by any street in any town on the river. The side of it which is left open, overlooking the river, ought to have a side-walk laid, of those flat rocks which can be so easily quarried at the bluff below the Catholic church; and there ought also to be a row of elm shade trees planted on that side, through the whole length of the town. Thus, Bench street may soon become one of the pleasantest promenades in the world.

These superlative expectations were doomed to disappointment. The first side walk was laid in 1851 on Third Street between Cedar and Minnesota. Bench Street, as a name and a thoroughfare, disappeared.

But the town was about to experience a boom in population and importance. For nearly a decade of years the steamboats plying between St. Louis and Fort Snelling had been calling at St. Paul's Landing to discharge freight and passengers, tourists and immigrants, and soon its streets were filled with a motley crowd in which the voyageur and half-breed in picturesque garb and the blanketed and painted Indian mingled and fraternized and in which hostile Indian tribes slaughtered one another. Immigrants came in increasing numbers bringing tents and bedding to provide temporary housing quarters until permanent dwellings were available.[4] The town became more and more a center of trade, a focus for business that increased with the development of the surrounding territory. It began to shed the swaddling clothes of infancy and put on the garb of maturity.

Most of the business of the city came by steamboat from the South and ox cart from the North. The latter increased considerably between 1851 when one hundred and two Red River carts came to St. Paul and 1858 when six hundred brought furs from the North and took back groceries and provisions.

These carts were two-wheeled vehicles, made of wood and leather, without iron, drawn by oxen hitched singly with raw hide harness and driven by half-breeds in picturesque garb. It took thirty days to make the trip between Pembina and St. Paul and sometimes longer due to the condition of the roads. The staple food of the drivers was pemmican, raw buffalo meat dried and powdered, mixed with tallow and pressed into bags made from buffalo hides. The cars squeaked terribly for want of oil in the axles.

In 1854 when the city was incorporated there were three dailies—The Pioneer, The Democrat and The Minnesotian—and the next year two others made their appearance—The Times and The Free Press. All travel was by boat and stage. The Milwaukee and Chicago Railroad did not reach Prairie du Chien till 1857 on its way to St. Paul. In 1851, however, St. Paul was ready to receive its first bishop.

First Bishop in the Northwest

More than a year elapsed before the Holy See acted on the petition of the prelates of the Seventh Provincial Council of Baltimore, held in May, 1849, asking for the erection of a new diocesan see in Minnesota Territory and the appointment of Father Cretin, missionary and Vicar General of Dubuque, as first incumbent. The delay was caused by the revolutionary disturbance in Rome which forced Pope Pius IX into exile at Gaeta, near Naples, on November 24, 1848, from which he did not return until April 12, 1850. During this time there was no meeting of the Sacred Congregations to transact the business of the Church. As soon as order was restored the petition of the American bishops was given due consideration and the Bulls of erection of the Diocese of St. Paul were issued on July 19, 1850, and four days later Father Cretin was named Bishop. He received the Bulls of appointment towards the end of September and records the fact that "he was no less astonished than all others at such a message". Before accepting it he

'took counsel of God and of experienced men,' had recourse to prayer and meditation, and 'believing that more labors than pleasures and more humiliation than glory awaited him in that new Diocese, where everything was to be built up, he submitted his shoulders with trembling to the cross.'

Among those whom he consulted on this grave matter was Father Ravoux, pastor of St. Peter's and in charge of the little flock in St. Paul, who urged him not to hesitate to accept the appointment and told him it would be a serious sin not to submit to the will of the Supreme Pontiff. Evidently Father Ravoux changed his mind on this point when, nearly twenty years later, he petitioned the Holy Father to revoke his own appointment as first Vicar Apostolic of Montana.

Before his consecration, in fact before he definitely decided to accept the appointment, Father Cretin wrote the Society for the Propagation of the Faith in Paris to ascertain whether he could rely on it for the financial help indispensable for a diocese in which everything had to be created, a diocese, as he explained, extending from Lake Superior to the Missouri river and from the Iowa state line to the Canadian border. Within that immense territory there was only one priest for the whites within a radius of one hundred miles from St. Paul, and only two missionaries for thirty thousand savages. Funds would be needed for the erection of a Cathedral, a residence for the bishop and clergy, schools for boys and girls, funds to educate clerical students, to support missionaries among the Indians, to purchase property that would be a source of revenue for the church later on—all of which would cost over 130,000 francs or $26,000.[5] The diocese had a Catholic population of about three thousand. The answer received from the Society was:

We are very sorry, but you came too late; our funds are spent; there is a large deficit in this year's receipts; and we have promised more than we can fulfil.

Far from being grieved at this refusal he was pleased with it for he thought he had found an excuse for refusing the appointment. Bishop Devie of Belley thought otherwise. The Apostles, he reminded the Bishop-elect,

began the conquest of the world with nothing, and the first bishops of America did not have the help of the Propagation of the Faith. Therefore, prepare yourself immediately for your consecration, and do not lose any more time in deliberation and hesitation.

He felt, however, that the Society would help him as far as possible with the limited funds at its disposal.

The Bishop's Youth and Training

An apostolic man was Joseph Cretin, first Bishop of St. Paul. In his veins flowed the blood of ancestors who were martyred for the faith. A grand uncle, Benoit Poncet, a Carthusian Monk, who refused to apostatize in the days of the Commune was executed on the guillotine. His parents, Joseph Cretin and Mary Jane Mery, were characterized by deep piety and staunch adherence to the Faith. Their home sheltered proscribed priests who said Mass on its hidden altar and dispensed the sacraments to those who gathered in secrecy for the celebration of the Holy Mysteries. His mother spent some time in prison because of her religious convictions. Among their descendants were holy priests and devoted nuns whose lives edified the people and merited graces for the Church in France at the close of the revolution.

Joseph, the youngest of four children born to this devoted couple, first saw the light of day at Montluel, in the department of Ain, France, on December 10, 1799,[6] and was baptized soon after birth, if not on the day itself. There is no record of his baptism due, no doubt, to the religious persecution of that revolutionary period. Montluel, a typical French village that traces its history back to the Roman era, is about twelve miles east of Lyons on the picturesque road to Geneva in Switzerland. His father, an inn-keeper and baker, was a man of competence and prominence in the community, whose ancestors came from Lorraine; his mother was a native of Montluel whose parental home not infrequently offered sanctuary to hunted priests.

Young Joseph received first Communion on Trinity Sunday, May 12, 1812; was educated in the primary and presbyteral schools of Montluel and Courcieux; made his classical studies in the preparatory seminary of Meximieux; his philosophical at L'Argentière and Alix and his theological at St. Sulpice in Paris which he entered on October 20, 1820. He received

Minor Orders on December 21, 1821; subdeaconship on June 1, 1822 deaconship on May 4, 1823; and priesthood on December 21, 1823.

In the meantime Montluel, formerly in the Diocese of Lyons, became part of the reorganized Diocese of Belley[7] of which Joseph also when ordained subdeacon became a subject under the jurisdiction of the Right Reverend Raymond Devie, its first bishop from 1823 to 1852.

During his first year as a seminarian in St. Sulpice Joseph Cretin devoted much time and attention to his personal sanctification, and to that end wrote "Method and Practices for the Sanctification of all my actions and for spending the whole day in union with O. L. J. C.".[8] The book, five by four inches, bound in leather, contains sixty-three pages, stitched to the cover, and written in a clear, bold hand, sometimes very small, but always perfectly legible, a work of love, no doubt, to which he evidently attached great importance. On the title page is the injunction: "You are earnestly requested not to read further on. XXX, L.J.C., 1821"

The means of sanctification to be employed are set forth as follows:
1st. Often to think that God is my first principle and my last end; that from Him I have received all my faculties, to be used for His glory; that all the actions directed to any other end, are not only lost for heaven, but that they also bring on the withdrawal of His grace, frequently sin, and its punishment. God is a jealous God; He searches the heart and the loins.
2nd Often to ask myself when passing from one exercise to the other, what am I about to do? What am I doing, for whom and what purpose?
3rd. To propose to myself as model of my actions, sometimes our Lord, sometimes the B. V., or St. Joseph, or St. Louis of Gonzaga. To ask myself: how would they have performed this action? spent this recreation?
4th. To perform the present action as if the last of my life.
5th. To act as if there were but God and myself on earth.
6th. To see in my superiors and in my fellow students only our L. J. C.
7th. To examine after each action the human motives that may have crept into my intention. If I find myself guilty, I shall humble myself before God, ask His pardon and impose some penance upon myself, such as to kiss the ground, recite a pater and ave, or pinch myself, etc.
8th. Frequently to ask of God to make me more humble, more void of self; to utterly destroy in me self love; to often tell him that I wish to do nothing but for His love and His greater glory.
I may (with advantage) propose each day to myself one of these motives.

This rule of life was not merely for seminary days but for all the years of his priestly and episcopal career and how faithfully he observed it those who lived with him and knew intimately his daily life could attest.

Father Cretin had just passed his twenty-fourth birthday when he was ordained in the chapel of the episcopal residence at Belley, the same chapel where, twenty-eight years later, he was to be consecrated first Bishop of St. Paul by the same prelate. His first Mass was said at midnight on Christmas eve in the Church of St. Stephen in Montluel in presence of the members of his family, all of whom received Holy Communion from his hands. The assistant priest was the Reverend John S. Bazin, later a missionary in Alabama, and third Bishop of Vincennes,[9] Indiana. At a later hour Father Cretin celebrated another Mass in the Church of Notre Dame in the same city.

In the Home of Voltaire

A few days afterwards he was sent as curate to Ferney, near the Swiss canton of Geneva, the home of Voltaire, the infidel leader of the anti-christian hosts of the eighteenth century, between 1758 and 1778. The town was a stronghold of Calvinism. During the French Revolution little of the Catholic faith survived in it. But a new era dawned for it when the Diocese of Belley was reorganized and Bishop Divie made his first pastoral visit to it in November, 1823. It was the one parish in the diocese where there was an organized community of Protestants.

The only chapel in the town, once owned by Voltaire, was a small stone structure entirely inadequate to the needs of the parish, and Father Cretin was commissioned by his bishop to solicit subscriptions throughout France for a larger one, a task which he completed with eminent success. The new church was consecrated on November 8, 1826,[10] in presence of a notable gathering of prelates, civic officials, priests and laity from the neighboring towns in France and Switzerland. Bishop Devie was the consecrator and celebrated the Mass, the Archbishop of Besançon preached and Father Cretin was master of ceremonies. Five years later he was made pastor of the parish. In the meantime he founded and directed a college for boys—now a flourishing institution[11] which ranks among the foremost of its kind in France—and withstood the fury of a mob that pillaged a convent and threatened to destroy the college, by rallying to his aid the students and the better element of the population. His sincerity of soul, unfailing charity and urbanity of manner disarmed prejudice and won universal respect and sympathy. He was esteemed by all for his civic and religious virtues and his success in imparting religious instruction. He was a diligent director of souls, prudent and tactful, firm and inflexible when duty required it and rigid in complying with its demands. "He taught his fellow-Catholics the lesson of virile courage in the defense of civic and religious rights. He was brave and aggressive when bravery and aggressiveness were needed."

During all the years at Ferney Father Cretin was obsessed with the thought of being a missionary in pagan lands. He yearned to go to Cochin China to be a martyr like his friend, Father Chanel, S. M., who was put to death by the savages of Futuna in Western Oceanica. He offered his services to a Bishop in China and was already on his way to the seaport to sail for the Orient when he was overtaken by his father and compelled to abandon his pious design. His dream of a missionary career was to be realized but not in the manner he expected. In 1838 Bishop Loras of Dubuque, his former professor and friend at Meximieux, came to France seeking recruits to evangelize the vast territory confided to him in Iowa which then comprised Minnesota and part of the Dakotas. After much importuning the Bishop of Belley gave Father Cretin permission to leave the diocese, temporarily,[12] and go to America. He refused to give him "full and entire permission" to sever all connections with it.

A Missionary in Iowa

Secretly, almost furtively, without a word to family or friends, he left Ferney on August 15, 1838, for Le Havre where he joined Bishop Loras, Father Pelamourgues, and four subdeacons—Lucien Galtier, Augustine Ravoux, Remigius Petiot and Jacques Causse—for the voyage across the Atlantic. After forty-five days of a stormy passage they landed in New York. The subdeacons were sent to Mount St. Mary Seminary in Emmitsburg, Md., to prepare for ordination and learn English, while Bishop Loras and Father Cretin journeyed to St. Louis, via Philadelphia and Pittsburgh, by train, canal boat and stage,[13] arriving at their destination on December 3, 1838, where they were forced to remain all winter waiting for the opening of navigation on the Mississippi. They did not pass the months in idleness but gave missions[14] and retreats in English which Bishop Loras spoke fluently and in French. On February 9, 1839, Father Cretin went to Harrisonville, Ill., thirty miles south of St. Louis, to amplify and perfect his knowledge of English, to study American ways and the condition of religion in rural parishes. It was the scene of his earliest missionary labors in America. Here he first preached in English on Sunday to the Catholics of the neighborhood. "Both these saintly prelates edified and charmed the Bishop (Rosati) and all whom they met with their exemplary presence, their learning and zeal in teaching and administering the sacraments". Bishop Loras and Father Cretin reached Dubuque by boat on April 19, 1839. The following Sunday the Bishop was installed in his see. He appointed Father Cretin Vicar General and pastor of the Cathedral parish while he and Father Pelamourgues of Davenport made a trip to Fort Snelling in April, 1839, where he said Mass for the first time in what is now the Archdiocese of St. Paul, gave spiritual comfort to the little group of Catholics in that vicinity and promised to send them a priest the following year.[15] On the Bishop's return preparations were made for the consecration of St. Raphael's Cathedral on August 15. In the evening of that day Father Cretin preached on the spiritual and temporal blessings granted to the faithful in our holy temples in presence of a capacity audience of Catholics and non-Catholics.

The new Vicar General was a remarkable man whose talents and culture were only equalled by his kindness of heart, industry and deep humility. He was busy about many things. He "was much engaged in the Cathedral, had the principal direction of a higher school established at Dubuque, (which developed into the present Loras College) where he was frequently one of the professors, and also attended several missions in the territory including Garnavillo, Guttenberg, New Vienna and Fort Atkinson, where churches were built".[16] He also visited scattered families on the Mississippi and Chippewa rivers, riding a small black pony that could travel sixty to seventy miles a day—a spirited animal which more than once threw its reverend rider heels over head.

He came to Prairie du Chien in 1839 but his duties as Vicar General required him to spend considerable time in Dubuque. In Prairie du Chien he erected the first church of St. Gabriel. In September, 1841, he made a trip up the Mississippi as far as St. Peter's where Father Galtier was pastor, his first visit to Minnesota.

In addition to his duties at Dubuque and Prairie du Chien Father Cretin was appointed a special missionary among the Winnebagoes[17] by Bishop Loras and, at the behest of his saintly superior, braved the dangers of the wilderness and endured the privations of frontier life to civilize and christianize the untutored savages. He began his apostolic labors among them in 1843 when Father Petiot was driven from their reservation at the instigation of Reverend David Lowry, a Presbyterian minister, who was the sub-agent. At that time Father Cretin was in his forty-fourth year and found it quite difficult to master the Winnebago tongue which he finally succeeded in doing in order that he might the better labor for their conversion and protect them against dishonest traders and unscrupulous liquor venders. He made many trips from Prairie du Chien over the military road to Fort Atkinson on the Turkey River where the reservation was located. His reception from those in authority was far from cordial. He met with opposition from Lowry who was finally removed from office by President Tyler in 1844. Father Cretin was recommended for the position as "a highly intelligent and useful man and universally respected by all classes", but Governor Chambers refused to consider him. Nor would the Governor permit Father Cretin to establish a school even at a distance of several miles from the reservation, although the Indians clamored for Catholic missionaries and teachers. The Governor and the Protestant element in charge of the agency could not appreciate the Catholic viewpoint regarding the salvation of immortal souls, especially Indian souls, and there was undoubtedly bigotry on the part of those who did not want the redmen to come under the influence of Catholic teachers. Notwithstanding the opposition, Father Cretin built a log school on the Turkey River at some distance from the Fort and carried on his work for a time. He records the fact that it bore fruit and when he returned to Dubuque he regretted that there were no Indians to be converted as he had under his charge "only civilized people such as they are". He loved the work among the Winnebagoes in spite of the physical discomforts of which he spoke in a letter to his sister—living in Indian houses, devoured by gnats and endangered by rattle snakes. The Directory for 1847 made note of the fact that "He has to bear every kind of opposition, even from the Government, which forbids him to keep any school; or, if allowed, it is on inadmissable terms". He found the Indians well disposed and anxious to have the ministrations of priests rather than of the ministers favored by the government. Nor did he lose interest in their welfare even after the Government bought their lands in 1848 and removed them to Long Prairie in Minnesota, destined to be the scene of his episcopal labors.

In the letter to his sister above referred to he stated in unequivocal terms his attitude towards worldly possessions.

> For myself I have no intention of possessing a home in this world. I shall not be caught in the snares of the evil one through the allurements of worldly possessions. It would be easy for me for a small sum to acquire possession of a large farm in the most pleasant, fertile and healthy part of the country; but let me repeat again, I came into this country for no such contemptible purpose.

Nearly sixty years after Father Cretin left Prairie du Chien a parishioner [18] who knew him very well recorded her reminiscences and impressions of him:

> So pious, so full of zeal, so benign in manners. Such fatherly love and kindness towards all the people to whom he made frequent visits, and when there was discord or ill feeling in families or among neighbors it was always settled amicably . . .
> His zeal knew no bounds, although encumbered by many duties, yet he wanted more, would sacrifice anything, undergo any hardships or privations for the glory of God. Always prompt on sick calls day or night, no matter what the weather was, and in many cases no conveyances and had to walk, not a word, not a murmur. He taught two schools, a day school for girls and a night school for boys, both schools aggregated about 60 or 75 pupils.

She referred to his mission among the Winnebagoes on Turkey River where the Protestant minister in charge put all kinds of obstacles in his way, but soon the mission was "running in good shape". He made numerous converts and had a catechism class of 40 or 50. The removal of the Indians to another part of the country put an end to his mission work.

> His diet was of the most abstemious kind and he would deny himself the minutest comforts of life. His couch was nothing but a thin coverlet

spread on the boards. His meals were mostly bread, butter and potatoes. He lived alone and did his own cooking . . . All virtues and attributes of a Saint were conspicuously blended in his nature.

At an earlier date Father Mazzuchelli, O.P., in his "Memoirs," p. 265, paid Father Cretin the tribute of saying that his charity, zeal, learning, his entire holy and blameless life at Prairie du Chien from 1841 will be forever held in benediction by that people, for whom he labored so earnestly to fix deep into their souls an enlightened piety. To him is owing almost all the spiritual good wrought in the parish of St. Gabriel and also the present fine condition of the church which combines an elegant simplicity with solidity and spaciousness.

Iowa was made a state in 1846 but Minnesota and eastern Dakota continued to be part of the Diocese of Dubuque. In that year Bishop Loras sent Father Cretin to Europe to seek funds and priests for the diocese. He sailed from New York on the "Hibernia" on February 17 and landed in Liverpool whence he traveled through France, Switzerland and Italy and was received in audience by the Holy Father. In Rome he met Cardinal Newman, the famous English convert and writer. On his return he brought with him five seminarians—J. G. Reffe, B. M. Poyet, A. Hattenberger, J. B. Villars and Louis DeCailly who was a nephew of Bishop Loras. Of his visit to Ferney in December, 1846, he wrote: "I was truly overcome by the interest and attachment of which all my old parishioners without exception gave me testimony: even some fanatical protestants came to greet me very cordially".[19]

During the gold rush to California Father Cretin wanted to accompany the people from Iowa who helped to swell the tide of emigrants to the West but the Bishop would not give permission. He remained in Dubuque during the cholera epidemic ministering to the stricken while Bishop Loras was attending the Seventh Provincial Council of Baltimore where action was taken regarding the founding of a new diocese in Minnesota Territory. During that time he had to reprimand the Catholics of the Cathedral parish for their failure to support the church, and to cope with the rebellious members of the congregation who demanded a German priest to minister to them.

Bishop of St. Paul

When the petition for the division of the Diocese of Dubuque by the erection of a new episcopal see in St. Paul was favorably acted upon by the Roman Congregation Father Cretin reluctantly decided to accept the appointment as its first bishop and went to France for consecration at the hands of Bishop Devie of Belley. The function took place on January 26, 1851,[20] the co-consecrators being the Right Reverend Stephen Marilley, Bishop of Lausanne, exiled from his diocese in 1848 by the

Protestant government of the Canton of Fribourg, and the Right Reverend G. Chalandon, Coadjutor to the Bishop of Belley.

On a post-consecration visit to Ferney the new bishop was presented with a massive gold cross and chain by his former parishioners as a testimony of their affectionate regard. The Minnesota Democrat for July 8, 1851, said that the Bishop while in Europe had been very successful in obtaining funds for a new Cathedral.

Before his return the Bishop secured two priests for the new diocese[21] —the Reverend Francis de Vivaldi, Canon of Ventimiglia in Italy, exiled in France, and Reverend Denis Ledon, curate of Nantua in the diocese of Belley; three subdeacons—John Fayolle, Edward Legendre and M. Rochette; and a cleric in Minor Orders—Marcellin Peyragrosse. The Bishop and his companions were detained three weeks at Le Havre either through delay in obtaining Father Ledon's exeat from the Bishop of Belley, or in the hope of getting an economical and comfortable ship. On May 29, 1851, the feast of the Ascension, in the chapel of the convent of Ingouville where they were guests of the Sisters of St. Thomas, the Bishop ordained Fayolle, Legendre and Rochette deacons and Peyragrosse subdeacon. On June 4, they sailed on the steamer "Humboldt", landed in New York on the 17th., and reached St. Paul on the feast of the Visitation, July 2, 1851, "and with effusion of heart he addressed and blessed his flock in a very poor frame chapel". He brought with him, among other things, a beautiful chalice presented by the Children of Mary of Avignon, bearing the inscription on the base, "Remember the Children of Mary of Avignon", which, he promised, "will not leave the Cathedral".

While in Le Havre the Bishop wrote the Society for the Propagation of the Faith that he had received word that the two Canadian missionaries among the Indians at Pembina, Fathers Belcourt and Lacombe, would be forced to leave their mission unless immediate help were forthcoming. They had received only one hundred dollars in three years and that from Canadian sources. There were two chapels in the mission thirty-six miles apart ministering to twenty-five hundred souls of whom five hundred were Indians and the rest half-breeds. With his own hands Father Belcourt had built two cabins, one for a church too small to accommodate the people and the other for a residence, and the Indians were well disposed. Furthermore, he was in need of funds to reprint a grammar in the Sioux language which he had composed some years before and much in demand by missionaries. He also had a dictionary in Sioux ready for the press. Bishop Provencher had helped to support these priests for years.

On landing in New York he wrote his friend Senator Jones of Iowa that he would neglect nothing to promote education and morality in St.

Paul. "My intention is to start soon a little college on a good footing".

On arrival in St. Paul, July 2, 1851, on the "Nominee" from St. Louis the Bishop and his party were met by Father Ravoux, the only priest in the area since 1844, and a group of citizens eager to see a Bishop for the first time, and the installation took place that evening in the enlarged log chapel, 40 by 18, the first Cathedral of St. Paul.

"The arrival of the Bishop at St. Paul", according to the Minnesota Pioneer of July 10, 1851, "was hailed with considerable enthusiasm by our Catholic fellow-citizens. In the evening large numbers assembled at the log chapel on the bluff, to see him and hear his voice. Religious ceremonies appropriate to the Church were performed. The Te Deum and Magnificat were chanted, and the Bishop addressed the congregation, both in English and French. He said that the purpose of his mission and residence among them was their religious and temporal welfare. The services closed with the Bishop's benediction on the congregation."

Father de Vivaldi, in a letter to the Central Council of the Society for the Propagation of the Faith, dated Long Prairie, June 5, 1852, describes the event as follows:

> The news of our arrival having been circulated among the Catholics, who, partly Irish and partly Canadian, compose the majority of the people, our chapel and the surrounding space was filled on the same evening with people assembled to hear the voice of the chief pastor and receive his blessing. We sang the Te Deum and his Lordship delivered so pathetic a discourse that he moved all present to tears.[22]

What manner of man was the new Bishop? The people saw a stockily-built prelate of medium height and middle age, rather corpulent, of pleasing appearance and address, with a benign countenance, high forehead, receding hair and kindly eyes behind large glasses, a man inured to the hardships of missionary life and unafraid of the difficulties confronting him in the new diocese. As they learned to know him better they recognized in him a dignity of bearing, a graciousness of manner and a calm assurance that made him master of any situation. A journalist, J. M. Newson, in "Pen Pictures of St. Paul and Biographical Sketches of Old Settlers" published in 1886, page 269, described him as

> a fine and intellectual man, with a very pleasant face, and a serene yet subdued expression. He was partially bald, wore glasses and had all the politeness of the French. He dressed in his ministerial garments, and was very devotedly attached to the Church, of which he was the honored head.

> Bishop Cretin had come into a poor inheritance.

> He knew better than any one else the rude and uncultivated vineyard which God and His Church had assigned to him to cultivate. It required apostolic zeal and resources, and Heaven's sustaining power, to draw fruit from the wilderness and create, as it were, an organized church for the Northwest.[23]

He had seen the majestic bluffs of Minnesota before; her vast extent, her mighty rivers and her Indian tribes were not unfamiliar to him. He could not foresee the future but he had confidence in God and was happy in the apostolic simplicity and poverty with which he inaugurated his episcopate.

St. Paul was a small village newly reclaimed from the wilderness. The material assets of the diocese consisted of the log Cathedral in St. Paul —the 1841 original of Father Galtier and the 1847 addition of Father Ravoux—and small churches in St. Peter's, St. Anthony and Pembina. The clerical personnel already in the field was made up of Father Ravoux at St. Peter's, near the see-city, and Fathers Belcourt and Lacombe at Pembina in the northwest corner of the Territory, a Catholic population of about a thousand in a total population of six thousand whites and thirty thousand Indians.

The vast territory under his jurisdiction was approximately one-third fertile prairie over which the savage Sioux and thousand of buffalo roamed, and two-thirds primeval forest harboring all kinds of wild animals. There were thousands of lakes teeming with fish, three mighty rivers—the Mississippi flowing south into the Gulf of Mexico, the Red River of the North winding its way to Lake Winnipeg, and the St. Louis flowing into Lake Superior and thence through the St. Lawrence to the distant Atlantic. In its northern area lay as yet undiscovered deposits of iron ore of immense extent and fabulous richness.

In a letter published in the Boston Pilot, October 11, 1851, the Reverend James Moran, who arrived in St. Paul shortly after Bishop Cretin, makes this observation about the state:

> I have never seen better land in my life—well-watered and heavily timbered for several miles, and then interspersed with beautiful prairies —in fine, it is the best farming country in all America. Nothing can exceed the wheat, oats, corn, potatoes, and all kinds of vegetables . . . the country also abounds with fish and wild fowl of every description. There is medicine in the very air over St. Paul's.

If men would work, says the St. Paul Pioneer for May 13, 1852,

> the whole region might be like a garden waving with luxuriance and groaning with plenty . . . there is no part of the world combining in such perfection all the requisites for successful and profitable farming: we mean good land, pure water, healthful climate, and a high cash market at home.

It is worthy of note that when Bishop Cretin came to St. Paul he brought with him a number of small apple trees, originally imported from France, and planted them in the garden back of the Cathedral where they grew and flourished and produced a yearly crop of "splendidly flavored fruit" according to the editor of the St. Paul Dispatch who, in the issue of October 10, 1863, said he was presented with a sample.

"The perfection to which they have been brought proves conclusively that with proper care as fine an apple can be raised in this state as in any other of the Union".

The new Bishop was not a total stranger to the people to whom he was sent nor to the diocese entrusted to his spiritual care. The Minnesota Democrat said of him:

> Many of our citizens are well acquainted with Bishop Cretin. He spent some time in this territory shortly after his arrival in the United States. Those who know him well, and of different sects, represent him as a highly educated and excellent man and an American in all his sympathies and warmly attached to the free institutions of the country.

Bishop Cretin was too stout-hearted to be dismayed at the prospect that unfolded itself before him. He had done missionary work in Iowa and knew what to expect. He lost no time in useless repining but set to work with unselfish dedication to develop the resources of the diocese and plan for future growth. He realized that it was incumbent on him to lay deep and secure the foundations of the Church in the Northwest, to instruct the people under his care to the best of his ability and the limit of his resources, and to initiate the traditions of devoted service to the least of the brethren and of enlightened administration destined to be the motivating force and inspiration of his successors and their co-workers. His motto was "all things to all men". He set an example of personal sacrifice and self-denial by living in a log shanty, 18 feet square and far from comfortable, behind the Cathedral and taking his meals for a time at least in a nearby rooming house.

He began at once to train the young levites brought from France and prepare them for ordination. In the vestry of the log Cathedral, the first seminary of the diocese, he put the finishing touches to their education and in due time Fayolle, Legendre and Peyragrosse, were promoted to the priesthood. Nothing is known of Rochette except that he was "detained on his way hither".[24] He dropped out of the picture completely.

Shortly after his installation the Bishop appointed Father Ravoux, who resided at St. Peter's, Vicar General; Father Ledon pastor of the Church of St. Anthony near the falls of that name; and placed Canon de Vivaldi in charge of the Winnebago mission at Long Prairie about one hundred miles to the north.

Prior to his arrival that portion of the Diocese of St. Paul lying between the Mississippi and St. Croix rivers was under the jurisdiction of the Bishop of Milwaukee. By indenture made August 26, 1851, between John Martin Henni, Bishop of Milwaukee, and Joseph Cretin, Bishop of St. Paul, for and in consideration of one dollar, the receipt of which was thereby acknowledged, the former deeded to the latter

all and singular the lands, tenements and real estate of every norm and nature whatever, within the Territory of Minnesota, according to the bounds of said Territory now established by law of which the said party of the first part now stands seized, whether it be in absolute fee simple or for any other or less estates.

This deed transferred the church property formerly under the control of the Bishop of Milwaukee to the Bishop of Saint Paul.

From Log Chapel to New Cathedral

The Bishop realized at once that a larger Cathedral was necessary than the one on Bench Street hill and with characteristic energy began the construction of a combined church, residence and school at Wabasha and Sixth Streets on the property bought by Father Ravoux before his arrival. During the building of it one of the center beams of the second story broke for want of proper support and crashed down with all the other beams into the basement, knocking holes in the unfinished walls. Fortunately no one was seriously injured but the work was retarded for some time.

A month after taking possession of the see he wrote the Society for the Propagation of the Faith that the new building, 84 by 44 feet in size and three stories high, would be ready for occupancy in October. The basement was of stone, the upper stories of brick. It would cost $5,000 towards which he had advanced $2,000 from his patrimony and $800 he had borrowed in the hope that the Society would reimburse him. He would be seriously embarrassed if it did not come to his aid. He added that the non-Catholics were favorably disposed to the Church, that Americans were coming into the Territory in large numbers and that immigrants would soon follow. There were four churches in the village, one of them a gothic episcopal furnished with an altar, tabernacle, communion table and candelabra that would lead "even the elect" to think it a Catholic Church. He was in dire need of missionaries for the Indians and had to pay part of the debt on one of his churches, St. Anthony of Padua, near the falls of that name.

When the new combination church-residence-school building was dedicated in the autumn of 1851 the Bishop, clergy and seminarians took possession of their quarters on the third floor where the Bishop occupied a small corner room. The church was on the second floor and the first floor or basement was set apart for the library, kitchen, dining room and school rooms for the seminarians transferred from the vestry of the log chapel which now became a school for girls under the direction of the newly-arrived Sisters of St. Joseph of Carondelet who, at the request of the Bishop, came from St. Louis to make a foundation in the diocese and organize the first school for girls, the forerunner of the present St. Joseph's Academy.

The Bishop's interest in education prompted him to open a school for boys on the first floor of the new building, taught by Fathers Legendre and Peyragrosse, and among the enrolled pupils were John Ireland and Thomas O'Gorman destined to accomplish so much for the welfare of the Church in the Northwest. In 1855 four Brothers of the Holy Family came from the Diocese of Belley to take charge of the school and establish a novitiate for their community.[25] Brother Cyrille was the Superior and Brothers Ernest, Mary Leo and Timothy, the other members of the community. In the second year there were twenty boys in the upper grades and forty in the primary as well as one hundred in a free school. The Holy Family community did not prosper. Few subjects entered the novitiate and these were dismissed when the Brothers were dispersed shortly after the Bishop's death. Brother Cyrille became a priest of the Congregation of the Holy Cross at Notre Dame, Indiana—the Reverend J. C. Carrier.

The four Sisters of St. Joseph who arrived in St. Paul on November 3, four months after the Bishop came, lost no time in opening a school for girls in the vestry of the log chapel and took up their abode in a small frame shanty on the river bank with the most primitive accommodations.[26] It had but one room with a shed kitchen in the rear and sleeping quarters for the Sisters in the attic reached from outside by means of a ladder. The school prospered. Before spring there were several boarders living in a small outhouse and the school had to be moved into the log chapel. Such was the uninspiring beginning of the splendid work done by the Sisters of St. Joseph in the Northwest as part of the magnificent school system inaugurated by Bishop Cretin under such unfavorable auspices and developed by his successors to its present state of perfection.

Financial Aid For Catholic Schools

Soon after Bishop Cretin's arrival in St. Paul the vexing question of financial aid for sectarian schools was threshed out in the Territorial Legislature. At the request of the Bishop, Daniel J. Fisher, a seminarian, drew up a petition asking for an amendment to the school law to enable Catholic schools to participate in the school fund. During the fourth session of the legislative assembly petitions were presented asking financial aid for Catholic schools, and referred to a special committee of three for consideration. On February 16, 1853, this committee, consisting of Messrs. Murray, Olivier and Ludden, introduced a bill providing state support for religious schools and recommended its passage, believing that it was the best way to reconcile the existing law with individual liberty and freedom of conscience.

After due discussion and debate by the members of the House of Representatives the Bill passed its first and second reading, was printed and engrossed, but was refused a third reading on February 28 by a vote of twelve to five, the affirmative votes being cast by Messrs. Lott, Murray, Noot, Olivier and Rolette. Thus ended the first of many attempts made in Minnesota to obtain a share of public funds for Catholic schools. In this as in every other instance Protestant bigotry could claim the victory.

The effort made by Bishop Cretin to subsidize his schools from the public treasury, to which Catholics contributed their proportionate share, may have been suggested by what took place in New York in 1839, when Archbishop Hughes successfully opposed the efforts of the Public School Society, a private corporation, to oust religion from the schools; but his request for state support for Catholic schools was denied. Bishop Cretin was, no doubt, familiar with this as he had visited New York several times between 1838 when he landed in America and 1852 when he was on his way to Washington to secure a share of the money appropriated by Congress for the education of the Indians in Minnesota.

Nor did Bishop Cretin forget the redmen who formed such a large portion of his diocesan charges. His interest in their temporal and spiritual welfare never flagged till the day of his death. As a priest in the Diocese of Dubuque he had ministered to them and would have been content to spend himself and be spent for them. His interest in the Winnebagoes did not cease with their transfer to Long Prairie, so-called "from the form and nature of the land that lies in the middle of it", but, on the contrary, increased. Even before he came to St. Paul as its first Bishop he had written Senator Jones of Iowa, whom he held in highest esteem as a friend, asking if the Government would entrust the care of a school among them to Catholic teachers, pay them a salary and provide the necessary funds to feed and clothe the Indians and thus help rescue them from their miserable condition. He promised not to interfere with the Government officials or the traders. He did not receive a favorable answer to his request. He knew that Lowry had been appointed Superintendent of the school at Long Prairie and he could expect nothing but opposition to his efforts to give the savages a religious upbringing. The agent at the reservation was J. E. Fletcher who, in the spring of 1851, before the Bishop's arrival, had been removed from office and Major Fridley appointed to succeed him. This was no improvement for the latter was accused of appropriating Government and tribal property and allowing others to use it for private purposes.

The Long Prairie Winnebago Mission

One of Bishop Cretin's first acts on coming to St. Paul was to send a priest to preach the gospel to the Winnebagoes and one of the pioneer Sisters of St. Joseph to prepare the children for the reception of the sacraments. He had to deal with government representatives in charge of the agencies and they were not always cooperative. Too often they resented the efforts of the missionaries to improve the condition of the Indians materially and spiritually. Many of the agents preyed upon the wards of the government and enriched themselves at the expense of those whom they were supposed to induct into the ways of civilization. Through the agent the Bishop had to deal with the Government and not infrequently the negotiations took an interminably long time and involved all kinds of red tape. There was no Catholic Indian Bureau to which he could refer his problems and through which he could present his case to the head of the department of Indian affairs. Very often after putting forth his best diplomatic efforts he had to confess defeat. Before he came, the Winnebagoes from Fort Atkinson on Turkey River in Iowa had been removed to Long Prairie where the Government had established an agency. The Bishop sent Canon de Vivaldi to open a mission[27] in the new reservation in July, 1851. At the time he had full and justified confidence in the Canon who was a priest of excellent reputation and brilliant attainments and for a time all went well.

On his arrival in Long Prairie Canon de Vivaldi said Mass in a miserable hut destined for his habitation. He made a poor frame building into a chapel dedicated to Our Lady of Seven Sorrows. Catholics were few. There were about 20 families of half-breeds poorly instructed in their religion; but the Indians were well-disposed and he baptized twenty catechumens after midnight Mass on Christmas morning. Prior to that, on All Saints' day, a class of boys and girls from the Metis or half-breed families was admitted to first Communion. In a letter to the Bishop, which required eighteen days to reach St. Paul, he wrote that he was in the wilderness "with only 3 francs, 1 pair of well-worn boots and no means of transportation". Nevertheless, he made a trip to Crow Wing and back which required two days. He asked the Bishop to give the bearer of the letter a few bottles of Mass wine as his supply was running short.

After Christmas the Canon availed himself of a sick call sixty miles from Long Prairie to pay a visit to St. Paul to ask the Bishop for a confrère and two sisters of St. Joseph to aid him in the work among the Winnebagoes. He also invited the Bishop to visit the mission and confirm a class of neophytes on the feast of the Epiphany. The Bishop accompanied him back to the mission taking with him Marcellin Peyragrosse, a subdeacon, and Sister Scholastica Vasquez. It was a two days' journey by sled, the only mode of conveyance. On the way back the Canon asked permission to go ahead to prepare the people for the coming of the Bishop. He and Peyragrosse mounted a sled drawn by a spirited horse which, on crossing a stream in a dense forest, shied and overturned the sled dislocating the Canon's arm. Peyragrosse tried in vain to pull it back into place. An Indian who witnessed the accident ran back to the cabin in which the Bishop was spending the night and told him of the mishap. The Bishop immediately sent his two Indian guides to bring the priest to his abode and, after five attempts, "an unskilled doctor" succeeded in putting the arm back in place. The next day the Bishop reached Long Prairie and the Canon arrived the day after. The Bishop confirmed "upwards of thirty persons" and returned to St. Paul, taking Peyragrosse with him. Sister Scholastica found a home with the Lequier family whose daughter was her companion and assistant while she was preparing a class of Indian children for first communion on March 25, 1852, after which she returned to her convent in St. Paul.

Father Vivaldi wanted a resident community of sisters and prepared a home for them, 18 by 20 and one story high. In July three Sisters of St. Joseph—Cesarine Mulvy, Scholastica Vasquez and Simeon Kane— arrived at Long Prairie and opened a school with an enrollment of twenty-three on the first day. Each was to receive forty dollars a month, while Father de Vivaldi received sixty and a farmer fifty. Major Fridley, the Government agent, did not welcome the missionary nor the sisters but put obstacles in their way, refusing to pay the stipulated salaries for their support and to provide food and clothing for the children.

In the meantime Bishop Cretin had attended the First Plenary Council of Baltimore which opened on May 8, 1852, in Archbishop Kenrick's house, and at its conclusion went to Washington and applied for one-half the $12,000 allotted to Minnesota for work among the Indians. He had a conference with the President who, though anxious to cooperate with Catholics in their efforts to civilize the Indians, was afraid of Protestant criticism. However, the Bishop's claim was allowed and on his return to St. Paul he entered into a contract[28] with Governor Ramsey, Superintendent of Indian Affairs for Minnesota, on behalf of the United States Government, to educate in the school on the Winnebago reservation as many children of both sexes, of full or mixed Indian blood, between the ages of five and eighteen, as would present themselves, furnish them with such clothing and board as they had been receiving, with books, stationery and other school supplies, instruct them in the English language in the branches of a common school curriculum according to their capacities and as the school superintendent shall direct, for the sum of seventy-five dollars a year for each pupil in attendance, to be paid quarterly by the agent.

In addition to school work the boys were to be instructed in agriculture and in the practical use of farm implements according to their ability and tastes, and the girls trained in the various branches of housewifery.

including sewing, knitting and weaving. He also agreed to cultivate the school farm by the labor of the scholars and use the produce for the support of teachers and pupils.

Neither the Government nor the Winnebago tribe would be held responsible for any excess of expenditure over and above the stipulated amount, except that the Government would guarantee the sum of two thousand dollars a year, in quarterly payments, to meet the salaries of teachers should the attendance of scholars not produce that amount at the rates agreed upon. The Bishop would appoint the Superintendent and teachers and pay their salaries.

The agreement was to continue in force for five years; but the Government reserved the right to cancel, annul and terminate it at any time for good cause made known to the Bishop in writing.

The Bishop considered this contract "very favorable to the Indians and to the interests of the Government". He wrote to Senator Jones

> I took charge of the school at some conditions very disinterested on our part and promised to apply more than two-thirds of the money appropriated by the Government for the school, for provisions and clothing for the school, not keeping the salary of laboring men for the teachers. I have appointed Superintendent of the school an excellent clergyman, De Vivaldi, an accomplished scholar and gentleman who has a great influence over the half-breeds and Indians. I sent two Sisters and will send two male teachers later to induce the scholars to cultivate the fields, confident to succeed in spite of the demoralization and prejudices introduced by the former system.

In the winter of 1853 the sisters' house and part of the school were destroyed by fire and the latter was repaired and used as a dwelling. The opposition of the agent and intertribal relations worked against Father de Vivaldi's success. In addition to that the Bishop had to reprimand him for carelessness in money matters, accusing him of incurring foolish expenses, buying on credit and contracting debt against the Bishop's orders. He was laboring under great difficulties as is evident from the report of his mission contained in the Catholic Almanac for 1854 which described the situation in the previous year: Father de Vivaldi

> has under his direction the school of the tribe. Between sixty and ninety children are in daily attendance at this school, and are improving much under many respects, mainly through the zeal, charity and patience of three Sisters of St. Joseph. A great deal more would have been done for this tribe if the liberal intentions of the government had not been frustrated by the dishonest opposition of the ex-agent, Mr. Fridley. He has refused until now to deliver the money handed to him more than eight months ago to pay the teacher and furnish the scholars with provisions and clothing. The Bishop of St. Paul has been obliged to advance a good deal of money to prevent the teacher and scholars from starving, and he has not yet recovered a cent.

In the meantime, in his perplexity about the future of the Winnebago and other Indian missions, Bishop Cretin sought the aid of religious orders, among them the Trappists near Dubuque whom he knew to be successful cultivators of the soil and whom he considered well qualified to teach the Indians how to farm, which was more necessary than to teach them how to read and write. "The Trappists are the only religious body notable for their ability in that line." It appears that the Trappists at first agreed to come, for he wrote Governor Ramsey that they were willing to take charge of the school and of the mission. He was ready to turn over to them the $6,500 received from the Government for the current year, with the assurance of a like subsidy for five years. But for some reason, perhaps because of a change of superiors, they finally decided not to accept the invitation. In a letter to Bishop Loras on March 10, 1853, he wrote that the Trappists whose reason for refusing he could not understand would acquire more of a reputation and more glory for the monastery if they sent four or five monks to a mission among the savages, and that if they made a foundation in his diocese they would attract novices and "should be able easily to erect an abbey".[29] He added, "I am going to address myself to the house in Kentucky".

In May, 1854, when Father de Vivaldi's debts reached the sum of five thousand dollars the Bishop sent Father Fisher to take charge of the mission; and the next year when the Winnebagoes were transferred to a new reservation at Blue Earth, Father de Vivaldi went with them and the Sisters of St. Joseph, with the exception of Sister Cesarine, returned to St. Paul. He continued in charge of the Indian school for a year during which it was taught by the Sisters of the Love of God, a community which he founded in 1855 and placed under the direction of Sister Cesarine. Again he ran the mission into debt and Bishop Cretin was asked to pay. Before long it had to be closed and Father de Vivaldi, dismissed by Governor Gorman, disappeared from the scene.

The Canon's Picturesque Career

In a letter to Bishop Loras, dated December 28, 1855, Bishop Cretin wrote: "Our Canon causes me trouble enough with his foundations of orders and villages. He throws himself into an abyss of debts; he begs by letter; he had a great many Indian children at his school, but it is hunger which attracts them and the provisions which they receive. No one bothers much about their christian education".[30]

There is no mention of the mission of Long Prairie in the Catholic Almanac for 1856 because it had been transferred to Blue Earth. The Almanac for 1857 is a reprint of that of 1856. In the Directory for 1858 there is no mention of Blue Earth or of missionary work among the Indians except the statement that "The Winnebagoes, Sioux and Chippewa Indians earnestly desire the assistance of missionaries". The name of Father de Vivaldi is not listed on the roster of priests in the United States, nor is it found in any subsequent issue. The last mention of him in the Diocese of St. Paul is in the Almanac for 1857 where he is stationed at Blue Earth among the Winnebagoes and "has under his direction and the superintendence of the Bishop of St. Paul a numerous school of Indian children instructed by some sisters". The Almanac for 1859 and subsequent years says the "Winnebago mission is attended from Mankato".

In 1856 Bishop Cretin wrote the Society for the Propagation of the Faith at Lyons that Father de Vivaldi had left the diocese and hinted that his heart as well as his head had gone wrong. The Canon entered the Diocese of Milwaukee and had a parish at Plattsville, Wisconsin, from the summer of 1856 to October, 1857, when he was placed in charge of St. John's Church, Green Bay, which he left suddenly in June, 1858, and thus ended his missionary labors in the United States.

After a picturesque career in the world, during which he served a term as American Consul in Brazil by appointment of President Lincoln, he dropped out of sight entirely until January, 1883, when he went to Buenos Aires whence the Archbishop sent him as a missionary to Chubut in Patagonia till 1890, when he returned to Europe expecting to be named Vicar Apostolic of that region. He met Archbishop Ireland in Rome in 1892 and shortly afterwards appeared in St. Paul on his way to St. Cloud to claim certain lands under litigation in the courts but was unsuccessful. On his return to France he said Mass in a convent in Paris where he died early in the twentieth century.

How impractical and visionary the Canon was is evidenced by a letter[31] written to the Boston Pilot from Blue Earth on January 10, 1856, a few months before he left the diocese. He outlined plans for the founding of a city, to be known as Piopolis in honor of Pope Pius IX, from whom "so many marks of paternal affection were received by me in Portici, 1849, and since I have been among my dear Winnebagoes".

This city of the future was to be populated exclusively by Catholic families "who desire their altars and their hearth-stones to be held sacred and secure, and who prefer the benefits of Catholic peace and quiet to the quarrels, troubles, agitations, and bloody riots of Know-nothingism".

He claimed to have secured a large tract of fertile land in the vicinity of Lake Elysian, on the western shore of which Piopolis would be laid out. He proposed to build a chapel dedicated to the Immaculate Conception or the Immaculate Heart of Mary, and an academy for young girls to be taught by the Sisters of the Love of God, whom he founded, whose motherhouse would be located there. Two blocks would be reserved for a church, two for a hospital, two for the Holy Father, one for a free school, and one for each bishop in the United States. A town lot would be given free to each of the first two hundred families settling in the city. Native Americans (Indians) would be their neighbors, mild kind and peaceful, as he could testify for he had labored among them for five years and had baptized many of them especially during the past three months. What a misfortune that Piopolis was destined to be nothing more than a dream!

When the Bishop came to the diocese the exterior of the frame Church of St. Anthony was completed but it was unfurnished and without provision for a resident pastor. Father Ledon who took charge of it in July, 1851, built a two-room addition to the rear to serve as living quarters. The Bishop dedicated the church July 20, 1852, and preached to the congregation. It was the second church dedication in the diocese, the first being that of the Cathedral in the previous autumn. During his pastorate Father Ledon took care of the Catholics living in the Dayton Settlement, walking thither and carrying the Mass kit on his back. He said the first Mass in the locality and his successor, Father Fayolle, likewise said Mass there for the scattered Catholics of the Settlement. Father Ledon ended his pastorate in 1855 when ill-health forced his retirement. He was pastor of the Cathedral for a couple of years and spent a winter in the south before returning to France where he died in 1881 as pastor of the parish of Mezeriat in the Diocese of Belley not far from the Seminary of Meximieux which he visited frequently while Father (now Monsignor) Guillot was a member of the faculty.[32]

Shortly after his arrival in St. Paul Bishop Cretin petitioned the Holy See, through the Sacred Congregation for the Propagation of the Faith, to sanction throughout his diocese the observance of the four holydays of obligation observed in the dioceses of St. Louis and New Orleans. The document,[33] written in Latin, on August 20, 1851, set forth the difference of practice in this regard in the two sections of which the diocese was composed. In the eastern section, detached from the Diocese of Milwaukee, eight holydays were observed, namely, the Circumcision, Epiphany, Annunciation, Ascension, Corpus Christi, Assumption, All Saints and Nativity: in the western section, taken from the Diocese of Dubuque, only four—Ascension, Assumption, All Saints and Nativity. These four feasts had been sanctioned in the French Concordat of 1801 for the Church in France, and the custom passed to the French colonies and was adopted by the Territory of Louisiana of which the dioceses of New Orleans, St. Louis and Dubuque formed part.

The reply of the Sacred Congregation conveyed the news that in an audience with the Holy Father on October 3, 1851, Pope Pius IX was pleased to grant the favor in the same form and terms as the concessions made to the dioceses of St. Louis and New Orleans.

Catholic Temperance Society

The year 1852 was a very busy one for the Bishop. It began with the organization of the Catholic Temperance Society on January 11 in which he took the greatest personal interest. He had taken part in a similar movement in Dubuque. It is interesting to note that the first Catholic Total Abstinence Society in America was organized by Bishop Loras in 1839 and, as Minnesota was then part of the diocese, we share in that glory. Bishop Loras expected his priests to practice and preach total abstinence from alcoholic beverages. Personally Bishop Cretin was a strict total abstainer, a zealous apostle of the movement and a good deal of a prohibitionist. In a letter to his sister he wrote on March 2, 1841, "I have not tasted wine for more than eight months; and still I am in perfect health". He could also bear testimony to the good done to others by temperance societies. In the same letter he writes;

> Intemperance is rapidly disappearing; saloons are being closed and beginning to disappear altogether . . . Temperance Societies grow and flourish in the country; a vow is taken never to drink a single drop of any intoxicating liquor; and as a rule this vow is faithfully kept; and the members of these societies enjoy good health . . . Miners and farmers now drink only water and they are stronger than before. It is a great mistake to consider wine as absolutely necessary. Vineyards might just as well be abandoned; in ten years their product will have very little value.

He was too optimistic as he was to learn later to his sorrow.

When Bishop Cretin reached the scene of his future labors in the summer of 1851 St. Paul was a frontier village and, like most of the primitive outposts of civilization, the abode of a motley population to many of whom strong drink was the elixir of life. He was quick to read the signs of the times and quick to apply an efficacious remedy for existing evils. He realized the absolute necessity of making an effort to diminish the evils attributable to the drink-loving propensities of his flock, and as a means to that end he founded the Catholic Temperance Society[34] which Catholics over twelve years of age were invited to join by taking the prescribed pledge. He was the Treasurer of the Society and Fathers Ravoux, De Vivaldi, Ledon, Legendre, Fayolle, Peyragrosse and Moran were members.

There was a growing sentiment in favor of prohibition in the community and the Catholic Temperance Society joined with others in petitioning the Legislature to pass a law restricting the sale of intoxicating beverages in the Territory. This sentiment in favor of prohibitive legislation bore fruit on March 6 when the Maine Liquor Law, as it was called, was enacted by the Legislature. It made the manufacture, possession or sale of liquor a penal offence to be severely punished. The measure was submitted to popular vote on April 6 and became the law of the land by "an overwhelming majority". Ramsey County gave a vote of 528 for and 496 against the measure. "In the evening", says the Minnesota Pioneer, of April 8, 1852, "the four church bells pealed the merry chimes of victory over the deadliest foe of human society and human happiness that ever desolated a state or territory". Among the bells rung in commemoration of the event was that of the Cathedral which did not please the anti-prohibitionists and especially the man who donated it. He called on the Bishop and did not hesitate to upbraid him for showing sympathy with the movement. The law was later declared unconstitutional and repealed by the Legislature on March 3, 1855.

From the beginning the Temperance Society was handicapped by the necessity of conducting its business in French and in English and, in August, 1852, it was deemed advisable to divide the society into two branches according to nationalities rather than form two distinct organizations. Two large ornamental tablets hung inside the door of the Cathedral bearing the names of the members of the Temperance Society.[35] They were rolls of honor for the Bishop and the early Catholics of St. Paul. On one of them was the name of John Ireland, future Archbishop of St. Paul. The two branches existed for about a year; but gradually the society lost its corporate unity although many remained faithful to the pledge. The general decay of interest in temperance work was due to the fact that more momentous questions were beginning to occupy public attention. The political disturbances preceding the Civil War and the upheaval and bloodshed incident to it were decidedly unfavorable to temperance activity and for more than a decade after Bishop Cretin's death no effort was made to revive the temperance movement in Minnesota.

But Bishop Cretin was loyal to the cause while he lived. His well-known views brought him into conflict with the saloon element and on one occasion, we are told, as he was passing a public house, the German proprietor invited him in and "insulted" him by offering him a glass of beer.[36] The Irish, when they heard of it, wanted to wreck the saloon, but the Bishop calmed them by saying that the proprietor did not know what he was doing. The Bishop preached what he practiced and practiced what he preached, kept no liquor in his house either for himself or for his guests, spoke on the question from the pulpit and platform, attended the meetings of the society to encourage the members and by word and example labored unceasingly for the promotion of sobriety and the formation of a truer and higher standard of private and public virtue.

Temperance Among Catholic Indians

It is rather surprising to learn that, during the forties of last century when Bishop Loras and Father Cretin were promoting the cause of total abstinence in the Diocese of Dubuque, similar efforts by missionaries among the Indians were fruitful in good results. For that we have the testimony of Reverend Otto Skolla, O.F.M., who left his Austrian homeland with the approval of his Superior and came to Father Baraga's mission field in the vicinity of Lake Superior to labor among the Menominee Indians in the decades following 1843. In a report[37] made to the Minister General of his order in 1852 he refers to the temperance movement among the Indians in the following terms:

> The virtue of temperance has done a great deal in North America to promote morality and restrain and root out vice, not only among the devout Irish where the movement first began and succeeded admirably well against drunkenness, but among other nationalities in North America, Catholic and non-Catholic, and especially among the Catholic Indians. In each congregation where it is introduced and adopted, societies are formed, and the organization itself is called the Temperance Society, that is, for abstinence from liquor. In order that the Indians might be disentangled from all dangers to the soul and thereby be able to devote themselves without hindrance to the worship of God in the Catholic religion, it was my custom to advise them before receiving baptism that, if they desired to love and serve God, they would give up all drinking parties and drunkenness, and, as was fitting for new Christians, would join the temperance society to further the salvation of their own souls and give good example to other nationalities.
>
> After the Indians had been baptized and their names registered at the font, I asked each of them separately, "Do you seriously intend to subscribe to temperance and abstain from ship-wine and fire-water? For how many years, or for what length of time do you intend to enroll"? Generally the response was in favor of adopting temperance for from five to ten years, and sometimes for life. This promise of temperance, based on the grace of God and a good-willed resolve, was faithfully observed. But the Indian women, even while still pagan, seldom use liquor. I have often heard them say, "No drop of wine or other liquor has ever passed my lips". Nevertheless, they are very zealous in encouraging their husbands to abstain from drink. They as well as the men join the temperance society, not because they need it, but to give good example to their husbands, to add to their words the force of their own temperance as observed (by their husbands), and finally to put to shame the fickleness of their men lest they ever lapse into their former bad habit under the urge of refractory nature. As the Indians are so led along the path of temperance, they gradually begin to detest what once they desired so avidly. For as soon as they notice that liquor (commonly called Whisky in English, and in Indian Ishkotewabo) is being smuggled into

their neighborhood or any hut of their tribe, they are so incensed that they go into the hut, break the urns, pitchers and bottles, and pour out the liquor, and in return give the owner no payment except a stiff rebuke.

Diocesan Affairs

The Bishop founded the St. Joseph Conference of the St. Vincent de Paul Society[38] to aid the poor and enhance the spiritual life of the members by visitation of the sick and destitute, which he never failed to do himself, and by personal contact showed Christian sympathy for those in need and gave them financial aid in the most unobtrusive manner. The charter members were W. B. McGrorty, A. L. Larpenteur, Charles W. Williams, William Markoe, W. J. Brownson and L. P. Cotter, the Secretary. It was incorporated on November 16, 1856. When the golden jubilee was celebrated Markoe and Larpenteur were the sole survivors of the original signers.

On May 9, 1852, Bishop Cretin was present at the First Plenary Council of Baltimore which lasted until the twentieth. He deemed it a privilege to take part in such an august assembly of prelates and legislate for the general welfare of the Church in America. He visited Washington and while there wrote to the Treasurer of the Propagation of the Faith and told him of the progress made in his diocese. Several parishes had been organized and missions set up, but much more could be done if he had the funds. It was a continual struggle against heresy and paganism to preserve the faith of Catholics who had come from all parts of the country, and to convert the 30,000 savages under his jurisdiction. He needed priests and brothers but could not afford to ask for them for want of means to support them. The Senate had ratified the treaty concluded the year before with the Indians and 21,000,000 acres of land were now offered to first-comers for two or three cents an acre, without a down payment for four or five years, and after that for a dollar and a quarter an acre for full possession. This had brought a great influx of immigrants, two or three hundred a day, mostly Catholics. It was impossible to provide spiritual ministration for them, spread out as they were over an area of one hundred and fifty miles from St. Paul.

While in Washington he put in a claim for half the $12,000 allotted each year for the education of the Indians in Minnesota who prefer priests for teachers. Even the government admits that priests have greater influence with the Indians than ministers. The President, he found, would like to help Catholics, but Protestant influence was strong, aggressive and scheming, and the Catholic vote was only beginning to count in elections. However, the following year the Government agreed to place at his disposal $6,000 annually for five years for the education and support of the Winnebagoes.

On February 8, 1852, Bishop Cretin made a report[39] on the condition of the diocese to the Propagation of the Faith in connection with the budget requirements for the year. There were 6,000 Catholics and 25,000 Indians in the Territory. In the previous year twenty adult conversions had been recorded and eight hundred Easter communions distributed. There were eleven priests in the diocese; two churches and three chapels; the beginning of a seminary and a school taught by the Sisters of St. Joseph. The most he could expect in the way of revenue was one thousand dollars from pew rents and collections, and he needed nearly $20,000 for clergy support, the building of churches and schools and work among the Indians. A great influx of immigrants was expected in the spring necessitating more priests and churches.

His dependence on the Propagation of the Faith induced him to try to establish a branch of the Society in the diocese, but he found it the part of prudence to defer it for a time because Catholics were poor and many appeals were made to them for funds for new churches, the support of the clergy and the needy.

In the summer of 1853 he sent Father Ravoux to Europe with John Ireland and Thomas O'Gorman whom he placed in the Seminary of Meximieux to begin their studies for the priesthood. They were the first fruits of Catholicity in the diocese and it gave him great encouragement. He did not live to welcome them on their return; but he was looking to the future. He planned to open five missions among the Indians, build a church in St. Paul and three in other localities, as well as an addition to the convent school to accommodate twenty more boarders. A hospital for the Sisters of St. Joseph was nearing completion that would also serve as a novitiate for the congregation. The Bishop was much consoled with the progress made in seven months and had every reason to be.

In a letter to Bishop Loras, dated March 10, 1853, he wrote,
all our missionaries are doing well and getting along well. None of them is giving me the least trouble just now. Next Saturday, the vigil of Passion Sunday, I shall ordain an American priest who will do well I think. I am confident that he will not cause any trouble; he is modest and he has good sense.

He referred to Daniel J. Fisher of New York whom he had invited to St. Paul in 1852, and who returned to the East a few years after his ordination. In the same year the Bishop began to publish in Catholic papers accounts of Minnesota's rich soil, great crops, and healthful climate where bilious fevers are unknown. He described its millions of acres of fine prairie, bordered with timber, with small lakes and streams, awaiting the coming of immigrants and their families.

The hospital he built is the oldest institution in Minnesota for the care of the sick. As early as 1851 Doctor Day, a physician of the village, formed a company to build a hospital, secured a site, fenced it and hauled a quantity of building material, chiefly stone, to it, but was unable to go further. For a consideration he sold the property and material to Bishop Cretin. But the greater portion of the ground for the hospital was donated by Hon. H. M. Rice.[40] In the fall of 1853 the construction of a four-story stone building was begun on the site now occupied by the central portion of the present St. Joseph's Hospital, erected in 1895. Despite scarcity of workmen and material it was completed in about a year and opened for the reception of patients. The major portion of its cost was borne by the Bishop himself who expended on it the greater part, if not all, of the ten thousand francs of his patrimony sent from France in that year.[41] He had, therefore, every right to be regarded as the founder of the hospital and he was so considered at the time, as evidenced by the observation made by the Minnesota Democrat in its issue of February 14, 1855.

> This charitable institution has been founded at the expense of the Right Reverend Bishop of St. Paul for the relief of the sick, without regard to creed or country. Not one cent has been asked or received for its erection from this community, so that the object for which it is now devoted may be changed should it not receive adequate support. No fixed revenue is as yet secured for its maintenance.

The same paper describes a visit made to the hospital by a member of its staff when it was caring for nine patients at the rate of one dollar a day.

> We went over the whole building and were much gratified and pleased at the neatness, convenience and care with which the interior arrangements had been set up for the sick or disabled stranger or citizen of our city.[42]

The Sisters of St. Joseph were placed in charge of the institution and made an enviable record of unselfish and devoted service in the care of the sick during the cholera epidemic of 1855-56.

Before it was completed the old log chapel on Bench Street had to be used as a hospital for the victims of the cholera epidemic many of whom arrived on the river boats and had to be segregated.

A free school for girls, maintained in a brick building erected near the hospital was opened on January 1, 1855, with an attendance of thirty pupils and was used for that purpose until the present St. Joseph's Academy was available in 1863.

On June 27, 1854, Bishop Cretin declared his intention to become a citizen of the United States, certifying that he arrived in the country on or about October 8, 1838, and has since resided therein and intends to remain in it, and willingly renounces allegiance to "Louis Napoleon the 3rd, Emperor of France".

Regulations for Parishes

In October, 1855, Bishop Cretin issued regulations for the temporal administration of the parishes in the diocese.[43] They obligated the pastor to keep a regular and detailed account. of the receipts from Sunday collections, donations and subscriptions as well as of the disbursements for parochial purposes. The Bishop appointed a committee of two or three members of the congregation to assist and advise the pastor in the management of the temporalities of the parish. No debt of more than one hundred dollars could be contracted in any year without the written authorization of the Bishop or the Vicar General. The salary of a pastor was $600.00; that of an assistant $400.00, and the latter must bear one-half the expense of the house unless he prefers to pay for his board and lodging. The parsonage is for the free use and occupancy of pastor and assistant, and all altar vessels, vestments and linens belong to the parish and are for its use and benefit. If there be no parsonage the pastor received an additional one hundred dollars for house rent. There should be a parsonage in every permanent congregation. An annual report should be submitted to the Bishop and a copy kept by the pastor for the information of the people. These rules were applicable to the larger parishes where Mass was said regularly on Sundays and festivals.

The first St. Patrick's day celebration[44] of which there is any record was that of 1853 when upwards of three hundred men joined in a procession wearing green scarfs over their right shoulders and sprigs of shamrock in their hats. The parade formed at the church after Mass and marched through the streets to the stirring notes of fife and drum. According to the Minnesota Pioneer it was "a magnificent affair, not the least impressive part of which was the Irish Catholic Temperance Society, with their temperance badges in addition to the other regalia. The Society was organized by the Right Reverend Bishop Cretin more than a year ago and by whose fostering care it continues to prosper". After the parade and a supper prepared by John Rogers, speeches, songs and toasts were the order of the evening in which many non-Catholics participated.

In 1855 the Bishop suffered a severe loss in the untimely death of Father Peyragrosse who was called to his reward on May 7, in the third year of his consecrated life—the first priest to die in the diocese. He was beloved by all for his devoted zeal, unbounded charity and exemplary life.

Bishop Cretin presided at the first reception[45] of postulants into the Sisterhood of St. Joseph in the old brick church on the corner of Sixth and Wabasha at the six o'clock Mass on Sunday, May 27, 1854, when Louise LeMay from Lotbinière, in the Province of Quebec, Canada, received the habit. "The novelty of the situation made her forget the name she was to take in religion, and when she reminded the celebrant of her plight, he opened his ordo, and as it was May 27, the feast of St. Gregory, the name was selected for the new sister". Next morning she left for the Winnebago mission in Long Prairie to work among the Indian children.

Her sister, Julia LeMay, received the habit and was given the name of Sister M. Pauline at the close of the annual retreat on September 30, of the same year. The first English-speaking postulant, Rose A. Cox, received the habit on the feast of the Ascension, May 17, 1855, and the name Sister Ignatius Loyola. This was the first reception after the opening of the novitiate at St. Joseph's Hospital.

The first religious profession took place on March 25, 1856, when Sister Marcelline, a novice from St. Louis, completed the prescribed two years of training in the novitiate and was allowed to pronounce her vows, and Margaret Grace who had entered the postulate in July, 1855, received the habit and the name of Sister Peter Richard in honor of the Archbishop of St. Louis, the Most Reverend Peter Richard Kenrick.

During the early days the Bishop obliged the sisters to attend every service in the church and thus give good example to the congregation. For that purpose it was often necessary for them to make the trip from their convent to the church several times a day and this involved considerable hardship especially in the winter season. The Bishop, fearing they might not have sufficiently comfortable foot wear for such constant travel, presented each sister with a pair of high arctic overshoes on New Year's day, 1855, and on the following St. Joseph's day, his patronal feast, sent his team and box sled to bring them to the church through a raging blizzard.

Just before the next new year he gave them another present when he sent to the convent a three year old girl whose father had died during the cholera epidemic and whose mother had been frozen to death in her miserable shanty. This little girl became the petted child of the sisters for a few years till she was adopted by Mrs. General Shields.

Appeal for Immigrants

The question of immigration occupied much of Bishop Cretin's time and thought, as it became more and more evident that the crying need of the diocese was an increase in Catholic population. As Vicar General of Dubuque he had cooperated with Bishop Loras in his efforts to attract settlers to the rich farmlands of Iowa and Minnesota by writing letters to the Boston Pilot, the New York Freeman's Journal and European papers in an effort to direct the stream of immigration to the West and away from the congested areas of eastern cities where so many eked out a precarious existence. As a result many prosperous settlements were founded in Iowa and Southern Minnesota.

A few weeks after he arrived in St. Paul—on July 23, 1851—a treaty was signed at Traverse des Sioux between the United States Government and the Sioux Indians who owned all the territory west of the Mississippi whereby they ceded to the United States 21,000,000 acres of land which was then opened to settlement by the whites. It marked the beginning of a new era in the history of the Northwest and the Bishop took advantage of the opportunity to attract immigrants to the lands made available to colonists. He adopted the methods found so successful in Iowa and in letters to the press appealed for settlers and painted attractive pictures of homes to be had in the North Star State. As a result the Catholic population of Minnesota more than doubled, and soon he had the happiness of welcoming increasing numbers of French, Irish and German immigrants who took up lands along the Mississippi, Minnesota and St. Croix rivers and laid the foundation of future prosperity for themselves and the state. Most of the Irish who came West were forced to leave their native land by the famine of 1848 and subsequent years. They came by the hundreds of thousands and by 1850 forty-four percent, it is said, of the foreign-born population of the United States was of that nationality. There is little definite information about the Irish settlements in Minnesota in the fifties of last century. There is mention of an Irish colony at Jessenland as early as 1854, but little is known about it. But the Dohenys and the Youngs were not the first Irish settlers in Minnesota. Hugh Derham of County Meath settled in Rosemount in 1850, where he had no near neighbors and the railroad was two hundred miles away, as he told John Sweetman when the latter visited him in 1880. General Shields, who became a resident of Minnesota in 1857, invited Irish Catholics to settle in Shieldsville, where the fertility of the soil, and the scenic beauty of lake and forest combined to form an earthly paradise. "This action of General Shields", writes Honorable William J. Onahan, in "A Chapter of Catholic Colonization" (Acta et Dicta, 5:1, July, 1917) "may be said to have powerfully influenced in directing the attention of the Irishmen, East and West, to the possible advantages of Minnesota as a place for settling". Twenty years afterwards there were 250 families in the locality; and Kilkenny, Erin and Montgomery, were formed out of it.[46] The French Canadians who were the pioneers of the western states continued to come in large numbers. French traders, explorers and missionaries had blazed the trail and colonists came in their wake and settled on the land. As early as 1720 there were German settlers in the lower Mississippi valley and subsequent to 1848 they came to Minnesota, the Dakotas and other western states and began to till the soil and raise families. They were a thrifty people who made the German name honored and respected. Many Germans came to Stearns County as a result of the efforts made by Father Pierz, a missionary among the Chippewas and early settlers, who wrote a pamphlet in 1855 for the purpose of attracting German farmers to Minnesota and especially to Stearns County, where "settlers will, with little care and labor, secure in a short time beautiful farms and a most perfect and satisfactory home". To him must be given credit for the predominantly German Catholic population of that county. In glowing terms he described the soil, climate, lakes, rivers, forests and farms and pictured Minnesota as the Promised Land for the German farmer. The resulting influx of Catholic settlers enabled the Bishop to write to the Propagation of the Faith that, in 1855, twenty thousand Catholics had come into the diocese and that the number would be doubled the next year, a prophecy that proved true for at the time of his death there were fifty thousand Catholics under his jurisdiction, served by twenty priests in twenty-nine churches and thirty-five stations.[47]

The budgetary requirements for 1855 amounted to $35,000 for the ordinary work of the diocese. The greatest need was for a college to educate boys attending non-Catholic institutions where their faith was endangered. He needed eleven missionaries for three nations of Indians, the Sioux, the Chippewas and the Winnebagoes. A dozen parishes had been organized in two years in new places and three Indian missions were flourishing. He had asked several congregations—among them the Capuchins and the Jesuits—to establish other missions among the Indians, but in vain.

Father Pierz Comes to Minnesota

When Bishop Cretin took possession of the diocese the Sioux and Chippewa Indians far outnumbered the white population and he had to provide missionaries for them. He sent an urgent appeal to Father Pierz, a noted missionary among the Indians of Michigan, who knew the language of the redmen, their customs and habits, begging him to come and preach the gospel to them. Father Pierz arrived in St. Paul on June 18, 1852,[48] was welcomed by the Bishop and sent to the Chippewas along the upper waters of the Mississippi. He established a mission at Crow Wing, a few miles from the present Brainerd, an Indian trading center, destined to become what may not inaptly be regarded as the Indian capital of Minnesota, where he began the work of evangelizing with his customary zeal and vigor. In one year he converted nearly all the redmen of the vicinity and built a log and, later, a frame, church which was well filled on Sundays with whites and Indians. He asked for four priests and sufficient funds to establish several missions among the Sioux. The work among them was costly as he had to pay for guides and intepreters at the rate of five dollars a day.

Father Belcourt, likewise, had asked for two additional priests for work among the Indians and half-breeds in and around Pembina in the Red River Valley. Among the whites it was a constant struggle to offset Protestant propaganda directed especially against children through the public schools. The Bishop tried to counteract it by bringing the Brothers of the Holy Family from France to open a boys' school in 1855.

In 1853 Father Pierz went to Mille Lacs where he converted Chief Gegonebi, his warriors and their families, and started a church which was completed the following year. Then he went to Fond du Lac, near the first rapids of the St. Louis river, fifteen miles west of the present Duluth. It had been an Indian village long before the advent of the white man in the Lake Superior region and was in close proximity to rich hunting grounds and an abundance of fish at certain seasons. He also visited Belle Prairie and said Mass in the home of Anton Bisson till a log chapel was erected two years later. In the early fifties Sauk Rapids was an important settlement, the stopping-place for stage coaches between St. Paul and Fort Ripley, near Crow Wing. In June 1854, Mass was celebrated for the first time in the log chapel of the village by Father Pierz.

In 1855 Father Pierz left Crow Wing on an extensive missionary journey through new settlements in the surrounding country. He visited St. Joseph's in February and officiated at the home of J. H. Linnemann. Three years later a church was opened in that locality and a mission preached by Reverend Father Weninger, S.J. In the same year he built churches at Wakefield, St. James Prairie and St. Augusta where Father Weninger gave missions to the people. But the burden of ministering to the Indians and whites became too great for the aging missionary and he suggested that Bishop Cretin write to the Abbott of St. Vincent's Benedictine Monastery in Pennsylvania and ask assistance from the community. As a result three Benedictines were sent to Minnesota—Fathers Demetrius de Marogna, Bruno Riss and Cornelius Wittmann. The two last named were ordained by Bishop Cretin on May 17, 1856.[49] The Bishop accompanied them to Sauk Rapids where they arrived on May 21. They soon crossed the river to St. Cloud, and built a small log house and a chapel that served as a center whence they ministered to the spiritual needs of the Catholics scattered far and wide in small groups throughout the present flourishing Diocese of St. Cloud. Father Cornelius was its first pastor.

We are indebted to the Benedictine Forum, Volume 1, No. 4, July 23, 1917, of St. John's, Collegeville, for the following data about the missions of the Benedictine Fathers during the episcopate of Bishop Cretin: When Father Cornelius became first pastor of St. Cloud the congregation numbered between fifteen and twenty families. He finished the log church begun by Father Pierz, attended some fourteen families at St. Augusta, built a log chapel and, in 1859, a frame church, the log building being used as a school house. In 1856 Father Bruno was stationed at St. Joseph where he completed the log church begun by Father Pierz, added a log residence, and made the mission a center from which others were attended. He also visited St. James, founded by Father Pierz, established a mission at Richmond, attended Holy Cross and Ley Settlement, now known as St. Martin, and visited Spring Hill, once known as Gau's settlement. Father Clemens organized the parish at Meier's grove in 1857, celebrated the first Mass at St. Nicholas the same year, visited New Munich and built a small log church there the next year. In October, 1856, the missionary band was increased by the arrival of Father Alexius Roetzer who was placed in charge of Sauk Rapids where Father Pierz had built a log chapel, together with the Irish settlement known as Brennan's Place in Benton County; Pleasant Valley in Sherburne County; St. Augusta in Stearns County; Clear Lake and St. Michael in Wright County; and Forest City in Meeker County.

In the fall of 1857 the Benedictines opened St. John's Seminary at the original foundation on the Mississippi south of St. Cloud with five students. In 1866 the College and Monastery were permanently located at Collegeville, north of St. Cloud. In 1858 it was made an independent priory with Father Benedict Haindl as first Prior, and eight years afterwards was elevated to the rank of an Abbey with the Right Reverend Rupert Seidenbusch as first Abbot.

The Benedictines were a godsend to Bishop Cretin and his successors. Following their arrival Father Pierz returned to Crow Wing and labored among the Indians scattered between Fond du Lac and Leech Lake. In a letter, dated January 5, 1857, to Reverend M. Kristan, pastor of Vace, Carniola, he made the following statement:

> I have reached the seventieth year of my life. In three years I have established ten new missions in the district entrusted to my care. With God's aid I have built two churches for the Indians, two for French Catholics, and six large churches for the German settlers in the most fertile country on the Sauk River. The German congregations are now in charge of the Benedictine Fathers. The French missions I shall give to a French missionary; and . . . consecrate the last decade of my eighty years entirely to the conversion of the Indians.[50]

Of this devoted missionary who may not inaptly be considered the founder of the Diocese of St. Cloud, of the Benedictine community of St. John's and the principal factor in the colonization of Stearns County, Archbishop Ireland said, on the twenty-fifth anniversary of the erection of the Diocese of St. Cloud:

> First in time, as first in zeal and in the output of energy, was the great missionary of Northern Minnesota, Francis Pierc . . . He it was who

ministered to the spiritual wants of the white-faced pioneers, traders or searchers of homes, when no other priest was within scores of miles, he it was who, aware of the wealth hidden in the soil of Stearns County, undertook to make this region a garden of Catholicity and with might and main worked to bring hither Catholic settlers. Wielding a facile pen, gifted with poetic fancy, skilled in description, he filled week after week, the columns of German papers in America and in Europe with vivid picturings of the region, beckoning hither all who craved for happy homes, who foresaw in the cultivation of the land prosperity for themselves and their children. At the call of Father Pierc there came crowds of settlers, sturdy sons of Rheinland, Westphalia, Bavaria, until a new Germany rose in Stearns County—a new Germany permeated to the core with that strong Catholic faith and energy racy of the Catholic population of those historic provinces of the older Germany.[51]

Progress in the Diocese

Early in the third year of his episcopate Bishop Cretin was consoled with the progress made on the hospital, orphanage and novitiate, all separate and independent units. He had used his own money to complete the work. He had asked several religious orders to come to his assistance but none responded favorably. By the end of the year he could declare that the diocese had experienced a growth for which he had not dared to hope. The population had increased rapidly, attracted by the richness of the soil and the salubrity of the climate. The majority of the immigrants were from New England and prejudiced against the Church. Their schools were attended by Catholic children and many were in danger of losing their faith. The Presbyterians were building a college (Macalester) to cost $100,000 not far from the city, and the Methodists were erecting one (Hamline) to cost $120,000, all secured by subscriptions, and with the avowed intention of stopping the progress of Catholicism. To counteract this influence Catholic schools, even a college, were a necessity.

In the Catholic Almanac for 1854, which refers to the condition of the Diocese of St. Paul in 1853, we read:

The New Englanders, pretty numerous in St. Paul, have imported from their former home their narrow eastern prejudices against liberty of conscience and the freedom of education. In the name of liberty, as understood by them, they disregarded, last year, numerous petitions on that subject, and defeated a bill claiming that each denomination should be authorized to have schools of their own, supported by the public funds, provided these schools be well conducted, and although religious instruction should be given there; they thought proper to compel parents to pay taxes for schools that their conscience and their pastors forbid them to profit by. There is no hope to obtain anything this year from our legislature, neither from the School Commissioners, for our numerous schools. These gentlemen would do well to take some lessons of liberality from their neighbors in Dubuque and Galena.

The Bishop had established the Society for the Propagation of the Faith in the diocese but all he received was $90.00 from three parishes. The receipts of the diocese from pew rent and other sources amounted to $1,700, and he needed $25,000 for projected religious works, to defray the cost of bringing six missionaries from Europe and to open new missions among the Indians. There were ten thousand Catholics in the diocese served by nine priests in five churches and six chapels. Three schools were under the direction of the Sisters and there was a college for boys in the episcopal residence, taught by two priests.

The first fruits of this institution as a nursery of vocations for the priesthood were John Ireland and Thomas O'Gorman whom he had sent to France to complete their education. They were the first seminarians of the diocese and set a high standard of intelligence, piety and unwearying activity for all who came after them. Bishop Devie of Belley had promised to educate them in one of his seminaries without cost to the diocese, and, when they completed their classical education, Fathei Colin, Founder of the Marists, assured the Bishop that his community would continue their education until they reached the priesthood in the Marist Scholasticate at Montbel midway between La Crau and Hyères in Southern France. When they completed their studies they returned to St. Paul for ordination by Bishop Grace, the former on December 22, 1861, and the latter on November 5, 1865. Both were to do notable work for the Church as priests and bishops.

On his return from France in 1854 Father Ravoux brought with him four French and three German seminarians—George Keller, Valentine Sommereisen, Francis Hurth, Anatole Oster, Claude Robert, Louis Caillet and Felix Tissot—all of whom reached the priesthood in due time, five being ordained by Bishop Cretin and the other two by Bishop Smyth of Dubuque after Bishop Cretin's death. In later years one of the group, Louis Caillet, used to tell with much amusement how Father Ravoux laid down a stringent code of rules and regulations for his charges on shipboard, and how his plans to establish a miniature seminary, as it were, on the high seas were sadly upset by the innocent pranks of two of the younger seminarians bent on whiling away the tedium of a voyage extending over forty-five days.

German Catholic Parish

During the fifties the Catholic German population of St. Paul had grown quite rapidly and was clamoring for a church of its own. In 1853 the Bishop commissioned the Reverend Michael Wurtzfeld, an assistant at the Cathedral, who had come from an eastern diocese for his health, to organize a parish for them and donated two lots as a site for the proposed church. The cornerstone of the original Church of the Assumption[52] was blessed on August 15, 1855, by the Bishop assisted by Fathers Ravoux, De Vivaldi, Ledon, McMahon and Robert. In it was enclosed a tin box with a parchment record of the event. The pastor, Father Keller, preached in German and addresses were delivered by the Bishop, Governor Gorman and Father De Vivaldi (in French). There was a procession from the Cathedral to the site, with singing by the choir and band-playing and a return to the Cathedral after the function. The Bishop contributed a twenty dollar gold piece to the collection. The church was opened for divine worship on May 25 of the next year and placed in charge of Father Keller. It was "a very beautiful church of stone" to the building of which seven prosperous farmers of the parish contributed one hundred dollars each. In the meantime Father Wurtzfeld returned to the East and became pastor of the parish of Clearfield in the Diocese of Erie where he died on December 17, 1870. Father Keller remained at the Assumption till January 1, 1858, when it was entrusted to the Benedictines until 1912 when they exchanged it for the parish of St. Bernard in the eastern suburbs of the city and the diocesan clergy once more assumed charge of it.

At the St. Patrick's day celebration in 1855, the health of good Bishop Cretin having been proposed, the Governor of the Territory, W. A. Gorman, Esq., said in response:

> It is now near a quarter of a century since this excellent man first came to the valley of the Mississippi, with the Bible in one hand, and the Holy Cross of the Savior of the world in the other, to preach the gospel of Christ, and establish the Church in this then vast wilderness. Nothing but his pure love for religion could ever have induced him to deprive himself of the ease and comfort he could have enjoyed in his native land, as he is from one of the most honorably distinguished families in France. But a high sense of duty gave him energy to push forward in his holy mission, his faith never failing, never shaking, never flagging. When he had sown the seeds of a true faith, he still pushed forward to other and more distant fields of labor in the wilderness. Traveling by night and by day through the vast wilderness and prairies of the West—making the green earth his bed, and the blue canopy of heaven his covering, his labors everywhere have been crowned with success. It was Bishop Cretin who emphatically planted the seed of the Church in the valley of the upper Mississippi. His whole life in the West has been a type of purity, morality and religion worthy of imitation by all who may come after him.[53]

In the summer of 1855 the suffragan bishops of the Province of St. Louis were summoned to attend the first Provincial Council which opened in that city on October 7 under the presidency of Archbishop Kenrick. Bishop Cretin was present with Bishops Loras of Dubuque, Henni of Milwaukee, Miles of Nashville, and O'Regan of Chicago. The Council enacted some very important legislation for the government of the Church in the dioceses presided over by these bishops.

At the beginning of that year Bishop Cretin was able to report to the Central Office of the Propagation of the Faith that a dozen parishes had been organized in two years in new places; five convents for religious had been erected; a community of Brothers of the Holy Family had come from France, and three flourishing missions were established among the Indians.

Bishop Cretin's First Pastoral

On February 17, 1855, Bishop Cretin issued a Pastoral Letter[54] to the clergy and laity of the diocese which was a call to prayer and repentance during the lenten season, "the acceptable time and the day of salvation", during which they were exhorted not to receive the grace of God in vain.

It is replete with quotations from Holy Scripture calling upon the faithful to turn to the Lord, to remember death, to avoid sin, to cultivate virtue, to comply with the laws of the Church, to obey their prelates and pray for all who are in authority over them.

All were exhorted to sanctify the Sunday, even though they were too far from a church to assist at Mass, by avoiding servile works, reading good books, teaching their children catechism and staying away from non-Catholic services. He warned parents against sending their children to Protestant schools if it were possible to patronize Catholic schools. All must respect the rights and liberties of others and safeguard their own. "Do honor, by your honesty, industry and sobriety, to the great country that Catholicity alone can preserve from total ruin, as being the only religion out of the control of man".

He concluded by laying down the regulations for the lenten season, urging all to comply with the paschal precept between the first Sunday of Lent and Trinity Sunday, and suggesting that public services and religious instructions be held in every parish at least twice a week.

Diocesan Statistics

The Directory for 1855, page 242, gives detailed information about the new churches and their location:

Three other log and frame churches have been erected on the banks of the upper Mississippi at Sac (Sauk) Rapids, Belle Prairie and Platte River. The right bank of the St. Peter river is settling fast with Irish emigrants and many German Catholic families have selected good land on the bank of the Mississippi, above the Falls of St. Anthony, where churches will be erected. There were four students of theology in the seminary attached to the Bishop's house and four others in other Dioceses, besides a numerous school for boys under the superintendence of Father Peyragrosse in the spacious and elegant rooms of the lower story of the Bishop's house.

Ten more priests were urgently needed, as well as a church in St.

Paul to cost $10,000. He would not dignify with the name "church" the hall in which Holy Mass was said for the faithful of the Cathedral parish. He also announced that the collection for the Propagation of the Faith for 1854 amounted to $188.00, of which one parish, struggling with a debt of $1,000, gave $77.00.

The burden of debt continued to harass him as the budget for diocesan requirements grew with the passing years. The total revenue was now $3,000 but the expenses amounted to $16,000 and he was alarmed. There were 22,000 Catholics under his jurisdiction, ministered to by thirteen priests, one of whom was native-born, in seventeen churches. The Easter Communions had risen to 55,000. Ten churches were under construction and in need of furnishings. The population of the state was trebling every year and half the increase was Catholic. Priests were so urgently needed that he thought of going to Europe in search of recruits but could not afford to do so. He finally decided to authorize Father Bobad, a priest of the Congregation of the Missions at Lyons, to make an appeal in his behalf.

He learned from Protestant papers of the "enormous sacrifices" made by the sects to build colleges and schools to which many Catholic children go with danger to their faith. It was incumbent on him to provide schools taught by sisters and brothers at great expense and he asks, "How long can I stand it"? Catholics from Ireland, Germany and Canada were coming in such numbers that he was obliged to neglect the Indian missions for want of priests, and as a result a prominent mission among the Sioux had fallen into Protestant hands, and another under Catholic control for six years was endangered because the director, Father de Vivaldi, had incurred a debt of $4,000 in spite of the orders of the Bishop who was now importuned to pay it. Father de Vivaldi had left the mission and if the Bishop were obliged to pay the debt, it would ruin the mission and the diocese and the Indians would be left without religious instruction. He had to engage a lawyer to ward off threatened prosecution before the case was settled. He felt that he was compromised in the eyes of the government by failure to pay the debt, for Father de Vivaldi maintained that the Bishop had no right to give him an order as he was directly under the Pope. He borrowed money without the Bishop's knowledge, bought on credit and forgot to pay.

As an indication that St. Paul was growing "prodigiously" he states that he had to change the location of the cemetery three times owing to the extension of the city limits. It cost four thousand dollars to purchase another site of sixty acres about three miles distant, the present Calvary cemetery.

The Society for the Propagation of the Faith had been established in all the parishes and missions since 1856. Owing to the lamented death of Father Peyragrosse, the director, on May 7, 1855, the receipts for the year amounted to only $26.00.

He was much edified with the piety of the faithful during the Holy Week services and especially on Holy Thursday and Good Friday when the church was filled almost continually even though it could accommodate only about one-fourth of the congregation. He had to suspend the work on the new Cathedral, begun in 1853, rather than contract debts which he could not pay and for which he could not afford to borrow as the interest rate was fifty percent, and the property of the defaulting debtor could be sold without mercy.

Visitation of the Diocese

Throughout his episcopate the Bishop personally attended to most of the work in the Cathedral parish. The writer of a letter on February 19, 1853, says: "The Bishop has charge of the church and the priest who is assisting him has nothing to do".[55] Notwithstanding that, the Bishop made periodic visits to other parishes saying Mass, preaching and confirming. He continued to do so almost till the day of his death. Anatole Oster, a deacon, records the fact that during the last two years of the Bishop's life, he accompanied him quite frequently on these parish visitations and was often called upon to act as an interpreter in hearing confessions in the German language with which the Bishop was not familiar.[56] From time to time he was bidden to preach at confirmation or on the occasion of a cornerstone laying and to do so in English with which he was not too conversant. On one occasion the Bishop said to him: "When you preach, always bear in mind that you represent the Bishop and speak as you think he would speak". In 1855 the Bishop visited Faribault in Rice County and stayed at the home of Alexander Faribault where he heard confessions, celebrated Mass and made plans for the first church, dedicated to St. Anne, and opened for religious services the next year. As late as July, 1856, the Bishop and his deacon made a four hundred mile journey in a horse-drawn buggy over rough road to Fort Ripley where the Bishop said Mass in the post chapel for some days and preached to the soldiers. The country was sparsely settled, houses were few, and they spent the nights wherever they could find shelter. On the way they paid a visit to Father Pierz at Belle Prairie and discussed missionary accomplishments and prospects among the Chippewas.

Other trips took them to St. Mary's Town (near Shakopee), Mankato and Brownsville, with a side trip to Dubuque for what proved to be Bishop Cretin's last visit to his former superior. They returned through Caledonia, Rushford, Chatfield, Winona, Buckley Settlement (near Rochester) and Shieldsville. In Brownsville the Bishop refused to say

Mass in a room used as a saloon, but asked and received permission to do so in a large house owned by a Protestant woman who gave them breakfast afterwards. On these trips the Bishop not infrequently slept in a bunk or on a straw pallet on the floor with his traveling bag as a pillow and his overcoat as a coverlet. Nor did he neglect the most distant parish of Pembina and its missions which he was unable to visit in person. He was fully aware of the splendid work done by Father Belcourt who had spent nearly a decade of years in and around Pembina and St. Joseph, thirty miles west (now Leroy, N. D.). When his assistant, Father Lacombe, decided to join the Oblates in Canada, Father Fayolle was sent to replace him, until his recall to succeed Father Ledon in the pastorate of St. Anthony in 1855. In 1858, Father Goiffon, who was ordained in France on June 2, 1852, and came to St. Paul on November 7, 1857, after Bishop Cretin's death, was sent by Father Ravoux, Administrator, to the Red River Valley to assist Father Belcourt and be his successor from 1859 to 1861.

New Cathedral Project

The plans which Bishop Cretin made as early as 1853 for the erection of a larger and more pretentious Cathedral on the corner of St. Peter and Sixth Streets in the same block as the existing church, bore fruit when the cornerstone was laid with solemn ceremony on July 27, 1856, by Bishop Timon of Buffalo, who had preached the annual retreat for the clergy. Bishop Cretin did not live to dedicate the new edifice to divine worship. A newspaper write-up[57] of the new Cathedral said that the basement is 175 feet long by 75 feet wide. When the steeple is added, it will make the whole length of the building 200 feet. The steeple is to be 250 feet high, and built of solid stone from foundation to spire. It was to be the largest and most imposing temple of religion west of Chicago. Those who remember the old Cathedral know how it was shorn of this glory; and it is doubtful that a steeple of such proportions was even contemplated in the boom days of the middle fifties of last century.

The cornerstone of the Cathedral, the largest stone in the building and the first one laid on the rock foundation, was seven and half feet long, two feet nine inches wide and eight inches thick, and another stone of equal dimensions rested on it. A cavity hollowed in the center of these stones received a copper box, 12 by 6 by 3 inches in size, containing a parchment record of the ceremony of blessing the cornerstone written by Father Oster, a United States cent of 1853, two Canadian coins of 1837 and 1854, a French centime of 1853 and another copper coin with no definite markings. The copper box was made by Jeremiah C. Prendergast, one of the parishioners, who sealed it and placed it in the cornerstone in 1856 and lived to remove it therefrom fifty-eight years afterwards when the building was demolished.

The inscription placed in the cornerstone, written in Latin by Father Oster, is translated as follows:

> In the year of Our Lord one thousand eight hundred and fifty-six, under the pontificate of Our Holy Father, Pius IX, Right Reverend Joseph Cretin, D. D., first Bishop of the Diocese of St. Paul, Minnesota, United States of America, and the Right Reverend John Timon, D. D., Bishop of Buffalo, officiating, Franklin Pierce, President of the United States, Willis A. Gorman, Governor of the Territory of Minnesota, on the XI Sunday after Pentecost, 27th day of July, after High Mass about midday, this cornerstone has been solemnly laid.[58]

In the autumn of 1856 the walls of the Cathedral were twelve feet high.

In connection with the project of building the third Cathedral of St. Paul, initiated several years before work actually began, the committee in charge published a list of contributors—individuals and firms—as well as "the sums promised and paid" to the building fund from November, 1852, to September, 1855.

The committee canvassed the city for subscriptions and secured promissory notes in which the signers pledged themselves "to pay the members of the committee for the erection of the Catholic Church in St. Paul, the sum of $ .... each month from the first of April, 1855, until the first of January, 1857". Attached to this are the names of the subscribers together with the total sum pledged and the amount paid. The list contains 186 names, a fine showing for these early days. Among them are the names of Richard Ireland, father of Archbishop Ireland, John O'Gorman, father of Bishop O'Gorman, and Rev. F. de Vivaldi, the noted missionary among the Winnebagoes. All the subscribers have passed away and most of those who knew them in the flesh, but the descendants of some of these old families are still to be found in the city of St. Paul.

The note at the end of the list says:

> All the receipts did amount on the 1st of September, 1855, to $1,349. All the expenses for quarrying and cutting stones, canal & cet. to $1,551.84 cts. Those who have not paid anything are invited to remember their promises. The work shall be stopped until the money comes. The fifth part of it is done.

The Catholic Bulletin, which published the list in its issue of October 25, 1913, made this pertinent comment.

> It may seem strange to some that a fifth part of the work of constructing the Cathedral had been completed when only $1,349 had been received from subscribers. This sum was a mere bagatelle in comparison with the cost of the Cathedral. But we must remember that the greater portion of the funds for the erection of the building was received from the

Society for the Propagation of the Faith in France. This society dealt very generously with the early missionaries in the United States and large sums were received from it for many years for the carrying on of missionary work in the diocese. Were it not for the financial assistance given by this society the present Cathedral of St. Paul could not have been erected and equipped for the work of religion more than sixty years ago. No doubt, the Catholics of those days contributed as generously as their means allowed; but they were far from rich and the sum of their contributions towards the Cathedral was small in comparison to the cost of the structure.

During his episcopate Bishop Cretin received from the Society for the Propagation of the Faith 208,925 francs, or about $41,785, part of which was spent in building the third Cathedral. Before his successor arrived an additional 40,000 francs or $8,000 was received by Father Ravoux, the Administrator.

On April 16, 1855, Bishop Cretin accepted with gratitude the offer of August L. Larpenteur "one of our most respected citizens and an edifying member of our Catholic congregation" to solicit from his friends in St. Louis and elsewhere funds for the erection of the proposed Cathedral. "The greatest confidence may be relied in the gentleman bearer of these presents", wrote the Bishop who promised perpetual prayers for the benefactors of the church.[59]

On December 14, 1856, the Bishop ordained Father Oster, the last levite whom he raised to the priestly dignity. It was the third ordination of the year. On May 17 the Reverends Cornelius Wittmann and Bruno Riss of the Benedictine Order received the sacred unction of the priesthood and the former lived to celebrate his golden jubilee, the last of the priests ordained by Bishop Cretin to pass away. On July 27, he ordained Father Mehlman.

On St. Patrick's day, 1856, "The Benevolent Society of the Sons of Erin", organized a few months previously and chartered by the Territorial Legislature, celebrated the patronal feast of Ireland by attending Mass in the Cathedral and listening to a sermon by Bishop Cretin. After Mass the procession re-formed and the members paid their respects to the Sisters of St. Joseph, Governor Gorman and ex-Governor Ramsey before reaching their hall where several addresses were delivered. It was Holy Week and the usual dinner was deferred till Easter Monday when two hundred and fifty men and women assembled in the City Council chamber where the guests included Bishop Cretin, the Chief Executive and his predecessor. The President of the Society, John O'Gorman (father of the future Bishop of Sioux Falls) presided, and the following toasts, drunk in cold water, were responded to: "Pius IX and the American Hierarchy" by Bishop Cretin; "The President of the United States", by Governor Gorman; "The United States, Our Adopted Country", by ex-Governor Ramsey; "The Day We Celebrate", by L. P. Cotter (father of the future Bishop of Winona); "Ireland, Classic Land of Our Fathers", by William Murphy; and "The Patriots of '98", by W. B. McGrorty.

On November 16 of the same year "The Benevolent Society of St. Paul" was formed under the direction of Bishop Cretin and a constitution and by-laws adopted. The committee in charge of the work of organization was composed of W. B. McGrorty, A. L. Larpenteur, C. W. Williams, W. Markoe, and W. J. Brown, with L. P. Cotter as Secretary.

The feast of All Souls was selected as the day on which the bodies of the dead would be transferred from the old cemetery to the new. The Bishop celebrated Mass in the mortuary chapel—a gothic structure thirty feet square by twenty high—in the cemetery where St. Joseph's Academy now stands, "after which he broke his fast with bread, cheese and sweetened water" and with the clergy and laity set out in procession to the present Calvary cemetery with the bodies of the dead, that of Father Peyragrosse in the lead, who died on May 7, 1855, the first priest of the diocese to go to his reward. On arrival at their destination, as Father Oster relates,[60] the Bishop "consecrated" the burying ground "with all the ceremony prescribed by the Ritual" although there is no documentary evidence to bear out that statement. In his "Reminiscences, Memoirs and Lectures", page 63, Father Ravoux who was present on the occasion states that the cemetery was "blessed" by the Bishop. It was probably the usual ritualistic blessing given a newly-opened cemetery, especially as the Bishop was far from well. The bodies were laid in their final resting-places and all withdrew. The ordeal was very severe on the Bishop, whose general health had begun to show signs of enfeeblement. In his last letter to Bishop Loras, written on December 15, 1856, he said: "I do not know what will happen to me soon, but my health is rapidly declining on account of insomnia." For some time prior to that he had been much troubled with asthma and now evidence of dropsy began to appear.

In connection with the transfer of bodies from the site of the present St. Joseph's Academy to Calvary cemetery, it is interesting to note that the first to purchase lots in the former cemetery were Louis M. Olivier, John Bell, John Rogers and Charles Bazille. Before the bodies of their dead were removed to Calvary a portion of it "was set aside and platted in an exact reproduction of the former one and the bodies were exhumed and buried again in the corresponding lots in Calvary".[61]

The Bishop's Last Letter

The last letter written by the Bishop was to Monsigneur Chalandon, Bishop of Belley, and was begun three days before he died and finished before he passed away. It was forwarded to its destination by Father Ledon. In it the Bishop admits that he suffered intensely from dropsy for three months and does not sleep two hours consecutively. He had been forced to give up the work of the ministry. But the needs of the diocese were great and preoccupied him night and day. The Catholic population had doubled in a year and now there were more than 50,000 in the diocese and only nineteen priests. He thought seriously of building a preparatory and major seminary under one roof for the time being. A college would be attached and would furnish good professors. It would cost $5,000. The last words he wrote were: "We have two new missions".

A copy of this letter was sent by Father Ravoux to the Propagation of the Faith in Paris, with the budget for the current year made out by the Bishop before he died. Diocesan resources were less than $8,000; there were 5 stone and 15 frame churches, 2 chapels and an unfinished Cathedral, for the completion of which but little could be expected from the Catholics who were poor.

The report made out in his own fine handwriting is dated February 19, 1857. After estimating the budget for the year for the support of the diocesan clergy; for the traveling expenses of missionaries coming from Europe; for interest on the debt; for the expense of existing and prospective institutions—amounting to $18,000, he recalled the most pressing needs of the Diocese and, as it were, in a last will and testament, expressed the desire of his paternal heart in the following words:

> In view of the urgent need of recruiting the diocesan clergy, and of the difficulty of procuring subjects from Europe, there is no other recourse than to found a college to train a native clergy. I have thought, if circumstances permit, of using the hospital for that purpose, and then either to build a new hospital on another site or change its purpose which would necessitate the construction of a new one at a cost estimated at three or four thousand dollars. The founding of a college will prevent a great number of youths from being corrupted who, because there is no high school for Catholics, frequent Protestant schools. An orphanage likewise is sorely needed but, with mounting costs, it, too, will require a similar amount.

These were the last expressed sentiments and wishes of the saintly Bishop of St. Paul "always full of zeal for the glory of God and the salvation of souls" as he was about to leave the world at the close of five years and eight months of an apostolic administration. He had already made his last will and testament.[62] It was

> done and signed at St. Louis on the 17th. day of October 1855, at double copies for one to be kept into the hands of the Most Reverend Archbishop of St. Louis, and the other into the hands of the Rev. Mr. Ravoux.

He bequeathed to Father Ravoux and to Father Ledon,

> both living in the Territory of Minnesota, all the properties, lands, monies,

furnitures, goods, horses, cattle, etc., found in my possession at the moment of my death and whose titles or deeds will be found among my papers, in my safe at St. Paul, with the obligation on their part to comply with the following condition, namely,

to transfer the above mentioned properties to his lawful successor in the episcopal see of St. Paul; to expend one hundred dollars, "and not a cent more" for funeral expenses; to have one hundred dollars distributed among the clergy of the diocese of St. Paul for two hundred Masses for the repose of his soul; and to have an anniversary service in the church of St. Paul once a year for twenty years.

One paragraph states:

I do not think proper to make any private donation or bequest to any body, although many persons are very dear to me. I hope these friends will not forget to pray for my soul.

A note incorporated into the will says: "This last will of mine concerns only whatsoever I possess in America, and not what I am yet owning in France". And again: "I declare that up to the present day I owe nothing to anyone either for the affairs of the Diocese of St. Paul, either for my own private affairs".

·On the margin of both sides of this document there is a pencilled notation saying "This is not the last will of the Rt. Rev. Bishop Cretin". No later will was ever produced. That the foregoing was his last will and testament seems to be borne out by the statement made by Archbishop Kenrick of St. Louis in a letter to Father Ravoux in which he says that the "late Bishop (Cretin) made a will here in 1855 when at the late Council. A copy was left with me and another with Bishop Loras who sent his to Father Ravoux for probate".

Father Ledon, one of the executors of the will, left St. Paul shortly after the death of Bishop Cretin, spent a few months in the South and returned to France. Letters of administration were granted to Father Ravoux on March 17, 1857, and the estate of the late prelate was transferred to him on November 3, 1858, when he was discharged from his trust.

Illness and Death

We condense the story of the last illness and death of Bishop Cretin as told by the Benjamin of his diocese.[63] Notwithstanding his enfeebled condition the Bishop directed Anatole Oster's retreat for ordination and examined him in the practical duties of the ministry. During the night of December 13-14 he was very ill, nevertheless he ordained the young levite the next day. It was his last ordination ceremony. On Christmas eve he celebrated the midnight Mass; and on January 26, 1857, the sixth anniversary of his consecration, he said Mass at five o'clock, and for the last time, in his room.

After that he grew worse. The dropsy progressed rapidly, and to pre-vent suffocation the physicians made two punctures on January 27 and 29 which appeared to relieve him considerably. But for several days the illness made alarming headway. When hope of recovery was abandoned the last sacraments were administered by Father Ledon, rector of the Cathedral, after which he addressed his final message to the sorrowing group at his bedside: "In my life I have asked neither for health nor sickness, for riches nor poverty, for success nor failure; but only that the will of God be done. In the long night when I cannot sleep I pray for you".

About two weeks before his death he asked to receive the holy Viaticum and Extreme Unction. He received them sitting in his chair; all the clergymen residing in St. Paul and several other persons were present. He said to us that if he had asked for those sacred rites, it was not for fear of any immediate danger, but that being the pastor of the faithful, he felt also bound to give them an example and not to wait to the last for the reception of those sacraments.

On the day before his death, which was Saturday, Father Oster was summoned to Mendota to take the place of Father Ravoux absent in Faribault. Before leaving he went to the Bishop's room to bid him good bye and to ask his blessing. The Bishop was so weak that Father Oster had to help him draw his hand from under the coverlet. "It is the last time", said the dying prelate, "but we must meet in heaven". The next day, Sunday, February 22, while the seven o'clock Mass was being said in the Cathedral he grew worse so rapidly that Father Ledon was hurriedly summoned to give him the final absolution before he died. His death was immediately announced to the congregation and evoked tears and sobs. When Father Oster arrived home that evening the body of the deceased, robed in pontifical vestments, lay in the coffin ready to be brought to the church. He had attained the fifty-eighth year of his life, the thirty-fifth of his priesthood and the sixth of his episcopate.

Further details of his last illness and death are given by one of his attendants, Louis E. Caillet, a seminarian, who was alone with him when he passed away.[64]

Our late beloved bishop died after two months of the most painful disease. In the midst of the most intense sufferings he never was seen to manifest the slightest impatience, never a complaint was heard from his lips.
In the thought of Jesus crucified he found a source of patience and fortitude. Often when in the most agonizing pains, he was heard to repeat these words, "O my Jesus why should I complain when I think of all you have endured for me. I suffer, but did you not suffer more? You had not all those comforts which I have; my bed is soft, yours was the hard wood of the cross; I have wine sweetened with sugar, etc., and you had only vinegar and gall. What are my pains compared with what

you suffered from those nails that pierced your hands and feet, from that crown of thorns, etc., etc".

His favorite reading was the chapter of the kingly way of the Cross in the Following of Christ. Day after day he would have us read it to him and when we would express a wish to change, he would tell us: "Read the kingly way of the Cross, ever the way of the cross, you can find nothing better". During these long sleepless nights he would often say to us, "Now my children since you cannot sleep do meditate on the sufferings of our beloved Savior".

In the midst of his pains he would entirely forget himself to see to the comforts of others and if anything saddened his heart it was the fear of causing others to suffer something. One day we were very much surprised to hear him complain, it seemed as though he was becoming impatient. I went to him and asked him to tell me what was the cause of his depression, he answered "I am so long sick", then added, "not for myself do I speak so, but for yourselves, I feel that I (am) now uselessly ruining your health".

No sooner would the most acute pains leave him than he would begin to work with his letters, etc. On the very eve of his death as he enjoyed comparative ease, he asked us to help (him) to go to his table and began to write, although his sight was so dim that he hardly could see and when we remonstrated with him that he was injuring himself, that he should rest, etc., his answer was, "my children, let me work. I feel able and while I feel so, work I must, we know not how long it will last".

On the morning anniversary of his consecration he celebrated in his room and for the last time the holy sacrifice of the Mass. I forget what day it was. His death although it had been expected for weeks took us by surprise. On the morning of the day in which it occurred there was no apparent change in his situation. All went to Mass except one of his attendants, (it was on Sunday). He requested that person to help him to sit on the edge of his bed, had his table brought near him, then began to thank him most affectionately for the attention paid him during his illness, expressing his ardent wish that God might reward him. Those words were the last he uttered; his attendant seeing him lean on one side thought (he) was fainting and caught him in his arms and thus our beloved bishop closed his eyes to the world.

On the day of the funeral the weather was so inclement that only the priests of St. Paul could attend. Protestant ministers asked the privilege of being present at the obsequies. The funeral procession wended its way to Calvary cemetery, the ministers of the Mass in their sacred vestments, the clergy in cassock and surplice. The Catholics walked to the graveyard; the non-Catholics brought up the rear in carriages.

A correspondent of the Boston Pilot in its issue of March 21, 1857, wrote about the funeral:

There were not less than fifteen hundred persons in the procession which followed the remains of the late Bishop Cretin to the grave. The funeral was the most imposing of the kind that has ever taken place in this city; and, if it was emblematic of nothing else, it proved the true devotion cherished by the mourners towards the lamented Bishop. The Shield

Guards, the Benevolent Sons of Erin, St. Vincent de Paul Society, the St. Joseph Society, the Sisters of Charity, and all the societies and schools under the auspices of the Church were out with all their members to pay a parting tribute to his memory. Four hundred and thirty-five men and boys, and three hundred and twenty-five ladies and girls followed on foot, while 170 vehicles of all kinds, averaging four persons each, made up the remainder of the solemn cortege. Altogether, a living assemblage of nearly 5,000 persons witnessed the passage of the procession, notwithstanding there was on the ground a disagreeable accumulation of water from the melting snow. The whole procession occupied nearly three-quarters of an hour in passing a given point. On the whole, it was a sight seldom witnessed, and long to be remembered by the participants. . . The Bishop sustained a high reputation for learning, piety and christian benevolence, and has been greatly instrumental in promoting the growth and prosperity of the Catholic Territory of Minnesota.

The pall bearers were C. W. Williams, Patrick Ryan, Dr. J. A. Vervais, Francis Meissel, E. N. Larpenteur, Richard Ireland, William Markoe, Thomas Daly, John O'Gorman, Thomas Grace, Mathew Flood and N. Hendy: the marshalls, W. J. Brownson, John Bell, Firman Gayeau and W. B. McGrorty: the armorial bearers, S. M. Olivier and Patrick Nash.

The esteem in which the deceased prelate was held by the citizens, irrespective of class or creed, was evidenced by the manifestation of grief caused by his death. He was regarded as a saint by all and especially by the members of his flock to whom he was in very truth the good shepherd who knew his sheep and watched over their spiritual welfare with the devotedness of another Christ.

No one grieved more over the death of Bishop Cretin than his devoted sister in the family home at Montluel. On June 17, 1858, she wrote a letter to her boys, John Ireland and Thomas O'Gorman, in the nearby seminary:

My mind and my heart are there (in St. Paul) night and day. My prayers, my sighs and my tears are for the needs of that diocese and for yours. . . . My brother loved it so much that he gave his life for it. I, too, love it, and I pray continually for all its needs.

A few months after his death Father Ravoux informed the Secretary of the Propagation of the Faith:

Monsigneur Cretin is no longer in the world. He was ripe for heaven and God called him to Himself to reward him for his works . . . Our loss is great and almost irreparable. He lived like an apostle, he died a martyr, because he suffered for three months the horrible torments of a disease with the same patience and resignation that the martyrs suffered who are honored with public veneration by the Church.

Remains Transferred to Memorial Chapel

His body was interred in a vault in Calvary Cemetery which he had bought and blessed, and remained there in undisturbed repose until October 10, 1884,[65] when it was transferred to the crypt beneath the gothic mortuary chapel built, at the direction of his successor, on the highest point of ground in the cemetery. On that day the coffin was taken from its resting-place and, preceded by a procession in which Bishops Grace and Ireland, twenty-five priests and 1500 people participated, borne to the chapel in which a Mass of Requiem was celebrated by Bishop Grace and the sermon preached by Bishop Ireland who described the life and labors of the deceased prelate, paid tribute to his distinguished services to the Church as first Bishop of St. Paul, and concluded by saying that Bishop Cretin, "broken down in health, a cold wintry day, returned from blessing the cemetery where he now sleeps, to end his days by a holy death".

After the service the coffin was reverently lowered into the crypt destined to receive the bodies of the future bishops of the diocese, where it remained until 1888, when it was reinterred in a nearby plot reserved for the burial of his successors. The grave is marked by a granite slab, 4 by 9 feet and 8 inches thick, lying on the ground and bearing the following inscription: Sacred to the Memory of Joseph Cretin, First Bishop of St. Paul, Born in Montluel, France, A. D. 1799, Died in St. Paul A. D. 1857. How beautiful upon the mountains are the feet of him that bringeth good tidings, and that preacheth peace. Isaias LII, 7. May he rest in peace.

When the remains were placed in the crypt of the mortuary chapel, one of the finest specimens of pure gothic architecture in the Northwest, a mural tablet was erected in a niche beside the altar with an inscription in Latin of which the following is the English version:

To the Memory of
JOSEPH CRETIN

A man of most eminent virtue, and of great apostolic zeal, who, having been on the 26th. day of January, 1851, consecrated the first Bishop of St. Paul, ruled the Church in this State during six years amid many difficulties and in a manner most praiseworthy; commenced in the Year of Grace, 1856, the building of the Cathedral, proved himself a most devoted servant of the Blessed Virgin Mary, and beloved of God and man, fell asleep in the Lord the 22nd. day of February, 1857.

THOMAS L. GRACE

his successor in office, albeit unworthy, has erected this memorial.

The Mortuary Chapel was dismantled in the summer of 1949, but nothing remained of the memorial tablet erected in 1884. It was made of plaster of Paris with gilded lettering at a total cost of thirty-one dollars and twenty-five cents. It disintegrated long before the chapel was torn down.

An editorial in the Northwestern Chronicle for October 16, 1884, written by Bishop Ireland, eulogizes the deceased prelate.

> The Diocese of St. Paul was singularly blessed in its founder. The fragrance of his virtue will perfume its history; his example will be a continuous and potent lesson to its clergy and its laity . . . 'The Little Saint' he used to be called by his fellow-students and his masters. Even at that early period of his life, he arrived at heroic sanctity and practiced penances that recall the hermits of the Theban deserts . . . All the Catholics in the Territory did not go much over one thousand . . . In his zeal he was a second St. Paul whose words 'I am made all to all' he took as his episcopal motto . . . When not engaged in works of zeal, he was to be found in prayer before the Blessed Sacrament. His charity towards the suffering and the poor was unbounded. Patience and mildness marked all his relations with his fellow-men. No one ever knew him but to love him for his rare goodness of heart, his noble sentiments, his child-like though dignified simplicity. He reproduced in the privacy of his life the highest examples of christian abnegation—wearing instruments of penance, seldom taking rest even at night save by slumbering a few hours in a chair or on a sofa . . . Zeal ever tempered with prudence reflected a mind stored with rich knowledge and capable of the widest range of thought . . . He was a firm believer in the great future of Minnesota and of the Diocese of St. Paul. The thorough education of the priesthood in piety and learning he deemed an essential work for the establishment of the faith in America. Bishop Cretin was a saint—and a saint such as this America needs in the nineteenth century.

Shortly after Bishop Cretin's death Archbishop Kenrick of St. Louis wrote Father Ravoux:

> The afflicting but not unexpected news of the death of your late saintly and devoted Bishop has been received here with profound regret by all his friends and by none more so than by myself.

Ten years after Bishop Cretin's death Father Ravoux wrote:

> His ardent zeal and charity for his fellow men, his constant labor, his mildness, his sincere humility and spirit of prayer, were strong and convincing proofs to us all that in his mind, in his heart, he had only two objects in view—the glory of God and the sanctification of souls.[66]

Thirty-three years after the death of Bishop Cretin Father Ravoux, than whom few, if any, knew him better, wrote in his "Reminiscences and Memoirs":

> Omnia omnibus factus sum was the motto engraved on his seal, and in fact the first Bishop of St. Paul, like the Apostle of the Nations, was "All to All." All those who have been well acquainted with him are convinced that he constantly walked in the footsteps of St. Paul by zeal, piety, charity, humility, incessant labor and patience in suffering; not only after his consecration, but also when a priest, when in the seminaire and in the colleges. (p. 62)

A Saintly Prelate

Father Oster who was closely associated with Bishop Cretin during the latter years of his life furnished many interesting details of the daily routine and occupations of the prelate.[67] He met the Bishop for the first time on June 16, 1854, as one of the group of seminarians brought from Europe by Father Ravoux. The Bishop was teaching catechism in the church and training the children to sing hymns and canticles in French and English. The Bishop was a skilled musician with a fine voice who loved congregational singing and did his best to teach the people to sing at Mass and Benediction. The Bishop was an early riser. He said Mass at five o'clock on week days and at seven on Sundays. He usually assisted at another Mass or heard confessions. At half past five on week days the priests, students, brothers and other members of the household assembled for morning prayers and meditation, followed by other Masses. He was always present at evening devotions in the church and made several visits to the church every day. During his life he made it an invariable practice never to leave the house or return to it without paying a visit to the Blessed Sacrament.

He was in the habit of attending to his own room. He made his bed which was narrow, provided with head and foot boards, and, when made up, looked like a common lounge. He swept and dusted his room, shook out the loose slips of carpet and put them down again, read and studied at night by candle light. He split his own wood and carried it to this room and would not allow others to wait on him. He often worked in the garden and helped to operate the treadmill used to cut wood. He was not above playing a joke on those who were taking their exercise on it, by pushing a stick of wood tight against the saw and laughing at their futile efforts to keep the mill in motion. He visited the poor and sick, Catholic and non-Catholic, with impartial regularity and found ways and means of helping the needy in the most unostentatious manner. For instance, he would express interest in a piece of bric-a-brac and, when it was offered to him, he accepted it but managed to leave a gold piece in its stead. He was a model of charity in word and deed and never complained about the inconveniences of frontier life. Even in his last illness he would not use a feather tick to make his bed less hard.

As a young priest in Dubuque he was disturbed whenever a day passed without appreciable suffering; and he gave up writing to his only sister on Sunday as an additional sacrifice. His letters have a pious tone for the most part, with little news of value; but homilies or sermons are frequent. There is a constant stressing of humility and fear of pride running through them like a golden thread. He makes light of the dangers to which he is exposed and of the opposition he meets in the line of duty.

"At Cretin's death", wrote the late Dr. Guilday, "Minnesota could boast of a perfectly organized church".[68] The mustard seed of faith sown in fertile soil by Bishop Cretin produced a bountiful harvest in due season as evidenced by a comparison of the statistics of priests, parishes and institutions in the diocese when he arrived with those at the conclusion of his pastoral career.

Diocesan Statistics

From "The Metropolitan Catholic Almanac and Laity's Directory" for the year of Our Lord 1850—which gives the statistics for 1849—we take the following summary from the Diocese of Dubuque to which the greater part of Minnesota Territory then belonged:

Churches and Clergy

St. Peter, Minnesota Ter., St. Peter's Church—Rev. Augustin Ravoux. The same clergyman attends Lake Pepin Settlement, St. Vincent's Church, and also St. Paul's, in Wisconsin. (p. 130)

Sioux Mission, above the Falls of St. Anthony, St. Francis Xaverius. This mission has languished on account of the intercourse of the whites with the Indians, and the introduction of spirituous liquor among the latter. The Church of St. Francis Xavier has been transferred to Lake Pepin, where several Catholic settlers have collected. It is visited occasionally by Rev. A. Ravoux, of St. Peter's. (pp. 130-131)

Pimbine Mission, Minnesota Territory, Church of the Assumption. This settlement is composed of 500 half-breeds from Red River. Rev. Geo. Ant. Bellecour and Rev. Albert Lacombe. These two clergymen attend several Indian missions in those remote northern regions. (p. 131).

To this we add the report from the Diocese of Milwaukee which had jurisdiction over the section of Minnesota Territory between the Mississippi and the St. Croix rivers.

Churches and Clergy, Minnesota.

St. Paul's, town of St. Paul's—Rev. Anthony Godfert. Instructions in French and English.

The adjoining stations of Pig's Eye and Gervais settlements, near the Falls of St. Anthony, as well as Bruce's and Prell's settlements, on Lake St. Croix, are visited from St. Paul's. (p. 123)

The Father Godfert referred to was ordained in Dubuque in 1842 and sent to assist Father Ravoux at Little Prairie, but owing to disagreement with his superior he was recalled and later permitted to affiliate with the Diocese of Milwaukee. He never lived in St. Paul but probably visited it occasionally before Bishop Cretin came. Father Ravoux is listed as attending St. Paul from his home parish in Mendota.

Contrast the foregoing with the report made by Bishop Cretin at the end of his first half-year in the diocese. The Directory for 1852, after noting the erection of the diocese in July, 1850, and the consecration of Bishop Cretin in January, 1851, lists seven parishes with resident priests, and three missions attended from the Cathedral, besides two priests in charge of a seminary and school in the see-city, making ten clergymen in all, including the Bishop. We subjoin the list:

Churches and Clergy

Minnesota Territory

St. Paul's—Rt. Rev. Joseph Cretin, D. D., Rev. Patrick Moran. Sermon in English and French.

The Bishop having arrived in his diocese only in July last, no church has yet been erected at St. Paul's. The faithful meet at present for divine service, in a large building, (stone and brick), which also serves for a seminary and school, and for the residence of the clergy.

St. Peter, St. Peter's—Very Rev. Augustine Ravoux. Sermon in English, French and Sioux.

Falls of St. Anthony, St. Anthony's—Rev. Louis Ledon. Sermon in French and English.

Little Canada, St. John's—Rev. Victor Fayole. Sermon in French and English.

Long Prairie, ... Rev. Francis de Vivaldi, Canon. Sermon in French and Winnebago.

Pimbina, Church of the Assumption—Very Rev. Jos. Bellecourt. Sermon in French, English and Chippewa.

Mandola Mission, ... Rev. Louis Lacombe. Sermon in Chippewa and Mandole.

Still Water, ... visited monthly from St. Paul's.

Point Douglas and Wabasho, are also visited from St. Paul's.

INSTITUTIONS

A seminary and a school are conducted at St. Paul's under the direction of Rev. Edward Legendre and Rev. Marcellin Peyragrosse.

The Sisters of St. Joseph, from St. Louis, are daily expected, to open a school at St. Paul's.

The Archconfraternity of Our Lady of Victories, is organized at St. Paul's and in other parts of the diocese.

The Society of St. Vincent de Paul is to be established in St. Paul's this winter.

The cornerstone of a Cathedral will soon be laid, which it is expected will be completed before five years. Many Catholic missionaries will be employed among the Sioux, as teachers, if a portion of the $12,000 annually appropriated for school purposes, can be obtained from the government. It is the wish of the Half-breeds and most of the Indians, to have the services of Catholic clergymen.

RECAPITULATION

Churches	7
Clergymen	10
Seminary	1
School	1

This report was communicated by the Rt. Rev. Bishop.

Two priests had been ordained during this period—Rev. James Moran of the Cathedral in the East and Rev. John Fayolle, pastor of Little Canada, in St. Paul.

The Metropolitan Directory for 1857, the year the Bishop died, says in a footnote that the information on the "Diocese of St. Paul's" is "reprinted from last year" and therefore, gives the statistics for the year 1855. It shows that ten churches were built in three years and three priests aggregated to the diocesan clergy. In addition, six other log and frame churches were erected in new settlements between Sauk Rapids and St. Anthony and Mendota and Wabasha but no regular services were given them. We list the new parishes and missions:

St. Paul, Assumption of the B. V. M. stone church (Ger.)—Rev. G. Keller. The Catholic population of St. Paul may amount to 2,500 souls, composed mainly of Irish, Germans and Canadian French.

Taylor's Falls—visited from Still Water, as well as three or four other places on the other side of the St. Croix river. The whole Catholic population of these different places may be estimated at about 900 souls.

Hastings and Point Douglas, Guardian Angels. A large frame church on a fine block—Rev. Mr. McMahon. The Catholic population three miles around may be set down at 500 souls.

Wabasha, on Lake Pepin, old log church—visited sometimes from St. Paul.

Brownsville, Houston County. The Catholics of this neighborhood amounting to 600 are erecting a church in the town and are visited from La Crosse by Rev. J. Tappler. From this place to Wabasha, on the western side of the Mississippi, there are five or six numerous settlements which are preparing materials for the erection of several churches.

Faribault Town, on Canon river, St. Ann's—visited from St. Paul.

Credit River, St. John the Baptist. Rev. Thomas McManus. Congregation nearly all Irish, more than 900 souls.

Marystown, St. Mary's Visitation, three miles from Chacoupee. German settlement visited from St. Paul. 700 souls.

St. Peter's, frame church, St. James'—Irish settlement, 500 souls visited from the Indian Mission.

Mankato, St. Philip's—German settlement, about 400 souls visited from Winnebago Mission.

Gessenland, near Anderson, St. Thomas'—Irish settlement, number of souls about 300. Visited from St. Paul.

Sauk Rapids, St. Luke's—visited once a month, 200 souls.

St. Cloud, St. Clotilda—German congregation, about 400 souls. A clergyman is soon to be sent there.

Belle Prairie, St. Andrew's—Rev. Francis Pierz. French Canadian congregation, about 300 souls.

Crow Wing, St. Francis Xavier—Rev. Mr. Pierz. Half breed and Canadians about 210 souls.

INDIAN MISSION

Blue Earth, among the Winnebago Indians, Our Lady of Seven Dolors. Rev. Canon Francis de Vivaldi, who has under his direction and the superintendence of the Bishop of St. Paul, a numerous school of Indian children, instructed by some Sisters.

Remark—Six other log and frame churches have been erected in some new settlements between *Sauk Rapids* and the *Falls of St. Anthony* and between Mendota and Wabasha, but no regular service has been yet organized.

INSTITUTIONS

Theological Seminary. There are four students of theology in the Seminary attached to the Bishop's house; four other students are preparing for the holy ministry in other dioceses.

Brothers of the Holy Family—to take charge of the boys' school—to establish a novitiate.

Sisters of St. Joseph. Their house affords spacious room for more than one hundred day-scholars and a good number of boarders.

Sisters of the Propagation of the Faith, Pimbina, Minnesota. These sisters, seven in number, have 100 pupils.

An Hospital, at St. Paul—room enough for a novitiate for the Sisters, for an orphan asylum, and many patients.

Temperance Society and Benevolent Society.

Most of the members of the Society of the Living Rosary, and of the Archconfraternity of the Sacred Heart of Mary, have formed a charitable confraternity for the relief of the poor and of the sick, the religious instruction of children, and the decent support of the sanctuary.

The Directory for 1858, which gives the statistics for the year 1857, at the beginning of which the Bishop died, lists fifty new church and stations, making a total of 29 churches and 35 stations attended by 20 priests, ministering to a Catholic population of 50,000. There are two communities of men—the Benedictines with four priests and six lay brothers; and the Brothers of the Holy Family, four in number, Cyrille, Leo, Timothy and Ernest, with Brother Cyrille, Superior, in charge of a high school with 20 pupils; a primary school with 40; and a free school with 100. The Benedictine Nuns with four professed sisters and three novices have been added to the religious communities for women. There are three clerical students; free schools in almost every parish where priests reside; and select schools at Mendota and Stillwater. Mother Protase is Superior of St. Joseph's Academy in St. Paul; Sister Scholastica of St. Mary's school in St. Anthony; and Sister Seraphine of St. Joseph's Hospital, St. Paul.

The Northwestern Chronicle for March 12, 1878, reports that La Semaine Religieuse de Bourg, France, makes pleasing reference to the memory of Bishop Cretin when recording the death of Reverend M. Bertrand, his successor in Ferney:

The works begun by Abbe Cretin in Ferney, have been blessed by Almighty God and are today in a most prosperous condition. His college occupies some ten priests and is one of the most flourishing institutions in the Diocese of Belley, so rich in numerous and important institutions. His name survives in Ferney, and secures still today the esteem and the affection of its inhabitants.

The memory of Bishop Cretin is preserved in St. Paul by Cretin High

School, Cretin Avenue, the western boundary of the College of St. Thomas and the eastern of the St. Paul Seminary, one of whose residence buildings is called after him.

In the museum of the Catholic Historical Society in the Archbishop Ireland Memorial Library of St. Paul Seminary are preserved Bishop Cretin's pectoral cross, crucifix and the penitential chain worn around his body; two ambrotypes, a photograph and two large paintings of him; the manuscript of the Method of Sanctification composed by him in 1821 for his own guidance; a rule of life, "Directeur Spirituel", composed by his sister, Clemence; the diploma of Bachelor of Letters granted him by the University of France on April 4, 1829 (which establishes the date of his birth at Montluel, France, December 19, 1799); his "Memorialis Tabella" or diary relative to the erection of the Diocese of St. Paul, his consecration and arrival; his letter of July 5, 1851, appointing Father Ravoux Vicar General; faculties granted to Father Ravoux on December 27, 1855; a set of green vestments presented to Father Oster about the time of his ordination; Biblia Sacra "Edit A. D. 1597"; 62 autograph letters to relatives (1812-57); 14 letters from the Propagation of the Faith in Lyons and Paris (1851-55); 4 autograph and 4 typewritten budgetary reports; and 15 typewritten copies of letters to the Propagation of the Faith in Lyons and Paris.

We cannot better conclude this desultory sketch of the life and works of the first Bishop of St. Paul than by quoting from the sermon preached by Bishop Ireland at the re-interment of his remains in the Mortuary Chapel in Calvary Cemetery, on October 10, 1884.

> Bishop Cretin did little that the world would call great, but he did much that is great before heaven.
>
> He was a saint, a man of God, one of those high born souls that the Master sends from time to time upon the earth to inspire us by their holy lives and deeds with a love for supernal things, and an ambition to follow them upon the royal road of spiritual perfection.
>
> Born in France in 1799 of a family noted for its piety and deserving well of the church for loyal services during the regretable scenes of the French revolution, Joseph Cretin was even as a boy and as a student known to be called a saint.
>
> Bishop Cretin's passion was a love for God. This was manifest from his sermons, his daily conversation, his frequent prayer. This divine love gave tone to his entire life as a christian and a bishop. He practised earnestly and continuously the virtues which should endear him to his Savior and make him a follower of this great model. Humility, meekness and self-denial were his choice virtues. As a bishop he was distinguished for burning zeal which was always tempered by prudence and intelligence. He loved the diocese of St. Paul with a fondness that betokened the tenderness of a mother for her first-born. How he labored and wrote, and talked, and planned for the development of the diocese! He built the Cathedral, the hospital, opened schools, invited hither communities of nuns, estab-

lished societies.   He was often in St. Paul without a priest to assist him.
The poor and the infirm found him often at their door.   He was unceasing
in preaching the word of God.   The people were poor, the country new,
and many of the Bishop's plans were beyond his power of realizing them.
They are remembered, however, as showing his wide range of mind, his
judicious forecast of the future.   As he intended to do, so we to-day may
do.   He had unbounded confidence in the future of Minnesota and of the
diocese of St. Paul, and he worked in view of this great future; he sowed
and we reap.

The First Chapel as Enlarged by Father Ravoux in 1847

Chapter VII

THE WIDOWED DIOCESE AND ITS ADMINISTRATOR

1857-1859

THE death of Bishop Cretin in what should have been, humanly speaking, the maturity of his power and influence as a religious leader was a great blow to the nascent Diocese of St. Paul. Six years of planning, planting and toiling, of unwearying labor, suffering and self-denial had gone into its upbuilding. Like St. Paul, his patron and model, Bishop Cretin had sown the mustard seed of faith in the soul of aborigine and immigrant, watered it with his tears, cultivated it with anxiety and solicitude and waited patiently and hopefully for God to give the increase.

Like most "doers of the word" he was not privileged to gather the harvest; but is it too much to believe that before death summoned him from the arena of his episcopal labors "his dimming eyes saw the mine of the future open and the golden veins appear"? In a few short years he had accomplished wonders under most trying circumstances and he builded better than he knew. He died in harness a martyr to duty, crowning a busy life with a holy death. He left a goodly heritage to his successors and they proved not unworthy of the trust.

For two and a half years no priest was found willing to take up the crozier that slipped from his relaxing grasp. In the meantime the burden of administration fell upon the shoulders of his Vicar General and friend, the Very Reverend Augustine Ravoux, than whom no one had a better or more comprehensive grasp of diocesan affairs and potentialities.

Early in March, 1857, Father Ravoux received a letter[1] from Archbishop Kenrick of St. Louis, appointing him Administrator of the Diocese until a new bishop was installed. In the letter the Metropolitan says:

By special faculty from the Holy See each Bishop, where there is no regular chapter, is empowered to nominate one or more clergymen, who, in the event of his death, should take charge of the see until the successor is appointed. It should be done in writing.

The Bishop should have also left a written document, containing the names of three clergymen whom he would recommend to be proposed to the Holy See, from among whom a successor might be appointed. This document should be prepared in duplicate; one copy of it to be sent to the Cardinal Prefect of the Propaganda, and one copy to be transmitted to the Archbishop.

No such documents were found.

On receiving notice of his appointment as Administrator Father Ravoux determined to carry out as far as possible the policy of the deceased prelate. No one was better qualified than he for the position; no one more familiar with the development and needs of the diocese. He had been a missionary among the Sioux whose language he spoke with ease and fluency, with whose customs and mode of life he was familiar from long and intimate contact, whose spiritual welfare he sought as a Hound of Heaven. He was pastor of the village chapel when the first bishop arrived and was intimately associated with him during the whole of his episcopal career. He had been pastor for more than a decade of years in the first residential parish of the diocese, and was admirably qualified for the new role he was called upon to play in the broader field of diocesan administration.

On July 15, 1858, he received from Pope Pius IX his faculties as administrator of the diocese,[2] and in that capacity devoted the greater part of his time and energy to the task of completing the third Cathedral. Owing to lack of funds he stripped the edifice of all the architectural adornment of the original plan and concentrated on a plain, substantial building with little more than four walls and a roof. The structure was 173 by 70 feet in dimensions, with eleven windows in each of the lateral walls, two smaller windows in the façade with a rose window above the main entrance. There were two additional doors in front reached by a broad series of stone steps. Besides the organ and choir loft there was a gallery supported by columns all around the interior walls, extending above the side altars in the sanctuary where it formed reserved and lattice-screened sections for the sisters who could assist at Mass without being seen by the congregation. The sanctuary, a circular recess, four feet above the floor of the nave, projected into the body of the church giving an air of compactness to the whole interior. The building "was more remarkable for its massiveness and a certain imposing boldness than for any special architectural merit."[3]

The financial depression of 1857 put an end to the orgy of speculation that characterized the previous five years during which there was an unprecedented boom in real estate due in no small degree to the tremendous influx of immigrants and the unusually large investment of eastern capital in St. Paul property. As a result new towns sprang into existence over night and cities, on paper, multiplied "faster than the wild locust of Egypt". Unprincipled speculators sold lots in swamps and under water to innocent victims. The man who did not own a corner lot was a nonentity and the man who had one a millionaire. The wave of speculation, well underway before 1855, assumed huge proportions in 1856 and culminated in the panic of 1857 caused by the failure of the Ohio Life Insurance and Trust Company on August 24 which brought disaster to the whole country with the resultant hard times. People were land-poor. There was no business, no immigration, no courage, no hope. Notes fell due and mortgages were foreclosed. Money was scarce and interest rates excessively high. Before the depression the value of city property had risen to $6,437,285, almost doubling in a year, and the population had correspondingly increased to a conservative estimate of between 5000 and 6000.

The panic dealt a staggering blow to the Cathedral building project. Work ceased for a time. The total amount collected from its inception to Bishop Cretin's death was only $3,820.50.

Third Cathedral Opened

Work was resumed on June 14, 1857, and did not cease until the edifice was under roof. On June 13, 1858, the church was opened for divine service although unfinished and unplastered. The collection on that day amounted to $428. During the summer the basement was plastered and made ready for Mass and at midnight on Christmas Eve there were two thousand present at the Holy Sacrifice and five hundred approached the Communion table. The total receipts from local sources to July, 1859, when the second Bishop was installed, were $10,108.20, and the disbursements to January 1, 1860, amounted to $33,647.94, leaving an indebtedness of $23,539.74, the greater part of which was paid by moneys received from the Propagation of the Faith, from pew rent, etc., amounting to $18,987.59, leaving an actual indebtedness of $4,552.15.[4]

On March 28, 1858, the Reverend Anthony Pelamourgues of Davenport, Iowa, was named successor to Bishop Cretin and as soon as he received official notification of his appointment he wrote Father Ravoux on May 22, apprising him of the fact and appointing him Vicar General of the diocese in which, as Bishop-elect, he could, according to a letter received from Archbishop Kenrick of St. Louis, exercise all the faculties of a Bishop except ordination and confirmation.

I appoint you my Vicar General and I send you all the faculties which I have received from Rome. You can then act as Vicar General of St. Paul

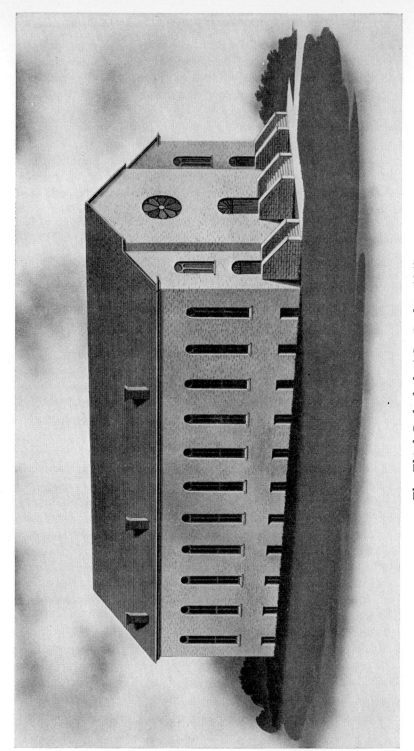

The Third Cathedral of St. Paul in 1858

till my resignation is accepted; and if not accepted I hope you will be to
me a counsellor during the rest of my days. You will be the only priest
having the powers of Vicar General in the diocese of St. Paul. . . I have
far more confidence in your wisdom than in mine.[5]

The Bishop-elect made a trip to Rome for a personal appeal to the
Holy Father and succeeded in having the appointment revoked.

As Administrator Father Ravoux officiated on December 8, 1858, at the
reception of Ellen Ireland and Ellen Howard, first cousins, into the
sisterhood of St. Joseph in which they were destined to play very
important parts in the development of the community. They were given
the names of Seraphine and Celestine. It was the first time that two
postulants were received at once. Father Ravoux preached a sermon
said to have been "much more impressive than many an eloquent one
heard since at similar occasions".[6]

Father Ravoux was one of the signers of the Pastoral Letter of the
Second Provincial Council of St. Louis, dated September 12, 1858, dealing with the jubilee of 1860 proclaimed by Pope Pius IX in an allocution
to the Cardinals on "his return from his late auspicious journey through
the States of the Church" and giving the conditions for gaining the
indulgences—reception of the sacraments, three visits to a church or
churches, a day of fast, and alms for the propagation of the faith. The letter also dealt with the question of vocations to the priesthood and christian
education, admonished the faithful to be loyal members of the Church
and not patronize schools where their faith is endangered.

A correspondent of the Boston Pilot, in its issue of April 17, 1858, gives
an account of the St. Patrick's day celebration[7] in which a procession,
led by a band and made up of the St. Paul City Guards, the Benevolent
Society of the Sons of Erin and many other organizations, marched to
the Cathedral for Mass and a sermon by Father McManus and then
paraded through the streets to the armory where they listened to a program of music and addresses. The writer continues: "Education is diffused throughout the state; and religion has made and continues to
make great progress; churches have been erected and others are in
course of construction in many places . . . Our new Cathedral is progressing very finely. The building is now being roofed and when completed
will be a splendid church edifice".

In the early part of 1859 Father Ravoux erected a stone building, 73
by 50 feet in size, and three stories high, on Third Street as a source of
revenue for the diocese, at a cost of $7,000, half of which was met by
diocesan funds and the balance with borrowed capital.[8] It was known
as the Catholic Block and was afterwards sold to the City of St. Paul
for municipal purposes.

New Parishes

During the interregnum the parish of the Assumption in St. Paul was placed in charge of the Fathers of St. Benedict with the Reverend Demetrius de Marogna as pastor: and the parish of St. Mark in Shakopee, authorized by Bishop Cretin, began its existence in the new church in 1857. A new parish for the Germans in St. Anthony came into being in October, 1858, when the first Mass was said in the Church of St. Boniface by Reverend Demetrius de Marogna, O.S.B., pastor of the Assumption Church in St. Paul. It was the second parish in St. Anthony, and was served by diocesan priests until 1874, when it was assigned to the Benedictines by Bishop Grace.

St. Felix parish in Wabasha was organized in 1858 by Father Tissot sent by Father Ravoux. During all these years it has had only four pastors —Fathers Tissot and Trobec and Monsignors Wurst and Bartholome.

The cornerstone of the Church of the Guardian Angels in Hastings, the most flourishing river town between St. Paul and Dubuque, was laid on June 20, 1858, by the pastor, Rev. J. K. McMahon, who also preached the sermon on the Marks of the True Church. The new edifice replaced a frame church which had become too small for the congregation. It was built of cut stone, front and spire, in Gothic design, 125 by 60 feet in dimensions, with five turrets on each side. [9]

A few settlers in the Minnesota valley, under the direction of Father Bruno Riss, O.S.B., formed the nucleus of the parish of the Guardian Angels in Chaska. For a time Mass was said in Catholic homes until the church was ready for occupancy in 1860. Since 1876 the parish has been under the direction of the Franciscan Fathers to whom it was entrusted by Bishop Grace.

The new church at Marysburg was blessed in December, 1858, by Father Sommereisen who walked twelve miles from Mankato to say Mass for the scattered Catholics of the locality many of whom came on foot to be present at the opening. [10]

The news of the appointment of Reverend Thomas Langdon Grace of Memphis, Tennessee, as Bishop of St. Paul, and of his reluctant acceptance of the honor was as sweet music to the ears of Father Ravoux, for it meant his speedy return to the ranks of a laborer in the vineyard without administrative responsibility. He was present with two others from St. Paul at the consecration of the Bishop-elect in the Cathedral of St. Louis on July 24, 1859, and returned with him to witness his installation in the unfinished Cathedral of St. Paul, and to retire from the position of Administrator after two years and five months of executive control. He was immediately appointed Vicar General and pastor of the Cathedral, retaining the latter position until Father Caillet was named his successor in 1861.

Spiritual Adviser of Condemned Sioux

The Sioux Indians had the utmost confidence in Father Ravoux not only while he labored among them as a missionary from the fall of 1841 to the spring of 1844 but when, as resident pastor of St. Peter's, he made periodic visits to their encampments, and for a score of years after he had any official connection with them.

This was shown when he was chosen as spiritual adviser by 33 of the 38 Indians condemned to death for their leadership in the uprising of 1862.[11] Armed with a letter of recommendation from Brigadier General Sibley of the military department he arrived in Mankato where they were confined on Friday, December 19, and presented his credentials to Colonel Miller who gave him every facility for seeing and instructing the prisoners, who numbered over three hundred. The 38 who were to pay the extreme penalty had not yet been separated from the others. The sentence of death was read to them the following Monday when Father Ravoux, accompanied by Father Sommereisen of Mankato, and two Protestant ministers, Williamson and Riggs, were present. Colonel Miller told the condemned men that there was no hope of a reprieve and advised them to choose a spiritual adviser, Catholic or Protestant. Without hesitation 24 of them selected the Black-robe, notwithstanding the fact that the ministers had been associated with them for twenty-five years, knew their language even better than Father Ravoux and had rendered them good service during their confinement. Three of the twenty-four were half-breeds—Jean Baptist Campbell, Henri Milord and Hypolyte Augé—who had been baptized but had not received their first Holy Communion. Later on ten others joined the class of instruction conducted by Father Ravoux, one of whom refused to be baptized with the others. After several days of instruction he baptized thirty-one and gave Holy Communion to the three half-breeds on December 25. Three others were baptized by the Presbyterian minister. Father Ravoux spent Christmas day with the neophytes, accompanied them to the scaffold, erected outside the jail, and prayed with and for them until they were launched into eternity. The Catholic Historical Society has the list he made of the 31 whom he baptized and the three to whom he gave Holy Communion.

In this connection Father De Smet, the Jesuit missionary among the Indians in Dakota Territory and elsewhere, wrote,

There has been a great outcry in the United States against the execution of these prisoners of war, who seemed to be given over to the vengeance of the whites of the frontier. The unhappy Indians are often wronged, insulted and outraged beyond measure by the whites, and there is no recourse open to them for the obtaining of justice. Driven to desperation, they dig up the war hatchet and utter the cry of vengeance against these whom they considered their enemies.[12]

During the year 1863, Father Ravoux frequently visited an encampment of some 300 Sioux families on the bank of the Minnesota river near Fort Snelling where he was welcomed by them for they had heard of what he had done for their friends executed at Mankato. He baptized 184 children, many of whom died soon after, and a man one hundred years old.

On another occasion, in November 1865, he received into the Church by baptism and Holy Communion Chiefs Shakopee and Medicine Bottle, walked with them to the place of execution and prayed with them until the fatal moment. Commenting on this the St. Paul Pioneer of November 12, 1865, said:

> Shakopee and Medicine Bottle were visited in their cell at an early hour by Father Ravoux, their spiritual adviser, who administered to them the sacrament, and remained in conversation with them until they were taken out. They had passed a good part of the night in repeating their prayers, and now as the hour of execution approached, they seemed more and more absorbed in their devotions, and in listening to Father Ravoux, who was earnestly engaged in conversation with the doomed chiefs in their own tongue.

And further, when they were prepared for execution, the Pioneer says:

> They held their hands firmly and we could not notice a finger tremble. Father Ravoux stood up with them, still conversing with them. The prisoners commenced again speaking their prayers which they scarcely ceased until they dropped from the gallows.

Episcopal Honors Declined

Father Ravoux may not inaptly be regarded as the founder of the Church in Minnesota. He was in the state a decade before the Diocese of St. Paul was erected. For seven years he was the lone sentinel of Rome in the upper reaches of the Mississippi with no priestly neighbor nearer than Dubuque on the south and St. Boniface beyond the Canadian boundary on the north. His record as a missionary and administrator was recognized by Pope Pius IX who, towards the end of February, 1868, appointed him Titular Bishop of Limyra[13] in Lycia and first Vicar Apostolic of the newly-erected Vicariate of Montana, an honor which he declined in a letter to Cardinal Barnabo, Prefect of the Congregation of the Propaganda, on July 15, in which he enumerated thirteen diseases from which he suffered, among them rheumatism, palpitation of the heart, short-sightedness, an affection of the throat and other internal complications.[14]

Notwithstanding this multiplicity of physical ailments he reached the ripe age of ninety-one, dying in 1906, in the first month of the sixty-seventh year of his priesthood.

There was considerable delay in accepting his resignation of the Vicariate of Montana due, no doubt, to the preparations being made for holding the Vatican Council; and his fear of an unfavorable outcome was heightened, rather than allayed, by the receipt of a letter[15] from Father Pelamourgues who was attending the Council, dated Rome, December 30, 1869, in which he said:

I think that you already know the reasons which you have given to Rome to decline the Episcopate, have not been sufficient, and I would not have written to you on this subject if Father Ireland had not requested me to do it.

Having had the occasion to see Cardinal Barnabo, he told me that you would be forced to accept, and when I told him that your health was very weak, he answered me that if you would die, you would be a martyr of obedience. His Eminence told me that you had not sent back the Bulls, but that you had only written. In such case I would advise you to come immediately to Rome with the Bulls; here you could expose your reasons to the Holy Father, and if he insists that you should accept, you could be consecrated here; and at all events, you would be present at the Council, which certainly will last till the month of June, and perhaps a longer time. Another reason for making this voyage, is that you could find some French priests, who would follow you to these missions, and as you ought to be convinced of it, the French priests would be the best for these savage countries. If I was not so old, I would ask to follow you, but I propose to finish my days in France. If I could be of some use, write to me.

On receipt of this letter Father Ravoux wrote Bishop Miege, Vicar Apostolic of the Indian Territory, residing at Leavenworth, Kansas, also in attendance at the Council, on January 20, 1870, asking him to intercede with the Holy Father in his behalf. On March 13, Bishop Miege informed Father Ravoux that he had discussed the matter with Monsignor Simeoni, Secretary of the Propaganda, who assured him that he would again refer it to his superiors. Bishop Miege was of the opinion that the petition would be favorably acted on, as it was soon after.

Father Ravoux was honored with the purple of a Domestic Prelate of the Papal Household[16] by Pope Leo XIII on March 1, 1887, and he invested himself with the robes of office with no more ceremony than the sprinkling of his cassock with holy water.

A Venerable Figure in St. Paul

About that time the following description of him appeared in McGee's Illustrated Weekly,[17] a description, the accuracy of which recalls him vividly to the diminishing number of priests who knew him in the later years of his life and held him in affectionate regard.

His benevolent features, ascetic without touch of harshness; the attenuated frame, tall beyond the ordinary, but now bent with years and hardships; the coat, almost a cassock in length and closely buttoned; the broad-brimmed, low-crowned felt hat, and inevitable walking stick—this is the unmistakable outline of a St. Paul landmark that is probably to the Protestant 'old-settler' as it certainly is to the Catholic, the most affectionate living memory that binds the populous, and busy center of the old Indian and Territorial days, when Abbe Galtier built the humble log church on the Bluff that gave this superb young city of the Upper Mississippi its name and its first impetus. Father Ravoux's health is not feeble, but much broken. He suffers from the labors, privations and inseparable exposures of his early missionary life, but there is no complaint. Fragrant in purity, inexorable though sweet in rebuke, and 'no respecter of persons' where admonition should follow, he is a glorious type of those apostolic men—a Dubois, a Bruté, an England, a Varela, and a Sudarini —that Europe gave our missionary land, the memory of whose burning charity, loving labors, and virtues is fast passing into tradition, though still cherished in the remembrance of our immediate parents, who knelt to them in blessing and whose faith was nourished at their hands.

General Sibley in a lecture on the Early History of Minnesota in Ingersoll Hall on January 15, 1867, referred to Father Ravoux as

A man of singular purity of life and character, of deep piety, disinterestedness and zeal. . . .since his arrival in the Northwest this good priest has always exercised a most salutary influence over both the Indian and white population.[18]

Another writer calls him "a grand venerable specimen of an old-time Catholic priest".

After retiring from the active work of the ministry he wrote his "Reminiscences, Memoirs and Lectures", published in English in December, 1890, and in French in February, 1892. Had he written them twenty years earlier, when the dates and events with which they deal were fresh in his memory, they would have provided an invaluable source of information about frontier conditions and the pioneer days of the Church in the Northwest. But even as it is they are not devoid of interest for the facts they chronicle, the personages with whom they deal and their description of some of the hardships and consolations of life among the Indians before there was any organized Catholic activity in what is now the State of Minnesota. At the time he wrote them his mental and physical powers were on the wane and they contain a considerable amount of matter not pertinent to a historical narrative.

His last will and testament was executed on January 11, 1898, and witnessed by Reverend William Colbert of the Cathedral Staff and John

P. O'Connor, Executive Secretary of the Diocese. He bequeathed his library to the St. Paul Seminary and the remainder of his estate to the Diocese of St. Paul on condition that it defray the cost of his funeral, not to exceed eighty dollars, have fifty low Masses said for the repose of his soul and use the balance for the education of aspirants to the priesthood. The historical documents, manuscripts and souvenirs found among his effects are now in the Catholic Historical Society Museum in the Archbishop Ireland Memorial Library of the St. Paul Seminary.

Monsignor Ravoux was an honored guest and distinguished personage at the ceremonies commemorating the fiftieth anniversary of the coming of the first Bishop of St. Paul on July 2-3, 1901. With the exception of the Reverend Albert Lacombe, O.M.I., of Midnapore, Alberta, in Western Canada, who also occupied a special place at the function and who was located at Pembina when Bishop Cretin came to St. Paul, Monsignor Ravoux was almost the sole connecting link between the pioneer past and the golden age of Catholicism in the Northwest.

Death and Obsequies

He continued to hold the honored position of Vicar General under Bishop Grace and Archbishop Ireland until the year 1892,[19] when the infirmities of advancing years postulated a respite from official duties that he might enjoy the otium cum dignitate to which he was so justly entitled. He occupied his room at the Cathedral residence, 19 West Sixth Street, until a short time before his death when he was taken to St. Joseph's Hospital where he passed away peacefully on January 17, 1906, six days after his ninety-first birthday and twelve days after the sixty-sixth anniversary of his ordination.

The solemn obsequies were held in the Cathedral which he had built and with which he had been associated for half a century, on Saturday, January 20. It was thronged with people of all classes, conditions and creeds who knew the deceased and wished to pay a tribute of respect to his memory and of appreciation for his long and laborious life and his services to God and country. Among them were members of the Territorial Pioneers, the Old Settlers' Association, nearly a hundred city and county officials, distinguished citizens, priests and sisters who occupied reserved places in the front pews. A band of white-haired octogenarians served as a fitting escort for the funeral cortege.

Bishop O'Gorman of Sioux Falls officiated at the Solemn Mass of Requiem, assisted by Father Lawler, pastor of the Cathedral, as archpriest, Fathers Heffron, Rector of St. Paul Seminary, as deacon, Genis of White Bear, as subdeacon, and Schaefer of St. Paul Seminary as master of ceremonies. Father Gibbons, pastor of St. Mary's, had general charge of the arrangements. An impressive feature of the service was the music chanted by the seminarians assisted by the vested boys' choir of St. Francis de Sales Church directed by the pastor, Father Bajec. The solemn Dies Irae was sung alternately by these groups. It was the first time a boys' choir sang in the Cathedral.

The Archbishop who preached the sermon was visibly affected by the significance of the occasion on which the monitor of his youth, the companion of his priestly years and his former Vicar General was about to be laid to rest in the silent abode of the dead. He recalled the personages and events of the early days and the life and labors of the deceased among the Sioux for three years during which he followed them from camp to camp, from Kaposia to Cháska, from Traverse des Sioux to Big Stone Lake, and later, from Mendota to Vermillion and Pierre in the Dakota Territory, enduring cold, hunger, fatigue and braving countless dangers to bring them the blessings of civilization and the consolations of the gospel of Christianity. He mastered their language, wrote catechetical and doctrinal books, and learned to love them. He was often poor, often destitute, but always happy in his work of saving souls.

He bought the property on which the Cathedral stands, welcomed Bishop Cretin to St. Paul as its first Bishop and served him and his successors with exemplary fidelity and devotion in an official capacity for over fifty years. On the death of Bishop Cretin he became administrator of the diocese until the arrival of Bishop Grace. In 1866 the bishops of the Plenary Council of Baltimore proposed him for Vicar Apostolic of Montana, but. owing to ill-health, he returned the Bulls of appointment and begged the Holy Father to release him from the burden. He edified all by his spirit of recollection, his life of prayer and his devotion to the Blessed Sacrament. He loved his God, his fellowmen, his city and his country. While he admired progress he often turned wistfully to the past and regretted whatever would rob him of its vision. He was a man of God, of faith, hope and charity. His old parish reaching from the Iowa line to the Canadian border and from the Mississippi to the Missouri, with its handful of soldiers and traders, is now the abode of two millions of people, among whom seven bishops and six hundred priests preach the gospel he preached to the untutored savage.

Monsignor Ravoux, he continued, was
the sole survivor of the Church in Iowa and Minnesota. During his long career as a priest, he was ever a good and holy priest. A man of duty he was in a supreme degree. The voice of duty was ever listened to and ever obeyed by him. He adhered with unwavering inflexibility to his conscience. . . .Our saint is gone—these were the words parting from the lips of many as the funeral cortege moved through the crowd. Peculi-

arities of nature he had; eccentricities of temperament were not removed from him, more particularly in his later years. But what were these but merest accidents, leaving the soul intact in its love for God, in its unsullied splendor of purity and of saintliness. . . .May the Church in the Northwest be ever mindful in thought and in fact of his apostolic zeal and his abiding loyalty to duty.[20]

The pallbearers were Fathers Remy of St. Louis Church; Heider, O.S.B., of the Assumption; Quinn of St. Patrick's; Koering of the House of the Good Shepherd; O'Neill of St. Michael's; Majer of St. Adalbert's; Riordan of Rochester; Kennedy of Belle Plaine; Plut of Shakopee; Kenny of Northfield; Tichy of New Prague and Andre of Minneapolis.

After the Mass the remains were borne in solemn procession to Calvary cemetery where they rest near the graves of the pioneer bishops whom he served and among the priests whom he had known during his long and busy life.

The following tribute to him and his work appeared in the St. Paul Pioneer Press shortly after his death.

The zeal and piety of Father Ravoux were exerted with benefit to the manners and morals of the settlers. A large number of the half-breeds, descendants of men who had forgotten the teachings of their faith, were gathered by him into the fold of the church, and baptized in the faith of their fathers. Marriage was once more sanctified by religion. Birth began to be regarded as the inauguration of a soul, and death its resignation to a forgiving God. And over all the simple people of these days, in whose hearts the priest touched mysterious chords of awe, and love, and reverence, never touched before, he held the same sway of gentleness and goodness. . . .The extent of their reclamation from the state of demoralization was apparent in the state of society which prevailed here at the period of our Territorial organization. The sanctions of the Church were accepted by the people as social laws, and the sacredness of family ties and social thrift took the place of beastly and reckless dissoluteness of manners which had prevailed before. On a summer Sunday the little log church upon the hill (in Mendota) was the central figure of a pleasant picture. Too small to hold the crowds that flocked to it, the reverent worshippers knelt in ranks upon the grass outside the window—the red-belted and moccasined voyageurs mingling with the tawny groups of children rescued by the Church from barbarity.

Most Rev. Thomas L. Grace, O.P., D.D.
Second Bishop of St. Paul
1859–1884

Chapter VIII

THE LIFE AND TIMES OF RIGHT REVEREND THOMAS LANGDON GRACE, O.P., D.D. SECOND BISHOP OF ST. PAUL

1814-1897

THE second Bishop of St. Paul, the Right Reverend Thomas Langdon Grace, O. P., D. D., was born in Charleston, South Carolina, on November 16, 1814,[1] the eldest son of Pierce Grace and his wife, Margaret Grace, who was no relative of her husband. He was the first native son of South Carolina to be ordained or consecrated and hailed from the diocese over which the Right Reverend John England ruled from 1820 to 1842. On his mother's side he could trace his lineage back to the Norman Conquest through one of the most ancient and honorable families in Ireland with large estates in Kilkenny. Among his ancestors were the Barons of Courtstown,[2] friends of King Charles 1, and opponents of Cromwell before being exiled to France. A Grace's regiment fought with spartan courage at the Battle of Aughrim on July 12, 1691. In later times the Grace family was connected with the most noble houses of England and was distinguished for its patronage of literature and the fine arts.

His father and mother were married on February 1, 1810, at the home of the bride's father, Thomas Grace of Newchurch, County Kilkenny, Ireland. He was 22, she 18. In that year they sailed for Charleston, South Carolina, where Thomas was born. He had three brothers and three sisters. The family was in Augusta, Georgia, in 1815. James Grace,[3] a granduncle of the Bishop, was an officer in the navy and distinguished himself in the storming of Quebec under General Wolfe; his granduncle, Richard Grace, had an official position in the Irish parliament that went out of existenece in 1800; his uncle, Patrick Grace, in religion Brother Barnaby, made his profession in Mount Melleray, Ireland, on November 1, 1839, came to New Melleray, near Dubuque, on July 16, 1849, with the monks who founded the institution, and died on July 8, 1884;[4] a first cousin, John Grace, studied for the priesthood but was not ordained. He emigrated to New Orleans where he opened a grammar school; another first cousin, Catherine Grace, was Mother Superior of a convent in Harrisburg, Pa.; another first cousin, William Grace, was Local Registrar of the High Court of Justice in Lindsay, Ontario, Canada; still another first cousin, Very Reverend W. J. Dunne, ordained in Sydney, Australia, in 1843, was Vicar General of the Diocese of Hobart Town, Tasmania, where he died March 7, 1883, after nearly forty years of missionary life. In April, 1875, he visited Bishop Grace in St. Paul on his homeward journey from a trip to Ireland and Rome.[5]

The Bishop's father was a man of scholarly attainments, a teacher by profession, and an officer in the United States Army in the war of 1812-1814. He gave his children the benefit of a good education. "The United States Catholic Miscellany" of August 24, 1850, edited by the Reverend James Corcoran, a classmate of Father Grace in Rome, referring to the rumored appointment of the latter to the proposed Diocese of Monterey, California, says that "Mr. Grace is a native of Charleston whence his family emigrated to the West Indies while he was yet of tender age", but does not say how long they remained there. Later on the family moved to Pennsylvania and thence to Ohio, settling in Cincinnati where Thomas attended Bishop Fenwick's College.

There is no record of the time or place of his birth or baptism in St. Mary's Church, Charleston, the only church whose records go back to the beginning of the nineteenth century. In the Book of Receptions and Professions of St. Rose's Priory, Springfield, Kentucky, it is stated that he was a native of Pennsylvania; but Archbishop Ireland who knew the facts better, perhaps, than any one else, maintained that this was because the family had moved from South Carolina to Pennsylvania and thence to Ohio shortly before Thomas entered the Dominican Novitiate.

In early youth Thomas received the grace of a vocation to the religious life, entered St. Rose's Priory and Novitiate, received the habit on June 10, 1830,[6] with five others, two of whom were Ottawa Indians, and made his profession on June 12, 1831, as a member of the Order of St. Dominic, in presence of the Prior, Father Stephen Hyacinth Montgomery. His solid but unostentatious piety and his intellectual brilliancy moved his superiors to send him to the Minerva College, Rome, in June, 1838,[7] to complete his studies for the priesthood. He was approved for deaconship on May 1, 1839, for priesthood on November 22, and was ordained on December 21 by Cardinal Patrizi, twenty-two years before his distinguished successor in the See of St. Paul, Archbishop Ireland, reached that goal at his hands and thirty-six years before he elevated him to the episcopal dignity.

Owing to ill-health Father Grace had to leave Rome in 1840 and was sent to Perugia in Umbria,[8] where he pursued post-graduate studies for five years, attaining the Dominican degree of S. T. Lr. in October, 1844. On his return to the United States in January, 1845,[9] he was appointed to the faculty of St. Rose's, made sub-Prior of the community and probably did missionary work from time to time in Kentucky.

On the Mission in Tennessee

In 1846, at the earnest request of Bishop Miles, O. P., first Bishop of Nashville, Father Grace was made a member of the staff of St. Peter's parish in Memphis, Tennessee,[10] to help in parochial work while the pastor, Father McAleer, was in attendance at the Sixth Provincial Council of Baltimore as theologian to Bishop Loras of Dubuque, and there he was destined to remain until his appointment as second Bishop of St. Paul, a period of thirteen years, for ten of which he was pastor. "Here he won the hearts of all by his zeal, virtues and priestly deportment, as well as by his kindly manners, charity, manly spirit, learning and eloquence. Memphis has yet to have any clergyman who has been more generally or profoundly loved, admired and esteemed than was he".

The Church of St. Peter, the only one in the city, was a substantial brick building, 70 by 30 feet in dimensions, costing $5,000, erected in 1843 and dedicated three years later at the first ceremony of the kind in Memphis, in presence of a large congregation the majority of whom were Protestants.

When Father Grace became pastor in 1849 he was alone in Western Tennessee for a year except for occasional help from some of his brethren. As the congregation increased in numbers he realized the need of a more commodious church and on May 25, 1852,[11] asked for bids for the construction of what the Catholic Telegraph of Cincinnati, in its issue of December 18, 1852, told its readers was to be "one of the most splendid edifices west of the Alleghanies . . . it is to have two towers, each one hundred feet high, surmounted by a chime of bells". The new church was dedicated on January 24, 1859, with imposing ceremonial by Bishop Miles and a sermon by Right Reverend Martin J. Spalding, Bishop of Louisville. Bishop Elder of Natchez and several clergymen were in the sanctuary. The church is a stately Gothic brick structure still regarded as "one of the finest ecclesiastical edifices in the South". To that the writer can bear witness as he had the privilege of saying Mass in it in 1929, during the pastorate of Reverend William R. Lawler, O. P., P. G.

The flourishing condition of the parish was due to the energy, zeal and unremitting activity of the pastor who was appointed Vicar General for the western part of the diocese on March 3, 1857. Few enjoyed as great a reputation for learning, eloquence and prudence.

"The New York Truth Teller" in 1850, reported that the name of Father Grace was on the terna for the proposed Diocese of Monterey in California, but, as a matter of fact, it did not appear on that list nor on the one for the same diocese in 1853.[12] When Bishop Miles was consulted about the matter he replied that Father Grace was a very worthy and efficient clergyman but too young and not in orders long enough. "This," he added, "is the only objection that could be made against him".[13] However, his name was sent to Rome for the proposed Diocese of Quincy, Illinois. Archbishop Kenrick of St. Louis, in a letter to Bishop Loras, dated October 27, 1853, said "I have this day sent the following names to the Sacred Congregation for the vacant See of Quincy—Rev. Charles P. Montgomery, O.S.D., of Zanesville, Ohio; Rev. Thomas L. Grace, O. P., of Memphis, Tenn.; and Reverend Leonard A. Obermeyer of St. Vincent's Church, Baltimore". The new diocese was erected July 29, 1853, but never organized and remained attached to Chicago until January 9, 1857 when the see was transferred to Alton.

Shortly after he became pastor of St. Peter's, Father Grace invited the Dominican Sisters of St. Catherine of Siena from Kentucky to open a school in Memphis and six sisters came on January 1, 1851, the first community of religious women to make a foundation in the diocese. They opened a school for girls in the old home of General Coe and named it St. Agnes Academy at the suggestion of the pastor. It became one of the foremost girls' schools in the South. The next year Father Grace sent a number of orphans to be cared for by the sisters and they founded an orphanage at Gracewood Farm a few miles outside of Memphis. When the name was changed to St. Peter's Orphanage it continued under the direction of the Dominican Sisters until 1884 when the Sisters of Nazareth took it over.

Elevation to the Episcopate

Father Grace was considered for Coadjutor Bishop of Nashville in 1858, but it was generally understood that he "would not accept the honor of the miter without compulsion".[14] He accompanied Bishop Miles, as his theologian, to the Seventh Provincial Council of St. Louis, to which ecclesiastical province Nashville belonged, in September, 1858, and it was at this meeting that his name was placed at the head of the list of three priests from among whom the Holy Father would probably select the second Bishop of St. Paul. The others on the terna were the Reverend Joseph Melchir, V. G., of St. Louis, Mo., and the Reverend

Lucien Galtier of Prairie du Chien, Wisconsin, the first resident pastor of the Diocese of St. Paul from 1840 to 1844.

The letter and decree of the Sacred Congregation of the Propagation of the Faith, nominating Father Grace, reads as follows:

> Since the Reverend Anthony Pelamourgues has declined to accept the office of Bishop of St. Paul in the Archdiocese of St. Louis to which he was elected, the eminent Fathers of the Congregation of the Propaganda de Fide, in meeting assembled on December 16, 1858, supplicated His Holiness to appoint Thomas L. Grace, O. P., to that see. At an audience on January 13, 1859, Pope Pius IX graciously consented and ordered that the Apostolic Letters in the form of a brief be sent to this distinguished religious.[15]

In due time the Bulls of appointment, dated January 21, 1859, reached Father Grace, but he returned them to the Holy See praying to be relieved of the burden. On June 10 they were sent back to him with a peremptory command to accept. The Reverend Joseph A. Kelly, O. P., Provincial, wrote in his diary of June 10, 1859, "Father Grace has just received his bulls for St. Paul's the second time. He must go now. Roma locuta est. Causa finita est".[16]

Father Grace bowed to the will of the Supreme Pontiff and was consecrated in St. Louis Cathedral on Sunday, July 24, by Archbishop Kenrick with Bishops Miles of Nashville and Duggan of Chicago as co-consecrators. The Bulls were read by Reverend Louis Power, O. P., Vice-President of Sinsinawa Mound College. Several bishops, the Very Reverend Provincial of the Dominicans, Father Jarboe (President of Sinsinawa Mound College), and other members of the Order were present. The sermon was preached by Bishop Duggan. Among those who witnessed the ceremony were three priests from St. Paul, one of whom was Father Ravoux, Administrator of the diocese. The new bishop was "the first son of the Palmetto State, that has ever been raised to a Bishopric in the Church".

The Catholics of St. Peter's parish and the citizens of Memphis in general were grieved when they heard that Father Grace had been summoned to another field of labor. He had endeared himself to all by his blameless and exemplary conduct as a priest, his enlightened influence as a citizen and his irreproachable bearing as a gentleman. A week before his departure the parishioners presented him with an address in which they extolled his zeal, example and eloquence which had contributed so much to the advancement of the Church and won the respect of all citizens irrespective of class or creed. They begged his acceptance of a purse as a tangible expression of their appreciation of his work and of their high regard for him personally. In reply he expressed his gratification to know that his efforts had met with their approval; but he attributed much of his success to his co-laborers and to the people in general. The pain of separation was alleviated by the expressions of regard he had received not only from Catholics but from Protestants. He thanked them for the generosity of their gift, one of many testimonials presented in a less formal manner, and assured them of his interest in their welfare and in the continued prosperity of Memphis and its people among whom he had lived so long and to whom he was bound by many and strong ties.

The letter of the ten bishops at the Provincial Synod of St. Louis, dated September 12, 1858, presenting the names to the Sacred Congregation of the Propaganda contains the following reference to him:

> For the episcopal See of St. Paul in Minnesota we designate, Rev. Father Thomas Grace of the Order of Preachers, about 40 years of age, born in this region of honest Catholic parents, pursued his studies in the Convent of Santa Maria Sopra Minerva in Rome and made a reader of his Order, he engaged in the work of the missions, he preaches eloquently, he is skilled in business affairs and is notable for piety and is beloved by the faithful of the long flourishing Diocese of Memphis where he built a great and beautiful church.[17]

Installation in St. Paul

Immediately after his consecration Bishop Grace left St. Louis by the "Northern Belle", arrived in his see-city on Friday, July 29, and was escorted by a large group of citizens from the landing at the foot of Jackson Street to the episcopal residence to vest for his installation. The function is thus described by an eye witness, C.P.L. (L. P. Cotter, father of Bishop Cotter of Winona) in the Boston Pilot, August 13, 1859:

> His arrival had been expected and preparations were made to give him a heartfelt, enthusiastic welcome, such a one as would prove that our hearts were none the colder for a residence in this far-northern clime.
> The clergy from this city, and from various places in the diocese, assembled at the Cathedral in the evening, accompanied by a numerous train of acolytes, bearing a large crucifix and lighted tapers, followed by the conference of St. Vincent de Paul, the Ladies Society of the Living Rosary, and numerous delegates from the congregation, embracing American, Irish, German and French. The procession proceeded to the Bishop's residence, where His Lordship, in full pontificals, with mitre and crozier, was received under a richly ornamented canopy, supported by four members of the Conference of St. Vincent de Paul.
> The "City Guards", Capt. John O'Gorman, were drawn up in open order, and as the Bishop passed through their ranks, presented arms, and when the procession returned to the Cathedral, the "Guards" took their appointed station in the center aisle. The solemn "Te Deum" was sung by the choir, Benediction of the Blessed Sacrament was given, and the Bishop took his seat upon the throne provided within the sanctuary. The act of homage was then made, the clergy advancing one by one to the throne, kneeling, and kissing the Apostolic ring, as a pledge of submission to their

spiritual father. The earnest and cordial obedience tendered showed how affectionate was their reverence. The entire congregation then knelt and received the apostolic benediction, and thus closed the solemn act of installation. As the Bishop was fatigued from the effects of travel, his address was deferred until Sunday, and he was escorted by the clergy, societies and military, in the same order of procession, to the residence, after which the large assemblage, numbering some six or seven thousand, dispersed, pleased beyond measure, and full of glad anticipations for the future.

A large number of citizens, Protestant and Catholic, men of rank and position, influential and otherwise, waited upon the Bishop as soon as his arrival was known, to bid him welcome to Minnesota, and, as people met on the streets afterwards, the talk was of the new Bishop—such a noble personage, so elegant in his manner, so charming in his conversation, and then everyone was anxious to hear him preach.

Sunday came and the Cathedral was filled to overflowing; there were at least five thousand persons present. The celebration of High Mass proceeded, the choir was excellent, and the Bishop ascended the pulpit, all eyes were directed towards him. He preached from the text! "Beware of false prophets who come to you clothed as sheep, but who are inwardly as ravening wolves",—and such a sermon, so clear, lucid and expressive, nothing vague or indefinite—but the most profound knowledge of the system of church government, and the economy of God's providence to fallen man, wrought out so naturally, logically and consistently, and treated as only a master mind, and educated Catholic, can handle such a subject. Protestants who were present (and they were numerous) some, too, who have ere now sat in the councils of the nation, and others ambitious of distinction, socially and professionally, all felt the power and influence of his genius. Many went on their way with the intention of returning frequently to hear him; and may the Almighty instil into their hearts a desire to learn more of the great truths inculcated by the Catholic Church, with the grace of conversion and final perseverance. How cheered and encouraged were the members of the congregation. . . .

The good Bishop appears, under God, to be a great agent to work a future for Minnesota. From this time will commence a new era, fruitful in good works, for there is much work to be done, and the laborers are few. Churches and schools to be erected, missions to be extended, teachers to be provided who are competent to educate our youth in the English language and in the truths of Christianity, as well as secular knowledge, and above and beyond all, pastors to be procured to serve the ministry, either from beyond our borders, or by the more tedious process of founding and maintaining a collegiate and scholastic institution at home—to say nothing of arousing the faithful, the tepid and the indifferent, to the practice of many virtues and pious customs interwoven in the Church.

A Protestant writing of the event said that the new prelate was received at his see with outward marks of reverential welcome.[18] All the bells of the Catholic churches of St. Paul announced his arrival and great numbers of the citizens and military escorted him in his carriage to his episcopal residence. In the evening the Cathedral was thronged by the faithful and others to assist at his first celebration in his diocese of Pontifical Vespers. May these consoling demonstrations be the auspicious commencement of a bountiful harvest in his apostolic labors.

Bishop Grace's first concern, like that of every newly-installed Ordinary, was to ascertain the condition of the diocese and its prospects and plan for future development.

Only the basement of the Cathedral had been plastered and used for divine service and he made arrangements for the finishing of the interior of the superstructure and the addition of transepts to strengthen and support the long, unbuttressed walls lest their weight cause the foundation to bulge inward and threaten the stability of the edifice. These transepts were largely ornamental, but in later years one of them provided an additional classroom for the parish school and the other the cemetery office with an entrance on St. Peter Street. So serious was the threat to the foundation that the Bishop decided not to permit a full basement in any church authorized by him but only a limited excavation for the furnace. This accounts for the absence of a full basement in old St. Mary's, St. Paul, and the Immaculate Conception in Minneapolis.

He appointed the Very Reverend Augustine Ravoux Vicar General of the Diocese, and named Father Demetrius de Marogna, O. S. B., pastor of the Assumption Church, Vicar General for the German parishes, an office he held until his death in 1869, when Father Clement Staub, O. S. B., his successor, was named in his place.

Before starting on a visitation of the diocese in the early autumn he had to make provision for extra classrooms in the Cathedral basement to relieve the congested condition of the school in the old church and residence facing Wabasha Street. Then, too, St. Joseph's Academy on Bench Street was over-crowded and, as no funds were available for the erection of the proposed new academy on the site of the old cemetery vacated in 1856, he solved the problem by transferring the sisters and their pupils to St. Joseph's Hospital on Ninth Street where there was more room than was required for the limited number of patients who, in turn, found ample accommodations in the vacated academy. This arrangement continued until 1863 when the first wing of the present St. Joseph's Academy was ready for occupancy. The hospital building was then restored to its normal use and the orphans formerly housed in it were given a home of their own erected in 1860.

Constitutions of the Diocese

About six weeks after his installation—on September 8, 1859—Bishop Grace communicated to his priests the Latin text of the "Constitutions of the Diocese of St. Paul[19] of which we append a free translation of its ten paragraphs:

1—We accept the decrees of the two former Provincial Councils held in St. Louis and give them the force of law in this our diocese;

2—We adopt and promulgate in the Diocese of St. Paul all the decrees of the Councils of Baltimore approved by the Holy See and command that they be observed in their entirety;

3—We most strictly prohibit in every case whatsoever the hearing of the confessions of women in the priest's house and, if the priest cannot go to the church to hear them, we command that they be deferred to a later date;

4—We order confessionals to be set up in mission churches regularly visited by the priest and, where no church or chapel exists, in homes designated by the bishop for the celebration of Mass;

5—We strictly enjoin the priests of the diocese not to carry the Blessed Sacrament about with them, under any pretext whatsoever, unless actually on a sick call, and we declare those who disobey suspended ipso facto;

6—To preserve and enhance the orderly government of the diocese we make our own the decree issued on September 11, 1858, by the Very Reverend A. Ravoux, then Administrator of the diocese, namely, that no priest is permitted to administer the sacraments within the territory of another priest unless invited by him to do so or authorized by us in writing. Each priest has jurisdiction only within the limits of the district committed to his care. If he is in doubt as to whether it is his own territory or not he can act as if he had jurisdiction;

7—We likewise make our own another regulation promulgated by the Very Reverend Administrator on September 11, 1857, to the effect that all the priests of the diocese before beginning the erection of a church obtain the written approval of the Ordinary as well as a deed to the property on which the church or chapel is to be erected. This document must be drawn up in accordance with the laws of the church in the United States;

8—Every priest in charge of a parish must procure a book in which to record and describe all the property belonging to the church, ascertaining what portion is subject to taxation and what is exempt, and all the contents of the church of the value of three dollars and over;

9—When there is grave question of a marriage contracted before a civil magistrate we decree that it be handled in the following manner: if the contracting parties entered into it maliciously and in contempt of church and pastor, they must do public penance in accordance with the ninth decree of the Second Provincial Council of St. Louis, approved by the Holy See and in the following manner. At the Solemn Mass on a Sunday or holyday the pastor will, from the pulpit, announce to all the people the names of the married couple and in their name and with their consent beg pardon of the congregation for the scandal they gave. Then and only then may they be admitted to the sacraments;

10—Since we read in the Council of Trent that bishops must make provision in each parish for teaching children, at least on Sundays and other feast days, the rudiments of faith and obedience to God and their parents by those to whom the duty belongs and, if necessary, compel them to do so by ecclesiastical censure, all privileges and customs to the contrary notwithstanding, we order all pastors, religious and diocesan, to teach the children themselves or, if that cannot be done, to provide competent teachers on all the aforesaid days even if only one child be present, as the Sacred Congregation of the Council has it.

Given at St. Paul from our episcopal residence on the 8th day of September, the feast of the Nativity of the B. V. M., A. D., 1859.

✠ Thomas L. Grace,
Bishop of St. Paul

Visitation of the Far-Flung Diocese

When these changes were effected the Bishop made preparations for a visitation of the diocese. He realized that he had been assigned an extensive field of labor with a scattered population of about fifty thousand Catholics, ministered to by twenty-seven priests in charge of thirty-one churches and ninety missions. There were three students for the priesthood—John Ireland and Thomas O'Gorman in France and Edward Walters in this country—all of whom were ordained in due time, the first two for the Diocese of St. Paul, the third for the Diocese of Fort Wayne, where he died comparatively young. There was one hospital, two parochial schools, an academy and a novitiate. Transportation facilities were very meagre, limited to canoe, ox-cart, stage coach and pony, unless one preferred to walk. The railroads which now gridiron the state had not reached the West. The Indian was still a picturesque figure: his hunt-lands had not yet been seriously threatened by the incoming whites: his war-cry could still be heard. But the advancing tide of immigration was flowing further and further into the State every year and priests, churches and schools had to be provided for Catholic colonists. It was imperative that the Bishop learn the situation from personal visitation and actual observation of the territory and contact with priests and people.

In September he began the official visitation of the parishes accompanied by Father Ravoux.[20] In each parish he celebrated Mass, preached and confirmed. In St. Anthony he confirmed 43; in Little Canada, 97; in Hastings, 47; in Wabasha, 18; in Winona, 70; in Stillwater, 70; in Palestine (near the present Osseo), 69; in New Treves, 25; in Faribault, 20; in St. Cloud, 59; in St. Joseph, 142; a total of 660. To these we add the 247 confirmed in the Cathedral, "which has just been completed", on the third Sunday of Advent, of whom 12 were converts;[21] the 80, including 3 converts, confirmed in the Church of the Assumption on the fourth Sunday; and the 100 confirmed in the Church of St. Peter, Mendota, on February 8, 1860; a total of 1087. The more distant parts of the diocese were reserved for a later visitation.

This first visit to the country districts, the forerunner of many he was to make during his episcopal career, gave him a good idea of the conditions prevailing in the settlements outside St. Paul. He realized that the diocese, though new and vast, was far from a cheerless waste. It was destined to be a land flowing with milk and honey. The soil covered with the mold of a thousand years was fertile and well adapted to the cultivation of cereals of all kinds. The streams and lakes were bordered with heavy timber. The climate was salubrious. The tide of immigration had set in and was to reach its flood during his episcopate.

First Pastoral Letter

Towards the end of the visitation he issued his first Pastoral Letter to the clergy and laity.[22] It was dated November 9, 1859. Thanks to the efforts of Father Busch of the St. Paul Seminary we have the text as published in the Catholic Telegraph of Cincinnati, Ohio, on the twenty-sixth of that month.

The Bishop began by assuring priests and people that he had made every effort to obtain full and accurate information about the diocese by a visitation of all but a few of the parishes inaccessible in the fall season, and he was consoled by the cordial and generous reception received everywhere from the clergy and by the evidence of good will on the part of the faithful. The diocese was peopled with immigrants "composed almost entirely of children of the church", of different nationalities hungering for the Bread of Life. Through no fault of their own, but owing to insurmountable circumstances many had gone beyond the reach of the pastor's voice, and priests were unable to follow them not because of a want of zeal but because they were too few in number. He recalled the devoted laborers of the past some of whom were still active. More apostolic priests were needed to minister to the growing congregations and to seek those who had become estranged from the Church as well as those outside the fold because of inherited prejudices. The virtuous lives of Catholics and their good example are the best recommendations of the faith to the unbeliever.

The written word should be utilized as a medium for instructing non-Catholics through a wider diffusion of Catholic books and periodicals and as an antidote to the publications against the Church with which the country is flooded. The laity, too, should take a more lively interest in their religion and use their talents, influence and position to enlighten their non-Catholic fellow-citizens by explaining and defending, whenever necessary, the dogmas of our holy faith and thus add to the number of the faithful.

For the promotion of piety and charity he recommended the societies already existing in the diocese and asked that their membership be increased many fold. He bade parents watch over their children, the "precious trust" confided to them by God, and form their character by home training and family example. "Expose not their faith to danger; look to the purity of their morals". Increased vigilance is necessary if the children are obliged to attend non-Catholic schools.

He reiterated the words of his predecessor, Bishop Cretin, who, in his Pastoral Letter of February 17, 1855, besought his people to respect the rights and liberties of others and assert their own, to abstain from party strife and preserve their independence. Catholics, as such, should not seek privileges but should demand their rights under the Constitution which guarantees equality of rights to all its citizens, and by honesty, sobriety, industry and respect for law and order show themselves worthy citizens of the Republic. Their rights will be respected by others if they themselves respect them and never consent to sink or sacrifice them in the interests of any political organization. The right of suffrage should be held sacred and exercised conscientiously for the good of all citizens and of the country. The virtue and morality of Catholics should be the greater as their faith is holier than that of other men.

Catholics and Partisan Politics

The issuance of this pastoral occasioned a friendly exchange of letters [23] between Bishop Grace and James A. McMaster, Editor of the Freeman's Journal of New York, one of the most influential Catholic papers of the time, in which the Bishop outlined the role a Catholic newspaper should play and expressed his views on the effect of partisan politics on Catholic interests.

In opening the correspondence the Bishop said:

> I hold that Catholic papers exclusively religious are comparatively of little service to the cause either of the Catholic religion or of the rights of Catholics; that secular journals animated with Catholic spirit and speaking to the country at large—taking part in the discussion of all public questions and measures, are the kind of papers demanded by the times, and they should be free to give their views and opinions upon all subjects and advocate or oppose the claims of any party or any measure as in their own judgment seems to be good.

In the second category he listed the Freeman's Journal which he regarded "as the most efficient paper we have".

In commenting on the political allegiance of Catholics he deplored their "unquestioning submission and undeviating adherence" to the Democratic party "regardless alike of its policy, its principles, its measures and its men". They place party success above the common good, whereas the "well being of the country, the public good and private rights of all depend upon the intelligent political action of its citizens as individuals", exercising the prerogative and duty of examining and discussing all questions of policy and government and forming their own judgment without reference to what the party leaders may dictate. The blind subservience of Catholics to a party, whether right or wrong, cannot fail to engender feelings of hostility against them and the church and cast upon their religion the odium for whatever evils may result. Such a partisan attitude deprives Catholics of the consideration due them because of their numbers and, since their loyalty to the party is taken for granted, no effort is made to ascertain their views on questions affecting the general welfare of the country, of which they are citizens. That they will vote with the party is taken for granted. In their blind devotion to party they lose sight of their individual rights and the general good.

It gratified McMaster to learn that the Bishop's idea of a Catholic paper coincided with his own and that the policy of the Freeman's Journal met with his approbation. He deplored, however, the tone of so many so-called Catholic papers whose treatment of many topics misled their Catholic readers and prejudiced non-Catholics who might read them.

While he agreed with the Bishop "as to the degraded political position occupied by Catholics at large throughout the country", he differed with him as to the cause and the cure. He did not think that "party allegiance had anything to do with it". It was rather their utter want of political conscience and principle and their unscrupulous pursuit of office for the sake of the money involved. While Catholics do not possess influence in proportion to their numbers, they receive all the consideration they are entitled to in view of their political intelligence. They can be depended upon to vote the party ticket unless they see a chance to better themselves financially by a temporary defection from its ranks. He regarded the political activity of Catholics "as the result of their character —not vice versa", and can see no remedy for this deplorable situation "except in the effort to make them, in their whole conduct, act more as men with individuality and conscience and less like dumb driven cattle".

In closing he pays a compliment to the Bishop by adding:

I have rejoiced at your appointment to a See that, whatever the momentary embarrassments of temporal affairs, is destined in a few years to be so important in numbers and position. I rejoice, too, in seeing another added to the Hierarchy who is capable of understanding the age and the country. If God does not raise up such men, who will freely accept everything of the country that is not opposed to the principles of the Church, some of us may live to see the opportunity of planting the Catholic religion in our soil passed never to return.

In a subsequent letter, written after he had received a copy of the Pastoral Letter, he thanks the Bishop for having written that part of the Pastoral "that speaks of the duty we owe our fellow countrymen not of the faith". He echoes the sentiment expressed by Father Hecker of the Paulists who, after reading the Pastoral, said: "Thank God for a Bishop so alive and so fully posted on the age in which we live".

That McMaster continued to hold Bishop Grace in high and affectionate regard is evidenced by the following excerpt from a letter written on October 27, 1876.

> I hold it as a constant regret that I have not had the privilege of seeing you, and having your counsel, and conversation, in regard to Catholic interests. . . There will be opportunity, in heaven, for us to understand how it has been that I have, for over twenty years, had so great an admiration for you, and why you, so often, have shown a friendship for me, of which I have not felt myself deserving.

On August 15, 1860, a new society was formed in the Cathedral parish for the purpose of collecting funds for the education of poor boys for the priesthood. It was called the "Young Catholics Educational Society", the members of which contributed one dollar a year for that purpose. The Bishop was very much pleased with their interest in a project vital to the future of the diocese and encouraged them by speaking about it from the altar and expressing the hope that similar societies would be organized in all the parishes of the diocese.[24]

Early in the year 1860 the Bishop lectured on "Human Rights" before a large and appreciative audience under the auspices of the St. Vincent de Paul Society and so excellent was the impression made on all who heard him that he was asked to deliver another address on a similar topic before a group of women of St. Paul's Episcopal Church for the benefit of the free hospital maintained by them. It attracted another large and interested audience and was delivered in "an easy and fluent manner without any attempt at oratorial display", and won the approval of the community "without regard to nation, party or sect".

Concern For the Indians

On August 14, 1860, six chiefs and thirteen braves of the Medewakanton bands[25] of Sioux Indians at the lower Sioux agency in Minnesota wrote Bishop Grace craving for themselves, their people or tribe, that "a clergyman of the order of the black gowns" and no other minister, be stationed among them to instruct and educate their children as they had full confidence in them and hoped the Bishop would grant their request.

Considerable correspondence passed between the Bishop and the

Bureau of Indian Affairs.[26] He wrote Superintendent Cullen of his desire to comply with the wishes of these wards of the Government and requested permission to cooperate in improving their condition and training them to habits of civilized life, offering to provide priests and sisters if the Government would grant an allowance to help meet the expenses thereby incurred. He pointed out the importance of religion in any educational program that might be adopted.

In forwarding this letter to W. P. Dole, Commissioner of Indian Affairs, Cullen assured the Bishop that "it has always been the policy of the Government to extend every facility to religious denominations in their efforts to christianize the Indians", and promised his cooperation.

The Bishop's requests and recommendations continued to be ignored and he wrote President Lincoln describing the efforts he had made to reach an agreement with the Indian Bureau and asking that, in the new policies and measures to be adopted by the Government, the expressed preference of the Indians for "Black Gowns" be respected and that he be allowed to cooperate with the Government in providing for their spiritual as well as their temporal well being.

This letter, turned over to Senator Rice, and, through him, to the Commissioner, received the scant courtesy of a brief reply in which he was informed that "the Sioux have heretofore had such schools and missions as were deemed by the Office commensurate with their wants", that there was no preference for or against any religious bodies proposing to help them and that all action in regard to the matters mentioned in the Bishop's letter would have to be deferred "till the Sioux shall have been located in the new country in which they are about to be removed in accordance with the action of Congress touching the same". There the matter rested indefinitely.

On March 11, 1863, a treaty was concluded between the United States Government and the Chippewas of the Mississippi and the Pillager and Lake Winnebigoshish Bands of Chippewa Indians, and Bishop Grace was appointed one of the Board of Visitors by I. P. Usher, Secretary of the Interior, by letter of May 9, 1863. The duty of the Committee as outlined in the seventh article of the Treaty was "to attend the annuity payments to the Indians and to inspect the fields and other improvements and to report annually thereon, on or before the first day of November, and also as to the qualifications and moral deportment of all persons residing upon the reservation under authority of law". The Bishop was also asked to ascertain "the number of acres prepared for cultivation under former treaties, and the condition of same, upon the several reservations ceded by treaty of 11th. March, 1863, and also upon Leech, Cass and Winnipie Lakes reservations, etc., which objects you will consider included particularly in your instructions herewith". The other members of the Commission were the Right Reverend Henry B. Whipple, Bishop of Minnesota, and the Reverend Thomas S. Williamson, Davenport, Iowa.

In its report the Board approved the general provisions of the treaty and urged an early appropriation of the money to complete the transfer. It also reported that the Chippewas were displeased because the greater part of the allottment was paid in currency instead of in coin.

The report must have been satisfactory for, on September 15, 1864, President Lincoln named Bishop Grace and the other two a Board of Visitors to the Red Lake and Pembina bands of Chippewas which the sixth article of the Treaty of October 2, 1863, with those Indians, and the amendments thereto, concluded at the City of Washington on the fifth day of May, 1864, stipulated should be provided for them.

A similar communication from James Steele, Acting Commissioner of Indian Affairs, was sent on September 16, to the Bishop advising him that the annuity payments would be made on the first of October and asking him to be present.

In reply the Bishop declined to accept the appointment. "These Indian reservations", he wrote on October 1, 1864, "lie hundreds of miles beyond all routes of travel; no conveyances can be got except at great cost. The communications between the reservations of the several bands required to be visited is only by way of Indian trails on foot or through lakes and swamps on canoes of bark. Add to this the trouble and expense of camp equipage and necessary attendants. The labor and bodily inconvenience the visitation entails, I would willingly undergo, but it is not reason to expect that the commissioners should defray with their time allowances the entire material cost of the service.

"In the expedition last year to the reservation at Mille Lacs, Gull Lake and Leech Lake an ambulance with driver, tent and camping equipage from Crow Wing were furnished the Commissioners by General Sibley".

The Bishop once more turned his attention to diocesan affairs. The need of a more commodious residence for himself and the clergy became more and more apparent as the months went by and in 1860 he began the construction of it on a site adjoining the Cathedral at 19 West Sixth Street. It was a oblong three-story, grey stone building, with an extension in the rear for kitchen and housekeepers' quarters, but with meager accommodation from the standpoint of modern comfort and conveniences. The Pioneer and Democrat of November 25, of that year, refers to it in the following terms:

> In all essential elements of durability, convenience and architectural finish it is, perhaps, ahead of any other building in Minnesota. . .The splendid cupola on the top of the main building, the cornices and all the wood work on the outside of the building corresponding in finish and color with the stone work, present an appearance of elegant architectural completeness which reflects great credit on the mind that conceived as

well as on the hands that executed it. . . .Such buildings not only add beauty and grace to our utilitarian city, but convey to strangers an exalted idea of the architectural taste and refinement of our citizens, and we hope those who contemplate erecting good residences next season may profit by and if possible improve upon the example.

The new residence was considered palatial in its day but it lacked even the facilities of an ordinary bathroom until 1896; and was heated by wood or coal burners in each room until 1910, when a steam heating plant was installed by Bishop Lawler. It served as the residence of the Ordinary, his Coadjutor and the Vicar General until the early nineties when Archbishop Ireland moved to 977 Portland Avenue, and of the pastor and priests of the parish until 1914 when it was dismantled with the Cathedral.

In the Red River Valley

Towards the end of 1860 the Bishop received a letter[27] from Father Oran of St. Boniface, dated December 10, informing him of the serious accident that had befallen one of his priests, Father Goiffon of Pembina, who, returning from St. Paul in October, had his feet frozen during a severe blizzard which overtook him a few miles from his destination and caused the death of his horse. He was delirious when rescued, his clothes had to be cut off him and he had to be taken to St. Boniface where he suffered the amputation of the right leg below the knee and of the left foot at the ankle. He recovered but was the unwitting cause of the destruction of the episcopal residence and the Cathedral with all their contents.

Bishop Grace soon realized that he had not ceased to be a missionary when he put on the miter. He had left one mission station to enter into a larger and more onerous one where he had to supervise and direct the activities of his priests and make provision for future development. He was anxious to familiarize himself with the hardships and trials incidental to missionary life in the more remote parts of his new field of labor. Accordingly, he and Father Ravoux undertook a journey to the most northerly part of the diocese to visit the missions in the Red River valley.[28] They left St. Paul on August 1, 1861, for St. Cloud whence they made a side trip to Belle Prairie where Father Pierz was stationed, and the Bishop confirmed thirty persons in the small but neat parish church.

At Crow Wing on the feast of the Assumption a class of fourteen, of whom three were Indians, received the same sacrament. Returning to St. Cloud the travelers resumed the journey by stage coach through St. Joseph, Richmond and the valley of the Sauk river where a colony of German immigrants brought out by Father Pierz tilled the rich, loamy soil. The journey over corduroy roads and through treacherous swamps was beset with great discomfort. They crossed the vast watershed whence three rivers seek the sea in different directions—the St. Louis flowing northeasterly into Lake Superior on its way to the Atlantic Ocean; the Red River turning and twisting in its northerly journey to Lake Winnipeg; and the Mississippi descending to the warm waters of the Gulf of Mexico. After many hardships they came to the bank of the Red River and had to wait several days at Georgetown for the boat that would bear them to their destination, Pembina, a straggling village of swarming half-breeds and Indians living in tepees, tents and bark lodges on the western bank of the river. In addition to these there were half a dozen French families, the most prominent of which were those of Joseph Rolette, then absent at the Selkirk Settlement, and of Joseph LeMay, United States Collector of Customs, at whose home the Bishop and Father Ravoux were hospitably entertained. The congregation of about three hundred souls was in charge of Father Goiffon whose sufferings in a blizzard the previous year had evoked the sympathies of Europeans as well as of Americans of all classes. Despite the handicap of an artificial limb and foot this devoted missionary was active in the ministry, traveling from settlement to settlement saying Mass, preaching, administering the sacraments and zealously guarding the faith and morals of the people living in the village and on the broad plains to the West. On Sunday the Bishop sang High Mass, at which Father Ravoux preached, and then confirmed eight persons. The church was a rude log building but not without an air of neatness inside.

Pembina was subject to periodic inundations from the river and many of the settlers sought higher ground in the vicinity of Turtle Mountain about thirty miles west where a village called St. Joseph, later Walhalla, had grown up. As the travelers approached it they were met by a cavalcade of two hundred riders dressed in the costume of Red River hunters who, having dismounted to receive the Bishop's blessing, conducted him and his companion to their destination. It was a community of about one thousand half-breeds living in well-built houses interspersed with sturdy stockades to serve as a protection against the sporadic raids of the Sioux to whom all the surrounding country belonged by right. This was the extensive feeding-ground of the buffalo which supplied the means of sustenance for the inhabitants, while the broad, fertile prairies remained untilled. The villagers, like those of Pembina, came originally from the Selkirk Settlement in Canada and lived by the products of the chase. They were fine specimens of physical strength and prowess. For a week Fathers Ravoux and Goiffon preached a mission to the congregation, at the close of which the Bishop confirmed a class of forty-five and was greatly edified with the fervent faith and piety of the people, their devotion to the Church and reverence for the clergy.

This was the end of the journey and the most northerly part of the immense Diocese of St. Paul. Bishop Grace was the first Ordinary to visit it officially. He promised Father Goiffon an easier charge and, after expressing himself as well pleased with all he had seen and heard, returned to Pembina with Father Ravoux. Before resuming the homeward journey they decided to pay a visit of courtesy to Bishop Taché of St. Boniface to thank him, the clergy and sisters for the devoted care and generous hospitality lavished on Father Goiffon during his serious illness. Bishop Taché was absent in Quebec but they were hospitably entertained by the clergy. They were shown the ruins of the Cathedral and of the episcopal residence destroyed by fire the previous year because of special preparations being made to provide a supply of candles for a fitting wake for the supposedly dying Father Goiffon. They visited the college for boys, and the academy for girls conducted by the Grey Nuns as well as the orphanage under their direction and learned about the missions of the Oblate Fathers that extended to the polar regions, two thousand miles north of the city. They returned home by steamboat on the Red River and stage coach overland and reached St. Paul on September 30 after an absence of two months and an expenditure of $289.50 for the trip.

In the meantime Bishop Grace "gave the pastoral care of the missions of Pembina and St. Joseph with all their dependencies to the Oblate Fathers from across the line, who took charge of them in October, a charge they faithfully fulfilled until the 9th of April, 1877".[29] The Reverend P. Andre "was duly installed as pastor and officiated in that capacity until August 31, 1864". He was followed by others during the next thirteen years.

The St. Paul Daily Press, Sunday, October 6, 1861, refers to their return "after a long absence, during which they have been unremittingly employed in providing for the advancement of the great cause of religion in the western country. They were everywhere received with that affectionate regard to which they exhibit such irresistible claims by their amiable and paternal deportment. May they be long preserved to us to witness wonders in the diffusion of the Catholic faith still more stupendous than those for which they have hitherto labored so successfully".

In this journey the Bishop and his Vicar General followed for the most part the route of the ox-cart caravans between St. Paul and Pembina taken by Father Goiffon on that memorable but disastrous return trip to his mission in October, 1860.[30] He had been summoned to St. Paul by Father Ravoux for consultation and on his way home left the slow-moving caravan on his spirited horse and hastened ahead in an endeavor to reach his destination before the feast of All Saints. He was overtaken by a blizzard and spent five days under a mantle of snow beside his frozen horse, from whose juicy rump steaks he drew the nourishment that sustained his life until his feeble cries attracted the attention of some members of the caravan he had set out with who at first thought the black object against the white snow was a dog. He was hurried to Pembina where an effort was made to thaw out his frozen limbs. When gangrene set in he was hauled on a dogsled to St. Boniface for surgical attention, and taken to the Bishop's residence where in two major operations his right leg was amputated below the knee and the other at the ankle removing the greater part of the foot. Hemorrhage set in, all hope of recovery was abandoned and the last sacraments were administered. The story goes that the Sisters in charge of the domestic arrangements in the Bishop's house were making candles for the anticipated wake when, through the carelessness of a servant, the tallow caught fire and the house and the Cathedral were burned to the ground with all their contents. Another version is that the fire was caused by the "igniting of a soot-pan". The dying priest was carried on a thin mattress from his room and laid in the snow. The cold stopped the hemorrhage and he finally recovered and was a pastor in the Diocese of St. Paul for more than forty years before death overtook him. Bishop Grace recalled him from the North and placed him in charge of Little (now, New) Canada.

As soon as the Bishop had dispatched the work and correspondence that accumulated during his absence in the North, he set out for a week's visit to the parishes in Houston County in the southern part of the state for confirmation and other religious functions.

At Caledonia he found a large Catholic population of Irish and Germans, with the former in the majority, a frugal, thrifty and prosperous people, in need of a larger church to accommodate them. He confirmed 54 persons on October 20. The Brownsville parish was composed, likewise, of Irish and German farmers with few Catholics in the town. Here, too, the church, though quite neat, was too small for the needs of the congregation. A class of 68 children and adults was presented for confirmation on October 22. The church in La Crescent served a congregation of industrious Irish people living on fertile farms and prospering. The sacrament of confirmation was administered to 11 persons.

On Sunday, October 27, he dedicated the new and substantial stone Church of St. Bridget (Simpson) built by Rev. M. Prendergast as a house of worship for a congregation of industrious and thrifty Irish, pious and zealous. It is about seven miles from Rochester. The Bishop was well pleased with the results of this visitation and the hearty welcome given him by priests and people.

The journeys above described were the first of many long and arduous trips undertaken by Bishop Grace in the twenty-five years of his episcopate during which he familiarized himself with every part of the diocese, providing priestly ministration for the increasing body of the faithful, opening new parishes, confirming, lecturing, unsparing of self and unmindful of hardship. Like a faithful shepherd he watched over his flock, provided for their needs as far as his limited means permitted and was an apostolic missioner in the full sense of the word.

The first religious reception at which Biship Grace officiated after his installation was scheduled for the feast of the Purification, February 2, 1860. Two young women—Mary Williams, a graduate of St. Joseph's Academy, and Johanna Shelly, a graduate of St. Anthony School—had entered the novitiate of the Sisters of St. Joseph in 1859 and were ready to receive the habit of the congregation. While they were on retreat the Superioress was stricken with a serious illness and received the last sacraments on January 30 and lest, in case of death, the reception would be indefinitely postponed, the date was advanced and they received the habit the following morning and the names of Sister Agnes Veronica and Sister Aloysia. "A more sorrowful reception was never witnessed and a more doleful recital of the 'Te Deum' was never heard". Sister Aloysia contracted a cold and died in 1863, the second death in the St. Paul community.

Ordination of Father Ireland and Others

At his first ordination Bishop Grace elevated to the priesthood Reverends Edward Essing and Pius Bayer on November 8, 1860; and the following year, on Sunday, December 22, the fourth Sunday of Advent,[31] he ordained John Ireland who returned from France to be promoted to that august dignity in his adopted land, and among the relatives and friends who had followed his career with deep interest and legitimate pride since his departure from St. Paul in 1853. The ceremony took place in the then new Cathedral far from completed. In its sanctuary Father Ireland said his first Mass and there he began his priestly career. With the Cathedral he was associated all his life, and none experienced more genuine sorrow than he when the ruthless fiat of progress made it necessary to dismantle it in 1914, when its incomparable successor loomed high above the city from the brow of St. Anthony hill. When the Civil War broke out young Father Ireland offered his services to his country and served as Chaplain in the South until his health failed, and he was mustered out and appointed to the staff of the Cathedral of which he was made pastor in 1867 in succession to Father Caillet, the founder and first pastor of St. Mary's in Lower Town. Father Ireland also acted as Secretary to Bishop Grace when Father Oster was made pastor of Burnsville (Byrnesville) and missions in that year.

Two other ordinations of early days are worthy of note, those of James Trobec on September 3, 1865, and of Thomas O'Gorman on November 5, of the same year. Both were elevated to the priestly dignity by Bishop

Grace in the Cathedral and both said their first Mass at its altar. Both were destined to reach the episcopate, the former as Bishop of St. Cloud on September 21, 1897, and the latter as Bishop of Sioux Falls on April 19, 1896.

Towards the close of 1861, Captain O'Gorman, father of the future Bishop O'Gorman, marched at the head of his company of Catholic volunteers to the sanctuary railing of the Cathedral to assist at Mass before setting out for the South to take part in the Civil War.[32] They stood throughout the service with their caps on and grounded arms at the elevation. It was one of the first military Masses which were not infrequent during the war years and since.

At the beginning of the Civil War there was the usual criticism of the Government and its policy and considerable dissatisfaction with its recruiting program. One D. A. Robertson, writing to Captain Earle S. Goodrich, said that it was known that "quite a large class of our population is avowedly hostile to the necessary enlisting measures of the Government which all loyal men should applaud for the suppression of the Southern rebellion".[33] It was reported in certain quarters that Bishop Grace, being a southerner, sympathized with this hostility. The report was utterly unfounded and unqualifiedly unjust to him. Although a southerner by birth and education, and one who had long worked among the people of the South, no one was more sincere in his allegiance to the Federal Government during the trying days of the Civil War.

In the course of a newspaper interview the Bishop said that he took no part in public affairs but had always encouraged his people to obey the Government and submit to the draft and volunteer. "I have always encouraged my people to enlist in defense of their country. I have discouraged them from trying to avoid a draft—and that any of them have thought of doing so I know only from rumor—and have always told them that they have enjoyed the protection of the Government and ought to be ready at all times to defend it".

On one occasion he wrote a letter to the priest in charge of a certain parish where Irish and French Catholics contemplated resistance to the proposed draft, "if there was any truth in the rumor, to discourage the movement in every possible way, and to impress upon the Catholics there a sense of their duty to obey the Government and the laws of the country; that their conduct might be that of good and loyal citizens". He authorized Father Ireland to speak to the people from the Cathedral pulpit and admonish them not to offer resistance to the draft but to obey the law as a patriotic and religious duty.

Early in 1862 Bishop Grace posed a difficulty[34] to the Sacred Congregation of Rites, saying that in his small diocese it often happened that there was not a sufficient number of priests to fill all the positions at

Pontifical Mass; and he asked whether it would be proper to have the deacon and subdeacon sit at the throne beside the bishop in place of the deacons of honor or would it be better to have seminarians, or even larger altar boys, in surplice, attend at the throne to perform the duties of the assistant deacons?

The reply of the Sacred Congregation, No 3114, dated March 22, 1862, was that when, because of the paucity of priests, it would be difficult to supply all the officers of a Pontifical Mass, it would be permissible for the deacon and subdeacon of the Mass to sit at the throne with the celebrating bishop. There they could perform the duties usually assigned to the deacons of honor which are little more than putting the mitre on and off, and removing or replacing the gremial. When both deacon and subdeacon so assisting are away from the throne, as just before the Gospel, the gremial and mitre can well be attended to by the master of ceremonies, who has this same function at this point when Pontifical Mass is celebrated at the faldstool.

The First Preparatory Seminary

Like his predecessor, Bishop Grace was vitally concerned about the recruiting of priests for the sacred ministry of the altar and, in the latter part of November, 1862, he opened a school,[35] known as the "Ecclesiastical Preparatory Seminary of St. Paul", on the second floor of the old Cathedral building which once served as a church and placed it in charge of William Markoe,[36] a convert from the episcopalian ministry, who acted as headmaster until the institution was closed in July, 1867. Twenty-three pupils were enrolled, among them John Shanley, later, Bishop of Fargo. Father Oster, the Benjamin of Bishop Cretin's anointing, was spiritual director as well as teacher and trained the boys for the service of the altar in liturgical chant and in the singing of the lamentations and prophecies during Holy Week. He won the esteem and affection of the boys by taking keen interest in all their occupations and an active part in their amusements, even to participating in snow-balling. He organized them into a sodality of the B. V. M. and taught them to recite the Little Office and sing the Ave Maris Stella. From time to time he took them on picnics to Father Robert's at Mendota and Father Goiffon's at Little Canada. It is probable that Thomas O'Gorman, a deacon, was a member of the faculty for a few weeks before ordination in 1865.

The head-master received the munificent salary of twenty-five dollars a month for ten months in the year. He was on duty from 9 A. M. to 5 P. M. with a two-hour intermission at noon.

This preparatory seminary was discontinued or rather merged with the Cathedral school in 1867, and no longer known under a separate name. About that time St. John's College was founded by the Benedictines at Collegeville and the students of the diocese were sent to it and other seminaries for their theological training. St. John's had been given the status of an Abbey in June, 1866, because "owing to a certain want of authority the Priors did not so far succeed in bringing unity of action and conformity of discipline under the Fathers there stationed".[37]

The cornerstone of St. John's was laid by Bishop Grace on July 19, 1866, and when it opened its doors the following year five pupils of the St. Paul institution were enrolled, among them John Shanley who had spent a year in St. Vincent's Seminary, Cape Girardeau, Missouri, and Joseph B. Cotter, destined to be the first Bishop of Winona, who had studied at St. Vincent's in Pennsylvania. The total enrollment for that year at St. John's was fifty-one. The next year it increased to eighty-four of whom forty were studying for the diocesan priesthood and the Benedictine Order.[38] In subsequent years students for St. Paul Diocese were found in Milwaukee, Montreal, Dublin, Paris, Louvain and elsewhere. On September 8, 1885, St. Thomas Aquinas Seminary opened in St. Paul with twenty students in theology, seven in philosophy and twenty in the classical department. Bishop Grace's dream for a diocesan seminary had at length been realized under his successor, but during his episcopate he never lost sight of the goal nor did his interest in the project abate. It was destined to be an unrealized ambition. That it was always an objective was evidenced by the fact that, as early as November 14, 1866, he purchased a forty-acre farm on the shore of Lake Johanna for a diocesan institution. "Some day I hope to build a seminary there", he told Ralston Markoe. More than half a century later that piece of land, and an additional forty acres, was selected as the location for Nazareth Hall, the preparatory seminary of the Archdiocese, and thus was realized in a measure the dream of the second Bishop of St. Paul.

To meet the expense of surveying, plotting and future maintenance of Calvary cemetery the Bishop issued regulations fixing the average price of burial lots at fifteen cents a square foot, with a small advance for those in more desirable locations and a slight reduction for those less favorably situated. The charge for opening and closing a grave for an adult was fixed at six dollars and for that of a child under ten years of age at five dollars. What a contrast to the cost of similar services nowadays.[39]

Bishop Grace was vitally interested in bringing immigrants to the state and settling them on its fertile farms. On May 12, 1864, the Minnesota Irish Emigration Society was formed to encourage and promote Irish immigration to the Northwest and, under his auspices and through its efforts, thousands of Catholics were attracted to Minnesota's productive prairies. Father Ireland was President, Dillon O'Brien, Secretary, and other influential Irish citizens were among its officers and active members, and as a result of their labors the Catholic population was materially increased. Many who had settled in the congested areas of the cities in the East were induced to leave their unwholesome surroundings and establish themselves and their children on the rich farmlands of the West amid the woodlands and beside the lakes and streams of the new state in the upper regions of the Mississippi. For years this society carried on its work quietly but effectively under the direction of its chosen officers and with the approbation of Bishop Grace, by issuing circulars to Irish immigrants in the East in which the attractions of Minnesota as a suitable location for Catholic homeseekers desiring to lay the foundation of future prosperity, were set forth somewhat in detail. As a result its secretary could state with truth that "hundreds of Catholic families have come to this state, who were induced to do so by our representations".[40] The primary object of the society was "to improve the moral and social position of our countrymen in America". Dillon O'Brien, the cultured and efficient Corresponding Secretary, traveled and lectured extensively in its behalf. In 1869 an attempt was made in St. Louis to organize the Irish Catholic Colonization Association to establish colonies in the West but nothing came of it. Later on a similar organization was brought into being in Chicago under the auspices of the American Hierarchy and it functioned for a number of years with very beneficial results.

In all of these projects Bishop Grace took a personal interest and not infrequently presided at the meetings. But for the most part he remained in the background and inspired others to do the work. He came to rely more and more on Father Ireland, especially after his consecration as coadjutor, and encouraged him to throw himself heart and soul into the colonization movement of which he became the inspiring leader and indefatigable worker. He was the energizing force behind the movement the story of which will be told in a subsequent chapter.

Three Sisterhoods Welcomed

Bishop Grace's interest in education prompted him to invite the Sisters of St. Dominic of Sinsinawa, Wisconsin, to take charge of the Immaculate Conception school in Faribault, and on St. Dominic's day, August 4, 1865, five sisters arrived in St. Paul—Sisters Josephine Cahill, Gertrude Powers, Veronica Powers, Imelda Hertzog and Benvenuta McCullough. The Bishop welcomed them, accompanied them to their destination, named their future home Bethlehem Academy and placed Sisters Veronica and Benvenuta in charge of the classes to be started in the basement of the church the following September. To aid the parish in meeting the obligations incurred by opening a school, the Bishop delivered a lecture on St. Patrick's day that was long remembered by those fortunate enough to hear it. The local paper described the Bishop as "an able and eloquent speaker, a man of rare talent and liberal views, to whom it was a pleasure to listen" and added that few persons in Minnesota, lay or clerical, surpass him as an able and finished scholar and orator.

During the next decade two other communities of religious women were invited into the diocese. At the suggestion of Father Ireland the Bishop asked the Sisters of the Good Shepherd to establish a home for wayward girls in St. Paul and on May 20, 1868, four of them arrived in the city from the Provincial House in St. Louis—Mother Mary of St. Bernard Flinn, Sisters Mary of St. Francis de Sales Carey, Mary of St. Dosithea Hayes, and Mary of St. Gabriel Corrigan. They were driven to the Bishop's residence where he and Father Ireland greeted them with words of welcome and encouragement, and conveyed them to their modest home, a frame building of eight rooms at Fort and Smith Streets, where they began their work of compassion, education and social regeneration. In May of the next year they purchased the St. Paul College built by the Presbyterians but never occupied and, in addition to a day school, opened a reformatory for unfortunate females, a protectorate for wayward girls, a Magdalen house, and a home for friendless young women of unblemished character whom they cared for until suitable employment could be procured. The new institution, located at 90 Wilkin Street, has been occupied by the Little Sisters of the Poor since the Sisters of the Good Shepherd made their third and final migration to Mount Eudes in May, 1883, where they are housed in a commodious monastery well adapted to their needs, with a modern wing for the Magdalen community. It is the Provincial House of the order in the Northwest.

Five years later, at the request of the Bishop, Father Caillet, pastor of St. Mary's, invited the Sisters of the Visitation of St. Louis to make a foundation in St. Paul. When he received an affirmative answer to his request he went to St. Louis to escort them to their future home. Six Sisters arrived in 1873 and took possession of the modest "two-story house with a window or two" prepared for their reception at 318 Somerset Street in Lower Town. The pioneer group consisted of Mother Mary Agatha Russell and Sisters Alphonsus McMahon, Clare Rogers, Magdalen Applebe, Clementine Shepherd and Martina Corby. At the end of eight years they outgrew the original quarters and bought the Litchfield residence on upper Robert Street, added a new wing for school purposes, and remained there until 1913, when they migrated to the modern and well-appointed Convent and Academy at Grotto and Fairmount Streets, built for them by a daughter of the late James J. Hill in exchange for their second home in the down-town area. The last of the original group, Mother Clementine, a convert, passed away on January 21, 1918.

After the Civil War Bishop Grace wrote Archbishop Spalding of Baltimore[41] for advice as to how to deal with the Germans in his diocese who, without consulting him, were "making arrangements for purchasing ground for the purpose of a cemetery to be used by the German people exclusively", notwithstanding the fact that the diocese already had a cemetery "of large extent and much expense in putting and keeping it in good order". Knowing that this would cause "great dissatisfaction among other Catholics, American, Irish and French", he asked whether he should "let the Germans go on with their project or oppose it, and how oppose it effectively without danger of scandal". The Archbishop's answer is not available, but it is a matter of record that the St. Joseph Aid Association purchased a tract of forty-seven acres at Randolph and Hamline Avenues, St. Paul, for a burying ground for German Catholics although it was never used for that purpose. It is now the site of St. Joseph's Orphanage.

Nine years later he wrote Archbishop Gibbons of Baltimore urging the de-Germanizing[42] of the Milwaukee Province by the naming of Bishop Spalding of Peoria as Coadjutor to Archbishop Henni with the right of succession. At the Provincial Council held in Milwaukee on September 4, 1878, Bishop Grace was the sole non-German prelate and it was only with the utmost difficulty that he succeeded in having the name of Bishop Spalding put on the list of candidates for that position. The only objection urged by the others was that he was not a German, though he spoke German fluently. Bishop Grace was assured by Father Kundig, the Vicar General, that it was "a false impression, if any such existed, that the German people would not be satisfied with any other than a German Bishop for the succession". There was, he said, already among the intelligent and influential German Catholics of Milwaukee, a leaning towards Bishop Spalding in view of this appointment of a coadjutor. . . . The fact that he was familiar with the German language would be sufficient to remove any objections that might be entertained. However, the succession of German bishops continued till 1930 and now four of the five bishops in the Milwaukee Province are non-German.

Bishop Grace's de-Germanizing policy was not without precedent in the Church in the United States.[43] As early as 1853 Archbishop Cajetan Bedini, Papal Nuncio to Brazil, who visited this country on his return from South America, in his report to the Cardinal Prefect of the Propaganda, opposed the project of appointing German Bishops for American sees as likely to bring disaster to the Church. Bishop Grace likewise urged his coadjutor to oppose this tendency to staff the Church in America with bishops and priests of foreign extraction committed to this nationalizing policy.

On December 8, 1864, Pope Pius IX issued his famous encyclical

"Quanta Cura" which, with its Syllabus of Errors, caused a loud, persistent and bigoted outcry in the Protestant world. It had for object to warn the faithful everywhere against the dangers that threatened the Church and society because of the pernicious errors and evil maxims of the day. In a series of eighty previously censured propositions the Syllabus reiterated the Church's condemnation of the current evils of atheism, rationalism, indifferentism, socialism, communism, freemasonry and various kinds of religious liberalism—the chief errors prevalent in a rationalistic century and aimed at undermining religion, morality and society. The sense of these propositions was misunderstood and misinterpreted by Protestants unfamiliar with the context from which they were taken and from which alone their true meaning could be gathered. To eradicate these false doctrines and vicious tendencies the Holy Father called upon the faithful to unite in a jubilee of prayers, sacrifices and good works and granted special indulgences during any month of the year 1865 designated by the bishop for the people under his jurisdiction.

Bishop Grace issued a Pastoral Letter,[44] his second, on Trinity Sunday and, in conformity with the terms of the Pontifical Brief, appointed the month between July 9 and August 8, inclusive, for the gaining of the jubilee indulgences by the Catholics of St. Paul, leaving it to the discretion of the pastors outside the city to designate a more favorable month for that purpose, provided it fell within the year. He said that most of the errors condemned in the Syllabus were

> long since proscribed by the Church, but revived under new names, or disguised in the general statement. The propositions censured do not all imply heresy, but something wrong, or false, or unjust, or injurious, or dangerous, and they are censured under these qualifications. Several of the propositions, whilst true under certain restrictions, are condemned as false when erected into absolute principles; others again, while legitimate under given circumstances, are declared erroneous when stated for universal application.

He outlined the conditions for gaining the indulgence: two visits to the Cathedral and the Church of the Assumption for the faithful in St. Paul, or to the parish church or the chapel in convents and academies, and the recitation of prayers, such as the Litany of the Saints or of the B. V. M., or five Our Fathers and five Hail Marys, for the intention of the Holy Father; fast and abstinence on Wednesday, Friday and Saturday of one week; reception of the sacraments for adults and the making of a good confession for children not yet admitted to first communion; the giving of an alms through the poor-boxes provided for that purpose, to be equally divided between local charities and the education of candidates for the priesthood.

New Parishes Founded

In the meantime the growth of the Catholic Church in St. Paul kept pace with the progress of the city. As the frontier trading post welcomed new accessions to its population the number of Catholics also increased. Throughout the state, likewise, there was a proportionate growth in numbers among Catholics as new immigrants joined the ranks of its citizens. For several years after Bishop Grace's arrival the Cathedral afforded ample accommodations for the English-speaking members of the fold; but gradually the need of another church began to assert itself. There was an agitation for a new parish in what was then and for many years afterwards called "Lower Town" which had rapidly developed into a residential district, attracting to itself the better class of citizens seeking a favorable location for their homes. The Catholics among them were at considerable distance from the Cathedral and a new church became a necessity for their accommodation. In the summer of 1865 Bishop Grace issued a call[45] for a meeting of those interested in the project and shortly afterwards a site was secured and Father Caillet, pastor of the Cathedral since 1861, was assigned to the new parish, placed under the protection of St. Mary. The cornerstone of the new church was laid on Pentecost Sunday, May 20, 1866, by the Bishop who also preached the sermon in which he emphasized the significance of the event and exhorted the parishioners to cooperate in bringing the work to a speedy and successful conclusion. The completed edifice of limestone was dedicated to divine worship on Sunday, July 28, 1867, and was a center of vitalizing Catholic life until the locality became undesirable because of the encroachment of commerce and a new parochial plant in a more favorable district, not far removed from the original site, was set apart for the service of God on February 12, 1922.

In less than a decade after the Bishop's arrival the parish of St. Anthony near the falls of that name had grown in population and importance. Many of the parishioners lived on the west side of the Mississippi and had to cross the suspension bridge for Mass on Sunday and for schooling on week days. At Bishop Grace's direction the pastor, Reverend John McDermott, purchased two lots in the Town of Minneapolis and erected a frame building for a school,[46] opened on December 8, 1866, by the Sisters of St. Joseph who resided at the Convent of St. Mary in St. Anthony, and made the trip across the river and back each school day. They were Mother Celestine, the directress, and Sisters Ignatius and Cecelia. In less than a month they registered one hundred and twenty-nine pupils. Mass was said occasionally in this school for the accommodation of the Catholics in the neighborhood, as, prior to its erection, probably, it had been said in Catholic homes in the vicinity.

Owing to the rapid growth in the population of Minneapolis, as the nascent town was named in 1855, a new parish became a necessity and, in October, 1868, the Bishop authorized the Reverend James McGolrick, recently ordained in Ireland and stationed at the Cathedral, to found a parish under the aegis of the Immaculate Conception of the Blessed Virgin Mary. In the rear of the school, but opening into it by folding doors, Father McGolrick erected a frame building, known as the "shed church", which served the congregation as a house of worship until replaced by a stone edifice on Third Street at Third Avenue, North, the cornerstone of which was blessed and placed in position by Bishop Grace on July 9, 1871, and which was dedicated on New Year's day of 1873.

The Bishop had promised to officiate on that occasion but when the time came he refused to attend the ceremony because of the manner in which the town had been placarded with posters announcing the event—a form of publicity to which he strenuously objected. In his absence Father Tissot of St. Anthony's blessed the church, Father Venn of Henderson celebrated the Solemn Mass and Father Ireland preached the sermon.

The new Church of St. Joseph in Red Wing was dedicated [47] on Trinity Sunday, July 11, 1865, by Bishop Grace, assisted by Fathers Caillet and Tissot. The site was bought in 1860 by Father Tissot who had charge of the Catholics in Wabasha and Goodhue counties. Shortly after the dedication Bishop Grace appointed Reverend C. J. Knauf first resident pastor with missions at Belle Creek, Cherry Grove and Belvidere.

On October 19, 1868, Bishop Grace signed a contract for the erection of a church at Rocky Run in Winsted township, the original church of the present Holy Trinity parish at Winsted.

Bishop Grace was one of the forty-eight prelates in attendance at the Second Plenary Council of Baltimore in October, 1866. Six months previously he had received a copy of the agenda and expressed his great joy on hearing of the convocation of the council "from which much is to be hoped for the interests of religion in our country".[48] He suggested to Archbishop Spalding "the advisability of publishing in this country the decrees of the Council of Trent regarding clandestine marriages" as an effective means to prevent the intermarriage of Catholics with Protestants.[49] His experience led him to believe that "it would be a blessing for time and eternity, if nearly every marriage contracted before a Protestant Minister or a civil magistrate could be declared null"; and he suggested that the declaration of Benedict XIV on the question of marriages in Holland and Belgium might be held in force. The Council was presided over by Archbishop Spalding of that city as Delegate Apostolic, and issued decrees concerning the orthodox faith; the hierarchy and the government of the Church; ecclesiastical property; the sacraments and discipline; religious orders; the education of youth; books and newspapers. He was one of the signers of the Pastoral Letter[50] issued by the Fathers of the Council on October 21; and, likewise, a patron of the Catholic Publication Society of New York, approved by the Council "to supply the Catholics of the United States with religious reading in a cheap, popular form". During the year it published a million copies of twenty tracts of which seven hundred thousand were put in circulation and sixty thousand distributed gratis to hospitals and prisons. It planned to purchase a headquarters when sufficient funds were available. Among the priests of the Diocese of St. Paul who contributed to the project were Fathers Oster, Ireland, Caillet, Keller, Murray, Venn, Berghold and Sommereisen.

First Official Visit to Rome

On Easter Monday, April 22, 1867, Bishop Grace, accompanied by Father Ravoux, started on his first Ad Limina visit to Rome to be present on the occasion of the eighteen hundredth anniversary of the martyrdom of St. Peter and at the canonization of several saints. He sailed from New York on the "City of Baltimore", arrived in Queenstown, Ireland, on June 7, and reached his destination on June 18, one of four hundred prelates, of whom twenty-five were from the United States, and one thousand priests assembled in the Eternal City. The Holy Father in his address to them announced his intention to hold an ecumenical council at a date not yet decided upon.

Before leaving St. Paul Bishop Grace wrote a Pastoral Letter[51] to the clergy and laity stating that his main purpose in making the trip abroad was to secure priests for the diocese.

> We had indulged the hope of being able to establish a seminary for the diocese with the faculty and Board of Directors from among our own clergy; but the pressing needs for the services of the clergy in other departments, together with our limited resources, has compelled us to postpone the undertaking until circumstances will be more favorable.

There were at the time a hundred thousand Catholics in the diocese cared for by fifty priests in one hundred and eleven churches and seventy-nine missions; there were eleven seminarians, and the need for more priests was quite evident.

During the Bishop's absence Father Oster, Secretary and Chancellor, was Administrator of the Diocese and Vicar General.

On the return journey the Bishop traveled through France, Ireland and other countries in quest of recruits for his diocese and arrived home on August 16.[52] He was met at the depot by the Catholic societies and escorted to his residence where an address of welcome was read by

Captain M. J. O'Connor, and in reply thereto the Bishop spoke briefly about his visit to the Old World, after which all repaired to the Cathedral where a solemn Te Deum was sung and Benediction of the Blessed Sacrament imparted. On the following Sunday at High Mass, the Bishop gave a more detailed account of his visit to Italy and other European lands.

The Parochial School Problem

During the Bishop's absence in Europe a petition signed by eight hundred Catholics was presented to the School Board of St. Paul on June 24, 1867, praying for financial aid for the parochial schools,[53] proposing to place them under the direction of the Board as far as secular education was concerned, giving the Board full authority to enter and inspect the schools at all times and to examine teachers and texts, provided the Board would recognize these schools and grant them, according to the number of scholars, their due proportion of the school fund. In this connection it was shown that the Catholic schools had an enrollment of one thousand pupils; the total receipts from tuition, collections and donations from September, 1866, to July, 1867, amounted to $2861.00, while the expenditure for teachers, janitor services and repairs came to $3921.10, leaving a deficit of $1,060.10.

In its reply the Board said:

> We cannot establish or support any school in which there is a religious test required as a qualification for the teacher, nor can any money be drawn from the treasury for the support of such schools, without a violation of the constitution of the State.

The reply quoted an opinion obtained from the Attorney General who declared that

> under the constitution and laws of the State I do not think the said request can be complied with. These provide generally that education at the public school shall be strictly secular, and I cannot see how under the principles of our government a system of free schools under denominational influence can be supported at the public expense for that necessarily involves the taxation of the citizens for the propagation of religious tenets conflicting with his own, a proposition manifestly opposed to all our ideas of civil and religious liberty.[54]

Evidently the reply was based on the false assumption that the Catholic religion was to be taught as part and parcel of common school education; that a religious test was required of teachers; that it compelled citizens to support a religious minority against their consent, and that a preference was to be given by law to a certain religious worship. Nothing of the kind was asked, suggested, or even thought of. The schools were offered to the Board not as Catholic but as public schools over which the Board would have full control. After school hours Catholic children could receive religious instruction. This was the germ of the Faribault School Plan of the early nineties.

But the matter was not allowed to rest there. In June of the next year Fathers Ireland of the Cathedral, and Staub of the Assumption parish again petitioned the Board of Education to adopt a plan "by which, while the rights of your Board are guarded, no impediment will be placed in the way of Catholic parents participating in the privileges of the school system. In other places a plan such as we desire has been agreed upon. . . . We have school houses, teachers and scholars. What is needed in order that our schools be recognized by your Board?" Once more the petition was denied, but the agitation continued for several years.

Early in 1868 the Catholische Volkszeitung of Baltimore carried an item to the effect that forty-two of the fifty-two priests in Minnesota were German.[55] As a matter of fact only twenty-two were German while eight were Slovenian and Bohemian and twenty-two Irish, French and American. Of thirty-six diocesan priests ten were German, eight Slovenian and Bohemian, and eighteen French, Irish and American; of sixteen members of religious orders twelve were German, and four Irish and French.

"The Catholic Mutual Benefit Society of St. Paul" was organized in April, 1868,[56] for the benefit of its members and the cultivation of a social and fraternal spirit, with the following officers: President, Mark Costello; 1st Vice-President, P. H. Kelly; 2nd Vice-President, James Cleary; Secretary, J. J. Egan; Treasurer, Patrick Keigher; an appointed Board of Directors and an Auditing Committee. It had the hearty approval of the Right Reverend Bishop.

A few months after Bishop Grace's return from Rome he issued a pastor letter designating the time for holding the triduum proclaimed by Pope Pius IX as a period of prayer and sacrifice to avert the dangers menacing the Holy See from the Italian forces. It could be held at any time between May 1 and October 17 and was to feature daily Mass followed by the Litany of the Blessed Virgin, and afternoon or evening devotions at which the Litany of the Saints was to be recited and Benediction given. Offerings, too, were to be made for the Holy Father.

Synods: Formal and Informal

Amid the distractions of an active life Bishop Grace did not forget or neglect the spiritual side of his apostolic ministry. During his episcopate five formal synods[57] were held in the Cathedral—the first on June 10, 1861; the second on September 24, 1863; the third on July 14, 1873; the fourth on August 24, 1875; and the fifth on August 27, 1877. In all of them salutary regulations were adopted and promulgated for the spiritual well being of religion within the diocese. Each of them was preceded by a retreat of eight days held in the episcopal residence under the direction of Reverend A. Damen, S. J., (for the first); Reverend Stephen Ryan, C. M., (for the second); Reverend Gaudentius Rossi, C. P., (for the third); Right Reverend Michael Heiss, (for the fourth); and Reverend Augustine F. Hewitt, C. S. P., (for the fifth).

The first synod was attended by eighteen diocesan and four Benedictine priests. The Reverend Michael Prendergast was appointed Promoter and the Reverend Anatole Oster, Secretary.

Seventeen diocesan and two Benedictine priests were in attendance at the second synod, and two diocesan priests, laboring in the Indian missions, were excused. The Reverend Michael Prendergast was Promoter, Reverend Thomas Murray, Procurator, and Reverend Anatole Oster, Secretary.

The roll call of clergy at the third synod showed forty-nine diocesan priests present and five legitimately excused, two Benedictines and two Oblates. The Very Reverend Augustine Ravoux was Promoter and the Reverends Anatole Oster and John Ireland, Secretaries.

Forty-six diocesans and five regulars were present at the fourth synod, with five diocesan priests excused. Father Ravoux was Archdeacon and Fathers Oster and Ireland, Secretaries.

The fifth synod was attended by fifty-nine diocesan priests, with Father Ravoux as Archdeacon and Father Oster, Secretary. Bishop Ireland also was present.

The first synod promulgated the decrees of the Councils of Baltimore approved by the Holy See and of the two Provincial Councils of St. Louis and made them of obligation in the diocese. It also dealt with the clergy and their functions; the necessity of keeping registers of baptisms, confirmations and deaths as well as inventories of parish properties and whatever is used in the service of the altar; receipts and expenditures; the administration of ecclesiastical goods; stole fees; collections for the Propagation of the Faith; parish schools and catechetical instruction; cultivation of vocations to the priesthood and support of the seminary; and the administration of the sacraments.

The second synod legislated about the clergy and ecclesiastical administration; the sacraments and other sacred rites; the rules to be observed in the exposition and benediction of the Blessed Sacrament; and affirmed the binding force of the decrees of the first synod.

The third synod regulated the use of wax candles in the Holy Sacrifice of the Mass; made "McCaffrey's" Baltimore Catechism official for the diocese; and forbade the holding of dances under the auspices of the Church and of Catholic societies for the benefit of church, school, or other religious purpose.

Copies of a booklet containing the official records and the decrees of these three synods are preserved in the archives of the Catholic Historical Society of St. Paul in the Archbishop Ireland Memorial Library at the St. Paul Seminary.

The fourth synod established seven deaneries and appointed deans: St. Paul, (Father Ireland); Minneapolis (Father Tissot); Burnsville (Father Oster); Belle Plaine (Father Kennedy); Mankato (Father Schnitzler, S.J.); Faribault (Father Genis); Winona (Father Plut). It decreed that priests' housekeepers, unless they are near relatives, must be over thirty years of age; that no priest act as doctor or surgeon under pain of suspension, ipso facto; that the regulations in force regarding the Cathedraticum be maintained.

The fifth synod added four new deaneries: Shakopee; Rochester; Caledonia; Jefferson (in Dakota Territory); forbade priests to enter saloons except for grave and urgent reasons and to drink therein under any pretext; decreed that all churches in the diocese be incorporated within six months in accordance with the civil law of the State of Minnesota and in the form and manner set forth in an appendix to the decrees.

In addition, two informal synods were held: the first on August 26, 1867, and the second on August 24, 1878. In the first it was agreed that each priest, whether diocesan or regular, having the care of souls, would determine the amount of Cathedraticum according to the number and resources of the churches under his care and transmit it to the Bishop at the beginning of each year. The amount should be not less than one twenty-fifth of his income. If not paid during the current year it should be sent not later than Easter of the next year.

In the second informal synod it was resolved that no festivals, picnics or fairs in aid of a church or religious society be permitted on Sunday; that dancing and the use of wine, beer and alcoholic beverages be forbidden, as well as the sale of intoxicating drinks for the benefit of church, school or any other purpose directly or indirectly connected with religion.

With the exception of a synod held during the regime of Archbishop Ireland on August 16, 1893, of which there is no record in the Archdiocesan Archives, no other synod was convoked in the diocese until 1939 when, under the direction of Archbishop Murray, one was held in St. Mary's Chapel of the St. Paul Seminary at the close of the diocesan retreat and was attended by all the clergy, both diocesan and regular. No report of the proceedings has been published.

In April, 1874, Bishop Grace authorized the building of a church dedicated to St. Peter in Delano to replace the original church erected in 1865 in what is now the parish cemetery. There was opposition on the part of those who lived near the church "in the country"; but it gave way to the Bishop's decision announced on April 6, 1874, by Father

Steinacker of Watertown, whom he commissioned to make it known to the people. The cornerstone was laid on June 15 by Father Steinacker assisted by Rev. I. Schaller of St. Michael. It was attended by the French from the old church in the country and the German and Polish Catholics in Franklin and neighboring townships, and soon it had to be enlarged.

In the afternoon of July 4, 1877, Bishop Grace laid the cornerstone of St. Mary's Church in Lake City which was opened for divine service in December, 1879. On the morning of that day Father O'Gorman celebrated Mass in the frame church erected in 1866, at a cost of $1,800, by Father Tissot of Wabasha, and preached at the ceremony in the afternoon. The first resident pastor of Lake City was Father Hermon who came in 1869, bought a rectory and the lot on which the present church stands. Reverend Francis A. Quinn who succeeded Father Hermon, built the church of which the bishop blessed the cornerstone. It was 53 by 100 feet in size, with stone basement, brick superstructure and a tower fifty feet high topped by a frame steeple and cross.

Catholic Papers Come Into Being

Bishop Grace had always been a strong advocate of the Catholic press and urged his people again and again to support it and help extend its influence. Shortly after the close of the Civil War a proposal to found a Catholic newspaper in St. Paul was made to him by Father Ireland and he accepted it without hesitation even though it did not fully harmonize with the view expressed some years previously in a letter to McMaster of the Freeman's Journal. When John Crosby Devereux resigned his commission in Company G. of the Third Minnesota Regiment and took up residence in St. Paul he renewed acquaintance with Father Ireland whom he had known as a Chaplain in the South. At Father Ireland's suggestion he agreed to start a Catholic weekly newspaper.[58] Before embarking on the enterprise, however, he thought it well to ascertain the need for it by canvassing the Catholic population. Armed with a letter from Father Ireland he made a six months' tour of the state soliciting subscriptions at the rate of three dollars per year to be remitted if and when the first issue of the proposed paper appeared. He returned with six hundred and forty subscriptions, nearly half of which were never paid for by the subscribers. The prospects seemed favorable to Bishop Grace and Father Ireland and it was decided to embark on the venture. Bishop Grace suggested the name, "The Northwestern Chronicle", and gave office room in the Catholic block rent free. The meager supplies necessary to equip the plant—a few fonts of type, bought in Chicago, and several pieces of office furniture—were procured and arrangements made to have the press work done by the St. Paul Pioneer. Devereux was editor, reporter, foreman, bookkeeper, solicitor for advertising and subscriptions. It was the first Catholic newspaper in the state and it required almost heroic courage to undertake such a project with the country in the grip of post-war inertia.

The first issue appeared on November 6, 1866,[59] and was mailed to subscribers of record who had promised to pay three dollars a year for it. Later on the price was reduced to two fifty. It was a five-column, eight page paper but at the beginning of the third year it was enlarged to six columns.

One of the most successful of the early solicitors for subscriptions was Richard Richards who came from Pittsburgh for his health. He made the acquaintance of Mayor O'Neil of Milwaukee who, on a visit to St. Paul, met Mr. Devereux, became interested in the Chronicle and promised to aid the project in his home city. Richards went to Milwaukee and, with the cooperation of the Mayor, secured three hundred and fifty subscriptions. The Mayor solicited the county officers and sent policemen with Richards to call on all the Catholics on their beat.

The Chronicle was the personal property of Devereux and neither Bishop Grace nor Father Ireland was financially interested in it. The Bishop used it as a medium of communication with the clergy. Devereux remained in full charge until 1875. For a time Manly Tello had a half-interest which he eventually sold to John Cullen. For six months Dillon O'Brien was editor at one-half the profits—but there were no profits. William Louis Kelly, a lawyer from Kentucky and afterwards a Judge of the District Court for over thirty years, was connected with the publication for two or three months, writing a column or two a week, at a salary of a hundred dollars a month.

At the end of a decade of struggle, when the paper had seven hundred and forty subscribers, Devereux sold it to Bishop Ireland for two thousand dollars and when all his obligations were satisfied he had eighteen dollars left, the net proceeds of these years of strenuous work. Two or three years after the Chronicle had come under his control, Bishop Ireland asked Devereux how he managed to keep it going and get it out on time. In subsequent years the Chronicle had a number of clerical editors among them Fathers John Shanley, John Conway and Ambrose McNulty, and Archbishop Ireland was called upon to meet the annual deficits until 1900 when the paper was sold to the Catholic Citizen of Milwaukee and issued from the office of that publication until 1935 when it went out of business.

A year after the Northwestern Chronicle appeared "Der Wanderer",[60] a German Catholic weekly, was launched in St. Paul by a number of German Catholics, under the leadership of the Benedictine Fathers of the Assumption Church, who decided to found a weekly newspaper in the German language to keep alive and enhance the traditions of their faith and fatherland and to serve as a medium for the diffusion of Catholic news and views among Catholic citizens of German origin and descent. The first issue appeared on November 16, 1867, and it has been published continuously down to the present. During these eighty-five years it has had but three editors: Francis Fassbind (1867-83); Hugo Klapproth (1883-99); and Joseph Matt (1899-). The Wanderer Printing Company was organized as a partnership, but became a corporation in 1888. It has had but three Presidents: Reverend Clement Staub, O. S. B., Mr. Nicholas Bures and Mr. Joseph Matt (since 1914). In the course of time it became increasingly difficult to make a success of a Catholic weekly in the German language because all too many of the younger generation of German Americans did not read, speak or understand the language of their forefathers; and it seemed the part of prudence to make provision for the future by issuing an English edition of the paper under the name of "The Wanderer", the first number of which appeared on January 8, 1931, with the approval of the ecclesiastical authorities. Since then both papers have been issued from the same press, owned and controlled by the corporation, and under the same management. Mr. Matt has associated with himself his two sons who relieve him of the business details and leave him free to carry out the editorial policy. He is undoubtedly one of the best known, most competent and scholarly German editors in the country. "Der Wanderer" came under interdict in Germany during the Hitler regime because of its outspoken and persistent criticism of Naziism in all its forms and tendencies. Several years ago Mr. Matt was made a Knight of St. Gregory by the Holy See in recognition of his distinguished services to the Church, and on the fiftieth anniversary of his editorial career was honored with a testimonial by his host of friends in St. Paul and throughout the state.

Not to be outdone by the Irish and Germans, M. D. Michaud of St. Paul founded "Le Canadien", a weekly newspaper in French which appeared for the first time on August 15, 1877, and continued until June 19, 1903, when it was merged with "Le Courier de l'Ouest" (1896), "Le Courier de l'Illinois" (1868), and "La Voix du Peuple" (1900), to form "Le Courier-Canadien" published in Chicago. On October 15, 1883, Le Canadien was purchased by a stock company and edited by different persons, among them Mr. A. Martin, a journalist of wide experience, who greatly improved it by giving more attention to Catholic matters. Incomplete files are in the newspaper room of the Minnesota Historical Society.

Six years afterwards, on May 2, 1883, "L'Echo de l'Ouest", a weekly newspaper for the French Catholics of Minneapolis and vicinity, was issued for the first time by Zephirin Demeules and Louis Laramee, the proprietors, and attained a circulation of upwards of twenty-five hundred subscribers who paid a dollar and a half yearly. Mr. Demeules died in

1898 and his son, Augustin, took charge of the publication with his sister-in-law, Mrs. Marie Lenoir, as editor. Augustin died in 1928 and the paper was discontinued on January 4, 1929. Almost complete files of the paper, beginning with Volume 2, No. 38, are in the Minnesota Historical Society Building.

"The Celtic World," a weekly newspaper, advocating the deliverance of Ireland from English rule and the policy of the Land League, made its bow to the Irish citizens of Minneapolis and the Northwest on Saturday, December 3, 1881. It was edited and controlled by McCann, Wood and Co. and issued from the office of publication, 7 South Second Street. It gave prominence to Catholic news. "Our tone, indeed, as far as religion is concerned, will be eminently Catholic. Patriotism and Catholicity will, in the Celtic World, go hand in hand." Before the end of the year it was issued by the Celtic World Publishing Company. In less than three months Thomas Wood was editor. In May, 1882, he associated himself with Charles G. Early who assumed the management of the paper until it ceased publication on December 9, 1882. A complete file is preserved in the Minnesota Historical Society newspaper room.

Nearly twenty years after the appearance of "Der Wanderer" another national Catholic weekly was founded in Minneapolis—"The Irish Standard".[61] It began its journalistic existence as "The Northwest Standard" the first issue of which came from the press on Saturday, November 7, 1885, a four-page paper whose main object was "to urge the Irishmen of Minneapolis and the Northwest in general to uphold the patriot's (Parnell's) hands in his fight with British tyranny, to defend the interests of our people ignored and insulted by a prejudiced and bigoted press, to guard the sacred interests of our Church, to assist labor in its war against capital". After five months, during which it was said to be an "extraordinary success" the name was changed to "The Irish Standard", with Edward O'Brien as editor and proprietor and John O'Brien, Jr., as business manager. The first issue under the new name appeared on April 17, 1886, and it was published continuously until June 19, 1920. Roger Vail was connected with it in an editorial capacity from 1900 to 1910 and it exerted no inconsiderable influence among Irishmen and their descendants for it never lost sight of its objective, namely, "to unite the Irish people and advance their interests as a whole and to resent any slur that might be cast upon the Irish race".

On July 18, 1866, Bishop Grace administered confirmation to 16 boys and 24 girls in the log chapel of New Munich; and on July 20, 1868, to 26 boys and 18 girls; and again on July 1, 1872, to 6 boys and 18 girls.

In November, 1868, the feast of the Immaculate Conception was made a holyday of obligation and the privilege of celebrating it on the following Sunday revoked.[62]

Catholic Total Abstinence Movement

The Catholic Temperance Society organized and fostered by Bishop Cretin ceased to exist as a corporate body before he passed away. It was contemporaneous with his episcopal career. His successor, Bishop Grace, although not unmindful of the benefits to be derived from total abstinence, did not make any effort to resurrect it. Nothing was done, perhaps nothing could be done, until after the Civil War.

The visit of Father Mathew to America in 1849-51 may be said to have inaugurated a new era in temperance work in the United States. During his tour he gave the pledge to over half a million people, and temperance societies sprang into being in the chief cities of the country. In the course of time many of them ceased to exist because of lack of leadership and enthusiasm for the cause. In the late sixties there was a revival of interest when the Second Plenary Council of Baltimore called attention to the havoc wrought by intemperance and urged bishops and priests to make war against the evil and bring about a reform of the liquor traffic.

In response to this appeal the priests of America began to preach and practice total abstinence from intoxicating beverages and thus was laid the foundation of a crusade against the use as well as the abuse of liquor and the drinking habits of society, which, in the latter part of the nineteenth century, wrought untold good for people in all walks of life.

Bishop Grace was present at the Council but he made no special effort to organize his people in opposition to the drink traffic. It is to his credit, however, that, when the movement was started by others, he put no obstacle in their way but rather gave fullest approval and encouragement to their efforts.[63]

The first to raise the standard of total abstinence in the Diocese of St. Paul after the Civil War was the Reverend Daniel V. McGinnity, a priest of the Milwaukee diocese, temporarily in charge of the parish of Belle Plaine, who formed a total abstinence society among his parishioners on December 1, 1868. It had a membership of one hundred and seventy within a month after organization. Father McGinnity was elected President, James Kilduff, Vice-President, John Henry, Secretary, and Philip Wagner, Treasurer. This first total abstinence society in the diocese was quickly followed by others and thus was inaugurated a new campaign against indulgence in intoxicating beverages of which Father Ireland was destined to be the foremost champion and recognized leader not only in Minnesota but throughout the United States.

Father Ireland hastened to follow the example set by Father McGinnity and on January 10, 1869,. organized the Father Mathew Society of the Cathedral parish with an initial membership of forty-six which in a very short time climbed to one hundred. Patrick Nash was elected President, Honorable John B. Brisbin, Vice-President, James Ackers, Treasurer, and Michael T. Ryan, Secretary. Similar societies were formed in Minneapolis, Hastings, Rochester and many other localities in the state.

The Father Mathew men made their first appearance in public in 1869, when they joined with other organizations in celebrating St. Patrick's day by assisting at Mass in the Cathedral and paying a courtesy call on Bishop Grace to whom an address was read. In replying thereto His Lordship said among other things

> The pleasure (of greeting you) is heightened by seeing among you so- cities whose object is the most legitimate and praiseworthy. I refer es- pecially to one—the Father Mathew Total Abstinence Society. Long may it continue to grow and flourish. And I hope every one of you will make himself an apostle of temperance. In proportion as that movement spreads, sin, wretchedness and poverty will disappear. Endeavor to make it a success and under its influence the great monster evil of our times must be done away with.[64]

While no steps were taken without Bishop Grace's approval the real head of the movement was Father Ireland and the story of his uncom- promising attitude, successful leadership and phenomenal success will be told elsewhere.

On January 6, 1869, the feast of the Epiphany, Bishop Grace received the perpetual vows of three Sisters of St. Benedict in the parish church of Shakopee and preached the sermon. They were Sisters Scholastica Kerst of St. Paul, Benedict Klein of Shakopee, and Xavier Pendy of Belle Plaine, all residing in St. Gertrude's Convent.[65]

In the autumn of that year Bishop Grace purchased a large oil paint- ing[66] of the Descent from the Cross and hung it on the rear wall of the Cathedral sanctuary behind the main altar where it remained until the building was demolished in 1914. The painting was executed in Sweden by Lehmann, a noted artist, who copied this masterpiece of Daniele da Volterra, the favorite pupil of Michaelangelo. It showed several life-size figures in the foreground and others in the background. The color is admirable in harmony, depth and richness of tone. The painting cost $300, about one-quarter of its real value.

It was taken to the new Cathedral and, after being retouched, hung for several years in the ambulatory behind the high altar from which it was removed when the organ was installed. It now hangs in an obscure corner behind one of the great piers near the Chapel of St. Joseph.

Dedication of New Churches

During these years the diocese had grown in population by leaps and bounds largely as a result of the immigration program initiated and fostered by Bishop Grace, and many new churches had to be erected to meet the needs of the faithful whose numbers had kept pace with the over-all increase. The Bishop was kept busy dedicating churches and administering the sacrament of confirmation.

In October, 1866, he dedicated the new Church of St. John the Baptist in Byrnesville, a frame structure, 70 by 40, designed by the temporary pastor, Reverend Thaddeus Stephens, and built on a commanding site. It was the forerunner of the Church of St. John the Baptist in Savage, which replaced it after the fire which reduced it to ashes on February 2, 1902.

On December 15 he dedicated the Church of St. Stephen, Anoka; and early in the next year, on February 10, he delegated Father Ravoux, V.G., to officiate at the dedication of the new gothic church at Inver Grove, 70 by 40, with octagonal sanctuary and tapering tower. The Bishop blessed the Church of St. Michael, West St. Paul, on September 29, 1867; and the new Stations of the Cross in the Cathedral on April 3, 1868, at which Father Ireland preached. Then he began a visitation of the diocese with confirmation in the Cathedral the following month and spent the summer going from parish to parish administering the sacrament until September 16 when he brought the visitation to a close in the Church of St. Gertrude, Forest City. On December 27, 1868, he dedicated the Church of St. Louis for the French Catholics of St. Paul; and on June 27, 1869, the Church of the Guardian Angels in Hastings, after which he celebrated High Mass, assisted by the pastor, Father Halton, Father Knauf of Red Wing, and Father Hermon of Lake City, who preached the sermon. In the afternoon he assisted at vespers and gave benediction before returning to St. Paul. The church in Hastings was begun in 1865, is 120 by 50 feet in size, and was complete except for the tower.

On July 22 he blessed and placed in position the cornerstone of the Church of the Holy Trinity, Rollingstone, of which Reverend C. Robert was pastor. On August 15, 1869, he dedicated the Church of St. Mary of the Purification at Marystown, a stone structure, 90 by 34, with a steeple 75 feet high and stained glass windows. On July 24, 1870, he dedicated the Church of St. Joseph in Minneapolis, assisted by Fathers Hillmer, pastor of St. Boniface Church, McGolrick of the Immaculate Conception and Tissot of St. Anthony of Padua.

In 1871 he dedicated the log Church of St. Nicholas at Belle River built by Reverend Ignatius Tomazin who remained in charge until August, 1873, when Reverend John Schenk of Long Prairie succeeded him. Ten years later the parish was entrusted to the Benedictine Fathers.

The first consecration of a church in the diocese took place at Clinton (St. Joseph), Minnesota, on June 29, 1871, when Bishop Grace performed that ceremony in the Church of St. Joseph assisted by Father Clement Staub, O.S.B., Vicar General for the Germans. The sermon was preached by Reverend C. Koeberl. The next day, after a Mass celebrated by the Right Reverend Abbot Seidenbusch, 165 persons were confirmed. The

Bishop rode ninety miles in a stage coach to be present on that occasion.

In the office of the Register of Deeds for Dakota County in the court-house at Hastings there is a record of the purchase of General Sibley's house in Mendota [67] by Bishop Grace on September 28, 1868, for the Sisters of St. Joseph who had opened a school for girls in it in December of the previous year. It is the oldest private residence in Mendota, built by the General in 1834, and occupied by him until his removal to St. Paul in December, 1862. It was known as the Immaculate Conception Convent until 1878 when the school was closed because it was not self-supporting. During these years the sisters taught the boys in the public school under an arrangement comparable to the Faribault School Plan of the early nineties. After the Sisters of St. Joseph retired from Mendota the convent was taken over by the Sisters of Mercy who conducted an Industrial School for girls until 1882.

The Vatican Council and Its Sequel

In October, 1869, Bishop Grace made preparations to attend the Vatican Council with Father Ireland, but as he was ready to depart he received from the Holy Father an affirmative answer to his petition to be allowed to absent himself from its deliberations "on account of the pressing cares of the diocese".[68] He authorized Father Ireland to represent him as far as possible at the Council. Before Father Ireland left St. Paul on October 13 he was presented with a substantial check by his friends to help defray the cost of the trip. He was accompanied to Rome by John Shanley who was enrolled in the Propaganda College to study for the priesthood. Father Ireland returned to St. Paul on May 14, 1870.

The Council did not complete its deliberations. It was forced to adjourn by the disturbances in the City of Rome which robbed the Church of its patrimony and made the Pope a voluntary "prisoner" in the Vatican. The breach of the Porta Pia in September, 1870, had repercussions around the world. All Christendom was aghast at the barefaced rape of the States of the Church and vehement protests surged up from all parts of the Christian world. In December of that year Pope Pius IX issued an encyclical condemning the usurpation of the Pontifical States by the Italian Government and repudiating the thirteen so-called guarantees [69] in the Terms of Reconciliation between the King of Italy and the Pope, by which the Italian Government sought to prove to Europe and the world that Italy respected the sovereignty of the Pope in conformity with the principle of a free church in a free state.

"We announce publicly and openly declare that, faithful to Our office and to the solemn oath which binds Us, We neither consent nor will consent to any project of conciliation which in any manner whatsoever destroys or lessens Our rights, which are the rights of God and of the Holy See; nor yield to or acquiesce in the unjust demands which are addressed to Us". The perpetrators of this outrage incurred "the greater excommunication and the other censures and ecclesiastical penalties published by the holy canons, apostolic constitutions and the decrees of General Councils and particularly of the Council of Trent".

In St. Paul the call for a demonstration on behalf of the Pope, as a protest against the spoliation of the States of the Church and the hampering of his spiritual functioning, was signed by sixteen men representing the Irish, German and French societies. The resultant meeting was held in the Cathedral on Sunday afternoon, January 22, 1871.[70] Special trains brought numerous delegations from most of the parishes outside the city. They were met on arrival by the local organizations and, despite a blinding snowstorm, escorted in a procession of several thousand men to the Cathedral which was crowded beyond capacity.

Bishop Grace, Abbot Seidenbusch and twenty-three priests were present. John S. Prince was elected chairman and, after an inspiring address by Bishop Grace, a long and detailed protest against the spoliation of the Holy See by the Piedmontese army was read by William Markoe in which he denounced Victor Emmanuel, King of Sardinia, unjustly styled King of Italy, and his sixty thousand soldiers who had violently seized the City of Rome and made the Pope a prisoner in the Vatican. Addresses were also delivered by Abbot Seidenbusch, Fathers Ravoux and Ireland, W. L. Kelly, F. Fassbind, Dillon O'Brien and Peter O'Connor. The protest and a full report of the demonstration were forwarded to the imprisoned Pontiff.

Under date of July 28, 1870, Bishop Grace sent the following letter to the clergy of the Diocese:[71]

"Rev. and Dear Sir:

"It has been our desire to see established, in accordance with the recommendations of the late Council of Baltimore, among the clergymen of the Diocese, ecclesiastical conferences of theological societies, the object of which would be to stimulate priests to the study of the sacred sciences, and by a mutual interchange of ideas, obtain among them, on practical questions, a salutary unity of action. We believe that the time has come, when we can, with prospect of success, imitate in this matter the efforts of older Dioceses. In this view we have resolved to invite the priests of the Diocese to come together at our episcopal residence, St. Paul, on the 24th day of August, and on that occasion to advise with them on the preliminary steps for the permanent establishment of a 'Diocesan Theological Society'".

✠ Thomas,
Bp. of St. Paul.

Was such a society formally organized? What success did it have? How long did it continue in existence? These are questions for which we seek in vain for an answer. There is no further reference to the Society in the available records of the diocese.

In 1871 Bishop Grace summoned the Christian Brothers[72] to take charge of the Cathedral school for boys and on November 2 they began to teach in what developed into the Cretin High School on St. Peter and Main streets. There were many demands for their services but, owing to the scarcity of Brothers, it was impossible to comply with most of them. Exceptions were made in favor of the Assumption School of which they took charge in 1875, and of St. Mary's in Lower Town where they remained from September 4, 1876 until June, 1891, nine years after they withdrew from the Assumption school. In 1882 the Brothers were twelve in number while the combined student body totalled six hundred and sixty-eight, including the younger boys taught by the Sisters of St. Joseph. When the old Cretin High outlived its usefulness, teachers and pupils were transferred to the new institution at Randolph and Hamline Avenues which was dedicated by Archbishop Dowling in 1928.

Indian Affairs

A letter from General Charles Ewing, Catholic Commissioner for Catholic Indian Missions, dated March 15, 1873, informed Bishop Grace that the Chippewa Agency in his diocese was vacant and, in view of the fact that most of the Indians were Catholic, he thought it desirable that the agent should be of that faith and asked whether or not he should make application for the appointment of a Catholic to that position.[73] Inferring that the Bishop would reply in the affirmative he asked to be informed of the date of establishment of the first Catholic mission among them and if it had been continuous; as well as the date on which any Protestant mission had been founded among them and if it had been continuously attended. He also asked whether or not the Bishop was prepared to provide the schools of the agency with competent teachers under government pay.

In reply to this communication Bishop Grace wrote, on March 21, an eight-page letter,[74] assuring the General that it was not only desirable, but very necessary, that a Catholic agent be appointed to secure the rights of the Catholic Chippewas and do justice to the expressed preference of the tribe for Catholic missionaries to instruct their children and themselves. He called attention, likewise, to the large number of half-breeds, or mixed bloods, descendants of the old voyageurs who intermarried with the natives, whose wishes should be respected.

The Chippewas retain vivid traditions of the Jesuit missionaries who labored among them from a very early date; of Bishop Baraga at Fond-du-Lac on the St. Louis River in 1836; of Father Belcourt at Pembina in 1848; of Father Pierz at Crow Wing in 1852. Since 1850 half a dozen priests have visited the Indians at regular intervals, often from four to six months at a time, and their successors are still among them.

Under the direction of the American Board of Missions, Protestant ministers came between 1832 and 1835, but retired before 1850 without leaving perceptible fruit. The Episcopalians attempted to establish missions at Leech Lake and Gull Lake in 1851-2 but had to abandon the attempt a few years later, and now they have only "deacon" Johnson at White Earth.

For fourteen years, at the earnest solicitation of the Indians, Bishop Grace had proposed to send priests and sisters to educate them if the Government would provide lodging and the "simplest maintenance", but without avail. He was still willing and anxious to do so.

The three agencies in Minnesota—Leech Lake, Lac-qui-parle, and White Earth—had been under the control of Protestant agents, Presbyterian and Episcopalian. And now "it would be but small justice to Catholics to allow them the agency at White Earth", which is vacant, where Catholic Indians and half-breeds are quite numerous and where no small inducements are held out to seduce them from the faith. The priest who visits White Earth has commenced a church and will take up his residence there in due time.

In a letter, dated March 24, 1873, Bishop Grace requested the Honorable Alex. Ramsey to use his influence to obtain the appointment of a Catholic agent at White Earth; but from past experience he was not encouraged to hope that his claim and preference would receive consideration at Washington. White Earth reservation is the central focus of Catholic missionary work among the Chippewas.

Mr. Ramsey interviewed the Secretary of the Interior and recommended favorable consideration of the policy suggested by Bishop Grace. The final result is not recorded in our diocesan annals.

The Catholic Union and the Industrial School

For some time the need of an organization through which the combined strength and activity of the diocesan societies could be mustered and made effective whenever necessary had been felt, and measures to provide it were taken on December 8, 1872, when Bishop Grace met with the St. Vincent de Paul societies of the Cathedral and St. Mary's parishes. It was decided to form the "Catholic Union of the Diocese of St. Paul"[75] to cement more closely the different societies under diocesan control and create a more intimate union among Catholics in general. The Bishop, Father Ireland and others spoke in favor of such an organization and it was voted to ask the societies to send delegates to a sponsoring meeting. On January 13 of the next year thirteen delegates from

eight societies met under the chairmanship of Bishop Grace. A Constitution was adopted and ratified at a meeting held on February 10 when
the organization was formally launched, "to bind more closely together
the various Catholic societies of the Diocese for the more effective support of our Holy Mother the Church and for the promotion of general
Catholic interests". It was composed of members from all the societies but
interfered with the activities of none. At this meeting several priests and
laymen spoke in favor of the project and the following officers were
elected: President, William Markoe of St. Paul; first Vice-President, A. L
Larpenteur of St. Paul; second Vice-President, Anthony Kelly of Minneapolis; third Vice-President, N. F. Kranz of Hastings; Secretary, William
L. Kelly of St. Paul; Treasurer, Mathias Koch of St. Paul. A committee
was appointed to draft by-laws to be voted on at a meeting on the second
Monday of March.

A year later, through its executive council, the Union which, in the
meantime, had accomplished "an immense amount of good" took up the
proposal, made by Father Ireland and approved by Bishop Grace, to erect
a Catholic Protectory and Industrial School for boys to be placed under
the direction of the Christian Brothers. Such a school was a necessity to
keep Catholic boys out of the State Reform School, a proselytizing institution, where they lost their faith, or off the public streets where they
were led astray by bad companions and into mischief of all kinds. It
would be a home not only for wayward boys but for orphans and the
mentally retarded where they would be given a Catholic education and
taught the rudiments of trades and mechanical pursuits with a view to
making them useful members of society.

It seems that when Father Ireland attended the National Total Abstinence Convention in New York he visited West Chester Protectory to
familiarize himself with its method of operation and results, and was so
much impressed with its accomplishments that he suggested the erection
of a similar institution in St. Paul. Bishop Grace offered to donate a
quarter section of land [76] owned by the Diocese a few miles outside the
city limits on the Dodd Road towards Mendota as a site for the buildings.
It was undulating prairie land with a small lake in the center and was
considered an ideal place for such an institution. As a preparatory move
to expedite the project "The Catholic Industrial School of Minnesota"
was incorporated on January 4, 1874, with Bishop Grace, William L.
Kelly, Thomas Grace, Louis Demeules, George Mitsch and Mathias
Koch as incorporators. Through the Catholic Union an appeal for cooperation and support was made to all Catholic societies and to Catholics in
general and a modest sum was realized. But soon the idea of building on
the "Bishop's Farm" was abandoned and a new site purchased on the
east bank of the Mississippi in the midway district, the William Finn
farm, where now the College of St. Thomas stands. It comprised four

hundred and fifty-two acres of wooded land in Reserve Township and was bought on May 2, 1874, for $56,500. For two years efforts were made to raise money to pay for the property and erect the proposed building. To help pay for the land a drawing for prizes was held in December of the next year under the management and control of six reputable citizens, four of whom were non-Catholic. Financially, the affair was a grand success, netting sufficient funds to pay for the land and erect the buildings. It is interesting to note that the Cathedral school,[77] in whose name fifty-five shares in the distribution, as it was called, were bought by parishioners won the first prize—the Underwood property on Summit Avenue valued at $20,000. Work was scheduled to begin the next spring. Finally in the fall of 1876[78] a three-storied frame building, 34 by 52 feet in dimensions, with full stone basement, rose on an eminence near Summit Avenue and not far from the river. Three Brothers of the Order of St. Francis—Augustine (Superior), Michael and Thomas—took charge of it in the following spring and operated it for about two years when it was closed and a new institution opened in the vicinity of Clontarf in Swift County, as a school for Indian and white boys under diocesan management. It functioned for about twenty-five years. The original structure in the midway district, enlarged and brick-veneered, became the administration and residence building of St. Thomas Aquinas Seminary opened on September 8, 1885.

When the Industrial School closed for lack of support not later than 1879, the Corporation sold two hundred and seventy-five acres of the original purchase to Bishop Ireland who paid the balance due on the notes held by Mr. Finn except $23,000. Knowing that the Bishop was endeavoring to establish a seminary Finn cancelled the remaining notes on July 11, 1880, and agreed to accept in lieu thereof a life annuity of five hundred dollars a year. On September 6, 1883, he sold an additional forty acres to the Bishop for thirteen thousand dollars; and in his last will and testament, dated March 16, 1889, bequeathed all his property to Archbishop Ireland and made him executor with the concurrence of his wife for whom due provision had already been made.

The first issue of a "Monthly Calendar" for the Cathedral congregation appeared in February, 1873, as a guide to the activities of the parish. It listed the hours of Masses on Sundays at 6, 7:30, 8:15, 9, and Solemn High at 10:30, with Sunday school, vespers and benediction at 2:30 and evening devotions at 7:30, at which instruction in christian doctrine and talks on timely topics as well as congregational singing were featured. At the first two Masses seat-holders—and every one should have a seat— were expected to put five cents in the collection box and at the other Masses ten cents. Baptisms were at 2 o'clock. Week day Masses at 6, 7:30 and 8:15; confessions on Saturdays from 10 to 12 in the forenoon, from 3 to 6 in the afternoon, and from 7:30 to 10 in the evening. No confessions of children were heard in the evening.

The Directory of Societies listed the St. Vincent de Paul, meeting at 10 A. M. on Sundays in the Cathedral; the Perpetual Adoration Society, requiring one hour of adoration a week from its members; the Living Rosary Society, a charitable organization for married women; the Crusaders' Total Abstinence Society for young men; the Father Matthew Total Abstinence Society for their elders; the Sacred Thirst Total Abstinence Society for women; the St. Paul Cadets for school children pledged to total abstinence; the St. Agnes Society for young women who looked after the side altars, visited the sick and made clothing for the poor; the Altar and Sanctuary Society charged with the care of the main altar and sanctuary, the vestments, linens and decorations; the Sacred Heart Society for devout adorers of the Blessed Sacrament; and the Cathedral Choir, meeting for rehearsals on Tuesday and Friday evenings of each week.

Then as now it was necessary to call attention to those who came late to Mass. "Observe" says the editor (no doubt, Father Shanley), "and you will see not only right and left-handed people but behind-handed people—always late for Mass".

An almost, but not quite, complete duplicate of this "monthly calendar" appeared in 1893.

Division of the Diocese

Many matters of more far-reaching consequences than the Industrial School project occupied the attention of Bishop Grace during the year 1874. In mid-March of that year a meeting of the Bishops of the Province of St. Louis, comprising ten suffragan dioceses, was held at St. Louis at which he was present. Among other things it petitioned the Holy See for the creation of three new dioceses—Peoria, Davenport and Kansas City—and prepared lists of priests from which the future bishops might be chosen. It is not improbable that at this meeting the Holy See was petitioned to divide the Diocese of St. Paul. The Freeman's Journal of New York, quoted in the Northwestern Chronicle of May 23, said:

> The Right Reverend Dr. Grace, Bishop of St. Paul, Minnesota, whom a distinguished Minnesotian, himself a Protestant, described to us, some years ago, as 'the foremost gentleman and most beloved citizen of Minnesota' has earnestly asked, in the interests of religion, that a new diocese may be erected in that vast, thrifty and important state. This wish of Bishop Grace, it is understood, has been recommended to the Holy See, with the approbation of the St. Louis Provincial Council.

The predicted division of the diocese took place with the issuance of the Papal Brief on February 12, 1875, erecting the Vicariate of Northern Minnesota comprising more than half the state. On Sunday, May 30, the

Right Reverend Rupert Seidenbusch, O. S. B., Abbot of St. John's, Collegeville, was consecrated Titular Bishop of Halia and Vicar Apostolic of the new territory with residence at St. Cloud. Owing to the absence of Bishop Grace in Rome, the consecrating prelate was Bishop Heiss of La Crosse, and the co-consecrators, Bishops Fink of Leavenworth and Dwenger of Fort Wayne. The sermon was preached by Bishop Hennessy of Dubuque. Among those present was the Right Reverend John Ireland Vicar Apostolic-designate of Nebraska.

The new Vicariate included all the Diocese of St. Paul north of the southern boundary of Chisago, Isanti, Sherburne, Stearns, Pope, Stevens, and Traverse counties in Minnesota, and of Richland, Ransom, La Moure, Logan and Burleigh counties in North Dakota—about two-thirds of the original area of the diocese. It extended from the Mississippi and St. Croix on the East to the Missouri and White Earth rivers on the West and from the aforesaid southern boundary to the British possessions on the North. Within this territory there were 44 priests—sixteen diocesan and 28 religious; 42 churches and 40 missions; one religious order of men and three of women; and a Catholic population of 18,500.[79]

After the division, St. Paul had 112 priests of whom 87 were diocesan and 25 belonged to religious orders. There were 168 churches and 52 missions; six religious orders of men and ten of women; 22 seminarians and a Catholic population of 115,000.

The erection of the Vicariate of Northern Minnesota was followed on August 12, 1879, by the creation of the Vicariate Apostolic of the Dakota including all the territory between the western boundary of the present Minnesota and the Missouri river, is what is now the two Dakotas. It was entrusted to the Right Reverend Martin Marty, O. S. B., first Abbot of St. Meinrad's in Indiana, who was consecrated Titular Bishop of Tiberias on February 1, 1880, and took up his residence in Yankton, South Dakota. He had under his jurisdiction 12 priests, 20 churches and chapels, 3 hospitals and four academies. These divisions took from Bishop Grace five-sixths of the original area of his diocese, leaving him only 27,515 square miles.[80]

On June 4, 1872, Bishop Grace blessed the cornerstone of the present Assumption Church in St. Paul which replaced the original structure built in 1855. After the ceremony there were two sermons, one in English by the Bishop, the other in German by Abbot Wimmer of St. Vincent's Abbey in Pennsylvania. Two years later, on October 18, 1874, the Bishop officiated at its solemn consecration, the second time the sacred rite was performed in the Diocese. The ceremony took place in presence of the clergy and a large concourse of the laity. At its conclusion the Abbot Seidenbusch of St. John's preached in German and celebrated Pontifical Mass and Bishop Grace preached after the first gospel. It was a memorable day for the German Catholics of the city for whom the parish was organized twenty years before. The new church, 180 by 90 feet in dimensions, was built of stone, with twin towers 200 feet high. The plan was prepared by Mr. Riechel, architect to the King of Bavaria. For some years the parish had been in charge of the Benedictine Fathers and at the time of consecration the pastor was Reverend Clement Staub, O. S. B.

The Fathers of the Society of Jesus were given charge of SS. Peter and Paul parish in Mankato in February, 1874.[81]

Appointment of a Coadjutor

An event of transcending importance to the diocese and, eventually, to the Church in America occurred in 1875, namely, the consecration of the Reverend John Ireland as coadjutor to Bishop Grace. A Papal Brief of February 12 of that year named him Titular Bishop of Maronea and Vicar Apostolic of Nebraska, in succession to the Right Reverend James O'Gorman, O. C. S. O. As soon as the news reached St. Paul Bishop Grace, fearful of losing the most energetic and promising priest under his jurisdiction, set out for Rome to make an appeal in person to the Holy Father to revoke the appointment and leave Father Ireland in St. Paul as Coadjutor Bishop. The Pope took the matter under advisement and finally decided to grant the request. Word of this decision reached Bishop Grace at Lourdes and, as a mark of gratitude, he vowed to place under the protection of Our Lady of Lourdes the next church dedicated in the diocese which happened to be the one now known as Notre Dame de Lourdes in Minneapolis in 1877.

In the meantime Father Ireland had returned the Apostolic Brief to the Prefect of the Propaganda together with an autograph letter to Pope Pius IX, dated April 22, 1875, submitting his resignation of the Vicariate Apostolic of Nebraska. At the same time he wrote Bishop Grace in Rome enclosing the Papal Brief and his letter to the Pope.[82] "You will perceive from reading this letter", he wrote to the Bishop, "I enter into no details as to the reason of my resignation, taking the liberty to refer to your statement of the case. I entertain no doubt whatsoever as to the final results . . . I put Nebraska entirely out of my mind and settle down quietly into my old attachments to Minnesota".

The brief and letters were lost in the wreck of the steamer "Schiller" off the Scilly Islands, near England, and two months later recovered by a diver and returned to Father Ireland on June 10, 1875, through the Post Office department. They are preserved in the archives of the Catholic Historical Society of St. Paul. The parchment was slightly damaged by the salt water but the type is still legible. One wonders what Bishop Grace thought when he received no word from his prospective coadjutor. The mystery was not solved until the documents were returned to St. Paul.

In due time the Holy See named Father Ireland Titular Bishop of

Maronea and coadjutor to Bishop Grace and the latter consecrated him in the Cathedral on December 21, 1875, almost the fourteenth anniversary of his ordination. No details of the ceremony are found in the Northwestern Chronicle for that week although it promised to give a full account of the function, as well as a verbatim report of the sermon of Father O'Gorman who was the preacher on the occasion.[83] In the current issue it advised its readers that "We give in full the eloquent address of our talented young priest Father O'Gorman of Rochester . . . We might add that we have described the consecration proper without availing ourselves of the able reports of the city journals, that the correctness of the ceremonial might be assured to our readers . . . The consecration ceremonies of Bishop Ireland, matter of four columns, published in the Chronicle were mailed to eastern exchanges". In the Chronicle there is no mention of the fact that Bishop Grace officiated nor are the names of the co-consecrators given nor any detail about the ceremony except that his two sisters, Sisters St. John and Seraphine, were present in the Cathedral. Probably the four-column account was mislaid before the issues of the year were bound for future reference. That it was sent to exchanges is evidenced by the fact that it appeared in the New York Freeman's Journal of January 1, 1876, from which we have taken the details elsewhere found in this volume.

In connection with the event the Northwestern Chronicle of December 25, 1875, mentions that the non-Catholic friends of the new Bishop presented him with an address and a set of the Encyclopedia Brittanica; the Catholics with a purse of $1,400 and an episcopal ring; the temperance societies with $800.00; Bishop Grace with the crozier; the Cathedral school with a pectoral cross; St. Agnes Sodality with a ring and miter; the Sisters of St. Joseph's Academy with the miter worn at the consecration; the Sisters of the Good Shepherd with a rochet and alb; the Sisters of the Orphan Asylum with the sandals.

It was about this time or, perhaps, earlier, that Bishop Grace dedicated the diocese to the Sacred Heart of Jesus, the first bishop in America to take such action. This is referred to in a letter written by McMaster of the Freeman's Journal on October 27, 1876, in which he asks the Bishop to "be so kind as to commend me to the Sacred Heart that you were the first bishop in America to dedicate your diocese to". The dedication took place probably on the third Sunday in September and each year thereafter the Bishop issued a letter to his diocesans asking them to appeal to the Sacred Heart for the triumph of the Church over the world and for an increasing personal devotion to this symbol and source of His great love for mankind. In this connection the Northwestern Chronicle of August 26, 1892, refers to the fact that Miss Mary T. Cramsie, prominent in temperance work and for years an officer of the Sacred Thirst Society, had written a poem "in memory of the dedication of the Diocese (to the Sacred Heart), December 8, 1873". This would seem to fix the day and year definitely.

In that case, Bishop Grace must have anticipated the action of the Sacred Congregation of Rites which, on April 22, 1875, issued a decree[84] in which Pope Pius IX, in response to innumerable petitions from prelates, priests and faithful beseeching him to consecrate the whole world to the Sacred Heart of Jesus as a means of arousing and increasing devotion thereto, approved and indulgenced a prayer for that purpose and asked the Ordinaries of all dioceses to commend the devotion to their flocks. He decreed that on June 16, 1875, the bicentenary of the revelation made to St. Margaret Mary Alacoque, this prayer be recited for the propagation of devotion to the Sacred Heart.

In May, 1876, Bishop Grace administered the last rites of the Church to former Territorial Governor, Willis A. Gorman, born of presumably Catholic parents but affiliated during life with the Episcopal Church, who was buried on May 23 from the Cathedral.[85]

On February 5, 1877, the Bishop sent a communication to the clergy, with copies of a letter from Rome announcing the forthcoming Golden Jubilee of the consecration of His Holiness Pope Pius IX, on May 21, 1877. He suggested that the faithful be encouraged to make offerings for the Holy Father as a tribute to his personal worth and an expression of veneration for his person and for the exalted office he holds as Supreme Pontiff of the Church. The names of the contributors would be inscribed in an album to be presented to the Pope together with the combined offerings as a tribute of loyalty from the diocese. He gave assurance that all names sent him would be recorded and all contributions forwarded before the date of the official celebration.

Bishop Grace was one of the distinguished guests present at the observance of the two hundredth anniversary of the discovery of the Falls of St. Anthony by Father Hennepin under the auspices of the Minnesota Historical Society on July 3, 1880, when the event was commemorated with a grand parade and public exercises on the campus of the University of Minnesota in Minneapolis.[86] The occasion was graced by the presence of public officials of state and nation and such other distinguished churchmen as Archbishop Taché of St. Boniface, Manitoba, Bishop Laflèche of Three Rivers, Quebec, and Bishop Ireland. The orator of the day was the Honorable Cushman K. Davis, Senator and former Governor. Brief addresses were made by the Honorable Alexander Ramsey, Secretary of War and first Territorial Governor of Minnesota, General W. T. Sherman and Bishop Ireland who came to the defence[87] of

Father Hennepin and sought to vindicate him from the charge of making a false claim to the discovery of the lower Mississippi leveled against him by those who accepted at its face value the story of that venture told in his "New Discovery" published at Utrecht in 1697. Utilizing the scholarly research done on that book by the well known historian, John Gilmary Shea, the Bishop pointed out discrepancies in the text and asserted that the pages of that volume, recounting the story of the alleged discovery, were evidently an interpolation after it came from the press and, therefore, could not be rightfully attributed to Father Hennepin whose description of his voyages in the New World are so faithfully and accurately detailed in his "Description of Louisiana", published in Paris in 1683, soon after his return from his memorable voyages in New France and his visit to Minnesota.

Bishop Grace Advocates Catholic University

Bishop Grace was one of the earliest and most consistent advocates of a Catholic University for America, and helped to bring it to a successful issue. In fact, he is said to have originated the idea and worked behind the scenes for its realization. "In his great mind originated the idea of a Catholic University of America" declared Bishop Shanley in the sermon preached at his obsequies in presence of prelates who were in a position to know the facts. At a meeting in St. Paul Bishop Grace strongly urged Bishop Spalding to get behind the project, to go actively ahead. As early as 1880 Bishop Spalding wrote to Archbishop Elder of Cincinnati, "Bishop Grace of St. Paul has begged me to undertake some such work; at least to make the attempt; and as he is a holy man, I have thought it might be the will of God".[88] For two years Bishop Spalding wrote and spoke and entreated before his labors were rewarded. At a meeting of the Bishops of the Province of Milwaukee in the spring of 1884 Bishop Grace proposed the founding of a Catholic University or, rather, a higher seminary for Philosophy and Theology, but did not receive much support from his brother bishops. He championed the idea of such an institution "long before most of the American Bishops". He suggested that Seton Hall College, South Orange, N. J., be bought for that purpose. He applauded the statement made by Bishop Spalding in his sermon at the close of the Third Plenary Council of Baltimore on December 7, 1884: "We have laid the foundation of an institution which, under God's providence, is destined to grow into an American Catholic University, the measure of whose usefulness, the grandeur of whose scope, and the fruitful blessings of which cannot be forecast by the mind".[89] He entered heart and soul into the project and no one rejoiced more than he when it received the cachet of approval by Pope Leo XIII

and became a reality with the opening of its doors for the inauguration
of class-work on November 19, 1889. He was unable to attend the ceremony of the cornerstone laying on May 24, 1888. "The condition of my
health is so uncertain", he wrote Cardinal Gibbons on May 16, 1888,
"that I have concluded that it would be imprudent for me to leave home".
He was glad that so many bishops promised to attend the ceremony and
by their presence encourage "an undertaking which I consider the most
momentous for the interests of religion and the Church in this country".

His interest in the Catholic University as an institution for advanced
studies in philosophy, theology and kindred subjects stemmed in large
measure from his cherished hope of one day having a seminary under
his own control to train and mould the future priests of the diocese
according to the mind of the Church. It was destined to be an unrealized
ambition; but he never lost sight of the goal. He dreamed of it; he prayed
for it; he spoke about it; he made appeals for it; it was the theme of
many letters to the clergy. As late as 1881, a few years before his retirement, he reminded priests and people that "the most essential (of several
diocesan works) is the work of providing for the education of young men
for the holy ministry. The establishment of a home seminary, which we
have had at heart for many years, we are obliged still to postpone, in
view of the inadequacy of the means to insure success and permanency
for the undertaking".[90] He added a P.S.: "We would earnestly suggest
whether it would add to the encouragement of the faithful, if the names
of the pastors were found more generally among the contributors to this
very important diocesan work, through means of which many of them
have been enabled to accomplish their pious desire to be enrolled in the
ministry".[91]

That year's collection for the seminary, from September 1, 1881, to
September 1, 1882, amounting to $6514.84, was little more than sufficient
to meet the cost of maintaining twenty-nine students in nine seminaries,
namely, the Grand Seminary, Montreal; St. John's, Collegeville; St.
Francis, Milwaukee; the American College, Louvain; St. Vincent's,
Latrobe, Pa.; St. Bonaventure's, New York; All Hallows, Dublin; St. Sulpice, Paris; and Meximieux, France. The tuition and expenses amounted
to $4613.12.[92]

The balance was so small that there was no possibility of accumulating
a fund sufficient to justify the hope of establishing a local seminary for
many years, if at all, unless a large donation were forthcoming from an
unsuspected source, which was just what happened before the St. Paul
Seminary became a reality. Bishop Grace lived to see the realization of
his life dream under his successor, and he rejoiced with a great joy.

In its issue of December 20, 1880, the St. Paul Pioneer Press listed the membership of all the religious denominations in St. Paul together with the cost of their church properties. We subjoin the list for the Catholic parishes:

Cathedral of St. Paul	3360	$132,000
Church of the Assumption	4760	150,000
Church of St. Mary	2360	35,000
Church of St. Louis	1760	13,500
Church of St. Stanislaus	1000	2,500
Church of St. Joseph	700	12,000
Church of St. Michael	800	9,000
	14740	354,000

Bishop Grace was very much opposed to the participation of women in political, civil and national organizations no matter how worthy the cause. He was convinced that their sphere and proper place was the home and not the hustings or the arena. The formation of women's leagues is not to be encouraged. On one occasion at least he expressed himself very forcibly on this matter.

In reply to the address of the societies that called to present their respects on St. Patrick's day, 1881, he said, among other things:

There is one thing here in St. Paul, of which I beg you will allow me to withhold my approval. It is the forming of ladies leagues. There is something about the calling out of mothers and daughters from their homes at night to form leagues and hold meetings that does not seem right. The movement I know did not originate with the women themselves. It is in opposition to all their womanly instincts. It is an infringement upon the sacredness of home life. It gives a rude shock to those domestic virtues which we should ever be careful to cherish. If you desire the cooperation of woman in this movement, leave her to cooperate in her own way. You need not be assured of her sympathies with her suffering country and suffering sisters at home. These sympathies are as strong as yours. . . Leave her to express these feelings by word and act in ways of her own, which she knows full well, and constrain her not to adopt the rough, unfamiliar ways of men, by holding public meetings for discussion.

In the early part of June, 1881, he was saddened by the news of the tragic death of one of his priests, Reverend Daniel Hayes, pastor of the Church of St. Stephen, Anoka, who with his lay brother, was suffocated when a lamp exploded and caused a fire in the home of a Mr. Malone in Corcoran, one of the missions attended by Father Hayes, whither he had gone to say the monthly Mass.[93] Father Hayes was about twenty-nine years of age. He was ordained by Bishop Grace on October 28, 1876, the last ordination at which he officiated, and was for a short time assistant to Father Genis at Faribault. On June 5, 1877, he was appointed to the Immaculate Conception Church in Minneapolis whence in January of the following year he was transferred to Anoka. The funeral took place on June 13, 1881, at which his brother, Reverend John T. Hayes of Cheyenne, Wyoming, officiated.

The new brick Church of St. John in Little Canada, a monument to the zeal of Father Goiffon, was dedicated by Bishop Grace on Sunday, June 19, 1881. The Mass was said by the pastor, the Bishop preached in English and Father Ravoux in French. The church was 80 by 35 feet in size.

On June 20, 1881, Bishop Grace presided at a meeting in St. Mary's school of the German Catholics of "Lower Town" belonging to St. Mary's parish who sought authorization for the erection of a parish exclusively for themselves, and permission was given for the founding of the parish of the Sacred Heart on Dayton's Bluff under the direction of Reverend Charles Koeberl who was appointed pastor.

From time to time Bishop Grace was obliged to reassert the teaching of the Church in regard to Catholic participation in sectarian services. On May 10, 1883, he sent a letter to the clergy requesting them to announce to their congregations that

> those Catholics who take part in Protestant and non-Catholic religious services by singing in church choirs will be excluded from the sacraments. Should any of those persons present themselves at the communion rail the priest is strictly ordered to pass them by and not administer to them the Holy Sacrament.[94]

Bishop Grace's Silver Jubilee

On July 24, 1884, Bishop Grace celebrated the twenty-fifth anniversary of his consecration with a Pontifical Mass in the Cathedral in presence of a large gathering of prelates and priests and a congregation that taxed the sacred edifice as, perhaps, never before in its history.[95] Very Reverend Augustine Ravoux, V. G., was assistant priest; Reverends A. Plut and L. Caillet, deacons of honor; J. Trobec and J. B. Cotter, deacon and subdeacon of the Mass; A. Oster, master of ceremonies, assisted by Reverends P. Danehy and J. Shanley.

Seated in the sanctuary were the Most Reverend Michael Heiss, Archbishop of Milwaukee; Most Reverend A. Taché, Archbishop of St. Boniface, Manitoba; Right Reverends Rupert Seidenbusch, O.S.B., Bishop of St. Cloud; F. X. Krautbauer, Bishop of Green Bay; J. L. Spalding, Bishop of Peoria; John Vertin, Bishop of Marquette; Kilian Flasch, Bishop of La Crosse; John Ireland, Coadjutor Bishop of St. Paul; Abbott Alexius Edelbrock, O. S. B., of Collegeville; and Monsignor T. J. Capel of England. The priests of the diocese and many from neighboring dioceses occupied seats in the body of the church.

For several days the women of the parish had been busy decorating the Cathedral and well and tastefully had they done their work. The main entrance was spanned with a beautiful arch ornamented with crosses, flowers and foliage. Palm leaves, wreaths and festoons of evergreens were arranged on the pillars of the nave and on the sanctuary wall behind the altar. On both sides of the main aisle was suspended in large letters of green the motto: Ad Multos Annos. The main altar was ablaze with lights and banked with flowers. Overhead was an arch bearing the inscription: Dominus Conservet Eum et Vivificet Eum. The Bishop's throne was tastefully decorated for the occasion. As early as eight o'clock a large crowd had gathered before the entrance awaiting admission. At nine the doors were thrown open and soon the church was filled to capacity. Every nook and corner in the nave and galleries was occupied and standing room was at a premium. Many had to go away, or stand in the streets to catch a glimpse of the procession.

Father Danehy, the cross-bearer, led the way accompanied by two acolytes bearing lighted candles, then the altar boys, Christian Brothers, priests to the number of one hundred in cassock and surplice; the Monsignor and the Abbot; the Bishops and Archbishops, the ministers of the Mass and finally the venerable Jubilarian blessing the people as he passed up the aisle.

The choir under the leadership of Professor Manner was supported by Seibert's full orchestra and the music was in keeping with the festive occasion and its deservedly high reputation.

The sermon was preached by Right Reverend John Lancaster Spalding, Bishop of Peoria, who paid a glowing tribute to the apostolic zeal, fruitful ministry and saintly life of the distinguished Jubilarian whom he extolled as a model bishop whose successful administration of a missionary diocese reflected great credit on himself, redounded to the welfare of religion and the honor and glory of God.

> Your generous heart, guided by a mind thoroughly trained and enlightened, has been an unfailing source of strength and courage to your priests and people, to whom by word and example you have preached sobriety, justice, charity and unselfish devotion to the interests of religion and civilization. . .
>
> Nor do I know in the church in the United States a prelate who more ardently desires to elevate the standard of intellectual culture. . .You were the first to approve and to lend the wisdom and the experience which are yours, to what else would have been meaningless or had died without an echo (the Catholic University of America?) . . . Looking beyond the sphere of official cares and local interests you have sought to further every righteous cause and to encourage all efforts, even the feeblest, to promote the progress of religion and society. . .We turn to the future with confident hope, and raise to God our most earnest prayer that He keep you in health and vigor yet many years, and that the salutary and ennobling influence of your life and example long continue to be a source of many blessings to your clergy and your people, and of encouragement to all who struggle for right and cherish the hope of better things.

After the Mass the Te Deum was intoned by the Jubilarian and taken up by the choir, voicing a magnificent upsurge of gratitude from the hearts of the faithful for the graces and blessings bestowed on their venerable Chief Pastor and on the diocese during the period of his administration.

At the close of the banquet in the Metropolitan Hotel an address from the clergy was read by the Reverend James McGolrick of Minneapolis, substituting for the Very Reverend Father Ravoux, Vicar General, fatigued by the lengthy ceremonies of the forenoon. It began with a reference to the changes in the diocese since Bishop Cretin came with a few missionaries to the sparsely populated Territory. At his death twenty-seven priests attended to the spiritual needs of the faithful, where now there are three flourishing dioceses.

> Under your gentle sway education and religion have gone hand in hand, keeping pace with the unparalleled material growth of the great North-west. Every movement for the welfare of Catholicity had its inspiration from you, and grew beneath your fostering care. In times of trial and of difficulty your earnest words infused new life into those whose hearts were almost wearied in the work. . .Today a Catholic population of well nigh two hundred thousand souls look to you for spiritual direction, and find in all their efforts for the good and the true your ready sympathy and timely aid. . . . Two hundred and fifty churches and stations attended by over one hundred and fifty priests, supply the needs of a constantly increasing Catholic people; with these have arisen the usual helps and aids to Catholic life—hospitals, asylums and protectorates which tell how dear to your soul is the Christian treasure of the poor, the friendless and the orphan. The schools, academies, societies, confraternities and sodalities which everywhere cover your diocese, and foster the growth of sound Catholic doctrine amid the rising generation, bear testimony to your loving care, and promise well for the future of Catholicity in the Diocese of St. Paul.

The address was accompanied by a purse of three thousand dollars, a testimony to the generosity and filial devotion of the clergy.

In his reply the Jubilarian disavowed all right to the praise bestowed on him and said that only a small amount of the credit for the growth and prosperity of the diocese could be placed to his account.

> Reference has been made to the great activity in conducting the affairs of the diocese, the enlarged views, the spirit of enterprise and the energy in carrying forward works of improvement or reform. How much of this is due to one whom I need not name it is not necessary to say; but I will say that in these respects the Bishop and the Diocese of St. Paul have had far more than is implied in the name of the Coadjutor.
> There is another to whom is due in no small degree whatever of success has attended the administration of the diocese. Stationed here as a missionary priest at an early period he prepared the ground and laid the foundation of what was to be the future diocese of St. Paul. He is still among us. He has lived to see the diocese what it now is, and what it has become in great measure under his counsel and careful solicitude. We see but realized what were, not the dreams, but the almost sure expectation based upon his sound judgment and prudent foresight.

The priests, too, had a large part in this work. Most of them have been pioneers, have gone through the toils and borne the privations and hardships of frontier missionary life. The churches in which the people prayed and the schools in which the young have been instructed are the fruits of their toil and sweat. The regular clergy have rendered efficient service, especially the Benedictines, the first to labor in the wilds of Minnesota and to whom the diocese owes a debt which shall be ever gratefully acknowledged in its annals. The religious communities of women have devoted themselves to the service of God and the neighbor in teaching and training the young and ministering to the sick. Above all, the honor and glory must be given to God who gave the increase.

Father Goldsmith of Chippewa Falls responded in behalf of the Metropolitan, Archbishop Heiss, and referred to the fact that Minnesota was once part of Wisconsin and that priests of the Milwaukee diocese labored in the diocese of St. Paul in the early days.

Archbishop Taché of St. Boniface spoke in French which, he said, was at once time quite generally spoken in St. Paul and was still understood by many. He claimed to be connected through Joliet, of whom he was the sixth lineal descendant, with the Mississippi valley and the Northwest Territory for two hundred years. He felt an interest in the diocese and entertained a warm personal regard for its Bishop.

Bishop Spalding, in a brief address, said among other things:

No one has come to these festivities with sentiments of greater admiration and love for the venerable Bishop Grace than I. I watched his work from afar. I have perceived all that was high and noble in Bishop Grace.

Monsignor Capel offered the greetings of one who, like themselves, was deeply interested in Holy Mother Church and admired the distinguished Jubilarian.

Bishop Ireland was called upon to respond to the toast of the clergy of the diocese. Before doing so he said:

I rise in obedience to the call of the Reverend clergy; but I regret that I am compelled to utter a word on this occasion. My relations both while a priest and a bishop with Bishop Grace have been too close, too intimate, too endearing to permit me to speak during the observance of this solemn jubilee. I would fain view my own life as part and parcel of his—the streamlet gladly mingling its waters with the great river and lost in it unseen. To address you in my own name, I fear, breaks the fancy of this cherished oneness. No personal regard of honor would I admit today. Honor for me is the reflected ray from the glories that cluster on the brow of him whom you with me fondly call our father. Yes, my life has been one with his. Not only has there been sweetest unity of hearts; but unity of minds and unity of labors. Our planning and methods for the extension of God's kingdom have been the same; and if in the execution of the work a seeming separateness appeared visible, it was only thus far, that the physical effort may have at times fallen on me, the inspiration and the direction have always been the fruit of his generous love and his matured thought. My past has been, through him, secure and happy, and my future suggests to me no fears, because whatever otherwise may be the changed conditions of my life, with God's blessing, he will for many and long years be still near to inspire and direct my counsels and my undertakings. . . .

He thanked God that heaven had blessed the diocese with a clergy so pious and so learned, so zealous and so disinterested. With such priests it is easy to accomplish glorious deeds ready as they are at the first invitation to rally round their bishop in the war for truth and justice and charity, even leading him on the field of battle in their fervent zeal for religion.

In the evening, despite a severe downpour of rain, there was a grand parade of Catholic societies to the Cathedral where the address from the laity was read by John D. O'Brien in which he expressed sentiments of affection and veneration for the beloved prelate and recalled the important part he played in the development of the diocese from a frontier see to the commanding position it holds in the Church in America. The honorable position of the Catholic laity is due to his wise administration and paternal solicitude in providing schools which are among the best in the country. He made a presentation to the Bishop on behalf of the faithful.

Two little girls from St. Joseph's Orphan Asylum, clad in white, ascended the sanctuary steps and presented an ornamented white silk cushion on which rested a purse with a generous contribution. In his reply the Bishop commented on the important part played by the laity made up of people of all nationalities, most of them humble and poor, but with a living, fervent faith that kept them secure amid the allurements of the world and the striving for social advantages. By their cooperation with bishop and priests they had a large share in all that was accomplished in the past twenty-five years. In the address he said there was a passage "which he could not admit except in a limited sense. The credit of much of the work done in the diocese was due to another, not to himself. Both in conception and execution the work was Bishop Ireland's own. All he could claim was that he gave the work his hearty approval and concurrence".

At the close Bishop Ireland delivered a short address.

Throughout the festivities and in all the tributes paid to Bishop Grace citizens of all classes and creeds vied with the clergy and their Catholic fellow-citizens in showing their appreciation of the sterling worth and civic virtues of St. Paul's most distinguished citizen.

Bishop Grace Resigns His See

A week later Bishop Grace made public his resignation[96] of the See of St. Paul in favor of his coadjutor, Bishop Ireland, in the following letter:

To the Clergy and laity of the Diocese of St. Paul:

Owing to our advanced age and increasing infirmities we have found the duties of the episcopal office so very onerous that we seriously for some time past entertained the thought of asking the Supreme Pontiff to be relieved of them. The sense of our inability longer to fulfill these duties in a manner satisfactory to ourself or as efficiently as they might be discharged, was no small addition to the cares and anxieties necessarily attendant upon the administration of the Diocese. The growth of the Diocese in the large increase of the number of priests, churches and institutions, has added proportionately to the weight of the burden, while our ability to bear it has grown less with failing health and increasing years. These reasons presented in earnest prayer to the Holy Father have moved him to graciously grant our petition. Rt. Rev. Bishop Ireland under his appointment as our coadjutor, succeeds to the title and office, with its incumbent duties, of Bishop of St. Paul. He enters upon the office not a stranger to the Diocese but fully acquainted with the condition of its affairs. The deep love we have for the diocese, for its clergy and people, which has strengthened with years, gives, indeed, poignancy to the separation, but we are consoled in the assurance that in Rt. Rev. Bishop Ireland clergy and people have one whose affection for them is as our own, and that with his well known piety, zeal, energy and abilities, the Diocese will be all the more prosperous under his administration.

✠Thomas L. Grace.

At the time of his resignation—although the area of the diocese had been reduced by five-sixths through the erection of two Vicariates—there were 147 priests under his jurisdiction, of whom 119 were diocesan, ministering to a Catholic population of about 130,000 in 195 churches and 51 stations; there were ten churches in St. Paul compared to two when he was installed and seven in Minneapolis where there was but two when he arrived; there were 29 students preparing for the priesthood in American and European seminaries; 6 religious orders of men and 14 of women laboring zealously under him. There were 10 academies and boarding schools for young women; 2 hospitals ministering to the sick; 5 asylums and protectories caring for orphans and other neglected children. In addition to seven Conferences of St. Vincent de Paul, there were Catholic Total Abstinence societies, confraternities and sodalities for men, women and children in nearly all the parishes.

What a change from the conditions that prevailed in the diocese when he came to administer its temporal and spiritual affairs! It was then "a wild region, without railroads, with many missions accessible by sleds drawn by dogs in winter time", with 27 priests and 31 churches, two of which were in the see-city, 97 missions and stations, and a Catholic population of 50,000 souls. What a phenomenal increase in twenty-five years in all of which he had played a significant role as guide, counsellor and wise administrator. What a bountiful harvest had rewarded the efforts of himself, his clergy and religious, to sow the seeds of faith in the souls of his flock scattered throughout the vast region entrusted to his care, to inculcate the binding obligations of the moral law and lay the foundations of the prosperity and prospects now enjoyed by the Church. Well might the aging Bishop feel entitled to a respite from labor and responsibility during the years that yet remained to him.

Although the Bishop had lost some of the vigor and robustness of his earlier years, he was well preserved and actively engaged, up to the time of his resignation, in managing the affairs of the diocese. He was recognized as a most convincing and graceful speaker, a learned theologian, and one of the ablest prelates in the Church in America. He was always most kind and affable in his relations and intercourse with all who came in contact with him, officially and otherwise; and no one could be more admired and beloved than he was not only by the members of his flock but by all who knew him. He was easily the first citizen of St. Paul and was held in highest esteem and reverence by the clergy and religious of the diocese.

At the time of his resignation Bishop Grace was interested in the construction of a memorial chapel and mausoleum for Bishop Cretin and his successors in Calvary cemetery. In fact the idea and its execution were entirely his own. On a knoll in the center of the cemetery he caused to be erected an octagonal building, twenty feet in the clear, of Dresbach stone, surmounted by a dome topped by a gilded cross six feet high. On the main floor was a chapel with an altar facing the door on the north and beside it a memorial tablet inscribed to his predecessor. It was made, probably, of plaster of Paris for it cost the modest sum of twenty-five dollars and the gilded letters added six and a half dollars to the amount.

The mortuary chapel was dedicated by Bishop Grace on October 10, 1884, in presence of a large number of priests and about fifteen hundred people. After the ceremony he celebrated a Requiem Mass for the repose of the soul of Bishop Cretin whose remains had been exhumed and placed before the altar where they were viewed by the faithful. The sermon was preached by Bishop Ireland who paid a tribute to the saintly life and shining virtues of Bishop Cretin whom he had known as a boy and by whom he was sent to France to prepare for the priesthood. He chose for text, "The just shall be in everlasting remembrance", the seventh verse of the one hundred and eleventh psalm. After the service the coffin was lowered into the vault. On the outside of the casket was a silver plate bearing the inscription, "Right Reverend Joseph Cretin, first Bishop of St. Paul. Died February 22, 1857"; and on the inside near the head another plate with the words, "Remains of Right Reverend Joseph Cretin, first Bishop of St. Paul. Died February 22, 1857. Transferred to the vault October 10, 1884".

On August 12, 1884, Pope Leo XIII appointed Bishop Grace Bishop of Mennith, in Palestine, and, as it was a titular see, he was not obliged to take up residence therein. He was one of the two Vicars General of the Archdiocese of St. Paul from 1888 to 1892, the other being Monsignor Ravoux who in the latter year, according to the Catholic Directory, terminated a tenure of over forty years as second in authority in the diocese under Bishops Cretin and Grace and Archbishop Ireland.

From 1884 to 1890 Bishop Grace continued to occupy his modest quarters in the Cathedral residence with his successor and the priests assigned to duty in the parish. During these years he went on confirmation tours, dedicated churches and performed other episcopal duties at the request of the new Bishop. For his services he received a salary of $1200. He was not in very affluent circumstances. On the occasion of his silver jubilee of consecration he was presented with a purse of $3,000 by the clergy of the diocese and received an offering of $1,084 from the laity. This constituted his entire wealth with the exception of $3,038.07 to his credit in the bank, five shares of stock in the Catholic Colonization Association, five in the Industrial School Distribution, three lots in Rosedale Park and one in Merriam Park—not a very imposing financial showing after twenty-five years of an active life in the episcopate. From the Colonization stock he received an annual dividend of thirty dollars from 1884 to 1891 when he sold it for five hundred and thirty dollars.

Although his health was not very robust for several years he was well preserved and showed the keenest interest in everything that appertained to the diocese and was au courant with the activities and developments in the church not only in the United States but throughout the world. In 1892 he resigned as Vicar General, two years after retiring to St. Thomas Seminary to pass the remainder of his life in seclusion, prayer and preparation for the final summons.

On February 27, 1885, he wrote Cardinal Simeoni, Prefect of the Sacred Congregation de Propaganda Fide, requesting him to thank His Holiness for releasing him from the pastoral charge of the Diocese of St. Paul.[97] However, he did not wish to sever all connections with his former diocese. For various reasons and especially for his greater spiritual good it seemed expedient that he continue to reside in the diocese in as much as he and Bishop Ireland were of one mind and got on well together.

It is quite true, he continued,

that by your letter of July 31, 1884, No. 3389, you make it clear that I need have no scruple about remaining outside the convent of my religious community, nevertheless, in view of the prescription of Benedict XIII, 'Custodes', regarding the obligation of religious bishops who resigned or were deprived of their diocese, returning to their monastery, for peace and tranquility of conscience I humbly ask whether or not this constitution obliges me, in spite of the fact that I have been appointed to a diocese in partibus infidelium.

In regard to dress I pray that while I remain in the diocese I be allowed to dress as secular bishops do, in as much as the white habit of a Dominican is with great difficulty kept clean and neat and is less suited to this part of the country than the ordinary garb. I would be eager to return to the monastery were it not that it seems best to remain in the diocese. However, in all these things I submit to the will of God whom to obey is salvation and life.

A few months later, on July 11, Cardinal Simeoni remitted to him the Apostolic Brief appointing him Titular Bishop of Mennith, a suffragan see of Scythopolis in Palestine, assuring him that His Holiness, having accepted his resignation, did not wish him to be deprived of an episcopal title. At the same time he made known that, for the peace and tranquillity of his conscience, the Pope granted him the privilege of living outside his monastic cloister and wearing the customary garb of members of the hierarchy.

In the early months of 1886 Bishop Grace petitioned the Holy See to grant him permission, while living, or in his last will and testament, to devote to pious uses whatever gifts were presented to him, a permission granted on April 11, through the Secretary of the Propaganda; and ten years later, on December 8, 1896, he was dispensed from the daily recitation of the breviary because of his advanced age of eighty-two and his mental debility.[98]

He was present at the first Plenary Council of Milwaukee from May 23 to 30, 1886.

He officiated at the early Mass at the first celebration of the feast of St. Thomas in the newly-established St. Thomas Aquinas Seminary on March 7, 1886, gave Holy Communion to the students and assisted at the High Mass at which the sermon was preached by Reverend James J. Keane, pastor of St. Joseph's Church, St. Paul.

When the Diocese of St. Paul was raised to metropolitan dignity in 1888 Bishop Grace was honored by promotion to the Titular Archbishopric of Siunia,[99] a suffragan of Sebaste in Armenia. When the news of his elevation to archiepiscopal rank reached St. Paul no one was more delighted than the clergy at the honor confirmed on him whose life was given to "the advancement of God's Kingdom and to the welfare, temporal and spiritual, of mankind".[100]

He visited St. Thomas Seminary for the first time after his elevation on October 9, 1889, with Archbishop Ireland and Bishop-elect McGolrick of Duluth. After dinner the students gave an entertainment in his honor and presented him with an address of congratulation to which he responded in fitting terms, thanking them for their good wishes.

The Bishop's Bookkeeping

From the beginning of his episcopate Bishop Grace kept an itemized account of receipts and disbursements in two small note books,[101] six by three and a half inches in size, in which he entered whatever money he received and the purpose for which it was expended. The final entry was made on January 2, 1897, a few weeks before he died.

From the first of these note books the cover is missing as well as several pages containing the entries prior to 1868; but from June of that year the various items, especially the expenditures, are assigned to months and days.

The cathedraticum, or offerings for his personal support and livelihood, constituted the main source of revenue during his episcopal career. The amounts contributed are listed in the names of the priests until December, 1882, after which they are credited to the parishes. Following his resignation of the see in 1884 the word "salary" is substituted for "cathedraticum" until 1890, when "pension" is used to connote the salary of $1,200, and an allowance of $300 a year for board and lodging which he paid to the President of the Seminary at the rate of $100 every four months, beginning with May of that year.

The Cathedraticum which, in 1868, amounted to $868.40 increased year by year to $2,329.94 in 1883, making an average annual offering of about $1,600. From 1875 to 1884 he gave his coadjutor $1,000 a year for his personal support.

The expenditures fill many more pages than the receipts. Among them are personal items for clothing, medical care, books, magazines, cigars, tobacco, snuff, stamps, stationery and travel on official business in the diocese. He seldom went beyond its confines. The balance of the expenditures may be listed under the head of "charity" including regular contributions to the ordinary run of applicants who find the clergy easy marks; to poor families and individuals whom he knew; to fairs for orphans, parishes and institutions; to St. Vincent de Paul Conferences; to working girls' and newsboys' homes; to the Catholic Truth Society; to sufferers from Minnesota fires and Red River floods; to religious communities in the diocese; to the non-Catholic mission program of the Paulists and Cardinal Manning's work in London; to Castle Garden Refuge for Irish immigrant girls; to the upkeep of the seminary grounds, etc.

Archbishop Grace was present at the celebration of the first patronal feast of the new Seminary of St. Paul, that of the Conversion of St. Paul, on January 25, 1895.

His will is dated October 19, 1876. In it he requests that his personal and official debts, if any, be paid, and bequeathes his estate to Bishop Ireland. It is witnessed by Fathers Ravoux, Shanley and Bruton. With truth he could have anticipated the statement of another distinguished Archbishop who, in his last will and testament, declared:

I have always considered it my duty, as a priest of Jesus Christ, to have no personal belongings whatsoever, beyond the books, clothing and the like utilities, called for by my daily life; and I am happy to be able to declare that substantially such has always been my condition, and that such it is today. Any personal revenue that has been mine has been held and used solely to meet the appeals of charity, which have never failed to be equal to the total of my income. For that end alone I ever had, or have now, a bank account—simply as a means for sending such contributions. Hence, if there happens, at the time of my death, to be any balance to my credit in the bank, it belongs to any charity claimants who may apply for it.[102]

For nearly seven years Archbishop Grace lived a life of retirement and prayer in St. Thomas Seminary, edifying all by his humble demeanor, his unaffected simplicity and saintly life. Each morning he said Mass at a private altar; and on the feast of the Immaculate Conception it was his custom to celebrate the community Mass for the students and give them Holy Communion. He made it a rule to be present at the commencement exercises each year and at other public functions. In his daily walks about the grounds he noted improvements that might be made and provided the funds to carry out his ideas. He had labored diligently and devotedly during his active life and now in its evening he made preparations for the coming night wherein no man can work.

As a student in St. Paul Seminary the writer often saw Bishop Grace strolling about the grounds of St. Thomas College accompanied by his factotum, Danny Donahue, and a dog, or in pensive mood in the vicinity of Lake Mennith, named after his titular see, an artificial pond which dried up long ago. Not infrequently the Bishop would be seen on the green sward near Shadow Falls looking across Summit Avenue towards the St. Paul Seminary, the realization of his dream for a diocesan seminary. He thanked God, no doubt, that he had been permitted to see the blessed day, and with the consciousness of work well done he could say, with the aged Simeon, "Now thou dost dismiss thy servant, O Lord, according to thy word in peace".

Towards the end of 1896—a few weeks before he died—Archbishop Grace paid a visit to St. Rose's Convent in Kentucky for the first time in more than forty years, to revisit the scenes of his youth, where he had made his novitiate more than half a century before and where he began his priestly career. One can imagine the joyous welcome he received from the community. It gave him great pleasure to note the progress made by the institution during the intervening decades. It is said that this was the first occasion in the more than ninety years of its existence that the Priory entertained an Archbishop. On his return to St. Paul he felt oppressed with the weight of eighty-two years and began a more intensive preparation for the final summons which, he felt, could not long be delayed.

Death and Obsequies

In the beginning of February of the next year he was taken sick and, when the illness became acute, he was removed to St. Joseph's Hospital where all that devoted medical skill and nursing care could do was done to prolong the life of the venerable patient. But it was not to be. The imperious summons to another world could not be disobeyed; and he had an ache for eternity. He received the last sacraments with edifying evidence of fervent faith and in a spirit of profound resignation to the will of God no matter what the outcome. On Monday, the twenty-second, he began to sink rapidly, Archbishop Ireland was summoned and, surrounded by several priests and sisters, began the recitation of the prayers for the dying to which the patient responded, remaining fully conscious to the end. He died without a struggle, like candle light fading into darkness, calmly and peacefully, in full possession of his faculties till the last breath. It was the fortieth anniversary of the death of his predecessor, Bishop Cretin. He had often expressed a wish to die on that day and his wish was granted.

After death his body, robed in pontificals, and placed in a solid oak casket covered and lined with black broadcloth, was borne to the hospital chapel where it lay in state for two days during which it was viewed by thousands of people of all classes, conditions and creeds who came to pay tribute to his personal worth and give evidence of the high esteem in which they held one who was the friend of all.

On Thursday the remains were taken to the Cathedral escorted by a procession of two hundred laymen from the different parishes and societies of the city and a large concourse of people. It was met at the entrance by the priests and the students of St. Paul Seminary who preceded the coffin to the sanctuary where it was received by the bishops and officiating priests and placed before the altar for the last time. The Office of the Dead was chanted by the seminarians and clergy. A Solemn Pontifical Mass of Requiem was celebrated by Archbishop Ireland and the responses sung by a group of seminarians and men from the choirs of the city under the direction of Father Simon of St. Paul Seminary and John Gehan, choirmaster of the Cathedral.

The sermon was preached by Bishop Shanley of Fargo whom the deceased had known as a boy, whom he had sent to Rome to complete his studies for the priesthood, whom he had appointed pastor of the Cathedral in succession to Bishop Ireland in 1875, and at whose consecration he had assisted as a co-consecrator in 1889.

After outlining Bishop Grace's career prior to his elevation to the episcopate, the preacher said in part: [103]

On the arrival of Bishop Grace in St. Paul in 1859 religion in Minnesota was in its infancy. The venerable Bishop Cretin had done much to plant

the church firmly in this portion of the Northwest . . . But in 1859 the
plans for the development of this diocese were still incomplete. To the
second bishop, Thos. L. Grace, it was left to carry them into effect. St.
Paul was a frontier village, Minneapolis a grain field, a few towns there
were on the Mississippi and in the valley of the Minnesota and the Red
River of the North. Two churches—this Cathedral, then unplastered, and
the old Church of the Assumption—more than sufficed for the Catholics of
this place . . . The diocese boasted one institution of beneficence—St.
Joseph's Hospital—one parish school connected with the Cathedral. The
number of clergy to minister to the wants of the Catholics scattered over
the vast tract between the St. Croix and the Missouri rivers was totally
inadequate to the work. They numbered seventeen . . . The people, few in
number, were poor in this world's goods. Means of inter-communication
were lacking. From his few priests and his laity he could expect little
financial assistance. Everything to be done and little or nothing with
which to do it. Behold the task before Bishop Grace.

How admirably he succeeded during his rule of 25 years over this see we
all know. He saw the grain of mustard seed grow into the wide-spreading
and vigorous tree of today, and to Thomas L. Grace is its healthy growth
mainly due. The growth of the church in his diocese was his incessant
care. For it he labored, for it he prayed. . . Little heeded he the sayings
and the doings of men beyond his jurisdiction. Thoroughly did he realize
the importance of the trust confided to him—the salvation of the souls over
whom the Holy Ghost had appointed him to rule. Filled with the sense of
his duty, he scrupulously made his diocese his home, absenting himself
from his post of duty only a few times—once for a few weeks when his
health was impaired, twice to attend plenary councils in Baltimore, and
two visits to Rome—the last one in 1874 for the purpose of securing as his
coadjutor with the right of succession to the See the then pastor of the
Cathedral, the present Metropolitan of this province. The needs of the
diocese required and received his closest attention. There were priests
to be procured, young men to be chosen and educated for the sacred
ministry, missions and parishes to be formed, churches, schools, hospitals
and orphanages to be erected and supported, money to be raised for all
these purposes, confirmation to be administered from Pembina to Yankton
and from Stillwater to Bismarck. Among the souls under his care, objects
of his tenderest love, were the poor Indians, at that time more numerous
than now and nearly all pagans—surely enough to deter the boldest and
strongest man. Yet, with a courage born of faith, he undertook the work,
and blessed by divine providence the work succeeded, so that at the day
of his death, after thirty-eight years of prayer and toil, he had the consolation to see six well established dioceses in the territory over which he
once presided, and governing these sees were five bishops whom he
looked upon as his own children, and who loved him as a father.

Bishop Grace was pre-eminently a man of duty, and because of his sense
of duty he succeeded. He was a man of broad ideas, foreseeing the future needs and greatness of the church in this country and ever suggesting
wise measures for advancement. This statement may appear exaggerated
to some who seldom saw or heard of him. He sought no notoriety. He
shunned publicity, and loved to do his work for God through others, his
being the directing mind. Many of the most beneficial works of religion
in this province, and even in this country, though popularly unassociated

with his name, are in great measure the fruit of his wisdom and initiative. In him every measure for the upbuilding of St. Paul and of the state found a firm and generous friend and promoter, and I question whether in church or state there was one more highly esteemed, or whose word carried greater weight, than Thomas L. Grace. . . .In his great mind originated the idea of the Catholic University of America. . . .

In his private life Bishop Grace was most saintly. He seemed to live for God, to always feel that he was in the presence of God. The hours of the day were arranged most regularly, and every hour well employed. Arising at five each morning, he spent an hour in holy meditation, six o'clock found him at the foot of the altar vesting for the celebration of the Holy Sacrifice of the Mass, after which his thanksgiving was always long and fervent. Then followed the various and exacting duties of the day, always performed promptly and properly. At five in the evening the Bishop was kneeling for his daily hour of advocation before the Blessed Sacrament, and at half past seven the devout members of the Cathedral congregation saw their saintly bishop near the Blessed Lady's altar reciting the rosary. . .

Bishop Grace was a model of piety to his priests, and he was to them a true father. . .His charity to the poor was boundless. Himself possessed of little, he gave of his store with unsparing hand to God's poor. . . .In his death the poor have lost their best friend. . . .He, like the late Cardinal Manning, often said that a bishop should die poor. Bishop Grace died poor. His wealth was spent in works of charity among the poor.

His death was the death of a servant of God, full of resignation to the divine will, and not without a holy joy that the day of rest and reward was at hand. There has passed away from this earth a man of whom we can truly say that the world is better because he lived.

The writer was present at the obsequies in the Cathedral and, after the Mass and absolutions, witnessed the following incident. The hearse containing the casket turned off Sixth and came to a halt on St. Peter Street while the carriages were being lined up for the funeral procession. The one occupied by Archbishop Ireland was next to the hearse. The day was bitterly cold and Danny Donahue shivered as he stood beside the hearse and gazed with tear-dimmed eyes at the coffin containing the mortal remains of his friend. The Archbishop saw him and, leaving his carriage, gathered the little old man into his strong arms and bore him to a seat beside him and took him to the cemetery. It was a significant gesture on the part of the great Archbishop revealing an unsuspected facet of his character.

The long funeral cortege proceeded slowly to Calvary cemetery where all that was mortal of the second Bishop of St. Paul was laid to rest beside the grave of his predecessor, Bishop Cretin, in the sacred enclosure reserved for the clergy, to await the clarion call of the resurrection. A granite slab similar to that above the vaulted grave of the first Bishop of St. Paul marks his last resting-place. It bears the following inscription:

SACRED TO THE MEMORY

OF

THOMAS LANGDON GRACE

SECOND BISHOP OF

ST. PAUL

BORN IN CHARLESTON, S. C.

A. D. 1814

DIED IN ST. PAUL

A. D. 1897

MERCY AND TRUTH HAVE MET EACH OTHER

JUSTICE AND PEACE HAVE KISSED

PS. LXXXIV. 11.

MAY HE REST IN PEACE

In the course of an obituary notice the Northwestern Chronicle of February 26 said:

Bishop Grace was always a close student and was profoundly learned. In the days of his vigor he was an orator of the first order, and his sermons were noted for perspicacity of expression, beauty of language and force of delivery. In the earlier years of his administration he was heard in public as well, having lectured before the state legislature by request. Always of gentle and winning ways, and kind and benevolent disposition, he was, at the same time, full of dignity of carriage and demeanor; to him it was the dignity of his office he was maintaining, but in the estimation of others it was the dignity of the man also, and set well upon him, matching the nobility of his character. A cultured, courteous gentlemen he was, in the very best sense of that term. A leading characteristic of Archbishop Grace was his singular humility which brought him, indeed, the increased respect and esteem of his fellowmen. He was in nothing proud and in his daily walk he ever imitated the meekness of his Master. He always possessed the deep regard, respect and veneration of all without distinction of race or religion. In the eyes of his fellow citizens, Catholic and non-Catholic, he was the perfect man.

The St. Paul Daily Dispatch, February 24, 1897, had the following reference to the Bishop's death which it said

removes another of the great men who have spent the larger part of their brave and christian lives in assisting and helping to carve an empire of Christian civilization from the wilds of the Northwest.

Forty years ago he came here to share in the toils, perils and privations incident to frontier and pioneer life, and to labor in a Christian mission, and he lived to see what were then mere isolated, widely separated missions among the Indians, and in widely scattered white settlements, a compact, prosperous, law-abiding community of new states of the Union. Much of this development of Christian civilization was due to his own influence, his teachings, and his personal guidance, and the result of his unselfish Christian heroism and example.

His life was one full of work and care for the holy cause for which he was ordained a Christian priest. He was truly a shepherd and pastor of the flock in this wide area, brought from savagery to civilization and Christianity; and the noble influences which were felt in his long and eventful lifetime and by his example will continue for all time to come for the great good of the generations who will follow him, and who piously cherish and revere his gracious memory.

A writer in the National Cyclopedia of American Biography, Volume IX, pp. 225-6, pays Bishop Grace the following well-deserved tribute:

In all movements for the betterment, temporal and local as well as spiritual, Bishop Grace was foremost in his advocacy, and ever ready with all the helps at his disposal. . .
Among all the distinguished prelates who have graced the hierarchy of America, none has more worthily fulfilled the ideal of citizen, priest and christian. While staunch and unwavering in his devotion to the church in all her rites and doctrines, his broad love of humanity and fervid patriotism hesitated to limit the sphere of his influence for good, and he joined hands heartily with all who were seeking in any way to uplift and benefit society. Many of the notable improvements in the development of the City of St. Paul had his substantial aid and all met with his encourage-, ment.

In his sermon at the last Mass in the old Cathedral, which he celebrated on August 31, 1914, Archbishop Ireland paid tribute to his predecessor, Bishop Grace, in the following words:

He was so faithfully present on his throne, Sundays and holydays during the twenty-five years of his episcopal service. The thousands still live who knew Bishop Grace. Was he not the good Bishop? Mild and sweet-mannered, of piety angelic, of ardor of love for God's Church, of whole-souled willingness to spend himself in the service of his flock, so prudent in counsel, so anxious that others should do as he was doing, yea, better than he himself was permitted to do. Good Bishop Grace. . . In fond remembrance of you your old throne in the old Cathedral will have the place of honor in the sanctuary of the new.

The Catholic Journal of Memphis in an obituary notice says:

Archbishop Grace may be said to have been a true pioneer in the christianizing of the Northwest. When he took his seat as Bishop of Minnesota his see included all of that state and ranged through the Dakotas. The Bishop was familiar with the Indians and did much to civilize them. His work carried him over thousands of miles of territory. He traveled through blizzards and storms on horseback and his tireless energy was rewarded by his having lived to see a wild prairie converted into a great and progressive section of the country, with boundless wheat fields and populous cities.

The Forgotten Bishop

Notwithstanding these encomiums, the verdict of contemporaries, Bishop Grace is undoubtedly the forgotten bishop of the Diocese of St. Paul. Scarcely a record of anything he said or did is to be found in its archives; nor has history done justice to his memory and achievements.

And yet he was in his day one of the greatest prelates in the Church in the United States. Why this unmerited oblivion? Why the failure to give him a niche peculiarly his own in our diocesan annals? Is it because he was overshadowed by the fame of his protege and successor? Or is it the result of his innate modesty and self-effacement, so timid of the public eye, which shunned publicity and sought only to do the work of God through others while he remained in the background although his was the directing mind and hand? He was in the world, it is true, but not of it. He carried the atmosphere of the cloister into the busy arena of every day life and action, and kept his thoughts fixed on God in the midst of its incessant calls of duty during fifty-eight years of priesthood and prelacy. In his daily round of toil he sought not the applause of men but the approval of his conscience, the sole guide and arbiter of his life.

He began his episcopal career in St. Paul when Minnesota was in its infancy and about to experience the full impact of the westward frontier movement that populated its fertile prairies with tens of thousands of immigrants, and which reached its zenith before he laid aside the crozier of authority to seek well-merited rest. He bore the burden of the day and the heats, he experienced the privations and perils incidental to pioneer life in the Northwest and made common cause with the clergy, religious and laity who, under his direction, laid the foundations of the Catholic Church in the North Star State; he bore the brunt of the hazards and inconveniences to which all immigrants were subjected in founding new homes on the western prairies.

His task was to build upon the rather meager foundation laid by his apostolic predecessor in toil and tears; and nobly and successfully he wrought for the welfare of religion by organizing parishes, erecting churches, schools and other institutions for the material and spiritual well being of the people entrusted to his shepherding, and seeking and assisting to the limit of his ability the other sheep not of the fold, without regard to class, creed, condition or racial origin. When he came to the diocese he found a Catholic population of fifty thousand ministered to by twenty-seven priests in thirty-one churches and ninety missions, with two sisterhoods and one religious order of men as auxiliaries. When he resigned the active administration of the diocese after twenty-five years of an arduous episcopate, that had seriously undermined his health, he bequeathed to his successor a well-equipped diocese staffed by one hundred and fifty priests, diocesan and regular, in charge of two hundred churches and sixty missions serving the spiritual needs of two hundred thousand Catholics, notwithstanding the fact that four-fifths of the original territory had been placed under Vicars Apostolic. The four seminarians studying for the diocese when Bishop Cretin died had increased to twenty-nine, the religious orders of men had grown to six and the sisterhoods to thirteen—a goodly harvest, indeed, from the seed of faith scattered in virgin soil by Fathers Galtier and Ravoux and watered and tended by Bishop Cretin; and the Church was even then bourgeoning with the promise of more glorious expansion into the golden era of power and influence soon to be realized.

A providential man was Bishop Grace, a prelate of brilliant intellectual attainments, a learned theologian, a profound student of contemporary events at home and abroad, thoroughly conversant with religious trends and tendencies in America and Europe, a linguist familiar with Latin and Greek, speaking Italian as fluently as a native, and capable of ministering to the Indians in their own dialects.

He was a convincing and graceful orator of more than ordinary ability to sway an audience. His sermons were models of literary excellence and elegance, noted for lucidity of expression and profundity of thought— the flash of the gem coupled with its solidity. He spoke with a fluency, ease and unction that commanded attention. Unfortunately little that he wrote, except a pastoral letter or two and a few letters to contemporaries, have been preserved. He merits well of the diocese and posterity, but no monument perpetuates his memory or enshrines his name except one of the original colonies, Graceville, founded by his successor and named in his honor, a residence at the St. Paul Seminary called after him and a modern business block on the old Cathedral property in the downtown district.

His charity and kindness were proverbial; his benevolence and humility recognized and admired by all; his courage and justice befitted one born to rule. He was dignified in carriage and bearing, gentle and winning in all his ways. He was strict and impartial where principle was at stake; and he never shirked or postponed a duty through human respect. He sought no positions of honor and, in meetings of the hierarchy, was known to ask to be excused from those to which he was entitled by seniority. The Northwestern Chronicle of April 29, 1882, commenting on one of these instances remarked that he never excused himself from the six o'clock Mass at home and the comfort it gave him to administer the Bread of Life to his beloved people. He was all things to all men and gave freely of counsel, service and substance to every worthy cause whether civic or religious; he paid little attention to politics or parties, but was patriotic to the core.

He was regarded as a saint by everyone and beloved by Catholic and non-Catholic alike. In private life he followed a daily horarium which found him at the altar shortly after day break ready for Mass, and before it many times during the day for visits to the Lord of the Tabernacle, the recitation of the Rosary in private and public, a holy hour and many other devotional exercises. He was at the beck and call of everyone who sought his advice or help; his charity to the poor and needy was bound-less and no one, however unworthy, appealed to him in vain.

The clergy, religious and laity of the present owe a debt of gratitude to Bishop Grace for what he accomplished under the trying circum-stances of pioneer days, with meager material resources, for the propaga-tion of Catholicism among the aboriginal inhabitants, the early colonists and their successors, our forefathers in the faith, as well as for the tradi-tions of devoted zeal and sacrificing labor which made the Diocese of St. Paul a stronghold of the Church in the Northwest.

The pectoral cross and episcopal ring of Bishop Grace, a silver goblet presented to him on June 29, 1859, a stole and crucifix that belonged to him are in the Catholic Historical Society's museum,[108] as well as the diary of a trip to the Red River valley in August and September, 1861; two personal account books from June, 1868, to January, 1897; a letter of July 16, 1865, subdelegating to Father Ravoux the faculties granted him by the Holy See on January 4 of that year; a similar letter dated June 28, 1871; a power of attorney in favor of Father Ravoux on March 29, 1875; a crayon picture; a portrait painting; a three-quarter length photo in a gilt frame; and an illuminated address from the faculty and students of St. John's, Collegeville, on the occasion of his silver jubilee.

Most Reverend John Ireland, D.D.
First Archbishop of St. Paul
1884–1918

Chapter IX

THE FIRST ARCHBISHOP OF ST. PAUL
MOST REVEREND JOHN IRELAND, D.D.

1838-1918

IT WOULD require several volumes to do anything like justice to the long and eventful career of the Most Reverend John Ireland, first Archbishop of St. Paul, to describe even in brief outline the signal services he rendered to Church and State in the land of his adoption, to recount with anything like adequate detail and accuracy even the chief events of a life, every moment of which was filled with the insistent calls of duty, public and private, civic and religious.

For more than half a century he was a dominant figure in the religious, social and political life of the United States—a churchman than whom no prelate was more highly esteemed by all classes and creeds; a states-man whose breadth of vision and grasp of events made him a valued counsellor in national affairs; a patriot whose loyalty to his country was second only to his love for God.

John Ireland, son of Richard Ireland and Judith Naughton, was born in the village of Burnchurch, County Kilkenny, Ireland, and baptized[1] on September 11, 1838, in the parish church of Danesfort. The baptismal register does not give the date of birth, nor is it signed with the name of the officiating clergyman, who was the parish priest, Reverend Edward Cavanagh; and the sponsors were John Naughton and Mary Marnell. He was the second eldest child in a family of six—two boys and four girls —Mary Anne, John, Elizabeth, Ellen, Judith and Richard, who died of typhoid shortly after his arrival in St. Paul. Their father was a carpenter, well educated, especially in Mathematics and Irish History, with the latter of which he was thoroughly conversant. He was a lanky, raw-boned man, stern and strict with his family and held in awe[2] by his nephews and nieces, but withal kind and benevolent. His eldest son, the Arch-bishop, resembled him in build and character; children and others, even the clergy, stood in awe of him. Mrs. Ireland was the motherly type, placid, unruffled, easy-going, a deeply religious woman of fine judgment and rare tact whose interests were centered in home and family. From his father—tall, sinewy, vigorous, impulsive, opinionated—the future Archbishop derived the rugged constitution, keenness of intellect, strength of character and determination of will which were his dominant characteristics. From his mother—known as "Julia" because she did not like "Judith"—he inherited the deeply spiritual nature and love for work which, blended with the paternal traits, admirably equipped him—physically, intellectually and spiritually—for the brilliant career which the future held in store for him.

At an early age John was sent to the village school where he made rapid progress in his studies. He learned easily and had a very retentive memory. But he was not to complete his education in the land of his birth. The years of famine that marked the close of the second quarter of the nineteenth century in Ireland proved disastrous to the country, not only because of the number who died from starvation and disease, but more so because of the forced emigration of so many hundreds of thousands of its population. In the spring of 1849 Richard Ireland determined to leave the land of his birth and seek his fortune in America. He landed in New York, accompanied by his youngest sister, Nancy, and set out for Burlington, Vermont, where he found work as a carpenter. In the autumn of 1850 his wife and family joined him and they remained for nearly a year in Burlington where John went to school. The next migration brought them to Chicago, Illinois, where they resided for upwards of a year, during which John attended St. Mary's school, under the direction of Father St. Cyr. In Chicago they renewed acquaintance with John O'Gorman and his family, who had come from Kilkenny some time previously, and together they decided to settle in the Northwest. In April, 1852, they left Chicago and traveled by easy stages to Galena, Illinois, where they boarded the steamer "Nominee" for St. Paul, landed at the foot of Jackson Street on May 20 and decided to make the then frontier village their home. The two families found a temporary abode in a one-story frame house at Fifth and St. Peter Streets, till they bought lots and built their own homes, the Irelands on Fifth Street where the Young Women's Christian Association now stands.

First Seminarian of the Diocese

When the Ireland family arrived in St. Paul the log chapel of Father Galtier had been superseded by a more commodious building that served as church and school, and residence for the bishop and clergy. The original log chapel housed a school for girls taught by the Sisters of St. Joseph of Carondelet who had just spent their first winter in the Territory. The village was struggling to cast off the swaddling clothes of infancy and to lay the foundation of a prosperous future. Log cabins were beginning to yield to frame and even to brick structures. The population had grown to a thousand and immigrants were arriving by the hundreds in search of homes and security on the fertile fields of the new Territory, beside its countless lakes and on the banks of its winding rivers. Minnesota was a haven of promise to families like the Irelands and O'Gormans who had fled the famine and misery of their native land and were anxious to begin a new future, to establish a permanent home and gain a competency in the land of their adoption.

Less than a year before their arrival St. Paul had welcomed its first Bishop, the Right Reverend Joseph Cretin, whose apostolic zeal, gentle disposition and love for the poor had already endeared him to all the inhabitants. The Ireland and O'Gorman families were welcomed by him, and soon John and Thomas, the eldest sons, attracted his attention by their intelligence and piety. They were enrolled in the Cathedral school. He made them altar boys, members of his household, as it were, and, under his tuition, they made rapid progress in their studies and especially in Latin. The saintly prelate, aware of the great need of priests to minister to the growing Catholic population committed to his care, was quick to detect the trend of their thoughts and aspirations and soon convinced himself of the genuineness of their vocation to the religious life. One day, according to the story told with variations by each of them in after life, he called them in from recreation and, having assured himself of their desire to become priests, bade them kneel before the altar of the Blessed Virgin in his humble Cathedral and dedicated them to the service of God as the first seminarians of the Diocese of St. Paul.

In 1853 they were sent to France under the personal care of the Reverend Augustine Ravoux, Vicar General of the Diocese, and placed in the preparatory seminary of Meximieux (Ain) in the Diocese of Belley.

Years later the Archbishop, in reminiscent mood, would give an amusing account[3] of the journey to France under the chaperonage of Father Ravoux, the memory of which never faded from his mind. The whole village turned out to see Johnny Ireland and Tommy O'Gorman aboard the steamer that was to take them to Galena on the first lap of the journey. They were lively and mischievous youngsters who made friends with all the passengers. On one occasion Father Ravoux caught them eating part of a watermelon that had fallen on the deck and broken into several pieces and accused them of stealing it (and went to the grave convinced of it). He reprimanded them and told them they were not fit to be priests and that he would put them off the boat at Prairie du Chien where they were to meet Father Galtier. They actually packed their grips though they were not fully convinced that he meant what he said.

He changed his mind when they changed conveyances for Chicago. In New York they stuffed their pockets with overripe, juicy peaches bought with money received from the Bishop and friends in St. Paul, and when they boarded the train for the wharf Father Ravoux sat in the narrow seat with Tommy and the juice of the crushed peaches ran over his clothes to his horror and disgust and their secret amusement. In Paris he took from Johnny a bottle of wine given him by the mistress of the boarding house where they stayed and put it in his trunk. Before reaching Lyons the bottle broke and the contents saturated his effects much to their concealed enjoyment.

At Meximieux the French boys were astonished to find that the American lads, far from being savages, were very much like themselves and their interest in them abated.

At the end of his course John Ireland, a deacon, returned to America in August, 1861, and at Prairie du Chien, where he assisted at Sunday Mass, he was too timid to call on the pastor who had preached what he called an excellent sermon. He spent the afternoon walking up and down the river bank waiting for the boat. In St. Paul he was met by Father Oster who put him in a room and forgot about him. He finally mustered up courage to meet the housekeeper who made him feel at home. One wonders why he did not go to his own home. He was ordained four months afterwards.

Meximieux and Montbel

While the boys were in France they were not forgotten by their friends in St. Paul. Every year in the month of November Jean Lallier,[4] a basket-maker, who lived with his sister in a cabin on stilts on what is now Cedar Street, then a bog, visited the Catholics and took up a collection to be sent to Meximieux at Christmas. He lived to welcome them on their return and to see John Ireland installed as Archbishop of St. Paul. Jean Lallier had the reputation of being a very saintly man. Every Sunday he took up the collection at the early Masses in the Church of St. Louis and then hastened to the Cathedral to do the same at the nine o'clock Mass. He was very kind to the clergy and especially to young priests arriving in St. Paul. When Father Guillot came in 1883 and was appointed assistant to Father Oster, in Austin, Lallier took him to the train, bought his ticket and gave him a lunch in a paper bag.

During their residence in Meximieux Johnny and Tommy received several letters from Father Ravoux. In one of them, written on July 31, 1857, after the death of Bishop Cretin, he exhorted them to

continue to pattern yourselves after the models you have before you in the persons of your professors and superiors and to mould yourselves in the ecclesiastical virtues so necessary if you would work efficaciously in the labor of the Lord Jesus. The field is yours; the harvest is plentiful, but the workers are few in number. . .Happy the missionary, happy the priest who, separated from the rest of men, and chosen by God for the glory of His name and the salvation of his brothers, devotes himself entirely, with all his abilities, and with soul and body to the fulfillment of his vocation. . .

My most sincere regards to Miss Cretin and all her family. You have, in France, a good mother. Pray God that she may live a long time on this earth for the glory of His Name; for her good works spread near and far the good odor of Jesus Christ. The Diocese of St. Paul will never forget the name and the virtues of its first Bishop, Monsigneur Cretin, and the kindness of Madamoiselle, his sister, will never be erased from our memory.

Why did Bishop Cretin send these boys to Meximieux in Belley? First of all, it was his natal diocese; but there was another reason and a rather important one for the bishop of a diocese as poor as St. Paul was in those days. When Bishop Devie of Belley consecrated his former priest, Joseph Cretin, first Bishop of St. Paul, he offered to educate, free of cost, any boys of his missionary diocese who showed signs of a vocation to the priesthood; and that is why these boys were sent to the classical seminary of Meximieux. In this nursery of learning and piety John Ireland remained four years, completing in that time a classical course[5] which usually took eight years, giving evidence of that keenness of intellect, retentiveness of memory and intensive application to study which characterized his whole career. When he was graduated he won nearly all the prizes, the one he appreciated most being the first prize for "French Oration".

One who knew him better than anyone else said he "was mentally quick and mentally deep at the same time; to want to learn a thing was to learn it; his grasp was instant and deep".

We have evidence of his industry and application while in Meximieux in two manuscripts—an index and a copybook, both hand made, 8 by 11 inches in size, sewn in paper covers, that of the notebook made from the New York Freeman's Journal and Catholic Register, August 24, 1861.

The index has 76 pages of references to books in Latin, French and English, bearing on 242 religious topics arranged in alphabetical order. Several topics have a page of references; others a line or two.

The notebook, written in French, is inscribed "Cahier d'Instruction Religieuse a Jean Ireland 1856-57". It comprises forty-four pages of a course of religious instruction given during his last year at Meximieux, dealing with the Mosaic religion and its divinity; the integrity and truth of the Pentateuch; the authority and genuineness of the gospels; the Christian religion and the proofs of its divinity drawn from the fulfilment of the Old Testament prophecies by the Messiah, and especially by the miracles and resurrection of Christ. The writing is neat, legible and characteristic. Two similar note books are preserved in the archives of Meximieux, one inscribed with the name of John Ireland, the other with that of Thomas O'Gorman, mementoes of two of its distinguished graduates.

At the end of the course in Meximieux John Ireland went to the Marist Scholasticate[6] at Montbel in the south of France where he made one year of philosophy and three of theology. Montbel was not even a village. It was an estate given to the Marist Fathers by a benefactor, and located midway between La Crau and Hyères, not far from Toulon. It was customary for the graduates of Meximieux to study philosophy at the other preparatory seminary in Belley and theology at Bourg. Why did Bishop Cretin send John Ireland and Thomas O'Gorman to Montbel to complete their course? Father Colin, founder of the Society of Mary, or the Marists, and many of his confreres had studied with Bishop Cretin and, at his request, they offered to educate, free of cost, the levites of his far-off diocese. Among young Ireland's companions in the scholasticate were the Most Reverend Archbishop Redwood of Wellington, New Zealand, Bishop Chatron of Osaka in Japan, Father Gros, one of the early pastors of the Church of St. Louis in St. Paul, and Brother Germain, afterwards Archbishop of Toulouse. At the completion of his seminary course John Ireland returned to St. Paul to receive ordination at the hands of the Right Reverend Thomas L. Grace, the successor of Bishop Cretin, in the Cathedral on December 22,[7] 1861. It was a memorable occasion for him, his family and friends who had followed his career with interest during his sojourn in France.

Civil War Chaplain

With all the ardor and intensity of a nature supernaturalized by grace the young priest entered upon the duties of his sacred calling. The people soon realized that a new force had been injected into the spiritual life of the community, and day by day Father Ireland found new avenues for the exercise of his apostolic zeal. He became all things to all men that he might save all. Looking beyond the confines of his allotted field of labor he divined the need of priests to minister to the soldiers engaged in the struggle for the preservation of the Union. Several months before his ordination the flame of civil war had been enkindled in the United States. The cry of secession had been heard in the South. Freedom or slavery became the issue. Fort Sumpter had fallen. President Lincoln had issued a call for volunteers. Minnesota was the first to respond when Governor Ramsey pledged one thousand men. The undisciplined tread of raw recruits was heard in the land. The North was swept by a mighty wave of patriotism. In ten weeks after the fall of Sumpter on April 14,

1861, one hundred and eighty thousand volunteers were under arms, but the issue was not decided for four years of strife, bloodshed and misery to determine once and for all time that the nation of the Founding Fathers was to endure, one and undivided, and without the ugly and un-Christian institution of slavery.

The flame of patriotism burned brightly in the soul of the newly-ordained Father Ireland. He could not shoulder arms in defense of his adopted country; but he could and did offer his services as a chaplain to minister to the soldiers engaged in the struggle for the permanence and perpetuity of the Union. In due time he received from Governor Ramsey, at Bishop Grace's request, his commission as Chaplain and was assigned to duty with the Fifth Minnesota Volunteer Infantry fighting in the South. He shared the hardships of the soldier's life and the dangers of severe fighting under the leadership of General Rosecrans, who gave the Fifth Minnesota the credit for saving the day at Corinth in 1862. It was on this occasion that, according to an oft-repeated and, doubtless, apocryphal story, Chaplain Ireland carried a supply of ammunition to the front and cheered the soldiers on to victory. If it be true, it was the only such exhibition of "manly intrepidity on the firing line" by a Chaplain during the Civil War.

During this trying period Chaplain Ireland wrote letters to his family in St. Paul and they were sacredly guarded as mementoes of that epoch in his life by his sister, Mother Seraphine, afterwards Provincial Superior of the Sisters of St. Joseph; but, unfortunately, shortly before her death in 1930, she burned them notwithstanding the appeal made to her to preserve them for their historical value.

One letter, descriptive of the Battle of Corinth, which he was afterwards to call a "most important battle" because of the part played by his regiment and the strategic value of Corinth, was written to the Editor of the St. Paul Press and published in the issue of November 1, 1862, because of its local interest. It is a report of Chaplain Ireland of the Fifth Minnesota regiment written from Corinth, Mississippi, October 23, 1862.

We have within the past week, returned to Corinth after having hotly pursued Van Dorn and Price over hills, vales, under sunshine and rain, by the most circuitous routes, for over the distance of one hundred miles. A little rest is at last granted to us; we need it badly; and we believe we are not undeserving of it. Ever since the 18th of August we have been on active duty. . .On the night of the 3rd. we quietly took our rest in one of the central squares of Corinth. . .The shells were bursting over our heads before daybreak on the morning of the 4th. The rebels charged Fort Robinette under the galling fire of our infantry which outflanked them. . .

He describes the battle of Corinth on the fourth, in which the Fifth

Minnesota alone saved the city. Everyone is proud of the regiment, he wrote, and

> Great is our renown in the army. The other regiment fully appreciates our valor; our praise is on every tongue. . .Minnesota may well be proud of the doings of her children. . .she ranks high for the bravery of her sons. They had able and gallant leaders. Their bravery during the contest was most praiseworthy.   Col. Hubbard and Lieut. McGrorty, quartermaster, kept up the supply of ammunition. . .no danger of our men being short of cartridges. . .(Does not this dispose of the story of his rushing ammunition to the front?)
> Our ranks are somewhat thinner than when we sailed down the Mississippi.   Some have been discharged, some fell victims to various diseases. . .The health of our men at present is excellent, they are fully acclimated, all ready to do battle anew for the cause of liberty, all inspired with true patriotic views, they are just the men we want.   May the all-ruling Providence, the God of armies, watch over them and bring them back safe to their own sweet home in Minnesota, or open to them the gates of His heavenly kingdom, if some are yet called upon to die the death of the brave.

After the battle he was missed by the regiment and when found was in an improvised hospital on the outskirts of the city comforting the wounded and dying and holding burial services for the dead. He often visited hospitals at considerable distance from his headquarters.

For a couple of days after the evacuation the Fifth Minnesota went into camp by a dirty rivulet called Clear Creek, and the soldiers built a rude altar with a canopy of bushes and saplings and the Chaplain talked to them in such a soldierly way that he attracted the attention of even the most indifferent, to such an extent that they cheered him when he ended. He was one of the most popular officers in the regiment.[8]

A member of Company C, Fifth Minnesota, C. B. Keller of Albert Lea, vouches for the fact that on one occasion in Western Tennessee he found Chaplain Ireland ministering to a soldier and his nurse, John G. Godley, who had been stricken with small pox,[9] providing food and drink for them, both of whom ultimately recovered.

His letter of resignation from the service, dated March 19, 1863, assigns as the determining motive for his action, not his impaired health due to an attack of enteric fever, but the need Bishop Grace had for his service to minister to the spiritualities of a large congregation, and the reduced number of Catholics in his regiment which did not warrant the continual presence of a Catholic chaplain. Thirty years afterwards he wrote, in the third person, the story of his war experiences for a book published by Reverend Peter P. Cooney, C. S. C. He considered the years spent in the army the "happiest and most fruitful" of his ministry. Though he did not fight, he inspired others by his fearlessness in the face of danger.

Chaplain Ireland's fidelity to duty under the most trying circumstances, his courage in the face of danger, his endurance of the privations incident to military life and his patriotic spirit inspired the men of his regiment with heroic courage and won their undying respect and love. Before long he was the idol of the regiment. After a year's service he was stricken with fever while on duty with the Fifth Minnesota at the siege of Vicksburg, one of the turning points of the war, and, on the order of his physician, supplemented by the request of his bishop, returned to the more congenial climate of Minnesota where he soon regained his normal strength and vigor. Throughout his life he gloried in the fact that he had served his country in the Civil War; and his services were officially recognized in later years by his appointment as National Chaplain of the Grand Army of the Republic whose conventions he attended whenever possible and with whom he delighted to associate whenever occasion offered. During his episcopate he took advantage of confirmation tours and other religious functions to meet the Civil War veterans in the smaller towns of the state and they, in turn, rallied around him and usually arranged a meeting in the town hall to hear "Comrade" Ireland recall the brave days of old and inculcate lessons of patriotism and love of fellowman irrespective of class, condition, color or creed. He would forego any pleasure and endure any discomfort for a chance to address the old soldiers; and he insisted that the local pastor make arrangements for such a meeting. No man with a knowledge of Chaplain Ireland's services to the nation in the days of her crises dared to challenge his patriotism or belittle his religion. If one were foolhardy enough to attempt it he never sought a second encounter. The Chaplain who displayed "manly intrepidity on the firing line" at Corinth did not need any one to furnish weapons to defend his faith or ward off attacks on his religion. He was quite able to defend himself whenever necessary and he never shirked an opportunity to do so.

Return to the Diocese

On his return from the South he resumed with zest and vigor his duties in the Cathedral parish and also acted as Secretary to Bishop Grace. In 1867 he succeeded Father Caillet, founder and first pastor of St. Mary's Church in Lower Town, as pastor of the Cathedral, a position he held until 1875 when he was consecrated Titular Bishop of Maronea and Coadjutor to Bishop Grace.

In December, 1866, Father Ireland spoke out boldly against efforts to organize a regiment of Fenians in St. Paul at a meeting in Ingersoll Hall addressed by Judge McCormick who called upon him, as a "Killarney" priest, to act as secretary. In refusing the request he said: "I have been a Fenian at heart for several years and desire the deliverance of

Ireland as much as any one but now is an inopportune time to attempt it". He characterized Fenianism as a "humbug", if not a "swindle". "To excite men to give money to a most fruitless cause, to push an Irishman to ruin and death, without any shadow of hope of doing good is an act morally wrong".[10] He believed in Fenianism as long as it could possibly do any good for Ireland. He had followed its growth and development, conversed with its earnest upholders and come to despise and distrust it, as most of the real friends of Ireland did. His view was that of his ecclesiastical superior, Bishop Grace, who, in a St. Patrick's day address, declared the movement to be

> an arrant humbug originating with unprincipled men whose only object was their own self-interest to be subserved at the expense of their honest, patriotic and generous countrymen. It was based upon the credulity of Irishmen who often acted first and reflected afterwards. All attempts to carry out the plans of its leaders would end in disaster to those engaged in it and it had already injured the innocent in Ireland whose oppressions had recently been increased in consequence.

During his early priesthood Father Ireland traveled on foot over wide areas of the state in his spiritual ministrations to the scattered flock and often slept on the floor of a farmer's shack with his suitcase for pillow and his overcoat for covering.[11] He made several trips to Waverly Mills, Watertown and Delano in the late sixties over poor roads, often mere trails. On one of these trips, in 1866, he walked to Waverly Mills carrying his suitcase and Mass kit, and on the way to Watertown became lost on the cross roads and trails of the Big Wood country. Before he could decide which way to turn to reach his destination the singing of a French hymn reached his ears and, tracing it to its source, he came to a small frame church in the cemetery not far from the present Delano where he found a congregation celebrating the feast of Corpus Christi as they were accustomed to celebrate it in Alsatia and Bavaria. He surprised them by entering, preached a sermon and conducted the service to the end, after which he continued his journey. The church had been erected the previous year by a small group of Catholics, who were merged in St. Peter's congregation of Delano in 1874.

He was the first priest to visit the White Earth Reservation[12] and administer the sacraments there. This was in 1868 when, as a member of the government commission to select lands for the Chippewa Indians to be transferred to the reservation from Crow Wing where Father Pierz had established a mission in 1852, he baptized several children of Patrick Quinlan and his full-blooded squaw wife. The reservation is in Becker and Norman counties, two hundred miles northwest of St. Paul, and fifty miles east of Fargo. It comprises thirty-six townships of excellent agricultural land.

More than twenty years afterwards, on Sunday, March 24, 1889, he again visited the reservation,[13] as Archbishop of St. Paul, accompanied by Father Shanley, pastor of the Cathedral, and preached at the Mass celebrated by Father Thomas, O. S. B., the Indian missionary, who interpreted the sermon. An Indian council was held in the afternoon at which the Archbishop presided and again spoke, inviting the redmen to take the total abstinence pledge for five years. Thirty-three warriors took the pledge for life and, with all the chiefs, formed the local total abstinence society of White Earth and received badges from the Archbishop. To show his appreciation the Archbishop provided two fatted beeves for the tribal dinner the next day.

He preached on December 8, 1868, at St. Joseph's Academy when his sister, Elizabeth, received the habit of the Sisters of St. Joseph and the name, Sister St. John. Father Ravoux, V. G., officiated as delegate of Bishop Grace.

The Total Abstinence Movement

In the years after the Civil War Father Ireland noted with dismay the ravages caused among the members of his flock by over-indulgence in strong drink and he sought an efficacious means to remedy the evil. At last he found it in the formation of total abstinence societies[14] whose members pledged themselves to abstain from all intoxicating beverages for the honor and glory of God and the welfare of themselves, their families and fellowmen.

While it is true that Father Ireland was not the founder of the Total Abstinence Movement in Minnesota—that honor belongs to the Reverend D. V. McGinnity, a priest of the Diocese of Milwaukee, temporarily in charge of the parish of Belle Plaine—it is conceded by all that he was its most noted advocate and most successful leader. He took up the work with such energy and enthusiasm that his name became inseparably linked with the cause, not only in Minnesota but throughout the nation. He was known as "The Father Mathew of the Northwest", "The Apostle of Total Abstinence"; and his great heart rejoiced at the betterment wrought in the condition of the people as a result of the crusade of which he was the recognized leader. Spurred on by the action of Father McGinnity he organized the Father Mathew Total Abstinence Society of the Cathedral parish on January 10, 1869, and thus inaugurated a movement which was carried on with such vigor and success that in a very few years this heroic form of temperance had its advocates and adherents in practically every parish of the diocese.

He laid no claim to priority as the father or originator of the movement. Addressing the delegates to the first State Convention of the Father Mathew Societies of Minnesota assembled in St. Paul, January 10, 1872, he "complimented Belle Plaine upon being the first parish in Minnesota where a temperance society was formed, and he was glad to know that there was not in Belle Plaine a single Irish whiskey seller". Thus publicly did he acknowledge that he was not the founder of the total abstinence movement in Minnesota of which he was the inspiration and leader for two score years. But this does not minimize the fact that he is rightly considered its father and most ardent advocate throughout America. It was owing to his earnestness, zeal and enthusiasm for the cause that total abstinence spread so rapidly in Minnesota and gained so many devoted adherents. 'Twas his voice and pen that made it known and practiced by tens of thousands: 'twas his example and consistent advocacy of it which swelled its ranks with new recruits and gained for him, even in the early days of the crusade, an honored niche in the temple of the world's great leaders. "A sower of infinite seed was he, a woodman who hewed towards the light".

He was a tower of strength to the cause in its infancy; and he stood loyally by it through all the vicissitudes of the fifty years of its existence. His connection with it began on the eighth of January, 1869. Let him tell the story in his own words.

In an address delivered on the twenty-sixth anniversary of the establishment of the Father Mathew Society of the Cathedral parish, he thus describes the inception of the work of organization.

Twenty-six years ago we gathered together in the old brick chapel then standing on the corner of Sixth and Wabasha Streets, and organized a Father Mathew society. . .I am said to be the founder of that society and that is true in the sense that I published the call for the organization, and that I had the great honor to be the first member—the first one who took the pledge, yet the inspiration to form the society really did not come from myself. Seven good, generous—too generous—men were assembled together on the previous Friday evening in a very popular saloon on Minnesota Street. They drank and treated one another; but a gleam of good christian sense dawned upon their minds and one said: 'We ought to stop lest we be ruined'. Another said: 'Let us go and see Father Ireland, and organize a temperance society'; and a petition with seven names upon it was actually gotten up in that saloon, and, candidly, the keeper of the saloon was one of the signers. The writing was a little tremulous. One was commissioned to bring me the petition, and as he opened the door of my room he was not very steady on his limbs, and he nearly fell, but he soon recovered himself and said; 'I have a petition for you'. I read the petition and without a moment's hesitation said: 'Yes, a society will be organized'. So at the High Mass on the following Sunday I said: 'I have been asked to form a temperance society. I cannot refuse to listen to a request of this kind, so with God's help a society will be organized'. And at four o'clock that afternoon fifty men signed the pledge, and the Father Mathew society was born.

"In response to a call from a number of Irish citizens, and addressed to the Rev. John Ireland, a most influential and numerously attended meeting was held at the Cathedral school house, for the object of organizing a temperance society". Such was the first public announcement of the fact that on January 10, 1869, a Father Mathew total abstinence society was formed in the city of St. Paul. Under the guidance and inspiration of its founder, the Reverend John Ireland, the good work thus inaugurated bore fruit in nearly every parish of the far-flung diocese. The good seed sown in the fertile soil of Catholic self-denial flourished like the mustard tree and yielded an abundant harvest. Since that day the total abstinence movement has passed through many changes. It experienced the cyclical ebb and flow characteristic of waves of reform; but notwithstanding these vicissitudes its light was never extinguished, its efficacy as a means of promoting sobriety and right living never ceased to be felt throughout the diocese, until the prohibition amendment to the Constitution became the law of the land. Then, unfortunately, the movement died an unnatural death.

Father Ireland presided at the initial meeting and Dillon O'Brien acted as secretary. Father Ireland's was the first name on the roll of honor and forty-one others followed it. Temporary officers were chosen, a committee was appointed to draft a constitution and by-laws and the work of organization was completed on January 24, when the proposed constitution and by-laws was adopted and permanent officers elected as follows: President, Patrick Nash; Vice-President, Honorable John B. Brisbin; Secretary, Michael T. Ryan; Treasurer, James Ackers. With that as a beginning the movement was launched and spread throughout the diocese.

From the beginning Father Ireland was closely identified with the movement, both local and national. He called to order the delegates to the first state convention of the Father Mathew societies of Minnesota in St. Paul on January 10, 1872, the third anniversary of the establishment of the first society in the Cathedral parish. Twelve of the fifteen societies in the state were represented by delegates, among whom were fifteen priests. Patrick Nash was elected chairman and James G. Donnelly secretary. An address to the Irish citizens was read by Dillon O'Brien and the draft of a constitution and by-laws presented by C. M. McCarthy was adopted. The new organization was known as the Father Mathew Total Abstinence Union of Minnesota. C. M. McCarthy was elected President; Edward O'Connor, corresponding secretary; James G. Donnelly, recording secretary; and Maurice Gleason, Treasurer. Father Ireland was appointed Spiritual Director by Bishop Grace. President McCarthy was sent as a delegate to represent the society at Baltimore where the Catholic Total Abstinence Union of America was organized on February 22, 1872, at a meeting attended by two hundred delegates from twelve states in the Union representing twenty-eight thousand members. President McCarthy reported fifteen societies and one thousand members in Minnesota.

Fathers Ireland and Cotter made their first appearance at the Third National Convention in New York, October 8-9, 1873, when the former was elected first Vice-President, a position which he held until his elevation to the episcopate in 1875, when he was succeeded by Father Cotter, who later on became National President.

To broaden the sphere and influence of total abstinence Father Ireland organized the "Temperance Crusaders of St. Paul" in the Cathedral parish on April 21, 1873, for young men between the ages of sixteen and thirty. It flourished for many years and did a world of good in saving and rescuing young men from the demon of strong drink.

He made it a point to attend the meetings of the local societies as frequently as possible to encourage the members by his presence and counsel, as well as state and national conventions, in all of which he was an earnest worker and a tireless advocate of the spiritual and material value of total abstinence to the individual. On his first appearance at the national convention in New York in 1873 he gave "a glowing account of the temperance cause in Minnesota and stated that already there were about twenty-five societies in the state; that in the Diocese of St. Paul they had resolved that not a single English-speaking parish should be without its temperance society". At that convention he was elected chairman of the committee on address to the Holy Father.

At the third convention of the Minnesota Union in Winona on May 6, 1874, he supported a resolution asking the temperance societies in the East to take an interest in temperance emigrants from Ireland on their arrival in this country and give them not merely advice and encouragement but pecuniary assistance, if necessary, in all of which the Minnesota Union would help. At this meeting the name of the organization was changed from "Catholic Total Abstinence Union of Minnesota" to "Catholic Total Abstinence Union of the Diocese of St. Paul".

As a result of the recommendation made at the fourth National Convention held in Chicago in October, 1874, the St. Paul Union appointed an Immigration Bureau to receive, protect and direct immigrants on their arrival in St. Paul and furnish prospective settlers with reliable information about the localities in which to settle and answer enquiries about local conditions and prospects.

Father Ireland was chairman of a committee appointed by the National Union to present an address to Archbishop Manning of Westminister, "the great teetotaler of the age", on the occasion of his elevation to membership in the College of Cardinals in 1875. "Your immediate field of labor", it said, "is the City of London, but in fact you are laboring for the whole English-speaking world, and if Total Abstinence today produces such wondrous fruit throughout England, Ireland, Australia and

America, we are convinced, in the hands of God, you are the chief motor of this unparalleled revolution for good, which it is given to our day to witness".

Promoted to the Episcopate

In the meantime other events in the Diocese of St. Paul challenge our attention.

When, in a formal rescript[15] "given at Rome, at St. Peter's on the 2nd. day of September in the year 1869", Pope Pius IX granted Bishop Grace's petition to absent himself from the General Council of the Vatican, "without any scruple of conscience" on account of the pressing needs of his diocese, Father Ireland was deputed to represent him in that distinguished gathering of prelates and priests from all parts of the world. He arrived at his destination in October, 1869, and met and mingled with the members of the hierarchy destined to mould the course of the Church for half a century. Two American prelates—Archbishops Spalding of Baltimore and Alemany of San Francisco—were on the committee that guided the question of infallibility through the Council. Shortly after the ballot, the American prelates voted to admit to their deliberations the procurator of Bishop Grace of St. Paul, the youthful Father Ireland, and Abbot Boniface Wimmer of St. Vincent's Abbey, Latrobe, Pa., and a committee was appointed to bring the status of procurators before the Council itself, where it was decided that they might be present at its deliberations but could neither speak nor vote. Thus in silence, as listener and observer, did the future Archbishop of St. Paul make his debut in the affairs of the Universal Church. The favorable impression he created because of his character and ability was evidenced by his appointment as Titular Bishop of Maronea and Vicar Apostolic of Nebraska on February 12, 1875, in succession to Bishop O'Connor who died in 1874. When word of his nomination reached St. Paul Bishop Grace was deeply distressed at the thought of losing the counsel and assistance of the most prominent and promising priest of his diocese, and he decided to go to Rome at once and make a personal appeal to the Supreme Pontiff to appoint Father Ireland Coadjutor Bishop of St. Paul with the right of succession to the see.

On April 22, 1875, Father Ireland returned the Papal Brief to Pope Pius IX together with an autograph letter in Latin begging the Holy Father to revoke the appointment.[16]

Beatissime Pater,
Ad pedes Sanctitatis Vestrae provolutus, dum gratias ago quod me, licet indignum, in episcopum Maroniensem in part. Infid. et vicarium apostolicum Nebracensem in Statibus Americae Foederatis, uti per litteras apostolicas constat, benigne volueru promovere, veniam suggerendi peto,

in spiritu tamen omnis humilitatis ac obedienciae, impedimenta gravia adesse ne dictum officium, nisi saltem cum maxima difficultate, possim suscipere. Quae impedimenta Revmus ac Illmus D. D. Episcopus Sti. Pauli, Thomas L. Grace, sub cujus ditione ecclesiastica usque nunc degi, coram Sanctitate Vestra viva voce evolvet. Ipsi et mihi certo gratissimum erit, si precibus nostris benigne annuens, Sanctitas Vestra me in parte supradicti officii ab omni ulterioris obligationis vinculo eximere dignetur. In hujus gratiae spe fundatus, litteras apostolicas, quibus et episcopus Maroniensis et vicarius Nebracensis constitutus sum, in manus Sanctitatis Vestrae remittere praesumo.

Deum precans ut diu sospitem Pontificem nostrum maximum servet, et apostolicam benedictionem pro me infimo servo petens, me subscribo

Sanctitatis Vestrae

Humillimum ac obsequentissimum filium,
Joannes Ireland
Sti. Pauli, in Minnesota,

Ad Summum Pontificem.   die 22a. Aprilis, A. D. 1875

On the same day he wrote to Bishop Grace then in Rome.

St. Paul, April 22, '75.

Rt. Rev. & dear Bishop—

I enclose all the long-expected documents, together with my letter of resignation to the Holy Father. As you will perceive from reading this letter, I enter into no details as to the reasons of my resignation, taking the liberty to refer to your statement of the case. I entertain no doubt whatsoever as to the final results. I put Nebraska entirely out of my mind & settle down quietly into my old attachment to Minnesota. God grant that it may be all right, & according to His merciful designs!

There is one reflection I would make in the case, which calms me very much. I never by any direct acting or choosing of my own have fashioned my destiny: it has been always apparently fashioned for me, & it has been all the better with me. I can well allow the same rule to obtain for my future that has guided me in the past. In this whole present affair, it would be a hard task for me were I myself to decide alone what I should do. My consolation is that it is all in your hands, & not in my own.

I presume you will leave Rome shortly after having received this letter. My next one will be addressed to you in Ireland. . .

Most respectfully, &c
J. Ireland

The packet containing these letters and the Apostolic Brief was lost in the wreck of the steamer "Schiller", near the coast of England, but later recovered by a diver. The letters were returned to Father Ireland on June 1, 1875, through the Post Office department and are preserved in the museum of the Catholic Historical Society in the Ireland Memorial Library of the St. Paul Seminary. Bishop Grace must have wondered why he did not hear from Father Ireland in a matter of such importance to both of them. Nor could Father Ireland enlighten him until the recovered letters were returned to him. The parchment of the Brief is quite wrinkled but the writing is legible and the letters are intact.

Bishop Grace left Rome before he received an answer to his petition. He was at Lourdes when the news that it had been granted reached him, and in gratitude for so favorable an outcome to his prayers, he promised to dedicate to Our Lady of Lourdes the next church in his diocese, a promise he fulfilled when the church under that name was opened in Minneapolis in 1877 for the French people.

First Episcopal Consecration in St. Paul

The most important event in the early history of the Diocese of St. Paul, next to the erection of the diocese itself and the coming of its first Bishop, was the consecration of the Right Reverend John Ireland as Titular Bishop of Maronea and Coadjutor to Bishop Grace with the right of succession. It took place in the Cathedral on December 21, 1875, fourteen years, less one day, from the date of his ordination in the same church. Bishop Grace officiated on both occasions. The day of consecration was a gala day for the Catholics of the diocese and indeed for all the citizens, irrespective of church affiliation, for all knew the work Father Ireland had done for the inculcation of religious and civic virtue and all rejoiced at the honor conferred upon him.

The ceremony was attended by a congregation that filled the sacred edifice as, perhaps, never before, and crowded the steps and sidewalks in the vicinity with people of all classes and creeds eager to catch even a glimpse of the unusual function.[17] It was the first time such a ceremony had ever taken place in St. Paul, the beginning of many similar events in the history of the venerable Cathedral and its successor. The Cathedral was elaborately decorated for the occasion with festoons of evergreens and pendent floral wreaths. From the galleries hung banners of state and city total abstinence societies, with Papal and American flags prominently displayed. Above the main altar a motto was suspended: Dies Tuos In Sua Pace Disponat. A brilliant star jetted its rays from among the surrounding tapers on the altar banked with flowers.

The procession from the adjoining residence entered the Cathedral led by cross-bearer with acolytes, censer-bearers followed by the altar boys; Reverend clergy, numbering nearly one hundred; Abbot Edelbrock of St. John's with Benedictine attendants; Bishops Borgess of Detroit and Krautbauer of Green Bay and Archbishop Henni of Milwaukee with chaplains; the assistant consecrators and attendants; the Bishop-elect in rochet and mantelletta; deacons of honor; subdeacon, deacon and assistant priest; and Consecrator.

The Bishops and Archbishops were seated in the sanctuary; the clergy in the pews in front of St. Joseph's altar; the Bishop-elect and attendants at the altar of the Blessed Virgin.

Bishop Grace was the consecrating prelate, assisted by Bishops Heiss-of La Crosse and Seidenbusch of St. Cloud; the assistant priest was Father Ravoux, the deacons of honor, Fathers Stukenkemper, O. S. B., of St. John's and Plut of Winona; the subdeacon of the Mass was Father McGolrick and the deacon Father Caillet; Father Oster was master of ceremonies, assisted by Fathers Shanley and Cotter; the reader of the Pontifical Brief was Father Trobec and the preacher Father O'Gorman, who took his text from the gospel according to St. Matthew, chapter 28, verses 18 to 20. The sermon theme was the transmission of the apostolic office. As the Savior sent the Apostles in olden days so today a successor of these Apostles sends another with the plentitude of the apostolic spirit. The Church thus provides for the perpetuation of her life. In the Church there is a hierarchy, a body of men acting in concert towards one another and a power of which this body of men is the depository. The Twelve encompassed the earth and left disciples to continue their work and make it fruitful to the end of time. The apostolic body branched out into the episcopacy, the successors of the apostles multiplied to rule the local churches. These scattered apostolic messengers were welded into one under the rule and guidance of a chief, the Pope, appointed by Christ. The papacy is the unity of the church as the episcopate is its universality. The bishops were dowered with power by the Holy Ghost and thus the Church was established as a spiritual kingdom. The world in its opposition to this spiritual force fails to take into consideration the power from on high with which the human messengers of Christ have been endued. The Church cannot be understood by those who stop at the human element and forget the indwelling Holy Ghost. Without this, how account for her rise, her preservation, her position in history, her influence on civilization, her antagonism to the spirit of the world, her persecutions, her triumphs, her internal and external life throughout the ages? If the church did not draw its life from God it could not have withstood the assaults of nineteen hundred years.

The preacher recalled the day of the new bishop's ordination and, beyond it, the day in 1852 when he first set foot in St. Paul, "a humble village slowly straggling up these river bluffs", the happy days in France; but he would "let the veil of memory cover the past in secluded privacy". He ended the sermon with these words:

Look up and around you. These pendent banners, emblems of a cause in which you have been a leader, are here to appreciate your work, to honor and thank you. The clergy of the Diocese of St. Paul, whose shining light you have been, surround you with their cheering pledge of obedience and love. And our beloved Bishop, whose right arm you have been, now bestows upon your more vigorous youth a share of his responsibilities and labors, and transmits to you the mantle of the first Bishop of St. Paul, Joseph Cretin of revered memory.

Child and heir of such saintly ancestry! Take up your father's mantle.

Assume the burden that heaven imposes upon your shoulders.   Grasp your crozier and rule the flock committed to you.   Before you is opened a field worthy of your energies and your zeal.   Labor like a good soldier of Christ until the moment when the jeweled mitre shall be transformed into the crown of eternal glory.

The ceremony proceeded with due solemnity, unrolling before the eyes of the rapt congregation, majestic vistas of the era of faith and preluding the triumphs of the not-distant future for the church in the Diocese of St. Paul. The father, mother and sisters of the newly-consecrated bishop were witnesses of the ceremony and rejoiced because of the exceptional honor conferred on the family. Towards the end of the solemn and significant rite the new Bishop, accompanied by the co-consecrators, blessed the congregation among whom he had lived and labored for so many years, while the people gave reign to their pent-up emotions in the happy tears that flowed down their cheeks while the Te Deum was chanted by the choir in a glorious outburst of harmony in union with the surcharged feelings of the people.

After the ceremony dinner was served to the prelates, clergy and guests in the Cathedral residence under the catering of the Metropolitan Hotel. In the evening the Total Abstinence societies held a torchlight procession in honor of the event, called upon the new bishop and presented him with a purse as a tangible expression of filial respect and affectionate regard.

Prior to the consecration the delegates to the fifth National Convention of the Catholic Total Abstinence Union of America, held in Cincinnati, Ohio, October 6-7, 1875, offered him "the heartfelt congratulations of the representatives of five hundred Catholic Total Abstinence Societies on your elevation to greater dignity, and a higher sphere of usefulness in our Holy Church".

The consecration cemented a most intimate relationship between the two bishops marked, on the part of Bishop Grace, by an increasing admiration for the strength of character, intellectual ability and determination of his youthful coadjutor, and on the part of Bishop Ireland by a devotion to his superior characterized by the reverence and respect of a son for the best of fathers. The elder Bishop's life was, in a measure, merged in that of the younger in which, as it were, it renewed its youth and, because of this interaction of personalities, they planned and labored, with one mind and one heart, for the advancement of religion and the expansion of the Church in the diocese so dear to both of them. By advice and counsel the elder prelate channeled the ardent and impetuous zeal of his protege between the banks of prudence and moderation, curbing his tendency to disregard or override all obstacles to reach the goal envisioned by him. For nearly a decade of years this intimate relationship continued until, in the providence of God, the time was ripe for the younger to receive the reins of full authority from the relaxing hand of the elder, and assume personal responsibility for planning and achieving still greater conquests for the honor and glory of God not only in the diocese but throughout the country.

Ten days after Bishop Ireland's consecration the St. Paul Daily Pioneer Press published the value of all the church property in the city, listing therein seven Catholic churches with an appraised valuation of $176,000, namely, the Cathedral ($60,000); Assumption ($85,000); St. Mary's ($15,000); St. Michael's ($5,500); St. Louis ($4,500); St. Joseph's ($3,500); St. Stanislaus ($2,500); and five institutions appraised at $69,000—St. Joseph's Academy ($20,000); House of the Good Shepherd ($20,000); Catholic Orphanage ($12,000); St. Joseph's Hospital ($10,000); and the Visitation Academy ($7,000). This valuation was considered very low, less than half the cost of these churches and institutions.

Within a year after Father Ireland's elevation to the episcopate the Catholic Total Abstinence Union had this to say about him:

> A valuable man to the Irish race in America is the young Bishop of St. Paul. He has their real interests at heart. He has the courage to give them good advice, whether palatable or not, and spends his life and influence in behalf of their amelioration. . .He has already peopled two counties, Swift and De Graff, in Minnesota with his countrymen. Comfort, temperance and good hope mark their condition.[18]

On Sunday, January 7, 1877, Bishop Ireland blessed the new bell[19] donated to the Church of the Immaculate Conception by the total abstinence societies of Minneapolis. It weighed three thousand pounds and cost nine hundred dollars. The Bishop was assisted by the pastor, Reverend James McGolrick, and his assistant, Reverend Daniel J. McMullan, in the chanting of the psalms and responses and, after the singing of the liturgical prayers, sprinkled the bell with holy water and fumed it with incense.

On the exterior of the bell is inscribed the prayer: Populus Tuus Convocatus Per Me Confortetur In Domino, (May thy people called by me to the house of prayer be strengthened in the Lord). This is followed by the designation of the donors: The Gift of the T. A. Societies of Minneapolis in Honor of the Immaculate Conception, and the date, 1876.

This bell rang the daily Angelus in pleasing musical tones and summoned the faithful to Mass and other religious devotions until it was transferred to the Basilica of St. Mary in 1914, where its function is confined to the ringing of the Angelus at noon and in the evening. It is operated by hand and has worn out many ropes and, no doubt, the patience of many sextons during three-quarters of a century. It had the rim of its great oak wheel renewed at least once in recent years.

Coadjutor Bishop

Bishop Ireland entered with zeal on his new duties during the year 1876 and in his visits to the different parishes for the purpose of administering confirmation or officiating at some other religious function, he did not forget to urge total abstinence upon those who had not yet embraced it. As a consequence he added many names to the rolls of existing societies and many new societies to the roster of the diocesan union. The principal societies organized by him were in Carver and McLeod counties.

He invited the Paulists to give a series of missions in the parishes during the autumn and winter of that year which heralded a renewal of interest in temperance work such as their previous missionary tour had evoked. At the close of the mission in Rochester he paid his first visit to that parish after his consecration with Father McGolrick and, in the course of an address, predicted that "the day was not far distant when the great vice of intemperance would be driven from every hamlet within the Diocese of St. Paul". It was on that occasion that the total abstinence pledge was administered for the first time to women and thus was inaugurated a new phase of the movement destined to accomplish untold good for the cause. Soon it was taken up in every parish and women total abstainers began to vie with men in carrying on the good work. The influence of total abstinent mothers, wives and sisters, in the home became a potent factor in the dissemination of total abstinence principles among the men and their example was largely instrumental in keeping husbands, sons and brothers, faithful to the obligations they had assumed.

The year 1876, therefore, witnessed a great revival of temperance work in the diocese with a correspondingly large increase in the number of professed adherents of the cause. With it the first period in the history of the total abstinence movement in the Diocese of St. Paul came to an end. It was the period of growth during which the mustard seed developed into a giant tree whose branches spread in all directions from the parent trunk.

It was preliminary to the golden age of total abstinence when it could be said, as Bishop Ireland told his beloved Father Mathew Society towards the end of the year, "There was not a parish in the Diocese of St. Paul where the cause was not flourishing".

In connection with the Total Abstinence movement a Catholic Mutual Insurance Association was incorporated in 1878 for the purpose of giving financial assistance to the widows, orphans and other heirs of the deceased, by assessing each member a dollar or a dollar and a half depending on his age at the time of admission, with the proviso that the total amount would not exceed one thousand dollars. It met with such success that its benefits were extended to all men from twenty-one to fifty who could pass the physical examination and were willing to pay the annual fee of three dollars a year in addition to the assessments. A board of directors, of whom Bishop Ireland was one, managed the affairs of the Association which soon had members in all parts of the state.

At the fifth annual Diocesan Convention held at Stillwater on June 21–22, 1876, the roster of the Union contained the names of fifty-five societies with a total membership of four thousand two hundred. The delegates resolved to establish an official board of immigration to further the work of colonization by corresponding with prospective settlers and finding suitable homes for them and their families. They also requested all subordinate societies to contribute to the fund for the erection of a fountain in Fairmount Park, Philadelphia, under the auspices of the National Total Abstinence Union, to commemorate the centennial of American independence—a project which reached its culmination on July 4, 1876, when the Memorial was dedicated with imposing ceremony and a monster parade of Total Abstinence Societies, viewed by Archbishop Wood of Philadelphia, Bishop Quinlan of Mobile, Bishop Ireland and other prominent personages among whom were John Lee Carroll, Governor of Maryland, and Governor Hartranft of Pennsylvania, who delivered addresses.

Bishop Ireland's personal interest in the work never flagged. He was always ready to aid it with voice and pen and presence at meetings of the local societies, the diocesan and national unions, whenever possible. In this he had the cordial approval of Bishop Grace who had the cause "greatly at heart" as he told the delegates to the National Convention held in St. Paul in August, 1882, "The public sentiment of the world", he added, "is fast concentrating itself upon the necessity of arresting the growth of this great evil of intemperance . . . I am glad of the spontaneous uprising against intemperance which is one of the greatest evils of the day".

In the course of an admirable address at one of the sessions of this convention Bishop Ireland defined the basis of the total abstinence movement.

> We do not say that the moderate use of intoxicating liquors is in itself wrong and sinful; we are not Manicheans. We do not propose to take from others against their will the rights allowed them by nature and nature's God to use within legitimate bounds wine, beer or whiskey. But neither do we acknowledge as resting upon ourselves an obligation to use these liquors, and we claim the God-given right to abstain as our own free choice from such use.

Shortly after the convention adjourned the liquor dealers of St. Paul, to the number of one hundred and twenty, met in secret conclave on August 30, 1882, for the purpose of forming a Minnesota State Association "for the protection of personal liberty".

The Bishop was one of the speakers at the banquet which closed the thirteenth annual Convention of the Diocesan Union held in Minneapolis in June, 1884, and at the fourteenth National Convention in Chicago in August of that year.

During the Third Plenary Council of Baltimore, which practically commanded all Catholics to join the total abstinence movement and admonished pastors to root out the evil of Sunday drinking by "threatenings and penalties whenever it becomes necessary", a special meeting of the National Union was held in Washington under the presidency of Reverend James M. Cleary of Kenosha, Wisconsin, at which Bishop Ireland declared that a total abstainer was

> the soldier of religion, the apostle of the Church, the guardian of home and family. Better than charitable societies which supply wants arising from poverty are total abstinence societies which prevent the existence of poverty. Seventy-five percent of poverty is due to intemperance. He also lashed out vigorously at the saloon-keepers who he said were 'tools of the devil'.

The official backing of the Third Plenary Council gave steady grounds for Catholics everywhere to join in the movement and, with non-Catholic groups, to do battle against drunkenness, the inveterate enemy of society in America.[20]

In September, 1885, W. P. Rand of Chicago, gave Bishop Ireland two thousand dollars as the nucleus of a fund for a series of lectures on temperance to be given throughout the country by a prominent and capable speaker. Father Cotter of Winona, the National President, was appointed and during the next year he delivered seventy-three lectures in the principal cities of the United States and gave the pledge to 22,732 persons. The societies under whose auspices he lectured incurred no expense except the cost of the hall. At the sixteenth National Convention held in Notre Dame University in August, 1886, it was decided to continue the series and Bishop Ireland, Bishop Spalding, W. P. Rand and W. J. Onahan were appointed a committee to supplement the fund by raising six thousand dollars a year to finance the project in subscriptions of one hundred dollars or smaller amounts to be paid before January 1, 1887. Mr. Rand was named Treasurer of the fund.

Papal Brief of Approval

At this convention delegates from 661 societies representing 43,991 members were in attendance. At the closing session Bishop Ireland declared that the total abstinence movement was recognized by the Third Plenary Council of Baltimore and had "the unqualified approbation of Rome". Thus the Church had officially rid itself of all possible reproach that she in any way encouraged the liquor traffic as conducted in America. But something more significant in the way of approval of the movement was in the offing. Shortly after Bishop Ireland returned from Rome in 1886 he was the recipient of a brief from His Holiness Pope Leo XIII giving the official approval of the Church to the total abstinence movement. Because of its importance it is here given in full in English dress:[21]

To Our Venerable Brother, John Ireland, Bishop of St. Paul, Minnesota.

Leo XIII, Pope

Venerable Brother: Health and Apostolic Benediction.

The admirable works of piety and charity by which Our faithful children in the United States labor to promote not only their own temporal and eternal welfare but also that of their fellow-citizens, and which you have recently related to Us, give to Us exceeding great consolation. And above all We have rejoiced to learn with what energy and zeal, by means of various excellent associations, and especially through the Catholic Total Abstinence Union, you combat the destructive vice of intemperance. For it is well known to Us how ruinous, how deplorable is the injury both to faith and morals that is to be feared from intemperance in drink. Nor can We sufficiently praise the prelates of the United States who recently in the Plenary Council of Baltimore with weightiest words condemned this abuse, declaring it to be a perpetual incentive to sin and a fruitful root of all evils, plunging the families of the intemperate into the direst ruin, and drawing numberless souls down to everlasting perdition; declaring moreover that the faithful who yield to this vice of intemperance become thereby a scandal to non-Catholics, and a great hindrance to the propagation of true religion.

Hence, We esteem worthy of all commendation the noble resolve of your pious associations, by which they pledge themselves to abstain totally from every kind of intoxicating drink. Nor can it at all be doubted that this determination is the proper and the truly efficacious remedy for this very great evil; and that so much the more strongly will all be induced to put this bridle upon appetite, by how much the greater are the dignity and influence of those who give the example. But greatest of all in this matter should be the zeal of priests, who, as they are called to instruct the people in the word of life, and to mould them to Christian morality, should also, and above all, walk before them in the practice of virtue. Let pastors, therefore, do their best to drive the plague of intemperance from the fold of Christ by assiduous preaching and exhortation, and to shine before all as models of abstinence, that so the many calamities with which this vice threatens both Church and State, may by their strenuous efforts be averted.

And We most earnestly beseech Almighty God that, in this important matter, He may graciously favor your desires, direct your counsels, and assist your endeavors; and as a pledge of the Divine protection and as a testimony of Our paternal affection, We most lovingly bestow upon you, Venerable Brother, and upon all your associates in this holy league, the Apostolic Benediction.

Given at Rome, from St. Peter's, this 27th day of March, in the year 1887, the tenth year of Our Pontificate.

Leo XIII, Pope.

Speaking of the importance of this Brief the Moniteur de Rome says:

This Brief has a very great importance for the Church in the United States.

The sad ravages caused by alcoholism in certain regions are well known. We know from the avowal of the Prelates in the Third Plenary Council of Baltimore—echoing that of the Fathers in preceding Councils—that amongst the Catholics of the United States intemperance is the most fatal and most dreadful scourge. The Prelates and clergy of the United States, urged by the exhortations of Plenary Councils, and by the approbation given to them by the Holy See, are making admirable efforts to remove this vice, the source of so many evils. They have been enabled to group the faithful who have the zeal and courage to oppose the evil, not only into parochial temperance societies, but also into a National Union, which counts nearly a hundred thousand members, all men, and all devoted Catholics, who are as the army of morality and good order in the country. To provide against danger and to give good example, they impose upon themselves the obligation of abstaining totally and from all kinds of intoxicating drinks; for experience has shown that, for the habit of drunkenness and ordinarily even for the inclination to this deadly habit, the only effective remedy is total abstinence. Many priests, and even several Bishops and Archbishops, touched by the necessities of their flocks, have put themselves at the head of this great moral movement, inspiring in the multitude the courage of a saving abstinence not only by their exhortation, but also by their example. Among these devoted chiefs of this popular reformation Msgr. Ireland, Bishop of St. Paul, Minnesota, is known everywhere as the most energetic and the most powerful by his influence. The laudatory Brief which the Holy Father has addressed to him is therefore a merited encouragement. The approbation of the Vicar of Jesus Christ will give to this work of zeal, charity and social wisdom, an increase of authority and influence not only in America, but wherever the sad plague of intemperance prevails.

The Colonization Movement

Side by side with the total abstinence movement and closely interwoven with it was the work of systematic colonization in which Bishop Ireland played a most important role. He was, in fact, the originator of the program on a diocesan and national scale. By voice, pen and active participation he guided its deliberations and took a personal interest in directing its affairs until its purpose was achieved and flourishing colonies attested its worth.

When Bishop Cretin came to St. Paul in 1851 there were about a thousand Catholics under his jurisdiction, the majority within a radius of one hundred miles from the see-city. Beyond that was an unexplored wilderness, the home and hunting-ground of savages who far outnumbered the whites. When he died after an episcopate of less than six years the Catholic population was more than fifty thousand. The increase was due in large measure to his efforts to attract new settlers to the Territory of Minnesota as he had done for Iowa during the twelve years of his apostolic labor in the Diocese of Dubuque.

When Minnesota became a Territory on March 3, 1849, it was in possession of its original inhabitants. St. Paul, Stillwater and St. Anthony were small villages and the other settlements mere hamlets. The total population was under five thousand. When the lands west of the Mississippi were thrown open to settlement in 1852 the tide of immigration set in with irresistible force. Covered wagons moved slowly over the bluffs and across the prairies and steamboats loaded with immigrants crowded the St. Paul Landing. The Atlantic seaboard sent its vanguard of colonists among whom were representatives of nearly every nation of northern Europe. The redman's wigwam soon gave place to the white man's cabin.

It was at this juncture that Bishop Cretin came to Minnesota to organize the Church along diocesan lines. His first care was to make provision for priests to minister to the Catholics already in the Territory and then to add to the number of the laity as speedily as possible. He adopted the plan used in Iowa and appealed through Catholic papers in the East for an increase in the Catholic population of the new diocese. In this he met opposition from Archbishop Hughes of New York who deplored and discouraged all organized movements to promote westward migration though he favored the migration of individuals and families. His attitude was unfavorable to the growth of the Church in the West. With others he emphasized the loneliness of life on the prairie and the danger of loss of faith where churches were few and far between. Were it not for this biased attitude, Archbishop Ireland wrote in later years,

the Catholic Church would be immensely more prosperous in all the Western States than ever again she can hope to be, and tens of thousands of Catholic families would have gained happy homes and an honorable competence upon the land, instead of having gone down to ruin in the fierce maelstrom of large cities.

Bishop Cretin was not daunted by this opposition much as he deplored the shortsighted policy. He continued his efforts to attract settlers to his immense diocese, and soon they came at the rate of hundreds a day, the majority of whom were Catholics, to take possession of the millions of acres recently opened up to homesteading.

In his annual report to the Society for the Propagation of the Faith he insistently appealed for larger allocations of funds to meet the demands of an ever-increasing influx of Catholic immigrants for new parishes and additional priests. In March, 1855, he wrote[22] that the Catholic population would probably double in the next six months; and a year later he declared that it had trebled. St. Paul alone had eight thousand souls of whom three thousand professed the Catholic faith. He had to change the location of the cemetery three times because of the expanding growth of the city. Some months more than twenty thousand immigrants sought homes in the state of whom almost half were Catholic. Forty churches would be necessary to accommodate them had he sufficient priests to staff them. When he died in February, 1857, there were more than fifty thousand Catholics in the diocese but only nineteen priests.

There was a group of Irish at Jessenland in the Minnesota valley as early as 1852—tombstones in the cemetery bear that date—and a few years later General Shields founded a colony at Shieldsville in Rice County which formed the nucleus of several other settlements in the vicinity, such as Kilkenny, Erin and Montgomery. In twenty years Shieldsville grew to two hundred and fifty families of sober and industrious farmers and developed, under the leadership of Reverend John J. Slevin (1880-1900), into a recognized stronghold of total abstinence with the largest parochial society of men in the United States.

The efforts of Bishop Cretin to draw settlers to Minnesota were ably seconded by Father Pierz, a missionary among the Indians in the northern part of the diocese, who was instrumental in bringing thousands of German immigrants from the eastern states and Europe to the fertile fields of Stearns County, making it the Catholic stronghold it is today. As a result, there was a large Catholic German population in that county when Bishop Grace arrived in St. Paul in 1859 as second Bishop of the Diocese.

It was during his episcopate that the colonization movement was organized on a diocesan basis and developed into a national undertaking. From the episcopal residence and from the Cathedral pulpit fervent appeals went forth again and again inviting immigrants to the fertile fields of Minnesota. The bishops who encouraged settlers to seek security on the land as well as the priests who ministered to them in their isolation taught them by word and example "the patient and hopeful courage required of the inhabitants of the wilderness". In this work none was more active, persevering and successful than the youthful Bishop Ireland.

On his forced return from the battlefields of the South where he served as chaplain during the first year of the Civil War, Father Ireland became interested in the work of colonization of which he was destined to be the inspiring leader and forceful director for a score of years. With the approval of Bishop Grace he launched the Irish Emigration Society on May 2, 1864, for the purpose of inducing settlers to come to Minnesota to establish new homes for the ones they were forced to abandon in Ireland because of the famine. Many thousands of exiles from Erin had settled in the cities along the Atlantic seaboard in surroundings quite unfavorable to their moral and material welfare, and the society proposed to offer them homes in more congenial surroundings to begin life anew. Father Ireland was elected President and Dillon O'Brien, Secretary, and through their endeavors many were induced to come to Minnesota and make it their permanent home. The society circularized the Irish in the East and three years later its secretary could say with truth that "hundreds of Irish families have come to this state who were induced to do so from our representations". The primary object of the society was to improve the moral and social position of Irishmen in America.

After his elevation to the episcopate in 1875 Bishop Ireland determined to promote the cause of Catholic colonization on a larger scale and in a more systematic manner. On April 10, 1876, he organized the Catholic Colonization Bureau, with a non-profit feature, to carry out his plans, and the following year the Catholic Colonization Land Stock Company to help finance worthy applicants without means to purchase farms for themselves and their families.

He selected Swift County[23] as the field of his first operations and when they proved successful in demonstrating the value of his program, he extended the work to other parts of the state and established colonies in Nobles, Big Stone, Murray and Lyon counties. The method of procedure was substantially the same in all cases.

In Swift County he secured an option for two years on all the lands controlled by the St. Paul and Pacific Railway, amounting to 117,000 acres, and opened them up to prospective settlers who could purchase farms only through him. As this land was intermixed with vacant government land for settlement under the preemption and homestead acts he practically controlled the entire county of twenty-one townships with the village of De Graff as its center and Clontarf seventeen miles west of it. He selected a site for the church in De Graff, commissioned Father McDermott of Litchfield to begin building operations in the spring and, later on, appointed Father Swift resident pastor, to direct and advise the immigrants and minister to their spiritual needs.

The land was rolling prairie suited for tillage, interspersed with meadows for grazing and cattle raising and abundantly supplied with water. Its black soil was capable of producing generous yields of wheat, corn and potatoes. The land sold for from one dollar and a quarter to three dollars and a half per acre depending on its distance from the village and the railroad.

Two weeks after the plans were announced settlers began to arrive and soon sixty thousand acres were bought and occupied. Each quarter section represented a family and additional land could be acquired by the grown-up sons who planned homes of their own. Before taking a claim the settler had to have four hundred dollars for buildings, farm implements and stock and for the support of the family until the first harvest was gathered. Each settler paid a fee of five dollars for every quarter section to help finance the colonization company. In a short time forty farms were under cultivation near De Graff.

This was the beginning of the extensive and successful colonization movement in Minnesota which brought hundreds of Irish, French, German and Polish farmers to the State, and Bishop Ireland became noted as a colonizer as well as a leader of the total abstinence crusade which made its influence felt in the colony. An official of the United States Land Office in Litchfield bore testimony to "the intelligence, integrity and good order manifested by the colonists in their business relations with the office"; and he could recall no instance in which one under the influence of liquor had been in the office.

Before the end of the year there were churches in De Graff and Clontarf, centers of prosperous settlements, where more land could be had at reasonable prices. The cost of developing the colony, though considerable, had been met by the fees paid by the farmers and the sale of choice sections at increased prices.

Notwithstanding the success of his initial experiment Bishop Ireland had not escaped criticism. With all the advantages that are offered to our colonists, he wrote to the Freeman's Journal as early as April 6, 1876,

> I am sure that before the first year will be over, not a few of them will have severely censured me for having invited them to Minnesota. Nevertheless, with the certainty of this censuring before me, I do not hesitate to call to our Minnesota prairies those who have no permanent homes, and who are relying for their support on their daily toil in the service of others. The future will reward me; after two years all those who will come, if they are sober and industrious people, will bless me for having been instrumental in getting them homes on the land. It is their children, however, yet more than themselves, that will be benefited most plentifully. God's church, too, will reap her harvest out of this colonization movement. She will have her share of this vast and fertile country, upon which, otherwise, her standard would not have been planted.

The chartered Land Stock Company proved its worth by aiding poor but industrious settlers to obtain farms, implements and stock on which it held a lien until the borrower paid in full and obtained a clear title to his holdings. The funds for this purpose were provided by the sale of shares in the company at ten dollars each.

In the meantime settlers continued to flock to the Swift County colony and soon there were several hundred families from all parts of the United States. On the question of immigration the State Convention of the Total Abstinence Union declared: "We can point with pride to one such noble effort fully carried out and now in successful operation, namely, the colony of the Right Reverend Bishop Ireland".

Catholic colonization in Minnesota was no longer an experiment. The encouraging success of the De Graff colony induced Bishop Ireland to secure seventy thousand acres of railroad land in Nobles County near Adrian where the Reverend C. J. Knauf was pastor, and offer it to Catholic settlers. Before the end of 1878 twenty-two thousand acres had been sold to immigrants and as much more to private parties. A church and a school had been built and the pastor was kept busy answering enquiries from Irish and German Catholics in the East. In May, 1880, only two farms were unsold and two years later Father Knauf had a congregation of two hundred and fifty families.

In 1878 Bishop Ireland bought eighty acres as a townsite for a new colony in Graceville[24] named after Bishop Grace. A temporary church was built by Reverend T. Ryan and during the first three months of 1879 the Bureau located one hundred and seventy-five families, many of them from southern Minnesota and Iowa, within a radius of six miles from the village. A more substantial church was erected by Reverend A. V. Pelisson. Bishop Ireland contracted for an additional fifty thousand acres of railroad land and placed one hundred families on it the first year. By 1880 there were four hundred families in the parish, fifty of whom had come from Minneapolis.

A tragic incident[25] threatened for a time the future not only of the Graceville colony but of the movement itself. Through the friendly intervention of Monsignor Nugent of Liverpool three hundred and nine destitute people from the wilds of Galway were sent to his friend, Bishop Ireland, who had promised to provide for "several families" and had collected two thousand dollars to aid them. For that purpose fifty farms had been set aside in Graceville. When they arrived in St. Paul in July, 1880, thirty families were sent to Graceville and provided with homes, equipment and supplies for two years. The rest of the group found work in the city. The new colonists had been fishermen all their lives and knew nothing about farming, nor did they want to learn. Their improvidence aroused the ire of their neighbors and alienated the sympathy with which they had been welcomed. The new-comers were shiftless medicants who expected to be supported by Bishop Ireland and his agents. The winter was unusually severe and, notwithstanding the generous provision made for them, the report was spread abroad by malicious tongues anxious to see the colony fail, that they were starving and freezing. When the inspectors came to verify their claims they hid the food and clothing furnished them and proclaimed they had been victimized. When the Pioneer Press of St. Paul published the true story sympathy for them rapidly evaporated. Most of them were finally transported to St. Paul where they settled in what came to be known as the "Connemara Patch" in St. Mary's parish under Dayton's Bluff. The few who remained in the colony became successful and prosperous farmers. The Connemaras were far from typical of the regular colonists;[26] and, ultimately, no harm came to the colony which in 1881 had four hundred families bravely and hopefully advancing to independence.

Another colony was opened in Murray County where the town of Avoca[27] was platted in 1878 and fifty thousand acres of unsurpassed farming land made available to settlers. The Reverend C. Robert was put in charge of the parish. At Fulda another colony was located and a third near Iona where Reverend M. McDonnell of Batavia, N. Y., bought five thousand acres as a site for the Sacred Heart Home for destitute children and had an agricultural farm for its support.

John Sweetman, a wealthy Irishman, purchased twenty-five thousand acres in the vicinity of Currie in 1881 and colonized it with seventy families.[28] He revisited Ireland and returned with more settlers. He set apart ten acres for a church which he built at a cost of $10,000. It was placed in charge of Reverend Joseph O'Keefe and was dedicated by Bishop Ireland on September 23, 1883. The land sold at an average of six dollars an acre, of which one-tenth was paid in cash and the balance secured by note with interest at six percent. Title was given when the note was paid.

In July, 1879, the Colonization Bureau opened 45,000 acres of fine farming land in the vicinity of Minneota in Lyon County[29] to purchasers at from five to six dollars an acre. The first settlers came in the spring of 1880. The Reverend M. J. Hawley was resident pastor.

Later in that year Canon Van Hee, a Belgian priest of the Diocese of Liverpool, and his brother, Angelus, secured land for a Belgian colony near Grand View (Ghent) six miles east of Minneota, and a group of Flemish farmers came in the spring of 1881 and were followed, in 1883, by Hollanders and Germans and a sprinkling of Canadians under the spiritual direction of Reverend Jule E. DeVos. During the next year churches were built in Minneota and Ghent.

The example of Bishop Ireland and the success of his colonization program induced other members of the hierarchy to take a practical interest in the work. A meeting was held in Chicago on March 17, 1879, for the purpose of putting the movement on a national basis. Bishop Ireland and nineteen delegates from Minnesota and representatives of most of the Catholic societies of the United States organized "The Irish Catholic Colonization Association of America" to assist worthy people of limited means to secure homes on the land. It was a stock company with a capital of $100,000 divided into shares of one hundred dollars each. Bishop Spalding of Peoria was elected President; Anthony Kelly of Minneapolis, Vice-President; W. J. Onahan of Chicago, Secretary; W. J. Quan of Chicago, Treasurer; and an executive board of seven Bishops and seven laymen whose duty it was to devise ways and means to locate Catholic colonies in the western states. At the meeting $10,000 was subscribed and an additional $14,000 in the evening after addresses by Bishops Spalding, Ireland and O'Connor (of Nebraska), John Boyle O'Reilly of Boston, Reverend D. J. Riordan of Chicago and General Lawler of Prairie du Chien. The Association was incorporated under the laws of the State of Illinois and began at once to negotiate for the purchase of lands in Nobles County, Minnesota, and Greely County, Nebraska, and many applications were received from prospective buyers.

Early in the next year Bishops Spalding, Ireland and O'Connor visited many of the eastern cities in the interest of the Association whose capital stock had not been fully subscribed and brought the total sales to about $80,000. They delivered lectures urging Irish Catholics and others to migrate to the West and take up farming in Minnesota and Nebraska where cheap fertile lands were still available. They maintained that in five years it would be very difficult to find sufficient land for a colony in the West.

In March of that year Bishop Ireland wrote Archbishop Gibbons: "The colonization movement, so far seems to be a success . . . due to the countenance the movement received from the foremost members of the hierarchy to whom we are under many obligations".

In a letter,[30] dated August 31, 1880, Bishop Ireland, writing to an unnamed correspondent in behalf of "The Irish Catholic Colonization Association of America", asked for the reservation of "a portion of your lands" for new settlers. He stated that he had been working single-handed for four years in the field of colonization, and during that time had control of 110,000 acres of land in Swift County; 50,000 in Big Stone and Traverse; 75,000 in Nobles; 60,000 in Murray; 45,000 in Lyon; and had settled, either on government or railroad land, 800 families in Swift County, 400 in Big Stone and Traverse, 300 in Nobles, 200 in Murray, and 70 in Lyon where he had begun to operate only very lately. What he had done single-handed the national organization should be capable of doing tenfold, as it numbered among its directors Cardinal Gibbons of Baltimore, several members of the hierarchy, and prominent lay men of the standing of John Lawler of Prairie du Chien and Anthony Kelly of Minneapolis. Only last spring it had opened a colony in Nebraska and its success has been very great.

A few years later Peter Leary who was in Minnesota in 1885 told a gathering of temperance men in London that he had visited the colonies of Bishop Ireland in which "not a sup of drink was sold". These colonies did not consist entirely of people from Ireland but of Irishmen from the cities of the Atlantic seaboard who bought farms of one hundred and sixty acres and were now comfortable and happy. He had never seen anywhere "so much intelligence, so much energy, or so much real happiness" as he saw in these sober Irish colonies of Minnesota and all because drink was prohibited by law.

Bishop Ireland maintained a deep, personal interest in the work of colonization in Minnesota and beyond its borders for a score of years until the administrative burden of the diocese made such constant and insistent demands on his time and energy that he was obliged to withdraw from actual participation in the planning and directing of its policies. New problems were clamoring for solution and, as immigration had apparently reached its zenith and would continue of its own momentum, he felt that the objective had been attained and he could devote his attention to more pressing concerns.

That his interest in the work never flagged was evidenced by his presence at the Northwestern Immigration Convention in St. Paul on November 19, 1895, when he delivered a forceful address on the agricultural and mineral resources of the State, and suggested the formation of a permanent organization to furnish information to prospective immigrants from Europe in search of homes for themselves and families. He attended a similar meeting in July of the next year at Dawson where he pictured the independence of the farming population and declared it a mistake for young people to flock to the cities in search of the competence offered them by the rural areas. No state in the Union, he said, offers greater opportunities to immigrants than Minnesota.

Nine Busy Years

The nine years of Bishop Ireland's coadjutorship were busy ones for him. More and more of the administrative work of the diocese fell to his lot. He was busy with confirmations, church dedications and other religious functions. His reputation as a preacher spread far and wide. In the Cathedral he occupied the pulpit on the first Sunday of the month, on special occasions and usually gave a series of lectures during the lenten season and at other times when circumstances seemed to demand them, which were heard by large congregations among whom were many non-Catholics attracted not only by the eloquence and impressiveness with which he delivered his message, but by the cogent reasoning and substantial content of his sermons. These discourses were published in the Northwestern Chronicle and were often gathered into pamphlets which enjoyed large circulation. His work for temperance brought him nationwide recognition and his leadership in Catholic colonization made him known beyond the Atlantic.

On August 11, 1876, he made an official visit to Yankton[31] in the Dakota Territory where he said Mass in the courthouse for several days, administered confirmation to forty persons, and completed arrangements for the building of a church in a central location. Before he left twelve hundred dollars were subscribed for the new project.

He had been a member of the Minnesota Historical Society for many years and had taken a personal interest in its work. He was anxious to cooperate with it in gathering into its archives the records of the founders of the Catholic Church in Minnesota and, as early as November 11, 1867, presented to the Society a handsomely-framed photograph of Bishop

Cretin[32] that had been tinted by Falkensheid; and five years later an enlargement of a small but clear ambrotype of Father Galtier found in possession of a family in Prairie du Chien. The enlargement was made by an artist named Hyde and paid for by Father Ireland and Charles Williams, secretary of the Historical Society. These pictures are the ones with which we are familiar from reproductions. In January of the next year (1877) he was elected President of the society for one year but during his long life retained membership and interest in it.

On February 22 of that year he celebrated a Pontifical Mass of Requiem for Bishop Cretin on the twentieth anniversary of his death and during the lenten season preached a series of sermons on "The Church and History" in the Cathedral.

The Catholic Standard and Times of Philadelphia announced on December 24, 1881, that

> steps have been taken to engage the Academy of Music for Bishop Ireland who will come from Minnesota next April to lecture for the Archdiocesan Union. Bishop Ireland is one of the leaders of our movement—bold, popular and eloquent. He knows how to stir up the hearts of the people. He is a bright star among the Catholic hierarchy of the world and our Union may well be proud of him.

Throughout his life Bishop Ireland cherished a profound admiration and veneration for the pioneers of whom he may not inaptly be regarded as one of the most distinguished. At a complimentary banquet tendered Governor Hubbard on January 9, 1882, the Bishop, responding to the toast, "The Early Pioneers of Minnesota", said, among other things:[33]

> It is but two centuries ago since the man who was to bear to civilization the first tidings of the existence of the Northwest painfully urged his canoe up the waters of the Mississippi, and for nearly a century and a half after Hennepin's discovery, this land remained still in the undisputed possession of the buffalo and the Indian. Only in 1819 was the United States flag unfurled in Minnesota to protect the forerunners of commerce upon her plains; only in 1841 was the corner block laid in the construction of the humble chapel which was to lend its name to the future metropolis; only in 1848 was a civil government accorded to Minnesota, when Minnesota's name was first mentioned in the halls of Congress. . .
> Father Hennepin after his return to Europe, wrote, 'There are scarcely any countries in the world more fertile. Nothing is wanting that is necessary for life. It can be thus judged how easy it is to found great colonies there' . . . The messengers of the Gospel, outstripping in their daring for Christ's sake the endurance and courage of the trader in his search for the spoils of commerce, were not unworthy followers of the Apostle of the golden era of the Church.

In May, 1882, the Northwestern Chronicle published "The Apostolic Church", a brochure containing a series of lectures on the Church and one on Divorce, preached by the Bishop in the Cathedral during the previous Lent. Referring to it the Ave Maria said: "As far as we know

'The Apostolic Church' is his first venture in a literary way, but we trust most sincerely that it will not be his last". It goes on to say, "Than Bishop Ireland few, if any, of our bishops have a wider reputation as an advocate of temperance and Catholic colonization. He has made a name for himself that will not soon be forgotten". Two years later his lecture on "Culture and Progress" was included in a series of addresses and essays by prominent orators and writers in "Questions of the Hour" published by Hickey and Company of New York.

On June 1, 1882, Governor Hubbard reappointed him[34] Colonel and Chaplain-General of the Minnesota National Guard as a token of the high esteem in which he was held by the Governor personally, and as a prominent representative of the Catholic Church, whose record as a Chaplain in the Civil War was characterized by unusual bravery in the face of danger and most devoted loyalty to the Republic. The appointment was renewed on January 31, 1884.

On October 24, 1882, the Bishop preached at the solemn consecration [35] of the recently-completed Abbey Church of St. John, Collegeville, commemorating the twenty-fifth anniversary of the arrival of the Benedictine Fathers in Minnesota. The church is a brick structure in Romanesque style, 150 by 146 by 62 feet in size, with two towers and a sanctuary ample enough for all liturgical ceremonies. The church and the main altar were consecrated by Bishop Seidenbusch of St. Cloud, who also sang Pontifical Mass, with Reverend Othmar Erren, O. S. B., deacon, Reverend Clement V. Gamache, subdeacon and Reverend Alfred Meyer, O. S. B., master of ceremonies. The Pieta altar of the dead Christ was consecrated by Abbot Innocent of Atchinson, Kansas, and the altar of St. Benedict by Abbot Boniface of St. Vincent's, Pa. A sermon in German was preached by Dr. Zardetti of St. Francis Seminary, Milwaukee. Bishop Grace was among the prelates in attendance.

An interesting story, illustrative of Bishop Ireland's ability to withstand hardship and fatigue and make the best of a trying situation,[36] is told by his friend, Monsignor Nugent of Liverpool, who with him and Coadjutor Bishop Ryan of St. Louis, had to pass a night in a small railway station in a country town waiting for an early morning train. Bishop Ryan and Monsignor Nugent sat up all night as uprightly in their dignity as drowsiness and fatigue would permit. Bishop Ireland "took a quick survey of the accommodations, buttoned his coat up to his throat, flung his gripsack into a corner, and without further preliminary, stretched upon the floor and went soundly to sleep on his improvised pillow. In the morning he started to his feet, gave a sweeping stretch to his tall, active frame, drew his hands rapidly over his eyes and was fully prepared and refreshed for a new day's labor". He had learned how to take the bitter with the sweet during the Civil War.

As Chaplain-General of the Minnesota National Guard Bishop Ireland preached at a field Mass celebrated by Father McGolrick at Camp Hubbard, White Bear Lake, Minnesota, on Sunday, July 16, 1882. Referring to the army he said:

> Here honor and duty reign supreme. Rebellion and insubordination are unknown. . . .Self-denial is inculcated and practiced in submission to law and order. . . .The army is the home and school of patriotism. . . .Love of country, warm and disinterested, is the soul of civil society. I recall these principles because on them is based the necessity for religion. . . Religion imperiously demands the allegiance of every man.[37]

The altar was decked in military style with United States flags encircling it in graceful festoons, swords and bayonets massed on both sides of the crucifix, with Irish and American flags for the background. Governor Hubbard, Commander-in-Chief of the National Guard with his staff was on the gospel side and the officers of the companies present in camp on the epistle side. At the gospel the artillery presented arms and also at the elevation, cannon pealed and another salute was fired when the Bishop gave the blessing.

The Bishop preached at the conferring of the Pallium on Archbishop Heiss of Milwaukee on April 23, 1882, and the Milwaukee Sentinel of the following day said that the sermon was long, the house large, and the speaking difficult, but he succeeded in making himself heard throughout the Cathedral as he traced the origin of the Pallium to St. Peter and discussed at great length the nature, organization and functions of the Church.

At the end of the year 1882[38] the Diocese of St. Paul had 172 churches, and 55 stations ministered to by 99 diocesan and 26 regular priests. Nine of the parishes were in St. Paul and six in Minneapolis. There were six religious communities of men and twelve of women, one hospital, five orphanages and protectories and a Catholic population of 125,000. On July 5 of the next year the Diocese as incorporated with Bishop Grace, Father Ravoux (Vicar General), Father Shanley (Chancellor), Bishop Ireland and Father Koeberl as incorporators and members of the Board of Directors, under and pursuant to the provisions of chapter 34, title 4, of the general statutes of Minnesota. The document was witnessed by Thomas D. O'Brien and D. A. Reilly.

Bishop Ireland and Bishop Chatard of Indianapolis were co-consecrators when the Right Reverend Patrick W. Riordan was elevated to the episcopal dignity as Coadjutor to the Archbishop of San Francisco by the Most Reverend Archbishop Feehan in St. James Church, Chicago, on September 14, 1883. The ceremony was attended by 12 bishops and 100 priests and the sermon was preached by Bishop Spalding of Peoria.

On February 28, 1884, he recommended the Reverend J. A. Stephan

THE FIRST ARCHBISHOP OF ST. PAUL

of Jamestown, North Dakota, for Director of the Bureau of Catholic
Indian Missions, instituted by the Third Plenary Council of Baltimore,
in succession to Father Brouillet because "he is well acquainted with
the best workings of the Bureau, has lived for several years among the
Indians and has the advantage of knowing personally several of the officials in Washington",[39] and he was appointed to the position by Cardinal
Gibbons.

One of his last official acts as Coadjutor Bishop was the consecration[40]
of the Church of St. Mary, Stillwater, then as now in charge of the Benedictine Fathers, on July 20, 1884. It was the third church in Minnesota
to be so honored, the others being the Church of St. Joseph, St. Joseph,
and the Church of the Assumption, St. Paul.

Bishop of St. Paul

The resignation of Bishop Grace on July 31, 1884, after a quarter of a
century of active administration of the spiritual and temporal affairs of
the Diocese of St. Paul, placed the youthful and energetic coadjutor on
the throne of authority and opened up to him a wider field of activity,
one offering greater scope for the unusual intellectual and administrative
ability with which he was dowered. It marked the beginning of a career
of exceptional service to Holy Mother Church in the diocese and
throughout the country and ultimately gave him an international reputation as a churchman and statesman of commanding power, ability and
prestige.

It may not be out of place to reproduce the highlights of a contemporary's pen-picture[41] of the youthful Bishop of St. Paul at the threshold
of his administrative career.

> No man in the Northwest has filled up the measure of his usefulness so
> completely and so grandly as Bishop Ireland. No name in history will glow
> with greater halo and warmth for good acts conceived, performed and
> reiterated than that of him who, coming from the ranks of the poor and
> lowly, has ever sought to elevate his own nationality and, through it,
> the whole world. Dealing with the material as well as the spiritual
> elements of our existence, he reached down into the great heart of human-
> ity and induced thousands to climb the ladder of respectability, healed
> many a broken heart and dried many a tear of sorrow. Like his Master
> he goes among publicans and sinners, seeking the purification of the inner
> man, pointing out the path that leads to temperance, prosperity and
> happiness, raising the fallen, encouraging the weak, and guiding the
> footsteps of the faltering. No man has such a strong hold on the affections
> of his people as he has, and no living bishop of any denomination has
> done more towards the advancement of the whole human family.
> The Irish citizens of St. Paul, once the hewers of wood and the drawers
> of water, are now among the most wealthy, honored and respected mem-
> bers of the community because of the influence and persistent efforts of

Bishop Ireland which, however, have not been exerted exclusively for his own people but for all classes of citizens, for he will unite cheerfully with ministers of any denomination to effect a lasting public good.

He was the very first to make the colonization movement in this state successful and practical by establishing three settlements of Irish farmers all of whom are prospering. No spirituous liquors of any kind can be sold on the lands they occupy. His consistent and unwearying efforts in favor of temperance has won for him the highest regard and respect not only of his own people but of a large class of American men and women who differ with him in their theological views.

Bishop Ireland is tall, slender, intellectual-looking, with sharp features and a bright, expressive face, giving one the impression of an active business man. As a public speaker he is clear, concise, logical, argumentative and eloquent; as a bishop he is devoted to his church, but tolerant, fair and dignified; as a citizen he is public-spirited and wide-awake to the interests of his adopted city; as a man, possessing all the essential elements of true manhood, Bishop Ireland has no peer.

The months that followed his accession to the see of St. Paul were busy ones. His first act was to appoint the Reverend James C. Byrne, ordained in Rome in 1883, and assistant at the Church of the Immaculate Conception, Minneapolis, to the position of Secretary where he remained until he was named pastor of that church in 1890 in succession to Bishop McGolrick and made its first and only irremovable rector.

On August 29, 1884, he dedicated the first church as Bishop of the Diocese, that of St. Francis de Sales in St. Paul, built by Father Stariha at a cost of $13,000, a brick structure, 135 by 54 feet in dimensions, with a front tower and steeple rising to a height of 130 feet. The festive sermon was preached in German by Father Plut of Shakopee, and at the close of the ceremony the Bishop spoke in a complimetary vein of the fine work done by the pastor who had also built a rectory and a school at a cost of $4,500.

In the afternoon of the same day he dedicated the Holy Rosary school in Minneapolis in charge of the Fathers of St. Dominic. In the course of his sermon he said: "Secular instruction is good as far as it goes, but it does not go far enough. The fact that it stops short of religion excludes the thought of the life to come".

The German Benevolent Catholic Societies of the United States met in National Convention in St. Paul and at the opening Mass in the Cathedral on September 5, 1884, the Bishop delivered the sermon in the course of which he said:

Our non-Catholic fellow-citizens are generous and liberal in their bearing towards the Church. There is in Minnesota no bigotry, no unfair discrimination. It is a Minnesota legislature that first placed on the statute books a liberty of conscience bill which honors beyond all words the North Star State and puts her in the front rank of freedom-loving and freedom-giving communities.

The Catholic Directory for 1884 gives the diocese a Catholic population of 130,000 which was far too small in view of the birth rate in the State. In 1883 there were 6,450 infant baptisms in the diocese which, multiplied by 32.5, the ratio of births to population, gives 209,625. On this reckoning the Catholic population was not less than 200,000.

At the annual gathering of the Army of Tennessee at the Hotel Lafayette, Lake Minnetonka, on August 14, 1884, Bishop Ireland was assigned the toast "The Golden Northwest" and, replying thereto, said, according to the Northwestern Chronicle for August 28, 1884:

> I speak unselfishly in my praises of our warriors. I am not one of them. I never drew a sword, or ordered a charge for the salvation of the country. Often, it is true, on tented fields, I cheered by soothing words, the tired soldier and in religion's name, I pointed towards heaven where he should see the reward of duty loyally performed and of sacrifice patiently suffered. I belonged to the peaceful and peace-loving wing of the army, the non-combatants. But slight as must have been the military honor attaching to the office of chaplain, it has ever since been a cause of pride to me that even to that slight extent did I participate in the labors and victories of the great war. . .
>
> The United States is today the powerful nation, whose sons surpass in liberty, in wealth, in social happiness, men of all other climes, whose mandate the first principalities of Europe receive in an obedient spirit because, from the Atlantic to the Pacific, from source to mouth of our giant river, along iron-paved highways, nearly 4000 miles in length the one flag flutters to the breeze intact and unsullied—the immortal Stars and Stripes.

Attendance at Councils

The Third Plenary Council of Baltimore opened November 9, 1884. Among the prelates in attendance were Bishops Grace and Ireland accompanied by Fathers Trobec and McGolrick. Bishop Ireland preached in the Baltimore Cathedral on Monday evening, November 10, on "The Catholic Church and Civil Society". It was a telling exposition of the teachings of the Catholic Church and of the facts of her history in their relation to social authority and to civil and political liberty.

> The Catholic Church commands and consecrates patriotism. The true Catholic must needs be the true patriot. In the eyes of the Church loyalty to country is loyalty to God; patriotism is a heavenly virtue, a high and holy form of obedience; the patriot dying for his country wears the halo of the martyr. . .The most valued aid given to the Republic by the Church is not her direct enunciations on liberty, but her powerful labors in the cause of religion, of purity, of honesty, of all the heavenly virtues that build up the Christian man and the Christian family.[42]

The Council was a very important event in the history of the Church in America. It was attended by seventy archbishops and bishops, as compared with the forty who were present at the Second Plenary Council. "Each of the prelates present represents a center of religious activity and of widening influence", said the Baltimore American, and

> from this it is manifest that the Catholic Church is sinking its roots deeper

and deeper into the soil of American civilization. The present Plenary Council is a living testimony of its truth.

Two days after the Council closed, December 9, 1884, Bishop Ireland and a group of men, chief among whom were John Gilmary Shea, Richard H. Clarke, Charles G. Hebermann, the Reverends James H. McGean and R. L. Burtsell, met in the Catholic Protectory, New York, and founded the United States Catholic Historical Society[43] to collect and preserve historical material relating to the origin, growth and development of the Catholic Church in the United States, to publish essays, documents and rare books relating to the above and maintain a historical library and museum.

The Catholic Directory for 1884, the year Bishop Ireland assumed charge of the diocese, gives the following statistics of priests, institutions and religious communities under his jurisdiction. There were 147 priests of whom 119 were diocesan and 28 regular; 195 churches and 51 stations; 29 seminarians; 6 religious communities of men and 14 of women; 2 hospitals, 5 asylums and protectories; 10 academies and boarding schools for young women; 7 St. Vincent de Paul Conferences; Total Abstinence societies, Rosary societies, sodalities and confraternities of the Sacred Heart in nearly all parishes and a Catholic population of 130,000. At that time the diocese comprised the southern part of the state below Chisago, Isanti, Sherburne, Stearns, Pope, Stevens, and Traverse Counties, an area of 27,515 square miles. When the Diocese of Winona was erected in 1889 it reduced the area to 15,233 square miles, with 114 diocesan and 27 regular priests; 95 churches and 60 missions; 1 theological seminary with 120 students; 2 hospitals; 3 orphanages with 210 inmates; 1 industrial school; 64 parochial schools with an attendance of 1100 pupils. The previous year there had been in the Archdiocese, as it was then called, 7,670 baptisms, 1,517 marriages and 2,467 deaths.

On July 1, 1885, Bishop Ireland officiated at the dedication of the new Ryan Hotel on Robert Street at Sixth, the most modern in the Northwest, and delivered an address. It is still one of the leading hotels of St. Paul.

The first Provincial Council to promulgate, explain and adjust to the needs of its component dioceses the laws framed and adopted by the Third Plenary Council of Baltimore, was that of Milwaukee which opened in St. John's Cathedral on Sunday, May 23, 1886,[44] and continued in session one week. It was attended by the Metropolitan and the bishops of the suffragan dioceses, seven in all, from Northern Michigan, Wisconsin, Minnesota, and the Dakotas, representing 800 priests and 500,000 Catholis. Archbishop Heiss was the celebrant of the Pontifical Mass and Bishop Ireland preached on "Councils in General and the Present Council". In addition to Bishop Ireland the Diocese of St. Paul was represented by Bishop Grace, Fathers Shanley and Plut as theologians, Father O'Gorman, President of St. Thomas Seminary, and the Abbots and heads of all the religious orders in the Province. On Tuesday evening Father O'Gorman preached on "The Unity of the Church".

During the sessions the bishops met and discussed ecclesiastical matters for the Province and decided to issue a Pastoral Letter dealing with the sanctification of the individual; the Christian education of children; the new catechism; the training of lay teachers to supplement the work of the religious; the formation of sodalities for youths; Catholic newspapers; capital and labor; and the education of the clergy.

Bishop Ireland read an address to Archbishop Heiss in which he said:[45]

> We have put the Church before our people as the great moral force in the land, the home of divine authority and filial obedience, the strength and salvation of the social order. Our deliberations have been free, friendly, prompted by zeal and love. Our decrees, as far as human sight can go, have been wise and prudent.

Rome, France and Ireland

While in Rome in connection with the founding of the Catholic University of America Bishop Ireland commemorated the twenty-fifth anniversary[46] of his ordination on December 21, 1886, in the American College where he celebrated Pontifical Mass and was honored with a literary and musical program by the faculty and student body. A congratulatory address was read by one of the students and poems in Latin, English, German, French and Italian, to all of which he responded in an address expressive of appreciation for the honor shown him. Why did he always celebrate the anniversary of his ordination on December 21st instead of the 22nd? Was it because his predecessors Bishops Cretin and Grace were ordained on December 21?

Pope Leo XIII signalized the occasion by sending a special Apostolic Blessing through Monsignor Della Volpe, Master of the Chamber to His Holiness. It was rumored that the jubilarian would soon be made an Archbishop. He was in Rome for the Consistory at which Archbishops Gibbons of Baltimore and Taschereau of Quebec were given the Red Hats on March 10, 1887. They had been created Cardinals on June 7 of the previous year.

While the Bishop was in Rome his father died in St. Paul on March 18, 1887, after an illness of many months and was buried from the Cathedral three days later. He was notified immediately and is said to have sent the laconic but significant cablegram: "No wake". Father Howard of Alton, Illinois, a nephew of the deceased, sang the Solemn Requiem with Fathers Danehy and Fitzpatrick as deacon and subdeacon and Father Gibbons master of ceremonies. The sermon was preached by Father McGolrick. Richard Ireland was born in Kilkenny in 1805 and took up his residence in St. Paul in 1852. The Bishop's mother died on March 27, 1895, at the age of eighty-seven.

While awaiting in Rome the arrival of Cardinal Gibbons to complete the negotiations for the launching of the Catholic University, Bishop Ireland paid a visit to Montluel[47] in France, the birthplace of Bishop Cretin. On February 20 he preached in French in the Church of Notre Dame in that city, describing the flourishing condition of the Church in America and especially in St. Paul, paying tribute to Bishop Cretin and his labors for the good of religion in the diocese of which he was the first bishop, and appealing to the faith and patriotism of his hearers to be loyal to their religious convictions. In the afternoon he presided at a meeting of the Children of Mary and, in response to an address, urged them to reproduce in themselves the life and virtues of the Blessed Mother. He also visited the parish cemetery and prayed at the tombs of the Cretin family.

The next day he was the guest of the pastor, l'Abbe W. Caron, who invited twenty priests who knew John Ireland in seminary days at Meximieux. The pastor welcomed him in a felicitous address to which the Bishop responded with warmth, thanking him and his friends for the honor paid him and the opportunity of renewing acquaintance with friends of his seminary days.

He returned to Rome and on March 18 was received in farewell audience by His Holiness and the next week left the Eternal City on his homeward journey.

Before doing so, however, he prepared a paper on emigration in general and Italian emigration[48] in particular to assist the Propaganda in studying the problem in regard to Italy. "The Italian Emigration Society" had already been organized along the lines of the St. Raphael Society in Germany, with the Bishop of Piacenza as President. It proposed to have a priest residing at each port of embarcation to assist emigrants, and one in New York, probably at Castle Garden, to meet and welcome them on arrival in the New World.

On the return journey to America Bishop Ireland spent some time in his native land with his friend, Monsignor Nugent of Liverpool. He lectured in Dublin, visited Maynooth College where he found that 350 of its 480 students were total abstainers, preached in the Redemptorist Church in Limerick, was presented with an address from the Central Council of the League of the Cross in Cork where he lectured on "The Irish in America", and sailed from Queenstown on Sunday, May 1, for New York.

Events at Home

In an interview[49] given the press on landing he said that the project of a Catholic University for America had received the cordial approval of the Pope and that Bishop Keane of Richmond, still in Rome, would be the first Rector of the institution.

In regard to the Knights of Labor, in whose behalf he had protested against their condemnation, he said:

> It is decided in Rome that the Knights are not to be condemned, and all censures against them, such as those formerly existing in Canada, have been withdrawn. But the action is negative. No positive approval was asked for or will be given and, of course, should the Knights in future do anything as a society contrary to the rules of natural justice or the laws of the Church, they will be liable to condemnation. Furthermore, the Church implicitly recognizes the right of the laboring classes to organize for the legitimate protection of their rights.

He was pleased, likewise, with the brief of Pope Leo XIII on Total Abstinence which caused a sensation in England, Ireland and on the continent.

His arrival was eagerly awaited in St. Paul and when he landed in the depot on May 14, he was greeted by Bishop Grace and a delegation of priests and laymen but, at his own request, there was no formal reception. When he reached the Cathedral residence he was presented with a new carriage and a span of spirited horses as a "trifling testimonial", following an address by John D. O'Brien on behalf of his host of friends.

The next day, Sunday, at the High Mass, preceded by a Te Deum, he occupied the throne and beside him was Monsignor Ravoux in his newly-donned robes of a Domestic Prelate of the Papal Household. In his sermon the Bishop gave expression to his sentiments of joy and gratitude for a safe return to his beloved St. Paul in comparison with which no place he had visited was so beautiful, no church grander than the Cathedral, no river more majestic than the Mississippi. He had visited Rome and the Pope who expressed abiding interest in the Church in America and blessed the Total Abstinence movement. He spoke of the Catholic University soon to be opened in Washington with the approval of the Holy Father, and of the Knights of Labor whose threatened condemnation had been averted largely through its own efforts though he did not say so.

In the afternoon he drove to St. Thomas Seminary with Bishop Grace and Monsignor Ravoux for a visit with the faculty and students. After supper he was welcomed with addresses in English, French, German, Polish, Slavonic, Bohemian and Latin and an informal program of musical numbers. In his response to the enthusiastic greetings of the students he assured them that he had thought of them and the seminary during his trip abroad and had purchased "many thousand valuable books" for its library.

In September, 1887, he was elected Vice-President of the National Conference of Correction and Charities at its annual convention in Omaha the first week of the month.

In August, 1888, Archbishop Ireland preached at the Golden Jubilee[50] of ordination of the Very Reverend Edward Sorin, C. S. C., founder of Notre Dame University at South Bend, Indiana, and Superior General of the Congregation of the Holy Cross. Father Sorin had been a chaplain in the Civil War and won golden opinions from all for his bravery and patriotism, to both of which the Archbishop paid tribute in his sermon, and made the following touching and impressive reference to the beauty and efficacy of devotion to the Mother of God, as cultivated by the Jubilarian.

> He loved Her with childlike simplicity and ardor; all his projects were brought to Her altar to be blessed by Her, before he sought to put them into execution. His efforts were unceasing to obtain that others love Her and commend themselves to Her intercession. Need we wonder at the success of his labors with this powerful Protectress praying for him? How much he has done to extend through the country this sweet devotion to Mary, I need not lose time in telling. Mary's Journal, the 'Ave Maria', weekly goes from Notre Dame to scores of thousands of Christian homes, and hundreds of practices of piety are made common that otherwise would not be known, and ten thousand acts of love are uttered that Heaven otherwise would not have heard. Of course, in the hurry of our American life, in the manifold labors which we are called to undertake in the service of souls, the danger is lurking nigh that the interior life be forgotten and we become as sounding brass. A most effective remedy is devotion to Mary, with all its supernal fragrance, and all its sweet inspirations to piety and holiness.

On September 6, with Postmaster General Dickinson and Congressman McDonald, the Archbishop paid a visit to the Capitol in Washington and, although visitors are not permitted on the floor of the House of Representatives during debate, he was admitted and greeted with great cordiality by the members and granted the privileges of the chamber, notwithstanding the rule.

The Knights of Labor

Archbishop Ireland played a very important role in averting the condemnation of the Knights of Labor,[51] an organization of working men founded in 1869 by Ulrick S. Stephens, a member of the Masonic order, who gave it a ritualistic initiation, oath-bound secrecy, grips, passwords, signs and symbols. It had for object to bind working men into a compact union to protect and enhance their rights against "big business" determined to hold them in subjection and bondage through low wages, long working hours and poor housing conditions. It grew slowly at first but reached the zenith of its numerical strength and influence about the middle eighties of last century as a fraternal organization of laboring men under the leadership of Terence V. Powderly, its President from 1879 till 1891. Powderly was a practical Catholic and, when he joined the Knights in 1876, was well aware of the attitude of the Church towards secret societies and anxious that the organization should not continue under her ban. From the beginning of his term of office he labored to eliminate the oath of secrecy and finally succeeded in 1882. But the other Masonic aspects of the ritual remained and the Church continued to regard the Knights with suspicion. The membership rose to nearly 700,000 in 1886 of whom about one-tenth were Catholics. Many of the bishops were opposed to it because of the veil of secrecy which enshrouded its activities and because of its alleged radical character. Bishop O'Hara of Scranton, of which Powderly was Mayor for three terms largely because of the support of the Molly McGuires, condemned the Knights and efforts were made to deter Catholics from joining their ranks.

In Canada Archbishop Taschereau of Quebec took action against them in 1883 when he referred the matter to Rome and, acting on the replies received from the Holy See, brought about their condemnation in 1886, and Catholics were forbidden to seek or hold membership.

> On account of the principles, organization and statutes of the Knights of Labor Association, that association is to be relegated among those which are prohibited by the Holy See, in accordance with the instruction of the Supreme Congregation, given on 10th of May, 1884.[52]

Cardinals Manning in England and Gibbons in the United States felt that the condemnation was injudicious and would militate against the Catholic Church by presenting her before the world as the "friend of the powerful rich and the enemy of the helpless poor"; and the latter consulted with President Powderly and asked him to appear at a meeting of the Archbishops in October, 1886, and tell them exactly in what the obligation of secrecy consisted. He readily agreed to do this, presented the ritual and assured the prelates that a mere pledge of secrecy and not an oath was enjoined upon the members; that the secrecy had for object to protect their business from enemies and did not interfere in any way with the duties and obligations of the members as Catholics and citizens. Only two out of the twelve Archbishops voted for condemnation. The others commissioned the Archbishop of Baltimore to make representations to the Holy See and present a memorial in behalf of the Knights asking, what then seemed impossible, namely, that the condemnation imposed on them in Canada be revoked or, at least, not extended to the United States. Archbishop Gibbons agreed to represent the American Hierarchy in the negotiations.

The next year he sailed for Europe to receive the Red Hat and present the plea on behalf of organized labor, a lengthy memorial which Bishops Ireland and Keane, who were in Rome in connection with the proposed Catholic University, helped him to prepare and translate into French.

The memorial,[53] dated February 20, 1887, and presented to Cardinal Simeoni, Prefect of the Congregation of the Propaganda, made note of the fact that "out of the seventy-five archbishops and bishops of the United States, there are but five who desire the condemnation of the Knights of Labor, such as they are in our country".

The memorial did not ask papal approval of the Knights but that the condemnation obtained by the hierarchy of Canada, forbidding Catholics to become members of the Union, be not extended to the United States for the following reasons: namely, that there is no oath-bound initiation in the organization; no secrecy inimical to the interests of Church or State; no promise of blind obedience; no hostility to religion, to the Church, to the country, its authority or laws; no danger to the faith of Catholics who are not exposed to evil influences in the organization other than those they meet in every day life; nor are the violence, strikes and clashes that occur from time to time between labor and capital attributable to the Knights any more than to any other labor unions. Furthermore, the Knights are well disposed towards the Church, the President being a practical Catholic and not a Mason. The organization is a necessary and efficacious means for obtaining from their employers and safeguarding the just rights of the working class. Moreover, if the Knights are condemned the Church will lose the right to be considered a friend of the workingman and of all who seek justice for him and the amelioration of his condition, and Catholics will be alienated from her and will be tempted to join secret societies.

The letter addressed to Cardinal Gibbons by Cardinal Simeoni on August 29, 1888, brought the good news that

. . .the Knights of Labor may, for the present, be tolerated. The Sacred Congregation only requires that the necessary corrections be made in the statutes of the organization, in order to explain what might otherwise be obscure, or be interpreted in a wrong sense. The modifications should, especially, be made in those passages of the preamble of the rules which refer to local associations. The words which, in these passages, savor of Socialism and Communism must be construed in such a manner as to make them express simply the right given by God to man, or rather to mankind, to acquire by legitimate means, respecting, always, the rights of property enjoyed by every one.

The Sacred Congregation praised highly the resolve of the Bishops of the United States to take heed lest there creep into the Knights of Labor and similar organizations anything contrary to justice and honesty or not in conformity with the instructions given as to the Masonic sect.[54]

This letter shows that the Church in her wisdom safeguards with equal and prudent solicitude the rights of individuals and families, is anxious to ameliorate the lot of the working man and has a special tenderness for the masses. By the time this letter was received the Knights of Labor had begun to disintegrate owing to internal dissentions and the membership had fallen from 800,000 to 200,000.

As early as March 6, 1887, Bishop Ireland had assured Bishop Gilmour of Cleveland that "the Knights will not be condemned in Rome. This fact is as good as settled".

The German Question

The people of the United States are a blend of many races. Every nation has contributed its quota to the melting-pot from which has emerged the homogeneity of our population with all that makes it distinctly American. The immigrants of early days clung tenaciously, as was but natural under the circumstances, to their national language, their racial traits and customs. In the course of time, as was inevitable, the ties that bound their descendants to the land of their forefathers became weakened and in some cases obliterated. The struggle for adjustment to conditions so vastly different from those of the old world was long and bitter and the end is not yet. Many of the elements in the melting-pot proved refractory and difficult of assimilation.

The Catholic Church played a not unimportant role in this process of assimilation and amalgamation. At the beginning of the immigration movement the Catholic newcomers, from other than English-speaking countries, needed spiritual ministration in their own language, for they were unfamiliar with the English tongue which has always been the language of America. Notwithstanding diversity of speech and custom, the different nationalities lived together in peace and harmony, putting up with the hardships of all kinds inseparable from the life of pioneers in a new land.

After the founding of the Republic difficulties and misunderstandings arose about the rights and liberties guaranteed by the Constitution, and among the German Catholics especially there was engendered a feeling that they were being discriminated against by those in authority in the Church. They wanted priests who spoke their mother tongue, schools in which the teaching was in German and parishes and dioceses presided over by German pastors and bishops.

In the frontier diocese of St. Paul Bishop Cretin procured the services of Father Wurtzfeld who celebrated a special Mass in the Cathedral on Sundays for the German Catholics of the city and preached in German. But they were not satisfied until, in 1855, the Bishop established the parish of the Assumption exclusively for them although the Cathedral was just as accessible to them as was the new church.

In Bishop Grace's time the Germans bought a cemetery of their own although there was plenty of room for them in the existing cemetery.[55]

It was much the same in other parts of the country, if we are to judge by the report made to Rome by Archbishop Bedini, Papal Nuncio to Brazil, to the effect that "the division of the Church into national or racial centers was bound to bring disaster". He asked the Holy See not to permit it. This tendency Bishop Grace protested against in his own Province of Milwaukee,[56] and only by the greatest effort did he succeed in getting the name of Bishop Spalding, who spoke German fluently and was acceptable to most of the German priests, on the list for coadjutor to Archbishop Heiss.

In later years Archbishop Ireland had difficulties with the German priests of his diocese and he tried to solve the problem by placing German congregations in charge of Slovenian priests who spoke German. He was destined to play a most important role in opposing the efforts to segregate the German people in parishes, schools and dioceses under the administration of German pastors and bishops in the later decades of the nineteenth century. He became in fact the central figure in the struggle to prevent the Church in America and the Republic itself becoming a loosely-knit aggregation of nationalities each preserving its racial characteristics and mother tongue.

In several places the German clergy banded together in a Priester-Verein for the removal of the alleged grievances under which they labored. Eighty-two German priests, regular and diocesan, of the Archdiocese of St. Louis over which Archbishop Kenrick presided, signed a petition on July 31, 1884, to Cardinal Simeoni, Prefect of the Propaganda, praying that priests in charge of German parishes in the Diocese of St. Louis be placed on an equality with the English-speaking pastors, although they were well treated in the diocese which had a German Vicar General who was quite nationalistic. They were unsuccessful in their efforts.

Bishops Gilmour of Cleveland and Moore of St. Augustine sent a memorial to the Propaganda on October 2, 1885, declaring that the Germans did not want to attend the same church as other Catholics, especially the Irish, which caused a conflict that was detrimental to the interests of religion. The establishment of Priester-Vereins, if not initiated by Peter P. Cahensly who visited the United States in August, 1883, may have been suggested and influenced by him. He was the Secretary and moving spirit of the St. Raphael Verein in Germany and during his stay in this country visited localities as far west as St. Louis.

The Milwaukee Petition

In November, 1886, a more detailed "Relatio"[57] bearing on this question, written by Reverend P. M. Abbelen of Milwaukee and read and approved by Archbishop Heiss of that see, was presented to the Sacred Congregation by the author who claimed full responsibility for its contents. It dealt with the relation between the German parishes and the Irish (English-speaking) parishes in North America, listed the grievances of the former and petitioned the Sacred Congregation of the Propaganda to grant relief from them.

At the time the petition was presented to the Propaganda Bishop Ireland and Bishop Keane of Richmond were in Rome as the representatives of the American hierarchy for the purpose of discussing with the Holy See the preliminaries for the founding of the Catholic University of America, and they were permitted by the Congregation "to present a few observations upon the German question in the Church in the United States", and to offer a counter memorial[58] in which they contended that the granting of the petition in question "would be disastrous to the Church in the United States".

Taking up the allegations one by one they pointed out that the same rights are scrupulously accorded to the German parishes and irremovable rectorships that are accorded to all others; that, when they have a choice of priests, the Bishops appoint a pastor who answers to the expressed desires of the majority, if not all, the parishioners whatever their nationality, and they permit all Catholics, whatever their racial origin, to send their children to any Catholic school; that the descendants of Germans who wish to join an English-speaking parish be allowed to do so without the formal permission of the German pastor or bishop; that no attempt is made by English-speaking priests or bishops to suppress the use of the German language or discourage German manners and customs; that to require Bishops who do not understand German to appoint a German Vicar General could not be done without according a similar privilege to other nationalities.

In the meantime the petition had been submitted to the American hierarchy and they declared the accusations false and unjust, protested the secret manner in which the matter had been treated, and asserted that special legislation along the lines proposed in the petition would introduce into the American Church a pernicious spirit of nationalism, arouse conflicts among the faithful and hostility towards the Church on the part of their fellow-citizens. They suggested that the whole question be submitted to the Holy See for final adjudication with a view to correcting abuses wherever they exist, and that any special legislation found necessary be fully discussed by all whom it affects before being enacted.

Many of the bishops wrote or telegraphed their opposition to the petition and these protestations came not only from English but from Belgian, Dutch and even German bishops and were presented to the Holy See by Bishops Ireland and Keane.[59]

The answer of the Propaganda[60] was given on June 8, 1887, in a communication to Cardinal Gibbons from the office of the Secretary, in which it was decreed that bishops may erect several independent parishes in the same territory and declare one or more of them immovable if, in their prudent judgment, it be necessary for "the sake of the salvation of souls"; that parents have the right of sending their children to any Catholic school they please; that the Congregation "will never consider" directing bishops as requested in the petition, but allow them to provide as best they can for immigrants and their children in the matter of language. The Cardinal was asked to communicate these resolutions to the Archbishops of the United States.

This decision, however, did not put an end to the agitation among certain groups of German priests in this country for the protection of their language and customs. They received help from Germany through the efforts of Peter Paul Cahensly who in 1883 established the St. Raphael Verein to provide for the spiritual welfare of foreign language groups, chiefly German, in the United States and who in that year visited many places in America where he added fuel to the fire of nationalism burning in the breasts of the members of the Priester-Verein. He returned to Germany determined to labor more assiduously for the welfare of the Germans in America.

At the International Congress of the officers and delegates of the St. Raphael Verein held in Lucerne on December 9, 1890, the Holy See was petitioned to provide for the spiritual and material wellbeing of immigrants to the United States by authorizing the formation, wherever possible, of national parishes in charge of priests of that nationality or, in default of such priests, of priests who would be strictly obliged to teach the truths of Catholicism in the language of the group; by establishing parish schools in which the national language would be taught; by founding societies and associations to help preserve the faith and language of each nationality; by providing bishops of each nationality, special seminaries to educate priests for the emigrant, and St. Raphael Vereins for their protection.

The Second Memorial

A second or amended memorial was sent to Cardinal Rampolla on June 30, 1891, in which it was asserted that the leakage in the Church in America was not less than 16,000,000, an increase of 6,000,000 over the estimate of the previous year. This loss, it was asserted, was due to lack of protection for emigrants on their outward journey, insufficient priests and parishes of their own nationality, exorbitant pecuniary demands made on them, lack of national parish schools and societies and a disproportion of national bishops.

This memorial merely summarized the long and detailed one presented by Father Abbelen and rejected by the Propaganda in 1887. After consultation with the American bishops the Holy Father rejected this petition on the ground that the granting of its demands, especially in the appointment of bishops, would create a strong public sentiment against the Church on the part of Americans. It was vehemently denied that there was any great defection from the Church among Catholics or that American institutions were hostile to the faith.

One of the most active opponents of Cahenslyism, as the movement was called, was Archbishop Ireland who saw the fallacy of the arguments adduced in its favor and who, in an interview in the Pioneer Press of St. Paul, denied that the German Catholics were neglected, for the bishops try to provide priests of foreign language for people of foreign birth. The bishops have no more notion of making the Catholic Church in America Irish than they have of allowing it to be made German. The Bishops of America were fully able to ward off a foreign invasion and maintain the Church on thoroughly American lines, and not allow the country to be partitioned at the good pleasure of foreigners. The inspiration for the work in Europe came from an American clique of the Priester-Verein which made an attempt several years ago to obtain control of Catholic affairs in America. The great body of German priests and laity are loyal to the Church in America.

Archbishop Corrigan of New York charged Cahensly with "total misconception of American institutions" and said if the memorial were adopted "it would result in incalculable harm to religion".

Cardinal Simeoni, writing to Cahensly said his request was "impossible of realization".

The editor of the Northwestern Chronicle wrote

It is injurious to religion and introduces foreignism into the United States. Foreigners should fall into line with the principles of American life—national and ecclesiastical. This country gives them a free asylum. Let them respect it. Why should these countries try to influence the formation of ecclesiastical policy here?

On June 28, 1891, Cardinal Rampolla notified Cardinal Gibbons that the Holy See had no intention of granting the requests of the St. Raphael societies and Cahensly for the appointment of national bishops in the United States.

But the spirit of Cahenslyism died hard. It was much in evidence at the Fifth National Convention of the German-speaking Catholics at Buffalo, N. Y., during the week of September 20, 1891. Before the convention opened the members of the Priester-Verein met to scrutinize all documents and censor all matters to be brought before the delegates. Its President, Father von Muhlsiepen, V. G., of St. Louis, presided at the sessions. On Monday evening, September 21, there was a grand parade in which all the German priests took part. The spires of the ten German-

American Catholic churches in the city were like pillars of fire for the illuminated procession in which streams of rockets, Roman candles and thousands of torches formed an arch of fire for the fifteen thousand marchers. One Buffalo priest said those who did not turn out were neither German nor Catholic and should have their names stricken from the parish rolls.

The next morning Archbishop Katzer of Milwaukee pontificated and Bishop Zardetti of St. Cloud preached a dramatic sermon in which he told his hearers that they must adhere to America as to a bride but were bound to remember their motherland and speak its language. He closed with a tribute to the Stars and Stripes. The first session was open to priests only, the others to priests and laymen in which the latter took little or no part.

Among the resolutions was a protest against any interference with parochial schools and any cry of foreignism raised against the race; a demand for the retention of the German language; an expressed hope for the future based on a central union of German young men's societies.

Cahensly was present to emphasize his plan for providing German parishes with German priests, teaching German in school, perpetuating German traditions, and filling diocesan sees with a proportionate number of German bishops.

Visit of Cardinal Gibbons

A pleasing incident in the autumn of 1887 was the visit of His Eminence Cardinal Gibbons to St. Paul, his first as a member of the Sacred College of Cardinals to which he had been elevated that year.[61] The eminent prelate was on his way to Portland, Oregon, to bestow the Pallium on the Most Reverend Archbishop Gross on Sunday, October 9. Accompanied by the Reverend Placide Chapelle, Rector of St. Mathew's Church in Washington, His Eminence arrived in St. Paul on the afternoon of September 29 and was formally welcomed that evening at a banquet in the Ryan Hotel attended by a distinguished gathering of clergymen and citizens eager to give public testimony to their appreciation of the services rendered to Church and State by the distinguished visitor. The banquet was preceded by a reception at which the priests were presented to His Eminence by the Archbishop, who also presided at the dinner and introduced the speakers. The formal address of welcome was read by Judge Kelly of which the Cardinal made a gracious and complimentary acknowledgement.

The toast of "The Pope" was responded to by Honorable W. J. Onahan of Chicago; "America" by Senator Davis; "Minnesota" by Governor Rice; "Father Hennepin" by Honorable T. V. D. Heard; "Political Institutions of America" by Honorable J. W. Willis; "Education" by Father O'Gorman; "The City of Minneapolis" by President Northrup of the University of Minnesota; "The City of St. Paul" by Honorable W. P. Murray.

The next evening an address, beautifully engrossed and artistically inscribed, was presented to His Eminence by John D. O'Brien on behalf of the C. T. A. U. of Minnesota in Crusaders Hall to which the Cardinal made a gracious reply. During the day he was received at St. Joseph's Academy in company with Archbishop Ireland and was presented with an address.

Saturday evening was reserved for St. Thomas Seminary where he was cheered by the student body and, after dinner, welcomed by an address in Latin read by Thomas F. Gleeson on behalf of the faculty and students. He was presented with an engrossed copy. In his reply he congratulated faculty and students on the fine work done in the recently-opened seminary under the direction of Archbishop Ireland and expressed bright hopes for the future of the institution.

On Sunday he presided at the Solemn High Mass in the Cathedral and preached to an overflow congregation. His departure from the city that evening was made the occasion of a special outburst of farewell cheering from the crowd that gathered at the depot to bid him godspeed.

At the opening of the Annual Convention of the German-speaking Catholic societies of Minnesota, at Chaska on September 16, 1888, the Most Reverend Archbishop presided at the Solemn High Mass celebrated by the Reverend Michael Rich, O. F. M., Rector of St. Joseph's College, Teutopolis, Illinois. During the Mass Father Anselmus Muller, O. F. M., preached in German on "Catholic Faith" and after Mass the Archbishop addressed the congregation and delegates, speaking candidly about the use of the German or any other foreign language [62] by the people of America. They should speak it at home, among themselves and to their children as part of a liberal education, the key to rich and abundant literary treasures and as serviceable in business and social relations. The children, however, should learn English well, because it is the language of the country, its laws and business. They are Americans and English must be given an honored place in their education. Their training in religion should be given in English as well as in German for the objections against the Catholic faith come largely from English-speaking people and they must be answered by Catholics well versed in their religion and capable of explaining and defending it in the language of the country.

The Archbishop and the Colored Race

Shortly before his elevation to the Archiepiscopal dignity Bishop Ireland approved the purchase of the Swedenborgian church on Market Street as a chapel for the colored Catholics of St. Paul. It was renovated, furnished, placed under the patronage of St. Peter Claver and served, as a mission from the Cathedral, by the pastor, Father Shanley. Prior to that time their religious education had not been neglected. After the Civil War Father Ireland had instructed the colored people in their religion in the brick school on Wabasha Street at Sixth and the work was continued by Father Shanley in the basement chapel of the Cathedral. In the spring of 1886 the little brick church opposite Rice Park on Market Street was rented and used for divine worship until it was finally purchased for their very own.

The Archbishop's attitude towards the colored race was forcibly stated by him on the occasion of a concert given in Cretin Hall by the St. Peter Claver Sodality in June, 1889, when he addressed the three hundrd whites and one hundred negoes who patronized it.

> There was a time when there was a foolish notion that white people were much superior to those of any other color and there could be no competition between them in art, science or learning. I would like to see white men and women of the same cultivation who could surpass the black people we have heard. When we look upon what the race has accomplished in but a quarter of a century we must admit there is a future before them. . . .All the black men want is fair play; that given they will care for themselves. . .The equaltiy of man is an American principle: it is also religious teaching. . .We are all brothers in Christ, and brothers do not look at color or race.

The President of the Sodality, Samuel F. Hardy, was one of the nine pioneers of St. Peter Claver parish and instrumental in founding the National Congress of Colored Catholics in 1889.

Again the Archbishop emphasized his stand on the negro question when he adddressed a large audience of colored people in Cretin Hall on Monday, April 7, 1890, as reported in the Northwestern Chronicle for April 11:

> There is but one solution of the problem, and it is to obliterate absolutely all color line. . .Open up to the negro as to the white man, the political offices of the country, making but one test, that of mental and moral fitness. Throw down at once the barriers which close out the negro merely on account of his color from hotel, theater and railway carriage. Meet your negro brother as your equal at banquets and in social gatherings. Give him, in one word, and in full meaning of the terms, equal rights and equal privileges, political, civil and social. . .
> My solution of the negro problem is to declare that there is no problem to be solved, since we are all equal, as brothers should be, and we will, in consistency with our American and christian principles, treat alike black and white. I know no color line, I will acknowledge none. . .The time is not distant when Americans and christians will wonder that there ever was a race prejudice.

The New York Tribune of May 23, 1890, paid tribute to the Catholic Church for not tolerating prejudice and exclusion grounded on racial differences.

Archbishop Ireland is roundly abused by southern journals for declaring that no church is a fit temple of God where a man, because of his color, is made to occupy a corner. He spoke as a consistent Roman Catholic when he denounced the shame and scandal of putting negroes in corners and lofts of churches of his communion, and of closing the doors of Catholic institutions against unfortunates of the colored race. To the honor of that Church be it said that prejudice and exclusion founded upon race have never been tolerated in the established practice of its ministrations to mankind. Its gospel has ever been a gospel of social equality in the sight of heaven.

The statement above referred to, namely, that "No church is a fit temple of God where a man because of his color is made to occupy a corner", was made by the Archbishop in the course of a sermon preached in St. Augustine's Church for negroes in the nation's capital, attended by senators, congressmen and others prominent in official life.

> Religion teaches that we cannot be pleasing to God unless we look upon all mankind as children of one Father in heaven. . .Let christians act out their religion and then there is no more race problem. Equality for the colored is coming.

He urged the colored people to be industrious, to purchase homes, to respect law and order, to educate themselves and their children, and to keep insisting on their rights. The color line, he said, must go and soon too. The line will be drawn at personal merit. The doors of all Catholic institutions must be opened to colored Catholics.

He reiterated his stand at a meeting held in the Market Hall in St. Paul on June 30, 1890, to honor Father Tolton, then the only negro priest in the United States:

> I pronounce for full religious, civil and social equality. . .Let there be no color line, but let the colored man be treated by man as he is treated before the religious laws of God and the civil laws, which are grounded upon the principles of the American Constitution. As a christian, an American, I hate any distinction made upon the sole basis of color and during my life I have never ceased to do all in my power to eradicate the evil, and so long as I have life and action I shall never cease to live and to act with the same end in view.

On January 1, 1891, the Archbishop was asked to deliver the principal address before the Afro-American League at the Emancipation Day celebration, an address reported at great length in the daily press of St. Paul as well as in full in the Northwestern Chronicle for January 9. The gist of it was that he would claim for the black man what he claimed for the white man—equality before the law. He would blot out the color line, break down all barriers, grant no immunity before the law to a white man violating the sacred personal rights of the negro, and in all public gatherings, in all public resorts, in halls and hotels, treat the black man as we treat the white man.

Towards the end of the year he again appeared before the public at a meeting in the St. Paul Market Hall in a plea for equal rights for the colored race. The Northwestern Chronicle for November 20, reported his address as follows:

> This prejudice against a race of men is unworthy of human reason—of those calling themselves Christians, and especially is it unworthy of the American people. . .In the past quarter of a century the black men have given the lie to all the enemies of their race. . .I doubt if an equal number of white men on this globe, reduced as they have been by servitude, would have made the progress of our American negroes. . .
> The Civil Rights Association will test certain state laws which mark out these differences between the races. . .It does seem to me that such law cannot find defence in the federal courts of our government. If it is set aside there is a great triumph for civil rights. The prejudice may remain, . . .but this will not be sanctioned by the Constitution, and gradually it will melt away, and soon we in America will be a united people, a Christian people, and a noble people.

When the new St. Peter Claver Church was dedicated on December 18, 1892, the Archbishop declared he had long wished to open a church for the special use of his colored brothers, not because he thought they should worship apart from their fellow-Catholics, but as a "temporary expedient" for their convenience, lest they be embarrassed by attending a church where they might be made to feel unwelcome because of their color. From the days of his youthful priesthood, he said

> I have felt myself drawn towards them and as opportunity offered and other time-taking occupations permitted, I have labored for them and induced others to labor for them. Their sad lot drew me towards them; and my sense of justice interested me in their service. I saw them in slavery. I rejoiced in my soul when slavery ceased; I will rejoice in my soul when this social prejudice shall cease, and in the meantime I will work in the name of humanity, of religion and patriotism to kill it out.

The New Metropolitan

The most important event of the year 1888 was the elevation of the Diocese of St. Paul to metropolitan rank and the appointment of John Ireland as its first Archbishop. It was a fitting recognition of the growing importance of St. Paul as a Catholic center and of the zeal and achievements of its Ordinary. The resolution of the Congregation de Propaganda Fide making St. Paul an Archdiocese was presented to the Holy Father by the secretary in an audience on Sunday, April 29, and duly confirmed by His Holiness. The decree[63] was signed by Cardinal Ledochowski on May 4, 1888, and the Bull appointing its first Archbishop on the same day.

"Of Our own accord, and from Our own knowledge and after mature deliberation We divide the province of Milwaukee by Our apostolic authority, in virtue of these present letters, and by that same authority We erect a new ecclesiastical province, raising by these present letters the Diocese of St. Paul into an Archdiocese, and We assign to it as suffragan churches the Vicariates Apostolic of Dakota and Northern Minnesota.

"Wherefore, holding you in special regard and love, with the advice of Our brothers, the Cardinals, in the plentitude of Our apostolic power, by virtue of these present letters, We elect, institute and declare you Archbishop of the above-named Church of St. Paul lately proclaimed by Us to be a metropolitan church, and We commit to you fully the government and administration of this church in things spiritual and temporal".

The Bishops of the Province of Milwaukee in Provincial Synod had asked that a new archbishopric be established in that region by dividing the Province of Milwaukee and making the Diocese of St. Paul an Archdiocese. This was done; and to the new Province were assigned as suffragan sees the Vicariates Apostolic of Northern Minnesota and Dakota, while Milwaukee was left with La Crosse, Green Bay and Marquette.

St. Paul was the thirteenth ecclesiastical Province in the United States and comprised the states of Minnesota, North and South Dakota.

The Pallium of his new dignity was postulated by Monsignor O'Connell at the Consistory of June, brought from New York by Bishop Keane and presented to him at Notre Dame with a speech from His Eminence of Baltimore, and conferred on him on September 27 at an impressive ceremony[64] in the Cathedral by his predecessor, Bishop Grace, Titular Bishop of Mennith, and soon to be promoted to the Titular Archbishopric of Siunia. The ceremony was graced by the presence of Bishops Taché of St. Boniface, Canada, Spalding of Peoria, Seidenbusch of St. Cloud, Cosgrove of Davenport, Flasch of LaCrosse, Vertin of Marquette, Hennessy of Dubuque, Ryan of Alton, Burke of Cheyenne, Bonacum of Lincoln, Marty of Yankton, Keane of Richmond, hundreds of priests from Minnesota, Wisconsin and the Dakotas, and an immense gathering of the laity, all of whom rejoiced in the honor so worthily conferred on the distinguished Archbishop whom they knew and loved.

The Mass was celebrated by Bishop Marty, with Father Caillet as assistant priest, Fathers Trobec as deacon and Cotter as subdeacon. The Chaplains to the Archbishop were Fathers O'Gorman and E. Walters of Fort Wayne, Indiana. The sermon was preached by Bishop Keane from Matt. XIII, 31-32, (the parable of the mustard seed), in the course of which he dwelt on the action of divine faith in the direction of society and the growth of the Church, especially in the Northwest, as evidenced by the history of the Diocese of St. Paul, to the administration of which Archbishop Ireland brought "the holiness of a saint, the wisdom of a statesman, and the energy of a Leo".

At the end of the sermon Father Danehy brought the Pallium from the sacristy on a golden salver and placed it on the altar, covering it with a silken veil. After Mass Archbishop Ireland and Bishop Grace, vested in full pontifical robes, resumed their seats while Father O'Gorman read the Papal Brief in Latin and in English. Bishop Grace then ascended the altar steps and sat on the faldstool. The Archbishop, accompanied by his chaplains, knelt at the foot of the altar, took the oath of office and of allegiance to the Holy See. Bishop Grace placed the sacred Pallium on the shoulders of the kneeling prelate who gave his blessing to the people, after which the Te Deum was sung, and the inspiring ceremony brought to a close. Dinner was served the bishops and clergy in the Ryan Hotel. A cablegram from the Pope brought a special blessing from the Supreme Pontiff.

In the evening a reception was tendered to the new Archbishop in the Ryan Hotel before which the prelates and priests, in thirty-seven carriages, drove through the city which was illuminated by order of the City Council as a tribute to the new Archbishop. A portrait of His Grace, painted by Gregori, and presented by the faculty and students of Notre Dame University to express their congratulations and good wishes, was on exhibition in the parlor of the hotel. The function was a memorable event in the annals of the Church in the Northwest, one long remembered by the citizens of St. Paul, to all of whom, irrespective of religious belief, the Archbishop had endeared himself by the signal services rendered to society at large and to the individual in particular.

The combination church, school and residence built by Bishop Cretin in 1851, was dismantled[65] in August, 1889, to make room for a business block, the Schuneman & Evans dry goods emporium of later years. On the Sunday before the work of demolition began commemorative services were held in the Cathedral at which the Archbishop bade a feeling "good bye" to the lovable old pile which for thirty-eight years had been a landmark in the city. It was once "a stately, magnificent edifice" to the people of St. Paul. He saw it for the first time in May, 1852, when he and his family arrived in the city which then had a population of about one thousand. It stood on the corner of the block at Sixth and Wabasha Streets, the rest of which was a garden. In its second story church Bishop Cretin said his daily Mass and pontificated on the great feasts of the year. He preached at every Mass, at vespers on Sundays and holydays and also at the evening service. The sermons were in French and English. He encouraged congregational singing, led by himself. He was a fine musician and it was his delight to sing. In its school room on the first floor the Archbishop sat and studied with Thomas O'Gorman and many of the older priests and Catholic citizens. When it was erected it was the only Catholic church in the village; now, in 1889, there are nineteen in the city that has grown up around it.

With the opening of St. Thomas Seminary in 1885 a new suburb began to develop in the western section of the city between Snelling Avenue and the Mississippi river. The Archbishop owned considerable property in that locality, having purchased the Finn farm with a view to the building of a diocesan seminary for the exclusive education of the clergy, and he was most interested in the development of the area and anxious that people should build homes in it. The great problem was the need of ample and cheap transportation; and he proposed the extension of the street railway from the heart of the city, along Grand Avenue to the river, passing through the grounds of Macalester College at Snelling Avenue and running within a block of the St. Thomas property at Cretin and Summit Avenues. The Church Progress[66] of St. Louis announced that Bishop Ireland and another man signed a contract in June for the construction of an electric railway with overhead wires and that the company backing them expected to spend several million dollars in establishing a new suburb. The Reserve Electric Motor project opened offices in St. Paul to receive subscriptions towards a proposed bonus of $250,000. Macalester College gave a right of way, 660 by 80 feet through its property, and $6,500. Property owners were to pay a certain percentage of their subscriptions when the steel rails were laid as far west as Cleveland Avenue and the balance in equal installments in three, six and nine months—all of which would be void if the line were not completed by July, 1890. In July, 1889, the Archbishop took advantage of a trip to Providence, R. I., to preach at the dedication of the new Cathedral, to investigate rapid transit problems in several eastern cities with a view to improving the St. Paul system.

In due time there was a civic celebration at the opening of the line for traffic and by degrees the suburb became more and more desirable as a residential district. Five years later St. Paul Seminary at the end of the line opened its doors for the enrollment of students for the diocesan priesthood and St. Thomas Seminary became a high school and college for boys.

Triple Consecration

The elevation of the Diocese of St. Paul to metropolitan dignity portended the erection of new dioceses in the territory comprised within the Province thus established. A decree of the Propaganda approved on September 16, 1889, and confirmed by the Pope on September 29, established five suffragan sees—Sioux Falls, St. Cloud, Duluth, Fargo and Winona.

To Sioux Falls was assigned the whole of South Dakota admitted to the Union on November 2, 1889. Jamestown was made the see-city of a diocese that comprised all of North Dakota which attained statehood on the same day. St. Cloud, Duluth, Winona and St. Paul parcelled the State of Minnesota among them. Duluth was given the northern portion with eighteen counties; St. Cloud a tier of sixteen counties south of it; St. Paul twenty-six in the central areas; and Winona twenty-one north of the Iowa line and south of the St. Paul belt.

Bishop Marty, Vicar Apostolic of the Dakotas, was made Bishop of Sioux Falls, with residence in that city; and the Diocese of St. Cloud was formed from part of the Vicariate of Northern Minnesota with Bishop Zardetti as its first bishop. The other three—Duluth, Jamestown and Winona—were new sees and the Right Reverends James McGolrick, John Shanley and Joseph B. Cotter were appointed the first bishops and consecrated at a unique ceremony in the Cathedral of St. Paul on the feast of St. John the Evangelist, December 27, 1889, by Archbishop Ireland assisted by Archbishop Grace and Bishop Marty as co-consecrators.

Only once before in the history of the Catholic Church in the United States had three bishops been elevated to that dignity at the same ceremony. On October 30, 1853, Right Reverends James Roosevelt Bayley for Newark, John Loughlin for Brooklyn and Louis de Goesbriand for Burlington were consecrated in New York by the Most Reverend Cajetan Bedini, Apostolic Nuncio to the Court of Brazil, on his way back to Rome from his diplomatic mission.

The triple consecration [67] in St. Paul was unique in that the three priests elevated to the episcopal dignity were from the Archdiocese and for three newly-erected sees within the Province. Since then one other consecration of three bishops at the same time took place in Chicago on March 7, 1949.

The Cathedral of St. Paul, the scene of the ceremony, never looked more beautiful with its Christmas decorations, profuse floral wreaths and sanctuary banked with flowers and brilliant with lighted tapers. Among the prelates present on that occasion were two Archbishops, thirteen bishops, two monsignors, three hundred priests, many seminarians and thousands of the laity admitted by ticket, among whom the relatives and friends of the bishops-elect occupied a reserved section in the front pews of the church.

Father Oster was assistant priest at the Mass; Fathers Maurice E. Murphy and James Trobec, deacons of honor; Fathers Charles Keoberl, deacon, and Patrick Kenny, subdeacon.

The choir was augmented by Seibert's Orchestra and the seminarians from St. Thomas Seminary sang the proper of the Mass. The sermon, preached by the Reverend Walter Elliott, C. S. P., had a national rather than a local bearing in as much as it dealt with the mission of the Church in America and the role which Catholics must play in bringing her teaching to the attention of non-Catholics. Before concluding he described the office of a bishop and his duties.

Father O'Gorman read the Pontifical Brief for Bishop-elect McGolrick, Father Byrne for Bishop-elect Cotter, and Father Gibbons for Bishop-elect Shanley.

The ceremony continued from ten thirty to three in the afternoon when dinner was served at the Ryan Hotel for the prelates, priests and invited guests. After the viands had been disposed of Father O'Gorman read an address and made a presentation to the new bishops on behalf of the clergy of the Archdiocese to which the bishops responded. The toast "Leo XIII" was assigned to Monsignor O'Connell, Rector of the American College in Rome; The Diocese of St. Cloud" to Bishop Zardetti; "Our Country" to Bishop Marty; "The Province of Milwaukee" to Bishop Flasch of La Crosse; "Our Visitors" to Bishop Hennessy of Dubuque; "The Catholic Total Abstinence Union" to Father Cleary; "The Bureau of Catholic Indians" to Father Stephan; "The Diocese of Duluth" to Father Buh; "The Diocese of Winona" to Father Wurst; and "The Diocese of Jamestown" to Father Conaty.

The following day the new bishops and others were guests of St. Thomas Seminary where an address was read by John A. Ryan. In due time the bishops were installed in their respective dioceses and began the work of organization and development. They had to plan from the ground up and their success was little short of phenomenal. Their chief concern was to get priests in sufficient numbers to minister to the scattered Catholic population under their care. They were not daunted by the magnitude of the task that confronted them; they faced the future with confidence in God and the results more than justified their faith in His providence.

The Centenary of the Hierarchy

The month of November, 1889, was significant for the Catholic Church in the United States. It witnessed three important events—the one hundredth anniversary of the establishment of the hierarchy in the person of John Carroll, first Bishop of Baltimore; the inauguration of the Catholic University of America at Washington; and the holding of the first Lay Catholic Congress. Almost the entire hierarchy attended these functions.

The centennial celebration took place in the Baltimore Cathedral on November 10. Archbishop Williams of Boston sang the Pontifical Mass on the opening day and Archbishop Ryan of Philadelphia preached the sermon. This was followed by a banquet at which addresses were delivered by Archbishop Satolli, the papal representative at the opening of the University, Cardinals Gibbons and Taschereau, Bishop Montes d'Oca of Mexico City and Archbishop Ireland who responded to the toast "Our Country". In the evening Archbishop Heiss of Milwaukee officiated at vespers and benediction and Archbishop Ireland preached on "The Mission of Catholics in America",[68] dwelling on the possibilities and duties of the century then opening and the role which the Church, through its priesthood and laity, is to play in the new age.

The first Catholic Congress of laymen was sandwiched in between the celebration of the centenary of the establishment of the American hierarchy and the dedication of the Catholic University. It convened in Baltimore on November 11 and 12

> to counsel and deliberate on subjects and affairs of common Catholic interest, and for the mutual social benefits to be derived from the intercourse and opportunities afforded by such a meeting. . .and by mutual interest and united action make laymen better Catholics and therefore better patriots and greater lovers of the country.[69]

The Congress had ecclesiastical approval and sanction and was attended by a representative body of Catholic laymen from all parts of the country. It was devotedly Catholic and loyally American.

Cardinal Manning was the first to suggest the holding of a laymen's congress in London but it did not materialize. The idea caught on in America and was energetically advocated by Archbishop Ireland and other members of the hierarchy. It had, likewise, the blessing of Leo XIII. The call was issued by the Honorable W. J. Onahan of Chicago, general chairman of a committee on organization consisting of three members, the other two being H. J. Spaunhorst of St. Louis and D. A. Rudd of Cincinnati, assisted by a group of forty men from all parts of the United States, one of whom was William L. Kelly of St. Paul.

The Congress opened with a Pontifical Mass in the Baltimore Cathedral on Monday, November 11, celebrated by Archbishop Corrigan of New York, at which the address of welcome to the delegates was delivered by Archbishop Gross of Oregon City who summarized the history of the Catholic Church in the United States during the previous one hundred years.

After Mass fifteen hundred delegates assembled in the Concordia Opera House, twenty-three of whom were from St. Paul, two from Minneapolis and six from other parts of Minnesota. John F. Prince of St. Paul was one of the Vice-Presidents. The meeting was called to order by Mr. Onahan and prayer offered by Archbishop Ireland. The Honorable John Lee Carroll, former Governor of Maryland, was elected temporary presiding officer. A message from the Pope was read and addresses delivered by Governor Carroll, Cardinal Gibbons and Honorable Daniel Dougherty of New York. Several other speakers addressed the delegates during the two days' sessions and thirteen papers were read, the most important of which were John Gilmary Shea's on "Catholic Congresses"; Major H. F. Brownson's on "Lay Action in the Church"; Charles J. Bonaparte's on "The Independence of the Holy See"; and William L. Kelly's on "Religion in Education".

Before adjournment it was decided to hold an international congress not later than 1892 in Chicago.

Archbishop Ireland in the closing address urged the delegates to carry back to their homes the enthusiasm for lay activity engendered by the congress and exert every human effort to practice and spread the sacred truths of Catholicism.[70]

Cardinal Gibbons said that at first he was opposed to the holding of a congress in connection with the centennial fearing there would not be sufficient time to dispose of the subjects presented for consideration, but he was compelled to listen to the solicitation and representations made by some of his honored friends in the western part of the country under the leadership of such a champion of faith and country as the Archbishop of St. Paul.

Judge O'Brien of New York presented the platform on which Catholic laymen were expected to stand in their propagation of divine truth and defence of the Church.

The Catholic University

In view of Archbishop Ireland's lifelong efforts on behalf of education for clergy and laity, it is not to be wondered at that he took a deep personal interest in the founding and upbuilding of the Catholic University of America, and gave to that undertaking his heartiest cooperation and unwavering support. His predecessor, Bishop Grace, is credited with having first suggested it, according to the statement made by Bishop Shanley in his sermon at that prelate's funeral in February, 1897. However that may be, the idea of founding a Catholic University, as the keystone in the arch of the Church's educational system in the United States, took definite shape at the Third Plenary Council of Baltimore in 1884 when it was decided to launch the project.

Prior to that there had been considerable discussion about it among the hierarchy. The idea of such an institution was given some consideration in the Second Plenary Council held in 1866 and it was suggested that a school already existing be made the nucleus of it. During the next decade there was a growing sentiment in favor of it; and the Reverend John Lancaster Spalding, later, Bishop of Peoria, wrote several letters in advocacy of what he called a theological high school for the graduates of diocesan seminaries, and even professed willingness to become a teacher in such an institution for a few years or devote his whole life to it. "I shall be delighted to beg, work or do anything as the servant of the bishops if

276 THE CATHOLIC CHURCH IN THE DIOCESE OF ST. PAUL

they will but write saying let us make the effort". His idea at the time was to begin with a college for post-graduate studies in philosophy and theology.

As Bishop of Peoria he received encouragement and backing from Bishop Grace and his coadjutor, Bishop Ireland, who probably derived from his venerable superior some of the zeal and enthusiasm he displayed in pushing the project to a successful termination. Bishop Ireland was one of its earliest and most consistent advocates, if not its co-founder with Bishop Spalding. From the inception of the undertaking he gave of his time and energy to its realization. Indeed it would seem that, were it not for his advocacy of it, the University would not have come into existence when it did. When other prelates, notably Archbishop Gibbons of Baltimore, and Bishop Keane of Richmond, were in favor of postponing further consideration of it, he persistently refused to yield to the opposition and enheartened the others to keep up the agitation till the goal was reached. Bishop Spalding, too, was unremitting in his advocacy. By voice and pen he tried to convince the older members of the hierarchy of the need of a school of higher studies if the Church in the United States would maintain and enhance her prestige for scholarship among the clergy. He suggested the possibility of securing Mount St. Mary's Seminary in Cincinnati for a theological school which might ultimately develop into a Catholic University. The plan would be to purchase the institution, appoint a board of directors and admit only the most promising graduates of our seminaries. His insistence brought the project to the attention of the American hierarchy. In a letter to Archbishop Elder of Cincinnati, dated September 16, 1880, he said that Bishop Grace of St. Paul had begged him to undertake such work, at least to make the attempt, "and as he is a holy man I have thought it might be the will of God".

No serious step was taken to carry out Bishop Spalding's suggestion till the Third Plenary Council of Baltimore met in November, 1884, which was attended by Bishops Grace and Ireland and the majority of the hierarchy. Bishop Grace, who was a firm believer in the necessity of a Catholic University of America, had spoken in favor of such a project at a meeting of the Bishops of the Province of Milwaukee some time before but did not receive much encouragement.[71] Most of them thought that the objective could be attained by improving the course of studies in the provincial seminaries.

Shortly after the opening of the Council a very definite impetus was given to the project when Miss Mary Gwendoline Caldwell, a wealthy young woman of New York, offered $300,000 for the establishment of "a national Catholic School of Philosophy and Theology" for seminary graduates, under the direction of a committee of bishops, but unaffiliated with any other institution, and uncontrolled by any religious order. She was to be considered the founder.

The subject was discussed at length in the Council and there was not a little difference of opinion among the prelates in regard to its necessity, location and value to the Church in America. The majority favored it at least in a general way. In his sermon at the close of the Council on Sunday evening, December 16, 1884, Bishop Spalding, after reviewing the work done in its sessions, declared prophetically "We have laid the foundation of an institution which, under God's providence, is destined to grow into an American Catholic University".

Miss Caldwell's gift was accepted as the nucleus of a fund for the proposed institution and a committee of her selection was formed to further the project, consisting of Archbishops Gibbons, Corrigan, Ryan, Williams and Heiss, and Bishops Ireland and Spalding with Monsignor Farley of New York as secretary and three laymen—Eugene Kelly of Baltimore, Reuben Springer of Cincinnati and William Drexel of Philadelphia. They favored an institution like the Dunboyne of Maynooth, near a large city to serve as the principal seminary for the United States. At a meeting in New York on January 26, 1885, Bishop Ireland proposed that Washington be selected as the seat of the University, a proposal rejected in favor of Seton College, South Orange, New Jersey, with the proviso that Miss Caldwell be consulted. Bishop Ireland suggested that it be called the Catholic University of America and, when Bishop Spalding found a site in the nation's capital, that became the paramount issue after Bishop Wigger of Newark withdrew the offer of Seton College.

Bishop Ireland became restive under the delay lest interest in the project wane throughout the country and he wrote Archbishop Gibbons "I feel deep interest in the University both for the merits of the project itself and for the sake of the Council whose honor is staked upon the realization of all its measures".[72] He almost reproached the Archbishop for his seeming inaction and in this he had the support of Bishop Spalding.

At the meeting on May 7, 1885, the committee decided on Washington as the site and Bishop Ireland urged that an option be taken on the Middleton property at the east gate of the Soldiers Home which was finally bought for $29,000 paid by Miss Caldwell. He and Father Chapelle of St. Mathew's Church were asked to attend to the details of incorporation. Two of the lay members of the commitee had died—Springer and Drexel—and M. Jenkins of Baltimore, B. W. Farren of Philadelphia and T. E. Waggaman of Washington were elected as well as Bishops Keane of Richmond and Marty of Yankton. Bishops Ireland and Spalding were responsible for the choice of Washington and Archbishop Gibbons and others gave grudging consent.

Bishop Spalding wrote the appeal for the endowment of professorial chairs and burses and asked contributions from Catholics of means towards "the first work of general and national significance undertaken by the Church in this country". It was the first official announcement of the project to the American people.

In the meantime the Pope had approved the project and expressed the hope that it would be carried to a speedy conclusion. Bishops Ireland, Keane, Spalding and Marty were authorized to canvass the dioceses for contributions, but they met with a cool reception in many places. Archbishop Corrigan, among others, was not sympathetic.

At the meeting in Baltimore on May 12, 1886, the question of a Rector was discussed and the choice was left to the Archbishops of Baltimore, New York, Philadelphia and Boston. Their choice was Bishop Spalding who refused the honor. They then chose Bishop Keane of Richmond who demurred because he felt that he did not possess the necessary qualifications but, under pressure, consented, but the choice was not divulged until the approval of the Holy See was secured.

Bishops Ireland and Keane were delegated to lay the matter before the Holy See and entrusted with letters to His Holiness and Cardinal Simeoni, Prefect of the Propaganda, asking for encouragement and approbation of the undertaking. They sailed from New York on October 30, 1886, and when they arrived in Rome were confronted with evidence of an alleged lack of unanimity among the American bishops regarding the project,[73] the site and the expense of supporting the institution in addition to the cost of the American College. The opposition was centered in Archbishop Corrigan and Bishop McQuaid, his mentor. All these objections and arguments were answered in a document presented to the Holy See but nothing definite was done until Archbishop Gibbons came to Rome in 1887 to receive the Red Hat. When the opposition in Rome became very strong Cardinal Gibbons and Bishop Keane favored abandonment of the whole project, but Bishop Ireland protested indignantly against "so cowardly a surrender to so unworthy an opposition" and his advice prevailed. Up to this time the Cardinal took little more than a passive interest in the project, a hesitancy he displayed in other cases, until sentiment in favor of it crystallized. Only after the official approval of the Holy See in 1887 did he give the project whole-hearted support.

On Easter Sunday, April 10, 1887, Pope Leo XIII issued a Brief approving the University as requested by the American Hierarchy under whose authority and protection it must always remain, who will direct its whole administration, system of studies and discipline,[74] and appointing Bishop Keane Rector who toured Europe to gather ideas on the course of studies, the faculty and administration. A special committee was appointed to prepare the statutes and select professors, consisting of Archbishop Ryan, Bishops Ireland, Keane, Marty and Spalding and Father Chapelle. Building operations were begun in 1887, and the cornerstone was laid on May 24, 1888.

In December, 1887, Bishops Ireland, Keane and Spalding made a special appeal for financial aid in a circular to the clergy and visited a few cities in January and February of the next year to solicit more generous subscriptions from well-to-do Catholics.

The dedication[75] of Caldwell Hall, the nucleus of the University buildings, was scheduled for Wednesday, November 13, 1889, at 10:30 o'clock. The formal procession had to be abandoned because of a downpour of rain, and the Chancellor, Cardinal Gibbons, after the singing of the Veni Creator by a choir of 250 voices from St. Mary's Seminary and St. Charles College, passed along the corridors, sprinkling holy water and saying the ritualistic prayers. At noon the Mass of the Holy Ghost was celebrated by Archbishop Satolli and the sermon preached by Bishop Gilmour of Cleveland who said that the University was dedicated to the cultivation of the "science of sciences—the knowledge of God". While this was taking place in the chapel Father Fidelis of the Cross (James Kent Stone) addressed the large gathering that could not be accommodated inside on "The Vitality of the Church, a Manifestation of God".

Dinner for 250 special guests was served in the hall beneath the chapel and 1,400 were accommodated in the refectory. During the program of speeches President Harrison and his suite entered and were greeted enthusiastically by the diners.

At the close of the dinner toasts were proposed. The first was to "Our Holy Father" to which Archbishop Satolli responded with ciceronian eloquence. "Our Country and Her President" was replied to by the Honorable James G. Blaine, Secretary of State. "Our Sister Universities" evoked a speech in French from the Canadian Cardinal. "The Hierarchy of the United States" was honored by Cardinal Gibbons who thanked the President, the Vice-President and the members of the Cabinet for their presence and the interest it evidenced.

Archbishop Ryan in a witty speech sketched the character of the leaders of the hierarchy and dubbed Archbishop Ireland "the Consecrated Blizzard of the Northwest". John Boyle O'Reilly's poem "From the Heights" brought the festivities to a happy and fitting close.

At the afternoon program Bishop Virtue of Portsmouth, England, and Monsignor Gadd of Salford, in the name of the Catholics of Great

Britain and Ireland living in Rome, presented to the University a marble bust of St. Thomas, the patron of Catholic schools, as an expression of interest in the institution and of good wishes for its success.

The formal inauguration of the course of studies took place in the late afternoon with addresses by Bishop O'Farrell of Trenton, substituting for Bishop Spalding who was ill, and Monsignor Schroeder, Dean of the Faculty, who spoke in Latin. That evening a spiritual retreat began under the direction of the Rector and Father Hogan, S. S., for the student body of thirty-one priests and six laymen and nine students of the Congregation of St. Paul the Apostle. Among the students were Reverends Patrick J. Danehy and Joseph F. Busch of the Archdiocese of St. Paul.

Bishop Grace of St. Paul was too indisposed to attend the dedication which was the culmination of his hopes and dreams and prayers for the educational welfare of the Church in America.

The establishment of the Catholic University was a triumph for Archbishop Ireland who, perhaps, more than any other member of the hierarchy, except Bishop Spalding, realized the need of such an institution "to provide" as Leo XIII so aptly expressed it in his Apostolic Letter of March 7, 1889, "instruction in every department of learning to the end that the clergy and laity alike might have an opportunity to satisfy fully their laudable desire for knowledge"; to improve and coordinate the Catholic school system in the United States; to maintain a high standard of Catholic scholarship; and to impress on the Catholics of America the value of an educational training obtained under the auspices of the Church.

From the beginning the Archbishop of St. Paul was a member of the board of governors and helped to map out the program of the institution and guide its destiny during the years of struggle and expansion. He aided it by every means in his power and fostered every project calculated to extend the sphere of its usefulness. He took a justifiable pride in the success with which the undertaking was blessed during the first twenty-five years of its existence, rejoiced in the recognition accorded it by the leading secular universities of the country, and looked forward with confidence to a future signalized by still more meritorious service to religion and education in the United States. From the beginning students from the Archdiocese were enrolled in its theological courses and almost from the beginning scholarly priests of the Archdiocese occupied professorial chairs in different departments and were among the recognized leaders of its faculty. Suffice it to mention the names of Doctors O'Gorman, Shields, Turner, Ryan (whom the Catholic Historical Review for October, 1945, calls "its most distinguished alumnus and professor") and Barron, all of whom, except Dr. O'Gorman, began their professorial careers in the St. Paul Seminary. Each was without a peer in his special line of work and each added to the name and fame of the University as a center of Catholic thought and influence.

The Catholic Truth Society

One of the most important and permanent results of the Catholic Congress held in Baltimore in 1889 was the founding of the Catholic Truth Society[76] in St. Paul, the first in America, on March 10, 1890, at the Archbishop's residence with nine charter members. The following officers were elected: President, M. W. Cole of St. Paul; Vice-President, Roger Vail of Minneapolis; Corresponding Secretary, William F. Markoe of Minneapolis; Recording Secretary, M. A. Stapleton of St. Paul; Treasurer, C. W. Copley of St. Paul; Censors, Reverend J. C. Byrne of Minneapolis and Reverend P. R. Heffron of St. Paul. The first Board of Directors was made up of J. W. Cresson, C. W. Copley, H. C. McNair, J. C. Nolan, M. A. Stapleton and M. W. Cole of St. Paul, and Roger Vail, Charles Larpenteur and W. F. Markoe of Minneapolis.

An office was opened in the Catholic Block and soon a publishing company was organized to flood the country with Catholic literature. The business of the Society was transacted by a Board of Directors of seven members elected annually who held monthly meetings alternately in St. Paul and Minneapolis. Any one could join the society by sending in his name and address and a fee of one dollar for yearly dues, for which he was entitled to special rates on books and other publications of the society. The object of the society was to give practical expression to the belief of the members that the mission of the Church in the United States was "to make America Catholic", by securing the cooperation of Catholics in disseminating Catholic literature in the form of short timely tracts on the fundamental teaching of Catholicism; by a prompt and systematic correction of misstatements or slanders against the Church; by publishing reliable news about Catholic events; by the circulation of books, tracts, pamphlets and newspapers; by lectures on Catholic topics; by supplying the inmates of jails and reformatories with Catholic reading.

The society was known as "The Catholic Truth Society of Minnesota" to distinguish it from a similar society in Canada; but, as a matter of fact, it was the Catholic Truth Society of America, and its publications bear the imprint "American Series of Publications, No. . . . ." The official prospectus issued at the beginning of the second year asks that all correspondence be addressed to "The Catholic Truth Society of America". The corresponding secretary's third annual report uses the same name; but most of the official reports retain the original name.

Enquiries for copies of the constitution and by-laws were received from all over the country and Kansas City, Kansas, was the first to form a local branch on June 2, 1890.

The first quarterly report showed that four articles on Catholic doctrine, fifteen correcting slanders and misstatements and twenty-three items of reliable Catholic news had been published in the daily press of the Twin Cities, an aggregate of thirty columns in all, for which no charge was made by the papers. Twenty-four articles relating to the society appeared in the Northwestern Chronicle and were copied in many Catholic papers. The society sold sixty-four Catholic books and many pamphlets by local priests refuting calumnies.

Two public lectures were given under the auspices of the society, one by the Reverend J. C. Byrne on "Calumnies Against the Catholic Church", and the other by Reverend Thomas O'Gorman on "How Catholics Come to be Misunderstood". Both were published in pamphlet form.

The second quarterly report issued in October showed that the society had a membership of 223 (including 14 women), of whom 115 were in St. Paul, 26 in Minneapolis and 30 throughout the state. Promoters were appointed in several parishes and committees named to take charge of special book sales in the churches. 14,000 copies of original pamphlets and leaflets had been sold out of a total of 41,000 published by the society and 21,000 copies of a prospectus had been distributed.

By the end of the year there were 294 members enrolled and new conferences had been formed in Worcester, Mass., with nine charter members, and in Newark, N. J., with five. Twenty-five copies of Catholic papers and as many magazines were distributed each week in the county jail and the workhouse in St. Paul and in the Old Soldiers' Home in Minneapolis.

During the first quarter of 1891 the membership rose to 493 representing 33 states with 294 in Minnesota. There were 69 women enrolled. The first annual lecture was delivered by Honorable W. J. Onahan of Chicago. The number of pamphlets, tracts and leaflets published by the society rose to 61,800 and 23,000 prospectuses were distributed. Arrangements were made to publish one pamphlet a month. Bishop Grace contributed the sum of fifty dollars to the society to further its work.

During the second quarter 11,945 pamphlets were circulated and 1,400 copies of the papal encyclical on the Condition of Labor were mailed to prominent members of the trades and professions. New members were enrolled from Ontario, Manitoba, Hawaiian Islands, Belgium, and 39 states of the Union, making a total of 602.

On December 21, 1891, the Minneapolis Conference of the Catholic Truth Society was formed with William F. Markoe, President; J. J. Collins, Vice-President; M. W. Meagher, Corresponding Secretary; J. J. Sinnott, Recording Secretary; J. C. Scallen, Treasurer; and Reverend J. C. Byrne, Censor. The 61 charter members grew to 81 in three months.

The second annual report showed 24 societies affiliated with the parent organization which had published 58,500 copies of original pamphlets during the year, secured the publication of 109 articles in secular papers and attained a membership of 911 of whom 415 were in Minnesota.

The third annual report, March 10, 1893, showed a membership of 1169 in 43 states of the union, in Canada, Belgium, Italy and the Hawaiian Islands, and 21 auxiliary societies in different parts of the United States. It announced the holding of a National Convention during the week of the Second Catholic Congress of the laity at the World's Fair in Chicago.

The last annual meeting in 1894 abolished the membership fee and consequently no formal organization was maintained thereafter. Many features of the work were discontinued except the distribution of pamphlets. Twenty-nine original pamphlets had been issued and distributed by the thousands. During these four years 280 articles had appeared in the public press; 356,000 pamphlets and leaflets had been printed, and 328,560 distributed.

Finally, in 1895, it was decided to merge with the International Catholic Truth Society of Brooklyn, N. Y., founded by Monsignor W. F. McGinnis, and all electrotypes, unsold pamphlets, tracts and leaflets, were shipped to its headquarters. This merger was necessitated in some measure by the financial depression of the early nineties and, perhaps, more so by the burdensome demands made on the busy men who were carrying on the work of the Society without remuneration. During the first years of its existence it did a world of good in breaking down anti-Catholic prejudice by the correction of erroneous statements and notions about the Church and the dissemination of her true doctrines through the printed word.

The fifth, and last, annual report, dated March 10, 1895, shows that, while no new pamphlets had been published, 40,000 copies of previous pamphlets and leaflets had been reprinted and 30,700 circulated, leaving on hand a complete assortment of all pamphlets and leaflets amounting to 26,150 of the former and 13,000 of the latter. The receipts for the year amounted to $589.86 all of which, together with a balance of $100.46, from the previous year, was disbursed for printing, mailing, etc., except $71.09 on hand when the Society closed its books and disposed of its possessions.

Events in St. Paul

On his return from the triple celebration in the East the Archbishop of St. Paul visioned a parish for the French Canadians residing in West St. Paul[77] and asked the Marist Fathers in charge of St. Louis Church to assume the direction of it. Father Gros, pastor of the parish and superior of the community, sent Father John Chareyre to say Mass for them in St. Michael's Church and ascertain the need, if any, for a separate parish. After several months of investigation and negotiation it was decided that there was no demand for a French parish in that locality and the matter was dropped. Father Chareyre was appointed Professor of Philosophy in St. Thomas Seminary and later on in the St. Paul Seminary where he remained till the spring of 1896.

The Northwestern Chronicle for April 18, 1890, announced that the Most Reverend Archbishop had established his residence at Chatsworth and Leslie Streets "far from the center of the city", but would maintain his office in the Cathedral residence where he would be accessible to callers whenever he was in the city. On August 15, 1892, Leslie Street was changed to Portland Avenue from Victoria Street to its western terminus.

The public records disclose the fact that the premises at 977 Portland Avenue, corner of Chatsworth, was conveyed[78] to the Archbishop on November 11, 1892, by Eugene and Gertrude C. Nehl, and by him deeded to the Diocese of St. Paul on December 25, 1893, for a consideration of one hundred dollars. This would indicate that he occupied the house for two and a half years before buying it.

On Sunday, April 27, 1890, the Archbishop was present at the laying of the cornerstone of the Sacred Heart Cathedral in Davenport, Iowa, and thence proceeded to the East for a ten-day visit in Washington and Baltimore.

The Blessing of the Right Reverend Bernard Locnikar, O. S. B., as Abbot of St. John's, took place in the abbey church on August 27, 1890, in presence of a distinguished gathering of prelates and clergy. The ceremony was performed by Bishop Zardetti of St. Cloud and the sermon preached by Bishop Shanley of Jamestown. The Most Reverend Archbishop Ireland was present together with Bishops Ryan of Buffalo, Cotter of Winona, Flasch of La Crosse, Vertin of Marquette, and Abbots Innocent of Atchinson, Frowin of Conception, Finyan of St. Meinrad's and Archabbot Andrew of St. Vincent's. The function was followed by a banquet and toasts responded to by the visiting prelates.

An important event of the summer of 1891, reported in the Northwestern Chronicle of July 21, was the visit of Archbishop Satolli to St. Paul where he arrived on Tuesday, July 25, after a month's tour of the West as far as the Pacific coast in the private coach generously placed at his disposal by Mr. Hill, President of the Great Northern Railway. A public reception in his honor was held at the Ryan Hotel attended by the Bishops of the Province and others, a large number of priests and about fifteen hundred people all of whom were greeted by the distinguished visitor. This was followed by a banquet at which an address of welcome was read by C. D. O'Brien on behalf of the Catholic laity to which the guest of honor responded in a Latin address translated into English by Father O'Gorman of the Catholic University who accompanied him on the trip. Archbishop Satolli celebrated Pontifical Mass in the Church of the Assumption the following Sunday.

During the first week of August Archbishop Ireland preached the clergy retreat for the Diocese of Davenport; and on the Sunday evenings of the month of September delivered a series of lectures on the Papal Enyclical "On the Condition of Labor" in the Cathedral of St. Paul which was crowded to the doors by interested listeners.

On September 30, 1891, he attended the silver jubilee of consecration of Bishop Hennessy of Dubuque in St. Raphael's Cathedral at which four Archbishops and nine Bishops were present together with hundreds of priests and thousands of the laity. The sermon was delivered by Archbishop Ryan of Philadelphia. The celebration ended with a dinner in the Hotel Julien at which toasts were honored by Archbishops Ireland and Feehan, Bishop Chatard of Indianapolis and Reverend D. S. Phelan, editor of the Western Watchman of St. Louis, to all of which the Jubilarian responded, thanking those who had honored him with their presence on the auspicious anniversary.

One of the first letters written by the Archbishop after his elevation to metropolitan rank asked for more generous collections for the education of young men for the diocesan priesthood in St. Thomas Seminary. The letter, dated November 4, 1888, says that the Archdiocese needs at least fifteen new priests every year and funds for their education must be available. There are 160 diocesans and 30 regulars engaged in the work of the ministry. The previous year's seminary collection of $8,336.68 left a deficit of $5,814.20 in the fund which should be at least $20,000 to meet the current expenses of the institution, and another $70,000 is needed to endow the professorial chairs. He suggests that scholarships of $4,000 each be founded and the faithful be urged to make bequests to St. Thomas in their wills.

Archbishop Ireland was credited with preventing the Hall-Fitzsimmons prize fight[79] in St. Paul in 1891, a fight promoted by local groups with public sentiment behind them. Non-Catholic ministers and others had tried in vain to stop the bout before Archbiship Ireland brought influence to bear on Governor Merriam who invoked the power of the state when local officials, derelict to duty, had previously agreed to allow the fight to proceed. This showed that the laws against prizefighting could be enforced despite the apathy of public sentiment. It is said that the late James J. Corbett of San Francisco, afterwards heavy weight champion, was on hand to view the fight and when he heard it had been called off wanted to know "who . . . is this John Ireland?"

In September, 1891, the Archbishop made the following priests irremovable rectors[80] of their respective parishes: Father Stariha of St. Francis de Sales, St. Paul; Father Byrne of the Immaculate Conception, and Father O'Reilly of St. Anthony, Minneapolis. A few years previously he had named Father Caillet irremovable rector of St. Mary's in St. Paul. Three of these parishes continued to be irremovable rectorships—St. Mary's, St. Francis and St. Anthony. The Immaculate Conception, for some reason, ceased to be one after Father Byrne's departure.

On February 20, 1892, the Holy See received a memorial[81] from the Right Reverend Anthony Racine, Bishop of Sherbrooke, in the Province of Quebec, on behalf of the French Canadian Bishops, relative to the religious welfare of the French Canadians living in the United States, in which it was stated that these immigrants were of different nationality and language from the Catholics with whom they associated, and special means should be taken to provide them with religious instruction in French. The memorial did not suggest the appointment of French bishops in the United States but left the question open, though it gave the impression that the French Canadian Catholics in the United States did not receive due consideration from the hierarchy. In view of the controversy on this point, decided against the Germans, no favorable action was taken in the matter.

Neverheless, the memorial was regarded as an unwarranted interference in the affairs of the Catholic Church in the United States. It was supposed to be kept secret but was published in Rome and Chicago. Its description of the moral and religious conditions in the United States was a gross and unwarranted exaggeration of facts. It was a calumny to say that Canadian Catholics in this country were not treated with fullest justice. The memorial was addressed in a special way to the Bishops of New England where so many thousands of Canadian French had settled.

Catholic Charities Bureau

One of the dominant characteristics of the Bishops of St. Paul was their love for the poor and underprivileged. Not only did they organize societies, such as the St. Vincent de Paul, to provide food, clothing and other necessities for them, but they exemplified in their own persons the finest traits of Catholic charity. Bishop Cretin was known as the father of the poor and noted for helping them in the most unostentatious manner, giving of his meager resources to aid individuals and families in distress.

We have noted elsewhere the record of Bishop Grace's benefactions. The appeals of the poor were never unheard. To the extent of his ability, Bishop Grace left no one unaided. So, likewise, Archbishop Ireland had his pensioners who came at regular intervals to his office in the old Cathedral residence, the friends of better days, the "financially embarrassed" and others in need of help to eke out an existence in a cold and unsympathetic world. Archbishop Dowling did not let the left hand know what the right did in relieving distress; and Archbishop Murray's motto of "All I Have Is Yours" is lived up to in the fullest measure by collecting money, food and clothing for the victims of depression, unemployment, world wars, and upheavals of nature.

Archbishop Ireland fostered the work of the St. Vincent de Paul Society, attended the meetings of its conferences and counselled a broadening of its relief program. So anxious was he that no worthy person suffer want, that he supplemented its work by forming a special society, known as the Catholic Central Bureau,[82] to provide for the stranger within the gates, the floaters and the transients who infest all large cities.

It was organized in 1887 with an office on St. Peter Street in the transept of the old Cathedral under the management of Lorenzo J. Markoe and Joseph Roupf. Its purpose was to supply information to strangers and visitors and give temporary relief to those who were not cared for by the St. Vincent de Paul Society or other agency. It had a board of directors of four members—C. M. Crowley (chairman), J. P. O'Brien, B. Wurst and H. de Wallace—under the direction of the Archbishop.

During the year 1890 it handled 826 applications for relief. The receipts amounted to $952.54 and the expenses to $970.00, for board, lodging, cash loans, transportation, clothing, medicine, etc. The paid-up subscriptions for 1890 amounted to $922.00 of which the Archbishop gave $100.00, J. J. Hill $80.00, Archbishop Grace $25.00.

The budget of $800.00 for 1891 provided very modest salaries for the managers, a horse and buggy to aid them in their work, the cost of printing, fuel, etc. Its work was in some respects a duplication of that of the St. Vincent de Paul conference and it had only a brief existence.

In the first decade of the twentieth century the National Conference of Catholic Charities was organized and Archbishop Ireland appointed a City Missionary for St. Paul in the person of Reverend John R. Power, assistant pastor of St. Mary's Church, who was commissioned a Probation Officer by Judge Orr of the Juvenile Court to look after the Catholic children who came before him, and to represent the St. Vincent de Paul Society in dispensing charity.[83] He was succeeded in 1908 by Reverend James Donahoe, assistant pastor of the Church of the Immaculate Conception in Minneapolis, who for several years had taken an interest in the work of the juvenile and police courts in that city, and who continued the work begun in St. Paul and amplified it until 1915, when he was appointed pastor of the newly-established parish of St. Bridget in Minneapolis. He was the first delegate from the Archdiocese to the National

Convention of Catholic Charities in Washington where he met the recognized leaders of the movement. It was during his tenure of office that the first home for friendless girls was established in 1910 in the former Mealey residence on St. Peter Street under the auspices of the Guild of Catholic Women, an institution that developed into the modern and commodious Guild Hall on Western Avenue. During the 1911 and 1913 sessions of the State Legislature Father Donahoe was credited with turning the tide in favor of the Mothers' Pension bill, the Police Women's bill, the Child-placing bill and others regulating the distance between boarding schools and taverns and granting legal custody of inmates to state-inspected and registered institutions.

Father Donahoe was succeeded in the office of City Missionary by Reverends L. F. Ryan, W. W. Finley, W. P. O'Reilly and J. F. Doherty, the latter of whom studied sociology at the Catholic University of America the better to carry on the work until it was systematized and legally incorporated at the beginning of the episcopate of Archbishop Dowling. Prior to that the salary of the City Missionary was paid by the Chancery Office and the work was sustained by voluntary contributions from interested friends, the St. Vincent de Paul Society, the Guild of Catholic Women and other groups. The City Missionary lived at the Cathedral residence, and on Sunday said Mass at Fort Snelling for the soldiers and civilians.

In the meantime similar arrangements were made for Minneapolis. In 1905 Judge Waite of the Juvenile Court requested Archbishop Ireland to appoint a priest to take charge of the delinquent Catholic children who appeared before his court, and Reverend W. Luby was set aside for the work with the title of City Missionary. He was succeeded by Reverend M. A. McRaith who worked in this field until 1918. They resided at the Immaculate Conception rectory and moved to the Pro-Cathedral residence with the parish clergy in 1914. Their salaries were paid by the Chancery Office, and the funds for the support of the work were provided by voluntary donations and by the Conferences of the St. Vincent de Paul Society. They were succeeded by the Reverend W. P. Driscoll under whom the Catholic Central Bureau was incorporated by Archbishop Dowling.

Conversion of the Scandinavians

For years Archbishop Ireland gave serious consideration to the conversion of the Scandinavian population of Minnesota. He was quite familiar with the question in all its bearings.

In a letter to Cardinal Gibbons, under date of December 5, 1889,[84] he writes that Minnesota is practically the Scandinavian state of the West. Swedes constitute about one half of the Scandinavian population. Norwegians and Danes make up the other half, the Norwegians, however, being three times more numerous than the Danes.

There are in Minneapolis 60,000 Scandinavians and 300,000 of them in the whole state. They are intelligent, industrious, aggressive. They are always largely represented in the legislature and in various state and municipal offices. Ten years ago they were addicted to drunkenness; but their ministers have worked hard for temperance and they are now the most temperate element of our general population, next to the Irish-Americans. I have not seldom spoken in their temperance meetings. They learn English rapidly. In view of their present numbers, and their future influence, too much importance cannot be attached to any question relating to them.

They are, nearly all, Lutherans of the old school—though Methodism has made, since their arrival in America, some progress among them. Believing as they do nearly all our dogmas, claiming the same sacramental system, and freed in America from social pressure and local traditions under which they suffer at home, I have always believed that the Church rightly presented to them would gain among them many adherents. It has long been my conviction that the chief effort for the conversion of the Scandinavians should be made in America—whence a Catholic spirit would reach their countrymen in Europe. We have in Minnesota some few Scandinavian converts in almost every mission. I have myself in the course of my ministry received a score of them into the Church.

To do good among the Scandinavians we need priests of their own tongue, and priests with peculiar gifts of soul. The Scandinavians are intelligent, and they will have to be reasoned into belief. The priest must be learned, and eloquent; he must be one who attracts by his sermons. He must be zealous and active, one, who as a true apostle will go from place to place, lecture in hall or church, distribute books.

We have made serious efforts to have men. Fifteen years ago we obtained from the Brignole-Sala College of Genoa, a Norwegian and Swedish priest, a convert. He was eloquent and had in St. Paul crowds to hear him. . . .He is now in charge of a German Catholic Church in Detroit. Five years ago I obtained a Swedish priest from Louvain; but he was no preacher: he has since died. I have now studying for this diocese three young Norwegians, in the Jesuit College of Copenhagen, selected purposely for me by the Vicar-Apostolic of Norway. But, of course, years and years must go by before they will be fit for work, even if they do persevere. You see, I have not been forgetting the Scandinavians. In other dioceses, nothing, I think, has been done. Indeed it is so difficult to do anything, that bishops cannot be blamed.

Last winter, a former student of Propaganda, Rev. Eric Wang, now in charge of the Catholic mission of Christiania, came to Minnesota to visit his relatives, who had emigrated hither. He was exactly of my type of Scandinavian missionary. He gave several lectures in Minneapolis, and his people talked seriously of building a church for him, if he would remain. He was anxious to stay. But his superior desired him to return to Christiania. Now if Cardinal Simeoni will order at once Father Wang to St. Paul, I will support him, and aid him in his work in every possible way. A test can be made, as to what the hopes may be for ultimate success. Please urge upon the Cardinal the sending of Father Wang to St. Paul. Without his presence in the West, nothing worth talking of can be done.

If the suggested appeal were made to Cardinal Simeoni it was barren of results. Nor did any of the students of the Jesuit College do missionary work in the diocese as far as the records go. A few years later, however, George A. Arctander of Minneapolis, a Norwegian convert, entered St. Paul Seminary, was ordained on November 11, 1896, for the Archdiocese of St. Paul, by Bishop Shanley of Fargo, and was engaged in parochial work in the Twin Cities until 1902, when he became a member of the Diocesan Mission Band and gave missions not only in the diocese but throughout the Northwest until 1907, when he was appointed pastor of the Church of St. Andrew, St. Paul, where he died rather suddenly in September, 1909.

In 1890 the question of providing chaplains for the Army and the Navy was a cause of grave concern to the members of the hierarchy. Priests to fill these positions were not to be had. The few who offered to serve were either unfitted for such work or sought the aid of politicians to secure the appointment. One applicant for a chaplaincy in the Navy gave as a reason for seeking the position the need of a sea voyage for the benefit of his health.[85] An application sent to President Harrison was referred to Archbishop Ireland before being acted on. It was finally decided that a commission of Archbishops with Cardinal Gibbons as chairman would present names for the chaplaincies in the Army and the Navy; and the necessity of filling the vacancies with a proportionate number of priests was on the agenda for the next meeting of the Archbishops.

The following year the Archbishop again addressed the Cardinal on the need of Catholic chaplains. He had to confess that he had found no applicants. "Better by far", he added, "to have no Catholic chaplains than to have unfit men".[86] He was alluding to one who was about to be court-marshalled.

Ten years later the Archbishop was informed by President Roosevelt that four Catholic chaplains were to be appointed. The Cardinal was to name one; Archbishop Corrigan another; and the other two were to be selected by the Archbishop of St. Paul from the West. The President wanted only first class priests. One indifferent Catholic chaplain would harm all others and lower the morale of the group.

The Faribault School Plan

From the beginning of the Diocese of St. Paul efforts were made to obtain from the public treasury financial aid for Catholic schools. Bishop Cretin and his friends as early as February, 1853, failed to muster enough votes in the Territorial Legislature to pass a bill giving state aid to sectarian schools.

In the first decade of Bishop Grace's episcopate the St. Paul Public

School Board was offered the administrative control of the parochial schools in the city on condition that it defray the cost of their upkeep and maintenance as a unit of the public school system—an offer which was rejected because it meant the diversion of public funds for the support of religious schools.

In these early days even as now the patrons of Catholic schools had to contribute their share of taxes for the support of the public schools in addition to building, maintaining and staffing their own schools. It was quite natural that they should become restive under the burden of double taxation and seek ways and means of remedying the discrimination. Most of the parents of the children attending the parochial schools found it difficult to pay even the modest tuition asked of them and as a result few, if any, of these schools were self-supporting.

Such was the condition of the Immaculate Conception school of Faribault in 1890. The Reverend James J. Conry had just been appointed pastor of the parish and in taking inventory found that there was insufficient revenue to meet the ordinary expenses of the parish, pay interest on the debt, and maintain the school and its teachers. The tuition was only fifty cents a month for each pupil and, as many were too poor to pay even that amount, the Dominican Sisters in charge received little more than a bare subsistence. Something had to be done to meet the severe drain on the resources of the parish.

To make matters worse the four rooms in the school were not fully occupied while the public schools were overcrowded. The advisability of closing the school was seriously considered when Martin W. Shields, Editor of the Faribault Pilot, suggested to Father Conry that it might be feasible to do what had been done in Scott County, where he had been superintendent of schools before coming to Faribault, namely, lease the school to the Board of Education with the proviso that the Sisters be retained and their salaries and all expenses of administration paid out of public funds.

Father Conry accepted the suggestion and, with the approval of Archbishop Ireland, approached the members of the Board of Education with whom he was well acquainted—George W. Batchelder, M. H. Keeley, A. E. Hoven, H. Chafee and County Superintendent, S. B. Wilson—to ascertain their reaction. At a meeting held on Saturday evening, August 22, 1891, he verbally submitted the proposition to place under their control the Immaculate Conception school with its equipment and grounds. They were rather surprised at the offer and deferred action till the following Wednesday when, at a special meeting, they decided to ask Father Conry to submit the proposition in writing which he did on August 26 when it was voted unanimously to accept it. The members felt that they should be commended "for broad-minded liberality and for manifesting their ability to deal with so vexing an educational problem, from a purely educational standpoint".

Father Conry's letter[87] was as follows:

Faribault, Minn.,
August 26, 1891.

To the Board of Education of the City of Faribault—

Gentlemen: I have been informed by a member of your board that you wished me to state definitely in writing the proposition I submitted to you on the evening of the 22nd inst., and to which you gave courteous attention. As an American interested in obtaining for the future citizens of the Republic the greatest advantages consistent with the common good, I beg leave to comply with your request and again submit (this time in writing) the proposition submitted on the evening of August 22, 1891, repeating with your permission a few of the reasons at that time submitted therefor, viz.:

That the children at present enrolled in the schools of the Immaculate Conception parish may receive the benefits that result from an American training in all that term implies; that these children may thus receive in their civic training a perfect preparation for the duties and the responsibilities of American citizenship, thereby enhancing the renown of this city among its sister cities of the commonwealth, as a great educational center; and that our custodians of the public schools may receive from the state and county appropriations that additional per capita tax which the commonwealth wishes them to receive, and which at present they fail to receive because of the maintenance of separate schools.

I herewith subjoin the proposition: In consideration of one dollar ($1.00) I agree to place under control of the board of education of the City of Faribault the school building and all its equipment, at present known as the parish school of the Immaculate Conception Church, with the grounds upon which the school is located, the same to be used by said board for educational purposes under such conditions as that board may determine to be for the best interests of all concerned.

Confidently trusting the matter, gentlemen, to your discretion and judgment, I remain,

Respectfully yours,
James J. Conry.

It is only fair to Father Conry to believe that the letter was written hurriedly and without the remotest conception of the importance it was to acquire in the immediate future. It was loosely put together and words and phrases employed which, on more mature consideration, would have been eliminated or modified. No wonder that Archbishop Ireland admitted that "the priest at Faribault bungled things somewhat and in his desire to avert Protestant bigotry used some expressions which Catholics can well criticize".[88]

This letter formed the whole basis for the now famous Faribault School Plan which was never intended to be more than an experiment made necessary by local conditions and which, if it proved successful, might be extended to other parish schools in similar circumstances.

The new arrangement went into effect on August 31, 1891, when the Immaculate Conception school, thereafter known as the Hill school, resumed the work of another year with the Board of Education agreeing to operate and manage it as part of the public school system. The contract was on a yearly basis and could be rescinded by either party thereto at the end of that period. Each of the three teaching sisters received forty dollars a month instead of the twenty-five theretofore paid whenever it was available. They were subject to examination by the school board as were the pupils and they were put on a level with the public school teachers. The school remained the property of the parish but was for all intents and purposes a public school from nine o'clock in the forenoon to half past three in the afternoon each school day during which the ordinary branches of a secular education were taught, and after that the children were given religious instruction for half an hour. All the expenses of the school for salaries, upkeep and maintenance were paid by the County, as well as a nominal rental of one dollar a year.

It seemed to be a very equitable arrangement. It is true that crucifixes and other emblems of religion were removed from the class rooms before the actual transfer took place, but this was done not because of any order or suggestion of the school board, but on the advice of prominent Catholics who feared that the presence of such emblems might cause unreasoning criticism and militate against the success of the plan. Nor did the pastor have anything more to say about the method of conducting the school than he had about that of any other public school.

In the meantime the plan was adopted by the Board of Education of Stillwater in favor of St. Michael's school handicapped by the need of sufficient funds to carry on its work in an efficient manner. The board leased the school for one dollar a year and conducted it as any other public school in the city. Here, as in Faribault, religious instruction was given the pupils after the regular school hours.

Both schools flourished as never before. New furnishings were provided by the state; new equipment installed; and the people, no longer responsible for the support of the school, were able to make more generous contributions for church purposes, and the parishes to pay their debts. The plan was simple, satisfactory, and safe for Catholic consciences and complied with the letter and spirit of the civil laws regarding schools.

It may be well to state that this experiment was not new even in Minnesota. It had been in operation for years in a number of schools in the Diocese of St. Cloud under conditions less favorable to the Church.

In other parts of the country, likewise, a similar arrangement had been in effect for many years. It had its origin in Poughkeepsie,[89] New York, where, in the year 1873, Reverend F. J. McSweeney, pastor of St. Peter's Church, proposed that the parish schools be placed under the Board of Education as far as secular teaching was concerned, the Board to pay a dollar a year rent for each of the buildings and furnishings and keep them in repair and insured; establish a public school in each building and have absolute and unrestricted control of them during school hours; select, employ and pay proper teachers to instruct the children in secular knowledge. The pastor insisted that the children be taught christian doctrine either before or after school hours. Either the pastor or the board could terminate the lease at the end of any scholastic year on thirty days notice.

Father McSweeney's successor, Father Nolan, was enthusiastic about the plan which flourished under Cardinal McCloskey, Archbishop of New York, and his successor, Archbishop Corrigan. It was taken as a model for the Faribault plan. In the memorial presented to the Holy See by Archbishop Ireland in defence of the Faribault plan he declared that it was "in operation in eight localities of the Diocese of Archbishop Katzer of Milwaukee who also established it in his former Diocese of Green Bay. It obtains in a great number of the schools of Bishop Zardetti in the Diocese of St. Cloud where it was the accepted system in German Catholic settlements throughout Stearns County; in the Diocese of Savannah, Bishop Becker has it in operation in all the Catholic schools of his episcopal city. The Fathers of the Society of Jesus have applied the same plan with great success in the parish of Connewago in the Diocese of Harrisburg; it also obtains in the dioceses of Albany, Erie, Buffalo, Rochester, Peoria, etc., etc."

It would seem, therefore, that Faribault and Stillwater were in excellent company and might confidently look forward to a period marked by harmonious relations between Catholics and Protestants as a result of the satisfactory solution of their educational problems. Such, however, was not to be the case. The smooth working of the system was not to continue indefinitely. While serious and fair-minded men regarded the plan with favor, Protestant ministers in St. Paul and throughout the state professed to see in it a surrender of the public schools to the Catholic Church, "a clever trick of the Archbishop of St. Paul to capture the public schools for the Church of Rome". They went so far as to say that there was a tacit understanding that the nuns would use the school to teach catechism, and that children were being segregated according to religion.

In Stillwater certain Protestant citizens protested the action of the school board and threatened legal proceedings to revoke the contract. A group of ministers in Minneapolis made a similar demand on the ground that the arrangement was a complete victory of the Catholic Church over the State.

It was, perhaps, reasonable to expect such an attack from Protestants but hard to understand why Catholics, especially German Catholics, should react so viciously and violently against the plan as if it meant the elimination of all parochial schools, unless they feared, which seems to have been the case, that the teaching of the German language would be completely banished from Catholic schools and with it all knowledge of their cherished national customs and culture. Nor were the fears without foundation in fact. The "Bennett Law" enacted by the Wisconsin legislature required that English be taught in all state schools for at least sixteen weeks each year to make it possible for all prospective Americans to speak the English language—the language of America. They assumed that it was Archbishop Ireland's objective to foist the Faribault School plan on all Catholic parishes in his diocese and as far as possible in the country, and they rose in protest against what they considered an attack on their rights as Catholics to have their children educated in Catholic schools where the German language and culture would be perpetuated. If other nationalities made similar claims, as they would have a right to do, America would be a babel of languages, disunited and disorganized. The German papers accused Archbishop Ireland of heresy and disloyalty to Catholic interests, but said nothing about the German Catholics of Wisconsin who had adopted the plan, particularly in Ozaukee and Washington counties, where the district school was taught by German sisters and supported by public money. Thus the Archbishop "found himself in a singular predicament . . . between two enemies—one Catholic, one Protestant". If he placated the one, he aroused the other.[90] He was made the object of concerted and violent attacks by opponents of the school plan. Even his religious orthodoxy was called in question. They recalled an address he delivered in July, 1890, before the delegates to the convention of the National Education Association in St. Paul, on "State Schools and Public Schools", in which he granted the state the right to establish schools and compel the attendance of children at some school, and praised its liberality in offering gratuitous instruction to all, irrespective of creed, color or condition of life. He went on to point out the most serious defect of the public school, namely, the tendency to eliminate religion from the minds and hearts of the youth of America. It is because of this that Catholics must have parish schools. They would not be necessary if the parish school were made "in every respect a state school". He cited the plan in operation (since 1873) in Poughkeepsie, N. Y., where the parochial schools are leased to the board of education for a nominal sum and incorporated into the public school system. The teachers are engaged and paid by the board; teachers and pupils examined; state books used; and visitation by the Superintendent of public instruction welcomed.

There was a tacit understanding that so long as the Catholic teachers passed their examination and did their work efficiently and loyally under control of the board they should not be replaced by teachers of another faith. During school hours no religious instruction is given.

He proclaimed himself not only a friend but "an advocate of the state school"; he praised the state for affirming "its resolve that within its borders no cloud of ignorance shall settle upon the minds of the children of its people". It is safe to say that "no other speech like it on Catholic and State schools had ever been uttered in the United States by an Archbishop".

The address aroused a storm of criticism and evoked protests from Catholics who thought that he was abandoning the parochial school in favor of what they considered "Godless" schools or at least in which the religion of the majority, namely, Protestantism, in one form or another, would be taught. It started a controversy among Catholic religious leaders which "was without parallel in American Catholic history in point of extent, intensity and bitterness of feeling".

Complaints were made to Rome about his heterodoxy in setting aside the decrees of the Plenary Council of Baltimore regarding Catholic schools and their necessity for the true education of the young. These unfavorable reports were for the most part based on garbled extracts from the address or quotations taken from the context, and Cardinal Gibbons was requested by Cardinal Rampolla, Secretary of State to His Holiness, Pope Leo XIII, to express his opinion on its orthodoxy, which he did after consultation with Archbishop Ireland who maintained that his enemies had "labored very industriously to misrepresent that address". The Archbishop declared that he had endeavored to obtain the cooperation of the state by insisting on the necessity of religion in its schools, with provision for the maintenance of denominational schools for minorities unwilling to accept the religious teaching of the majority. Far from deploring the existence of parochial schools he had gone so far in his diocese as to lay upon parishes "rather unbearable burdens in order to give them schools". As a matter of fact there were sixty-three Catholic schools in the diocese with 12,000 in attendance and in many places not provided with parish schools the teachers in the local schools were Catholic and no danger threatened the religious welfare of the children in attendance.

On December 30, 1890, Cardinal Gibbons sent a detailed report to Leo XIII which he regarded as a "full vindication of Archbishop Ireland", and for a time all was quiet on the western front, until the Faribault plan brought into the forum of public discussion in a very definite way the question of religion in education and of state funds for denominational schools.

A couple of months after the inauguration of the Faribault plan Dr. Bouquillon, a distinguished professor of the Catholic University at Washington, issued a pamphlet entitled, "Education: To Whom Does It Belong?", a pamphlet[91] which had no direct connection with the Faribault plan but which came from the press at such an inopportune time as to give rise to the suspicion, if not the conviction, that it had been inspired by Archbishop Ireland, an accusation which he flatly denied. "I knew nothing of Dr. Bouquillon's pamphlet until I saw it in print". As a matter of fact it was written at the request of Cardinal Gibbons and was, as Monsignor Guilday described it, "a purely abstract exposition of principles independent of circumstances of time or country".

Dr. Bouquillon's thesis dealt with "the right to educate, the reason to educate, authority over education and liberty of education. These he considered from the fourfold point of view of the individual, the family, the state and the church". His closing paragraph gave answer to the question: "Education: To Whom Does It Belong?" "It belongs to the individual, physical or moral, to the family, to the State, to the Church, to none of these solely and exclusively, but to all four combined in harmonious working, for the reason that man is not an isolated but a social being. Precisely in the harmonious combination of these four factors in education is the difficulty of practical application". It was a vindication of the State's right to educate her children and compel their attendance at school.

Dr. Bouquillon's conclusions were challenged by Father Holaind, S. J., in a brochure entitled, "The Parent First", which called for "A Rejoinder to Critics" from the learned doctor in which, according to the editor of the Catholic World, he "made it even more unmistakably clear that his doctrine is in perfect accord with the judgment of the ecclesiastical authority".

Others entered the lists. Bishop Chatard of Vincennes, while agreeing in the main with Dr. Bouquillon, thought he gave the state too much authority and that Father Holaind had answered him in "a solid and able manner". Dr. Messmer, professor of Canon Law at the Catholic University and Bishop-elect of Green Bay, considered both pamphlets excellent—the one dealing with theoretical principles, the other with the practical application.

At a meeting of the Archbishops at St. Louis on November 28, 1891, in connection with the silver jubilee of consecration of Archbishop Kenrick, Archbishop Ireland was asked to explain the Faribault plan to the assembled prelates which he did so fully and satisfactorily that they were satisfied but passed no judicial opinion on it.

The secular press took notice of this meeting, and the New York Herald printed what purported to be the "inside" story, at which, it asserted, the pamphlets of Dr. Bouquillon and Father Holaind were discussed. Archbishop Ireland in an interview in the Herald for December 14, 1891, denied that there had been any discussion and in terse and vigorous language explained the fundamental conception of the Faribault plan, reviewed the pamphlets in question and threw down the gauntlet to his opponents, the German-American followers of Cahensly, the Jesuits in America and Italy, and Archbishop Corrigan of New York with whom he was in disagreement on many points of church policy in the United States. The concerted attack on Archbishop Ireland from these quarters made it imperative that he go to Rome to vindicate his orthodoxy before the highest court in the Church. There is some evidence that the prelates at the St. Louis meeting foresaw this eventuality and suggested that he present the matter in person to the Roman authorities.

In the meantime Bishop John J. Kain of Wheeling, West Virginia, at the request of Cardinal Simeoni, Prefect of the Propaganda, wrote a fifteen-page letter in French explanatory of the Faribault plan which he characterized as "a step in the right direction, towards the lifting of the double tax from heavily burdened Catholic shoulders". He reviewed favorably Dr. Bouquillon's pamphlet and declared that the Jesuits were "starting a campaign against the Archbishop of St. Paul and are the allies of the Germans who attacked this prelate principally and especially because he is against their anti-American spirit". The letter proved very gratifying to the Archbishop of St. Paul who declared that it was "written admirably".[92]

The most persistent and venemous attacks on Archbishop Ireland and his so-called liberal views on Catholic education were contained in the Civilta Cattolica, edited by Father Brandi, S. J., of Rome and they continued even after the final decision was given. The Pope expressed disapproval of these attacks and told Archbishop Ireland to attach no importance to them.

On February 21, 1892, Archbishop Ireland had an audience with Leo XIII lasting "exactly one hour"[93] and was promised "several others". He was quite encouraged by the friendly attitude of the Pontiff and of many others prominent in church affairs in the Eternal City.

On March 1, Cardinal Gibbons wrote a letter in French to the Holy Father in which he gave a detailed report of what transpired at the meeting in St. Louis at which Archbishop Ireland had explained the Faribault plan to the Archbishops. He declared that none of those present offered a word of criticism and many approved the plan, among them Archbishop Williams of Boston who congratulated the Archbishop of St. Paul and wished that the schools of his diocese had such an agreement with the public school authorities. The plan had so many advantages, wrote His Eminence, that opposition to it must be attributed to malice or ignorance. It had been in operation in a dozen dioceses before it had been adopted in Faribault and Stillwater and no one thought of raising objection or accusing the bishops and priests of unfaithfulness to their mission and treason to the Church. But passions were stirred up as soon as Archbishop Ireland acted because he had bitter enemies even in Rome and the silence of the Holy See had been and will be interpreted as a virtual condemnation of his conduct and views.

The Famous Memorial

Archbishop Ireland presented and defended his case in a memorial[94] of twenty-five typewritten pages, addressed to Cardinal Ledochowski, Prefect of the Propaganda, who, with Cardinals Rampolla, Vannutelli, Seraphini, Zigliara and Parocchi, composed the special committee appointed to hear the case and give the decision.

The memorial dealt with the practical difficulty confronting him in the Diocese of St. Paul. He denied that he inspired or knew anything about Dr. Bouquillon's pamphlet before it came from the press and asserted that the Faribault school agreement had been entered into before it appeared. It was an administrative action in which, following the dictates of conscience and judgment, he did what he believed best for the cause of Catholic education in the diocese. He had no thought of reflecting on the system of parochial schools in the United States, for that was decided by the Third Plenary Council of Baltimore and the Instructions of the Congregation of the Propaganda on November 24, 1875, which he had done his best to carry out.

In his address before the delegates to the National Education Association convention in St. Paul in July, 1890, he admitted all that he could in favor of what was good in the public school system but pointed out its deficiencies, advocated the claims of religious and especially of Catholic education, deplored the existence of double taxation and asked the State to provide a remedy by giving financial aid to Catholic as well as Protestant schools.

In the Faribault and Stillwater school plan he had no intention of dealing with the practical school problems of other bishops, but tried to meet a difficult situation in his own diocese in the best possible manner.

He went on to say that in Minnesota, a new state of the Union since 1858, the Catholic population consisted almost entirely of immigrants and their children. In Faribault almost half the population of 7,000 is Catholic and there are three parishes one of which, the Immaculate Conception, has about 1,300 souls, mostly farmers and laborers depending on a daily wage. The total annual parochial expenditure is $4,400.00, of which $1,260.00, or nearly one-third, is for school support—a heavy burden for the people.

In Stillwater conditions are about the same. It has a population of 10,000, and there are also three parishes, one of which, St. Michael's, has to spend $2,150.00 for the maintenance of the school in addition to $4,150.00 for the parish of two thousand members nearly all of whom are laboring people.

Here, as in Faribault, there was question of closing the school and sending the children to the public school, or leasing it for one dollar a year to the public school board and receiving support from public funds, with provision for the teaching of religion before or after the official school day. As a result these schools are now more flourishing than ever.

This was not a new or untried system for it had been in operation in Poughkeepsie, New York, for eighteen years and in a dozen other dioceses for shorter periods of time, as well as in England and Ireland with the approval of the bishops and to the entire satisfaction of all concerned.

The opposition aroused in St. Paul was due in no small degree to the fear of Protestant ministers and their followers that Catholics were about to capture the public schools for the Church, and they demanded that the plan be set aside.

Another attack was launched by the German Catholics who maintained that the plan involved an abandonment of the parochial schools. In reality, they feared that any departure from the present system of Catholic schools would militate against the perpetuation of the German language and old-world customs and traditions fostered by their parochial schools. In many dioceses under the jurisdiction of German bishops this very plan is in operation, and they fear that its extension to all schools would be the deathknell of their efforts to keep alive the German language and promote German culture in America, while other bishops are trying to make the rising generation American citizens in the fullest sense of the term regardless of their racial descent.

He pointed out that only a third of our Catholic children are in Catholic schools and that the Council of Baltimore makes no provision for the two-thirds in public schools. To build sufficient schools for the latter would impose an unbearable financial burden on Catholics most of whom belong to the laboring class. What has already been done was made possible by the sacrifices willingly made by our religious teachers, mostly sisters, not all of whom are able to meet the qualifications demanded by the state of all teachers. Most of the parochial schools are free and are patronized by the middle and lower classes while the well-to-do Catholics prefer to send their children to private schools not all of which are Catholic.

He answered the objections and criticisms of his enemies in dignified and convincing language and begged the Holy See "once and for all to free me from my enemies, to vindicate my conduct, to allay the apprehensions or may be reprisals of the American people, particularly at this moment when it is the policy of our Holy Father to pursue a policy of reconciliation with the spirit of Republicanism".

The memorial was prepared by Archbishop Ireland, but edited and revised[95] by Monsignor O'Connell and Reverend Humphrey Moynihan, a student of the American College for the Archdiocese of St. Paul, to bring it more into harmony with the requirements for presentation to the Congregation. In its final form it retained as much as possible of the phraseology distinctive of its author. The memorial was presented some weeks before the decision was reached by the Congregation on April 21 and approved by the Pope on the same day, but not officially communicated to Archbishop Ireland until April 30. It is evident that he learned of the favorable decision before receiving official notification for, on April 27, he wrote the Reverend James C. Byrne, pastor of the Immaculate Conception parish in Minneapolis, the famous letter in which he declared that "the so-called Faribault plan is now favorably allowed in spite of Germans and Jesuits". The decision is "tolerari potest" which means canonically "is fully allowed" . . .

Father Byrne was blamed[96] for giving this letter to the press, although, as a matter of fact, he did not do so, and for years afterwards he did not enjoy the full confidence of his superior. But time healed the breach and for many years before the Archbishop's death Monsignor Byrne was Vicar General of the Archdiocese.

The following is a translation of the official Latin communication giving the Propaganda's decision[97] in the famous controversy:

"In special congregation of the Propaganda, held on the 21st of April, 1892, to consider the question what judgment is to be formed of the arrangement entered into by Archbishop Ireland concerning the two schools at Faribault and Stillwater, Minn., in this case they decided to reply affirmatively and without derogating from the decrees of the Councils of Baltimore on parochial schools; that the arrangement entered into by Archbishop Ireland concerning the schools at Faribault and Stillwater, taking into consideration all the circumstances, can be tolerated. In an audience held on the same day, His Holiness deigned to approve the resolution of the Cardinals given above".

The friends of Archbishop Ireland were jubilant but his enemies persisted in their opposition by questioning the full import of the words "tolerari potest". The Civilta maintained that the decision had reference to the two schools in which the experiment was in force and did not justify its extension to other schools unless express permission were given. Archbishop Ireland in an interview in Rome declared that the Civilta was "in no way the organ of the Vatican"; that Cardinal Ledochowski "formally, both verbally and in writing, repudiated these interpretations" and "that the Faribault plan is allowed and approved as far as the Bishop's arguments can be approved and is permitted in all cases where independent parish schools are maintained with difficulty . . . Cardinal Ledochowski's letter imparting the decision was clear. I replied to it on May 18, saying the decision filled my heart with joy since it responded admirably to the needs of the American Church. . . . A practical code for particular conditions—I take home with me a great act, immortal hope and imperishable gratitude.[98]

After two years the Immaculate Conception school in Faribault was returned to the control of the parish because the public school board, disregarding the protest of Father Conry, substituted Protestant teachers for two sisters; and St. Michael's in Stillwater ceased to be a unit of the public school system of that city after a successful year because a local Protestant clergyman kept up agitation against it and the board would not renew the contract. The Archbishop thought the resolution of the Board "was adopted through a misunderstanding and remains open to reconsideration".

The Faribault Democrat of September 15, 1893, declared that "the work has been greatly and persistently misunderstood, and not only the board but Father Conry also has been subjected to much unjust and unfair criticism."

In September, 1893, the Archbishop issued a statement about the much-discussed plan in which he said it was stronger "in promise of future health . . . than at any preceding time". Its suspension in Faribault was temporary and made on his advice; but the plan was in successful operation in other places in the state and beyond it. Its acceptance indicates a hopeful growth of mutual good will and necessary forbearance among different classes of citizens. It has met with opposition from extremists, Catholics and non-Catholics, as was to be expected, but Rome's decision had put an end to overt opposition among the former. The Faribault plan survives as "an augury of an era of greater peace and conciliation".

About the same time he addressed a letter to the Paris Universe protesting against assertions made by "some French Journals" to the effect that he had lost favor in Rome and had been warned to give up his cherished school plan. "No monitum (warning) has been addressed to me and there is no indication that the good will of the Holy See has been withdrawn from me. . . . The decree of Tolerari Potest remains in the sense attributed to it by the Cardinal Prefect of Propaganda. I am now engaged in extending it to certain parishes in my diocese, which find themselves in those circumstances and conditions which will justify the decree".

It demanded almost superhuman courage on the part of the Archbishop to follow his convictions, to accept the abuse and vilification heaped upon him during this and other controversies without a word or sign of anger, complaint or resentment, as Father Wallburg of Cincinnati pointed out in a letter to Monsignor O'Connell on March 15, 1904, but fearless and undeterred to walk on serenely to the accomplishment of his design. The Faribault plan is on record, he wrote, and will go down in history, and when some future day the Church will be forced to accept it, he will be gloriously vindicated. It requires a high degree of courage to proclaim one's convictions and principles in the face of ridicule and opposition.

As far as the records show the Faribault School Plan ceased to operate in the Archdiocese when St. Mary's school in Waverly became an exclusively parish school in 1904, at the end of eleven years as a consolidated parochial and public school.

One of the most unrelenting opponents of Archbishop Ireland, especially on the school question, was Bishop Matz of Denver. He said that he would see his right hand withered before he would adopt the Faribault plan in the diocese. His attitude may be gleaned from the fact that on August 28, 1891, he laid down the following law for the people of his diocese:

For the future no children will be received for first Communion and Confirmation who have not, for at least two years, been attending the parish school or some other Catholic school, and we reserve to ourselves the right to judge whether the reasons are sufficiently grave in certain cases, to allow an exception to this regulation.

Archbishop Satolli wrote him a letter sharply disapproving his attitude, and the Bishop said he had modified the ruling though there was no public record of it. Archbishop Satolli instructed Father Malone of the "Colorado Catholic" that the ruling was to be ignored as a harsh and injurious measure and empowered him to announce its abrogation.

Shortly afterwards the Bishop of Denver issued a pastoral letter emphasizing the Baltimore decrees, and exhorting Catholic parents to send their children to a Catholic school, and added

Though wilful disobedience to these decrees will not subject parents to any ecclesiastical penalty or disability, they are not, therefore, to regard such violation as free from sin. The Apostolic Delegate entertains no doubt of our perfect loyalty to his authority and unfeigned respect for his person as the representative of the Vicar of Christ, Leo XIII.

Diocesan and Other Events

The fiftieth anniversary of the dedication of the log chapel of St. Paul was officially commemorated on Sunday evening, November 1, 1891, in the Cathedral, its second successor, with a sermon preached by the Most Reverend Archbishop, than whom no one was more familiar with its history. When he came to St. Paul in 1852, as a boy of fourteen, the log chapel was intact, together with the addition put to it by Father Ravoux in 1847. It was dear to him because of its association with Bishop Cretin and the early pioneers, of whom he was one of the most distinguished. He reviewed the events that led to its erection by Father Galtier, described it as he remembered it, spoke of Father Ravoux' connection with it from 1844, of the removal of the original portion threatened with collapse in 1856, and of the use of the addition as a convent chapel by the Sisters of St. Joseph until 1864 when they migrated to the new Academy in the suburbs. He recalled the growth of the diocese since 1850—twenty parishes in St. Paul, fifteen in Minneapolis and hundreds in the rural districts. But he was interested in the future and tried to visualize the city as it would be fifty years afterwards. "What will it be in 1941? I confess to a wish to be present at the centennial celebration, to see on the first of November, 1941, the city of St. Paul and the diocese of St. Paul. My soul shall crave from God on that day the privilege to roam the streets of my beloved city and to listen to the Te Deum in its majestic Cathedral".

Little did he dream (or did he?) that he would not only see the majestic Cathedral of the future, but would plan, build and dedicate it on a then unvisioned pedestal in his beloved city, and, during the same decade, do what no other Archbishop had ever done in America, if not in the world, namely, plan, build and dedicate a magnificent Basilica, only a little less monumental, in the sister-city of Minneapolis, to stand for future ages as symbols and types of the more enduring monuments, not builded by hand, nor made of bronze nor granite, formed and fashioned in the souls of the people entrusted to his shepherding during more than half a century of consecrated service to God and humanity.

While the Archbishop was in Rome in 1892 the Osservatore Romano deplored the attacks made on him by certain German and Italian newspapers which accused him of being opposed to the temporal power of the Pope. They gave garbled quotations from his sermons and addresses and attributed to him views he never held. In this connection the Osservatore calls attention to the sermon preached by him in the St. Paul Cathedral on the occasion of the sacerdotal jubilee of His Holiness, in which he dwelt on the greatness of the Papacy and eulogized the pontificate of Leo XIII, asserting that the Papacy must be independent of all foreign powers and influence. There is, declared the Osservatore, no more ardent and zealous upholder of the Pope and his policy than the Archbishop of St. Paul and none more devoted to the person of His Holiness.

On August 25, 1892, during the annual retreat for the clergy of the Archdiocese an association was formed among the priests, the members of which agreed, on being notified by the secretary of the death of one of their number, to say, as soon as convenient, three Masses for the repose of his soul. At that time the association had a membership of 108. The Reverend A. Oster was elected secretary. Four years later the membership had risen to 151. Father Oster was made perpetual secretary and issued a list of members, for it was optional to join or not. The following year 14 new members were added. Each member was asked to pay twenty-five cents on joining to meet the cost of stationery and stamps and no further assessment was levied until the fund was exhausted. The members were requested to notify the secretary of the death of a fellow priest and he issued a notice to all. On the death of Monsignor Oster in 1910 the Reverend P. M. Jung was made secretary, and when he passed away the obituary notices were sent out from the Chancery Office as at present and all diocesan priests, after ordination, automatically became members. In 1949 an incomplete list of the deceased priests from the beginning of the diocese was printed, giving the dates of death arranged according to months. This list in handy form is posted in the sacristy as a reminder to all who celebrate Mass in that church to pray for their souls. In 1951 an attempt was made to obtain the names and obituary notices of all the priests buried in the parish cemeteries of the diocese as it was constituted when erected, and as it was until the subdivisions into new dioceses restricted its area, but the results were so unsatisfactory that no list even approximately complete can be made.

On Sunday, February 5, 1893, the Archbishop dedicated the Church of St. Joseph in Sioux City, Ia., of which Father Fowler was pastor, and preached on "Religion, a Necessity of Mankind", before a congregation of fifteen hundred who crowded its nave while many more were unable to find entrance. In the evening he delivered a lecture in the Seavy Opera House to a capacity audience. On Monday evening he was tendered a reception and banquet by the business and professional men and the Protestant ministers of the city at the Mondamin Club at which E. H. Hubbard presided. The guest of honor spoke on "American Citizenship: Its Duties and Obligations" in which he answered the attacks of atheists and agnostics, and was loudly applauded by his hearers.

The Most Reverend Archbishop Ireland was present in St. Raphael's Cathedral, Dubuque, at the solemn investiture of Archbishop Hennessy with the Pallium of his new authority which was conferred by Cardinal Gibbons after Pontifical Mass by Archbishop Satolli on September 17, 1893, at which the sermon was preached by Archbishop Ryan of Philadelphia. Present at the ceremony were ten archbishops, twenty-one bishops, five monsignori, the clergy of the Archdiocese, visitors from outside and a congregation that taxed the capacity of the Cathedral. After the investiture a banquet was served to four hundred prelates and priests at Mount St. Joseph College at which, following an address and presentation from the clergy, Archbishop Satolli responded to the toast "The Holy Father"; the Archbishop of St. Paul gave an address on the "Hierarchy of the United States"; the Archbishop of New York on "Church and Country". In the Opera House that evening at a public reception tendered to the new Metropolitan an address was delivered by Archbishop Ireland on "The Catholic Church and Our Times", and Father Nugent of Liverpool made an effective plea on behalf of temperance. Before returning home Archbishop Ireland held a reception for two hundred priests and laymen and a large number of Protestant ministers.

His Eminence Cardinal Manning had promised to read a paper on Total Abstinence at the World's Fair in Chicago in June, 1893, but died before its opening. Archbishop Ireland took his place and in the course of his paper said:

> Total Abstinence differs in meaning from Temperance. Total Abstinence is the plenary abstention from the use of alcoholic beverages, Temperance allows moderate use of them. The mere use of intoxicating beverages is not a physical or moral wrong. The wrong is in the abuse or immoderate use.

On June 2 he presided at the opening session of the World's Congress of Social Purity and read a paper.

Archbishop Satolli, accompanied by Doctors O'Gorman, Pace, Shahan and Grannan of the Catholic University, arrived in St. Paul on June 23, 1893, for a brief visit before going to the Pacific Coast in the private car of Mr. Hill to acquire an accurate idea of the West from personal observation and contact with bishops, priests and laity. Archbishop Grace joined them and they visited Helena, Great Falls, Spokane, Everett, Seattle, Tacoma, Portland, San Francisco (where they spent six days), Salt Lake City, Butte and Yellowstone Park. During the trip they met ten prelates, hundreds of priests and thousands of the laity. Archbishop Satolli gave an interview to the Seattle Post-Intelligencer in which he vindicated Archbishop Ireland's position on the school question.

"The Church and the Age"[99] was the topic chosen by Archbishop Ireland as the subject of his discourse at the episcopal silver jubilee of His Eminence Cardinal Gibbons in the Baltimore Cathedral on the evening of October 18, 1893. The ceremony brought together a group of thirteen archbishops, fifty bishops, hundreds of priests and an overflowing congregation of the laity. It began with Pontifical Mass celebrated by the Jubilarian at which Archbishop Corrigan of New York preached on the dignity and office of a bishop. It was at the vesper service chanted by Archbishop Redwood of New Zealand that the Archbishop of St. Paul preached on the Church and the Age and extolled the Jubilarian as the loyal churchman, the patriotic citizen. He declared and proved that "between the Church and the age, properly understood and properly interpreted, there is no disagreement". It was an epoch-making discourse in which he described democracy as struggling towards a higher plane of social and intellectual life in which it has the encouragement and friendship of the Church seeking to effect a closer bond of union and cooperation between the clergy and the people, thus bridging the chasm that would otherwise separate the Church from the Age.

Writing to a friend in Rome on November 6 the Archbishop said his sermon was making "an immense sensation" and that it was approved very highly by the Apostolic Delegate.

One who heard the discourse wrote of him as follows in the Boston Pilot:

> Archibshop Ireland is a very embodiment of intelligent, concentrated and irresistible energy. He is totally devoid of self-consciousness; the dominant idea being simply to stamp the thought which has impressed his own soul on the souls of his hearers . . . a faithful son of the Church, he is no less a son of his own century. He has the spirit of the Apostle who dared the perils of the sea and the wilderness, the scoffs of the cultured heathen and the treachery of apostate brethren in spreading the faith; but he would speed the gospel ships with steam and set up electric lights in the wilderness, and storm the strongholds of error with the battering rams of the printing press.

The Honorable Theodore Roosevelt, Civil Service Commissioner of New York, lectured in Boston on March 15, 1893, on "True Americanism and the Public Schools" which he characterized as "the nurseries from which spring the future masters of the Commonwealth", and denounced as the enemies of these schools all who discriminated against people on religious grounds, also the American Protective Association and Know-nothingism as repugnant to true Americans, who have a right to be proud of the great men who stand as exponents of the different creeds on American soil and the leaders of religious thought. He added: "Every true American, Catholic or Protestant, should be glad that there lives in the United States so stout a champion of Americanism as Archbishop Ireland, the only Bishop, by the way, in existence who is entitled to wear that badge of nobility, the button of the Loyal Legion".

At the jubilee celebration of the Father Mathew Total Abstinence Society of St. Paul, the second organized in the diocese, the Archbishop told the story of its origin and continued,

> There was a time when to drink was fashionable, when it was regarded as a proof of good fellowship, when one was looked upon as a miser and un-sociable who did not drink, and the weak ones were carried away by the torrent of evil, but today these are looked upon as the true heroes who dare to abstain. It is no longer fashionable to be a saloonkeeper. The few who now go into the business are not fond of it and want to get out of it as soon as they can.

On January 16, 1894, at an informal meeting at the residence of Father Keane twenty-one priests of the Twin Cities decided to form the Minneapolis Clerical Conference for the study of Catholic religious problems. Father Caillet was elected President; Father Genis, Vice-President; Father O'Reilly, secretary and Fathers Keane, Kenny and Cleary a committee to select subjects for discussion and assign papers. It met in the rooms of the Brownson Club on the afternoon of the third Tuesday of every month. At the meeting on February 20 Father John Andre read a paper on "Marriage and Its Solemnization"; and at the next meeting his nephew, Father Gabriel Andre, read one on the "Forty Hours". There is no further reference to its existence or activity.

The North American Review for October, 1894, carried an article from the pen of Archbishop Ireland on "The Catholic Church and the Saloon" in which he commented on the decree[100] issued by Bishop Watterson of Columbus, Ohio, on March 1, 1894, withdrawing approbation "from any and every existing Catholic society, branch or division thereof in the diocese that has a liquor-dealer or saloon-keeper at its head or anywhere among its officers", and forbidding a new Catholic society or new branch of an old organization to admit to membership any person engaged, "as principal or agent, in the manufacture or sale of intoxicating liquors". Furthermore, saloon keepers who persist in conducting their business in an unlawful manner or in selling liquor "on Sundays either openly or under any sort of guise or disguise, in violation of the civil law, and to the hurt of order and religion and the scandal of any part of the community" are to be refused absolution.

One of the societies appealed to the Apostolic Delegate who affirmed the binding force of the decree as "not only being in harmony with the laws of the Church, but also reasonable and necessary to the honor of the Church. . . . Those things which the Right Reverend Bishop has commanded in his decree I approve, and I decide that they are to be observed".

Though confined to one diocese, wrote the Archbishop, it is a victory over the saloon for the whole United States. The reasons for the decision are weighty and cogent. It brands saloon-keeping as a disreputable business and the saloon keeper as one who must be kept aloof from places of honor and distinction in the Church, and the saloon as a baneful nuisance for which the Church must show its disapproval. It is true that Catholic theology does not teach that saloon-keeping is in itself a moral evil, or sin, but as ordinarily conducted, it is productive of many evils and is responsible for the awful intemperance which is the physical and moral plague of our time. It personifies the vilest elements of modern civilization and menaces the peace of the family, the material, moral and intellectual welfare of the people, and the free institutions of the Republic. The Catholic Church stands on record before the country as the determined foe of the American saloon.

The St. Paul Seminary

The year 1894 witnessed the fruition of the aspirations and strivings of Archbishop Ireland and his predecessors to have a diocesan seminary exclusively for the education of priests. Nine years previously he had founded St. Thomas Aquinas Seminary but it was not devoted entirely to the training of young men for the priesthood, but had, likewise, a classical department for lay students. It was the best solution of the problem of Catholic higher education for young men possible at the time and under the circumstances, and the first successful attempt made in the diocese to educate priests in the environment in which they were to work after ordination. The Archbishop visioned a further goal—a theological seminary in the strict sense—and it was made a reality through the munificence of James J. Hill, President of the Great Northern Railway, who gave the sum of $500,000 for that purpose. He was induced to do this either because of a sermon preached by the Archbishop in St. Mary's Church at which he was present, or, what is more probable, because of his long and intimate friendship with Father Caillet, the pastor of St. Mary's, to which his wife and family belonged. There was a report in those days that Mr. Hill had offered the money to the City of St. Paul for a public library under certain conditions which the city was unwilling to accept or fulfill, and that he then decided to use it for the building and endowing of a seminary for the education of priests.

In October, 1890, the Archbishop issued his annual appeal for funds for the support of St. Thomas Seminary which showed a deficit of $7,875.93, and announced this princely gift which was to be "devoted to the erection of buildings for the exclusive use of the theological students and for the perpetual endowment of professorial chairs, the number of which will in this manner be increased beyond all that otherwise would have been possible for us and in fullest compliance with the most advanced requirements of the Church in this country and in this age. The new theological seminary will be ready for use, it is expected, in the autumn of 1892".

In the issue of November 5, 1890, the Northwestern Chronicle confirmed the reports appearing in the local press that "our esteemed citizen, President James J. Hill, has consented to build and endow an institution of learning, costing at least $500,000, in the interests of higher education for the Catholic priesthood and that the selection of the site is left to the Archbishop of St. Paul". In an editorial comment it adds that the buildings will be completed and the plan fully realized within two years, "when will be opened the greatest educational enterprise and the greatest monument to generosity ever witnessed in the State of Minnesota".

The hopes and plans for a speedy completion of the project did not materialize, and it was not until September 6, 1894, that the seminarians from St. Thomas, to the number of sixty-five, took possession of the new institution, the six buildings of which were not quite ready for occupancy nor all the facilities and modern conveniences available for use. The dining room was unfinished and the students had to march to St. Thomas College for their meals and put up with many other inconveniences for several months. But the faculty members were in readiness and classes were started. The Right Reverend Louis E. Caillet, former pastor of the Church of St. Mary in St. Paul, and Vicar General of the diocese, was the first Rector, and the faculty consisted of the Reverends J. Soentgerath (Dogma), A. Cestelli (Moral), N. McCaffrey (Ethics), J. Chareyre (Philosophy), H. Moynihan (Apologetics), P. Danehy (Scripture), F. J. Schaefer (Church History), and Mr. J. A. Hartigan (Science).[101]

The new seminary had one unique feature, namely, two rooms—a study and a bedroom—for each student, and for that thanks are due to Mr. Hill who, when the Archbishop protested that one room was sufficient, retorted, "Two rooms or none, Archbishop. Take your choice". It was Hobson's choice. The St. Paul Seminary is still unique in this regard. In each of the residences—there were but two in the beginning—there were seventy-five such suites and a similar arrangement obtained for the professors in the Administration Building.

On June 8, 1895, the first public ordination was held in the Aula Maxima, or auditorium in the class building, which for a number of years served as a temporary chapel, when twenty-five students received the several Holy Orders, including six for the priesthood. Some months before five others had been elevated to the priestly dignity for Sunday service in the parishes, while continuing their studies in the seminary.

The new seminary was formally dedicated[102] on Wednesday, September 4, 1895, with an out-door Pontifical Mass celebrated by the Most Reverend Francis Satolli, Apostolic Delegate to the United States, with Father Heffron as archpriest, Fathers Keane and Solnce, deacons of honor, Fathers Soentgerath and Danehy, deacon and subdeacon, and Father Schaefer, master of ceremonies, assisted by Father Turner just aggregated to the teaching staff. Mr. and Mrs. Hill occupied seats in the front of the congregation. After Mass the celebrant blessed the buildings in the manner prescribed by the ritual. A choir of two hundred voices from the parishes in St. Paul, augmented by the Danz Orchestra, and under the direction of John Gehan, choirmaster of the Cathedral, with Mrs. Shawe at the organ and Miss Collins at the piano, sang the responses of Gounod's Messe Solennelle of St. Cecilia. The following prelates occupied seats in the improvised sanctuary: Archbishops Ireland and Grace of St. Paul; Kain of St. Louis; Hennessy of Dubuque; and Bishops Keane of the Catholic University; Brondel of Helena; Chatard of Vincennes; Vertin of Marquette; Scannell of Omaha; Schweback of La Crosse; Dunne of Dalles; Matz of Denver; Cotter of Winona; and McGolrick of Duluth; Abbot Peter Engel, O. S. B., of Collegeville; and Monsignors Ravoux of St. Paul; Nugent of Liverpool; O'Bryen of Rome; and McMahon of Washington. A luncheon was served at noon for the prelates, clergy and distinguished guests.

In the evening there was a public meeting in the Aula Maxima at which the Most Reverend Archbishop presided. He read congratulatory messages from Pope Leo XIII and Cardinal Gibbons and introduced the following members of the faculty, Fathers Soentgerath, Danehy and Moynihan, who delivered addresses; Father Sheran also of the faculty read his dedication ode. Bishop Keane spoke on behalf of the Catholic University of which he was Rector. Archbishop Satolli delivered an address in Latin which was translated by Dr. O'Gorman. After that Mr. Hill, who was greeted with an ovation, formally presented the seminary to the Archdiocese of St. Paul in the name of his Catholic wife of whom it may be said, he added, "Blessed are the pure of heart". The Archbishop accepted the magnificent gift in the name of the Archdiocese, and paid a glowing tribute to the donors for their generosity and for the truly christian spirit that animated them in providing so well-equipped an institution for the education of the priestly leaders of the future, whose influence will extend far beyond the domain of religion and make itself felt in many ways throughout the communities in which they live and labor.

On Thursday evening a reception was held in honor of the Apostolic Delegate, local and visiting dignitaries and clergymen at the palatial residence of Mr. and Mrs. Hill on Summit Avenue, and thus was brought to a fitting close one of the most important and significant celebrations in the religious history of the Northwest.

The articles of incorporation of the St. Paul Seminary were signed by Archbishop Ireland, Father Stariha, Vicar General, Bishop Cotter of Winona, John D. O'Brien of St. Paul and Anthony Kelly of Minneapolis.

The Constitution and Rules[103] for the government of the Seminary, drawn up by the Most Reverend Archbishop, provided for its financial management by a Board of Directors, organized under the laws of the State of Minnesota in conformity with the wishes of the Founder, in whom title to all its property is vested. The government of the Seminary, in educational and spiritual matters, is in the hands of the Ordinary and exercised in due conformity with the laws of the Church.

The rules and regulations prescribed by the Ordinary for the government of the Seminary in all its departments are its statutes to which adherence is required. The appointment of all officials of the Seminary and members of the faculty is in his hands, as well as the general direction of studies, in matter and method, and the discipline, and nothing in contravention thereof can have the force of rule or custom.

The immediate government of the institution is entrusted to the Rector, the Vice-Rector, the Spiritual Director, the Deans and the Counsellors, whose duties are outlined. These officials, together with two professors chosen annually by the Ordinary, constitute the Council of the Seminary which meets regularly on the first Monday of each month or more frequently at the call of the Rector.

The unanimous vote of the members of the Council is necessary for the promotion of students to orders, their dismissal or other extraordinary punishment. They make recommendations as to the best method of enforcing discipline and promoting the general welfare of the Seminary, decide on the time of examinations and the methods of conducting them, with final action reserved to the Rector and the Ordinary.

At the beginning of each scholastic term, and before ordinations and examinations, meetings will be held to which all officials and professors will be invited, and all matter discussed by them will be referred to the Council for final action.

The Constitution and Rules can be changed only by the authority of the Ordinary of the Diocese.

The Archbishop and the Seminary

Archbishop Ireland was not only the founder and father of the Seminary but its inspiring guide for a quarter of a century. His vibrant personality dominated it from the beginning. The ideals he cherished were the pillar of fire by night and of cloud by day that moulded its course through the formative years to the maturity of the present. He played the stellar role not only in the founding but in the fashioning of the institution and its program of intellectual and spiritual development. The future alone can tell how far-seeing and comprehensive his vision, how penetrating and accurate his diagnosis of the ills of the day that warred against the Church, and how efficacious and healing the antidote he prescribed, namely, an intelligent and holy priesthood to challenge a world estranged from God and make the Christ of Galilee live and reign once more among the sons of men.

Aided by the princely generosity of the Empire Builder of the Northwest, he drafted the preliminary plans of the seminary, charted its course, mapped out its curriculum, selected and prepared its faculty, presided at its dedication, and bade it God speed on its mission of enlightenment and sanctification.

In the beginning, at least, in deference to the views of Mr. Hill, the Archbishop felt constrained to give science a more prominent place in the curriculum than theretofore deemed necessary for aspirants for the priesthood. For more than a decade of years the scientific department flourished and well-equipped laboratories were maintained. Side by side with Theology he enthroned the Natural Sciences which relate the wisdom and power of God in the material order as Revelation speaks of His mercies in the supernatural. The study of science and religion would prove that there was no conflict between them except in the minds of men who mistook their dreams for the principles of religion or of science. Theology, the primary study of the seminary, cannot ignore the civil, natural and social sciences. "Professors and priests think as I do on the matter", he wrote to Bishop Keane, Rector of the Catholic University of America, on July 23, 1895.

He scouted the idea that diocesan priests could not staff and conduct a seminary as efficiently and successfully as regulars and he lived to prove, beyond the possibility of a doubt, to the doubting Thomases of the hierarchy that it could be done. He laid down strict rules for professors and students that none dared to disobey. He would have the members of the faculty give good example to the student body not only by fidelity in attending class and due preparation for the exposition of the subjects assigned them, but by regular attendance at the spiritual exercises on Sundays and holydays of obligation. The professors were forbidden to accept any engagement that would take them away from Solemn Mass and vespers on these days. Rather would he allow a parish to go without Mass on Sunday than permit a faculty member to be absent from his accustomed place on that day. The professors were inclined to regard this regulation as rather stringent, but they recognized the Archbishop's reasons for the rule and obeyed it; and who shall say it was not for the best interests of all concerned? It saved the professors from the importunities of the pastors and enabled them to bring undissipated energy to their professional tasks.

From the opening day the Archbishop was the energizing force and directing spirit of the institution. It was the core of his heart, his child of predilection. He visited it frequently—on an average of once a week when in the city—and took a personal interest in every detail of management. Twice a year he presided at the examinations, not as a spectator, but as an active participant, and not infrequently astonished the other members of the examining board with the depth and accuracy of his knowledge of the subject under discussion.

On his every visit he gave a half hour conference to the student body, opening his heart and revealing his mind freely, fully and familiarly, in his discussion of the problems of the day and of the spiritual life as reflected in the priestly office. These conferences were masterpieces of erudition, thought and expression and inspired his hearers with the ambition to live up to the lofty ideals of priestly conduct which he portrayed so eloquently and convincingly. He urged the young levites to be above all else men of prayer and self-denial, to cultivate a passion for study, to be priests after God's own heart, fit ministers of the gospel, other Christs in very truth. He spoke with the persuasive eloquence of a man of God and his words bore fruit in youthful hearts seeking to know the will of Most High in their behalf.

Years afterwards a student, John F. Duggan, who took notes of these lectures, published them in the San Francisco Monitor of which he was editor, and in the Ecclesiastical Review for October, 1939, (Vol. 101, pp. 289 & ff.) and thus preserved for future generations the matter, if not the form, of a series of conferences given by the Archbishop during his years in the seminary. He assembled the more important of them under three heads: The Priest as a Gentleman; The Priest as a Scholar; and The Priest as a Saint. Under these captions the Archbishop discussed Vocations to the Priesthood; the Formation of Character; the Value of Good Manners in the Home, in Church and on the Street; the Virtue of Truthfulness; Intellectual Leadership; the Art of Public Speaking; the Philosophy of Style; Methods of Study; the Value of Notebooks; the Study of Foreign Languages; the Supernatural Life; the Spirit of Self-denial; Mortification of the Senses; Total Abstinence; Pride and Humility, and cognate topics.

On his every visit he also opened his heart and mind to the assembled faculty, giving them the benefit of his garnered wisdom. He spoke of the projects in which he was engaged; his plans for the future of the Seminary and of the Diocese; his discussions with the learned men of the day; theological and spiritual publications; the political situation in the United States and Europe; the religious outlook at home and abroad and the thousand and one problems engaging the thinking minds of the leading men of his day and generation. The professors marvelled at the wide range of his knowledge of the Sacred Sciences, his profound grasp of world problems, his judicial appraisement of men and movements. He was a tower of strength to them in the example he gave of persevering effort, resolute self-reliance and optimistic determination in the face of obstacles which seemed almost insurmountable. He had the indomitable courage of his convictions and the confident assurance of one who knew full well that

"Immortal things have God for architect,
And men are but the granite He lays down".

The Seminary of St. Paul honored itself by dedicating to his memory its new library on October 19, 1950, during the centennial year of the erection of the diocese which he loved with every throb of his heart, and served with every fibre of his being.

During these visits he dined with the faculty and student body, listened to the sermons and reading in the refectory, insisted on the correct pronunciation and enunciation of the English language, took part in the seminars and other public meetings and in a hundred other ways showed his determination to make the St. Paul Seminary the leading institution in the country for the training of recruits for the priesthood in America. For several years it was his custom to invite the deacons to an informal dinner at his residence to get better acquainted with them, to study them at close range, to draw them out in conversation, to note their timidity or forwardness. Who shall say how much these meetings with the great Archbishop of St. Paul influenced the lives of these young men in after years? It taught them how informal and democratic true greatness and genuine nobility can be.

His personal interest in the Seminary and all that concerned it did not mean that he neglected the other institutions of the diocese which had grown to maturity under his guidance. He exercised constant supervision over all of them. He visited them frequently, especially in the later years of his life, when he found it increasingly difficult to concentrate on his literary work in the afternoon. Next to St. Paul Seminary the colleges of St. Thomas and St. Catherine were special objects of his paternal solicitude. Scarcely a week passed without a visit from him and not infrequently more than one. The sound of his carriage as William reined the team to a halt before the front entrance was the signal for every one to be on the alert. Quickly the word went round. "The Archbishop is here". The program was the same for all—a talk to the student body, supper in the common dining room, a visit of an hour or more with the faculty, all of whom were expected to be present. The discussion covered a wide range of subjects, theological, philosophical, scientific, literary, with all of which he showed an astonishing familiarity. It was a pleasure to listen to his sparkling conversation, a steady stream of fascinating talk, interspersed with witty sallies that were never flippant. There was a personal magnetism about him that held the undivided attention of his listeners who could not help admiring his remarkable versatility. No one was too unimportant to be noticed by him. He tried to draw everyone into the conversation. It was an education to hear him tell of the important persons he had met, the places he had visited, the projects in which he was engaged, the plans for diocesan expansion and for the welfare of the church at home and abroad, the political situation as it affected the well-being of Church and State, and the hundred and one personal and official interests that absorbed his time and attention.

Time will vindicate Archbishop Ireland's right to be considered the greatest prelate the Church in America has produced. When shall we see his like again? He loved the Church and he loved America with all the fervor of consecrated service. Religion and patriotism were duties enjoined by divine command, and he stood as a Gibralter against whatever would minimize or endanger their sway over the hearts and minds of men.

Recognition of Mr. Hill

An official and memorable recognition of Mr. Hill's munificent contribution to the cause of priestly education in the Archdiocese of St. Paul came in the form of a letter addressed "To the Illustrious Sir, James J. Hill" from His Eminence Cardinal Rampolla, Papal Secretary of State, who, under date of May 28, 1892, wrote in the name of Pope Leo XIII, expressing appreciation of his most generous gift of 2,500,000 francs for a new theological seminary. It gave His Holiness the greatest satisfaction; and he prayed God to reward this magnificent deed of beneficence. As a testimony of personal esteem Pope Leo offered a portrait of himself "in the belief that it will be acceptable to yourself and your honorable family".

Nor were the priests of the Archdiocese unmindful of the debt of gratitude they owed Mr. Hill for the provision made through his generosity for the education of their successors. At the close of the annual retreat on August 29, 1896, they presented him, through Father Danehy, with an address in which they gave expression to their gratitude for his munificence in founding the St. Paul Seminary as a training school and nursery of the priesthood, and testified to the high esteem in which they held him personally. The address was engraved on four plates of solid silver, hinged booklike, by two solid silver rings, and enclosed in a velvet-lined mahogany casket, 14 by 10 by 4 inches in dimensions. On the exterior of the casket are five solid silver plates on each of which is an engraving illustrative of the seminary and its work. The plate on the top of the casket has in each of its four corners and midway at the sides, representations of the original six seminary buildings. At the head of the plate in the middle is a cross in the clouds symbolizing religion. At the foot in the middle is the U. S. shield, flags and eagle, symbolizing patriotism; and in the center is an inscription telling what the casket contains. The other four plates are mounted on the sides of the casket. The first represents Christ giving the Apostles the commission to teach; the second St. Paul, the patron of the seminary; the third a globe, compass, retorts, etc., surmounted by a burning lamp of knowledge and having on each side an open volume marked "Genesis" and "Mathew" emblemizing, respectively, secular and religious science; the fourth represents the Ten Commandments on two tablets of stone symbolizing divine and human law. The address contains 1150 words; and the design was conceived by Father John Dolphin who supervised its execution.

This artistic casket and contents are preserved in the historical museum in the Archbishop Ireland Memorial Library of the St. Paul Seminary.

Twenty years later, on November 27, 1912, the faculty and students of the seminary tendered a reception to its founder. It took the form of an evening dinner, at which Mr. Hill was guest of honor, attended by the Most Reverend Archbishop, Bishop Lawler and a number of priests and prominent laymen. After dinner all repaired to the Aula Maxima where a literary and musical program was rendered. In the meantime Mrs. Hill, accompanied by Mr. and Mrs. Walter Hill, arrived and were present during the program.

The Archbishop, in a brief speech, voiced the sentiments of gratitude and appreciation that animated the members of the faculty and the students towards the guest of honor in whose name he thanked him for his munificent generosity. Mr. Mathias M. Hoffmann read an address summing up the activities of Mr. Hill during the past half century and emphasizing the value of what he had done for the seminary. After the musical program rendered by the seminary choir, Mr. Michael P. Bourke read an essay on "The Catholic Seminary".

Mr. Hill was greeted with prolonged applause as he rose to acknowledge the tribute paid him and the reception tendered him. He expressed satisfaction with the work the seminary was doing in preparing priestly leaders to train upright citizens conscious of their duty to God and fellow men. The responsibility that rests on the priest is very great and as long as he does that faithfully all is well. The program was reported in the Catholic Bulletin for December 7.

The St. Peter Claver Sodality for colored Catholics, organized by Colonel Sam Hardy, held its fourth annual banquet on January 23, 1894. The Sodality began with sixteen members and rose to one hundred and sixty. It helped to build St. Peter Claver's Church at a cost of $14,000, for a congregation which numbered four hundred. At the banquet plates were laid for four hundred among whom were one hundred women. J. B. Talbot was toastmaster and the guests included the Most Reverend Archbishop, Father Casey, the pastor, Fred McGhee, a prominent attorney of the parish and Colonel Hardy. In the course of his address the Archbishop said he had watched the growth of the congregation with pride and he congratulated it on the evidence of culture and progress made by the colored race. In view of its beginning "no other race on earth at any time, under any circumstances, had equalled or could surpass their achievements". He wished to see Catholic negroes first in all movements for the advancement of the race.

On April 4, 1894, the Archbishop delivered an address on the "Duty and Value of Patriotism" before the New York Commandery of the Loyal Legion, and on April 6 on the "Catholic Layman" at a banquet in honor of Honorable W. J. Onahan of Chicago, who had recently been the recipient of a high honor from Rome—Knighthood in the Order of St. Gregory—because of his sterling Catholicity and his services to the Church over a long period of years.

At a convention of teachers engaged in the education of Indians[104] held in the State Capitol during the week of August 13, 1894, the Archbishop pleaded for a better understanding of the Indians and a fuller realization of the possibilities of civilizing them. They can be taught truth, sobriety and gentleness. The first objective should be to christianize them and let religious instruction go hand in hand with secular education and a training in the industrial branches suitable for their mode of life—agriculture and trades for the boys and home-like arts for the girls. He paid tribute to those engaged in the work.

Catholic Students at the University of Minnesota

The religious welfare of the Catholic students at the University of Minnesota had been an object of solicitude to Archbishop Ireland for more than a quarter of a century prior to his death. He was not unaware of the menace to their faith that lay in some of the teaching of that institution because of the secularism and anti-Catholic prejudices which increased with the lengthening years of its existence. The first evidence of the recognition of the danger on the part of the Catholic students themselves came at the beginning of the last decade of the nineteenth century.

On Sunday, May 24, 1891, a number of them from the University[105] called on the Reverend James C. Byrne, pastor of the Church of the Immaculate Conception in Minneapolis, to discuss the advisability of forming a literary and social club, and asked him to give them a series of lectures on Catholic doctrine to offset the anti-religious character of much of the teaching of the University. They found him not only sympathetic but enthusiastic about the project. He hailed it as an important step in the right direction and, in a spirit of cooperation, offered the use of a room in the parish house for the meetings.

A temporary organization was effected and a committee, consisting of E. B. Kinney (Law, '92), chairman, J. McKenna (Med., '93), secretary, John Brown (Law, '92), and J. Murphy (Acad., '93), appointed to draft a constitution and by-laws. At a subsequent meeting a permanent association was formed; and any Catholic young man or woman in attendance at the University was declared eligible for membership. The association met every Sunday afternoon in the parochial residence for instruction in Christian Doctrine and discussion of topics bearing on class work in the University. A group of twenty was present at the meeting on October 4, when a paper on J. H. Newman was read by William McNamara and Father Byrne gave a lecture on "Plato and His School".[106] There was promise of an increase of twelve for the next meeting on October 11. Occasionally the program was varied by the reading of papers by the members, but at every meeting Father Byrne gave a lecture on a religious or semi-religious topic to those in attendance, an average of about twenty-five.

When Father Byrne left the parish in September, 1892, to assume the Presidency of St. Thomas College, the group met for a time in the Immaculate Conception school; but as no priest took any special interest in the work the organization began to languish and finally died. It is difficult to realize that no priest took interest in it in view of the fact that the Reverend James J. Keane, who succeeded Father Byrne, is said to have delivered lectures to the association several years later when it was revived on the University campus. Father Keane was well aware of the dangers that threatened the faith of the Catholic students and it is quite unlikely that he would have failed to show interest in the organization had he been invited to do so or if the meetings were held in his school even for a short time after he came to the parish. The enthusiasm for the movement may have waned under new officers for, had they contacted Father Byrne, the founder and first moderator, he would certainly have continued to aid them and could very easily have called to his assistance the members of the College faculty.

Attempts were made in 1898 to revive the association as a social club devoted largely to dancing; but the idea of a permanent organization to promote the spiritual welfare of the Catholic students was never lost sight of. On March 18, 1900, thirteen (or was it twenty-four?) students held a meeting to form an organization to promote the religious and social well being of the Catholic young men and women in attendance at the University, and subsequently a constitution and by-laws were adopted and officers elected. It is not probable that any of the leaders were connected with the association formed in 1891 or even knew of the efforts made by their predecessors. Some of them may have taken part in the attempt made in 1898 to revive interest in the work.

The new association had for object to promote the spiritual welfare of the Catholic students. The members undertook no propaganda among their fellow students of other denominations, but confined their efforts to uniting their co-religionists in a body to strengthen their faith by open profession and sound doctrine and provide for their entertainment and social intercourse. The meetings were held every Sunday afternoon at four o'clock usually in the Young Men's Christian Association. The Spiritual Director delivered lectures on religious topics, and other priests and laymen, at his invitation, on literary and scientific subjects, all emphasizing the Catholic viewpoint. Receptions were held at the beginning of the semesters and outings and excursions provided at the end of the year. Banquets were held separately for men and women at first, but later on they were combined with beneficial results.

One of the members of the organizing group was George V. McLaugh,- lin, now an attorney in Minneapolis, but Owen McElmeel, then recently from Iowa, was the moving spirit.[107] Temporary officers were chosen and two committees elected, one to prepare a constitution and by-laws, the other a program of activities. The name chosen was the University Catholic Association. Permanent officers were elected at the beginning of the fall semester and the religious instruction, a most important part of the program, was given by priests from the Twin Cities who freely gave of their services. There was no official Spiritual Director until 1902 when Reverend Patrick Danehy, pastor of the Church of St. Stephen in Minneapolis, was appointed by Archbishop Ireland. He was succeeded by Reverend Humphrey Moynihan of the St. Paul Seminary faculty until 1904, when the pastors of the Church of St. Lawrence near the University campus were assigned that work and continued in that capacity until 1915 when the Paulist Fathers took charge of the parish.

From the beginning it was the ambition of the association to have a home of its own and with that end in view it filed articles of incorporation on March 18, 1903, and placed its government in the hands of nine directors elected from the student body and the faculty. From this group the permanent officers were chosen.

The purpose of the incorporation was to provide a legal entity to take charge of the building project. The incorporators were Owen P. McElmeel, George V. McLaughlin, Edward O'Brien, Edward Tuohy, Joseph Murphy and Andrew McCarthy. The officers were: President, Owen P. McElmeel; Vice-President, John Layne; Secretary, Josephine Cornish; Treasurer, Augusta McGuire. Nine directors were elected annually. The by-laws provided for annual communion in a body on the third Sunday of March; and, when amended in 1911, twice a year—during Advent and at Easter. The association grew rather slowly in numbers from the original nucleus in 1900 to eighty-nine in 1905, over two hundred in 1911, and six hundred, almost every Catholic student, in 1917.

To supervise and direct the building program a Board of Trustees, drawn from different parts of the Northwest, was selected and a campaign, the first of its kind in the United States, undertaken to raise the necessary funds to meet the estimated cost of $15,000. Appeals were made to the Catholic alumni of the University and others and pledges to be paid in three years solicited with the understanding that work would not begin until the entire fund was on hand. A site was purchased across from the University campus in the autumn of 1903 for $3,900 and a down payment of $2,400 made, leaving a balance of $1,500 in the form of a mortgage which hung as a sword of Damocles over the association until it was finally paid in full in 1918.

In the meantime the vital and necessary work of the association was carried on by the Spiritual Director and priests drawn largely from the St. Paul Seminary and the College of St. Thomas, one of the most active and zealous being Father Moynihan who for years gave a course of lectures in Apologetics and kindred branches every Sunday afternoon in the Y. M. C. A. Very often he had among his listeners the beloved President of the University, Dr. Northrup. Other lectures on scientific, literary and historical topics from the Catholic viewpoint were given by priests and laymen invited by the Spiritual Director. These were interspersed with social functions, outings, excursions, receptions and banquets at which addresses were delivered by men and women prominent in the business and professional life of the community.

The building project remained a dream and was finally abandoned. In January, 1920, to meet the objection of the University which did not wish to have its name associated with any denominational project, the name of the organization was changed to "Students' Catholic Association" and in 1925 to "Newman Club", when a residence at Fourth Street and Thirteenth Avnue, S. E., was purchased for $16,000, called Newman Hall, and opened for student activities on March 21, 1926, during the time the Paulists served as Spiritual Directors. In 1939 the spiritual direction was turned over to a diocesan priest, Reverend Louis W. Forrey, who, in turn, gave place to the present Spiritual Director, Reverend Leonard P. Cowley.

In 1928 the Newman Hall became the property of the Archdiocese of St. Paul and is now in charge of the assistant Spiritual Director, Father Wagner, who resides in the building, while the Spiritual Director is pastor of St. Olaf's Church in Minneapolis, and in charge of a new building project for the club. The Hayes property, bordering the University campus was acquired some years ago and a building with a chapel and other features is in course of construction.

Sermons and Addresses

The year 1895 was a busy one for the Most Reverend Archbishop who, in addition to the administrative work of his growing diocese culminating in the formal dedication of the St. Paul Seminary for the education of the diocesan clergy, had a heavy schedule of addresses at public functions and meetings. On Washington's birthday, February 22, he delivered an address on "American Citizenship" before the Union League of Chicago, and two days later spoke at a reception in his honor at Notre Dame University. He appeared before the Minnesota Congregational Club at Park Avenue church in Minneapolis on March 25, where he repeated his address on "American Citizenship" before a large audience. He was present at the commemoration of the golden jubilee of ordination of Archbishop Williams of Boston on May 16 and 17. The Pontifical Mass was celebrated by the Jubilarian and the sermon preached by Bishop Bradley of Manchester. In the evening there was a reception and banquet at which Archbishop Ireland delivered an address; and on June 17 he chose "Liberal Education and the Church" as the subject of his sermon at the golden jubilee of the University of Notre Dame. On July 31 he lectured on "Patriotism" in the armory of the University of Wisconsin at Madison before three thousand people in connection with the celebration of "Minnesota Day" at the Columbian Catholic Summer School holding its first annual meeting in that city. It opened on July 14 and closed on August 4. It held its sessions in the Fuller Opera house. It had lately been organized as a summer school for Catholics under the presidency of Bishop Messmer of Green Bay who, on the opening day, celebrated Pontifical Mass in St. Patrick's Church at which Bishop Chatard of Vincennes preached the sermon. Another Pontifical Mass was sung in St. Raphael's Church by Bishop Shanley of Fargo at which the sermon was delivered by Father Dempsey of Detroit. St. Paul was represented among the lecturers by the Reverend P. J. Danehy who gave a series of five lectures on Sacred Scripture, and Judge William L. Kelly who lectured on the missionary explorers of the New World. The school proved very successful for several years from the viewpoint of attendance and interest.

On April 14, 1896, the Archbishop preached at the funeral of Bishop Ryan of Buffalo, N. Y., who, for twenty-eight years, had occupied the position of Chief Pastor of that diocese. He was the successor of Right Reverend John Timon, first Bishop of the diocese (1847-67), who laid the cornerstone of the third Cathedral of St. Paul in 1856 after preaching the annual retreat for the diocesan clergy presided over by Bishop Cretin.

Five days later he preached at the consecration of his boyhood companion in St. Paul and in the Seminary of Meximieux, Right Reverend Thomas O'Gorman, Bishop-elect of Sioux Falls, S. D., in St. Patrick's Church, Washington, D. C., in presence of the Apostolic Delegate, Archbishop Satolli, and the élite of the District of Columbia. In the course of his sermon he outlined the role of the episcopate in the divine provision for the government of the Church and in its specific care for the diocesan priesthood. Religious orders are founded to meet extraordinary emergencies and do special work. They obey directly the behests of the Pope.

This takes them largely from the jurisdiction of the bishop who has no part in their training and cannot rely on them for the work of the diocese, whereas the diocesan clergy depend on the bishop and he counts on them to minister to the faithful under his jurisdiction. They are the sons of the diocese and, for weal or woe, have sworn enduring fealty to it. The intrinsic sacredness of the priesthood and the dignity of the ministry of saving souls demand that they be as learned and holy as the religious. This was not said in a spirit of antagonism to the religious orders but to clarify the relation between them and the bishop of the diocese in which they labor.

In May, 1896, he delivered a lecture on "Patriotism" before the Loyal Legion of St. Louis and was rather severely criticized for his attitude towards arbitration as if he made a plea for war rather than for patriotism. He explained his meaning by saying that war evokes and stimulates patriotism and that, in case of universal arbitration, some other spring and source of this noble virtue must be found. It rests with the advocates of arbitration to show that under the regime of their ideas patriotism does not suffer. He did not discuss arbitration but raised the question. War, he said, in defence of patriotism and national honor is condemned neither by religion nor reason.

In a letter to be read in all the churches of the diocese on Sunday, August 30, 1896, the Archbishop declared that "henceforth the parish schools in the English-speaking parishes will be free to all pupils attending them. No stipend will be exacted or required from any pupil". The cost of maintaining the school must be taken from the receipts of the parish. The only exception was in favor of Cretin High School for boys, an institution under the direction of the Christian Brothers who depend on tuition for the running of the school, and similar institutions for the education of girls.

On October 16, 1896, he made a patriotic address at the encampment of Lafayette Post of the G. A. R. in the masonic temple, New York, where he was introduced by Admiral Meade, Commandant of the Post.

The Church and Modern Society

Two volumes of lectures, addresses and articles, under the general title of "The Church and Modern Society," hand down to posterity the noblest sentiments of religion and patriotism uttered by Archbishop Ireland during the score of years between 1884 and 1904. They appeared towards the end of 1896 and in 1904 and are dedicated to the Sisters of St. Joseph in the sense that

Whatever pecuniary profit is derived from the sale of The Church and Modern Society is offered as a gift to the Sisters of St. Joseph of St. Paul, to aid them in defraying the expenses of building their Academy and College for the higher schooling of young women. The price paid for The Church and Modern Society will be a tribute, much less to the merits of the book, than to the intelligent and self-sacrificing zeal of the Sisters of St. Joseph during the last half century in the cause of education and religion.

Volume one contains a seventeen-page Introduction and fourteen discourses delivered during the decade prior to 1895. At the end of the Introduction he says:

> Whatever the occasion which led up to these lectures and addresses, whatever the lines of thought upon which they are constructed, they never took me away, I wish to believe, from the spirit, or the responsibilities of my priesthood. The priest, and because the priest, I was the citizen. As the priest and as the citizen, I held it my duty to contribute my mite, as opportunity permitted, to the pleasure or the improvement of fellow-man, to the welfare, passing or permanent, of country and society. I hope I have been right: I crave indulgence if I have been wrong.

Volume two contains fourteen sermons or lectures and three articles written for the North American Review. The subject-matter of these volumes covers a wide range of thought and activity and illustrates

> various points of contact between the Church and Society which the conditions of modern times make possible, and which, it does seem neither the friends of the Church, nor those of Society, can afford to pass over with an unobservant eye.

The keynote of these volumes, according to the Liverpool Times, is that

> for the sake of the world the Church must be in close contact with life and must face the living issues of the age and follow all the relations of man with the principles of the Sermon on the Mount and bring to bear on the world the vivifying energy of christian ideas.

The first volume was prepared for publication by the Reverend H. Moynihan and the writer during the summer of 1896, and when the suggested changes in the manuscript were placed before the Archbishop for final approval or disapproval, he protested vigorously that they modified, if they did not eliminate, much of his characteristic style and phraseology. In the end he usually capitulated, for he had great respect for Father Moynihan's literary judgment and taste.

The twenty-fifth anniversary of the arrival of the Christian Brothers in St. Paul was commemorated at a banquet and a reunion of former graduates, at which an alumni association was formed, on November 16, 1896, in Cretin Hall. George T. Redington was elected President of the Association; John F. McCauley, Vice-President; W. J. Conway, Secretary; and John Melady, Treasurer. The President read an address to the Brothers to which the Director of the school, Brother Emery, responded. Under the toastmastership of Dr. H. J. O'Brien, Reverend

James Fitzpatrick, pastor of the Church of St. James, spoke on behalf of
the City of St. Paul; John A. Ryan (a student of the St. Paul Seminary
and an alumnus) on "Catholic Education and Citizenship"; Thomas D.
O'Brien on "When We Were Boys"; Reverend Charles Corcoran on "The
Church"; W. J. McCabe on "The Young Man of Today"; Father Lawler,
pastor of the Cathedral, on "Our Schools". The Most Reverend Archbishop described the original one-room "Catholic School", as it was
called, on Sixth and Wabasha Streets, and dwelt on the disinterestedness
and ideals of the Christian Brothers, praised the boys of the olden days
and expressed the hope that the young graduates would distinguish
themselves in all walks of life. He regretted that he could not recall the
names and characteristics of the classmates of his boyhood days in
1852-3.

Sixteen conferences of the St. Vincent de Paul Society reported at a
meeting in Cretin Hall on December 13, 1896, under the chairmanship of
Captain M. J. O'Connor, at which the Archbishop gave an address. He
reviewed the history of the society since its foundation in 1840 and its
establishment in the diocese of St. Paul in 1855 under the direction of
Bishop Cretin, by John Brownson, A. L. Larpenteur and William Markoe.
He urged the members to renewed efforts on behalf of the needy and
more personal visits to the poor. The conference in Minneapolis formerly
belonged to the Particular Council of St. Paul but recently it established
one of its own.

In a lecture on "Conscience: The Mainstay of Democracy," delivered
before the Cleveland Chamber of Commerce on May 13, 1897, Archbishop Ireland declared that conscience is the test and guide of democracy and its perpetuity. It is the Nation's safeguard.

> The greatness of America is her democracy; the peril of America is her
> democracy. . .America honors manhood, consecrates its rights and endows
> it with the freedom that it needs to develop its unborn power and satisfy
> its loftiest ambitions. America is the nation of the people. All men are equal
> in citizenship. . .No civil or political privilege is reserved for the few, no
> civil or political inferiority is allotted to the many. . .It is said that people
> will abuse political power: that democracy is for gods not men and is
> destined to failure even in America. Democracy requires constant care
> and vigilance. In America it has undergone trials to prove its right and
> power to live. Conscience will give democracy immortality. There is a
> divinity within us—conscience—an element in the formation of good ci-
> tizenship. The true greatness of a country lies in men of conscience.

The Archbishop preached at the Solemn Requiem Mass in Chicago
for the Right Reverend Thaddeus Butler, Bishop-elect of Concordia,
Kansas, who died in Rome a few days before the date set for his consecration in August, 1897, and was a guest of the pastor of the Church
of St. John at Eighteenth and Clark Streets. He began his sermon with
the solemn declaration, "Nothing exists but God and the soul".

Americanism

Americanism, a heresy of the nineties of last century, is all but forgotten. It has little more than historical significance for us. Probably it never would have been heard of were it not for the prominence of Archbishop Ireland, the most notable personage involved in it. After his victory in the Faribault school controversy there was a breathing-spell during which no great problem confronted the Church in America, and then all at once a cloud no bigger than a man's hand appeared above the horizon. It grew and darkened and carried the threat of a storm which eventually broke.

It was occasioned by the publication in France of a translation of Father Elliott's life of the Reverend Isaac Hecker, Founder of the Paulists, which appeared in 1891 with an introduction by Archbishop Ireland. The translation was made by Mlle de Guerines at the request of Count de Chabrol who admired Father Hecker and America.

The French edition was revised by Reverend Felix Klein of the Catholic Institute of Paris who wrote the preface, dated June 5, 1897, in which he lauded the spiritual teaching of Father Hecker regarding the submission of the individual soul to the guidance of the Holy Ghost, and the need of active rather than passive virtues to meet the religious conditions of the modern world and sanctify it.

The book passed through seven editions in a short time without causing more than a ripple on the sea of the religious and literary world of France though its orthodoxy was questioned in some quarters. It would probably have been forgotten like many another book were it not for an address entitled "Americanism According to Father Hecker", by Monsignor O'Connell, Rector of the American College in Rome, at the International Catholic Scientific Congress at Fribourg in August, 1897, in which he praised the Americanism of Father Hecker and drew a distinction between its political and its religious meaning, aspects and implications. The former referred to the God-given rights of men to the life, liberty and pursuit of happiness guaranteed by the Constitution of the United States and "the loyal devotion that Catholics in America bear to the principles on which their government is founded", the latter to the liberty enjoyed by the Church in America unhampered by the intrusion of the State into its spiritual affairs, compared with the restrictions placed upon it in countries where Church and State are united. The Church in America is free to recognize the authority of the Pope, and Bishops to communicate with the Holy See without interference by the civil authorities. This involved a quasi-separation of Church and State which redounded to the advantage of religion. Father Hecker's Americanism postulated new methods of approach to non-Catholics, the adaptation of Catholic doctrine to the needs of the modern world under the duly constituted authority of the Church and in obedience to the internal action of the Holy Spirit.

This address furnished occasion for attacks on Father Hecker's teaching and its sponsors. Two disgruntled French clerics, neither of whom had any love for America—the one because he knew nothing about her institutions, the other because he had been dismissed from the chair of Canon Law in the Catholic University—wrote a series of articles criticizing the book and questioning Father Hecker's orthodoxy. They were the Reverend Charles Maignen of the Congregation of the Brothers of St. Vincent de Paul, who wrote under the name of "Martel", and the Reverend George Peries who signed himself "St. Clement", whose articles in "La Vérité Francaise" caused considerable comment. They attacked Father Klein's preface as destructive of the supernatural life, and Americanism as "one of the greatest dangers that menaces the Church". At the same time Jesuit preachers in St. Sulpice and Ste. Clotilde denounced Father Hecker and his Americanism. Newspapers in France, Belgium, Switzerland and Rome took up the controversy and it was debated pro and con in the daily press and in learned reviews. The Jesuits, Dominicans and Franciscans joined in the free for all. Father Maignen's articles were published in a volume entitled: "Le Père Hecker: Est-il un Saint" (Is Father Hecker a Saint?), Paris, 1898, for which Father Peries is believed to have supplied much of the material. Father Maignen claimed neither its merit nor paternity. It was characterized as "inaccurate, biassed, vitriolic and venemous". The Archbishop of Paris refused to grant the Imprimatur but Father Albert de Lepidi, O. P., Master of the Sacred Palace of the Vatican, affixed his signature which seemed to give the book a semi-official authority.

The battle was on. From this distance one is at a loss to understand the acrimony of the controversy. Many admired Father Hecker, it is true; but no one, much less the Church, regarded him as a saint or dowered with infallibility. He had founded a religious community to put his theories in practice and for a long time it specialized in missions to non-Catholics.

His critics contended that he advocated a new mode of christian life by following the inspiration of the Holy Ghost without regard to the external guidance of the Church; that in making converts the Church should relax her ancient rigor, water down certain points of doctrine and give them a meaning different from that recognized by the teaching office of the Church; that the natural virtues, as contrasted with the supernatural, were more in accordance with modern requirements and active, rather than passive virtues more suitable for our day; that religious vows were alien to the spirit of the new age.

Since Archbishop Ireland had sponsored the original life and Father

Klein the translation they were singled out as the objects of special attack. The friends of the Archbishop insisted that he come to Rome to defend himself and prevent the condemnation of the book which, according to rumor, was imminent. They did not want it dignified by being put on the Index.

Cardinal Satolli who had praised Father Elliott's work, but whose first friendship for the Archbishop, yielding to pressure from others, had cooled, and Cardinal Mazzella were appointed a committee to study the question and it was currently believed they would bring in an adverse decision.

In the meantime the Archbishop had learned on good authority that Archbishop Corrigan of New York had "actually congratulated Lepidi". On October 26, 1898, he wrote Monsignor O'Connell that "Maignen's book remains unheard-of in America . . . several Catholic publishers . . . refuse to touch the unclean thing". Some said the Pope wanted him to come to Rome; others that he was ordered to come, which he denied very emphatically.

The Archbishops of the United States would not join in a protest to Cardinal Rampolla, but left Archbishop Ireland to fight the battle alone which he was quite capable of doing as they knew from experience. Archbishop Corrigan voiced a timid protest on behalf of the Paulists but the brunt of the battle fell on Archbishop Ireland.

Apparently, Archbishop Ireland did not realize the seriousness of the situation for he did not go to Rome for six months after he was advised to do so in July, 1898. He protested[108] to Cardinal Rampolla, Secretary of State, as did also Cardinal Gibbons, Bishop Keane and Monsignor O'Connell, that Father Lepidi's Imprimatur gave the book "the almost official approval of the Vatican", "an importance it did not otherwise deserve" and was a vicious attack on respectable prelates "who obey the least word from Rome". Cardinal Rampolla replied that the Holy Father had the matter under consideration and would pass judgment in due time.

Apostolic Letter on Americanism

He arrived in Rome in January, 1899, too late to prevent the issuance of the Apostolic Letter, "Testem Benevolentiae" (Proof of Friendship), which Pope Leo XIII addressed to Cardinal Gibbons and the American Hierarchy, on January 22. The Archbishop saw the letter for the first time in the Osservatore Romano on February 21. He maintained that it was based on an Americanism conjured up by fanatics and put before the Pope. "The words of the letter allow us to say that the things condemned were never said or written in America, not even by Hecker, but were set afloat in France as 'Americanism' "[109] This was borne out by a statement made in a letter to Mrs. Storer in August, 1900, that the Pope told him to forget the letter on Americanism "which has no application except in a few dioceses in France".

In an interview with Cardinal Rampolla the Archbishop was told that the letter had been toned down and softened "in the beginning and in the end" out of deference to him. The body of the letter was written by Cardinal Mazzella and Father de Lepidi.

The letter examined and rejected certain opinions attributed to Father Hecker on the manner of leading a christian life and considered the consequences that flowed from them. It warned against the contention that the new age "demanded a relaxation of old-time morality, that external spiritual guidance should be set aside, that religious vows are alien to the spirit of the times". The natural virtues are not to be unduly emphasized over the supernatural nor is there to be a distinction made between the active and the passive virtues. The letter concluded with a brief exhortation to unity.

In regard to the word Americanism it said that

if by that name be designated the characteristic qualities which reflect honor on the people of America; or if it implies the conditions of your commonwealths, or the laws and customs which prevail in them, there is surely no reason why We should deem that it ought to be discarded. But if it is to be used not only to signify, but even to commend the above doctrines, there can be no doubt that our Venerable Brethren, the bishops of America, would be the first to repudiate and condemn it, as being especially unjust to them and to the entire nation as well. For it raises the suspicion that there are some among you who conceive of and desire a Church in America different from that which is in the rest of the world.[110]

This letter put an end to "the most notable controversy in American Catholic history". Archbishop Ireland was the first to applaud its teaching and accept its direction.

With all the energy of my soul I repudiate and condemn all the opinions that the Apostolic Letter repudiates and condemns—all those false and dangerous opinions to which, as the letter says, certain persons give the name of Americanism; I repudiate and condemn these opinions without any exception, as literally as Your Holiness repudiates and condemns them; with all the more readiness and cordial joy that never for an instant have my Catholic faith and my understanding of the teachings and practices of the Holy Church permitted me to open my soul to such extravagances.[111]

This was the line of thought taken by the majority of the secular press. Other bishops of the United States made it clear that, whatever departures from the same might have occurred, they had not become either widespread or systematic as they had been made to appear in the interpretation put upon the Life of Father Hecker in the preface to the French translation. Most of the bishops denied that there was any of the condemned Americanism in the Church in America. They were all but unanimous in testifying that Father Hecker never countenanced any deviation from or minimizing of Catholic doctrine. His loyalty to the Holy See was unquestioned and none spent himself more generously than he in upholding its dignity and extending its sway.

In his letter the Archbishop emphasized the Pope's view, and Cardinal Rampolla, while assuring him that the Holy Father never intended to condemn real Americanism, declared that he "had rightly interpreted the meaning of the Pope" and urged him to make the fact known.

Father Klein assured the Pope of the suppression of his book, "The Life of Father Hecker" and rejected without exception or reservation the errors which had been condemned.

Most people who knew or heard of Archbishop Ireland took it for granted that, because of his record in the Civil War, he was a member of the Grand Army of the Republic but, as a matter of fact, he did not become a "comrade" until August 25, 1897, when the ceremony took place in the rooms of the Lafayette Post of New York, when he was inducted by Past Commander-in-Chief Lawler and received the official button from Corporal Tanner. Congratulatory addresses were made by General Howard and Past Commander Lawler. The Archbishop expressed his pride and appreciation of the honor conferred upon him. He had been a member of the Loyal Legion for many years and had just taken part in the national encampment of the Grand Army of the Republic at Buffalo. In May, 1898, he became a member of Acker Post of the G. A. R.

In July, 1897, the Archbishop publicly denied a statement made by Father Malone of the "Colorado Catholic", that he had entered into a political bargain or deal with H. H. Kohlsaat of the Chicago Times-Herald, whereby he was to have a certain influence with the administration in consideration of his letter in behalf of the Republican ticket in the fall of 1896. The Archbishop declared that neither directly nor indirectly, remotely nor proximately, had Kohlsaat asked him to aid in the election of McKinley to the Presidency of the United States. The letter in question was written at the urgent request of a score of the leading business men of St. Paul, who urged him to depart from his rule of non-interference in purely political matters, by making public in his own way his views on the burning questions then before the electorate, the most important of which was the free coinage of silver advocated by William Jennings Bryan, candidate for the Presidency on the Democratic ticket. This he did on October 12, 1896, in what was regarded as the most important pronouncement of the year, a singularly clear and able analysis of the Chicago platform. The letter, in which he justified his right as a churchman to take part in political controversy whenever questions of moral issue, social order, the prosperity of the people, the integrity of the nation, and the honor of the community were involved, was published in full in the Catholic Herald of New York on October 24. It declared that the free and unlimited coinage of silver dollars, at the ratio of sixteen to one, as legal tender in the United States would undermine the financial stability of the country and bring about a business depression far beyond anything yet experienced. But that menace to the financial security of the nation was subordinated to the denial of the President's right to send troops to any state in the Union to quell a riot and protect federal interests, unless requested by the Governor of such state, and to the plank menacing the non-partisanship of the Supreme Court, the palladium of American liberty. The letter turned the tide of votes in favor of William McKinley who was elected President.

Bishop Trobec's Consecration

A significant event of the year 1897 was the consecration[112] of Right Reverend James Trobec as third Bishop of St. Cloud on September 21, the feast of St. Matthew, Apostle and Evangelist. It took place in the Cathedral with Archbishop Ireland as consecrator and Archbishop Katzer of Milwaukee and Bishop Vertin of Marquette assisting. Father Stariha was archpriest, Fathers Lawler and Keane deacons of honor, Father Smalian deacon of the Mass and Reverend J. Seliskar, a seminarian and nephew of Bishop Trobec, subdeacon. Father Schaefer was master of ceremonies assisted by Fathers Moynihan, Turner and Colbert. The Apostolic Brief was read in Latin and in English by Reverend P. Danehy of the St. Paul Seminary faculty. The music of Gounod's Messe Solennelle was under the direction of John Gehan, Choirmaster of the Cathedral, with Mrs. F. L. Hoffmann at the organ.

The sermon was preached by the Right Reverend Joseph B. Cotter, Bishop of Winona, on the text "As the Father hath sent me I also send you" in which he emphasized the perpetuating ministry of the Church of Christ founded on apostolic succession and described St. Matthew, the dauntless bishop and writer of the first gospel, as a worthy exemplar for the new prelate whom he had known so long and whose career in the priesthood was a guarantee of a fruitful episcopate.

Seated in the sanctuary were Archbishop Hennessy of Dubuque, Bishops Schweback of La Crosse, Scannell of Omaha, McGolrick of Duluth, Shanley of Fargo, O'Gorman of Sioux Falls, Monsignors Nugent of Liverpool, Bauer of St. Cloud, Caillet, V. G. of St. Paul, and Dr. Reiner, Rector of St. Francis Seminary, Milwaukee. Monsignor Ravoux was too ill to attend. There was a very large attendance of the clergy, diocesan and regular, the seminarian body and a congregation of the laity that filled the venerable edifice to the doors.

The solemn religious rite was followed by a banquet in the Ryan Hotel at which Father Byrne, President of the College of St. Thomas, was toastmaster. Addresses were delivered by the Most Reverend Archbishop who dwelt on the significance of the ceremony of the forenoon, Monsignor Nugent on "Our Holy Father", Father Stariha on "The New Bishop", Bishop Shanley on "Our Country", Bishop O'Gorman on "The Province of St. Paul", Father Heffron on "The St. Paul Seminary", Father Lawler on "The Clergy of the Archdiocese", and Father Jones, pastor of the Cathedral of St. Cloud, on "The Diocese of St. Cloud", to all of which the newly-consecrated prelate responded in a brief address expressive of appreciation of the honor conferred upon him and of gratitude to all who had helped to make the occasion the most memorable of his life.

On September 28, the day of his installation he was greeted by a large gathering of priests and laymen on his arrival in St. Cloud, and escorted to the Cathedral of the Holy Angels where he was seated on the throne by Archbishop Ireland who, in the course of his sermon, dwelt on the unity and harmony prevailing in the Church in America notwithstanding the diversity of racial descent, language and customs of the faithful. Each country contributes its share to the Church and to America and all their people are Americans at heart. An address was presented by Father Gregory, O. S. B., on behalf of the clergy. H. C. Waite was spokesman for the English-speaking and B. Reinhardt for the German-speaking laity. The ceremony was followed by a dinner and reception in the Grand Central Hotel.

The new Bishop began his apostolic career by a visitation of the diocese and did not relax his vigilance until his resignation of the see was accepted by the Holy Father in 1914, when he was appointed Titular Bishop of Lycopolis and administrator of the diocese until his successor, the Most Reverend Joseph F. Busch, was installed the following year.

The Christmas season of 1897 was made memorable by the visit[113] of Archbishop Martinelli, the Apostolic Delegate, and his entourage, Drs. Rooker, Pace and Bishop O'Gorman. They arrived in St. Paul on December 24 and were met by the Archbishop and a welcoming committee of laymen. The Apostolic Delegate pontificated in the Cathedral on Christmas day and Bishop O'Gorman preached. The Archbishop welcomed the Delegate officially. In the evening the Delegate officiated at Vespers in the Church of the Immaculate Conception, Minneapolis. The following Sunday he was the celebrant of the Pontifical Mass in the Church of St. Francis de Sales in St. Paul and listened to a sermon in German by Father Klein. In the evening an informal reception was held at the residence of the Archbishop for the faculty and students of the St. Paul

Seminary. On Monday evening a dinner was given by the Archbishop for His Excellency at which Archbishop Langevin of St. Boniface, Manitoba, Bishops Cotter, McGolrick, Shanley and several clergymen—fifteen in all—were present, and on the following evening the Delegate was greeted at a dinner in the Archiepiscopal residence by Archbishops Hennessy of Dubuque, Katzer of Milwaukee, Langevin of St. Boniface and Bishops Scannell of Omaha, Bonacum of Lincoln, Shanley, O'Gorman and Trobec, Fathers Rooker and Pace of Washington, Keough of Milwaukee and Cleary of Minneapolis. On Wednesday evening there was a reception at the Seminary at which Father Danehy read an address of welcome. On New Year's eve he was given a public reception and dinner by the laity at the Ryan Hotel at which C. D. O'Brien presided and D. W. Lawler gave the address of welcome to which His Excellency responded. He was in St. Paul for twelve days and such a series of receptions, banquets and visits was never before witnessed in the Twin Cities. Catholic and Protestant vied with one another in honoring the Pope's representative and he was fairly dazzled.

Archbishop Ireland as a Diplomat

The year 1898 was the memorable year of the Spanish-American war during which Archbishop Ireland had his brief diplomatic career in the cause of peace as the representative of Pope Leo XIII. It was also a year of crisis in the history of the United States as a nation, the beginning of a new era in its national life. For many decades there had been unrest in Cuba, a dependency of Spain in the western world. Finally there was a revolt against Spanish misrule which brought about the establishment of the Republic of Cuba in 1895. Spain sent General Weyler to suppress the uprising and his drastic measures brought suffering and death to thousands on the Island and threatened the vested interests of the United States in its plantations, mines and railroads. The sympathy of Americans was aroused and food and medical supplies were rushed to the suffering Cubans.

When McKinley became President in 1896 he demanded that the deplorable conditions in Cuba be remedied; and local autonomy was promised by Spain but rejected by the insurgents who wanted independence. The tension of the situation was aggravated by the destruction of the battleship Maine in Havana harbor on February 15, 1896, with a loss of 260 officers and marines for which Spain was held responsible, though it was afterwards proved that she had nothing to do with it. The martial spirit of this country was aroused and the clouds of war gathered on the horizon.

The Pope was called upon not to arbitrate but to exercise his diplomatic influence to settle the difficulty by persuading Spain to change her attitude towards the Cubans. At his request, transmitted through Cardinal Rampolla and Bishop Keane, then in Rome, on March 27, 1898, Archbishop Ireland, a friend of President McKinley and of the administration, was asked to take whatever measures he deemed necessary to preserve peace, and he went to Washington towards the end of March believing that war between the United States and Spain was not inevitable despite the general clamor for reprisals against that country. His special task "to obtain from Spain an armistice to Cuba".[114] Tremendous pressure had been brought to bear on Spain by the Pope to grant it but without success. The Archbishop was soon in touch with the Vatican and President McKinley, working behind the scenes and through others. He rarely visited the White House but dealt with the President through emissaries. Spain hesitated to grant the armistice except on condition that the United States withdraw its fleet from Key West[115] which, of course, the President would not dare do, although he was for peace. Congress was bent on declaring war. Some of the leaders thought that a war, a successful war, against no matter how weak an adversary, might enable them to ride into the White House at the next election. The Archbishop was well aware of the delicacy of his mission, and that more time than he had at his disposal was necessary to convince the Queen Regent of Spain of the seriousness of the situation, and the necessity of granting an armistice if she would prevent war between the two nations. President McKinley was persuaded to withhold his final message to Congress for a few days, which he did despite the pressure brought to bear on him by the jingoes. Spain finally yielded when, on April 10, General Blanco was given authorization to proclaim an armistice, but it was too late to avert war. The President was aware that Spain had granted a "suspension of hostilities" before he sent his message to Congress on April 11, but he was not a strong executive and could not withstand the pressure brought to bear on him. All negotiations ceased. War was an actuality.

How did Archbishop Ireland feel about the outcome? He felt that Congress had gone back on the President, on all the friends of peace; that if he had been asked by the Pope to intervene two months earlier he would have succeeded.[116] He risked everything "to serve the Vatican". It was to his credit that he worked for peace as long as peace was possible, "to have been chosen by the Pope to speak for him, to have accomplished so much with Spain and other foreign countries". As it was, Cardinal Rampolla thanked him for all he had done. Official Washington recognized the fact that he had done "wonderful work for peace".[117] But since the die was cast he was for war, for the Stars and Stripes, for there was no question of his patriotism. He was an American through and through, and came out of the ordeal without compromising his church or his patriotism. "I am keeping up my Americanism . . . it is my pièce de resistance and I will not let it go".[118] He was convinced that the war would result in a stronger and larger navy and enable the United States to reach out for new territory; that the Philippine Islands as well as Cuba and Porto Rico would be retained by America, for public opinion had definitely tended in that direction. But even if the United States would decide not to hold Cuba and the Philippines the Church in these countries would be organized on American lines. "In the settlement of Church affairs in Cuba and the Philippines", he wrote to Monsignor O'Connell,[119] "Rome should yield gracefully to a separation of Church and State and merely seek full liberty and the possession of her present temporalities. If the Cubans have their own way, there will be wholesale confiscation. America must be looked to as the protector of the possessions of the Church. The bishops in Cuba should be properly instructed in this matter."

But the Vatican was not pleased because he had not succeeded. It would make no allowance for failure. "To be misunderstood by those whom I was serving so loyally and for whom I was risking my reputation as an American—it is dreadful. It does look as if Madrid or Rome worked against me".[120] He was never fitted to play the role of a diplomat. He was too impulsive, too anxious to reach the objective by brushing aside all obstacles to be a good diplomat. His first idea was to "stay at home". He knew that the chief element of success—time—was lacking, but he was hopeful to the last. He lost hope before the President did. McKinley relied on his party to sustain him. The House members were with him but the Senate was for war by a strong majority.

In connection with the resignation of Bishop Keane as Rector of the Catholic University of America in 1896, rumors appeared in the American press to the effect that Cardinal Gibbons, Archbishop Ireland and other American prelates had incurred the displeasure of the Holy See. Cardinal Satolli told the correspondent of a New York paper that such reports were wholly devoid of foundation. He wrote the Archbishop summarizing the report he had made to the Holy Father on American church affairs at an audience after his return to Rome.

> I did not fail to speak at length of yourself and to narrate to him how sincerely and loyally you are devoted to the Holy See and to the person of the Holy Father himself; with what zeal and success you labor incessantly in all things that may be to the advantage of the Catholic Church in the United States. I added that your zeal and success will surely increase in the future.

On December 3 Cardinal Rampolla sent a cablegram to the Apostolic Delegate in Washington authorizing him to "deny all such falsehoods which are the product of reprehensible manoeuverings".

In an interview with the Roman correspondent of the New York Sun Cardinal Satolli said

> I have nothing but a sentiment of profound veneration of friendship and of gratitude towards Cardinal Gibbons, Archbishop Ireland and Archbishop Corrigan. These have, each in his own degree, a great solicitude and sincere wish for the progress of the Church and the common well being of the country.

Epochal Controversies

The decade of years following the elevation of Bishop Ireland to metropolitan dignity were, in a measure, crucial years for the Church in America, because of the epochal controversies waged during that period in which he played the stellar role. The hierarchy was divided into two camps—the liberals and the conservatives—the former led by Cardinal Gibbons, Archbishop Ireland, Bishop Keane and others, the latter by Archbishop Corrigan, Bishops McQuaid and Wigger and their friends. There was no question of doctrinal differences but of policy, whether to hold the letter of the law as sacred as its spirit, or to adapt the Church's teaching to the needs of the new age, not by minimizing the doctrinal content of revelation but by emphasizing the religious tenets, however fragmentary, held in common by the Church and the sects rather than the differences which tended to separate them from one another. These different viewpoints developed a line of cleavage, and in some cases almost a personal antipathy, between the recognized leaders of the different groups, and especially between Archbishops Ireland and Corrigan, which was a source of scandal to the laity. Both prelates were dowered with more than ordinary intelligence but differed radically in personality, temperament, character and viewpoint. The Archbishop of New York was quiet and retiring, persistent and uncompromising, and firm when firmness was required. The Archbishop of St. Paul was impulsive, dynamic, opinionated, and determined to reach the visioned goal at whatever cost. He did not seek a fight but when called upon to do battle for a cause wanted to win. There is little doubt that the opposition between them was fostered by camp followers, ardent partisans and fool friends. One feared that the other would outgeneral him for a higher position in the estimation of Rome and ultimately bear off the alluring Red Hat. They should have known, as unprejudiced onlookers knew, that such a triumph was for both or neither and it proved to be for neither.

It was natural that the liberalizing Archbishop Ireland should be the focus of more controversies than the conservative Archbishop Corrigan, despite the fact that he had a diocese which did not compare with New York in wealth, population or influence. He was "a ten-thousand horsepower dynamo driving a one-thousand horsepower plant".

The struggle between the two groups may be said to have started during the Third Plenary Council of Baltimore in 1884 when the question of founding a Catholic University was up for discussion. It had been debated pro and con for a score of years and there was a great diversity of opinion as to its necessity, importance and location. Bishops Ireland and Spalding were its most enthusiastic proponents and they finally converted the majority of the other bishops to their way of thinking and ultimately succeeded in bringing the project to fruition in 1889.

In the meantime the question of condemning the Knights of Labor, after the example of the Canadian hierarchy, evoked a difference of opinion among the American bishops. Some were for prohibiting Catholics from joining the union while others, among them Cardinal Gibbons, Archbishop Ireland and Bishop Keane, worked successfully to prevent the ban of Rome's disapproval being placed upon the Knights and thus enhanced the reputation of the Church as the friend of the laboring man.

The Faribault school plan proposed by Archbishop Ireland raised a storm of protest from bigoted Catholics who thought he was undermining, if not destroying, the parochial school system, and from non-Catholics who were convinced that his aim was to take over the public schools. An experiment to make religious training available to Catholic children attending public schools was magnified into an attempt to make these schools Catholic. In two words, "Tolerari Potest", the Holy Father, showed how wrong both parties were.

Before the school controversy was settled the Archbishop was called upon to lead the opposition to Cahenslyism which advocated the appointmen of bishops of different nationalities to care for immigrants by making provision for teaching them in their national language, perpetuating their racial traits, customs and traditions and thus preserving their individuality as a class apart from the citizens about them. He was the first to see that it struck at the life of the country as a whole and set up innumerable petty factions prejudiced against one other and ignorant of the principles of the government under which they lived.

At the close of the European trip in which he won recognition for his school plan, the Archbishop was called upon to spread republican principles among the royalists of Paris in pursuance of the Pope's plan to bring the support of the Church to the side of the existing government. His Holiness wanted the people and the Church to support the French Republic but the decree met with resistance. On his way from Rome Archbishop Ireland stopped in Paris to champion the cause of the Republic by an informal lecture on "Choses d'Amerique"[121] in the Hall of the Geographical Society on the evening of June 18, 1892, which took the city by storm. He did not touch on the existing state of affairs in France but on the beauties and benefits of the republican form of government in the United States. The cream of French society constituted the audience and he was called upon for interviews by the press which spread his teaching through France.

The establishment of an Apostolic Delegation in the United States was feared by the bishops for many years but it was destined to come sooner or later. The sending of Archbishop Satolli as the representative of the Vatican to the centennial of the establishment of the American hierarchy and the dedication of the Catholic University was the entering wedge. His presence in the same capacity at the World's Columbian Exposition in Chicago confirmed the impression. At first Archbishop Ireland was not in favor of it, but when he was given to understand that it was inevitable he championed it, and did all he could to pave the way for the acceptance of the first Apostolic Delegate. He knew it was useless to kick against the goad when Rome had spoken. Attacks were made on the Delegate in the public press, and several prelates talked against him, but Archbishop Ireland ultimately maintained that the Delegation was a great success in America. The Delegate was discouraged by the attacks and thought seriously of returning to Rome, but was prevailed upon to remain.[122]

Archbishop Satolli was his friend, at least in the beginning. He came to St. Paul to be briefed about religious conditions in the United States: but the friendship cooled with the inevitable misunderstandings of the years and, though there was a rapprochement later on, the fine edge had been dulled. The Archbishop welcomed him when he came to announce the mind of the Pontiff in regard to the school question. At the annual meeting of the Archbishops at the residence of Archbishop Corrigan in New York in November, 1892, plans were discussed for the religious instruction of Catholic children in the public school. Archbishop Satolli was present with his secretary, Monsignor O'Connell, Rector of the American College in Rome. The distinguished visitor addressed the gathering and laid before the Archbishops the Pope's views on the school question. Where there were Catholic schools he decreed that Catholic children attend them though there was to be no compulsion. In addition, the Holy Father desired that the work of the Church be carried on in harmony with the government in all matters where cardinal doctrines of religious belief were not directly involved. In commenting on the meeting Archbishop Ireland said that the address of Monsignor Satolli had been put into his mouth by the Pope before he left Rome and the controversy is finally settled. He declared that Archbishop Satolli had amplest powers to settle disputes between bishops and clergy and his decision is without appeal. His authority is universal, showing the Pope's fullest confidence in him. He may soon be vested with the authority and powers of an Apostolic Delegate. His mission has been productive of good. He has brought peace and tranquility to the Church in America.

Father McGlynn and Henry George

The Archbishop maintained that the suspension of Dr. McGlynn, pastor of St. Stephen's Church, New York, by Archbishop Corrigan was a comparatively insignificant incident exaggerated out of all proportion to its real importance by the popular interest it evoked. Father McGlynn espoused the cause of Henry George who advocated certain novel economic theories and went on the hustings to support his candidacy for the mayoralty of New York City. He refused to heed the admonitions of Archbishop Corrigan who disapproved of the socialistic writings and theories of Henry George, was removed from his parish, ordered to Rome by Pope Leo XIII, but refused to obey the summons and was excommunicated. His partisans formed the Anti-Poverty Society which he addressed every Sunday until Christmas, 1892, when he was absolved from censure by Archbishop Satolli after he presented a statement of his opinions on moral economic matters which was judged to be not contrary to Catholic doctrine as set forth in the encyclical "Rerum Novarum". He expressed regret for his lack of respect for ecclesiastical authority and was appointed pastor of St. Mary's Church, Newburgh, N. Y., in 1894, where he remained until his death in 1902.

On one occasion while he was excommunicated he called on Archbishop Ireland at the Fifth Avenue Hotel who did not refuse to see him lest it embitter him and smother whatever good sentiments he had. As a matter of fact the Archbishop found him rather well disposed and got him to promise to postpone indefinitely his anti-poverty discourses and await patiently whatever action Rome might take in his behalf.

A year later, after his reconciliation, the Archbishop saw him again and found him smarting under the ostracism to which he was subjected, so much so that the Archbishop thought it not improbable that he would break out again. He did what he could to restore Father McGlynn's confidence by inducing Bishop McGolrick to invite him to Duluth for a series of lectures.

Henry George's "Single Tax" theory advocated a tax on land value solely, to the exclusion of other taxation by the same state. This tax should supersede all others and be exacted only on valuable land exclusive of the improvements made on it. His book was actually before the Sacred Congregation of the Index "at the request of an American Bishop", but its condemnation was prevented largely through the efforts of Archbishop Ireland who, as early as March, 1888, in a letter to the Moniteur de Rome, brought out strongly that George's doctrine was dead and buried beyond resurrection, unless imprudent notice was taken of it by men well-meaning but not observant of the march of ideas. He invoked the aid of Bishops Marty and Spalding and wrote Cardinal Gibbons to do all he could to prevent the condemnation, and to the Cardinal Prefect of the

Congregation that "the good of religion demanded absolutely that George be left in oblivion". To his friend, Monsignor O'Connell, he wrote "I do hope you will keep George off the Index". His efforts were successful and soon the incident became a matter of history. He was likewise opposed to the condemnation of Mivart whose articles on Hell were placed on the Index in 1893. When the London Tablet made the announcement the Archbishop wrote Cardinal Gibbons on August 10 of that year, "if this be true, thought in the Church will evermore slumber".

Three Secret Societies

No sooner was the Knights of Labor freed from danger of condemnation by the Roman authorities than a new problem confronted the American hierarchy, namely, that of forbidding Catholics to join certain secret societies. The Masonic sect was already officially condemned, and an effort was made in certain quarters to place under the ban of the Church the Knights of Pythias, the Oddfellows and the Sons of Temperance, societies of recent origin.

The Knights of Pythias, a fraternal and benevolent society, was founded in Washington in 1864 by Masons; the Oddfellows, also benevolent and fraternal, was introduced into America from England in 1819; the Sons of Temperance originated in New York in 1842 to make permanent the temperance movement of the time. It featured life insurance, sick and death benefits.

None of these societies was secret in the sense that its ritual, purposes and activities could not be made known to competent civic and ecclesiastical authorities; and hence the decree of the Holy Office did not condemn them under censure, but asked the bishops to warn the faithful against joining them and refuse the sacraments to those only who joined in spite of the warning and refused to leave them.

Many of the bishops were opposed to the condemnation of these societies on the score that there was nothing in their ritual or practices antagonistic to the Church and her teaching. Archbishop Ireland was among the first to voice a protest. Writing to Cardinal Gibbons on March 20, 1889, he said: "In reply to the question—'Should the Oddfellows and the Knights of Pythias be refused the sacraments?' I beg leave to state as my opinion that these societies should be tolerated. I am opposed to condemning societies unless there appear clear reasons for such action. As much liberty as is at all consistent with principles should be allowed Catholics: methods seemingly arbitrary irritate men and drive them from the Church. So far as I know the societies of Oddfellows and the Knights of Pythias, I have not perceived anything intrinsically wrong with them. I would however mildly dissuade Catholics from belonging to them".

He and the other prelates were amazed and saddened beyond expression by Archbishop Satolli's letter saying that the Pope wished the condemnation of these three societies to be promulgated. In protest the Archbishop once more wrote the Cardinal "I am as certain as I can be that there is no reason to condemn those Societies; and that the publication of the condemnation will do the Church in America immense harm . . . the bishops will be placed in a ridiculous position when they know not why these societies, which they must condemn, are worthy of censure. Few things occurring within the last decade of years have annoyed me so much as this condemnation, and the setting aside included therein of all regard for the episcopate of America".[123]

The Cardinal Archbishop of Baltimore and several other members of the hierarchy voiced their objection, especially to the promulgation of the decree, and at length the Apostolic Delegate was moved to adopt their views. In the meantime the Archbishop of St. Paul wrote Archbishop Satolli through his secretary, Dr. Rooker, that he was ready to have the societies alter whatever was objectionable in their rituals provided he knew what it was. He would visit the chiefs of the societies and was sure that as soon as the objections were stated they would be found to be non-existent. He also wrote Cardinal Rampolla saying that he would not publish the decree until he heard from him. Several months elapsed before he received an answer that discouraged him, yet, reading between the lines, as he wrote Cardinal Gibbons on March 14, 1895, it showed some rays of light and hope, for it plainly indicated that the bishops who had promulgated the decree were wrong and had it not been for these premature promulgations all would be well.

At length Cardinal Gibbons received word that the bishops were not obliged to publish the decree and the Archbishop hastened to thank him for freeing them from an obligation that would have done incalculable harm to the Church and to souls.

A new decree was issued on January 13, 1896, allowing nominal membership in these societies at the discretion of the Apostolic Delegate who was authorized to grant it on four conditions, namely, that the member joined in good faith; that there be no scandal; that grave pecuniary injury would result from withdrawal; that there be no danger of perversion. In addition, the Delegate usually required that the member remain away from the meetings and the lodge hall, pay his dues by mail or through a third person and, after death, that the society have nothing to do with the funeral.

Catholics and the Parliament of Religions

The participation of Catholics—prelates, priests and laymen—in the Parliament of Religions in connection with the World's Columbian Exposition in Chicago in 1893, under the so-called liberal wing of the American hierarchy, was the cause of dissension among church leaders and ultimately evoked a rebuke from Rome. Archbishop Ireland felt that there should be some very definite participation by Catholics in the Exposition, and a lay congress, the second in the United States, was held in connection with it, to consider the "Social Question" as outlined by Leo XIII in his encyclical on that subject, "Catholic Education" and "The Independence of the Holy See", on which papers were read and discussed, as a sequence to a series of papers bringing out the historic facts of the discovery of America, the roles played by Columbus and Queen Isabella, and the results of this discovery. This program[124] was carried out between September 4 and 9, 1893. The "Parliament of Religions" was a different matter. It was part of the World's Congress Auxiliary of the Columbian Exposition and representatives of all faiths were allowed to expound their religious beliefs and exhibit their sacred books. It was nothing more or less than a comparative study of religions in a friendly non-controversial atmosphere. On Catholic day Archbishop Ireland spoke on "The Fitness of the Catholic Church for the Actualities of the Present and the Development of the Future", emphasizing the part played by the Church in the formation, preservation and promotion of democracy, liberty and true progress. Many of the bishops did not favor Catholic participation in the Parliament of Religion and Archbishop Satolli, the representative of the Vatican and the official guest of the Exposition and of the nation, looked askance at it. Pope Leo tolerated it with prudent silence but afterwards declared that " it would seem more advisable that Catholics should hold their conventions separately" while opening its sessions to all-comers. Thereafter Catholics were not permitted to participate in such gatherings nor to sympathize with their object.

Bishop Keane Deposed

It came as a great shock to Archbishop Ireland and to others as well to learn that Pope Leo had summarily removed Bishop Keane from the rectorship of the Catholic University. The only reason assigned in the letter of September 15, 1896, was that it was customary "that they who were appointed to preside over Catholic Universities should not hold the office in perpetuity". He had filled the position for nine years.

The deposed rector was given a choice of remaining in the country as the occupant of an archiepiscopal see or taking up his residence in Rome as consultant in one or other of the sacred congregations. At first he decided to remain in America without any official position whatsoever, but later on went to Rome, was made Titular Archbishop of Damascus, Canon of St. John Lateran and Consultor to the Propaganda.

In many quarters there was more than a suspicion that his removal had been engineered by Cardinal Satolli, whose friendship for him and Archbishop Ireland who had taken him under his wing, so to speak, where he came to America, had cooled under the influence of the more conservative leaders in the Church. Some attributed Bishop Keane's deposition to his alleged liberalizing tendencies and his not infrequent appearances in public under Protestant auspices. Whatever the reason it was a fait accompli.

Archbishop Ireland felt that "an enemy hath done this", or, rather, that several had conspired to give the impression that the Holy Father looked with disfavor on him and his friends. But he bowed to the inevitable and, in an interview, declared that the Holy See was but enforcing "a rule which generally obtains in other Roman Catholic Universities", the reasons for which were obvious; but it did not necessarily mean that Bishop Keane would not continue to be associated with the University in some capacity that would permit him to exercise his zeal and influence in its behalf. In that, however, he was mistaken. Before the end of November it was announced that the Reverend Thomas J. Conaty of Worcester, Mass., had been appointed Rector of the institution.

Archbishop Ireland's efforts to vindicate Bishop Keane bore fruit when, on July 24, 1900, the latter was appointed Archbishop of Dubuque.

Modernism

In view of the important role played by Archbishop Ireland in the "phantom" heresy of Americanism, it is not surprising that he should be numbered among those who were supposedly tainted with the "synthesis of all the heresies" known as Modernism.

Whatever justification there may have been for considering Modernism indigenous to Europe, to Italy and France especially, there was little or none for thinking it widespread in America. Few, if any, even among the intellectuals, had heard of it before the Encyclical "Pascendi Dominici Gregis" was issued by Pope Pius X on September 8, 1907, due to the fact, probably, that the tainted doctrines with which it dealt were of slow growth and rather widely diffused. But in a few weeks after the appearance of the Encyclical, Modernism was the subject of discussion on the street and in the marketplace in the words and phrases not of the theologian but of the ordinary man. The press, secular and religious, devoted much attention and space to it, and platform lectures and pulpit sermons gave it sudden and wide publicity. All were anxious to know what the new heresy was that had caused such a stir and drawn down upon itself the solemn condemnation of Rome.

There were those who traced the origin[125] of Modernism to the religious revolt of the sixteenth century, while other maintained that it had its root in the philosophy of the French Revolution. Whatever its origin it was difficult to give a satisfactory definition of it. Pascendi Gregis said it was the sum and substance of all modern "isms" which it synthesized for the first time, bringing them out of the night of the speculative into the light of day. Father Loisy was one of the best known of those whose orthodoxy was questioned. He taught that "the original constitution of the Church is not immutable, but the christian society like human society is subject to perpetual change". He had many devoted followers among his students who were loath to believe that there was anything uncatholic in his teaching. Father George Tyrrell, S. J., of England was looked upon as a leading exponent of these heterodox views.

The Pope's letter gave a methodical explanation of Modernism, examined its causes and effects, sought the necessary remedies for it and made application of them in a series of practical and energetic measures. It was condemned because it did away with the rational foundations of all religious faith, destroyed the possibility of all religion, natural and revealed, and made divine truth nothing more than the speculative description of human feelings; rejected the Bible and its historical value as a record of supernatural or miraculous events; taught that Christ was man, not God, and had no mediatorial character; interpreted the dogmas of faith as expressions of mere subjective experience; recognized no Church founded by Christ, nor sacramental system instituted by Him; and accepted an agnosticism subversive of all knowledge of ultimate reality, natural or divine. It involved a complete denial of the miraculous.

All this was in direct opposition to the teachings of Christianity and the only course open to the Catholic Church, as the guardian of revelation and the custodian of a divine trust, was to condemn it officially as it did in the Papal Encyclical which required all priests—preachers, professors, confessors, pastors—to take an oath according to a formula which reprobated the principal modernistic tenets.

As soon as the Encyclical was published Cardinal Gibbons wrote Pope Pius X expressing agreement with the Sovereign Pontiff in the condemnation of these errors and obedience to the regulations laid down for their suppression. Archbishop Ireland and the other members of the Board of Trustees of the Catholic University did likewise, and asserted their determination to make a survey of its library for modernistic books and a recommendation in regard to them.

In the North American Review for April, 1908, Archbishop Ireland published an article on "The Dogmatic Authority of the Papacy", in answer to one that appeared in the previous December issue from the pen of Charles Johnston who raised the question of the dogmatic despotism of the Papacy, as evidenced in the Encyclical on Modernism. The Archbishop maintained that the encyclical was a defence of religious truth against certain vital errors that had come into vogue, inside and outside the Church, in modern times, and a condemnation of the "New Theology", as it was called in England, where the Protestant, R. J. Campbell, and the Catholic, George Tyrrell, S.J., were its leading protagonists. The starting-point of Modernism, he declared, was the assumption that, of itself, human reason is powerless to establish either the existence of God as a transcendent reality or the divinity of the person and mission of Christ.

This "New Theology" which regards God as unknown and unknowable and effaces the divine in revelation and in the Church was solemnly condemned by Pope Pius X, not in the exercise of a dogmatic despotism, but as the official guardian of the deposit of revealed truth. The encyclical thus protects the whole fabric of the Christian Religion in its vital principles and its foundation stones in history and human reason.

In connection with the Encyclical we have an undated, typewritten article of six pages entitled, in the handwriting of Archbishop Ireland, "The New Theology—Modernism",[126] in which he praises the twentieth century for its discoveries, inventions, industries, commerce and educational ambitions, not because they are modern but because they mirror the goodness and power of God whose existence the Modernists deny. In the field of religion, he writes, there is talk of new theologies which ruthlessly push aside all that is old and medieval as unfit for man abreast of the ages. Nor do they stop short of God whom they relegate to the regions of the unknown and unknowable, together with Christ whom they consider a mere man, the gospels which are myths, the Church which is a human institution with its dogmas and sacramentals which are only opinions and symbols, religion a mere sentiment of the human mind, and the supernatural a superstition of olden times.

Against those, he says, the Pontiff inveighs, condemning modernism in religion in all its varied phases, restoring God to His rightful place in the universe, vindicating the divinity of Christ and His Church, her teaching and sacraments. He challenges the modern world from the fortress of the living God and His divine Son, proclaiming anew with authoritative voice the spirituality and immortality of the human soul and the divine character and mission of the Church which is the oracle of unchanging truth.

Friars Land Question

Although Archbishop Ireland failed to prevent a declaration of war between the United States and Spain he never wavered in his conviction that it could and should have been averted. He had the consciousness of having worked well and prudently in behalf of peace even though by so doing he had risked his reputation as an American. During the war he was the loyal patriot ever ready to advance the interest of his country at whatever cost. At no time had he any doubt about the ultimate outcome of the struggle. America would win. When she did he felt that she had passed through a crisis during which she had attained to international stature. Although she did not wage a war of conquest she had acquired colonies and public sentiment was in favor of retaining them.

The Treaty of Paris, signed December 10, 1898, put an end to the war, it is true, but it offered no solution for the problems arising out of it, the most important of which concerned the Catholic Church in the Philippine Islands, her rights and possessions. The Philipino Catholics were under the rule and influence of Spanish bishops and priests so closely identified with the government as to be considered its agents. They were members of religious orders—Dominicans, Franciscans, Augustinians, Recollects and Jesuits—all of whom, except the Jesuits, controlled large estates on which the natives were rent-paying tenants. The Friars, as they were called, failed to develop a sense of responsibility and independence among the people and earned their dislike, especially after the abortive insurrection of 1896. The native clergy, too, were opposed to the Friars who never placed them in positions of authority in the Church.

How to deal with the religious situation in the Islands and what to do about the Friars and their holdings were two of the knotty problems that had to be solved by the American Government. The Treaty of Paris protected the Friars in their rights and property. The native clergy wished to throw off their yoke; and the Filipinos dreamed of independence from Spanish rule in Church and State.

A commission, headed by Jacob Gould Schurman, President of Cornell University, was appointed in January, 1899, to deal with the situation and recommended that the Friars be replaced by native priests, that the land held by the religious orders be returned to its original owners and that religious toleration be proclaimed. The second commission, under William H. Taft, reached the Islands June 4, 1900, to establish a civil government. It, too, recommended the expulsion of the religious orders, except the Jesuits, and the substitution of American priests for the Friars which, of course, was impossible. The Americans thought there could be no pacification of the Islands as long as the Friars remained.

On the whole, however, the new government showed respect for the rights and liberties of the Church, recognizing the evident fact that the Philippine Islands was a predominantly Catholic country. That the Friars were there to stay had been pointed out by Archbishop Ireland in an article in the Independent of September 29, 1898. Governor Taft wanted the support of American Catholics in his work, especially in the field of education. "The more Catholic teachers who have taught in public schools we can get, the better, if they are up to the average in teaching capacity".[127] He adopted the Faribault School plan which permitted the clergy or their representatives to go into the schools at certain hours and teach religion to the pupils whose parents wanted them to have such a training.[128] At that time Archbishop Ireland, who was not personally acquainted with Governor Taft, wrote him that the proposed solution of the religious problem in the schools of the Islands was "so just and prudent". In return the Governor regretted that the Archbishop was not the Apostolic Delegate "to assist in the work of pacification". Few Catholic teachers applied, though efforts were made to enlist their help.

Early in the spring of 1902 Archbishop Ireland, at the request of Cardinal Rampolla, who had previously expressed the Pope's "vivo desiderio"[129] that he do what he could for the protection of Catholic interests in the countries lost to Spanish domination, began negotiations with the American Government to effect a settlement of the question of the Friars and their lands, as the representative of the Vatican, so that "no one could accuse him of a personal intrigue in the delicate and difficult matter he was undertaking".[130] He was asked to make known to the Holy See, in a positive but unofficial way, the wishes of the United States Government. He had a talk with President McKinley on the church question in the Philippines who asked him to take the matter up with Elihu Root, Secretary of State, and, early in August, 1901, he approached Mr. Root to ascertain the wishes of the government. Before anything could be done President McKinley was assassinated on September 21 and Theodore Roosevelt succeeded to the Presidency. He was inclined to look with favor on the proposal to deal directly with the Vatican, but contended that there was no precedent for the sending of a commission to Rome to negotiate a business deal with the Pope. The Archbishop reminded him that "great men make precedents", and the case was won.

On February 23, 1902, a commission, with Governor Taft as chairman, was named to proceed to Rome to treat with Leo XIII on the future of the Friars' property. The other members of the commission were Judge Smith of the Supreme Court of Manila, Bishop O'Gorman of Sioux Falls, and General Porter of the American army. Bishop O'Gorman reached Rome on May 4 to prepare the way for the others. There was no unfavorable reaction from Protestants because their leading papers, the Independent and the Outlook, as well as prominent members of both parties in Congress approved the plan.[131] It was considered a wise and statesman-like act to treat with the effective owner of the property in question. Some of the New York clergy and of the leading Catholics protested, mainly because they feared that the success of the program would assure the Red Hat for the Archbishop of St. Paul.[132] In the meantime the plan was jeopardized by the appointment of Archbishop Sbarretti of Havana as Apostolic Delegate Extraordinary to the Philippine Islands. He was persona non grata to the American Government and President Roosevelt, who was incensed at the move, asked Governor Taft to protest the appointment. As a result the new Delegate was detained in Washington on his way to Manila. The commission reached Rome on May 31 and was received by Cardinal Rampolla on June 2 and by the Holy Father in solemn audience on June 5, to whom Taft presented an autographed letter from President Roosevelt and eight volumes of his literary works in a white Morocco leather case with the Papal coat of arms engraved on top, and gave details of his mission and its purpose. While Judge Taft's mission was not a diplomatic one, but "simply a business transaction with the owners of property in the Philippines", as Secretary Root described it, his credentials gave him greater powers than those usually conferred upon ambassadors.

The Pope was disposed to deal with the matter in the broadest spirit of cooperation to safeguard the rights of the Church and the interests of the United States in the Philippines. The points were discussed in detail. The commission asked for the removal of the Spanish Friars, except the Jesuits, which the Holy See refused to grant, and the request was withdrawn. A commission of five Cardinals was appointed to study the problem and it was finally agreed that the specific questions of lands, corporations, trusts and religious properties be left for settlement between Governor Taft and the Apostolic Delegate to be appointed, and the final audience was granted the Commissioners on July 21, 1902. A new Apostolic Delegate, Archbishop Guidi, replaced Archbishop Sbarretti.

"The Taft mission is a success", wrote Archbishop Ireland to Monsignor O'Connell on September 7. "The President is well pleased with it. So is the country. In fact the attitude of the country in the whole matter is magnificent. It is a precedent: going to Rome will no longer be going to Canossa".

The following month he expressed his disapproval of the coming of Archbishop Falconio as Apostolic Delegate to the United States, an appointment which would undoubtedly make "a most unfavorable impression" on Roosevelt and Taft. "Sending a Friar to Washington is a bit of diplomacy which in the present circumstances passes my comprehension. Such an act is being taken by the country as a slap in the face to Taft and the whole administration. I am annoyed and discouraged beyond my ability to speak".[133]

In the final negotiations the Friars asked $14,000,000 for their holdings and Governor Taft countered with an offer of $6,000,000. After several years of discussion a compromise was reached and $7,543,000 was ultimately agreed upon. Claims against the American government for damages to churches and religious institutions as a result of the occupancy of them by the military during the war were satisfied by a payment of $363,000 divided among several dioceses. Much of the damage, it was shown, was caused by the insurrectoes.

In connection with the pious or charitable trusts of which there were four, Governor Taft suggested to the Vatican that the matter be submitted to arbitration; but the Pope ordered that it be left to the decision of the Governor and the Apostolic Delegate, Archbishop Guidi, who recommended that the Government retain control of one of them, the Hospital of San Lazaro, and relinquish all claim to administering the others.

President Roosevelt appreciated what the Archbishop had done to effect a settlement. As early as June 3, 1902, he said to him: "There is none to whom I feel under such obligations as to you for no other (member of the hierarchy) has rendered as great a service to the country as you".

At the close of the negotiations Archbishop Ireland wrote President Roosevelt, under date of December 23, 1903: "Permit me to congratulate you on the happy termination of the Friar question in the Philippines. With the sale of the lands, and the installation of Americans as bishops in the Islands, the religious pacification is complete. There is no further room for agitation in the States or in the Islands".

The next year, in May, Archbishop Guidi said in a letter to the Archbishop of St. Paul: "The sale of those lands is a great profit both for the interests of the Church and for those of the State, and for the pacification of these islands. Without the efficient cooperation of Gov. Taft, without his tact, his condescension and even patience I could not have gone on in my efforts to have the sale made".

Several years later Governor Forbes of the Philippine Islands said: "The purchase of the Friar lands was the successful solution of a difficult problem. . . . It laid the foundation for the present harmonious and mutually beneficial relations of the Church and the Government of the Islands".[134]

The Cardinalate

The success of the Taft mission to the Vatican must be attributed in largest measure to the influence, genius and planning of Archbishop Ireland. It gave renewed life to a report already circulated in America that the Archbishop of St. Paul would soon be made a member of the Sacred College of Cardinals. If a Roman prelate had done for the Church a tithe of what the St. Paul prelate did during more than a decade of years there would be little question of the reward. The Archbishop was not unaware of the efforts made at home and abroad to prevent such a consummation. He could not be held responsible for the way in which his name was bandied about in ecclesiastical circles and in the press in connection with the expected honor, as it was to be for years to come.

Friends and foes were on the alert, the former to promote his cause by well-meant, if futile efforts, the latter to decry his claims to such recognition.

After his elevation to metropolitan dignity in 1888 he was frequently mentioned as a worthy candidate for such an honor; and the longer the expected honor was deferred the greater was his annoyance at the publicity given the rumors in the press of the nation.

As early as 1892 his friend, Richard C. Kerens of St. Louis, assured Cardinal Gibbons that President Harrison said it would be gratifying[135] to him and the United States represented by his government if Archbishop Ireland were raised to the dignity of a Cardinal as representative of the American Republic, but he would not be warranted in writing a letter to that effect. Not long afterwards Mr. Kerens asserted that he had dictated[136] the points of a letter which the Secretary of State, James G. Blaine, addressed to Cardinal Rampolla requesting such an honor for the Archbishop of St. Paul. Cardinal Gibbons was induced by Father Magnien, the Sulpician Rector of St. Mary's Seminary, to write a letter[137] in favor of Archbishop Ireland's promotion and send it to Monsignor O'Connell, Rector of the American College in Rome, for presentation to the Holy Father, and was informed by the Papal Secretary of State that the letter pleased Pope Leo who, however, had not committed himself as the Consistory had been deferred.[138]

The crux of the matter was undoubtedly the difficulties between Archbishop Ireland and the Archbishop of New York. This was assigned as a reason why there would be no American Cardinal in a cablegram to the London Chronicle copied by many papers in this country. Rome could not choose the one and overlook the other. Each had claims to such an honor—Archbishop Corrigan because of the wealth and influence of his archdiocese, Archbishop Ireland because of his personal worth and outstanding achievements. The papers kept the matter before the public so much that Archbishop Ireland expressed the belief that "the fuss will keep the Cardinalate away from him (Archbishop Corrigan) and me".[139] He felt "ashamed before the country" and begged all the correspondents "to drop me, to forget that I live".

In the meantime other friends of the Archbishop had not been idle. Theodore Roosevelt when Governor of New York wrote President McKinley to request the Red Hat for his friend, Archbishop Ireland. His cousin, Maria Storer, and her husband, Bellamy, were active in the Archbishop's behalf and conveyed the President's wishes to the Holy Father. Governor Taft of the Philippine Islands wrote Mrs. Storer on May 19, 1901, about his interest in the Archbishop's promotion. The Storers were charming and influential people. Mr. Storer was Ambassador to Madrid and afterwards to Vienna and through them the Archbishop met many cultured and socially prominent people in Europe and elsewhere, and they were most anxious that he be made Cardinal.

Towards the end of 1900 the Archbishop received from Monsignor O'Connell and others some sort of assurance[140] that he was to be made Cardinal, one of two Americans to be so honored in the near future. If it be true, the Archbishop wrote to Monsignor O'Connell, on November 16, of that year, "it is the closing of a singular and protracted drama" and emphasizes "a most remarkable revolution of ideas and tendencies". He would await the official declaration before accepting it as true. "I am still not without my doubts". Should it prove to be true it would be the official seal of approval on his triumph in the Faribault school case for, despite what his foes thought of the Tolerari Potest, "America knows we have triumphed and rejoices with us and the whole American press stood nobly by us".

A private letter of Governor Taft in which he expressed his opinion about the good impression which the conferment of the Red Hat on Archbishop Ireland would produce was indirectly sent to the Pope who held it "in great account".

Bishop O'Gorman in a memorandum regarding the Taft mission to the Vatican said that the "success of the negotiations would of course redound to the honor of Archbishop Ireland, and secure him the hat".

When Theodore Roosevelt became President he asked the Storers to speak to the Pope viva voce in favor of Archbishop Ireland's elevation to the Cardinalate, but later became alarmed at the effect this action, if known, might have on the American public and denied he had done so. He reiterated that denial in a letter to "Dear Maria" on December 14, 1905, in which he asserted that he had "always and unequivocally refused, directly or indirectly, to ask for the appointment of any man as Cardinal", and rebuked her for taking advantage of her husband's position as Ambassador to Vienna to make overtures to the Pope in behalf of the candidacy of Archbishop Ireland, threatening to recall Bellamy, which he did by a "brutal cable" in 1906.

Whatever hopes the Archbishop may have cherished after the death of Archbishop Corrigan in June, 1902, were blasted when he was passed over in the Consistory of January 30, 1903, when only one Cardinal, an Italian, was created. The Pope was no longer confronted with the dilemma of creating two American Cardinals or making a choice between the Archbishop of New York and the Archbishop of St. Paul. In failing to honor the survivor, Leo XIII showed little gratitude for the loyal and unselfish services rendered to the Church by Archbishop Ireland for nearly a score of years.

The Archbishop's friends, from the President down, were disappointed. They had believed that the Pope really meant to confer the Red Hat on the Archbishop during his pontificate, but deferred action in the belief that he would live many years more and there was plenty of time. As a matter of fact His Holiness had given assurance to the Archbishop's friends that "We shall not forget him", but in the June Consistory the Archbishop was not one of the three, two Italians and an Austrian, added to the Sacred College.

The election of Pius X to the Supreme Pontificate put an end to the hopes of Archbishop Ireland and his friends for the time being at least, for during this pontificate the Archbishop was virtually an exile from the Vatican. When his friend, Salvatore Cortesi, the Roman correspondent of the Associated Press, broached the subject of Archbishop Ireland's promotion to the Sacred College, to the new Pope the Pontiff's benignant face hardened and a cold light came into his eye as he replied, "There is no room in the College of Cardinals for the representatives of Americanism". The Pope's attitude was definitely shown when, in the Consistory of November 11, 1911, he honored three Americans with membership in the Sacred College—Cardinals O'Connell, Farley and Martinelli, the last named a naturalized citizen. Many were disappointed that Archbishop Ireland was not among the chosen few.

It may be that an incident which took place in Rome in 1906 contributed not a little to his failure to attain the goal of his ambition. After September 20, 1870, when the troops of King Victor Emmanuel breached the Porta Pia, there was a distinct line of demarcation engendered between those who acquiesced in the new status of the Pope as a voluntary "prisoner" beyond the Tiber and those who protested against it. The former were known as the "Whites", and the latter as the "Blacks", a situation which persisted until the Treaty of the Lateran in 1929. Not only were the members of the Roman nobility divided into two well-defined camps but the diplomatic corps accredited to the Vatican and the Quirinal as well. They did not recognize one another in a social way.

Hence it caused little short of a sensation when the American Ambassador, Henry White, gave a private dinner in honor of Archbishop Ireland which was attended by Cardinals Vannutelli (Vincenzo), Satolli, Martinelli and Mathieu and several officials of the royal court. The press took notice of it as did Cardinal Oreglia, Dean of the College of Cardinals, who sent a sharp reprimand to his offending brethren calling their attention to the precedent they had violated, and assuring them that the relations between the Vatican and the Quirinal had undergone no change. This proved embarrassing to the guest of honor and did not make him more of a persona grata to the Holy Father than he had been.

There are those who, like Maurice Francis Egan in "Ten Years Near the German Frontier", maintained that the attitude of the Kaiser Wilhelm had not a little to do with the failure of Archbishop Ireland to gain the Cardinal's hat. The Kaiser had no love for the Archbishop who had stamped out Cahenslyism, and rendered abortive every attempt of the Kaiser to interfere in the government of the Catholic Church in America, by keeping Catholic German immigrants faithful to the Fatherland—aut Kaiser aut nullus. Then, too, the Archbishop was a friend of Cardinal Rampolla against whom Austria had exercised the veto in the consistory that elected Pope Pius X. Moreover, the Archbishop had been the emissary of Pope Leo XIII in his efforts to reconcile the Catholics of France to the Republic. Under these circumstances the elevation of Archbishop Ireland to the Sacred College would be regarded as an insult on the part of the Pope not only to the Prussian ruler but to the Bavarian and the Austrian Courts as well.

A number of the Cardinals—the Vannutelli, Falconio, Lega, Agliardi, Gasparri, Gasquet and others—wanted him made a Cardinal in 1914 and thought that the honor would surely come to him in 1915, under Pope Benedict XV, who said Archbishop Ireland would have been made a Cardinal "over ten years ago had it not been for the death of Leo XIII" and added, "I shall put the matter right, you may be sure". But he did not do so even in the consistory of 1916 when he gave the Red Hat to Cardinal Sbarretti, at one time persona non grata to Archbishop Ireland and the American Government.

However, Benedict XV was finally prevailed upon to "put the matter right" at the next Consistory, but the Archbishop was seriously ill and never recovered. The writer was assured by His Eminence Cardinal Vincent Vannutelli in 1927 that the elevation of Archbishop Ireland to the Sacred College of Cardinals had been definitely determined upon. Cardinal Cerretti gave a similar assurance to the late Bishop Kelley of Oklahoma City-Tulsa. The Northwestern Chronicle for November 16, 1918, quoted the "Corriere d' Italia" to the effect that "the Sovereign Pontiff had formally decided to create Monsignor Ireland a Cardinal at the next Consistory".

That Archbishop Ireland deserved the Red Hat no one will deny; that it would have been the merited crowning of a life of devotion to the Church and her interests no one will question. It would have been the accolade of supreme approval for his outstanding work for God and country. It would have meant little to him personally, for he cared nothing for honors save in so far as they opened up new and broader spheres of action and afforded him additional opportunities to labor for the good of religion. He valued them, not for their intrinsic worth, but as incentives to a fuller dedication of self to the higher purposes of life. He cared neither for praise nor blame provided conscience pointed out the path of duty which he was to follow to the eternal goal. The assurance of the Red Hat was not much comfort to the dying Prelate. Red Hat or not he was the unique Archbishop Ireland.

The Outlook for October 9, 1918, made the following pertinent comment:

> His critics said that Archbishop Ireland was ambitious. That is probably true. Most men who are good for anything are ambitious. We do not doubt that it was a real, and perhaps bitter, disappointment to him not to receive the Cardinal's hat. He was not one to fall under the condemnation of Christ in the saying, 'Woe unto you when all men shall speak well of you'. His vigorous participation in the great questions of the day probably prevented the Vatican from giving him the promotion which his services had earned. But he earned what was much better— the reverent affection of thousands of his fellow-citizens for his life of unselfish service and courageous warfare. Patriot and priest, Archbishop John Ireland well deserves the grateful remembrance in which he will be held, not only by the membership of his own Church, but by all who love a patriotic and devoted fellow-American.

Events At Home

The consecration of the Right Reverend Alexander Christie, pastor of the Church of St. Stephen, Minneapolis, as Bishop of Victoria in Vancouver Island, Canada, was an important event in the history of the St. Paul diocese. It took place in the Cathedral on June 29, 1898. Archbishop Ireland was the consecrating prelate with Bishops Brondel of Helena and Shanley of Fargo as co-consecrators. The sermon was preached by the Reverend James M. Cleary, pastor of the Church of St. Charles in Minneapolis; Father Lawler was assistant priest; Fathers Heffron and Cahill deacons of honor; Fathers Dolphin and Shea deacon and subdeacon of the Mass; and Father Schaefer of the St. Paul Seminary, master of ceremonies. The function was graced by the presence of several bishops, hundreds of priests and a large congregation of the faithful. It was the fourth ceremony of the kind in the history of the diocese. A banquet was served at the St. Paul Seminary at which Father Lawler acted as toastmaster and the Archbishop and Bishop Brondel gave addresses. On behalf of the priests of the diocese Father Cleary presented a testimonial to which the new Bishop responded.

Father Christie had been pastor at Waseca when the Diocese of Winona was established in 1889, but elected to remain in the Archdiocese of St. Paul and came to Minneapolis as founder and first pastor of the Ascension parish in 1890. Four years later he was appointed to the pastorate of the Church of St. Stephen in the same city. He took possession of his diocese in July, 1898, and was promoted to the archbishopric of Oregon City (now, Portland), February 12, 1899, and died April 6, 1925.

There is a story behind these bare facts. During a visit to Helena,

Montana, whither he went on the advice of his physician in 1897, Father Christie's affability, charm and ability as a raconteur won the friendship of Bishop Brondel who proposed him for the vacant see of Victoria to which he was appointed without the knowledge of Archbishop Ireland. It had an unexpected sequel. When Archbishop Gross of Oregon City (now, Portland) died on November 14, 1898, Bishop Brondel aspired to be his successor, but the Archbishop of St. Paul intervened and Bishop Christie was transferred to the widowed Archdiocese.

The Reverend Michael Dougherty said his first Mass in the Cathedral on December 18, 1898, and Bishop Shanley of Fargo, whom he had served as an altar boy when the Bishop was pastor, preached the sermon in the course of which he said that Father Dougherty was the ninth boy from the parish to be ordained a priest, the others being Archbishop Ireland, Bishop O'Gorman, Reverend Edward Walters (who died a few years previously in the Fort Wayne Diocese), Bishop Cotter, Bishop Shanley, Reverends James Fitzpatrick of Minneapolis, Charles Corcoran of Stillwater, and Jeremiah Prendergast, S. J. Father Dougherty was ordained for the Diocese of Fargo and, after its division in 1910, was in Bismarck diocese until his death.

Archbishop Ireland was one of the principal speakers at the "National Jubilee of Peace" held in Chicago on October 18, 1898, in token of the gladness and gratitude of the nation for the peace and glory of victory at the close of the Spanish-American war. The meeting of more than 5,000 people took place in the Auditorium hall and was attended by President McKinley and his cabinet and presided over by the Honorable George R. Peck of Chicago. The Archbishop chose for his subject "War and Peace"[141] in which he described the horrors of even a necessary war, which evoked the prowess of the American soldiers and their patriotism and which, by its triumph over Spanish arms, had not only liberated Cuba but had given America a place in the sun and made brighter the hope of universal peace through international arbitration.

Joan of Arc Celebration

One of the greatest of Archbishop Ireland's orations was delivered from the pulpit of the Cathedral of Orleans in France on May 8, 1899, on the 470th anniversary of the deliverance of that city by Joan of Arc, of Domremy, as the heroic Maid of Orleans.[142] He was selected for the great honor by the Archbishop of Orleans who admired "the fervid, virile eloquence of the Archbishop of St. Paul. We know that he, once a soldier himself, will do ample justice to the militant Maid of Orleans. Then he is the nearest approach to our own Bossuet that the Church has today". It was a memorable occasion. The celebration opened with a salute of twenty-one guns and the ringing of all the bells of the city. At ten o'clock the municipal and other bodies entered the Cathedral which was fittingly decorated for the occasion. Among those present was a descendant of the family of Joan of Arc, Captain Delgatto, stationed at Marseilles. The Archbishop spoke in French. After the Mass all went in procession to the old Fort of Tourelle stormed and captured by Joan and her army on May 8, 1429, in the assault of which she was wounded by an arrow. When the dismayed English garrison withdrew from Orleans she ordered a Te Deum sung in the Cathedral for the deliverance of the city. The route from the Cathedral to the old fort was lined with soldiers and in the procession marched the city officials, the fire brigade, societies and citizens. After the visit all returned to the Cathedral for a solemn Te Deum and in the evening there was a torch light procession and fireworks.

Five thousand of the social and intellectual élite of France heard the Archbishop's discourse, among them Bishop O'Gorman and Bellamy and Maria Storer, his intimate friends.

A Triumphal Tour

After this memorable address Archbishop Ireland began what proved to be a triumphal tour through France, Belgium and the British Isles on his return journey to America. In his letters to Monsignor O'Connell,[143] he speaks of the banquets at which he was the distinguished guest, the speeches he delivered, the receptions with which he was honored. In Paris he had "dinners without end" and offers of dinners and receptions which he had to refuse for lack of time. He received a tremendous ovation at the Church of Ste. Clotilde in the heart of Faubourg St. Germain where he delivered the panegyric on the Saint on Trinity Sunday, May 14. He also lectured before a large audience where Ferdinand Brunetière, of the Revue des Deux Mondes presided, in which he declared that "practical religion today must be energizing and effective". The Paris Debats complimented him on his sermon at Ste. Clotilde for his eloquence and marvellous acquaintance with the French tongue.

> Archbishop Ireland has a wealth of language and a variety of correctness in the use of expression which even many French orators do not possess and he is capable with his bold evangelical ideas of stirring great multitudes.

The Daily Chronicle of London characterized as a memorable utterance the sentence in which he said: "Let us by all means be careful not to take away one iota from the faith, but let us also be sure not to add to it ideas and interpretations which are binding upon nobody". The writer adds that this is what "Roman churchmen" are prone to do and "it is interesting to watch the struggle of Archbishop Ireland and his friends against these forces of reaction . . . the Archbishop is treading on delicate ground which may break under his feet".

The correspondent of the New York Journal said the Archbishop administered quite a shock to the "ancien regime" at Ste. Clotilde's. The ears of the aristocratic worshippers in that historic edifice were not attuned to such doctrine as he expounded—a democratic sermon, breathing of the equality of man and other sentiments foreign to the Faubourg. The old nobility were told that they were behind the times in clinging to a superseded and false ideal. The age is a living and not a dead age and it had needs which it was their christian duty to satisfy. "Noblesse oblige" entails obligations of nobility to recognize the rights of the proletariat and uplift the masses. Human freedom and brotherhood were the keynotes of an impassioned address.

In Brussels the Archbishop dined with the King, the Comte de Flandre and the Storers with all the haut ton, and gave a conference to the "Jeunesse Catholique" attended by the élite of the city. He preached in Ste. Gudule before a capacity audience. At Louvain he dined with the Rector and addressed the students of the American College and had to refuse an invitation to speak to one thousand students of the University. He notes, "If ever Americanism were alive, it is alive in Brussels and Louvain as manifested in talks with me and honors done me".[144] At Brussels "the whole aristocracy—ministers, senators, deputies, clergy, even the Nuncio, even two Jesuits—put no limit to that enthusiasm. . . . Americanism triumphs, and no one speaks of the opposition but to censure its vileness". He returned to Paris and was formally received by President Loubet at the Palace de l'Elysée.

In the midst of all he yearned to be back in America, away from turmoil.

Mon Dieu! What a sad visit mine was to Rome. I wish these three months were blotted out of my life story. However they revealed to me realities heretofore hidden. . .I think I shall never again visit Italy. I am more than tired of it.

In Paris he had to spend some time in a hospital caring for a sore arm and a black eye "the result of a fall from a runaway". Thence he went to his old seminary of Meximieux for a visit of a few days and returned to Paris to issue his letter on Americanism in which he took high ground, avoiding allusion to persons "whom we must despise".[145] Then, entirely re-made in spirit, with the Pontine fevers gone from every fibre of his soul, he set out for Calais on June 26 and was welcomed in England by Catholics and non-Catholics. He was tendered a reception at the Catholic Union, where he met the leading Catholics of the country—Denbigh, Bute, Ripon, Barry, Lilly, Ward and others under the presidency of the

Duke of Norfolk and delivered an address. He decided to keep in touch with them as never before.

The New Era of London in a sketch of his life wrote that in him

We find the ideality of Dante combined with the eloquence and political energy of Savanorola. . .Rome, Paris, London and Brussels have tendered him the homage of their deepest respect and admiration. Kings and Presidents have paid him court. The highest representatives of Church and State, the world's aristocracy of rank and intellect have hung upon his lips whether he has spoken in private conference or at a great public demonstration such as the recent centenary at Orleans.

His "grand tour" of the British Isles closed on July 19 with a temperance lecture in Cork[146] where three bands and thousands of people escorted his jaunting car through the streets. It was his warning to the land of his birth. Ireland's aspirations, he told his great audience, are being blighted by the curse of drink. He bade them renew the work of Father Mathew and organize total abstinence societies. He appealed to the priests to be leaders in a new crusade and further the cause of sobriety, for Ireland sober is Ireland free.

The next day he sailed from Cork. For three days his mind was filled with thoughts of Europe and its triumphs, then it turned to America with the activities there awaiting him and once again he was an American in feeling and impulse as if he had not crossed the ocean. Then he reviewed the "grand voyage" drawing to a close.[147]

Beginning at Milan and ending at Cork, and from one end to the other, 'des triomphes eclatants'. Everywhere the social élite, the scholarship, the statesmanship, anxious to do me honor. It is hard to say which place excelled. I would say—for heart, Milan and Paris—for éclat, Brussels and London. London was a most unexpected revelation to me. The Catholics there were superb, the Protestants scarcely less so: Choate and the Americans wondrous in their attentions. In Brussels royalty did its best and Louvain was admirable.

And then he asked himself what the cause, what the meaning?

One thing is sure—Americanism reigns and the 'Civilta' and its adherents make no impression on the world, save the Archbishop of Paris and the Jesuits of Paris and London—all of whom I scorned. Orders were sent out from the General in Rome to the Jesuits of Paris and London to shun me. I have this from the most reliable inner source. Hence the Parisian Jesuits animosity which has recoiled upon the society in the anger of the young men.

On The Home Front

On his arrival in St. Paul he became immersed in the work of the diocese, "working hard and knowing of no country outside of America . . . I have totally forgotten Rome, never again to think of it, never again to see it".[148] All talk about Americanism had subsided though he could not help being angry with the two men who had "belied America"—

Archbishops Corrigan and Katzer—who had admitted the existence of erroneous opinions, while six denied it—St. Paul, Baltimore, Boston, St. Louis, San Francisco, and Philadelphia. Four—Baltimore, San Francisco, St. Louis and Boston—denied it so strongly that Rome dared not publish their letters. Three did not write at all—Chicago, Dubuque and Santa Fe, while three—Cincinnati, Portland and New Orleans—wrote neutral letters.

President McKinley was the guest of honor of the Marquette Club of Chicago at its annual banquet in the Auditorium on October 7, 1899. On that occasion Archbishop Ireland spoke on "The American Republic" which he characterized as

> the embodiment of our highest civic and political concepts, the best form of organized democracy revealed in humanity's history, to which she claims homage from her own citizens as much as she draws to herself the attention of the world. Her democracy and her organization of her democracy—behold the glory of the American Republic.[149]

The last priest ordained by Bishop Cretin—the Right Reverend Anatole Oster—was invested with the purple robes of a Domestic Prelate by the Archbishop on October 26, 1899, at the St. Paul Seminary of which he was Spiritual Director. Pontifical Mass was celebrated by Bishop Shanley with Fathers Robert as archpriest, Kane of Rush City deacon, Egan of Watertown subdeacon, and Schaefer master of ceremonies. The papal rescript was read by Father Stariha, V.G., and the sermon preached by the Archbishop. Bishops Cotter, McGolrick and Trobec were in the sanctuary, and a large number of priests, alumni of the Seminary, and others were present as well as the members of the faculty and the student body.

In the name of the citizens of St. Paul the Commercial Club held a reception in honor of the Archbishop in November, 1899. The President, Mr. Hamlin, presided and addresses were delivered by Mayor Kiefer, Judge Flandreau, Bishop Gilbert of the Episcopal Church and M. D. Munn on behalf of the club membership. In reply the Archbishop said that the honors shown him abroad were in large measure a tribute to an American who took pride in being a citizen of America, familiar with the spirit, aims and hopes of its institutions.

> In no city of America is there less evidence of religious strife or dissension than in the City of St. Paul. In no state of America has this happy condition of affairs been so strongly marked as in our own state of Minnesota. I pray that this evening's assemblage symbolize the history of our future as it factfully reflects the history of the past.

Paris, Rome and Meximieux

The statue of Lafayette, designed by Paul Bartlett, and presented by the United States to France as an inspiring testimonial of friendship from one Republic to another, was unveiled in Paris on July 4, 1900. It was paid for by the pennies of the children of America aided by a generous donation from the American Government, and was erected in the Place du Carrousel in Paris. A commission of distinguished American citizens of which Mr. Robert J. Thompson of Chicago, who first proposed such a tribute, was secretary, cooperated with Mr. Ferdinand W. Peck, General Commissioner of the United States to the French Exposition of 1900, and selected Archbishop Ireland as the speaker at the ceremony of unveiling the statue. Their choice was approved by President McKinley in a letter to the Archbishop on June 11, 1900. On that occasion the Archbishop delivered one of the greatest orations of his career.[150] He spoke in French from a notable rostrum, an international pulpit, and the whole world lent an attentive ear to his discourse, in which he paid tribute to Lafayette as the friend of America, the true soldier of liberty and its defender.

From Paris the Archbishop made a short visit to Rome to comply with the requirements of the Holy Year and was received in audience by the Pope who expressed satisfaction at the attitude of the American government and of President McKinley towards the Church.[151] Before leaving Rome he attended a function at which the Holy Father was present and twenty-one members of the Sacred College of Cardinals. The Pope asked him what he would tell the American people on his return home, and he improvised a speech in French for twenty minutes which held the Pope and Cardinals spellbound as he spoke glowingly of the devotion of American Catholics to the Holy See and their desire for a united church, independent of any temporal power. He described liberty under the American flag, and set forth the necessity of the Pope, as head of Christendom, being free and independent of the civil power, "so as to be, in fact as well as of right, the sovereign teacher and ruler of all nations and peoples, without special dependency on any special nation or people".[152]

On his homeward journey he stopped in Paris and at a meeting in the Elysée Palace Hotel received from Jules Cambon, French Ambassador to the United States, then on a visit to France, the insignia of a Commander of the Legion of Honor to which he had been nominated. The insignia is a five-rayed cross suspended from a leaf of laurel and oak by a crimson ribbon. A distinguished group was present for the function, among them General Horace Porter, American Ambassador to France, Viscount de Vogue of the French Academy, and Ferdinand Brunetière, editor of the Revue des Deux Mondes. The Legion of Honor is an order of merit instituted by Napoleon Bonaparte as a recognition for special military and civil services. It is the highest honor France can confer and few foreigners attain it. It was bestowed upon the Archbishop as an expression of gratitude for his eulogy on Lafayette and his panegyric on Joan of Arc.

From Paris he went to his beloved Meximieux and was asked to give an address[153] to the clergy of the Diocese of Belley who were on retreat, in the course of which he dwelt on the salient characteristics of the priest living in the modern world and meeting the impact of its paganism. To be victorious in the strife the priest must be imbued with apostolic zeal and inspired by love for souls, a hero, a saint and an apostle. He must not allow himself to become pessimistic nor discouraged with the world-wide prevalence of evil and unbelief, and retire to the sacristy to save his own soul. He must not lose faith in the promise of Christ to be with him all days even to the consummation of the world, but go down into the arena to do battle for souls, resolved to conquer or die. He must live in the present, unregretful of the past. He must go to the people and by his knowledge of the truths of faith and the elegance of his diction win them from their idols. All that is necessary to convert the world is the gospel of Jesus Christ. The world is never so cold or so cruel that it will not respond to the love of a zealous priest who knows his flock by name and goes after them in the conviction that it is souls that count, souls for whom Christ shed His precious blood, and that He "will demand an account of those souls if we have failed to do all that we can to gain them".

It was a stirring appeal to leave the sheltered ways of the past and launch out into the deep where souls were struggling with temptation and sin and rescue them from the destroyer. The need of this type of priest was brought home to his hearers in the following decade when Combes and his ilk tried to throttle the Church in France.

He sailed from London on the Majestic on October 10 and gave two lectures on board on "The Duty of Capital and Labor" in which he advocated toleration, justice and charity, and asked capitalists to give laborers sufficient wages to enable them to live decently.

Archbishop's Vote and Interview

On landing in New York the Archbishop was besieged by reporters from the city newspapers anxious to know how he intended to vote at the coming election. In reply thereto he gave following interview on October 20:

How do I intend to vote? It cannot at first sight but seem more or less impertinent for any citizen to tell the public how he intends to vote. In voting each citizen obeys the dictates of his own sense of civic duty; he should simply do this and leave to others to do likewise. However, since a certain number of newspapers have undertaken to say how I intend to vote, and in doing so have misinterpreted my intention and have not been unwilling to make political capital out of my supposed vote, I will give to the question—how I intend to vote—a categorical and unmistakeable reply. I intend to vote for William McKinley and Theodore Roosevelt.

In giving my vote for the candidates of the Republican party, I am satisfied in my own conscience that I serve the best interests of the country at home and abroad, that I contribute to the maintenance of the country's material prosperity and of peace and good will between the several classes of its population, that I aid the country in bringing about the safest and most honorable solutions of the complex problems which confront it as a result of the late war and in retaining for itself the exalted position which it holds at present commercially and diplomatically before other nations of the world. I trust no further doubts will be expressed as to how I intend to vote.

The local papers made reference to the fact that he had just returned from Europe and had made an interesting statement concerning the Vatican's view of the attitude of the American Government towards the Catholic Church in the Philippine Islands and in Cuba. They quoted him as saying that he had several audiences with the Pope and the Cardinals, who were not unwilling to have their opinions on that subject made public.

In one of the audiences granted him by Pope Leo XIII His Holiness said,

We are well pleased with the relation of the American Government to the Church in Cuba and the Philippine Islands. The American Government gives proof of good will and exhibits in its acts a spirit of justice and respect for the liberty and the rights of the Church. The reports We receive from Bishops and others indicate this. Difficulties of detail occur as a consequence of war and of newness of complexions. But We understand such things. We have confidence in the intelligence and the spirit of justice of the American Government, and believe that the future will not lead Us to a change of sentiment towards it. Under the American Government there will be due respect for rights of property and conscience. You will thank in My name the President of the Republic for what is being done.

Furthermore, Cardinal Rampolla, Secretary of State to His Holiness, told the Archbishop he was at liberty to make known to the American people the views of the Pope, and revealed to him that

on no less than three different occasions petitions were sent to the Vatican, in the name of the Filipino leaders, to have opened between them and the Vatican direct official relations, but that the Vatican always refused to listen to such petitions out of consideration for the American Government . . . The Church needs in Cuba and the Philippines the cooperation of the American Government for the protection of its rights and liberties, as, indeed, the American Government needs the cooperation of the Church for the pacification of these countries.

Cardinal Gotti, as Superior General of the Carmelite Monks, had established three houses of the Order in Cuba before the American ocupation and he told the Archbishop that recent letters from his community assured him that they enjoyed under the present administration of the Island full liberty; that they have undisturbed possession of all their properties; that they were never in better position to labor for the progress of religion and the salvation of souls.

The Archbishop went on to say:

The authorities in Rome are informed to a degree that both astonished and pleased me about matters religious and political in the Philippines and in Cuba; and as they have the interest of the Church in these countries most deeply at heart, and know far better than we in America could know what the rights of the Church are and how best such rights may be defended, Americans—Catholics and others—may safely accept their judgment of things, and not give themselves further needless trouble about the religious conditions of the Philippines or of Cuba.

As a plain matter of fact, the only safety which the Catholic Church at the present time has in the Philippines for the possession of her properties and for the lives of her priests is the protection afforded by the American flag; and all this is fully understood and fully recognized.

The jubilee indulgence for the Holy Year commemorating the opening of a new century held in Rome in 1900 was extended to the Catholic world for six months during 1901, each bishop determining the time for his own diocese. Archbishop Ireland selected the period between March 15 and September 15 and set forth the conditions for gaining the indulgence—confession and communion (different from the annual confession and paschal communion prescribed by the Church), visits to four churches each day for fifteen days, either continuously or separately (including one's parish church and three others) and prayers for the extirpation of heresy and schism and the exaltation of the church. The number of visits was "considerably lessened" for a congregation or society which, led by the pastor, went in procession in the country places or through the streets. Confessors were given special faculties to absolve in reserved cases, to commute vows and grant dispensations.

The Northwestern Chronicle in its issue of June 22, 1901, published a list of the parishes in St. Paul and the dates of their organization: The Cathedral, 1841; Assumption, 1855; St. Mary's, 1867; St. Stanislaus, 1872; St. Michael's, 1874; St. Joseph's, 1875; St. Adalbert's, 1880; Sacred Heart, 1881; St. Francis de Sales, 1884; St. Patrick's, 1884; St. John's, 1886; St. Mathew's, 1886; St. James, 1887; St. Vincent's, 1887; St. Agnes, 1887; St. Luke's, 1888; St. Peter Claver, 1888; St. Mark's, 1889; St. Bernard's, 1890; St. Casimir's, 1893; St. Andrew's, 1896; Holy Redeemer, 1899.

Towards the close of 1901 the Archbishop promised to write a short introduction—one of several by different authors—for a new translation of Horace in which he would deal with his philosophy, poetry, wit and charm and the delight a mature mind takes in reading this classic and the reason for that delight. Shortly before that Monsignor O'Connell of the

American College in Rome sent him a copy of a new edition of Horace which pleased him very much as he was a life-long student of the classics.

About that time he received a very cordial invitation from the Archbishop of Damascus to visit Lebanon and the Church in Syria and make a tour of the Holy Land, and was guaranteed a very pleasant, profitable and interesting itinerary. The pressure of diocesan duties prevented his acceptance of the invitation. He never visited the Holy Land.

The National Educational Association met in annual convention in Minneapolis in July, 1902, and the Most Reverend Archbishop delivered an address before the delegates on July 9 on "Devotion to Truth: The Chief Virtue of the Teacher",[154] in which he declared that

> the teacher is by profession the apostle of truth and the guardian of the human mind. . .The search of truth is the search of the divine. . .the search of truth is an act of religion. The profession of teaching is the priesthood of truth; where the teacher speaks there is sanctuary—the sanctuary of truth; and the sense of the Divine should permeate the atmosphere. . .Let the teacher do well his duty: let the pupil be properly formed, and great will be the America of tomorrow, devoted will it be to truth.

He also insisted upon the value and importance of clean and honest journalism.

> If I were to choose where, outside the classroom, for the general welfare of humanity, I should have devotion to truth prevail, I should name the newspaper. The newspaper is today preeminently the mentor of the people. It is read by all; it is believed nearly by all; its influence is paramount; its responsibilities tremendous. Its province is to narrate facts, to give the truth, nothing but the truth, and all the truth.

Diocesan Golden Jubilee

The solemn commemoration of the golden jubilee[155] of the erection of the Diocese of St. Paul should have been held on July 19, 1900; but the Archbishop was then in Europe and it had to be postponed until the next favorable date, July 2, 1901, the fiftieth anniversary of the arrival in St. Paul of the Right Reverend Joseph Cretin, its first Bishop.

Early in the year committees of priests and laymen were appointed to map out, in detail, a religious and civic program worthy of the event. The general committee of priests was composed of Fathers Lawler (chairman) Byrne (secretary) O'Reilly, Gores, Jung and McNulty, assisted by an auxiliary clerical committee on diocesan album and jubilee fund. The general committee of laymen had for chairman, T. D. O'Brien, secretary, William O'Gorman, and treasurer, Frank Machovec, assisted by committees on history, speakers, music, invitations, parade, finance, printing and badges, hall and decorations, etc.

The principal features of the religious celebration on July 2 were the Pontifical Mass on the St. Paul Seminary grounds with Bishop McGolrick celebrant and Archbishop Ireland preacher; presentation of the Jubilee Fund and Diocesan Album at 3 P. M.; laying of the cornerstone of St. Mary's Chapel at 4 P. M. by Bishop Trobec, and sermon by Bishop O'Gorman; and on July 3 Solemn Requiem Mass in the Cathedral for the deceased priests and people of the Province; a grand parade of parish organizations and independent societies followed by a monster meeting in the St. Paul auditorium in the evening.

The Jubilee Mass was celebrated at an improvised altar on the grassy hillside between the Administration Building and the Mississippi river not very far from the place, "a league below the Falls of St. Anthony of Padua," where, more than two hundred years earlier, Father Hennepin beached his canoe. The green sward sloping in natural terraces towards the river, was divided into nave and transepts by rows of stately elms and oaks and provided accommodation for the congregation of about ten thousand present on the occasion, in addition to two archbishops, seven bishops, four hundred and fifty priests and seminarians. Two venerable clergymen, Monsignor Ravoux and Father Lacombe (of Western Canada), who were in the diocese when Bishop Cretin arrived, were special guests and centers of attraction at the function.

"Fifty years of Catholicity in the Northwest" was the theme of the Archbishop's sermon in which he sketched the history of the diocese, paying a special tribute to Monsignor Ravoux and Father Lacombe, and eulogizing their successors, the priests of the diocese, and the faithful Catholic laity trained by them.

Pope Leo XIII honored the event with an autograph letter to the Archbishop imparting the Apostolic Blessing to him, the suffragan bishops, clergy and faithful of the Province.

At the end of the midday dinner in the seminary refectory, two presentations were made in the name of the clergy of the diocese—the one a leather-bound memorial album, the other a jubilee fund for the benefit of the College of St. Thomas. The memorial album,[156] in four large volumes, told in pictures the story of Catholicity in Minnesota and the Dakotas prior to 1851; of Hennepin naming the Falls of St. Anthony; of the log chapels of Mendota, St. Paul and Pembina with their pastors, Fathers Galtier, Ravoux, Belcourt and Lacombe; and of pioneer Bishops Loras and Henni who exercised spiritual authority over the original territory of the diocese.

Then followed a graphic account of the origin and development of every parish in the Archdiocese, with pictures of the priests who served them, the churches, schools and other institutions within their boundaries, together with names and dates and a skeleton history of each as well as of the colleges, academies and other religious institutions in the diocese.

The volumes, with leaves 28 x 20 inches in size, are five inches thick bound in hand-tooled American leather and enclosed in an artistically carved oak case on casters, with a reference index. The presentation was made by Father O'Neill, chairman of the committee of priests charged with the work.

Following him Father Stariha stepped forward to present a purse of $80,000 subscribed by the clergy to aid the College of St. Thomas. In accepting these gifts the Archbishop, deeply moved, made a feeling reply on behalf of the Archdiocese for whose benefit they were intended, and told his hearers how much the occasion meant to him for his whole life had been bound up with the diocese and its progress. "I can wish, for no greater blessing to the Diocese in the next fifty years than that those years be in zeal for the glory of God and the salvation of souls, as the fifty years that are closed today. ... Fifty years hence! Fortunate will the Diocese be if, then, its priests endow it, in proportion to their number and to the measures of their ability, as richly as they endow it today".

Undoubtedly the most important event of the jubilee day in its significance for the future of the diocese was the blessing of the cornerstone of the new chapel under the invocation of the Blessed Virgin Mary. It crowns a knoll between the Administration building and Summit Avenue and in its chastely ornate style of architecture presents a pleasing contrast to the classic simplicity of the other buildings. It is 156 feet in length, 58 in width, with a cross surmounting the gable 58 feet from the ground. The exterior walls are of Kettle river sandstone with Bedford stone trim. The interior, basilicar in type, is modeled after St. Paul's Outside the Walls in Rome.

Bishop Trobec officiated at the blessing and laying of the cornerstone in presence of a large gathering of clergy and laity and Bishop O'Gorman preached the festive sermon in which he referred to the pioneer missionaries, the first preparatory seminary established by Bishop Cretin and of which he and the Archbishop were graduates, its successor, St. Thomas Seminary, and went on to describe the aim and program of the major seminary of which the proposed chapel is to be the very soul, "since here he (the seminarian) comes in contact with Christ, whose dwelling it is".

The Solemn Requiem Mass in the Cathedral the next day was sung by Bishop Shanley, its former pastor, and the seminarian choir. In the sanctuary were Archbishops Ireland and Christie, Bishops Scannell, McGolrick, Trobec, Glennon, O'Gorman and Eis. The sermon was preached by the Archbishop who emphasized the spiritual claims on the living of "the dead ... who still rule our spirit from their tombs", whose heritage we enjoy and whose deeds should not be forgotten. He dwelt lovingly on the old memories and touched upon the practical lessons which the past transmits to the future.

The ceremonies of the morning which ended the religious observance of the jubilee gave place to the civic festivities of the evening. There was a grand parade of Catholic societies in eleven divisions, with thousands of men participating from all the parishes of St. Paul and cheered by 30,000 spectators along the line of march. It took over an hour for the procession to pass the balcony of the Cathedral residence from which the Archbishop and other dignitaries reviewed the marching ranks.

The parade ended at the auditorium where the public mass meeting was presided over by Thomas D. O'Brien who, after brief introductory remarks and the reading, in Latin and in English, of the autograph letter of the Pope by Bishop O'Gorman presented Judge William L. Kelly who made the principal address reminiscent of the Catholic history connected with the founding of the diocese by Bishop Cretin and descriptive of its growth during half a century.

One of the pioneer settlers, Honorable William P. Murray, a non-Catholic but sympathetic observer of the early struggles of the Catholic Church in the Northwest, spoke of the religious conditions prevailing in St. Paul fifty years before and of his acquaintance with Bishops Cretin and Grace, Father Ravoux and other pioneers. He was followed by August L. Larpenteur, a resident of St. Paul since 1843, who knew the old voyageurs, traded with them, and saw the beginning of organized government in Church and State.

On behalf of the French citizens Judge E. W. Bazille spoke briefly of the part taken by French explorers and colonists in the development of Minnesota, and Herman Nienstedt reviewed what the Germans had done for the spiritual and material advancement of the Northwest.

Bishop Shanley spoke of Bishop Cretin and his successors and warmly praised the role they played in the religious development of the city and state. In a brief address the Most Reverend Archbishop congratulated the Catholics on the part taken in the Golden Jubilee and on the success of the meeting and ventured the prophecy that "the victories of the past half century would lead up to more glorious triumphs in the half century upon which the Church in Minnesota had just entered". The speakers were applauded by a capacity audience of Catholic and non-Catholic citizens who entered whole-heartedly into the festive spirit of the occasion.

After the singing of the "Star-Spangled Banner" by the audience, led by a chorus which had rendered several selections during the evening, the gathering dispersed and the celebration of the golden jubilee of the erection of the Diocese of St. Paul passed into the realm of history.

Diocesan Mission Band

The project of a Diocesan Mission Band of priests to give missions, retreats, triduums, etc., to Catholics and to preach the gospel to non-

Catholics, was under consideration by Archbishop Ireland as early as 1894, but priests were too few to permit him to set aside even the nucleus of such a group. However, the matter was not forgotten, but held in abeyance till the summer of 1901, when he deputed the Reverend Joseph F. Busch to represent the Archdiocese at the first conference for missionaries to non-Catholics held at Winchester, Tennessee, under the auspices of the Paulist Congregation which had been founded for the purpose of preaching to non-Catholics wherever they could be brought together and supplying them with Catholic literature.

The next year the St. Paul Diocesan Mission Band was formally organized with Father Busch as superior and the Reverend George A. Arctander, a convert from Lutheranism, as associate. They took up residence in the St. Paul Seminary and carried on their work in the Archdiocese and the Province of St. Paul from September first through the winter to June thirtieth of each year. The work was supported by voluntary offerings from the people to whom they preached, especially Catholic congregations. The first mission was given in the Church of St. Peter, North St. Paul, during the week of September 7, 1902.

From the beginning it was the Archbishop's intention to provide a permanent headquarters for the Band in a parish not too far distant from the Twin Cities. Such a location was found in Excelsior[157] on the shore of Lake Minnetonka, in the autumn of 1903, when the Universalist church in that village was brought for $2,200, remodeled, and formally opened for divine worship, under the patronage of St. John the Baptist, on Easter Sunday, 1904. It had a seating capacity of 230, amply sufficient for the accommodation of the twenty Catholic families residing permanently in the parish and of the Catholic summer visitors who spent their vacations or week ends in the lake area. Two Masses were said on Sundays during the summer and one in winter. At the end of the second year the entire cost of the church property and improvements, amounting to nearly $5,000, was fully paid. The priests of the mission band received no salary from the parish, but the surplus, after meeting current expenses, was used to defray the cost of maintaining the mission house.

Father Busch built the mission house at his own expense on a plot of ground opposite the church overlooking the lake from the rear and it was ready for occupancy on Christmas eve, 1905. It served as headquarters for the missionaries as long as the group continued to function. There they spent their leisure time between missions and were charged with the spiritual direction and care of the parish.

During the first three years seventy-five missions[158] were given in parish churches and in public halls where no church existed; five thousand copies of Father Searles' "Plain Facts For Fair Minds" were distributed free of charge to non-Catholics, and from thirty to forty converts received into the Church each year. Five thousand dollars worth of religious literature was purchased by Catholics.

Father Arctander retired from the Mission Band in 1907 to accept the pastorate of the Church of St. Andrew in St. Paul where he died in September, 1909. He was succeeded by the Reverend Francis J. Lang, a graduate of the Apostolic Mission House in Washington, who remained with the organization until 1909. In the meantime the Reverend John H. Peschges of the Diocese of Winona, joined the band in 1908, and the Reverend William Colbert from the same diocese in 1909.

The Mission Band continued to operate until May 19, 1910, when the superior, Father Busch, was consecrated second Bishop of Lead, South Dakota, and the Reverend James M. Reardon of the faculty of the St. Paul Seminary, was appointed his successor. Fathers Peschges and Colbert were recalled to their diocese during the summer and the Mission Band ceased to function because the Archbishop was not in a position to assign others priests to the work.

Father Reardon remained in charge of the parish until December 31, 1910, when the Reverend Thomas Cushen was appointed pastor. Some years later the Mission House was bought from Bishop Busch by John Hennessey, a local business man, who occupied it for a few years as a residence and then sold it for use as a rest home for aged people. Bishop Busch was transferred from the See of Lead to the Diocese of St. Cloud in 1915. Father Peschges died Bishop of Crookston on October 20, 1944. Father Colbert died on February 11, 1948, after many years of faithful pastoral service in the Diocese of Winona. The Reverend Francis J. Lang is pastor of the Church of St. Anthony, Minneapolis, and Monsignor Reardon of the Basilica of St. Mary in that city.

The Catholic Extension Society of the United States was organized in 1905 by the Reverend Francis Clement Kelley of Lapeer, Michigan, under the patronage of Archbishop Quigley of Chicago, which soon became its headquarters. The bishops in the missionary area of the South and Southwest especially hailed it as a godsend; but many of the bishops in the East and in the more prosperous dioceses in the West, not realizing from personal experience the need for such a society, withheld official approval. Among the latter was Archbishop Ireland to whom the new venture did not appeal from the beginning. He was asked by the Founder to release one of his priests to serve as General Secretary of the Society but refused. Nor would he permit public appeals for support to be made in the churches, though he did not object to solicitation by letter, or lectures by representatives of the Society in high schools and academies or before interested groups.

He was not fully aware of the generous monetary contributions made to parishes in the Province of St. Paul through the suffragan bishops until, towards the end of his life, he paid a visit to the Extension office in Chicago, spent a day inspecting the set-up, asking questions and looking over the records and thus finding out for himself that over a quarter of a million dollars had been poured by Extension into seven of the suffragan dioceses. On his return to St. Paul he wrote Father Kelley commending the Society and its purpose.[159] In this way, by actual contact with its work, he and many other bishops became converts to the cause of Extension and realized the importance of the work it was accomplishing.

The Catholic Historical Society

The preliminary meeting for the organization of the Catholic Historical Society of St. Paul[160] was held in the St. Paul Seminary on April 25, 1905, with the Most Reverend Archbishop, the Bishops of the Province of St. Paul, the Abbott of St. John's and many priests in attendance. The Archbishop presided and explained the object of the meeting. The Catholic Church in the Northwest, he said, had passed the formative period of growth and development and clergy and laity are in position to study her history and draw inspiration from the lessons it inculcates. The proposed society will endeavor to interest them in this important work and encourage each one to record whatever fact he may be able to glean regarding the origin and spread of Catholicity in his locality. Its object, therefore, will be to collect and preserve materials of all kinds—books, papers, manuscripts, documents, souvenirs, etc.—relating to Catholic activity not only in the Province of St. Paul but in the Northwest.

We owe it to the past, he continued, to gather and correlate all available information about the progress of the Church in this part of America and thus rescue from oblivion the noteworthy incidents in the lives of her pioneer missionaries and laymen.

We owe it to the present, not less than to the future, to be conversant with the various factors which, in the past, contributed to the upbuilding of the Church in the Northwest in order that we who are to erect a superstructure on the foundation laid by our forefathers in the faith may labor intelligently for her advancement and welfare.

The charter members were: Archbishop Ireland, Bishops McGolrick of Duluth, Cotter of Winona, Shanley of Fargo, O'Gorman of Sioux Falls, Trobec of St. Cloud, Stariha of Lead, and Abbots Engel of St. John's and Wehrle of Richardton; Monsignor Oster, V. G., of Mendota; Reverends J. J. Lawler, Jerome Heider, O. S. B., J. M. Solnce, T. J. Gibbons, A. McNulty, F. X. Bajec, P. M. Jung, F. X. Gores, A. Ogulin, W. L. Hart of St. Paul; Reverends J. C. Byrne, J. O'Reilly, F. Jaeger, J. Andre, Othmar Erren, O. S. B., of Minneapolis; and Reverends P. F. Heffron,

F. J. Schaefer, J. Campbell, B. Feeney, J. M. Reardon, J. A. Ryan, J. Seliskar, D. Hughes, N. Stubinitzki, and A. Ziskovsky of St. Paul Seminary; and Reverend H. Moynihan of the College of St. Thomas. Of these only three survive—Fathers Reardon, Hart and Ziskovsky.

A constitution and by-laws was adopted. The name of the organization was "The St. Paul Catholic Historical Society", later (in 1913) changed to "The Catholic Historical Society of St. Paul" as it is at present. Its primary object was to collect and preserve materials of all kinds—books, papers, pamphlets, manuscripts, maps, documents, and souvenirs of historic interest—relating to the Catholic history of the Province of St. Paul; and secondary, to gather and correlate and preserve all available information concerning the history of the Catholic Church in the Northwest.

The membership was to be of three kinds: Active (comprising the bishops, abbots, priests and Catholic laymen of the Province of St. Paul); Corresponding (made up of persons within or without the Province interested in the Society to the extent of making regular contributions of any kind); Honorary (composed of persons who manifest a very special interest in the Society and its purpose and are chosen by the active members at a regular meeting).

The officers would consist of an Honorary President (the Ordinary of the Archdiocese of St. Paul), a President, two Vice-Presidents, a Secretary and Librarian and a Treasurer, as well as a Board of Directors elected by the active members, twenty-five in all, including one from each of the suffragan dioceses and from the abbeys of Collegeville and Richardton, in addition to the Archbishop and Bishops of the Province and the Abbots who are ex-officio members.

General meetings were to be held semi-annually on the first Wednesday after Easter and the second Wednesday in November. The executive body would meet at the call of the President on the first Wednesday of January, March, May and October, and ten constituted a quorum. The annual election of officers followed the regular meeting after Easter.

The officers elected were: Honorary President, the Archbishop of St. Paul; President, Reverend F. J. Schaefer; First Vice-President, Reverend J. J. Lawler; Second Vice-President, Reverend Jerome Heider, O. S. B.; Secretary and Librarian, Reverend J. M. Reardon; Treasurer, J. Seliskar. All the priests present were elected to the Board of Directors. Monsignor Flynn of Madison, S. D., was chosen to represent the Diocese of Sioux Falls; Father Conaty of Grand Forks, N. D., the Diocese of Fargo; Monsignor Nagl, V. G., of St. Augusta, Minnesota, the Diocese of St. Cloud; Father Corbett of Duluth, the Diocese of Duluth; and Father Hoffmann, O. S. B., St. John's Abbey at Collegeville.

In due time a library and a museum were opened and "Acta et Dicta" was launched as the official organ, containing reprints of original documents; historical papers; a chronicle of current events; obituary notices; partial lists of library books and manuscripts and museum objects of historic interest.

The first issue of "Acta et Dicta" appeared in July, 1907, and it was issued annually thereafter till 1911 when it lapsed for four years, was resumed in 1915 and continued till 1918, inclusive.

In 1912 the Society was reorganized [161] and incorporated with a Board of five trustees and such other members as the Board might elect. After 1918 the Society was inactive, but it was not extinct, as the Board of Directors retained office and the library and museum were maintained, though few additions were made to them.

In July, 1916, the first four chapters of the Life of Bishop Cretin by Archbishop Ireland appeared in Acta et Dicta and eleven additional chapters in the two subsequent issues.

The Society was revived [162] under Archbishop Murray at a meeting in St. Paul Seminary on November 7, 1932, called to order by Father Reardon, second Vice-President of the Society as officered prior to 1918. The report of the Treasurer, Father Schaefer, showed it to be in good financial condition with assets amounting to $6,730.06, most of which was a bequest to the Society from the Right Reverend Anatole Oster, and no liabilities. It was voted to resume publication of Acta et Dicta and issues came from the press in October 1933, 1934, 1935 and 1936, when it ceased to appear and has not been resurrected. It would not be fair to lay the blame for its discontinuance on any one individual; but scholars regret that such an interesting and promising magazine should be allowed to die through apathy on the part of those who should be active in the work it was intended to foster. Provision should be made for the collection of source material and its proper custody until such time as Acta et Dicta is resurrected.

Cathedral Building

The project of building a new Cathedral of St. Paul to replace the commodious but unpretentious and architecturally unimpressive church in the down-town area was in process of incubation many years before its inception. The third Cathedral of St. Paul, unplastered and unfinished, was opened for divine worship on June 13, 1858, and served the needs of the parish and of the Diocese, and as a center of impressive ecclesiastical ceremonies, until it was demolished in 1914. It became outmoded with the growth of the city in population and importance and the corresponding increase in the number and prestige of its Catholic citizens. When the Diocese of St. Paul was raised to metropolitan dignity in 1888 a new impetus was given to the project. It became a matter of common belief that a new Cathedral in a prominent locality, remote from the business section and in the direction of Minneapolis, was imperative. Several sites were proposed but no decision was made for over a decade of years.

Owing to the growth in population and importance of the Midway District as a business center lying between the two cities it was thought that the future Cathedral should be located somewhere in that area. As a matter of fact a site considered quite suitable for that purpose and lying to the north of St. Thomas College was prominently mentioned and for years regarded as the logical location for a Cathedral for the Twin Cities.

In 1887 Bishop Ireland purchased the Wann property[163] on Summit Avenue at Victoria Street and it was popularly believed that it was being considered as a site for the proposed Cathedral. It ultimately became the location of St. Luke's Church and rectory. The diocese also owned a block on the corner of Western and St. Anthony Avenue which many regarded as an excellent location for an imposing church.

The Archbishop believed that the two cities would soon be one, if not as a corporation, at least in every other respect and he was disposed to look favorably on the suggestion that the new Cathedral be erected in "Federal City"[164] as the Midway area was called at the time. It was reported that the new Capitol would be built on a commanding site in that district. He was inclined to leave the selection of a site to the Catholic people provided that it be in a prominent locality, remote from the business section of St. Paul, towards Minneapolis, and that $500,000 be on hand for the undertaking. The Wann block, known as the Cathedral property, had its advocates who believed that within five years, with the contemplated improvements, it would be in the center of a large population, and be a suitable setting for a grand Cathedral facing Summit Avenue.

That the Archbishop had in mind the project of building a new Cathedral we learn from an interview given by the Most Reverend John J. Keane in Liverpool in the early part of 1889 in which he said that the Archbishop deferred it in order that "the work in behalf of Higher Education (the Catholic University at Washington) might have a better chance of progress".[165]

So the matter rested until Holy Thursday night, March 31, 1904, when the Archbishop, grieved at the impossibility of providing adequate accommodations in the old Cathedral for the immense concourse of people who wished to attend Holy Week services, decided that the time had come to think seriously about the construction of a new Cathedral which he had theretofore been inclined to leave to his successor.[166] He was then in his sixty-sixth year and the prospect of building a cathedral, adequate to the needs of the people and commensurate with the prestige of the Archdiocese, was not an alluring one, but he was a prelate of big ideas, broad vision and tireless energy, who maintained that a man was in his prime at seventy, and the prospect, with the planning and hardship it entailed, did not daunt him. On that night the die was cast and the new Cathedral project was born. It was destined to be the crowning achievement of his long and fruitful episcopate, the last great work undertaken by him for the honor and glory of God and the furtherance of the interests of religion. Before he passed away he had the happiness of dedicating to the service of the Most High a Cathedral of monumental proportions, of unusual architectural splendor and unique symbolism whose massive dome dominates the city from its stately eminence on St. Paul's crowning hilltop.

On that Holy Thursday night he answered in the affirmative the question that had confronted him for some time: "Has not the time come for a great Cathedral in St. Paul?" Fortunately the fates were propitious. For several years a magnificent site on the brow of St. Anthony hill, known as the Kittson property, bounded by Summit, Dayton and Selby Avenues, had been the object of litigation which had just been settled by the court. The property was now available and on April 9, 1904, it was purchased for $52,500 by C. H. F. Smith and H. C. McNair acting for the Archdiocese. It proved to be a matchless pedestal built by nature for a monumental church and the Archbishop could declare with truth, "Seldom has an act of mine received such universal approval as the selection of that site".

No time was lost in getting underway. On July 15 he addressed a letter to a number of intelligent and zealous Catholic laymen requesting them to serve as a Board of Counsellors. The first meeting was held in Raudenbusch Hall on July 28 at which they were present as well as the city pastors. The Archbishop presided and spoke of previous cathedrals and their building, the evident need of a new one, and placed a limit of five years for the contemplated work. Several laymen spoke, among them A. L. Larpenteur who was a member of the committee selected by Bishop Cretin to build the third Cathedral opened in 1858. An executive committee of nine members was chosen by the Archbishop; and E. L. Masqueray was named architect. He was a laureate pupil of the "Ecole des Beaux Arts" of Paris who had spent two years in Italy studying church architecture and several years in the ecclesiastical department of the Bureau of National Architecture in Paris working on the restoration of the great French cathedrals.[167] No happier choice could have been made for he was recognized as one of the foremost architects of his time. Before opening an office in St. Paul he spent four months in France visiting her great cathedrals and consulting renowned architects.

Louis W. Hill was appointed Treasurer of the Executive Committee and John B. Meagher, Secretary.

A campaign for subscriptions began immediately with priests and laymen as solicitors in the city and country parishes. The list of subscribers was headed by Foley Brothers who gave $40,000, followed by Louis W. Hill and C. H. F. Smith with $20,000 each. At the beginning of November, 1905, $302,500 had been pledged and the Archbishop was very much enheartened by the response to his appeal. By December first another fifty thousand had been added.

On November 15 the committee approved the tentative plans of the architect, ordered the site cleared of houses and plans made to break ground in the spring of 1906. Savings banks of metal were distributed to the children to gather their contributions to the fund in pennies, dimes and quarters and their gifts were supplemented by offerings made by the candidates for Confirmation in all the parishes for several years.

The final design for the sacred edifice was approved on January 8, 1906, and by the first of March the subscriptions totalled $435,200.[168] The Reverend P. J. Boland of Litchfield was given a temporary assignment as chief director of the subscription campaign with residence at the Cathedral rectory.

In the meantime news of the gigantic undertaking had spread beyond the diocese and encouraged other bishops to initiate similar projects or stimulated their activity on work already begun. The neighboring city of Minneapolis was in the throes of erecting a magnificent church to replace the stone structure of the Immaculate Conception about which we shall have something to say later on. In fact it was an era of cathedral planning and building. Plans were being drafted for new cathedrals in Los Angeles, Salt Lake City, Portland (Oregon), Helena, Boise, Denver, Great Falls; and actual construction had begun in St. Louis, Pittsburgh, Richmond, Omaha, Harrisburg, Newark and Seattle.

On July 4, 1906, a mammoth picnic for the benefit of the undertaking was held in the State Fair grounds at which addresses were delivered by the Archbishop and Governor Johnson and a contest for a set of vestments staged between the parishes in St. Paul divided into two groups according to population and resources. In the larger group St. Joseph's won the prize and St. Patrick's in the smaller. The sum of $9,600 was realized. By that time the subscriptions totalled $524,200.

When the site was surveyed it was found to be too restricted for the projected building and its approaches. The Kittson property was only 233½ feet wide by 293½ deep, whereas the plans called for a building 274 feet long and 214 wide. Additional property could not be bought in the rear owing to the prohibitive price asked for it, and it was necessary to purchase ground on the south side of Summit Avenue for $29,500 and move the avenue ninety feet in that direction, reducing its curvature and thus providing room for suitable approaches. This work was undertaken at once; and the first contract for grading the entire site and building one-half the foundation walls was awarded to Lauer Brothers of St. Paul for $72,250 in September, 1906. By this time one-half the diocese had been canvassed and the subscriptions stood at $550,000.

The approved plans called for a church whose outside dimensions were 274 feet in length, 214 at the transepts, with a façade 140 feet wide by 130 high, twin towers 150 feet high, a dome 120 feet in diameter topped by a cross 280 feet above the grade. There were to be twenty-four large windows in the dome; and the seating capacity of three thousand was later reduced to twenty-seven hundred.

By this time the cream of the subscriptions had been gathered and there was an ominous lag in the returns. To offset this the Board of Equalization, made up of the consultors and deans, met under the direction of the Archbishop and decided upon a minimum "expectation" from each parish. The pastors were notified of the change in the plan of campaign, and urged to meet the "expectation" as speedily as possible.

Cornerstone Laying

Early in 1907 it was decided to use Rockville granite from the quarries near St. Cloud for the foundation and crypt which were brought up to the water table during the year. When it became evident that the progress of the work would permit the laying of the cornerstone on June 2 of the next year, elaborate plans were outlined for that important event, the spectacular feature of which was an immense parade of representatives of all the parishes of the Archdiocese and others from outside.

June 2 was a perfect day from the viewpoint of weather. The sun shone brightly and all nature was garbed in green with flowering plants in profusion. To accommodate the crowds pouring into the city by train and other conveyance hourly Masses were said at the Cathedral, St. Mary's, Assumption and St. Louis churches. For the first time in forty years and more there was no Solemn Mass in the Cathedral.

Early in the afternoon the Reverend Clergy, who had assembled at St. Joseph's Academy, set out in procession[169] for the residence of Mr. Hill where four Archbishops and thirty Bishops with their chaplains joined the ranks, and proceeded to the site where they were met by Governor Johnson, Mayor Smith, Senator Clapp and other state and city officials and assigned reserved seats on the reviewing stand, to witness the parade of thirty thousand Catholic men marching under the banners of the Church and Catholic societies, a grand outpouring of devoted Catholics in which the entire state took part, a parade which will long be remembered as the greatest ever held in the city with the possible exception of that of the G. A. R. in 1896. It comprised a platoon of mounted police, veterans of the Civil War, old settlers, cadets from the College of St. Thomas, societies and parish organizations from outside the diocese of St. Paul, parishes and societies from Minneapolis and the surrounding towns, the parish of Mendota (the oldest in the diocese), parishes outside the Twin Cities and parishes and societies of St. Paul. The final section was made up of the different divisions of the Ancient Order of Hibernians and the Knights of Columbus.

The streets for blocks around the Cathedral site were thronged with people eager to catch even a glimpse of the proceedings. It was estimated that the function brought 60,000 visitors to the city for that day, the most notable gathering of the kind in the history of the Northwest. For that day St. Paul was the mecca of that vast gathering of Catholics who came to witness the crowning act of fifty years' effort from the mission days on the Indian frontier to that memorable hour with its promise of future greatness. In this demonstration non-Catholics stood shoulder to shoulder with their fellow-Catholic citizens to share in the joy of witnessing the laying of the cornerstone of a magnificent temple of religion in a favored land.

The copper box placed in the cornerstone was 6 x 12 x 14 inches in size and contained, besides copies of the current editions of newspapers and other periodicals, records and souvenirs of historical importance and a parchment written in Latin setting forth the details of the ceremony in the usual form of such documents.

The cornerstone was blessed and placed in position by the Right Reverend James McGolrick, Bishop of Duluth, assisted by Dr. Heffron as deacon, Dr. Moynihan as subdeacon and Dr. Schaefer as master of ceremonies, and a choir of eighteen seminarians under the direction of Reverend Leo Gans. The religious ceremony ended with the blessing of the foundations and the sprinkling of them with holy water.

The Summit Avenue side of the cornerstone displayed an inscription in Latin of which the following is a translation:

1841-1907

"Succeeding to the lowly chapel—built of old by the river bank—from which our fair city received its glorious name, this noble temple rises; a solemn testimony to the growth of Holy Church, a generous offering of love and gratitude to the Almighty God, of all things Lord and Ruler".

On the Dayton Avenue side the stone declares, in English translation:

"To God in Unity and Trinity. The sacred, auspicious stone of this metropolitan temple, bidden to bear the name of St. Paul, was duly laid on the second day of June, A. D., 1907. To restore all things in Christ".

When the actual ceremony of laying the cornerstone ended the Most Reverend Archbishop rose and read a congratulatory cablegram from Pope Pius X and a telegram from President Roosevelt, after which he delivered an address of historic import and religious significance, and then introduced Judge E. W. Bazille as chairman of the civic portion of the program. Addresses were delivered by Mayor Smith, Governor Johnson, Senator Clapp and Judge Kelly. The ceremony was brought to a close by the firing of a salute by Battery A., First Artillery, Minnesota National Guard, after which the seminarians intoned the Te Deum which was caught up by prelates, priests and people in a glorious outburst of praise and gratitude to God for an ever-memorable day in the religious annals of the Northwest.

Receipts and Disbursements

From time to time statements of receipts and expenditures were issued for the information of interested parties. The following shows the financial status[170] from the inception of the work to December 31, 1909:

Receipts		Disbursements	
Diocese of St. Paul....	52,500.00	Original site.........	52,500.00
City parishes.........	174,912.66	Additional land......	31,512.22
Country parishes.....	223,264.08	Summit Avenue change	10,384.07
Special subscriptions..	106,387.29	Construction to date	
Bequests from wills...	2,893.52	and Architect's fees...	454,847.02
Confirmation offerings.	5,997.25	Office, collection exp.	
Picnic, July 4/06.....	9,600.00	and Salaries.........	12,524.52
Miscellaneous........	2,179.88		561,767.83
Total.....	577,734.68	Balance on hand,	
		1/1/10	15,966.85

The old Cathedral parish subscribed $73,366.00 prior to December 31, 1908.

Total cost of Cathedral (estimated).........	1,657,590.27
Resources in sight from parish "expectations"	1,317,757.13
Deficit....................	339,833.14
Another statement gives the receipts in full to	
12/31/11...............	781,334.88
Disbursements to same date..............	778,812.64
Balance on hand..........	2,522.24

On July 18, 1912, the granite cross crowning the façade was blessed by the Archbishop and hoisted into position in presence of a large gathering of interested spectators, to whom the Archbishop preached a sermon. The cross weighs five and a half tons, stands ten and a half feet high, with horizontal arms five feet two inches in width. It rests on a pedestal one hundred and fifteen feet above the main floor.

The total receipts to that date amounted to $862,388.05 and the disbursements to $858,342.73. The granite for the entire section, including towers and dome cost $473,310.00.

In the autumn of 1912 it was thought that, for lack of funds, it would be necessary to leave the dome uncompleted till a later date; but the citizens of St. Paul appointed a committee to solicit funds among the business firms interested in seeing the work carried to completion according to the plans, and the sum of $100,000 was realized and presented to the Archbishop in January, 1913, and as a result the work was carried on so expeditiously that the last stone was set on the apex of one of the turrets that adorn the dome on December first of that year. It was blessed by the Archbishop who delivered an address on the occasion thanking all who had contributed to the result and expressing his gratitude to Almighty God for the successful completion of a work of such magnitude. He had literally watched the Cathedral grow stone upon stone, had made almost daily trips to the dizzy heights on which the workmen labored and showed himself a most interested spectator of the work during its progress. All that now remained to mark the completion of the last detail in connection with the exterior was to bless and hoist the steel cross to the apex of the magnificent dome and anchor it securely by steel supports to the metal plates belted in position to receive it. That ceremony took place on May 18, 1914. The cross is fourteen feet high, six inches square, with eight foot arms. The top of the cross is three hundred feet above the floor of the nave, is illuminated at night, and can be seen from afar as one approaches the Cathedral bulked against the sky.

Another statement issued as of February 10, 1916, showed the total cost of the Cathedral to that date to be $1,631,527.27 of which $541,113.29 was for granite and $34,968.00 for structural iron.

Other large items of expense were the cost of putting in the foundation and floor, $228,940.33; the walls and piers, $177,902.03; towers, dome and front steps, $102,351.02; statuary, (models and carving), $32,300.00; copper roofing, $71,356.42; heating and ventilating system, $49,687.00; ceiling and railings, $57,620.22; power house, tunnel, etc., $19,349.95; pews, $13,663.75; windows and frames, $13,617.58; roof tile and chapel roofs, $20,055.13; tile flooring, $12,697.42. The architect's fees amounted to $80,927.64; salaries and other expenses to $24,032.21.

Farewell to Old Cathedral

Before the exterior of the new Cathedral was completed it became necessary to demolish the old Cathedral[171] to make room for contemplated improvements at Sixth and St. Peter streets. Two days were set apart for the final services in the venerable edifice. On Sunday, August 30, 1914, Pontifical Mass was celebrated by Bishop O'Gorman of Sioux Falls before a congregation that taxed every available foot of space in the church. In the front pews sittings were reserved for about one hundred of the pioneer settlers of all creeds and nationalities who had witnessed the laying of its cornerstone on July 27, 1856. The rest were more recent settlers and members of the parish. In the sanctuary were Archbishop Keane of Dubuque, Bishops McGolrick of Duluth, Trobec, retired Bishop of St. Cloud, Lawler, pastor of the Cathedral, and several priests. The sermon was preached by Archbishop Ireland; and the Cathedral choir had charge of the singing. In the evening Bishop McGolrick officiated at Pontifical Vespers and Bishop Lawler preached. Solemn Benediction brought the service to a close in presence of a capacity congregation and all the prelates who had attended the morning Mass.

The following day, Monday, August 31, the last Mass was said in the venerable building by Archbishop Ireland who also preached the sermon. In the afternoon Bishop Lawler and the priests of the parish moved to their new homes on Dayton and Selby Avenues, in the rear of the new Cathedral.

The cornerstone of the old Cathedral, the first stone in the foundation, blessed by Bishop Timon of Buffalo on July 27, 1856, was lifted from its place on October 2, 1914, and from it was taken the copper box with its contents. The box was removed by Jeremiah C. Prendergast, who had made it, sealed it and placed it in the cornerstone fifty-eight years before. He opened it in presence of the Archbishop and a group of priests at the Archiepiscopal residence on October 6. Water had seeped in and ruined the parchment documents it contained; all that remained was a few copper coins. The box and coins were given to the Catholic Historical Society of St. Paul.

Dedication of New Cathedral

After the demolition of the old Cathedral the people of the parish worshipped in the new Cathedral school until Palm Sunday, March 28, 1915, when the Archbishop said the first Mass in the unfinished Cathedral at six A. M. and preached to a congregation that filled it to completion. Twenty-five hundred received Holy Communion, the first being his sister, Mother Seraphine, Provincial of the Sisters of St. Joseph; and at the eight o'clock Mass 2000 members of the Ancient Order of Hiberians and of the Ladies Auxiliary approached the sanctuary rail. The Archbishop blessed the palms and, at the Pontifical Mass celebrated by Bishop Lawler, delivered another sermon. In the evening there was Solemn Benediction of the Blessed Sacrament at which Father Reardon, Editor-in-Chief of The Catholic Bulletin, officiated.

The formal dedicatory ceremony took place on April 11 when the Archbishop blessed the new edifice, after which Bishop McGolrick celebrated Pontifical Mass and Bishop O'Gorman preached. In the evening

Bishop Trobec officiated at Solemn Vespers and Benediction and Archbishop Keane preached.

Up to April 9, 1915, the total cost[172] of the Cathedral and grounds was $1,591,102.21; the total receipts from subscriptions amounted to $1,120,990.35, and from other sources $397,200.00, leaving a deficit of $72,911.86. A special appeal was made in the hope of wiping out the deficit before the dedication and $51,607.01 was collected leaving a red figure of $21,241.85.

In 1914 several stones from the staircase turret of the Chateau de Rouen in which Joan of Arc was imprisoned were sent to New York to be built into the pedestal of her statue in that city.

When Archbishop Ireland was in New York in 1916 he met Dr. George Frederick Kunz, President of the American Scenic and Historic Preservation Society, whom he had known since 1892, and expressed a desire to have one of the stones for the French chapel dedicated to St. Remy in the new Cathedral, and he received assurance that his wish would be granted. On March 18, 1916, he wrote Dr. Kunz suggesting that the stone be sent by freight and in January, 1917, it arrived and its receipt was acknowledged by the Archbishop who promised that "It will be preserved sacredly in the new Cathedral of St. Paul. One of the chapels is to be known as the French chapel and in one of its walls the memorial from Rouen will be safely and religiously ensconced, visible to all and receiving from all sentiments of love and gratitude for the great virtues symbolized in the life of Joan".

In finishing the interior of the Cathedral Archbishop Dowling substituted St. John the Baptist for St. Remy and the Little Flower for St. Anscar and the Joan of Arc stone was incorporated into the interior wall of the chapel of the Little Flower on the gospel side where it protrudes about an inch and carries a bronze plaque with the following inscription: "This stone from the Castle of Rouen, France, where Joan of Arc was prisoner. A. D. 1431".

The new Cathedral is in the "Classical Renaissance" style of architecture, an adaptation of the original plan of St. Peter's as designed by Bramante and Michaelangelo but without the long nave added by Maderna. In its main proportions it is the Greek Cross type of architecture, the central feature being the magnificent dome at the juncture of nave and transept.

Mr. Masqueray, the architect, died May 26, 1917, and was buried from the Cathedral at a Mass celebrated by Bishop O'Gorman at which the Archbishop preached.

The Pro-Cathedral of St. Mary

The erection of a Cathedral is usually a work of sufficient magnitude and expense to absorb the time, energy and resources of the Bishop of a diocese while it is being planned and built. No bishop in the history of the Church in America built the equivalent of two cathedrals at the same time except Archbishop Ireland who was no ordinary prelate. He would shoulder a second burden like unto the first and at the same time. As soon as the ambitious project of building a Cathedral in St. Paul was inaugurated he decided to erect in Minneapolis what he misnamed a Pro-Cathedral scarcely less massive, imposing and costly to take the place of the Church of the Immaculate Conception which had become quite unsuitable for church purposes because of its location and surroundings, and he lived several years after dedicating both of them. The growth of the city and the changes brought about by commercial expansion made it evident that a new edifice would have to be built sooner or later at some distance from the old site. The encroachment of wholesale houses and manufacturing plants had forced the people to migrate to the outlying districts and, perforce, the church must follow them.

The Reverend James J. Keane, pastor of the parish at the beginning of the century, was so fully convinced of the need for a new church that he bought a piece of property on the northwest corner of Ninth Street and Mary Place (now La Salle Avenue) on September 16, 1901, for $30,000. It was found inadequate for the larger project on which the parish embarked a few years later and was sold on April 16, 1907, at an advance of $5,000.

Under his successor, Reverend Thomas E. Cullen, the first public announcement of a new church was made by Archbishop Ireland on Christmas day, 1903, when, preaching in the Church of the Immaculate Conception, he outlined the plans for a new structure and asked the cooperation of the parishioners in providing Minneapolis with a church which would stand in the same relation to the city as the new Cathedral to the Archdiocese, an edifice which would be a striking symbol of the value and significance of religion to the individual and the community. In other words, what he called a Pro-Cathedral which would be "distinctively the Bishop's Church".[173]

The congregation was not enthusiastic because property had already been bought for a parish church, but early in the new year a committee of one hundred men was appointed to carry on an educational campaign among the parishioners to acquaint them with the details of the project and arouse their interest in it. Other committees were appointed to formulate plans, decide on the probable cost, secure the most favorable site and map out the financial campaign.

The first choice of a location was the McNair and Wilson properties on Hawthorne Avenue at 13th Street, bought for $30,000 on May 11,

1904. Later on it was deemed unsuitable and, on July 1, 1905, it was sold to the Sisters of St. Joseph for St. Margaret's Academy, a high school for girls.

The final choice of a site was the commanding knoll on Hennepin Avenue, where it curves gracefully to the south, a site which, in perspective, elevation, accessibility and other external qualities of beauty, is without peer in the city as a pedestal for the majestic church which now crowns it.

There was no question about the architect. Mr. Masqueray was chosen and he decided that a great church along the general lines of those of Aquitaine and Perigord in France with the wide nave would be artistically appropriate and well adapted to modern religious conditions in the United States.

The first estimate of the cost of the proposed church was $250,000, and many thought that too high. Not so the Archbishop who visioned the growth and influence of Minneapolis and prevailed on the committee to authorize an expenditure of half a million dollars, part of which would be contributed by the other parishes of the city and of Hennepin County which, for that reason, would be exempted from any contribution towards the new Cathedral. As a matter of fact, before the plans were finally approved the cost of the exterior alone was not much under a million dollars.

The first step in the actual inauguration of the work was taken on June 21, 1905, when Lawrence S. Donaldson, a prominent merchant of Minneapolis and a member of the parish of the Immaculate Conception, bought the southern half of the block on Hennepin Avenue between 16th and 17th Streets, from the Thomas H. Pewter's estate for $45,000 and deeded it to the corporation.

The plan finally adopted called for a granite church in modern Renaissance style, with a massive rectangular dome surmounting the sanctuary, and twin towers flanking the main entrances. It was decided to use Rockville granite for the whole building but finally Vermont granite was substituted for the superstructure. The plans called for a building 274 feet long (the same as the Cathedral) by 120 wide and a façade 140 feet high, with towers rising 120 feet above the floor.

On August 7, 1907, ground was broken for the foundation by Archbishop Ireland who turned the first spadeful of earth in presence of the building committee, invited guests and five thousand people. The work of excavation and construction was carried on so expeditiously that all was in readiness for the cornerstone laying [174] on May 31 of the following year.

Blessing of Cornerstone

On that day the weather was all that could be desired and a vast but orderly multitude filled every inch of available space in the vicinity of the site, responsive to the emotions evoked by the event. Thirty thousand marched in the parade that preceded the ceremony and required nearly two hours to pass the reviewing stand. It was led by a platoon of mounted police and details of ten men from the G. A. R. and Co. F. of the National Guard acting as an escort for the Stars and Stripes. It was made up of representative groups from all the parishes in the Twin Cities and vicinity. The sons of eight nations marched side by side under the bond of a common faith. The music was furnished by a large number of bands marching with the different units. The parishes in St. Paul marshalled twelve thousand men in the wake of a float, representing the Galtier log chapel of 1841 drawn by six white horses decorated with plumes and flags and escorted by twelve pioneers. This section was followed by four hundred and fifty cadets from the College of St. Thomas.

The Minneapolis section comprised fifteen thousand marchers at the head of which was a float drawn by eight white horses representing Father Hennepin, the discoverer of the Falls of St. Anthony and the first white citizen of the metropolis, seated in a canoe, surrounded by Indians from the White Earth Reservation in Northern Minnesota and escorted by twenty braves and several squaws dressed in full tribal costume. Then came the students of De La Salle High School and delegations from a number of suburban parishes.

The line of march was along Hennepin Avenue and Papal colors, American flags and parish banners lent color and variety to the parading units as they passed in front of the reviewing stand from which the Apostolic Delegate, Most Reverend Diomede Falconio, Archbishops Ireland, Glennen and Christie, twelve bishops and hundreds of priests viewed it as well as Governor Johnson, Mayor Haynes, James J. Hill and many other distinguished citizens.

Amid the plaudits of the mighty throng the cornerstone was blessed and lowered into position by the Apostolic Delegate assisted by Reverends James O'Reilly as deacon, Othmer Erren, O. S. B., as subdeacon and Francis J. Schaefer as master of ceremonies. The responses were sung by the students of St. Paul Seminary.

The southeast cornerstone bears an inscription in Latin of which the following is a translation:

TO GOD, GREAT AND GOOD.

"The cornerstone of this Pro-Cathedral Church, dedicated under the title of Mary, Mother of God, Virgin conceived without the primal stain, and destined to adorn the city of Minneapolis, was laid with solemn rite on the thirty-first day of May in the Year of Our Lord 1908".

On the southwest cornerstone the following is engraved in Latin:

"In the year of Our Lord 1680 Louis Hennepin, the pioneer standard-bearer of the Christian faith, while traversing regions hitherto untrodden by the footsteps of civilization, paused in admiration at the falling waters hard by the city of the future and adorned them with a saintly name transmitted on the pages of history.

"In the year of grace 1908 the faith of Louis Hennepin gloriously ripened into this magnificent temple".

At the conclusion of the liturgical ceremony the Most Reverend Archbishop read congratulatory messages from His Holiness Pope Pius X and President Theodore Roosevelt and preached the festive sermon from the text; "Jesus Christ, yesterday and today, and the same forever" (Hebrews XIII-8), after which he presented W. P. Devereux, vice-chairman of the executive committee, who, in turn, introduced Governor Johnson, Mayor Haynes, James J. Hill and Frank Gross who delivered brief addresses, and the civil portion of the ceremony was brought to a close by a discourse from the chairman, the singing of "Holy God, We Praise Thy Name" and the National Anthem. The prelates and several invited guests were entertained at the residence of L. S. Donaldson, and the priests at St. Margaret's Academy.

Financial Statement

The contract for the superstructure of white Bethal granite from Vermont—including walls, towers, dome, steps and copper roof—was awarded to the Leighton Building Company of Minneapolis for $480,631.00, in June, 1909. It was estimated that the building would cost $820,010.00, to be met by the "expectations" from the parishes in Hennepin County and other sources which amounted to only $632,136.00, leaving a deficit of $187,873.00. It was thought that the work would be completed by January, 1913. As a matter of fact the first Mass[175] was said by the pastor, Father Cullen, on Pentecost Sunday, May 31, 1914, the sixth anniversary of the laying of the cornerstone. The Most Reverend Archbishop preached the sermon. In the evening a sacred concert was given and a lecture delivered by the Reverend William Patton, O. M. I., pastor of St. Mary's Church, Winnipeg, Canada.

Prior to that a civic celebration,[176] commemorative of the approaching completion of the Pro-Cathedral, was held in the month of November, 1913. A series of lectures was given on the Sunday evenings of the month —the first by the Archbishop on "Why Church and Church-Going People?"; the second by Honorable John Barrett of Washington, D. C.,

General Director of the Pan-American Union, on "America and the Sister-Americas—A Mighty Opportunity"; the third by Honorable Bird Coler of New York, who choose for his subject "The Hour and Its Opportunities"; the fourth by Archbishop Keane of Dubuque, whose topic was "The Social Problem"; the fifth by Professor Talcot Williams of Columbia University of New York, who discussed the problem of "Universal Peace".

The general trend of the discourses was in harmony with the purpose of the civic celebration, the speakers emphasizing the necessity of civic righteousness in the highest type of American citizenship, the need of a more exalted conception of civic duties and responsibilities if they would serve the best interests of city, state and country. The lectures set forth the Pro-Cathedral as a center of civic betterment even before it was dedicated to the religious purpose for which it was erected.

In addition, the famous Paulist Boys' Choir of Chicago, "The Champion Church Choir of Christendom", gave concerts in the afternoon and evening of November 27, under the direction of the Reverend W. J. Finn, C. S. P. They were rare musical treats. The spacious auditorium of the church was filled to capacity at the lectures and concerts which were followed with close attention and much profit.

The formal dedication of the Pro-Cathedral took place on the feast of the Assumption, August 15, 1915. The Archbishop officiated at the ceremony and preached the sermon at the Solemn Mass celebrated by Father Cullen. The church had been used for divine services since it was informally opened on May 31, 1914.

The financial statement [177] as of May 31, 1914, the date on which Mass was said for the first time in the new church, showed receipts of $774,646.83 and disbursements of a like amount. The receipts comprised the following items:

The parish of the Immaculate Conception....	$215,801.42	
Other parishes of Minneapolis.............	130,731.00	
Rural parishes of Hennepin County........	24,906.25	
Special subscriptions....................	44,485.00	
L. S. Donaldson (for the site).............	45,000.00	
The Archbishop (as a loan)...............	13,000.00	
Confirmation offerings...................	960.00	
Mortgage loans........................	250,000.00	
Bills payable...........................	49,763.16	$774,646.83

The disbursements were as follows:

Cost of the crypt........................	71,158.30
Granite for the superstructure.............	303,124.00
Price of the property....................	45,000.00
Contractor's bid........................	184,557.62
Architect's fees........................	18,812.04
Heating system........................	34,387.00
Models and statuary....................	32,698.87

Interest on loans........................	29,864.23	
Floors (stone and wood)................	10,224.00	
Pews, altars and confessionals.............	6,972.00	
Insurance, salaries, rent, printing, etc........	37,848.77	$774,646.83

The eighteen parishes in Minneapolis owed $26,961.00; and the sixteen in rural Hennepin County $6,039.00, a total of $33,000.00, which offset a like amount due on contracts as of August 1, 1914.

The "expectation" from the city parishes varied from $1,500.00 to $20,000, depending on size and financial standing, and in the rural areas from $500.00 to $4,000.00. All these parishes were exempted from contributing to the construction of the new Cathedral in St. Paul.

The new edifice was far from complete on the day of dedication. The exterior walls and the ceiling were finished and the pews and a temporary altar installed. An architect's design for finishing the interior was accepted before the first world war began in 1917 and bids about to be called for; but nothing further was done until the early twenties when, under the Right Reverend James M. Reardon, P. A., the present pastor, the work of erecting the massive Main Altar and baldachin, sheathing the interior walls with stone and furnishing the sacred edifice was begun and carried to a successful conclusion in five years at a cost of upwards of seven hundred thousand dollars. A new residence and a sacristy were erected in 1927-28 and the last installment of the indebtedness paid in 1940 as a preparation for the solemn consecration of the Basilica of St. Mary, as it was officially re-named from the beginning of 1926, on June 27, 1941.[178]

The dimensions of the completed building are: length, exclusive of front steps, 274 feet; width, 120 feet; height from grade to nave ridge, 95 feet; dome, 61 feet square outside and 48 inside; height to foot of cross, 187 feet; cross, 13 feet; front towers, 133 feet high and 22 feet square; height from nave floor to ceiling, 75 feet; height from sanctuary floor to dome ceiling, 138 feet; nave, inside piers, 140 x 82 x 75 feet; nave ambulatories, 155 x 10 x 20; sanctuary ambulatories, 62 x 10 x 67 feet; vestibule, 84 x 10 x 20 feet; chapels, 8 x 12; baptistry, 11 x 14; sacristy, 28 x 45 feet.

"The American Architect" of New York, for July 13, 1910, devoted several columns to a description of the Cathedral of St. Paul and the Pro-Cathedral of Minneapolis and carried fifteen plates of architectural drawings. It concluded:

"The two Catholic Cathedrals, the drawings of which are herein published for the first time, will be, when completed, noteworthy achievements in church buildings for any period; in extent and splendor they promise to surpass anything yet attempted in ecclesiastical work in the United States".

Another tribute, even more laudatory and, because unexpected, welcome, than that of "The American Architect" was paid to these buildings by "The Builder" of London, England, in the issue of June 16, 1911, which may not inaptly be considered a Masqueray, Cathedral and Pro-Cathedral number. This authoritative organ of English architecture devoted the greater part of its space to a description of these immense structures and of the career of their renowned architect. Five pages of views were included.

Diocesan Events

At the annual encampment of the G. A. R. held in Minneapolis in August, 1906, Archbishop Ireland was elected Chaplain-in-Chief and on Sunday, August 12, during the encampment he preached in the Church of the Immaculate Conception on "Love of Country—Civic Virtue".

At the golden jubilee of the founding of the Church of the Assumption, St. Paul, on October 21, 1906, the Archbishop pontificated and addressed the congregation after Mass. The festive sermon was preached by Reverend A. Brockmeyer, O. S. B. The Right Reverend Peter Engel, O. S. B., Abbot of St. John's, brought the celebration to a close with Pontifical Requiem Mass the following morning.

In December, 1906, the Archbishop took advantage of the conflict raging in France between the Catholic Church and the "Grande Nation" to set forth the situation in its causes and probable effects during a sermon preached in the Cathedral on "The Church and State in France"; and on Washington's birthday he delivered a patriotic address under the auspices of the Minnesota Society of the Sons of the American Revolution.

Cemetery Sunday became an annual observance throughout the diocese after its institution on the third Sunday of September, 1908. It had for object to assemble the faithful in their respective cemeteries in the afternoon to take part in religious exercises—a sermon and prayers—for the souls in Purgatory in general and for their deceased relatives and friends, in the early autumn when the weather is usually mild and pleasant rather than on All Souls day at the beginning of the winter season. This custom has been kept up during the intervening years.

The recommendation of the bishops of the Province of St. Paul that two more dioceses be erected in the Northwest was sent to the Apostolic Delegate in August, 1909, and forwarded to Rome for action by the Holy See. The petition was favorably acted on early in the new year and Crookston in the northwestern corner of Minnesota and Bismarck in western North Dakota were established. The former was taken from the Diocese of Duluth and comprised that portion of Minnesota west of the eastern boundaries of Hubbard and Beltrami counties and north of the southern lines of Clay, Becker and Hubbard counties. The latter comprised all of North Dakota west of the easterly lines of Simmons, Burleigh, McLean and Ward counties.

On September 12, 1909, the Archbishop preached on the twenty-fifth anniversary of the dedication of the Cathedral of the Holy Angels, St. Cloud, at a Pontifical Mass celebrated by Bishop Trobec.

On Columbus day he delivered an address on the "Catholic Laity" under the auspices of the Knights of Columbus in Pittsburgh, Pa.

In April of the following year he gave the principal address on "Farming in Minnesota" before the delegates at the first Minnesota Conservation Agricultural Development Congress in St. Paul.

At the annual clergy retreat in August, 1911, the fiftieth anniversary of the Archbishop's ordination, the priests of the diocese pledged a gift of $100,000 which he promised to devote to the building of the Cathedral and the Pro-Cathedral. Of this amount only $38,399 was paid before April 15, 1913, when the Archbishop in a letter reminded those who had not paid in full that, before the public, he was credited with having received the full amount and asked them to make good their pledges.

The Sixfold Consecration

Thursday, May 19, 1910, is an ever-memorable day in the annals of the Archdiocese of St. Paul, an occasion of historic interest without parallel in the Catholic Church in America, and "an event rarely surpassed or paralleled in the history of the world for 2000 years". It witnessed the consecration in St. Mary's Chapel of the St. Paul Seminary of six bishops to fill and amplify the ranks of the hierarchy in the Province of St. Paul.[179]

It is true that the event was surpassed in the number of participants when Pope Pius X consecrated fourteen bishops at the same ceremony to replace the members of the French hierarchy who had obeyed the Government rather than the Church, but they were for the whole of France and not for one ecclesiastical province as in St. Paul. Besides, the six bishops were priests of the Province and all of them, but two, of the Archdiocese itself.

The series of causes which led up to the sixfold consecration in St. Paul had its inception when Bishop Stariha resigned the see of Lead on March 29, 1909. Then followed the deaths of Bishops Cotter of Winona on June 27, and Shanley of Fargo on July 16, of that year, thus vacating three suffragan sees. On January 7, 1910, two new dioceses—Crookston in Minnesota and Bismarck in North Dakota—were erected by the Holy See; and some time previously the Most Reverend Archbishop petitioned for an Auxiliary to aid him in his administrative work.

For these vacancies and new sees six bishops were appointed between December, 1909, and May, 1910. The Reverend James O'Reilly, pastor of the Church of St. Anthony, Minneapolis, was notified of his appointment as Bishop of Fargo on December 18, 1909; Reverend John J. Lawler, pastor of the Cathedral, was named Titular Bishop of Greater Hermopolis and auxiliary to the Ordinary of St. Paul on February 9, 1910; Very Reverend Patrick R. Heffron, Rector of St. Paul Seminary, was appointed to the see of Winona on March 4, 1910; Very Reverend Timothy Corbett, pastor of the Cathedral of Duluth, Right Reverend Vincent Wehrle, O. S. B., Abbot of the Benedictine Monastery, Richardton, N. D., and Reverend Joseph F. Busch, Superior of the Diocesan Mission Band, Excelsior, Minnesota, were named for the sees of Crookston, Bismarck and Lead, respectively, on April 9, 1910.

The Most Reverend Archbishop was the consecrator with Bishops McGolrick and Trobec as co-consecrators and Bishop O'Gorman as preacher. The officers of the Mass were: assistant priest, Father Gibbons of St. Mary's Church, St. Paul; deacons of honor, Fathers Byrne of St. Lawrence, Minneapolis, and Rulquin, S. M., of St. Louis, St. Paul; deacon of the Mass, Father Ogulin of St. Bernard's, St. Paul, and subdeacon, Father Othmar Erren, O. S. B., of St. Joseph's, Minneapolis; master of ceremonies, Father Schaefer of St. Paul Seminary. The seminary four-part choir, under the direction of Father Missia, rendered suitable music for the services.

A committee of priests was appointed to provide for the large number of visiting clergymen expected, and of laymen to assist in the incidental preparations for the event, as well as a reception committee of forty prominent men from the Twin Cities. Over a thousand invitations were mailed to prelates, priests, relatives and close friends of the bishops-elect as well as to leading Catholics and non-Catholics and the capacity of the chapel was overtaxed.

Among the distinguished prelates who honored the occasion with their presence was the Most Reverend Diomede Falconio, Apostolic Delegate to the United States, who occupied a throne in the sanctuary opposite that on which the celebrant of the Mass was seated.

The Bishops-elect assembled at the Seminary on May 18 for the administration of the episcopal oath of office and the blessing of the six sets of insignia to be bestowed in the morrow's ceremony. At the midday meal the seminarians presented two commemorative addresses—one in Latin and the other in English—embodying their congratulations and best wishes and their appreciation of the honor conferred on the seminary by the selection of St. Mary's Chapel as the scene of the notable event. This was followed by an address by the Most Reverend Apostolic Delegate. Bishop-elect O'Reilly, for himself and the other bishops-elect, thanked the Delegate for his presence and spoke in terms of cordial appreciation of the reception given by the seminarians.

May 19 was a perfect day and the spacious grounds of the Seminary were arrayed in a garb of springtime verdure that was a delight to the visitors. Five hundred and fifty priests assembled for the function in addition to the Apostolic Delegate, two Archbishops (Ireland and Messmer), fourteen bishops, two abbots, nine monsignors, Governor Eberhart and his staff in brilliant uniforms with the cadet corps of the College of St. Thomas as guard of honor for the prelates.

The sacred rite was conferred on the chosen candidates with all the pomp and circumstance of the imposing ritual of the Church; and the memory of it will live in the minds of all who were privileged to behold the Church of God thus amply renewing and renovating her universal and indefectible mission. From the reading of the Papal Bulls to the singing of the Te Deum the interest and admiration evoked by the impressive service were absorbing and undiminished.

The sermon of Bishop O'Gorman, in its matchless diction, recounted the history of the Church's growth in the Province of St. Paul from the pioneer missionary days to the culminating glory of the present when, instead of one bishop and three priests and twelve hundred Catholics at the organization of the diocese, there are now a Metropolitan, eight bishops and six hundred thousand Catholics. It traced the growth and development of the Church in the United States from the days of Bishop Carroll of Baltimore to the youngest bishop in the ceremony of the morning. It dwelt on the episcopate and its powers through whom this expansion is manifested and secured, and described the solemn and significant liturgy of the Church as it unrolled before them.

The ceremony lasted four and a half hours; and at its conclusion a banquet was served to the new bishops and the visiting prelates, priests and distinguished guests by the clergy of the Archdiocese in a large tent on the Seminary grounds. Places were reserved for six hundred and twenty-eight persons. The Archbishop presided with the Apostolic Delegate on his right and Governor Eberhart on his left. At the end of the meal he read a message of congratulation from the Holy Father and made the welcome announcement that, owing to the lateness of the hour and the exhausting demands of the long ceremony, there would be no toasts honored by speeches. He thanked all for their presence and interest and assured them of the gratitude of the new bishops for the courtesy and kindness shown them at the beginning of their episcopate.

This was the last consecration at which Archbishop Ireland officiated, a fitting climax for the series of five similar functions at which he had imposed hands on thirteen bishops, all priests of the Province and all but two of the Archdiocese.

In the evening there was a public reception for the six bishops at the Seminary which was attended by about three thousand persons, an appropriate ending for an eventful day in the Catholic history of the Northwest.

Visit of Cardinal Vannutelli

In September, 1910, the twenty-first International Eucharistic Congress was held in Montreal, Canada, for the first time on this side of the Atlantic. Among the distinguished prelates who took part in it was Archbishop Ireland who had the happiness of meeting an old and valued friend of many years' standing, His Eminence Cardinal Vincent Vannutelli, Papal Legate to the Congress, whom he invited to visit St. Paul before returning to Rome, an invitation which was graciously accepted by the eminent prelate, destined to succeed his brother, Cardinal Sebastian Vannutelli, as dean of the Sacred College of Cardinals.

The visit of a Cardinal of the Roman Curia is always an event of historic importance the more so if, in addition to the exalted position he occupies, he is distinguished for long and faithful service to the Church as a diplomat and counsellor of the Holy Father. Such was Cardinal Vannutelli who paid a visit[180] of courtesy and friendship to Archbishop Ireland on September 20, 1910. His coming was a memorable event for the Catholics of St. Paul not only because they entertained a noted Prince of the Church, but because St. Paul was the first city in the United States to have an opportunity to honor such a distinguished personage.

On the way west from Montreal His Eminence spent a few days in Winnipeg and St. Boniface as the guest of the Most Reverend Archbishop Langevin of the latter city. He arrived in St. Paul the morning of Tuesday, September 20, accompanied by the members of his suite: Monsignor Michael Lega, Secretary of the Roman Rota; Monsignor Tampieri of the Papal Secretariate of State; Right Reverend Prince de Croy; l'Abbe Gelase Uginet, Secretary to the Cardinal; Commandatore Kelly of New York, a Knight of the Cappa e Spada (cape and sword); Count Galileo Vannutelli, nephew of His Eminence; Count Cogiatti and Emil Heberk. Right Reverend D. J. O'Connell, Auxiliary Bishop of San Francisco, accompanied the party from Montreal. They were met at the depot by the Archbishop, Bishops O'Gorman and Lawler, a large number of priests and a reception committee of one hundred laymen who escorted them to the Cathedral where His Eminence said Mass in presence of Archbishops Ireland and Christie, Bishops Lawler, O'Gorman, Carroll, O'Connell and many priests and a congregation that filled all available space in the venerable edifice. The escorting laymen occupied a reserved section in the front pews. During the Mass the children's choir of the Cathedral sang appropriate hymns. As the Cardinal left the Cathedral he was enthusiastically cheered by the crowd gathered outside to catch a glimpse of him. He and his suite breakfasted in the Cathedral residence as the guests of Bishop Lawler.

The Cardinal and his party were taken to the new Cathedral where His Eminence placed the "Vannutelli stone", a large lintel of granite, on the southwest door of the transept. After a brief visit to the residence of the Archbishop, they proceeded to the St. Paul Seminary for luncheon and were met at the main entrance to the grounds by the St. Thomas College cadets drawn up in military formation, and the seminarians, who lined the driveway from Summit Avenue to the Administration Building, and greeted him with the cheers of Evviva Pio Decimo! Evviva il Cardinale Vannutelli! He was received by the Rector and faculty and a group of the older priests of the diocese and nearly a dozen bishops of the Northwest. One hundred and twenty priests and the laymen's reception committee occupied seats in the body of the refectory at luncheon. The Archbishop welcomed His Eminence on behalf of the faculty and student body and Mr. Martin P. Weidner, a student of the Archdiocese of Chicago, read a Latin address and presented an embossed copy of it to His Eminence as a souvenir of the visit. The Cardinal thanked the Archbishop and the students for their cordial reception and congratulated the latter on the special advantages they enjoyed in the St. Paul Seminary. All retired to the chapel where the Apostolic Blessing was imparted by His Eminence after which he held a reception in the parlors of the Administration Building.

Then followed a visit to the College of St. Thomas where he was received by the members of the faculty and the cadets drawn up in the attitude of salute. Cannon boomed as the Cardinal appeared on the balcony to review the college battalions in their manoeuvers and military formations. Cadet Lieutenant Coughlin read an address in Latin expressive of appreciation of the honor conferred on the institution by the visit of such an eminent Roman Prelate and the Cardinal replied briefly in Latin.

At St. Catherine's College, to which His Eminence and other distinguished visitors repaired, an address in Italian was read by Sister Clara and the Cardinal replied in the same language and spoke interestingly of the Montreal Congress at which he presided as Papal Legate. Before leaving to return to the residence of the Archbishop he bestowed the Apostolic Benediction on the sisters and their pupils.

At six o'clock a banquet was tendered by the laity to His Eminence and the members of his entourage in the St. Paul Hotel at which two hundred Catholic laymen were present.

Governor Eberhart and Mayor Keller were among the twelve thousand who greeted the distinguished visitor and the members of his suite at a mass meeting in the auditorium over which Archbishop Ireland presided. A welcome from city and state was voiced by the Mayor and the Governor; the Honorable C. D. O'Brien spoke on behalf of the laity. The Archbishop paid a warm tribute to His Eminence before introducing him to the thousands who had assembled to greet him. The Cardinal who spoke in French expressed gratitude for the fine reception tendered him by the Catholics of the city and his pleasure to be able to visit St. Paul and its distinguished Archbishop. The address was translated by the Archbishop who did not fail to interpret the sentiments of His Eminence in such a way as to leave no doubt about their genuineness. This brought to an end a very busy day in which the distinguished visitors were allowed very little time for rest.

The second day was no less strenuous given over as it was to visits to St. Joseph's Academy, the Visitation Convent, the State Capitol, where they were received by the Governor and his staff, Cretin High School, Little Sisters of the Poor, St. Joseph's Hospital and the Good Shepherd Convent. At noon they were served luncheon at the home of James J. Hill, after which a visit was paid to the Pro-Cathedral in Minneapolis where His Eminence set the "Vannutelli stone" in the wall of the baptistery of the new edifice. Brief vists were made to St. Margaret's Academy, De La Salle High School, and St. Mary's Hospital, after which they returned to the residence of the Archbishop for a final dinner before taking train for Omaha to spend a day with Bishop Scannell. Archbishop Ireland and Bishop O'Gorman accompanied them.

The Catholic Bulletin

The summer of 1910 saw the culmination of a project which the Archbishop had in mind for some time and which he officially announced at the clergy retreat in August, namely, the founding of a Catholic newspaper to serve not only as the official organ of the Archdiocese, but as a medium for the inculcation of religious truth and the dissemination among the laity of a more adequate and intelligent knowledge of the teaching, practices and history of the Church. He had always been a staunch advocate of the Catholic press, for he realized the invaluable assistance which a vigorous and well-conducted Catholic newspaper can render to the Church in this age when, in spite of its boasted enlightenment and progress, the truths of Catholicism and its moral injunctions are so inadequately understood by the masses and so little considered in the affairs of every day life.

At the close of the retreat he summoned the Reverend James M. Reardon, Superior of the Diocesan Mission Band and former member of the

St. Paul Seminary faculty, and appointed him Editor-in-Chief to organize, edit and publish The Catholic Bulletin[181] as the new publication was called. It was to serve as the official organ of the Province of St. Paul, for the suffragan bishops, with one exception, accepted it as such for their respective dioceses.

In September an office was opened in room 315 Newton Building, at the corner of Fifth and Minnesota Streets in St. Paul. In addition to the Editor, the original staff consisted of Joseph A. Blanchard, business manager, Benjamin P. Kolesky, advertising solicitor, and Miss Agnes M. Reardon, bookkeeper and stenographer.

The Archbishop appealed to priests and people to support the new publication and help extend the sphere of its influence as an exponent of the Church's teaching.

Under date of November 9, 1910, he wrote to the clergy: "I feel that the establishment of the Catholic Bulletin is among the most important of the works in which Providence has allowed me to have a part. I feel that I am doing a signal service to Holy Church in calling earnestly upon the priests of the diocese to give it most efficient aid".

The response was immediate and generous. The first issue came off the press of the Willwerscheid and Roith Company on January 7, 1911, and was mailed to twenty-five hundred paid subscribers.

High official approval was given the project in the following letter[182] from the then Apostolic Delegate:

> Washington, D. C.,
> January 23, 1911.

Most Rev. Archbishop Ireland,
Your Grace,

Please accept my sincerest best wishes for the success of the "Catholic Bulletin", the new Catholic weekly published in St. Paul.

There is no doubt that the Bulletin, being under your wise direction, will find favorable reception not only from the people of your vast Ecclesiastical Province, but also throughout the United States and wherever the English language is spoken; and, cordially, I cherish the hope that it will be productive of great good. May God bless the undertaking.

> Your obedient servant in Xt,
> ✠ D. Falconio,
> Apostolic Delegate.

The Archbishop took the greatest interest in the new venture, watched over it with a vigilant eye, wrote editorials on topics of current interest and before he passed away had the happiness of knowing that his efforts for the spread of Catholic truth, through the medium of a diocesan paper, had borne abundant fruit.

The only instruction given the editor was to publish an interesting, well-written and well-edited Catholic newspaper, non-political and non-controversial, which did not necessarily reflect the Archbishop's views on any subject. With the exception of what he himself wrote, he never saw, nor asked to see, a line of any editorial or article that appeared in The Catholic Bulletin until it came from the press. He was not a carping critic, but never failed to make helpful suggestions. It was a pleasure to work with him. He had the happy faculty of allowing one to whom he assigned a special work to use his own judgment in doing it.

One strict injunction, however, he laid down, that, under no circumstances whatsoever, should a word of encomium be published about him, or a laudatory reference made to his preaching or activities in the columns of the paper, A diocesan organ, he maintained, was always prone to refer to the sermons of the Ordinary as "most eloquent and impressive masterpieces", and he would have none of it. As a matter of news, it was permissible to state that the Archbishop preached on this or that occasion, but no excerpt from the sermon could be published unless he furnished the copy.

He never set foot inside the office of publication; but he was always accessible for comment or suggestion on any matter connected with the news at home or abroad. At no time did he insist that his views be made the views of the paper. In this regard the editor had fullest freedom and his fullest confidence.

Father Reardon continued in full charge of The Catholic Bulletin even after his appointment as Irremovable Rector of the Church of St. Mary in August, 1916, when the Reverend Charles F. McGinnis of the faculty of the College of St. Thomas was named Associate Editor, and did not relinquish control until October 11, 1922, when, more than a year after his appointment to the pastorate of the then Pro-Cathedral of St. Mary, he turned over to his successor, the Reverend John R. Volz, the subscription list of upwards of twenty-five thousand, twelve hundred dollars in cash and bonds, a well-equipped office and no unpaid obligations.

The office of publication was transferred to the Chancery building and Father Volz remained in charge until January 31, 1925, when the paper was placed under the control of a lay editor and since then it has been just another Catholic paper without definite editorial policy.

Fairbanks and Roosevelt Incidents

Early in the year 1910 the Honorable Charles W. Fairbanks, former Vice-President of the United States, arrived in Rome during the course of a European visit, and was scheduled to address the Methodist Association which for years had been engaged in a vigorous and vicious attack on the Catholic Church in an effort to discredit it in the eyes of the Italian people. When application was made on his behalf for an audience with Pope Pius X it was refused. Immediately there was an outcry against the Holy See on the part of the Methodists and their friends who regarded the rebuff as an act of unpardonable discourtesy. But His Holiness did not yield and Mr. Fairbanks left Rome without meeting the Pontiff.

The refusal of the Holy Father received widest publicity in the United States and indignant protests appeared in many newspapers at what was characterized as a wanton insult to a distinguished American.

Archbishop Ireland took up the cudgels in behalf of the Holy See and, in an interview[183] given the Associated Press in Chicago on February 8, clarified the situation.

People in America may easily misapprehend the circumstances in Rome which led the Vatican to refuse an audience with the Holy Father to Mr. Charles W. Fairbanks, after he, a former Vice-President of the United States, would have made a public address before the Methodist Association of that city. Most likely Mr. Fairbanks himself did not fully realize the meaning which Romans would attribute to his address.

It was not a question of Mr. Fairbanks being a Methodist or going to a Methodist church in Rome for Sunday devotions. It was a question of appearing to give fullest approval to the work of the Methodist Association in Rome.

American Methodists in Rome are active and—I may readily say—pernicious proselytizers. The Methodist Association is not in Rome to serve and meet American Methodists, but to pervert from the Catholic faith all those upon whom they can bring influence to bear.

I was in Rome last winter and I made a very particular study of this Methodist propaganda. . .

The purpose of the work of the Methodist Association in Rome is confessed openly. The means employed are by no means honorable. They take advantage of the poverty of the poor of Rome.

The books circulated and displayed in the windows of their book stores are slanders against the Catholic faith, the Holy Pontiff at Rome and a misrepresentation of the whole Catholic system. The success of the movement is far from adequate to the efforts put forth and the money expended. They do not make permanent Methodists of Italian Catholics.

Now a public address by a former Vice-President of the United States before the Methodist Association can have no other meaning in the eyes of the Roman public than the approval of America of the propaganda of the Methodist Association. Had the Holy Father, guardian of the spiritual interests of the Catholic Church of the world, smilingly welcomed Mr. Fairbanks to an audience on the following day, in what other position would he appear to be than giving his approval to the propaganda of the Methodist Association before which the address had been given?

It was simply impossible for the Holy Father, in his official position as the Sovereign Pontiff of the Catholic Church, to do aught else than to say politely to Mr. Fairbanks:

I cannot receive you and accord you the honors due you in all other circumstances as an American and a distinguished representative of a great republic!

One arm of combat which those Methodists use in Rome, as I know from personal observation, is to create the impression that Methodism is the great faith of the American Republic and that the Catholic Church is merely an Italian institution.

There are in Rome Protestant American churches for the benefit of Americans that put forth legitimate efforts, mind their own business, and make no war on the Catholic Church. What I have said of the Methodists in Rome does not apply to the other churches there. I have in mind the Protestant Episcopal chapel on the Via Nazionale and its former rector, Dr. Nevins, a man whom I was pleased to call a friend and whom I was always glad to meet.

I shall leave for New York tomorrow, and I shall be pleased to answer the Methodists here or in the East at any time. I cannot make it too plain that I am not attacking the entire Methodist church, but merely the Methodist Association in Rome. I am not too old to enjoy a fight when the occasion requires it.

Two months later former President Theodore Roosevelt, on his homeward journey from Africa where he had hunted big game, reached Rome and, when he would not give assurance that he would not visit the Methodists, the Holy Father refused him an audience. After the Fairbanks incident the Holy See feared that Mr. Roosevelt might, unwittingly and in good faith, be led into showing open sympathy with and friendship for this hostile center of aggression against the Catholic Church. When he asked for an audience, therefore, the wish was courteously expressed that he would avoid being drawn into the objectionable position of appearing publicly to support the offensive campaign against the Pope. He refused all conditions and agreements and thus allowed the possibility of his accomplishing what would be offensive to His Holiness. No other course was open to the Vatican but to refuse him an audience.

Before coming to Rome Mr. Roosevelt had accepted an invitation to hold a reception in the American Embassy on April 6 for all Americans in Rome. He was so annoyed by the publicity given to the Pope's refusal to grant him an audience, which he regarded as personal and not to be publicised as it was, that he called off the reception. He was moved to do this by an attack made on the Catholic Church by the Reverend B. M. Tipple, pastor of the American Methodist Church in Rome, because he did not propose to be used as an occasion for such an unprovoked assault. The reception had been arranged by the American Ambassador, Mr. Leishman, to enable Americans in Rome, irrespective of religious faith, to meet the former President on neutral ground. Mr. Roosevelt was exceedingly annoyed that a personal incident should have incited an exhibition of the religious hostility which he so greatly deprecated. He would not play into the hands of Reverend Mr. Tipple in an attack on the Papacy, said Archbishop Ireland, in commenting on the cancellation

of the proposed meeting between Mr. Roosevelt and Pope Pius X. He
reiterated the stand he took in connection with the Pontiff's refusal to
see Mr. Fairbanks and maintained that the Holy See could not act otherwise in dealing with any one, however otherwise illustrious and worthy,
who was likely to give public recognition of any kind to the work of
the Methodist Association. He quoted with approval the words of Cardinal Merry del Val, Secretary of State to His Holiness, who told the
Associated Press that

> It is not a question of religion. Mr. Roosevelt might have gone to an
> Episcopalian, Presbyterian, or any other church, except the Methodist, and
> delivered an address there and he could have been received by the Pope
> even on the same day. But he could not be received when it was suggest-
> ed that after the audience he intended to go to the Methodist church in
> Rome, which is carrying on a most offensive campaign against the Pontiff.

Mr. O'Loughlin (the former President's secretary) was asked by
Cardinal Merry del Val, "Can you guarantee that Mr. Roosevelt will not
visit the Methodists here?" And his reply was, "I cannot. Indeed, I
believe that Mr. Roosevelt is just the man to go there. He will do as he
pleases".

On this point Archbishop Ireland had this to say: [184]

> For my part I differ with Mr. O'Loughlin. I believe that, brought face
> to face with the situation in Rome, as created by the Methodist propa-
> ganda, Mr. Roosevelt would not have addressed the Methodists. He wrote
> his telegrams in Cairo away from the seat of war, and refused to bind
> himself to his movements before he was on the ground. But, once in
> Rome, face to face with the situation, such as his quick intuition into
> things would have soon revealed it, he would not have thought of leaving
> the Vatican to repair to the camp of its virulent foes. That is Mr. Roose-
> velt as, I think, I know him. At the same time, I comprehend the posi-
> tion from which Cardinal Merry del Val measured his duty. He had to
> be guided by the situation as it loomed up around him in Rome; by
> the knowledge he had of local circumstances. He could take no risk;
> principle was at stake. And so he demanded assurance that, whatever
> was likely to happen, the honor of the Holy See was safeguarded.

The Archbishop went on to cite numerous instances of the type of
bigoted warfare carried on by the Methodists in Rome against the
Catholic Church by quoting the "Evangelista", the organ of the Methodists in Rome, and the "Asino" which he called "the filthiest of publications."

The Archbishop was publicly attacked[185] by the Reverend Benjamin
Longley, Superintendent of the St. Paul District of the Methodist Episcopal Church, who declared that the Archbishop did not know the situation
in Rome, and by Bishop Robert McIntyre of the Southern Minnesota
Conference of the Methodist Episcopal Church, who used such vile and
intemperate language that the Archbishop was justified in declaring

that Bishop McIntyre would be at home preaching in the Methodist church in Rome or editing "Evangelista" and its recognized ally "Asino", more than in lecturing in Methodist or non-Methodist temples in America. "I stand upright straight before men who deal in facts or arguments. I run away from mud-slingers".

He added that, if a slight had been intended by the Holy See, which is inconceivable, "We in America who respect Mr. Roosevelt and who love the Republic, would, unfalteringly, stand by Mr. Roosevelt and by our country".

When the storm had subsided the Most Reverend Archbishop received from Cardinal Merry del Val a letter[186] in which the Secretary of State to His Holiness gives the inside story of the Holy See's refusal to grant an audience to Mr. Roosevelt. We reproduce it in full as it clarifies the situation.

SEGRETERIA DI STATO
  DI SUA SANTITA

Private

My Dear Lord Archbishop,

So many thanks for your kind letter of May 13th. There is just one point which I should like to call your attention to, not for the purpose of controversy, but for your information and as deserving your consideration. The point is Mr. Roosevelt's public and marked demonstration of friendship and sympathy with Fera and the Italian Freemasons from whom he received and welcomed significant honours. If anything was required to justify the position of the Holy See, it was this, and there was only one opinion here in Rome in regard to that. It was so striking and eloquent that most people were convinced that I had foreseen it or that I had been informed previously of Mr. Roosevelt's intentions. As a matter of fact I was not. But of course had Mr. Roosevelt been received by the Holy Father and then followed up with these demonstrations, a very grave insult would have been offered to the Holy Father. As you are aware the Masons here, especially those, are the most heinous and blasphemous adversaries of Religion, of the Holy See, etc, politically, socially, and are the avowed enemies of Christianity in every way. It is precisely because the Methodists here go hand in glove with these Masons, that they are so objectionable. Hence, as a matter of fact, Mr. Roosevelt did accomplish what was just as bad or worse than showing friendship for the 20 Settembre Methodists. Many believe that he thought we had them in mind when the hope was courteously expressed that nothing similar to the Fairbanks incident would crop up to prevent the audience, and that as he had already taken an engagement with Fera, he could not or would not undertake to give any assurances; for if he did not intend honouring the Methodists, he was already committed to something just as bad or worse. We had not foreseen this, but in view of what has taken place, had Mr. Roosevelt been received by the Holy Father, the position of the Holy See would have been most painful. I understand that Mr. Leishman is a Jew and a Freemason. Judging by his despatches published in the "Outlook" he tried to excite Mr. Roosevelt rather than make things easy. I mention all this for your information and in order that you should be able to realize better what all the circumstances were in connection with this unpleasant occurrence.

    With kindest regards and esteem, I am, dear Lord Archbishop

Yours devotedly in Xt.

R. Card Merry del Val.

26 V. 1910

The Foreign Mission Field

At the Easter meeting of the American hierarchy in 1911 the question of founding and fostering a seminary in America for the education of priests for the foreign mission field was on the agenda for discussion and it was formally approved.

The idea of such an institution had been incubating for several years in the minds of two priests—Fathers James Anthony Walsh, Director of the Propagation of the Faith for the Archdiocese of Boston, and Thomas Frederick Price, the Tar Heel apostle of North Carolina. They met during the International Eucharistic Congress in Montreal in 1910 and pooled their resources—an idea and no means to realize it. But the idea was pregnant with import from on high and they felt that ways and means would be found to actualize it. They placed the matter before Cardinal Gibbons who, on March 25, 1911, wrote a letter calling it to the attention of the hierarchy who approved it officially and authorized Fathers Walsh and Price to bring it to the attention of Cardinal Gotti, Prefect of the Sacred Congregation de Propaganda Fide, which was done in due time, and papal approval for the project obtained from Pope Pius X on June 29, 1911.

The first Foreign Missionary Seminary, under the direction of diocesan priests, was established at Maryknoll, New York, and proved to be the work of God in its phenomenal success as a training school for foreign mission work, not only in the Orient, but, as the result of war, throughout the world. It gave impetus to similar institutions, one of the most successful of which, originating as the Maynooth Mission, became the St. Columban Foreign Mission Society, founded by Bishop Galvin of Hangyang, China, with regional headquarters near Omaha, Nebraska. To each of these is loosely aggregated a society of missionary sisters who serve as teachers, doctors, nurses, etc., in the foreign mission field.

When the founding of a foreign mission seminary was proposed Archbishop Ireland pointed out one of the most potent effects of such an institution on the Church in America when he said: "The time has come when no excuse can be offered for further abstention from a participation in this holiest of works. A Foreign Mission Seminary will be of inestimable value to seminaries having for their prime object the formation of priests for the ministry in America itself".[187] How right he was the intervening years have amply demonstrated.

His successors have given high approval and personal encouragement to the work of these foreign missionary societies. The Archdiocese of St. Paul has supplied and continues to supply a large number of priests and sisters for the foreign mission field. Furthermore, local headquarters for carrying on the work have been established in St. Paul by the Columban Fathers, and in Minneapolis by the Maryknoll Fathers, with the formal approval of Archbishop Murray who has encouraged the work in every possible way. The Twin Cities have become the recruiting center for foreign missionary activity throughout the Northwest.

The Archbishop and The Knights of Columbus

The St. Paul Council of the Knights of Columbus was organized on February 22, 1899, the first west of Chicago. For more than a decade of years it carried on its work in rented quarters awaiting the day when it would be numerically strong enough to shoulder the financial burden involved in the erection of a home of its own. It was one of the first councils in the Order to reach that goal. In the early months of 1912 it purchased a plot of ground, 110 by 120, on Smith Avenue, between Fifth and Sixth Streets, for a club house costing $105,000. Work began in the spring and everything was in readiness for the laying of the corner-stone [188] on Sunday afternoon, July 14. The local knights and visiting members of the Order met at the club rooms on Cedar Street and marched in procession to the Cathedral residence, 19 West Sixth Street, whence they escorted the Most Reverend Archbishop and Bishop Lawler to the new building, where a large crowd had gathered and a number of priests assembled to participate in the ceremony.

At three o'clock the Reverend Clergy in cassock and surplice, preceded by the acolytes and cross-bearer and followed by Bishop Lawler and his chaplains, Fathers Donahoe and Heinz, and the Archbishop accompanied by Fathers Gaughan of Minneapolis and Gleeson of St. Paul, proceeded to the cornerstone where the choir, directed by Professor Bruenner, sang the Veni Creator, at the conclusion of which the Most Reverend Archbishop blessed the cornerstone which was set in position under the direction of Father Reardon, master of ceremonies. The choir sang another hymn as the procession re-formed and marched to the speakers' platform on Fifth Street. Two addresses were delivered, one by the Archbishop, the other by the Honorable John W. Willis, Past Grand Knight of the Council, who was introduced by the Honorable Thomas D. O'Brien, its first Grand Knight and the first State Deputy of Minnesota. Judge Willis spoke of the Catholic ideals and prophetic vision of Christopher Columbus, the patron of the Order, and of the purpose of the new club house not only as a center for the activities of the knights but for the service of the public without distinction of creed or nationality.

The Archbishop prefaced his address on "The Typical Christian" with a eulogistic reference to the Knights of Columbus whom he congratulated on their new home which "as its rising walls foretoken, is to be, in ample proportion and artistic architecture, worthy of their noble association and of the high purpose to which it is pledged. The blessings of the Church have been invoked upon the cornerstone, upon the whole achievement which it symbolizes, and no less upon the good works of religion and Christian benevolence to which birth will here be given. . . . The beginnings are ominous of a bright and prosperous future; from our hearts do we pray that coming years be rich in fruition as the present day is rich in hopes and promises.

"The ideals and purposes of the Association known as the Knights of Columbus are worthy of all commendation. As a Bishop of the Church I prize and praise them, and to the carrying out of them into effective realization I am most willing to lend my earnest and continuous cooperation.

"I take pride and pleasure in stating as a fact that, so far as my observations of men and things teach me, in Minnesota and in the country at large, the ideals and purposes embodied in the constitution and rules of the Association are no mere words or theories, that, wherever they work, the Knights of Columbus make the loyal effort to rise in practice to the high altitude of their profession, to be in all things what they propose to be, typical Christians, typical sons and soldiers of Christ's Church—loyal in word and in act to its teachings, responsive to its aspirations, generous in defence and support of its interests and its enduring welfare."

The new building, three stories high with full basement, contained club rooms for the knights, a spacious auditorium for public gatherings, a fully-equipped gymnasium with swimming pool and baths. It was completed in due time and became a center of civic activity under the auspices of the St. Paul Council.

With its facilities it served as an adequate setting for the National Convention of the Order held in St. Paul the week of August 3, 1914, when the Supreme Officers, Directors and delegates of four hundred thousand members met for one of the most successful gatherings in its history up to that time.

The commodious auditorium of the club house served admirably for the exemplification of the ceremonial of the Fourth Degree for a class of three hundred and fifty knights on the afternoon of August third, under the direction of Henry C. Soucheray, Master of the Fourth Degree for Minnesota and North Dakota. At the evening banquet in the St. Paul Hotel, J. F. T. O'Connor of Grand Forks, N. D., presided and toasts were responded to by Deputy Supreme Knight Carmody of Grand Rapids, Michigan, Supreme Master Reddin of Denver, Right Reverend M. Fallon, Bishop of London, Ontario, Thomas D. O'Brien, Grand Knight of the local council, and Honorable William L. Kelly who read an original poem on "The Dream of Father Marquette".

On August 4, the Supreme Officers, Directors, delegates and their friends assisted at a Pontifical Mass celebrated by Auxiliary Bishop Lawler in the old Cathedral. Among those present were four of the original incorporators of the Order—Daniel Colwell, William M. Geary, Dr. M. C. O'Connor and Cornelius P. Driscoll, as well as two Past Supreme Knights—John J. Phelan of Bridgeport, Connecticut, and John J. Cone of New Jersey. The other Past Supreme Knight, Edward L. Hearn, was detained in the East. The sixty members of the K. of C. Choral Club of St. Louis, Mo., sang the Mass. It was one of the last significant gatherings in the old Cathedral which was dismantled at the end of the month.

The sermon, too, was significant.[189] It was preached by Archbishop Ireland who took for his theme "The Typical Catholic Layman in America", in the course of which he declared, "I cannot over-value the nobleness of the ideals that are yours, the wealth of the power you may put into the service of religion through the diffusion of those ideals among the whole membership of the Church, as trusted auxiliaries in the fulfilment of her divine mission, her organized chivalry, ever first and foremost where her call is heard, or her banner leads . . .

"From you, her imperial guard, the Church demands an act of intelligent faith, the vital condition of supernatural life, of membership in Christ's mystical body, the assent of the intellect to truths, principles and facts that have distinct and absolute entity, in themselves, outside of and separate from the human mind. This faith rejects the so-called Modernism condemned by Pope Pius X, teaching that the soul itself, is the source, the creative agency of man's belief and life. Catholic faith demands objective truths that exist and have being independently of the human soul, in themselves, and outside the intellect that is asked to see them, to accept them, and feed upon their splendor and beauty. This faith postulates dogma, the specific statement of a principle or a fact enunciated by Christ and reiterated by His Church, the rejection of which is the rejection of a divine truth contained in the deposit of revelation, a denial of the existence of Him who gave the revelation".

The Mass was a fitting farewell tribute to the old Cathedral which had witnessed so many memorable functions during its long and eventful career. The local Knights of Columbus were hosts, so to speak, to the last significant event within its hallowed walls in which Catholics from practically every diocese in America were present to bid it a fond fare-well before the hammer of the destroyer reduced it to rubble a few weeks after the convention.

One afternoon during the convention was reserved for a visit to the new Cathedral where the Most Reverend Archbishop explained to the delegates the symbolism enshrined in its design and purpose, and con-ducted them on a tour of the immense building whose imposing site and architectural beauty had evoked their admiration.

Epochal Legal Victory Over Bigotry

The convention was significant from another point of view. It was held close on the heels of the epochal legal victory over bigotry won by the Fourth Degree, Knights of Columbus, when, on Wednesday, July 29, a jury at Waterville, Minnesota, returned a verdict of guilty of criminal libel against A. M. and G. E. Morrison, father and son, editor and publisher of the "Mankato Morning Journal" of Mankato, Minne-sota, who had charged E. M. Lawless, editor of the "Waterville Sentinel", with having taken the bogus Knights of Columbus oath, printed and circulated by the Menace of Aurora, Mo., and distributed by anti-Catholic organizations in immense quantities for several years in Canada and the United States. The perpetrators escaped legal action as long as they accused the Knights in general and not a particular individual of taking the alleged oath. They were emboldened by their supposed im-munity; but sooner or later some one made a slip. That happened when the Morrisons accused Mr. Lawless of taking the oath. An action for criminal libel was instituted in Waterville; and the trial was a sensational one[190] from more than one point of view. It was presided over by a Protestant Judge, George J. Dressel. The District Attorney who prose-cuted the case was Francis J. Handsel of Montgomery, Prosecuting Attor-ney for Le Sueur County, assisted by Attorney Hessian of Le Sueur. The defendants were represented by Owen Morris of St. Paul. The foreman of the jury was Reverend Thomas Billing, the resident Methodist min-ister of Waterville, and the Reverend H. E. Chapman, pastor of the local Congregational Church, was a witness for the prosecution in the matter of publication.

The surprise of the trial, showing the intense interest it evoked throughout the Order, was the appearance on the witness stand of two of the Supreme Officers. Dr. E. W. Buckley of St. Paul, Supreme Physi-cian, testified that Mr. Lawless was initiated into the Fourth Degree under his jurisdiction as Master of the Fourth Degree for Minnesota and took the usual obligation as part of its ceremonial or degree work.

William J. McGinley, Supreme Secretary of the Order, and official custodian of the ceremonial text and matters appertaining to the degree work, placed a copy of the obligation of the Fourth Degree in evidence, and it was made part of the records of the trial. Furthermore, he emphasized the fact that the Knights of Columbus was not an oath-bound society and that no member was asked to take more than an obligation which any gentleman and citizen might conscientiously take.

The defendents made no attempt to establish the authenticity of the bogus oath; but threw themselves on the mercy of the court. The jury returned a verdict of guilty, read by the Reverend Thomas Billing, and the court imposed a jail sentence of thirty days without the option of a fine. An appeal was taken to the District Court where the defendents pleaded guilty and were fined $25 each which they paid. Thus, this so-called "oath" was proved to be the foulest kind of a bigot's libel.

The official text of the "Obligation of the Fourth Degree", taken by the Knights of Columbus thus became a matter of public record, and was printed for the first time in The Catholic Bulletin in the issue of August 8, 1914.

> I swear to support the Constitution of the United States.
> I pledge myself as a Catholic citizen and a Knight of Columbus, to enlighten myself fully upon my duties as a citizen and to conscientiously perform such duties entirely in the interest of my country and regardless of all personal consequences. I pledge myself to do all in my power to preserve the integrity and purity of the ballot and to promote obedience and respect for law and order. I promise to practice my religion openly and consistently, but without ostentation, and to so conduct myself in public affairs and in the exercise of public virtue as to reflect nothing but credit upon our Holy Church, to the end that she may flourish and our country prosper to the greater honor and glory of God.

A Name For The Twins

For twenty-five years and more the question of a united city at the head of navigation on the Mississippi was the subject of periodic discussion and debate in business and professional circles, but without practical results. Among the earliest and most consistent proponents of such a union was Archbishop Ireland. He gave serious consideration to the possibility of it when there was question of selecting a site for the new Cathedral which he wished to be as central and accessible as possible. He was most anxious that the Twin Cities form one municipality, a metropolitan center unrivalled for strategic position and promise of future expansion, a city which in a few years would count more than a million people, a center of cultural pursuits, a leader in commercial enterprise. He believed they would soon be one politically as they were already one commercially and socially.

His views were expressed in an editorial in The Catholic Bulletin of December 9, 1911, in which the advantages of such a union—the gain in prestige and power, the new life, ambitions and interests to be thereby engendered—were declared to be beyond dispute. Newspapers as far away as New York considered the union an assured fact before many years.

In view of that it was necessary to have a name for the new-born metropolis that would embody past traditions and future aspirations. He suggested "Paulopolis", a name that recalled the olden days of the two partners in this proposed wedlock, a name born of Latin and Greek classics befitting a city with an illustrious university. Other names had been proposed—Twin City, Geminopolis, St. Anthony, Mendota—all lacking the euphony and significance of Paulopolis. He was shocked and chagrined beyond further expression when the Kansas City Star suggested "Minnehaha"—"Minne" for Minneapolis and "Ha-ha" for St. Paul. That ended the attempts to find a suitable name for a city that was never born, for twins that did not wish to be siamesed, but preferred to live in friendly rivalry without thought of other than the physical union provided by nature.

Life of Bishop Cretin

For several years before his death Archbishop Ireland cherished the hope of finding time to write the life of Bishop Cretin whom he knew in boyhood and whose memory he revered with filial affection and reverence. But the work of administering an Archdiocese of such growing importance and influence, of building churches, schools and other institutions to meet its increasing needs, as well as the ceaseless demands made upon his time and energy by extra-diocesan projects and functions compelled him to defer what he considered a labor of love until the last years of his life.

In the meantime he had accumulated all available historical data for such a work. On his visits to France he had secured more than a hundred autograph letters of Bishop Cretin to his sister and other members of the family, and to the Society for the Propagation of the Faith in Paris and Lyons describing the conditions and needs of his frontier diocese, and had gathered and collated every scrap of information from any source about him and his work in the Diocese of Belley, in Dubuque and St. Paul.

The first installment of the projected biography was published in Acta et Dicta (Vol. IV, No. 2, pp. 187 & ff.) for July, 1916; and subsequent installments appeared in the issues of that publication for July, 1917, and 1918. Unfortunately death took the pen from his nerveless fingers before he completed the work. The fifteen chapters that appeared in print are a mine of information not only about the boyhood, youth and priestly life of Joseph Cretin before he arrived in America, but about religious conditions in France during the Reign of Terror and subsequent civil disturbances in the first half of the nineteenth century.

The first installment of four chapters deals with the birth of Joseph Cretin in Montluel, France, in 1799; the French Revolution and the Church; the recruitment of the clergy through presbyteral schools such as Joseph Cretin attended; the seminaries of Meximiex, l'Argentière, Alix and St. Sulpice where he prepared for the priesthood.

The second installment of seven chapters tells of his spiritual life at St. Sulpice, his ordination and first Mass at Montluel; his appointment to Ferney, first as curate, then as pastor; his work in that stronghold of Calvinism; the church and college he built; his personal virtues; and his friends among whom were the Curé of Ars and Blessed Pierre Chanel, the martyr of Futuna.

The final installment consists of four chapters dealing with Bishop Loras of Dubuque; Father Cretin's farewell to France; his voyage from Havre to St. Louis, Missouri, in 1838, and the last lap of his journey to Dubuque.

The illness with which the Archbishop was attacked in September, 1917, which caused his death a year later, prevented his completing the work of love on which he had set his heart and to which he had devoted the scant leisure of less than two years.

As was to be expected from one who was not a trained historian, who regarded Bishop Cretin as a saint and was an apologist for France despite her many shortcomings and her persecution of the Church, the biography is eulogistic. His friendly eye could see no fault in his subject. It contains none of the references which scientific biographers delight to incorporate in their works; but the facts set forth can be verified from the letters of Bishop Cretin and reliable histories of the period with which it deals.

Diocesan Functions And Growth

There was no celebration of the golden jubilee of the Archbishop's ordination in 1911, on December 21, the day he always regarded as the anniversary of that significant event.

My reasons for not wishing any demonstration in honor of the event, he told the Cathedral congregation in his sermon the next Sunday, were many but chiefly the day was too sacred to me, and I wished to cherish memories of the days long ago when, as a young levite, I knelt at yonder altar and with the hand of Bishop Grace on my head took the vows which day by day and year by year since that time I have tried to keep sacred. . . .Of all the priests at that altar that memorable day not one remains but myself. . .Father Oster the last died a year ago.

He paid tribute to the pioneer Bishops Cretin and Grace and to the twenty families who built the log Cathedral at a cost of not more than

$75.00 as well as to the larger number who built the third Cathedral at a cost of $40,000.

When Bishop Stariha resigned the see of Lead in 1909 he retired to his native home in Austria. Under date of September 2, 1911, he wrote Archbishop Ireland from Laibach in Krain, that he had visited the grave of Father Pierz, a famous missionary in Minnesota and a colonizer of note, and found that the headstone above it bore the inscription: "Rev. Fr. Xav. Pirc, born Nov. 20, 1785, ord. 1813, worked in the diocese 22 years, in the Indian missions of North America 38 years, returned to live here 7 years. Died Jan. 22, 1880". He added that the correct spelling of the name was Pirc, taken from his baptismal record. In the new Slovenian literature the name may be written Pirec.[191] Some years ago the bodies were removed from the St. Christopher cemetery to a new location and all traces of the final resting-place of Father Pierz have been lost.

Six new parishes were organized in the diocese in mid-year of 1912: St. Cecilia's (the twenty-sixth in St. Paul) by Reverend F. X. McDermott; Sacred Heart, Robbinsdale, (the twenty-third in Minneapolis) by Reverend W. H. Blum; St. Joseph's, Montevideo (formerly a mission of Renville) by Reverend John Fahey; St. Peter's, Forest Lake, by Reverend Thomas F. Gibbons, with missions at Taylor's Falls and Franconia; Sacred Heart, Murdock, (a mission of De Graff) by Reverend W. P. Walsh; and St. Mathias, Wanda, (a mission of Lamberton) by Reverend Joseph Jagemann, with Clements as a mission. These changes were reported in the diocesan organ for June 29 and July 6.

Spiritual retreats for men and women were announced in a letter of June 2, 1913. The retreat for men would be held in the St. Paul Seminary from Thursday evening, June 26, to the following Monday morning, under the direction of the Reverend Walter Elliott, C. S. P., Superior of the Paulist Mission House in Washington, D. C.; and the retreat for women at St. Joseph's Academy on the same dates under the leadership of the Right Reverend John P. Carroll, Bishop of Helena, Montana.

Quadrennial Methodist Conference

The quadrennial conference of the Methodist Episcopal Church held its sessions in Minneapolis in May, 1912. In order to focus public attention on its meetings it did not serve its purpose to enter upon a calm and intelligent discusion of the questions of church policy which would naturally engage the attention of such a representative body. An orderly and sane method of procedure would not satisfy the blatancy of a sect which sees no notoriety in the peaceful discussion of problems that concern its own welfare.[192] Strife must be stirred up; an object of attack must be found; and the guns of Methodism must be trained upon an enemy conjured up by the perfervid imagination of its leaders. It attacked the President and the Catholic Church. President Taft, it seemed, had disregarded "the expressed wish and prayer of the christian manhood and womanhood of the nation" by permitting Secretary of Agriculture Wilson to address the International Congress of hop-growers and brewers. In their eagerness to arrogate to themselves a monopoly of the "christian manhood and womanhood of the nation" the Methodist delegates forgot that others, not a whit less patriotic than they, but with a more intelligent concept of their duty as American citizens, saw no harm in the formal recognition given the organization by the authorities in Washington so long as nothing was done or said contrary to the provisions of the Constitution and the honor of the Republic.

The attack on President Taft whetted the appetite of the Methodists for a more bitter assault on the Catholic Church. They denounced the Ne Temere decree which safeguards the sacred character of christian marriage as "an insult to many Protestant homes . . . a defiance to our national laws regulating marriage".

Had they read the provisions of the decree they would have learned that it legislates for Catholics only and has nothing to do with the marriage of Protestants. Nor does it minimize in any way the effects of the civil enactments regarding the marriage contract.

But that was mild compared with what was to follow. Bishop Burt made an envenomed attack on European Catholicism which he characterized as pagan in its conceptions, doctrines and traditions. He referred to Catholic festivals in Italy as Bacchanalian feasts and claimed that all educated Italians had turned away from the Church in disgust, for Roman Catholicism was not christianity.

He was ably assisted by Reverend Walling Clark, for twenty years Superintendent of the Methodist mission in Italy, who asserted that the Italians knew nothing about the Bible until a Methodist colporteur brought it into Rome in the wake of Victor Emmanuel's troops. Another doughty leader, Dr. W. F. Rice, declared that the Catholic Church "deprives its members of the right to read the Holy Bible".

Reverend J. T. Stafford, delegate from Great Britain and Ireland, described the deplorable situation in these countries where Methodists had to combat Anglicanism in England, Presbyterianism in Scotland and Catholicism in Ireland which was in the grip of an "alien religion" and where Methodism was "begirt on every hand by hostile forces". In fact, the whole world was depraved except where the flickering candle of Methodism had been lighted.

Nor was South America forgotten. Here, too, were universal ignorance of the Bible, neglect of religious observances, breaches of the moral law, vice, poverty and superstition, all chargeable to the Catholic Church. "The very sanctity of the marriage tie has been for centuries a matter of barter by the prevailing ecclesiasticism and the exorbitant pecuniary demands of the priesthood".

This was the sum and substance of the alleged information put before the delegates to the conference by their acknowledged leaders. But these unfounded and oft-refuted calumnies did not go unchallenged. These purveyors of falsehood and slander forgot they were in a city where Catholics were numerous, intelligent and on the alert to resent calumnies against the Church, her doctrines and priesthood. Above all did they forget that the great Archbishop Ireland was a watchman on the towers of Israel, a staunch, undaunted advocate and defender of the doctrines and rights of the Church; and when he entered the lists to challenge their statements and insist on proof for their assertions they regretted their hardihood in crossing swords with this champion of truth and honesty. In a series of articles in the daily press he marshalled facts and figures, dates and documents in such formidable array that these cowardly defamers ran for cover. The David of fact slew the Goliath of falsehood, and enheartened every right-thinking man irrespective of creed or condition. The Archbishop knew Italy and its Catholics, their familiarity with the Vulgate, for sale in every bookstore in the peninsula, their loyalty to the Church as shown by the recent census. He vindicated the faith of the Irish people whose love for the religion preached by St. Patrick had comforted them in the trials they had to undergo for fifteen hundred years. He quoted extensively from the statutes of the Church in South America to refute the charges based on the alleged mercenary demands of the clergy, to show the true status of the marriage tie, the morality of the laity and clergy. In a scathing denunciation of their hypocrisy he challenged the Methodist leaders to refute his statements. He silenced their guns so effectively that all controversial matters were put in cold storage during the rest of the conference. The sessions lasted nearly a month. It was more like a political gathering than a religious assembly. The good men among the delegates resented the charges made against the Catholic Church with such utter abandon and disregard for even the semblance of truth, but they were powerless to stem the tide of vituperation. When challenged by the Archbishop their leaders had recourse to silence and in that they showed good sense as they were in no position to answer his smashing indictment. They showed themselves cowardly falsifiers of truth and base detractors of a religion which gave no cause nor excuse for their unchristian assaults.

. During the conference little, if any, thought was given to doctrinal matters. No pronouncements regarding the teaching of Methodism were made. No profession of faith emanated from the assembly. Many of the delegates did not observe the canons of even ordinary propriety when dealing with the Catholic Church. The climax came when some of the delegates who were loudest in denouncing the immorality of the South American clergy were caught in surroundings which proved them to be not above suspicion in their personal lives.

Towards the end of the conference the Archbishop wrote to his dear friend, Cardinal Gibbons, "Where duty calls I am always ready to step to the front. I could not allow the enemy to speak insults and lies against the old church without challenging them to battle. There was no direct reply to my letters; but in the last sessions of the conference efforts on the part of the more bellicose members to renew the war were quashed by the majority as soon as spoken.

"You are correct in noting a recrudescence of anti-Catholic feeling in the country. There is no doubt of the fact that violent bigotry is stalking through the land and, financially, is richly supported. I fear the waves will be badly ruffled for a time at least".[193]

Diocesan School Board

The Diocesan School Board was organized by the Most Reverend Archbishop in 1890 with 8 members under the chairmanship of Father Caillet. From 1896 to 1904 the Deans were additional members. It was reorganized in 1911 with Fathers Gibbons, (President), Byrne and Jung of St. Paul, and Erren, O. S. B., Cullen, (Secretary), and Harrington of Minneapolis. During the year three committees of two each visited all the parish schools in the Archdiocese. In their first annual report they declared they had inspected the schools and examined the pupils in the various branches of the curriculum and found that good, serious work was being done. The teachers were zealous, efficient and ambitious, the school buildings well kept, the furnishings and equipment adequate. Twenty-one pastors returned statistical statements of the number of pupils enrolled, the average attendance and the number of boys and girls.

The report recommended greater emphasis on religious training, with catechism and bible history the most important part of the curriculum; no change in text books unless recommended by the board; the teaching of singing by note not memory; emphasis on fundamentals not fads; competitive examinations for all schools; exhibit of parochial school work at the State Fair in 1913; assignment of home work for pupils by teachers; uniformity of opening and closing dates and holidays, with Tuesday after Labor Day as the annual opening day and about mid-June the closing; and the observance of national and state holidays.

The sixteenth hundredth anniversary of the peace and recognition given to the early church by Emperor Constantine in A. D. 313, was officially commemorated by a jubilee proclaimed by Pope Pius X and made known to the faithful of the Archdiocese by the Archbishop in a letter, dated June 25, 1913, in which he set forth the conditions for gaining the indulgences, namely, confession, communion and six visits to a church or churches depending upon the locality. In St. Paul the parish church, the Cathedral and the Assumption; in Minneapolis, the Pro-Cathedral and St. Joseph's in addition to the parish church. In localities where there are three churches two visits must be made to each; and where there is only one six visit must be made to it. The indulgences were applicable to the souls in Purgatory. An alms for the benefit of the House of the Good Shepherd must also be given. The jubilee closed on December 8.

At the golden jubilee celebration in honor of Monsignor Plut pastor of the Church of St. Mark, Shakopee, on February 12, 1915, the Archbishop in the course of his sermon said that there were only four clergymen in Minnesota who had been actually engaged in the work of the ministry for more than fifty years—himself, Bishop Trobec of St. Cloud, Monsignor Buh of Ely, and the Jubilarian.

The Catholic Educational Association held its twelfth annual meeting in St. Paul from June 28 to July 1, 1915, under the auspices of Archbishop Ireland who preached at the Pontifical Mass celebrated in the newly-opened Cathedral on June 29. The St. Paul Hotel was the local headquarters and the sessions were held in the Cathedral school with the exception of the public meeting on the evening of June 30 in the St. Paul Municipal Auditorium at which addresses were delivered on Catholic topics by Father Cleary of Minneapolis, Honorable Pierce Butler of St. Paul, Honorable Julius Coller of Shakopee, Very Reverend H. Moynihan, President of the College of St. Thomas and the Right Reverend John P. Carroll, Bishop of Helena, Montana.

Diocesan Society For The Propagation Of The Faith

The Society for the Propagation of the Faith in the Diocese of St. Paul is almost as old as the diocese itself. It was established by Bishop Cretin in 1853, when the sum of ninety dollars was received from three parishes. The collection rose to $188.00 in 1854 and dropped to $26.00 the following year owing to the death of the director, Father Peyragrosse. The Bishop's idea was to show appreciation, even in a small way, for the assistance which the Society in Paris and Lyons gave and was giving for the support of the works of religion in the diocese. During his lifetime the Bishop received nearly $42,000 and an additional $8,000 was given to Father Ravoux as Administrator after the Bishop's death. Between

1852 and 1864 the allocations amounted to 356,925 francs or about $70,000. For many years after that the Society continued to be a benefactor.

Father Oster, ordained in 1856, acted as an unofficial director of the Society for many years. One of his small record books, in possession of the Diocesan Office, shows entries totalling $82.00. For the first fifty years and more the amounts forwarded to the parent office were comparatively small owing to the many demands made on the faithful for the building of churches, schools and other institutions, as well as for the support of the needy, underprivileged and orphans of the diocese.

The diocesan branch of the society was formally established in 1916 by Archbishop Ireland who, in a letter,[194] dated June 12 of that year, appointed the Reverend James A. Byrnes of the St. Paul Seminary faculty Diocesan Director, authorizing him to carry out and foster the "most noble, most holy" purposes of the society by "obtaining financial help for the missions of the church in non-christian lands, wherever these lands be situated on the surface of the globe". In contributing for this purpose "the Diocese of St. Paul is paying a debt—not merely one of charity, but also one of strict justice". He assured the Director that he would have the generous support of his fellow-priests in whatever measures he adopted to obtain contributions from individuals and parishes in the diocese for the support of home and foreign missions.

An office was opened in the St. Paul Seminary and much of the clerical work done by the seminarians until it was moved down town for a couple of years before being finally located in the old Chancery building on Dayton Avenue. The annual report for 1918 showed receipts of $39,325.64, which included $3,495.92 received from the Holy Childhood Association, through which the parochial school pupils made their offerings for the propagation of the faith. Father Byrnes remained in charge of the work even after his appointment as Superintendent of Catholic Education in 1920 by Archbishop Dowling who, in 1927, reorganized the society in conformity with the decision of the hierarchy, approved by Rome, to allocate sixty percent of the receipts to the foreign missions and the balance to the home missions to aid struggling dioceses in the West, South and Southwest which theretofore had to rely on contributions made by individuals or the Extension Society. In October, 1927, he named Reverend James A. J. Troy, recently incardinated into the diocese, assistant to Father Byrnes as field agent to promote the work in the parishes and elsewhere. Father Troy was director from September 1, 1928, to October 29, 1933, and was followed by Fathers Prendergast, (1933-47), Walsh (1947-8), Cashman (Neil) (1948-51) and Jennings (1951-). The society housed in the Chancery Office since that building was opened, was moved in 1951 to the former residence of the Most Reverend Archbishop, 226 Summit Avenue.

The Father Mathew of the Northwest

After his elevation to metropolitan dignity the demands made upon Archbishop Ireland's time and energy by the growing importance of the diocese and the national and international problems of the Church made it increasingly difficult for him to devote much attention to the total abstinence movement. That did not mean that his interest in it flagged in the slightest degree. Rarely was he able to attend a national convention; seldom did he miss the annual meeting of the diocesan union. To the former he usually sent a letter expressive of his continued interest in and hearty sympathy with the work, urging the delegates to speak out strongly, to act bravely and make the cause more effective for the social and moral elevation of the people.

The decade between 1880 and 1890 may not inaptly be regarded as the golden age of the movement in the Diocese of St. Paul, if not throughout the country. He was the recognized national leader to whom all looked for guidance and inspiration, and he did not fail them.

He welcomed the delegates to the twelfth national convention in St. Paul in August, 1882, and at the Solemn Mass in the Cathedral delivered a scathing denunciation of intemperance and a ringing challenge to united, persistent, organized work for total abstinence as the only antidote for the evils of the liquor traffic. Twelve years later, at another general convention held in his see-city, he felt justified, as a result of "more mature thought and better observation", in reasserting in a stronger tone his conviction that "the enemy of the family, country and church, the enemy of God, is intemperance".

On the former occasion the St. Paul Pioneer Press of August 4, 1882, paid him a deserved tribute for his zealous and indefatigable efforts to bring about a radical change in the drinking habits of the Irish Catholics of the city, and his eminent success in changing them from a "disorderly and rowdy element of the community" into a "temperate, orderly, industrious, thrifty" and God-fearing people, to such an extent that it was very rare "to find an Irishman saloon-keeper in St. Paul", where "Irish Catholics probably contribute, in proportion to their numbers, fewer patrons of the saloon than any other part of the population".

This result was brought about by his unqualified denunciation of intemperance as the "master evil" of society that preyed especially on the laboring classes who, if they would abstain entirely from drink, would be enriched materially as well as spiritually. High license and strict enforcement of the laws regulating the liquor traffic do much to lessen the attendant evils but nothing short of personal total abstinence can eradicate them. His views were largely incorporated in the decrees of the Third Plenary Council of Baltimore[195]—where there is a whole chapter on "The Promotion of Temperance"—in response to a memorial drafted by a committee headed by Father Cotter of Winona asking for legislation on the liquor question. This legislation prepared the way for the Brief of March 27, 1887, addressed to Bishop Ireland by Pope Leo XIII to which reference has already been made.

In an address to the delegates at the national convention in St. Paul in 1894 the Archbishop paid tribute to his valiant cooperators without whom he could have done little and added: "I have given my whole soul to the cause of Total Abstinence. Whenever I can I speak for it; whenever I can I fight for it; and whenever I can I pray for it". He related for the first time the incidents that led to the issuance of the Brief. On his way to Rome in 1886 he paid a visit to Cardinal Manning in London and asked him to request from His Holiness a strong, authoritative letter that would be an incentive to greater effort among Catholic total abstainers, and His Eminence agreed to do so. At the audience with Pope Leo XIII the Archbishop dwelt on the grand work being done by total abstainers in the United States, and the Holy Father asked him to prepare a memorandum on the subject relating in full the nature of the movement, its prospects and ambitions and the means employed to attain its goal. "I assure you I put my heart in that paper; and I put in it also the truth". His Holiness was delighted with the result and the Archbishop begged him to write a letter on the subject to Cardinal Manning. The Pope said, "I will write a letter, but I will address it to you". The letter was written but, before it was officially signed, it was sent to the Archbishop "to know if it was strong enough".

Commenting on this Papal Brief Bishop Keane of Richmond said it took a man like Bishop Ireland to "put the whole meaning and whole object of the Catholic total abstinence movement beyond misunderstanding, to make it clearly appreciated, to win for it the hearty esteem and the earnest cooperation of the Holy See . . . He converted the Pope".

Meanwhile the work of total abstinence in the diocese went on with varying degrees of success. Between forty and fifty societies of men, women and cadets paid per capita tax to the local and the national unions. A number of others were unaffiliated with either one, and hundreds of individuals had pledged themselves to lives of sobriety without joining any society. Some of the older societies fell by the wayside largely through the apathy of their officers and new ones filled the breach. It was difficult to maintain enthusiasm for the movement and more so to enroll new recruits. The total membership did not exceed three thousand nor did it go above that figure during the next decade in which two new unions, one in Duluth and the other in Winona, were separated from the parent organization and grew apace.

In the midst of his preoccupations the Archbishop found time to write an article for the October issue of the Catholic World in 1890 in which he declared that

> Intemperance is our misfortune. It, as nothing else, paralyses our forces and awakens in the minds of our non-Catholic fellow-citizens violent prejudices against us. . .Catholics nearly monopolize the liquor traffic; Catholics loom up before the criminal courts of the land, under the charge of drunkenness and other violations of law resulting from drunkenness, in undue majorities; poorhouses and asylums are thronged with Catholics, the immediate or mediate victims of drink; the poverty, the sin, the shame that falls upon our people result almost entirely from drink. . .The Theobald Mathews are few and these few are timid.

At the national convention held in Boston in 1889 the Reverend James M. Cleary of Kenosha, Wisconsin, later of Minneapolis, suggested that the Catholic Total Abstinence Union of America endow a Father Mathew Memorial Chair in the Catholic University at an estimated cost of $50,000 to be subscribed by the subordinate unions and their individual members. Archbishop Ireland was among the first to contribute. Many of the subordinate units of the Diocesan Union followed his example and $1,051.00 was realized. Eventually the sum of $25,000 was accepted by the University as a partial endowment and the chair established in 1893. It provided for a professorship of mental and moral science and required that two of the yearly public lectures be on a subject akin to the great work to which Father Mathew consecrated his life and be known as the Father Mathew lectures.

Early in March, 1896, the Most Reverend Archbishop received a merited tribute [196] to his total abstinence campaign from a distant land in the form of a letter from C. S. Adama van Scheltema of Arnhem, Holland, dated February 26, telling him that "in the land of Sykdam, our Holland, at last the Roman Catholics are awakening to see the value of total abstinence. The majority of the awakened are yet only pleading for total abstinence from gin and all distilled spirits, but a few, as Mr. van Birning, are total abstainers as you and I have been for many years.

"From the Union Signal I know that in the painful struggle against alcoholism you are not averse to joining hands with Protestants; as I for fifty years was never averse to do the same with Roman Catholics. In 1863 we had a general congress in Hanover, where more than twenty priests were present and they and I were in fullest sympathy. Unhappily that is not the case here. In 1844 I became an abstainer from spirits only, but very soon experienced how little influence it had on the working classes. In 1861 I was the first to try total abstinence from all intoxicating drinks as the best means of influencing the working and poor people. For twenty years I was an only one among all Protestant ministers and, as far as I know, among our Catholic clergy. Since 1882 others have followed and, in 1895, a Dr. Alphonsus Ariens lifted the abstinence banner and opened a battle against gin . . ." Mr. van Scheltema says he translated the Archbishop's speech at the Congress of Chicago and many of Cardinal Manning's works; and his life of Father Mathew has been published in full in a Flemish paper by a Belgian priest. What is needed is an English Temperance Alliance where all can stand together. For the present that is impossible as priests and ministers stand so much aloof; but we are advancing, as a younger generation shows another spirit.

The central figure at the Hartford convention in 1901 was Archbishop Ireland who appealed to the delegates to support the project of writing the history of the total abstinence movement in the United States. He was chairman of the committee appointed for that purpose at the Chicago Convention in 1899, but for two years nothing had been done to initiate the work. The time had come to take a decisive step and it was voted to entrust the task to Reverend Edward McSweeny of St. Mary's College, Emmitsburg, Md., and a former President of the Seminary of St. Thomas Aquinas of St. Paul, for which five thousand dollars would have to be raised by subscriptions from the subordinate unions, each one of which was asked to place an order for ten or fifteen copies of the projected history and pay for them in advance. At the Dubuque convention the next year he urged the unions to fulfil their promises in order that the history might be available at an early date. It was finally distributed in 1907.

The Seminary Apostolate

A new phase of total abstinence work was inaugurated with his approval and blessing when, on March 27, 1900, the students of St. Paul Seminary organized the St. Paul Clerical Total Abstinence Society[197] and adopted a constitution and by-laws. It was the first society of the kind formed in any seminary in the country, the forerunner of a dozen similar societies organized in other seminaries largely through the efforts of Father Siebenfoercher of Cincinnati who devoted many years to that apostolate.

The purpose of the society was to enroll the students and alumni of St. Paul Seminary under the banner of total abstinence in an organization that would encourage and assist them, directly and indirectly, to refrain from the use of intoxicating beverages of all kinds, and equip them for participation in the total abstinence crusade when engaged in the active work of the ministry, by a thorough study of the liquor question in all its phases. During the year papers dealing with different aspects of the drink problem were read and discussed. The society relied on the moral courage and strength of character of its members for the keeping of the pledge and for doing all they could, by word and example, to prevent or cure intemperance in others. The students were expected to retain regular membership in the society for at least five years after ordination and might continue indefinitely by giving notice of their intention to the secretary. The society, with a membership of forty-five, was reported at the convention in Dubuque in 1902 and at subsequent conventions until 1910 when it had a membership of sixty-six. At that convention Father Siebenfoercher reported similar societies in eleven seminaries with a total enrollment of 588. During the same period the Cadets of St. Thomas College, under the spiritual direction of Reverend J. Dunphy, had grown in numbers since first reported at the national convention in Pittsburgh in 1903, and remained on the roster for several years. With the Seminary society it was described by Father Siebenfoercher as the "most progressive on the roll".

The St. Paul Clerical Society flourished until the year 1920, had a large and influential membership among the students and faculty and raised up a generation of total abstaining priests among the graduates of the institution.

The approval and blessing which Archbishop Ireland bestowed on the St. Paul Clerical Total Abstinence Society was given likewise to the Priests' Total Abstinence League of America[198] instituted at Pittsburgh, Pa., on August 7, 1903, whose primary object was to encourage apostolic work along the lines of total abstinence for all priests rather than a reformative one for those not pledged to sobriety. It was organized along the lines of the Sacred Heart Priests' League for the Promotion of Total Abstinence founded at Cincinnati, May 31, 1899, under the personal initiative and supervision of Archbishop Elder for the priests of his diocese. Archbishop Ireland had requested that his name be placed on the list beside that of Archbishop Elder.

Father Siebenfoercher was elected President of the new society and the Reverend John T. Mullen, D. C. L., of Boston, Secretary. The charter members were Archbishops Elder, Ireland and Ryan, Bishop Canevin of Pittsburgh, and fifty-nine priests, three of whom, Fathers Cleary, Egan and Reardon, represented the Archdiocese of St. Paul. At the next meeting held in St. Louis, on August 11, 1904, the roster contained the names of seven Archbishops and upwards of three hundred priests from thirty-six dioceses in the United States and three in Canada; and had received the high approval of Archbishop Falconio, the Apostolic Delegate who, in a letter to Father Siebenfoercher, dated Washington, November 21, 1903, declared that he had no doubt that it would prove to be "one of the most efficacious means for the preservation of the abstemious, and for the reformation of those who have become victims of intoxicating drink." He expressed appreciation of "the self-abnegation of those priests who embrace total abstinence in order to inculcate more effectively, both by word and example, the holy virtue of temperance".

The unqualified approbation of Rome given by Pope Leo XIII was supplemented by his successor in 1912, when he warned the National Union of the danger of affiliating with the Prohibition or any other political party, because it would interfere with the aim of the Union which depends on moral suasion for the promotion of total abstinence. To encourage the members Pope Pius X granted them plenary indulgences on the day of enrollment, the feast of St. John the Baptist or any other patron of the society and on any four days designated by the Ordinary of the diocese "once and for all", as well as numerous partial indulgences. In reality this was the renewal of indulgences granted as far back as 1888 when Archbishop Ireland designated Christmas day, Easter Sunday, the Sunday following June 24, the feast of St. John the Baptist, and the feast of the Assumption for the diocese.

The interest of Archbishop Ireland in the total abstinence movement never flagged during his long and active life. He was the first to take the pledge in St. Paul when the Father Mathew Total Abstinence Society of the Cathedral parish was organized on January 10, 1869, and he kept it faithfully and religiously during his lifetime. No liquor was kept in his house; none was served at his table, nor did he leave his pledge at home when he traveled abroad. His name was on the roster of the temperance society founded and fostered by Bishop Cretin, which hung inside the door of the second Cathedral of St. Paul. No sacrifice of time or energy was deemed too great for the cause. For ten years after the organization of the Father Mathew Society of the Cathedral parish he never missed a Sunday evening meeting. The writer recalls very vividly his insistence, even to the last year of his life, that the annual rally of the Diocesan Union be not dispensed with, that the meeting be held in a public hall, usually the old State Capitol at Wabasha and Exchange Streets, that a program of musical numbers and addresses be prepared, that he be notified of the time and place of the assembly that he might encourage, by voice and presence, those interested in the cause to keep up the good work and gather recruits about its standard. While he lived we dared not omit the annual meeting under pain of his displeasure. Towards the end it was little more than a rally of the remnant and friends of the old Father Mathew society whose ranks grew thinner with the passing years. It was a token convention of the old guard that never died till the great leader passed away.

The Archbishop did not believe in prohibition[199]—though he never made an address or wrote a line against it—except as a last resort and a drastic measure, because it was an infringement of personal rights and liberty and, therefore, liable to lead to serious abuses. In this he was right. He looked upon prohibition as "altogether a question of public expediency, relying for its solution on the degree of needs for severe measures, and on the degree of probability that these measures shall be enforced". . . . He differed from "those prohibitionists who look upon any restrictive measures short of absolute prohibition as wrong and immoral." He opposed the abolition of the canteen in the Army because of the protection from outside temptation it affords the soldiers who would find a way to procure liquor if it were not available within the post. He was an ardent supporter of high license in Minnesota and in any other state where nothing better could be obtained.

When the Prohibition Amendment to the Constitution was ratified in 1920 the advocates of total abstinence were lulled into a false security. They thought there would be no further need to continue the crusade, but in this they were woefully disappointed.

His Eminence Cardinal Gibbons raised his voice in vigorous protest against the ratification of the Amendment. He was denounced by its advocates and criticized even by its opponents for his description of the moral evils that would follow in the wake of its incorporation into the Constitution. Many thought he was unduly perturbed over a movement which promised so much for the promotion of individual and national sobriety. Congressman Volstead of Minnesota, author of the amendment, became the patron saint of the prohibitionists who won the day. Their victory was short-lived, though they would not admit they had opened a Pandora's box. The attitude of the Cardinal was vindicated by the moral turpitude and resultant disregard for law and order traceable to this "noble experiment". Archbishop Ireland never favored the amendment, and he died before it was ratified by the votes of two-thirds of the states of the Union.

The enforcement of prohibition was impossible; its repeal was logical. The need for a resumption of a campaign of total abstinence is more imperative now than ever before. Another Father Mathew of the Northwest is needed to arouse us from our lethargy and inaugurate a new crusade against the demon of drink.

Churchman and Statesman

As a writer and apologist Archbishop Ireland stood in the front rank of American ecclesiastics. For more than four decades of consecrated activity, during which he took no vacation from the work of the ministry, his facile pen, virile and trenchant, was always at the service of Church and Country, ever ready to defend the cause of truth wherever it needed a champion. The claims of religion to an impartial hearing before the bar of public opinion made an especial appeal to him, and he never failed to take advantage of an opportunity to place the doctrines of the Church in their proper light and bearing before his fellow citizens of every condition and creed. He wrote for Catholic and non-Catholic alike. To the former he appealed with all the authority of a recognized leader of the Church, enunciating divine truth in all its fulness and certainty; to the latter he spoke with the logic and persuasiveness of a religious teacher who understood the yearning of the human heart for "the things that are above" and who had a message worthy of their acceptance. He never minimized one jot or tittle of the deposit of faith; but he possessed a peculiar power of placing the doctrines of the Church before the non-Catholic mind in their most alluring garb, and of showing the harmony that exists between the fundamental dogmas of religion and the basic principles of the Constitution. He sought no religious controversy; but whenever the Church was attacked in her teaching, practice or policy, he stepped into the arena armed with irrefutable arguments in support of her claims and many a valiant adversary went down to defeat before his vigorous onslaught. No critic of the Church ever challenged him to a second debate. They recognized his superior intellectual equipment and as gracefully as possible withdrew from the field. The collection of his most important essays and addresses which he gave to the world under the title of "The Church and Modern Society" represents his mature thought on the subjects with which they deal. The masterly discourses of his later years were published in pamphlet form by The Catholic Bulletin.

Archbishop Ireland was a noted preacher as well as a vigorous writer. As a priest he won fame as a pulpit orator and attracted to the Cathedral, of which he was pastor, congregations which taxed the seating capacity. By study and training extending over many years he developed and perfected his natural ability and fluency as a speaker, and joined to fecundity of thought a grace of expression and an unction of delivery which made him a much-sought-after preacher on great occasions throughout the country. For many years he preached on the first Sunday of the month in his Cathedral and many of his most important pronouncements were made on these occasions. There was an earnestness and impressiveness about his delivery which captivated the audience and held them spellbound during the longest discourse. His object was not to charm but to convince and he did both. He spoke in a loud somewhat harsh voice, distinctly, deliberately, impressively, with sweeping, often ungraceful gestures. He wrote out his sermons and addresses in long hand and memorized them verbatim. He had an extraordinarily retentive memory and never made use of manuscript or notes.

A National Figure

No sketch of Archbishop Ireland's life and activity could make any pretension to completeness without a reference, however brief and fragmentary, to the part which he played in national affairs. He was regarded by all as one of the most devoted and patriotic of American citizens. He gloried in America and her institutions; he loved her starry flag and constitution which he considered the text-book of freedom, the bible of the rights of men forever. He was unalterably opposed to any drastic change in that sacred document and outspoken in opposition to all radical demands for the recall of judges. He rejoiced in the opportunities for material success which his adopted country offered to all and in the freedom of worship which she guaranteed to even the humblest of her children. He had taken part in the struggle which preserved the Union and earned the right to serve the Republic with all the devotion of his great heart. Next to God he loved America. In him religion and patriotism went hand in hand, and necessarily so. He could not conceive of a deeply religious man who was not a true patriot, especially if that man professed allegiance to the Catholic Church. He embodied in himself the highest attributes of a churchman and the noblest qualities of a citizen. No man dared to impeach his patriotism because of his religion; nor to challenge his religious sincerity because of his love for the land of his adoption. He looked upon all men as brothers whatever their creed, color, condition or country of origin. He came up from the ranks of the lowly, laboring class but he had no grudge against the rich and powerful. He was the friend of the workman and of his employer. He spoke with balance when discussing the clashing interests of capital and labor. He deplored the unorganized and helpless condition of unskilled labor, but he condemned with equal vigor acts of violence and picketing on the part of labor unions and urged individual freedom for employer and employee. He was a member of the Labor Board of Conciliation and Arbitration for the whole country, attended its meetings whenever possible and prepared himself by reading and study to take an intelligent part in its deliberations.

For many years Archbishop Ireland was a national figure, a statesman of more than ordinary ability, whose counsel was sought by men of prominence in every walk of life and especially by the leaders of the Republican party to which he owed political allegiance. For many years he was a tower of strength to his party in the National Capital; and had he chosen the political arena rather than the religious world as the theater of his activity, there is no position within the gift of his fellowmen, short of the Presidency itself, to which he might not have attained. His ability to divine the trend of events, to estimate men and measures at their relative values, to map out a course of action, to advocate a cause before the public, enabled him to wield an immense influence in national affairs.

Early in life there dawned upon him the realization that if all Catholics, and especially all Irish Catholics, belonged to the Democratic party, they would wield no influence in government circles when that party was not in power. He decided to throw his lot in with the Republicans in order that there would be some one at court to plead the cause of the Catholic Church and defend her interests when they held the reins of power and dispensed patronage. He became influential in the councils of the party, was an intimate friend of many of its leaders and was consulted by them on all important questions of public policy. In not a few instances he safeguarded the rights of the Church by forestalling legislation detrimental to her welfare. He had his finger on the pulse of public opinion, knew when to speak and when to be silent. Through his influence with the President and his advisers he was able to effect a settlement of the problems arising out of our occupancy of the Philippine Islands and won golden opinions from all true Americans. Many other signal services did he render to the nation during nearly half a century of unwearying activity for the public welfare. The most distinguished men of the country paid tribute to his worth and rejoiced in his friendship. They knew that he had no selfish ambitions; that he sought no personal honors; that he cared neither for praise nor blame when duty mapped out a course of action; that he had in view only the interests of the Church which he desired to put above all political parties, the queen of all, the servant of none.[200]

St. Paul was on the itinerary of nearly all men of distinction who visited America during the latter half of his life. They deemed it an honor to be received by him, and a privilege to sit at the feet of the Gamaliel of the Northwest for the discussion of world problems. He welcomed their coming not as a tribute to his personal worth, but to the church of which he was a recognized leader.

During all these years he was untiring in his efforts to promote the material and spiritual well being of his flock. New parishes were formed; more imposing churches erected; hospitals and charitable institutions increased in numbers and efficiency and religious growth and expansion were fostered in every way. He never lost sight of the needs of his diocese. The rapidity with which it developed under his enlightened leadership and its increasing importance as a center of virile Catholic thought and activity, owing to his personality, gave him ample opportunity for the display of his talents as churchman and statesman.

In a little more than a quarter of a century the number of diocesan priests increased from 130 to 302; of priests of religious orders from 29 to 56; of churches with resident pastors from 117 to 208, while missions decreased from 95 to 66; of parochial schools from 63 to 102; of pupils in these schools from 11,748 to 25,730; of seminarians from 160 to 210; of academies for girls from 4 to 10 with 2,597 pupils. St. Thomas College had an enrollment of 1,050 and St. Catherine's 354. The total number of pupils under Catholic instruction amounted to 31,411. There was over 1,200 sisters of different religious orders in the Archdiocese.

But the diocese did not absorb all his attention. He was filled with solicitude for all the churches of America and of the world, for he recognized no diocesan nor national boundaries when there was work to be done for the Master. Many important problems clamored for attention at home and abroad and many complex questions demanded discussion and action, and he gave of his time and energy to their solution.

The pity is that men of such heroic stature and nobility of soul must pay the debt of nature while their work, humanly speaking, is yet uncompleted. Those who knew Archbishop Ireland intimately were well aware that many projects for the good of religion and the welfare of the Church were in germ in his mind when, for the first time in eighty years of uninterrupted activity, the premonitory symptoms of a serious illness suggested a respite from the ceaseless round of duty. He would not, however, be convinced that they were more than indications of a passing indisposition. He could not realize that the weight of four score years must be reckoned with in all his planning for the future. He must be about his Father's business. And so he did not relax until the vigorous constitution was undermined, until the once rugged body refused to bear the burden he would impose on it. But even then he could not believe that the breakdown was final. He chafed under the enforced idleness and loss of precious time, for the bodily weakness had not affected the brain. His mind was as alert as ever and he retained his intellectual vigor until the last moment of life.

The End of a Noble Life

In the early autumn of 1917 Archbishop Ireland suffered an acute attack of lumbago to which he was subject. Usually a few days of complete rest—at most a week or two—sufficed to restore him to normal health. At best he was not a very patient sufferer. This first serious illness was an unwelcome interruption in his normally busy life and he bewailed the loss of time it entailed from his accustomed routine of duties. But this attack was more serious than usual being complicated by a severe cold which he was unable to shake off as he had done on previous occasions. He was advised to slow up his work but refused to do so. It was the beginning of the end though he and others knew it not. After a few weeks there was a noticeable improvement in his condition; but he complained about the loss of time which must be made up in some way. He was warned about the danger of a relapse but paid no heed till a more severe attack laid him low. He would not go to the hospital but remained in his home under the care of his devoted housekeeper, Miss Annie McDevitt, who had been in charge of his household for many years and had learned how to humor him. He became gradually reconciled to a longer and more tedious convalescence. The months dragged on slowly and he chafed under the restraint put upon him. He was urged to seek a warmer climate and at length yielded to the importunities of his friends. On January 8 he left for St. Augustine, Florida, accompanied by Bishops O'Gorman and O'Reilly, the latter of whom remained with him after the former returned home. The weather was far from pleasant. In a letter to the Chancellor from the Hotel Ponce de Leon on January 21 he complained: "The weather is just bearable. Yesterday it was 70 in the hot sun for a few hours, but the nooks and corners were very cold and chilly. No substantial change is looked for for a few days to come".

Early in 1918, as a consequence of World War 1, a more detailed and comprehensive course of military instruction was prescribed by the War Department for every college in which a senior unit of the Reserved Officers' Training Corps had been established. In St. Thomas College, affected by this ruling, new courses were organized and additional instructors secured. Two West Point cadets were added to the staff of the Commandant, Captain McNeal, and the first installment of $15,000 of government subsidy received for use of the cadets recommended by the College. At that time the Archbishop was in the Southland with Bishops O'Gorman and O'Reilly recuperating from illness. During his sojourn he urged the people of his diocese to contribute generously to the Third Liberty Loan in support of the effort of the country

> to carry still further towards a happy and full accomplishment the gigantic task imposed upon her. Catholics have thus far made a worthy record in every department of war work. . .a Catholic community without the record of having subscribed its full quota of the loan would be a dishonor to the Catholic Church. See to it that there is no such community in the Archdiocese of St. Paul.

He was saddened by the news of the death of his life-long friend, Bishop McGolrick of Duluth, who passed away on January 23 of an acute attack of indigestion. Mother Clementine of the Visitation Convent, whom he had known since she came to St. Paul, died two days earlier, the youngest member of the band of six pioneer sisters who founded the community in St. Paul in 1873 and the last of them. The thought of death obtruded itself on him with sobering effect. Another reminder of death came to the Archbishop with the announcement of the death of Most Reverend John J. Keane, retired Archbishop of Dubuque, on June 22, 1918. They had been intimately associated with each other in the work of the church for over three decades of years. An understanding friendship made them one in mind, heart and effort in every movement for her welfare in the United States.

His sojourn in the Southland brought only temporary relief. He yearned for the salubrious climate of Minnesota and early in the spring he returned to St. Paul, but too ill to resume active duty. He was comforted by the receipt of a letter[201] from his friend, Theodore Roosevelt, from New York, dated April 26:

> My Dear Archbishop Ireland,
>   I don't know whether you will be able to read this, but at least I hope that whoever does read it, will tell you that I have written. You are one of our really great American figures. This country owes you very much. I feel not only deep concern and sympathy for you because of my long friendship, but also as an American because you have been one of the greatest influences for good in our American life.
>   With very hearty and earnest hopes for your complete recovery,
>   Ever yours,
>   Theodore Roosevelt.
>
> His Grace,
> Archbishop Ireland,
> St. Paul, Minnesota

One of his last official acts was to procure the honor of Knighthood in the Order of St. Gregory for four prominent Catholic laymen—C. H. F. Smith and Timothy Foley of St. Paul, and L. S. Donaldson and Morris McDonald of Minneapolis, as a token of official ecclesiastical approval and recognition of their work for religion and their benefactions to the Church in the Archdiocese. The notification reached him by cablegram on July 13.

A few months after he received the honor of Knighthood of St. Gregory Timothy Foley gave $100,000 to the College of St. Thomas "for the erection of a dormitory for young men preparing to enter the St. Paul Seminary", to provide not only accommodations for a large number of candidates for the Seminary but to give them the care and special training which future seminarians require in their early years. It will make possible special exercises of piety and lessons in the spiritual life as part of the daily routine and thus help to mould priestly minds and hearts. The gift was contingent on the raising of an endowment of $150,000, the income of which was to be applied to defray the expenses of the students destined for the ministry. It formed the nucleus of the fund for the erection of the preparatory seminary, known as Nazareth Hall, which was one of the most notable projects of the episcopate of the Most Reverend Austin Dowling who succeeded Archbishop Ireland in the see of St. Paul.

In the meantime negotiations for the purchase of an official residence for the Archbishop near the Cathedral had reached a successful termination and the house at 226 Summit Avenue directly across the street, the home of Amherst H. Wilder, the philanthropist, was acquired for $50,000 and made ready for occupancy and the Archbishop took possession of it during the week of July 22. It also served as Chancery Office. It was a great improvement on the house he occupied for more than twenty-five years at 977 Portland Avenue. The rooms were large and airy with accommodations for a number of guests. The dining room pleased him very much. It provided space for many more guests than the one in his old home and he was delighted at the prospect of being able to entertain on a more elaborate scale than formerly. But it was not to be. He regretted that he had not moved to the new residence many years before when a change from the old home was suggested. It was pathetic to see him sitting on the lawn in the sun, gazing wistfully across Summit Avenue at the magnificent Cathedral constructed under his direction, a stooped, emaciated figure wrapped in a warm cloak. During the summer he grew perceptibly weaker though now and again his former vigor reasserted itself and he took an interest in current events. Recurring weak spells left him in a more feeble condition. Except for short periods of unconsciousness his mental faculties remained unimpaired. He lingered through the summer months until the autumn leaves began to turn when he took to bed never to leave it.

As the end approached anxious watchers at his bedside noted the gradual ebbing of his strength and realized that the end was not far off. The ravages of an illness extending over the greater part of a year had gradually undermined the robust constitution which had sustained the physical exactions of eighty years of intense activity; and as the summer drew to a close it became apparent to the attending physicians that the resources of medical science were wholly inadequate to prolong the precious life beyond a few weeks.

The patient, too, had come to realize that his sickness was unto death and gradually gave up the struggle for life. He surrendered himself unconditionally into the hands of his Creator and in perfect submission and complete resignation to the divine will awaited the end. "It is the will of God", he said; and commended to the care of the Most High his beloved diocese and its institutions, the clergy, religious and people, as well as the projects, completed or otherwise, which he had undertaken for the honor and glory of God and the welfare of religion.

On Monday, September 3, he received Extreme Unction from the hands of his boyhood friend, Bishop O'Gorman. When, finally, it was apparent that his span of life was limited to a few hours at most, the faithful watchers by his bedside redoubled their prayers for a happy death and favorable judgment. The physicians and attendants marvelled at the vitality which he displayed up to the last moment. He seemed conscious of what was going on about him and from time to time rallied sufficiently to recognize by a feeble attempt at a smile—for he could no longer speak—his intimate friend, Bishop O'Gorman, his sister, his secretary and a few of the priests. A privileged group knelt in prayer through the long watches of the last night, the last three nights in fact, and as the subdued repetition of the Rosary, the Archbishop's favorite devotion, touched the mystic chord of memory his feeble hand was seen to move slowly across the coverlet to clasp the beads that rested on his breast.

At 3:55 A. M. on Wednesday, September 25—fourteen days after his eightieth birthday—death came quietly, almost imperceptively. There was no agony, just a falling asleep, as of a candle fluttering into darkness. Without a tremor of the body the soul of Archbishop Ireland— distinguished prelate, honored citizen, great statesman, true friend— passed to its eternal home, and soon the pallid features settled into repose as if in normal sleep, lifelike in death. At the bedside when the end came were his sister, Mother Seraphine, Provincial of the Sisters of St. Joseph, Sister St. Rose, her assistant, Bishop Busch of St. Cloud, Fathers Byrne, Vicar General, Welch, Secretary and Chancellor, Bajec, Reardon, Crowley and Ryan, Doctor Greene, one of the attending physicians, Miss McDevitt, the housekeeper, Miss Cook, the stenographer, and the nurses. As they left the house of death the bell of the Cathedral tolled the Angelus of a new day saddened by the death of this distinguished prelate.

At once the announcement of his death pulsated from St. Paul to all parts of the continent and along the ocean bed to distant lands and evoked tributes of respect and tears. For a week the news had been momentarily awaited.

Funeral Arrangements

The remains of the deceased were prepared for burial by O'Halloran and Murphy. As soon after death as possible the body, vested in pontifical robes, lay in state in the reception room of the residence, 226 Summit Avenue, which had been transformed into a mortuary chapel, where it was viewed by the diocesan clergy, visiting prelates and priests, members of the religious communities and a steady stream of citizens of all ranks and denominations. The seminarians in groups of four took turns in watching beside the bronze coffin and chanting the prescribed prayers of the ritual; and each morning several Masses were celebrated on the altar before which lay the remains of the illustrious dead.

A meeting of the priests of St. Paul was held in the Cathedral school early in the afternoon of September 25 for the purpose of making arrangements for the funeral, and for the reception and accommodation of the large number of bishops and priests from all parts of the country who were expected to attend the obsequies. Committees were appointed and the details of the ceremony discussed. It was decided to hold the funeral on Wednesday, October 2, at ten o'clock, and to bring the remains in solemn procession to the Cathedral on Tuesday, place the body in state before the high altar in charge of a guard of honor and admit the public to view the deceased for the last time.

The Right Reverend Bishop O'Gorman, senior Bishop of the Province, appointed Very Reverend Father Byrne Acting Administrator of the Diocese and gave him general charge of the funeral arrangements.

Under the direction of the Reverend L. F. Ryan, pastor of the Cathedral, the sanctuary and altar, throne and pulpit were suitably draped for the solemn occasion and a section of pews in the middle front of the church set apart for the relatives, pallbearers and special guests.

The Reverend Alois Ziskovsky of St. Paul Seminary was placed in charge of the ceremonies incident to the occasion and under his expert direction arrangements were perfected to make the funeral of the distinguished prelate one of the most imposing and impressive ever seen in the United States.

As soon as possible after the death of the Archbishop an announcement of the fact and of the date of the funeral was sent to the Cardinals, the Apostolic Delegate, the Archbishops, Bishops and other prelates in the United States and to members of the Canadian episcopate; and shortly afterwards telegrams of condolence and appreciation poured into the Chancery Office from the members of the hierarchy, public officials of the state and nation, representatives of foreign governments, and men prominent in the business and professional worlds, all testifying to the widespread sorrow evoked by the death of our beloved Archbishop.

On every side there was evidence of sincere grief. The city of St. Paul, by proclamation of Mayor Hodgson, took cognizance of the loss of its most distinguished citizen by placing the flag on the city hall at half-mast until after the burial; and on the day of the funeral the flag on the State Capitol was lowered. All business in the state and municipal departments was suspended from ten to twelve o'clock to enable the officials and others to attend the obsequies. Business in St. Paul and Minneapolis ceased for five minutes at noon on the day of burial as a mark of respect.

During the time between the death of the Archbishop and the funeral, Solemn Masses of Requiem were celebrated in the different churches and institutions of the Archdiocese and many fervent prayers and Holy

Communions offered up by the faithful for the happy repose of his soul.

On Tuesday, October 1, the remains of the Archbishop were borne in solemn procession to the Cathedral almost directly across Summit Avenue from his residence. At nine o'clock the seminarian choir of eighty voices, under the direction of Reverend Francis Missia, marched from the Cathedral rectory to the episcopal residence where they were met by the Very Reverend James C. Byrne, Administrator. The choir sang the De Profundis and, as the remains were carried to the Cathedral, the Miserere. The cadets from the College of St. Thomas, drawn up in double line from the house to the church, acted as an escort and a large number of priests took part in the procession.

The honorary pall-bearers were six priests from Minneapolis: Reverends J. M. Cleary, T. E. Cullen, Othmar Erren, O. S. B., J. Harrington, T. S. McGovern, O. P., and E. T. Mallon, C. S. P. The active pall-bearers were Messrs D. A. Murphy, Pierce Butler, J. W. Willis, L. E. Shields, M. W. Waldorf, F. Maron, F. Buchmeier and H. H. Gillen.

When the cortege reached the Cathedral the choir sang the Subvenite. The body was met at the entrance by the Cathedral clergy and borne to the sanctuary where it rested in state until after the services on the following day. A Solemn Mass of Requiem was then celebrated by Father Byrne, assisted by Fathers Wilbee of Minneapolis as deacon, Roy of St. Paul as subdeacon and Ziskovsky as master of ceremonies. The responses were sung by the seminarian choir and the Mass attended by the children of the higher grades of the parochial schools of St. Paul, the pupils of St. Catherine's College, St. Joseph's Academy, the Visitation Academy and Cretin High School. Through the courtesy of Commissioner Wunderlich of the department of education, permission was given to the Catholic children above the fifth grade in the public schools to attend the services. The Cathedral was thronged with the children in charge of their teachers, each school having its own reserved section. The sermon was preached by Very Reverend H. Moynihan, President of St. Thomas College, who had been closely associated with the deceased prelate for more than a score of years.

After the Mass the pupils viewed the remains of the dead Archbishop, their benefactor and friend; and throughout the day and far into the night a continuous stream of people of all classes, conditions and creeds, visited the Cathedral while a special guard of honor composed of the Fourth Degree Knights of Columbus of the Twin Cities, and the Ancient Order of Hibernians kept vigil during the day and night and until the hour set for the funeral the following day.

Tuesday evening at eight o'clock the clergy of the diocese and the seminarians assembled in the sanctuary and chanted the Office of the Dead. Palestrina's Miserere and Haydn's Libera were sung by the choir

Wednesday, October 2, the date set for the funeral, was an ideal autumn day. The sun shone from an unclouded sky; the air was crisp and bracing. At an early hour people began to assemble at the Cathedral to await the opening of the doors at nine o'clock or to secure a point of vantage from which to view the clergy procession scheduled for half past nine. The dignitaries from all parts of the United States and from western Canada assembled in the archiepiscopal residence, while the diocesan clergy, visiting priests and seminarians met at the Cathedral rectory on Selby Avenue. Promptly at half past nine the procession started. The order was: acolytes, altar boys, seminarians, Christian Brothers, Priests, Monsignors, Mitred Abbots, Bishops and Archbishops, followed by the celebrant of the Mass and the ministers. It moved slowly down Selby Avenue from the Cathedral residence through a vast concourse of people which filled every available foot of space in front of the Cathedral; and as it wheeled into Summit Avenue the prelates joined the ranks and between two lines of cadets from the College of St. Thomas the procession slowly ascended the broad granite approaches to the Cathedral and passed into the sacred edifice where places had been reserved for all, either in the sanctuary or in the front pews. Eight Archbishops, twenty-nine Bishops, eleven Monsignors, about seven hundred priests and two hundred seminarians took part in the procession.

Reservations had been made in the nave of the Cathedral for the relatives of the deceased prelate; the diocesan sisterhoods; the Knights of St. Gregory—Messrs. C. H. F. Smith and Timothy Foley of St. Paul; L. S. Donaldson and Morris McDonald of Minneapolis; Lieutenant Renard of the French High Commission; Loyal Legion of which the deceased was commander; G. A. R. of which he was an honored member; Garfield and Acker Relief corps; Territorial Pioneer Association; Cathedral and Pro-Cathedral Building committees; state and city officials; U. S. Army and Naval officers. Governor Burnquist and other state officers and department heads, about fifty in number, attended the services in a body with a military escort under the command of Adjutant General Rhinow. An equal number of city officials, headed by Mayor Hodgson, were present as well as the judges of the Supreme, District and Municipal courts. Hamline University (Methodist) suspended classes during the funeral as a mark of respect.

The Pontifical Mass of Requiem was celebrated by the Most Reverend Thomas O'Gorman of Sioux Falls, S. D., Senior Bishop of the Province, assisted by the Very Reverend Francis J. Schaefer, D. D., Rector of the St. Paul Seminary, as arch-priest, the Reverend J. J. Howard of Springfield, Illinois, a cousin of the dead Archbishop, as deacon, the Very Reverend H. Moynihan, D. D., President of the College of St. Thomas, as subdeacon, and Reverend A. J. Ziskovsky of St. Paul Seminary, as master of ceremonies. The Requiem Mass was strictly Gregorian and was sung by a select choir of seminarians.

Archbishop Keane's Sermon

The sermon[202] was preached by the Most Reverend James J. Keane, Archbishop of Dubuque, who had served as a priest of the Archdiocese for many years before he was elevated to the episcopate. He chose as his text, "O Lord, thou hast tried me, and hast known me" (Psalm 138-1). It was not an eloquent discourse though he had an outstanding subject; it was not an oration such as the Bishop of Meaux would have given on a similar occasion, but it was marked by sincerity and a deep feeling of personal bereavement. It dealt with the chief events in the career of the deceased prelate, reviewed in broad outline the dominant achievements of his long and busy life during which he had wrought wonders for church and country, and labored as a good soldier of Christ. It brought into orderly relief the striking events of a life distinguished by rare talents, strenuous endeavor, high ideals, notable achievements, exceptional gifts of mind and heart, a remarkable memory and a physique equal to the tremendous demands of a zeal for souls and a zest for work that finally undermined his robust constitution. He referred to the multiple activities undertaken for the glory of God, the benefit of religion and the welfare of his fellowmen. Brilliant talents, lofty ideals and spiritual vigor marked him for inspiring leadership. He extolled his distinguished services as chaplain in the Civil War; his phenomenal success as an ardent advocate of total abstinence and a recognized leader in the cause of temperance; his successful promotion of Catholic colonization; his opposition to all forms of foreignism in the Church in America; his forceful advocacy of the true principles of religion and social life as taught by the Church. He dwelt on the important role the deceased Archbishop played in the negotiations preliminary to the Spanish-American war and in the settlement of the Friars' lands question in the Philippine Islands. Religion and patriotism were twin passions with him. His loyalty to the Holy See was unfaltering; his devotion to the Church and the Republic unchallengeable; his freedom from the stirrings of vulgar ambition unquestionable. His was the active life of an apostolic bishop who had scant leisure for the intellectual pursuit of knowledge in which, were his life less strenuous, he would have won distinction.

In his private life he was a model of every priestly virtue. His living apartments were less commodious and comfortable than those of the majority of his priests. His fare was the simplest. He took little rest and no recreation. He was at the call of every one whom he could serve. He was regular in everything and in nothing more than in his religious duties and devotions. Even when, as often happened, the duties of the day held him captive till midnight, he invariably began his Mass at six o'clock in the morning after due preliminary exercises of piety. His great devotions were to the Blessed Sacrament, which he visited regularly, and to the Blessed Virgin, whose rosary he prayed with the confidence of a child. He had no great attachments save such as came of his faith.

After the Mass the five absolutions prescribed by the rubrics were pronounced by four Archbishops—Most Reverends J. J. Harty of Omaha, J. J. Glennon of St. Louis, S. G. Messmer of Milwaukee, G. W. Mundelein of Chicago—and by the celebrant of the Mass, Bishop O'Gorman.

At the close of the service, as the body was borne from the Cathedral, the choir sang the Miserere and the Benedictus. The honorary pall-bearers were six priests from St. Paul: Reverends P. O'Neil, E. Vinas, S. M., J. Rynda, V. Nelles, O. F. M., F. X. Bajec and T. F. Gleeson. The active pall-bearers were: Messrs. T. D. O'Brien, A. Schaller, J. J. Regan, F. Schlick, W. D. Dwyer, M. H. Foley, F. W. Sullivan and E. W. Buckley.

It had been suggested to him while living that he be interred in the crypt of the magnificent granite Cathedral he had built and dedicated, which would be as fitting a monument for him as St. Paul's in London is for its architect, Sir Christopher Wren, but he rejected the suggestion by saying that he wanted to be buried beneath the green sward in the sunshine of Calvary Cemetery beside his anointed predecessors, with the pioneer priests, religious and faithful.

The funeral cortege formed outside the Cathedral and the body of the first Archbishop of St. Paul was borne, by way of Summit Avenue and Lexington Boulevard, to Calvary Cemetery where it was laid to rest beside his predecessors, Bishops Cretin and Grace, where a grave with a bricked interior was prepared to receive it. Most of the prelates and clergymen and the Governor and his staff accompanied the body to the cemetery in automobiles. The prescribed service at the graveside was conducted by the Most Reverend Bishop O'Reilly of Fargo; the responses and the Benedictus were chanted by a choir of twenty seminarians; the final prayers were said in the vernacular by the Reverend Thomas E. Cullen, pastor of the Pro-Cathedral, Minneapolis, after which the dignitaries present sprinkled the coffin with holy water, and all withdrew.

In the spring the grave was covered with a granite slab, four by nine feet in dimensions and eight inches thick, similar to those that mark the last resting-places of the pre-deceased bishops and his parents. It bears the following inscription:

SACRED TO THE MEMORY OF JOHN IRELAND
FIRST ARCHBISHOP OF ST. PAUL
BORN IN KILKENNY IRELAND, A. D. 1838
DIED IN ST. PAUL, A. D. 1918
HE WAS RENOWNED EVEN TO THE UTMOST PART OF THE
EARTH, AND HE GATHERED THEM THAT WERE PERISHING.
1 MAC. 111-9
MAY HE REST IN PEACE

The funeral procession was the largest ever seen in St. Paul, and one of the most imposing of its kind ever witnessed in the United States. It was a well-deserved tribute of respect and admiration for the great Archbishop Ireland, who, for nearly half a century, was the dominant personality of the Catholic Church in America and a tower of strength to the Republic in all that made for true progress and enlightenment. All who witnessed it realized that it was a fitting expression of genuine sorrow for an illustrious leader who deserved well of Church and State, whose death was an almost irreparable loss to the highest and holiest interests of the nation which he served with such enlightened zeal and unselfish devotion.

Hundreds of messages of condolences were received in St. Paul from all parts of the country and from European lands, testifying to the genuine sorrow evoked by the death of the distinguished Archbishop of St. Paul.

Let it suffice to put on record two of them—one from the President of the United States, the other from the Cardinal Primate and hierarchy of the land of his birth.

"I mourn the death of Archbishop Ireland. He was a great patriot as well as a great churchman. He was an old and valued friend, and moreover, when with him I felt I was in the company of a great ecclesiastical statesman of the old type in point of ability, and yet abreast of modern American thought. His death is a great loss and leaves a very real blank in American life".

Theodore Roosevelt.

"In the death of the Archbishop of St. Paul our country mourns the loss of an illustrious son. His career as a great churchman, a courageous statesman, and an intrepid advocate of Temperance, was eagerly followed in his native land. Love of the country of his birth mingled in him with love of America; and the Archbishops and Bishops of Ireland, in annual meeting assembled, tender their heartfelt condolence to the clergy and laity of St. Paul under the heavy load of sorrow which the death of their great Archbishop has entailed".

October 8, 1918.

✠ Cardinal Logue, Chairman.

✠ Robert Brown, Bishop of Cloyne, ⎫
✠ Denis Kelly, Bishop of Ross, ⎬ Secretaries.

MOST REVEREND AUSTIN DOWLING, D.D.
Second Archbishop of St. Paul
1919-1930

Chapter X

THE DOWLING DECADE
MOST REVEREND AUSTIN DOWLING, D. D.
SECOND ARCHBISHOP OF ST. PAUL
1868-1930

THE death of Archbishop Ireland was a distinct loss to the Church. He was one of the most prominent members of the hierarchy, a leader for more than twenty-five years and, with the possible exception of Cardinal Gibbons, the best known and most influential churchman not only in this country but throughout the world outside of Rome itself. He was the last of the great prelates of his generation and had few, if any, equals in the history of the Church in America. Men of his stature are not produced every generation nor century. By voice and pen he strove to promote, advance and defend the most sacred interests of the Church which he served with all the intensity of his deep and abiding faith in her divine origin and purpose.

His death left a void in the ranks of the hierarchy which it was difficult to fill. The question was who would take his place. There were the usual conjectures about his successor among clergy and laity. The merits and accomplishments of the prelates who might be considered for the position left vacant by his death were discussed pro and con, and not a few were mentioned who would seem to have a presumed title to his throne.

Towards the middle of January Bishop Dowling of Des Moines was a guest of his friend and Metropolitan, Archbishop Keane of Dubuque, and in the course of the visit, more for the purpose of keeping up conversation than in the hope of getting definite information, he asked the Archbishop who, in his judgment, was most likely to be appointed Archbishop of St. Paul.[1] The Archbishop replied that, as far as he knew, it would be Bishop So and So, mentioning the name of one whom he considered the logical choice. Nothing more was said about the matter. The next morning's mail brought to the desk of the Bishop of Des Moines a letter from Archbishop Bonzano, the Apostolic Delegate, notifying him that he, Austin Dowling, had been appointed successor to Archbishop

Ireland. Naturally he was somewhat surprised, not to say perturbed, for he was not the bishop mentioned in the conversation of the previous evening. With considerable misgivings he reluctantly accepted the promotion and began to make preparations for his departure from Iowa to Minnesota.

The Most Reverend Austin Dowling was born in New York City on April 6, 1868,[2] the son of Daniel Dowling and Mary Teresa Santry, recent immigrants from Ireland, and was baptized Daniel Austin on April 19, by the Reverend William Everett in the Church of the Nativity, the sponsors being Frederick and Mary Shepherd. He had an only sister who became a member of the Sisters of Mercy in Providence and outlived him twenty years.

With his family young Austin moved to Newport, Rhode Island, where he attended the Academy of the Sisters of Mercy before going to Manhattan College conducted by the Christian Brothers from which he was graduated in 1887, and ever afterwards gloried in the fact that he was a "Brothers' Boy". He had for fellow students the future Cardinals Hayes and Mundelein. After three years of a theological course in St. John's Seminary, Brighton, Mass., he was sent to the Catholic University in Washington to complete his studies and was ordained on June 24, 1891, by Bishop Harkins in the Providence Cathedral. He returned to the Catholic University for an additional year of post-graduate work for a Licentiate in Theology before engaging in parochial duties for a short time, after which he spent two and a half years as Professor of Church History in his Alma Mater, St. John's Seminary, whence he was recalled to edit the Providence Visitor from February, 1896, to October, 1898, and succeeded in placing it in the front rank as a Catholic weekly.

He was one of the leading workers in the New England Catholic Historical Society which was organized in Boston in 1900, and ceased to function in 1904; one of the five co-authors—four priests and a layman —of "The History of the Catholic Church in the New England States" published in Boston in 1899, and regarded as "one of the few worthy attempts at a provincial history of the Church in America".[3]

During his assignment at St. Joseph's Church (1896-1904) he spent part of a year in European travel and wrote the "History of the Diocese of Providence". A brief pastorate (1904-5) in St. Mary's Church, Warren, R. I., where he familiarized himself with the Polish language the better to minister to a portion of his flock, prepared him for the rectorship of the Cathedral of Sts. Peter and Paul where he remained from July 3, 1905, until his consecration as first Bishop of Des Moines. He accepted this promotion with reluctance as he thought he was being exiled to a western territory of which he had scarcely heard.[4] While pastor of the Providence Cathedral he had befriended Bishop Keane of Cheyenne,

Wyoming, who made more than one tour through the East collecting funds for his frontier diocese, and the friendship thus engendered endured during life, and the western prelate, then Archbishop of Dubuque, may have suggested Father Dowling's name when there was question of securing an energetic occupant for the new see of Des Moines erected in his Province.

The Bishop-elect was consecrated on April 25, 1912,[5] in the Cathedral of which he had been rector for seven years, by Bishop Harkins, assisted by Bishop Davis of Davenport and Bishop Walsh of Portland as co-consecrators. The Most Reverend Archbishop Keane of Dubuque preached the sermon.

Bishop of Des Moines

The Diocese of Des Moines to which he was assigned was erected on August 12, 1911, and comprised 12,466 square miles of territory taken from the Diocese of Davenport. It had a Catholic population of 25,000 ministered to by sixty-one priests in fifty-four parishes and twenty-five missions; three hospitals; three academies for girls; and sixteen parochial schools with an attendance of 1,579 pupils.[6]

Almost immediately after his consecration Bishop Dowling set out for the West and was enthroned in St. Ambrose Cathedral on the first of May by Archbishop Keane of Dubuque, after which the clergy pledged obedience to him as their Chief Pastor. At the conclusion of the ceremony the visiting prelates and the clergy were tendered a banquet in the Grant Club. In the evening there was a public reception in the Berchel Theatre at which Governor Carroll welcomed him on behalf of the state, Mayor Hanna for the city and J. H. Sullivan for the Catholic citizens. Monsignor Flavin, whom he appointed Vicar General, added a word of greeting and good wishes on behalf of his brethren of the clergy, after which the new Bishop acknowledged the compliments paid him and voiced his appreciation of the welcome extended him in an appropriate address which made an excellent impression on all who heard it.[7]

He began at once a visitation of the diocese and in a few months was familiar with every part of it and cognizant of its most pressing needs. He set to work to organize it with consummate skill and met the various demands on his time and energy with placid courage and ability, and discharged the duties of his high office with the "distinction and dispatch of a master mind". By his kindness and simplicity he won the hearts of priests and people.

For nearly seven years he labored with patient industry to build up the territory confided to his care and lay the foundation for future growth and development. His interest in education was shown by the founding of a Catholic college for the training of young men in an effort to develop an educated laity. He bought the Iowa Baptist College in September, 1917, for $170,000 and placed it in charge of diocesan priests.[8] It consisted of four substantial buildings on a ten-acre tract in the residential district of north Des Moines and was opened as a high school on September 11, of the following year with Very Reverend G. J. Toher as President, and an enrollment of 119 students of whom 12 were graduated the next June. It became a junior college in 1922 under Bishop Drumm. The name was changed from Des Moines Catholic College to Dowling College in 1935. The collegiate department was discontinued in 1941 when the students were called to the armed forces in the second world war. It is now known as Dowling High School under the presidency of Very Reverend T. J. Costin.

He also provided additional facilities for the education of young women. He founded new parishes, called to his aid religious orders to supplement the work of the diocesan clergy and local sisterhoods, fostered missionary endeavor at home and abroad, enhanced and defended the rights of the Catholic body and inspired confidence and prudent self-assertion in all.

He issued regulations for the teaching of Christian Doctrine in the diocese beginning with the year 1916-17.[9] In parishes with schools twenty-five minutes a day for five days a week had to be set apart for that work in all grades up to high school. During this period hymns might be sung and instructions given on religious topics other than the text of the catechism; but as a general rule the time was to be devoted to direct catechetical work.

In parishes without schools a minimum of forty hours of instruction in catechism during the school year was imperative. It was left to the pastor to determine the days on which the classes were to be held, and he was to do the work himself wherever possible. If lay teachers were employed the pastor had to train them first. In missions the teaching was to be done by lay teachers prepared by the pastor. The official text was the Christian Brothers series of graded catechisms.

Shortly after his arrival in Des Moines he acquired possession of the palatial mansion of the late Jefferson F. Polk, known as Herndon Hall, for his official residence.[10] It was of stone and brick construction, erected in 1893 at a cost of $175,000 in a park of five acres. It was appraised at $90,000. The owners had been made aware that the Bishop would not pay more than $20,000 for a residence and they offered it to him on condition that he donate that sum to the sisters in charge of Mercy Hospital to endow four beds in perpetuity for the sick poor of Des Moines.

In his official report[11] to the Holy See on the status of the Church in the Diocese of Des Moines, dated March 20, 1919, Bishop Dowling states that the people came to the locality as immigrants in 1845. The Catholics among them were few and found it difficult to fulfil their religious duties because of the dearth of priests who regarded it as exile or punishment to be sent to such remote localities. The Bishop lived in Dubuque and seldom visited the smaller communities owing to the distance. The land was fertile and well adapted to agricultural pursuits but nevertheless many Catholics sold their farms and moved to the cities or lost the faith if they did not become enemies of the Church. Even in 1919 the number of Catholics in the diocese was small and their influence almost negligible in civic affairs.

When the diocese was erected in 1912 there were only 25,000 Catholics in the territory, ministered to by 61 priests. In 1919 the number had grown to 35,000 with 80 priests. During these seven years four parochial schools had been built in the see-city and five in other parts of the diocese; four new parishes had been formed and fourteen churches erected at considerable expense; the Jefferson Polk home had been purchased as a residence for the Ordinary in 1912; and six years later a college on a commanding site and equipped with solid and new buildings, at a cost of $170,000, opened for the sound Catholic education of boys and the cultivation of vocations to the priesthood. All the parishes are rural except those in Des Moines (115,000) and Council Bluffs (35,000), the largest with a population of 2,000 and the smallest with one hundred and thirty souls. A religious community, the Passionists, have made a foundation in the diocese; and there are nine communities of women with a membership of one hundred and seventy-five. The Protestants are mostly Methodists, Campbellites, Lutherans and Baptists with a sprinkling of other denominations.

Second Archbishop of St. Paul

On January 14, 1919, he was notified privately by the Apostolic Delegate of his appointment as Archbishop of St. Paul and on January 31 the news was made public. Half the priests of the diocese accompanied him on the special train which carried him to St. Paul and he was met at Faribault, fifty miles from the city, by a large delegation of his future priests and many laymen. Here he made his first address in the diocese to the parochial school children, their teachers and the large group of the laity who had come to the station to greet him.

He was installed on March 25 on the historic throne so recently vacated by Archbishop Ireland and welcomed, on behalf of the clergy, religious and laity, by the Administrator, Monsignor Byrne, to whose greetings the new Archbishop responded in felicitous terms.

> I came here this morning to this high post of authority, of honor and of grave responsibility, by the command of that Supreme Pontiff who has the

solicitude of all the churches and the homage of all the faithful. My first thoughts, my first words, must be an expression of love and loyalty to the Holy See which, disregarding my unworthiness, has lifted me up to this exalted station and has confided to me the care and government of this great Archdiocese. I owe the best that is in me, however insufficient that may be, to the great work assigned me, and it shall be my endeavor, in the interpretation of the mind of the Holy Father, to hide my own short-comings and thus to make my ministrations a benediction to the diocese. And though I am meeting you for the first time I feel I may, without hesitation or reservation, add your suffrages to mine in the name of all—clergy and laity of the Archdiocese of St. Paul, which, with singular devotion, has always manifested the deepest veneration for and established the most intimate relations with the Holy See. Your faith is known abroad, splendid in its fervor, marvellous in its works, unswerving in its allegiance to the Head of the Church. If I sought for any confirmation of your loyalty, I could find it readily in the open-hearted generosity of your reception of me—the unknown, the unexpected, the undistinguished successor of the great Archbishop Ireland. I can bear you witness that from the first moment of my appointment, now seven weeks ago and more, to this there has been but one chorus of welcome, of submission and of allegiance—the more agreeable to me because I discovered in it nothing that was personal to me but only the expression of your faith and confidence in the great Mother Church of Christendom, the standard of our orthodoxy, the interpreter of our morality, the seat and source of ecclesiastical authority. Thus auspiciously do we begin in the ancient way the intimate relations of a Bishop with his flock; and the guarantee of the church's future in these parts is not the Church's possessions here, magnificent as they are, not the swarming throngs that fill our churches and by their generosity maintain them, but rather the purity and integrity of our faith whose symbol is our devotion to the Holy See.

That devotion has become a tradition in this great Archdiocese handed down from Bishop to Bishop—from Cretin to Grace, from Grace to the illustrious Ireland. Please God, in my hands, it shall grow no less but greater.

Your thoughts this morning as my thoughts turn to that majestic figure whom those who knew him can never forget, whose presence seems to hover about this wonderful building, the crown of his life, the child of his dreams, and now his fitting monument. No man can ever fill his place in this community, in this gateway of the Northwest. Few may aspire to fill it in the nation. You who have known him all your lives as Bishop and as citizen have probably stood too close to him to understand what he has meant to the country at large.

For us who saw him from afar he loomed large as the most significant figure in the Northwest. A great Bishop and first and last devoted to his spiritual work he became the interpreter of political democracy first to his flock and then to the world.[12]

He was assisted at the Pontifical Mass which followed by Monsignor Byrne as archpriest, Fathers Viñas, S. M., as deacon, Cieminski as subdeacon and Ziskovsky as master of ceremonies. Fathers Moynihan, President of the College of St. Thomas, and Schaefer, Rector of St. Paul

Seminary, attended the Archbishop at the throne. The music of the Mass was rendered by the seminarian choir under the direction of Father Missia.

After the installation a banquet was served in the Knights of Columbus hall under the direction of a committee of priests. The Very Reverend James M. Cleary was toastmaster and addresses were delivered by the suffragan Bishops, except Bishop O' Gorman who was ill, and whose place was taken by Father Desmond of Huron, South Dakota. Archbishop Messmer of Milwaukee spoke of the strong ties that unite the Provinces of Milwaukee and St. Paul. The function was brought to an appropriate close with a fine address by the new Metropolitan.

Reception and Functions

The souvenir menu[13] was a work of art in the form of a program-booklet designed by the noted architect, John T. Comes of Pittsburgh, who drew the plans for St. Luke's and St. Mark's churches in St. Paul. Under an elaborate cover design it recorded on its four inner pages the programs of the installation, the noonday banquet and the civic reception in the auditorium in the evening.

The citizens of St. Paul and vicinity turned out en masse for the public reception which was opened with the singing of America by the audience accompanied by the Cretin High School orchestra. The Honorable T. D. O'Brien presided and welcomed the new Archbishop, recalling the past glories of the archdiocese entrusted to his care. Addresses were given by Governor Burnquist in behalf of the State of Minnesota, Mayor Meyers of Minneapolis, Mayor Hodgson of St. Paul, Charles E. Vasaly, Chairman of the State Board of Control, and Senator Julius Coller of Shakopee. The final address was delivered by the new Archbishop who thanked the audience for the tribute paid him which he accepted not as due to himself but to the exalted office he held as the successor of the first Archbishop of St. Paul.

There were other receptions and functions, tributes from different organizations in the diocese, as well as a thousand and one demands on his time before he received the Pallium—postulated in Rome by his friend, Very Reverend J. A. Walsh, co-founder of Maryknoll—at another ceremony in the Cathedral on May 27, when he was invested with that symbol of his new dignity by Archbishop Keane of Dubuque, and his former Professor at the Catholic University, Bishop O'Gorman of Sioux Falls, preached the sermon.

The ceremony was graced by the presence in the sanctuary of Archbishops Keane of Dubuque and Mundelein of Chicago, all the suffragan bishops and six others from neighboring dioceses, Abbot Engel of Collegeville, ten Monsignors, hundreds of priests and sisters and a congregation that filled every inch of space in the vast Cathedral. At the end of the Pontifical Mass celebrated by Archbishop Keane the Pallium was conferred on the kneeling Metropolitan; and after the ceremony prelates and clergy repaired to the Aberdeen Hotel where dinner was served and addresses made by the three Archbishops.

One of the first acts of the new Archbishop was to appoint as Vicar General one of the oldest and most respected priests of the Archdiocese, the Right Reverend Monsignor John J. Slevin, pastor of the Church of the Immaculate Conception in Faribault, who served in that capacity with singular devotion and efficiency until his lamented death in 1924, when he was succeeded by the Chancellor, the Right Reverend Thomas A. Welch, whose tenure of office ended with his consecration as Bishop of Duluth on February 3, 1926.

A month before Archbishop Dowling's arrival, on February 20, 1919, the Minnesota Council of Catholic Women was formed at a convention held in St. Paul and attended by delegates from the Catholic women's societies of the state. Mrs. W. J. O'Toole of St. Paul was elected President and Mrs. L. S. Donaldson of Minneapolis Vice-President and committees were appointed to draft a constitution embodying its purpose and by-laws for its efficient functioning. The new Archbishop graciously granted his approval and blessing to the organization which has done yeoman service for the Church during the intervening years.

The Archbishop officiated at the dedication of the new chapel of the College of St. Thomas on May 29, and celebrated the first Pontifical Mass on its marble altar. The festive sermon was preached by Bishop Lawler of Lead, South Dakota. The chapel was designed by E. L. Masqueray, architect of the new Cathedral, and built under the direction of Archbishop Ireland at a cost of about $80,000, provided by the Most Reverend Archbishop himself, to give the institution a house of worship large enough to accommodate the student body and ample enough in its sanctuary for the carrying out of the liturgical ceremonies in an impressive manner.

The summer months were spent on confirmation tours, in visitations and conferences to enable him to ascertain the condition of the Archdiocese and plan future development. He was a keen observer and was soon quite familiar with the situation and ready to build on the foundation laid by his predecessors.

National Catholic Welfare Conference

In the latter part of September the first annual meeting of the American Hierarchy was held at the Catholic University in Washington. Ninety-three Archbishops and Bishops attended, at their head, Cardinal Gibbons, sole survivor of the prelates present at the Third Plenary Council of Baltimore in 1884, at whose suggestion they met in the National Capital. A committee on Catholic Affairs and Interests had been appointed at the meeting of seventy-seven bishops held the previous February, in connection with the celebration of the Golden Jubilee of His Eminence, to suggest ways and means of capitalizing on the united spirit and effort of Catholics during the first world war, and its report was on the agenda for the September meeting. The result of the deliberations was the formation of the National Catholic Welfare Council[14] to take the place of the National Catholic War Council, organized in 1917, which had supervised and unified Catholic patriotic activities during the war years. It was to be a voluntary association of the members of the hierarchy, without mandatory or legislative power, to take common counsel on matters of general import for the welfare of the Church in the United States, and, through a common spirit of cooperation, serve and promote the cause of Catholic unity. It had for objective to further the religious and social welfare of the Church in America; to aid the Catholic press; to promote Catholic publicity; and to assist home and foreign mission work. In a word, its sole purpose was to provide regularly and efficiently for all the interests of the Church in the United States.

An Administrative Board of seven prelates, headed by Archbishop Hanna of San Francisco, was elected to prepare a program of future activity. The other members were Archbishops Dougherty of Philadelphia and Dowling of St. Paul, Bishops Muldoon of Rockford, Russell of Charleston, Canevan of Pittsburgh, and Schrembs of Toledo. Five departments were organized, namely, Education, Social Work, Press and Literature, Lay Societies, and Home and Foreign Missions. Archbishop Dowling was elected Treasurer of the parent body and Chairman of the Department of Education, positions which he filled efficiently and continuously for nearly ten years until ill-health forced his resignation. He played a prominent role not only in the organization of the Council but in the conduct of its affairs and in October, 1928, published an article in the American Ecclesiastical Review in which he described the formation, aim and purpose of the Council, as it was called until 1923, when it was changed to Conference in deference to the wishes of some of the bishops and at the suggestion of the Roman authorities.

In January, 1923, Archbishop Christie of Oregon City (now, Portland) appealed to the N. C. W. C. for assistance in defending the parochial schools of Oregon against the attacks of bigoted opponents. As Chairman of the Education Department Archbishop Dowling planned much of the strategy employed in the long fight against the iniquitous law placed on the statute books of that state by a vote of 115,506 to 103,685 during a wave of bigotry fomented by the Ku Klux Klan, and which threatened not only all private and especially Catholic schools in Oregon, but jeopardized the existence and liberty of all Catholic schools in the United States. It made guilty of a misdemeanor any parent who failed to send his child, between the ages of eight and sixteen, to a public school. "It was grounded on a philosophy of education which held that the child belonged first to the state even before he belonged to his parents.[15]

To Archbishop Dowling fell the task of arranging for the conduct of the case, its financing and the engaging and direction of counsel. The Supreme Court of the United States declared the law unconstitutional in June, 1925. From the viewpoint of the Catholic Church it was one of the most important litigations in her history and the outcome was a triumph for the principle of freedom in education and religion.

Under the direction of its Chairman the Department of Education was the most vigorous opponent of the various schemes for the federalization of education submitted to Congress; and it gave genuine aid to Catholic schools and colleges as a clearing-house for technical information of all kinds.

Towards the close of his life Archbishop Dowling set forth the objectives of the Department of Education over which he presided for a decade of years.

> The Catholic school represents one of the major interests of the Church in America. Over 2,500,000 children are now attending these schools, which range from the primary grades to the university. The Department of Education of the National Catholic Welfare Conference was organized to meet the needs of this school system for advice and assistance, which could be supplied adequately only by a well-staffed and scientifically conducted central clearing-house of educational information. It functions through a Bureau of Education which gathers statistical data, makes surveys, places teachers and professors, and stimulates knowledge of and interest in the progress of the Catholic school. It acts, likewise, as a connecting-link between the Catholic school system and national organizations of an educational character and the federal Bureau of Education. Moreover, since the private school is subjected to attacks on many sides, the Bureau keeps in close touch with educational legislation, State and Federal, and organizes a defense of the rights of the religious school whenever such rights are likely to be jeopardized by unfriendly legislation. The Bureau of Education of the National Catholic Welfare Conference is a purely advisory body, exercising no control over the Catholic system, which is governed locally. Its advice is gratuitous, and the best obtainable, due to the simple fact that its executive committee is made up of the leading Catholic educators in the United States, who serve without pay or expense, in the sole interest of better Catholic schools.[16]

When Archbishop Dowling came to St. Paul there were 93 parochial schools in operation in the diocese. One of his first moves was to provide for their supervision, coordination and standardization by appointing the Reverend James A. Byrnes, of the St. Paul Seminary faculty, Superintendent of the Bureau of Education under which the elementary and the high schools have since functioned and developed.

Catholic Charities Organized

With the advent of Archbishop Dowling the work of charity in the diocese was systematized by the incorporation of bureaus in each of the Twin Cities.

As a result of a meeting of priests and laymen in Minneapolis the Catholic Central Bureau came into existence in December, 1919, with Reverend W. P. Driscoll, City Missionary since 1918, as Director, who added a social worker from Chicago to the staff.[17] In 1920 the Bureau was licensed by the State Board of Control to make permanent placement of children in homes for adoption; and the next year it opened the Economy Shop on East Hennepin Avenue to help the poor and needy. In 1922 it assumed responsibility for the intake and discharge of unwed mothers at the Catholic Infant Home and also of all children of Hennepin County entering the Catholic Boys Home in Minneapolis, the Catholic girls' and St. Joseph's Orphanages in St. Paul. In the same year it became a participating agency of the Community Chest. In 1936 the name was changed to the Catholic Welfare Association and Father Driscoll continued to direct its activities until 1938, when he was transferred from the parish of the Holy Family in St. Louis Park, of which he had been pastor since 1925, to the new parish of Christ the King, and was succeeded by Reverend T. F. Meagher under whose direction the staff of thirty social workers has handled 4671 children, 2350 unmarried mothers, 5000 delinquents, and placed 1200 children in foster homes.[18] The Director spends the forenoon of every day in the Court House looking after delinquent boys and girls and arranging for their probation. He has the confidence of the judges and their cooperation in rescuing youths of both sexes from environments that would lead them from the path of rectitude. Funds for the work are provided not only by the Community Chest but by state, county and city welfare agencies as well as by interested individuals and firms, members of the Catholic Charities Guild and friends who organize and promote sporting events.

The Bureau of Catholic Charities in St. Paul was incorporated on December 17, 1920, with the Reverend J. F. Doherty in charge.[19] Its purpose is to centralize and coordinate all Catholic charities in St. Paul and Ramsey County, find homes for the adoption of orphans, homeless, abandoned, neglected and dependent children and act as their legal guardian. Its office is in the Amherst H. Wilder Charity building which furnishes heat, light, janitor service and maintenance free to charitable organizations. It has a staff of twenty-nine social workers engaged in the preservation, spiritual and physical rehabilitation of family life and the care of dependent children. Its operating budget for 1950 in these departments was $175,471.83 of which all but $36,011.83 was allocated by the Community Chest. The lamented death of the first Director in November,

1928, was followed by the appointment of his brother, Reverend R. W. Doherty, to the position which he has filled most acceptably since then. The five rooms occupied by the Bureau in 1930 have expanded to twenty-two in 1950 and the agency staff includes, besides the Director, three case supervisors, seventeen case workers and a clerical staff of eight. It holds membership in the National Conference of Catholic Charities, the Minnesota State Conference of Social Welfare, and the Child Welfare League of America. In 1950 the family department had a case load of 907 families of whom 632 were closed out during the year, leaving 275 families carried over into 1951. In the child welfare department 741 children received care and supervision during 1950 and 512 were on the list at the beginning of the next year.

Archbishop Ireland Educational Fund

At the first anniversary requiem for his predecessor at which Archbishop Dowling officiated and preached, he called attention to the propriety of commemorating the memory and achievements of this distinguished churchman in some fitting way. He said many suggestions had been offered, among them one to erect a life-sized statue on a pedestal in front of the Cathedral. He made reference to the splendid work done by the late Archbishop in providing educational facilities for the youth of the Archdiocese, and suggested that an attempt be made to develop, coordinate and consolidate this educational system to provide for greater efficiency, by erecting a Preparatory Seminary for aspirants to the priesthood, a Normal School for the training of the sister teachers of all the communities engaged in school work in the diocese, high schools at strategic points for the graduates of the parochial schools and others who may wish to patronize them, a system of complete supervision for all educational institutions, and a permanent fund, the income from which would care for the up-building of all our educational institutions. He said the parish priests had already been consulted and were enthusiastic about the project. In initiating the campaign the Archbishop commented on the substantial support already given by the clergy and said that he would soon make an appeal to the people. He set forth the purpose he had in view, namely,

> to defend christian education in this Archdiocese by bringing together the various unrelated units of our existing educational work and building them up into an organism all christian and Catholic in its inspiration and its aim. To do so on a scale equal to our needs and the cause we design thus to establish, we need first of all men and women of consecrated lives, of trained minds, of supple character, ready to adjust their plans to the exigencies of our time and place. We need the laity both men and women—the more cultured they are the more useful they will be—to counsel with us, to take their part in teaching, but above all to be the interpreters

of our endeavors to a world which is frequently hostile to us because it usually misunderstands us. Lastly we need money and if we are successful in making our own people comprehend what christian education may and should achieve, we shall need a great deal of money but only on condition that there is a great deal of interest.[20]

The first step towards the realization of this ambitious program was taken in July, 1920, when the Reverend Thomas A. Welch, Diocesan Chancellor, was placed in charge of it. The preliminary work involved the taking up of an accurate census in all the parishes and the appointment of committees of priests to plan and supervise the details of the campaign. The first public meeting was held in the College of St. Thomas on September 7 when several hundred guests were entertained at dinner by the Most Reverend Archbishop. Each parish was represented by the pastor and two laymen.

The Archbishop presided and explained the project and said that the goal set for the campaign was $5,000,000 for the upbuilding and strengthening of the educational forces of the Archdiocese. It would be known as the Archbishop Ireland Eduational Fund. Other speakers on the program were Pierce Butler, Edward Foley, Julius Coller, Thomas D. O'Brien and Neil Cronin. It was announced that the priests of the Archdiocese had already contributed $170,000.

What He Have — What We Need

As a preparation for the campaign five leaflets[21] were distributed showing "What we have—What we need" in the way of parochial, high and normal schools, colleges and seminaries. In the respective leaflets the present status and future requirements of our diocesan system were clearly stated.

The Archdiocese has 96 parochial schools—21 in St. Paul, 14 in Minneapolis and 61 in the country—with an enrollment of 23,000—8,000 in St. Paul, 7,000 in Minneapolis and 8,000 in the country—about one-half the number of Catholic children who should be in parish schools. These schools represent an investment of $3,000,000 and are staffed by 550 religious teachers. It needs more parochial schools to provide adequate and uninterrupted religious training for the fifty percent of Catholic children in public schools, and a capital fund of $150,000 for organization, supervision, uniform text books and standards. The need was for Catholic rather than parochial schools.

The Archdiocese has one parish high school for girls in the Twin Cities and 6 for boys and girls in the country with an enrollment of 432. It has 7 "pay" high schools in the Twin Cities, 3 for boys and 4 for girls, with an enrollment of 1299 boys and 1075 girls. It needs many free high schools in the cities and the rural districts to place the advantages of Catholic higher education within easy reach of every graduate of a diocesan grade school, of which there will be more than 2,000 in June, 1921.

The Archdiocese has no normal school to take over from the religious communities the burden and expense of educating their subjects for school work. Very often they have to attend state high schools and the salary they receive does not provide for pedagogical training. Most of the 550 teachers have received normal training and some of them are certified. It needs a normal school under diocesan supervision, with adequate equipment, a competent staff and sufficiently high standards to receive recognition from the proper authorities, where the sisters may be trained at a minimum of cost to their communities for the work they are to do in the diocese. This will require $400,000 even if it is only a day school, for there must be a fund to take care of any deficit.

The Archdiocese has two colleges—St. Thomas and St. Catherine's— the former with 8 buildings, equipment and a campus of 55 acres valued at over one million dollars; the latter with 5 buildings, equipment and property appraised at $655,250. The former has a faculty of 49 professors and an enrollment of 1052; the latter is staffed by 35 sisters and has 370 students in attendance, all that can be accommodated under existing conditions. Both institutions need additional buildings, better equipment and larger endowments. The Rockefeller Foundation for the Advancement of Education has promised St. Catherine's $100,000 on condition that it raise $200,000 in the Archdiocese.

The Archdiocese has a provincial seminary, dedicated to St. Paul, which cost it nothing because it was the gift of Mr. Hill, with 8 buildings, 34 acres of ground and a total valuation of $600,000, with an attendance of 182 students, of whom 50 are studying for the Diocese of St. Paul compared with 56 twenty-five years ago. It needs more vocations to provide 15 or 20 priests each year for St. Paul and for that it must have a preparatory seminary, a boarding school, to strengthen vocations and train aspirants for the priesthood. A substantial endowment is necessary as a majority of the students come from the ranks of the poor who can give very little financial assistance. Such an endowment will require 85 burses or scholarships of $6,000 each, to provide the minimum of $500,000 required to meet the anticipated deficit of about $25,000 annually.

The proposed educational fund of $5,000,000 will provide more parochial schools and additional equipment for existing schools: centralized high schools in various sections of the Archdiocese; a normal school for the training of sisters; new buildings and equipment for the colleges of St. Thomas and St. Catherine; a preparatory seminary for young men studying for the priesthood; complete supervision for all educational institutions; and a permanent fund, the income from which will care for their most pressing needs.

In regard to St. Thomas College it was pointed out that, until 1900, it had but a single building, costing $65,000, and 99 students, with 15 professors, whereas it has now 8 buildings worth $1,000,000, an enrollment of 1,052 and a teaching staff of 49. Twenty-five years ago the revenue was $19,381 and the expenditure $19,132, whereas the last year's receipts amounted to $242,053 and the disbursements to $240,158.

St. Catherine's College had 6 enrolled students in 1905 while its present student body numbers 370, and the institution represents a conservative value of $650,000. It has a faculty of 18 M. A.'s, 5 Ph. D's, and 8 Licentiates in Music.

Results of the Campaign

The plan of campaign as outlined was a simple one but required no inconsiderable amount of detailed planning and close supervision to make it a success. The Archdiocese was divided into five districts in which the campaign would begin on five consecutive Sundays starting on October 24. On the first two Sundays in each parish priests would explain the general plan of campaign and dwell on the purpose for which the funds were to be used and make an appeal for generous contributions. The priest who preached on the third Sunday would do the actual soliciting in the parish with the cooperation of the pastor. The program was also explained in a letter to the clergy. All pledges were to be paid within five years.

The clergy were the first to respond. As early as May, 1920, the Archbishop stated that one hundred and sixty-four priests had pledged $130,000; thirty-four had paid in full and ten had given $1,000 each. In order not to work a hardship on the junior clergy he agreed to credit all payment on their seminary indebtedness to the educational fund, provided they were received before January 1, 1921. Many took advantage of the concession. On January 31, 1922, 267 priests had pledged $207,287.63 and paid $148,987.63.[22] Of these 95 contributed $120,500 in sums ranging from $1,000 to $6,000 each. The Archbishop gave $10,000.

Any person or parish contributing the sum of $6,000 would be credited with a burse for the education of a candidate for the priesthood in the projected preparatory seminary. The parish of St. Canice, Kilkenny, was the first to subscribe such a burse in addition to the $27,000 pledged to the general fund.

During the summer of 1923 seminarians called upon delinquent subscribers in an effort to clean up outstanding balances.

At the end of the five-year period, in September, 1925, a report from the Chancery Office showed that the sum of $4,392,872.50 had been pledged by 45,551 persons of whom 21,898 had made no payments. Unpaid pledges amounted to $1,700,000. As a result of an effort made to collect some of the delinquent pledges, the number was reduced before the end of the year to 5,375 in St. Paul; 6,303 in Minneapolis; and 9,042 in the country. The individual pledges averaged nearly $100.00. No report has ever been made of the actual amount of cash paid into the Archbishop Ireland Educational Fund nor of the actual disbursements. As far as known the Fund earmarked $1,280,000 for the construction and partial endowment of the Preparatory Seminary known as Nazareth Hall; allotted $200,000 to the endowment fund of the College of St. Catherine which had called off its campaign for that purpose in deference to the educational program of the Archdiocese; gave $150,000 to St. Thomas College to secure the bequest of $100,000 made by Timothy Foley of St. Paul, who died on May 25, 1920, for the erection of a preparatory seminary on the grounds of that institution, a condition that had to be complied with in three years under pain of forfeiture; subsidized the De La Salle School building program in Minneapolis to the amount of $200,000, and made a similar donation to Cretin High School in St. Paul, both of which are diocesan properties.

Nazareth Hall, planned in 1921, was erected on the shore of Lake Johanna, outside the corporate limits of the Twin Cities, on a plot of ground consisting of ninety acres, forty of which were bought in 1866 for $800 by Bishop Grace who recorded on the deed that "this property will at some time be used for a diocesan institution". It is really a group of six buildings in one.[23] The main structure has a frontage of 422 feet, with an imposing square tower 105 feet high. The north wing has a depth of 277 feet. The chapel lined with Numidian marble is entered from the tower and has a seating capacity of 300, with a crypt underneath for daily Masses. The building has accommodations for over 200 students and there are adequate grounds for outdoor sports.

It was opened for the reception of students on September 12, 1923, when it was dedicated by the Archbishop in presence of a large group of priests. At the dinner he was presented with a check for $13,000 to defray the cost of the main altar which, together with the chapel, was consecrated by him on September 8, 1924.

Nazareth Hall was the apple of his eye and woe betide the priest or layman who dared to utter an uncomplimentary syllable about the institution, its architecture, location, purpose, faculty or product. Every other institution in the diocese was a step-child, seldom visited except officially. At Nazareth Hall a suite of well-furnished rooms was set apart for him to which he retired from time to time to rest and recuperate and breathe the invigorating suburban air.

School of Social Studies

Shortly after his arrival in St. Paul Archbishop Dowling asked the N. C. W. C. to send one of its field agents to organize an Archdiocesan Council of Catholic Men. P. W. O'Grady came as the official representative and addressed meeting of the clergy and laity, at which the Archbishop presided, to acquaint them with the purpose of the organization and its method of functioning. As a result the Twin Cities Council of Catholic Men was formed with units in St. Paul and Minneapolis, each with its own staff of officers. On January 4, 1922, Michael B. Hurley of Pine City was elected President of the St. Paul Council; Carl Klaproth, Vice-President; Frank Rosenthal, Financial Secretary; and Frank Mosbrugger, Treasurer, who soon gave place to C. E. Robertson. The Minneapolis Council, on January 6, elected E. J. Loring, President; Jacob Kunz, Vice-President; Henry Riley, Financial Secretary; and Ben Brombach, Treasurer. The Reverend Thomas A. Welch, Chancellor, was appointed the Archbishop's representative for St. Paul; and Reverend James M. Reardon, pastor of the then Pro-Cathedral of St. Mary, for Minneapolis. P. W. O'Grady was named Executive Secretary, and addressed meetings in several parishes in the interests of the Council.

When the Twin Cities Council was ready to function a request was sent to the national headquarters for a program, but none was forthcoming and it was told to devise its own. The result of its deliberation and planning was a course of lectures and studies so comprehensive that it was adopted by the parent organization and became known as "The Twin Cities Plan".[24] Lectures were delivered by priests and laymen prominent in the religious and civic life of the community, and the same series was given in each of the cities except in the case of the Archbishop who, to show his interest in the movement, delivered twelve lectures on the "High Points of Church History" in the College of St. Thomas midway between the two cities and equally accessible to both. These lectures were given between January and April, 1922, and attracted an average audience of seven hundred. They were informal or family talks delivered in a conversational tone and taken down by a stenographer and transcribed for all who desired copies.

The other lectures were given in the Assumption and in St. Mark's school halls in St. Paul, and in the Pro-Cathedral school auditorium in Minneapolis. During 1922-23 sixteen lectures[25] were delivered on such widely different subjects as "The Infallible Church", "The Boy Problem and Its Solution", "Censorship and Free Press", "The Confessional", "The Church and Labor", "The Massacre of St. Bartholomew's Day", "The Spanish Inquisition", "The Catholic Church and Miracles", "Organic Transformism", "Ludwig Windthorst", "The Church and Science", and "William Emmanuel Ketteler", by the Reverends C. F. Cremin, R. E.

Nolan, J. C. Harrington, J. T. Blankert, J. Seliskar and others of equal repute for scholarship.

Those single lectures were fitted into a framework of instructive courses[26] on "Popular Apologetics" by the Reverend Humphrey Moynihan; "Economics" by Reverend M. McRaith; "Elements of Christian Philosophy" and "Popular Psychology" by Reverend J. Seliskar; "Philosophy of Social Life" by Reverend J. A. Schabert; "Civics" by Honorable Judge Oscar Hallam; "Public Speaking" by Professor Rarig of the University of Minnesota; "Sacred Scripture" by Reverend A. Ziskovsky; and "Ancient Rome" by Reverend P. F. O'Brien. A small entrance fee was asked and a minimum price placed on printed or mimeographed copies of the lectures; and meetings were held two or three evenings each week while the school was in session.

The promoters were convinced that the Twin Cities School of Social Studies, as it was called, was filling a long-felt want in Catholic educational work by presenting the truths of faith to the laity in a pleasing and instructive manner; but at no time was the attendance commensurate with the effort put forth by the lecturers and the sponsors. Perhaps an exception should be made for the course given by the Most Reverend Archbishop.

In the early months of 1923, between January 8 and April 2, the Archbishop gave a very interesting course of twelve lectures on "The Reformation in England" in the St. Thomas College auditorium, and drew large audiences because he was recognized as an authority on that subject. An additional lecture was given on "The Church in America". The lectures were well received by all who had the privilege of hearing them. The officers made every effort to enkindle enthusiasm for the work of the school and to maintain its popular appeal. Weekly luncheon meetings were instituted and were well attended as was the first annual dinner in the Commodore Hotel, St. Paul, on May 5, 1923, at which the Archbishop presided. In his address he emphasized the importance of the work done by the school and urged the members to maintain their zeal for it. It was decided to have a fall term from September 9 to December 23, and a winter term from January 6 to April 20. Similar courses were pledged and all lectures were to be submitted in manuscript for publication and distribution.

Admiral Benson's Visit

One of the most important features of the first year's activity was the sponsoring of a lecture[27] on Sunday afternoon, November 12, 1922, in the St. Paul Auditorium, by Admiral William S. Benson, supreme head of the Navy during the first World War and Chief of Naval Operations, as well as President of the National Council of Catholic Men. He was introduced by the Archbishop and made a stirring appeal before a capacity audience for nation-wide Catholic Action to counteract the evil tendencies and combat the aberrations of modern American life. He praised the National Council of Catholic Men as an organization for which there was crying need, whose objectives could be attained only through its subordinate societies and the alertness and intellectual acumen of their individual members. After the meeting an informal testimonial dinner was given in the Athletic Club attended by four hundred guests. The musical program was rendered by a chorus of five hundred voices from the parochial schools. Mr. Hurley was toastmaster and addresses were given by Archbishop Dowling and Professor Jamieson, State Deputy of the Knights of Columbus, to which Admiral Benson responded. The Hennepin-Minneapolis Council of the Knights of Columbus held a reception for him the next day at which he delivered a similar address.

At the close of his address at the dinner for the Admiral Archbishop Dowling asked the men, "What are you going to do about it"? The answer was given shortly afterwards when the executives of the Twin Cities Council met in Minneapolis, under the Chairmanship of E. J. Loring, and decided to resume the program of the School of Social Studies which had been interrupted by the misunderstanding about the meaning and scope of the sponsoring organization, the National Catholic Welfare Council.[28] The implications of the word "Council" caused some prelates in the United States to fear that the organization intended to legislate for the Church in America as a General Council does for the Church Universal, which, however, was far from the original intention. A committee consisting of Archbishop Moeller of Cincinnati and Bishop Schrembs of Cleveland hastened to Rome and gave definite pledges and assurances to the Holy See, and it was finally agreed that the word "Conference" be substituted for "Council". Pope Pius XI expressed the wish that there be no change in the program. Under these circumstances the work of the School of Social Studies was resumed and plans made for lecture courses extending over twenty weeks.

A New York lawyer wrote the Director on December 15, 1923, that he took the material for an address before a large audience from the printed lectures of the School of Social Studies, and was given an ovation such as he had never before received. This was encouraging and indicative of the widening influence of the school through the diffusion of its booklets.

In a letter published in The Catholic Bulletin, September 15, 1923, the Archbishop declared that the School of Social Studies was "an earnest attempt to develop a spirit of enquiry and of study among Catholic men and women". It was still frankly an experiment, but proposed to increase the number of its courses and the length of its sessions. "None will watch the experiment with more sympathetic interest or eager hopes than I and I wish its sincere supporters and patrons every success".

He promised to give a series of lectures on "The Elizabethan Era of the English Reformation" in the early months of 1924, but was unable to do so because of his Ad Limina visit to Rome where he was received in private audience[29] by the Pope on January 31. On the feast of the Conversion of St. Paul he preached in the Church of Santa Susanna at the Mass celebrated by Cardinal Georgi, and returned to St. Paul about the first of April.

The School of Social Studies continued to function with more or less success for several years but finally went out of existence, leaving the Minneapolis Director and the Executive Secretary responsible for the indebtedness incurred by the printing of the lectures and other incidental expenses. In an effort to meet these obligations it was decided to organize a pilgrimage to Ste. Anne de Beaupre, in the Province of Quebec, and in the latter part of June, 1924, pilgrims from all parts of the Northwest, to the number of two hundred and thirty, set out for the shrine and were the recipients of so many extraordinary favors that it was decided to make the pilgrimage an annual event as it has been for more than a quarter of a century. The headquarters of the movement, known as the Hennepin Travel Bureau, was in Minneapolis until 1942, and every year a group of the clients of good Ste. Anne journeyed to her favorite shrine. It was not long before visits to other shrines in Canada and elsewhere were added to the itinerary and side trips made to Cap de la Madeleine, St. Joseph's Oratory in Montreal, Kateri Tekakwitha's shrine at Caughnawaga, the North American Martyrs' shrines at Midland, Ontario, and Auriesville, New York, near the scene of Father Jogues martyrdom. Since the central office was moved to Chicago in 1942, the number of annual pilgrimages has increased and the shrine of Our Lady of Guadaloupe in Mexico City and shrines on the Pacific Coast, as well as Fatima, Lourdes and Rome for the Holy Year of 1950, were added and the organization elevated to the rank of a Confraternity affiliated with the mother shrine of Ste. Anne, and placed under the patronage of distinguished members of the hierarchy in Canada and the United States. For several years a special pilgrimage for the sick and handicapped has been a feature of the work.

On March 2, 1923, Father Cullen, President of the College of St. Thomas, wrote a letter[30] to Archbishop Dowling requesting the Board of Trustees of the College to authorize the establishment of a Law School for students who wished to become lawyers, and who, in that case, would remain at the College for the full course in the liberal arts and a grounding in Catholic Philosophy while pursuing the prescribed studies for a degree in law. He informed the Archbishop that local judges and attorneys were enthusiastic about the proposal.

He estimated the annual cost of such a course at $6,550, made up of $1,000 salary for a secretary, $2,700 for lecturers' fees, $2,500 for a suitable library, $250 for printing and stationery, and $100 for incidentals. The cost would be met by an attendance of sixty students paying a tuition fee of $100 and $10 for registration. He asked permission to organize the school and appoint a dean and a secretary.

The Most Reverend Archbishop and the Board graciously granted the request and the school began to function with classes in the afternoon from three-thirty to six-thirty. The Honorable T. D. O'Brien of St. Paul was appointed Dean and Francis D. Butler of the firm of Doherty, Rumble, Bunn and Butler of St. Paul, Secretary. In 1925, he was succeeded by Owen P. McElmeel who took over the administrative work of the school. The lecturers were attorneys of repute from St. Paul and Minneapolis. Mr. McElmeel prepared a petition to the Supreme Court asking accreditation as a full-time law school with the required three instructors—G. W. C. Ross, T. L. O'Hearn and himself—on a full-time basis, which was granted. For several years the school maintained a high standard of scholarship and efficiency, as evidenced by the success of its graduates in the Minnesota State Bar examinations to which they were admitted on a parity with the graduates of the University of Minnesota Law School. The attendance did not exceed thirty-five or forty at any time. With the transfer of the College to the Holy Cross Congregation in 1928, Professor Ross, who had succeeded Judge O'Brien as Dean in 1926, was given full charge of the school whose administration became progressively difficult during the depression years until it was discontinued in 1933.[31]

On July 27 of that year the Board of Trustees of the College appointed one of their number to confer with Dean Frazer of the University of Minnesota regarding the treatment to be accorded former students of the St. Thomas Law School, and he was assured, as he reported at the meeting on August 7, that every consideration would be shown them and that the University "would accept the report of Mr. Ross of the Faculty of St. Thomas in their regard"[32].

While Archbishop Dowling was in Rome in 1924, it was announced by the Chancery Office that the six members of the Board of Consultors and the Chancellor of the diocese had been made Domestic Prelates of His Holiness at his request. The Consultors thus honored were the Right Reverend Monsignors Moynihan, Byrne, Cleary, O'Neil, Jung and Ogulin, and the Chancellor was Monsignor Welch. The Papal Rescripts were issued on February 5. In due time all were formally invested with the purple robes of the new dignity.

Official Report on Catholic Schools

In the meantime the office of the Superintendent of Catholic Education, created in the fall of 1919 with the appointment of Reverend James A. Byrnes of the St. Paul Seminary faculty, had been opened.[33] To prepare himself for the work Father Byrnes spent several months in the East, where he consulted Dr. Shields of the Catholic University at Washington, and other recognized leaders in pedagogical work, visited different dioceses to study the organization and program of their educational units, and returned to familiarize himself with conditions in the Archdiocese. When the Archbishop Ireland Educational Fund was established a sum of money was set apart to defray the expense of the office without taxing the schools for its support.

The official report[34] for 1920-1921, a lengthy, comprehensive and scholarly review and exposition of the Catholic educational system in the Archdiocese, showed that there were 28,226 pupils under instruction in 142 parochial and private schools, grade, high and commercial. Of these 13,926 were boys and 14,300 girls. Twenty-one parochial schools in St. Paul had an enrollment of 11,547; eleven in Minneapolis, 7,081; and in the country parishes, 9,598. Fourteen sisterhoods taught 27,013; the Christian Brothers, 663; and 550 were in attendance at St. Thomas Academy.

At the beginning of the school year in September, 1921, the Sisters of St. Joseph had under their charge 11,326 children; the School Sisters of Notre Dame, 5,506; the Sisters of St. Benedict (St. Joseph, Minnesota), 2,870; the Dominican Sisters (Sinsinawa, Wisconsin), 1,727; the Sisters of Christian Charity, 1,354; the Sisters of St. Francis (Rochester, Minnesita), 798; the Franciscan Sisters (Milwaukee, Wisconsin), 876; the Franciscan Sisters (Toledo, Ohio), 1,360; the Poor Handmaids of Jesus, 91; the Felician Sisters, 773; the Benedictine Sisters (Duluth, Minnesota), 50; the Visitation Sisters, 128; the Ursuline Sisters, 76; the Sisters of the Good Shepherd, 78; the Christian Brothers, 663; and the faculty of St. Thomas Academy, 550, a total of 28,226.

The Catholic school enrollment accounted for little more than half the Catholic children of school age in the diocese, for 25,000 were in public schools because of lack of room and dearth of teachers in Catholic schools.

The Superintendent proposed the establishment of a Normal School to train teachers in the philosophy and history of education, to give them a foundation of Catholic pedagogical principles as a background for evaluating the importance of the educational tendencies of the day. Trained diocesan priests were needed to foster the academic life of the school, and community supervisiors and free principals to direct and oversee the work of teachers and pupils.

To provide adequate medical service he recommended the employment of five trained nurses for the schools in St. Paul and three for those in Minneapolis. He also asked for the adoption of an approved list of text books with a certain amount of latitude for the teaching staff in the choice of them. Secondary education facilities in the diocese were quite inadequate as there was a great lack of high schools.

On July 23, 1922, the Archbishop officiated at the laying of the corner stone of the new De La Salle High School in Minneapolis, which cost $250,000, to modernize and bring up to date the facilities for training the graduates of parish schools under the Christian Brothers. The completed structure was dedicated[35] on March 11, 1923. The old school founded in 1900, following an abortive attempt made in 1889-91 to open a school for boys in the Immaculate Conception parish, had become outmoded and a more commodious and modern one was imperative if it would continue to make progress. As already stated the Archbishop Ireland Educational Fund gave $200,000 to the project. It was not till 1949, under the direction of Archbishop Murray, that work on a new residence and chapel for the Brothers was undertaken and a building costing $300,000 made possible by funds provided by the parishes in Minneapolis. The new home was dedicated on February 26, 1951, by Auxiliary Bishop Byrne. On the two previous days it had been thrown open to the public for inspection.

Educational Congress and Yearly Mass

To focus attention on the parochial schools and their work the Archbishop asked the Superintendent of Education to hold an educational congress[36] in the College of St. Thomas, featuring an exhibition of the handiwork of the pupils of grade and high schools. It was held on Saturday and Sunday, June 10 and 11, 1922. Fifty display booths lined the walls of the armory which was tastefully decorated for the occasion, and distinguished priests and laymen were invited to address large audiences at the various sessions. It opened on Saturday forenoon with a meeting at which the Very Reverend Thomas E. Cullen, President of the College, presided and introduced Dr. F. E. Harrington, Health Commissioner of Minneapolis, who stressed the necessity of physical culture for school children. He was followed by the Archbishop who dwelt on the need of religious training and emphasized the inalienable right of the Church to provide schools for her children and thus surround them with the proper Christian influences. A choir of 500 voices provided entertainment at the different sessions.

In the afternoon there was a championship baseball game between the winners in the parochial tournaments in the Twin Cities, namely, St.

Vincent's for St. Paul and Holy Cross for Minneapolis. The game was witnessed by an immense crowd, and St. Vincent's won by a score of 15 to 0. The Twin Cities parochial teams marched around the stadium led by the Cretin High School band after which the Archbishop presented the trophies to the champions and to the winners of the different divisions in both cities.

On Sunday Pontifical Mass was celebrated by the Archbishop at ten o'clock with Very Reverend James C. Byrne as archpriest, Reverends W. Busch and L. Kucera as deacons of honor, J. Doherty and R. E. Nolan as deacon and subdeacon of the Mass and A. Ziskovsky master of ceremonies. Admission to the chapel was by ticket but nevertheless it was thronged with the pupils of the upper grades, their teachers, visiting sisters from all parts of the Northwest and friends of the institutions. The responses were chanted by a choir of one thousand boys from the parochial and high schools. In a brief sermon the Archbishop explained the meaning of the symbols and liturgy of a Pontifical Mass.

At the afternoon session, presided over by Very Reverend H. Moynihan, Rector of St. Paul Seminary, the Reverend J. A. Melody of Chicago deplored the loss of reverence in the people of America. He defined reverence as "the sense of truth in practice" and asserted that seventy-five percent of the children of America know nothing of religion except what they pick up in the most casual way. Bishop Busch of St. Cloud developed the idea of education with reference to life and emphasized the value of religion in the everyday activity of the individual.

The Honorable John W. Willis presided at the evening session and introduced the Reverend A. B. C. Dunne of Eau Claire, Wisconsin, who developed the theme of christian educational ideals. He was followed by the Honorable P. H. O'Donnell of Chicago who compared Greek and Roman pagan ideals of life and conduct with the divine splendor of christian teaching and its influence on humanity. The congress was brought to an official close by the Archbishop who thanked all who contributed to its success and summed up the results as a triumph for Catholic education in this part of the country.

The educational Congress was the second function of the month that emphasized the importance of parochial schools in the mind of the Archbishop. A few days before it convened he inaugurated the custom of celebrating a Pontifical Mass for the pupils of the four upper grades of the parochial schools before the close of the school year, in the St. Paul Cathedral and in the then Pro-Cathedral of St. Mary in Minneapolis, for the purpose of familiarizing them with the ceremonies and the Gregorian chant. The pupils assembled several times for preparatory rehearsals before the date set for the Mass under the baton of Father Missia of the St. Paul Seminary who directed the massed choirs of several thousand boys and girls. At each Mass a sermon explanatory of the liturgy was preached and the children sang the proper and the common. The two churches were over-crowded with the pupils and their teachers and no one else was admitted. On all these occasions the Archbishop spoke to the children and exhorted them to understand and practice their faith openly and fearlessly. The arrangements for these functions were in the hands of the Superintendent of Catholic instruction and they were an annual feature until the health of the Ordinary made it necessary to omit them.

The Archbishop's love for children was proverbial. He was always happy with them, and the youngsters soon learned not to stand in awe of him. He loved the people, too, and on more than one occasion deplored the fact that his position and duties prevented his mingling more frequently and freely with them.

At the beginning of his course of lectures on "The English Reformation", under the auspices of the School of Social Studies, in the College of St. Thomas, on January 8, 1923, he confided to his audience:

> My great desire is to be with you. I confess that there is nothing that I have to do that I like better than to be near the people, to meet them and to talk with them. . . And that is not merely a personal sentiment, although there is involved in it the fact that I never quite reconcile myself to the fact that I was withdrawn from the people when I was made a bishop. I had all my life as a priest lived close to the people, knew them and knew them intimately, and then suddenly I was put in a position where it seemed impossible to get close to them and where, no matter what effort I made, either they would not believe me or for some other reason they did not take me seriously when I told them I would like to know and share intimately in their lives.

Nevertheless he was not unmindful of their limitations as Catholics and their diffidence in asserting their religious convictions. He would have them proud of their religion, not apologetic, but militant in defence of it. On the same occasion he said:

> I scarcely need to enlarge upon that subject, how much I have at heart the development of our people intellectually, and by that I do not mean that they are not developed intellectually from a Catholic viewpoint. And there are many reasons why they should not be.
> In the first place, Catholic literature is more or less remote from them, they have to seek it out. The literature of the land, of the country and of the language is not Catholic, either historically or in its present development. Our people are, we say many times, merely emotionally Catholics and yet are apologetic Catholics. They seem to feel as if there was something that they were holding back, that you have to apologize for the Church, while, as a matter of fact, it is the great constructive force. . . that has gone on from century to century, has entered intimately into the lives of the people, has never refused the struggles or the challenges of the times, and has held its course calmly and triumphantly.

He deplored the fact that Catholics are indifferent to sermons; that they prefer a Mass where there is no sermon or only a very short one; that they do not read Catholic literature; nor love the Mass as such and go there to meet God. Our churches are crowded, it is true, but are Catholics able or prepared to meet the challenge of the age and give a reason for the faith that is in them?

His solicitude for the youth under his care was manifested not only by the multiplication of institutions of learning but in other ways. He encouraged and authorized the formation of Catholic Boy Scout troops to supplement the work already done along that line in many parishes. In this connection it is interesting to note that long before there was a separate Catholic Scout movement the first church-sponsored scout troop,[37] the George Washington Troop, was organized in September, 1910, by the Reverend William L. Hart, pastor of St. Mark's Church in Merriam Park. It was the first Catholic scout troop in St. Paul and, possibly, in the country. Troops were formed in other parishes but there were no coordinated attempts to increase their number or efficiency until "Scouting Under Catholic Auspices" received its impetus under the direction and fostering care of the Most Reverend Francis Clement Kelley, Bishop of Oklahoma City and Tulsa.

One of the most distinguished priests of the Archdiocese, the Right Reverend James M. Cleary, celebrated the golden jubilee of his ordination on July 9, 1922, by officiating at a Solemn High Mass in the Church of the Incarnation, Minneapolis, which he founded and of which he was pastor. The festive sermon was preached by Archbishop Dowling in presence of Archbishop Keane of Dubuque, several monsignors, a large group of priests and a congregation that taxed the capacity of the church. At the evening banquet in the Radisson Hotel, at which Archbishop Dowling presided, addresses were delivered by Archbishop Keane, Monsignor O'Hearn of Milwaukee, Father Dunne of Eau Claire, Fathers Reardon and Cullen, Governor Preuss and Mayor Leach, all of whom congratulated the Jubilarian on his exemplary priestly life and fruitful ministry. He was especially noted for his work in behalf of total abstinence.

Ad Limina Report

When Archbishop Dowling made his first Ad Limina visit to Rome in 1924, as Archbishop of St. Paul, he made a report[38] of twenty pages to the Holy See on the material and spiritual condition of the diocese which we summarize as follows:

The Diocese comprises thirty counties of the State of Minnesota, with an area of 15,233 square miles and a population of 1,140,653 of whom 275,000 are Catholic. Most of the diocese is given over to agricultural pursuits. Eighty percent of the faithful live within fifty miles of St. Paul and all are of the Latin Rite except two small congregations of Maronites numbering six hundred souls in all.

The faithful are served by 361 priests of whom 317 are diocesan and 44 belong to religious orders. There are 207 parishes with resident pastors and 50 missions. 25 parishes are in charge of religious orders. 50 priests are engaged in teaching, 12 in the St. Paul Seminary, 11 in Nazareth Hall preparatory seminary and 27 in the College of St. Thomas. 18 priests in the diocese were once members of religious orders; some are incardinated, others are not. Four priests are studying in the Catholic University in Washington, one in the Catholic Institute in Paris and one in Rome.

In the past five years the Archbishop ordained 46 priests and has had to employ 7 from outside dioceses. There are at present 60 students for the diocese in the Major Seminary out of an enrollment of 125 in Theology and 54 in Philosophy from 24 dioceses; and 130 in the Minor Seminary which is located about ten miles from St. Paul and has its own faculty. It was opened in September, 1923.

St. Paul Seminary is located in a wooded area of thirty-four acres on the bank of the Mississippi. It has invested funds that yield $30,000 a year which, with the tuition of the students and the annual collections taken up in the parishes, enables it to meet expenses. It has no debt but considerable repairs will have to be made soon.

The Chancery Office, erected in 1923, is a commodious building of fire-proof construction with convenient offices for the material and spiritual administration of diocesan affairs.

In 1923, 951 out of 3,022 marriages, or nearly thirty percent, were mixed.

There are seven communities of men in the diocese:
Benedictines, with 11 priests in charge of 6 parishes;
Franciscans, with 11 priests in charge of 10 parishes;
Dominicans, with 9 priests in charge of 1 parish;
Oblates of Mary Immaculate, with 5 priests in charge of 5 parishes;
Paulists, with 3 priests in charge of 1 parish;
Marists, with 5 priests in charge of 2 parishes;
Christian Brothers, with 22 Brothers in charge of 2 high schools.

There are eleven communities of religious women:
Sisters of St. Joseph, with 342 sisters in charge of 1 college, 5 high schools for girls, 40 parish schools, 3 orphanages and 2 hospitals;
School Sisters of Notre Dame, with 157 sisters in charge of 28 parish schools;
Benedictines, with 73 sisters in charge of an orphanage and 14 parish schools;

Franciscans, with 69 sisters in charge of 12 parish schools;
Dominicans, with 49 sisters in charge of 7 parish schools;
Visitation, with 22 sisters in charge of an academy for girls;
Christian Charity, with 44 sisters in charge of 6 parish schools;
Ursulines, with 9 sisters in charge of an academy for girls;
Little Sisters of the Poor, with 30 sisters in charge of 2 Homes for the
Aged;
Handmaids of Jesus Christ, with 21 sisters in charge of a hospital and
a Home for the Aged;
Felicians, with 21 sisters in charge of 2 parish schools;

The Cathedraticum amounts to about $12,000 a year; and the diocese
has a debt of $435,000 created when the Cathedral was built, and which
will be paid little by little through rents from the property it owns in
the heart of the city.

He might have added that during the first world war 14,645 of his
Catholic subjects served in the armed forces and 319 made the supreme
sacrifice on the altar of patriotism. This was a little less than one-sixtieth
of the total number of Catholics who participated in the war and of
whom 16,000 shed their blood in defence of the things America holds
dear.[39]

Diocesan Teachers College

From the beginning of his episcopate the Most Reverend Archbishop
was anxious to provide the best educational facilities for the sisters in
charge of the parochial schools; but ways and means were not available
until the summer of 1925 when the daughters of James J. Hill bought their
Father's residence from the estate for $90,300, and presented it to the
Diocese of St. Paul on condition that it be conducted for fifty years as
a Normal School for the teaching sisters.[40] The gift was accepted and
the building dedicated to its new purpose on October 8, when it was
blessed by the Archbishop who expressed the hope that the school would
be in operation the following year. As a matter of fact it opened as the
St. Paul Diocesan Institute for its first session on January 8, 1927, with
more than three hundred sisters of teaching communities in the Twin
Cities present. Two hundred and fifty registered for regular classes on
Saturdays, a new and promising development in the educational system
of the Archdiocese. Six lecture courses were conducted by professors
from the St. Paul Seminary. In his address the Archbishop discussed the
aims and hopes of the Institute and said that the present courses are
experimental, looking to the day when a fully-equipped and staffed
Normal School must be available to relieve sisters from the burden of
vacation work. The Reverend James A. Byrnes, Superintendent of Catholic instruction, was in charge of the Institute and its program which

offered six weeks of standardized training in a curriculum that embraced all the courses given in the best state normal schools and, in addition, a course in religion. The school functioned under the charter of the College of St. Thomas with which it was affiliated and was empowered to grant credits of college grade to all who completed the course. The faculty was composed of sixteen instructors, all specialists in their fields, drawn from the St. Paul Seminary, St. Thomas College, religious communities of women, and laymen.

When the first regular summer school session began on June 20, 233 nuns registered for the six-weeks' course. They came from Minnesota, North and South Dakota, Iowa and Wisconsin. They were the pioneers in a movement which redounded to the educational progress of the parochial and high schools of the Northwest, the forerunners of thousands who have been graduated from the institution during the intervening years.

At the annual meeting of the American hierarchy at Washington in September, 1925, it was voted to organize the American Board of Catholic Missions to receive and disburse all funds allocated by the Society for the Propagation of the Faith for the maintenance of the Home Missions in the United States, amounting to forty percent of the total income to be devoted to missionary work. The other sixty percent was for the support of the Foreign Missions.

His Eminence Cardinal Mundelein of Chicago was elected President, Bishop Noll of Fort Wayne, Secretary, and Bishop Kelley of Oklahoma City and Tulsa, Treasurer.

Two years later Archbishop Dowling announced the reorganization of the Society for the Propagation of the Faith along more methodical and progressive lines to promote missionary zeal and endeavor in the diocese. Annual membership was fixed at one dollar; special at ten, and perpetual at fifty. He placed Reverend J. A. Troy in charge of field work under Father Byrnes the Diocesan Director.[41]

Good Will Movement

The publication of a Good Will or Tolerance Edition of the Minneapolis Daily Star on November 24, 1925, was the culminating feature of a movement which had its inception in the early part of the year when W. C. Robertson, editor of the Star, wrote an editorial calling for a broader spirit of toleration and good will among the citizens in religious, political, commercial, professional and social life.[42] He followed it up by inviting half a dozen clergymen of different faiths to a conference for the discussion of ways and means to further this object. It was suggested that a Good Will organization be formed and an appeal made to the citizens for cooperation. The approval of the leaders of the different religious groups was sought and freely given. Archbishop Dowling gave cordial approbation to the program. Several luncheon meetings were held at which plans were discussed and a program mapped out. It was agreed to ask Mayor Leach to issue an official proclamation setting apart the week of May 17, 1925, as Good Will Week, which he did, and asked churches, schools, clubs and civic leaders to cooperate. The Mayor was Chairman of a committee of which four clergymen were Vice-Chairmen and prominent citizens were members.

On Sunday of that week practically every clergyman of the city preached on the subject of tolerance and every afternoon and evening a pastor or layman, including the Governor of the State and the Mayor of the city, spoke over WCCO on the value of tolerance. In addition, a speaker was assigned to each of the luncheon clubs and civic organizations for a brief talk on the subject. On Friday noon, May 22, a mass meeting was held in the Garrick Theatre which was addressed by twelve clergymen of as many denominations and most of the addresses were afterwards broadcasted from Dunwoody Institute. Arrangements for this observance were perfected by a committee of three laymen and five clergymen — a Catholic priest, a Jewish Rabbi, a Lutheran, a Congregational and a Methodist minister. In the meantime weekly luncheon meetings had been held by the committee and so pleasant were the associations that it was suggested that a permanent Good Will Club be formed.

When the Club was revived in the fall it was proposed that the Minneapolis Daily Star issue a good will edition to be supervised and edited by five clergymen. The date selected was November 24 and the editorial board consisted of Father Reardon, pastor of the then Pro-Cathedral of St. Mary; Dr. Dewey, pastor of the Plymouth Congregational Church; Rabbi Matt of Ardath Yeshurnan Synagogue; Dr. Stark, pastor of Emmanuel Lutheran Church; and Dr. Smith, pastor of Simpson Methodist Episcopal Church and an expert cartoonist, whose cartoon for the edition showed the spirit of tolerance closing Pandora's box and imprisoning again the evils of the world which intolerance had permitted to escape. Every item of news and advertising and every feature that went into the paper was scrutinized by the clerical editors, each of whom furnished a signed editorial dealing with the religious, social, political, or racial angle and implications of tolerance, and making earnest pleas for increased good will and understanding among people of all creeds and callings. These editorials were said to be "masterpieces of exposition, logic and diction".

Commenting on the experiment Editor Robertson said:

The interest which these reverend gentlemen took in their work and the harmony and cooperation they manifested was most inspiring. It is a most difficult task, of course, for men unfamiliar with the newspaper game to handle something like eighty columns of news and feature matter from eight o'clock to twelve-thirty, but they managed to read and edit every line of it. I might say that the waste basket did a very flourishing business also.

And he adds: "I have never been connected with an enterprise which I believe has been of such real value to the newspaper itself and to the community".

The unusual experiment attracted attention in newspaper circles throughout the country and as far away as London.[43] The comments were invariably most favorable and optimistic.

One of the noteworthy results of the Good Will movement was the opportunity it afforded the clergymen of the different denominations in Minneapolis to fraternize with one another; to discuss topics of common interest; to urge a more sympathetic regard for one another's views both civic and religious; to emphasize the basic principles of christian life and conduct; to coordinate the forces of good in opposition to the powers of evil; to stress the necessity of equality before the law in civic and religious matters and respect for the sacred rights of others, by safeguarding for them the fullest measure of political liberty and religious freedom, to the end that no one be deprived of his prerogatives because of conscientious convictions. The attainment of these objectives postulates an absence of racial antipathy, political rancor, social ostracism, religious animosity and economic injustice, based on the fundamental recognition of the Fatherhood of God and the brotherhood of men.

In his Lenten letter[44] to the clergy on February 18 for the Holy Year of 1925, the Archbishop called attention to the fact that Lent tests

the quality of our faith and reveals to us the defects of our ministry. It means prayer and mortification. Priests must preach mortification by example. The character of our ministry is the most cogent reason for the decline of faith among our people, for their tepidity, indifference and apostasy. The priest who gives his people the impression that he is primarily a business man and only incidentally a distributor of the sacraments and a preacher of the word of God, need not wonder if his people have no sense of spiritual values and no Catholic sense.

Lent challenges priests to be the typical Catholics of their parishes. They are bound to observe it even if no one else does. He will give up even legitimate comforts and indulgences and unite mortification and prayer and will keep the doors of the church ever open for preaching, prayer and dispensing of the sacraments.

He reminded the clergy that 1925, was a year of jubilee which stressed the duty, privilege and compensations of prayer and furnished an occasion to obtain for themselves and their people the full measure of spiritual refreshment which the Church provides for her children especially in Lent.

In announcing the extension of the Jubilee to the whole world he set forth the conditions for gaining the indulgence, namely, the reception of Penance and Holy Communion (apart from the Easter duty and annual confession); visits to four churches on each of five days and prayers for the intention of the Holy Father. In St. Paul the churches were the Cathedral, the Assumption, St. Louis and St. Mary; in Minneapolis, the Basilica, St. Stephen's, the Incarnation and Holy Rosary. He reminded them that the intention of the Holy Father was for the propagation of the faith; for peace and concord among nations; for a disposition of the holy places in Palestine in accordance with the rights of the Catholic Church. The indulgence could be gained for one self and for the Holy Souls.

Diamond Jubilee of Diocese

On August 1, 1925, The Catholic Bulletin published a special edition to commemorate the Diamond Jubilee of the erection of the Diocese of St. Paul, and featured an article from the pen of the Archbishop in which he traced the prodigious growth of the Church from pioneer days, and challenged priests and people to emulate the faith and achievements of their forefathers and, under improved conditions, build upon the foundations laid in poverty and hardship. It is worth reproducing in its entirety for form, matter and historic content:

The Brief by which the diocese of St. Paul was erected bears the date of July 19, 1850. It is signed not by Cardinal Lambruschini, the prefect of the congregation of Propaganda, but by Archbishop Piccheoni "substitutus". When in the following December Bishop Cretin arrived in Paris on his way back to his native diocese of Belley, where he was to be consecrated, he saw the need of verifying the signature of his brief through Cardinal Ferrari, Nuncio Apostolic to the French Republic, who attested on the document itself that it was indeed "the true signature of the Most Illustrious and Most Reverend Lord Angelo Piccheoni".

It was an hour of great anxiety for the Church. The Holy Father had returned to Rome only in the previous April after an exile of two years. The foundations of Christian Rome seemed shaken. St. Peter, facing revolution and strife in the old world, turned to St. Paul, struggling with poverty and the chaos of all beginnings in the new.

After the interval that spans ages in the abdication not so much of kings and emperors as of the ruling ideas of the old order, St. Peter still sits under his dome in Rome receiving the loyal pilgrims of all quarters of the globe as calmly as if the lowering clouds of a modern day were not rumbling with the thunders of a new revolt; and St. Paul beyond the seas in distant Minnesota keeps his anniversary under a dome that in the fraternal rivalry of the apostles recalls in queenly grace and the calm security of possession that other dome by the side of the Tiber.

Bishop Cretin's Task

When Bishop Cretin landed in July, 1851, on the verdant banks of that settlement on the Mississippi to which Father Galtier's log cabin chapel had by the merest chance—yet surely not unguided by Providence—given a name, even his missionary's heart must have sunk at the rudeness of the diocese that was to be his. If it were only the Indians he was to evangelize!—the Indians so idealized in the early 19th century by the romantic school of nature worshippers to which Jean Jacques had given a vogue and also by the French missionaries who, driven from France in 1790, had found the redskins more amenable to their tongue and their zeal than the other inhabitants of the United States! But it was neither Indians nor French Canadians that awaited him when the full measure of his task grew upon him.

Revolution in Europe, financial disturbances in this country, famine, poverty, disorder were filling the tides of immigration to the full and Minnesota was a bright spot in the El Dorado which beckoned to the young and the adventurous to begin life afresh in a new world.

When the first bishop of St. Paul died in 1857, he doubtless thought that Minnesota was destined to be one of the most populous states in the Union. The dream of its explorers and exploiters in the 50's was dissipated by a series of events which, occasioned by Civil War, ended in developing the great transcontinental railroads and incidentally in opening up the farther west.

The tradition of the diocese of St. Paul is a missionary one. The memory of pioneer days is still vivid. Evidences of the straitened circumstances and pitiful poverty of the beginnings are even yet not hard to find, though they are rapidly disappearing. The material fabric of the Church at the present day symbolizes the heroic scale of its faith—rude, unfinished, imposing like the great cathedral whose dome rides the skyline like a halo above the city to which it has given a name. Its unfinished interior, which is being but slowly clothed with the glory that it challenges, tells of its high faith and its most confident hopes.

Not a diocese in the country holds in its hands the elements of a more complete educational system than does St. Paul—seminary, colleges, preparatory seminary, high schools, 45 parish schools in the Twin Cities out of a possible 50 in parishes large and small, and 66 more in country parishes with the ferment of school enthusiasm manifesting itself on all sides.

Parochial Activities in the Cities

The building program of the diocese has been on a prodigious scale in recent years. Not to speak of the Cathedral which has been an almost continuing operation since its inception—the three finished chapels of St. Peter, Our Lady and St. Joseph, and the monumental high altar with the great sacristy have been completed within the decade. The chancery building and the clergy house in the rear of the Cathedral, notable and costly structures, are but just erected.

The Pro-Cathedral of St. Mary in Minneapolis, in undertaking to finish its interior in stone and marble, is engaged in a work that will run into the hundreds of thousands while the finishing of the sanctuary, chapels and ambulatory of the Cathedral, which is presently to begin, is a work of great magnitude. In the decade St. Mark's fine church in St. Paul and practically all the 20-room school have been built. The Church of St. Luke, which promises to be one of the finest in the country, is even now being erected. St. John's parish has built itself a new church. New schools have been erected in the parishes of St. Andrew, St. Bernard, the Blessed Sacrament, St. Casimir, St. Cecilia, St. Columba, St. Mary, the Nativity, while a new school and hall are rising in the Sacred Heart parish. The same activity has been displayed in the parishes of Minneapolis. Within the ten-year period new churches have been erected in the Incarnation parish and that of Our Lady of Perpetual Help. Combination schools and churches have been provided in All Saints parish, the Annunciation, St. Bridget, St. Hedwig, St. Lawrence and at the present moment in St. Anne's and St. Thomas parishes, while schools have been erected in St. Helena's and the Holy Name, not to speak of La Salle high school on Nicollet Island. Meanwhile the Sisters of St. Joseph have practically built up St. Catherine's College in the ten-year period, its most recent achievement being the great college church whose basement serves as a library to the institution. The important college chapel of St. Thomas falls within this period, as does the drill hall and theater.

Unique in its way is Nazareth Hall at Lake Johanna, a building which in the elaboration of its design and the completeness of its detail suggests one of the great monumental structures of the past.

In other fields Catholic enterprise has not been inactive. St. Mary's Hospital in Minneapolis is a structure that falls within this prodigious ten-year period, as does also the great wing to St. Joseph's Hospital in St. Paul and the new nurses' house which is presently to be undertaken by the same institution. The Infant asylum on Dale Street, purchase and construction, is a product of the last decade. Even now the Provincialate of St. Joseph's Sisters is erecting at their place on Randolph Street, a new chapel and home for the aged sisters.

Outside the Twin Cities

Outside the cities churches have been built at Buffalo, Columbia Heights, Sacred Heart, Faribault, Farmington, Litchfield, Maple Lake, Marshall, Montgomery, Morton, Mound, Osseo, Prior Lake, Rosemount and Tracy, while churches are even now building at Le Sueur, Olivia, Murdock, and White Bear Lake. Combination schools and churches are not so popular in country parishes, but at Hopkins and St. Mary's, New Ulm, and South St. Paul there are three very recent interesting structures of this type. Schools have been erected in Clara City, Hampton, Lamberton, Loretto, Medina, St. Adalbert's, Silver Lake, Wabasso. A large addition was made to the Holy Trinity school in New Ulm for high school purposes, while a new separate high school and gymnasium is going up in Bird Island. Parish schools at this moment are being erected in the Immaculate Conception parish in Faribault, in Northfield and North Mankato.

It is not only in the number of building operations but in the solidity and the character of the edifices that the significance of all this laborious and expensive activity can be found. The zest of the effort leaves no time to make comparisons with other times or places. A spirit almost of impatience to be up and doing—a disposition to consider all that is being done in the nature of "a plant"—as something whose fruition awaits God's blessing and the coming years—is manifest on all sides. The golden days are not the memories of the diocese, hallowed though they be, but the days that are to come. Out of the past come voices to cheer us, to stimulate us against the faintheartedness that the prospect of new and increasing labors adumbrates. In dark days our forbears "carried on". They kept the faith, they fought the good fight, they insured what success we note. Shall we not gladly take up what they laid down and in the sight of all that has been done do our part to continue the work of those who, with the invocation of St. Paul on their lips, sowed the seed of the faith which now seems to be whitening for a harvest.

Holy Name Diocesan Union

In the course of time the Archbishop turned his attention to the Holy Name societies which were uncoordinated in their activity. At a meeting in the Ascension Club, Minneapolis, in June, 1926, the Archdiocesan Union was organized for the purpose of bringing the individual parish societies under one government and extending their influence by the formation of new branches in parishes where the society did not exist.[45] James Kirby of the Incarnation parish was elected President and the Reverend J. P. Aldridge, O. P., Prior and pastor of the Holy Rosary parish, was appointed Spiritual Director. The next year he was succeeded by the Reverend John Dunphy, pastor of the Ascension Church, and at a meeting in the St. Thomas College auditorium, attended by six hundred members from twenty-one parishes, plans were made for more efficient work for the coming years. To that end it was decided to hold a public rally of Holy Name men on the athletic field of the St. Thomas College on June 17, 1928. There was an unusually large gathering of people from the Twin Cities and vicinity on that sunny Sunday afternoon to take part in the first rally of the Holy Name societies in this part of the country. Four thousand men from twenty-two parishes — more than half the membership of the Union — paraded before the reviewing stand from which Archbishop Dowling blessed them as they passed, each group carrying its parish banner and American flags. Father Dunphy presided and after the parade the Archbishop addressed the gathering in which there was a large number of the clergy, complimenting the Union on the fine showing made by the individual societies and expressing the hope that such a rally be made an annual affair. The gathering dispersed after Benediction of the Blessed Sacrament. The second annual rally was held in the same place on June 16, 1929, when, owing to illness, the Archbishop could not attend, and the address was given by the Right Reverend James M. Cleary, pastor of the Church of the Incarnation, Minneapolis. The third rally was on the spacious parade grounds of Fort Snelling Military Reservation on June 8, 1930. A special feature was the presence of a group of Indians in tribal costume led by the Reverend Philip Gordon of Centuria, Wisconsin, a member of the Chippewa tribe. Two years later, on June 11, 1932, the Holy Name

Union held its annual rally on the State Fair grounds in the Midway district at which 7,000 men, wearing the regalia of the Society, marched in review before the new Archbishop of St. Paul, the Most Reverend John Gregory Murray, and were cheered by 30,000 spectators in the grandstand. Father Dunphy presided, the Archbishop made an address and the gathering dispersed after Benediction of the Blessed Sacrament. Since then the annual rallies have been held in the State Fair grounds and under favorable weather conditions as many as thirty thousand viewed the parade and cheered the marchers. On November 18, 1937, at his own request, Father Dunphy was replaced, as Spiritual Director, by the Reverend W. A. Brand, pastor of the Church of St. Peter in Richfield, under whose fostering care the Holy Name Union has grown in numbers and influence, and a varied program featuring a holy hour of adoration is carried out in June of each year.

Rural Life Conference

Archbishop Dowling gave the principal address at the closing session of the third annual meeting of the Catholic Rural Life Conference in the Ryan Hotel, St. Paul, on October 14, 1925, in which he discussed the place of "The Rural Parish" and its role in the economy of the Church. Bishop Muldoon of Rockford, Ill., presided. Other speakers dwelt on the economic status of American agriculture.

The first session of the Conference was held in the St. Paul Seminary where Solemn Mass was celebrated in St. Mary's Chapel on October 12, at which the sermon was preached by the Reverend Thomas R. Carey of Lapeer, Michigan, the National President. It was followed by a meeting in the Aula Maxima presided over by Reverend J. Harrington of the seminary staff and at which papers dealing with the students' mission crusade in rural parishes, were read and discussed. The other meetings were held in the Ryan Hotel and an interesting series of addresses by prominent leaders in the field of rural problems presented. Among the speakers was Father O'Hara of the Archdiocese of Portland who presented "A Catholic Rural Program". Other topics dealt with religious vacation schools; religious correspondence courses; vocations from rural areas; Catholic racial groups in rural America; and census-taking in country parishes.

In was one of the largest and most important conferences since the first awakening of active interest in the rural life movement through the efforts of Reverend E. V. O'Hara of the Rural Life Bureau. It was under the general direction of Bishop Muldoon, Chairman of the Special Action Department of the NCWC. In all the papers and discussions the need of Catholics showing greater solicitude for those who live on farms and in small country towns was insisted upon. Only in this way can the faith make progress and the drift to the city be stopped. There were delegates from fifteen states present and the evening meetings were open to all interested in the problems of rural life.

On December 13, 1925, the Catholic Education Association, through its commission for the standardization of Catholic colleges and secondary schools, at a meeting in Chicago to prepare a list of institutions fulfilling its requirements, approved St. Thomas and St. Catherine's colleges in St. Paul; St. Mary's and St. Teresa's colleges in Winona; and St. John's University in Collegeville.

First Minor Basilica in America

During the year 1924 Archbishop Dowling suggested, as others had done before him, the propriety of changing the name of the Pro-Cathedral of St. Mary because, in the first place, it was an ecclesiastical misnomer in as much as it was never a Pro-Cathedral in the true sense of the term and, in the second place, it was commonly referred to as the "Pro", an undignified title for a magnificent church dedicated to the Blessed Virgin. It was suggested that the only way in which a change could be effected with propriety was to have the church designated a Minor Basilica which could be done only by the Holy See. No action, however, was taken until April, 1925, when the pastor was authorized by the Archbishop to take the matter up with the Roman authorities.

The following petition[46] drafted by His Eminence Cardinal Sbarretti and Right Reverend A. E. Burke, P. A., first President of the Catholic Church Extension Society of Canada, then residing in Rome, was sent to the Holy Father through the Sacred Congregation of Rites which had jurisdiction in such cases:

PRO-CATHEDRAL OF ST. MARY
MINNEAPOLIS, MINNESOTA

Beatissimo Padre,

Il sottoscritto, Reverende Giacomo M. Reardon, Rettore della Pro-Cattedrale di Santa Maria, nella Citta di Minneapolis, Arcidiocesi di San Paulo, negli Stati Uniti d'America, umilmente prostrato ai piedi della Santita Vestra, ardisce esporre quanto appresso:

A causa di una presunta rivalita tra due citta gemelle, S. E. il Revmo. John Ireland, defunto Arcivescovo di San Paolo, giudico conveniente construire due grandi chiese: una che venne chiamata Cattedrale di San Paolo, e che e la vera cattedra dell' Arcidiocesi; l'altra sul fiume, in Minneapolis, ed alla quale venne dato il titolo di "Pro-Cattedrale di Santa Maria";

Che per quanto riguarda la chiesa di Minneapolis questo titolo non solo non e adatto, ma non puo nemmeno trovare alcuna spiegazione ecclesiastica, ne piace ai sacerdoti e alle persone che vi assistono tanto che tale denominazione vienne spesso abbreviata nel semplice prefisso "Pro", con evidente perdita di dignita e del rispetto devuto alla Benedetta Virgine Titolare;

Che, se pure aleuna ragione esisteva per tale Titolo quando questo venne dapprima conferito, questa e ormai interamente scomparsa, e tutti desiderano ardentemente di avare la loro splendida Chiesa chiaramente denominata, sotto la protezione della Madre di Dio, la piu grande di tutti i Santi;

Con l'approvazione dell' Ecellenza Revmo. Austin Dowling, Arcivescovo di San Paolo, il cui benestare quindi e qui allegato, il sotto scritto umilia alla Santita Vestra la preghiera di remuovare la parte non desiderata del titolo, facienda abbandonare le parole "Pro-Cathedral," e portando la magnifica chiesa alla dignita di una Basilica Minore, con tutti i diretti e privilegi.

Umiliato ai piedi Santita Vestra si Sottoscrive,
Giacomo M. Reardon
Pastore della Pro-Cattedrale di Santa Maria.
Visum et Approbatum.
✠Augustinus Dowling
Arcivescovo di San Paolo.

Minneapolis, Minnesota,
Stati Uniti d'America,
20 Aprile, 1925.

Considerable delay was encountered by the shunting of the petition from the Congregation of Rites to the Consistorial, before it was determined that the former had jurisdiction, and by hesitation to establish a precedent by granting the favor. At that time there was no Minor Basilica in the United States.

The first public reference to the proposed change of name was made by the pastor at the Pontifical Mass celebrated by the Archbishop on Christmas morning, when it was announced that Pope XI had graciously deigned to honor the Pro-Cathedral by elevating it to the rank of a Minor Basilica, the first in the United States. The Pontifical Brief,[47] dated February 1, 1926, and signed by His Eminence Cardinal Gasparri, Secretary of State to His Holiness, is herewith appended in its English translation:

PIUS XI, POPE AND BISHOP

For Lasting Remembrance of the Event:

Conspicuous in the City of Minneapolis, within the territory of the Archdiocese of St. Paul, stands the church dedicated to St. Mary, right noble in its structure and specimens of art, the building whereof, as well as of a Catholic school for boys and girls erected at considerable expense, was undertaken and completed by the late lamented John Ireland, Archbishop of St. Paul, a prelate most worthy of remembrance and renown. The Church of St. Mary is rightly and deservedly reckoned among the leading churches of the Archdiocese of St. Paul.

Whereas, Our Beloved Son, James M. Reardon, its present Rector, has made humble request of Us, that We vouchsafe to raise the sacred edifice in question to the dignity of a Minor Basilica, thereby superseding its present title of Pro-Cathedral, We, of Our full knowledge that the aforesaid church is wholly worthy of this distinction, both by reason of the piety of its worshippers as well as by the splendor of its ritual and the richness of its adornment, have deemed it well to accede to the wishes expressed in this regard, and We are further moved thereto by the crowning approval and high recommendation of Our Venerable Brother, Austin Dowling, Archbishop of St. Paul, as well as of Our Beloved Son Donatus Sbarretti, Cardinal Priest of the Holy Roman Church.

Wherefore, having given the matter most careful and serious consideration along with Our Venerable Brother, Anthony Cardinal Vico, Bishop of Porto and San Rufina and Prefect of the Sacred Congregation of Rites, We, of Our own proper motion, after sure knowledge and mature deliberation and from the fulness of Our Apostolic power do, by tenor of these presents, raise to the singular title and dignity of a Minor Basilica St. Mary's Church in the City of Minneapolis and Archdiocese of St. Paul, Minnesota, hereby superseding the title of Pro-Cathedral hitherto in current use; and We grant unto it all the privileges and tokens of honor which pertain to Minor Basilicas as of right.

This, then, is Our behest and decree, that these presents be and continue to be always sound, valid and effective; that they obtain and maintain their effect whole and entire; that they be, both now and hereafter, ample authorization for those whom they concern or shall concern; that thus it must be duly judged and defined; and that if aught else over and above these presents should happen to be attempted by any person or by any authority whatsoever, whether knowingly or unknowingly, the same will be null and void — everything to the contrary notwithstanding.

Given at Rome, at St. Peter's, under the Fisherman's Seal, on the first day of February in the year 1926, being the fourth of Our Pontificate.

P. Cardinal Gasparri,
Secretary of State.

From this it is evident that no church may arrogate to itself the title of Minor Basilica.[48] The distinction is bestowed only by Apostolic Letter, bearing the Seal of the Fisherman, and carries with it certain rights and privileges, such as the use of a pavilion and bell and the wearing of the Cappa Magna by the Canons, if any, attached to the church. By time-honored custom a Minor Basilica also has the right to a coat-of-arms and a corporate seal.

The pavilion or canopy has the form of a large umbrella so constructed that it cannot open more than half way. It is composed of twelve alternate stripes of red and yellow each with a braided and fringed pendent of the other color, the whole supported by ribs fastened to a wooden handle topped with a gilded metal ball and cross. The pavilion which forms part of the coat-of-arms is the distinctive emblem of a Basilica.

The bell, not more than six inches in diameter at its rim, is mounted on an elaborate framework or belfry of metal or carved wood and fixed on a banner pole. The pavilion and bell are carried in procession by laymen and when not in use are prominently displayed in the sanctuary.

A Basilica, as such, is not dowered with spiritual privileges above those of an ordinary church; but can obtain them by having recourse to the proper authorities. The Basilica of St. Mary is one of the most highly indulgenced churches in the United States by virtue of its affiliation with St. John Lateran and St. Mary Major in Rome and Our Lady of Mount Carmel in the Holy Land.[49]

Furthermore, a Pontifical Brief of March 5, 1927, grants to the faithful who visit the Basilica of St. Mary on the first Sunday of every month in perpetuity a Plenary Indulgence on the usual conditions of confession and communion and prayer for the intention of His Holiness.

The other Minor Basilicas in the United States are: Our Lady of Victory, Lackawanna, N. Y.; St. Josaphat, Milwaukee, Wisconsin; the Cathedral of the Assumption, Baltimore, Md; the Monastery Church of Conception Abbey, Conception, Mo.; the Abbatial Church of St. Mary of Gethsemani, Louisville, Ky.; and the Church of San Francisco de Asis, (Mission Dolores) San Francisco, California.

First Consecration in New Cathedral

The first and only consecration ceremony[50] during the episcopate of Archbishop Dowling, and the first in the new Cathedral, took place on February 3, 1926, when the Most Reverend Thomas A. Welch, Vicar General of the Archdiocese, was consecrated Bishop of Duluth in succession to Bishop McNicholas, O. P., promoted to the Metropolitan See of Cincinnati. Archbishop Dowling officiated as consecrator with Bishops Busch of St. Cloud and O'Reilly of Fargo as co-consecrators. The sermon was preached by Archbishop McNicholas. A banquet was served in the St. Paul Hotel at the end of the ceremony and a generous purse presented to the new Bishop on behalf of the clergy of the Archdiocese. The following day a large group of prelates and priests accompanied Bishop Welch to Duluth where he was installed in the Cathedral of the Sacred Heart by Archbishop Dowling who also preached the sermon, and the clergy and laity of the diocese of Duluth gave the Bishop a royal welcome. A banquet was served in the leading hotel and addresses delivered by prominent members of the clergy and the laity to which the new Bishop responded in an appropriate speech thanking all who had contributed to the solemnity and pleasure of the occasion.

Distinguished Visitors

After the twenty-sixth International Eucharistic Congress held in Chicago in June, 1926, a group of eight members of the Pontifical Commission that accompanied the Papal Legate, His Eminence John Cardinal Bonzano, paid an unofficial visit to St. Paul on the return trip from the Pacific Coast and were the guests of Archbishop Dowling on Sunday, July 18.[51] They were: Monsignor (afterwards Cardinal) Camillo Caccia-Dominioni, Maestro di Camera of His Holiness Pope Pius XI; Monsignor Carlo Resphighi, Prefect of Apostolic Ceremonies; Monsignor Rocco Beltrami, Rector of the Pontifical Italian Emigration College; and two laymen: Nobili Pius Franchi de Cavalieri, first of the Chamberlains of Cape and Sword, and Commendatore Francisco Pacelli, Attorney of the Papal Court. These official members of the Pontifical Commission were accompanied by others who belonged to the private suite of His Eminence—Monsignor Charles Grano, Master of Pontifical Ceremonies; Canon Angelo Bina, private Secretary of the Cardinal; and Reverend Thomas F. Tierney his English Secretary. This constituted the most important mission that ever represented a Pope in America. During their brief sojourn they visited the Cathedral, the Chancery Building, St. Paul Seminary, St. Thomas College, Nazareth Hall, St. Luke's Church, the Basilica of St. Mary and other institutions before continuing their journey to Chicago in the late afternoon.

The lay retreat movement under the auspices of the Diocesan Teachers' College proved more successful than anticipated in the number that attended the exercises held on week-ends during the lenten season. At the close of the first retreat in 1928, a Catholic Retreat League was formed at the social gathering held on Easter Sunday after the communion breakfast for the purpose of popularizing the movement. The second annual reunion[52] took place on May 8, 1929, in the college dining room and the list of speakers included Archbishop Dowling, Judge Hughes of Hibbing, and Father Boyle, C. S. C., of the College of St. Thomas.

Six week-end retreats were held during the Lent of 1930,[53] four of which were preached by Father Connolly of St. Paul Seminary and the others by Reverend D. J. Ryan, Rector of the Sacred Heart Seminary, Detroit, Michigan.

The College had accommodations for thirty retreatents who paid ten dollars each for the privilege of attending the exercises.

The honor of preaching the festive sermon at the sesquicentennial celebration of the founding of the city of San Francisco on October 10, 1926, was accorded to the Most Reverend Archbishop of St. Paul. The function took place in Mission Dolores Church in that city at a Mass celebrated by His Eminence Patrick Cardinal Hayes of New York. In the course of his sermon[54] the Archbishop deplored the indifference of American Catholics until very recently towards the propagation of the faith and attributed it to their absorption in parochial affairs to the exclusion of the broader concept of the Universal Church. After the celebration he visited Los Angeles with the Cardinal as the guest of Archbishop Cantwell and was honored with a reception by the Newman Club in the Biltmore Hotel.

Rural Vacation Schools

During the decade of Archbishop Dowling's episcopate much attention was given by Catholic educators to the question of religious education in rural schools, the object of which was to supplement the instruction given at Mass and in the home when the children were unable to attend a parochial school during the year. These religious vacation schools, as they were called, were established in the Archdiocese of St. Paul in the middle twenties and produced very satisfactory results. They were taught for the most part by sisters in the church sacristy, parish hall or in a house not too distant from the church. Where sisters could not be obtained lay persons did the work under the direction of the pastor. Instructions were given in catechism, bible history and Catholic practices as a preparation for the reception of the sacraments of Penance, Holy Communion and Confirmation. Many of the children came from homes ten to twenty miles from the church, thus showing the interest their parents took in the project. The pastors, too, gave fine cooperation to the diocesan authorities.

A report published in The Catholic Bulletin, July 16, 1927, showed that seven hundred and twenty children were receiving instruction in Catholic doctrine in eight schools, as follows:

In Buffalo there was an average attendance of one hundred and twenty-five from four to fourteen years of age taught by the Sisters of Notre Dame of Mankato, six days a week for four weeks. Sixty of the children came from the country, within a radius of seven miles.

The vacation school in Belle Creek was opened in 1924, under the direction of the Sisters of St. Joseph from St. Paul. Seventy pupils attended a two-hour session a day for six days a week for several weeks in the parish hall.

In Cannon Falls the Sisters of Notre Dame from Hampton taught fifty-four children from six to fifteen years old in the church and sacristy.

In Corcoran where the school was opened in 1925 the Sisters of Notre Dame taught eighty-three children from six to sixteen years of age in the church and hall and lived in a rented house.

The school in Lamberton was opened in 1922 and held in the parish hall where seventy-three children received instructions at daily sessions for several weeks. Some of them came from ten to twenty miles distant, and ranged in age from five to fourteen.

In Redwood Falls eighty-five children from seven to sixteen were taught by four lay teachers from the Normal School.

In Vermillion one hundred and one children from nine to fifteen were taught by the pastor and a layman in the district school and the church basement.

In Rush City there was an average attendance of ninety from seven to sixteen years old taught in the parish hall by three Sisters of Notre Dame, and in North Branch, a mission, forty children were taught in the church.

In Marysburg a vacation school was conducted for two weeks by lay teachers.

Other schools were opened was soon as sisters or lay teachers became available.

On May 12, 1927, Monsignor Ladeuze, Rector Magnificus of Louvain University, wrote Archbishop Dowling asking him to accept an honorary doctorate in Sacred Theology [55] from the institution, on the five hundredth anniversary of its founding which was to be solemnly commemorated the following year. The honor was accepted by the Archbishop of St. Paul with due appreciation of the compliment paid him by this venerable and renowned educational center, but he was unable to be present in person when the degree was formally conferred in June, 1928. He was one of several distinguished American prelates—among them Bishop Lawler of Lead, Bishop Kelley of Oklahoma City and Tulsa, and Bishop Murray of Portland, Maine—singled out for this special and coveted distinction.

One would think that the Archbishop's training and acumen as a historian before coming to the West would cause him to take the deepest personal interest in the Catholic Historical Society organized under his predecessor on April 25, 1905, and publishing the "Acta et Dicta" for many years. But during his episcopate he evinced not the slightest concern for it or its work, and nothing was done to collect documents bearing on the history of the diocese, or gather souvenirs or write papers to perpetuate the memory of the lives and deeds of the bishops, priests and laymen who laid the foundation of our religious prosperity in the Northwest.

St. Thomas College in Alien Hands

At the beginning of October, 1927, the Very Reverend Thomas E. Cullen resigned the Presidency of the College of St. Thomas and was appointed pastor of the Church of St. Stephen in Minneapolis, and the Reverend John P. Foley of the College faculty was named acting President on October 13, a position which he held until July, 1928, when he was named pastor of the Church of the Immaculate Conception in Faribault.

It came as a complete surprise to priests and people to learn that the College of St. Thomas had been turned over to the Holy Cross Congregation, South Bend, Indiana, in the summer of 1928, for a five-year period with the option of renewing or terminating the contract at the end of that time. The transfer was resented by the clergy, alumni and laity as contrary to the constitution and tradition of the institution and its best interests, a direct challenge to the diocesan priests who had administered its affairs and taught in its class halls since it was founded in 1885, built it up to its prosperous condition and were quite able to continue the management of it. However the deal was consummated and nothing could be done about it at the time.

One of the reasons assigned for turning the administration of the College over to the Holy Cross Fathers was that the number of diocesan priests was too few to meet the expanding needs of the institution which, during the year just closed, enrolled 435 students in the collegiate department and 315 in the military academy and had a faculty of 24 priests and 25 laymen.

The change in administration alienated in large measure the interest and support of the diocesan clergy and many friends of the institution, and the breach was widened by the attitude of the newcomers who professed to be able to found a new Notre Dame in the Northwest and make it a success without the aid of the priests of the diocese. The Holy Cross Fathers assumed the administration of the institution but retained the former faculty, adding to it a couple of their own men. Most of the teaching was done by the diocesan clergy and whatever standing the college had during the five years of the new tenure was due largely to their efforts. Many changes were introduced on the score of modernization, new policies adopted, new methods outlined. The old administration building, the original structure on the campus, was dismantled and a new headquarters facing Summit Avenue erected at a cost of $300,000. Appeals were made privately to laymen supposedly able to contribute generously but not a tithe of its cost was realized. The balance was paid by an assessment on the clergy and the parishes at the end of the five-year period when the arrangement was discontinued and the College returned to diocesan control.

According to the agreement[56] made and entered into, on July 9, 1928, by and between the College of St. Thomas, the Congregation of the Holy Cross and the Archbishop of St. Paul, the Congregation, on July 17, 1928, took over the control of the College, its buildings, equipment and furnishings, its property, real and personal, to use, manage and operate for educational purposes for a period of five years ending July 16, 1933, through the administrative officers appointed by the Superior General of the Congregation.

The Archbishop agreed to permit the diocesan priests on the faculty to remain or replace them, whenever necessary, by others equally qualified.

The Congregation agreed to operate the College as economically as possible with the ordinary revenue and the interest from the endowments; but any deficit was to be charged to the College.

At the end of five years a contract might be entered into for the permanent alienation of the College, conveying to the Congregation, in fee simple, the title to its real estate, buildings and contents and all its endowments.

If the Congregation withdrew during or at the end of five years it would be reimbursed for any expenditure of community funds made for the improvement of the College.

This agreement, equivalent to a lease, was signed by Archbishop Dowling on behalf of the College and of the Archdiocese and by the Very Reverend James A. Burns, C.S.C., Superior General of the Congregation.

In addition to the foregoing conditions which Father Burns laid down in a letter to Archbishop Dowling on July 3, 1928, he stated that either party to the agreement might withdraw at any time after giving one year's notice to the other party, and that, while the agreement lasted, no other Catholic College or University would be permitted in or near the Twin Cities. To this the Archbishop agreed and promised "not only for myself but, in so for as I can control or counsel my successors, in their name also, that no other Catholic College for young men shall be permitted in the diocese".

The new administrative officers were: Reverend Matthew Schumacher, President; Reverend William A. Bolger, Vice-President; Reverend James J. Boyle, Prefect of Religion; Reverend James H. Callagan, Prefect of Discipline; and Reverend William Cunningham, Dean of Studies.

Visit of Cardinal Cerretti

A distinguished visitor during the Christmastide of 1928 was His Eminence Bonaventure Cardinal Cerretti, returning from the Antipodes where he was Papal Legate to the International Eucharistic Congress in Sydney, Australia,[57] He was accompanied by Count Edward L. Hearn, Overseas Commissioner of the Knights of Columbus in Rome, and Reverend Vincenzo Lorenzo, his secretary. The Cardinal celebrated midnight Mass on Christmas eve in the Chapel of the Presentation at the

Motherhouse of the Sisters of St. Joseph in St. Paul, and resided at the Diocesan Teachers College with his secretary. Count Hearn was the house guest of the Most Reverend Archbishop, and was present at the High Mass in the Basilica of St. Mary on Christmas day and dined with the clergy. His Eminence also visited the principal diocesan institutions and the Honorable P. H. Rahilly and family, Lake City, Minnesota.

From the time the Cardinal landed in San Francisco reports appeared in the public press that a settlement of the Roman Question involving the relations between the Pope and the King of Italy was imminent, and that a treaty was soon to be ratified by the Papacy and the Italian Government bringing to an end the abnormal situation between the Vatican and the Quirinal that had persisted since 1870.

A semblance of truth was given to these reports by the anxiety of His Eminence to be back in Rome early in February and his willingness to accept rather poor accommodations for the trans-Atlantic voyage. As a matter of fact he arrived in Naples on February 4 in time to reach Rome before the Treaty of the Lateran was signed on February 12. In this connection it is interesting to read what Bishop Kelley of Oklahoma City and Tulsa says in "The Bishop Jots It Down" (pp. 266-76) regarding the part he played in the preliminary conversation with Premier Orlando of Italy during the negotiations leading to the signing of the Treaty of Paris in 1921.[58] The writer was a guest of Bishop Kelley in January, 1929, when he received a letter from Cardinal Cerretti from New York, asking him to write the official story of his part in the earlier negotiations in which he served as intermediary between Premier Orlando and the Holy See. This report, translated into Italian, appeared later in a magazine published in Milan. When the official announcement[59] of the settlement of the Roman Question was made, there was no mention of the part played by Bishop Kelley or Cardinal Cerretti whom he had contacted on reaching Rome after his interview with Premier Orlando in Paris. But Premier Mussolini mentioned it when he made the announcement of the Treaty to the Italian Parliament. As soon as the official report of the signing of the Concordat reached St. Paul a special thanksgiving Mass was celebrated in the Italian Church of the Holy Redeemer at which Archbishop Dowling preached on the Roman Question and its solution.

In a letter dated February 17, 1929, the Archbishop formally promulgated the rules laid down by the Church on the question of dances[60] for parish purposes, and asked that they be read to the congregation on the Sunday before Lent and posted in a conspicuous place for all to read. No dances can be held in buildings used for parish purposes, neither in the church, school, residence, hall nor in any place directly under control of the church; no priest or pastor is permitted to be present at them nor can the proceeds be accepted for the parish treasury. The pastor cannot allow or give permission to any society or sodality, bearing the name of the church or in any way connected with it, to hold dances for any purpose. If it does so, attention must be called to it from the pulpit and parochial sanction withdrawn.

The dances to which reference was made were mixed dances between men and women or youths of both sexes, not esthetic dances by school children for school entertainments.

Marshal Foch Honored in Death

On March 26, 1929, Marshal Ferdinand Foch, Generalissimo of the allied armies in the first world war, was buried in Paris. His body lay in state in the great Cathedral of Notre Dame until the final absolution after the Pontifical Mass of Requiem celebrated by the Cardinal Archbishop of Paris, and thence borne through streets thronged with his mourning fellow countrymen to its tomb in Les Invalides.

Simultaneously with his obsequies in Paris, with due allowance for difference in time, five thousand men and women, civilians and military, crowded the Basilica of St. Mary and its environs in Minneapolis to pay the final tribute of respect and prayerful homage to the soldier-hero of the world and its most distinguished Catholic at a Solemn Requiem Mass under military auspices.[61].

This was the distinctive and most appropriate feature of a city-wide commemorative observance in honor of Marshal Foch under the direction of the Foch Memorial Committee of the American Legion posts of Minneapolis.

The day began with a salute of twenty-one guns in his honor at early dawn in Fort Snelling, the highest possible military salute, and paid to no foreigner since the death of Lafayette. At the parade ground, adjoining the Basilica, where the citizens of Minneapolis, eight years before, heard him eulogized as the greatest military genius of modern times, the 151st Field Artillery fired a salute every half minute during the day.

The Basilica was appropriately decorated for the solemn occasion. In front of and above the main altar hung the Stars and Stripes of America and the Tricolor of France. Behind the altar and around the sanctuary were displayed the flags of the other allied nations, of Great Britain, Canada, Belgium, Italy and the rest. Small American flags were suspended from the columns of the nave. The statues draped in lenten purple added a further solemn note to the occasion.

At the head of the center aisle, outside the sanctuary gates, stood a catafalque draped with the Tricolor and in front of it a black-bordered easel on which rested a picture of the dead marshal taken sixty days after the signing of the armistice. On the catafalque lay a draped saber and a French helmet. Two lighted candles kept sentinel watch at each side of it and two guards from the Third Infantry stood at rigid attention during the service, presenting arms at the consecration of the Mass.

Civil and military leaders occupied reserved sittings in the front pews, among them Governor Christiansen, Mayor Leach, in the uniform of a Brigadier General, Colonel Sweeney, Commandant of Fort Snelling, and Adjutant General Walsh—each with his staff.

The color guard was the first to enter the church carrying the Stars and Stripes and the flags of the American Legion posts. Behind them marched the members of the Legion, Veterans of Foreign Wars, Disabled American Veterans, Red Cross nurses in white uniforms and blue capes lined with scarlet, Boy Scouts and Fourth Degree Knights of Columbus in uniform.

The American flags borne in the procession were massed before the sanctuary rail on the epistle side and the standards of the Legion posts and of the Third Infantry on the gospel side. As the procession entered the church the organ poured forth the stirring strains of the Marseillaise. The bright March sunlight streamed through the glorious stained glass windows and lent additional color to the scene within the Basilica.

The church was crowded as never before or since. Every inch of available space in nave, balcony, ambulatory and even behind the wrought iron grille was taken and several hundred who sought admission had to be turned away for want of room.

The Solemn Mass of Requiem began at nine o'clock with Father Reardon, pastor of the Basilica, as celebrant, Fathers Cullen of St. Stephen's, as deacon, Dunphy of the Ascension, as subdeacon, and Brand of the Basilica staff, as master of ceremonies. A boys' choir of fifty voices, under the direction of Father Missia, with Professor Beck at the organ, sang the responses of the Mass.

After the gospel Father Reardon delivered the sermon in which he dwelt on the signal service rendered to mankind by Marshal Foch, one of the greatest military geniuses of all ages and a devoted Catholic. He challenged the statements of those who deny that a loyal Catholic can be a patriotic citizen and cited the example of this little grey man of God, whose life and achievements were an outstanding refutation of the charge. "Not to me, O Lord, but to Thy name give glory" was the keynote of his life.

After Mass the absolution was given at the catafalque, the priests returned to the altar, the soft notes of taps echoed through the church, and when they faded into silence the organ pealed forth the opening notes of the Star Spangled Banner which was taken up by choir and congregation. The procession re-formed and marched from the church and a detachment from the Third Infantry presented arms as the Governor and the Mayor left the sacred edifice.

A complete description of the celebration with pictorial accompaniment in a specially-designed folder[62] inscribed with the names of the Mayor of Minneapolis, the celebrant and ministers at the Mass and the Chairman of the memorial committee (Frank H. Bellew) was sent to Madame Foch, as a suitable souvenir of the only memorial service held in the United States in memory of her famous husband on the very day on which his remains were laid to rest beside the tomb of Napoleon Bonapart in the heart of Paris.

Diocesan and Other Functions

The death of Archbishop Keane of Dubuque, his friend and former Metropolitan, brought a sense of personal loss and poignant sorrow to the heart of Archbishop Dowling. The sad event occurred on August 2, 1929.[63] He was present at the obsequies in St. Raphael Cathedral when the Solemn Mass of Requiem was celebrated by Bishop Duffy of Grand Island, who accompanied the deceased when he went to the West as Bishop of Cheyenne in 1902, and preached the sermon in which he paid deserved tribute to the missionary zeal, fruitful ministry and personal worth of the distinguished churchman who had been summoned to his reward.

When Archbishop Dowling resigned the office of Treasurer of the NCWC and the Chairmanship of the Department of Education in November, 1929, his resignation was accepted with regret and the following resolution adopted by the Board of Directors:

His Grace, the Most Reverend Austin Dowling, Archbishop of St. Paul, has been a member since its organization of the Administrative Committee, NCWC; he has been also the Episcopal Chairman of its Department of Education, and for an equal length of time has served as treasurer of the NCWC.

His thorough understanding of the problems and questions of the day; his zeal in the work of his office; his devoted interest in the promotion of the spiritual welfare of the Catholic body, have made him a leader and a guide in this work of ours. Only his own conviction that through ill health he can no longer serve has led us to accept his resignation.

This resolution is a testimony of our appreciation. We hope and pray that Our Lord in His great goodness may restore health and strength to the Archbishop of St. Paul, that he may yet and for years to come personally give of his wisdom and his devotion to our deliberations.[64]

For the first time in the history of the Archdiocese the "Bene Merenti" medal[65], bestowed by the Holy See on laymen and women who have deserved well of the Church, was conferred on Miss Helen Oswald Graham of Red Wing, Minnesota, by the Most Reverend Archbishop on August 12, 1929, at a ceremony held in the home of her niece, Miss Helen Coughlin of Minneapolis, in recognition of forty-seven years of devoted service as organist in the Church of St. Joseph in Red Wing.

In connection with the fiftieth anniversary of his ordination Pope Pius XI proclaimed a Holy Year in the form of a universal jubilee ending December 31, 1929, and enriched it with ample indulgences to be gained for oneself or for the souls in Purgatory as often as one complied with the requirements set forth in the pontifical rescript.

Archbishop Dowling promulgated the Holy Year to his diocesans and prescribed the conditions under which the indulgences could be gained, namely, the reception of Penance and Holy Communion; fast and abstinence on two days not otherwise of obligation; two visits to each of three churches in St. Paul (the Cathedral, the Assumption and the Holy Redeemer) and in Minneapolis (the Basilica, St. Stephen's and Holy Rosary); in the country districts six visits to the parish church unless there were two or three churches in the locality when the visits were pro-rated among them; six visits to the convent chapel for religious; a dispensation from the number of visits for societies making them in a body. During these visits prayers were to be said for the conversion of sinners, the extirpation of heresy and schism, peace and concord among Christian rulers, and for the exaltation, freedom and prosperity of the Church. In addition, an alms must be given for a pious purpose through the Society for the Propagation of the Faith. None of the ordinary indulgences were suspended during the Holy Year. A special indulgence of seven years and seven times forty days could be gained by all who visited the Blessed Sacrament and prayed for the Pope's intention, and a plenary if the practice were continued for a year. All priests were granted the personal right of a Privileged Altar.[66]

The campaign for health and nursing service[67] for the children of the parochial schools in Minneapolis, similar to that given the pupils of the public schools, was won by the Federation of Mothers Clubs after a long and hard-fought struggle, when the Board of Education and Taxation allocated six thousand dollars to the Board of Public Welfare to inaugurate on January 1, 1930, this public service in the twenty-one parochial schools in the city. Great credit is due the Federation for bringing about this change of attitude towards the parish schools on the part of the Health Department. Registered nurses are now assigned to these schools as well as to the public schools. At first it was a full-time service but of late years, owing, no doubt, to a dearth of competent nurses, the service is confined to a couple of days each week.

In what proved to be his last address to the faculty, visiting clergy, senior and honor students of the College of St. Thomas on its feast day, March 7, 1930, the Archbishop said:

> The College of St. Thomas has done a great work for this diocese, and for the entire state of Minnesota, and it will always be a sacred memory. Our youth have to receive the best that can be given them. The best in

education, the best in equipment, the best that any father or mother might expect for their son. I say this to you this day not as if I were inaugurating a money drive, or even remotely thinking of any such thing, but I am glad to find before me this day so many priests of this diocese. I have said to them many times that for years and for times to come the Church in this country will be carried on the shoulders of the priests. We want to see St. Thomas succeed. It has done well. If the days to come measure the achievements of the past it will do wonderfully well.

Obsequies of Mother Seraphine

On June 25, 1930, the Archbishop was called upon to pontificate at the obsequies of Mother Seraphine, the surviving sister of the late Archbishop Ireland, who, for thirty-nine years, was Provincial Superior of the Sisters of St. Joseph of Carondelet who taught her as a little girl just arrived in the frontier village of St. Paul, and whose community she entered in 1858 at the age of sixteen. In 1921 she resigned her official position in the community and lived in retirement, but not inactive, in the cell-like room she had occupied for many years in St. Joseph's Academy. There she was stricken with what proved to be her first and last serious illness extending over a period of several years, but critical for about two, during which she intensified her preparation for death and, with exemplary resignation to the will of God, yielded her soul into the hands of her Creator on Friday, June 20, in her eighty-eighth year of life and seventy-second of religious profession.

Her funeral took place from the majestic Cathedral of St. Paul built and dedicated by her illustrious brother, and to her the greatest church in the world, on Wednesday, June 25. The Most Reverend Archbishop was assisted at the Solemn Requiem by Monsignor Moynihan, Rector of St. Paul Seminary, as archpriest; Fathers Ryan, Rector of the Cathedral, and Cullinan of Nazareth Hall, as deacon and subdeacon; Kotouc of St. Stanislaus, and Schaefer of St. Mathew's, as deacons of honor; and Bandas of the St. Paul Seminary as master of ceremonies.

In the sanctuary were Bishops Busch of St. Cloud, Welch of Duluth, Mahoney of Sioux Falls and Kelly of Winona, as well as Monsignors Guillot, Cleary and Byrne, Fathers Egan, Geraghty and Ryan of Fargo Diocese, many other priests and hundreds of sisters, among them Reverend Mother Agnes, the Superior General, and Sister Columbine of St. Louis, Mother Clara, the Provincial Superior, and her assistant, Sister Grace Aurelia, as well as the Mother Superiors of fifty houses of the Sisters of St. Joseph in the Northwest and elsewhere.

The honorary and the active pallbearers were chosen from among the senior sisters of the community who had been more or less intimately associated with the deceased in the government of the Congregation.

Before the absolution the Archbishop, addressing the crowded congregation, spoke of the deceased as

our first parishioner and most distinguished Catholic, who, like St. Genevieve of Paris, was mother to the City of St. Paul which she saw grow from
a frontier village in 1852 to a thriving and prosperous commercial center.
She was distinguished for her faith, her piety and her love of Christ; a
human being with a mother's heart and an exemplar for her sisters in religion; a valiant woman with a love of poverty and, like her illustrious
brother, indifferent to the little comforts to which even the most self-
denying might lay claim. Like him she dared greater things for God and
her beloved community, as he for his beloved diocese. Her memory is
enshrined with his on the diptychs of the Archdiocese of St. Paul and held
in benediction by her community.[68]

Leaflet Missal and Catholic Digest

During 1930 the project of publishing and distributing the "Leaflet
Missal"[69] containing the complete text of the Sunday Mass, with rubrical
notations and explanatory notes, was launched in St. Paul by two of the
younger diocesan priests, Reverends Paul Buzzard and Edward F.
Jennings, and proved a very successful venture. By means of it the
ordinary Catholic can follow the Mass with ease and spiritual profit.
It is, as one bishop wrote, "A practical method for bringing our people
into intimate and intelligent contact with the Mass". He was one of many
from all parts of the country who praised the zeal and ingenuity of the
editors for having devised such a simple and effective method of putting
the Mass within reach of the faithful. During the intervening years the
"Leaflet Missal" has grown in popular appeal and found its way into all
parts of the country. It is furnished to subscribers in monthly installments, and many churches keep a supply in special stands near the doors
and available to parishioners and others, either free of charge or for a
few cents each.

The weekly issue averages 90,000 copies; the Christmas edition is
450,000 (printed in lots of 1,000,000); the Nuptial Mass and ceremonies
sells at a rate of 100,000 per month; and the Mass for the day of burial at
20,000.

Six years afterwards these enterprising young priests associated themselves with the Reverend Louis A. Gales in originating the Catholic
Digest,[70] the golden thread of Catholic thought culled from more than
three hundred publications carrying articles written from the Catholic
viewpoint. It is the first venture of the kind in the United States. The
initial issue of 15,000 came from the press in October, 1936, from the
office of publication in the basement of the Chancery building. In seventeen months the press run expanded to 52,500 copies of sixty-four
pages. During the intervening years its size has more than doubled and
improvements have been made in type, paper, illustration, and general
make-up. It now owns its own building—two stories with full basement—

at 41 East Eighth Street, St. Paul, which has become too small for its needs, and arrangements are under way to purchase a more commodious headquarters with more ample facilities for handling the monthly issue of 551,000 copies, of which 200,000 are sold in churches and 75,000 on news stands throughout the country. It recently opened an office in New York.

In September, 1940, the Catholic Digest began the publication of an edition in Braille, sent free to the blind, and financed by donations from interested readers. This was followed during the next decade by several editions in foreign languages: the Spanish in Buenos Aires, Argentina; the British and Irish in Dublin, Ireland; the French in Paris, France; the German in Aschaffenburg, Germany; the Dutch in Louvain, Belgium; the Italian in Milano, Italy; and the Japanese in Tokyo, Japan. An edition in the Spanish language, "Lo Mejor del Catholic Digest", will appear in October, 1952. It will be published and printed in the United States, and sent to subscribers in the twenty countries of Latin America between the Rio Grande and Cape Horn. Its editorial direction and advertising pages will be under the supervision of a competent staff of Latin Americans. Subscriptions for any and all of these can be sent to the home office for self or friends abroad. The Catholic Digest carries no advertisements, has no agents and sells on its merits.

Diocesan Affairs

One of the last letters written by Archbishop Dowling to the clergy—the last about Nazareth Hall—is dated September 6, 1929, and sets forth the financial condition of that institution in the following words:

> The difference between what students have been able to pay and the cost of maintenance during the six years of the institution's existence has been $165,000.00. Last year, alone, the sum was over $30,000.00. This money is taken from our investments and the annual collection. Our investments are not equal to the burden of the school's deficit.[71]

Since then no report of the institution's financial condition has been given to the clergy. Each year a printed list of the burses valued at $6000 each and their beneficiaries is sent to the priests by the Chancery Office. The list for 1951 shows that there are 93 burses paid in full—41 from the priests of the Archdiocese: 46 from the laity, and 6 from parishes. Besides these there are 42 incomplete burses—19 from the clergy, 21 from the laity and 2 from parishes. A few of the completed burses are inactive because the interest goes to the donors.

The Most Reverend Archbishop wrote a foreword for the second annual year book issued under the auspices of the Federation of Mothers' Clubs of Minneapolis early in the year 1930 which contained a history of the

Catholic High Schools of Minneapolis, namely, St. Anthony's which graduated its first class in 1880; St. Margaret's (1907), an offshot of Holy Angels which opened in 1876; and De La Salle which began in 1900, as the successor to and continuation of a Brothers' school opened in 1889 and graduating its first and only class in 1891. The book also mentioned other Federation projects, such as welfare work, school survey, city-financed nursing projects, physical education and art programs.

In the preface Archbishop wrote:

> The best thing the Federation has done—and already in its existence it has done notable things of permanent value—has been to convey to a relative-ly small number of mothers the wholesome and inspiring ambition to par-ticipate in the Church's labors for christian education in this Arch-diocese.[72]

A free clinic for needy children—the first established by a privately owned hospital in Minneapolis—was opened in St. Mary's Hospital on January 21, 1930, with the approbation of the Most Reverend Archbishop, when five hundred persons inspected the new quarters and equipment.[73] It had fifty beds for patients, from infancy to fourteen years, the hospital staff—doctors and nurses—would care for all patients registered at the clinic and all hospital equipment was at their disposal. The project was sponsored by St. Mary's Guild, a group of men and women who pay ten dollars a year for membership. The clinic is located in the old portion of the hospital which had been renovated and furnished with the latest appliances for the work. There are five private detention rooms to prevent contagion. No charge is made for any unable to pay; otherwise a nominal fee is expected.

A regional meeting of the Catholic Conference on Industrial Problems[74] in which the Archbishop took great interest, met at the Ryan Hotel, St. Paul, on Monday and Tuesday, June 2 and 3, 1930, for the discussion of the ethical phases of labor, wages and employment by nationally recognized authorities. The Archbishop welcomed the delegates at the first session, presided over by Reverend John Doherty of the Catholic Charities Bureau, St. Paul. Addresses were delivered by Father Glenn, Director of Charities of Duluth, William F. Schilling of Northfield, a member of the Federal Farm Board, Mr. Doyle and Mr. Doig. The afternoon session was presided over by Mr. Joseph Matt, Editor of Der Wanderer, when George Lawson, Secretary of the Minnesota Federation of Labor, Miss Florence Monahan and Father Bolger, C. S. C. of St. Thomas College, appeared on the program. Judge O'Brien was chairman of the evening meeting when other problems connected with labor and wages were discussed.

Father Driscoll of the Charities Bureau of Minneapolis was chairman of the forenoon session on Tuesday and E. A. Prendergast of Minneapolis was toastmaster at the banquet in the evening when Reverend John A. Ryan of the Catholic University, Washington, and Dr. John A. Lapp of Marquette University, Milwaukee, delivered addresses, and also the Archbishop who urged Catholics to make a study of labor and unemployment problems in the light of the Church's teaching and realize that "justice is not a mere custom or problem of the moment but that it is eternal". During the sessions Drs. Ryan and Lapp took part in the discussions, emphasing the moral aspects of the problems under consideration in view of the papal encyclical on the labor question.

Arrangements for the conference were in the hands of Fathers Doherty and Driscoll, aided by Judge McNally, Francis Gross and Miss Linna E. Bresette, Field Secretary for the national organization.

The last ordination ceremony[75] at which Archbishop Dowling officiated was held on Monday, June 9, 1930, in the St. Paul Cathedral, the first in that majestic edifice. Prior to that time all such ceremonies took place in St. Mary's Chapel of the St. Paul Seminary, which could accommodate only a limited number of persons, mostly members of the immediate families of the young levites promoted to the priestly state on that occasion. It was decided to give the general public an opportunity to witness the imposing event by holding it in the Cathedral which was filled with spectators. On that occasion twenty young levites were raised to the priestly dignity, thirteen for the Archdiocese, four for the Diocese of Winona, one each for Duluth, Omaha and Boise. Among them were members of the first class of graduates from Nazareth Hall, many of whom were from the Twin Cities and that added to the joyful significance of the occasion. Twenty-five others were advanced to the order of subdeacon. There was a large attendance of the clergy from St. Paul and other dioceses.

The Archdiocese of St. Paul was officially represented in Omaha at the Sixth National Eucharistic Congress[76] which opened on September 23, 1930, and continued for three days. A special train carrying a large group of pilgrims, under the direction of Fathers Doran of Minneapolis and Keefe of Anoka, reached Omaha in time for the opening Mass celebrated by the Apostolic Delegate to the United States, Archbishop Fumasoni-Biondi, in St. Cecilia's Cathedral at which Archbishop Beckman of Dubuque, preached. Among the pilgrims was Monsignor Moynihan, Rector of St. Paul Seminary, who, on the afternoon of the second day, read a paper on "The Blessed Sacrament, the Nourishment of Divine Life in the Soul".[77] The program of the Congress followed the usual lines of such gatherings and drew thousands of the laity and hundreds of clergymen from all parts of the country. It was sponsored and directed by the Ordinary of the Diocese, Most Reverend Bishop Rummel. Its most distingushed pilgrim and visitor was his Eminence Cardinal Mundelein, Archbishop of Chicago, who, at the public demonstration in the Creighton Stadium on Wednesday evening, September 24, delivered an address on "The Blessed Eucharist and Catholic Action."

During Archbishop Dowling's episcopate twenty new parish schools were opened and at his death the system included three high schools for boys, six for girls, seventeen parochial high and one hundred and thirteen grade schools with an attendance of 35,000 children. The Chapel of the Presentation, costing $375,000, built by the Sisters of St. Joseph to commemorate the Diamond Jubilee of their coming to St. Paul, the connecting link between the Provincial House and the Novitiate, was dedicated by him in March, 1927.

His Eminence Cardinal Hayes of New York, accompanied by his secretary, Monsignor Stephen Donahue and his friend, George McDonald, a Commander of the Order of the Holy Sepulchre, spent Wednesday, October 8, 1930, in St. Paul en route to San Francisco from Notre Dame where he dedicated a new school building. He was the guest of the Most Reverend Archbishop and visited some of the churches and institutions in St. Paul and in Minneapolis. In San Francisco he was scheduled to preach on Sunday, October 19, at the concluding Mass of a week's celebration in honor of the diamond jubilee of St. Ignatius College—an outdoor Mass in the new stadium which was built to accommodate fifty thousand people.

For the first time in the history of the diocese a conference of the parochial sodalities of Our Lady was held at the College of St. Thomas on Sunday, November 16, 1930, with the approval of the Most Reverend Archbishop though he was too ill to attend the sessions.[78] Eighteen hundred sodalists gathered for the meeting, which was under the direction of Father Lord, S. J., of St. Louis, the National Director. Solemn High Mass was celebrated in the College chapel at which Father Lord preached to a congregation that filled every inch of available space with an overflow on the campus. In the course of his sermon he told the delegates that the object of the sodality was "to give women of the world an opportunity to work for Christ through their parishes, for the good of souls, their own and others". The celebrant of the Mass was Very Reverend F. J. Schaefer, Pastor of St. Matthew's Church, St. Paul, assisted by Fathers Cogwin of St. Stephen's Church, Minneapolis, and Plaschko of St. Matthew's Church, St. Paul, as deacon and subdeacon respectively. Father Rolwes of Columbia Heights was master of ceremonies.

Immediately after Mass the delegates met in the armory for a session which lasted till five o'clock with time out for dinner in the college dining hall. Father Boyle, C. S. C., Director of religion at St. Thomas College, introduced Father Lord who, with Miss Dorothy Williams of St. Louis, General Secretary of the National organization, conducted the meeting at the close of which it was decided to form an Archdiocesan Union. To that end group meetings were held in Minneapolis on Monday evening and in St. Paul on Tuesday evening at which the combined attendance was about seven hundred. These were followed by a leadership meeting in the Midway on Wednesday attended by one hundred prefects and delegates from the twenty-five sodalities in the Twin Cities and suburbs who voted to form a Union. Miss Mary Gleason of Minneapolis was elected temporary chairman to act until permanent officers were chosen at the first meeting of the Union, on Tuesday, December 9, 1930.

In the early days of the depression the Archbishop decided to foster and promote the construction of new buildings for diocesan, parochial and institutional purposes to the amount of $1,532,000, as a contribution to the relief of unemployment. The sum would be far greater were it not for the large-scale building operations of the previous decade. Several major construction projects were undertaken in the Twin Cities and additions to schools and other parochial equipment in the country districts. These plans were amplified and brought to a happy fruition under his successor, Archbishop Murray.[79]

Father Hennepin Memorial

It was a matter of keen regret that Archbishop Dowling was too ill to take part in the ceremonies commemorative of the two hundred and fiftieth anniversary of the discovery and naming of the Falls of St. Anthony by Father Louis Hennepin, the Belgian Recollect missionary and historian, on July 4, 1680. The celebration took place on Sunday, October 12, 1930, six weeks before the Archbishop passed away.

For nearly a decade of years the Knights of Columbus of Minnesota had been making plans and seeking ways and means for erecting a monument to Father Hennepin, the first white citizen of Minneapolis; but it was not till 1930 that they were in a position to carry out the project. Then it was decided that the memorial would take the form of a heroic copper statue of the missionary-explorer robed as a Franciscan friar, holding aloft a crucifix and resting on a granite pedestal of artistic design. The statue, cast in Geislengen, Germany, from a design made in America, was erected on a triangular plot of ground donated by the Basilica of St. Mary on Hennepin Avenue, and faced in the direction of the original waterfall. A copper tablet, modeled after Douglas Volk's painting of Father Hennepin discovering the Falls of St. Anthony and forming part of the mural decorations of the State Capitol, was set into the front of the pedestal, and appropriate inscriptions chiseled on the other sides.

The religious ceremony[80] began with Pontifical Mass in the Basilica at 10 o'clock celebrated by the Most Reverend Francis C. Kelley, Bishop of Oklahoma City and Tulsa, assisted by the Reverend T. E. Cullen, pastor of the Church of St. Stephen, as Archpriest, Fathers Dunphy of the Ascension parish and Doran of Litchfield as deacons of honor, Jennings and Brand of the Basilica staff, as deacon and subdeacon, and Hauer of the Basilica as master of ceremonies. In the sanctuary were Archbishop Sinnott of Winnipeg, Manitoba, Canada, a dozen Monsignors and priests. Fourth Degree Knights of Columbus in regalia served as a guard of honor. The church was filled as seldom before and thousands stood outside during the Mass and sermon brought to them by loud speakers.

Among the distinguished laymen who occupied reserved seats in the front pews were Count Lantscheere, first Secretary of the Belgian Embassy in Washington and representative of the Prince de Ligne, Belgian Ambassador to the United States; Governor Christiansen and his staff; Mayors Kunz of Minneapolis and Bundlie of St. Paul; Mr. Orren E. Safford the Belgian Consul; representatives of the Civic and Commerce Association; state and local officers of the Knights of Columbus; and men prominent in the commercial and professional life of the city and state.

The sermon was preached by the Reverend James M. Reardon, pastor of the Basilica, and the responses at the Mass were sung by the vested choir of the church.

After the Mass the Fourth Degree Knights of Columbus and the Basilica Boy Scout Troop 111 formed in line and led the procession of distinguished guests and clergy to the site of the monument where the statue was unveiled by the Reverend Cyrinus Schneider, O. F. M., pastor of the Church of the Sacred Heart, St. Paul, and a member of the religious order to which Father Hennepin belonged. As the veil fell from the statue and disclosed the artistic figure of the great missionary there was enthusiastic and prolonged applause from the large gathering that packed all available space in front of the Basilica and extended down Hennepin Avenue and Wayzata Boulevard. The memorial was blessed by Archbishop Sinnot after which the dignitaries of church and state assembled on a platform on the Basilica steps, decorated with American, Papal, French and Belgian flags. Father Reardon presided and read the following message from Cardinal Pacelli, Secretary of State to His Holiness, Pope Pius XI:

His Holiness Pope Pius XI rejoices in the tribute of honor rendered to the memory of the great priest and explorer Father Hennepin by the erection of a monument in the City of Minneapolis. With all the affection of his heart he imparts the Apostolic Benediction to His Grace, the Most Reverend Archbishop of St. Paul, to the Knights of Columbus of the State of Minnesota, to the Catholic people of the City of Minneapolis and of the entire Archdiocese of St. Paul.

An address was delivered by the Honorable Thomas D. O'Brien of St. Paul, first State Deputy of the Knights of Columbus in Minnesota, who said that Father Hennepin came not to acquire fortune or territory but to win souls for Christ. And so it is today that we dedicate a shaft to a gentle hero, willing to give his life if in return he might have the privilege of baptizing even one Indian baby.

He was followed by Count Lantscheere who said:

I come as the representative of my sovereign, His Majesty, the King of the Belgians, to join with you in this celebration in honor of Father Hennepin. And I thank you on behalf of the Belgian nation, for this impressive tribute to that Belgian priest who was first to plant the cross in this vicinity and dedicate the waters of your Falls of St. Anthony.

Where he set up an humble altar there has risen the Basilica of St. Mary. Where he found a primeval forest, we find the great and thriving metropolis of the Northwest. The falls which he discovered in their unbridled strength, have become a mighty industrial force harnessed to provide the necessities of mankind.

All this was not the work of Father Hennepin, but it was he who was the first to blaze the trail for those who followed in his footsteps; for those who, under the hand of God, have made this spot a great center of civilization, of industry, and of christianity. It is as pioneer explorer and priest that we honor him today.

At the conclusion of the program the vested choir sang "Holy God, We Praise Thy Name"; and the prelates, priests and other distinguished guests were entertained at luncheon in the Basilica residence.

In the afternoon there was a civic program in the Municipal Auditorium at which Governor Christiansen presided and addresses were delivered by distinguished speakers. Count Lantscheere read a lengthy address written by Prince de Ligne, the Belgian Ambassador, who was unable to appear in person.

In the evening the Knights of Columbus of Nicollet Assembly were hosts at a banquet in the Nicollet Hotel attended by nearly eight hundred guests. The principal feature of the program was an address on "Hennepin and Early Catholic Days in Minnesota" by the Right Reverend Humphrey Moynihan, Rector of St. Paul Seminary, after which greetings were given by Archbishop Sinnott, Bishop Kelley, Count Lantscheere, Judge O'Brien and J. E. Corrigan, Master of the Fourth Degree for Minnesota. It was a fitting climax for a memorable day which witnessed the greatest religious and civic function in the history of the Church and city since the laying of the cornerstone of the Basilica in 1908.

As a sequel to the celebration, His Majesty, the King of the Belgians, by Royal Decree of December 8, 1930, conferred the decoration[81] of "Officer of the Order of Leopold II" on Father Reardon and Mr. Edward C. Gale, chairman of the civic group sponsoring the public meeting in the Auditorium on the afternoon of October 12. The decoration was conferred in the name of King Albert, by Orren E. Safford, Belgian Consul for Minnesota, at a meeting held in the Elks Club on March 9, 1931, under the auspices of the Hennepin-Minneapolis Council, Knights of Columbus, and presided over by J. Earle Lawler, State Deputy of the Order in Minnesota.

A few years afterwards, in 1939 to be exact, those in charge of the Hennepin celebration in Minneapolis were asked by the officers of the Royal Archeological Circle of Ath in Belgium[82] to cooperate with them in commemorating the three hundredth anniversary of the birth of Father Hennepin at Ath in 1940, on which occasion it was proposed, among other things, to issue a popular edition of his works to make him better known to the people of his native land, and erect a suitable monument. It was the wish of the promoters that a commitee, of which Archbishop Murray would be chairman, be formed in the United States to cooperate with the local committee under the high patronage of His Eminence Cardinal Van Roey, Archbishop of Malines, and the Premier of Belgium. It was also suggested that a duplicate of the statue of Father Hennepin in Minneapolis be erected in his native city. Before any arrangements could be made the second world war broke out and the project has not been revived.

Religious Progress in the Diocese

During these years the general work of the Archdiocese did not lag. There was growth and development on all sides. The Archbishop kept in touch with every phase of parochial and educational activity. He visited the parishes regularly for the administration of the Sacrament of Confirmation and attended other parochial functions and encouraged priests and people to be solicitous for the general welfare of the Church as well as for the local institution. It was during his episcopate that Ireland Hall was built on the campus of St. Thomas College as a residence for professors and students, and Mendel Hall erected at St. Catherine's College to provide up-to-date facilities for scientific studies and research. The main altar was installed in the Cathedral, the gift of Mrs. George E. Slade, daughter of James J. Hill; the sanctuary was finished in stone, marble and bronze; the Cathedral was completed by the addition of a sacristy at the rear of the sanctuary, begun April 15, 1924, and ready for use in May, 1925; three of its chapels were finished; the residence of the clergy on Selby Avenue, begun March 25, 1924, and occupied

December 7, 1924, and the Chancery Building on Dayton Avenue, begun in the spring of 1922 and ready for occupancy in March, 1923, were added to complete the group. Throughout the diocese many new churches, schools, rectories and other institutions were built to round out existing parish plants or provide for an increase in Catholic population.

A comparison of the statistics given in the Catholic Directory for the year 1918, when Archbishop Ireland died, and for 1930, when his successor passed away, shows that there was an increase in the number of diocesan priests from 302 to 368 and of priests of religious orders from 56 to 61, while the total number of churches in residential parishes and missions decreased from 274 to 257. Seminarians increased by 5 to a total of 215, with 165 students in the preparatory seminary which did not exist in 1918. The number of pupils in Catholic schools of all kinds increased from 30,661 to 35,841. There was an increase of 311 in the number of sisters but a decrease of 34 among novices and postulants. The orphans decreased by 153, and the inmates of homes for the aged by 29. During this period the Catholic population increased from 265,000 to 280,346. In 1930 there were 7042 infants baptized and 772 adults, 2583 marriages performed and 2620 deaths recorded.

Illness and Death

During the last three or four years of his life Archbishop Dowling's health was seriously impaired due to the fact that his heart was not functioning normally, and the resultant circulatory disorders gave rise to complications which brought him to death's door on several occasions.[83] He had a serious illness in 1927, was ordered south for a rest in 1928, and returned to spend some time in the Mayo Clinic. During the summer of 1929 he collapsed while on a confirmation tour and a critical illness resulted. For a time he rallied sufficiently to leave his bed and walk unaided, and his friends were encouraged to hope that his life would be spared, but it was not to be. Pneumonia set in, a congestion of the lungs resulting from a weak heart. He was cheered and comforted by the receipt of a message from the hierarchy assembled in annual meeting in Washington, and signed by Archbishop Hanna, Chairman of the Administrative Board.

> The members of the hierarchy of the United States, in meeting assembled, send you the expression of their great affection, their joy because of your improved health, and their prayers that you may soon be restored to your vigor and again take your place in our council.[84]

A month before he died, on October 31, 1930, the only living member of his family, Sister Antonine of the Sisters of Mercy of Providence, R. I., and intimate friends, among others Father Walsh co-founder of Maryknoll, were summoned to his bedside for a farewell meeting. Calling them by name he blessed each one, gave a final message to them and, through them, to his flock.

> I am nothing. God is everything. The mercies of God are wonderful. How good He is to me, a sinner, to have you, my friends and dear ones, about me now. I bless you. I pray for you all.[85]

He lapsed into unconsciousness four hours before his peaceful death in the late forenoon of Saturday, November 29, 1930, at his residence on Summit Avenue, directly across from the Cathedral.

His body robed in purple vestments with pallium, pectoral cross, ring and white miter, was placed in a bronze casket in the drawing room of his residence, turned into a mortuary chapel with a temporary altar on which Mass was said on Tuesday morning for his sister, who had returned to the East and did not reach St. Paul till after his death, and members of the household, as well as on Wednesday morning before it was transferred to the Cathedral for the children's Mass celebrated by Father Ryan, pastor of the Cathedral. Over five thousand children and their teachers from the upper grades of the parochial schools were accorded this privilege because of the deceased prelate's love for them. The sermon was preached by the Right Reverend Monsignor Moynihan, Rector of St. Paul Seminary.

During the day the body lay in state in the Cathedral. It was estimated that not less than fifty thousand people viewed the remains. Students from the major and the minor seminaries kept watch during the day and at night the diocesan clergy took over. The Knights of Columbus formed a guard of honor in relays of eleven every half hour till ten at night. Then the Knights of St. George in full dress uniform kept vigil until six o'clock in the morning when the Knights resumed their watch.

On Wednesday evening the solemn Office of the Dead was chanted by priests and seminarians. The burial service was set for the following day, Thursday, December 4, at ten o'clock. At that hour four archbishops, twenty-nine bishops, two abbots, and seventeen monsignors took their places in the sanctuary and 450 priests, 223 seminarians, 510 sisters, 22 christian brothers and city and state officials occupied reserved sections in the nave of the immense Cathedral.

The Solemn Mass of Requiem was celebrated by Bishop Welch of Duluth, assisted by Fathers Schaefer of St. Matthew's Church as archpriest, Ryan of the Cathedral as deacon, Crowley of Nazareth Hall as subdeacon and Ziskovsky of St. Paul Seminary, as master of ceremonies. The responses were sung by the seminarian choir under the direction of Father Missia. The sermon as preached by Archbishop McNicholas of Cincinnati, and the final absolutions were given by Archbishops Glennon of St. Louis, Beckman of Dubuque, Stritch of Milwaukee and Bishops Busch of St. Cloud and Welch of Duluth.

The Final Tribute

In the course of his sermon Archbishop McNicholas paid tribute to the many admirable qualities of mind and heart of the deceased prelate, and recounted his service to the Church in America.

Archbishop Dowling, he said, was

as simple as he was sincere. . .as open-hearted, as honest, as approachable as a child. . .his transparent honesty made him shrink from anything that even suggested a pose. . .his essential simplicity never changed. . . the graces of the priesthood and of the episcopacy but supernaturalized his gifts. . .he loved his priests. . .he wished them to come to him freely with their perplexities and problems. . .he thought of himself always as one of them, as their spokesman, their leader. . .he never became entirely reconciled to the separation from the people which was the inevitable result of his devotion to the duties of his pastoral office. . .it was his delight to mingle freely with them, to know their thoughts, to help them in their difficulties, to protect them from imposition. . .throughout all his priestly and episcopal years his absorbing theme was the Church . . .the divinity of the Church was the noonday sun of his life. . .he was totally devoid of personal ambition. . .he thought of the episcopal office only in terms of responsibility. . .he had ever before him the unassailable position of the Church and her uncompromising attitude towards moral wrong. . .he welcomed most cordially any views that were constructive, even though they were entirely at variance with his own. . .
In his relations with all outside the fold of the Catholic Church Archbishop Dowling was ever governed by the broadest charity, which, however, never betrayed him into sacrificing one jot or tittle of Catholic principle. He was ambitious for the Church. . .he wanted the non-Catholic learned world to look up to her, to be compelled to go to her as the source of sane and sanctified scholarship. He was ambitious for a learned priesthood. . .that all should appreciate and profit by priestly learning. . . he was an ardent American; but in his true Americanism he considered his native land in relation to the Church. . .his compelling love for the Church made him earnestly desire that our government should know the Church as she really is, that it should recognize her ennobling principles, the strength of her moral code, the sanity of her laws and of her discipline. . .
He was kind, lovable, approachable, patient and forbearing to an almost incredible degree in personal matters, but instant and fearless in his defence of the rights of the Church. Naturally impatient of everything that meant a display of bad judgment in those serving the Church, he imposed upon himself always the restraint of silence. He was ever the gracious and cultured prelate. Generosity and hospitality will be associated with his name while his memory lives.
The twelve years of a truly apostolic episcopacy exercised in this Archdiocese are twelve glorious pages in the history of the Church of the Northwest.[86]

During the Mass thousands who could not find even standing room in the Cathedral waited outside in a drizzling rain until the funeral cortege departed, in a three mile procession, for Calvary cemetery where the final prayers were said in Latin by Bishop O'Reilly of Fargo, and in English by Monsignor Moynihan after which the casket was lowered into a brick and cement vault beside his predecessors in the clergy plot; and in due time a granite slab similar to those above the remains of the other prelates, was placed over his final resting-place with the following inscription:

SACRED TO THE MEMORY OF AUSTIN DOWLING

SECOND ARCHBISHOP OF ST. PAUL

BORN IN NEW YORK CITY A. D. 1868

DIED IN ST. PAUL A. D. 1930

THE WISE MAN WILL SEEK OUT THE WISDOM OF ALL THE

ANCIENTS AND WILL BE OCCUPIED IN THE PROPHETS

ECCLI. XXXIX–1

MAY HE REST IN PEACE

Archbishop Dowling was the fourth Ordinary of the diocese to be laid to rest in Calvary Cemetery in which, during the seventy-four years of its existence, 50,000 burials were recorded up to November 19, 1930. It comprises one hundred acres of land, sixty of which were added to the original forty bought by Bishop Cretin in 1856, to take the place of the cemetery that occupied the site of the present St. Joseph's Academy, from which the bodies were removed on November 2 of that year, and taken in procession to the new location on Front Street.

The first Catholic cemetery in St. Paul adjoined the log chapel on Bench Street, the site of which had been donated by two of the early settlers.[87] In it eleven persons were buried before 1849. It was abandoned in 1853 when the second cemetery at Marshall and Western Avenue was acquired. In this cemetery Father Peyragrosse, who died on May 7, 1855, was buried and his was one of the bodies taken to Calvary cemetery in 1856. He was, therefore, the first clergyman to be buried in Calvary. The second was Bishop Cretin on February 26, 1857, who was followed by Fathers Bernier on August 31, 1857, McManus on April 2, 1864, and Tomazevic on October 27, 1867. Since then 10 monsignors and 86 diocesan priests have been buried there. The average age of the former was 77.6 years and of the latter 54.16.

The Diocese of Providence, R. I., where Archbishop Dowling served as a priest, paid the last tribute of prayerful respect for his life and achievements at a Pontifical Mass[88] celebrated in the Cathedral of Sts. Peter and Paul on December 11, 1930, by the Most Reverend Bishop Hickey, assisted by Monsignor Blessing, V. G., as archpriest, Fathers McKitchen and O'Reilly, as deacon and subdeacon, Doran and O'Toole, as deacons of honor, and Collins as master of ceremonies. The Mass was attended by fifty priests, and over a thousand people, including the students of St. Xavier Academy and Tyler parochial school. Sister

Antonine, the only surviving member of Archbishop Dowling's family, was present. After the Mass Bishop Hickey spoke feelingly of Archbishop Dowling's love for the Church, his fruitful ministry in the local diocese and in the West and characterized him as a national champion of Catholic education. The responses of the Mass were sung by the boys' choir of the Cathedral.

A Forceful Preacher

Within the diocese as well as beyond its limits the Most Reverend Archbishop was recognized as an eloquent and forceful preacher and lecturer with an unsurpassed ability to clothe his thoughts in elegant and fascinating phraseology, and he was much in demand as a speaker at home and abroad. Usually he spoke without notes or manuscript and most of his sermons are lost to posterity. He was in constant demand as a preacher but did not allow it to interfere with his diocesan work. His writings, said the Providence Visitor of February 2, 1912, "were characterized by clearness of style, depth of thought, and a dash of humor that easily charmed the reader, and endeared him to men of letters".

Besides his sermons and addresses at dedications and similar functions in the diocese, he preached on many other occasions the more important of which were:

In the St. Paul Cathedral on the first anniversary of the death of Archbishop Ireland, September 18, 1919; at the banquet in the College of St. Thomas inaugurating the Archbishop Ireland Educational Fund campaign on September 7, 1920; at the Sixth Annual Convention of the Catholic Hospital Association in St. Paul on June 24, 1921; at the Christian Brother golden jubilee banquet in the Ryan Hotel, St. Paul, on November 21, 1921; at the Archdiocesan Educational Congress in the College of St. Thomas on June 11, 1922; at the golden jubilee of Monsignor Cleary in the Church of the Incarnation, Minneapolis, on July 9, 1922 and at the evening banquet in the Radisson Hotel; at the golden jubilee of the Sisters of the Visitation, St. Paul, on August 12, 1923; and at the Regional Catholic Industrial Congress, St. Paul, on June 3, 1930.

Among the notable occasions on which Archibshop Dowling spoke outside the diocese may be mentioned the following:

The dedication of St. Joseph's Cathedral, Sioux Falls, S. D., May 7, 1919; before the Crevecoeur Club, Peoria, Ill., February 22, 1921; obsequies of Bishop Trobec in the Cathedral of St. Cloud, December 18, 1921; consecration of Most Reverend Joseph G. Pinten as Bishop of Superior in St. Peter's Cathedral, Marquette, Mich., May 3, 1922; dedication of the Sacred Heart Church, Washington, D. C., December 10, 1922; consecration of St. Patrick's Church, Fall River, Mass., October,

1923; consecration of the Cathedral, Helena, Montana, June 2, 1924; feast of the Conversion of St. Paul, in the Church of Santa Susanna, Rome, January 25, 1924; National Conference of Catholic Charities at Des Moines, Iowa, September, 1924; National Convention, Knights of Columbus, Duluth, Minnesota, August 4, 1925; installation of Archbishop McNicholas in the Cathedral, Cincinnati, Ohio, August 12, 1925; consecration of the Church of St. Mary, Oswego, N. Y., September 13, 1925; dedication of Cleveland Seminary, October 25, 1925; obsequies of Bishop Carroll of Helena, Mont., December 2, 1925; installation of Bishop Welch in the Sacred Heart Cathedral, Duluth, February 4, 1926; the International Eucharistic Congress, Chicago, Ill., May 29, 1926; centennial of the founding of the Diocese of St. Louis and consecration of the new Cathedral, June 30, 1926: consecration of Most Reverend Francis M. Kelly as Auxiliary Bishop of Winona, June 9, 1926; sesquicentennial celebration of the founding of the City of San Francisco in the Mission Dolores Church, October 10, 1926; obsequies of Bishop Muldoon, Rockford, Ill., October 12, 1927; silver jubilee of Archbishop Keane, Dubuque, Iowa, October 27, 1927; funeral of Bishop Heffron, Winona, Minn., November 28, 1927; tribute to Bishop Shahan on resigning the rectorship of the Catholic University of America, Washington, D. C., 1927; convention of the Central Verein of America, St. Cloud, Minnesota, 1928; obsequies of Archbishop Keane, Dubuque, Iowa, August 7, 1929.

Diocesan Institutions Dedicated

The ten years of the Archbishop's active life in St. Paul were busy ones if we are to judge by the material progress of the diocese indicated by the number of churches, schools, educational and charitable institutions dedicated by him. We append a summary of the more important of these functions.

On May 29, 1919, he dedicated the new chapel at the College of St Thomas and sang the Pontifical Mass at which Bishop Lawler of Lead South Dakota, preached; on May 20, 1920, he blessed the new Monastery for the Magdalen community of the Sisters of the Good Shepherd, Moun Eudes, St. Paul, the gift of Mr. and Mrs. Timothy Foley, a three-story structure, 124 by 30 feet in size, housing forty-seven Magdalens; on September 11, 1921, he laid the cornerstone of the Church of St. Mary St. Paul; on July 23, 1922, he blessed the cornerstone of the new De La Salle High School, conducted by the Christian Brothers in Minneapolis and dedicated it on March 11, 1923; on May 21, 1922, he officiated a the blessing of the cornerstone of Nazareth Hall Preparatory Seminar at Lake Johanna and delivered an address after Bishop McNicholas c Duluth preached the festive sermon, and on September 8, of the follow ing year dedicated the institution and consecrated the chapel on whic occasion Bishop McNicholas again preached; in the spring of 1922 he inaugurated the building of the Chancery Office in the rear of the Cathedral on Dayton Avenue, which was ready for occupancy in March, 1923; on December 17, 1924, the Cathedral rectory on Selby Avenue, begun March 25 of that year, was occupied by the pastor and his assistants; and the Cathedral Sacristy, begun April 15, 1924, was finished in May of the next year; on October 7, 1924, he dedicated the Chapel of Our Lady of Victory at the College of St. Catherine, celebrated Pontifical Mass and Father Cullen, President of the College of St. Thomas, preached the sermon; on October 8, 1925, he dedicated the Normal School for sister teachers, the gift of the daughters of the late James J. Hill; on May 13, 1926, he was honored with an official reception at the Newman Hall, 1228, 4th Avenue, South East, Minneapolis, which had been formally opened for the benefit of the Catholic students of the University of Minnesota on May 8; on May 26, 1926, he consecrated the Mother of God Shrine at Nazareth Hall, a Bedford stone structure, 28 by 15 feet in size, with a marble altar, erected in memory of a benefactor of the institution; on August 28, 1926, he blessed and laid the cornerstone of Seton Guild in Minneapolis at 207 South 9th Street, and spoke at a program presided over by Monsignor Cleary and at which other addresses were delivered by Mayor George E. Leach and E. L. Somerville, a member of the Board of Directors of the institution; on October 3, 1926, he officiated and preached at the dedication of the Church of St. Luke, St. Paul, of which the Right Reverend James C. Byrne, Vicar General, was pastor; on March 19, 1927, he dedicated the Motherhouse of the Sisters of St. Joseph on Randolph Avenue, St. Paul, erected to commemorate the seventy-fifth anniversary of their arrival in the diocese, an institution costing $375,000, and on the same occasion blessed the new chapel of Our Lady of the Presentation in connection with it, officiated at the Pontifical Mass and at the reception into the community of 28 postulants and the taking of vows of 22 novices; on April 16, 1927, he laid the cornerstone of the new St. Andrew's Church, St. Paul, and on December 4 of the same year officiated and preached at the dedication of the sacred edifice which cost $150,000, and will seat 510 persons; on August 27, 1927, he dedicated Mendel Hall, the new science building of the College of St. Catherine, a five-story structure, 231 by 65 feet in dimensions; on October 9, 1927, he officiated at the dedication of the new grade school for the parish of the Ascension in Minneapolis, built under the direction of Reverend John Dunphy; on Christmas day, 1927, he had the happiness of celebrating Mass in the completed sanctuary of the Cathedral; on June 10, 1928, he officiated at the dedication of the new Cretin High School in St. Paul, which cost $625,000, of which $200,000 was contributed by the Archbishop Ireland

Educational Fund, $300,000 by the parishes in St. Paul, $35,000 by the Christian Brothers, $50,000 by the late Mrs. James J. Hill, and $40,000 by the sale of the old school property; on April 28, 1929, he dedicated the Church of St. Boniface in Minneapolis, in charge of the Benedictine Fathers, and the Abbot of St. John's, the Right Reverend Alcuin Deutsch, O. S. B., preached the sermon; on August 1, 1930, he blessed the memorial oratory and statue of St. Teresa in the Catholic Boys' Home, Minneapolis, furnished by Mr. Hubert Kelly, a member of the Orphanage Board, in memory of his wife, and after the ceremony officiated at Benediction in the local chapel and preached a sermon in which he made a plea for assistance for the orphans and traced the history of such institutions in the United States; on May 30, 1930, he dedicated the new addition to St. Joseph's Academy in St. Paul.

National Catholic Historical Convention

The twelfth annual convention of the Catholic Historical Association of the United States was held in the Nicollet Hotel, Minneapolis, during the week of December 28, 1931, concurrently with the annual meeting of the American Historical Society. It took place during the interregnum betwen the death of Archbishop Dowling and the coming of Archbishop Murray, under the administration of Monsignor Byrne. The sessions were largely attended by priests, sisters, layman, teachers and students from the Catholic academies and colleges of the vicinity. It was under the direction of Reverend Peter Guilday of the Catholic University, General Secretary of the Association, assisted by Father Reardon, General Chairman of the local committee on arrangements.

The evening before the official opening of the convention Dr. Guilday lectured before the Knights of Columbus and their guests on "A Catholic Chapter in American History", called their attention to the importance of the convention and invited them to attend the sessions.

The general theme of the convention, "The Catholic Church in Contemporary Europe", was discussed in nine papers prepared by prominent educators in the field of Catholic history and proved interesting and instructive to the large audiences that heard them.

The President of the Association, Professor Carlton J. H. Hayes of Columbia University, chose for the subject of his address, "The Significance of the Reformation in the Light of Contemporary Scholarship".

The following message was sent to the convention by the Most Reverend John G. Murray of Portland, Maine, who was to be installed as Archbishop of St. Paul on January 27, 1932:

> Regretting my inability to attend the sessions of the Catholic Historical Association convention I beg to congratulate the officers on the intensely interesting program prepared and to express my appreciation of the hospitality extended by the people of my future jurisdiction. To all who

are assembled for the meeting I wish an abundance of profit from their devotion to the great science which Leo XIII proclaimed the 'mistress of life and the light of truth.' [89]

In his annual report Dr. Guilday referred to the early history of the Church in the Northwest.

The Catholic landmarks of Minneapolis and St. Paul are among the oldest in our country; and many are the Catholic names linked inseparably with the story of the advance of civilization, culture and religion in this part of the great old Northwest Territory—Groseilliers and Radisson, the earliest explorers; Hennepin and his companions, Michael Accault and Anthony Augelle; the traders, Nicholas Perrot and Pierre Charles Le-Sueur; the Jesuits, Joseph Jean Marest, Michael Guignac and Nicholas de Gonner—to mention but a few of the pioneers who explored and evangelized this part of our land during the two centuries which preceded the arrival of the first regularly appointed priests—Father Lucien Galtier, who built the first log chapel in 1841, dedicated to St. Paul, the Apostle of the Gentiles.[90]

He spoke of the arrival of Bishop Cretin in 1851 when there were only one thousand Catholics in the diocese which six years later had fifty thousand; the coming of the Sisters of St. Joseph; the building of Catholic schools and hospitals; the organization of St. Vincent de Paul Conferences and Catholic Temperance societies—all of which followed this auspicious beginning of juridic ecclesiastical life. "When the saintly Cretin died in 1857, Minnesota could boast of a perfectly organized church".

He referred to Bishop Grace and his work; to Archbishop Ireland who died in 1918, "after forty-five years of active social and religious leadership not alone in the Northwest but in the country at large"; to Archbishop Dowling who, as Bishop of Des Moines, mapped out the broad general lines of the work of the Catholic Historical Association in 1919; and to Archbishop Murray who, as Auxiliary Bishop of Hartford, was one of the sixty-eight founders of the Association and who, as General Chairman of the committee, made the preliminary arrangements for the convention of the Association held in New Haven, Connecticut, in 1922.

Officers elected were: President, Dr. James F. Kenney, Ottawa, Canada; First Vice-President, Dr. Constantine E. McGuire, Washington, D. C.; second Vice-President, Rt. Rev. E. J. McGolrick, Brooklyn, N. Y.; Treasurer, Rev. J. K. Cartwright, Washington, D. C.; Secretary, Rev. P. Guilday, Washington, D. C.; Archivist, Miss J. Lyon, Catholic University, Washington, D. C.

MOST REVEREND JOHN GREGORY MURRAY, S.T.D.
Third Archbishop of St. Paul
1932—

XI

TWENTY YEARS OF PROGRESS
MOST REVEREND JOHN GREGORY MURRAY, S.T.D.
THIRD ARCHBISHOP OF ST. PAUL

1877—

The Most Reverend John Gregory Murray was born in Waterbury, Connecticut, on February 26, 1877, the son of William Murray and Mary Ellen Connor.[1] His father hailed from Carrickmacross, County Monaghan, Ireland, and his mother was a native of Maryborough, Queen's (Leix) County. He was baptized on March 1, 1877, in the Church of the Immaculate Conception, Waterbury, received his first Holy Communion in St. Patrick's Church in that city on November 27, 1887, and was confirmed in the same church on September 8, 1888, by the Right Reverend Lawrence Stephen McMahon, fifth Bishop of Hartford. He was educated in the public schools in the elementary, grammar and high grades, graduating from the Waterbury High School on April 11, 1895. He then entered the College of the Holy Cross, Worcester, Mass., and was graduated with the degree of Bachelor of Arts in June, 1897. He distinguished himself by quick intelligence and steady diligence in his studies and was sent to Louvain, Belgium, to complete his preparation for the priesthood for which he had manifested a vocation from the days of youth. He matriculated at the American College, Louvain, in October, 1897, and resided there until July 15, 1900. He followed the theological course in the Schola Minor of the Jesuit College from October, 1897, to July, 1898; in the Schola Minor of the University of Louvain from October, 1898, to July, 1899; and in the Schola Superior of the University from October, 1899, to July, 1900. He was ordained to the priesthood on April 11, 1900, for the Diocese of Hartford, Connecticut, by the Right Reverend Bishop Van der Stappen, Auxiliary to the Cardinal Archbishop of Mechlin. During his residence in Louvain he hung up a record for exceptionally high scholastic attainments, a gentle, generous disposition and a manliness of character that won for him a reputation as an exemplary student that has persisted till the present. He is still fondly remembered as "the good John Murray".

507

On his return to the United States he was appointed, on September 1, 1900, Chaplain to the Hartford County Jail and Professor of Greek, Latin and German in St. Thomas Preparatory Seminary, built by Bishop Tierney, where he remained until October 3, 1903, when he became Chancellor of the Diocese of Hartford with residence in the Bishop's house, 140 Farmington Avenue, until November, 1922. He was appointed Titular Bishop of Flavias and Auxiliary to Bishop Nilan of Hartford on November 15, 1919, and consecrated on April 18, 1920, by the Most Reverend John Bonzano, Titular Archbishop of Mitilene and Apostolic Delegate to the United States, assisted by Bishops Nilan of Hartford and Shahan, Rector of the Catholic University of America, as co-consecrators. The sermon was preached by the Right Reverend Monsignor Thomas S. Duggan, Editor of the Catholic Transcript from 1897 to 1945. He continued to live at the Bishop's house until November, 1922, when he was appointed pastor of St. Patrick's Church in Hartford and went to reside in the parish.

The duties of Auxiliary Bishop and of pastor of a large parish absorbed most of his energies until he was promoted to the residential see of Portland, Maine, on May 29, 1925, and installed therein as its fifth bishop, on October 12 of that year.

During his residence in the Diocese of Hartford he helped to organize the Catholic Historical Association in 1919 and was one of the sixty-eight founders. He was General Chairman of the local committee that supervised the arrangements for the annual meeting of the Association in New Haven during the last week of December, 1922.

Bishop of Portland

During his six years in Portland, Maine, he organized thirty-one new parishes by placing resident pastors in former missions, and encouraged the erection of parochial schools wherever possible. In Bangor a central high school was built at a cost of $800,000. In the Cathedral parish a new elementary school was erected in 1927 and a Guild hall that houses the Chancery Office, the Bureau of Charity and other offices as well as a large gymnasium.[2]

The Cathedral rectory was entirely modernized and, on the occasion of the Diamond Jubilee of the Diocese and the sixtieth anniversary of the dedication of the Cathedral, the building itself and its chapels were completely renovated. A Diocesan Director for the Propagation of the Faith and a Superintendent of Schools were appointed, assigned work and officers. "The Church World", the diocesan weekly paper, was founded and circulated in the parishes.

In June, 1927, he attended the celebration of the five hundredth anniversary of the founding of the Catholic University of Louvain, a brilliant event which brought together from all parts of the world eminent prelates, famed scholars, and leading educators. He was one of the recipients of the degree of Doctor of Sacred Theology "honoris causa", an honor very rarely bestowed.

A comparison of the diocesan statistics in the Official Catholic Directories for 1925 and 1931 shows that the number of diocesan priests increased from 167 to 216; churches with resident pastors from 95 to 126; and parish schools from 56 to 58; while the number of mission churches was reduced from 73 to 57 and of stations from 168 to 80 due to the elevation of many of them to parochial status. He was an active member of the National Catholic Welfare Conference and for several years treasurer of the organization.

He manifested a great love for the missions and tried to make the people mission-minded as a means of strengthening their faith and making them more active in the propagation of the gospel at home and in foreign fields.

He was beloved by all the citizens irrespective of class, color, racial descent or religious affiliation. He was helpful and cooperative in all movements for the public welfare, interested in every project for the spiritual and material advancement of the community and encouraged a wholesome respect for law and order. He was recognized as a leader not only in the religious world but in the civil domain. He was cited by the Forty and Eight Voiture of the American Legion of Portland as an outstanding citizen and given the privilege of honorary membership in the organization. He was likewise a member of the advisory committee of such cited citizens formed by Post 17 in that city.

It is no wonder, then, that not only the priests and the Catholic laity but the citizens in general heard with dismay that the dynamic and beloved bishop had been called to another field of labor. While they rejoiced at the well-merited promotion to the Archiepiscopal Throne of St. Paul, they regretted that it would take him from among them. Plans were made for a series of farewell meetings[3] and demonstrations of affectionate regard. The clergy tendered him a banquet in the Hotel Lafayette at which one hundred and fifty guests surrounded the festive board. They presented him with a pectoral cross of celtic design in green gold set with African tourmaline and a ring with Siberian amethyst as a token of high personal regard and of appreciation for the work he had done in the diocese during the six years of his incumbency.

Seven hundred men attended a communion breakfast at which he presided; and five councils of Catholic women held a reception for him in the Cathedral Guildhall. They praised him for his latest contribution to diocesan institutions, the Cheverus Dental Clinic, opened a few days previously, for the benefit of the Catholic school children. It is recognized as one of the finest in the New England States.

At a dinner in his honor the Knights of Columbus presented him with a traveling bag as a token of appreciation and in reply he assured them that he came to Maine "determined never to make a law, impose a regulation, or administer a rule, unless the evil became so rampant that such action was necessary. I came determined to let matters be guided by the goodness of your hearts ... and I have not been disappointed ... You have lived up to every expectation I had and have fufilled my every hope".

The Pontifical Bulls appointing him Archbishop of St. Paul were issued on October 29, 1931, and as soon as the news was flashed to the Midwest, Monsignor Byrne, pastor of St. Luke's parish, St. Paul, and Administrator of the Diocese, and Monsignor Moynihan, Rector of the St. Paul Seminary, hastened to Portland to greet him, to make known to him the joy with which the announcement of his nomination was received by his future diocesans and to assure him of a royal welcome when he came to take possession of his see.

When the day came for his departure from Portland five hundred citizens gathered at the railway station to bid him a final farewell and a delegation of sixteen priests accompanied him to his future home in Minnesota. He was met in Chicago by a group of priests and laymen from the Twin Cities and escorted to St. Paul. On his arrival in the Union Depot he was welcomed by an immense throng eager to catch a glimpse of their new spiritual leader who, after the formalities of reception were over, went immediately to the Cathedral for a visit to the Blessed Sacrament, after which he reviewed the program for the morrow's functions and retired for the night to the episcopal residence directly across Summit Avenue.

From Maine to Minnesota

In the early forenoon of Wednesday, January 27, 1932, the new Archbishop was officially received[4] at the entrance to the Cathedral by the pastor, Reverend L. F. Ryan, who presented the crucifix to be kissed, and by Monsignor Byrne who offered the holy water sprinkler with which the incoming prelate asperged himself and the ministers of the Mass and was then incensed by the Administrator. The procession reformed and moved up the center aisle to the spacious sanctuary where two Archbishops—McNicholas of Cincinnati and Beckman of Dubuque—thirty-four bishop and abbots and a score of monsignors awaited him in their places, while five hundred priests and seminarians and four hundred sisters of different religious communities were accommodated in the pews beyond the sanctuary rail. A congregation of about five thousand filled the immense church and an additional fifteen hundred waited patiently outside.

A few minutes after his arrival in the sanctuary the Apostolic Briefs, three in number, were read in Latin and in English by the Chancellor, Reverend R. E. Nolan. The first, directed to the new Archbishop, informed him that the Holy See had entrusted to him the "care, government and administration of the Church of St. Paul in matters spiritual and temporal, with all the rights and privileges, duties and obligations pertaining to this pastoral office" with the firm hope and confidence that, sustained by the hand of God, the Church under his charge would be advantageously administered through his paternal activity and fruitful zeal, and would show greater growth from day to day in both the spiritual and temporal domains; the second, to the clergy and laity, exhorted them to welcome, support and respect the new Archbishop, give obedience to his salutary admonitions and commands and show reverence for his person, that he might find in them devoted children and they in him a kind father; the third, to the suffragan bishops, notified them of the appointment of the new Metropolitan and exhorted them to render him obedience according to the canons, that in union with him rich fruits might be garnered for the good of souls.

When the reader descended from the pulpit, the Administrator chanted a prayer and the Apostolic Delegate, Archbishop Fumasoni-Biondi, took the new Metropolitan by the hand and seated him on the Cathedra or throne of teaching authority in the Archdiocese, after which he delivered an address stressing the new prelate's numerous qualifications for the high office to which he had been elevated, and assuring priests and people that their joy on this occasion would develop into admiration, esteem and love as they came to know and appreciate the spiritual qualities of the new Chief Pastor placed in authority over them.

The Archbishop was then greeted by Monsignor Byrne with a formal address in which, after a reference to the deceased bishops of the diocese, he declared that its spirit was one of deep and abiding loyalty to the Holy See, and pledged the homage and obedience of the clergy and the faithful to their new Spiritual Chieftain.

In his inaugural sermon Archbishop Murray voiced his trust in the power of God and the guidance of the Vicar of Christ and pledged his utmost to serve the Church, his brethren in the hierarchy, the people entrusted to his keeping and the citizens without exception who would offer him the opportunity to associate himself with them in the cause of God and country. The clergy then approached the throne and kissed the ring of their new Archbishop in token of homage and loyalty. It was a memorable scene not likely to be soon forgotten by those privileged to witness it.

At the Pontifical Mass which followed the Archbishop was assisted by Fathers L. F. Ryan as archpriest, M. J. Casey and M. A. Schumacher,

C. S. C., as deacons of honor, J. Cieminski as deacon of the Mass, J. A. Corrigan as subdeacon and A. J. Ziskovsky as master of ceremonies. The Apostolic Delegate was attended by Fathers Cullen and Reardon and had for master of ceremonies Father Schaefer. The Mass and ceremonies were broadcast over KSTP by Father Peters, C. S. P., and over WCCO by Father Busch.

After the Mass a banquet was served to five hundred and ninety prelates and priests in the St. Paul Hotel at which Father Cullen, pastor of the Church of St. Stephen in Minneapolis, presided as toastmaster. The toast to "The Holy Father" was responded to by the Most Reverend Apostolic Delegate; to "Our Country" by Monsignor Cleary; to "The Province of St. Paul" by Bishop Lawler; to "Our Diocese" by Father Ryan, pastor of the Cathedral. At the close of the program Archbishop Murray made gracious acknowledgement of the tributes paid him by the various speakers and of the courtesy shown him since his arrival—omens of the happy relations to exist between them in the future.

In the evening at the Athletic Club the alumni of Holy Cross College gave a dinner at which the guests of honor were Archbishop Murray and the Reverend John Fox, S. J., President of the institution. It was attended by the visiting graduates and many from different parts of the Midwest who rejoiced that the College had given its first Archbishop to the Church in the United States.

The Archbishop was guest of honor at a civic reception held the following evening in the Municipal Auditorium where fourteen thousand persons greeted him with prolonged applause as he took his seat on the stage. The Honorable T. D. O'Brien presided and, after a program of addresses by state and city officials, the Most Reverend Archbishop delivered an address on "Good Citizenship" which was frequently interrupted by applause and favorably commented on by all who heard it.

Prominent among the decorations at the Cathedral, in the dining hall and the auditorium was the coat-of-arms[5] of the Archbishop, a composite of that of the Archdiocese of St. Paul and of his personal crest. The dexter side, the left as one faces it—that of the Archdiocese—shows the sword of the spirit cleaving the waters of the Mississippi, three impaled crosses —one of which is the hilt of the sword—honoring the Blessed Trinity, with the heraldic miter at the summit of the seal.

An eagle, rampant, symbolic of St. John the Evangelist, his patron saint, surmounts the central portion of the sinister or personal side; a dove in profile represents St. Gregory and three stars in a field of blue are the heraldic device of the Murray family. Rising behind and above the sinister is the crozier. The whole is surmounted by the ecclesiastical hat with cords and ten pendent tassels on each side, and below all the motto: Mea Omnia Tua (all that I have is yours).

Religious and Social Affairs

On the Sunday following his installation, January 31, His Excellency pontificated in the Basilica of St. Mary[6] in presence of nearly fifty priests of Minneapolis, the Christian Brothers of De La Salle High School, the Sisters of St. Joseph from St. Margaret's Academy and elsewhere and a congregation that taxed the capacity of the church. He was welcomed by the pastor, Father Reardon, on behalf of the parishioners and by Monsignor Cleary, pastor of the Church of the Incarnation and Dean, in the name of his fellow priests of the city. In his sermon the celebrant praised the zeal of the clergy and the faith of the people, complimented them on their magnificent church, comparable to any in the Old World, and assured them of his desire to be of service to them in every possible way. At the dinner which was served in the Basilica residence he met the priests personally and spoke to them with paternal benevolence.

These formal and official functions were followed by a series of luncheons and dinners given by civic and fraternal organizations and groups to welcome His Excellency and give their members an opportunity to meet him personally.

At noon on the day after his installation he paid his first visit to the St. Paul Seminary and was entertained at dinner to which a large number of guests had been invited. An address of welcome was read by Louis McCarthy, a seminarian, and Monsignor McDonough, who had been his Vicar General in Portland, spoke of the loss sustained by that diocese in the transfer of its beloved bishop to the Midwest. The Archbishop greeted the faculty, guests and seminarians in an inspiring address which was loudly applauded.

The business men of St. Paul tendered him a reception and dinner at the St. Paul Hotel on February 1; and a week later, under the auspices of the Civic and Commerce Association, a thousand business men and women of Minneapolis met him at a complimentary luncheon in the Radisson Hotel. It was the first time in the history of the Association that such a tribute was paid to a churchman. Addresses were delivered by Mayor Anderson, B. B. Sheffield, President of the Association, and Bishop McElwaine of the Episcopal Church who assured the guest of honor of a hearty welcome and fullest cooperation in all efforts for the betterment of the city and the state. In his response the Archbishop praised the citizens of Minneapolis for having already developed three outstanding qualities: character, culture and civic spirit, in order to maintain leadership, not only in the county and in the state, but in the nation at large—a leadership that redounded to the honor of all who participate in the responsibility of this common citizenship. After the luncheon there was an informal reception where the guests met in fraternal and cordial amity.

On February 3 the national, state and local officers of the Knights of Columbus gave a dinner in his honor in the St. Paul Hotel at which the Supreme Knight, Martin Carmody of Grand Rapids, Michigan, presented a check for one thousand dollars as an expression of appreciation, and addresses were delivered by Reverend John McGivney, the Supreme Chaplain, and a life-long friend, and others. Four hundred guests applauded the Archbishop's address.

Similar tributes were paid him by the local Councils of the Knights of Columbus; and the members of Nicollet Assembly, Fourth Degree, of Minneapolis, had him as their special guest at a dinner in the Radisson Hotel for the annual observance of Washington's birthday. He told the assembled Knights that George Washington had the distinction of a constructive leadership unequalled by any other hero in the field of government and deserved a tribute of love and gratitude from every human heart that cherishes the God-given right of self-development.

Official Appointments and Activities

As soon as the ceremonial pomp of the installation and the festivities incident thereto—and they were many and varied, for civic bodies as well as Catholic societies and groups manifested their good will, welcoming sentiments and spirit of hearty cooperation by receptions and dinners—His Excellency settled down to the official duties and exacting demands of his new position. He appointed the Right Reverend James C. Byrne, pastor of the Church of St. Luke, St. Paul, Vicar General of the Archdiocese, and made no changes in the rectorship of the Cathedral nor in the staff of the Chancery Office. He took up his residence in the house occupied by his predecessors, 226 Summit Avenue, directly in front of the Cathedral, where he remained for five and a half years before vacating it to provide accommodations for sisters attending the summer school of the Diocesan Teachers College, and taking up his residence in more circumscribed quarters in the Cathedral rectory, 239 Selby Avenue, where he has since lived with the priests of the parish and of the Chancery Office.

In the course of a few weeks he appointed to membership on the Board of Consultors[7] the Right Reverends J. M. Cleary, pastor of the Incarnation parish, Minneapolis, P. O'Neill of St. Patrick's, A. Ogulin of St. Agnes, and Reverends F. J. Schaefer of St. Matthew's, A. Kotouc of St. Stanislaus, and J. A. Corrigan of St. Mark's, all of St. Paul.

In the midst of the joyous festivities he was called upon to offer his first Pontifical Mass of Requiem in the Church of the Guardian Angels, Hastings, for the repose of the soul of the pastor, Reverend C. F. McGinnis, a former professor of St. Thomas College and associate editor of The Catholic Bulletin, at which the sermon was preached by Mons-

ignor Byrne. The body of the deceased was taken to Chicago for inter-
ment in the family plot. A few days previously he presided at the
obsequies of Reverend Francis L. Kelly, O. P., in the Church of the
Holy Rosary, Minneapolis. The Mass of Requiem was said by Father
Kearney, Provincial of the Order, and burial was in St. Mary's Cemetery.

The first ceremony of religious reception and profession at which the
Most Reverend Archbishop officiated after his installation was held in
the chapel of the House of the Good Shepherd, St. Paul, on February 21,
when two postulants received the choir habit of the sisterhood and one
novice made her profession. The Archbishop was the celebrant of the
Mass and during the ceremony, following his sermon, was assisted by
the chaplain, Father Barron, and several priests, all of whom were
invited to dinner and privileged to visit the Magdalens in their community room.

About a month later, on Saturday, March 19, the feast of St. Joseph,
he officiated at a similar ceremony in the chapel of the Presentation at
the Provincial House of the Sisters of St. Joseph, when nineteen novices
pronounced their first vows and twenty-two postulants were clothed with
the habit of the sisterhood and given their names in religion. The Archbishop preached after the Solemn Mass celebrated by the Right Reverend J. C. Byrne, V. G., and with the visiting clergy was entertained
at dinner after the ceremony.

The first confirmation[8] administered by Archbishop Murray was in the
chapel of St. Margaret's Academy, Minneapolis, on Sunday, February 23,
where he confirmed a class of deaf mutes who had followed the exercises
of a week's retreat preached in the Basilica of St. Mary by Reverend
E. J. Gehl of St. John's Institute for the Deaf, St. Francis, Wisconsin,
which was attended by one hundred and twenty-five persons, seventy-
five of whom were deaf mutes and ten of whom were non-Catholics.
The Archbishop said Mass and preached to them and their friends
gathered for the occasion. His sermon was translated into the sign
language by Father Gehl. The class was presented by Reverend W. A.
Brand of the Basilica staff, chaplain of the deaf mutes of the Twin
Cities. After the ceremony a group picture was taken in front of the
Academy.

On the feast of St. Thomas, March 7, he pontificated in the College of
St. Thomas chapel preliminary to the dedication[9] of the new Arts and
Administration building fronting on Summit Avenue and erected at a
cost of upwards of $300,000. It houses the administrative offices, the
liberal arts and law school, the college and the law libraries, and club
rooms for the different campus organizations and activities.

The occasional sermon was preached by the Reverend R. G. Bandas
of the St. Paul Seminary faculty. The colorful procession of 250 uni-

formed cadets, 600 college men, members of the faculty in their academic robes and distinguished guests which preceded His Excellency and the ministers of the Mass to the chapel, was dispensed with after Mass because of the inclement weather and the Archbishop and his attendants hastened to the new building for the ritualistic blessing of its different rooms, after which dinner was served and addresses delivered by Monsignor Moynihan, Rector of the St. Paul Seminary, and Father Schumacher, President of the College. In the evening there was a public meeting under the auspices of the Alumni Association at which the Archbishop delivered the principal address wherein he visualized a new era for the College and expressed his hopes for an increase of inspiring leadership on the part of its graduates. On the previous day visitors were conducted through the building which is the very latest in design, arrangement and equipment. It was the first of several new buildings to be dedicated during his regime for the modernization of the institution and the development of its facilities as an up-to-date training school for Catholic young men. The O'Shaughnessy Hall and Stadium, and the Albertus Magnus Science Hall came into existence in a few years, and several others were planned.

On Tuesday, March 15, he was guest of honor at a noonday luncheon given by the Kiwanis Club of Minneapolis; and two days later at a similar function by the St. Paul branch of the organization. On the evening of St. Patrick's day he was present at the annual dinner of the Emerald Club in the Curtis Hotel in Minneapolis.

On Sunday, March 20, he attended the quarterly meeting of the Archdiocesan Union of the Holy Name societies in the Ascension Club, Minneapolis, at which four hundred members, many of whom were delegates from the thirty-nine affiliated units, were present for the annual installation of officers and for the discussion of plans for the rally in the State Fair grounds in June. He delivered an address in which he felicitated them on the good example they gave to their fellow-Catholics and to the citizens in general by their avoidance of the unbecoming use of the Holy Name, and exhorted them to add to their ranks the many more eligible men of the Archdiocese. After dinner in the pastoral residence he met the people of the parish at an informal reception in the auditorium of the club house.

His Excellency was guest of honor at the dinner and reception in the Radisson Hotel on March 28 under the auspices of the Twin City chapter of the International Federation of Catholic Nurses at which plates were laid for over two hundred. The principal speakers were Dr. Harrington, Commissioner of Health for the City of Minneapolis, Dr. Brady of the St. Paul Seminary and the Most Reverend Archbishop. The Federation was organized at Spring Bank, Wisconsin, in 1924. Twelve nurses from

St. Mary's Hospital, Minneapolis, and St. Joseph's Hospital, St. Paul, took part in its formation and Miss Kathryn McGovern, a graduate of St. Mary's, was elected President.

At a dinner and reception tendered him on April 19 by the Christ Child Society of St. Paul, the Most Reverend Archbishop was welcomed by Reverend Louis Pioletti, pastor of the Italian parishes of the Holy Redeemer and St. Ambrose. The various phases of the educational program of the society were described by Miss Eleanor G. Dowling, Director of the local unit. Miss Margaret Smith, President of the society, presided at the dinner which was attended by more than two hundred guests among whom were Fathers Schenk, Assistant Chancellor, and Doherty, Director of the Catholic Charities Bureau. The Archbishop congratulated the sponsors of the society on what had been accomplished and praised the efficient Director for the splendid work done among the Italian children of the neighborhood.

The twenty-fifth anniversary banquet of the alumni of De La Salle High School, Minneapolis, at which five hundred were served, was held in the school on April 20, under the toastmastership of Patrick Carr '10. Addresses were given by Monsignor Cleary, Fathers Dunphy and Reardon, Brother Cassian, the Director, Richard J. Dynes, President of the organization, Theodore Wiegand on behalf of the alumni and Bernard Van Demark of the class of '31. The Archbishop praised the Christian Brothers for their excellent work as educators according to the mind of the Church, her principles and ideals, and exhorted the alumni to make public profession of their faith whenever called upon to do so and reflect credit on De La Salle by their loyalty to God and country.

The Most Reverend Archbishop attended the semi-annual meeting of the Board of Trustees of the Catholic University of America on April 6, 1932, at which it was voted to organize the Friends of the Catholic University in accordance with the plan outlined by Pope Pius XI in his letter of October 10, 1929, for the purpose of educating clergy and laity in regard to the fundamental aims and immediate needs of Catholic higher education, and the ultimate development of a group of Catholic laymen interested in promoting Catholic pre-eminence in cultural fields. He and Archbishop Glennon of St. Louis were commissioned to direct and foster the organization in an effort to establish it in every diocese in the country. It was hoped that a membership of 300,000 could be secured the first year. The plan was gradually put into operation in most dioceses and the Ordinaries appointed chairmen to promote the work, but no great interest was aroused. Archbishop Murray appointed the Diocesan Chancellor, Reverend D. J. Gregory, an alumnus of the Catholic University, who held the position until his untimely death in

1947, when the present director, Very Reverend Gerald Baskfield, of St. Paul Seminary, was appointed.

On the first of May the Most Reverend Archbishop paid an official visit to St. Maron's Church, Minneapolis, where the Syrians worship according to the Maronite rite. He was met at the parish house by Monsignor Byrne, V. G., pastor of the Church of St. Luke, St. Paul, Monsignor Moynihan, Rector of St. Paul Seminary, and a group of civic officials who escorted him to the church where the pastor, Reverend Peter Aschkar, said Mass in the ancient rite and the Syrian choir sang the responses. The pastor welcomed His Excellency in an address in English and spoke to the people in their native tongue. The church, too small for the normal congregation, was crowded beyond capacity and hundreds, unable to enter, followed the service as well as possible from without. At the end of the Mass the Archbishop preached and administered the Sacrament of Confirmation to a class of seventy children and five adults.

After the ceremoney all repaired to the Nicollet Hotel where dinner was served to several hundred guests from St. Maron's and from the Holy Family parish, St. Paul. H. Aschkar, brother of the pastor, presided, and two papers were presented—one by Elias Curie, Director of the Syrian choir of St. Maron's Church, dealing with the history of the Maronite people, and the other by Jack Zenn on their history in the Northwest. Addresses were delivered by Monsignor Moynihan, Father Schabert of St. Thomas College, who assisted at St. Maron's on Sundays, Mayor Anderson of Minneapolis, Peter Isaacs of Holy Family parish, and Father Aschkar, after which the Archbishop expressed his appreciation of the honor paid him and of the pleasure it gave him "to break bread and eat salt" with a branch of the Semitic race which had been faithful to the Catholic Church for fifteen hundred years.

In the evening he confirmed thirty children in the Holy Family Church, St. Paul, at a ceremony witnessed by a congregation of five hundred in the church and two thousand on the outside. At the close of the day His Excellency said that the program was "one of the most touching and dignified since my coming to St. Paul".

Educational Institutions

In the month of April the Archbishop wrote a letter to the clergy calling their attention to the tenth opening of the Diocesan Teachers College for the training of the sisters teaching in parochial and other schools, urging them to make arrangements for the attendance of their parochial teachers in order that they might obtain advanced training in the technique of pedagogy, especially in the subjects which vitally affect the life of the child. In a similar letter to the diocesan sisterhoods he urged them to take advantage of the opportunity afforded by the College to give their teaching sisters a more scientific insight into the matter and method of the subjects which they teach in the schools. He pointed out that, under the direction of the Reverend J. A. Byrnes, Superintendent of Catholic instruction in the Archdiocese, many new subjects were offered by the curriculum during the coming session and an augmented faculty would be on hand to carry on the work efficiently from the opening of the courses on June 20 till the close on July 30. The additions to the curriculum comprised the study of modern Catholic poetry, the literature of asceticism, music, physical education, school room handicraft, supervision and improvement of instruction.

During a visit to his former diocese in Maine, whither he was called on business, he hastened to the bedside of his sick sister in Waterbury and thence to New York, where his fellow-alumni of Holy Cross College honored him with a banquet attended by 500 many of them outstanding men in public life, all of whom rejoiced at the metropolitan dignity bestowed on him by the Holy See and, through him, the reflected honor on their Alma Mater.

On his return from the East he fulfilled an engagement to deliver an address on "The Church of the Air" program over a nation-wide hookup of the Columbia Broadcasting System.[10] He chose for his subject "The Church and the University" and on April 30 spoke from the studios of WCCO in Minneapolis, dwelling on the commission given the Church of Christ to teach all nations all things for all time. While this refers primarily to doctrines of faith and morals, the Church must be ready to enter every field of thought and be a patron of all kinds of learning that she may reach all classes of men in all states of life for the purpose of bringing all to their eternal destiny. With the twin torches of faith and reason she must dispel the darkness of ignorance and illumine the minds of men in every country. He described the development of Christian schools under the fostering care of the Church from the second century through the Middle Ages, when they were founded and guided by her, and down to more recent times when Papal authorization was given to modern universities, including the Catholic University of America. He contrasted the Church's system of education in which knowledge is cultivated for the purpose of ennobling and perfecting the intellectual man, with the applied science of the present which has usurped the field of human thought and endeavor almost to the exclusion of philosophical and ethical science. A program of liturgical music was rendered by the Schola Cantorum of the St. Paul Seminary.

The Federation of Mothers' Clubs of Minneapolis had the Archbishop for honored guest at the eighth annual luncheon on May 3 in the Curtis Hotel which was attended by more than three hundred members from all sections of the city. Mrs. William Schwick presided and among the speakers were Father Byrnes, Superintendent of Catholic schools for the Archdiocese, Mrs. P. J. Frey, President of the Federation, and Mrs. Timothy P. Foley, President for the first six years of its existence. Monsignor Cleary introduced the Archbishop who paid tribute to the welfare work done by the Federation and the assistance it had given to the parochial schools of the city.

The Archbishop was given an opportunity to meet President Coffman of the University of Minnesota, members of the Board of Regents, the Deans of several colleges and the Knights of Columbus contact committee at a luncheon under the auspices of the Newman Club of the University at the Nicollett Hotel on April 3, when a thousand Catholic students gave him a rousing greeting. Father Peters, C. S. P., Chaplain of the Newman Club, presided and Dr. W. A. O'Brien of the University Medical School was toastmaster. President Coffman welcomed the Archbishop and pledged cooperation "in the common task which the education of youth places on us all alike". Dean Ford of the graduate school and J. A. Farley, President of the Newman Club, delivered brief addresses. In his response the Archbishop spoke of the University as an institution dedicated to the development of the highest type of citizenship by training leaders in independent thought and action. "The academic life and the life of the Church run so closely together that we must approach their service to the country in a united spirit of cooperation".

On June 4 he presided at the annual rally of the Diocesan Holy Name Union in the State Fair grounds when seven thousand members of the organization marched in parish groups, with Papal and American flags and society banners, before the reviewing stand on which he stood in Cappa Magna, with General John H. Hughes of Fort Snelling and Colonel C. J. Leonard, chief of staff, and blessed them as they passed. The colorful parade was witnessed by thirty thousand people in the grand stand who listened to his address after an introduction by Reverend J. Dunphy, pastor of the parish of the Ascension, Minneapolis, and Spiritual Director of the Union. Father Foley of Faribault led the renewal of the Holy Name pledge, and Father Dühr of Miesville officiated at Benediction of the Blessed Sacrament, at which the Knights of St. George formed the honor guard. It was the first of many similar demonstrations at which His Excellency presided during his long episcopate.

In the meantime he had made plans for a visitation of the diocese which called for confirmation in each parish and mission every three years, a program which he carried out with the utmost fidelity until Holy Week of the year 1947 when, on March 31, he was seriously injured in an automobile accident in front of the Cathedral which necessitated surgery and prolonged hospitalization in the Mayo Clinic at Rochester, Minnesota. Early in this period of inactivity he was given an Auxiliary in the person of Reverend James J. Byrne of the St. Paul Seminary faculty who was consecrated Titular Bishop of Etenna in the St. Paul Cathedral on July 2, 1947, by the Most Reverend Amleto G. Cicognani, Apostolic Delegate to the United States, assisted by the Most Reverends T. A. Welch of Duluth and F. J. Schenk of Crookston, as co-consecrators. The sermon was preached by the Most Reverend W. O. Brady, Bishop of Sioux Falls. The new Auxiliary was the second native of St. Paul to be consecrated, a member of St. Columba's parish and a graduate of Nazareth Hall, St. Paul Seminary and the American College, Louvain, Belgium. He taught in the College of St. Thomas before he was appointed to the Seminary faculty. He immediately took over the confirmation appointments of the Archbishop and substituted for him at all public functions until 1950 when His Excellency, restored to normal health and vigor, was once more able to resume his busy life, much to the delight of priests and people.

Diocesan Functions

The Encyclical Letter of Pope Pius XI, "Caritas Dei" of May 3, 1932, received widespread publicity in the diocese and evoked an explanatory letter from the Archbishop to the clergy giving detailed directions for carrying out the wishes of the Supreme Pontiff. The papal letter invited all Catholics and all men of good will to unite in a crusade of prayer and penance "to alleviate in some measure the terrible consequences of the economic crisis under which the human race is struggling". He enjoined an octave of reparation and consecrated mourning to be held in connection with the feast of the Sacred Heart of Jesus when all the faithful would unite in a "holy rivalry of reparation and supplication".

The Archbishop ordered a novena of prayer and reparation in every parish and mission beginning on the feast of the Sacred Heart with all-day exposition of the Blessed Sacrament, appropriate prayers and the reading of a portion of the Encyclical every evening before Benediction.

In connection with this program he ordered the organization of the crusade of charity prescribed by the Encyclical "Nova Impendit" of October 4, 1931, to solicit and obtain contributions of one day's income a month to be distributed in food, hospitalization, employment, etc., to the needy, regardless of creed or color, in cooperation with whatever agencies of relief existed in the locality. The parish would act as a unit or in connection with other parishes in the city or country area in complying with these regulations that succor might be given to all families and individuals in distress of any kind. There was to be no conflict with the Community Chest, the St. Vincent de Paul and similar organizations already engaged in the work of relief, but the closest cooperation was to be maintained and solicitation made to those who do not contribute to these agencies.

The silver jubilee of the laying of the cornerstone of the Cathedral of St. Paul was commemorated with a Pontifical Mass on Sunday, June 5, at which the rector, Reverend L. F. Ryan, preached, recalling the sacred memories of the day on which the event took place—the milling throngs that surrounded the site, the marching column of thirty thousand Catholic men passing before the reviewing stand where scores of prelates, hundreds of priests and representatives and spokesmen of city, state and nation paid tribute to them in eloquent addresses, the climax of which was the magnificent oration of the venerable Archbishop Ireland, then at the height of his career and oratorical powers.

During the intervening years the Cathedral had been gradually approaching completion. It has been a monumental work, the preacher declared, which in the Middle Ages would have been spread over centuries, but which in these modern days is done in decades. The sanctuary was completed with its seven bronze grilles, said to be unique in the world's history of bronze craftsmanship; the main altar, the soul of the Cathedral, in the center of the spacious sanctuary and the gift of Mrs. Norman Slade, lifts its majestic columns and baldachin towards the heavens. The sacristy, too, and the apsidal chapels have been finished; and the greater part of the interior walls have received their sheathing of golden Mankato stone.

The first Mass in the uncompleted structure was said by Archbishop Ireland on March 28, 1915; St. Peter's chapel, the gift of Mrs. James McCahill of Lake City, was finished in May, 1917; St. Joseph's chapel, donated by the Sisters of St. Joseph and their friends, a year later; and that of the Blessed Virgin Mary with funds provided by the Catholic women of the diocese, in 1919.

In the afternoon of the same day the annual celebration of the feast of St. Boniface was held when four thousand men and women of German ancestry, under the sponsorship of the German societies of the city, crowded the nave of the Cathedral, sang German hymns and listened to an address by the Most Reverend Archbishop in German and in English. Solemn Benediction was given by Monsignor Byrne. The details of the celebration were arranged by Father Schaefer of St. Matthew's Church and Monsignor Ogulin of St. Agnes. It was an annual event for several years.

Honors for the Clergy

During the month of May, 1932, three priests of St. Paul received notice of a rare honor conferred on them by King Victor Emmanuel III of Italy in recognition of their services to the Italian citizens of the Twin Cities. The announcement was made by Chevalier Attilo Castigliano, the Italian Consul in St. Paul.

The title of "Officer of the Order of the Crown of Italy" was conferred upon the Right Reverend James C. Byrne, Vicar General of the Diocese and the pastor of the Church of St. Luke, in recognition of his work among the Italians of the city since his return from Rome in 1883.

The same distinction was conferred on the Right Reverend H. Moynihan, Rector of St. Paul Seminary, a recognized authority on the works of Dante, the great Italian poet.

The Very Reverend L. F. Ryan, Rector of the St. Paul Cathedral, was made a "Chevalier of the Order of the Italian Crown" for his research work into the history of the Italians in Minnesota, his promotion of devotion to their patron saint and his cooperation in erecting the Christopher Columbus memorial on the State Capitol grounds in October, 1931.

The Italian residents of St. Paul gave a dinner in honor of the Most Reverend Archbishop in the Lowry Hotel on May 24 which was attended by one hundred and fifty guests. The Reverend Louis Pioletti, pastor of the Holy Redeemer and St. Ambrose churches, was toastmaster and addresses were delivered by Monsignors Byrne and Moynihan, Father Ryan of the Cathedral, Fred Ossanna of Minneapolis and Attilo Castigliano, the Italian Consul. The Most Reverend Archbishop in acknowledging the tribute paid him, praised the ideals, high intellectual and moral standards of the people of Italy and congratulated their representatives and descendants in the Northwest on their loyalty to the land of their adoption.

The Archbishop preached at the diamond jubilee of ordination of Monsignor Cleary in the Church of the Incarnation at a Solemn High Mass celebrated by the Jubilarian on Sunday, July 10, 1932. Five monsignors and fifty priests were present and fifty altar boys assisted in the sanctuary. A complimentary dinner was tendered the Jubilarian after the Mass and a reception followed on the church lawn at which tributes were paid by Mr. Brick, President of the Holy Name Society, and Mayor Anderson of Minneapolis. Monsignor Cleary came to Minneapolis from the Archdiocese of Milwaukee in 1892, built St. Charles Church of which he was pastor till 1909, when he organized the parish of the Incarnation in a sparsely settled district south of Lake Street and watched it grow to be one of the largest and best equipped in the city.

Later on in the summer the Archbishop preached at the consecration of his successor in the Diocese of Portland, the Most Reverend Joseph E. McCarthy, in the Cathedral of the Immaculate Conception in that city, where he was consecrated on August 24, by the Most Reverend M. F. McAuliffe, Coadjutor Bishop of Hartford, with Bishops Nilan of Hartford and Peterson of Manchester as co-consecrators.

In 1927 the Archbishop Ireland Educational Fund had $619,160.09 in its treasury and the income was used to meet the expenses of the Bureau of Education and the Diocesan Teachers College, and to allocate to the College of St. Thomas a yearly amount representing the partial income from a prospective endowment which the College must have to be recognized as an accredited institution. Before 1933 a yearly subsidy of $15,000 was given and, in addition, $140,979.03 was advanced out of the fund to meet the capital expenses incurred in the program of expansion begun in 1930. In 1934 the annual allotment to the College was raised to $20,000. In 1933 the Bureau of Education cost $6,741.00 and the Teachers College $3,771.56. On July 31, 1934, the Educational Fund was reduced by the foregoing expenditures to $455,377.67.

A few week after the foregoing statement about the Educational Fund was released, His Excellency issued a letter on the financial situation in the diocese, suggesting an equitable arrangement for solving the problem by setting aside a certain percentage of the ordinary revenue of a parish for the cathedraticum, clergy, seminary and orphan fund, and designating certain Sundays in the year for specific collections for diocesan and extra-ordinary purposes, such as the first Sunday of Lent for the Negro and Indian work; Easter Sunday for the Seminary; Pentecost for the Holy Father; the third Sunday of July for the Home and Foreign missions; the third Sunday of September for Nazareth Hall; the first Sunday of October for the orphans; and the first Sunday of Advent for the Catholic University of America.

From the beginning the Archbishop established a reputation for punctuality in keeping his appointments despite obstacles that would have deterred many another from making an attempt. The worst storms of a Minnesota winter have not prevented him from making a succesful effort to reach his distination in time and not disappoint those awaiting his arrival. Priests, children and people know that, if at all possible to brave the blizzard, the Archbishop will not fail them. Nothing but physical inability to do almost the impossible deters him from keeping his engagements in any kind of weather.

His first winter in the state was a severe test. There was much snow and blizzards were not uncommon. In the early part of November he had to resort to auto, bobsled, farm wagon and train to visit snowbound towns in the western section of the Archdiocese. Accompanied by the Chancellor, Father Schenk, he set out on a week's confirmation tour during which he ran into a heavy snowstorm before reaching Danvers. During the night the storm grew worse but that did not prevent his setting out the next day, during which he had to dig his way along almost impassable roads to Ortonville and Rosen and the following day to Nassau, Madison and St. Leo. Farmers with shovels were pressed into service to help clear the way. The road from St. Leo to Taunton was completely blocked to auto travel, and a farm sled and team of horses had to be commandeered to cover the nineteen miles of snow-bound road during which the horses lost their footing, the sled was overturned and the occupants precipitated into a snow bank. A fresh team of horses and a wagon were secured from a farmer for the remainder of the trip. On the return journey the Archbishop and his companion found it necessary to make the trip from Marshall, through Tracy, to Springfield by train in order to reach St. Paul in time to set out for Washington to attend the annual meeting of the Bishops of the United States.

In a letter addressed to the clergy on March 18, 1933, the Archbishop warned them against meddling in political affairs, quoting the decree of the Third Plenary Council of Baltimore which formulated into positive law the injunction of St. Paul to Timothy: "No one serving as God's soldier entangles himself in worldly affairs". The letter forbade "any priest, secular or religious, to discuss in public any question dealing with legislation of a political nature or affecting candidates for public office or concerning persons holding public office" unless there is question of "a religious or moral problem" in which case they must obtain the permission of the Ordinary.

The regulation applied also "to all Catholic societies, parochial, diocesan and national, and to all property owned or occupied by any Catholic Church corporation within the archdiocese, whether the property be assigned to the use of a Catholic or non-Catholic group".

Catholic Historical Society Reorganized

The Catholic Historical Society of St. Paul, established by Archbishop Ireland on April 25, 1905, to gather, preserve and publish information about the origin and development of the Catholic Church in the Northwest and especially in the Ecclesiastical Province of St. Paul, ceased to publish its official organ, "Acta et Dicta", in 1918 when its founder passed away. No effort was made to resume publication under Archbishop Dowling. When Archbishop Murray came to the diocese in 1932 he was asked to reorganize the society[11] as an agency for the collection and preservation of historical records—manuscripts, souvenirs, documents, books, relics, etc.,—about the beginning and growth of the Catholic Church in Minnesota, and authorize the resumption of its official publication as a medium for the dissemination of a knowledge of her past history, present status and future prospects.

He graciously agreed to do so and, with that end in view, called a meeting of the former officers of the society in the St. Paul Seminary on November 7, 1932, at which, as ex-officio President, he was the presiding officer. The following were elected to assist him: First Vice-President, Monsignor Moynihan, Rector of the Seminary; Second Vice-President and Secretary, Father Reardon of Minneapolis; Treasurer and Curator of the Museum, Dr. Schaefer of St. Paul; Assistant Secretary, Father Shanahan of the Seminary faculty; Editor-in-Chief of "Acta et Dicta" Father Busch also of the Seminary faculty.

The report of the Treasurer showed that the society was in a healthy financial condition, with assets amounting to $6,730.06, and a checking account of $314.00 made up of interest on the bonds it owned. It was voted to resume the publication of "Acta et Dicta" and the specific work of the society.

At a subsequent meeting Monsignor Byrne, V. G., of St. Paul, was elected to the Board of Directors and Fathers Connolly of the Seminary staff and Moelter of St. Thomas College were made members of the editorial board to assist Father Busch.

Volume VI of "Acta et Dicta" was issued in two numbers in October, 1933, and 1934; and Volume VII, likewise in two numbers, in October, 1935, and 1936; and then the society ceased to function. Its official organ died of inanition, and no one was willing to assume responsibility, much less blame, for its untimely and lamented death, or to prophesy or even guess when it would be resurrected. Those who are interested in Catholic historical research regard its early demise as a distinct loss to the Church in the Northwest.

In the encyclical letter, "Quadragesimo Anno", Pope Pius XI wrote; "the first and immediate apostles of the workingmen must themselves be workingmen". In compliance with that counsel and with the approval of Archbishop Murray, a Catholic labor school[12] was established in November, 1935, (one of the first in the nation), and the first classes were held in the school hall of St. Joseph's parish in Minneapolis. Later, they were moved to St. Bridget's and then to St. Stephen's to secure a more central location. Attendance was restricted to Catholic men and women who were members of labor unions. Formal classes were offered in Catholic social teaching, economics, parliamentary law and labor law. The average attendance on each class evening was well over one hundred.

Because of conditions begotten by the second world war classes were suspended from 1942 until 1946. Then the school in Minneapolis was reopened at St. Stephen's and a new school established in the Cathedral parish in Saint Paul.

Father Francis Gilligan of the St. Paul Seminary is the director of the schools and associated with him have been Fathers Edward Grzeskowiak of Nazareth Hall and Theodore Krebsbach, O. S. B., of St. Paul. They have been assisted by prominent labor officials and attorneys.

The aim of the schools has been to develop among workingmen strong Christian convictions about the social order so that they individually might spread those convictions and attitudes within their respective unions and thus lay a genuine foundation for the restoration of the social order. The schools were conducted quietly and, because of peculiar conditions, it seemed wise to avoid large public demonstrations. As one product of the schools some of the younger priests developed associations with labor leaders and thus have been able to render substantial service as mediators and arbitrators in industrial disputes.

St. Thomas College Restored To Diocese

The most important problem confronting Archbishop Murray at the outset of his administration was the future of the College of St. Thomas which his predecessor had handed over to the Congregation of the Holy Cross of South Bend, Indiana, by a contract[13] entered into on July 9, 1928, which called for renewal or termination at the end of five years. Notwithstanding this provision the Fathers of the Congregation, in charge of the College for the stipulated five years, labored under the impression that they would be allowed to remain permanently in control of the institution. "Holy Cross managed the College with the thought that its conducting of the College was to be permanent", wrote the President, Father Schumacher, on July 6, 1933. "The Fathers of the Holy Cross are not withdrawing of their own accord. They have asked to remain permanently". They made many alterations and improvements, dismantled the original administration building and erected a new one facing Summit Avenue at a cost of $288,765.63 on which only $75,000 had been paid. At the close of the scholastic year in 1933 the mortgage indebtedness of the College amounted to $250,000 in addition to $330,000 secured by notes. When the Archbishop learned, after repeated demands, that among the methods advocated by the Holy Cross Fathers to liquidate these obligations was one he could not countenance, he decided that it was imperative to restore the College to diocesan control and assume the indebtedness incurred during the five-year period ending July 16, 1933. The proposed plan called for the erection of a separate parish and "center of culture" in the neighborhood with the College chapel as the parish church. Such a parish, it was maintained, would do a great deal of good to certain types of individuals who would patronize it and it would be a source of revenue for the College. It was to be bounded on the East by Cleveland Avenue, on the North by Marshall Avenue, on the West by the Mississippi river, on the South by the College boundary extended to the river along Summit Avenue. A blue print of the collegiate parish in the archives of the Chancery Office makes Lincoln Avenue to Cretin Avenue and Summit Avenue the southern boundary. This request was based on the assurance given by the President that "at Marquette and Detroit the Jesuits are credited by the North Central Association with parish revenue as the equivalent of an endowment fund". The Holy Cross Fathers were willing to concede that the extent of the parish was "a minor consideration. The boundaries would include those families that are living on property that formerly belonged to the College".

On January 31, 1933, Father Burns, the Provincial, wrote Archbishop Murray that he understood that it was his wish that the Holy Cross Fathers continue in charge of the College and asked his views about a permanent agreement.

In reply the Archbishop wrote to Father Schumacher, President of the College, on April 11, after a meeting with the Board of Trustees, that it was advisable to determine beforehand the exact form of such agreement. To that end he asked if the Congregation would require a conveyance of the college property to itself or if it would remain a Minnesota corporation and a diocesan institution, and what assurance would the Congregation give that it would maintain the institution without appealing to the diocese for financial aid.

The answer to these questions came from Father Burns who, on April 17, assured the Archbishop that the title to the College would remain in the Minnesota corporation, and it would continue to be a diocesan institution, even though all the trustees would be members of the Congregation, which would accept full responsibility for the financial management of the institution.

As an apologia for the five-year tenure of office the President, Father Schumacher, issued a "Summary Financial Statement" to the Board of Trustees as of July 6, 1933, in which he maintained that the conditions, financial and otherwise, peculiar to the College were not created by his Congregation; that it was generally understood that extraordinary expenses would have to be incurred; that Archbishop Dowling authorized him to do whatever was essential to meet the pressing needs of the institution; that the Board of Trustees had approved what he did and also the mortgage loan to cover the work; that a new building was authorized by the Administrator, the Consultors and the Trustees; that the Holy Cross Fathers would never have undertaken the management of the College had any intimation been given that they were not to remain permanently; that the work they did "was not born of hirelings but came from the free sons of God"; that they had offered to assume every cent of the debt and carry out the building and development program but the offer was rejected, and they were returning to Notre Dame.

On the advice of his consultors the Most Reverend Archbishop asked the Holy Cross Fathers to withdraw, which they did reluctantly, and appointed the Very Reverend James H. Moynihan, a member of the faculty, to the Presidency of the institution.

At the time it was deemed inadvisable to launch a campaign to liquidate the debt; and it was suggested that an effort be made to obtain from the priests of the diocese an amount sufficient to meet the mortgage indebtedness, and defer the general campaign to a more opportune time. Accordingly, the priests were invited to contribute on the basis of a minimum of one thousand dollars for pastors and five hundred for all others with the suggestion that the sky was the limit for those in more affluent circumstances. By October 1, 1935, the personal contributions of the clergy had reduced the indebtedness from $630,000 to $500,000. The first report,[14] dated December 16, of that year showed that their contributions had reached the sum of $146,088.09.

In the meantime a campaign[15] had been launched among the alumni and friends of the college for the liquidation of the entire debt on the occasion of the Golden Jubilee celebration held on October 17, 1935. The Most Reverend Archbishop pontificated in the College chapel and the festive sermon was delivered by the Most Reverend Edwin V. O'Hara, Bishop of Great Falls, Montana, an alumnus of the institution. The religious observance was followed by a banquet in the Armory for the priests, alumni and three representatives of each parish, at which the project was outlined and the quotas for the parishes announced. The total of the proposed quotas amounted to $694,295.00. The highest amount, $25,000, was asked of three parishes—the Cathedral and St. Mark's in St. Paul, and the Basilica of St. Mary in Minneapolis—and a graduated scale was used for the other parishes. The quotas were to be obtained by a campaign conducted by pastor and people. Some of the parishes paid the assessment without an appeal to the parishioners. All returns were to be made not later than July 15, 1936. On that date, according to the Archbishop's letter of July 20, the contributions from the clergy amounted to $154,292.95 and from the parishes $164,422.04, leaving a balance of outstanding obligations amounting to $363,744.62. On November 5, 1936, the parishes owed $183,435.28 on their quotas. Another report, as of November 1, 1938, credited the clergy with $161,303.10 and the parishes with $257,342.60, a total of $418,645.70, which was paid on the debt, leaving an unpaid balance of $296,939.10. A final report on October 23, 1940, showed that the parishes had paid $304,348.02. Five parishes in St. Paul had paid in full; five in Minneapolis; and fifteen in the country.

Confraternity of Christian Doctrine

The decree issued by the Sacred Congregation of the Council on January 12, 1935, on the promotion of catechetical instruction was put into effect a few months later by the Archbishop who organized the Confraternity of Christian Doctrine,[16] under the direction of the Reverend R. G. Bandas of the St. Paul Seminary faculty, to carry out its provisions by the formation of study clubs to advance the religious education of adults, to train teachers for the release period work permitted by the statutes of Minnesota, to promote vacation schools in country parishes to be taught by sisters or other qualified teachers, and year-round programs of religious instruction for children attending the public schools. Confraternity summer schools for teachers' training and club leadership were held in St. Thomas College, St. Paul, and in St. Margaret's Academy, Minneapolis. 427 were enrolled in these courses from April 5 to July 17 and 1058 from June 14 to July 30 at the Confraternity Center, 281 Summit Avenue, St. Paul.

The Confraternity fostered a uniform program of religious instruction for all children attending public schools, assigning definite subject matter adapted to their age and intellectual capacity. For study clubs it also assigned certain subjects for each year. For the fall semester of 1937 the senior high schools of St. Paul showed an enrollment of 1349 for the release classes and of 619 for the junior high schools, while in Minneapolis the enrollment was respectively 1336 and 629.

The report on the vacation school activities for the first three years showed a constant increase in attendance in country parishes and a decrease in city enrollment offset by the larger number of pupils availing themselves of the release periods. In a letter to the clergy, dated January 13, 1938, the Most Reverend Archbishop stated:

> The experience gained during these three years emphasizes the importance of the work in behalf of our young people and also demonstrates the apostolic zeal of both lay and religious teachers in a cause so vital to the welfare of the Church and society, as well as to the individuals who are the direct recipients of guidance in the way of truth and virtue.[17]

The cultural activity of the Confraternity for the benefit of young men and women of more mature years took the form of a Choral Club under the direction of Reverend F. A. Missia of St. Paul Seminary, which made its first appearance at a concert in the St. Paul Municipal Auditorium on January 19, 1938, to the delight of a capacity audience. Similar programs were given in succeeding years.

Another feature of Confraternity work was the establishment of Catholic Youth Centers in St. Paul and Minneapolis in charge of directors to promote the aims and purposes of the movement, and to provide legitimate recreation for the young as well as for those of more mature years. The Catholic Youth Center of St. Paul was established in the former Knights of Columbus building, 150 Smith Avenue; and in Minneapolis in a private residence at 2120 Park Avenue, purchased for that purpose. They served as training schools for the equipment of teachers, lecturers and leaders whose services were at the disposal of parishes on educational and social programs.

An important phase of Confraternity work was that done through the Bureau of Publicity and Information, with Father Bandas as director, and headquarters at the Confraternity Center, 251 Summit Avenue, St. Paul. Its purpose was to cooperate with the Administrative Committee of the N. C. W. C. in disseminating Catholic truth concerning the Church, her teaching, policy and history, in relation to the problems of contemporary life, to enlighten public opinion, correct misinformation, misrepresentation and vicious propaganda through the public press, radio, theaters, schools, public lectures and other channels.

The St. Paul Confraternity of Christian Doctrine was incorporated on August 30, 1940, and canonically erected in every parish on September 8, 1948. The work is promoted by deanery meetings at regular intervals attended by the Archdiocesan officers and chairmen.

In keeping with the terms of the decree on the promotion of catechetical instruction issued on January 12, 1935, the Archbishop in a letter of March 25, 1936, ordered that vacation schools be held in all parishes from June 15 to July 12, unless a more convenient period be approved for certain parishes. All grade and high school children, not attending a parish school and who had not yet received first communion or confirmation, were required to attend and receive instruction from the pastor, the sisters or, in default of the latter, from intelligent laymen or women who could be induced to offer their services.

In this connection he asked the pastors to visit the homes of Catholic parents whose children were expected to attend and register them so that when the sisters came classes could be organized without delay. The classes were to be held in the church or school, if one were available, or in a public school in the forenoon or afternoon. Provision was to be made for the teaching sisters in a convent of their order, if available, even at a distance, or in the priest's house to be vacated by the priest for their use exclusively but not in a hotel or boarding house. If they were accommodated in a private house a bedroom and a dining room must be set apart for their exclusive use. They must not be asked to instruct adults, either men or women, investigate invalid marriages or do anything prohibited by the rules of their community.

The action taken by various national, state and county organizations, extending membership to groups devoted to the propaganda of birth control and sterilization, made it necessary for the Archbishop to call the attention of priests and people to the ethics governing the relationship of individuals and societies to any organized body adopting principles or policies in violation of the natural law. In a letter of August 6, 1935, he stated very emphatically that thereafter

no individual or group of individuals or society may accept or retain membership in any organization recognizing or supporting birth control or sterilization. Persons employed in any position that involves cooperation of any kind in the process of supporting, promoting or effecting either birth control or sterilization must withdraw from such employment. Physicians, nurses, social workers who contribute to the dissemination of knowledge or participate in any action designated to effectuate birth control or sterilization must be denied the sacraments, until they have agreed to repair as far as possible the injury done and guarantee to refrain from cooperation in such evil. Relief workers who may be commanded to propagate these evils for economic or social reasons must refuse to become agents of such anti-social and demoralizing activity.

All persons who have held membership in any society, conference or federation which has countenanced these evils by accepting them in policy or principle or permitting those professing these evils to associate themselves formally with such groups must send formal notice of withdrawal from the group.

He declared that "the small band of vicious propaganists who have captured the fancy or destroyed the morale of our social leadership do not represent the great body of American thought and morals". An antidote for their activity must be found in the organized force of sane thinking and sound ethics.

On December 21, 1937, Archbishop Murray issued a tentative schedule for a confirmation tour of the diocese extending over three years during which every parish would be visited. If the parish had a parochial school confirmation would be administered during the school year; if not, it would take place during the vacation school period. A similar schedule was issued triennially until he came under the doctor's care.

In making provision for the due observance of the Motu Proprio of Pius X on church music the Most Reverend Archbishop decreed that on and after the first Sunday of October, 1935, there would be in all the churches of the diocese a Solemn Mass or Missa Cantata not later than 11 o'clock with music approved by the Archdiocesan Committee on Sacred Music. The approved text was the "Liber Usualis" either in Plain Chant or modern notation with a short motet in Latin after the proper offertory to be finished before the celebrant was ready to sing the Preface. There was to be no organ accompaniment for the chant of the celebrant or ministers at the altar and all responses were to be made, preferably, without organ accompaniment. During Advent and Lent the use of the organ was prohibited, except on Gaudete and Laetare Sundays and when necessary to sustain the voices of the choir, and for all liturgical services from Holy Thursday to Holy Saturday. At weddings and funerals nothing was to be sung but what was in accord with the liturgy of such services, and the full text of the Dies Irae must be sung without omission or substitution and the chanting of the Libera after the Non Intres said by the celebrant. It was unlawful to sing anything in the vernacular at liturgical services of any kind. Whenever possible the vespers of the Sunday or of the feast should be sung unless the vespers of the B. V. M. were substituted for the vespers of the day. At Benediction only approved hymns were to be sung and at this and other non-liturgical services congregational singing should be strongly recommended. In all cases the organ must be played according to the rules of sacred music.

Visit of Cardinal Pacelli

The most distinguished church dignitary who ever came to St. Paul— none other than the Supreme Pontiff, Pope XII gloriously reigning, then His Eminence Cardinal Pacelli, Secretary of State to His Holiness, Pope Pius XI—arrived in a chartered airliner in the late afternoon of Monday, October 26, 1936, in the course of a hurried trip across the continent. He was accompanied by Auxiliary Bishop Spellman of Boston and Count Galeazzi, an official of Vatican City, and was met at the airport by Archbishop Murray and several bishops of the Province as well as by hundreds of the laity anxious to catch a glimpse of and receive the blessing of this famous member of the Sacred College of Cardinals. The assembled prelates were introduced to His Eminence who greeted each one with brotherly affection. The Cardinal paused before entering the airport station to bless the kneeling throng of people who had awaited his arrival; and then, headed by a motorcycle police escort, the procession of automobiles bearing the distinguished group, went directly to the archiepiscopal residence on Summit Avenue where bishops from six neighboring states had assembled to welcome him to the Northwest. All were entertained at dinner by Archbishop Murray and after a pleasant evening of informal chat retired for the night.

The following morning His Eminence celebrated a low Mass in the Cathedral at 8 o'clock. Thousands of persons of all ages and sexes filled the vast edifice as never before and thronged the streets in its vicinity to salute and welcome the eminent Cardinal so closely associated with Pope Pius XI in the government of the Church and receive his blessing.

When the impressive procession reached the sanctuary and His Eminence was seated on the throne the Archbishop ascended the pulpit and greeted the distinguished visitor with welcoming words.

We are profoundly grateful to Your Eminence for coming here to this part of the United States. Even though your passing is brief, nevertheless, it is much appreciated and we ask God to bless and strengthen you, to grant you length of years and to fortify you in mind and soul in the solution of the great problems that are presented to you in your special office sustaining the Vicar of Christ by your intimate association and by your exemplary manifestation of all that is ideal in the priesthood of Christ.

The Cardinal then spoke briefly in English of which he is a master as he is of several other languages.

On this unforgettable occasion I would like to address you at some length and to open to you my heart, but unfortunately I am not able to do it, as my plans call for long travel and I must today reach San Francisco.
I flew across the country to reach the West and I have come to St. Paul by the same extraordinary means in order to visit the beloved Ordinary of the Archdiocese of St. Paul, my dear and esteemed friend, Archbishop Murray.
I have come also to pay a tribute to the Most Reverend Archbishops and Bishops of all this region, to the earnest priests, the holy religious and the devout faithful, because I know that in you there dwells the spirit of the pioneer, the spirit of the missionary, the spirit of the middle West and the Northwest of this great and powerful nation.
I pray God to bless you abundantly and your labors and sacrifices for His greater honor and glory and for the salvation of souls. In the name of the Holy Father I am happy to bestow upon you all, upon your dear ones, and upon all those committed to your care, the Apostolic Benediction as a pledge of heavenly favors.[18]

The congregation knelt to receive the papal blessing, after which His Eminence celebrated a low Mass, made a brief thanksgiving and, after a light breakfast, hurried to the airport to resume his journey to the West, stopping at Cheyenne, Wyoming, on his way to San Francisco.

At the Mass His Eminence was assisted by the Very Reverends W. O. Brady, Rector of St. Paul Seminary and J. H. Moynihan, President of the College of St. Thomas, and Reverend G. Ziskovsky, master of ceremonies, assisted by the Cathedral clergy.

Sections of the Cathedral had been reserved for the priests vested in cassock and surplice, the sisters of the various congregations, the students of the College of St. Catherine, of the Academy of the Visitation, in academic caps and gowns, of the College of St. Thomas and by the pupils of the upper grades of the parochial schools, as many as could find place in the aisles and in front up to the sanctuary rail. The cadets of St. Thomas Military Academy and of Cretin High School formed a guard of honor between the Archbishop's residence and the Cathedral through which the procession filed into the church and returned after the Mass. The Archbishop, Bishop Spellman, Count Galeazzi, several other bishops and the priests of the Chancery Office, accompanied His Eminence to the airport, and the Archbishop had to decline a pressing invitation to join the distinguished party on its journey to the West because of confirmation dates that could not be changed.

On the tenth anniversary of the Cardinal's visit, the feast of Christ the King, a suitably-inscribed bronze tablet, depicting His Eminence preaching to the congregation, was affixed to the wall near the pulpit as a permanent memorial of the visit of him who is now our Holy Father Pope Pius XII.

The visit of His Eminence was said to be non-official, strictly private and personal, a relaxing and restful respite in a busy life, during which he would call on the American Cardinals in New York, Boston and Philadelphia, and make a leisurely visit to the more important sections of this great country about which he had heard so much. But so numerous were the invitations extended to him by members of the hierarchy, eager to have him visit their dioceses, that the restful sojourn he anticipated became a whirlwind tour by rail, auto and plane, from coast to coast during which he visited twelve of the sixteen ecclesiastical provinces, passed through sixteen states, met eighty Archbishops and Bishops, was greeted by hundreds of priests and religious and thousands of the laity eager to see and hear such a distinguished visitor and kneel for his blessing.

He landed in New York on October 5 and, after formal greetings, went directly to St. Patrick's Cathedral where he met Cardinal Hayes before retiring, for a brief rest, to Inisfade, the palatial home of Mrs. Nicholas F. Brady on Long Island, which was to be his official residence while in the country, and where a brilliant reception was held for him on Saturday evening, October 21, just before he left for the West. It was attended by Cardinals Hayes of New York and Villeneuve of Quebec and distinguished members of New York Society.

In Boston he was the guest of Cardinal O'Connell and Bishop Spellman who accompanied him on his tour of the United States with Count Galeazzi. He spent some days with Cardinal Dougherty in Philadelphia before going to Baltimore and Washington where he was entertained by the Apostolic Delegate, visited the Catholic University, Georgetown College, the Library of Congress, the headquarters of the N. C. W. C., and Mount Vernon where he placed a wreath on the tomb of Washington. In the Nation's Capitol he attended his only non-Catholic function, a complimentary luncheon tendered him by four hundred members of the National Press Club, to whom he made a brief address in the course of which he told them "the Holy Father appeals to you, who have great responsibility in reporting facts and in inspiring public opinion, to work for peace".

From New York he was borne by airplane to the West Coast stopping at South Bend, Chicago, St. Paul, Cheyenne and San Francisco, where he blessed the newly-completed Golden Gate bridge, before continuing to Los Angeles. On the return journey he visited St. Louis and Cincinnati with brief stops at Albuquerque, Amarillo, Wichita, Kansas City and Cleveland, arriving in New York in time to sail on November 9, after Mass in St. Patrick's Cathedral. He had luncheon with the President at Hyde Park on November 5. He was the recipient of honorary degrees from Georgetown, Fordham, Notre Dame and St. Louis universities, addressed large gatherings wherever he landed and, in spite of his frail appearance, stood the journey remarkably well.

His Eminence traveled over eight thousand miles by airplane in less than seven days, crossed the continent twice, got an idea of its vast extent by viewing industrial centers and farming areas, and noted the progress of the Church, her development and accomplishments, with all of which he expressed himself well pleased. He was mightily impressed with the flourishing parochial life of the Church, its beneficial social influences, its school system made possible by the extraordinary generosity of the faithful, the diffusion of frequent, even daily, communion and the close cooperation of clergy and laity in all that appertains to the welfare of religion. Before sailing for home he said, in a written statement,

> I am leaving America with gratitude in my heart to all with whom I have come in contact and with a prayer that Almighty God may continue to bless this great nation, that its citizens may be happy and prosperous, and that the influence of the United States may always be exerted for the promotion of peace among peoples.

Pope Pius XII is the first Pope who visited North America, but not the first to set foot on the western world. Pope Pius IX, as Abbate Giovanni Maria Mastaï Ferretti, spent two years, 1823-5, in Chili, South America, as Auditor of the Apostolic Delegate, Monsignor Muri.

Rallies, Conventions and Ordinations

A rally of the Girl Scout troops of twelve Minneapolis parishes was held in St. Stephen's Church on the afternoon of Sunday, March 12, 1937. It was arranged by Reverend R. E. Cogwin, assistant pastor of the parish, and Diocesan Director of scouting for girls, to commemorate the twenty-fifth anniversary of girl scouting. Five hundred uniformed

Girl Scouts carrying American and troop flags walked in procession from the school to the church, where they listened to an address by Archbishop Murray who traced the history of girl scouting from its humble beginning in Savannah, Georgia, with an initial group of twelve to its present strength of almost 400,000 throughout the country. He declared that the apostolic mission of Catholic Girl Scouts was "Scouting for Souls". They are the lineal descendants of the noble line of women who from the earliest days of the Church have assisted in carrying "the standard of the cross and a knowledge of the christian life to others". The Girl Scout movement is designed to bring together high-minded women and girls to further lofty ideals of life and conduct "by prayer, good works and spiritual activities, and along natural lines by striving to be courageous, self-reliant, patient and perservering". The ceremony was brought to a close with Benediction of the Blessed Sacrament at which Father Cullen, pastor of the parish, officiated. Several priests honored the function with their presence.

The twenty-third National Conference of Catholic Charities[19] to which Archbishop Murray was host during the last week of August, 1937, brought to St. Paul two Archbishops, eleven bishops and nine hundred delegates, leaders in charity and social work, from all parts of the country among whom were monsignors and priests, diocesan directors of charity, in addition to about one hundred delegates from Minnesota and the Northwest. The Superior Council of the St. Vincent de Paul Society met concurrently with it as well as the Conference of Religious of which Sister Katherine, O. S. B., of Duluth was chairman.

The convention opened with Pontifical Mass in the Cathedral at which Archbishop Beckman of Dubuque officiated and Archbishop Cantwell of Los Angeles preached. In the afternoon at 3 P.M., Mrs. James O'Neil of Faribault, President of the Minnesota Council of Catholic Women, presided at a meeting of Catholic women in the Auditorium at which Archbishop Murray gave the principal address. Daily sessions were held during the next three days at which were discussed such topics as Families and Children, Health, Youth Activities and social and economic problems. To acquaint the general public with the work of the Church in the field of charity three open meetings were held, two in the St. Paul Auditorium and one in the Minneapolis Auditorium. On Sunday evening Mayor Gehan welcomed the delegates and their friends on behalf of the City of St. Paul and His Excellency the Most Reverend Archbishop Murray in the name of the Archdiocese. Monsignor Wagner, Director of Charities for Cincinnati, gave the response, after which the presidential address was delivered by James Fitzgerald, Executive Secretary of the St. Vincent de Paul Society of Detroit. On Monday evening the principal address at the public meeting was delivered by Bishop Muench of Fargo. Bishop Shiel of Chicago was the guest speaker at the open meeting in Minneapolis on Tuesday evening. On Tuesday noon Archbishop Murray spoke over a nation-wide radio broadcast during the Farm and Home hour of the network of the National Broadcasting Company over WTCN. He was also the principal speaker at the banquet on Wednesday evening at the St. Paul Hotel where he dwelt on the importance of charity in the parish. To foster it is the prime responsibility of the pastor. Under his direction the people cooperate and the union of charity and faith begets genuine piety. Every Catholic should be actively engaged in the works of charity. Monsignor Corrigan, Rector of the Catholic University, spoke on the "Outlook for Charity". President Fitzgerald presided.

The Holy Father honored the convention with a message sent to Archbishop Murray and the Apostolic Delegate likewise sent a lengthy letter which was well received by the delegates. At the close of the session Monsignor O'Dwyer of Los Angeles was elected President for the next year.

While he seldom referred to vocations to the priesthood or religious life in his sermons or instructions when visiting a parish, the Archbishop was fully aware of the necessity of turning the minds and hearts of the young towards these goals. To that end he decreed that "in every Catholic school within the Archdiocese a novena and, if possible, a retreat, should be held before the end of the scholastic year to make the students conscious of their duty to determine their vocation and be disposed to use the means to fulfill it".

A unique event[20] took place in the Basilica of St. Mary on Sunday, October 3, 1937, at the 11 o'clock Mass, when the Most Reverend Archbishop Murray conferred the powers and prerogatives of the Holy Priesthood on Reverend Leo White, a member of the parish. It was the first time an ordination ceremony was held in Minneapolis. The Archbishop was assisted by Very Reverend W. O. Brady, Rector of the St. Paul Seminary, and Very Reverend J. J. Cullinan, Rector of Nazareth Hall, with Reverend George Zizkovsky of St. Paul Seminary as master of ceremonies.

Father White celebrated his first Solemn Mass in the Basilica the following Sunday at 11 o'clock assisted by the priests of the parish. The sermon was preached by Father Reardon. Father White graduated from St. Paul Seminary in June, 1936, but was too seriously ill to be ordained with his classmates. He was appointed to the faculty of Nazareth Hall.

A similar function[21] took place on Saturday, May 22, 1943, when the Reverend Eugene J. McCarthy was ordained in the Basilica by Archbishop Murray who had conferred the deaconate on him the previou.

day. The Archbishop was assisted by the priests of the parish. Father
McCarthy said his first Mass on Sunday, May 23, at 11 o'clock with Monsignor Reardon as archpriest, Fathers Brand as deacon, Quinlan as subdeacon and Gearty as master of ceremonies. Monsignor Reardon
preached the sermon and Fathers Shea of Nazareth Hall and Hughes
of St. Mary's Hospital were in the sanctuary.

Father McCarthy, a member of the Basilica congregation, began his
studies for the priesthood in St. Paul Seminary and completed them in
St. Augustine's Seminary, Toronto, Canada. He is engaged in parish
work in the Diocese of Gallup, New Mexico, under the direction of
Bishop Espelage, O.F.M.

Father McCarthy is the twenty-eighth priest from the Basilica
parish, eleven of whom have been called to their reward. The first was
Reverend Patrick J. Danehy, ordained in Montreal on December 16,
1881, who died on March 5, 1904, as pastor of St. Stephen's Church,
Minneapolis.

The nation-wide campaign to eliminate obscene literature from homes,
schools, libraries, news stands and trains had the Archbishop's unqualified
support. On February 12, 1938, he asked each parish to organize a committee to further the interests of the campaign by doing all in their
power to persuade public vendors of such literature to cease to carry
it in stock. This was in addition to the pledge of the Legion of Decency
taken annually since 1924 within the octave of the feast of the Immaculate Conception.

In connection with a decree of the Sacred Congregation on the
Discipline of the Sacraments issued on the feast of the Ascension, July
5, 1938, dealing in more detail with the regulation in Canons 1265 to
1275 concerning reverence for the Blessed Sacrament, and the method
to be followed in keeping It securely guarded in parish church and
convent tabernacle, he wrote: "To effect this act of reparation" (for
sacrileges against the Blessed Sacrament in recent years due to desecrated
temples and violated tabernacles) "in the Archdiocese of St. Paul the
priests are hereby directed to organize in every parish the Confraternity
of the Blessed Sacrament prescribed in Canon 711", and to exhort all
the members of the congregation—children, mothers, young women and
men—to join its ranks and fulfill its obligations.

The Archbishop cooperated whole-heartedly with the nation-wide
efforts to raise $2,000,000 from bishops, priests and laity to relieve the
more pressing economic needs of the Catholic University.[22] The diocesan
quota was fixed at $150,000 by the campaign manager sent from the East
who set up a special headquarters, and the solicitation took place between October 16 and 23, 1938, with the result that 154 parishes subscribed $45,153.89 and individuals $21,682.10, a total of $66,836.99 or

about forty-five percent of the quota. The drive did not arouse much interest. All felt that the diocesan goal was too high. No announcement was made of the actual amount of cash realized.

Three Bishops Consecrated

The Most Reverend Archbishop officiated at two of the three consecrations that took place since he came to the diocese. On August 24, 1939, he elevated to the episcopal dignity the Most Reverend William O. Brady, Rector of the St. Paul Seminary, as Bishop of Sioux Falls, South Dakota; and on May 24, 1945, he was the consecrating prelate at a double ceremony in which Most Reverend Francis J. Schenk, Rector of the Cathedral and Vicar General of the diocese, was made Bishop of Crookston, Minnesota, and Most Reverend James L. Connolly, Rector of the St. Paul Seminary, Coadjutor Bishop of Fall River, Massachusetts. In the former ceremony he was assisted by Bishops Cassidy of Fall River and Vehr of Denver, as co-consecrators, and the sermon was preached by Reverend James L. Connolly of the St. Paul Seminary faculty; and in the latter by Bishops Brady of Sioux Falls and Binz of Winona for Bishop-elect Connolly; and Bishops Welch of Duluth and Muench of Fargo for Bishop-elect Schenk. The occasional sermon was preached by Bishop Brady. As already stated he was unable to be present, much less officiate, at the consecration of his Auxiliary, Bishop Byrne, on July 2, 1947.

The local work of the Catholic Campaigners for Christ, founded by David Goldstein of Boston, a convert from Judaism, was inaugurated in the Archdiocese the latter part of June, 1937, by Reverend C. M. Carty, diocesan missionary, who traveled from place to place in a sedan with a trailer equipped with a loud-speaking system capable of reaching twenty thousand people. He preached from the trailer which served as an office open for the instruction of prospective converts or for the answering of questions about Catholicism forenoon, afternoon and evening. He began the work in the rural parishes, giving in each place a series of six lectures on the Church and the State, the Church and Labor, Family Life, the Bible, Confession, and kindred subjects, interspersed with a musical program. During part of the summer he was accompanied by Mr. Goldstein who was well known in the Twin Cities as a former lecturer on Socialism and allied topics under the auspices of the Knights of Columbus. Towards the end of the summer they came to the cities and addressed gatherings of non-Catholics, not large but interested. The lectures were educational, not controversial, though at times it was difficult to avoid taking issue with some of the hecklers. In a few localities bigotry showed its head and its votaries tried to foment religious prejudices; but on the whole, much good seemed to be accomplished before the campaign came to an end.

Anniversary Celebrations

The eightieth birthday of His Holiness Pope Pius XI was commemorated throughout the diocese on the last days of May, 1937,[23] by an outpouring of the faithful at the altar rail in thanksgiving for his providential guidance of the Church during the years of his pontificate. Upwards of 80,000 Holy Communions were received by the faithful and offered up for his intention and spiritual welfare. The result was cabled to the Vatican and acknowledged by Cardinal Pacelli who sent the papal blessing to all. Early in the next year the seventeenth anniversary of his coronation was to be celebrated, and the sixtieth of his ordination with a crusade of prayer to effect a realization of his purpose and intentions in the government of the Church, namely, the peace of Christ in the Kingdom of Christ. This crusade of prayer and good works was to begin the first Sunday of Lent and continue until Trinity Sunday, from February 26 to June 4, with daily prayers, Holy Communions, hours of adoration and a special collect in the daily Masses whenever the rubrics permitted. It was specified that the faithful give one day of labor each week, of suffering and of visits to the sick for his intention as well as a day's income for charitable purposes. The Pope died on February 10, 1937, and the foregoing program was changed to prayers for the eternal repose and refreshment of his soul, with a Requiem Mass in every parish to be attended by the faithful and the school pupils and a Pontifical Mass in the Cathedral for the clergy, religious and laity. After the funeral, prayers were ordered for the election of a worthy successor and the addition of a collect, pro re gravi, in the daily Mass until the result was known.

The one hundredth anniversary[24] of the birth of Archbishop Ireland was commemorated on Sunday, September 11, 1938, in the Basilica of St. Mary, when a bronze memorial, three and a half by five and three-quarters feet in size, attached to the front pier on the gospel side near the pulpit, was unveiled and blessed by Archbishop Murray before the Pontifical Mass at which he officiated, assisted by the clergy of the parish. The sermon, dealing with the life and activities of the first Archbishop of St. Paul, was preached by his former Auxiliary, Most Reverend John J. Lawler, Bishop of Rapid City.

The plaque shows a life-like, three-quarter face and bust of the Archbishop in bas-relief in a sunken panel garlanded with laurel leaves. The pectoral chain is modeled after the one he wore on ceremonial occasions. In the upper corner on his right is his coat-of-arms and on the left the coat-of-arms of the Basilica. Below the medallion are two flags with staffs crossed—the Stars and Stripes and the Church Flag, the latter recalling his services as a chaplain in the Civil War. The lower half of the memorial chronicles the chief events in his life: his birth in Ireland in 1838; his ordination in St. Paul in 1861; his consecration in 1875; his elevation to archiepiscopal rank in 1888; and his death on September 25, 1918. Then follows the scriptural tribute: "A great prelate who in his day pleased God and wrought wonderful things for the church".

The memorial is the gift of the Basilica of St. Mary and, with the exception of a rose window in its eastern transept, the only one in the Archdiocese.

A year later the twenty-fifth anniversary[25] of the first Mass in the Basilica was observed with a special service on Sunday, June 4, at which the Most Reverend Archbishop blessed a bronze memorial plaque, bearing a bas-relief of the church and a suitable inscription, before the Solemn Mass celebrated by Reverend T. E. Cullen, pastor of the Church of St. Stephen, who said the first Mass in the then Pro-Cathedral of St. Mary, on Pentecost Sunday, May 31, 1914. He was assisted by Reverend H. J. Scherer of New Ulm, who was deacon at the first Mass, and Reverend W. A. Brand of the Basilica staff, as deacon and subdeacon, respectively, with Reverend T. J. McNamara, also of the Basilica staff, as master of ceremonies. The Right Reverend H. Moynihan, pastor of the Church of the Incarnation, and Father Reardon, pastor of the Basilica, were deacons of honor to the Archbishop who preached the sermon.

Several synods were held during the twenty-five years that Bishop Grace ruled the Diocese of St. Paul. During the intervening sixty-six only two were convoked—one in 1893 by Archbishop Ireland and the other by Archbishop Murray in 1939. Of the former there is no record in the diocesan archives. The announcement of the latter was made to the clergy on June 14, 1939, and one week later it was convoked in St. Mary's chapel of the St. Paul Seminary during the annual retreat of the clergy. The sessions were held on June 21, 22 and 23, and were attended by the diocesan officials—the Vicar General and the Board of Consultors—the seminary rectors, deans and pastors, diocesan and regular, all of whom participated in a free and full discussion of matters pertaining to the synod. No official report of the deliberations was published.

Notable Rally of Catholic Boy Scouts

Since 1939 it has been customary to hold annual rallies of the Catholic Boy Scouts in different churches of the Archdiocese. They usually took the form of a vesper service at many of which the Most Reverend Archbishop presided and delivered the principal address to the assembled troops of the area and scout officials. They were under the auspices of the Archdiocesan Catholic Scout Committee. One of the most important was the vesper service[26] held in the Basilica of St. Mary on Sunday evening, March 23, 1941, because of the fact that the address was deliv ered by the Most Reverend Francis C. Kelley, Bishop of Oklahoma City-Tulsa, Episcopal Chairman of the National Committee on Scouting.

Before the meeting dinner was served in the Basilica school cafeteria to a number of invited guests including the Most Reverend Archbishop, Bishop Kelley, the chaplains of the scout troops, the Archdiocesan Scout Committee, and the officers of the Twin Cities scout area, all of whom had an opportunity to meet the distinguished visitor.

Eight hundred scouts from the twenty-five parishes of the city marched in procession from the Basilica school to the church carrying American flags and troop colors, accompanied by their parish committees, scout masters and executives. The church was filled with their friends and well-wishers. After an address of welcome by Father Reardon, His Excellency presented the Archbishop Ireland streamers and awards to the winning troops, and Reverend R. E. Nolan, Chaplain of the Archdiocesan Scout Committee, led in the renewal of the scout oath. In his inspiring address Bishop Kelley traced the scout movement from its origination by General Baden-Powell of England, who took counsel with Cardinal Bourne from the inception of the project, and many of the foundation stones of scouting are of Catholic origin. On them the Church built a superstructure of spiritual values and encouraged Catholic boys to join the movement which has grown to great proportions in the United States since it received the approval and encouragement of the hierarchy. The function was brought to a close with Solemn Benediction of the Blessed Sacrament.

Ban On Inter-Faith Activities

Under date of March 25, 1940, Archbishop Murray wrote a letter to the clergy which evoked considerable criticism on the part of non-Catholic leaders in various walks of life, when they became aware of its content and purpose. It forbade Catholic youths of both sexes in glee clubs, school choirs and similar organizations to participate in programs of worship in non-Catholic churches or to take active part in any non-Catholic ritual by singing or acting on any program religious in character or designed to provide support for non-Catholic religious activities.

Catholics may not be participants in the activities that imply profession of faith adopted by any religious or social organizations that are not Catholic, such as the Y. M. C. A., Y. W. C. A., the Hi-Y, the Girl Reserves, the Salvation Army, the Volunteers of America, nor may they enroll in the De Molay, the American Youth Congress, the Young Pioneers and a score of similar communistic organizations designed to alienate them from the Catholic religion or all religions.

The letter also forbade attendance at graduation exercises or baccalaureate addresses in non-Catholic churches, at public lectures and forums not approved by their pastors; nor may they take part in Bible reading, Bible interpretation, religious functions, devotional exercises, initiation ceremonies, chapel services, religious purpose programs, moral problem discussions under any auspices than that of the Catholic Church.

To allay the agitation this letter caused in Protestant circles the Archbishop agreed to meet at luncheon a group of ministers and leaders of the organizations banned in the letter, and answer fully and candidly any questions they wished to ask on these or other points of Catholic doctrine, policy or history, and that without knowing the questions before hand. The meeting was a very friendly one and the Archbishop had no difficulty in convincing them of the reasonableness of his attitude, which is that of the Church, and the only one possible under the circumstances. About seventy-five persons attended the luncheon, among them half a dozen priests, who were in admiration at the skillful and scholarly manner in which His Excellency met the challenge of his opponents and answered even historical questions without a moment's hesitation. The result was a triumphant vindication of the Church's attitude and teaching in regard to the participation of Catholics in any and all kinds of religious services and programs not under her auspices.

A rather rare liturgical function took place on the afternoon of June 30, 1940, when the Archbishop performed the rite of consecrating with the solemn pontifical blessing that portion of the new Resurrection cemetery at Mendota which had been graded and landscaped during the previous year, in presence of a large gathering of the clergy and laity who seldom or never before participated in such a ceremony. As a matter of fact the congestion of automobiles and busses converging on the cemetery made it impossible for many to reach it in time to witness the function. The site of the cemetery was purchased by Archbishop Dowling many years ago when the rapid filling of the Catholic cemeteries in the Twin Cities area made it imperative that provision for future burials be made while it was possible to secure land at a reasonable cost. Three hundred and fifty acres of rolling prairie just beyond the town of Mendota were purchased for the sum of $400,000 and surrounded by a wire fence. Only forty acres were consecrated, and already many burials have taken place in it. It is quite inaccessible except by automobile or bus, being nearly three miles from the nearest street car line across the river in Fort Snelling. This makes it very difficult for people to visit the graves of their departed relatives or friends; but, no doubt, this will be remedied in time.

At the end of the first decade of his administration Archbishop Murray could regard with satisfaction the progress made in the Archdiocese as evidenced by the statistics in the Official Catholic Directory for 1941 which showed that the number of diocesan priests had increased from

369 to 431 and of regulars from 65 to 75. The total number of churches with resident pastors had risen from 211 to 258, the increase being due in large measure to the elevation of missions to parochial status as the number of missions had decreased from 46 to 27. There were ten fewer young men in the major seminary but that was offset by an increase of 11 in the preparatory seminary. The enrollment in St. Thomas College increased from 581 to 792 and in St. Catherine's from 465 to 625. The three private schools for boys with 1,647 in attendance had increased to four with 1,883; and the seven high schools for girls from 1,188 to 1,336. The 16 parochial high schools had more than doubled their attendance to reach the total of 1,551. The 117 parochial grade schools had grown to 128 and the attendance from 31,170 to 33,089; and the grand total in all Catholic institutions of learning rose from 35,387 in 1929 to 39,707 in 1941. There were 1564 sisters and 70 brothers in the diocesan communities. The number of infant baptisms showed an increase of 1,645; the number of converts more than doubled in the decade and the Catholic population was 289,123, an increase of 7,825 over what it was when he arrived in the diocese. He had every reason to be proud of the result of his labors since he came to the Midwest. The progress it connoted was to be enhanced during the next ten years.

Ninth National Eucharistic Congress

One of the most important, significant and impressive events of the past decade in the Archdiocese of St. Paul was the Ninth National Eucharistic Congress[27] held in the Twin Cities from June 22 to 26, 1941, under the sponsorship of Archbishop Murray, a function honored by the presence of the majority of the American Hierarchy, many prelates from Canada and Mexico, hundreds of monsignors, priests and religious, and tens of thousand of the laity from all parts of the country, and especially from the Northwest. The invitation to hold the Congress in the diocese was tendered Archbishop Murray during the Eighth National Eucharistic Congress in New Orleans in the autumn of 1938, and the acceptance of it was signalized some months later when he authorized the preparation of a special musical program under the direction of Reverend F. A. Missia, Professor of Plain Chant in the St. Paul Seminary, as a preliminary to the training of an adult choir of one thousand voices drawn from the church choirs of the two cities, and of thousands of pupils from the parochial schools, to sing the liturgical responses at the Pontifical Masses during the Congress.

The immediate preparation for the Congress began in December, 1940, when the Most Reverend Archbishop appointed the Reverend James M. Reardon, pastor of the Basilica of St. Mary, Minneapolis, General Chairman, the Reverend William A. Brand, Chaplain of the Catholic Boys'

Home, Minneapolis, Executive Secretary, and Mr. Frank H. Delaney, Vice-President of the First National Bank of St. Paul, Treasurer, to plan and supervise the work of the Congress. They were assisted by twenty-two committees of priests, sisters and laymen.

The Holy Father honored the Congress by appointing a Legate a latere, His Eminence Dennis Cardinal Dougherty, Archbishop of Philadelphia, who was accompanied by the following members of his suite: Most Reverend Gerald P. O'Hara, Bishop of Savannah—Atlanta, Right Reverend J. Carroll McCormick, Chancellor of the Archdiocese of Philadelphia and Sir Aloysius Fitzpatrick, Private Chamberlain of the Cape and Sword, also of Philadelphia. The local members of the Papal Mission were Right Reverend James M. Reardon, P.A., of Minneapolis and Sir Ignatius A. O'Shaughnessy of St. Paul, Private Chamberlain of the Cape and Sword and Knight of the Holy Sepulchre. The Reverend Salvatore Burgio, C.M., was master of ceremonies to the Cardinal Legate.

The general theme of the Congress was "Our Eucharistic Lord Glorified by Sacrifice" based on St. Paul's Epistle to the Colossians (1:24), and involving an analysis and application of the Encyclical Letter "Miserentissimus Redemptor" of Pius XI on May 8, 1928. The Most Reverend Archbishop selected the topics to be discussed at each sectional meeting, appointed the presiding bishop, the bishop who read the paper and the episcopal discussion leader, as well as the Archbishops who preached at the Pontifical Masses.

The former episcopal residence opposite the Cathedral was selected as the headquarters of the Congress and the meeting place of the chairmen of the committees charged with special duties. An elaborate and detailed program was mapped out featuring a religious and a civic reception for the Papal Legate, Pontifical Masses, including a midnight Mass for men, and twenty-six sectional meetings at the State Fair grounds, transformed into a Eucharistic Center, a Maronite Mass at the Cathedral, a Byzantine-Slavonic Mass at the Basilica, holy hours for priests at the Eucharistic Center, for sisters at the Cathedral and the Basilica, and for the laity at the Municipal Auditoriums in the two cities, provision for daily Mass for visiting priests in the auditoriums and for the hierarchy in the St. Paul Hotel. The culminating feature of the Congress was the liturgical procession with the Blessed Sacrament from the Church of St. Andrew in St. Paul to the Repository in Como Park, where the parochial groups, societies and other organizations passed in review before the Archbishops, Bishops and priests guarding It, and thence to the Eucharistic Center for the final ceremony. Archbishop Murray carried the Blessed Sacrament from St. Andrew's to the Repository whence after the procession, the Apostolic Delegate bore It to the Eucharistic Center where It was received by the Papal Legate who gave the fina benediction to the kneeling throng, numbering over a hundred thousand who, despite a downpour of rain, remained till the last echo of the Divine Praises died in the distance. It was estimated that upwards of seventy-five thousand marched in the procesion which was witnessed by tens of thousands who braved the soaking rain of the late afternoon to get a view of this spectacular feature of the Congress. Among them were many non-Catholics who showed the utmost respect for the Eucharistic Lord and His bodyguard of marchers.

Shortly after midday His Holiness Pope Pius XII addressed the assembled units in a worldwide broadcast from Vatican City. Owing to local atmospheric conditions the Pontiff's address was followed with difficulty, but many present in the Cathedral in the fall of 1936 recognized his voice as he exhorted them to respond to the theme of the Congress by acts of sacrifice and reparation to the Eucharistic Lord.

The expense of the Congress was borne not by an assessment on the priests or the parishes nor by contributions from business men and firms of the Twin Cities—for they were not asked for one cent—but by the sale of a patented Congress Emblem to the faithful of the diocese for fifty cents apiece, thus placing the cost of the Congress where it rightfully belonged—on the individual Catholic. About $120,000 was realized from this source. Unsolicited donations from individuals and societies amounted to about $5,000, and concessions of all kinds brought in $35,000, making a total of $160,000. The disbursements amounted to $118,000, leaving a balance of $42,000 for the "Minnesota Eucharistic Society", incorporated under the laws of Minnesota on January 16, 1941, to foster, promote and extend in every way adoration of, and devotion to the Blessed Sacrament.

A handy volume of 295 pages was published in October, 1941, containing the history of the Congress, the sermons at the Masses, the addresses at the sectional meetings and other valuable information, of which about 3,300 copies were sold. Artistically bound volumes were presented to His Holiness, Pope Pius XII, the Cardinal Legate, the Apostolic Delegate and the Archbishop of St. Paul. Two hundred copies were reserved for future use in the library of St. Paul Seminary.

The day after the Congress the Basilica of St. Mary of Minneapolis was solemnly consecrated by His Eminence the Cardinal Legate who also consecrated the main altar, while seven other marble altars were consecrated simultaneously by the Apostolic Delegate (Sacred Heart altar), the Archbishop of St. Paul (St. Joseph's Altar), Archbishop Morison of Antigonish, Nova Scotia, Canada (St. Anne's Altar), Bishop Lawler of Rapid City, South Dakota (St. Anthony's Altar), Bishop Kelley of Oklahoma City-Tulsa, Oklahoma (St. John Baptist Vianney's Altar), Bishop Kelly of Winona, Minnesota (St. Teresa's Altar), and

Bishop Muench of Fargo, North Dakota (St. Mary's Altar at the rear of the Main Altar). After the consecration Archbishop Murray pontificated and preached to a capacity congregation. It was the largest consecration ceremony ever held in the United States. At its close the prelates, priests and special guests were entertained at luncheon in the Curtis Hotel.

Daily Exposition of Blessed Sacrament

In connection with the Eucharistic Congress and as a preparation for it the Most Reverend Archbishop authorized daily Exposition[28] of the Blessed Sacrament in the Basilica of St. Mary beginning May first, 1940. Later on the same privilege was granted to St. Lawrence Church and daily exposition continued for about a year. Shortly after the Congress the Reverend Peter F. Meade, pastor of the Church of St. Vincent, St. Paul, with ecclesiastical approval, organized the women of the parish into groups and assigned to each group one day of the week, during which its members would keep continuous vigil before the Blessed Sacrament exposed on the altar from early morning Mass till evening devotion. It was discontinued in the latter part of 1951 when Father Meade was hospitalized.

For a few years—from 1943 to 1948—the Reverend John P. Foley of the Immaculate Conception parish, Faribault, succeeded in interesting his parishioners in the devotion but finally had to discontinue it. The pastors of the seven churches in Dakota County inaugurated the devotion for one day a week in each parish but found it impossible to continue it indefinitely. At the present time the only parish church in the Archdiocese in which the Blessed Sacrament is exposed daily, from morning Mass till late at night, is the Basilica of St. Mary.

For more than ten years the privilege of daily exposition has been enjoyed by the Sisters of St. Joseph in the chapels of their Novitiate and of the Infirmary connected with St. Joseph's Hospital. In 1950 it was inaugurated in the Convent of the Sisters of the Cenacle in Minneapolis.

As soon as the Eucharistic Congress was over preliminary steps were taken to hold the second National Liturgical Week[29] in St. Paul under the patronage of Archbishop Murray, from October 6 to 10. The Reverend William Busch of St. Paul Seminary had charge of the arrangements and received the hearty support and cooperation of his brother priests. The function brought to the city several members of the hierarchy, priests from all parts of the country, sisters and laymen interested in liturgical problems. The theme chosen for discussion was "The Living Parish: One in Worship, Charity and Action". Each morning Mass was celebrated in the Cathedral at which a homily was preached and the sessions were held in the Catholic Youth Center for the reading and discussing of papers dealing with different phases of the theme. The sessions were well attended and proved profitable to all. The sermons, addresses and discussions appeared in book form shortly after the beginning of the next year. The cost of the meeting was borne by the clergy of the Archdiocese who contributed $2,257.00 to cover the expenses which amounted to $2,030.00, leaving a balance of $227.00.

Catholic Scouting Committee

As early as 1936 the Most Reverend Archbishop authorized the organization of the Archdiocesan Committee on Catholic Scouting and appointed Reverend R. E. Nolan of Hastings, Chaplain, Honorable Carlton McNally of St. Paul, General Chairman, and George A. Ghizoni of St. Paul, Executive Secretary. The Archdiocese was divided into six areas each with its chairman. On the sixth anniversary an elaborate report was issued, as of May 19, 1942, which conveyed the information that, during the six-year period, twenty-two general meetings had been held; seventy troops had merited the silken banner of the Archbishop Ireland Award for meeting the ten requirements of good scouting; and forty-three scouts had received the Ad Altare Dei award from November, 1940, when it was first made available, to May, 1942. This award consists of a bronze cross suspended from a ribbon in papal and national colors under a bar inscribed Ad Altare Dei that can be pinned to the uniform on the left breast. It is given to scouts who serve at the altar in any capacity, who know their religion and the proper Latin responses for the Mass, are punctual in keeping appointments and observe decorum in the sanctuary. In other words it in awarded solely for service rendered the Church by the scout on the authority of the Bishop of the Diocese, through the Diocesan Scout Committee and is usually presented at a religious ceremony.

The report goes on to state that many troops had adopted a war chaplain from this area and supplied him with missals, wax candles, scapular medals, playing cards, games, Catholic literature and cash.

During the Ninth National Eucharistic Congress in June, 1941, 1245 scouts and leaders were on duty in emergency and first aid stations in the Eucharistic Center and along the line of march of the final procession as well as in reception, information, messenger and publicity booths. The troops were presented with streamers by the Congress officials in recognition of their services.

Three Catholic Scoutmasters entered the ranks of professional scouting as executives. They were Eugene C. Krapf of the Basilica of St. Mary troop 111, Minneapolis; Leo V. McCarthy of Sacred Heart troop 232, Robbinsdale; and John C. Wells of the Immaculate Conception troop 6, Faribault. In September, 1946, Mr. Krapf was chosen by the National

Catholic Scout organization to set up a Catholic scouting program in Guam under the direction of the Vicar Apostolic, the Most Reverend A. W. Baumgartner, O. F. M. Cap.

The Archdiocese of St. Paul has always been noted for its loyalty to the Holy See and to the person of the Supreme Pontiff. The personal appeal has been intensified since the present Pontiff, Pope Pius XII, honored it with a visit as Cardinal Pacelli in 1936. It is not to be wondered at, therefore, that a very special effort was made on the occasion of the twenty-fifth anniversary of his episcopal consecration, to offer him a spiritual bouquet that would be a tangible manifestation of the love and reverence of priests and people, and an expression of affectionate regard.

On the anniversary, May 3, 1942, the Most Reverend Archbishop sent a radio telegram to Vatican City in which, as spokesman for five hundred priests, sixteen hundred religious and three hundred thousand laity, he presented "for transmission to Your Holiness" the following good works as a spiritual bouquet:

2,029 Masses offered by the clergy; 5,325 Masses requested by the laity; 299,078 Masses heard by the laity; 175,538 Holy Communions received; 93,276 Stations of the Cross; 369,578 rosaries; 63,371 hours of adoration; 1,048,555 hours of labor and suffering; 51,871 visits to the sick; 24,900 litanies; 10,393 visits to the poor; 833,503 ejaculations; 497,728 other prayers; $7,455.35 alms for the poor; $6,811.07 offerings for the missions.[30]

During World War II there was a great demand for chaplains[31] and each diocese was asked to release up to ten percent of its priests for service in the armed forces. Archbishop Murray invited "all the assistants in the Archdiocese to volunteer for service with the Armed Forces of the United States" and gave his priests to understand that any one meeting the requirements of the War Department, would be permitted to enter the chaplain corps. Over fifty were accepted and most of them saw service overseas. Three were rather seriously wounded in the line of duty but recovered. At the end of the war some elected to remain in the regular army. The others were given parishes in recognition of their patriotic services to the nation in time of crisis. Authorization to say three Masses on Sunday was given to one priest in every parish from which a chaplain was taken.

All but thirty parishes sent to the Chancery Office lists of the men and women in one or other branch of the service during the war. These lists show that 32,015 men wore the uniform, of whom 997 were killed and 1,151 women of whom 3 made the supreme sacrifice.[32]

The bureaus of Catholic Charities of the Twin Cities incorporate thirty years ago have for the scope of their operations the counties and cities in which they are located. With the start of World War II and the consequent dislocation of family life and responsibilities, applications for help from individuals and public agencies indicated the need of another agency to function outside the urban areas of the diocese.

The recognition of this need prompted the establishment of the Diocesan Bureau of Charities[33] which was incorporated as a child-placing and family agency under Minnesota statutes on May 29, 1943, and placed under the direction of Reverend Francis W. Curtin with offices at 226 Summit Avenue, St. Paul. The government of the corporation and the management of its affairs are vested in a Board of Trustees, twelve in number, presided over by the Most Reverend Archbishop and including five laymen from different parts of the rural area.

The purpose of the Bureau is to secure foster homes for orphans, homeless, delinquent, neglected or defective children and those surrounded by bad or immoral influences, and to rehabilitate the dependent families of those likely to become public charges. Its operation in the first half-year revealed its necessity as an agency in placing children in homes for adoption. In the three years prior to 1950 it handled a total of 2235 individuals of whom 1322 were adults and 903 children; and received in the same period, from the diocesan collections for charity in the rural counties, the sum of $35,585.60. The Director reported that "the study reveals a startling imbalance between the great amount of assistance given and the charitable contributions in support of the service".

At the close of the scholastic year in June, 1943, the Government asked the College of St. Thomas to introduce the Navy College program for the duration of the war and, accordingly, a change of schedule for collegians was put in force on July first, whereby they would follow an all-year accelerated course of studies that would make them eligible for graduation at the end of three instead of four years. The school year would have three semesters of four months each instead of two semesters. This brought about a large influx of new students and the Government had to provide temporary housing for the veterans. In the summer of 1946, the President announced that 72 houses were in process of construction and 9 more promised, a total valuation of $200,000. For the students of the Academy the usual course was adhered to without interference from the navy's program.

Post-war increase of enrollment in St. Thomas College and Academy made an expansion of facilities imperative. Additional housing had to be provided for veterans and their families and large accessions made to the faculty to meet the demands of the expanding student body. New buildings were projected and one of them, a science hall, had to be erected without delay at a cost of $1,341,561.43. It was dedicated with appropriate ceremony by the Auxiliary Bishop on September 1, 1948, following a Pontifical Mass celebrated by him in the college chapel at which he preached the sermon. The new building is known as the Albertus Magnus Science Hall and faces Summit Avenue in line with the Administration building with which it harmonizes in material and architectural design, and with which it is connected by an artistic archway. The completion of the science hall necessitated another campaign for funds announced by the Most Reverend Archbishop in a letter to the clergy on December 1, 1947, in response to which they contributed $87,039.16 as of January 20, 1949, and the parishes $1,192,450.58 of an assessed quota of $1,261,550.

The science hall, however, was not the only substantial building erected on the campus after the return of the College to diocesan control. In 1940, O'Shaughnessy Hall, a recreation center, was dedicated with impressive ceremony. It is the gift of Mr. Ignatius A. O'Shaughnessy of St. Paul, an alumnus, and houses a gymnasium, swimming pool, bowling alleys, billard room, basketball, handball and squash courts, medical examination rooms, class rooms and offices for the department of Physical Education. It is a modified form of Gothic architecture, constructed of Mankato and Bedford stone and harmonizes with the Administration building and Albertus Magnus Science Hall.

Archbishop Ireland Memorial Library

In September, 1944, the St. Paul Seminary celebrated the fiftieth anniversary of its dedication with a Pontifical Mass in St. Mary's Chapel celebrated by the Most Reverend Archbishop at which the festive sermon was preached by the Most Reverend Edward D. Howard, Archbishop of Portland, Oregon, the only alumnus made an Archbishop. After the dinner a meeting was held in the Aula Maxima presided over by the Rector, Father Connolly, at which several addresses were delivered and much enthusiasm displayed by the alumni who were present in large numbers. It was decided to signalize the event by providing the Seminary with a modern, fireproof library adapted to present and future needs and to name it the Archbishop Ireland Memorial Library. It was announced that a sum of money amounting to $30,600 had been accumulated as the nucleus of a fund for that purpose, and the alumni were asked to supplement it with offerings as generous as their means would permit. The Rector issued an appeal[34] which brought in $16,000 in cash and $5,000 in pledges from 245 alumni and friends, three of whom gave $1000 each. Plans and specifications for the proposed library were prepared and the site selected and surveyed. But the difficulty of obtaining material and workmen necessitated a delay in beginning actual building operations. It was not until January, 1949, that the contract was awarded.

The status of the project was made known to the clergy and other benefactors by a letter from the Archbishop, dated February 10, 1949, in which he reported that the original fund with accumulated interest had reached a total of $32,168.22, and that the response to the first appeal had added $36,401.50, a total of $68,569.72, of which $8,327.00 had been expended for architect's fees and a survey of the site. It was estimated that the library, fully equipped, would cost upwards of $400,000, to meet which it would be necessary for the 450 priests of the Archdiocese and the 900 in active service in other dioceses to contribute an average of $250.00 each.

The alumni in the episcopate contributed $8,020.00; the priests of the Archdiocese, $19,096.50; clergymen outside the Archdiocese, $6,475.00; and other benefactors, $2,180.00, as of February 1, 1949.

The St. Paul Seminary corporation is prohibited by its statutes from incurring indebtedness for any purpose and, consequently, the Most Reverend Archbishop had to assume personal responsibility for funds borrowed to complete and equip the memorial.

The library was dedicated by the Most Reverend Archbishop after the Pontifical Mass on October 19, 1950, commemorating the one hundredth anniversary of the erection of the diocese on July 19, 1850.

Accreditation of the Seminary

The accreditation of the St. Paul Seminary by other institutions of learning took place shortly after the celebration of the golden jubilee of its opening. The meaning and extent of these affiliations are set forth in the annual "Register" from which the following statement is condensed.

The St. Paul Seminary with its six-year course of studies was accredited by the North Central Association at its annual meeting in Chicago, March 25-30, 1946; it was approved as an institution for the education of veterans under the Servicemen's Readjusment Act of 1944 by the United States Government; it was approved on June 7, 1946, by the Department of Education, State of Minnesota, as an agency for the education of teachers for accredited Catholic High Schools and authorized to grant a High School Standard General Certificate to any seminarian who had obtained a B. A. degree and 18 semester credits in Education; it was pronounced qualified to grant the M. A. degree on February 28, 1947, by the Board of Review of the North Central Association.

On April 1, 1947, the Accrediting Board of the University of Minnesota declared that it would honor the M. A. degree granted by the Seminary whenever the holder of the degree is assigned to teach in an accredited institution; and eight days later, the Board of Trustees of the Seminary authorized the adoption of both the B. A. and the M. A. programs.

The St. Paul Seminary is accredited to the University of Minnesota by action of the Senate Committee on the Relation of the University to other institutions of learning and of the entire University Senate.

This accrediting of the Seminary by recognized agencies was sought in conformity with the prescriptions of the Congregation of Bishops and Regulars, May 10, 1947, and the Instruction of the Congregation of Seminaries and University Studies of August 28, 1948, which recommended the granting of legal academic degrees for the safeguarding of the liberty of choice of state, for the utility of priests, and for the prestige of Cathlic education.

All these, of course, are in addition and consequent to the power to grant academic degrees and issue diplomas in evidence thereof, given to the Board of Trustees of the Seminary by the statutes of the State of Minnesota when it was incorporated on September 2, 1895.

Diocesan Events

A new sisterhood—the Oblate Sisters of Providence of Baltimore[35]— was welcomed into the diocese on September 30, 1945, at a Pontifical Mass celebrated by His Excellency in St. Peter Claver's Church for the colored Catholics of St. Paul, where they opened a convent at 327 Fuller Street, next to the pastoral residence, and began the work of catechetical instruction while awaiting the building of a parochial school. They were the first Negro sisters in the diocese and Mother Barbara, Sisters Anthony and Celine were accompanied to their destination by the Superior General of the community, Mother Theresa, and a companion, who remained a few days in the city.

The Mass was attended by the leaders of inter-racial relations from cities outside the diocese, by civic, religious, business and labor officials as well as by the clergy. The Archbishop preached and after Mass there was a dinner followed by a reception for the new group in the parish auditorium. Since then a combined school and gymnasium has been opened at 1060 Central Avenue, West, with an initial enrollment of 225 pupils and several sisters have been added to the staff. The Reverend J. J. Luger is pastor of the parish.

The silver jubilee of the Archbishop's consecration fell on April 28, 1945, and the Holy Father took cognizance of it by sending a paternal letter, dated February 28, in which he said: "We cordially congratulate you on the observance of this sacred occasion in which We unite with you in thanksgiving to the Giver of all good gifts, and from Our heart wish every blessing for the welfare of yourself and your people".

There was no official celebration of the event but the clergy, religious and laity, in token of prayerful esteem and affection, presented a spiritual bouquet of 861 Masses said by the clergy; 4233 requested by the laity; 184,434 heard by the faithful; 89,118 Holy Communions; 30,000 stations of the cross; 151,479 rosaries; 158,853 litanies; 4527 hours of office; 62,938 visits to the Blessed Sacrament; 5,000 holy hours; 289,254 hours of labor and suffering; 30,676 visits to the sick and the poor; 1,030,400 other prayers; and 5,068,685 ejaculations. In a letter to the clergy on May 1, 1945, the Most Reverend Archbishop thanked them and, through them, all who had participated in the spiritual offering.

The St. Thomas College post-war expansion program, for the addition of new buildings and the improvement of existing facilities, was launched at a dinner given by the Archbishop to one hundred and fifty religious, civic, business and educational leaders on July 23, 1945, in the St. Paul University Club at which it was decided that a campaign for $3,830,000 be inaugurated in the immediate future under the general chairmanship of Mr. I. A. O'Shaughnessy an alumnus and benefactor of the institution. It was announced that an anonymous donor had pledged $100,000 in four annual installments as a nucleus for the fund.

The Board of Trustees authorized an appeal to a selected group of citizens throughout the country interested in the institution asking their help to make the campaign a success. A reputedly skilled manager was secured at a salary of $20,000 a year and the cost of on office staff. Pledges totaling $374,952.91 were recorded as of March 1, 1948, and $318,129.41 paid on them at an expenditure of $63,761. The results were so meager and disappointing that it was finally decided to call off the drive. In 1947, 274 alumni contributed $7,926.50, the interest on $300,000 at current rates and thus nearly doubled the endowment of $303,375.65. They also expressed their willingness to do this annually. In addition to that the alumni contributed $1,867.28 to their Association Fund.

The enrollment in the College in the autumn of 1947 was 2103, of whom 244 were boarders, 1028 day scholars and 831 out-of-town students living off the campus. 1959 were Catholics, 140 Protestants and 4 Jews. The Academy registered 568 students, of whom 173 were boarders, and 395 day scholars. 527 were Catholics, 27 Protestants and 14 Jews. The college faculty consisted of 30 priests and 104 lay teachers. 12 priests taught in the Academy and 49 laymen. The value of the plant was $4,374,491.[36]

In the meantime the College had put up a new science hall costing $1,350,000 and acquired from the Federal Public Housing Authority a classroom building, a cafeteria, a student activity building, three residence halls, housing 190 men, and 40 faculty and student houses, to all of which the College had title. They were insured for $457,200 and their installations and improvements cost $25,913.

The Official Directory for 1945 gave the Archdiocese a Catholic population of 294,861, and the state 526,785. There were 532 priests laboring in the diocese, 267 parishes, 25 missions, 146 chapels, 270 seminarians, 1109 college students, 3807 high school students, 35,393 pupils in parochial schools, 19,469 in vacation religious schools — a total of 59,778 under religious instruction. The sisters numbered 1740 and there were 50 Christian Brothers. 1,082 converts had been made the previous year and 10,809 were baptized.

The year 1947 brought two distinguished members of the Sacred College of Cardinals to St. Paul. On Sunday afternoon, March 2, His Eminence Conrad Cardinal von Preysing, Bishop of Berlin, addressed a capacity audience of Catholics in the St. Paul Municipal Auditorium and expressed his gratitude to them and their brethren in the United States for the providential help given the victims of the war in his country and elsewhere. He was entertained at the Cathedral residence by the Most Reverend Archbishop and the suffragan bishops and visited some of the churches during his short stay in the Twin Cities.

On Friday, May 30, His Eminence Eugene Cardinal Tisserant, Secretary of the Congregation for the Oriental Church, presided at a Solemn Mass in the Maronite Rite in the Cathedral, St. Paul, celebrated by the Right Reverend Peter Assemani, pastor of St. Maron's Church, Minneapolis. Cardinal Tisserant was on a visit to the priests and people of the Oriental Rites in the United States. He, too, paid a brief visit to some of the churches and institutions in St. Paul and Minneapolis.

Diocesan Consultors Honored

Early in April, 1947, it was announced officially that the Holy Father, at the request of the Most Reverend Archbishop, had honored the six Diocesan Consultors by elevating them to the dignity of Domestic Prelates and members of his household, entitling them to wear the royal purple and be addressed in speech and writing as Right Reverend Monsignor. This signal mark of papal and episcopal approval was conferred on the Right Reverends John Dunphy, pastor of the Church of the Ascension, Minneapolis; Joseph A. Corrigan, pastor of the Church of St. Mark, St. Paul; Aloysius Ziskovsky, pastor of the Church of St. Mathew, St. Paul; James Zachman, pastor of the Church of St. Francis de Sales, St. Paul; John J. Cullinan, pastor of the Church of St. Luke, St. Paul; and Vincent W. Worzalla, pastor of the Church of the Holy Cross, Minneapolis. The rescripts were dated March 3. The investitures, at which the Most Reverend Archbishop was unable to officiate, took place in their respective churches when the official robes—purple cassock, rochet, mantelletta and biretta—were blessed and bestowed at ceremonies before the Solemn Masses celebrated by the recipients. Each was honored at a dinner and reception by the people of the parish, relatives and friends.

In a letter to the clergy on December 1, 1947, the Most Reverend Archbishop announced that the College of St. Thomas had an enrollment of 2596 students and a faculty of 172 in its collegiate and academic departments; that its income for the previous year had been $1,288,937.42 and the disbursements $1,249,978.44; that the new Albertus Magnus Science Hall, begun in 1945, had cost $1,341,561.42; that $60,000 had been expended for the erection of buildings donated by the United States Government for the housing of war veterans and their families and valued at $180,000. All this was preliminary to the statement that the College had incurred an indebtedness of $1,275,244.16, which had to be paid by an assessment of $300.00 on the pastors and $100.00 on all other priests of the Archdiocese, in addition to a levy on the parishes according to their membership and financial standing. On February 27 of the next year, according to his letter of that date, the contributions from the clergy amounted to $67,770.16 and from the parishes $642,342.08, a total of $710,112.24 or a little more than one-half the indebtedness. In this letter he requested that the unpaid quota of each parish be borrowed from a bank and forwarded to the Chancery Office before the end of March, and allowed a weekly collection to be taken up in the parish until the loan with interest was paid in full. The final report was made by the Archbishop in a letter of January 31, 1949, wherein he stated that 370 diocesan priests out of 440 had contributed $85,009.16, and 266 parishes $1,192,450.58 or 93% of the outstanding obligations of the College. The remaining 17 parishes owed $82,473.60.

Assessments for other purposes placed on the Archdiocese during the year were as follows: $75,000 for the Bishops' Relief Campaign for the destitute victims of the world war; $130,000 for construction of the new North American College in Rome to replace the original building donated by Pope Pius IX in 1859 as a missionary project to provide priests for the United States; $67,000 for the completion of the Shrine of the Immaculate Conception at the Catholic University in Washington, a project for which $5,000,000 was asked and towards which $1,500,000 had already been paid from last year's collection on Mother's Day.

The Pontifical Work of Ecclesistical Vocations was inaugurated in the Archdiocese by Archbishop Murray in a letter to the clergy, dated March 31, 1948, in which he announced the program to be followed by all the parishes in carrying out the mandate of the Supreme Pontiff.

This Pontifical program had its origin on August 1, 1922, when Pope

Pius XI called on all who love the Church to promote vocations by every means in their power. The Sacred Congregation of Seminaries, to which the work was entrusted, prescribed, on January 24, 1928, that it be established in every parish throughout the world to foster vocations not only for the diocesan priesthood but for the religious life in general. A Motu Proprio of Pope Pius XII on November 4, 1941, assigned full jurisdiction to this Congregation which, by decree of September 8, 1943, set up the legislation governing the operation of the work in every parish, which had for object to spread abroad a clear and correct knowledge of the necessity and excellence of the priesthood; to promote the offering of Masses, prayer and works of penance and charity for an increase of vocations; to effect a union between the parish unit and the diocesan society and, through it, with the headquarters in Rome; to request priests to instruct the faithful in regard to the dignity and importance of the priestly office and urge them to increase their esteem for it by a study of authoritative works, and foster a desire for the religious life in general among the young. As a means to that end it prescribed triduums of prayer in schools, the observance of sacerdotal days, the offering of sacrifices and suffering as well as contributions for the furtherance of the work.

The work of the Pontifical Society for Vocations was initiated in the diocese on December 8, 1948, with a novena in preparation for the feast of the Immaculate Conception, which was designated Sacerdotal Day by the Most Reverend Archbishop in a letter to the clergy on November 22, and the faithful were urged to offer their prayers, sacrifices, labors, etc., for an increase of vocations for the priesthood. The Most Reverend James J. Byrne, Auxiliary Bishop of St. Paul, was named Diocesan Director and an office opened at 324 South Prior Avenue, St. Paul, where a library of books on vocations is being built up as a guide and model for similar libraries in the parishes.

Family Guild Retreats

In his solicitude for the spiritual welfare of the family His Excellency authorized the formation of a Family Guild[37] in the summer of 1946, and appointed the Reverend R. T. Doherty of the St. Paul Seminary, Spiritual Director. The primary purpose of the Guild is to labor for the restoration of christian family life, the sanctity and permanence of which is so seriously threatened by the secularism of the age in which we live. The Guild is composed of married couples who meet in groups of four to six once a month in homes or elsewhere to discuss family problems and strive to find a solution for them. They also contact other families and seek their cooperation in restoring the pristine glory of the home modeled after the Holy Home of Nazareth. Each of these parish groups is known as a cell and several of them constitute a section which may comprise as many as a hundred persons, and of which there are thirty-two in the Archdiocese, forming a federation which meets at St. Thomas College in the evening of the fourth Monday of every month. A representative of each section reports on the work done during the previous month and the federation makes plans for future activities.

Retreats, conferences and days of recollection are the most fruitful means employed to supernaturalize the family life in all its phases. Father Doherty has been very successful in popularizing the "Cana day" program and it has proved to be a prolific source of grace not only to husbands and wives but to engaged couples. For the latter it has been given the name of "Pre-Cana day", the first of which was held in St. Peter's Church, Mendota, on Sunday, August 29, 1948.

This latest evolution of the retreat movement for the laity was inaugurated in New York on March 23, 1943, when the Reverend John P. Delaney, S. J., gave the first retreat to a group of husbands and wives, whom he sought to make one in mind and heart through the exercises of a day of recollection to renew the ideals of their married life. He called them "Family Renewal Days", but they are now better known as "Cana days" because of their identification with the marriage feast honored by the presence of our Lord, His Blessed Mother and the Apostles. Cana clubs to the number of 112 have been formed in 23 dioceses and more than 100,000 married couples follow the exercises every year and 30,000 single persons attend pre-Cana conferences.

With the approbation of Archbishop Murray the first Cana day retreat [38] was conducted by Father Doherty on Sunday, September 22, 1946, in the Church of St. Peter, Mendota, the cradle of Catholicity in Minnesota and the oldest stone church in the Archdiocese, located on a high bluff overlooking the confluence of the Mississippi and Minnesota rivers, and easily accessible from either of the Twin Cities. Before the end of the Holy Year 76 such retreats were attended by 1836 couples. The Cana and the Pre-Cana day retreats are conducted on a monthly basis, the former on the second Sunday of the month, and the latter on the third.

The retreatants assemble in the parish hall at nine-fifteen, assist at Mass at nine-thirty and receive Holy Communion. After breakfast spiritual conferences are held before and after an early dinner and Benediction is given at four-thirty. The expense is met by the voluntary contributions of the retreatants.

The Holy Year proved to be banner year for the movement and St. Paul led all the other dioceses with 27 retreats attended by 729 couples.

In addition to this special form of Catholic Action for families and parish groups there is a somewhat similar movement along vocational lines. A Guild of St. Francis[39] for Catholic journalists, radio commentators and publicists was organized, under the moderatorship of Father Doherty, in November, 1947, to inculcate and cultivate the virtues of justice and charity in the dissemination of news and views through the media of their professions. Nearly two years later, in August, 1949, the St. Thomas More Guild [40] was inaugurated for Catholic lawyers who believe that "justice is the indispensable foundation of the State and of peace among the nations", and who deplore "the separation of law from ethics, morals, sound philosophy and God". Under the auspices of this Guild the custom of an annual "Red Mass" for members of the bench and bar was initiated on Sunday, September 25, 1949, in St. Thomas College when the Votive Mass of the Holy Ghost was celebrated to beg God's blessing and divine guidance on the administration of justice during the forthcoming judicial year.

With the cooperation of the Archdiocesan Council of Catholic women a new movement known as "Nazareth Conferences" has been inaugurated for parents and deals exclusively with the training of children in the home.

The Cana group of retreatants first conceived the idea of setting aside the first Sunday in May of each year for the special glorification of the Mother of God and, in 1947, the promoters met in St. Thomas College for that purpose. The devotion proved so stimulating and aroused so much enthusiasm that it was decided to transfer the celebration to the St. Paul Cathedral which was done on the first Sunday of May, 1948, when the rosary was recited by a large congregation. The next step was an outdoor procession in which the marching unit was the family and in which flags, banners and majorettes were conspicuous by their absence. All the parishes in St. Paul were asked to cooperate, and their groups assembled in the vicinity of the Cathedral and marched in procession to it reciting the rosary in honor of Our Lady of Fatima whose statue was carried by a group of marchers. So well had the function been publicized that upwards of twenty-five thousand persons took part in the procession or viewed it from the side lines. The Cathedral was filled to capacity for the Solemn Benediction which brought the service to a fitting close. The following years drew larger marching groups and more onlookers and, in order that all might be present at Benediction, a temporary altar was erected on the front steps of the church and from it the Eucharistic Lord blessed the thousands assembled before it to implore the intercession of His Blessed Mother in behalf of peace.

A number of Catholics from Minneapolis took part in the procession and were so impressed by what they saw, heard and experienced in the way of religious emotion, that they determined to have a similar celebration in their home city on the first Sunday of May, 1951. The time for preparation was rather short but nevertheless some eight thousand persons from the different parishes assembled near the parade ground and marched to the Basilica of St. Mary, each parish group reciting the rosary in unison until it came within hearing distance of the loud speakers when it joined with other groups in the responses.

A pleasing feature of the procession was the presence of a group of St. Thomas Military cadets, who led the way, uniformed nurses from St. Mary's Hospital, students of St. Margaret's and Holy Angels academies and De La Salle High School, altar boys with lighted candles and Fourth Degree Knights of Columbus who formed a bodyguard for the statue of the Blessed Virgin borne on the shoulders of a group of international exchange students attending Catholic colleges in the Twin Cities. The statue was placed on a pedestal behind the temporary altar within sight of the thousands who implored the aid of the Immaculate Mother of God for the restoration of peace among individuals, family and nations.

A police escort kept Hennepin Avenue free from traffic as the people congregated in front of the Basilica where an out-door altar had been erected on which the Blessed Sacrament was exposed from the beginning of the procession till It was lifted in final benediction above the kneeling throng. The weather was glorious and a unanimous wish was expressed for a repetition of the devotion the next year.

The first Catholic Men's Institute was held in the College of St. Thomas on January 30 and 31 and February 1, 1948, preliminary to the organization of the Archdiocesan Council of Catholic Men with constituent units in every parish and deanery. About 500 men and a group of priests and brothers participated in it, and listened to a series of addresses on the methods of forming and operating the council and kindred topics. James Mitchell, Executive Secretary of the National Council of Catholic Men, Washington, stressed the need of concerted action by a united body of Catholic laymen, under the direction of the bishops and Reverend P. Kenny, a consultant in the national office, explained the method of organizing the parochial units of the proposed council. Reverend E. Schmiedeler, O. S. B., Director of the Family Life Bureau of the National Council of Catholic Men, gave a series of four addresses on "The Adolescent Boy" in the home, the school, in social and personal life.

The call for the meeting was issued by the Most Reverend Archbishop on January 8, 1948, to put into operation the program outlined by Pope Pius XII in an address on September 7, 1947, to the members of the Catholic Action group assembled in Rome for the observance of the silver jubilee of its establishment by Pope Pius XI. He outlined a five-point program for this Catholic Apostolate under the heads of Diffusion of Religious Culture; Restoration of the Christian Family; the Spread of Social Justice; the Sanctification of the Sunday; and Loyalty and Truthfulness in Dealing with one Another.

At the close of the meeting the Archbishop appointed the following officers of the Archdiocesan Council; Roy Johnson of Minneapolis, President; Walter Matt of St. Paul, Treasurer; and J. Victor Jaeger of Minneapolis, Secretary. The Presidents of the thirteen deaneries were ex-officio Vice-Presidents. A second meeting of the Institute was proposed for June 18, 19 and 20.

"Founder's Day" at St. Thomas

"Founder's Day" was instituted at the College of St. Thomas on September 28, 1948, for the purpose of keeping alive among its alumni and its students, the knowledge of the all-important part played by Archbishop Ireland in founding the institution and opening it on September 8, 1885, for the reception of students preparing for the priesthood, as well as for others desirous of an education in the classics and sciences. It was a daring project in these far-off days when the maintenance of such an institution demanded great sacrifices on the part of Catholics, relatively few in numbers and far from rich in worldly possessions, when priests to staff it were not easily procured and their education for such a position rather costly. God blessed the undertaking and the courageous zeal of its founder, and in less than a decade of years a benefactor was found to provide a theological seminary for the education of priests distinct from the College, and the latter began the career of development which ultimately brought it to the position of prominence it now occupies in the educational world.

The commemoration took the form of a Pontifical Mass celebrated in the college chapel by the Most Reverend Archbishop Murray at which the sermon was preached by the Most Reverend Edwin V. O'Hara, Bishop of Kansas City, Mo., an alumnus of the College, who dealt with the ecclesiastical career of Archbishop Ireland and his work as the founder of the institution. Dinner for hundreds of the alumni and friends was served in the armory during which Archbishop Ireland's qualities as a civic leader were extolled in a paper prepared and read by Dr. Richard Purcell of the Catholic University of America, a professor in the history department of the College of St. Thomas from 1916 to 1920.

The next year the Pontifical Mass was celebrated in the armory to accommodate the larger group of alumni and friends desirous of attending and the sermon was preached by the Reverend James H. Moynihan, a professor in the College for thirty years, and its President from 1932 to 1944. After Mass dinner was served in the cafeteria.

In September, 1950, in a similar setting the Very Reverend L. F. Ryan of the St. Paul Seminary faculty, delivered the eulogy on the venerated founder of the College before an audience which taxed the capacity of the armory. It is the intention of the President and faculty of the College to make this commemoration an annual affair and thus perpetuate the memory of its distinguished sponsor and benefactor.

Mission Pageant

More than ten thousand persons sought admission to the Cathedral of St. Paul on Sunday afternoon, October 24, 1948, to show their interest in the mission work of the Church as portrayed by hundreds of boys and girls from the parochial schools dressed as missionary priests, sisters and brothers, but not more than half of them were able to participate in the ceremonies that took place under its magnificent dome and before its majestic altar where the procession ended. The bright autumnal sun shone down on a brilliant and colorful pageant never before witnessed in St. Paul, a pageant conceived and directed by Reverend W. J. Walsh, Diocesan Director of the Propagation of the Faith, and a former officer in the regular army. It had for object "to promote interest in the work of the society, to encourage vocations to the religious life by emphasizing the obligation of the Church in the United States to supply priests, nuns and brothers for the home and foreign missions". The children selected by the parochial schools from the members of the Pontifical Society of the Holy Childhood were dressed in miniature duplicates of the religious costumes worn by the members of the different congregations working in the mission fields throughout the world. More than thirty congregations were represented by the hundreds of children who took part in the pageant, "One World for Christ". The altar boys and the boys and girls representing the missionary groups assembled at the Diocesan Teachers College and those who represented the nations of the world at the St. Paul Priory. Led by the crossbearer, acolytes, and boy scouts carrying the massed flags of the nations they marched along Summit Avenue to the Cathedral and up the middle aisle to the sanctuary where they were reviewed by the Most Reverend Archbishop and the clergy assembled for the function.

The procession itself is thus described by a writer in The Catholic Bulletin of October 30, 1948: "One hundred and twenty-five little girls dressed as nuns led the procession; 85 little boys costumed as priests were next in line. There were 225 children in the native garb of mission lands and 75 Boy Scouts in full regalia.

"Scouts carried the massed flags of the nations and stacked them near St. Peter's chapel.

"A single blue banner stood nearer the altar rail. It bore the legend 'Pray for Russia'.

"Four hundred other children wore the uniforms of their respective parish schools.

"Two small boys from Holy Rosary parish in Minneapolis in the robes of cardinals, carried the flower-trimmed memorial volume inscribed with the names of perpetual members of the Society for the Propagation of the Faith.

"A six-year-old tot in the habit of a Passionist priest and a twelve-year-old lad wearing the habit of a White Father of Africa were youngest and oldest respectively in the procession of religious orders.

"Nearly 100 diocesan priests and 500 nuns were present".

In the procession were army and navy chaplains properly uniformed, three girls from distant Venezuela, pupils of Villa Maria Academy at Frontenac, and a number of Indian girls from northern Minnesota reservations. In spite of the youth of the participants and the distractions inevitable on such an occasion, the procession was a dignified and serious one and reflected credit on the marchers and those who trained them.

As soon as the children were seated in the pews the Most Reverend Archbishop preached on "The Four Marks of the Church" and expressed his appreciation to all who had any part in the demonstration, "to the little boys and girls here, as well as to the priests and sisters who by their presence demonstrate their devotion".

The children in the habits of the religious communities, His Excellency said, "give some insight into the infinite diversity of response to the grace of God in carrying out the apostolic commission, for they represent every race, every color and every degree of social and economic condition".

The ceremonies concluded with Solemn Pontifical Vespers chanted by the clergy and Benediction of the Blessed Sacrament sung by the Cathedral mixed choir.

Fullest credit for the success of the pageant must be given to Father Walsh who spent himself and was spent in the preparation of it. Every detail was mapped out by him and was carried out without a hitch. As soon as it was over he completed plans for another meeting, one long contemplated under the auspices of the Society of which he was Director, a regional gathering of the national officers and diocesan directors of the Society for the Propagation of the Faith and of the Holy Childhood Association under the patronage of Archbishop Murray, who entered heartily into his plans. It was convoked for Thursday, November 11, but a few days before the meeting, and while on a trip to New York to complete the final arrangements for it, Father Walsh was suddenly stricken with a heart attack and died on Sunday, November 7, at the home of a friend in New Rochelle, N. Y. His remains were returned to St. Paul and his funeral took place from the Cathedral on Friday, November 12, the day following the regional meeting which was held as scheduled. The Most Reverend Archbishop officiated at the Pontifical Requiem and the sermon was preached by Father Le Beau, a former army chaplain and friend of the deceased. The body was laid to rest in the Resurrection cemetery beyond Mendota.

The regional meeting was attended by Bishop McDonnell of New York, National Director of the Propagation of the Faith, Monsignor Boardman, the National Secretary, Father Ackermann, CSSP., National Director of the Holy Childhood Association and all the diocesan Directors of the Propagation Society from Minnesota, North and South Dakota, Wisconsin, Nebraska, Iowa and Michigan. It was overshadowed by the lamented and untimely death of Father Walsh to whom many tributes were paid by the delegates and by His Excellency at the luncheon in the St. Paul Hotel where the program was carried out along the lines planned by him.

The Nestor of the Clergy

An event unique in the history of the Diocese of St. Paul, and very rare in the Church in the United States, was celebrated at the Motherhouse of the Sisters of St. Joseph on September 1, 1948, when the chaplain of the institution, Monsignor Joseph Marie Guillot, attained the seventieth anniversary of his ordination to the priesthood, and the sixty-fifth of his apostolic labors in the diocese. Mass was said in the Chapel of the Presentation at 10:30 by the Most Reverend Archbishop who, in the course of his sermon, declared that the Jubilarian was the sole survivor of a group of apostles from Lyons and vicinity in France who, at various times during the past one hundred and twenty years, participated in organizing the church in the Midwest from Mobile, Alabama, to St. Paul, Minnesota, and who had rendered yeoman service to the faithful wherever their lot was cast. The celebration was private except for the presence of a large number of priests and sisters; and the clergy and the Jubilarian were entertained at dinner after the Mass.

Monsignor Guillot had passed his ninety-third birthday by nearly seven months and, except for impaired hearing, was in full possession of his faculties. He was born near Lyons on February 7, 1855, and in his youth had the unforgettable privilege of being blessed by the sainted Curé of Ars, which he always considered the outstanding event of his life. After his ordination in 1878 he taught in the Seminary of Meximieux for five years before coming to St. Paul and labored fruitfully in many parishes of the diocese, notably in Waverly where he built one of the finest churches in the rural area, and at Marshall before coming to Minneapolis in 1910 as pastor of the Church of Notre Dame de Lourdes. He was honored with membership in the Papal Household on January 11, 1913, and invested with the purple robes by Archbishop Ireland on April 6. He was appointed chaplain of the Motherhouse in 1919 and since then has been most faithful in the discharge of his duties. He had just been relieved of the obligation of saying the community Mass, but he continued to say Mass privately at a side altar, was in good health, received visits from his friends, read the newspapers, and kept in touch with what is going on in the world around him. He lived to commemorate the seventy-fourth anniversary of ordination although unable to say Mass for a couple of years.

Missionary Cooperative Plan

The Missionary Cooperative Plan[41] was inaugurated in the Archdiocese on February 5, 1949. It has for object to systematize the appeals for financial aid made by religious societies of men and women engaged in mission work at home and abroad. With the approval of the Most Reverend Archbishop the Diocesan Director of the Propagation of the Faith allocates to the missionary society a definite number of urban and rural parishes to be visited by its representative on a Sunday designated by the pastor of the parish. All applications are made to the Archbishop who examines the credentials of the applicant, investigates the merits of the appeal and ascertains the numbers of missions and institutions supported by the organization in the field of labor assigned it by the Holy See.

If the application be approved the society agrees to accept the assignment made by the Diocesan Director and not visit any other parish in the Archdiocese. Each pastor is asked to permit one missionary appeal to his people on a designated Sunday each year, but is free to allow others a similar privilege if he wishes. The proceeds of the collection are sent to the office of the Propagation of the Faith to be forwarded to the headquarters of the missionary society. When the solicitors are sisters the pastor makes the announcement and the sisters accept the offerings given by the people as they leave the church if no other method be devised. No missionary organization with professional solicitors for magazines or other merchandize is allowed to participate in the plan. In this way the office of the Propagation of the Faith serves as a clearing-house for all appeals of a missionary character and saves the pastor the importunities of unauthorized solicitors.

An unusual ceremony was witnessed in the St. Paul Cathedral or Sunday afternoon, September 11, 1949, when two Franciscan missionaries were assigned their field of labor and presented with their crucifixes.[42] It was arranged by Father Cashman, Diocesan Director of the Propagation of the Faith, and Father Elias Koppert, O. F. M., of the Sacred Heart Church in St. Paul. The missionaries were Fathers Ervan Reichert O. F. M., assistant pastor of that parish, and Raymond Francis Crowe O. F. M., a newly-ordained friar. Auxiliary Bishop Byrne presided and the traditional homily of advice was preached by Father Eligius Weir, O. F. M., Minister-Provincial of the twelve-state Franciscan Province of the Sacred Heart with headquarters in St. Louis, Mo. He described the mission field which he had just visited, gave the departing missionaries paternal advice and bade them God-speed. While they lay prostrate before the altar he read letters of obedience, official notifications that their superiors had approved their requests to be sent to a foreign mission country and deemed them worthy of that exalted vocation. He then blessed the crucifixes which were presented by Bishop Byrne to the youthful missionaries. The Itinerary was sung by the Friars and the versicles and orations by the departing missionaries. The ceremony was witnessed by a large congregation and was brought to a close with Solemn Benediction by Father Eligius assisted by Reverends George E. Ryan, rector of the Cathedral, as deacon, Neil S. Cashman, Director of the Propagation of the Faith, as subdeacon. The Cathedral choir sang the liturgical hymns.

The missionaries left immediately for their destination in Brazil, South America, seven hundred miles by airplane up the Amazon river from Belem, the port of entry. Eleven priests and three brothers are already laboring in the mission territory.

In the early years of his episcopate the Most Reverend Archbishop found it necessary to call the attention of his diocesans to the decree of the Church outlawing dances under her auspices for any purpose whatsoever and forbidding pastors to put into the parish treasury funds derived from such sources.

In the latter part of October, 1949, he took cognizance of the reiterated complaints of parents "concerning the dangers to which their children have been exposed at dances conducted under Catholic auspices". In a letter to the clergy he recalled the legislation of the Holy See on March 31, 1916, prohibiting Catholic priests, diocesan and religious, as well as all other Catholic clerics, from promoting, sponsoring or encouraging dances even for the benefit of pious projects and from being present at them, even if held under the auspices of the laity.

> If the Catholic laity sponsor dances it is their moral obligation so to organize the dance that it may not be open to indiscriminate attendance by persons both Catholic and non-Catholic who seek an opportunity to exploit every type of dance for immoral purpose.

Catholic societies or groups are forbidden to foster dances unless the attendance is limited to members of the organization, or to persons presenting an authorized invitation, or unless the name, address and parish affiliation of the applicants are enrolled in a register and the escort promises to be responsible for his partner from the time she leaves her home until she returns thereto.

The apostolic reverence traditional in the house of God is too often disregarded by women who appear in church with their heads uncovered, notwithstanding the legislation of St. Paul in the eleventh chapter of his first Epistle to the Corinthians concerning the obligation to have their heads covered when they enter church for any purpose. This Pauline legislation was formally expressed by the Sacred Congregation of Rites on July 7, 1876, in the following decree:

> All members of the female sex are obliged to cover the head when they assist at sacred functions or even when they pray privately in view of the altar although unseen on account of a grill.

The Most Reverend Archbishop emphasized the binding force of this decree in a letter of July 2, 1949, asking pastors to call it to the attention of the women of their congregations who are thereby obligated to cover their heads with a hat, veil or other cloth whenever they assist at Mass, benediction, processions of the Blessed Sacrament, ceremonies of first communion or confirmation, funerals and weddings, or whenever they pray privately in church.

Events of 1949

The year 1949 was Centennial Year commemorating the organization of the Territory of Minnesota on March 3, 1849, and Governor Youngdahl issued an official proclamation designating Sunday, October 9, as Centennial Sunday, and asking the different religious denominations to observe it as a day of prayer and thanksgiving for the unnumbered blessings, material and spiritual, with which the State had been enriched during the intervening century.

The bishops of the five dioceses in Minnesota decided to cooperate in this observance[43] by holding a novena of prayer from October 2 to 10, during which the family rosary was recited in every home "in thanksgiving to God for the spiritual and temporal blessings bestowed during the past one hundred years". They suggested that in every school the pupils be asked to participate in a program "to recall the Catholic missionaries and the pioneers".

On the Centennial Sunday itself the recitation of the Litany of the Blessed Virgin Mary was prescribed at the end of every Mass "to thank the Mother of God for her patronage of a hundred years and invoke her protection for the centuries ahead".

That prayer might be supplemented by sacrifice they authorized Bishop Schenk of Crookston to distribute a pamphlet to all Catholics telling them the story of Father Aulneau, the young Jesuit missionary massacred by the Sioux on June 5, 1736, not far from Fort St. Charles on the most northerly point of Minnesota, and asking a contribution to help erect at Warroad, the parish center nearest the place of martyrdom a memorial church to this first martyred priest within the present State of Minnesota. The pamphlet, written by Father Shanahan of Warroad, was distributed on October 2 together with envelopes addressed to the Bishop of Crookston for the offerings which were to be taken up the following Sunday. The amount realized was much less generous than the promoters hoped, but it was supplemented by collections taken up in many parishes by Father Shanahan himself, who was authorized by his bishop to procure plans for a church to cost about sixty thousand dollars, and begin the work of construction as soon as possible.

Under the patronage of the Most Reverend Archbishop and the sponsorship of the Catholic students of the University of Minnesota, with their chaplain, Reverend L. P. Cowley, in charge of arrangements, the thirty-fourth annual convention of the Federation of Newman Clubs met in Minneapolis for a three-days' session beginning Friday, September 3, 1949, with headquarters at the Radisson Hotel and St. Olaf's Church as the center and scene of Solemn and Dialogue Masses for the hundreds of priest-chaplains and delegates from more than five hundred Newman Clubs in the United States. The theme of the convention was "The Social Responsibility of Catholic Students". It included panel discussions on "Social Action", "Religion in Higher Education", "Club Programming", etc. Auxiliary Bishop Byrne preached at the Solemn Mass on Sunday and, at the dinner which brought the convention to a close, addresses were delivered by Bishop Kearney of Rochester, N. Y., Episcopal Moderator of the Federation, and Monsignor Tanner, Assistant General Secretary of the N. C. W. C., Washington. During the convention the Reverend J. E. Schieder, Director of the Youth Department of the N. C. W. C., told the delegates that the Newman Club chaplains were the unsung heroes of the Catholic Church in America because they faced opposition to their work from within and without during these hectic years, but notwithstanding that they were more willing than ever before to labor for the expansion and advancement of the Catholic religion in every section and area where they work.

The convention named Reverend L. P. Cowley National Chaplain of the Federation in succession to Father McPhillips, Chaplain of the Newman Club of the University of Michigan, Ann Arbor. The chaplains held a three-days' conference at the College of St. Thomas before the opening of the convention for the discussion of problems pertinent to their work with a view to making it more effective in reaching and influencing all Catholic students in secular institutions. The University of Minnesota had the largest Catholic student body of any university in America, about six thousand, approximately one quarter of the entire enrollment. Father Cowley, their chaplain, resides at St. Olaf's Church of which he is pastor, and his assistant, Father Wagner, at the Newman Club on the border of the university campus.

With the opening of the scholastic year in September, 1950, the Diocesan Teachers College began to function as the Department of Elementary Education of the College of St. Catherine, with the result that a four-years' course leading to a Bachelor of Science degree and a certificate to teach in the schools of the State of Minnesota, will be available to the teaching sisters and to young women attending St. Catherine's. Under this plan the courses in the liberal arts are given at St. Catherine's and most of the professional courses in education at the Diocesan Teachers College. In the future, four years of preparation will be required for certification of teachers seeking positions in the public schools of Minnesota; and the directed teaching of prospective teachers will be carried on in the parochial schools of St. Paul. Students beginning their preparation will enroll in the College of St. Catherine.

Originally the Diocesan Teachers College held week-end sessions and summer school courses for the training of teachers which developed into a full course for ten months of the year. For a number of years it has prepared lay teachers for positions in Catholic schools.

Provision For High Schools

As a preparation for the celebration of the centenary of the Diocese of St. Paul in 1950, an educational expansion program was initiated during the month of September, 1948, by the purchase of sites for two high schools for boys, one in St. Paul, the other in Minneapolis, and the transfer of a parochial school in St. Paul to a teaching community of sisters who conduct it as a high school for girls. The site for the high school in St. Paul is on St. Anthony Avenue in the block bounded by that avenue on the south, Syndicate Street on the east, Hamline Avenue on the west and Bohn Avenue on the north. The site for the Minneapolis school is on Fourth Avenue South, in the block bounded by that avenue on the east, Forty-second Street on the north, Forty-fourth Street on the south and Third Avenue on the west. The new high school for girls in St. Paul opened in September, 1951, in St. Luke's parish school, in the block bounded by Summit Avenue on the east, Victoria Street on the north, Milton Street on the south, and Portland Avenue on the west. It is staffed by the Congregation of Our Lady of Charity of the B. V. M., with headquarters in Dubuque, Iowa, who purchased it for $600,000 and began with the ninth grade and will add another each year until a full high school course is available. During the three years that elapsed before the school was opened the parish of St. Luke built a new and modern school on property adjoining the church on Summit Avenue, under the direction of the pastor, Right Reverend J. J. Cullinan. The

St. Paul site for the new high school for boys was bought from Brown and Bigelow and the Minneapolis site from Michael Kelly, former owner of the Minneapolis base ball club. Efforts are being made to procure the services of a religious community of priests to teach in these schools and building operations will not begin until the Most Reverend Archbishop has definite assurance that teachers will be available when the schools are ready. It is his wish that "every parish have a school of its own, or participate in the organization of inter-parochial schools convenient to all parishes, hence these plans for new inter-parish high schools, which will ultimately mean every Catholic child in a Catholic school".

The Archbishop's Jubilee

The month of April has always had a sacred significance for the Most Reverend Archbishop. During that month he was ordained and consecrated. On April 14, 1900, he was dowered with priestly power and on April 28, 1920, elevated to the episcopal dignity. When the fiftieth anniversary of his ordination and the thirtieth of his consecration were drawing near priests and people hoped to take advantage of them to show their appreciation of him personally and of the significant work he had done in the diocese during eighteen years. But he would not permit any public celebration of the events. All he would agree to was a Pontifical Mass in the Cathedral on the anniversary of his ordination which was attended by a congregation that taxed the capacity of the church. Four bishops were present—Brady of Sioux Falls, Schenk of Crookston, Ferrando of Shillong, India, and Byrne of St. Paul—with 250 priests, hundreds of sisters from different communities, and delegations from Catholic schools and colleges. After the gospel Auxiliary Bishop Byrne ascended the pulpit and voiced the congratulations and good wishes of the clergy, sisters and laity and surprised the Jubilarian by reading an autographed letter from His Holiness Pope Pius XII in which the Pontiff recalled his visit to St. Paul in 1936 and authorized His Excellency to impart the Apostolic Blessing to all present "provided that they observe the special regulations for the Holy Year of Jubilee".

> We felicitate you, Venerable Brother, on your long and fruitful performance of your sacred duties of shepherd and at the same time We beg of God to graciously bestow on you His gifts and consolation and to preserve you for many years in the service of your flock.

The Archbishop spoke briefly thanking God for the graces of ordination and consecration and the blessed fruitfulness of his sacerdotal and episcopal years and expressed his gratitude to the clergy, religious communities and laity for their cooperation and good wishes and especially for the spiritual bouquets offered for him.

The common of the Mass was sung by the children's choir of the Cathedral school assisted by thirty priests.

After the Mass the prelates were served luncheon in the parochial residence and the clergy in the Cathedral crypt.

Notwithstanding the Archbishop's positive refusal to accept a personal tribute of any kind, the priests felt that something tangible should be done to show their filial devotion and appreciation of all he had accomplished during the eighteen years of his chief pastorship in the diocese. The Consultors, knowing the attitude of the clergy and with due respect for the wishes of the Archbishop, approached him with the suggestion that he allow them to defray at least a part of the outstanding personal obligations amounting to $117,933.00 incurred during these years in meeting the demands of religion and charity for which no diocesan funds were available. He was finally prevailed upon to accede to their wishes, and an appeal made by them to the clergy on March 27, realized the magnificent sum of $67,333.00, thus reducing the personal indebtedness of His Excellency to $50,600.00. The presentation was made informally by the Consultors in the name of their fellow-priests and suitably acknowledged by His Excellency in a letter to the clergy, on May 24.

The Diocesan Centennial

The most significant religious event of the year 1950 was the solemn commemoration of the one hundredth anniversary of the erection of the Diocese of St. Paul on July 19, 1850. Since the actual date of the centenary came in mid-summer, when the schools were not in session and it would be impossible to assemble their pupils to participate in the liturgical observances, the Most Reverend Archbishop and the Consultors decided to postpone the culminating celebration in the Twin Cities till the week of October 15.

As a preparation for the due observance of the event the Archbishop directed a letter to the clergy on March 29 in which he said that

the observance of the Centenary of the Diocese of St. Paul includes a program of spiritual activities associated with the endeavor of the Holy Father to make this Holy Year the year of the great return and the great pardon, the restoration of spiritual life to the thousands of lapsed Catholics by their return to participation in sacramental union with Christ and the pardon of indifferent Catholics who are such in name only until they abandon a life of sin, seek forgiveness through sincere penance and resume the effort to develop a truly Christian character.

The celebration in the eleven rural deaneries began on Sunday, May 7, continued at intervals during the summer and ended on October 15. In each deanery there was a Pontifical Mass of reparation and thanksgiving and a sermon dealing with the centennial and its significance to which the clergy and the laity of the district were invited by the Dean and his committee who made the arrangements for their participation and entertainment. All the priests who could possibly be present assisted at the Mass and large congregations showed the interest of the faithful in the centennial observance.

Early in the year the general program[44] was mapped out and the pupils in the upper grades of the parochial schools and in the high schools were trained in the liturgical chant. The immediate preparation began with the opening of the schools in September and several group rehearsals were held before the great week of October 15 dawned, during which the jubilee functions would take place in St. Paul on Tuesday, in Minneapolis on Wednesday and in the St. Paul Seminary on Thursday. The program mapped out in the Archbishop's letter of October 10 was similar for each of the cities and called for a Pontifical Mass in the municipal auditorium in the forenoon and a public meeting in the evening, with sermons, addresses and musical numbers.[45] Provision was made for the celebration of daily Mass by the 336 clergymen who had signified their intention to be present at the celebration on the 48 altars available in the Cathedral, the St. Paul Seminary and the Catholic Youth Centers in St. Paul and Minneapolis.

The celebrant of the Pontifical Mass in the St. Paul Auditorium, on Tuesday, October 17, was the Most Reverend T. A. Welch of Duluth, the senior Bishop of the Province, at which the sermon was preached by the Right Reverend J. A. Corrigan, pastor of the Church of St. Mark, who gave a thumb-nail résumé of the careers and achievements of the five "singularly remarkable" prelates who "individually and collectively would adorn with lustre the pages of any century of ecclesiastical history". The officers of the Mass were chosen from among the senior seminarians with Reverend G. Ziskovsky in charge of the ceremonies. The proper of the Mass was sung by the seminarian choir of nearly three hundred voices and the common by six thousand children from the parish and the high schools of St. Paul under the baton of Father Missia with Father Schuler of Nazareth Hall at the organ. Five thousand people packed the balconies on the three sides and the overflow occupied the main floor behind the children's choir. Half a dozen bishops and hundreds of priests and sisters from the different religious communities were in attendance.

The Archbishop presided at the civic meeting on Tuesday evening where a few thousand people assembled to listen to the program of classic and modern music rendered by the St. Paul Catholic Choral Society directed by Father Missia with Father Schuler as accompanist, and to an address by the Right Reverend J. M. Reardon of Minneapolis in which he briefly recounted the principal events in the lives of Bishops Cretin and Grace who administered the affairs of the Diocese of St. Paul from 1851 to 1884. Several bishops occupied seats on the stage and a large number of priests were present in the audience.

A similar program was carried out in Minneapolis the next day. The celebrant of the Pontifical Mass was the Most Reverend James J. Byrne, Auxiliary Bishop of St. Paul, and the Reverend L. P. Cowley was the preacher. He declared that Bishop Cretin, first occupant of the St. Paul See, "had a passionate zeal to establish an educational system in the diocese that would guard the children against the ravages of intellect that were beginning to infest the minds of European youth"; and that his successors built a magnificent superstructure of educational institutions on the foundation laid by him. The ministers of the Mass were seminarians and Father G. Ziskovsky directed the ceremonies. The student choir sang the proper of the Mass and the common was sung by a massed choir of six thousand children from the parochial and high schools of the city. The rest of the auditorium was comfortably filled with the laity and several hundred priests and sisters.

After Mass the Archbishop and Bishops Welch, McCarty, Connolly, Fitzgerald, Byrne, Monsignors Costigan and Healy (of Rapid City Diocese) Fathers Hacker, V. G. and Gilligan of St. Paul Seminary, were entertained at luncheon in the Basilica residence.

At the civic meeting in the evening the Archbishop presided and the Very Reverend J. H. Moynihan of the Incarnation parish delivered an address in which he extolled the achievements of the three Archbishops of St. Paul in thir administration of diocesan affairs from 1884 to 1950. Archbishops Ireland and Dowling

ruled this diocese with consummate wisdom and prudence and with the sense of awful responsibility that they know who have the care of souls and all the churches. Both were great in administration. . .one drifting on the tide of immigration to a frontier village and watching it grow through long years into a great metropolis, grew himself into greatness and worldwide influence, crowning at last his city with a temple that vies with the great basilicas of the world. The other brought his great talents to complete with more generous resources the princely plans for the exaltation of religion that haunted his artistic fancy. Both were educators, men of the highest idealism. Both realized that the vision of God is the very essence of a noble life.

To Archbishop Murray must be given credit for

some of the marvellous progress of the diocese during the past twenty years. . .the astounding record of almost four score new parishes, new centers of Catholic life and worship, set up in these years. . .of the intensification of Catholic life through catechetics, of zeal and energy in the cause of Catholic Action. . .of solicitude for the problems of youth, of compassion for the needy and unfortunate.

The St. Paul Seminary was the scene of the final event of the centennial celebration on Thursday when the Most Reverend Archbishop offered Pontifical Mass in St. Mary's chapel in presence of Bishops Busch, Welch, McCarty, Mueller, Dworschak and Byrne, fourteen monsignors, the

Seminary faculty, three hundred priests and the seminarians who had charge of the ceremonies and sang the responses. The sermon was preached by the Most Reverend J. L. Connolly, Coadjutor Bishop of Fall River, Mass., and a former rector of the Seminary.

He made emphatic enunciation of

the cure for the perversities of our times. It is our faith. . .Christianity is not alone a creed but a culture. It is a way of life. It calls us to grow in Him who is the head, Christ Jesus. . .It is not enough that priests have an accurate knowledge of Divinity. Their lives must be affected by it. They must be able to impart it. They must believe as Bishop Cretin did when he trained seminarians in his household; as Bishop Grace did when he bought property for a seminary; as Archbishop Ireland did when he founded this institution; as Archbishop Dowling did when he planned Nazareth Hall; as Archbishop Murray does when he dedicates the new memorial library to house the rich source of secular and spiritual learning for the preparation of learned, zealous and devoted laborers in the vineyard of the Lord.

After Mass all repaired in procession to the new Archbishop Ireland Memorial Library which the Archbishop blessed with ritualistic exactness and, in presence of bishops and clergy assembled in the spacious reading-room, conferred, for the first time in the history of the seminary, the degree of Master of Arts on five of the priests ordained in June—Fathers Richard Moudry of Nazareth Hall; John Liebert of the Resurrection parish, Minneapolis; Leo Goblirsch of St. Agnes parish, St. Paul; Edward Baumann and Henry Tenhundfeld of the Latin School, Covington, Kentucky.

The prelates, local clergy and visitors were entertained at dinner in the seminary refectory and listened to a reminiscent address by Bishop Busch of St. Cloud, the nestor of the American hierarchy in years of life and length of consecration.

Towards the end of the year, at the request of the employees of parishes and institutions, the Most Reverend Archbishop in a letter, dated December 12, authorized the pastors and those in charge of institutions to ascertain whether or not their lay help wished to be included in the old-age and survivors' insurance system of the Government which up to that time excluded from its operation all who worked for religious corporations. If two-thirds of them expressed in writing a wish to take advantage of this social security provision for old age, the pastor or head of the institution had to apply to the nearest internal revenue office for the official blanks which the employees must sign, authorizing the employer to withhold from their wages the amount prescribed by the terms of the law, which is 1½% from 1951 to 1953, 2% from 1954 to 1959, 2½% from 1960 to 1964, 3% from 1965 to 1969, and 3¼% for 1969 and afterwards. Priests and religious are excluded from a participation in this form of old-age security.

The names and addresses of the employees who elect to participate in this plan must be mailed to the nearest internal revenue office, and at the end of each quarter the employer must send a check for the sum withheld from the employees' wages and an equal amount from the treasury of the corporation. This plan has been in operation for many years but its provisions were extended to the employees of religious corporations only this year. Each one receives a Social Security number which does not change if the holder seeks other employment.

During these two decades of progress twenty-five of the older parishes erected new churches, some of which are among the most imposing of the Archdiocese; others remodeled and enlarged existing buildings; and others planned to build anew or renovate when funds are available, or the cost of construction warrants. Eighteen of the older parishes, urban and rural, have built new and modern schools since 1932; others have enlarged or remodeled existing structures or plan to do so when the cost is less prohibitive. Many new convents, rectories and halls have been added to existing parish equipment.

The growth in religious vacation schools was most encouraging and consoling; and the number of pupils taking advantage of the release periods during these years augurs well for the Catholic education of children who, for one reason or another, or for no reason at all, are deprived of the blessing of a religious training in parochial schools. This notable advance was due to the development of the work of the Confraternity of Christian Doctrine to which His Excellency has always given whole-hearted support. In evaluating the progress made in the Archdiocese during these eighteen years it must not be forgotten that it took place under the adverse circumstances of the worst depression in the country's history and of the most savage and costliest of wars in which the nation has ever engaged, a war which taxed as never before the manpower and resources of its citizens.

The Second Decade

The second decade of Archbishop Murray's administration shows impressive results especially in the field of Catholic education.[46] Not less impressive from the material standpoint is his record in providing more ample opportunities and accommodations for the faithful to hear Mass and approach the Sacraments by opening new parishes and authorizing the construction of new churches in more accessible locations.

The number of parochial schools increased from 128 to 146 and the enrollment from 33,089 to 45,812; sixteen parish high schools with an attendance of 1,551 at the beginning of the decade increased to nineteen with 4,008 pupils. In St. Thomas College 1,624 young men were being educated, an increase of 832; and in St. Catherine's the enrollment rose from 625 to 955, making a total of 2,579 receiving a higher education under Catholic auspices. Special religious classes in vacation schools and release periods numbering 1,006, had an attendance of 23,570 which, with the 55,134 in Catholic educational institutions, brought the number under Catholic instruction to the all-time high of 78,704.

The number of priests in the diocese rose to 525, of whom 443 are diocesan and 82 regular, an increase of 12 of the former and 7 of the latter. The major and minor seminaries housed 533 students as compared with 381 ten years ago. The teaching staff in the Archdiocese comprised 62 priests engaged in full-time work, 44 christian brothers, 1,404 sisters and 328 lay teachers. The number of sisters increased from 1,564 to 1,978 in 33 religious communities. The baptism of infants mounted from 8,862 to 14,690 and of adults from 1,432 to 1,844 in the ten-year period.

Five general hospitals, an increase of two since 1942, ministered to 40,992 patients annually, more than double the number of that year. In addition, one special hospital with a bed capacity of 67 treated 289 during the year. The Catholic population grew from 289,123 to 369,660. This remarkable development was due to the vision and leadership of the Most Reverend Archbishop and the sustained cooperation of the clergy, religious and laity.

In every field of activity, spiritual and material, there was marked progress during the years between 1932 and 1952. New parishes[47] to the number of 83 have been opened in the Twin Cities and in the country districts. Of these 36 are in the rural areas—missions theretofore without resident pastors elevated to parochial status—with the addition of a school, completed or under construction, wherever justified by the number of children within their borders. Nineteen new parishes have been carved out of pre-existing parishes in St. Paul and vicinity and twenty-eight in Minneapolis and its suburbs. One new parish every two and a half months over a period of eighteen years surely establishes a record of worth-while activity in any diocese. The one, perhaps the only, alarming feature is the increasing Catholic population of the cities and the marked tendency to desert the farming areas for the bright lights of Broadway. The new city parishes had to build from the ground up, beginning with a combination church and school to meet the demands of religion and education, at the cost of staggering mortgage indebtedness assumed by parishioners most of whom had already built and helped to pay for the parent church and school, but who were not unwilling to begin over again to secure the future for the Church of Christ. The country missions, made parishes, had churches many of which required enlargement and renovation, and, in addition, the parishioners had to undertake the building of a school and a residence for the pastor and assume an indebtedness that taxed their resources. But they, too, had confidence in God and were prepared to make sacrifices for the good of religion.

Epilogue

A century closes: a century opens. The former has been stabilized in eternity: the latter faces an unrevealed future. A hundred years is a short time in the annals of christianity, a shorter in the history of humanity, a nothing in the unending hereafter.

A hundred years ago when Bishop Cretin, poor, unknown and unheralded, took possession of his frontier see, St. Paul was a straggling village, Minnesota a wilderness where the Indian war-cry preluded the scalping orgy, and the hardy colonist contended with the redman for the possession of his huntlands. When he died, six years later, the tide of western immigration had borne tens of thousands into the upper valley of the Mississippi, the only highway to civilization; and the one thousand souls who constituted his primitive flock had multiplied half a hundredfold. During his episcopate he made heroic efforts to reach his scattered people and was a bitter foe of the frontier saloon. He left an organized church, a growing priesthood, budding sisterhoods, a reputation for personal sanctity and a tradition of knowledge and righteousness as a goodly inheritance to his successors who built on this foundation a superstructure of ideals and accomplishments that have made the name of the Diocese of St. Paul a synonym for material and spiritual progressiveness beyond the seven seas.

Few missionaries in a new land have the consolation of reaping even a modicum of the harvest of their own sowing. Others come to gather the golden heads whose seedlings they did not cast into the furrow; but in the providence of God, they share the richness of the garnered grain with their benefactors. Bishop Grace saw the harvest whiten for the sickle and sent laborers into the vineyard. The 50,000 souls he inherited increased to 130,000 in twenty-five years and through his efforts 147 priests gathered the flock into 246 parishes and missions and fed them with the Bread of Life. Schools and hospitals multiplied, and six religious orders of men and fourteen of women helped to lighten the burden of his advancing years. The net was full almost to the breaking and twenty-nine levites were hastening to lend a helping hand.

When he would lay aside the crozier of authority, one whom he had chosen and trained, a goodlier than he, stood ready to ascend the vacated throne under whose benignly autocratic rule the diocese was to attain international stature and make the name of Archbishop Ireland synonymous with its own. The golden age of the Church of St. Paul was reached before the mid-century of its diocesan existence; and the leaders of Church and State, at home and abroad, found their way to the North-west to sit at the feet of Gamaliel.

The germ of every existing institution of which the diocese boasts today was planted by his hand in fertile soil and watered by his labors and prayers, his tears and sacrifices, during the three and a half decades of his consecrated leadership. For years he was the Nestor of the clergy in active service in the diocese; and the province into which it burgeoned was ruled by hand-picked suffragans who rendered filial homage to another John sent by God. When, full of years and merits, he was gathered to the fathers he was laid to rest, not beneath the majestic dome of the magnificent temple he had planned and built on the brow of St. Anthony hill, but under the grassy sward kept green by heaven's dew among the pioneers whom he loved.

A stranger came with apostolic mandate to enjoy the fruits of three score years and ten of planning and toiling and building, to shepherd the bereaved flock, to assume the sceptre of authority and sit in the teaching chair for a decade of years during which he amplified and enhanced the educational and cultural facilities for clergy, religious and laity, added to the number of priestly auxiliaries to meet the ever-increasing demands of the ministry, and joined with his brethren of the hierarchy in coordinating the activities of the Church on American soil through the administrative council of bishops of which he was a prominent official. He erected new churches and institutions, clothed with interior beauty unadorned walls and empty sanctuaries, and enriched the dwell-ings of the Lord with the beauty of the king's daughter. And yet, withal, he was a prelate of simple tastes and democratic mien, timid of the public eye, who sought not the applause of men, and few, save his intimate friends, found the pathway to his door. Archbishop Dowling was at the beck and call of all who had, or thought they had, a claim on his time or energy and when his spirit winged its flight to God, he, too, was laid to rest besides his predecessors on Calvary's verdant hillside.

From the Atlantic seaboard came another John, a charming and cultured churchman, to inaugurate the twenty years of material growth and spiritual progress that rounded out the first century of our diocesan existence, an apostolic prelate who viewed the people committed to his care as part and parcel of the Mystical Body of Christ and strove to make them cognizant of their dignity. With unassumed humility but with conscious power he placed himself in the van of the army of souls entrusted to his shepherding and, by exhortation and example, allured them to a brighter world and a fuller realization of their supernal destiny.

In the discharge of his apostolic duty he opened new parishes by the score and thus brought the sacramental ministrations of the Church to remote hamlets. He authorized the building of parochial schools wherever possible to insure Catholic training for the young. He summoned the pupils of secular schools to the study of religion during vacation days and thus laid the foundation of an intelligent and righteous generation.

From his viewpoint, which is that of the Church, the only education that counts is that which develops and enhances the life of the soul and gives the individual a fuller participation in the graces that supernaturalize his daily activity. The purified and ennobled life of the individual is reflected in the family circle, the state and the nation.

Archbishop Murray has emptied himself in the service of the faithful by multiplied Pontifical Masses in cramped sanctuaries, by continuous confirmation tours and canonical visitations, by solicitude for the young, the orphan, the underprivileged, the victims of war and pestilence. His charity embraces all and knows no limit. "All I have is yours" is his motto and, when personal funds are exhausted, he does not hesitate to borrow freely and generously to satisfy the needs of those who are in distress. A worthy successor is he to the four prelates who preceded him in the Diocese of St. Paul and an exemplar worthy of imitation by him who, in the distant day, we hope, will grasp the crozier as it slips from his relaxing hand.

The Diocese of St. Paul has every reason to be proud of the prelates whom the Holy Ghost has chosen to guide its destiny during the first hundred years of its organized existence; and, judging the future by the past, there is every reason to believe that the century upon which it has embarked will be no less prolific of material progress, spiritual development and exemplary leadership than the one to which it bids adieu today.

Chapter XII

PARISH CHRONICLES

In mid-year, 1948, questionnaires were mailed from the Chancery Office to all the pastors of the Archdiocese asking for detailed information about the origin and development of their parishes and missions and the responses have been tabulated.

The questionnaires asked for the early Catholic history of the locality; the names of the pioneers and their racial descent; the date of erection of the original and subsequent (if any) churches; the improvement and renovations in parish properties; the schools and other institutions under parish control; the names of the pastors and assistants and of the laity who played prominent roles in the religious life of the community; and the number, if not the names, of all who embraced the religious life. In a word, the questionnaires postulated a brief but detailed history of the important events in the life of the parish and of its missions.

This historical data has been condensed into a paragraph or two in the following pages. In many cases the information given in the questionnaires was supplemented by facts drawn from other reliable sources and compared with the comparatively small number of historical sketches preserved in the archives of the Catholic Historical Society in the St. Paul Seminary. Our first thought was to give the names of all the priests associated with each parish, but the lists were so incomplete that it was decided to mention only those who had signalized their pastorate in some important way.

The work of writing the parish sketches above referred to was begun during the administration of Mrs. Genevieve Rahilly Irwin of Lake City, President of the Minnesota Council of Catholic Women from 1927 to 1929, when a historical department was organized under the direction of the late Mrs. Jane Hughes Sullivan of Mankato. It had for object to rescue from oblivion the story of the early Church in Minnesota and since then a number of parochial and institutional histories have been gathered.

They were consulted in the preparation of the following sketches and the information therein contained checked with the more recent reports sent in by the pastors which were judged to be more reliable in regard to facts, names and dates.

CITY OF ST. PAUL

1841—CATHEDRAL OF ST. PAUL

It originated in the log chapel, 18 by 20, built under the direction of Reverend Lucien Galtier and dedicated by him on November 1, 1841, which became the first cathedral of the diocese on July 2, 1851, when Bishop Cretin was installed in its primitive sanctuary. It was succeeded in November of that year by the second

581

582   THE CATHOLIC CHURCH IN THE DIOCESE OF ST. PAUL

Cathedral on the middle floor of the three-story stone and brick building, 80 by 40, on Wabasha at Sixth Street which did duty until June 13, 1858, when the third Cathedral, 140 by 70, facing Sixth Street at St. Peter was opened for divine worship though unplastered and unfurnished, and served the needs of the diocese until it was dismantled in August, 1914. The congregation worshipped in the auditorium of the Cathedral school, 325 Kellogg Boulevard, until Palm Sunday, March 28, 1915, when the first Mass was said by Archbishop Ireland in the present granite edifice on Summit Avenue, between Dayton and Selby Avenues, which was officially dedicated by him on Sunday, April 11, of that year.

The Cathedral has had the following rectors: Bishop Cretin (1851-56) Reverend D. Ledon (1856-57); Reverend A. Ravoux, Administrator, (1857-59); Bishop Grace (1859-61); Reverend L. E. Caillet (1861-67); Reverend John Ireland (1867-75); Reverend John Shanley (1875-89); Reverend P. R. Heffron (1890-6); Reverend J. J. Lawler (1896-1916); Reverend T. J. Gibbons (1916, May-July); Reverend L. F. Ryan (1916-40); Reverend J. J. Cullinan (1940-2); Reverend F. J. Schenk (1942-5); Reverend G. E. Ryan (1945–).

The present Cathedral school had its origin in the pioneer school for boys opened in the second Cathedral basement by Bishop Cretin in 1852, which developed into the parochial school for boys and girls on the corner of Seventh and St. Peter Streets and was transferrred to its present location in 1912. The parish school has always been under the direction of the Sisters of St.Joseph of Carondelet.

The first residence for Bishop Grace and the clergy was built in 1860 and occupied until 1914, when Bishop Lawler, the pastor, moved to an old frame house in the rear of the new Cathedral on Dayton Avenue, and the assistant priests to a frame building at 239 Selby Avenue, the site of the present imposing brick residence occupied since December 17, 1924. It has been the residence of the Most Reverend Archbishop Murray since June 18, 1937, when he vacated the episcopal residence at 226 Summit Avenue, across from the Cathedral, to provide accommodations for sisters attending the summer school of the Diocesan Teachers College.

1856—CHURCH OF THE ASSUMPTION

The original frame church for the German Catholics of St. Paul was completed in 1856, under the direction of the Reverend G. Keller (1856-8), and the first Mass was said in it on June 1, by Bishop Cretin. It was transferred to the pastoral care of the Benedictine Fathers on January 1, 1858, with Reverend Demetrius de Marogna (1858-63) as pastor. A frame school for boys was built in 1860; the rectory in 1863 by Reverend Clemens Staub, O.S.B. (1863-73); and a stone school in 1867; the rectory was enlarged and brick-veneered in 1881 by Reverend Valentine Stimmler O.S.B. (1875-87). The present imposing stone church, erected in 1871, was consecrated by Bishop Grace on October 18, 1874. Eight Benedictine Fathers followed Father Clemens until 1912 when Reverend J. M. Solnce, a diocesan priest, became pastor and was succeeded by Reverend L. Haas (1916-35) when the present pastor Reverend J. Stelmes was appointed who built the substantial rectory and the new combined convent and grade school.. The first school, destroyed by fire in 1863, was rebuilt of stone and is now used as a meeting-place for German societies. A brick school was erected in 1887. The girls were taught by the Sisters of St. Joseph until 1885 when the Sisters of Notre Dame took charge. The Christian Brothers had charge of the boys from 1875 to 1882.

9 Benedictine and 2 diocesan priests, 6 brothers and 64 sisters are from the parish

1865—CHURCH OF ST. MARY

A new parish for English-speaking Catholics in Lower Town, at some distance from the Cathedral, was organized in 1865 by Reverend L. E. Caillet, pastor of the Cathedral, and placed under the patronage of the Blessed Virgin. The cornerstone of the new church was blessed on May 20, 1866, by Bishop Grace and the complete edifice dedicated on July 28, 1867, by the Reverend A. Oster, Administrator of the

Diocese during the absence in Europe of Bishop Grace and Father Ravoux, V.G. The sermon was preached by Reverend J. Ireland who also preached at the silver jubilee in 1893 and the golden jubilee in 1917 when a Pontifical Mass was celebrated by the Most Reverend Joseph F. Busch, Bishop of St. Cloud, who had been assistant in the parish. The first rectory was built in 1869 and occupied until 1902 when a more suitable house in the same block was purchased by Reverend T. J. Gibbons who succeeded Monsignor Caillet in 1893. In 1875 the chapel of the Sacred Heart was added to the west of the sanctuary.

A frame school was ready for occupancy in October 1869. It was enlarged in 1876 when two Christian Brothers from St. Louis were added to the faculty of three Sisters of St. Joseph to teach the boys. They remained till 1891. The first half of the new brick school was blessed on September 4, 1887, and the second four years later. In 1910 Father Gibbons was succeeded by Reverend J. A. Corrigan (1910-11), Reverend J. C. Byrne (1911-16), Reverend J. M. Reardon (1916-21) who, in 1919, sold the church property to the Great Northern Railway and bought a new site in May, 1921, for the combined church, school and attached rectory dedicated by Archbishop Dowling on February 12, 1922, during the pastorate of Reverend J. Dunphy (1921-25). On May 24, 1939, the new church and marble altar were consecrated by Archbishop Murray during the pastorate of Reverend B. F. Audus (1925-41). The seventy-fifth anniversary was celebrated on September 20, 1942, with Pontifical Mass by Archbishop Murray and a sermon by Monsignor Reardon. The pastor was Reverend D. J. Gregory (1941-7) who was succeeded by the present pastor, Reverend J. M. Pilger (1947–).

6 priests, diocesan and regular, and a large number of sisters are from the parish.

1868—CHURCH OF ST. LOUIS

The first church for the French Catholics of St. Paul, on Cedar Street at Tenth, was blessed by Bishop Grace on December 20, 1868, with Reverend G. Schmirer as pastor. Father Ravoux preached. The second church on Wabasha and Exchange Streets, bought from the Universalists, was dedicated on April 24, 1881, by Bishop Ireland. The parish was assigned to the Marist Fathers on August 4, 1886, shortly after the parish school was opened by Reverend C. Genis (1884-6) with the Sisters of St. Joseph in charge. The present church and rectory on Cedar Street were built during the pastorate of Reverend P. Rulquin, S.M., (1907-13) and dedicated on December 19, 1909, by Archbishop Ireland. The main altar of the church was consecrated by Bishop Lawler on November 30, 1911.

6 priests from the parish.

1868—CHURCH OF ST. MICHAEL

The first Mass was celebrated in St. Michael's Church on September 29, 1868, by Reverend J. Ireland, assistant at the Cathedral, to which it was attached as a mission. The first resident pastor was Reverend P. J. Gallagher (1879-88) who was succeeded by the Reverend P. O'Neill (1888-1944) and the present pastor, Reverend J. O'Neill (1944–). The church was enlarged by Father O'Neill in 1906, and the rectory built by him in 1903. The parish school was opened in September, 1884, with the Sisters of St. Joseph in charge and in 1910 the Welde home was purchased for a convent.

23 priests and 35 sisters are from the parish.

1872—CHURCH OF ST. STANISLAUS

The parish was founded by Bohemian and Polish immigrants. For the original church Bishop Grace donated the lot on which the school now stands and it was built under the direction of Father Bast, a Polish priest. The Bohemians were attended by Father Maly of New Prague. When Father Bast left the parish it was served by the Benedictine Fathers of the Assumption Church until 1874 when Father Steinacher, a Bohemian, came. He was succeeded by Reverend F. Tichy (1877-80) who bought lots for the first parish house which was completed during the pastorate of Reverend H. Povolny (1882-6). The Reverend J. Rynda (1886-

1924) erected a new church during the first year of his pastorate with a seating capacity of 450. It was destroyed by fire on April 9, 1934, while Reverend A. Kotouc (1924-39) was pastor. Mass was said in the parish hall till June 29, 1941, when the present brick church was completed in May of that year under the direction of Reverend W. J. Jiracek (1939–) at a cost of $100,000 and paid for in two and a half years. The first school was opened in 1886 in the original church by three School Sisters of Notre Dame. In 1902 it was replaced by a four-room brick school at a cost of $17,000. In the same year a brick parish hall was erected which cost $15,000. Increased attendance made it necessary to open two school rooms in the basement of the church and this was the situation until January 7, 1951, when an addition put to the old school made it possible to accommodate three hundred pupils with seven sisters.

The first residence, built in 1882, served the priests of the parish until 1941 when the present rectory was acquired and remodeled at a cost of $13,450. In 1886 a large room was added to the original rectory and was used as a parish hall until 1902.

7 priests, 1 brother and 7 sisters from the parish.

1875—CHURCH OF ST. JOSEPH

The parish was carved out of the Cathedral parish in the summer of 1875 and placed in charge of Reverend L. Lebret (1875-8). A brick-veneered church, 90 by 45, was erected on the corner of Carroll Street and Virginia Avenue and made ready for the first Mass on Christmas day. It was enlarged and renovated in 1887 and a school, taught by the Sisters of St. Joseph from the neighboring St. Joseph's Academy, was opened in the basement. The second pastor was Reverend Joseph O'Keefe (1878-80). His successor, Reverend J. W. Nealis, died in January, 1885, and was succeeded by Reverend J. J. Keane who, in September, 1886, was appointed Procurator of the newly-established Seminary of St. Thomas. He was succeeded by the Reverend Walter Raleigh (1886-95).

A new church, 105 by 93, at Dayton and Western Avenues, was planned by Reverend J. T. Harrison (1895-1903) at a total cost of $110,000 including site and furnishings. It was designed by E. J. Donahue for a seating capacity of one thousand. The contract for the foundation was awarded to E. J. Johnson for $13,-322.25 and work had actually begun when the parish was merged in the new Cathedral parish and all work ceased on the new structure which, later on, served as the foundation for an apartment building. Father Harrison was transferred to another parish and soon took up his residence in the Diocese of Seattle.

1879—CHURCH OF ST. ADALBERT

In 1879 a group of Polish Catholics bought the frame Church of St. Louis, 60 by 34, on Tenth and Cedar Streets, from the French congregation and re-erected it on a stone foundation at Charles and Galtier Streets. It was dedicated on November 20, 1881, by Bishop Grace who preached in English. Reverend Dominic A. Majer preached in Polish. The first resident pastor was Father Horbaczewski (1881-3). A frame school, 22 by 30, on the site of the first Sisters' convent was taught by a lay teacher till 1885. Church and school were enlarged in 1885 by Reverend D. A. Majer (1883-1911) who built a two-story brick convent in 1887 with the Sisters of St. Francis in charge till September, 1908, when the Felician Sisters replaced them. The cornerstone of the present church was laid on May 8, 1910. Monsignor Majer was the first Polish priest in America to be made a Domestic Prelate in May, 1906, and he was buried from the uncompleted church in March, 1911. He was succeeded by the Reverend P. A. Roy (1911-1950). The new church, 144 by 60, with transepts 84 feet wide, was dedicated by Archbishop Ireland October 8, 1911. It was redecorated in 1922. The second rectory replacing an older one, was on the site of the original convent. The old church, made into a parish hall, was destroyed by fire in 1915. The present pastor is Reverend Max J. Matz (1950–) who built a new convent and a new rectory in 1951.

5 priests and over 50 sisters from the parish.

1881—CHURCH OF THE SACRED HEART

The Reverend C. Koeberl said Mass on Christmas day, 1881, in the original frame church erected by him for the German Catholics on Dayton's bluff. The rectory was occupied a few days previously. The church was razed in 1946. A combination church and school and a new rectory were completed in April, 1926, under the direction of Reverend Gaudence Worm, O.F.M. (1924-30). The following diocesan priests had charge of the parish: Reverends C. Koeberl (1881-99) and F. X. Gores (1899-1909). The parish was given to the Franciscan Fathers on September 15, 1909, and nine members of the order have been in charge since then. The new school and modern priests' house were completed in 1926 and an imposing brick church erected in 1950 and dedicated on April 14, 1951, by Archbishop Murray, to complete the corona of parish buildings. The first combined school and convent, 60 by 40, was established in 1883. The Sisters came on November 21 and opened school the next day with 86 pupils. The present brick convent was occupied on March 19, 1904, by the School Sisters of Notre Dame who are in charge of the school. It was dedicated by Archbishop Ireland on November 29 of that year.

The golden jubilee was commemorated on May 29, 1932, with Pontifical Mass and sermon by Archbishop Murray.

1884—CHURCH OF ST. PATRICK

The first Mass was said in the old Rice school purchased by the pastor, Reverend D. Reilly, and moved to Case and Mississippi Streets in October, 1884. He built a frame church dedicated by Bishop Ireland on December 21, 1884—the eleventh church in St. Paul. The present combination church and school was erected on a new site in 1938 by Reverend R. Lee, the ninth pastor (1928–). The first parochial school was opened in the original church in 1885 and transferred to the basement of the frame church on October 5, 1888. It was taught by the Sisters of St. Joseph. The first frame school was erected in 1905 by the Reverend M. Quinn (1904-27). The present school was ready for occupancy October 20, 1938. An addition was completed in 1952.

4 priests, 2 brothers and 25 sisters from the parish.

1884—CHURCH OF ST. FRANCIS DE SALES

A frame church, 100 by 50, with sacristy, 24 by 50, was dedicated August 31, 1884, by Rev. J. N. Stariha (1884-1902) who built the rectory at the same time. Prior to the dedication of the church Mass was said in St. Stanislaus Church in the neighboring parish. The church was veneered with brick later on. The school was opened September 9, 1884; the convent completed August 28, 1886, at a cost of $2,083, to which the Sisters of Notre Dame moved from an annex of the school. They arrived from Milwaukee on September 2, 1884. The church was decorated, with the addition of new altars and an enlarged sacristy, in 1912-3 by Reverend F. X. Bajec (1903-31). The school was enlarged in 1905, a new one erected in 1937, and a new convent in 1950 by Rt. Rev. James Zachman (1931–) who was made a Domestic Prelate in 1947.

Father Stariha was consecrated Bishop of Lead, South Dakota, on October 28, 1902, resigned March 29, 1909, and died in Jugoslavia November 23, 1915.

Sister Mary Cherubim who came to the parish on September 2, 1887, taught sewing to the pupils for forty-seven years, retiring on her golden jubilee in 1934; and Sister Mary Agnes taught music and art from 1888 till 1933 when she was transferred to a less arduous post in Madelia, Minnesota.

17 priests, 3 brothers and 40 sisters from the parish.

1886—CHURCH OF ST. MATTHEW

The parish was formally organized on March 9, 1886, with Reverend A. Plut as pastor, who built a combination church, school, convent and a rectory in 1887. The first Mass was said in the basement of the present church on April 17, 1887. His successor, Reverend J. M. Solnce, turned the rectory into a convent. In 1897 the Reverend P. M. Jung began a thirty years' pastorate during which he built the school in 1902; enlarged and remodeled the church and convent in 1908. An addition to the school was built in 1929 by Reverend F. J. Schaefer (1928-32). The present pastor, made a Domestic Prelate in 1947, is Right Reverend A. Ziskovsky (1932—). The School Sisters of Notre Dame have charge of the parochial school.

10 priests, 2 brothers and 30 sisters from the parish.

1886—CHURCH OF ST. JOHN

The first church, a frame structure, was built in 1886 by Reverend L. Cornelius (Aug., 1886-June, 1887), and the present brick edifice in 1922 by Reverend T. F. Gleeson (1894-1929). The parochial school was opened in September, 1889, by Reverend J. Fleming (1887-94) with the Sisters of the Immaculate Heart in charge till September, 1892, when the Sisters of St. Joseph replaced them. The new rectory was built in 1927 by Father Gleeson and the new school in 1931 by Reverend J. E. Doyle (1929-45). The Reverend E. S. DeCourcy was made pastor in 1945.

6 priests from the parish.

1887—CHURCH OF ST. JAMES

The parish was incorporated on October 4, 1887, and the first church built in 1888 by the Reverend John Conway (1887-9). The first Mass was said on August 28, 1888, by the Reverend John E. Fitzmaurice, Rector of the Seminary of Overbrook, Pa., and the sermon preached by Reverend J. J. Keane, Rector of St. Thomas Aquinas Seminary. The church was dedicated on October 7, 1888, by Bishop Grace. The present church was erected in 1938 by Reverend W. Cashman (1936—). There were four pastors prior to him.

The school, opened in September, 1913, by Reverend J. O'Connor (1901-36), is taught by the Sisters of St. Joseph who reside at St. Joseph's Provincial House. The original rectory was built in 1889 and occupied until the present rectory was incorporated into the school addition of 1923.

10 priests, 8 brothers and 18 sisters from the parish.

1887—CHURCH OF ST. AGNES

Parish Masses were said in St. Adalbert's Church from October 9, 1887, to August 15, 1888, and then in the school basement. The temporary church was blessed by Archbishop Ireland on September 23, 1888. The present church was begun by Reverend J. Trobec (1887-97), later, third Bishop of St. Cloud, and completed on an enlarged foundation by Reverend J. M. Solnce (1897-1912). His successors were Reverends A. Ogulin (1912-33); F. Rant (1933-7); and J. C. Gruden (1937—) who built a combination grade and high school, a new rectory and a new convent.

The School Sisters of Notre Dame have been in charge of the parish school (grade and high) since 1888. The former rectory was bombed the night of November 4, 1917, and severely damaged but no one was seriously injured.

23 priests, 3 brothers and 90 sisters from the parish.

1888—CHURCH OF ST. LUKE

A frame church at Portland and Victoria was built in 1888, by Reverend J. J. Lawler (1888-96), later, Bishop of Lead. The present location at Summit and Lexington was acquired in 1917. Services were held in the church crypt by Reverend J. C. Byrne (1916-42) and the superstructure was completed in 1926. The first baptism in the parish was October 27, 1888, and first wedding on September 15, 1890. The first school opened October 29, 1904, with the Sisters of St. Joseph in charge; second (brick) September 25, 1931, both on original church site. A school site nearer to the church on Summit Avenue was bought on July 24, 1946 and the new school was ready for occupancy in September, 1951. The second school was sold to the Sisters of Charity of the Blessed Virgin Mary of Dubuque, for high school for girls and the ninth grade opened in September, 1951. The first con vent at 977 Portland Avenue (Archbishop Ireland's old residence) was occupied in 1918; the new convent at 1034 Summit was purchased in 1948. The first (rented) rectory was on the old site and occupied in April, 1889: the clergy reside in a house behind the church on Lexington Avenue since September, 1919. Right Reverend John J. Cullinan (1942—) built the new school and acquired the property between it and the church for a rectory which will be ready for occupancy in a few months.

15 priests, 4 brothers and 24 sisters from the parish.

1888—CHURCH OF ST. VINCENT

The first Mass was said by Father Raleigh in a small chapel erected by the St. Paul Conference of the St. Vincent de Paul Society in the rear of the present church on December 1, 1888. The chapel was enlarged and made a mission of St. Luke's parish and Mass said regularly by Reverend J. J. Lawler (later, Bishop of Lead, S. D.) until 1889, when he was succeeded by the first resident pastor, Reverend L. Cosgrove (1889-1910) who built the present brick church in which the first Mass was celebrated on Christmas day, 1897. The church was dedicated on May 7, 1898, by Archbishop Ireland who preached at the Pontifical Mass said by Bishop Trobec of St. Cloud. The first rectory, built by Father Cosgrove, was occupied on October 18, 1889; and the present one, built by Reverend M. I. J. Griffin (1922-40), on October 3, 1927. Reverend W. P. Walsh was pastor from 1910 to 1912; and Reverend T. E. Crowley from 1912 to 1922. The Reverend P. F. Meade (1940-52) obtained episcopal permission for daily exposition of the Blessed Sacrament in 1943. It was discontinued in 1951 when he became a patient at St. Joseph's Hospital. The Reverend C. Morgan was appointed pastor in June, 1952.

The school was opened in September, 1902, with the Sisters of St. Joseph, residing at St. Joseph's Academy, in charge.

10 priests, 3 brothers and 27 sisters from the parish.

1888—CHURCH OF THE MOST HOLY REDEEMER

As early as 1874 Father Shanley, assistant pastor of the Cathedral of St. Paul, held services occasionally for the twenty Catholic Italian families of St. Paul. From 1883 to 1888 his place was taken by Reverend J. C. Byrne. Reverend Father Cestelli of the faculty of the College of St. Thomas then said Mass for them in the basement of the Cathedral and ministered to them till 1896. Other priests carried on the work until 1899, when the Reverend S. N. Odone came from Italy to take charge on August 29 of that year. He found one hundred and fifty families and said the first Mass for them on October 1, 1899, in the renovated basement chapel of the Cathedral, which, on May 27, 1901, was officially named the Church of the Most Holy Redeemer by Archbishop Ireland. The parish was incorporated February 9, 1906. Father Odone lived at the Cathedral residence and continued the work until 1909 when there were three hundred families in the parish. A few years afterwards the parish of St. Ambrose was opened for the Italians living in the Bradley street district. When the old Cathedral was dismantled in 1914 the Italian congregation worshipped in the Assumption Church until the new brick Church of the Holy Redeemer on College Avenue was ready for occupancy. It was built under the direction of Reverend R. Balducci with St. Ambrose as a mission and was dedicated on January 9, 1916. The Church of St. Ambrose was closed for a time but was reopened in 1917 by Father Reardon, pastor of the Church of St. Mary, and, after several years, restored to its mission status.

The Reverend L. Pioletti became pastor of Holy Redeemer on December 24, 1924, and in the course of time paid off the debt, bought additional property, acquired a rectory and remodeled the parish hall. In 1950 he renovated and redecorated the church at a cost of $22,000. He was decorated by the Italian Government for his service in World War 1 and later on for promoting the welfare of Italian immigrants. He was likewise made an Honorary Canon of the Cathedral of Chieri by Cardinal Fossati.

1888—CHURCH OF ST. PETER CLAVER

The colored Catholics of St. Paul first worshipped in a rented church on Market Street which they afterwards bought where Reverend J. Shanley, pastor of the Cathedral, said Mass for a year prior to his consecration as Bishop of Jamestown on December 27, 1889. Other priests followed him till 1892 when the present frame church at Farrington and Aurora Streets was dedicated by Archbishop Ireland on December 18. The first resident pastor was Reverend E. Casey (1892-5). The rectory was acquired in 1902 by Reverend T. A. Printon (1897-1910). He was followed by Reverend S. L. Theobald, a colored priest, born in Georgetown, British Guiana, and ordained in the St. Paul Seminary in June, 1910. His successor was Reverend C. Keefe (1932-42). The golden jubilee of the parish was celebrated in 1942 by Reverend J. Luger (1942–) who bought the convent on December 4, 1943, for the Sister Oblates of Providence (colored) of Baltimore, who arrived on September 5, 1945. Property for a school and gymnasium was purchased on July 25, 1947, at some distance from the church, building operations began in the spring of 1950, and the dedication took place in August of that year.

1889—CHURCH OF ST. MARK

The first frame church, 120 by 60, was erected in 1889 under the supervision of Reverend J. J. Keane, President of St. Thomas Aquinas Seminary, and dedicated on December 15 by Archbishop Grace. Father Keane said the Mass and Father O'Gorman of the Seminary faculty preached. The first resident pastor was Reverend J. T. Harrison (1891-5). His successors were Reverends E. Casey (1895-7); J. M. Prendergast (1898 for six months); G. D. Doyle (1898-9); W. L. Hart (1900-11). They occupied temporary rectories.

The golden age of development began with the appointment of Reverend J. A. Corrigan as pastor in 1911. He built the school in 1913; the rectory in 1917; the new church in 1919; an addition to the school in 1921; the convent in 1928. St. Mark's Church was solemnly consecrated by Archbishop Murray on May 29, 1939. The pastor, a member of the Board of Consultors, was made a Domestic Prelate of the Papal Household in 1947 and invested with the purple robes of his new dignity on Sunday, May 25, of that year. The Sisters of St. Joseph have charge of the school.

31 priests, 7 brothers and 26 sisters from the parish.

1890—CHURCH OF ST. BERNARD

The parish was legally organized on April 11, 1890, with Father Bernard Locnikar, O.S.B., as temporary pastor. A combination church and school was erected in 1890 by Reverend A. Ogulin (1890-1912) and the school opened on February 22 1891, with three Sisters of St. Benedict in charge, and 220 children enrolled. The school attendance reached an all-time record of 1280 in 1934—the largest grade school west of Chicago. The convent was ready for occupancy on September 8 1893; the parish hall was built in 1896 and the rectory in 1900. The present church costing $102,000 and seating 1000 was dedicated on January 1, 1907, by Archbishop Ireland. A new convent was opened on September 30, 1911. The Father of St. Benedict succeeded Father Ogulin on November 7, 1912, with Reverend Pauline Wiesner as first pastor from 1912 to 1916; and during the pastorate of Reverend Raymond Basel, O.S.B., a new rectory replaced the older structure in 1939 The school was enlarged by Reverend Odilo Kohler (1944-48) and his successor Reverend Theodore Kresbach, O.S.B., built a parish hall in 1950.

11 priests and 45 sisters from the parish.

1892—CHURCH OF ST. CASIMIR

A combined church and school was erected in 1892 by Reverend H. Jajeski (1892-4, 1911-16). The present church was built in 1904 by Reverend C. Kobyliski (1899-1910). Four pastors served the parish until 1916, when it was given to the Oblates of Mary Immaculate and Reverend A. Stojar, O.M.I., was placed in charge of it.

The first school was built in 1893; the present in 1924. Franciscan Sisters taught in the school till 1908 when they were replaced by the Felician Sisters from Chicago. The first convent was erected in 1894; the second in 1926; and the rectory in 1895.

5 priests and 27 sisters from the parish.

1898—CHURCH OF ST. ANDREW

A frame church, belonging successively to different Protestant organizations, was bought by Father Cosgrove, pastor of St. Vincent's, moved to Hatch and Churchill Streets in Como and dedicated by Archbishop Ireland on September 18, 1898. It was attached to St. Vincent's as a mission until 1907 when Reverend G. A. Arctander (1907-9) was appointed first resident pastor. After his death on September 15, 1909, the Reverend T. A. Printon (1909-46) was named pastor. A combination church and school, donated by Timothy Foley of St. Paul, was erected in 1919 on a new and more central site. A house was purchased, remodeled and used as a rectory until 1950. The present church and convent were built by Father Printon in 1911. His successor, Reverend J. E. Doyle (1946–) moved into the new rectory beside the church in 1950. The School Sisters of Notre Dame are in charge of the school.

The procession which brought to a close the Ninth National Eucharistic Congress on June 26, 1941, started from St. Andrew's Church.

3 priests and 2 sisters from the parish.

1908—CHURCH OF THE HOLY CROSS

Authorization for the establishment of the parish of the Holy Cross was given by Archbishop Ireland for the benefit of the parishioners of St. Mark's who lived in the Hamline district, and an acre of land was bought on Sheldon and Capitol Avenues, opposite the Lutheran Seminary, and central for the neighborhood. The Archbishop approved the site and appointed Walter P. Confarr and John Feely, Jr., trustees who collected a thousand dollars towards the cost of the property. Before anything further was done the Archbishop decided to abandon the project and decreed that the property be disposed of and the contributions refunded. The territory is now comprised in the parish of St. Columba.

1911—CHURCH OF ST. AMBROSE

As early as August, 1908, Father Odone said Mass in the home of Signor A. DiBuci, near Phalen Creek, but, owing to the small attendance, the service was discontinued. On June 18, 1911, the Reverend R. Balducci, pastor of the Italian congregation, purchased the German Methodist Church on Bradley Street as a place of worship for the Italians in that area at a considerable distance from the old Cathedral on Sixth and St. Peter Streets, in the basement of which they worshipped. The new church was a brick structure, in gothic style, with a high tapering tower and a seating capacity of four hundred. It was thoroughly renovated, a sanctuary added, an altar and pews installed and a gallery built for the choir. When the improvements were completed the church, placed under the protection of St. Ambrose, was dedicated by Archbishop Ireland on Sunday November 19, 1911, after which Father Balducci celebrated a Solemn High Mass assisted by Reverends James Donahoe as deacon and R. Gullo as subdeacon, with Father Schaefer as master of ceremonies. After the gospel the celebrant preached in Italian and at the end of the Mass the Most Reverend Archbishop complimented the congregation on the new church and urged them to take advantage of the opportunities for spiritual development it afforded.

On August 18, 1912, the Reverend A. Comparini was appointed pastor and the Reverend James C. Byrne, pastor of the neighboring parish of St. Mary, preached in Italian, introducing him to the congregation. In the summer of 1914 he was succeeded by the Reverend H. D. Ciebattone pastor of the Holy Redeemer Church, of which it became a mission. When the new Holy Redeemer Church was opened in January 1916, St. Ambrose was closed for over a year when it was reopened after a mortgage indebtedness of $2,700 was collected and paid by the Reverend James M. Reardon, pastor of the Church of St. Mary, who retained charge of it till 1921 when his successor, Reverend John Dunphy, continued to serve the congregation until 1925, when it once more became a mission of the Holy Redeemer under the new pastor, Reverend Louis Pioletti, who, in 1930, doubled the original seating capacity of the church and bought fourteen lots in the vicinity as a site for the rectory and the parish school of the future. The parish has about four hundred and fifty families.

1912—CHURCH OF ST CECILIA

The church was built in 1912 under the direction of Reverend F. X. McDermott (1912-13) and had five pastors prior to April 24, 1944, when Reverend L. L. Klein, the present incumbent, was appointed. The school was erected in 1924 by Reverend J. E. Doyle (1916-29) and is staffed by the Sisters of St. Joseph who reside at St. Joseph's Academy. The present rectory was purchased in September, 1919. The parish was a mission of St. Mark's from 1908, when the first Mass was offered in the Odd Fellows' Hall by Reverend W. L. Hart, till 1912.

1 priest and 6 sisters from the parish.

1914—CHURCH OF ST. COLUMBA

The first Mass was said by Reverend Michael Casey, the pastor, in a small store on the corner of Hamline Avenue and Thomas Street, on September 16, 1914; and in the newly-erected frame church on October 24, 1915. The church was dedicated on November 21, by Archbishop Ireland. The school was built in 1922 and a wing added in 1931. It is in charge of the Sisters of St. Joseph who reside outside the parish. The rectory was occupied on November 26, 1918 and enlarged in 1951. The present stone church of unique design and distinguished by an Irish round tower as the distinctive feature of the façade, was dedicated by Archbishop Murray on Sunday, June 11, 1950.

Auxiliary Bishop Byrne, 17 priests and 20 sisters from the parish.

1916—CHURCH OF THE BLESSED SACRAMENT

The initial Mass in Hazel Park was said in a rented building by Reverend Joseph T. Barron, assistant at the Cathedral, on July 2, 1916. The first church was erected by Reverend W. W. Finlay (1916-46) who was appointed pastor in September, 1916. The church was dedicated on July 1, 1917, by Archbishop Ireland. The parochial school, the gift of Timothy Foley, was opened in September of the following year and taught by the Sisters of St. Joseph who reside at St. Agatha's Conservatory. It was dedicated on October 12, 1919, by Archbishop Dowling. The rectory was completed in 1919. In 1946 Reverend J. F. Cronin succeeded Father Finley and constructed the new brick and stone church of Romanesque type of architecture with clerestory and trussed ceiling which was dedicated on June 13, 1948, by Archbishop Murray.

1 priest and 4 sisters from the parish.

1918—CHURCH OF THE HOLY FAMILY

Prior to 1918 the Maronites of St. Paul worshipped in the basement of St Michael's Church. In that year a non-Catholic church was purchased, renovated and adapted to the Syrian-Maronite rite. The first Mass was said on Rosary Sunday 1918, by Reverend Paul Shade who came from Lebanon in September of that year Since then it has had six resident pastors and other priests have served for brief periods. Reverend Peter Aschkar planned a new church prior to his death in 1946 In May, 1948, the Reverend Joseph Ziade was appointed his successor and completed the plans for the new church the cornerstone of which was laid in April 1950, by Auxiliary Bishop Byrne. It was ready for dedication on January 28, 1951 when the Most Reverend Archbishop Murray officiated at the sacred rite and preached at the High Mass celebrated by the pastor. The church is of brick trimmed with Mankato stone. It has a red Spanish tile roof and a low square bel tower to the right of the façade as one enters. It has a seating capacity of 305 in nave, balcony and mothers' room. The altar is of white Italian marble flanked by pedestals supporting statues of the patron, St. Maron, and St. Theresa. The style of the church is reminiscent of the early Romanesque churches of Syria and Lebanon, the ancestral homeland of the parishioners.

1922—CHURCH OF THE NATIVITY

The parish was organized in 1922 with Reverend T. Moore as first pastor who said Mass in the St. Catherine's College auditorium from September 1922 to August, 1923, when the combination church and school was ready for occupancy. Mass was said in the school auditorium till April 16, 1939. The present stone church was completed in 1939. The school, taught by the Sisters of St. Joseph from the neighboring Motherhouse of the Congregation, was opened on September 14, 1923. The rectory was occupied on August 2, 1923. Father Moore died January 21, 1948, and was succeeded on February 6, by the Most Reverend James J. Byrne, S.T.D., Auxiliary Bishop of St. Paul, who completed a new convent in 1952.

5 priests and 15 sisters from the parish.

1926—CHURCH OF ST. THERESE

It was built by Reverend E. F. Casey of St. Thomas College in February, 1926, and served by him until 1933, when Reverend W. J. Gibbs became first resident pastor and built the rectory in 1935, and the parochial school in 1949, staffed by three Sisters of St. Joseph who reside outside the parish.

1931—CHURCH OF OUR LADY OF GUADALUPE

This parish serves Mexicans and their families and other Spanish-speaking residents of the Twin Cities. A building housing church, rectory, library and recreation center was purchased in 1931 by the first pastor, Reverend J. H. Guillemette (1931-7). He was succeeded by Reverend H. Dicks who died in 1942. The parish was incorporated on April 25, 1939. The present resident pastor is Reverend J. A. Ward (1942-). Mass was said in a rented store from February 22, 1931, to May 10, 1932, when the present combination church and rectory was ready for occupancy.

1936—CHURCH OF THE HOLY SPIRIT

The first Mass in the newly-established parish was said in Cretin High School auditorium on Sunday, October 11, 1936, by the pastor, Reverend G. W. Keefe, who erected a combination church and school in 1937 at a cost of $126,000. Four rooms were added to the school in 1939. The school was opened in September, 1937, with an enrollment of 322 pupils in charge of the Sisters of St. Joseph who reside at the Provincial House on Randolph Avenue. A temporary rectory was occupied for a year prior to August, 1937, when a residence was bought and remodeled at a cost of $6,600. The basement of a new church with an attached rectory was built on a new site and dedicated in 1950.

3 priests from the parish.

1939—CHURCH OF CORPUS CHRISTI

The first pastor, Reverend J. L. Westfall (1939-40) was succeeded by Reverend J. L. Guinney who built the church in 1940, and purchased the rectory. There is no parish school. Prior to 1939, Mass was said in a building at Como and Carter Avenues.

2 sisters from the parish.

1939—CHURCH OF ST. ROSE OF LIMA

Sunday services were held in the town hall of Rosetown for thirteen months before the church was ready for occupancy. The Reverend J. A. Abbott (1939-) erected the combination church and school, the latter staffed by the Servants of Mary of Ladysmith, Wisconsin, since it opened on September 15, 1940. The convent, costing $4,900 and the rectory, $7,500, were purchased by Father Abbott.

1939—CHURCH OF THE TRANSFIGURATION

Erected in 1939 by Reverend J. C. Normoyle, the pastor, who said the first Mass in Landy's cafe on August 15, 1939. First baptism, September 8, 1939. The rectory was purchased in the fall of 1939. Father Normoyle died in 1951 and was succeeded by Reverend B. Keany who is building a school.

1942—CHURCH OF ST JOSEPH (West St. Paul)

The parish was incorporated on October 12, 1942. A building was bought and remodeled for church purposes in 1942 by the pastor, Reverend J. H. Foran, who also remodeled another house to serve as a rectory. The first Mass was said on September 27, in the Sibley Junior High School, and on March 7, 1943, the church was blessed by Archbishop Murray. The school was opened in the autumn of 1949, with the Sisters of St. Joseph of Crookston, Minnesota, in charge. A new convent was provided for them in 1949, and a church and auditorium added to the school in 1951.

1 sister from the parish.

1945—CHURCH OF ST. LEO

The first Mass was said in the Highland Theatre on June 24, 1945. A combination church and school was begun by the pastor, Reverend B. H. Murray, in December, 1945, and the first Mass was said on Christmas Eve, 1946, in the basement, and in the upper church on February 2, 1947. The dedication took place on July 13, 1947. The rectory was completed in March, 1946, and the school opened in September, 1947, with the Sisters of St. Joseph in charge, who reside at the Provincial House on Randolph Avenue.

1946—CHURCH OF ST. PASCHAL BAYLON

The church and the rectory were built in 1946, by the pastor, Reverend J. V. Ryan. A new combination school and church auditorium was built in 1950, and the Sisters of St. Joseph occupied the temporary church converted into a convent.

1946—CHURCH OF THE HOLY CHILDHOOD

The parish was founded March 6, 1946. A combination church and school erected by the pastor, Reverend J. Buchanan, in 1947, was dedicated by Auxiliary Bishop Byrne on January 18, 1948. Prior to August 15, 1947, Mass was said for several months in a building in the State Fair Grounds. The rectory was occupied on June 1, 1947; the Sisters of Notre Dame in charge of the school moved into the convent on September 15 of that year.

1946—CHURCH OF THE PRESENTATION OF THE BLESSED VIRGIN MARY

Mass was offered for the first time in the Gladstone school on Sunday, January 27, 1946. A structure to serve as church and school was erected in 1947 by the pastor, Reverend R. A. Rutkowski. A residence was purchased on May 1, 1946, and daily Mass was said in the basement of it till Christmas Eve, 1947. The school was opened in 1949, by the Franciscan Sisters of Sylvania, Ohio, and the capacity of the school was reached in 1951.

1949—CHURCH OF THE IMMACULATE HEART OF MARY

First Mass was said on Saturday, May 14, 1949, at 1543 Summit Avenue by Reverend Raymond J. Reed, the first Sunday Mass in Midway Veterans' Hall and later at Grandview Theater. The combination church and school on Summit Avenue was dedicated in 1950. The pastor resides at 1525 Summit Avenue and the Sisters at 1543 Summit Avenue. Father Reed was recalled into service as a navy chaplain in 1951 and Reverend Paul Murray appointed administrator.

1949—CHURCH OF THE MATERNITY OF THE BLESSED VIRGIN MARY

The first Mass was said in a private home in the parish on February 27, 1949, by the pastor, Reverend Joseph C. O'Donnell, who built the combination church and school as well as a new rectory at the corner of Dale and Arlington Streets. The Sisters of St. Benedict staff the school which has an enrollment of 200.

1951—CHURCH OF ST. GREGORY THE GREAT

This new parish was placed in charge of Reverend Thomas R. Jude, who began the construction of a combined church and school in 1952.

CITY OF MINNEAPOLIS

1851—CHURCH OF ST. ANTHONY

It was begun in 1849 by Reverend Augustine Ravoux, a stone basement and frame superstructure, of which Reverend D. Ledon became first resident pastor (1851-5). He was succeeded by Reverend J. Fayolle (1855-60) who began the construction of the present stone church, 140 by 60 by 30, completed by Reverend J. McDermott (1860-6) and dedicated on July 21, 1861, by Bishop Grace. He was succeeded by Reverend F. Tissot (1866-87) who built the first parish school before he gave place to Reverend J. O'Reilly (1887-1910) who replaced the original front of the church with a red-brick, two-towered façade in 1887 which was dismantled by the present pastor, Reverend F. J. Lang (1945—) who also renovated the entire structure as well as the rectory and erected the stone shrine of Our Lady of Perpetual Help in 1947.

The first parish school was opened in 1853 by the Sisters of St. Joseph in a rented store. The next year it gave place to St. Mary's Convent and school on the site of the present St. Anthony Convent. The present school for grade and high school pupils was opened in 1915 during the pastorate of Reverend P. Kenny (1910-5) and replaced the earlier school erected by Father Tissot. The pastoral residence was built by Reverend E. J. Wilbee (1915-39) on the site of the original chapel. He was succeeded by Reverend M. O'Brien who paid off the indebtedness before his death on November 17, 1945.

14 priests, 3 brothers and 48 sisters from the parish.

1858—CHURCH OF ST. BONIFACE

The first church was erected in 1858 and Mass said in it by Reverend Demetrius de Marogna, O.S.B., pastor of the Church of the Assumption, St. Paul. The first rectory was built in 1861 by Reverend E. Gahr, O.S.B. (1859-63). From 1865 to 1873 the parish was in charge of diocesan priests of whom there were four, after which it was returned to the Fathers of St. Benedict. Since then there have been nine pastors. The present brick church was erected by Reverend M. Hermanutz, O.S.B., in 1928; the basement had been used as a church from 1899. The first school was opened in 1875 and enlarged in subequent years. The present school was built in 1905, and is conducted by the Sisters of Christian Charity. The rectory and the convent were built in 1912. Reverend Oswald Johannes, O.S.B., was appointed pastor in 1951.

8 priests, 2 brothers and 30 sisters are from the parish.

1868—BASILICA OF ST. MARY

It had its origin in the "shed" Church of the Immaculate Conception built in 1868 by Reverend J. McGolrick (1868-89) as an addition to the school opened in 1866 by Reverend F. Tissot, pastor of the Church of St. Anthony, and staffed by the Sisters of St. Joseph from the convent in St. Anthony parish. The second church of stone was built by Father McGolrick and dedicated on January 1, 1873. The brick school, begun in 1879, did duty till 1913 when the third, or Pro-Cathedral of St. Mary school, was opened at Sixteenth Street and Laurel Avenue. The third church (of granite) known as the Pro-Cathedral of St. Mary till February 1, 1926, when it was elevated to the dignity of a Minor Basilica, the first in the United States, was opened for divine worship on May 31, 1914, during the pastorate of Reverend T. E. Cullen (1902-21). The interior was completed and the sacristy and residence built between 1922 and 1927 by Reverend J. M. Reardon (1921—). The Basilica was solemnly consecrated on Friday, June 27, 1941, by His Eminence

Cardinal Dougherty, Archbishop Cicognani (Apostolic Delegate), Archbishop Murray, Archbishop-Bishop Morrison of Antigonish, N. S., Bishops Lawler of Rapid City, S.D., Kelley of Oklahoma City-Tulsa, Kelly of Winona and Muench of Fargo, N. D.

29 priests, several brothers and 45 sisters from the parish.

1870—CHURCH OF ST. JOSEPH

The original church was built in 1870 by Reverend J. Hillmer, pastor of St. Boniface parish, and blessed by Bishop Grace on July 24. It was a mission of St. Boniface until 1875. The present stone church was dedicated on September 15, 1889, by Archbishop Ireland. Since 1875 the parish has been in charge of the Fathers of St. Benedict from St. John's Abbey, Collegeville, Minnesota. Reverend A. Straub, O.S.B. (1883-1904) was pastor when the church was built. The first school was opened in 1875; the second in 1882; the third in 1897. The Sisters of Christian Charity were in charge from 1875 to 1876 when they were replaced by the Sisters of St. Benedict from St. Joseph, Minnesota. The present convent is a remodeled sanitarium. The first rectory was built in 1875, enlarged and remodeled in 1914, and brick-veneered in 1927. The present pastor is Reverend Permin Wendt, O.S.B.

The Most Reverend Bernard Kevenhoerster, O.S.B., Vicar Apostolic of the Bahama Islands, who died in 1950, 11 priests, 2 brothers and 38 sisters are from the parish.

1877—CHURCH OF OUR LADY OF LOURDES

The First Universalist Church was purchased on July 27, 1877, and placed under the patronage of Our Lady of Lourdes by Bishop Grace in fulfilment of a promise made at Lourdes in France in 1875. Reverend Pascal U. Brunel (1877-9) said the first Mass on July 29. Transepts, apse and vestry were added in 1881 by Reverend Z. L. Chandonnet (1879-84) and the enlarged structure, 130 by 65 feet, was dedicated by Bishop Ireland on November 13. In the following year a wooden gothic steeple-belfry was added and replaced in 1914 by a brick entrance. The combined school and convent, at considerable distance from the church, was erected in 1888 with the Grey Nuns of the Cross of Ottawa, Canada, in charge till 1906, when they gave place to the Sisters of St. Joseph. The rectory was completed in January, 1904, at a cost of $8,000. The Right Reverend J. Guillot (1910-17) was the last diocesan priest. The Marist Fathers succeeded him, eight in all, including the present past, Reverend P. Rietsch, S.M.

12 priests—6 diocesan, 4 Marists, 1 Benedictine and 1 Paulist—and 23 sisters are from the parish.

1878—CHURCH OF THE HOLY ROSARY

The original frame church at Fifth Street and Nineteenth Avenue, South, was bought from the Lutherans by the Reverend Thomas Power, O.P. (1878-81). The stone church on the present site was built in 1888, by Very Reverend P. A. Dinahan, O.P. (1886-9) and rebuilt after the fire of December 15, 1904, by Very Reverend J. Fowler, O.P. (1905-8). It was decorated in 1928 by Very Reverend J. P. Aldridge, O.P., and renovated by Reverend E. M. Cuddy, O.P., in 1949. 21 pastors have served it to the present time. There is a convent and a parochial school staffed by the Sisters of St. Dominic of Sinsinawa, Wisconsin.

24 vocations to the Dominican Order.

1882—CHURCH OF ST. ELIZABETH

The parish was established in November, 1882. A public school was bought and used as church and school until 1883, when the present church was built by Reverend P. Jeram (1882-5). Franciscan Sisters taught in the old school till 1887. The present school was erected in 1891 by Reverend B. Sandmeier (1885-98). The Sisters of Christian Charity are now in charge, and Reverend A. Mahowald (1943-), the pastor, renovated the parish buildings. Prior to the organization of the parish Father Meinulph Stukenkemper, O.S.B., pastor of St. Joseph's Church, said Mass on a week day from December 2, 1876 till 1882, in a school bought by the St. Vincent Society, and the Benedictine Sisters taught school from 1877 to 1881. 3 priests from the parish.

1884—CHURCH OF ST. CLOTILDE

The parish was organized on April 24, 1884, as an accommodation for the French people living west of the Mississippi river who found it inconvenient to assist at Mass in the Church of Notre Dame de Lourdes. It was placed in charge of Reverend Lucien Nougaret who bought a Protestant church in which to say Mass until he built the brick church on the corner of Lyndale Avenue, North, and Eleventh Street, in 1886, which was dedicated by Bishop Ireland on December 29, 1887. A brick rectory was built beside the church. In 1898, during the pastorate of Reverend Joseph Legardeur (1898-1901) the parish met with financial reverses and was re-organized under the name of St. Anne. It had nine pastors prior to 1902, when Reverend Damase Richard was appointed who established a new parochial center at Queen Avenue, North, and 26th Street in 1922, where he erected a parish hall used as a church until the present stone church was built. He also built a temporary rectory and moved into it in 1923. The old church was sold to a colored congregation.

1885—CHURCH OF ST. STEPHEN

The parish was incorporated June 10, 1885. A small frame church was used for several years before the present brown standstone church was erected in 1889-90, at a cost of $60,000, by Reverend P. Kenny (1885-94), and dedicated by Archbishop Ireland on May 10, 1891. The chapel was moved to Northeast Minneapolis. Father Kenny bought the rectory which served the needs of the clergy till 1932, when the present rectory about a block away was purchased for $26,000 by Reverend T. E. Cullen (1927-40). The school was opened in 1915 during the pastorate of Reverend J. H. Gaughan (1912-27) who also enlarged it in 1926. It is staffed by the Sisters of St. Joseph whose convent across the street was ready for occupancy in 1923. The present pastor is Reverend R. E. Nolan (1946—).

The second pastor of the parish was Reverend A. Christie (1894-8) who was consecrated Bishop of Victoria, Vancouver Island, Canada, in the Cathedral of St. Paul by Archbishop Ireland on June 29, 1898, and promoted to the Archbishopric of Oregon City (Portland) Oregon, on February 12, 1899.

1 priest from the parish.

1886—CHURCH OF THE HOLY CROSS

The first Mass was said in the frame chapel (built in 1851) bought from the Church of St. Anthony. A brick church was erected in 1892 by the Reverend J. Pacholski (1886-94). The present church was built in 1929 during the pastorate of Reverend J. F. Cieminski (1915-32). He was succeeded by the Right Reverend V. W. Worzalla (1932-51) who, in 1950, dedicated the new school, grade and high, to replace the brick structure built in 1894. A few years previously he had replaced the old convent with a new and modern building for the Sisters of St. Francis who staff the parish school. He was succeeded by Reverend J. F. Siegienski (1951—).

10 priests and 100 sisters from the parish.

1887—CHURCH OF ST. LAWRENCE

The original church was opened in November, 1887, by Reverend J. O'Reilly, pastor of the Church of St. Anthony (1887-1910). It was staffed by six diocesan priests, successively, until 1915 when it was given to the Paulist Fathers of New York who were to have charge of the Catholic students attending the University of Minnesota. The present combination church and school was erected between October, 1921, and February, 1922, during the pastorate of Reverend J. C. Allard C.S.P. (1920-6). The school was opened in September, 1922, under the direction of the Sisters of St. Joseph housed in the old St. Lawrence rectory until the new convent was ready for occupancy in September, 1926. The new rectory was completed in 1937 by Father Bradley, C.S.P. A new parish hall was built by Reverend J. Mitchell, C.S.P. (1946-52), who was succeeded by Reverend J. F. McLean, C.S.P.

1890—CHURCH OF THE ASCENSION

In 1890 the first frame church was built by the Reverend A. Christie (later, Archbishop of Oregon City) who was pastor for four years. His successor, Reverend J. Harrington (1894-1924) erected the first school in 1897; the present brick church in 1903; the gymnasium and club in 1921; the rectory in 1924, replacing a previous residence on the same site. His successor, Reverend J. Dunphy, built the present modern and commodious school in 1927, the new convent in 1949 to take the place of the residences bought and remodeled as a home for the Sisters of St. Joseph in 1916, and re-decorated the church in 1950. He was made a Domestic Prelate in 1947.

14 priests and several sisters are from the parish.

1891—CHURCH OF OUR LADY OF PERPETUAL HELP

The first frame church had for pastors Reverend F. Simonik (1891-2) and Reverend F. Hrachovsky (1892-1904) before Reverend J. F. Hovorka (1904—) was appointed who built the present church in 1922 and the rectory in 1924, replacing an older one. There is no parochial school but Dominican Sisters from Holy Rosary parish teach catechism.

3 sisters from the parish.

1892—CHURCH OF ST. CYRIL

The parish was incorporated February 23, 1891. The first pastor, Reverend J. L. Zavadan (1892-5) built the original church, dedicated by Archbishop Ireland on October 10, 1893, for the Slovak Catholics, and purchased an adjacent house for a residence. The present church, dedicated in September, 1917, was erected by Reverend F. Hrachovsky (1904-1919), who built the rectory in 1904. The parochial school, in charge of the School Sisters of Notre Dame, was opened in 1937, by the Reverend G. S. Dargay (1926—) and the new convent in the same year. Prior to 1904 Father Hrachovsky administered the parish for nine years while pastor of the Church of Our Lady of Perpetual Help.

3 priests and 9 sisters from the parish.

1892—CHURCH OF ST. CHARLES

A new parish at Thirteenth Avenue and Fourth Street, South, was organized in the fall of 1892 by Reverend James M. Cleary who came to the Archdiocese from Kenosha, Wisconsin. While the frame church and attached rectory were being built Mass was said in a neighborhood hall on Sundays until June 3, 1894, when they were dedicated by the Most Reverend Archbishop Ireland who preached at the Solemn Mass celebrated by his secretary, Reverend H. Moynihan. The ceremony was witnessed by 1500 people. In the evening the Archbishop preached at Vespers sung by Father Sandmeier. The first baptism was administered on December 11, 1892. The new church attracted large congregations due to the reputation of Father Cleary as a preacher and lecturer. He remained in charge until the summer of 1909 when he was commissioned to establish the new parish of the Incarnation at Thirty-eighth Street and Pleasant Avenue, South, and was succeeded by Reverend F. J. Lang who took possession on September 8. The building was struck by lightning in the early morning of June 4, 1914, and reduced to ashes together with its contents, except the Blessed Sacrament and the sacred vessels. The debt of $17,000 was paid by the insurance. The church was not re-built but the congregation assisted at Mass in St. Elizabeth's parish hall until September 8 of that year when Father Lang was appointed pastor of the Church of the Guardian Angels, Hastings. The last baptism was on August 24. The baptismal records were transferred to the Church of St. Elizabeth and all other records and documents sent to the Chancery Office for safekeeping.

1902—CHURCH OF ST. CLEMENT

It was originally a mission, known as New Boston, attended from St. Anthony's and Mass was said for several years in a frame church at Lowry Avenue and Quincy

Street, Northeast. It became an independent parish with the arrival of the Reverend R. J. Fitzgerald on April 2, 1902, who erected the present brick, stone-trimmed church, 113 by 68, at a cost of $45,000, at Jackson Street and 24th. Avenue, N. E., in 1913. It was dedicated on Sunday, May 24, 1914, by Archbishop Ireland, before the Solemn Mass celebrated by Reverend C. F. McGinnis of the College of St. Thomas. Father Fitzgerald administered its affairs until his death on August 8, 1941, when he was succeeded by the Reverend F. T. J. Burns, who renovated the church and pastoral residence. The main altar was donated by Mrs. J. E. Hennessy in memory of her deceased husband. Other furnishings were also donated. The old frame church became the first church of the newly-organized parish of St. Hedwig in 1914.

1906—CHURCH OF ST. MARON

The first church for the Maronites of the city, a residence at 321 Main Street, N. E., was purchased in 1906 by Reverend A. Eito (1906-7); the second, that of Our Lady of Mount Carmel, at 625 Main Street, N. E., in 1919, by Reverend E. El-Kouri (1916-21); the third built at 219 Sixth Avenue N. E., in 1948 by Right Reverend P. F. Assemani (1936—) to replace a temporary church in a public school building on the same site at a cost of $200,000 for church and rectory. Fourteen pastors have served the parish which is for Catholics of the Maronite Rite who number about 450. It is a shrine of Maronite saints. Three boys are preparing for the religious life—one in the Trappist Order, another in St. Paul Seminary and the third with the Christian Brothers. 106 members of the parish, or 18%, served in World War II.

1907—CHURCH OF OUR LADY OF MOUNT CARMEL

A chapel for the Italians of Minneapolis was opened in the Church of the Immaculate Conception during 1907 and placed in charge of Reverend R. Balducci (1907-9) who resided at St. Paul Seminary. Prior to that the spiritual needs of the Italians had been ministered to by Fathers Cestelli of St. Thomas College, Odone of the Holy Redeemer Church, St. Paul, and Serpaggi, assistant pastor of the Church of Notre Dame de Lourdes, Minneapolis. During the pastorate of Reverend A. R. Bandini (1910-4) a German Lutheran church at Main Street and Seventh Avenue, Northeast, was bought for $5,500 and blessed on Sunday, December 11, 1910, by Very Reverend F. J. Schaefer, Rector of St. Paul Seminary, who also celebrated the Solemn Mass at which the pastor preached. The congregation of over one hundred families worshipped there until 1919. The church was formally dedicated by Archbishop Ireland on January 28, 1912. The Reverend A. Comparini was pastor until 1916, when the Reverend J. A. Kern was placed in charge and resided at 625 Main Street, N. E., until 1919 when the church was sold to the Maronites who established a parish under the patronage of St. Maron with Reverend E. El-Kouri as pastor. The Italians were without a church of their own until 1938.

1908—CHURCH OF ST. FRANCIS OF ASSISI

The church, under the direction of the Franciscan Fathers, was located at 2827 Lyndale Avenue, North, with Reverend Odo Richardt, O.F.M., as pastor and Reverend Odilo Eichenseer, O.F.M., assistant. Crystal Lake in Hennepin County was a mission attached to it. There is no record of the building of a church or the holding of services in either parish. In 1909 the parish of the Sacred Heart, St. Paul, was given to the Franciscans (probably in exchange for the Minneapolis parish) and Father Richardt was placed in charge with Fathers Hubert Pfeil, O.F.M., and Ivo Beu, O.F.M., as assistants, and the parish of St. Francis of Assisi went out of existence.

1908—CHURCH OF ST. THOMAS THE APOSTLE

The original frame church was built in 1909 under the direction of the first pastor, Reverend M. O'Brien (1908-18) and the adjoining rectory in 1910. The present church and school on 44th Street, between Upton and Washburn Avenues, were erected in 1925 by his successor, Reverend J. P. Cleary (1918–). The Sisters of St. Joseph, residing at St. Margaret's Academy, are the teachers.

3 priests and 9 sisters are from the parish.

1908–CHURCH OF ST. PHILIP

A frame structure for church and school was built in 1908 by the first pastor, Reverend S. Zdechlik (1908-12). The parish hall was added in 1928 by the present pastor, Reverend F. J. Rakowski (1919–). The rectory was purchased in 1914 and the convent in 1921. The Franciscan Sisters taught the school from 1912 to 1920, when the School Sisters of Notre Dame took charge.

7 priests and 10 sisters from the parish.

1909––CHURCH OF THE INCARNATION

The Incarnation Institute (church and school) was completed in 1911 by the Reverend J. M. Cleary, founder and first pastor of the parish, who said Mass in a public hall prior to May 28, 1911, when the first Mass was said in the Institute. The present commodious brick church was opened under his direction on October 3, 1920. He built the modern rectory in 1912, and the convent for the Sisters of St. Dominic in charge of the school in 1923. His successor, Right Reverend H. Moynihan (1933-43) erected an additional school, with auditorium and gymnasium, in 1935, opened a kindergarten in a separate building in 1937, and founded the parish library which has over 5000 volumes. The present pastor is Right Reverend J. H. Moynihan (1943–) who was made a Domestic Prelate in 1951.

8 priests and many sisters from the parish.

1913–CHURCH OF ST. HELENA

The first church, a frame building, was erected in 1914 by the first and only pastor, Reverend O. Rowan (1913–). Prior to that Mass was said in a neighborhood hall from July to mid-October, 1913. The present fine stone edifice was dedicated in 1940. There is a parish school taught by the Sisters of St. Joseph who resided in the building till 1951 when the new convent, opposite the church, was completed. A four-room addition was put to the school in 1951. The rectory was built in 1925.

5 priests and 9 sisters from the parish.

1914–CHURCH OF ST. HEDWIG

First Mass in the parish, formed from the parish of the Holy Cross, was said by Reverend M. M. Klesmit, assistant at Holy Cross, on December 25, 1914, in the Holy Cross auditorium. The first church was the old frame church of St. Clement and Reverend A. Szczukowski was pastor from January 16 to May 27, 1915, when the present pastor, Father Klesmit, took charge. He erected the church and school in 1919, and said the first Mass on Christmas day. The rectory was built in 1918 and the convent in 1925 for the Sisters of St. Francis of Sylvania, Ohio, who have charge of the school since 1920. The parish was incorporated on March 6, 1914.

1 priest, 3 brothers and 14 sisters from the parish.

1915–CHURCH OF ST. BRIDGET

A frame church was erected in 1915 by the first and only pastor, Reverend J Donahoe (1915–) and dedicated by Archbishop Ireland on November 21. The rectory was built in 1919. The combination church and school was opened in 1922 and the auditorium has been used as a church since 1924 when the original church became too small for the growing congregation. The present convent for the Benedictine Sisters who teach in the school was erected in 1930.

3 priests and 12 sisters from the parish.

1916–CHURCH OF ALL SAINTS

The parish was established by Archbishop Ireland on August 15, 1916, with Reverend F. J. Matz as resident pastor (1916–), who said the first Mass on September 24, and recorded the first baptism on October 18. A combined church and school was erected and Mass said in it on September 29, 1918. The present church was dedicated on February 19, 1939, by Archbishop Murray. The rectory was purchased March 30, 1919, and the convent on April 8, 1918. The school, opened on September 3, 1918, is staffed by the Sisters of St. Francis of the Congregation of Our Lady of Lourdes, Sylvania, Ohio. A new convent was erected in 1951.

4 priests and 60 sisters from the parish.

1916—CHURCH OF THE HOLY NAME

The first Mass was said in it on December 5, 1916, by the pastor, Reverend P. R. Cunningham (1915-35) who, from the establishment of the parish, said Mass for the congregation in the chapel of the Catholic Boys' Home. It was dedicated on February 7, 1917 by the Most Reverend Archbishop Ireland. It cost about $15,000. In 1918 the rectory was built at a cost of $15,000 and in September, 1923, the school, an eight-room structure costing $98,000 and taught by the Sisters of St. Joseph, who reside at Holy Angels Academy, was opened. Father Cunningham was succeeded by Reverend T. Crowley (1936—) who has made plans for a new church yet to be erected.

3 priests, 2 brothers and 8 sisters are from the parish.

1922—CHURCH OF ST. ANNE

The original church, dedicated to St. Clotilde, was renamed St. Anne in 1898. A new parish was opened in North Minneapolis and placed in charge of Reverend D. Richard who had been appointed pastor of St. Clotilde's in 1902. With the approval of Archbishop Dowling, he built a brick parish hall to be used as a temporary church on Queen Avenue, North, at 26th., in which the first Mass was said on October 1, 1922, the school in 1926, the first convent in 1927 and the second in 1937 for the Benedictine Sisters in charge of the school. The present stone church on an adjoining site was completed in 1949 at a cost of $600,000 by Reverend A. J. Eichinger, Administrator since 1952. The first rectory was built in 1922 and the second in 1927. Father Richard lives in semi-retirement near the church as Pastor Emeritus.

9 priests and 18 sisters from the parish.

1922—CHURCH OF THE ANNUNCIATION

A combination church, school and convent was erected by the first pastor, Reverend F. J. Lang (1922-45). The first Mass was said on October 1, 1922, in Community House, 4301 Pillsbury Avenue, South, then in a store at 54th and Garfield, and in the new church October 18, 1925. The rectory was occupied December, 1923. First baptism October 1, 1922. School opened September, 1923, by the Sisters of St. Dominic who moved into a new convent in 1949. The present pastor is Reverend J. A. Byrnes (1945—) who decorated the church and remodeled the sanctuary in 1946 and built the new convent.

The territory comprised within the parish was formerly served from the Immaculate Conception parish until 1875, when the Benedictines opened a parish in Richfield. A monthly publication "The Annunciation Chronicle" carries the record of parish activities. It was probably the first church in the city to introduce the novena in honor of Our Mother of Perpetual Succor on October 15, 1933.

6 priests, 5 brothers and 10 sisters from the parish.

1924—CHURCH OF THE IMMACULATE CONCEPTION, COLUMBIA HEIGHTS

In 1924 a combination church and auditorium was built by Reverend G. Rolwes (1923-36). His successor, Reverend J. F. Lapinski (1936—) procured a new altar, pews and other furnishings in 1949; erected the school in 1938; the parish residence in 1949; and the convent in 1949 for the Sisters of St. Francis who conduct the school.

2 priests and 14 sisters from the parish.

1933—CHURCH OF THE RESURRECTION

It was built between August, 1933, and January, 1934, by the Reverend T. Sheehy who was in charge until his death in 1943. It was dedicated on January 7, 1934. He erected the school which opened in September, 1941. It is staffed by the

Sisters of St. Dominic who resided at the Holy Rosary Convent until 1944 when they moved into the rectory placed at their disposal as a convent in August of that year by the present pastor, Reverend W. A. Daly (1943–), who purchased the rectory he now occupies at 5420 Eleventh Avenue, South. The population of the parish in 1933 was 543 souls; in 1948 it was 1642.

1935—CHURCH OF ST. ALBERT THE GREAT

A church-school building was opened on September 9, 1935, with the Reverend J. R. Dooley, O.P., as first pastor (1935-42). The present commodious stone church with attached rectory, matching it in design and material, was dedicated by Archbishop Murray in 1949 during the pastorate of Reverend J. M. Nugent, O.P. (1948–). It was planned by Reverend R. M. Burke, O.P. (1942-48). Sisters of St. Dominic from Sinsinawa, Wisconsin, took charge of the school in August, 1935, and occupy the adjacent convent.

1937—CHURCH OF ST. AUSTIN

It was built in 1937-8 by Reverend J. A. J. Troy, its first and only pastor, and dedicated on June 25, 1939, by Archbishop Murray. The first Mass was celebrated on Christmas day, 1938. A combination convent and parish school in a different location was opened in September, 1950, and staffed by the Sisters of the Holy Humility of Mary. Father Troy was made a Domestic Prelate in 1951.

1938—CHURCH OF ST. CHARLES BORROMEO

The parish was founded on November 24, 1938, and the first Mass said in the home of Roy F. Miller on December 8. A brick building housing church, school and convent was erected in 1939 under the direction of the pastor, Reverend C. F. Doran (1938–). The first Mass was said on October 26 of that year and the school opened on September 15 by the Sisters of St. Joseph who now occupy the convent built on an adjoining lot in 1947. A pastoral residence at some distance from the church was purchased, enlarged, and made ready for occupancy in June 1939. An addition to the school was begun in June, 1952.

1 priest from the parish.

1938—CHURCH OF OUR LADY OF MOUNT CARMEL

A Protestant church was purchased and blessed on April 3, 1938, for the benefit of the Italian Catholics of Northeast Minneapolis, the successor of an earlier Italian church in another locality which was closed in 1919. Reverend L. Malley is pastor.

1939—CHURCH OF CHRIST THE KING

A combined church-school was erected in 1939 by the first and only pastor, Reverend W. P. Driscoll (1939–) who opened the school in September 1940, with the Sisters of St. Joseph in charge, and the rectory in the same year. The Sisters lived at Holy Angels Academy until 1952 when the pastor's residence was made ready for them. An addition of eight rooms to the school and a new rectory were completed in the same year.

4 sisters from the parish.

1940—CHURCH OF ST. LEONARD OF PORT MAURICE

Property for a church for the colored Catholics of South Minneapolis was bought by Reverend L. Hirman, the pastor, at 3615 Fourth Avenue, South, in February, 1940, for $4,500.00. On it was a duplex, the first floor of which was converted into a church and the second occupied as a rectory for about a year when it was sold. A new site on Clinton Avenue at Fortieth Street was acquired where a church was built and dedicated on June 15, 1941. Two houses were included in the purchase, one for a rectory, the other for a future convent for the Oblate Sisters of Providence who are expected to establish a catechetical center which will ultimately evolve into a parochial school.

1940—CHURCH OF ST. OLAF

The Protestant Church of the Redeemeer was bought in December, 1949, for a downtown Catholic Church. Before it was ready for occupancy the pastor, Reverend J. R. Coleman, said Mass in Seton Guild. He was succeeded by Reverend W. F. Murphy in January, 1941, and the church was dedicated on June 1. Reverened L. P. Cowley is pastor.

1940—CHURCH OF ST. MARTIN

A parish for the colored Catholics of North Minneapolis was established in 1940 when a site on Bryant Avenue, North, at Fifth Street, was bought by Father Hirman and a church and a rectory built. It was incorporated on July 27, of that year, and was a mission to St. Leonard's until 1942 when the Reverend F. J. Burns was appointed pastor. A benefactor paid the indebtedness on the church and rectory.

1941—CHURCH OF ST. KEVIN

It was built under the direction of the pastor, Reverend J. R. Coleman (1941—), who purchased a residence for a rectory. In 1951 an eight-room school was erected as well as a modern parochial residence with accommodations for three priests. A ten-acre plot provides playground facilities for the children and room for future expansion. The Sisters of St. Joseph are in charge of the school.

1945—CHURCH OF ST. MARGARET MARY

Mass was said in Glenwood Hills Hospital until the church was ready for occupancy in December, 1947. It was built by the pastor, Reverend J. A. Phelan (1945—), who took possession of the new rectory on July 1 of the next year. The church was solemnly blessed on January 11, 1948, by Auxiliary Bishop Byrne. A convent for the Sisters of St. Francis of Rochester who will have charge of the school was purchased on June 1, 1952; and the cornerstone of the school was laid by Bishop Byrne on the following July 6.

1945—CHURCH OF OUR LADY OF VICTORY

This new parish, organized November 8, 1945, embraces the territory of North Minneapolis bordering on the Mississippi river and extending North along the river to the Town of Brooklyn Center. It was incorporated by Reverend Joseph Musch, the pastor, on November 29, 1945. The first Mass was celebrated in the Camden Theatre December 23, 1945. The entire block bounded by Emerson and Fremont Avenues and 51st and 52nd Streets was purchased in February, 1946, and a temporary church constructed of military barracks erected for $5,000 at Colfax Avenue, North, and 53rd Street in Brooklyn Center. It was used for three years till the combination school and church auditorium became available for Mass at Christmas, 1948, and the school opened under the care of the Sisters of St. Benedict of Duluth with an enrollment of 240 children in September, 1948, increased to 400 in 1950. The new convent was opened to receive the Sisters in February, 1951, and the construction of the rectory began in October of that year.

1946—CHURCH OF ST. JOAN OF ARC

The Reverend M. A. Farrell, first and only pastor, built the church-school in 1947 and opened the school September 6, 1948, under the direction of the Sisters of St. Joseph of Crookston, Minnesota. The rectory, at some distance from the church, was purchased in September, 1946, and the convent in July, 1948. From September 22, 1946, to December 25, 1947, Mass was said in Eugene Field public school gymnasium. An addition of three school rooms was built in 1951 and a new rectory in 1952.

1 priest from the parish.

1946—CHURCH OF ST. FRANCES CABRINI

The first Mass in the parish was said in the Sidney Pratt public school on September 29, 1946, and in the new church on May 23, 1948, by the pastor, Reverend

B. Keany (1946-51). It was dedicated on June 27, 1948. The rectory was built with the church and is attached to the rear of it. There is no school but religious instructions are given every Saturday. The Reverend Henry Sledz became pastor in 1951.

1946—CHURCH OF THE GOOD SHEPHERD

The first Mass was said in a neighborhood cafe by the pastor, Reverend T. J. McNamara, on April 21, 1946. A temporary pre-fabricated church served also as a residence for the pastor till 1949, when a rectory was purchased at 1505 Fairlawn Way. Sunday school is taught by the Sisters of St. Joseph from St. Margaret's Academy. A new and more central site comprising eighteen acres has been acquired for future parish purposes.

1946—CHURCH OF THE VISITATION

The parish was incorporated August 28, 1946, and Mass said in the rectory, 4532 Dupont Avenue, South, September 17, 1946, and in Clara Barton school from September 22, 1946, by the pastor, Reverend R. E. Cogwin, until the combined church and school at Lyndale and 45th Street, South, was ready for Mass in the basement on Christmas day, 1947, and in the upper church on May 1, 1948. The school opened September, 1948, with the Sisters of St. Benedict from the St. Paul Priory in charge. The convent was ready for occupancy on July 20, 1948.

OUTSIDE THE TWIN CITIES

1840—CHURCH OF ST. PETER, MENDOTA

Mass was first said in a house given by J. B. Faribault to Reverend L. Galtier (1840-44), the first resident priest in Minnesota, and used as a church and residence till it collapsed in the summer of 1842. It was replaced by a combination frame church and residence blessed on October 2 of that year. He was succeeded by Reverend A. Ravoux who resided there until 1857. Prior to the installation of Bishop Cretin in 1851 Father Ravoux had charge of the log chapel of St. Paul, which he enlarged in 1847 and said Mass there every second Sunday until the Bishop came, when he returned to Mendota as pastor until 1857 when he was appointed Administrator of the diocese after the death of the bishop. The present stone Church of St. Peter was built by him in 1853, and the log chapel became a school taught by Mr. Deautinet. The Sisters of St. Joseph opened the Immaculate Conception Convent in 1867 in the Sibley house, bought by Bishop Grace in 1868, and taught the girls there and the boys in a brick school purchased by the parish, until 1879. A community hall was built in 1938 and the church decorated in 1940 by the present pastor, Reverend W. J. Harrington.

1 bishop (Most Reverend T. Corbett, first Bishop of Crookston (1910-38), several priests and sisters from the parish.

1843—CHURCH OF ST. FRANCIS XAVIER, LITTLE PRAIRIE (CHASKA)

While Father Ravoux lived at Little Prairie ministering to the Sioux, he built the church, 15 by 30, on the bank of the Minnesota river at a cost of $250 given him by Bishop Loras of Dubuque. It presented a neat appearance and had a shingled roof. In August of that year Bishop Loras sent Reverend A. Godfert, ordained in 1842, to assist Father Ravoux who had opened a little school to teach the Indian children to read the catechism in preparation for baptism. In the first three months of 1844 twenty-three Indians and half-breeds were baptized after which Father Godfert returned to Dubuque and the mission was closed. After his appointment as pastor of Mendota in 1844, Father Ravoux visited the mission occasionally until 1846, when the chapel was in danger of being burned by the Indians unless removed to another location. He sold it to the Catholics of Wabasha who dismantled it floated it down the Mississippi river and re-erected it as a place of worship. Bishop Loras gave forty dollars to help defray the expense of removal.

1848—CHURCH OF THE ASSUMPTION, PEMBINA

The parish of Pembina (now in North Dakota) became part of the original Diocese of St. Paul in July, 1850, prior to which it belonged to the Diocese of St. Boniface in Canada. A log church was built in 1848 by Reverend G. A. Belcourt (1848-59) who ministered to the five hundred half-breeds from the Red River and Indians of the vicinity for a decade of years. He was assisted by Reverend A. Lacombe (1849-51), Reverend J. Fayolle (1854-5) and Reverend J. Goiffon (1858-9). From 1853, when Father Belcourt made St. Joseph, thirty miles west, his headquarters, till his departure in March, 1859, it was a mission of St. Joseph administered by his assistants. When Father Goiffon took up his residence in St. Joseph, as successor to Father Belcourt, he continued to serve the people of Pembina. Bishop Grace sang High Mass in the Church of the Assumption on Sunday, September 1, 1861, and assisted by Fathers Ravoux and Goiffon, administered the Sacrament of Confirmation to eight persons. The Bishop described the church as "a rude log building but not without an air of neatness inside". In 1861 the parish was given to the Oblates of Mary Immaculate who retained charge of it till April 9, 1877. It was then part of the Vicariate of Northern Minnesota. It is now under the jurisdiction of the Bishop of Fargo.

1851—CHURCH OF OUR LADY OF SEVEN DOLORS, LONG PRAIRIE

Long Prairie, about one hundred miles north of St. Paul, was a government reservation for the Winnebago Indians transferred from Iowa in 1848. In July, 1851, Bishop Cretin sent Reverend Francis (Canon) de Vivaldi to the reservation to open a mission and school, which he did in a frame building transformed into a chapel. He admitted a class of Indians and half-breeds to first Communion on All Saints, baptized twenty catechumens on Christmas day and presented thirty persons for confirmation by Bishop Cretin on January 13, 1852. Sister Scholastica Vasquez and Miss Laquier, at whose home the sister lived, prepared a class of children for first Communion on March 25, after which the Sister returned to the Motherhouse of the Sisters of St. Joseph in St. Paul. Father Vivaldi built a convent, 18 by 20, one story high, for the Sisters of St. Joseph who, in July, 1852, opened a school for Indian children. In the winter of 1853, the convent and part of the school were destroyed by fire and the latter was repaired and used as a school and residence for the sisters. Difficulties arose between the government agent and Father Vivaldi and Father Fisher was sent to take his place in 1854. The next year the Winnebagoes were transferred to Blue Earth, the sisters returned to St. Paul, and Father Vivaldi went with the Indians and opened a school for them under the direction of a community of the Sisters of the Love of God which he founded. Father Vivaldi incurred debts in the name of the mission which displeased Bishop Cretin and he was dismissed by Governor Gorman and disappeared before the end of the year 1855. The Church of Our Lady of Seven Dolors was dismantled in the course of time and nothing remained but the cemetery to link the original foundation with the present Church of Our Lady of Mount Carmel, Long Prairie, through its predecessors, a log church, 20 by 24, built by Father Buh in 1868, and a frame church, 32 by 80, erected in 1871, and dedicated by Bishop Grace on August 22 of that year when he also administered confirmation, assisted by Fathers Pierz and Buh. Father Buh visited the parish every two or three months till 1874 when Reverend J. Schenk (1874-82) became pastor and it formed part of the Vicariate of Northern Minnesota. It is now under the jurisdiction of the Bishop of St. Cloud.

1852—CHURCH OF ST. JOHN THE EVANGELIST, LITTLE (NEW) CANADA

A log church was built in 1852 by Reverend J. Fayolle (1852-4) with attached rectory. It was torn down in 1890. The second, a brick church, 35 by 90, was dedicated on June 11, 1881, by Bishop Grace, during the pastorate of Reverend J. Goiffon (1861-82). The log church was remodeled for a rectory by Reverend L. Nougaret (1882-4). A new rectory was built in 1890 by Reverend F. Combette (1890-1) and made into a convent for the sisters in 1948 by the present pastor,

Reverend A. H. Durand (1940–), who built the new school in 1948 and remodeled the parish hall for a rectory. The school, dedicated on Sunday, August 1, 1949, by Auxiliary Bishop Byrne, is staffed by the Sisters of St. Francis of Assisi of Milwaukee.

Several sisters from the parish.

1852–CHURCH OF ST. FRANCIS, CROW WING

Crow Wing was an Indian trading-post at the confluence of the Crow Wing and Mississippi rivers, near Fort Ripley, to which Reverend F. X Pierz was sent by Bishop Cretin after his arrival in St. Paul on June 18, 1852. In one year he converted nearly all the Indians in the locality and built a log chapel and later a frame church for them and the whites who numbered about two hundred. It was his nominal residence until 1870, the center of his missionary activity among the Chippewas at Mille Lacs, Sandy, Cass, Leech and Red Lakes, which proved very successful because of the good dispositions of the Indians and their desire to have a "blackrobe" among them. In his time it was a flourishing town, the Indian capital of Minnesota. In the summer of 1858 Father Pierz visited Red Lake and placed Reverend Lawrence Lautishar in charge who was frozen to death on December 3 of that year while crossing the lake on his return from a sick call. Bishop Grace, assisted by Fathers Ravoux and Pierz, confirmed fourteen persons in the church on the Feast of the Assumption, August 15, 1861, and preached in English, French and Chippewa. During his missionary career in Minnesota Father Pierz built a number of log churches in Stearns County and elsewhere which were taken over by the Benedictine Fathers who came to the state in 1856. Father Pierz retired to Laibach in his native Carniola in 1873 and died on January 22, 1880. The site of the mission is owned by the Diocese of St. Cloud. When Brainerd became a railroad center, and the Indians were removed to reservations, Crow Wing was literally absorbed by Brainerd and only traces of basements and cemeteries remain to mark what was once the cradle of Catholicism in Northern Minnesota.

1852–CHURCH OF THE HOLY FAMILY, BELLE PRAIRIE

This mission was composed almost exclusively of French Canadians numbering about three hundred souls. The original log chapel was erected by Reverend F. X. Pierz and was the first church in what is now the Diocese of St. Cloud. He visited it periodically until 1865. On August 13, 1861, Bishop Grace confirmed thirty persons in the church assisted by Fathers Ravoux and Pierz. The Reverend Joseph Buh succeeded Father Pierz and had charge of the parish until 1877. During his frequent absences on missionary journeys he was assisted by the Reverend J. Trobec, (afterwards, third Bishop of St. Cloud), from May to September, 1866, and other missionaries until it was placed in charge of Reverend L. Chandonnet (1877-9) when it was part of the Vicariate of Northern Minnesota.

1852–CHURCH OF ST. ANNE, LESUEUR

The first Mass was said in March, 1852, in the home of Henry Cantwell, by the Reverend V. Sommereisen of Mankato, who attended the parish from 1852 to 1857. There is a record of the first baptism on June 12, 1859; of the first wedding on April 18, 1860; and of the first burial on March 23, 1862, before the first brick church was built in 1864 by Reverend T. Venn (1861-71). An addition was put to it in 1890 by Reverend P. Jung (1888-97). The present church on an elevated site was erected in 1925 by Reverend W. Cashman (1918-35) in English Gothic style. The rectory in English Manor type was built in 1927. The first rectory, the Doran residence, was bought in 1882 by the first resident pastor, Reverend M. Wurst (1880-7). It was too far from the church and he built another nearer the church in 1884. The school opened in 1882 in charge of the Sisters of Notre Dame from Milwaukee who lived in the building till June, 1902, when it was taken over by the Sisters of St. Joseph who established a conservatory in 1907 with grade, high and commercial departments. The present pastor is Reverend G. Hughes (1952–).

Five of the nineteen pastors became prelates—two Bishops and three Domestic Prelates. Bishop Busch of St. Cloud, in 1910; Bishop Duffy of Grand Island, Nebraska, in 1913; and the late Monsignors Kennedy of Belle Plaine; Wurst of Wabasha; and Jung of St. Paul.

5 priests and 16 sisters from the parish.

1853—CHURCH OF ST. JOSEPH, ST. JOSEPH (WALHALLA, N.D.)

Father Belcourt, pastor of Pembina, went to reside permanently at St. Joseph, thirty miles to the west, in 1853 and remained until March, 1859. He built a church, school, presbytery and grist mill (the first in North Dakota), founded the congregation of the Sisters of the Propagation of the Faith who taught the children of St. Francis Xavier school in French, English and Chippewa, and instructed the half-breed and Indian women in the faith. There were never more than seven half-breed sisters under the direction of Mother Francis Xavier. St. Joseph was the center of Father Belcourt's missionary journeys among the Indians of the western plains as far as the Missouri river and Devil's Lake until 1859 when he returned to his native province of Quebec and was succeeded by Father Goiffon (1859-61) who had Pembina for a mission. Bishop Grace, accompanied by Father Ravoux, visited St. Joseph in September, 1861, and at the close of a week's mission given by Father Ravoux assisted by Father Goiffon, sang High Mass on Sunday, the eighth of the month, and confirmed forty-five persons. The Bishop noted that "the Mass was well sung accompanied by the Melodion and the singing of some hymns in the (Sauteux) or Chippewa language was very sweet". Bishop Grace recalled Father Goiffon to St. Paul and gave the parish to the Oblates of Mary Immaculate who served it till April 9, 1877, when it was part of the Vicariate of Northern Minnesota. It is now within the corporate limits of the Diocese of Fargo.

1853—CHURCH OF ST. MICHAEL, STILLWATER

The original church was built in 1853 on Fourth Street, North, by the first resident pastor, Reverend D. J. Fisher (1853-6) and enlarged by Reverend T. Murray (1856-70) who built the rectory and started the school. Between 1849 and 1853 Fathers Ravoux and Peyragrosse said Mass in the homes of James Heffernan, Sr., Patrick Lloyd and Jacob Brown. On September 7, 1852, Bishop Cretin officiated at the wedding of John Sullivan and Catherine Donahoe. The present stone church, in Romanesque style, 80 by 140, with spire 190 feet high, was erected in 1875 by Reverend M. E. Murphy (1870-91) and dedicated by Bishop Grace on August 15 but not opened for regular services until the feast of St. Michael, September 29. The church was decorated and the sacristy enlarged in 1925 and a new main altar of marble installed in 1936 by Reverend C. Corcoran (1891-1943). It was redecorated and renovated in 1950 by Reverend D. F. McCarthy (1943–). A new school was built in 1875 costing $80,000 and a new rectory in 1898. In 1913 a more modern school was made possible by a donation from Maurice Clancy, a member of the congregation, for the erection of the Clancy Memorial School for grade and high school work. The golden jubilee of the parish was observed on September 29, 1925, when Solemn Mass was celebrated by the Right Reverend James C. Byrne, and the sermon was preached by Archbishop Dowling. In the evening there was a public meeting at which the principal addresses were delivered by Bishop O'Reilly of Fargo, and Father Corcoran. The following morning a requiem Mass was said by Reverend Maurice Casey and a sermon preached by Father Carlin, a former assistant in the parish. The church and the main altar were consecrated by Archbishop Murray on September 29, 1937.

3 priests, 2 brothers, 14 sisters from the parish.

1855—CHURCH OF ST. JOHN THE BAPTIST, BYRNESVILLE (BURNSVILLE)

The first Mass was said in this locality by Father Ravoux of Mendota in 1853 in the home of William Byrne (grandfather of the late Monsignor Byrne, V.G.) after whom the township was named. In the following year a log church was begun and completed in 1855 for a congregation of ten families to whom Fathers McManus and Oster ministered for a time. The first baptism recorded in the parish register is that of Edward McDonald at which Father Oster officiated on April 28, 1859. There are four monuments in the cemetery with 1855 engraved on them.

The first resident pastor was Reverend D. J. Fisher from December 19, 1859, to June 17, 1861. He was succeeded by Reverend J. Claude Robert (1861-6) who built the first rectory in 1865. From May 5 to August 16, 1866, Reverend J. Thaddeus Stephens, a priest from the East, was in charge of the parish and began the construction of a frame church, 40 by 70, designed by himself, on a commanding site near the cemetery laid out on higher ground behind it. The Northwestern Chronicle for November 4, 1866, says that Bishop Grace dedicated the church, which cost $8,000, in October of that year, but Mass was not said in it until December 16. The parish was without a resident pastor from August 16, 1866, till September 8, 1867, when Reverend A. Oster was appointed and remained in charge until October 27, 1878. He established the Apostleship of Prayer on December 2, 1867. From May 1 to August 15, 1878, Reverend Peter H. T. Ryan conferred three baptisms and collected about $1,200 for a new rectory. During these years the salary of the pastor was $450, out of which he paid the sexton. In 1882 the total receipts from all sources amounted to $821.00 and the expenditures to $765.00.

On November 18, 1878, Reverend P. F. Glennon began a pastorate of eighteen years during which the church was burned on April 13, 1883.

It was replaced at a cost of $6,000 on the original site and was blessed by Bishop Ireland on April 26, 1885, assisted by his secretary, Reverend J. C. Byrne, born in the parish, and Reverend F. McIntyre of Shakopee. On that occasion the Bishop preached, administered the total abstinence pledge to one hundred young men and confirmed fifty-five children. In October of that year the parish of Credit River was detached from Byrnesville of which it had been a mission and was thereafter attended from Prior Lake. The new rectory was occupied on September 14, 1889, and the old one sold for $1,200.

Another fire robbed the people of their church on Sunday, February 2, 1902, entailing a total loss except for an insurance of $7,000. In the meantime, less than a mile away, the village of Hamilton, soon to be named Savage after the owner of the famous pacing stallion, Dan Patch, acquired a railroad station and a place in the sun. The Archbishop decreed that the new church must be built in Savage and the rectory moved thereto. This took place during the pastorate of Reverend W. Rhatigan (1896-1903) and its future is told in the history of the Church of St. John the Baptist of Savage.

Bishop Grace confirmed on five occasions in the church at Byrnesville—July 19, 1868 (56 children); August 22, 1870 (28 boys and 36 girls); July 26, 1874 (65 boys and 58 girls); July 30, 1878 (35 boys and 35 girls); June 27, 1880 (47 boys and 99 girls). On January 26, 1896, Archbishop Ireland confirmed a class of 25 boys and 23 girls.

Some years ago the original church site of four and one-fifth acres was sold to Peter Kearney for $382, and three and one-third acres added to the cemetery at a cost of $201. When the railroad passed through the parish, it secured a right-of-way along the western border of the church property for one hundred dollars.

1855—CHURCH OF ST. GENEVIEVE, CENTERVILLE

The first church was built in 1855 by Reverend G. Keller; the second in 1859 by Reverend C. Robert; and the third in 1870 by Reverend J. Goiffon (1861-91). The present pastor is Reverend V. P. Dudley (1948–).

1 priest from the parish.

1855—CHURCH OF ST. VINCENT DE PAUL, OSSEO

A log chapel, 30 by 50, dedicated to St. Louis, was erected in 1855 by the pioneers at Palestine, and the next year Reverend F. Hurth became the first resident pastor (1856-60). The first Church of St. Vincent de Paul, a frame structure, 32 by 54, was completed in 1864 by Reverend C. Genis, and enlarged in 1880. A frame rectory was built in 1870 when Reverend F. J. A. Lechner came to reside in the parish. The cornerstone of the present brick church was laid on November 8, 1921, during the pastorate of Reverend H. J. Boerboom (1917–) and the edifice was solemnly dedicated on August 27, 1922, by Archbishop Dowling. The rectory was built in 1900 by Reverend L. Simon (1898-1903). A new parish house was completed in 1951, and a parochial school, in charge of the Sisters of St. Benedict from Crookston, opened in September, 1952.

1856—CHURCH OF ST. MARY OF THE PURIFICATION, MARYSTOWN

There is a tradition that a log chapel built in 1855 by Father Keller was destroyed by fire before completion. Two churches—one erected in 1857 and the other by the Benedictines in 1870—preceded the church built by the Franciscans in 1882. This church was completely destroyed by fire on February 28, 1917, and rebuilt before the end of the year at a cost of $23,183.43, by Reverend W. J. Skluzacek (1916-9), Bishop Cretin said Mass in the parish under a tree on Anton Pieper's farm in 1855, and blessed the original cemetery. The parish was in charge of the Fathers of St. Benedict from 1857 to 1871; of the diocesan clergy till 1876; of the Franciscans till 1909, when it was restored to the diocesan clergy. The school was built in 1893; St. Mary's rectory in 1910 replacing a one-room log rectory built in 1859; the convent in 1920 for the School Sisters of Notre Dame who have been in charge since that year. The present pastor is Reverend Henry Minea (1949–). 2 priests, 3 brothers and 35 sisters came from the parish.

1856—CHURCH OF THE GUARDIAN ANGELS, HASTINGS

A frame church, 30 by 50, was dedicated on November 2, 1856, by Reverend J. McMahon (1855-9). The present stone church, 145 by 100, was constructed in 1865 by Reverend F. Hurth (1861-8) who also built the first rectory. The second was erected in 1872 by Reverend J. Halton (1868-83). The church was remodeled and renovated by Reverend R. E. Nolan (1932-43). The school, built in 1872, was replaced in 1932 by a modern structure in charge of the Sisters of St. Joseph. The present pastor is Reverend P. J. Ryan (1943–). 10 sisters from the parish.

1856—CHURCH OF THE IMMACULATE CONCEPTION, FARIBAULT

The first church, dedicated to St. Anne, was built on land deeded to Bishop Cretin by Alexander Faribault on May 5, 1856. Before it was completed it was destroyed by fire on October 5, 1857.

In the spring of 1858 the Reverend George Keller was appointed pastor and erected a stone church, 100 by 50 by 32, dedicated to the Immaculate Conception, the first in the Diocese of St. Paul. He opened a two-room school in the basement in 1860 taught by Brother Ernest of the Brothers of the Holy Family of St. Paul, and lay teachers until 1865, when the Sisters of St. Dominic came and Sisters Veronica and Benvenuta took charge. A new bell weighing 1106 pounds was blessed by Bishop Grace September 17, 1866. It melted in the fire of 1900. Father Keller was succeeded in 1870 by Reverend A. D. Reville, O.P., who, in 1872, volunteered for service during the yellow fever epidemic at Memphis, Tennessee, and died of the dread disease, September 26, 1879. Reverend C. Sheve (1872-4) built the stone school in 1872—the first parochial school in southern Minnesota—which did service until 1925. The church was enlarged by the addition of a sanctuary, sacristy, and tower, and embellished by stained glass windows during the pastorate of Reverend F. Genis (1874-82) and rededicated by Bishop Grace, assisted by Father Ireland, on October 15, 1875. The improvements saddled the parish with a debt of $12,000 which was not paid for twenty years.

A brick rectory was built by Reverend T. O'Gorman (1882-5) who was named first Rector of St. Thomas Aquinas Seminary. A year later, during which the parish was administered by Reverend J. J. O'Connor, assistant, the Reverend J. J. Conry began a pastorate, ending February 2, 1900, made memorable by the famous Faribault School plan which was in operation for a couple of years. Before he left the parish the mortgage was burned.

In April, 1900, Father Slevin of Shieldsville was placed in charge and rebuilt the church after the disastrous fire of 1901, using the old walls. He built "three tabernacles", two in Shieldsville and one in Faribault. He was elevated to the dignity of a Domestic Prelate of the Papal Household in 1913, named Vicar General by Archbishop Dowling in 1919, and died on November 24, 1924. His successor, Reverend Oliver Dolphin (1925-8) had the present brick school ready for occupancy in the fall of 1925, and the new residence in the spring of 1926. The Reverend John P. Foley who was transferred to the parish from the Presidency of the College of St. Thomas, redecorated the church, remodeled the altars and for several years had the privilege of daily exposition of the Blessed Sacrament. For many years it had as a mission St. Edward's Church, Richland, now attached to the parish of Kenyon.

1 Bishop (Most Reverend Thomas A. Welch of Duluth), 6 priests and more than 50 sisters from the parish.

1856—CHURCH OF ST. PATRICK, SHIELDSVILLE

The original church of native lumber was built by the pioneers at a cost of $800, exclusive of material, in the fall of 1856 at the request of Bishop Cretin made known to them by Father Ravoux who, with other missionaries, said Mass in the homes of Patrick Hanlon, Jeremiah Healy and Michael Gavin, and who appointed the first trustees, James Carpenter and George McDonnell.

Father McCullough was the first resident pastor from 1867 to 1870, when Father Robert took his place for ten years. In 1880 Shieldsville Township had a population of 781 of whom 118 were in the village on the shores of Lake Mazaska, when the Reverend John J. Slevin (1880-1900) was appointed pastor and replaced the frame church with one of stone, 80 by 40, in 1882 at a cost of $16,000. It had a seating capacity of 620. He also built the rectory costing $1,000. On April 4, 1888, the church was struck by lightning and gutted by the ensuing fire. The old walls were used in re-building the new structure which was completed in December of that years in time for Mass on Christmas day. Father James J. Fleming who succeeded him gave place to Reverend John J. Molloy in 1909 who redecorated the church and built the parish hall. Father Molloy celebrated his diamond jubilee on June 28, 1951, and received an assistant for the first time in the person of Reverend John E. Joyce.

In the early seventies of last century there were two missions attached to the parish, one at Wheatland and the other at St. Michael's, three miles east of Montgomery, both of which have disappeared.

1856—CHURCH OF ST. PETER, ST. PETER

In 1856 Reverend V. Sommereisen of Mankato erected the first church which was lost to the parish during the depression of 1857, but redeemed by Reverend T. Venn of Henderson in 1863, completed by Reverend J. Zuzek (1865-78) and enlarged by Reverend J. Tori (1878-81). The present brick church was built by Reverend D. J. Moran (1908-18). In 1875 a school taught by the School Sisters of Notre Dame was opened and a convent provided for them. In 1877 the Sisters of St. Francis replaced them till 1892 when the school was closed. It was reopened in 1908 with the Sisters of St. Joseph as teachers. A new school was built in 192 by Reverend H. J. Jordan (1924-31) and later the School Sisters of Notre Dame were placed in charge. The present convent was bought and remodeled in 1922 by Reverend D. Sullivan (1919-23). The rectory was built in 1893 by Reverend P. Care (1892-1908) and remodeled by Reverend J. Ryan (1936—). One school now accommodates the children of St. Peter's parish and of the Immaculate Conception parish. Father Ireland had charge of the parish for a few months in 1863 and the school is called the "John Ireland School".

1 sister from the parish.

1856—CHURCH OF ST. MARK, SHAKOPEE

The first Mass was said on January 1, 1856, by Reverend G. Keller in the home of Anthony Entrup and the church was blessed in the autumn of that year by Reverend J. Mehlmann (1856-7); the second built by Reverend G. Scherer, O.S.B., (1865-8) was dedicated on December 8, 1868, by Bishop Grace, to which the tower was added by Reverend A. Plut (1876-86). The edifice was completely renovated in 1919 by Reverend M. Savs (1917-44). The school, 23 by 29, built in 1856, was staffed by the Sisters of St. Benedict from 1859 to 1878. They erected St. Gertrude's Convent and Academy in 1870 and occupied it till 1878 when they left Shakopee. It is now St. Francis Hospital under the direction of the Sisters of St. Francis. Since 1878 the School Sisters of Notre Dame have been in charge of the school. The second school was built in 1888 by Reverend P. Jeram (1886-9) and the present by Father Savs (1917-44). The first rectory was built during the pastorate of Reverend Benedict Haindl, O.S.B., (1887-8) and the present one by Reverend W. M. Stulz. Reverend H. J. Scherer is the pastor.

1856—CHURCH OF ST. MICHAEL, ST. MICHAEL

A log chapel, 18 by 32 feet, near Crow river, two miles east of present church, was built by Reverend Demetrius de Marogna, O.S.B., in 1856. It was replaced by a frame church near the present location in 1866. From it the community and the village took their name. The present brick church was erected in 1890-1 by Reverend R. Deustermann (1889-1904) and consecrated by the Right Reverend James McGolrick, Bishop of Duluth, September 29, 1892. It was decorated by Reverend A. Miks (1904-38) for the golden jubilee. The first resident pastor was Reverend Magnus Maria Mayr, O.S.B., (1862-5). The first diocesan pastor was Reverend G. Koering (1865-9). The present pastor is Reverend Henry Geisenkoetter (1951—). The first rectory was sold when the second, a frame building, was built by Reverend J. A. Schroeder (1877-89). The present was erected by Father Miks in 1913 and renovated by Father Ettel in 1950. A brick veneered school, 34 by 48 feet, and two and a half stories high, was erected in 1876 by Reverend I. Schaller (1871-7). Part of it was occupied as a convent by the School Sisters of Notre Dame from Milwaukee, who came on September 12, 1876, till 1899 when the entire building was given them and a new brick school built by Father Deustermann in that year. The present convent was erected by Father Miks and occupied by the Sisters on December 9, 1905, when the old one was demolished. The modern fireproof school was opened in September, 1940, by Reverend V. Schiffrer (1938-44). It cost $100,-000 and was free of debt in 1946, when the parish celebrated its 90th. anniversary.

The late Rt. Rev. Peter Engel, O.S.B., Abbott of St. John's, Collegeville, Minnesota; Rt. Rev. Cuthbert Goeb, O.S.B., Abbott of St. Mary's, Richardton, North Dakota; Rt. Rev. James Zachman, pastor of the Church of St. Francis de Sales, St. Paul; and the late Rt. Rev. Otto Zachman of Winona Diocese are from the parish.

22 priests, 2 brothers and 70 sisters from the parish.

856—CHURCH OF ST. PATRICK, INVER GROVE

A log church, built under the supervision of Father Ravoux, V.G., was used as a house of worship for ten years, before it was dismantled and the logs reconstructed into a large granary and barn on the farm of William Grace, Rosemount. This barn was brought by Thomas Corrigan in 1891 and the barn razed in 1907. The beveled, augered end of one of the logs, with its wooden peg in place, and a large bronze key of the original log church were presented to the Catholic Historical Society in 1951 by the Right Reverend Joseph A. Corrigan, pastor of the Church of St. Mark, St. Paul, a native of the parish of Inver Grove.

The new frame church, erected in 1866, was dedicated by Father Ravoux, as the delegate of Bishop Grace, on February 10, 1867, while the parish was attended by Father Genis from Mendota. The Northwestern Chronicle for November 24, 1866, says the church was 40 by 70 feet in size, had an octagonal sanctuary, stained glass windows, a tapering tower and cost $6,000. Father Ireland lectured in it on November 8, 1867, the proceeds amounting to $225. The rectory was built in 1879-80 by Reverend J. Andre, first resident pastor. The church was enlarged in 1894 by the addition of a chapel and a sacristy. On the first Saturday of September, 1919, church and rectory were completely destroyed by a fire originating in the belfry from defective wiring. The Blessed Sacrament, the sacred vessels and the parish records were saved. The church was not re-built. The insurance, now amounting to $9054.71, is in a savings account in the First National Bank of Rosemount. The Reverend M. M. Ryan was pastor when the church was destroyed. The parish records, prior to 1866, are kept in the Church of the Guardian Angels, Hastings, and in St. Peter's Church, Mendota, and the registers, since that date, are in possession of the Administrator of the parish of St. Agatha, Coates. The old cemetery on a knoll in the rear of the church is still used for burials.

2 priests (one of them, the Right Reverend Joseph A. Corrigan) and 4 sisters from the parish.

1857—CHURCH OF ST. PATRICK, CEDAR LAKE

It originated in a log chapel built in 1857 in which Father Maly said the first Mass. A year earlier Mass was said by Reverend D. J. Fisher in the home of Thomas Quill. Other priests from Shakopee, New Prague and Marystown, said Mass in Catholic homes before the present church was erected in 1873 under the supervision of Reverend C. J. Knauf, pastor of Marystown (1872-7). The parish is in charge of Reverend L. P. Bonin (1946—). It was made up of Irish immigrants in the beginning; the Germans came in 1930 and the Bohemians in 1938. There is no parochial school. St. Catherine's parish, Spring Lake, is a mission.

1 priest and 6 sisters from the parish.

1857—CHURCH OF ST. PATRICK, EDINA

Originally known as Cahill Settlement, it was incorporated as the village of Edina in 1888. The first settlers were from Ireland. Mass was said in the houses of John Duggan and John Burke by Father Fayolle of St. Anthony. A log church was built in 1857 and attended as a mission from the Church of St. Anthony of Padua, Minneapolis, by Reverend J. McDermott (1860-6), then by Reverend F. Tissot his successor, till 1868, when the Reverend J. McGolrick founded the parish of the Immaculate Conception in Minneapolis and had pastoral charge of Cahill Settlement until 1889. In 1884 the log chapel was replaced by a frame church on the present site, donated by Patrick W. Ryan. It was destroyed by lightning in 192 and rebuilt in that year by Reverend J. H. Gaughan, pastor of St. Stephen's, Minneapolis, of which it was a mission until 1932 when Reverend T. P. Ryan became first resident pastor (1932-4). The rectory at some distance from the church was bought in 1942 by Reverend G. E. Ryan (1941-4). Reverend V. Yany is the pastor.

2 priests from the parish.

1857—CHURCH OF ST. SCHOLASTICA, HEIDELBERG

The frame building erected in 1857 by Reverend B. Haindl, O.S.B. (1857-9) served as a church until 1905 when the present edifice was blessed by Reverend W. Skluzacek (1904-8). The parochial residence was built in 1902 by Reverend A Kotouc (1897-1904). The first school was erected in 1878 by Reverend F. Simonik (1877-97), but was discontinued after a short time. Reverend F. R. O. Haye is the pastor.

3 priests from the parish

1857—CHURCH OF THE IMMACULATE CONCEPTION, MARYSBURG

A log chapel was built in 1857 probably by Reverend V. Sommereisen of Mankato. The present church was erected in 1886 by the Reverend P. K. Ryan (188 6). Fifteen pastors are listed since 1867, when the Reverend F. Maly (1867-9 erected the first parish house which was replaced by the present rectory in 18 built by Reverend W. Dowling (1886-9). The parish hall put up in 1901 by Reverend P. J. McCabe (1895-1901) was destroyed by fire in 1902 and replaced in 1933 by Reverend A. Kryjewski (1931-47). P. M. Meagher deeded five acres for the cemetery in 1857 and two for the church site; R. Cleary deeded twenty acres to the parish; M. B. Farrell built the foundation of the church; and John Quirk hauled the bell by ox team from Mankato. The present pastor is Reverend Joseph N. Streff (1951–).

1 priest and 9 sisters from the parish.

1857—CHURCH OF ST. MARY, NEW TRIER

First Mass said on May 8, 1856, by Reverend G. Keller (1856-61) in the log cabin of J. J. Fuchs and on the same day he baptized, among others, F. X. Gores who became pastor of the parish in 1898 and died in 1909 while in charge of the Church of the Sacred Heart, St. Paul. A log chapel was erected in 1857 by Father Keller and replaced by a stone structure built in 1864 by Reverend P. Bayer which served till 1909 when the cornerstone of the present church was laid during the pastorate of Reverend N. Stubinitzky (1908-20). The school was taught by the Benedictine Sisters from 1865 till 1877; and the Sisters of Notre Dame from Milwaukee came in 1879. The first convent was built in 1870 and the new one in 1950. The original school was replaced in 1900 by the present school begun by Father Gores and completed by Father Haas (1899-1904). The rectory built in 1868 was replaced by a modern structure in 1922 by Reverend M. Doring (1920-32). The pastor is Reverend Nicholas Gillen (1951–).

3 priests and 35 sisters from the parish.

1858—CHURCH OF ST. WALBURGA, FLETCHER

It was originally a log chapel erected in 1858 in St. John's two miles south of the present location by Reverend Demetrius de Marogna, O.S.B. The present church was built in 1883 by Reverend I. Schaller, pastor of St. Michael's Church, St. Michael, of which it was a mission known as St. Walburga. It was enlarged in 1899 by Reverend L. Keukelink (1897-1905). It was assigned to the Oblates of Mary Immaculate in 1915 and is still in their charge, with Reverend A. H. Rosenthal, O.M.I., pastor since 1943. A log school in charge of a lay teacher was erected in 1865; and a frame building in 1885. The present brick school was built in 1902, and the Sisters of St. Francis of Milwaukee have been the teachers since 1904. The first rectory was built in 1885; the second a few years later; and the third in 1917 by Reverend J. Schulte, O.M.I. (1916-21) as a mission house for the Order.

1 priest and 5 sisters from the parish.

1858—CHURCH OF ST. WENCESLAUS, NEW PRAGUE

The log church, built in 1858, was destroyed by fire in 1863 during the pastorate of Reverend P. Maly (1861-6). The second church was completed in 1868 by Reverend A. Plut (1866-8). The third, begun in 1904 by Reverend F. Tichy 1880-96), was finished in 1907 by Reverend J. Cermak (1906-36) who now lives in retirement in a private house in the town. The first rectory was built in 1862 by Father Maly; the new one in 1873. The school, erected in 1878, has been taught by the School Sisters of St. Francis since 1884. The first convent was built in 1885: a new convent was erected in 1949 and the present school in 1914. In 1895 Father Tichy erected a mortuary chapel in the cemetery. The present pastor, Reverend C. M. Popelka, succeeded Father Cermak in 1936.

14 priests and 25 sisters from the parish.

1858—CHURCH OF ST. JOHN THE BAPTIST, JORDAN

The first church, 26 by 46, was built in 1858 by Reverend C. Wittmann, O.S.B.; the second, 30 by 80, in 1865 by Reverend A. Berghold; the third in 1889 by Reverend B. Schuetz, O.F.M. (1887-94). The first resident pastor was Reverend

Bruno Riss, O.S.B. (1860-1). The parish was placed under the Franciscan Fathers in 1875, and the present pastor is Reverend Samuel Martin, O.F.M. (1949–). The parish house was built by Reverend R. Deustermann (1873-5), and the school, erected in 1877, has been staffed by the School Sisters of Notre Dame since 1879. A convent was built near the school and a new residence in 1914. A modern school was opened in 1908 by Reverend H. Kuester, O.F.M. (1907-11).

8 priests and 33 sisters from the parish.

1858—CHURCH OF ST. JOSEPH, SCOTT COUNTY (JORDAN P. O.)

The first church was built in 1858 by Reverend B. Haindl, O.S.B., and the present, in 1873, by Reverend R. Deustermann (1873-5). Since then the parish has been attended by the Franciscan Fathers. A rectory was built in 1860 and the present one in 1921. It is occupied by Reverend Florian Thiel, O.F.M.

1858—CHURCH OF ST. GEORGE, WEST NEWTON

The log church, completed in 1858 by Reverend V. Sommereisen (1857-64), escaped destruction during the Indian outbreak of 1862, but was replaced by a frame church in 1871 under the supervision of Reverend A. Berghold of New Ulm. It was converted into a hall in 1892 when the present brick structure was erected by Reverend B. Beinhart (1883-1902). The first resident pastor was Reverend S. Mon (1879-83). The school and convent, erected in 1916 by Reverend F. Pozek (1905-47), are in charge of the Poor Handmaids of Jesus Christ from Donaldson, Indiana. The first frame rectory was built while the parish was a mission. The present brick residence was erected in 1900 by Father Beinhart. A new school was built in 1951. The Reverend A. L. Schwinn is pastor (1947–).

3 priests and 5 sisters from the parish.

1858—CHURCH OF ST. JOSEPH, MEDICINE LAKE

In early days it was known as St. Francis in honor of the pioneer, Francois Boucher, in whose home as early as 1854 Reverend D. Ledon said Mass. A log chapel, 24 by 32, was built in 1858, and the first Mass was said in it by Reverend F. Hurth, ordained by Bishop Cretin in 1856. The present frame church, 36 by 80, was completed in 1877 and dedicated by Reverend P. Boucher, a grand nephew of the pioneer, Francois Boucher. The parish was a mission until 1934 when Reverend N Finn was appointed pastor, but when he built the Church of St. Mary of the Lake three miles south of St. Joseph's, Reverend J. Allard became the first resident priest in 1935, and built the rectory in that year. There is no school and only seventy families in the parish.

1 priest from the parish.

1858—CHURCH OF THE GUARDIAN ANGELS, CHASKA

The history of the Catholic church in Chaska may be said to go back to 184: when, at the invitation of J. B. Faribault, proprietor of the Indian Trading Post a Little Prairie (Chaska), Father Ravoux established a flourishing mission among th Sioux and built a chapel, 15 by 30, which was dismantled three years later. Rev erend Bruno Riss, O.S.B. (1858-60) built a church in the west end of the village and Reverend Magnus Mayr, O.S.B. (1865-72) in the east end. They were fol lowed by a diocesan priest, Reverend W. Lette, from 1872 to 1876, when th parish was given to the Franciscan Fathers of whom there have been twelve be fore 1945 when Father Justinian Kugler came. The second church was burned i 1902 and rebuilt by Father Guido Knepper, O.F.M. (1895-1905). The paris house was erected in 1872; the school and the convent in 1878 for the Sisters c Christian Charity from Wilmette, Illinois; and the high school in 1925. The preser pastor is Reverend Lucius Hellstern, O.F.M. (1850–).

5 priests, 2 brothers, 29 sisters from the parish.

1858—CHURCH OF ST. VICTORIA, VICTORIA

A log chapel, built in 1858 by the parishioners on the site of the cemetery, w; served by itinerant missionaries till the present church was erected in 1871 by Re' erend M. Mayr, O.S.B., (1865-72), and enlarged in 1884 by Reverend O. Jansen, O.F.M. (1880-5). The first school and convent were built in 1877 for the Franciscan Sisters from Milwaukee who taught in it till 1890 when the Sisters of Christian Charity took over for ten years and were succeeded by the Sisters of St. Benedict in 1900. The new school was erected in 1913 by Reverend R. Moehle, O.F.M. (1908-14); the rectory in 1923 by Reverend H. Stotter, O.F.M. (1915-30). The Reverend Justinian Kugler, O.F.M., who came in 1950, died two years later.

5 priests and 6 sisters from the parish.

1859—CHURCH OF ST. BERNARD, COLOGNE

The first Mass was said in a private house in 1859 by Reverend Bruno Riss, and in the church by Reverend Cornelius Wittmann, O.S.B., at an unknown date. Both were from Shakopee. The first resident pastor was Reverend G. Scherer, O.S.B. (1864-6). The parochial school was built in 1876 by Reverend G. H. Braun (1876-88) and placed in charge of the Sisters of Notre Dame. The new brick school, costing $32,000 was erected by the Reverend P. Schirmers (1910-21). The present pastor is Reverend A. Heer (1950—) who is building a modern convent.

2 priests from the parish.

1859—CHURCH OF THE ASCENSION, NORWOOD

The first parish was organized in Young America, a neighboring village, in 1859 and a church, begun in 1863 by Father Stukenkemper, was completed three years later by Father Stern. It became too small and a new church was erected in Norwood in 1880 at a cost of $8,000 by Father Braun. It was served by Father Seubert of Cologne from 1888 to October, 1906, when Reverend M. Goevert was appointed resident pastor and built the rectory in 1908. The present brick church was erected in 1905 at a cost of $25,000, by Father Seubert. The interior was redecorated in 1925 by Father Remskar (1921-38). In 1942 a new brick residence was built by Father Galles (1938-48). The present pastor is Reverend A. Funke (1948—).

1859—CHURCH OF ST. BENEDICT, ST. BENEDICT

It was founded September 30, 1859, by Reverend Cornelius Wittmann, O.S.B., when he said Mass in the home of John Berndgen who, with Christ Busch, donated twelve acres for church purposes to Bishop Grace by deed filed February 26, 1861. The original congregation numbered 31 German families. The Benedictines withdrew in 1861 and the parish became a mission to New Prague under Reverend P. Maly (1861-6) who opened a log church, 18 by 24, in 1862. Father Plut of New Prague (1866-8) replaced it by a frame church, 30 by 45, in September, 867, at a cost of $42.00. A tower was added in 1869 by Reverend H. Povolny,).S.F., who furnished the church, built a school house, and lived there until June, 874, when he returned to Europe. At the request of Bishop Grace the Franciscans came to Jordan in July, 1875, and Reverend Guido Knepper, O.F.M., had pastoral charge of St. Benedict's until he was succeeded by Reverend Casimir Iueffe O.F.M. (1875-85) who planned the present church of brick and stone, enlarged the school in 1881 and added a convent for the Franciscan Sisters of Milwaukee who remained till 1888. The church was begun in 1887 by Reverend Benignus Schuetz, O.F.M. (1886-7) and completed by Reverend Otto Jansen O.F.M. 1887-92) and blessed on October 9, 1887. It cost $8,736.79. The new school was rected by Reverend Odo Richardt O.F.M. (1896-9) and blessed on September 4, 898. It cost $4,367.00, and is taught by lay teachers. The rectory was built by Reverend Agnellus Bleser, O.F.M. (1916-7). The present pastor is Reverend Godfrey iontkowski, O.F.M.

1 priest, 2 brothers and 21 sisters from the parish.

859—CHURCH OF ST. HENRY, ST. HENRY (LESUEUR COUNTY)

A log chapel, 28 by 18, was built by twelve parishioners in the Big Woods and he first Mass said by Reverend Cornelius Wittmann, O.S.B., of Shakopee on January 3, 1859. He visited it again in February, May and August, 1860. Bishop Grace ordered the church moved one mile west of the original site to a ten acre plot of ground. It was dedicated to St. Henry and the first Mass was said in it on September 1, 1861, for nineteen families. From February, 1862, to September, 1865, Reverend P. Maly of New Prague had charge of it and then Reverend J. Zuzek of St. Peter till 1878. In 1870 Father Zuzek built a frame church in which the first Mass was said in November. It was blessed on October 1, 1872. A steeple was added in 1876. The rectory was built in December, 1882, by Father Maly who became the first resident pastor (1882-9). In 1885 transepts were added to the church. Reverend J. C. Wagner (1918-37) renovated the church in 1920 and built the parish hall in 1923. In 1889 the congregation gave sixty-two families to the new parish of St. Mary, Le (Sueur) Center. The present pastor is Reverend John R. Fleming (1950–).

3 sisters from the parish.

1859—CHURCH OF ST. JOHN, SIBLEY COUNTY (BELLE PLAINE P.O.)

A log church built in 1859, and a frame church that replaced it ten yeras later, preceded the present church erected about 1885. This territory was originally served by priests from Mendota and Henderson who came via the Minnesota river. It was formerly a mission attended from Assumption. The first pastor to reside in the parish was Reverend W. Luby (1919-27) who built the rectory. A parish hall still in use was erected in 1875. The Reverend W. W. Weiers has been pastor since 1948.

2 priests and 2 sisters from the parish.

1860—CHURCH OF ST. THOMAS, CORCORAN

A church dedicated to St. Patrick was built in 1860 three miles east of Corcoran where there is an old cemetery; and one under the patronage of St. Thomas in June, 1862, three miles northwest of Corcoran adjoining a cemetery. They were merged in 1896 when the present St. Thomas Church was erected on a new site in Corcoran by Reverend Adam Coyle (1895-1903). Father Swift was the first resident pastor in 1875, but the baptismal records go back to 1868. The rectory was built in 1896, and the present cemetery opened. A basement was added to the church in 1922 by Reverend G. Vander Velden (1921-36) and new altars installed in 1924. The present pastor is Reverend H. V. Green (1946–).

1 priest and 1 sister from the parish.

1860—CHURCH OF ST. COLUMBKILL, BELLE CREEK

Belle Creek was a mission of Wabasha before the church was built in 1860 and of Red Wing after that date. It received its first resident pastor in 1878 in the person of Reverend W. T. Roy who had charge of Cannon Falls and Cherry Grove as missions. He was succeeded by Reverends J. O'Reilly, H. McDevitt and Father Ansbro until 1886, when Reverend R. J. Fitzgerald became pastor (1886-99) who erected the present brick church, and also the one in Cannon Falls. He was followed by Reverend J. H. Prendergast (1899-1912) who was given Goodhue as a mission in place of Cherry Grove which was attached to Pine Island, and Cannon Falls became an independent parish in 1905. He built the parish hall and beautified the cemetery, and was followed by Father Ennis and Father McAvay. The present pastor is Reverend Francis E. Smith (1935–).

1860—CHURCH OF THE SACRED HEART, BELLE PLAINE

The original church, built in 1860 by Reverend Bruno Riss, O.S.B., (1860-1) was dedicated to St. Martin but when the German members of the congregation seceded in 1869 and formed the new parish of SS. Peter and Paul, the church was placed under the protection of the Sacred Heart, and Reverend T. Kennedy (1867-1914) began his long pastorate of forty-seven years. He erected the present church in 1873 which was renovated by Reverend T. Minogue, his successor for a period of twenty-seven years. The first rectory was built by Father Kennedy and the present brick structure by Father Minogue. The Reverend D. J. Fisher was resident pastor from June, 1861, to June 3, 1862. Belle Plaine was founded in 1854 by French settlers who soon yielded to Irish immigrants. The Germans came in 1857. As early as 1858 Mass was said in the settlement by Reverend Cornelius Wittmann, O.S.B., in the home of Peter Stravens. At the time of the separation on national lines there were forty German families and seventy-two Irish. In early days the parish had its own school under the supervision of the Sisters of St. Benedict who left in 1882. Then the children attended the German school in charge of the Franciscan Sisters from Milwaukee from 1878 to 1888, when the Sisters of St. Benedict came. Reverend W. W. Finley has been pastor of the parish since 1946. It was in this parish that the first Total Abstinence Society of the Diocese of St. Paul was organized by Reverend D. V. McGinnity in 1868.

1 priest, 1 brother and 6 sisters from the parish.

1860—CHURCH OF ST. JOHN, UNION HILL

The first log church, built by the people in 1860, was not authorized by Bishop Grace; the second, also of logs, was built in 1865 on a different site and Mass was said in it once a month by Reverend P. Maly of New Prague. A set of vestments was given to the parish by Count Beisel of Cologne, Germany, some of whose domestics were among the settlers of Union Hill. The church was closed in 1866 because it was too small, not centrally located and too near Heidelberg. The third church, a large frame building, with a sacristy in the rear, was erected on another site in 1867 by Reverend A. Berghold of Heidelberg (1866-8), and the first Mass was said on July 15 of that year. The tower and bell were added by Reverend J. Schenk (1869-73) of Jordan. The school was built in 1873 by Reverend R. Deustermann (1873-75). In 1875 the parish was given to the Franciscan Fathers residing at Jordan and Reverend C. Cybulla, O.F.M., was placed in charge (1875-6). The present Gothic church in the form of a cross and seating 350 persons was erected in 1883 by Reverend F. Rechtiene, O.F.M. (1880-5) and dedicated by Bishop Grace on July 2, 1884. In 1910 a four-room residence was added at the rear of the church by Reverend H. Stotter, O.F.M. (1902-14). Four Franciscan Sisters came August 14, 1884, but as they had Mass only every second week on Friday, Saturday, Sunday and Monday, they were recalled to the Motherhouse in Milwaukee in August 1888. The school was destroyed by fire on December 26, 1894. The brick school, built in 1895 by Reverend O. Puthoff, O.F.M. (1885-98) was remodeled in 1915 to provide an auditorium by Reverend R. Holte, O.F.M. (1914-24). It was burned on January 5, 1920 and rebuilt in December of that year. It has lay teachers. The present pastor is Reverend Kenneth Gausmann, O. F.M.

5 priests, 1 brother and 14 sisters from the parish.

1860—CHURCH OF ST. MICHAEL, PRIOR LAKE

This locality was visited by Reverend A. Oster in the early days and he may have built the first frame church about 1860 which was destroyed by fire. The present church was built by Reverend J. Deere in 1921, as also the rectory in 1917. Reverend E. M. Barry is now in charge of the parish.

1 priest from the parish.

1860—CHURCH OF ST. JEANNE DE CHANTAL, CORCORAN

This church, the center of a French parish whose pioneers, Michael Patnode and David Dufort, came from Canada in 1860, is a mission of St. Thomas in the southwestern part of Corcoran township. The present pastor of both is Reverend J. V. Green (1946—). The church was badly damaged by a wind storm in June, 1952.

1860—CHURCH OF ST. PETER, CREDIT RIVER

The original frame church, built in 1860, in Spring Lake, under the direction of Reverend D. J. Fisher (1860-1) and served by seven other priests, was moved to

Credit River in 1919 by Reverend J. Deere (1906-36). It has been attached to Prior Lake as a mission since 1912.

4 priests from the parish.

1860—CHURCH OF ST. JOSEPH, HENDERSON

A large frame church was built in 1860 by Reverend V. Sommereisen of Mankato who said the first Mass in it. A two-story school and convent was erected in 1874 by Reverend A. Stecker (1874-81) and placed in charge of the School Sisters of Notre Dame, but was destroyed by fire in September, 1886, and not rebuilt. The present church was erected under the supervision of Reverend W. B. G. Jansen who was pastor from 1888 to 1899 and from 1902 to 1904. The Reverend J. H. Brennan came to the parish in 1936.

3 priests from the parish.

1860—CHURCH OF ST. JOHN THE EVANGELIST, DERRYNANE TOWNSHIP

The Catholic Almanac for 1861 mentions the Church of St. John the Evangelist in process of erection in Derrynane Township and visited occasionally by a missionary priest. The next issue—that of 1864—says the church is visited from New Prague; and in that year as well as in 1866 there is listed a St. John Church in Le-Sueur County also visited from New Prague. There is a record in the Register of Deeds office in Le Center stating that Thomas L. Clifford of Derrynane deeded to Bishop Grace, on January 6, 1860, a little more than five acres "provided that a church shall be erected and fit for public use on or before January 1, 1863". The church in Derrynane Township was a log church about two miles east of the present site with an adjoining cemetery still in existence from which nearly all the bodies have been removed to the new cemetery beside the present Church of St. Thomas. This church ceased to exist about 1866 when the Germans in the congregation seceded and joined the parish of St. John, Union Hill, and the rest built the Church of St. Thomas on the present site. This is evidenced by the fact that Bishop Grace deeded back to Thomas L. Clifford, on February 7, 1868, the land he had donated and the latter set aside the cemetery as sacred.

1861—CHURCH OF ST. MARY, WAVERLY

The earliest church of which there is record was erected in 1861 on the north shore of Waverly Lake on the Doerfler farm and in 1863 it was a mission of St. Michael's. Five years later a small church was built in old Waverly and services held regularly in it till 1872, when a new church was built on the site of the present edifice. The first rectory was built in 1874 by Reverend J. McDermott. Waverly was a mission of Watertown until August 10, 1884, when Reverend J Guillot was appointed pastor and remained for twelve years during which he built the present brick church, 138 by 43 feet, with two spires, which was dedicated on August 15, 1892, by Bishop McGolrick of Duluth. The present rectory, begun by Reverend E. Casey, was completed by Reverend P. J. Lucey (1898-1910). A building for school and convent was erected in 1885 and staffed by the Sisters of St Joseph who are still in charge but occupy a new convent built in 1923 by Reverend T. Moore (1910-23). In 1949 Reverend M. E. Keeler took charge of the parish.

2 priests and 13 sisters from the parish.

1861—CHURCH OF ST. MICHAEL, BELGRADE

The first church built in 1861 by Reverend V. Sommereisen of Mankato, and the second church some years later preceded the present edifice erected in 1899 by Reverend A. Miks of St. Peter (1897-1902). The first resident pastor was Reverend J. Zuzek (1866-78). Since 1907 it has been a mission of Nicollet of which Reverend Joseph Pendzimas is pastor since 1951.

1 priest from the parish.

1861—CHURCH OF ST. NICHOLAS, NEW MARKET

The first church of logs, built in 1861, was followed by a frame structure erected in 1871 by Reverend P. Bayer (1863-72) and enlarged by Reverend C. J. Knauf (1872-7). A chapel was added in 1900 by Reverend A. Berghold (1899-1906) who designed and erected an out-door Way of the Cross in 1905. The present church and rectory were built by Reverend M. Stukel (1906-22). The stained glass windows and the shrine of the Sacred Heart were installed by Reverend H. J. Minea. The first rectory and the first convent were built about 1879 by Father Kimel. The Sisters of Notre Dame came in 1916. The present convent was built by Reverend Henry J. Minea in 1950. The pastor in charge is Reverend Carl A. Renz.

4 priests from the parish.

1863—CHURCH OF THE IMMACULATE CONCEPTION, WATERTOWN

The first church was erected under the supervision of Reverend G. Scherer, O. S.B., of Waconia, at a cost of about one thousand dollars, on a site northwest of the present Cottage Hospital. Father Scherer ministered to the spiritual needs of the congregation for four years when the first resident pastor, Reverend C. Robert, came and, followed by Fathers Stern, Seel, Juskiewicz and Steinacher, served the parish until 1876, when a new church, costing five thousand dollars, was built under the direction of Reverend L. Weisler of Waconia. In 1879 the parish became a mission of Waverly and was attended by Fathers Kenny and Swift. Since 1882 the following have been in pastoral charge: Reverends M. Quinn (1882-3); J. Guillot (1883-6). who purchased and installed the inscribed bell in the church: J. Fitzgerald (1886); D. Jones (1887); M. Cauley (1886-96); J. Nugent (1896-8); M. J. Egan (1898-1900) and T. Rehill (1900–). The parish has been noted for its active Total Abstinence Society and its interest in the work of temperance since 1887.

1863—CHURCH OF THE ANNUNCIATION, HAZELWOOD

The first church was built under the supervision of Reverend G. Keller of Faribault in 1863, enlarged in 1874, 1881, 1903, destroyed by fire on June 24, 1913, rebuilt in the same year at a cost of $12,000, and dedicated by Bishop Lawler on June 16, 1914, after which a Solemn High Mass was celebrated by Reverend P. F. Meade, pastor of Northfield, of which it was a mission till 1940, when the present pastor, Reverend R. E. Russell, was appointed. He built the parish house in 1942; and the outdoor Grotto of Our Lady of Fatima was dedicated by Auxiliary Bishop Byrne on October 31, 1948.

1 priest and 8 sisters from the parish

1863—CHURCH OF ST. JOHN THE BAPTIST, DAYTON

A log chapel, near the old cemetery, two miles south of the present location, was built in 1863 by Reverend C. Genis (1863-6). A second and a third church nearer the present site gave place to the brick building erected at the beginning of the pastorate of Reverend C. A. Pettigrew (1902-34). It was renovated in 1937-38 by Reverend J. H. Guillemette (1937–) who in 1948 changed it into a combination church and school, the latter in charge of five Sisters of Notre Dame of Mankato, with 138 pupils enrolled. The church has had ten pastors.

1 priest and 1 sister from the parish.

1865—CHURCH OF ST. CATHERINE, SPRING LAKE

The parish was established in 1865 and the first church built by the only resident pastor, Reverend Alois Plut, in 1867. It was incorporated by Bishop Grace, Father Ravoux, V.G., and Reverend J. Knauf on February 19, 1877. The first church was burned and the present erected in 1896. It is a mission of St. Patrick's, Cedar Lake, attended by the pastor, Reverend Leon Bonin.

1865—CHURCH OF ST. MARY, STILLWATER

A Presbyterian church was bought on December 8, 1865 for $750.00 by Reverend A. Plut (1865-6), who for nine months had said Mass for the German Catholics in St. Michael's Church. The present brick church was completed in 1884 by Reverend A. Kuisle, O.S.B. (1883-95) at a cost of $20,000, and consecrated by Bishop Ireland on July 20, the third in the state to be solemnly dedicated to God. The first school was opened in 1872 with the Sisters of St. Joseph in charge till 1880. In 1882 the Sisters of St. Benedict came and lived in the school building. The new brick school was built in 1904. In 1887 work began on a new rectory and winter chapel to replace the frame residence bought in 1871 and was completed the next year. The present pastor is Reverend P. Meinz, O.S.B. (1940—).

4 priests, 1 brother and 11 sisters from the parish.

1865—CHURCH OF THE VISITATION, BRIGHTON, (SWAN LAKE)

A log church was built about 1865 under the supervision of Reverend J. Zuzek (1865-78) and the present structure by Reverend W. J. Skluzacek in 1912 after fire had destroyed the old church. It was a mission attended from St. Peter and, later, from Nicollet until 1942, when Reverend P. Berger was appointed resident pastor (1942-3). The rectory was purchased on August 16, 1942. The parish is also known as Swan Lake and the present pastor is Reverend Otto Neudecker (1951—). The mission of St. Nicholas, Middle Lake, is attached to it.

1 priest from the parish.

1865—CHURCH OF ST. HUBERT, CHANHASSEN

Reverend M. Mayr, O.S.B. (1864-72) built a log chapel in 1865; the Reverend W. Lette (1872-7) a frame church in 1873, with two-room rectory attached. A school built in 1881 was replaced with a more modern building in 1894. It was taught by the Franciscan Sisters from 1881 to 1888; the Sisters of Christian Charity from 1888 to 1895; the Sisters of St. Benedict from 1895 to the present time, and is under the direction of the pastor, Reverend Oswald Gasper, O.F.M. (1945—). Twenty-six pastors have served the parish.

5 sisters from the parish.

1865—CHURCH OF ST. PETER, DELANO

In 1865 a church was built by the parishioners outside Delano and attended by visiting priests; in 1874 another was erected in the village by Reverend F. Steinacher. The first resident pastor was Reverend D. Sacks (1875-84). The present church was erected in 1913 by Reverend M. Savs (1896-1917). The rectory was built in 1892; the first school in 1888; the second in 1929; the convent in 1929 and enlarged in 1948. The Sisters of St. Francis of Rochester, Minnesota, have charge of the school under the direction of Reverend F. P. Neumann (1936—).

1 priest from the parish.

1865—CHURCH OF ST. JOSEPH, RED WING

In the early days the Catholics of Red Wing were ministered to by Reverend F Tissot, residing at Wabasha, who had charge of Wabasha and Goodhue Counties In 1860 two lots were bought on which the present school is built, but the churcl was not dedicated until Trinity Sunday, July 11, 1865, by Bishop Grace assisted by Fathers Caillet and Tissot, after which fifty-five persons were confirmed. Shortl afterwards Reverend C. J. Knauf was appointed pastor of Goodhue County with residence at Red Wing, where he remained until 1872, when he was succeeded b Reverend J. H. Stariha (1872-84) who erected a convent and two-room schoc in 1873, and placed it in charge of three Sisters of Notre Dame from Milwaukee It was formally opened on November 4, 1873, with an enrollment of ninety pupil after a Solemn Mass celebrated by the pastor and a sermon by Father Trobec c Wabasha. When the present stone church was erected in 1878, at Sixth and Par Streets, the old one was annexed to the school, forming a third class room. F several years Father Stariha was assisted by Reverends A. Walter, A. Holzer an J. Meier in attending the missions of Belle Creek, Cherry Grove and Belvider

The old rectory built by Father Knauf on the school lot was too far from the church and Father Meier (1884-5) erected a new one adjacent to the church. In 1908 the Frederick Busch brick home on Seventh Street was donated to the parish by Mrs. Anna Busch as a convent for the Sisters of Notre Dame. A two-story brick school, costing $25,000, was dedicated by Bishop Busch on Sunday, September 8, 1910. Reverend Martin Donovan (1945–) is the pastor.

Most Reverend Joseph F. Busch (Bishop of St. Cloud), 6 priests and several sisters from the parish.

1865—CHURCH OF STS. PETER AND PAUL, GLENCOE

In 1865 Reverend Cornelius Wittmann, O.S.B. of Shakopee, bought a house and remodeled it to serve as a temporary church until replaced by a frame church erected in 1875 by Reverend R. Deustermann (1875-89). It was destroyed by fire on March 19, 1877. A new church, dedicated by Bishop Grace in 1878, was also destroyed by fire on October 13, 1889. It was replaced by the present brick church in 1890 under the direction of Reverend J. A. Schroeder (1890-2). The school was opened in 1878, as a one-room addition to the convent, and was under the control of the Sisters of St. Francis of Rochester. A frame school building erected in 1885 was veneered with brick in 1914 and still serves as the parochial school. Reverend Arnold Luger is the present pastor.

5 priests and 10 sisters from the parish.

1865—CHURCH OF ST. MARY, SHAKOPEE

St. Mary's Church was built in 1865 under the direction of Reverend A. Oster and attended as a mission from St. Mark's parish until 1878, when the Reverend J. J. Slevin was appointed pastor, remained two years and built the rectory. The tower and steeple were added in 1905 by Reverend H. McDevitt (1905-6), and stained glass windows put in by Reverend J. Fleming (1895-1900). The parish school was erected by Reverend M. McRaith (1928-50) who began the construction of an addition before he died, leaving the completion of it to his successor, Reverend H. J. Byrne (1950–). The school is taught by the School Sisters of Notre Dame.

1 priest from the parish.

1865—CHURCH OF ST. CANICE, KILKENNY

Mass was said in the home of Dennis Doyle in 1858 by Reverend G. Keller of Faribault and by others in subsequent years. The first church was erected in 1865 by Reverend M. Cauley, resident pastor; the second in 1880 by Reverend J. Fleming, his successor, who built the rectory in the same year. In 1910 the school and convent were completed by Reverend P. Carey with the Sisters of St. Joseph of Carondelet in charge who were later replaced by the Sisters of St. Joseph of Crookston. The present pastor is Reverend M. Reilly.

8 sisters from the parish.

1865—CHURCH OF ST. MARY, BELLECHESTER

A frame church built in 1865 by Reverend C. J. Knauf (1865-72) was replaced in 1877 by a stone edifice costing $16,000, by Reverend J. Stariha (1872-8), and the present church in 1926 by Reverend J. Zachman (1917-31) after fire had destroyed its predecessor. It was dedicated by Archbishop Dowling on July 17, 1927. On March 29, 1942, fire ruined the interior of this church and it was remodeled and rebuilt by Reverend F. L. Tschann (1934-43), and blessed by Archbishop Murray on November 24, 1942. The original church was changed into a school in 1877 and the School Sisters of Notre Dame took charge in 1881, when the first convent was erected. The present school and convent were built in 1902 by Reverend F. Roemer (1901-9); and the rectory in 1891 by Reverend I. A. Limberg (1889-1901). The pastor is Reverend Anthony Louis (1951–).

1 bishop (Most Reverend Peter W. Bartholome, Coadjutor Bishop of St. Cloud), 6 priests, 1 brother and 16 sisters from the parish.

1866—CHURCH OF ST. GERTRUDE, FOREST CITY

The Benedictine Fathers of St. John's Abbey, Collegeville, Minnesota, built the first church in 1866. It was a mission of Darwin till it was made a separate parish in 1946, when the rectory was built by Reverend M. Lawler. Reverend F. A. Welch is pastor.

1 priest from the parish.

1866—CHURCH OF THE NATIVITY, CLEVELAND

A frame church, without basement, was built in 1866 on the site of the present church by Reverend J. Zuzek (1865-78) of St. Peter, for a congregation of one hundred and fifty persons. The first resident pastor was Reverend John Tori (1878-9). It was a mission of St. Henry, Marysburg, and St. Peter, successively, until 1934. The present church was erected in 1893 by Reverend P. Carey of St. Peter who attended it as a mission from 1892 to 1908. The church was moved to a new site, donated by a non-Catholic, Mr. Hackelroth, in 1923 by Reverend C. McDevitt (1919-26). The interior was refinished in 1943 by Reverend H. V. Green (1942-6). The rectory was built in 1879 and occupied for part of that year by Reverend F. Niebling and part of 1887 by Reverend P. McCabe (1887-92). In 1908 Father Carey sold it for $125, and the new rectory was built in 1945 by Father Green. Mass was said before 1865 in the home of Peter McCabe whose son said his first Mass in the parish on July 3, 1887. On that occasion Father Pryor of Mankato preached in English and Father Maly of St. Henry in German. The Reverend F. X. Weninger, S.J. gave a mission in 1869, and a Father Daly, O.P., in 1878, and inspired three girls to join the Dominican Sisterhood. The settlers in 1860 were Irish from New England and Canada, and Germans from Illinois. The Bohemians came in 1920. Germans were largest in number, the Irish second and the Bohemians third. The present pastor is Reverend A. Cepress.

1 priest and 5 sisters from the parish.

1866—CHURCH OF ST. PIUS V, CANNON FALLS

A small stone church, the cornerstone of which was laid by Father Ireland in 1864, was completed in 1866 under the direction of Reverend P. Bayer who said the first Mass in it. Six years previously Mass was said in the home of Frank Wise by a missionary priest. The parish had a financial struggle after the Civil War from 1865 to 1890 during which only one Catholic family, that of Florian Carnal, settled in the vicinity. Father Bayer said Mass in the parish once or twice a year and, from 1873 to 1876, Reverend J. Pavlin prepared the children for first communion and took a class to Northfield to be confirmed by Bishop Grace in August, 1876, after which the parish became a mission to Belle Creek whence it was served by Reverends J. O'Reilly, H. McDevitt and R. J. Fitzgerald (1886-99) who built the present stone church in 1894, dedicated by Archbishop Ireland in February, 1895. Ten years later Reverend F. X. McDermott was sent to reside in the parish. He razed the original stone church and built the residence in 1907. The diamond jubilee was celebrated on July 19, 1939, during the pastorate of Reverend E. O'Connor (1936-45). Church and rectory were renovated and refurnished and a basement chapel, seating forty-seven, completed by Reverend E. Whelan (1945—) Mass is said once a month in the Mineral Spring Sanitorium five miles away.

2 priests and 7 sisters from the parish.

1866—CHURCH OF OUR LADY OF MOUNT CARMEL, BUDEJOVIE

This church was built for a colony of Czech Catholics on a site two and a half miles west of Montgomery under the supervision of Reverend A. Plut, pastor of New Prague, and was commonly known as the Budweis Church. From 1870 to 1874 it was in charge of his successor, Reverend H. Povolny, a Franciscan, and served by other priests—Father Kimel of New Prague and Father Simonik of Heidelberg—until 1881, when the parish of the Holy Redeemer in Montgomery was organized and included the Catholics of this parish and others in the vicinity. The church and cemetery remain, and the bell in the church tower still tolls for funerals from Montgomery.

1866—CHURCH OF THE HOLY TRINITY, NEW ULM

A small wooden church, begun February 6, 1858, was destroyed during the Indian uprising in August, 1862, before it was completed, for which the U. S. Government paid an indemnity of $325 in 1865. When the cornerstone of the first Church of the Holy Trinity, 97 by 36, was laid on September 1, 1866, by Reverend J. B. Zwinge, O.F.M., there were only twelve Catholic families in New Ulm. It was not ready for occupancy when the first pastor, Reverend A. Berghold (1869-90), came on January 10, 1869. It was dedicated on September 11, 1870, by Bishop Grace, with Pontifical Mass. Father Zuzek preached in German. Forty-five children received first Holy Communion and 159 were confirmed. Father Berghold bought a stable for a rectory in 1869 and it served for that purpose till 1901. A brick convent, built in 1872, dedicated to St. Michael, was used also as a school from 1874, when the Sisters of Christian Charity from Wilkesbarre, Pa., took charge of it till 1881 when a tornado on July 15 practically destroyed the church and unroofed the convent-school. The convent was repaired and the church rebuilt with an addition for the school which was occupied till 1905. St. Michael's Convent was owned by the Sisters till 1927, when the parish bought it for $40,000. The High School of New Ulm was opened in September, 1919, and an annex built in 1920. The name was changed to Holy Trinity High School in 1937. Work on the present brick church was begun March 29, 1890, and it was dedicated by Bishop Cotter on July 20, 1893, during the pastorate of Reverend J. A. Schroeder (1892-8). A new rectory was occupied on January 1, 1901, by Reverend B. H. Sandmeyer (1898-1910), and the present school was blessed by Archbishop Ireland on October 22, 1905. The golden jubilee of the parish was celebrated with a Pontifical Mass by Archbishop Dowling on June 15, 1919, under the direction of Reverend R. Schlinkert (1910-28); and the diamond jubilee in September, 1944, during the pastorate of Reverend H. J. Scherer (1928-48), with Pontifical Mass by Archbishop Murray. The present pastor is Reverend J. Ettel (1951—).

8 priests, 1 brother and 78 sisters from the parish.

1867—CHURCH OF ST. THOMAS, LE SUEUR P. O.

There is a tradition that, prior to the frame church, 36 by 60, without sanctuary rail or pews, built in 1867 under the direction of Reverend A. Berghold, a log church occupied the present site and after being removed therefrom stood in a neighboring yard and was used as a stable for many years. There is record of a baptism in 1859 which would seem to lend color to the belief of a primitive church, as well as a reference to a St. Thomas Church, Le Sueur County, in the Catholic Almanac for 1860. There is no mention of it in subsequent issues. It may have been closed by Bishop Grace because it was too near the church in Derrynane Township. Then, again, there is in the Register's office in Le Center the record of two deeds to fifteen acres of land given to Reverend A. Ravoux, Administrator of the Diocese of St. Paul, by Patrick Cassin and Patrick Ronan on February 2 and 3, 1858, probably the site of the present church which was built in 1883, during the pastorate of Reverend M. Cauley (1881-8) who also erected the priest's house occupied until 1938, when the modern rectory was built by Reverend D. Buckley (1935-46). The church was incorporated in 1882. Father Ravoux deeded the property to Bishop Grace on June 11, 1861, and the Bishop deeded it to the parish on February 4, 1884. The parish is six miles square. The church and the old residence were modernized by Reverend L. Carey (1904-18); and his successor, Reverend W. A. Dobbin (1919-29), decorated the church and erected new Stations of the Cross. The sacristy, razed by fire, was rebuilt by Reverend T. D. O'Connell (1929-35). The roof and steeple were damaged by a storm in the fall of 1949. Repairs and re-decoration, made under the direction of the pastor, Reverend M. Foy, cost about $8,000, partly covered by insurance.

3 priests and 12 sisters from the parish.

1867—CHURCH OF ST. TIMOTHY, EAST MAPLE LAKE

The Reverend I. Schaller of St. Michael, Minnesota, built a church, dedicated to St. Timothy, in this locality about 1867. From 1860 Mass was said from time to time in the homes of Patrick, Jerry and Timothy Desmond and Patrick Butler. Later on it was consolidated with the Church of St. Charles in Chatham to form the parish of Maple Lake. The rectory was built by Father Savey and, with the church, was torn down when the second church was erected in Maple Lake.

1867—CHURCH OF ST. PETER AND PAUL, LORETTO

The log church, 16 by 28, erected in 1867 by Reverend M. Mayr, O.S.B., of Big Crow River (1864-7), was replaced by a frame church, 30 by 35, in 1876, and the log chapel used as a school in charge of lay teachers. The present church was built in 1903 by Reverend A. Vanden Heuvel (1902-10). The first rectory was occupied in 1882 by Father Mayr who was pastor for the second time from 1880 to 1886, while living at Holy Name, and its successor by Reverend A. Kern (1912-21) who also erected the school staffed by the Sisters of Notre Dame whose convent was built by Reverend G. Kaufmann (1929-46) at whose death Reverend W. J. Michel was named pastor, the fifteenth to occupy that position.

2 priests and 11 sisters from the parish.

1867—CHURCH OF ST. BRENDAN, GREEN ISLE

Reverend T. Venn of Henderson built the first church in 1867, but Mass was said as early as 1857 by Father McManus of St. Paul in the homes of Thomas McMahon, Michael Nugent, John McGrann and Patrick O'Meara. In 1882 the present brick structure was erected by the first resident pastor, Reverend T. Ryan (1881-4) who also built the first rectory, replaced in 1891 by the present residence during the pastorate of Reverend John Hand (1884-1909). The Reverend J. Savage is in charge during the absence of the Reverend A. Doyle, who in 1949 returned to Ireland to regain his health after a pastorate of twenty-six years.

1867—CHURCH OF THE ASSUMPTION, ASSUMPTION

It was blessed by Bishop Grace on 1867. It was burned in 1935 and rebuilt by Reverend Jerome Campbell. The present pastor is Reverend Thomas Coleman.

4 priests from the parish.

1868—CHURCH OF ST. MICHAEL, MONTGOMERY TOWNSHIP

This church, built on a ten-acre plot of ground deeded to Bishop Grace by J. Frank Quinlan and wife of Le Sueur County, served as a house of worship for the Irish Catholics of the locality for nearly fifty years when it was closed and the congregation left free to go to Kilkenny or Montgomery though neither claims jurisdiction over them. It was located about four miles south of Montgomery and was incorporated on October 6, 1882. Bishop Grace deeded the property to the corporation on January 26 of the following year. About twenty years ago the church was sold for lumber, but the cemetery is still in use and looked after by a committee of laymen. In the early days the people were ministered to by priests from Shieldsville.

1868—CHURCH OF ST. NICHOLAS, CARVER

The church, built in 1868, by Reverend M. Mayr, O.S.B., has never had a resident pastor. It was served by the Franciscan Fathers residing at Chaska till 1917 at Sacred Heart Church, St. Paul, till 1931, and since then at Chaska, Reverend V Scherrer, O.F.M. acting pastor. The bell tower was added in 1880 by Reverend C Lohrbacher, O.F.M. A school with living quarters for the sisters was erected by Mrs. Susanna Zanger on grounds adjoining the church in 1876 and the Sisters of St Benedict had charge until 1881, when a Sister of Christian Charity took over, walking daily from the convent in Chaska for a year. From 1882 till 1917 the school was taught by lay teachers.

3 sisters from the parish.

1868—CHURCH OF THE JAPANESE MARTYRS, LEAVENWORTH

The first church was built in 1868 by Reverend A. Berghold of New Ulm of whic it was a mission until transferred to Sleepy Eye to which it was attached until 193 when it became an independent parish with Reverend F. Plaschko (1935-9) a pastor who built the church and rectory. The present pastor is Reverend H. Sterner (1948—).

1868—CHURCH OF ST. JOSEPH, ROSEMOUNT

Reverend A. Oster of Burnsville built the first church in 1868, three miles from the site of the present church on land donated by Thomas Hyland. It was destroyed by a cyclone on May 7, 1881, and rebuilt in the village the next year by Reverend M. Quinn (1878-82). The third church was erected in 1924 by the pastor, Very Reverend L. Carey (1918—). The rectory he occupies was built in 1905 by Reverend T. Moore (1903-10) to replace one erected by Reverend J. Glennon (1877-8) in the first year of his pastorate. Three Benedictine Sisters from Farmington teach catechism on Tuesday afternoon to the Catholic pupils of the consolidated school during the release period. Reverend James Furey is Administrator.

1 priest and 6 sisters from the parish.

1868—CHURCH OF ST. JOHN THE BAPTIST, ROCKY RUN

This was the mother church of Holy Trinity parish, Winsted, and was built about six miles west of it, under the supervision of Reverend C. Robert, a missionary of the early days, at the behest of a group of French Catholics of whom the leaders were Pierre and Adolph Crevier, Joseph Lemire, Antoine Rivard, Nicholas and Auguste Violet. It was 40 by 26 feet in dimensions; and the contractor was Auguste Violet. It is said that Father Ireland frequently came to the parish and said Mass in the church, walking the distance from St. Paul and visiting the scattered Catholic families along the way. Less than a year after the completion of the church a number of German Catholics belonging to the congregation petitioned Bishop Grace for permission to erect a more central church in Winsted which gradually absorbed the parent parish, and the church was closed after a brief existence. It was destroyed by fire of unknown origin some years ago, the foundations were removed and the site converted into a field. The only remaining landmark is the cemetery in which lie buried forty-two of the original parishioners.

1869—CHURCH OF SS. PETER AND PAUL, BELLE PLAINE

The first church, erected in 1869, was destroyed by a storm before completion. It was rebuilt by Reverend J. Schenk (1869-73), dedicated by Bishop Grace on December 8, 1871, and assigned to the Franciscan Fathers in July, 1875, and since then eighteen members of the Order have served the parish. The present church was erected in 1905 by Reverend R. Holte, O.F.M. (1899-1905), and blessed by Archbishop Ireland on November 12. The school was built in 1878 with the Franciscan Sisters of Milwaukee in charge for nine years when they were replaced by the Sisters of St. Benedict. In 1895 and 1907 additions were made to the original building and for several years it was attended by children from the neighboring parish. It is served by Reverend Conwan McCurren, O.F.M., residing at Jordan.

3 priests, 1 brother and 18 sisters from the parish.

1869—CHURCH OF ST. DOMINIC, NORTHFIELD

About the year 1865 Father Keller said Mass in the home of William Ryan and urged the few Catholics to build a church. A small frame church, without sanctuary, sacristy or steeple, was blessed August 4, 1869, the feast of St. Dominic, by Bishop Grace, who appointed Reverend R. Haase (1869-70) first pastor. A cottage was purchased for a rectory in 1875 by Reverend J. Pavlin, who added sanctuary, sacristy, pews, vestibule, and steeple to the church. In 1892 a new parochial residence was built by Reverend T. Gleeson (1890-4). The present brick church was erected at a cost of $32,800 in 1914 by Reverend P. F. Meade (1910-41) who also built the school which was opened in September, 1927, under the supervision of the School Sisters of Notre Dame. The church was dedicated by Archbishop Ireland on February 26, 1914. The present pastor is Reverend W. L. Howley (1942—).

3 priests and 8 sisters from the parish.

1870—CHURCH OF ST. BONIFACE, HASTINGS

A frame church was dedicated on November 13, 1870, by Reverend G. Scherer,

O.S.B. (1870-80) and the present church built in 1893 by Reverend O. Erren, O. S.B. (1890-1904), and dedicated by Archbishop Ireland on June 18. A temporary school used from 1872 to 1874, was replaced by one taught by the Sisters of St. Joseph till 1889 when the Sisters of St. Benedict were placed in charge. The new school was completed in 1917 by Reverend W. Schneppenheim, O.S.B. (1916-21) and the rectory, built in 1884, was remodeled into a convent in 1919, when a new rectory was built. The pastor is Reverend L. Beckwerth, O.S.B. (1950-) who built a new convent in 1951.

8 priests, 2 brothers and 17 sisters from the parish.

1870—CHURCH OF THE SACRED HEART, RUSH CITY

The first church was built in 1870 by Father Murphy of Stillwater; the second was begun in 1883 and completed in 1887 by Reverend P. Carey. The parish formed part of the Vicariate of Northern Minnesota from 1874 to 1889, and several parishes were carved from its original territory. The present brick church was erected in 1905 by Reverend R. V. Kennedy (1903-8) and rebuilt after the fire in 1939 by Reverend J. C. O'Hara (1938-40). The parish was served by twenty-two pastors up to 1947, when the Reverend R. J. Payant, the present incumbent, was appointed. The first rectory was built about 1875 by Reverend W. Wilkens (1874-8) and occupied till 1902 when a residence was rented until 1921, when the present rectory was constructed by Reverend J. T. Fitzgerald (1918-22). There is no parish school.

4 sisters from the parish.

1870—CHURCH OF THE GUARDIAN ANGELS, OAKDALE

Mass was said in the parish as early as 1857 by Reverend G. Keller and others down to 1870 when a frame church, 34 by 28, was built and served by visiting priests till 1885 when the Reverend F. X. Gores, first pastor, erected the present church and priest's house and ministered to the spiritual needs of the congregation till 1898. The church was dedicated by Bishop Grace on November 1, 1886. Reverend P. O'Neill has been in charge since 1937.

1870—CHURCH OF ST. LAWRENCE, FARIBAULT

In 1869 Bishop Grace gave the German Catholics of Faribault permission to form their own parish. A small frame church in which the first Mass was said on February 2, 1870, by Reverend C. Scheve, was built on a different site from that occupied by the present stone structure erected in 1876 by Reverend L. Zavatski (1875-6), enlarged and remodeled by Reverend V. Schiffrer (1933-8), and rededicated by Archbishop Murray on October 21, 1934. It was refurnished in 1946 by Reverend F. Tschann (1943-). A school was built by Reverend J. Van Leent (1881-8) and is taught by the Sisters of St. Dominic residing in the adjoining convent. The new school was erected in 1913 by Reverend F. H. Smalian (1912-22) and the convent in 1921. The present rectory was built about 1896 by Reverend F. Elshorst (1896-1910).

1 priest from the parish.

1871—CHURCH OF ST. LOUIS, WHEATLAND

As early as 1855 Father Ravoux said Mass in the settlement, then known as Centertown, in the home of Thomas Lambert who donated ten acres for the church built in 1871, about three miles north of the village on the shore of Cody Lake, a site now occupied by a public school. It was attended by Father Keller from Faribault for several years and then became a mission of Shieldsville with Mass every other Sunday. In 1903 the congregation was merged with that of the Immaculate Conception parish of Lonsdale, incorporated on March 11, 1903, and of which Reverend F. Bouska became pastor on September 8, 1905. At that time there were no more than twenty families in the Wheatland parish. The church was dismantled in 1916 and the land, with the exception of the cemetery, sold to Thomas Skluzacek Between 1860 and 1911 there were eighty-six burials in the cemetery of whom fifty-six have markers. One of the marked graves is that of Joseph Jack Fraser, half-breed Sioux known as "Iron Face", a United States scout and interpreter, who died in 1869 at the age of seventy. He made a heroic and successful effort to giv the alarm to Fort Snelling when Fort Ridgley was attacked by savages, and General Sibley placed the headstone over his grave. The early settlers of Wheatland were French and Irish, the former in the majority. One of the latter, Patrick Wilby, born in Ireland in 1817, built the first frame house in Wheatland in 1857 with lumber hauled from St. Paul. The Lonsdale church is located on his farm.

The Most Reverend Louis B. Kucera, Bishop of Lincoln, Nebraska, was born in the parish.

1871—CHURCH OF ST. THOMAS, JESSENLAND

There is a tradition in the parish of one, perhaps, two churches prior to 1871, built by Reverends V. Sommereisen of Mankato, and T. Venn who erected the present church in 1873. He was succeeded by Reverend J. W. Nealis (1873-80) who built the rectory in 1875, and under whom the first baptism, in 1874, was recorded. The church was notably renovated by Reverend A. J. Coyle (1913-23), Reverend P. J. Callanan (1932-44), and by the present pastor, Reverend W. P. Delaney (1944—). There is a record of an Irish settlement in Jessenland in 1854, and in the cemetery there are tombstones bearing dates as early as 1852. There is no parish school but Saturday religious classes are taught by sisters from the neighboring parishes.

1 priest from the parish.

1871—CHURCH OF ST. PHILIP, LITCHFIELD

The first church was a room in the rectory built by Reverend A. Hurley (1871-2). The frame building now used as a residence for the pastor was built in 1887 by Reverend P. J. Boland (1886-1931). The first church was built in 1882 by Reverend P. Kenny on the site of the present one erected in 1921 by Reverend P. J. Boland, decorated by Reverend C. F. Doran (1932-8) and again by Reverend E. J. Cogwin (1941-6). In 1935 Father Doran opened a catechetical school in a large brick house opposite the parochial residence and placed it in charge of four Sisters of St. Benedict from St. Joseph, Minnesota. It began with an enrollment of one hundred and one children in religious classes, release and otherwise, eighteen in kindergarten and sixteen in the music department. In a few years the number in the religious classes rose to three hundred and fifty-seven with twenty-four in the kindergarten. In August, 1947, property was bought for a new school by Reverend C. F. Foley (1946—). It is claimed that Mass was first said in the home of John Dougherty in 1859 by Reverend C. Wittmann, O.S.B.

3 priests and 3 sisters from the parish.

1871—CHURCH OF ST. AGATHA, VERMILLION

This frame church, 24 by 56, was erected by Reverend J. Halton for the Irish Catholics of the vicinity as distinguished from the Germans who had their own Church of St. John about four miles to the northeast. It was attended once a month by the priests from Mendota who served the Church of St. Patrick, Inver Grove, and the resident pastors who succeeded them in 1880. On the other Sundays of the month the people went to Inver Grove or Rosemount which was nearer. The original church was replaced by a larger one on the same site about 1899. This was struck by lightning twice, the second stroke being followed by fire which reduced it to ashes probably in 1913. It was re-built, under the same name, at Coates, on the railroad, less than a mile from the original site, and continued as a mission of Inver Grove until St. Patrick's church was burned in September, 1919.

2 priests (Right Reverend John A. and Reverend L. F. Ryan) and 3 sisters from the parish.

1871—CHURCH OF ST. MARY, WILLMAR

Reverend A. Hurley said the first Mass in M. P. Moran's store and built the first church in 1871. The parish was a mission of DeGraff until 1888 and of Litchfield until 1900, when the Reverend J. J. Molloy (1900—9) became the first resident pastor, built the rectory and bought ground for a new church. The church was rebuilt and enlarged in the nineties and again in 1921. A convent was purchased in

1939 by Reverend P. Kenny (1926–) and placed in charge of four Sisters of the Presentation from Aberdeen, South Dakota, who conduct a catechetical school. In 1926 Father Kenny built the present rectory to replace an older structure.

3 priests and 1 sister from the parish.

1872—CHURCH OF ST. COLUMBANUS, GREENLEAF

It was attended by Reverend Thomas M. Cahill from 1872 to 1874 as a mission of Litchfield to which it was attached until July, 1901, when it became a mission of Hutchinson. It was incorporated by Reverend Patrick J. Boland, pastor of Litchfield, January 17, 1896. There were no services held in the church from 1922 to 1937 when it was reopened. A new concrete building replaced the old wooden structure in 1950.

1872—CHURCH OF ST. NICHOLAS, MIDDLE LAKE

The Reverend J. Zuzek who built the church about 1872 had charge of the parish for twelve years. It has always been a mission, successively of St. Peter, New Ulm, Nicollet and now of Brighton (Swan Lake) and is attended by Reverend Otto Neudecker, pastor of Brighton. In early days it was a center of Catholic activities with outdoor processions on certain feast days and outside Stations of the Cross, the first in the locality. The first mission was held in 1881, according to the date inscribed on a mission cross made of black walnut from the local woods and preserved in the church.

1873—CHURCH OF THE ASSUMPTION, BEAR CREEK

This was a small church, built in 1873, four miles south of Silver Lake, by a group of Czech Catholics from eastern and southern Bohemia with accessions from other sections in Minnesota. Before that date itinerant missionaries said Mass in private homes, among them Father Stern (known locally as Father Huczda), a French priest whose name is unknown, and Father Juskiewicz. After the church was built Father Steinacher celebrated Mass in it from 1872 to 1875; Father Sulak, S. J. of Chicago, from 1876 to 1877; Father Povolny, pastor of Winsted, from 1878 to 1882, and the pastor of St. Adalbert's Church, Silver Lake, from 1882 to 1893, when his successor, Reverend F. Jiranek, was given charge of the Bohemian Catholics of Bear Creek. In the meantime the Czech population of Silver Lake had increased and the need of a church for them was apparent. On April 6, 1895, St. Joseph's Church was incorporated with Bear Creek as a mission and on Christmas day the Reverend J. Cermak took charge as pastor, built the church and the rectory the next year and remained until 1906. He was succeeded by Reverend W. J. Skluzacek who closed the mission church and dismantled it. The cemetery, opened in 1867, is still used for the burial of old Czech Catholic settlers.

1873—CHURCH OF ST. JOSEPH, MIESVILLE

The original church, built in 1873 by the Reverend G. Scherer, O.S.B. of Hastings, was torn down in 1908, a year after the present church was erected by Reverend J. Mies (1900-10). The latter was destroyed by fire in 1912 and rebuilt the same year by Reverend L. Keukelink (1910-28). It was redecorated in 1947 by Reverend F. J. Plaschko (1946-7). The first rectory was built probably in 1882 and the second in 1902 by Father Mies. Reverend G. H. Galles became pastor in 1948.

1 sister from the parish.

1873—CHURCH OF ST. JOSEPH, TAYLOR'S FALLS

The local community built a frame church in 1873. It was successively a mission of Stillwater, Rush City, Forest Lake and North Branch, until it was made an independent parish in September, 1948, with Reverend F. E. Shea as first pastor with the Church of St. Francis, Franconia Township, as a mission. The church was enlarged in 1942 by Reverend B. Murray. The present pastor is Reverend Oscar Winzerling.

1874—CHURCH OF ST. EDWARD, RICHLAND

The first Mass in Richland Township was said by Reverend G. Keller of Faribault in December, 1858, in the home of Mr. Moore and later in the homes of Andrew Malloy and Samuel Nolan. Ground for the church was donated by John Degnan and for the cemetery by Samuel Nolan. The present church was erected in 1874 by Reverend C. Scheve (1872-4), pastor of the Immaculate Conception Church, Faribault, of which it was a mission until 1944, when it was attached to Kenyon. The church was renovated in 1931 by Reverend P. J. Ryan, assistant pastor of the Immaculate Conception Church in Faribault. As a mission of Kenyon it is served by Reverend Francis M. Hayden. Before 1944 catechism was taught after Mass on Sundays; but since then on Saturdays and during the summer vacation by the Dominican Sisters of Faribault.

6 sisters from the parish.

1874—CHURCH OF ST. PATRICK, BIRCH COULEE

Before a church was built Father Berghold of New Ulm said Mass once a month in the home of Patrick Ryan. The church and pastor's house were erected one mile east of his place, in 1874, by Father Brennan; the second church was built three miles north of Franklin in 1898 by Reverend J. J. O'Connor of Morton of which it was a mission. It was destroyed by fire 1945 and rebuilt by Reverend M. A. Keeler of Franklin about 1946. It is smaller than its predecessor as the parish has dwindled from 125 to 30 families. In 1935 St. Patrick's became a mission to Franklin and is attended by the present pastor, Reverend Louis J. Heitzer (1950–).

2 priests and 10 sisters from the parish.

1874—CHURCH OF THE HOLY TRINITY, VESELI

The present church was erected in 1905 by Reverend A. Kotouc (1904-10) to replace a frame church built by the early settlers between 1874-8 and blessed by Reverend J. Simonik (1877-81). The first resident pastor, Reverend J. Pribyl (1881-2) was followed by twelve others prior to 1927 when Reverend R. M. Bastyr was appointed. The first school, erected by Father Pribyl in 1881 had lay teachers until 1912, when the School Sisters of St. Francis from Milwaukee came and the present school was built in 1916 by Reverend W. J. Jiracek (1910-21), and a new rectory and convent in 1926 by Reverend J. J. Bouska (1921-30). The first parish house was completed by Father Pribyl in 1881. Reverend Stanley J. Srnec is the present pastor (1950–).

7 priests and 4 sisters from the parish.

1875—CHURCH OF ST. JOSEPH, WACONIA

The first brick church was erected in 1875 in the parish which is said to date back to 1858. The name of Reverend G. Scherer, O.S.B., is found in the baptismal registers of 1861, 1864 and 1865. Others followed until 1894, when the parish was served by the Franciscan Fathers. The present church was built in 1900 by Reverend R. Moehle, O.F.M. (1899-1909). In 1909 the Franciscan Fathers left the parish to take over the Sacred Heart parish in St. Paul, and were succeeded by Reverend J. Stelmes (1909-35). The Reverend J. Kauer became pastor in 1950.

1875—CHURCH OF ST. STEPHEN, ANOKA

Reverend E. Arth said Mass on August 15, 1856, at the home of Peter Donnelly. In 1875 the Congregational church was purchased. The present brick church was erected in 1888 by Father Brennan; the rectory was built in 1905 by Reverend O. Dolphin. St. Anne's Convent was opened by the Sisters of Mercy in 1881 and taken over by the Sisters of St. Joseph in 1890, and by the Presentation Sisters of Aberdeen, South Dakota, in 1945. A new school was dedicated in 1950 by the present pastor, Reverend W. F. Murphy (1949–).

6 priests from the parish.

1876—CHURCH OF THE ASSUMPTION, RICHFIELD

The first church, dedicated to St. Valentine, was blessed by Bishop Grace in June, 1876. Ten years later it was destroyed by fire and rebuilt under the present name by Reverend B. Sandmeyer of St. Elizabeth's parish, Minneapolis, dedicated by Bishop Grace in June, 1887, and incorporated on July 13, 1891. In April, 1894, it was attached as a mission to the Bohemian parish of Our Lady of Perpetual Help, Minneapolis. A school taught by lay teachers was held in the basement of the church from 1887 to 1900 when a school and a convent were opened with the Sisters of St. Benedict in charge. A rectory was built in 1900 when Reverend B. Vonderlage became resident pastor. The Reverend P. Schmitz, O.M.I. (1916-50) built a larger school in 1917 and modernized it in 1946, as well as the rectory which was remodeled in 1923. The present pastor is Reverend Emil Twardochleb, O.M.I.

1 Mitered Abbot (Right Reverend Bruno Doerfler, O.S.B.), 6 priests, 2 brothers and 26 sisters from the parish.

1876—CHURCH OF ST. CHARLES, CHATHAM

This church was erected by Reverend I. Schaller of St. Michael's in 1876. Reverend C. Robert had charge of the parish from 1880 to 1885. In that year Father Savey succeeded Reverend J. A. Jacobs who had been pastor for a few months and in 1887 moved to Maple Lake where he had built a small church previous to that date and then a larger one torn down by Father Francis O'Brien.

1876—CHURCH OF ST. MARY, HELP OF CHRISTIANS, SLEEPY EYE

The original frame church, 40 by 70, was built in 1876 and opened in September of that year, by Reverend A. Berghold who, from 1869 to 1875, said Mass in different homes in the parish. The first resident pastor was Reverend H. B. Sandmeyer (1878-84). The church was enlarged in 1889 by Reverend J. Tori (1885-90). The fine new brick church, costing $68,000, begun in 1900, was completed two years later by Reverend W. M. Stulz (1900-14), frescoed and redecorated by Reverend A. J. Koller (1943–). The parochial school, built in 1883, served also as a residence for the Sisters of the Third Order of St. Francis of Rochester until 1911 when the old parish house, erected in August, 1879, was made available for them until their new convent was ready for occupancy in the spring of 1920. It cost $36,500 and was built by Reverend J. Klein (1914-24). The residence for the clergy was erected in 1904 by Monsignor Stulz at a cost of $15,000, and was remodeled by Reverend F. Rant (1928-33). The new school was completed in 1914 and cost $63,644.95; the first high school commencement was held in 1918. The science hall and auditorium were put up in 1939 for $90,000, under the supervision of Reverend Anthony Scholzen, and a new high school by Reverend Andrew Koller in 1951.

10 diocesan, 3 religious priests and 32 sisters from the parish.

1876—CHURCH OF ST. PATRICK, KANDIYOHI

The small church erected in 1876 was enlarged by Reverend P. J. Boland of Litchfield of which it was a mission until 1900, when it was attached to Willmar until 1933, when it became an independent parish with Reverend W. Murphy as resident pastor (1933-5). In 1943, during the pastorate of Reverend J. Lord (1941-7) it was made a mission to Regal, its former mission, which then became the home of the resident pastor, now the Reverend Bernard P. Schreiner.

1 priest from the parish.

1876—CHURCH OF ST. BRIDGET, DE GRAFF

The first church, dedicated to Our Lady of Kildare, was built in 1876 by Reverend F. J. Swift (1876-80) who also erected a larger church. In 1901 the fine brick church of the present was erected by Reverend W. P. Walsh (1900-10). A modern brick rectory was built in 1937 by Reverend J. Troy (1936-41). The present pastor is Reverend Melvin J. Blais.

1 priest and 1 sister from the parish.

1877—CHURCH OF THE HOLY NAME, MEDINA (WAYZATA P. O.)

A log chapel antedated the frame church built in 1877 by Reverend G. Keller. The first pastor was Reverend J. Czarnovski (1877-9). It had fifteen pastors prior to 1912 when the present church was completed by Reverend G. Scheffold, O.S.B. (1912-25) who also built the rectory after fire had destroyed the church and residence in 1911. The school was opened in 1913 with the Sisters of St. Benedict in charge. Reverend Edward Botzet, O.S.B., is the pastor.

3 priests and 4 sisters from the parish.

1877—CHURCH OF ST. BONIFACE, STEWART

A small frame church was built south of the village in 1877 by Reverend F. Andrew (1877-81). It was hauled to the town, rebuilt and enlarged by Reverend A. Kober (1883-92). The present brick church was erected in 1902 by Reverend S. Joerge, O.S.B. (1901-5). The school and rectory were built in 1927 by Reverend A. E. Rhode (1926-34). The school is under the direction of four Sisters of St. Joseph from Crookston, Minnesota. The present pastor is Reverend J. F. Stolz (1944—). All the records prior to 1893 were destroyed by fire in the fall of 1892.

1877—CHURCH OF THE MOST HOLY TRINITY, WINSTED

An iron cross stamped with the date 1869 is all that remains of the primitive chapel built in that year under the supervision of Henry Weinbach. Mass was said in it probably by Father Steinacher. A frame church was built in 1877 by Reverend H. Povolny, O.S.F. (1877-84) who also built the first rectory; the second church was erected in 1886 by Reverend F. Elshorst (1884-94) and enlarged and decorated in 1944 by Reverend W. Wey (1933-44). The school was taught by the Sisters of St. Francis of Rochester, Minnesota, from 1882 to 1901, when the Sisters of St. Francis of Milwaukee took charge. The second grade school was built in 1907 by Reverend I. Limberg (1901-8); the high school in 1926 by Reverend F. H. Smalian (1925-33); the rectory in 1902 by Father Limberg. The present pastor is Reverend F. J. Plaschko (1947—).

7 priests, 1 brother and 61 sisters from the parish.

1877—CHURCH OF ALL SAINTS, LAKEVILLE

The first church, 100 by 36, was built by Reverend A. Oster and attended by him from Rosemount. The present church was erected in 1932 by Reverend W. L. Hart (1919-38). The first resident priest was Reverend M. Quinn (1885-1904) and the present pastor is Reverend E. O'Connor (1945—). There is no school but three Sisters of the Divine Savior from Milwaukee have a convent in the parish and teach catechism during release periods.

1878—CHURCH OF THE SACRED HEART, FARIBAULT

The original church, 92 by 40, was erected by the people in 1878. The first resident pastor was Reverend J. Leonard (1879-80) who built the rectory replaced in 1905 by a more modern home constructed by Reverend E. Monge (1896-1918) who purchased a large residence for a school opened in September 1916 under the direction of the Sisters of St. Dominic from Bethlehem Academy. Reverend I. Domestici who was appointed pastor in 1919 and laid the cornerstone of the present church on March 7, 1922, resigned the pastorate in 1950 and was succeeded by Reverend J. A. Schabert (1950-51). The present pastor is Reverend Cecil T. Houle.

1878—CHURCH OF ST. ROSE OF LIMA, CHERRY GROVE

The stone church was erected in 1878 by Reverend J. Stariha of Red Wing and was a mission assigned to Belle Creek till 1890 and to Pine Island until 1939, when it was attached to Zumbrota and is now served by Reverend R. G. Dillon (1951—).

2 sisters from the parish.

1878—CHURCH OF ST. JOHN, DARWIN

It was built in 1878 by Reverend J. McDermott (1875-87) who said the first

Mass in it on December 8, and who also constructed the first rectory, replaced in 1912 by one erected by Reverend W. A. Dobbin (1902-17). St. Charles parish hall, now St. Joseph's hall, was built about 1895 by Reverend P. J. McCabe (1893-1901) and moved to its present location in 1900. The present pastor is Reverend J. J. Campbell (1945–).

2 priests and 5 sisters from the parish.

1878—CHURCH OF ST. MICHAEL, PINE ISLAND

It was built in 1878 under the direction of Reverend M. Bruton (1877-9). A new altar was put in the church in 1916 by Reverend O. F. Rice (1893-1919). The parochial residence was erected in 1920 by Reverend J. C. O'Hara (1919-30). The present pastor Reverend P. J. McCann was appointed in 1945. There is no school but the Sisters of St. Francis from Rochester, Minnesota, teach catechism every week.

1 Archbishop (Most Reverend James J. Keane, of Dubuque,) 1 priest and 1 sister from the parish.

1878—CHURCH OF ST. MALACHY, CLONTARF

The church and the rectory were built in 1878 by Reverend A. Oster (1878-98) who also built the second church in 1896. A hall was erected by the Hibernians in 1899. The present pastor is Reverend R. G. King (1933–).

3 sisters from the parish.

1878—CHURCH OF ST. RAPHAEL, SPRINGFIELD

The first church was begun in 1878 by Reverend A. Berghold of New Ulm, and completed by Reverend B. H. Sandmeyer in 1879 who said the first Mass in it before it was plastered or furnished. The first resident pastor was Father O'Haire (1881-2) and he has had fourteen successors. The present brick church was built in 1915 by Reverend H. P. Fey (1910-16). The first school was erected in 1900 by Reverend A. Wirth, O.S.B. (1898-1901); the second in 1940, at a cost of $81,000, by Reverend I. Schumacher (1928-51). Reverend W. M. Stulz (1883-5) purchased the first rectory in 1883; the second, built by Reverend L. Haas (1886-90), was moved to a new location, enlarged and brick-veneered for use as a convent by the Sisters of St. Francis in charge of the school. The present parochial residence was built in 1917 by Reverend F. S. Rant (1916-28). The Reverend V. Schiffrer succeeded Father Schumacher after his death in 1951.

2 priests and 11 sisters from the parish.

1879—CHURCH OF ST. ANNE, HAMEL

The church was built in 1879 by the parishioners before the arrival of Reverend Z. L. Chandonnet (1879-80), and its successor in 1934 by Reverend M. Masl (1918-47). The first rectory was built in 1879 for Father Chandonnet and the second in 1914 by Reverend J. Perigord (1914-7). The Reverend L. R. Morin was named pastor in 1947. The granite mausoleum of Dr. and Mrs. A. A. Laurent is built on the church property adjoining the parish cemetery.

2 priests and 1 sister from the parish.

1879—CHURCH OF THE HOLY TRINITY, WATERVILLE

It was built probably in 1879 by Reverend A. Christie of Waseca, afterwards Archbishop of Oregon City, Oregon. The first baptism took place February 19, 1880, and the first marriage on June 3. The first resident pastor was Reverend P. J. Lucey (1892-4) who built the priest's house in 1892. The Reverend J. MacCormac was named pastor in 1941, and built a new church in 1951.

1 priest, 2 sisters from the parish.

1880—CHURCH OF ST. MARGARET, HOPKINS

The settlement served by St. Margaret's Church, three miles southwest of Hopkins was started in 1867, by six Czech Catholic families, and Mass was said in private homes by Reverend H. Povolny, a Franciscan, in 1867, and by Reverend C. Augus tinsky in 1878. In 1879 Vaclav Dvorak donated land for a church and cemetery and labor for the erection of the former in which the first Mass was celebrated July 1, 1880, by Reverend F. Tichy of New Prague who continued to serve the mission until 1886, when Reverend J. Rynda of St. Paul, took charge until 1890. From that time until 1920 it was attended by the pastors of the Church of Our Lady of Perpetual Help, Minneapolis — Reverend F. Simonik for three years, Reverend F. Hrachovsky until 1904, and Reverend J. F. Hovorka until 1920. Father Hovorka said Mass there every two weeks for a congregation of nearly ninety families. In 1920 Archbishop Dowling decided to unite the Irish congregation of Hopkins with the Czech congregation of St. Margaret's in a new parish in Hopkins, which was done after some opposition on the part of the Czechs who, for a time, continued to assist at devotions in their own church conducted by the organist. The issuance of an interdict brought about their submission and in 1921 the Reverend C. E. Hovorka was appointed pastor of the new parish of St. Joseph, and the old Church of St. Margaret was torn down.

1 sister from the parish.

1880—CHURCH OF ST. MARY, ARLINGTON

It was erected in 1880 by an unknown priest, one mile from the present site and moved into town in 1894 by Reverend P. Rosen. It had eighteen pastors prior to 1926, when the Reverend J. Ellerbush was appointed. The parochial residence was erected in 1910 by Reverend F. Rant (1904-16).

1880—CHURCH OF ST. MARY, BECHYN

The first church was erected somewhere in the vicinity in 1880 by Reverend H. Povolny, O.F.M. of Winsted who said Mass in it three times a year from 1880 to 1887, and visited by eight other priests prior to 1910 when it was made a mission to Redwood Falls till 1932. The present church was erected in 1915 by Reverend J. J. Tomek. The first resident pastor was his brother, Reverend F. J. Tomek (1932-40), who built the rectory in 1932. Reverend M. Skoblik became pastor in 1948.

7 sisters from the parish.

1880—CHURCH OF THE HOLY ROSARY, GRACEVILLE

A temporary church was built by Reverend T. Ryan (1879-81). This church was torn down and replaced with a neater one by Father Pelisson; the third by Reverend C. Genis (1884-92) and the rectory about 1886. It is still in use. The church was burned in 1894 and a brick church erected by Reverend M. O'Brien (1896-1908) was dedicated in November, 1897, by Archbishop Ireland. It was decorated in 1946 by the present pastor, Reverend P. J. O'Connor, appointed in 1933. St. Mary's Academy and convent, a grade and high school, was built in 1900 and is conducted by the Sisters of St. Joseph. It took the place of a school for white and Indian girls established in 1886 and destroyed by fire in 1898.

5 priests and 4 sisters from the parish.

1880—CHURCH OF ST. AGNES, HEGBERT

The church was built in 1880 by Reverend A. Oster of Clontarf. It has always been a mission and has been attended from Clontarf since 1935.

1881—CHURCH OF ST. MARY, BIRD ISLAND

A chapel in the rectory built in 1881 by Reverend F. Elshorst (1880-1) was used for divine services till 1884 when a frame church was erected during the pastorate of Reverend A. Kober (1881-1902), and the modern brick church in 1951 by Reverend Stephen Adrian (1949—) who also built a new convent for the sisters. The second rectory dates from 1893. It was enlarged for the Sisters' convent in 1896 when the third pastoral residence was opened. A brick school was erected in 1898; a grade school in 1913; and a high school, costing $90,000, in 1925, by Reverend A. Scholzen (1910-33). The Sisters of St. Joseph teach in the school.

8 priests and 19 sisters from the parish.

1881—CHURCH OF ST. FRANCIS, BENSON

The first church, dating from 1881, was replaced by the present brick edifice in 1917 by the first resident pastor, Reverend P. M. Shea (1898-1947), who had built the rectory some years previously. The parish was incorporated on December 10, 1881. Reverend R. E. Doerrer has been in charge of it since 1947. Vacation school is taught by the Sisters of the Presentation since 1945.

3 priests and 12 sisters from the parish.

1881—CHURCH OF THE MOST HOLY REDEEMER, MONTGOMERY

In 1858 a church dedicated to St. Michael was built four miles south of Montgomery, and in 1868 a church dedicated to the Blessed Virgin two miles west of it by Father Plut of New Prague. The Reverend H. Povolny, O.F.M. erected a frame church in Montgomery in 1881, which served the Catholics of these parishes, which ceased to exist; and Reverend J. Pribyl, appointed first resident pastor (1881-8), built the rectory. A combination school and convent was put up in 1887 and from 1889 was in charge of the Sisters of St. Benedict. It was known as St. Agnes parochial school. The new parish house was built in 1895 by Reverend F. Pozek (1895-1905); a new St. Raphael School by Reverend E. Polasek (1905-37), who also built the convent in 1932, and the present church dedicated by Archbishop Dowling on November 25, 1924. A large addition to the school was begun in February, 1949, by Reverend F. J. Tomek (1946–).

3 priests and 12 sisters from the parish.

1881—CHURCH OF ST. BONIFACE, ST. BONIFACIUS

A log and a frame chapel were destroyed by fire prior to 1881 when the present church was built and enlarged by the Franciscan Fathers. The first resident pastor was Reverend F. Jaeger (1908-20) who built the priest's house in 1909, the present frame church in 1911 and the brick convent. The school, first taught by the Sisters of Christian Charity, is now in charge of the Sisters of St. Benedict. The Reverend K. Wohlfort was named pastor in 1944.

14 sisters from the parish.

1881—CHURCH OF ST. MARY, WHITE BEAR

Masses were said in the public school and in the Markoe residence from time to time by visiting priests between 1874 and 1881 when the original frame church was built by Reverend J. Goiffon (1881-3). It was unplastered and windowless when dedicated by Bishop Grace on August 15, 1881, and a packing case served as an altar. The parish comprised about two hundred and fifty souls in all. Bishop Ireland preached in the church on the first anniversary of its dedication. Several pastors ministered to the spiritual needs of the people prior to 1891 when Reverend D. F. Lee was placed in charge and two years later he enlarged the church by adding to its length and building a sacristy. At the beginning of the century the parish had about seven hundred souls and the Reverend P. R. Cunningham increased the capacity of the church and installed a better heating system. The parochial school was built in 1914 by Reverend P. J. Hart (1908-15) and placed in charge of the Sisters of St. Joseph who occupied a frame residence at some distance from the church before moving into a convent opposite the present church where they resided until November 29, 1925, when they moved to the new brick convent erected by Reverend J. Fahey (1915-36). During his pastorate a new church — a replica of the old stone Church of St. Mary in St. Paul — was built on a different site and presented to the parish by four daughters of the late James J. Hill who formerly worshipped in the latter church. It was dedicated on November 27, 1926, by the Right Reverend J. C. Byrne, who was pastor of St. Mary's in St. Paul, from 1911 to 1916. The pastor, Reverend Nicholas Finn, lives in a house beside the church and dedicated an addition of several rooms and a gymnasium to the school in 1951.

1882—CHURCH OF ST. JOSEPH, STILLWATER

The parish was organized for the accommodation of the French Canadian worker, in the lumber industry and with their departure it lost its national character and importance. The first pastor was Reverend Eugene Roy (1882-7). He had several successors at frequent intervals before Reverend C. Pettigrew came in 1895 and remained eight years. On June 16, 1897, the steeple of the church was damaged by lightning. The Reverend Jules Perigord (1917-9) met a tragic death, with the Benedictine pastor of the neighboring St. Mary's Church, in a collision between his auto and a train at Bald Eagle. He was succeeded by Father Vanden Bosch who, in 1938, gave place to the present pastor, Reverend W. C. Soulard, who renovated the church and beautified the grounds.

1882—CHURCH OF ST. JOHN, VERMILLION

The first church was built in 1882 by the German Catholics of the locality without the knowledge of Bishop Grace. It was within four miles of St. Agatha's for the Irish Catholics. Mass was said in it for the first time on March 11 of the following year by the pastor of New Trier who served it until 1891 when the Reverend J. J. Jacobs was appointed resident pastor. The present pastor is Reverend A. Kaesen (1911—) who built the new church in 1914, and the new rectory in 1923, replacing one built in 1886 by the people and against the wishes of the pastor.

3 priests and 10 sisters from the parish.

1882—CHURCH OF ST. EDWARD, MINNEOTA

The first church was erected in 1882 by Reverend L. Cornelius, and the second by Reverend W. J. Stewart on land bought in 1912 from Mr. O'Connor for $1,500, of which $700.00 was donated to the parish. The church was dedicated by Archbishop Ireland on October 11, 1914. Ill-health brought about the resignation of Father Stewart in 1925. He joined the Archdiocese of Los Angeles and was pastor of the church at Redonda Beach for several years before he took charge of a church at Long Beach. Some years later he died during a visit to Ireland. Rectory and school were built by Reverend P. Casey who died in 1949. The school was opened in September, 1938, under the direction of the Sisters of St. Joseph to whom the pastor turned over his own residence for a convent. Reverend A. Loosen succeeded Father Casey in the pastorate and on his death in October, 1951, Reverend Vincent Hope was named pastor.

1882—CHURCH OF ST. IGNATIUS, ANNANDALE

Prior to the erection of what is now the sanctuary and sacristy of the present church in 1901 and the completion of it in 1902, by Reverend T. G. Plante (1899-1903), there was a church near the cemetery three miles south of Annandale built by Reverend C. Robert in 1882 when the parish was incorporated. The first resident pastor was Reverend J. Darche (1898-9) who built the rectory which was replaced by a more modern residence in 1949 by the present pastor, Reverend P. Keany (1939—). In Clearwater, a mission transferred from Fletcher to Annandale, the Church of St. Luke was built in 1906 by Reverend C. Cavanaugh (1903-6). In 1909 it was made a mission to Monticello and in 1931 given a resident pastor.

1 sister from the parish.

1883—CHURCH OF ST. ANDREW, FAIRFAX

The original church was built in 1883 under the direction of Reverend J. Andre of Birch Coolee and the present brick structure, costing $40,000, in 1910 by Reverend J. J. Goergen (1903-31). It was dedicated by Auxiliary Bishop Lawler on June 23. The first resident pastor was Reverend C. C. Schmidt (1886-9). The children were taught in the old church from 1893 till 1898 when Reverend F. X. Bajec (1895-1903) built a Catholic hall which was remodeled into a school some years later and occupied until the new school was erected in 1927 by Father Goergen who also built the convent in 1905. The present rectory was built in 1891 by Reverend P. Rosen (1890-4). The family of the late Bishop Peschges of Crookston lived in this parish at one time. The present pastor is Reverend Joseph Neudecker (1950—).

8 sisters from the parish.

1883—CHURCH OF ST. MARY OF CZESTOCHOWA, FRANKLIN TOWNSHIP

The original church was erected in 1883 under the supervision of Reverend J. B. Renning as a mission of St. Peter's Church, Delano. The present church was built in 1914 by Reverend S. Zdechlik, pastor of St. Joseph's Church, Delano (1911-9). Its first resident pastor was Reverend A. Handzel (1940-2). The rectory was built by Reverend A. Wojciak (1942-8), and the present pastor is Reverend F. J. Poplawski (1948—).

1883—CHURCH OF ST. ANASTASIA, HUTCHINSON

In the early eighties of last century Father Ireland said Mass in the home of Leopold Steineke, a blacksmith. The first church, a wooden structure seating about one hundred people, was built in 1883 by the resident pastor, Reverend P. Boucher (1883-8) and moved to a site near the present church in 1891. A modern brick church was erected in 1923 by Reverend T. O'Brien (1910-24); the rectory, replacing an older house, by Reverend P. F. Meade (1901-9). From 1866 to 1883 the parish was visited periodically by priests of the neighborhood. The present pastor is Reverend Marion Casey.

2 sisters from the parish.

1883—CHURCH OF THE HOLY REDEEMER, MARSHALL

The first church was built in 1883 under the supervision of Reverend J. DeVos of Ghent (1883-6). The present church on a site at the other end of the town was erected in 1916 by Reverend G. E. Carlin (1914-41) and repaired and underpinned after his death by his successor, Reverend R. A. Neudecker (1941—), who began the erection of a new school in another location in 1949. It was dedicated Sunday, September 24, 1950, by Archbishop Murray. The first school was opened March 19, 1900, by Reverend J. Guillot (1898-1910) with the Sisters of St. Joseph as teachers. The first rectory was built by Reverend H. Victor (1890-3), and the present purchased and blessed in 1908 by Father Guillot. Father Ravoux said Mass in the early sixties of last century on the site of the first church.

4 priests and 14 sisters from the parish.

1883—CHURCH OF ST. LEO OF BURTON, ST. LEO

The first church was built in 1883 by Reverend E. Lee of Minneota; the second in 1896 by Reverend F. Jaeger of Marshall; the third, a stone structure, in 1940 by Reverend J. N. Gores, the present pastor (1933—), at a cost of $75,000. It is free of debt. The first Mass was said on Christmas day. The convent was bought in 1913 for the School Sisters of Notre Dame who teach in the school. From 1889 to 1913 the school was taught by lay teachers. The rectory was built in 1897 by Father Jaeger; the new school in 1903 by Reverend A. Rinke (1901-8); and an addition to it in 1926 by Reverend M. Dühr (1924-8).

2 priests and 24 sisters from the parish.

1883—CHURCH OF ST. JOHN CANTIUS, WILNO

A frame church was built in 1883 by Reverend R. Byzewski of Winona, and the first resident pastor was Reverend D. Koziolek, O.F.M., Chicago, from March to July, 1884. The present brick church was erected in 1901 by Reverend J. Andrzejewski (1897-1902). The first rectory was built by Reverend J. F. Cieminski (1902-7) and later changed into a school and convent for the Sisters of St. Francis of Rochester, Minnesota. The new rectory was built by Reverend A. Broszkowski (1923-7), and the Reverend A. J. Wojciak took charge of the parish in 1948, introducing the Sisters of St. Dominic to replace the School Sisters of Notre Dame who withdrew in 1947.

1883—CHURCH OF ST. MATHIAS, WANDA

In the early seventies of last century the Reverend Father O'Mahoney of Tracy said Mass in different Catholic homes in the locality and built the first church in 1883, three miles east of the present location; the second church erected in 1902 by

Reverend E. Polasek on the present site was destroyed by fire in 1907; and the present brick structure erected in 1910 by Reverend J. Jagemann (1910-5) who also built the rectory in 1912. A chapel in honor of Our Lady was donated in 1922 by John Pohlan. The present pastor is Reverend L. J. Bertrand (1944—) who redecorated the church, and built a parish school in 1951.

5 priests and 8 sisters from the parish.

1883—CHURCH OF ST. ELOI, GHENT

The original church built probably in the early eighties of last century, had for first resident pastor, Reverend J. DeVos, who came on June 27, 1883, and remained a year, but returned in 1885 and left again on April 10, 1885. The church was destroyed by fire on January 1, 1902, and the present brick church was erected in 1904 by Reverend E. Walsh (1903-5) and renovated by Reverend J. M. Pilger (1931-47). A school-convent was erected in 1901 and placed in charge of the Sisters of St. Joseph. The present four-room brick school was built in 1914, and the rectory in 1905 by Reverened H. V. Van Walleghem (1905-30), and renovated by Father Pilger. The present pastor is Reverend John Siebenand.

2 priests and 18 sisters from the parish.

1884—CHURCH OF OUR LADY, MANANNAH

Incorporated September 19, 1884, as a mission of Litchfield, it received Reverend Hugh McDevitt as its first resident pastor in 1886. He was succeeded by Reverend Michael Cauley in 1897 who remained until 1900 when it again became a mission of Litchfield. It was re-established as a parish with Reverend Francis X. McDermott as pastor in 1903 who also had Eden Valley as a mission. A year later Eden Valley became the parish and Manannah the mission till October, 1937, when it was restored to parochial status, with the Church of St. Columbanus in Greenleaf as a mission. Reverend R. F. Rypel is the pastor. It possesses a historic painting of Our Lady of Perpetual Help.

1884—CHURCH OF ST. FRANCIS, FRANCONIA

In early days Mass was said in the homes of the parishioners by visiting priests. With Taylor's Falls it was ceded to the Vicariate of Northern Minnesota in 1875 but restored to the Archdiocese in 1889. The parish was established in 1884 and attended from Stillwater, Rush City, Forest Lake and North Branch until 1948, when it became a mission of Taylor's Falls under the first resident pastor, Reverend F. E. Shea who was succeeded by Reverend O. Winzerling in 1951.

1884—CHURCH OF ST. JOHN THE BAPTIST, NEW BRIGHTON

The original church — that of St. Charles, Moundview — was built in 1884 by Reverend C. Genis of White Bear; the basement of the church of St. John the Baptist in New Brighton in 1902 by Reverend A. Szczukowski (1902-7) and the superstructure in 1922 by Reverend A. Kryjewski (1916-31). The rectory was built in 1903 and a new school in 1951 by its present pastor, Reverend Paul Koscielniak (1950—).

1885—CHURCH OF ST. MARY, TRACY

First Mass was said in the home of Patrick Summers in 1880 by Reverend E. Lee of Ghent, who built the church in 1885. The first resident pastor was Reverend D. Sullivan (1888-90). The present brick church was completed May 1, 1921, by Reverend H. Cahill (1914-52), at a cost of $73,000. It was free of debt in 1931. The first rectory was built in 1896 by Father Darche. On March 1, 1917, the Gould residence was bought; in March, 1919, the Donaldson residence nearer the church; and finally in February, 1937, the Robinson home, now the pastor's residence. In 1918 the high altar was donated by the pastor in memory of his brother, Reverend R. Cahill who died that year. The new church was dedicated by Archbishop Dowling on September 4, 1921. The parish was incorporated on July 18, 1896. The present pastor is Reverend Richard T. O'Connor, who is building a school.

3 sisters from the parish.

1885—CHURCH OF ST. JOSEPH, ROSEN

The first Mass in the locality was said in the home of Nicholas Karels about 1881 by Reverend A. Kober who built a frame church in 1885. It was attended as a mission from Madison prior to 1901, when it was attached to Nassau till 1911. The church was built in 1907 by Reverend A. Kaesen of Nassau (1905-11), enlarged and remodeled by the present pastor, Reverend E. M. Clemens (1948—) at a cost of one hundred thousand dollars. The first resident pastor, Reverend N. Gerstl (1911-21), built the rectory in 1911, and his successor, Reverend C. Pfeifer (1921-36) the school in 1927. The Benedictine Sisters of Crookston took charge of it in 1930.

2 priests, 1 brother and 15 sisters from the parish.

1885—CHURCH OF ST. CATHERINE, REDWOOD FALLS

Mass was said in the home of John O'Hara in 1870 by Reverend A. Berghold of New Ulm, and in other homes periodically till July, 1885, when the first church, 74 by 40, was erected under the direction of Reverend A. Ogulin of St. Peter, and attended by him as a mission until a resident pastor was appointed in the person of Reverend J. J. Woods in 1897. He built the rectory and several churches in neighboring localities before his transfer to Le (Sueur) Center in 1908. The present church, 44 by 120, was opened on March 7, 1915 by Reverend J. Tomek (1910-21) and dedicated by Bishop Lawler on November 16 of that year. It was renovated and refurnished by the Reverend G. O'Sullivan who has been in charge of the parish since 1931.

1885—CHURCH OF ST. ANDREW, GRANITE FALLS

The first church, dedicated by Archbishop Ireland on November 27, 1885, was built by Reverend A. Kober of Bird Island (1884-9) and named in his honor. The parish was a mission till 1938 when Reverend W. F. Murphy (1938-9) built the rectory. He was succeeded by Reverend E. G. Trainor under whose supervision the new church was erected in 1942, and dedicated on May 23, 1943, by Archbishop Murray. The parish was entirely free of debt on May 13, 1945.

2 sisters from the parish.

1886—CHURCH OF ST. MICHAEL, MADISON

The first frame church built by Reverend A. Kober in 1886, was struck by lightning and burned in 1903. The following year a brick church was erected by Reverend J. Klein (1904-10), destroyed by fire on August 15, 1913, and restored and enlarged in 1914 by Reverend V. Schiffrer (1911-20). It is recorded that the first Mass was said in the locality by Reverend J. C. Byrne (later, Vicar General) in 1884 in the home of M. S. McDonough. The rectory was built in 1890 by Reverend P. M. Schoenen (1890-1). There have been fourteen pastors (thirteen resident) before Reverend E. M. Frederick (1944—). The first was Reverend F. B. Reichel (1887-9). The existing brick school was built in 1914 by Father Schiffrer and is taught by the School Sisters of Notre Dame, whose convent was donated to the parish in 1912 by J. Kemers, Senior. A complete high school was maintained between 1921 and 1932 during the pastorate of Reverend H. J. Minea (1920-31), from which sixty-four students were graduated.

4 priests and 8 sisters from the parish.

1886—CHURCH OF THE IMMACULATE CONCEPTION, TREBON

This mission church was built by Reverend F. Pribyl, pastor of Montgomery, for the accommodation of a settlement of Czech Catholics in Erin Township, Rice County, ten miles southeast of Montgomery, and four miles from Shieldsville. The succeeding pastors had charge of them until Reverend W. J. Skluzacek officially closed the church; but the people still care for the building and the cemetery is kept in wonderful shape.

1886—CHURCH OF ST. MICHAEL, GAYLORD

The church was erected in 1886 by Father Stecher of Henderson of which it was a mission until 1942, when Reverend E. M. Clemens was placed in charge of it for one year. The presbytery was bought in 1945 by Reverend A. L. Schwinn (1944-7). The present pastor is Reverend Ambrose Siebenand, 1951—). It has Winthrop for a mission. The family of Bishop Schenk of Crookston lived in Gaylord ten years during which he began his studies for the priesthood.

1887—CHURCH OF ST. TIMOTHY, MAPLE LAKE

The first church was built about 1887 by Reverend F. Savey of Chatham who in that year moved to Maple Lake and had charge of the parish until 1903. He built a larger church, and the first rectory at his own expense and later sold it to the parish. The parish is a consolidation of the parishes at East Maple Lake and Chatham. The present church was erected in 1922 by Reverend F. C. O'Brien (1904-49) and was solemnly consecrated by Archbishop Murray on April 21, 1938. A few years later a cyclone caused $20,000 damage to the roof. The Reverend C. H. Morgan (1949-52), erected the modern parochial school in charge of the Sisters of St. Benedict from St. Joseph, Minn., and was succeeded by Reverend F. J. Barthelme.

1 priest and 3 sisters from the parish.

1887—CHURCH OF ST. MARY, SEAFORTH

The first church, dedicated to St. Henry, and three miles northeast of Seaforth, was built in 1887 by Reverend A. Berghold of New Ulm, on a five-acre plot of land donated by John Trost. Before that Mass was said in the homes of Lawrence Holton and Jerry Mooney by Father Berghold from 1879 to 1881, by Father Kielen of Madison from 1881 to 1887, and by others till 1900, when the present church was erected by Reverend J. J. Woods of Redwood Falls (1897-1908). It was attended by priests from the neighboring parishes until 1935 when Reverend John Stolz (1935-42) built the rectory in 1936 and became first resident pastor. He moved the church back from the street, added a basement and sacristy. The present pastor is Reverend A. J. Kern (1948—). The Sisters of Notre Dame from Wabasso teach the children on Saturdays and during vacation.

3 sisters from the parish.

1887—CHURCH OF ST. JOHN, HECTOR

Mass was offered on December 17, 1878, by Reverend C. H. Braun of Stewart, in the home of William Ebert and later on in other places for almost a decade before the parish was organized. The church was erected under the supervision of Reverend A. Kober of Bird Island in 1887 and attended by him until 1891 when it was attached to Stewart as a mission. The Reverend G. M. Van der Velden came to reside in the parish in 1905, remained for six years and in 1908 built the parochial residence. It was a mission of Bird Island a second time from 1915 to 1934 when the Reverend J. A. Ettel was appointed pastor who remodeled the altar and redecorated the church in 1935. The Reverend L. F. Ryan was assigned to the parish in 1946.

1888—CHURCH OF ST. JOSEPH, MONTEVIDEO

The Reverend A. Kober of Bird Island built the church in October, 1888. It was a mission of Renville till 1910, when Reverend J. Fahey (1910-5) became first resident pastor and built the rectory. The original frame church was razed a year after the present combination church and school was built in 1927 by Reverend C. H. Morgan (1925-31). The school continued from 1928 to 1931 under the direction of the Sisters of St. Benedict. Fifteen priests served the parish prior to the Reverend P. A. Colbert (1944—), who reopened the school in 1950, staffed with the Sisters of Notre Dame.

1888—CHURCH OF ST. ALOYSIUS, OLIVIA

A frame church was erected in 1888 by the first pastor, Reverend A. Kober (1888-96). His successor, Reverend T. Plante (1896-1904) built the parish house in 1897. A combined school and convent, the "Aloysianum", was built in 1914 by Reverend H. D. Pomije (1907-49) who also built the present fine church, costing $150,000, dedicated, virtually free of debt, in 1926, three altars of which were solemnly consecrated on August 27, 1947, by Bishops Schenk of Crookston, Kucera of Lincoln, and

Auxiliary Bishop Byrne of St. Paul. The school is taught by the Sisters of St. Joseph. In 1951 a new convent was built by its present pastor, Reverend Stanley Skluzacek (1950–).

2 priests and 7 sisters from the parish.

1888—CHURCH OF ST. MARY, CRYSTAL, NEAR ROBBINSDALE

A frame church built in 1888 for the German congregation was served by the Franciscan Fathers from Jordan – Father Florentine Kurzer to 1894; others to 1907; Father Keil of Wayzata till 1908, when the record ends. Baptismal registers to 1907 are available, and marriage records to 1908. There is an existing list of thirty families who belonged to the parish. The church was torn down but the hall is still used for meetings of the St. Jacob German Society. The small adjoining cemetery is used occasionally for burial of members of old families. The parish was merged with the parish of the Sacred Heart, Robbinsdale, in 1911 or 1912, and the territory included in the new parish of St. Raphael, Crystal, in 1951.

1889—CHURCH OF ST. ANTHONY, WATKINS

A log church, dedicated to St. Anne, stood two miles east of the present site and was built on the property of John Becker, under the direction of the Benedictine Fathers of St. John's Abbey who said Mass in the Becker home in the early seventies of last century; the second, dedicated to the Assumption, was built west of Watkins under Benedictine supervision. In 1889 the foundations of the present church were laid during the pastorate of Reverend Pius Schmidt (1889-95), and the superstructure completed in 1912 by Reverend A. Vilman (1902-23). In 1907 the Sisters of St. Benedict took charge of the school. The present pastor is Reverend J. L. Westfall.

5 priests and 10 sisters from the parish.

1889—CHURCH OF ST. ADALBERT, SILVER LAKE

A small frame church was built by the early settlers on the south side of the lake, and Mass said in it by missionary priests from 1878 to 1888. The present church was erected in 1889 by Reverend L. Tyszkiewicz (1888-94) and extensively renovated and improved in 1949 by Reverend J. Julkowski (1932–) at a cost of $60,000. The rectory built in 1898 by Reverend A. Zalewski (1897-1924) was modernized in 1938 by Father Julkowski. The school and the convent were opened September 4, 1919, by Reverend V. W. Worzalla (1924-32), with the Sisters of Notre Dame from Mankato in charge.

3 priests and 7 sisters from the parish.

1889—CHURCH OF THE IMMACULATE CONCEPTION, ST. PETER

The contract for building the church was let on April 11, 1889, during the pastorate of Reverend B. Sproll and the work done under the supervision of Reverend A. Ogulin (1889-90). The church was dedicated by Archbishop Ireland on December 8, 1889, when he administered the sacrament of Confirmation to 150 persons. Father Ogulin began the construction of a rectory completed by Reverend L. Haas (1890-7), enlarged and renovated under subsequent pastors. A frame school, 26 by 60, was opened on September 7, 1891, under the direction of the Sisters of St. Francis of Rochester, Minnesota, who remained in charge until the "John Ireland" school near the Church of St. Peter was opened in 1926 to serve the two parishes. The present pastor is Reverend E. Yunker (1944–).

1 priest and 3 sisters from the parish.

1889—CHURCH OF ST. JOHN, MORTON

In 1889 the Reverend J. A. Soumis (1888-90) built a frame church which was destroyed by lightning in 1922 and replaced by the present brick church erected by Reverend M. A. Condon (1918-30). The first Mass was said by Father Brennan in Patrick O'Neill's home in Henryville Township in 1873, and a church, unathorized by Bishop Grace, built on Michael Gerrity's farm by Reverend J. Andre in 1880 and later on recognized by the Bishop. The parish had fifteen pastors up to 1939.

when Reverend A. Schaefer was placed in charge. The rectory was built in 1892 by Reverend J. O'Connor (1890-1901). Morton was known as Birch Coolee until 1894 when the latter became a separate parish and St. Patrick's Church was built in 1898 by Father O'Connor.

2 priests from the parish.

1889—CHURCH OF ST. PETER, NORTH ST. PAUL

A church belonging to the Congregationalists was purchased on June 25, 1889, and attended every other Sunday by Reverend F. X. Gores of Oakdale (1888-98) and his successors until 1902, when the first resident pastor was appointed in the person of Reverend P. J. Lang (1902-18) who built the rectory in 1904; the church in 1917 which was completed and decorated in 1925 and 1948 by Reverend W. P. O'Reilly (1918—). The old church building was remodeled into a school and opened in September, 1917, by the Sisters of St. Joseph who had charge of it till 1928, when the Sisters of St. Francis from Rochester came. The convent was ready in February, 1922; the parochial residence in 1904; and the new school and the convent in 1929.

5 priests and 10 sisters from the parish.

1889—CHURCH OF ST. JOHN, APPLETON

Mass was said for the first time on May 11, 1880, by Father Brioty in the home of O. H. Poirier. The first church was dedicated by Archbishop Ireland on October 6, 1889. The present church was bought from the Universalists in 1910, and priests from Graceville ministered to the spiritual needs of the congregation from 1889 till 1914, when the Reverend M. A. Condon was named resident pastor (1914-8). The rectory was purchased in 1916. A summer vacation school of four weeks is conducted by the Sisters of St. Francis from Sylvania, Ohio. The present pastor is Reverend T. D. Szymanski (1945—). It has a mission — St. Joseph's Church, Halloway.

1890—CHURCH OF ST. WILLIBRORD, GIBBON

It was built in 1890 by Reverend P. Rosen of Fairfax, and remodeled in 1927 by Reverend W. Reuter (1919—). It was a mission of Fairfax until 1915.

1 priest and 2 sisters from the parish.

1890—CHURCH OF ST. FRANCIS, BUFFALO

The first church, 40 by 40 feet in size, was built in 1890, although the parish was incorporated on November 15, 1888, and thus separated from East Maple Lake from which it was attended by Reverend F. Savey who probably built the church. From 1887 to 1890 week day Mass was said in the O'Connor building by Father Swift of East Maple Lake and Father Savey of Chatham. The first resident pastor was Reverend F. Raquin (1892-3) who occupied a rectory behind the church. The church was enlarged in 1894 by Reverend T. Plante (1893-6). A new site was bought by Reverend W. H. Blum (1904-12) for $1,800, and he persuaded the Catholics of Pelican Lake to join the parish. The new church was built by Reverend J. A. Heinz (1912—) at a cost of $35,000, and in 1937, a school, costing $42,000, was erected and staffed by the Sisters of Notre Dame. The parish numbers about 250 families.

1890—CHURCH OF ST. CLARA, CLARA CITY

A small frame church, 37 by 30, was erected in 1890 by Reverend H. Victor (1890-4) of Marshall, and enlarged in 1895 by Reverend F. Jaeger (1894-8). The first resident pastor, Reverend A. Buckler, came in 1898, and built the rectory. The present church, costing $60,000, was dedicated on October 9, 1929, during the pastorate of Reverend A. J. Koller (1917-31). The school, in charge of the Notre Dame Sisters of Mankato, was opened on September 9, 1918. The Reverend Harold W. Hesse is the present pastor.

4 priests and 8 sisters from the parish.

1890—CHURCH OF ST. JOSEPH, RICE LAKE

The church, built about 1890, was destroyed by a wind storm. The present one was built in 1896 by Reverend J. Goiffon of Centerville; enlarged by Reverend M. Masl, also of Centerville, and decorated by Father Hammang (1939-45), a member of the faculty of St. Paul Seminary. The parish is attended by Reverend J. F. Checka (1945—) who resides at Nazareth Hall Preparatory Seminary, and completely renovated the church in 1950.

1890—CHURCH OF ST. MICHAEL, MORGAN

It was incorporated on November 8, 1890, by Reverend George Pax, pastor of Sleepy Eye, who attended it as a mission. In 1892 Reverend Bernard Vonderlage became resident pastor with Redwood Falls, Lamberton, Willow Lake, Sheridan, Madison, Yellow Bank and Westline as missions. By September, 1898, all the missions were established as parishes or allocated to other parishes. A school was organized and placed under the care of the School Sisters of Notre Dame who continued to have accommodations in the school building till 1951 when a new convent was built and the entire school building converted into class rooms. Reverend A. Leifeld is the pastor.

1891—CHURCH OF ST. GEORGE, GLENCOE

It was erected in 1891 by Reverend W. Rhatigan (1890-4); partly destroyed by fire on March 21, 1892, and rebuilt in 1894. Father Rhatigan built the priest's home in 1891, and Reverend P. C. Moloney (1916-46) remodeled it in 1923. The parish was originally part of the parish of SS. Peter and Paul. Reverend Robert Bastyr was appointed pastor in 1950.

1891—CHURCH OF THE HOLY REDEEMER, RENVILLE

The first church was built in 1891 by Reverend A. Kober, and the first resident pastor was Reverend F. J. T. MacEwan (1897-1902). The rectory, built in 1892, was remodeled in 1924 by Reverend P. J. O'Connor (1921-33), who erected the present church in 1926-7. A new residence was built in 1940 by Reverend C. Renz (1938-47). The church was decorated in 1948 by the Reverend D. J. Noonan who came to the parish in 1947.

1 priest from the parish.

1892—CHURCH OF THE VISITATION, DANVERS

The Reverend A. Oster of Clontarf, who said the first Mass in the district in 1885 in the home of Frank Donlan, supervised the erection of the first church in 1892, and it continued to be served from Clontarf until 1898, when it was attached to Benson and attended by Reverend P. M. Shea till 1915, when it received its first resident pastor in the person of Reverend J. Hurst (1915-26), who built the rectory in 1916. The present church was erected in 1931 by Reverend J. L. O'Neill (1927-35). Catechism is taught by the Sisters of the Presentation from Willmar. Reverend Joseph Esser (1952—) is the present pastor.

1894—CHURCH OF ST. ANDREW, ELYSIAN

It was incorporated on February 8 of that year by Reverend Patrick J. Lucey, pastor of the Church of the Holy Trinity, Waterville, of which it was a mission until it was attached to the parish of the Immaculate Conception, Marysburg, in 1947.

1894—CHURCH OF ST. THOMAS, ST. PAUL PARK

It was attended by Reverend Francis X. Gores, pastor of the Church of the Guardian Angels, Oaklade, from 1884 to 1897. The first baptism was conferred in April, 1885, and the first confirmation administered by Archbishop Ireland in July, 1888. It was attended from the Church of St. John, St. Paul, after the pastorate of Father Gores in Oakdale. The first church was named St. Patrick in Langdon. The parish was incorporated as the Church of St. Thomas, St. Paul Park, by Reverend John Walsh, pastor of the Church of St. Augustine, South St. Paul, January

27, 1903. For several years it was a mission attended from the St. Paul Cathedral. The church was renovated and modernized by the first resident pastor, Reverend Patrick J. Hart (1916-34), a former Army Chaplain in the Spanish-American War. who built the rectory and placed an ornamental fence around the property. The school and convent were set up in September, 1949, by the Reverend James L. Westfall and placed under the charge of the Sisters of St. Joseph of Carondelet. Reverend Charles Eggert is the pastor.

2 priests and 1 sister from the parish.

1894—CHURCH OF THE SACRED HEART, MURDOCK

A frame church was erected in 1894 by Reverend P. J. O'Connor of DeGraff of which it was a mission until 1912 when the present pastor, Reverend W. P. Walsh, took charge and built the brick and stone church in 1925, at a cost of $93,000. The first Mass was said in it on Christmas Eve and it was dedicated by Archbishop Dowling on May 6, 1926.

4 priests and 11 sisters from the parish.

1895—CHURCH OF ST. JOSEPH, LAMBERTON

It was built in 1895 by Reverend B. Vonderlage (1895-8), enlarged in 1904 by Reverend E. Polasek (1899-1905), and refinished in 1937 by Reverend G. H. Galles (1933-7). The rectory was built in 1900 by Father Polasek and enlarged in later years. The present pastor, Reverend G. J. Eischens came in 1947.

1 sister from the parish.

1895—CHURCH OF ST. MARY, HOPKINS

A wooden building, 20 by 42, with bell tower and steeple, was erected in 1895 by Reverend M. J. Egan, assistant pastor of the Church of the Immaculate Conception, Minneapolis, of which it was a mission until 1902, when Reverend M. Mahoney was appointed first resident pastor (1902-13). He purchased a rectory in 1902, which served the purpose for twenty years. His successor was Reverend B. F. Audus who was transferred to Kilkenny in 1920 when the parish was merged with St. Margaret's to form the present parish of St. Joseph.

1895—CHURCH OF STS. CYRIL AND METHODIUS, TAUNTON

Mass was said by the first pastor, Reverend A. Zaleski, on August 1, 1895, and the first baptism was administered on September 1, 1895. The present church was built by Reverend J. Dohmann in 1928 who, as pastor of Canby, had Taunton as a mission. Reverend John Pawelski is the present pastor.

1896—CHURCH OF ST. JOSEPH, SILVER LAKE

The first church was built by the Czech Catholics at Bear Creek, four miles south, in 1873 and ministered to by itinerant missionaries. In 1894 Reverend F. Jiranek, pastor of St. Adalbert's Church (1894-5), was the first resident pastor for the Bohemians of Bear Creek. He organized the new St. Joseph's parish, incorporated April 3, 1895. The present church was erected in 1896, and the priest's house completed by Reverend W. J. Skluzacek (1927-36) as well as a combination school and convent for the Sisters of Notre Dame in 1931. He also added a new sanctuary and transepts to the church. The present pastor, Reverend Robert Slechta, was appointed in 1950.

4 priests and 7 sisters from the parish.

896—CHURCH OF ST. LUKE, CLEARWATER

The first church was erected by Father Brogan of Foley (1890-1912); the second by Reverend C. Cavanaugh of Annandale (1903-6). It was a mission of Monticello before the coming of the first pastor, Reverend J. H. Kern (1927-31) who purchased the rectory in 1927. Reverend J. Krall was named pastor in 1939.

2 sisters from the parish.

896—CHURCH OF ST. AUGUSTINE, SOUTH ST. PAUL

The first church was erected in 1896 by Reverend J. F. Busch (1895-1896), now,

Bishop of St. Cloud, remodeled in 1914 by Reverend H. G. McCall (1910-26), destroyed by fire on March 31, 1923, and rebuilt in 1924. The school was opened in September, 1925, under the supervision of the Sisters of St. Dominic for whom a convent was purchased by Father McCall. The church was enlarged and refurnished in 1948 by the present pastor, Reverend T. F. Nolan (1946–). The rectory was bought in 1940 by Reverend J. O'Callaghan (1926-46) and enlarged in 1941.

2 priests and 10 sisters from the parish.

1896—CHURCH OF ST. DIONYSIUS, TYLER

It was blessed on October 27, 1896, by Reverend J. Darche of Tracy who personally constructed the altar still in use. On that occasion Father Darche celebrated a Solemn High Mass and Father McNally of Elkton, South Dakota, preached. It was enlarged in 1929 by Reverend G. O'Sullivan. It was a mission of Tracy till 1903 and of Lake Benton till 1940 when it received its first pastor, Reverend M. G. Harrington (1940-4) who purchased the present rectory. The Reverend W. J. Marks (1944–) was named pastor to succeed him. As early as 1880 Father Hanley of Minneota said Mass in the home of Mathias Dressen and other neighboring priests ministered to the Catholics of Tyler before the church was built. Since 1944 two Sisters of St. Benedict conduct a religious vacation school for three weeks in the summer.

1897—CHURCH OF ST. GENEVIEVE, LAKE BENTON

It was erected about 1897 by Reverend J. Darche of Tracy and the first resident pastor was Reverend A. Doyle (1903-10) who built the rectory in 1904. The Reverend Paul Gorman became pastor in 1950. It was formerly a mission of Tracy with Mass once a month.

1898—CHURCH OF ST. PETER, CANBY

The first church, built under the direction of Reverend F. Jaeger, was dedicated on June 29, 1898, and totally destroyed by fire with all its contents, except vestments and sacred vessels, January 27, 1926. It was originally a mission of St. Leo. The present brick church, costing $28,000, was dedicated on November 23, 1926, by Archbishop Dowling during the pastorate of Reverend J. Dohmann (1922-31). The sanctuary was added by Reverend P. Remskar (1914-22). The first resident pastor was Reverend F. J. Bouska (1903-4), and the present is Reverend T. Exley (1952–). The rectory was occupied at the end of October 1904. The church was decorated in 1940 by Father Coughlin (1937-44).

2 priests from the parish.

1899—CHURCH OF THE SACRED HEART, FRANKLIN

It was formerly part of the old Birch Coulee parish. A frame church was built by parishioners in 1899 when it was placed in charge of Reverend J. J. Woods of Redwood Falls. It was a mission of Morton from 1908 to November, 1935, when it received its first resident pastor, Reverend H. Byrne (1935-42), with Birch Coulee as a mission. In September, 1948, a full basement was added, an oil-burner installed and a parish hall fully equipped with facilities for instructing children, the church redecorated and the floor sanded. The rectory was purchased by Reverend M. A. Keeler (1943-7). The present pastor is Reverend Louis Heitzer (1950–).

2 sisters from the parish.

1899—CHURCH OF OUR LADY OF VICTORY, LUCAN

It was erected at Westline in 1899 by Reverend J. J. Woods of Redwood Falls and moved to Lucan in 1904 by Reverend E. Polasek of Lamberton. The first resident priest was Reverend V. Schatz (1905-11) who built the parish house in 1906. An addition — transepts, sanctuary and sacristies — was put to the church in 1919 by Reverend G. Vander Velden (1916-9). The Reverend M. A. Guetter was named pastor in 1946.

1 priest and 8 sisters from the parish.

1899—CHURCH OF ST. MARY, LE CENTER

In June, 1899, the Reverend P. Carey was appointed pastor of the new parish to be organized in Le (Sueur) Center and said the first Mass on June 5 in the public school. The cornerstone of the frame church was blessed and placed in position by Archbishop Ireland on August 15, and the completed edifice dedicated by Reverend F. Tichy of New Prague on December 12. Father Carey was succeeded by Reverend F. J. Hovorka (1902-3) who moved into the new rectory at Christmas. The parochial school and the convent for the Sisters of St. Joseph were ready for occupancy in January, 1915, during the pastorate of Reverend J. J. Woods (1908-31), and the total indebtedness liquidated in 1919. The church was redecorated and the altars remodeled by Reverend H. J. Minea (1939-46); and the golden jubilee was observed on August 11, 1949, under the direction of the present pastor, Reverend D. J. Buckley (1946–). Pontifical Mass was celebrated by the Most Reverend Archbishop Murray and the sermon preached by Reverend W. P. Delaney of Jessenland. An addition of four rooms was made to the school in 1951 and blessed by Archbishop Murray on Sunday, December 9.

2 priests and 13 sisters from the parish.

1900—CHURCH OF ST. MATHIAS, HAMPTON

It was erected in 1900 while a mission of New Trier, and attended by Reverend L. Haas till 1904, when it became an independent parish under the direction of Reverend R. Schlinkert (1904-10) who bought the rectory in 1906. which was replaced by the present brick house. A school was opened in 1918 by Reverend M. J. Dühr (1916-24) in charge of the Sisters of Notre Dame. A new school and a convent were erected in 1925 by Reverend V. Bozja (1924-31). Reverend L. Hoffmann was appointed in 1940.

1 priest and 6 sisters from the parish.

1900—CHURCH OF SS. PETER AND PAUL, IVANHOE

The first church was erected in 1900 by Reverend J. Andrzejewski of Wilno, of which it was a mission until 1907, and placed under the patronage of St. George, until Reverend P. Roy became pastor in 1907, and changed the name to SS. Peter and Paul. He was succeeded by the present pastor, Reverend S. F. Dobrenski, who built the rectory in 1913, and transformed the church into a parish hall. A new Gothic church, costing $160,000, was dedicated by Auxiliary Bishop Byrne on October 14, 1951.

1 priest and 1 brother from the parish.

1900—CHURCH OF ST. ANNE, WABASSO

Reverend J. J. Woods of Redwood Falls built St. Anne's Church in 1900. It was dedicated by Very Reverend J. Stariha, V. G., on September 27 of that year, and enlarged in 1915. As a mission of Morgan it was attended by Reverends M. Stukel till 1906; H. Leydeckers till 1909; F. Roemer till 1923; M. Moitzheim till 1935; F. Neumann till 1936; W. J. Skluzacek till 1938; P. Remskar till 1940; and Reverend T. H. Diehl, the present pastor. The School Sisters of Notre Dame have been in charge of the school since 1923. The rectory was built by Father Roemer in 1921. A new school was built in 1945 and a new church in 1951.

1 priest and 3 sisters from the parish.

1901—CHURCH OF ST. PAUL, COMFREY

The first church was erected in 1901 by Reverend F. H. Smalian, pastor of Lamberton. It was destroyed by fire on February 8, 1948, and re-erected by the Reverend H. B. Geisenkoetter (1944-51), at a cost of $180,000. The parish house was built in 1908 by Reverend J. F. Gleason (1905-8). The school was opened on October 1, 1917, with the Sisters of Notre Dame in charge, and the convent built in the same year by Reverend A. Ziskovsky (1908-21). Reverend Peter Berger is pastor.

2 priests and 3 sisters from the parish.

1902—CHURCH OF THE SACRED HEART, RAYMOND

It was built in 1902 by Reverend I. Schumacher and the first resident priest was Reverend W. Murphy (1936-8) who purchased the rectory. It was formerly a mission of Clara City and Willmar. Reverend A. T. Guillemette has been the pastor since 1948.

1902—CHURCH OF ST. JOHN THE BAPTIST, HUGO

The first church was built in 1902 by Reverend J. Perigord (1902-10), and destroyed by fire on February 12, 1947. The present church was erected under the supervision of Reverend L. J. Fortin (1947—). The rectory was built about 1904 by Father Perigord.

2 priests and 8 sisters from the parish.

1902—CHURCH OF ST. ALBERT, ALBERTVILLE

It was erected by Reverend W. H. Blum (1903-4) and transferred to the Oblates of Mary Immaculate in 1916 with Reverend J. Pothmann as pastor since 1934. The school was opened on September 15, 1915, with the School Sisters of Notre Dame in charge. The convent and rectory were built about the same time.

12 sisters from the parish.

1902—CHURCH OF ST. THOMAS, SANBORN

A public school was purchased in 1902 and used as a church served by the pastors of Lamberton and Comfrey till August, 1941, when Reverend N. Schmitt was named pastor. The rectory was built in 1942, and the new church blessed by Archbishop Murray December 19, 1946. It cost $24,000.

2 sisters from the parish.

1902—CHURCH OF ST. JOSEPH, CLEMENTS

It was erected in 1902 by Reverend Father Bergler (1902-6). The rectory was built in 1940 by Reverend N. Gillen (1939-44) who was succeeded by Reverend H Thissen. The parish was formerly a mission attended from Morgan.

5 priests and 7 sisters from the parish.

1902—CHURCH OF ST. JOSEPH, LEXINGTON

The parish was established in 1902 for the Polish Catholics in the vicinity and was attended as a mission by Reverend A. Kotouc (1902-4) and several Polish priest: until October 14, 1948, when Reverend J. Sliwa became first resident pastor. The rectory was built in 1906 by Reverend W. J. Skluzacek (1904-7). Two acres of land were donated by John Pelowski for church and cemetery. There is no school but th children are sent to schools in the neighboring parishes.

1902—CHURCH OF ST. JOHN THE BAPTIST, SAVAGE

When the Church of St. John the Baptist of Byrnesville, less than a mile fror Savage, was destroyed by fire on February 2, 1902, Archbishop Ireland decided tha the new church would be built in Savage through which the railroad passed. Ac cordingly, property was bought, the rectory moved from Byrnesville to it, and th construction of the new brick church begun in July of that year, at a cost of $11 497.00. The cornerstone was blessed on October 5 during the pastorate of Fathe Rhatigan which ended on September 12, 1903. He was followed by Reverend J. / Kane (1903-31) who completed the furnishing and decorating of the church an paid the final installment of the indebtedness on January 12, 1921. His successo Reverend T. J. Keane, (1931-8) built the parish hall in November, 1935, at an ou lay of $7,000. Reverend J. Vacek (1945-50) expended $20,000 in renovating an improving the church and other parish buildings. The parish still operates under tl corporate name of "The Church of St. John the Baptist of Byrnesville." In olde records the name is spelled Burnsville. The present pastor is Reverend A. J. Ziskov sky (1950–) who has assurance from the School Sisters of Notre Dame that they will assume charge of the parochial school in 1954 if it be ready for occupancy.

1 sister from the parish.

1902—CHURCH OF ST. JAMES, NASSAU

It was erected in 1902 by Reverend P. Lauer of the Diocese of Sioux Falls, on grounds donated by John P. Kanthak, Senior, and was remodeled and renovated in 1941 by Reverend F. Plaschko, who built the rectory in 1940, to take the place of one erected in 1902 and occupied till 1910. There are sixty-five families mostly German with a sprinkling of Irish, English and Polish. Ground for the cemetery was donated in 1902 by Albert Schuelke. In 1910 it became a mission of Rosen till the fall of 1939, when Father Plaschko was named pastor and was succeeded in 1946 by Reverend F. J. Barthelme who gave place to Reverend E. Wojtowicz in 1952.

1902—CHURCH OF ST. PAUL, ZUMBROTA

The few Catholic families of this locality were ministered to by priests from Red Wing and Belle Creek till the parish became a mission of Pine Island of which Reverend O. F. Rice was pastor who built the frame church of St. Paul which was dedicated in October, 1902, by Archbishop Ireland assisted by Fathers Rice, Fitzgerald, Gaughan and Prendergast. It was the seventh church in Goodhue County and has Cherry Grove as a mission, with Reverend R. G. Dillon (1951–) as pastor. The rectory was built in 1940 by Reverend George Campbell.

1903—CHURCH OF ST. BARNABAS, BARRY

The first church was erected in 1903 by Reverend M. Gallagher (1903-6) and the second by Reverend P. J. Barron (1906-21). It was destroyed by fire. The present church was built in 1931 by Reverend H. J. Byrne (1929-35) and the rectory by Reverend E. Coughlin (1935-7). The Reverend L. A. Keller came to the parish in 1949.

2 priests and 2 sisters from the parish.

1903—CHURCH OF ST. JOHN THE BAPTIST, EXCELSIOR

It was bought from the Universalists in 1903, reconditioned, and served by Reverend J. F. Busch (now, Bishop of St. Cloud) while Superior of the Diocesan Mission Band till June, 1910, and by his successor, Reverend J. M. Reardon, till December 1, of that year, when Reverend T. Cushen was appointed pastor who built the rectory in 1914, renovated the church in 1921, and added a new sanctuary ten years later. A parish church-school and a convent were built on another site in 1951, and staffed and occupied by the Sisters of St. Joseph. Father Busch erected the Mission House at his own expense in 1904 as headquarters for the Mission Band till 1910. It was sold and is now a rest home.

1 priest, 1 brother and 4 sisters from the parish.

1903—CHURCH OF ST. GREGORY, NORTH BRANCH

A frame church built in 1903 by Reverend R. V. Kennedy of Rush City was destroyed by fire in November, 1942. It was a mission attended from Rush City till 1935, when Reverend E. Coughlin was placed in charge of it. The basement of the new church was completed in 1943 by Reverend B. H. Murray (1940-4). The rectory was purchased in 1936, and Reverend J. B. Garvey was named pastor in 1944.

1903—CHURCH OF ST. JOHN, ORTONVILLE

It was built in 1903 by Reverend M. O'Brien of Graceville, of which it was a mission till 1914. The first resident pastor was Reverend J. A. Sullivan (1921-4). The rectory was built in 1926 by Reverend P. J. Callanan (1924-33). The present pastor, Reverend G. Campbell, came in 1943. It is said that the first Mass was celebrated in the home of Patrick Clarke in November, 1879, by Reverend J. Ryan.

1 priest and 1 sister from the parish.

1904—CHURCH OF ST. JOSEPH, DELANO

It was built under the direction of Reverend M. Savs, pastor of St. Peter's Church in the same city; and Reverend J. Smiech was appointed pastor (1904-7) who erected the parish house in 1905. In 1942 Reverend A. H. Handzel was named pastor.

2 priests and 8 sisters from the parish.

1904—CHURCH OF THE IMMACULATE CONCEPTION, LONSDALE

In 1904 the first church was erected by Reverend A. Kotouc, pastor of Veseli, and the present edifice was built by Reverend R. M. Bastyr (1936-46) and dedicated by Archbishop Murray on September 1, 1941. The rectory was built in 1907 by Reverend F. J. Bouska (1905-21) and the school in 1912, with the School Sisters of Notre Dame in charge. The Reverend C. C. Jirik was appointed pastor in 1948.

2 priests and 18 sisters from the parish.

1904—CHURCH OF ST. MICHAEL, MILROY

It was built in 1904 by Reverend E. Polasek of Lamberton, and in 1922 a full-size basement was added by Reverend A. Kern. It was a mission attended from Lucan from 1905 until 1939, when the rectory was purchased and Reverend D. Noonan became the first resident pastor (1939-47). Reverend P. J. McGuire is the present pastor (1948–).

2 priests and 1 sister from the parish.

1905—CHURCH OF ST. PETER, EDEN VALLEY

It was built in 1905 by the Reverend J. Powers (1906-10), who was then pastor of Manannah; and enlarged in 1917, by Reverend J. O'Callaghan (1912-26) who built the rectory in 1913. Reverend Ambrose R. Filbin is now pastor.

3 priests and 1 sister from the parish.

1905—CHURCH OF ST. JOHN THE BAPTIST, SEARLES

As early as 1859 a small church was begun in Cottonwood Township and completed in 1861. It was abandoned in 1869 when Holy Trinity Church was built in New Ulm. The property, except the little cemetery, was sold February 7, 1895. The first church erected in Searles by Reverend J. Stelmes (1905-6) was dedicated on June 24, 1906, destroyed by fire on March 30, 1935, and rebuilt by Reverend J. L. Neudecker (1935-47). The cornerstone was laid by Archbishop Murray September 15, 1935, and the first Mass said on Christmas Day, 1935. The school and convent were built in 1936 and blessed by Archbishop Murray on June 28 of that year. The School Sisters of Notre Dame are the teachers, since September 14, 1936. The rectory built in 1906, was partly destroyed by fire in 1935 and rebuilt the same year. The parish is in charge of Reverend O. J. Berg (1947–).

1905—CHURCH OF ST. PETER, FOREST LAKE

The Reverend J. A. Kane of Rush City (1895-1903) and his successor, Reverend R. V. Kennedy (1903-8) said Mass in Forest Lake prior to 1905, when the church was dedicated by Archbishop Ireland. It was a mission of Rush City until 191 when the first and only pastor, Reverend T. F. Gibbons, was appointed who built the parochial residence in that year, enlarged the church in 1922, installed new altars and an organ, the gifts of parishioners, and added a sub-auditorium at a cost of $20,000. The site for a school was purchased in 1948.

1 priest and 4 sisters from the parish.

1906—CHURCH OF ST. MARY, BEARDSLEY

It is asserted that there was a small frame church on the site of the present building prior to 1906, but when or by whom built is unknown. The church was erected by Reverend E. Gauvreau. The rectory was built in 1915, by Reverend P. Shanahan (1914-49). The Reverend H. F. Egan was appointed in 1949.

1 sister from the parish.

1906—CHURCH OF THE HOLY TRINITY, GOODHUE

It was erected in 1906 by Reverend H. J. Prendergast, pastor of Belle Creek, who said the first Mass in it on January 13.

1 priest from the parish.

1906—CHURCH OF ST. PAUL, WALNUT GROVE

It was built in 1906-7 by Reverend J. Byrne of Tracy, on a site donated by Mrs. Breckenridge of Rochester, and dedicated June 29, 1907, by Reverend Joseph F. Busch, diocesan missionary, who preached the sermon. It was a mission of Tracy until Reverend R. E. Russell was appointed resident pastor (1939-40), who bought the Allen house for a rectory for $2,200. The bell was consecrated on Sunday, December 21, 1941, by Archbishop Murray during the pastorate of Reverend A. Loosen (1941-8). The Reverend R. T. Aubart was named pastor in 1948.

2 sisters from the parish.

1907—CHURCH OF ST. MARY, OTTAWA

This was a mission of Le Sueur, five miles distant, organized by Reverend Richard Cahill, pastor of the Church of St. Anne, and incorporated on February 5, 1907, with Martin Schwartz (Secretary) and Frank Kilburg (Treasurer), as lay trustees. A stone church and three lots were bought from the Board of Trustees of the Minnesota Church Foundation (Episcopal) for seventy-five dollars on April 22 of that year, renovated and refurnished. Mass was said in it occasionally for a few years, then it was abandoned and finally sold for a private residence for one hundred dollars which was given to the Le Sueur parish. A bell, donated to the church by the Chicago Northwestern Railway, is now in the W. F. Schilling Hobby House, Northfield, Minnesota.

Only two financial reports are available—one for the year ending June 8, 1913, and the other for the following six months, which might indicate that the mission was abandoned about that time. A bill for livery service lists four trips between October 26, 1913, and January 25, 1914. The first report shows receipts amounting to $487.90, made up of a contribution of $404.00 from twenty-three subscribers, $53.89 from plate collections and $30.01 from festivals. The disbursements of $445.26 were for building materials and furnishings, leaving a balance of $42.64. The second report lists receipts of $263.42, from pew rent ($100.00), plate collections ($31.97), festivals ($88.81) and the balance on hand ($42.64). The disbursements were for the pastor's salary ($100.00), and incidentals ($29.56), leaving $133.86 in the treasury of the church. The mission is listed in the Catholic Directory from 1914 to 1926.

An attempt was made to establish another mission at Rush River, across the Minnesota River from Le Sueur, and Mass may have been said a few times in Catholic homes, but no church was erected. It is listed in the Catholic Directory for 1914.

1908—CHURCH OF ST PAUL, NICOLLET

Mass was said in the rectory purchased October 3, 1908, and remodeled for use as a church by Reverend F. Mazir (1907-9). The present church was erected in 1912 by Reverend W. J. Skluzacek (1910-5). The parish was incorporated in 1907, and is in charge of Reverend J. Pendzimas since 1951. It has St. Michael's Church, Belgrade, for a mission.

1908—CHURCH OF ST. MICHAEL, FARMINGTON

A mission successively of Rosemount, Northfield and Lakeville, until 1908, when became an independent parish with the Reverend J. F. Gleason as pastor for a few months. He was succeeded by Reverend J. R. Power (1908-18) who replaced the original frame church with the present brick structure, costing $18,000, on a different site and bought the adjoining house for a rectory. The new church was dedicated by Bishop Lawler on June 16, 1914, who preached at the Solemn High

Mass celebrated by Reverend O. Dolphin of Anoka, and confirmed a class of forty in the afternoon. A convent and catechetical center in charge of the Benedictine Sisters was established in 1940 by Reverend D. J. Moran (1918-43). The present pastor is Reverend G. A. Rogan (1943–).

1909—CHURCH OF OUR LADY OF THE LAKE, MOUND

An old schoolhouse and two lots were bought for $2,000 by Reverend F. J. Jaeger of St. Bonifacius, who organized the parish and said the first Mass on June 13, 1909 in presence of thirteen persons. As a mission of St. Bonifacius it was incorporated September 10, 1909. Father Jaeger was first resident pastor (1921-41). At first Mass was said once a month in summer until 1912, when it was said every Sunday. In 1915 Mass was said regularly throughout the year. The frame church was completed in the spring of 1923 at a cost of $18,000, and dedicated June 17, by Archbishop Dowling. The rectory was built in 1934, at a cost of $9,000. The next pastor was Reverend S. N. Hauer (1941-9), whom the present pastor, Reverend I. Morin, succeeded. The Presentation Sisters who came in August, 1939, to do catechetical work lived in the rectory which the pastor turned over to them until the convent was ready for occupancy on December 8, 1940. The parochial school was dedicated by Auxiliary Bishop Byrne in September, 1951.

1 priest, 1 brother and 1 sister from the parish.

1910—CHURCH OF ST. HENRY, MONTICELLO

A school house was bought in 1910 for use as a church by Reverend S. Kinkead (1910-2), and the present church, built in 1913, by Reverend T. Minogue (1912-4) was blessed by Bishop Lawler on November 23. It was enlarged and additional property bought by Reverend J. M. Pilger (1924-31). On June 19, 1936, Bishop Busch of St. Cloud, dedicated a new altar and tabernacle during the pastorate of Reverend G. W. Keefe (1931-6). The rectory was bought by Father Kinkead; the convent in 1937, by Reverend G. Vander Velden (1936–) and occupied as catechetical school by the Franciscan Sisters until 1941, when they were replaced by the Presentation Sisters of Dubuque, Iowa.

1 brother and 9 sisters from the parish.

1911—CHURCH OF THE HOLY NAME, VESTA

The first church was moved from Belview in 1911, by Reverend A. Schaefer Lucan, dismantled in 1935 by Reverend J. Stolz of Seaforth, of which Vesta was then a mission, and the present basement church built. The parish house was erected in 1945 by Reverend A. Leifeld. Since 1946 the Sisters of St. Joseph come from Marshall every Saturday to teach the children. Reverend Charles J. Stark now pastor.

1 sister from the parish.

1911—CHURCH OF ST. MARY, NEW ULM

The parish was founded September 26, 1911, and the property bought for $2848.17. The people worshipped in the basement of the Holy Trinity Church until the new church was ready for occupancy. On September 1, 1921, Reverend Anthony Losleben was appointed pastor and built the church-school and the convent in 1925 at a cost of $85,000. The first Mass was said on February 2, 1923. Father Losleben died in 1930. He was succeeded by Reverend John J. Goergen (1931-50) who, March 1, 1940, purchased the residence of H. L. Beecher, as a rectory to take the place of the outmoded building used as a residence from the beginning. The Sisters of Christian Charity have charge of the school. Father Goergen died a month after he celebrated his golden jubilee in June, 1950, and Reverend George W. Rolw was appointed to succeed him.

1911—CHURCH OF THE SACRED HEART, ROBBINSDALE

The church was built in 1911 by Reverend J. Harrington, pastor of the Church of the Ascension, Minneapolis, of which it was a mission, enlarged in 1927 by the first resident pastor, Reverend W. H. Blum (1912-31), renovated and decorated by the present pastor, Reverend F. J. Nolan (1931—). The rectory was built in 1912; the school in 1926; the convent in 1927, for the Benedictine Sisters who teach in the school. Transepts and sanctuary were added to the church in 1928.

6 priests and 11 sisters from the parish.

1912—CHURCH OF ST. MARTIN, ROGERS

It was erected in 1912 by Reverend M. F. Doring (1912-6), and the rectory built n 1924 by Reverend P. Schirmers (1922-5). A school was built in 1951 and staffed)y the Sisters of Notre Dame. Reverend Mark Otto is the pastor.

1 priest and 3 sisters from the parish.

913—CHURCH OF ST. AGATHA, COATES

The first baptism in the parish was administered on February 8, 1914, by Reverend '. J. McCabe, pastor of St. Patrick's, Inver Grove, from June, 1912, to December, 914, when he was succeeded by Reverend M. M. Ryan (1914-20). St. Agatha's vas made an independent parish in 1915 with Inver Grove as a mission, but the .ext year it reverted to its former status and so remained until St. Patrick's was lestroyed by fire in September, 1919, when Father Ryan took up his residence at Coates. After his departure the parish was administered by Reverend Thomas P. 'yan, of the College of St. Thomas, until his death in 1930. After an interval of a ear and a half the present administrator, Reverend M. J. Gillen, of the St. Thomas 'ollege faculty, took charge.

1 sister from the parish.

913—CHURCH OF ST. JOSEPH, RUSSELL

This was a mission of Marshall from 1913 to 1923, when it was abandoned and le church sold.

914—CHURCH OF ST. CLOTILDE, GREEN VALLEY

The first church was purchased from the Presbyterians and blessed by Reverend Guillot of Marshall, of which it was a mission till 1914. The present church was uilt by Reverend W. C. Soulard (1921-32). The Reverend R. T. O'Connor was istor from 1949 to 1952 when he was succeeded by Reverend R. Zwicky.

1 priest and 3 sisters from the parish.

16—CHURCH OF ST. BARTHOLOMEW, WAYZATA

The Reverend G. Scheffold, O.S.B., of Holy Name, who said the first Mass on ptember 10, 1916, in Wayzata Town Hall, built the church in 1916, and opened for divine service on Christmas Day, became the first resident pastor (1925-6), d bought the first rectory in 1925. The church was enlarged in 1924, and plans r a new church were prepared under the direction of Reverend L. Beckwerth, S.B. (1940-50). The new rectory was completed in 1942, and blessed on May 15, the Right Reverend Alcuin Deutsch, O.S.B., of St. John's Abbey, Collegeville. e pastor is Reverend Demetrius Hagmann, O.S.B., who plans to build a school.

1 priest from the parish.

16—CHURCH OF ST. GEORGE, LONG LAKE

Mass was said for the first time in Long Lake Hall (now Kogan's grocery) and er in the home of Samuel Rettinger whose wife was a Catholic. The church was cted in 1916 by Reverend G. Scheffold, O.S.B., of Wayzata, of which it was a ssion until the first resident pastor, Reverend W. J. Nolan, came in 1948. He oc- ied a temporary rectory purchased in the same year. The sanctuary was re- leled by Reverend Lambert Beckwerth, O.S.B., of Wayzata.

21—CHURCH OF ST. JOSEPH, HOPKINS

his parish is a consolidation of two parishes, one for the Bohemians (St. Mar- et's) and the other for the English-speaking Catholics (St. Mary's). Their histories are given elsewhere. The present St. Joseph's church-school, rectory and convent were built in 1922 under the direction of Reverend C. E. Hovorka (1921–). The school opened in 1923, with the Sisters of St. Joseph in charge.

1 priest and 11 sisters from the parish.

1921—CHURCH OF ST. JOSEPH, HALLOWAY

This church was incorporated at Edison, in Edison Township, Swift County, on September 12, 1921, and moved to its present location in the village of Halloway in October, 1944, by the pastor, Reverend R. Doerrer (1943-5). For thirty years prior to its incorporation the Polish Catholics of Edison Township were ministered to by the priests from the neighboring parishes who said Mass once a month in Catholic homes. In 1921 it was made a mission to Appleton under Reverend S. Julkowski (1921-7) who was succeeded by eleven pastors including the present one, Reverend T. Szymanski (1945–). The parish consists of thirty-four families.

1925—CHURCH OF THE HOLY ROSARY, NORTH MANKATO

A combination church and school was erected in 1925 by Reverend J. Freisleber (1924-48). The first rectory was occupied in 1925, and the present one completed in 1927, when the former was remodeled into a convent. The school is conducted by the School Sisters of Notre Dame and the present pastor is Reverend A. Schlad-weiler who was appointed in 1948 and built the new church.

1 brother and 10 sisters from the parish.

1926—CHURCH OF THE HOLY FAMILY, ST. LOUIS PARK

It was incorporated January 13, 1926, as a mission of the church of St. Joseph Hopkins, and attended by Reverend Cornelius Normoyle from the College of St Thomas assisting the pastor of Hopkins. The first Mass was said in a store near the Post Office. A frame building was erected and Mass said therein until Sunday, December 9, 1951. The auditorium chapel in the new school building and the school were blessed by Archbishop Murray, December 16, 1951. Reverend William Driscoll was appointed first resident pastor in October, 1926, and was succeeded by Reverend Michael Condon on June 1, 1938. Reverend Francis Wilkins came October 28, 1947, purchased a new rectory and gave the former residence for use as convent by the Servite Sisters who opened the new school in September, 1951.

1 sister from the parish.

1933—CHURCH OF ST. ANTHONY, REGAL

A basement church was built in 1933 by Reverend W. Murphy of Kandiyohi, of which it was a mission until 1943, when it was given the status of an independent parish with Kandiyohi as a mission. The parochial residence was purchased in April 1943, from Wallace Weidner. The present pastor is Reverend Bernard Schreine (1951–).

1935—CHURCH OF ST. MARY OF THE LAKE, MEDICINE LAKE

The cornerstone of this church was laid on September 8, 1935, during the incumbency of the founder and first pastor of the parish, Reverend N. C. Finn (1935-45) The church was decorated in 1948 by the Reverend T. P. Ryan (1945–). Th rectory is attached to the church.

1936—CHURCH OF ST. THOMAS MORE, LAKE LILLIAN

This parish was organized as a mission of the Church of the Sacred Heart, Raymond, in 1936, and the basement church was built in 1940.

1938—CHURCH OF ST. FRANCIS OF ASSISI, ST. CROIX BEACH

It was erected in 1938 by the Reverend F. E. Benz (1938-41) and is now charge of Reverend D. A. Roney (1952–).

1940—CHURCH OF ST. JUDE OF THE LAKE, MAHTOMEDI

This stone church was built in 1940 by Reverend J. F. Cronin (1939-46) who al purchased the building occupied as a parish house. The Reverend S. N. Hauer w appointed to the parish in 1950 who built the convent for the Sisters of St. Benedict of Crookston, who have charge of a catechetical school.

1940—CHURCH OF THE HOLY TRINITY, SOUTH ST. PAUL

It was erected in 1941 by Reverend J. F. Siegienski (1940-51) who, prior to December 8, said Mass in the Roosevelt School. The first Mass was said in the basement of the church December 8, 1941, and in the upper church March 7, 1942. The church was dedicated June 25, 1942, by Archbishop Murray. The rectory was blessed on July 20, 1941. There is no school but the Felician Sisters from St. Casimir's Church, St. Paul, teach catechism. Rt. Rev. V. W. Worzalla became pastor in 1951.

2 sisters from the parish.

1941—CHURCH OF ST. JEROME, NEW CANADA TOWNSHIP

The parish was first entrusted to Reverend J. L. Westfall who said Mass in the Edgerton School during August, 1940. Father Mingo of St. Paul Seminary said Mass for the people till December 28 when Reverend J. W. Brady was appointed pastor who erected the church in 1941. The rectory was completed in July of the following year when Father Brady was succeeded by Reverend F. Wilkins (1942-7). The present pastor is Reverend L. D. Kachinsky who came in 1947. A new school and convent were built in 1951.

1943—CHURCH OF ST. FRANCIS DE SALES, WINTHROP

It was begun in 1943 by Reverend E. N. Clemens of Gaylord and completed by Reverend L. Krzmarzick, his successor. Only the basement is finished for service. It is a mission of Gaylord of which Reverend Ambrose Siebenand is pastor.

1943—CHURCH OF ST. TIMOTHY, SPRING LAKE PARK

The Reverend T. D. O'Connell was appointed pastor on January 16, 1943, and said Mass in the Blaine School until the church was completed the same year. He bought a farm house for a rectory in 1944. Before that he lived at St. Stephen's parish house in Anoka. There is no school. St. Patrick's, Cedar Creek, is a mission.

1943—CHURCH OF ST. CHARLES, BAYPORT

A basement church was built in 1943 by Reverend F. J. Miller (1943—), Chaplain of the State Penitentiary, Stillwater. The Sisters of St. Joseph from St. Michael's Convent, Stillwater, teach catechism.

1943—CHURCH OF ST. MICHAEL, KENYON

The parish was incorporated in 1943 during the brief pastorate of Reverend M. Lawler. A large house with five city blocks was purchased in 1944 by the first resident pastor, Reverend A. M. Louis (1944-51), who transformed it into a combination church and residence and said the first Mass in it on February 13, 1944. Kenyon is a Norwegian settlement with few Catholics. The Dominican Sisters of Faribault teach catechism on Saturdays and during summer vacation. The Church of St. Edward, Richland, is a mission. Reverend Francis M. Hayden is the pastor.

1943—CHURCH OF ST. PETER, RICHFIELD

The first Mass was said in Holy Angels Academy on November 14, 1943, by Reverend W. A. Brand (1943—) and regularly on Sundays for the congregation till the combined church and school, begun in October, 1945, was dedicated by Archbishop Murray in 1946. The upper church was finished in 1950. The school was opened in September, 1946, by the Sisters of St. Joseph and additional rooms were provided in 1950. A rectory at 204 West 66th Street was purchased on November 10, 1943; and the new parish house bought from the Government, was moved to the present site, remodeled and occupied in 1950.

1943—CHURCH OF ST. GREGORY THE GREAT, LAFAYETTE

It was a mission of Gaylord till September, 1943, when Reverend E. M. Clemens was transferred thereto from Gaylord, bought a hall, 40 x 80, and remodeled it into a church in 1944. He purchased the rectory in 1943. He was succeeded by Reverend L. Krzmarzick. The Sisters of the Poor Handmaids of Jesus Christ, residing at St. George, teach catechism on Saturdays and during June, since 1943. A new rectory was built in 1950.

1944—CHURCH OF THE MOST HOLY TRINITY, ST. LOUIS PARK

Mass was said by the pastor, Reverend J. W. Brady, in May, 1943, in the Lilac Lanes Bowling Alley building and in the American Legion Hall from May to December, 1944, when the present basement church was ready for occupancy. The school was opened in September, 1945, with an enrollment of 178 pupils under the direction of the Benedictine Sisters from St. Joseph, Minnesota. The rectory and the convent and other buildings were purchased by the parish to secure additional ground and facilities.

1946—CHURCH OF ST. THERESE, DEEPHAVEN

This parish was part of St. John's parish, Excelsior, prior to 1946, when the church was erected by Reverend M. J. Otto shortly after he said the first Mass in the Groveland school on June 9. A rectory was built in 1951 by the present pastor, Reverend Francis E. Shea (1950—).

1946—CHURCH OF THE IMMACULATE HEART OF MARY, GLEN LAKE

It was opened on July 12, 1946, with Reverend T. R. Jude as pastor (1946-51) who said Mass in a quonset hut. It is now in charge of Reverend F. Fleming, who opened the school in September, 1952, with the Sisters of the Immaculate Heart of Mary in charge.

1946—CHURCH OF OUR LADY OF GRACE, EDINA

Mass was said in the Edina Theater until 1949, when the combination church and school with attached convent was built and dedicated in 1949, under the direction of the pastor, Reverend L. W. Forrey (1946—). The school is in charge of the Sisters of Mercy. A rectory, at some distance from the present site, was purchased in 1946 and occupied until 1949, when the pastor took up his residence in the new building.

1946—CHURCH OF ST. JOHN VIANNEY, SOUTH ST. PAUL

It was built by Reverend H. E. Whittet (1946—) who also purchased the rectory. A school was built in 1950.

1949—CHURCH OF ST. BRIDGET OF SWEDEN, LINDSTROM

The basement of the proposed brick church which will cost $48,000, was built in 1949 under the direction of Reverend J. B. Garvey of North Branch, of which it is a mission, and dedicated in July, 1950. The parish has only forty families. The locality is a center of Swedish protestantism.

1949—CHURCH OF THE NATIVITY OF THE B. V. M., OXBORO

The parish was organized in November, 1949, under the direction of Reverend M Larkin, who built the parish house in 1950. The combination church and school was dedicated by Archbishop Murray on September 9 of the next year, and the first confirmation administered in the afternoon of that day. The school is staffed by the Sisters of St. Joseph.

1950—CHURCH OF ST. JOHN THE BAPTIST, INTERLACHEN PARK

The parish was established in June, 1950, under the direction of Reverend J. F Vacek who built a combined church and school. The Sisters of Divine Providence of Kentucky assumed charge of the school in September, 1951.

1952—CHURCH OF ST. RICHARD, RICHFIELD

It was incorporated on January 21 and the first Mass was said in a public school on February 3 by the pastor, Reverend Alfred Longley, who had just completed ten years of service as an army chaplain. The parish embraces the territory south of the Minneapolis City line to 90th. Street, and west of Humboldt to France Avenue. Plans have been prepared for a combination church and school.

Chapter XIII

DIOCESAN INSTITUTIONS

Under this heading are listed, with brief descriptive paragraphs, the names of all the religious institutions established in the Diocese of St. Paul and approved by the Ordinary, if not under his direct control, since the beginning of its existence.

The information about existing institutions was furnished by, or at the request of, their official heads on questionnaires sent out by the Chancery Office, supplemented, whenever possible, by facts drawn from other reliable sources.

The sketches of institutions no longer in existence are based on the meager records in diocesan and other archives, newspapers and local histories, and may prove not uninteresting to readers.

CITY OF ST. PAUL

1851—ST. JOSEPH'S ACADEMY

This first educational institution in the frontier Diocese of St. Paul was established on November 10, 1851, in the original log "Palace" of Bishop Cretin by the four Sisters of St. Joseph—Mother St. John Fournier, Sisters Philomene Vilaine, Francis Joseph Ivory and Scholastica Vasques—who had just arrived from Carondelet, near St. Louis, Mo., and who opened a school for girls in the vestry of the log chapel, the first Cathedral, on Bench Street hill. Fourteen girls were enrolled the first day and before the next spring the attendance had increased to such an extent that the chapel itself had to be used for school purposes. A two-story brick school was erected in 1852 and housed the rapidly growing classes until 1858. When Bishop Grace arrived in 1859 he transferred the pupils to St. Joseph's Hospital, Ninth and Exchange Streets, with Mother Seraphine Coughlin as directress.

The present site of St. Joseph's Academy on Marshall Avenue was bought in 1860 and three years later the central unit was occupied as a boarding school, as it was far from the center of the city. It was incorporated in June, 1867, with academy and elementary departments, the latter ungraded until 1895. In the beginning the teaching was in English and French. By 1875 the academic classes were organized into graduating, intermediate, first and second class, and courses in music, art, cooking and sewing added. A wing for class rooms and boarders' quarters was added in 1877; and affiliation with the University of Minnesota obtained in 1899. An Alumnae Association was organized in 1901.

The boarding school was transferred to Derham Hall on Randolph and Cleveland Avenues in 1905 and the Academy became a day school. The elementary department was closed in 1926 to make room for an increased enrollment of high school students and the next year it was on the list of North Central Association's accredited high schools.

In 1930 two new buildings were added—the one a four-story class room wing with offices, laboratories, dining rooms, gymnasium and an auditorium seating more than nine hundred; the other a chapel and library. The local Superior is Mother M. Clara. There are on the staff 32 sisters and 10 lay teachers for an enrollment of 783 students. A number of sisters teaching in parochial schools reside at the Academy, making 80 in all.

1853—ST. JOSEPH'S HOSPITAL

This is the oldest hospital in Minnesota and was founded and staffed by four teaching Sisters of St. Joseph in 1853, at the request of Bishop Cretin. It was a brick building, four stories high. The following year three additional sisters came from St. Louis to care for the sick. The original structure was torn down in 1895 and replaced with a more modern building which, together with the west wing built in 1878 and the east in 1885, is still in use, but remodeled and modernized. In 1894 Mother Bernardine Maher (1884-1920) founded the training school for nurses. The present north wing was added in 1922 and the nurses' home in 1926. The institution was incorporated on April 16, 1895, with Mother Seraphine Ireland as the first President. The first interne, Dr. A. Gillette, came in 1885; and a school for nurses was established in 1894. The first operation in America for the complete removal of the gall bladder was performed in St. Joseph's Hospital by Dr. Justus Ohage, Sr., on September 24, 1886. There are now 40 sisters on the staff with Mother M. Antonius in charge. It has a capacity of 260 beds and 59 bassinets, with 118 student nurses, 140 clerical and professional, and 212 non-professional employees.

1853—ST. JOSEPH'S NOVITIATE

It was opened in the original St. Joseph's Academy on Bench Street and the first reception of the religious habit took place in May 1854, when Louise LeMay was admitted to the community as Sister M. Pauline. In the second reception, held in 1858, Ellen Ireland (Sister Seraphine) and her cousin, Ellen Howard (Sister Celestine), received the habit. The novitiate was transferred to the new St. Joseph's Academy in 1863 where it remained until 1912 when the recently-erected Novitiate on Randolph Avenue was opened and the first reception of the habit took place in the forenoon of August 15. The last Profession was held in the old novitiate on the afternoon of the same day.

1853—CATHOLIC ORPHANAGE

The cholera epidemic of 1853 made many orphans and they were temporarily housed in the newly-erected St. Joseph's Hospital. In 1859 Bishop Grace opened an orphanage for boys and girls in the first residence of the Sisters of St. Joseph adjoining the old academy on Bench Street where they were under the supervision of the Mother Superior of the hospital and of the academy. In the summer of 1863 both hospital and orphanage were re-established in St. Joseph's Hospital which had been vacated by the transfer of the pupils to the new St. Joseph's Academy on St. Anthony hill. Six years later the orphanage was incorporated and opened as a separate institution at Grove and St. Paul (now, Olive) streets in lower town. It had an average enrollment of eighty boys and girls under the care of eight Sisters of St. Joseph. When the orphanage in Minneapolis was opened in 1878, the boys were transferred thereto and the St. Paul institution was thenceforth reserved for girls. It was moved to the present location, 933 Carroll Avenue, in 1883.

1855—BROTHERS OF THE HOLY FAMILY

Early in 1855 four Brothers of the Holy Family from Belley, France, came to St. Paul on the invitation of Bishop Cretin to take charge of a boys' school and found a novitiate of their order. They were Cyrille (the Superior), Timothy, Mary Leo and Ernest. They opened a school in the basement of the second Cathedral building on Wabasha at Sixth Street and soon had a large number of boys under instruction. They received very meager support and a few entered the novitiate. The Bishop promised to help them when and if he received funds from the Society for the Propagation of the Faith. The Brothers were permitted by their rule to go singly with priests to act as sacristans and catechists. In 1856 Brother Timothy was sent to Father Belcourt at St. Joseph, west of Pembina, and Brother Mary Leo to Father Pierz at Belle Prairie, and Brother Ernest to Father Keller at Faribault in 1858 as teacher in the parish school. After the death of Bishop Cretin in February, 1857, the Superior General, Father Gabriel, recalled them to France. Brother Cyrille received permission to join the Congregation of the Holy Cross, South Bend, Indiana, was ordained to the priesthood as Reverend J. C. Carrier, and was Prefect of Religion at Notre Dame University. There is no record of what became of the others and no mention of the Institute in the Catholic Directory for 1861, indicating that they must have left the diocese in 1860.

The congregation was first established by Brother Gabriel Taboran in the Diocese of Saint Claude, France, in 1824, but it was not a success. A new foundation was made in 1827 at Hauteville; and about 1835 in the Diocese of Belley. It was approved by Pope Gregory XVI. The Superior General is elected for life and the only priests admitted are those needed to fulfil the sacred offices and direct the novitiate. In 1901 it had forty members engaged in foreign mission work.

1860—ST. JOSEPH'S PROVINCIALATE

The Provincial headquarters of the Sisters of St. Joseph was established in St. Joseph's Academy in 1860 with Mother Seraphine Coughlin as Provincial Superior. Death removed her within a year and her successor was Mother Stanislaus Saul. In 1882 when Mother Seraphine Ireland became Provincial there were eight houses in the Province and ten parochial schools, five of which were in St. Paul. In 1925 work began on the new Provincial house on Randolph Avenue and Mother St. Rose, who succeeded Mother Seraphine, took up her residence there. On August 10, 1949, it housed 92 professed sisters, 53 novices and 11 postulants. Mother M. Eucharista was Provincial Superior, Mother Deborah, local superior, Mother Edwina Mistress of Novices and Mother Bertha in charge of the postulate. In 1951 Mother Aquin was appointed Provincial Superior with Sister M. Bertha as assistant. Mother Aquin resigned in 1952 and was succeeded by Mother Bertha. There are 38 subordinate houses in the Archdiocese of St. Paul and 5 in the Diocese of Fargo.

1868—HOUSE OF THE GOOD SHEPHERD

Mother Mary of St. Bernard Flinn and three other Sisters of the Good Shepherd from the St. Louis Motherhouse came to St. Paul on May 19, 1868, and took possession of an eight-room frame house at Smith Avenue and Fort Street. They were welcomed by Bishop Grace, Father Ireland, Captain O'Connor, Charles Boyle and Mesdames Boyle, Slater, Akers and Withaus, who prepared the house for them. The first Mass was said by Father Ireland on May 21, the feast of the Ascension. In September they opened school in a house, 20 by 30 feet, which they bought and moved beside the convent, and placed Sister Mary of Blessed Margaret Ward in charge. On December 15, 1868, Mother Bernard, thirty years old, was installed as Superior by Bishop Grace assisted by Fathers Ravoux and Ireland. The last Mass was said in that convent on April 19, 1869, when the Sisters moved to the Baldwin College Building, 90 Wilkin Street, which they bought.

In 1871 they built an addition for the rehabilitation of wayward girls and for a preservation class and opened a private school for girls which was burned down in 1879. They supported themselves by laundry work, needle work and fine embroidery. The Novitiate was in St. Louis but they established a Magdalen community in 1878 with eight subjects.

In 1881 the sisters bought their present location on Mount Eudes comprising 27½ acres and moved to the new home in 1883. For a time water for the laundry and other purposes had to be hauled from a distance but ultimately Michael Doran, at his own expense, connected the institution with the city water supply and piped the house. The first resident chaplain, Father Ducunich, came in 1885; the novitiate was opened in 1886, when the first postulant was Miss Hughes, afterwards Mother Mary of St. Rose of Lima, the Provincial Superior who died in 1933. The present Provincial Superior (since 1933) is Mother Francis Xavier Hickey who celebrated the seventieth anniversary of her profession in 1951. There are 36 choir sisters, 48 Magdalens and 144 girls. There are seven subordinate houses throughout the West, in Omaha, Denver, Spokane, Helena, Seattle, Portland and Sioux City.

1871—CRETIN HIGH SCHOOL

At the urgent request of Father Ireland, pastor of the Cathedral, two Christian Brother—Brother Jucondian, Director, and Brother Porphyrus—came to St. Paul on November 2, 1871, to teach in the Cathedral school in the brick building on Wabasha at Sixth Street, opened in 1851 by Bishop Cretin. The next year there were 250 pupils in four classes and five brothers. They lived in the rooms on the third foor vacated by the bishop and clergy in 1860. The Brothers taught the Assumption school from 1875 to 1882, and St. Mary's from 1876 to 1891. In 1882 there were twelve brothers in the community and 668 boys under their care, the younger ones taught by the Sisters of St. Joseph. The Brothers' rooms and the chapel were gutted by fire in November, 1886. The new Cretin High School, at Sixth and Main Streets, was dedicated by Bishop Grace in March, 1889, but the Brothers resided in their old quarters till August of that year, just before the second Cathedral was dismantled. The twenty-fifth anniversary of their arrival was celebrated in 1896, and an Alumni Association formed at a banquet in honor of the event. In 1904 Cretin High was accredited by the University of Minnesota. It then had 500 students in twelve classes. The close association of the Brothers with the Sisters of St. Joseph who taught the lower grades since 1871 came to an end in 1914 when the new Cathedral school was opened to accommodate the grades. The cornerstone of the present Cretin High was laid on April 27, 1927, on an 11-acre tract of land at Randolph and Hamline Avenues and the building was ready for occupancy in September of the next year. The first commencement was held in it before the opening on June 10, 1928, when Archbishop Dowling dedicated it. During the previous year the classes were held in the old Webster Public High School on Laurel Avenue and Mackubin Street and the Brothers resided in a rented house on Holly Avenue. The four-year high school curriculum was established in 1914 and the military unit introduced in 1918. Cretin High had 24 directors prior to 1946. Among its graduates are the Most Reverend James J. Byrne, Auxiliary Bishop of St. Paul, the late Monsignor John A. Ryan of the Catholic University of America, and a large number of priests, both diocesan and regular.

1873—CONVENT OF THE VISITATION

Six Sisters of the Visitation Order came from St. Louis on August 12, 1873, at the request of Bishop Grace, and took posssession of a frame house at 318 Somerset Street, under the leadership of Mother Mary Agatha Russell. They were escorted by Father Caillet, pastor of St. Mary's parish, in which the convent was located, and Father Fenelon, Chaplain of the St. Louis convent. The first Mass was said in their new home on August 15 and closure regularly established. They opened a select school enrolling 27 pupils, and a month later the institution was incorporated. In June, 1881, the ten sisters of the community moved to a larger convent on upper Robert Street at Aurora Avenue. The attendance continued to grow and, on January 29, the feast of St. Francis de Sales, their patron, Archbishop Ireland blessed the newly-erected brick building to serve as a school when the frame building became the monastery. In June, 1913, the present Monastery and academy at Fairmount Avenue and Grotto Street was occupied by the 27 sisters of the community and it was blessed by Archbishop Ireland on July 2 of that year. There are 32 sisters under the direction of Mother Jane Margaret Cullinan, the present Superior, 6 lay teachers and 200 students.

1874—CATHOLIC INDUSTRIAL SCHOOL OF MINNESOTA.

It was incorporated January 4, 1874, as a home and trade school for under-privileged boys. The first site selected was the "Bishop's Farm" on the Dodd Road, now the Riverview Golf Course. It was abandoned when Bishop Grace bought the Finn farm of 452 acres in Reserve Township between Cleveland Avenue and the Mississippi for $56,500, on May 2, 1874, as the future home of the school. A building was erected in 1876, 34 by 52 feet, three stories high, and the school opened in the spring of 1877 in charge of three Brothers of the Third Order of St. Francis, with Brother Augustine as Superior and Brothers Michael and Thomas as assistants. It was operated for two years and never had more than twenty boys in residence. Later on it was reopened on a farm near Clontarf.

1877—ST. JOSEPH'S ORPHANAGE

It was opened in temporary rented quarters at Ninth and Robert streets, with six orphans taken from the Catholic orphanage on Grove and Olive Streets, and was in charge of lay persons. Later it was placed under Mother Benedict, O. S. B., (1877-1908) and Sister Agatha, O. S. B., from Shakopee. Larger quarters were rented opposite the Assumption rectory in the fall of 1877. A new orphanage was erected on property adjoining St. Joseph's Hospital at a cost of $9,000 in addition to the price of the land, $3,000, occupied on October 27, 1880, and blessed by Bishop Grace on December 9, of that year. The first Mass was said by Reverend Valentine Stimmler, O. S. B., pastor of the Assumption parish, on December 14.

The orphanage was incorporated on March 19, 1881. A school was opened in 1888. The present orphanage, on the forty-seven acre tract at Randolph and Hamline Avenue, cost $75,000, was opened on October 7, 1900, and dedicated on November 1. It has accommodations for 127, but, owing to lack of workers, the nursery was closed in 1948, reducing the number by 25. Since 1887, 3,150 children have been cared for. Financial support comes from the annual diocesan collection and the Community Chest. Children are admitted through the charity bureaus of the diocese and placed in homes through them. The present staff is composed of Sister M. Marcelline, Superior, and nineteen Sisters of St. Benedict who teach up to the end of the seventh grade. The pupils of the eighth grade are sent to the adjoining parochial school of the Holy Spirit parish. An 8-acre truck garden supplies the institution with fresh vegetables in summer and canned vegetables and fruit for winter. The Benedictine chaplain resides in a cottage on the grounds.

1883—ST. PAUL CATHOLIC ORPHAN ASYLUM

A four-story brick structure was erected at 933 Carroll Avenue to provide better accommodations for the girls from the old Catholic orphanage at Grove and Olive Streets in lower town who were transferred to it in 1883, when it was dedicated by Bishop Grace, assisted by a number of priests and the members of the Board of Directors. A boiler room and a laundry are in a separate building, and an addition was made to the main structure in 1911. The original building cost $34,694 and was out of debt when dedicated. It shares in the diocesan collection and the Community Chests of the Twin Cities. It is in charge of 11 Sisters of St. Joseph with Mother Agnes Patrice as Superior, and has 60 girls from three to sixteen years of age.

1883—LITTLE SISTERS OF THE POOR

They occupy the house vacated by the Sisters of the Good Shepherd in 1883 and devote themselves to the material and spiritual welfare of men and women over sixty years of age who have no visible means of support. The original accommodation for 150 has been increased to 185 by a recent addition and remodeling costing $300,000 donated by benefactors. Fifteen sisters have charge of the home with Mother Marguerite as Superior.

1884—ST. AGATHA'S CONSERVATORY OF MUSIC AND ART

It was first established in the Lick residence at Tenth and Main Streets near St.

Joseph's Hospital, and in 1886 moved to Judge Palmer's frame house on Exchange Street between Cedar and Wabasha. At first it was a kindergarten and music school but the growth of the latter forced the closing of the former. In 1892 a temporary frame addition provided rooms for the faculty and students. Classes in vocal music and expression were added in 1900. A new wing was built in 1901 to replace the temporary structure; and in 1908 the present commodious seven-story brick building was erected with an adjoining chapel. It is a home for the faculty members and for the sisters teaching in six parochial schools in the city. There are 92 sisters in residence and Mother M. Annetta is the Superior.

1884—ST. MARY'S HOME FOR GIRLS

This home for friendless and unprotected girls was opened at 571 Westminster Street, in April, 1884, in a frame house accommodating twelve persons. It was sponsored by a group of prominent women in St. Mary's parish each of whom undertook to raise one hundred dollars a year for its support. Funds for a year were subscribed before it was opened. The women took turns in managing it. It provided a home for girls temporarily out of work or seeking employment, was non-sectarian, with morning and evening prayers in common. The Board of Directors was supplemented by an executive committee of which Mrs. J. J. Hill was chairman. During the first year 248 girls were registered and meals and lodging provided for many more. An industrial department was opened to teach girls to sew and make garments. Miss Anne Veeley was the matron. Receipts for the first six months totalled $2.332.37 from donations, laundry, board of inmates, etc., and additional $1,300 had been set aside as the nucleus of a building fund.

Before the end of the year the home was committed to the care of the Daughters of the Immaculate Heart of Mary, who managed similar institutions in other cities. They did not wear a religious garb but a secular dress.

Before many years the home was moved to 318 Somerset Street, the original convent of the Sisters of the Visitation, where it provided accommodations for forty persons. The girls paid three dollars a week for board, lodging, medical care and had the free use of sewing machines. Those who were unemployed paid nothing but helped about the house and in the sewing room. The first Superior of the home was Miss Anne Sullivan who had charge till 1888 when she was succeeded by Madame Adele Perronno who supervised the institution until it was closed in 1896 after the death of Madame Nardin of Buffalo, N. Y., the American Provincial of the community.

Connected with the home was a day nursery where working mothers could leave their children to be cared for. It was opened in a house erected by the sisters at a cost of $2,400, in which Mass was said from time to time on an altar donated by Mr. and Mrs. Smith. From five to ten children were cared for daily.

1886—DEAF MUTE INSTITUTE

An institute for the education of deaf mutes was established in September, 1886, at 537 Mississippi Street under the supervision of Madame Boucher of the Daughters of the Immaculate Heart of Mary. It opened with one pupil, a girl, and before the end of the third year had an enrollment of 42 boys and girls. The boys lived in the institute, the girls at St. Mary's Home. In the early years of its existence the sign language was used as a medium of instruction, but later on the more improved methods of articulation used in similar institutions in Paris and Bordeaux were adopted. Lack of financial support forced its closing in 1893 and many of the pupils were taken to schools in Chicago conducted by the Daughters of the Immaculate Heart of Mary. On October 10, 1897, Father Gibbons, pastor of St Mary's Church, revived the work, organized the deaf mutes into a society and provided teachers to instruct them on the second Sunday of the month in the school hall. At one time it had a membership of sixty, from sixteen to eighty-three years of age, half of whom lived in Minneapolis. Professor Schroeder of St. Paul a deaf mute, was President, Miss Louise Smith of Minneapolis, Secretary, and

Father Gibbons, Spiritual Director. It continued till 1910 when Father Gibbons left the parish.

1893—ST. PAUL TABERNACLE SOCIETY

At a meeting of forty representative Catholic women of the Twin Cities held in the Aberdeen Hotel, St. Paul, on the first Friday of August, 1893, the St. Paul Tabernacle Society was organized, with the approbation of the Most Reverend Archbishop, by Mrs. Benjamin Thompson who was elected President and held office until March 30, 1911, when she resigned.

The purpose of the society as set forth in its constitution is "to make and furnish gratis to needy churches the vestments and linens necessary for celebrating the Holy Sacrifice of the Mass, giving Benediction, administering the sacraments, and, so far as the finances of the society permit, any article of church or altar furnishings".

The society is composed of sustaining and active members, the former paying three dollars a year and the latter, in addition to paying dues, assisting in making vestments and altar linens. It holds weekly meetings from the last Friday in September until the last Friday in April, inclusive, with regular monthly meetings on the last Fridays of these months to receive reports from the officers and transact other business. The work of each year begins with Mass and a day of recollection in the St. Paul Cathedral and in the beginning ended with similar exercises in the then Pro-Cathedral of St. Mary, Minneapolis.

The Society has carried on its beneficent work during the past fifty-eight years, meeting regularly in different places in down-town St. Paul, in the Cathedral rectory, and now for several years in the former residence of the Archbishop, 226 Summit Avenue.

The Spiritual Directors were Archbishop Ireland; Bishop Lawler; Reverends T. J. Gibbons, J. C. Byrne, L. F. Ryan and G. E. Ryan.

1894—COLLEGE OF ST. THOMAS

It began its existence on September 8, 1885, as the St. Thomas Aquinas Seminary for ecclesiastical and lay students, teaching theology and philosophy and a six-year classical course. The seminary department was transferred to the St. Paul Seminary in September, 1894. In 1885 there were 27 theologians and 39 in classics with Reverend Thomas O'Gorman as first President.

The College was incorporated on January 25, 1894, with 99 students during the Presidency of Reverend J. C. Byrne (1892-9). A two-year commercial course was added in 1895 and an English scientific course in 1897. The science hall was built in 1900 during the Presidency of Reverend John Dolphin (1899-1903).

The College came of age under Reverend H. Moynihan who was President from 1903 to 1921. The enrollment grew from 253 to 1,059 from 24 states in the Union, Canada, France, Mexico and the Philippine Islands. An Alumni Association was formed on June 2, 1903, with a roster of 113 names and John A. Hartigan was elected President. The class building (now the Academy building) was opened in October, 1903; the military drill hall in 1905; the infirmary in 1905 with a Sister of St. Joseph as registered nurse. Cardinal Vannutelli was received with military and academic honors on September 21, 1910. Ireland Hall, a residence building, was opened in September, 1912. It cost $127,500 and has 176 rooms for boarders. The armory was completed in 1914, at a cost of $80,000; and a chapel, 191 by 43, with transepts 80 feet wide in Byzantine style, in 1918, with seating capacity of 800. Its sanctuary is 31 by 39 feet in dimensions. In 1915 the high school department was separated from the college and became known as St. Thomas Military Academy. In 1910 the college conferred its first academic degrees. The institution has always been under the control and direction of the diocesan clergy except from 1928 to 1933 when the Fathers of the Holy Cross had charge of it, but even then the teaching staff, with few exceptions, was composed of diocesan priests. The Very Reverend Vincent J. Flynn is President.

1894—ST. PAUL SEMINARY

The diocesan seminary was made possible by a gift of $500,000 from Mr. James J. Hill, President of the Great Northern Railroad, in the autumn of 1890, which provided for the erection of the six original buildings and endowed the professorial chairs. It was opened on September 6, 1894, when sixty-five seminarians were transferred from the St. Thomas Aquinas Seminary. The faculty was made up of six priests and a layman. It was formally dedicated on Wednesday, September 4, 1895, by Archbishop Satolli, Apostolic Delegate, who celebrated the Pontifical Mass at which Father O'Gorman of the Catholic University of America preached. At a public meeting that evening in the Aula Maxima, presided over by Archbishop Ireland, Mr. Hill formally transferred the seminary to the Archdiocese of St. Paul in presence of a distinguished gathering of prelates, priests and laymen. The first Rector of the Seminary was Monsignor Caillet who has had seven successors with the present Rector, Very Reverend R. G. Bandas. Three of them have been elevated to the episcopate—Bishops Heffron, Brady and Connolly. One member of the original faculty, Most Reverend William Turner, was made Bishop of Buffalo in 1919. The first graduate to be so honored was Bishop Duffy of Grand Island (1913-31), now living in retirement. A third residence building was completed in 1913, a library building in 1951 and a convent for the Sisters of St. Joseph in charge of the domestic department in 1952, the gift of Miss Minnie Bell of St. Paul.

1904—DERHAM HALL

Derham Hall was opened as a convent and the first unit of St. Catherine's College, on December 26, 1904, by the Sisters of St. Joseph with Mother Hyacinth Werden as Superior and Principal of the high school in which classes began on January 5, 1905, and the first college courses in September of that year. It was incorporated as "College of St. Catherine" in May, 1913, and granted its first Bachelor degrees to two students in June, 1913. It shares its non-academic staff with the College. There are five sisters on the staff with Mother M. Antonine as President of the institution.

1905—ST. THOMAS MILITARY ACADEMY

As early as 1890 the St. Thomas military battalion was formed in St. Thomas Seminary with two companies—the Siunia and Mennith Light Guards. No uniforms were worn, equipment was meager and the battalion was short-lived.

Military training was inaugurated in 1905 when, at the request of the Reverend H. Moynihan the President, Father Reardon of the St. Paul Seminary faculty, and unofficial chaplain at Fort Snelling from 1902 to 1908, asked Colonel Robert Lee Bullard to send a drill master to the college. He assigned Sergeant Futherer to organize and drill the corps of cadets. Uniforms became obligatory and suitable training equipment was provided. In 1906 the Corps was recognized by the War Department and Lieutenant E. K. Massey detailed as full-time military instructor and additional equipment was issued by the Government. Military training was obligatory for all who were physically fit at St. Thomas College till 1922 when the St. Thomas Military Academy became a separate department. It was discontinued from 1928 to 1933 during the regime of the Holy Cross Fathers. During the first World War a Students' Army Training Corps was established. At the close of the war 1,100 alumni were serving in the armed forces, 300 of whom were commissioned officers. Seventeen died in the line of duty. In the second World War there were 5,000 alumni in the armed forces, 2,000 officers and one hundred and seventy-one paid the supreme debt of patriotism. At present there are seven priests and thirty-eight laymen on the staff and 558 students enrolled. The Very Reverend Vincent J. Flynn is President.

1905—COLLEGE OF ST. CATHERINE

This institution for the higher education of young women is conducted by the Sisters of St. Joseph. The site was bought in the nineties of last century and the first unit was called Derham Hall in honor of Hugh Derham of Rosemount who gave $20,000 as the nucleus of a fund for its construction. The first college classes opened in September, 1905, and it was incorporated in May, 1913. It was placed on the approved list of the Association of American Universities in 1917, when Mother Francis Clare Barden was Superior and Principal from 1910 to 1919. Sister Antonia McHugh was elected President of the corporation in 1919 and was Superior and Principal from 1931 to 1937. There are 65 sisters on the staff, 36 lay teachers, 779 students and 241 nurses in training.

Many new buildings have been added since Derham Hall was opened: Whitby Hall and Auditorium in 1914; Caecelian Hall in 1921; Our Lady of Victory Chapel in 1924; Mendel Hall in 1927; Fontbonne Hall (Health Center) in 1932; new power plant in 1937. In 1931 the Library School, the first Catholic Library School in the United States, was accredited; and in 1938 a Chapter of Phi Beta Kappa was established, the first in any Catholic College in America.

1906—THE GUILD OF CATHOLIC WOMEN

The Guild was organized on December 8, 1906, by twenty-five women who met in St. Luke's school under the chairmanship of Miss Caroline Beaumont (later, Mrs. Dr. H. J. O'Brien). Mrs. J. M. Bishop was elected President and Reverend Ambrose McNulty, pastor of the parish, appointed Spiritual Director. Its purpose was to relieve the distress of the poor by collecting, mending and distributing usable clothing, providing food for them and making visits to needy families to ascertain their material and spiritual wants. A constitution and by-laws were adopted in January, 1908. Weekly meetings were held in the school until 1911 when they were transferred to the Knights of Columbus hall on Cedar Street. Prior to that the members had become interested in juvenile court work under the direction of Reverend James Donahoe, City Missionary, who, in 1911, succeeded Father McNulty as Spiritual Director. As the membership increased the scope of the work broadened to include departments of Philanthropy, Social Action, Arts and Letters and Guild Hall. With the passage of the years came a diversity of operations and interests, originating in and emphasizing the general purpose of the organization as expressed in the Articles of Incorporation signed on February 21, 1912, namely: "Mutual counsel, philanthropic and educational work in accordance with Catholic principles". The Guild took part in every project for individual and civic betterment and was interested in legislation affecting the Church and the family. It cooperated with the Minneapolis League of Catholic Women in the management of the Infants' Home from September 20, 1917, when it was opened in the Larpenteur residence on Dale Street, St. Paul, until it was taken over by the Sisters of St. Joseph in 1920.

During the war years the Guild participated in Red Cross work, liberty loan drives and thrift campaigns. It was represented by the President, Mrs. R. A. Walsh, at the Chicago meeting of the Presidents of all Catholic Women's Leagues in September, 1917, which ultimately resulted in the formation of the National Council of Catholic Women at which she was elected the first President. On her return to St. Paul she helped to form the present Minnesota Council of Catholic Women.

In February, 1913, the Guild moved into new quarters in the Wilder Charity Building where it remained until 1927 and, after occupying temporary quarters for three years, found a permanent meeting-place in the new Guild Hall on Marshall Avenue. In 1914 the Guild had a paid-up membership of five hundred and seventeen.

On March 20, 1912, the Guild leased the Mealey residence, 574 St. Peter Street, as a home for working girls earning a small salary, and unprotected girls coming into the city. It had accommodations for twenty-five who paid from two to four dollars a week for room and board. In 1915 larger quarters became imperative and the Guild Hall, as it was called, was moved to the former Mannheimer residence, 215 Nelson Street (now Marshall Avenue), purchased for $18,000 and remodeled. It was dedicated by Bishop Lawler on January 19, 1916. It is a large brick and stone, three-storied structure, one block from the Cathedral and within easy walking distance of the down-town shopping center. An addition to the original building was opened on February 14, 1930, bringing its total capacity to seventy-five girls, earning not more than one hundred and fifty dollars a month, who pay from $7.50 to $9.50 a week for board and lodging. The Guild Hall operates under its own treasury and management and a board of fifty members. It is self-sustaining. Since 1932 two bequests—one from the estate of Mary T. Wagner, and the other from a trust fund left by Mrs. J. J. Hill, totalling approximately $18,000 in bonds and property—bring in a yearly income for the work of the organization. The Reverend Lawrence F. Ryan of the St. Paul Seminary faculty has been Spiritual Director since 1916.

1911—THE CHRIST CHILD SOCIETY

This is a branch of the original society founded in Washington by Miss Mary Merrick in 1886 to aid in the care and instruction of needy and underprivileged Catholic children. The St. Paul branch was organized on Monday, April 3, 1911, under the auspices of the Guild of Catholic Women at its monthly meeting in the Knights of Columbus Hall, to afford young women an opportunity to devote their spare time to looking after the material and spiritual welfare of the poorer class of Catholic children, especially among Italian immigrants, and in the Hospital for Crippled Children, for whom they provide the benefits of religion. The headquarters was finally established in the vicinity of St. Ambrose Italian Church on Bradley Street, St. Paul, where a settlement house has been operated for more than thirty years.

1917—CATHOLIC INFANTS' HOME

It came into existence on August 20, 1917, when its predecessor, St. Joseph's Home, was closed in Minneapolis. It occupies the old home of A. L. Larpenteur, a pioneer resident of St. Paul, 341 North Dale Street, and was under the direction of the Guild of Catholic Women of St. Paul and the League of Catholic Women of Minneapolis till 1920 when the Sisters of St. Joseph assumed the management of it. There are several sisters under the direction of Mother M. Aleda, the present Superior, and eight lay assistants.

There was a Catholic Infants' home in St. Paul as early as October, 1894, on the corner of Martin and Mackubin Streets, organized and conducted by a small group of women. It had no endowment but relied on voluntary contributions for its support. Physicians offered their services gratis and when nurses were not available the women assumed the duty of caring for the babies. It had 430 infants in its care during the first five years of its existence. A lawn fete was held for its benefit on July 1, 1898, attended by Bishops Cotter and Shanley and a number of the clergy as well as by a large gathering of the laity. Its total receipts for the first five years amounted to $10,390.24 and its disbursements to $10,132.81. The President was Mrs. M. F. Kennedy; first Vice-President, Mrs. T. Foley; second Vice-President, Mrs. M. Doran; Treasurer, Miss Sarah Dowlan; Recording Secretary, Miss Rose Donagh; Corresponding Secretary, Mrs. George Mealey.

1923—NAZARETH HALL PREPARATORY SEMINARY

This is the preparatory seminary of the Archdiocese of St. Paul, and was opened for the reception of students on September 12, 1923, with Reverend T. E. Crowley as Rector (1923-35). It was financed by the Timothy Foley bequest of $100,000 and the Archbishop Ireland Educational Fund and cost over $1,250,000. The cornerstone was laid on May 21, 1922, by Archbishop Dowling and the sermon preached by Bishop McNicholas of Duluth. It was dedicated on September 10, 1923, and was complete except for the chapel which, with the main altar, was consecrated September 13, 1924, by Archbishop Dowling. 125 students were enrolled the first year; and in 1949 there were 226. The present Rector is Very Reverend L. J. McCarthy, and there are 14 priests on the faculty. In twenty-five years it has given 185 priests to the church in the Archdiocese, 70 to that in other diocese, 1 to the Greek Rite and 13 to religious Orders. It most distinguished graduate is the Most Reverend James J. Byrne, Auxiliary Bishop of St. Paul.

1923—NAZARETH HALL CONVENT

The Sisters of St. Francis, whose Mother house is in Waldbreitbach, Germany, are in charge of the domestic arrangements at Nazareth Hall Preparatory Seminary since it was opened in 1923, and occupy a wing of the institution. Twelve sisters arrived on August 9 of that year. The present Superior is Mother M. Humiliana.

1927—ST. WILHELMINA'S HOME

This club, under the direction of the Bureau of Catholic Charities, was made possible by a donation from Miss Wilhelmina Coolbaugh of Chicago, and is named in her honor. The former home of the Christian Brothers, 205 West Sixth Street, was purchased and remodeled and provided accommodations for fourteen young Catholic working girls, struggling to be self-supporting and living apart from their homes and parental guidance. It was placed in charge of Miss Rosemary Tuttle of the Catholic Charities staff who, in 1928, was succeeded by Miss Ann Kaye, another staff member. The need for larger quarters was met by the purchase of the home of Edward Saunders, 323 Summit Avenue, in 1941. It has accommodations for twenty girls from sixteen to twenty-one most of whom are employed and earn an average of $125 a month and pay from $40 to 48.50 a month for board and lodging. Since the club was opened 825 girls have been enrolled and the average stay has been from six to eight months. The matron in charge is a trained social worker who advises the girls in all important matters. It is a home, not an institution, and its income is augmented by the earnings of a small endowment.

1932—ST. ALBERTUS HALL.

This is a house of studies for the School Sisters of Notre Dame who attend the Diocesan Teachers College, and a music studio. Five sisters reside there under Mother Margaret Mary the present Superior.

1933—ARCHDIOCESAN COUNCIL OF CATHOLIC WOMEN

It was founded by Archbishop Murray on March 25, 1933, to comply with the mandate of His Holiness, Pope Pius XI. In the following May the constitution was adopted and Mrs. Thomas P. Ryan was elected President. Several hundred women became interested in its program of Catholic Action, comprising the religious education of children and adults, participation in the lay retreat movement, the distribution of Catholic literature, the support of the Catholic press, the supervision of radio and movie programs and active personal charity. During the years it has taken articulate interest in community, national and international affairs. Mrs. T. F. O'Neil, its war-time President (1935-45), was succeeded by Mrs. M. R. Drennen (1945-48), and Mrs. W. J. Daly (1948-51). Auxiliary Bishop Byrne is the Moderator and each committee has a priestly adviser. Conferences are held several times a year not only in the Twin Cities but in the deanery centers of the diocese and themes adapted to the promotion of spiritual growth through Catholic Action on a social level discussed, as well as those which affect personal, family and youth activities. Panel discussions and workshops on organization, parliamentary procedure, discussion clubs, missions and international relations are held. The Council is represented on civic groups, such as the Community Chest, child welfare, housing and recreational projects, Red Cross, polio relief, veterans' hospitals and library board.

Since 1948 supplies for missions and post-war relief of an estimated value of $32,745.00 have been collected and dispensed through the Holy Father's storehouse, and $950.00 expended for new clothing and other supplies for the needy. Mrs. A. E. Dornbach was elected President at the convention held in 1951.

1935—ST. MARY'S HOME FOR THE AGED

A home for elderly people of both sexes sponsored by the St. Paul Federation of German Catholic Societies. When Mother M. Balthasara, Assistant General of the Congregation of the Franciscan Sisters of the Blessed Virgin Mary of the Angels, came to St. Paul in the spring of 1935, she said her congregation would assume the ownership and management of the institution, which is located across the street from the Church of the Little Flower. Ground was broken on March 19, 1936, and the first Mass said in the chapel on October 1 of that year by the Most Reverend Archbishop who dedicated the building the same day, and five sisters took up their residence in it. It had accommodation for 30 elderly persons who paid a moderate fee for board and lodging. The first Superior was Mother Humiliana. The building was enlarged in 1939 to accommodate about 70. It is now the Mother house of the community in the United States, with two subordinate houses in the Archdiocese—the Nazareth Hall Convent and the St. Francis Convent and Hospital in Shakopee—and one in the Diocese of La Crosse. The first American postulant came in 1940 and the next year three were invested with the habit. The present Mother Superior is Mother M. Laura and there are 11 sisters in the home.

1938—ST. MARY'S MISSION HOUSE

It was established in 1938 by the Missionary Sisters of St. Peter Claver to aid the Catholic missions of Africa no matter by whom conducted. The local "Sodality of St. Peter Claver" prints two monthly magazines—"Echo From Africa" and "The Negro Child" (both in English and Polish) as well as the "Claver Almanac" and other literature such as bibles, catechisms and religious books in the African languages. The congregation was founded in 1894 by Mother Mary Teresa Ledochowski who died in 1922, and has its Motherhouse in Rome. St. Mary's Mission House is staffed by ten sisters under the direction of Mother Carmela.

1941—OUR LADY OF GOOD COUNSEL FREE CANCER HOME

The Sisters of St. Dominic, Servants of Relief for Incurable Cancer, opened the home at 2076 St. Anthony Avenue in the Merriam Park district of St. Paul, in the summer of 1941, as a refuge, not a hospital, for patients afflicted with chronic cancer, without regard to sex, color, creed or race. The local telephone exchange building was bought for $18,000, remodeled and re-furnished at a cost of $80,000. It was dedicated by Archbishop Murray on December 3, after which he said a low Mass in the presence of twenty-five priests, the Mother General and eight members of the community. Since then it has given 85,727 days of free hospital care to 652 men and 742 women. 27 were negroes and 1367 whites; 689 were Catholics; 684 Protestants; and 21 Jews. Rev. George A. Reilly is the resident chaplain. The sisters in charge belong to the Sisters of St. Dominic of the Congregation of St. Rose of Lima, founded in New York in 1896 by Mrs. Rose Hawthorne Lathrop, which has a number of free cancer homes throughout the country.

1943—BENEDICTINE HOUSE OF STUDIES

The house on Summit Avenue was purchased about 1943 as a residence for the Benedictine Sisters from St. Benedict's Priory, St. Joseph, Minnesota, who attend the Diocesan Teachers College. The Superior is Sister M. Rudolpha, O.S.B.

1947—ST. GERTRUDE'S HOUSE OF STUDIES

The property was purchased from Mrs. Venetta O'Brien in February, 1947, by the Sisters of St. Benedict of Crookston, Minnesota, as a residence for their sisters attending the Diocesan Teachers College and other schools in the Twin Cities and for sisters on business trips or attending conventions, etc. During summer school there are about 35 sisters in residence; and from August to June rooms on the second and third floors are rented to other sisters or to respectable woman. On the staff there are two sisters under Sister M. Marcella, O.S.B.

1948—ST. PAUL'S PRIORY

The Priory was canonically erected as an independent priory of the Congregation of St. Benedict with pontifical status on June 22, 1948. Mother Loraine Tracy, O.S.B., was elected Prioress on that day. It was incorporated August 20, 1949, with Mother Loraine, President; Sister Alcuin Braun, O.S.B., Sub-Prioress, Vice-President;

Sister Luanne Meagher, O.S.B., Secretary; Sister Wilma Guetter, O.S.B., Treasurer; and Sister Mathias Sieben, O.S.B., Procurator. The first novices were clothed with the habit on June 13, 1949.

It has 184 sisters, 6 novices and 12 postulants in 17 subordinate houses in the Archdiocese. During the first year it reopened the catechetical school in Farmington, a new parochial school in the Visitation parish in Minneapolis, staffed 13 other parish schools, one catechetical school and an orphanage, and likewise the schools in the Immaculate Heart of Mary and the Maternity of the Blessed Virgin Mary parishes in St. Paul.

1950—FRANCISCAN HOUSE OF STUDIES

The Franciscan Sisters of the Immaculate Conception of Little Falls in the Diocese of St. Cloud, established a House of Studies at 365 Summit Avenue, for the members of their community who desire to study for degrees at colleges in the Twin Cities. Sister Mary Elaine, O.S.F., is the local Superior.

1951—OUR LADY OF PEACE HIGH SCHOOL

In 1948 the parochial school of St. Luke's parish was bought by the Sisters of Charity of the Blessed Virgin Mary of Dubuque for $600,000. They took possession in June, 1951, and, after making the changes necessary to adapt it to its new purpose, opened it as a high school for girls in the ninth grade. One grade will be added each year till the full four-year course is provided. Registration began as early as March 10, 1951. The Sisters bought a convent at 1035 Summit Avenue not far from the school, and Sister Mary Adorinus is the Directress.

CITY OF MINNEAPOLIS

1877—HOLY ANGELS ACADEMY

It was the outgrowth and flowering of the first convent opened by the Sisters of St. Joseph in Minneapolis on January 29, 1877, in the Ankeny home, Third Street, North, and Second Avenue, near the Church of the Immaculate Conception, by Mother St. John Ireland and Sisters Victoria and Martina. It was called the "White Convent" and, officially, Holy Angels. It was moved to the Skiles home on Fifth Street, between Hennepin Avenue and First Avenue, North, thence to the "Brown Convent" on Third Street, North, whence three classes graduated before its final migration to the Bassett property on Fourth Street, North, and Seventh Avenue, in 1881, when a boarding school was added and Sister Francis Clare was placed in charge of the high school. In subsequent years two additions were built and Sister Francis Clare succeeded Mother St. John in 1896 as second Superior. Mother Rosalia Hayes, the third Superior, was a graduate of the "Brown Convent". In 1907 when the locality became undesirable for a school the high school pupils were transferred to the newly-opened St. Margaret's Academy on Linden Avenue and Thirteenth Street. The Holy Angels Academy was the oldest private school for girls in Minneapolis.

1878—THE CATHOLIC BOYS' HOME

On February 18, 1878, Bishop Ireland presided at a meeting in the Immaculate Conception school to consider ways and means of establishing a Catholic Boys' orphanage in Minneapolis, and an association was formed to carry out the project. In March a wing of the Winslow House in St. Anthony, then unoccupied, on the site of the old Exposition Building and the present Coca-Cola offices, was rented for $350 a year, fitted up to accommodate two hundred orphans and placed in charge of Mother Angela Smythe, Superior of St. Mary's convent. Before the end of the year it was decided to transfer the orphans to the west side of the river and the Day homestead, Sixth Avenue, North, and Third Street, was purchased from Annie Kelly for $4,217.31 plus the cost of the repairs made after she acquired the property. It was renovated and enlarged to provide dormitories and class rooms for the boys brought from the former orphanage and those theretofore housed in St. Paul Catholic Orphanage. Mother Mary James, Directress of the Immaculate Conception school, was appointed Superior and the institution was incorporated on May 7, 1879, as "The Minneapolis Catholic Orphan Asylum". Mother Priscilla succeeded Mother Mary James in 1884, and served for three years, until the institution was transferred to the present Catholic Boys' Home at 46th Street and 10th Avenue, South, the site for which was bought from James Stanchfield in 1885 for $16,000. It comprised forty acres in the Town of Richfield adjacent to the West Side Catholic Cemetery (St. Mary's). The cornerstone of the first building costing $24,028, was laid on July 4, 1886, by Bishop Ireland and the completed structure dedicated by him on July 22, of the following year. Mother Mary Xavier Carroll, who succeeded Mother Priscilla in 1887, was the first superior and filled that office most acceptably until her death in 1906.

The first resident chaplain, Reverend H. McGolrick, was appointed in 1890. St. Francis Xavier chapel, erected at a cost of $18,000, was dedicated by Bishop Mc-Golrick of Duluth on August 30, 1908, and the sermon preached by Archbishop Ireland. A picnic on the grounds sponsored by the parishes in Minneapolis in July, 1913, netted $13,000. A new dormitory, including class rooms, dining room, etc., costing $60,000, was occupied in 1915; and a campaign conducted by Charles Sheffield of Cleveland, Ohio, from November 30 to December 11 of that year to liquidate the debt, brought in a total of $68,000 in pledges. During the regime of Archbishop Dowling the greater part of the acreage of the Home was sold. Another campaign for a new gymnasium netted $80,628.17 as of April 30, 1949. To this was added a bequest of $10,000 in the will of Maurice Schumacher; and the contract for the new building was signed April 24, 1951, with the stipulation that it be finished by September 21 of that year. It was blessed by Archbishop Murray on Sunday afternoon, December 2, 1951.

1883—ST. MARY'S HOSPITAL

The first Catholic Hospital in Minneapolis was opened by the Sisters of Mercy under the direction of Mother Mary Joseph Lynch in 1883 in the home of Captain Edward Murphy who died in 1865. It was in their charge until 1887 when the Sisters of St. Joseph secured the property and changed the name to St. Mary's Hospital, with Sister Ignatius Cox, Superior, and Sisters Irmena Doherty, Symphrosia Grace, Leonie Forest and Barbara Foley as nurses. The original frame structure was replaced with a four-story brick building begun in May, 1890. In 1898 Sisters Thecla Reid and Aloise O'Dowd of the nursing staff volunteered for service in the Spanish-American war with three sisters from St. Joseph's Hospital, St. Paul, and several from St. Louis and went to Camp Hamilton in Kentucky to care for 600 soldiers with typhoid and malaria. In December they were sent to Camp Gilman in Georgia and thence to Matanzas in Cuba until April, 1899, when they resigned their commissions and returned home. During the administration of Mother Jane Francis Bochet (1890-1906) a clinical laboratory for attending physicians was opened and a training school for nurses established.

It was at St. Mary's on July 19, 1914, that the first meeting was held which eventually resulted in the formation of the Catholic Hospital Association of the United States and Canada. A six-story brick building, 268 feet with wings at each end 180 feet in length was ready for patients on November 5, 1918; the nurses' home was erected in 1924, and the old hospital connecting these buildings was remodeled and set aside as a pediatric department. In November, 1944, St. Mary's X-ray Technicians' Training School was approved by the American Medical Association. It had been opened in 1942 and since then 26 have completed the course and seven were enrolled in August, 1949. The Superior of the community is Mother Martha, the Superintendent of the Hospital, Sister Harriet, and there are 51 Sisters on the staff and 377 lay helpers. During the year 18,705 patients were treated. On July 19, 1945, "Bethany", a recreation cottage for sisters was formally opened.

1888—ST. ELIZABETH'S HOME FOR YOUNG GIRLS

This was a branch of St. Mary's Home for Girls established in St. Paul in 1884 under the direction of Madame Perronno of the Daughters of the Immaculate Heart of Mary with headquarters in Buffalo, N. Y. It was opened at 903 Hennepin Avenue and in 1890 was moved to 828 Sixth Avenue, South. The Directress was Miss Catherine Sullivan under Madame Perronno who was the superior of both institutions. It had a more prosperous career than the St. Paul Home, but both were closed in 1896. The Reverend James M. Cleary said Mass on week days in St. Elizabeth's home while St. Charles Church was under construction.

1888—CONVENT OF THE GOOD SHEPHERD

It was located at 2650 Bloomington Avenue and opened on November 3, 1888, in a large house bought from Mrs. Carrie A. Wright for $23,000 by Mother Mary of St. Bernard Flinn, Provincial Superior of the community, who appointed Mother Mary of the Incarnation Crowe local Superior, a position she held until 1892 when she was named Provincial and returned to St. Paul. During the fifteen years of its existence it cared for and educated 349 delinquent girls, 62 of whom were sent by the Court and the rest by private commitment or voluntary placement. There were in all 92 girls in the Preservation Class prior to its discontinuance in 1893. The institution was supported for the most part by commercial machine sewing— shirt-making for Frank's in Minneapolis and Gettenberg's in St. Paul. On May 15, 1903, it was merged with the parent institution in St. Paul because its proximity thereto prevented the growth and development of the Provincial House. In 1902 the second Superior, Mother St. John Madden (1892-1903), celebrated the silver jubilee of her religious profession. There were six sisters in the convent when it closed. The Dominican Fathers of Holy Rosary Church were the chaplains.

The new chapel was blessed on Sunday, June 1, 1890, by Father Bloomer, O. P., assisted by Father Egan, O. P., chaplain, and Father Gmeiner of the Provincial House in St. Paul, who celebrated Solemn High Mass at ten-thirty at which the sermon was preached by Reverend C. H. McKenna, O.P. At the vesper service and benediction the sisters' choir chanted the psalms and hymns. The chapel, 28 by 50 feet in dimensions, cost one thousand dollars and had an artistically carved altar and stained glass windows. There was a cloistered section for the sisters of whom there were eleven in charge of forty young women and girls.

1891—ST. JOSEPH'S HOME FOR THE AGED POOR

This institution was incorporated on January 30, 1891, as a home for the neglected poor regardless of creed, color or race. It admits men and women over sixty years of age and has accommodations for 160 ministered to by 16 sisters under Mother Mary of St. James, the present Superior.

1900—DE LA SALLE HIGH SCHOOL

The first Catholic high school for boys in Minneapolis was opened in 1900 under the name of De La Salle high school by the Christian Brothers. It was made possible by a bequest of $10,000 from Anthony Kelly, a prominent Catholic merchant of the city, supplemented by a fund of $15,000 raised by the parishes. A site was bought from the King estate on Nicollet Island in the Mississippi and the school was opened on October 1, as the Hennepin Institute. The first Director was Brother Athanasius of Sebaste, assisted by Brother Lewis as teacher of the second class and Brother Levian Benedict as cook. There were fifty boys enrolled and an additional teacher, Brother Luperius Emery, came in 1901. The name was changed to De La Salle high school in 1902 and thirteen were graduated the next spring when Archbishop Ireland presided at the commencement. The Brothers resided in the school until 1914 when the rest of the King estate, including the house built about 1860, was acquired and the Brothers moved into the house which served them as a residence until the present modern home was ready for occupancy in

1950. In 1907 an addition costing $15,000 was made to the original structure; and on May 23, 1922 the cornerstone of the modern, commodious school was laid and the completed edifice dedicated on March 11, 1923, by Archbishop Dowling. It cost over $200,000. The school was accredited by the University of Minnesota in 1927 and by the North Central Association in 1929. Brother Mark is the Director of 19 Brothers and 5 lay teachers in charge of 802 students. Up to 1946, 27 De La Salle graduates became priests; 40 joined the Christian Brothers; and 85 lost their lives in World War II.

1907—ST. MARGARET'S ACADEMY

The block on which the Academy is located was bought by the Immaculate Conception parish from the McNair estate as a site for a new church but was found unsuitable for the purpose. It was sold to the Sisters of St. Joseph in 1906 and the three buildings fitted for school purposes. The academy opened as a grade and high school in 1907 when the pupils were transferred thereto from the old Holy Angels Academy, but it has been exclusively a high school for girls since 1920. It was accredited by the University of Minnesota in 1908 and is also a member of the North Central Association and of the Association of Catholic secondary schools of Minnesota. There are seventeen sisters and five lay teachers on the staff and 370 students. Mother M. Carmena is Superior and Principal.

1911—MINNEAPOLIS LEAGUE OF CATHOLIC WOMEN

In the spring of 1911 a committee headed by Miss Mary Chute waited on Archbishop Ireland and received his permission to begin social service work among the young Catholic women of Minneapolis, with the formal injunction that they open, as soon as possible, a down-town free employment and information bureau in charge of a secretary.

A group of about two hundred Catholic women met in Donaldson's tea rooms on November 16, of that year and, after due deliberation, voted to organize for the purpose of undertaking social, philanthropic and educational work among young girls earning small salaries and away from their normal home environment. At a meeting held on November 27 a constitution was adopted and officers elected as follows: President, Mrs. W. J. Moorhead; Recording Secretary, Mrs. G. V. Ziemer; Corresponding Secretary, Mrs. D. C. Dailey; Treasurer, Mrs. G. W. Hineline; and six Vice-Presidents — Mesdames W. J. Murphy, H. B. Sweetser, L. S. Donaldson, F. A. Gross, R. Evans and C. S. Brackett. Only one of these officers, Mrs. G. V. Ziemer, is living today, the sole survivor of the charter members of the League.

Immediately after organizing the League set up a free employment bureau, with housing and information service, in temporary quarters in the Kasota Building, Fourth Street and Hennepin Avenue. Evening classes for the Girls' Branch (afterwards, the Junior Catholic League) were held there as early as January, 1912. In the following July St. Mary's Hall was opened at 1344 First Avenue, South, and the employment and information office was transferred thereto. The Hall had accommodations for about twenty girls who paid from three to four dollars a week for board and room. The demand for admission soon became so great that in a little more than a year larger quarters had to be provided in a more commodious dwelling at 1608 Hawthorne Avenue, in the vicinity of the then Pro-Cathedral, which was purchased and operated as a rooming house for girls seeking employment in the city or temporarily out of work. The first matron, Miss Josephine Hegarty, was succeeded by Miss Marie Norton. An adjoining building on the property was rented for several years before being dismantled in the hope, never realized, that a modern and well-equipped home for girls would be erected on the site combined with an adjoining lot on the corner of Hawthorne at Sixteenth Street. St. Mary's Hall was sold in August, 1945.

The Girls' Branch, above referred to, was established shortly after the League was organized for the girls who were the beneficiaries of its social and educational work. In the course of time its complexion changed and, when the daughters of the members of the League gained the majority, in 1918, the name was changed to the Junior Catholic League which, under the direction of a chairman from the sponsoring organization, has done yeoman service in a social and educational way for its growing membership, and ranks high among similar organizations in the city.

The second project undertaken by the League was the opening of a cafeteria in 1913 at 720 Marquette Avenue where about four hundred meals were served at noon each day. In the evening classes in cooking, sewing, millinery, china painting and social graces, interspersed with lectures by prominent speakers, were held and they became so popular that additional space had to be rented. The League also looked after delinquent children, posted travelers' aides at the depots, cared for the sick and friendless and assumed charge of St. Joseph's Home for unwed mothers and their children for several years. The cafeteria and social center was transferred to 35 South Sixth Street in 1922 where the down-town headquarters was maintained until the remodeling of the building necessitated removal to a new location at 807 Hennepin Avenue, opened to the public on September 8, 1936. When the cafeteria was closed the next year the office of the League was moved to St. Mary's Hall on Hawthorne Avenue, where it remained until 1945 when the Hall was sold, after which the officers met in rented quarters until 1950, when the League purchased Seton Guild, 207 South Ninth Street, as a permanent headquarters for itself and for the Junior League. The new home was blessed by Archbishop Murray on January 15, 1951, after which Mass was celebrated in its auditorium by the Spiritual Director, Monsignor Reardon. During the Mass the Archbishop preached a sermon on the corporal works of mercy and congratulated the League members on their centrally-located headquarters.

1912—SETON GUILD

Seton Guild was founded by Miss Rose Kane (afterwards, Mrs. D. E. Virtue), a seceding member of the Minneapolis League of Catholic Women, who opened a club house and cafeteria at 206 South Fourth Street, in the fall of 1912, as a home for Catholic working girls, providing educational, recreational and social facilities for them. Classes in sewing, millinery, china-painting, choral singing, grammar, history, literature, dramatics and gymnastics were made available to all who wished to patronize them. As an adjunct, Seton Cliff on Phelp's Island, Lake Minnetonka, about twenty miles from Minneapolis, was dedicated as a vacation home for young women on June 21, 1914, by Father Jaeger of St. Bonifacius who said Mass at 11 o'clock. It soon had to be enlarged into a two-story modern club house to meet the demands for accommodations at moderate cost. In a few years the Guild found it necessary to seek larger quarters and a site was purchased at 207 South Ninth Street, and plans drawn for a new Guild Hall, costing about $50,000 towards which Mr. J. J. Hill contributed $10,000. The cornerstone was blessed and placed in position in the latter part of August, 1926, by Archbishop Dowling at a function presided over by Monsignor Cleary, the Spiritual Director. Addresses were delivered by the Archbishop, Mayor Leach and Edwin L. Somerville, of the Board of Directors. The Guild was opened the next year with a large enrollment in its classes, social groups and public forums for the discussion of topics dealing with Catholic doctrine and discipline. Mrs. Virtue continued in charge until her death on December 13, 1936, when Mrs. T. J. Foley became Executive Director until the summer of 1950 when the building was purchased by the Minneapolis League of Catholic Women as a headquarters for the senior and junior divisions and their activities. After renovation it was formally dedicated on January 15, 1951, by Archbishop Murray.

1912—ST. JOSEPH'S INFANT HOME

This home for the care of unwed mothers and their children was opened in a rented house at 2718 Stevens Avenue by Mrs. H. B. Sweetser, Dr. Ellen Magner and Miss Delia O'Connell who had charge of it for a new months before it was taken over by the Minneapolis League of Catholic Women as part of their philanthropic work. They received a monthly subsidy of $100 from Archbishop Ireland.

Several doctors, notably Dr. Arnold Hamel, gave generously of their time and services. After a year a larger house was rented at 2748 Cedar Avenue where the work was carried on until 1916 when it procured permanent quarters in "the Anchorage", the old Larpenteur home, 341 North Dale Street, St. Paul, and was under the joint management of the Minneapolis League and the St. Paul Guild of Catholic Women until 1920 when it was taken over by the Sisters of St. Joseph.

1915—MARGARET BARRY SETTLEMENT HOUSE

Shortly after the organization of the League of Catholic Women the members interested themselves in kindergarten and settlement work among the Italians and Syrians on the East Side and, in 1915, the Margaret Barry Settlement House was established at 759 Pierce Street, Northeast, at an outlay of $10,000, for work among the foreign-born population of the neighborhood and their children. An addition was put to it in 1922. It comprises a kindergarten, a club for boys with facilities for manual training, a department for girl with classes in cooking, sewing and other housewifely arts, a branch of the public library, dental, optical and other clinics. A nursery school with a daily attendance of thirty-six was opened in 1947. As an accommodation for the Catholics of the neighborhood Mass was said in the House on Sundays by the Paulist Fathers of St. Lawrence Church, and by Father Odone, a retired Italian priest residing at the St. Paul Seminary, and catechetical instructions given by volunteer teachers until the Church of Our Lady of Mount Carmel was opened in 1938. The work was originated and supervised by Mrs. Margaret Barry, a charter member of the League, after whom the house was called, until her death in 1944. She was assisted successively by the following head residents or executive directors: Mrs. Alice Leahy Shea until 1923; Mrs. Mollie Sullivan Augustine, her successor, until 1944; and since then Miss Florence Bentley.

On July 14, 1949, McCall's Magazine gave the League a sum of money to finance the operation of an experimental free playground, known as Yardville, using waste materials and modeled after similar playgrounds in Denmark and Sweden. On October 2, Yardville was opened under the supervision of the Margaret Barry Settlement House at Pierce Street, Northeast and Thirty-fifth and operated for a year and a half when the experiment was discontinued.

1931—ACADEMY OF THE HOLY ANGELS

The Academy of the Holy Angels at Nicollet Avenue and 66th Street, was opened in 1931 as a grade and high school, but the grade school was discontinued in 1947 when the parochial school of the adjoining St. Peter's parish was opened. It is now a school for resident and day pupils with an enrollment of 360. There are 22 sisters on the staff and three lay teachers. Mother M. Eileen is the Superior. A number of sisters teaching in parochial schools reside at the Academy.

1939—ST. MARY'S CONVENT

It was founded in June, 1939, by the Dominican Sisters of the Sick Poor officially organized in New York City in 1910 by Mother Mary Walsh (1850-1922), for free, generalized, visiting nurse service in the homes of the poor of any race, color or creed from whom they accept no fee or donation of any kind. The convent was blessed and the first Mass said in its chapel by the Most Reverend Archbishop Murray on September 5, 1939. It has a staff of four nursing sisters with Mother Catherine, O.P., as Superior, supported by an auxiliary organization and by voluntary contributions.

1949—CONVENT OF OUR LADY OF THE CENACLE

The Religious of the Cenacle, founded by Father Stephen Terme and Mother Therese Couderc (beatified in November, 1951) at La Louvesc, France, in 1826, came to Minneapolis in May, 1949, at the invitation of the Archbishop of St. Paul, to open a retreat house for women. The Dayton home, 2321 Blaisdell Avenue, was purchased for them by the Elizabeth Quinlan Foundation as a substitute for Miss Quinlan's home on Emerson Avenue, South, which had previously been offered to them but was found too small for their work. Seven sisters with Mother Clare

Gartland as Superior, took possession of the new convent and supervised the changes necessary to adapt it to its purpose. On November 23 it was blessed by the Most Reverend Archbishop Murray, assisted by several priests and in presence of a large number of the laity, at a ceremony which ended with the celebration of Low Mass by His Excellency. It is one of fifteen similar institutions in the United States and Canada and has accommodations for about thirty women for week-end retreats. It also makes provision for days of recollection for individuals or groups under the direction of a priest and with the cooperation of the sisters. The first retreat, which began on Thursday, November 24, was conducted by the Reverend James O'Neill, S.J., of Prairie du Chien, Wisconsin. Forty-nine week-end retreats were held during 1951 and an average of two days of recollection each week.

OUTSIDE THE TWIN CITIES

1853—CONVENT AND ACADEMY OF ST. FRANCIS XAVIER, PEMBINA

This institution was in charge of the Sisters of the Propagation of the Faith established by Reverend George A. Belcourt in 1853 to teach the half-breed and Indian children of his missions in Pembina and vicinity. It was located in St. Joseph on the Pembina river near the present Turtle Mountains, about thirty miles west of Pembina on the Red River. The sisters were half-breeds, never more than seven in number, who taught the children in English, French and Chippewa. In 1855 they had one hundred pupils in the Academy and planned, when circumstances permitted, to extend their sphere of operation to the visitation and care of the sick. Mother Francis Xavier was the Superior. The community ceased to exist when Father Belcourt left the mission in 1859.

1856—ST. JOHN'S ABBEY, COLLEGEVILLE

Three Benedictines from St. Vincent's Abbey, Latrobe, Pa., arrived in St. Paul on May 2, 1856, led by Father Demetrius de Marogna, and were welcomed by Bishop Cretin who, after ordaining the companions of the leader on May 17, 1856, took them to Sauk Rapids and gave them possession of a floorless chapel built by Father Pierz. The location was deemed unsuitable for their work and they moved across the Mississippi to St. Cloud and settled on a tract of land donated by William and Louis Rothkopf where they erected a small house and a church, and opened a school on November 10, 1857. A bill incorporating "St. John's Seminary" was signed by Governor Gorman on March 6, 1857. There was a defect in the title to the property given them and the headquarters was transferred to St. Joseph in March, 1858, and erected into an independent priory with Father Benedict Haindl as first Prior, who, in March, 1859, returned the institution to its original site in St. Cloud. In 1863 it was decided that they had no legal right to the property and, under the new Prior, Father Othmar Wirtz, a foundation was made about half a mile from the present Collegeville station whence, on February 1, 1867, the community migrated to its fourth and permanent location adjacent to Lake Sagatan and Watab river. In 1869 it was authorized to confer academic degrees and fourteen years later its legal title was changed to St. John's University. It was made an Abbey in 1866 with Right Reverend Rupert Seidenbusch as first Abbot, a position he occupied until he was consecrated Vicar Apostolic of the Vicariate of Northern Minnesota in 1874. The Abbey is in the Diocese of St. Cloud.

1857—ST. BENEDICT'S CONVENT AND ACADEMY, ST. JOSEPH

It had its humble origin in a frame annex to the log chapel built in St. Cloud, in 1856, by the Benedictine Fathers, where the Sisters of St. Benedict, recently arrived from Pennsylvania, began their teaching career in the Northwest on December 9, 1857, with an enrollment of twenty pupils. It was a plastered lean-to with a floor of split logs and two windows, and was occupied for about six years. The Sisters taught the four R's—reading, writing, arithmetic and religion, besides drawing, needlework, German, etc. They lived in rented quarters, known as the St. Cloud Convent, at some distance from the school. Later on the name was changed to St. Benedict's Convent.

In 1863 the Sisters accepted an invitation to transfer the school to Clinton, where St. Joseph's parish was the most prosperous in the settlement, now known at St. Joseph. They took possession of two log houses previously used as a church and a school, added a third, 30 by 56 feet in dimensions, and gave the institution the name of St. Joseph's Convent and Academy which, in 1868, was placed under the protection of St. Benedict. In the course of time the school prospered and ampler and better accommodations were provided for the boarders and day scholars in a new building, begun in 1879, and completed in 1883. It was the first unit in the cluster of modern, commodious and imposing buildings which constitute the present St. Benedict's College, recognized as one of the foremost Catholic educational institutions for girls, whose history is closely interwoven with that of the Vicariate of Northern Minnesota, erected in 1874, and its successor, the Diocese of St. Cloud, established in 1889.

1861—ACADEMY FOR GIRLS, WINONA

The Catholic Directory for 1861 lists a school for young girls in Winona, with one hundred pupils, under the direction of the Sisters of St. Bridget from the Motherhouse in Tullow, Ireland. There is no mention of it in the Directory for 1864. No directories were published in 1862 and 1863.

These sisters were members of a congregation founded by Dr. Delany, Bishop of Kildare and Leighlin, at Tullow, County Carlow, Ireland, on February 1, 1807, to teach young girls and orphans, the first of the Irish sisterhoods of the nineteenth century. It was approved on March 31, 1845, and finally in 1907. The Generalate was established at Tullow in 1889 and the Provincial for Ireland resides at Mountrath where the second foundation was made. The sisters came to the United States in 1851, to Wisconsin, Michigan and Minnesota. "The Democrat" of Winona, for November 17, 1860 says that the Reverend M. Prendergast had finished a building for the Sisters, two in number, who had a flourishing school. "The Republican" of that city on January 1, 1862, speaks of "The Catholic Mission School". These references may be to the school taught by the Brigidine Sisters, who are not mentioned by that name.

1862—ST. GERTRUDE'S CONVENT AND ACADEMY, SHAKOPEE

In 1862 the Right Reverend Abbot Boniface Wimmer, O.S.B., brought two choir sisters and one lay sister from St. Mary's, Pa., to Shakopee, where they opened a small convent and academy in a former barn on October 9, with Mother Maria Clara Vogel as Prioress and Sisters Mechtildis Richter and Adelaide as members of the community. In 1866 there were six nuns in the convent and they taught in the public school in the north of the town. In 1870 they erected, at a cost of $10,000, the stone building now known as St. Francis Hospital conducted by the Sisters of St. Francis from Germany. The incorporators were Mary K. Vogel, Catherine Richter, Catherine Kerst, Martha Klein and Ellen Pendy of the Order of St. Benedict of Shakopee. The officers of the corporation were: President, Mary K. Vogel (Sister M. Clara); Vice-President, Catherine Richter (Sister M. Mechtildis); Secretary, Catherine Kerst (Sister M. Scholastica). On January 6, 1869, Bishop Grace received the perpetual vows of three of the sisters in the parish Church of St. Mark—Sisters Scholastica Kerst of St. Paul, Benedict Klein of Shakopee, and Xavier Pendy of Belle Plaine. The Sisters had charge of schools at Shakopee (till 1876), Carver, Belle Plaine, New Trier and Minneapolis. The community grew slowly and, finding the work of the parish schools and the orphanage too much for their slender resources, the sisters effected a merger with the Sisters of St. Benedict of St. Joseph, Minnesota, on August 31, 1880. The orphans were transferred to St. Paul and one of the sisters, Mother Benedict, was the first Superior of St. Joseph's German Orphanage from 1877 to 1908, and had for assistant, Sister M. Agatha. The Shakopee convent was sold to the county for a home for the poor

1865—BETHLEHEM ACADEMY, FARIBAULT

Six Dominican Sisters of the Congregation of the Most Holy Rosary from Sinsinawa, Wisconsin, arrived in Faribault on August 5, 1865, accompanied by

Bishop Grace and took possession of a building donated by Major Fowler and remodeled it to serve as a convent, school and residence for students, which the Bishop named Bethlehem Academy. On September 3, the Academy opened for the reception of young girls and two of the Sisters began teaching in the parish school in the basement of the Immaculate Conception church. There was a small enrollment for four years and much suffering and privation had to be endured by the sisters. In 1869 Father Keller who had been instrumental in bringing them to Faribault procured a new residence for them on the corner of Second Avenue and First Street, Southwest, and more students came. In 1876 the sisters moved into the nucleus of the present residential section of the Academy which was incorporated in 1885 when it graduated its first class, among whom was Ellen Coughlin who, as Mother M. Samuel, was Mother General of the order for forty years prior to 1949. In 1900 the north wing was added and eight years later another wing. It was accredited by the University of Minnesota in 1910 and by the North Central Association in 1932. It was made co-educational in 1935 as the only high school under Catholic auspices in the city. The new Academy building, begun on August 15, 1948, was ready for occupancy on September 5, 1949, with accommodations for 500 students. The cornerstone was laid by Bishop Byrne who later dedicated the completed building.

1867—CONVENT OF THE IMMACULATE CONCEPTION, MENDOTA

It was opened in the old Sibley House in December, 1867, when four Sisters of St. Joseph came to reside there and began school the following January with 150 pupils. The girls were taught in the convent; the boys in the public school once a stone church belonging to the Presbyterians. The sisters taught both schools (the Faribault plan). Mother Pauline LeMay was Superior and her assistants were Sisters Ignatius Loyola Cox and Columba Auge who had charge of the boys. When the sisters withdrew from the public school they taught in the parish school till June, 1879, when they left the parish, and the Sisters of Mercy opened an industrial school. Among the students were Bishop Corbett of Crookston, Dr. Thomas E. Shields of the Catholic University, Washington, and several sisters. Bishop Grace attended the commencements.

1877—VILLA MARIA ACADEMY, FRONTENAC

Six Ursuline nuns left their Motherhouse in Alton, Illinois, on August 16, 1877, en route to Lake City, Minnesota, to found a mission. They reached Winona on August 24 and were met by Reverend Francis J. Quinn, pastor of Lake City, who brought them to their destination by rail the next day. They opened a school in the old church on Prairie Street and lived in a little house nearby. Times were hard and support meager. When Mother Liguori Curran was appointed superior she bought a house and remodeled it into the Academy of Our Lady of the Lake where classes began in September, 1880. In five years the registration exceeded the capacity and a new academy became imperative. In 1885 General Garrard, a non-Catholic, offered them 124 acres near Frontenac on the historic site of Fort Beauharnois built in 1727. The new academy was ready for dedication on September 8, 1891, when Archbishop Ireland officiated. It was named "Villa Maria" and the chapel was placed under the patronage of St. Michael the Archangel, as was the chapel in the old fort. The Reverend Walter Raleigh was the first resident chaplain from August 3, 1893, to June 15, 1904, when he died. After the opening of Villa Maria the Academy of Our Lady of the Lake at Lake City became Nazareth School for boys which closed several years ago.

On October 29, 1945, ground was broken for the new building, the cornerstone of which was blessed by Archbishop Murray on May 4, 1946, who officiated at the dedication of the completed structure on October 21, the feast of St. Ursula. The building, 206 by 38 feet in dimensions, with a wing for the chapel, contains class rooms, gymnasium, dormitory and other facilities for faculty and students. During the summer Camp Glengarda affords recreational facilities for girls. There are 22 sisters on the staff and Mother M. Stephen Chastant is the Superior. The

Reverend C. J. Farrell is resident chaplain since November 1, 1946, succeeding Father Ronayne who died the previous month after a tenure of thirty years.

1878—HOME OF THE SACRED HEART, IONA

This institution for the care of orphans from all sections of the country was founded by Reverend Martin McDonnell, born in Ireland in 1833 and ordained in Buffalo, N. Y., in 1854, who developed an interest in underprivileged children and determined to devote his life to their welfare.

With the approbation of Bishop Ireland, he bought five thousand acres of railroad land near Badger Lake in Murray County in southern Minnesota, and erected an orphanage which was formally opened in 1882 with five children. Two years later five others came. For support it relied on the industrial farm operated on a large scale by his brothers, Michael and Patrick. The boys, according to age and ability, were trained to work on the farm and care for the cattle, poultry and bees. The girls were taught domestic science and music and given an opportunity to attend the Mankato Normal School to prepare for teachers. All were paid a reasonable wage for their services; and when the boys left they were given an acre of land each and many of them secured farms in the neighborhood.

The town of Iona named by Father McDonnell, grew up in the vicinity, and he was pastor from 1878 to 1893 when ill-health forced him to retire. The orphanage was the center of business activity for the community and Father McDonnell was post master, merchant, druggist, banker, mayor, teacher and spiritual director. The people worshipped in the chapel of the Home until 1891 when the Church of St. Columba, so named by Father McDonnell, was erected. It was attended from St. James from 1893 to 1898 when it became a mission of Fulda. For many years its has had a resident pastor.

A larger and more modern Home, with 25 or 30 rooms, was erected on a site east of Iona in 1902 and blessed by Bishop Cotter, first Bishop of Winona, on September 26, 1904. The average number of orphans was about twenty-five.

The matron was Miss Crehan who had been a member of the Calced Carmelites in Batavia, N. Y., and known as Sister Mary Joseph. She tried to establish a branch of the Order in the West but was unsuccessful. She belonged to a well-to-do family and used her patrimony for the orphans. Some years after the turn of the century she bought thirteen acres of land on the outskirts of Mankato, built a new Home and transferred the ailing Father McDonnell and fifteen orphans thereto on April 16, 1910. Father McDonnell died the following September 24 and Miss Crehan in 1913. The orphans, from three to eighteen years of age, were sent to other institutions. During the twenty-eight years of its existence in Murray County the Home trained eighty children for useful careers in the world.

In January, 1884, Father McDonnell began the publication of a monthly magazine called "The Echo", a journal of religious and miscellaneous information, in the interests of the Home and kept it up for a couple of years.

1879—INDUSTRIAL SCHOOL FOR GIRLS, MENDOTA

It was opened in the Sibley House convent vacated by the Sisters of St. Joseph in 1879, by five Sisters of Mercy under the direction of Mother Mary Joseph Lynch They had forty children under their care in 1881-2. There is no mention of it in the Catholic Directory after 1883. Mother Lynch and the sisters (among them her niece, Sister M. Agnes Boland) came from Grand Rapids, Michigan, arrived in St. Paul on January 19, 1879, and went to Mendota. After her sojourn in Mendota she established the first Catholic Hospital in Minneapolis (now, St. Mary's), opened a small school in Anoka, which was acquired by the Sisters of St. Joseph in 189 as a boarding school for small girls and a day school for Catholic children o grade age.

1879—INDUSTRIAL SCHOOL FOR BOYS, CLONTARF

In 1878 the Board of Directors of the Catholic Industrial school in the Midwa district bought 2000 acres of land near Clontarf in Swift County for a ne industrial school to open in the spring of 1879. Temporary buildings were erected that year under the direction of Father Oster, pastor of the parish of Clontarf. Two Brothers—Malachy Shields and Alfonsus Moroney—came from Brooklyn in April, 1880, and in July three others—Leo Wall, Benedict Stephenson and Vincent Ryan, but there were no boys to be instructed. They secured temporary lodgings and harvested the crops. In 1881 Brother Benedict, the Superior, opened a private school in Clontarf and conducted it for over two years. Four more Brothers came in 1882 and the industrial school was opened. The first permanent frame building, 160 by 60, and three stories high was erected in October, 1883, and was amply sufficient for Brothers and pupils. By May, eight of the original Brothers had gone away discouraged at the prospect and only Brother William Osbelt was left. He had the courage to open a novitiate and seven men passed through it in four years.

On September 1, 1884, the name of the school was changed to St. Paul's Industrial Boarding school. It came under government control and 60 Indians were sent for whom the government paid from one hundred to one hundred and fifty dollars a year for board, lodging and tuition. A second residence, larger than the first, was built in 1885 and barns, granaries, etc., at a cost of $17,643.48, and the institution continued to be a success till 1895. Whites and Indians were enrolled in the proportion of one to six. The average attendance was 130. The boys were taught carpentry and other crafts, farming, stock and sheep raising. 3400 acres were cultivated. There were 21 farm buildings. Before the end of 1893 the Archbishop advanced $46,787.89 for land and buildings. There is no indication of the source of this money or whether he ever realized anything from the outlay.

In 1896 the Government decided to make no further appropriations for sectarian schools and no money would be available after 1900. The Government bought the school buildings and the land on which they stood in April, 1897, and in 1899 everything was dismantled and the project came to an end. In 1894 the Reverend Martin J. Egan was appointed resident superintendent and remained until the end.

1883—LORETTO HOSPITAL AND ST. ALEXANDER'S HOME, NEW ULM

St. Alexander's Hospital opened for patients on November 1, 1883, under the control of the Sisters of Christian Charity and as the result of an appeal made by Reverend Alexander Berghold, pastor of Holy Trinity Church. The original building was 36 by 36, two stories high, with basement, reception, operating and consultation rooms. An adjoining building of the same size was the convent of the sisters. They owned thirty-four acres of land much of which was under cultivation.

In October, 1884, the hospital was purchased by the Poor Handmaids of Jesus Christ for $7,000. In 1897 an addition, costing $16,000, was built and in February, 1912, the original structure was torn down to make room for a modern hospital costing $40,000 and the name was changed to Loretto Hospital. It was ready for occupancy in May, 1913, and was dedicated in June by Archbishop Ireland. The name of St. Alexander was retained for the home for the aged under the same management. There are 20 sisters on the staff and 27 doctors. The hospital has 20 patients and the Home 47 residents. For both institutions there are 56 full time and 26 part time employees. The Superior is Mother M. Confirma, R.N.

1883—ACADEMY OF THE HOLY CHILD, AVOCA

This school for Indian girls was operated until 1890 by six Sisters of the Holy Child from Philadelphia, and was then taken over by the Sisters of St. Joseph and the name changed to St. Rose's Convent. It was staffed by Sisters de Chantal Filteau, Lidwina Bradamus, Liguori Hunt and Francis Joseph Lemay. It was closed in 1902 and reopened three years later as St. Bernard's Hall for little boys. The superiors were Mothers de Chantal Filteau (1890-4); Hilda Tousignant (1894-7); Aloysia O'Dea (1897-1900); Leocadia Hayes (1900-2); Josepha Jarrett (1905-6); Antoinette Foley (1906-9); and Annunciata Connor (1909-10).

On February 12, 1910, the building was burned to the ground and not rebuilt. The sisters were recalled to the Motherhouse in St. Paul.

1886—CONVENT OF OUR LADY, GRACEVILLE

It was established by the Sisters of St. Joseph as a part Indian school for girls from Sisseton Agency and supported by the Government which paid $150.00 a year for each of twenty-five girls allotted to it. Additional support was received from Miss Katherine Drexel of Philadelphia. The Indian girls were housed in a separate building from the white girls and taught the branches of a common school education, housekeeping, dairying, sewing and knitting. The Government withdrew its aid from all private schools in 1896 and two years later on October 8, the institution consisting of four buildings valued at $12,000 on a tract of land valued at $4,500, was burned to the ground. The convent was rebuilt in 1900 and named St. Mary's and is still under the direction of the Sisters of St. Joseph.

1888—ST. JOHN'S HOSPITAL, WINONA

This small hospital, originally St. Joseph's Convent, a school for girls, was opened in 1888 under the supervision of Mother Jane Francis Bochet (1888-91) and a staff of three nursing sisters—Baptista O'Leary, Irmina Doherty and Thecla Reid with Sister Mechtilda Endres in charge of the domestic department. It had an average of twenty patients a day. Mother Aurelia McAndrews was appointed Superior in 1891. Two of the sisters connected with it died and were buried in Winona—Sister Marie Goodin on October 9, 1889, and Sister Carmena Lee on September 7, 1892. The institution was bought by the Sisters of St. Francis in 1894 and the site incorporated into the campus of the College of St. Teresa.

1928—OBLATE MISSION HOUSE, WHITE BEAR

It was established on September 15, 1928, by the Oblate Fathers of Mary Immaculate, with Father Meinwegen as the only resident till 1931. It was canonically erected on February 6, 1934, and Reverend Peter Bour, O.M.I., became Superior. The present Superior is Reverend Stanley Sergot, O.M.I. There are four priests in residence who give missions and help in parish work. The Mission House was moved to St. Paul in 1952. The Provincial headquarters is in Belleville, Illinois.

1938—ST. FRANCIS HOME AND HOSPITAL, SHAKOPEE

In the autumn of 1938 the old building first erected as St. Gertrude's Convent in 1862 and sold to the county as a home for the poor in 1880 was given by the county to become St. Francis Home with the proviso that the inmates continue to be cared for by the Sisters of St. Francis. It was remodeled and modernized and in November four Sisters of the Third Order of St. Francis, whose Motherhouse is in Waldbreitbach, Germany, began their charitable ministrations with about 45 old people and patients. In the spring of 1939 the first patients were admitted to the hospital. Mother M. Laetitia is the Superior with 6 sisters to staff the institution. A new and modern hospital was opened in 1952.

1945—HOLY TRINITY HOSPITAL, GRACEVILLE

The institution was purchased by the Missionary Sisters of St. Benedict of Norfolk, Nebraska, in October, 1945, under the direction of Mother M. Edburga, O.S.B., and twelve sisters who constitute the staff with 28 patients. It was formerly a non-Catholic hospital, known as the West Central Minnesota Hospital owned by a number of stockholders and operated by Dr. T. C. Oliver for thirty-one years.

1948—JESUIT RETREAT HOUSE, NORTH ST. PAUL

The Jesuit Fathers of the Missouri Province purchased the Waldorf estate on Lake Demontreville, near North St. Paul, in July, 1948. The first Mass was said on August 15 by Reverend Vincent Erbacher, S.J., who supervised the work of remodeling. On Thursday, November 18, Reverend Donald J. Keegan, S.J., the present Superior, began the first retreat for fifteen men. Up to July 21, 1949, 35 retreats were attended by 703 men. The retreats begin Thursday at 7 P.M. and end the following Monday at 6:15 A.M. There is no fixed charge; a voluntary offering is accepted. On June 29, 1949, Roy J. Johnson of Minneapolis was elected

President of the Laymen's Retreat League with four counsellors from St. Paul and four from Minneapolis. Fathers Keegan and an assistant give the retreats with occasional guest retreat masters.

1951—ASSUMPTION SEMINARY, CHASKA

The Province of Our Lady of Consolation, Friars Minor Conventual of Louisville, Ky., took over the Mudcura Sanitarium, 18 miles south of Minneapolis, on April 12, 1951, for a House of Studies for their students. The property comprises 120 acres and, in addition to the main building with 70 rooms, there are two residences, a dormitory, farm buildings and a garage. The main building was renovated to provide accommodations for the forty-two scholastics who began classes on October 5. It is known as the Assumption Seminary. Very Reverend Basil Heiser, O.F.M., Conv., was elected Guardian and Superior on July 26, 1951, and the first faculty consists of Fr. Owen Bennett, O.F.M., Conv. of Rensselaer, N. Y., Fr. Robert Bayer, O.F.M., Conv. of Carey, Ohio, and Fr. Donald Schiffli, O.F.M., Conv. of Terra Haute, Indiana. There are three brothers in the community.

Chapter XIV

APPENDIX

PRIESTS OF THE DIOCESE OF ST. PAUL ELEVATED TO THE EPISCOPATE

Seidenbusch, Right Reverend Rupert, O.S.B.: consecrated May 30, 1875; Titular Bishop of Halia and Vicar Apostolic of Northern Minnesota (1875-88); Titular Bishop of Halia (1888-95).

Ireland, Most Reverend John: consecrated December 21, 1875; Titular Bishop of Maronea and Coadjutor to Bishop Grace of St. Paul (1875-84); Bishop of St. Paul (1884-8); Archbishop of St. Paul (1888-1918).

Marty, Right Reverend Martin, O.S.B.: consecrated February 1, 1880; Titular Bishop of Tiberias and Vicar Apostolic of Dakota (1880-89); Bishop of Sioux Falls (1889-94); Bishop of St. Cloud (1894-6).

McGolrick, Right Reverend James: consecrated December 27, 1889; Bishop of Duluth (1889-1918).

Cotter, Right Reverend Joseph B.: consecrated December 27, 1889; Bishop of Winona (1889-1909).

Shanley, Right Reverend John: consecrated December 27, 1889; Bishop of Jamestown (1889-97); Bishop of Fargo (1897-1909).

Delany*, Most Reverend Patrick: consecrated December 10, 1893; Titular Bishop of Laranda and Coadjutor to Archbishop Murphy of Hobart, Tasmania (1893-1907); Archbishop of Hobart (1907-26).

O'Gorman, Right Reverend Thomas: consecrated April 19, 1896; Bishop of Sioux Falls (1896-1921).

Trobec, Right Reverend James: consecrated September 21, 1897; Bishop of St. Cloud (1897-1914); Titular Bishop of Lycopolis (1914-21).

Christie, Most Reverend Alexander: consecrated June 29, 1898; Bishop of Victoria, Vancouver Island, Canada (1898-9); Archbishop of Oregon City (Portland) (1899-1925).

Keane, Most Reverend James J.: consecrated October 28, 1902; Bishop of Cheyenne (1902-11); Archbishop of Dubuque (1911-29).

Stariha, Right Reverend John N.: consecrated October 28, 1902; Bishop of Lead (1902-9); Titular Bishop of Antipatride (1909-15).

O'Reilly, Most Reverend James: consecrated May 19, 1910; Bishop of Fargo (1910-34).

Heffron, Most Reverend Patrick R.: consecrated May 19, 1910; Bishop of Winona (1910-27).

Lawler, Most Reverend John J.: consecrated May 19, 1910; Titular Bishop of Greater Hermopolis and Auxiliary to Archbishop Ireland (1910-16); Bishop of Lead

(1916-30); Bishop of Rapid City (1930-48).

Corbett, Most Reverend Timothy: consecrated May 19, 1910; Bishop of Crookston (1910-38); Titular Bishop of Vita (1938-9).

Wehrle, Most Reverend Vincent, O.S.B.: consecrated May 19, 1910; Bishop of Bismarck (1910-39); Titular Bishop of Teos (1939-41).

Busch, Most Reverend Joseph F.: consecrated May 19, 1910; Bishop of Lead (1910-5); Bishop of St. Cloud (1915—).

Duffy, Most Reverend James A.: consecrated April 16, 1913; Bishop of Kearney (1913-7); Bishop of Grand Island (1917-31); Titular Bishop of Silando (1931—).

Welch, Most Reverend Thomas A.: consecrated February 3, 1926; Bishop of Duluth (1926—).

Brady, Most Reverend William O.: consecrated August 24, 1939; Bishop of Sioux Falls (1939—).

Schenk, Most Reverend Francis J.: consecrated May 24, 1945; Bishop of Crookston (1945—).

Connolly, Most Reverend James L.: consecrated May 24, 1945; Titular Bishop of Mylasa and Coadjutor to Bishop Cassidy of Fall River (1945-51); Bishop of Fall River (1951—).

Byrne, Most Reverend James J.: consecrated July 2, 1947; Titular Bishop of Etenna and Auxiliary to Archbishop Murray (1947—).

MEMBERS OF THE FACULTY OF ST. PAUL SEMINARY WHO BECAME BISHOPS

Most Reverends P. R. Heffron; W. O. Brady; James L. Connolly (see above). Turner, Most Reverend William; consecrated March 30, 1919; Bishop of Buffalo (1919-36).

MEMBERS OF THE FACULTY AND GRADUATES OF THE ST. PAUL SEMINARY WHO WERE MADE BISHOPS

Most Reverends F. J. Schenk and J. J. Byrne (see above).

GRADUATES OF ST. PAUL SEMINARY PROMOTED TO THE HIERARCHY

Most Reverends J. A. Duffy and T. A. Welch (see above).

Howard, Most Reverend Edward D.: consecrated April 8, 1924; Titular Bishop of Isauria and Auxiliary to Bishop Davis of Davenport (1924-6); Archbishop of Portland (1926—).

Kelly, Most Reverend Francis M.: consecrated June 9, 1926; Titular Bishop of Mylasa and Auxiliary to Bishop Heffron of Winona (1926-8); Bishop of Winona (1928-49); Titular Bishop of Nasai (1949-50).

O'Hara, Most Reverend Edwin V.: consecrated October 28, 1930; Bishop of Great Falls (1930-9); Bishop of Kansas City (1939—).

Kucera, Most Reverend Louis B.: consecrated October 28, 1930; Bishop of Lincoln (1930—).

Wosnicki, Most Reverend Stephen S.: consecrated January 25, 1938; Titular Bishop of Pelte and Auxiliary to Cardinal Mooney, Archbishop of Detroit (1938-50); Bishop of Saginaw (1950—).

Peschges, Most Reverend John H.: consecrated November 9, 1938; Bishop of Crookston (1938-44).

Ryan, Most Reverend Vincent J.: consecrated May 28, 1940; Bishop of Bismarck (1940-51).

Bartholome, Most Reverend Peter W.: consecrated March 3, 1942; Titular Bishop of Lete and Coadjutor to Bishop Busch of St. Cloud (1942—).

Mulloy, Most Reverend William T.: consecrated January 10, 1945; Bishop of Covington (1945—).

Sheen, Most Reverend Fulton J.: consecrated June 11, 1951; Titular Bishop of Cesariana and Auxiliary to Cardinal Spellman, Archbishop of New York (1951—)

Hoch, Most Reverend Lambert A.: consecrated March 25, 1952, Bishop of Bismarck (1952—).

*Archbishop Delany was ordained in All Hallows College, Ireland, in November, 1879, for the Diocese of St. Paul and, with the permission of Bishop Grace, became a member of the faculty as Professor of History and Canon Law until 1885, when he went to Australia and joined the Diocese of Ballarat. On February 6, 1888, at the request of Cardinal Simeoni, Bishop Ireland gave him his exeat. On December 10, 1893, he was consecrated Titular Bishop of Laranda and Coadjutor to Archbishop Murphy of Hobart, Tasmania, whom he succeeded on December 29, 1907, and died on May 7, 1926, in the seventy-third year of his life.

VICARS GENERAL OF THE DIOCESE OF ST. PAUL

	1851	1952
Very Reverend Augustine Ravoux		1851-7 and 1859-92
Very Reverend Demetrius de Marogna, O.S.B.		1860-9
Very Reverend Clemens Staub, O.S.B.		1869-76
Very Reverend A. Oster	April 22 to	August 16, 1867
Most Reverend T. L. Grace, O.P., D.D.		1888-92
Right Reverend L. E. Caillet		1893-7
Very Reverend J. N. Stariha		1897-1902
Right Reverend Anatole Oster		1902-10
Most Reverend John J. Lawler, D.D.		1910-6
Very Reverend James C. Byrne		1916-18
Right Reverend John J. Slevin		1919-24
Right Reverend Thomas A. Welch		1924-6
Right Reverend Patrick O'Neill		1926-30
Right Reverend James C. Byrne		1932-42
Very Reverend Francis J. Schenk		1942-5
Very Reverend Hilary B. Hacker		1945—

DOMESTIC PRELATES OF THE DIOCESE OF ST. PAUL

Right Reverend Augustine Ravoux	March 1, 1887
Right Reverend Louis E. Caillet	August 7, 1892
Right Reverend Anatole Oster	October 26, 1899
Right Reverend Alois Plut	May 10, 1906
Right Reverend Dominic A. Majer	May 10, 1906
Right Reverend Thomas C. Kennedy	July 26, 1906
Right Reverend Bernard H. Sandmeyer	May 12, 1909
Right Reverend John J. Slevin	January 11, 1913
Right Reverend Wendelin M. Stulz	January 11, 1913
Right Reverend Joseph M. Guillot	January 11, 1913
Right Reverend Francis Tichy	January 11, 1913
Right Reverend Humphrey Moynihan	February 5, 1924
Right Reverend James C. Byrne	February 5, 1924
Right Reverend James M. Cleary	February 5, 1924
Right Reverend Anthony Ogulin	February 5, 1924
Right Reverend Patrick O'Neill	February 5, 1924
Right Reverend Peter M. Jung	February 5, 1924
Right Reverend Thomas A. Welch	February 5, 1924
Right Reverend John Dunphy	March 27, 1947
Right Reverend Joseph A. Corrigan	March 27, 1947
Right Reverend John J. Cullinan	March 27, 1947
Right Reverend Alois Ziskovsky	March 27, 1947
Right Reverend Vincent W. Worzalla	March 27, 1947
Right Reverend James Zachman	March 27, 1947

Right Reverend James H. Moynihan .... April 6, 1951
Right Reverend James J. A. Troy .... August 9, 1951

PROTONOTARY APOSTOLIC

Right Reverend James M. Reardon .... June 18,1941

ORDINATIONS TO THE HOLY PRIESTHOOD

By Right Reverend Bishop Cretin in the Cathedral

Reverend John Fayolle .... September 20, 1851
Reverend Edward Legendre .... September 20, 1852
Reverend Marcellin Peyragrosse .... September 20, 1852
Reverend Daniel Fisher .... May 14, 1853
Reverend Thomas Murray .... September 23, 1854
Reverend George Keller .... September 23, 1854
Reverend John McMahon .... March 24, 1855
Reverend J. Claude Robert .... September 22, 1855
Reverend Francis Hurth .... March 8, 1856
Reverend Valentine Sommereisen .... March 8, 1856
Reverend Cornelius Wittmann, O.S.B. .... May 17, 1856
Reverend Bruno Riss, O.S.B. .... May 17, 1856
Reverend John H. Mehlman .... July 27, 1856
Reverend Anatole Oster .... December 13, 1856
  Bishop Cretin ordained 12 diocesan and 2 Benedictine priests.

By Right Reverend Clement Smyth, O.C.S.O., of Dubuque

Reverend Louis E. Caillet .... August 12, 1857, (in St. Paul)
Reverend Felix Tissot .... August 15, 1858, (in Dubuque)

By Right Reverend Bishop Grace in the Cathedral

Reverend Edward Essing .... November 8, 1860
Reverend Pius Bayer .... November 8, 1860
Reverend John Ireland .... December 22, 1861
Reverend Theodore Venn .... April 19, 1862
Reverend William Lette .... March 12, 1864
Reverend John Zuzek .... November 1, 1864
Reverend John N. Tomazevic .... November 1, 1864
Reverend Alexander Berghold .... November 1, 1864
Reverend Alois Plut .... February 12, 1865
Reverend Wolfgang Northmann, O.S.B. .... February 12, 1865
Reverend Gregory Koering .... July 30, 1865
Reverend Christian J. Knauf .... July 30, 1865
Reverend James Trobec .... September 8, 1865
Reverend Thomas O'Gorman .... November 5, 1865
Reverend Ignatius Tomazin .... November 5, 1865
Reverend Ferdinand Stern .... November 5, 1865
Reverend Francis A. Casper, O.S.B. .... February 11, 1866
Reverend Maria L. Nicolas .... April 25, 1866
Reverend Joseph M. Velle, O.S.B. .... February 2, 186
Reverend Prosper Maurer .... April 30, 1867
Reverend Alexius Edelbrock, O.S.B. .... September 29, 186
Reverend Joseph J. Hillmer .... April 19, 186
Reverend Francis J. Toplak .... June 30, 186
Reverend James Halton .... June 30, 186
Reverend George A. Schmirer .... June 30, 186
Reverend Thomas Cahill .... November 1, 186
Reverend Thomas C. Kennedy .... March 30, 186
Reverend Charles Koeberl .... March 30, 186

Reverend Anthony Holzer .... March 30, 1869
Reverend Valentine Stimmler, O.S.B. .... March 30, 1869
Reverend Rudolph Haase .... September 5, 1869
Reverend Maurice Murphy .... September 5, 1869
Reverend James A. McGlone .... April 10, 1870
Reverend Patrick K. Ryan .... April 10, 1870
Reverend James Schwebach (La Crosse) .... June 7, 1870
Reverend Boniface Mull .... December 27, 1870
Reverend Justus I. Barzez .... May 21, 1871
Reverend Joseph B. Cotter .... May 21, 1871
Reverend John Mullins .... May 21, 1871
Reverend Ignatius Schaller .... July 16, 1871
Reverend Francis J. A. Lechner .... July 16, 1871
Reverend John Nealis .... September 29, 1872
Reverend Simplicius Wimmer, O.S.B. .... September 29, 1872
Reverend Eric Peterson .... December 22, 1872
Reverend Alphonsus Kuisle, O.S.B. .... December 22, 1872
Reverend Vincent Schiffrer, O.S.B. .... December 22, 1872
Reverend Bernard Locnikar, O.S.B. .... December 22, 1872
Reverend Joseph L. Salzeder, O.S.B. .... March 16, 1873
Reverend John Pavlin .... March 16, 1873
Reverend Bartholomew Rajgelj, O.S.B. .... September 29, 1873
Reverend Michael Cauley .... September 29, 1873
Reverend Meinrad Senthard, O.S.B. .... September 21, 1874
Reverend Placidus Watry, O.S.B. .... September 21, 1874
Reverend Pancratius Maechren, O.S.B. .... September 21, 1874
Reverend Francis Pribyl .... March 27, 1875
Reverend Daniel F. Hayes .... October 28, 1876
   Bishop Grace ordained 42 diocesan and 14 Benedictine Priests.

By Right Reverend Bishop Ireland in the Cathedral
Reverend John Tori .... July 8, 1877
Reverend John Meier .... July 8, 1877
Reverend Max Wurst .... April 20, 1878
Reverend Bernard Sandmeyer .... July 25, 1878
Reverend Henry McGolrick .... October 6, 1881
Reverend Edward Duffy .... October 6, 1881
Reverend David Murray .... September 25, 1882
Reverend Edward Lee .... December 11, 1882
Reverend Patrick Kiernan .... July 27, 1883
Reverend Michael P. Lynch .... April 14, 1884
Reverend Anthony Ogulin .... September 19, 1884
   Bishop Ireland ordained 11 diocesan priests before the opening of St. Thomas Aquinas Seminary on September 8, 1885.

By Bishop Ireland in St. Thomas Aquinas Seminary Chapel
   November 5, 1885: Reverends Robert Hughes, Thomas J. Gibbons, I. Lauson, Patrick McTeague, Dennis O'Keefe.
   June 18, 1886: Reverends Patrick Dwyer, John T. Harrison, John Hannack, Leopold Haas, Louis Keukelink, James Pacholski, Joseph Soumis.
   August 10, 1886: Reverends Ignatius Limberg, Francis Savey.
   August 11, 1887: Reverends Robert J. Walsh, Patrick O'Connor, John Peters, Joseph Goergen, John Jacobs, Francis Reichel.
   June 10, 1887: Reverends Hugh J. McAvay, James J. Conry.
   June 14, 1888: Reverends John A. Kane, Thomas Gleeson, Denis Sullivan, Charles Mikula.
   April 6, 1889: Reverends James J. Treanor, John J. Sullivan, Methodius Slatinski.

June 8, 1889: Reverend Francis Windisch.
October 12, 1889: Reverend Charles Corcoran.
December 21, 1889: Reverend Stephen Condron.
March 22, 1890: Reverend Peter Schoenen.
May 31, 1890: Reverend Charles A. Pettigrew.
September 20, 1890: Reverend Francis X. Bajec.
November 15, 1890: Reverends Patrick Lucey, Francis Kosmerl, John Pivo, Alexander Zalewski.
March 14, 1891: Reverends Thomas E. Shields, James Connolly.
June 21, 1891: Reverend Joseph B. Illig.
December 19, 1891: Reverends Martin J. Egan, Patrick J. Hart, Nathaniel Mc-Caffrey.
October 2, 1892: Reverend Terrence Moore.
December 17, 1892: Reverends Mathias Bilban, Francis Hrachovski, Francis Jaeger, Anthony Vilman, Michael O'Brien, Patrick McDonough, Patrick R. Cunningham.
November 1, 1893: Reverend Gabriel Andre.
March 10, 1894: Reverend Robert Polasek.
August 17, 1893: Reverend Ferdinand Posek.
March 6, 1893: Reverend Owen F. Rice.
May 23, 1894: Reverend Patrick McMahon.
June 23, 1894; Reverends Jeremias M. Prendergast, Louis Grandchamp (Duluth), Philip Murphy (Duluth), Robert Condon (La Crosse).
December 10, 1894: Reverend Adam Coyle.

63 ordained in St. Thomas Aquinas Seminary by Bishop Ireland between November 5, 1885, and December 10, 1894.

In the St. Paul Seminary between January 1, 1895, and June 12, 1917, Archbishop Ireland ordained 266 priests.
Archbishop Dowling ordained 192 priests between June 1, 1919, and June 9, 1930.
Archbishop Murray ordained 213 priests between June 4, 1932, and June 8, 1946.
Auxiliary Bishop Byrne ordained 73 priests between June 8, 1948, and June, 1952.

CONSECRATED CHURCHES AND CHAPELS IN THE DIOCESE OF ST. PAUL

The Church of St. Joseph, St. Joseph, on June 29, 1871, by Bishop Grace.
The Church of the Assumption, St. Paul, on October 18, 1874, by Bishop Grace.
The Church of St. Mary, Stillwater, on July 20, 1884, by Coadjutor Bishop Ireland.
The Church of St. Michael, St. Michael, on September 29, 1892, by Bishop McGolrick of Duluth. (The crosses and candle-holders on the interior walls, the visible proof of consecration, were removed when the church was re-decorated in 1904 and never replaced).
St. Mary's Chapel, St. Paul Seminary, on May 24, 1905, by Bishop Cotter of Winona. (Pontifical Mass was celebrated by Bishop McGolrick of Duluth and the sermon preached by Bishop O'Gorman of Sioux Falls. Bishop Lenihan of Great Falls celebrated Pontifical Vespers and Archbishop Ireland preached).
The Chapel of the Annunciation, Nazareth Hall Preparatory Seminary, on September 8, 1924, by Archbishop Dowling. (Bishop McNicholas of Duluth preached and Bishops Lawler, Busch and Mahoney were present at the ceremony).
The Church of St. Michael, Stillwater, on September 29, 1937, by Archbishop Murray.
The Church of St. Timothy, Maple Lake, on April 21, 1938, by Archbishop Murray.
The Church of St. Mary, St. Paul, on May 24, 1939, by Archbishop Murray.
The Church of St. Mark, St. Paul, on May 29, 1939, by Archbishop Murray.
The Basilica of St. Mary, Minneapolis, on June 27, 1941, by His Eminence Dennis Cardinal Dougherty of Philadelphia, two Archbishops and five Bishops.

CONSECRATED ALTARS IN THE DIOCESE OF ST. PAUL

Main altar, Church of St. Louis, St. Paul, November 30, 1911, by Bishop Lawler.

Three altars in the chapels of the Cathedral of St. Paul by Archbishop Dowling, namely, St. Peter's on June 30, 1920; St. Joseph's on August 21, 1920; and Our Lady's on May 28, 1921.

The altar of the Mother of God shrine on the grounds of Nazareth Hall on May 26, 1926, by Archbishop Dowling.

The new altar of St. Mary's Chapel, St. Paul Seminary, on November 12, 1930, by the Rector, Right Reverend Humphrey Moynihan, delegated by Archbishop Dowling. (It is the gift of the priests and alumni and is made of Algerian onyx, with relics of Sts. Clementianus and Valerianus, Martyrs, enclosed in the sepulchre).

Seven altars in the chapels of the Cathedral of St. Paul by Archbishop Murray in 1933, namely, those of St. Anthony, St. Patrick, and St. John the Baptist on September 28, and of St. Boniface, Sts. Cyril and Methodius, St. Therese, and the Sacred Heart of Jesus on September 29.

The altar of St. Anne's Convent, Minneapolis, on November 4, 1939, by Archbishop Murray.

The main altar of the Church of the Holy Cross, Minneapolis, on May 30, 1940, by Archbishop Murray.

The main altar and two side altars in the Church of St. Aloysius, Olivia, on August 28, 1947, by Bishop Kucera of Lincoln, Bishop Schenk of Crookston and Auxiliary Bishop Byrne of St. Paul.

CATHOLIC CHAPLAINS IN THE ARMED FORCES

The following facts relative to the Catholic Chaplains who served in the Armed Forces of the United States, are taken from "United States Catholic Chaplains in the World War", published in New York, in 1924, by the Ordinariate of Army and Navy Chaplains.

In the Revolutionary War the Catholic Chaplains in the service, about one hundred, accompanied the units that came from abroad to aid the Colonies in their struggle against England. The same is true of the Catholic Chaplains in the war of 1812 and the early part of the Mexican War. In 1846 President Polk commissioned two priests selected by Bishops Hughes of New York, Portier of Mobile and Kenrick of St. Louis. In the Civil War about one hundred priests volunteered for service and were recognized as regular commissioned chaplains. Among them were Reverends John Ireland, Lawrence McMahon and Bernard McQuaid.

In the Spanish American War of 1898 twelve priests held commissioned rank. A few of the National Guard units which entered the Federal service at that time had their official chaplains, and some dioceses sent priests, in civilian capacity, with the troops from their states. The entire National Guard was mobilized by Federal order on the Mexican border in 1916; but there were only nine Catholic priests identified with them, of whom one was from St. Paul, Reverend W. J. Harrington, now pastor of the Church of St. Peter, Mendota, who served from September, 1916, to February, 1917.

When the United States entered World War I on April 6, 1917, there were sixteen priests in the Regular Army and nine in the National Guard. During the war the quota of Catholic Chaplains was raised from 24% to 37.8% till 1920 when it was lowered to 25%. When the armistice was signed on November 11, 1918, there were 1023 chaplains in active service with the Army, Navy or K. of C., and 500 approved applicants would have been commissioned on January 1, 1919.

On November 24, 1917, Bishop Hayes of New York was appointed Episcopus Castrensis to systematize and unify the chaplain corps at home and abroad. In 1924, ninety-six priests were in the service and two hundred in the Officers' Reserve Corps of the Army and in National Guard organizations.

In the first World War each diocese was requested to furnish a number of chaplains based on the total number of priests on its roster. The quota for St. Paul was 11 of whom 10 were in the service and 10 others had made application. In World War II 53 priests of the Archdiocese of St. Paul served the fighting men at home and abroad and 21 are now engaged in that essential apostolate.

The Civil War

Ireland, Reverend John, from May 10, 1862, to April 3, 1863.

Post Chaplains—Fort Snelling, Minnesota

Dolphin, Rev. John F., from 1888 to 1893.

Hart, Rev. Patrick J., from February, 1893 to April, 1898.

Spanish-American War

Hart, Rev. Patrick J., from April, 1898 to May, 1908.

Colbert, Rev. William, from April to November, 1898, and from June, 1901, to September, 1904.

Doherty, Rev. Francis B., from April, 1902, to October, 1920.

First World War

Cullinan, Rev. John J., from August 22, 1918, to August 19, 1919.

Harrington, Rev. William J., from July 1, 1917, to May 12, 1919.

Moran, Rev. David J., from August 26, 1918, to July 10, 1919.

Normoyle, Rev. Cornelius J., from August, 1918, to April 1, 1919.

O'Neil, Rev. Joseph L., from August 23, 1918, to June 16, 1919.

Troy, Rev. James J. A., from July 26, 1918, to August 20, 1920.

Knights of Columbus Chaplains

Burns, Rev. Francis T. J., from August, 1917, to January, 1919.

Hart, Rev. William L., from November, 1917, to March, 1919.

Jordan, Rev. Hilary R., from June to October, 1919.

Missia, Rev. Francis A., from June to September, 1917 and 1918.

Chaplains awaiting appointments when hostilities ceased

Reverends J. F. Cassidy; C. J. Farrell; J. T. Fitzgerald; E. P. Murphy; M. O'Brien; J. Sodja; A. V. Szczukowski; S. Winter.

Second World War

Adrian, Rev. Stephen J., from January 25, 1944, to July 12, 1946.

Ahern, Rev. Patrick H., from February 23, 1945, to September 12, 1946.

Bertrand, Rev. Aloysius F., from November 5, 1944, to

Blatz, Rev. Albert B., from February 1, 1944, to March 27, 1946.

Blatz, Rev. Roman T., from September 15, 1944, to

Bonin, Rev. Leon, from August 1, 1944, to August 1, 1946.

Brady, Rev. J. Wilson, from May 25, 1942, to May 5, 1943.

Buchanan, Rev. John J., from February 22, 1942, to September 26, 1945.

Cashman, Rev. Neil, from February 5, 1941, to December, 1945: from January 16, 1951, to

Cashman, Rev. Emmett, January 16, 1951, to

Clemens, Rev. Edward M., from October 19, 1949, to

Coates, Rev. Patrick W., from June 7, 1943, to May 28, 1946: from September 21, 1950, to

Dean, Rev. Harold J., from October 15, 1941, to December 7, 1946: from October 11, 1951, to

Eggert, Rev. Charles M., from October 28, 1942, to September 12, 1946.

Esser, Rev. Joseph F., from February 9, 1942, to September 15, 1945: from July 15, 1947, to October 31, 1949.

Farrell, Rev. Mark A., from June 23, 1942, to June 1, 1946.

Fenelon, Rev. Thomas F., from March 15, 1945, to August 1, 1946.

Filbin, Rev. Ambrose R., from March 7, 1942, to October 30, 1945.

Fleming, Rev. Francis J., from August 28, 1944, to July 15, 1946.

Forrey, Rev. Louis W., from September 30, 1942, to January 3, 1943.
Fortin, Rev. Lloyd J., from March 14, 1942, to May 1, 1946.
Gearty, Rev. Patrick W., from June 7, 1943, to September 2, 1946.
Grandpre, Rev. Edward A., from January 16, 1951, to
Henrich, Rev. Rudolph M., from December 5, 1942, to June 1, 1946.
Hesse, Rev. Harold W., from August 20, 1942, to June 1, 1946; from May 11, 1952, to
Hope, Rev. Vincent J., from November 5, 1942, to September 12, 1946.
Houle, Rev. Cecil F., from March 7, 1942, to October 31, 1945.
Howley, Rev. William L., from January 8, 1941, to November 23, 1945.
Jude, Rev. Thomas R., from April 17, 1944, to May 12, 1946.
Kachinsky, Rev. Leonard D., from July 8, 1942, to June 20, 1947.
Kasel, Rev. Joseph T., from March 12, 1942, to
Keany, Rev. Brian, from May 17, 1943, to May 28, 1946.
LeBeau, Rev. Walter L., from February 14, 1944, to May 15, 1946.
Longley, Rev. Alfred C., from March 7, 1942, to January, 1952.
McNamara, Rev. Thomas J., from March 7, 1942, to October 29, 1945.
Michel, Rev. William J., from September 15, 1944, to January 22, 1946.
Murphy, Rev. Terrence, from March 4, 1949, to
Musch, Rev. Joseph J., from May 7, 1942, to November 1, 1945.
Nolan, Rev. Rudolph E., from May 30, 1943, to February 1, 1946.
O'Neil, Rev. John J., from September 24, 1944, to
O'Sullivan, Rev. John J., from September 7, 1942, to October 13, 1945.
Otto, Rev. Mark J., from August 20, 1942, to April 18, 1946.
Powers, Rev. Stanley M., from October 1, 1944, to
Reed, Rev. Raymond J., from December 3, 1945, to August 12, 1946; from April 2, 1951, to
Robertson, Rev. Thomas J., from August 16, 1944, to October 7, 1946; from June 16, 1951, to
Rutkowski, Rev. Raymond A., from August 17, 1942, to January 22, 1946.
Ryan, Rt. Rev. Patrick J., from June, 1928, to
Savage, Rev. John L., from November 3, 1942, to January 22, 1946.
Schaefer, Rev. Roman J., from March 22, 1944, to
Schuck, Rev. David B., from June 10, 1950, to
Schumacher, Rev. Bernard F., from February 9, 1942, to December 31, 1945; and from August 16, 1948, to
Seefeldt, Rev. Wilbert T., from July 27, 1942, to February 7, 1946.
Thissen, Rev. Frederick W., from March 30, 1942, to December 31, 1945; and from August 12, 1946, to June 21, 1947.
Troy, Rev. James J. A., from May 15, 1941, to September 1, 1945.
Vashro, Rev. Robert A., from March 1, 1951, to
Weiers, Rev. Wilfred W., from February 1, 1944, to March 1, 1946.
Walsh, Rev. William J., from March 15, 1933, to November 1, 1947.
Westhoff, Rev. Donald, from June 6, 1949, to
Whittet, Rev. Harold E., from February 1, 1944, to July 12, 1946.

In Canadian Army
Murphy, Rev. Edward P., from 1918 to 1919.
Thornton, Rev. Francis B., from May, 1942, to June 1, 1946.

NEW PARISHES IN ST. PAUL

Name of Parish	Date of Organization or Incorporation
Holy Spirit	January 22, 1937
Our Lady of Guadaloupe	April 20, 1939
Corpus Christi	April 28, 1939

St. Leo .... June 28, 1939
Presentation of the B.V.M. .... February 11, 1946
Holy Childhood .... April 9, 1946
St. Paschal Baylon .... June 18, 1946
Maternity of the B.V.M. .... February 22, 1949
Immaculate Heart of Mary .... May 12, 1949
St. Gregory the Great .... July 17, 1951

NEW PARISHES IN VICINITY OF ST. PAUL

St. Francis of Assisi (St. Croix Beach) .... October 26, 1938
St. Rose of Lima (Rosetown) .... July 24, 1939
St. Jude (Mahtomedi) .... August 11, 1939
Transfiguration (Harvester Avenue) .... August 25, 1939
Holy Trinity (South St. Paul) .... June 30, 1940
St. Jerome (East County Road, A-2) .... February 17, 1941
St. Joseph (West St. Paul) .... October 12, 1942
St. Charles (Bayport) .... August 17, 1943
St. John Vianney (South St. Paul)................. July 22, 1946

NEW PARISHES IN MINNEAPOLIS

Resurrection .... June 18, 1933
St. Albert the Great .... March 9, 1935
St. Austin .... April 21, 1937
Our Lady of Mount Carmel .... March 20, 1938
Christ the King .... May 13, 1938
St. Charles Borromeo .... November 21, 1938
St. Leonard of Port Maurice .... January 15, 1940
St. Martin .... July 27, 1940
St. Olaf .... February 6, 1941
St. Kevin .... October 17, 1941
Our Lady of Victory .... November 8, 1945
Visitation of the B.V.M. .... August 24, 1946
St. Joan of Arc .... September 3, 1946
St. Frances Cabrini .... October 10, 1946

NEW PARISHES IN MINNEAPOLIS SUBURBS

St. Joseph (Medicine Lake) .... July 10, 1934
St. Mary of the Lake (Medicine Lake) .... October 12, 1935
St. Timothy (Spring Lake) .... February 23, 1943
Holy Trinity (St. Louis Park) .... June 7, 1943
St. Peter (Richfield) .... October 29, 1943
St. Margaret Mary (Golden Valley) .... January 30, 1946
Our Lady of Grace (Edina) .... February 18, 1946
Good Shepherd (Tyrol Hills) .... December 31, 1945
St. Therese (Deephaven) .... June 3, 1946
Immaculate Heart of Mary (Glen Lake) .... July 12, 1946
Nativity of the B.V.M. (Oxboro) .... November 1, 1949
St. John the Evangelist (Interlachen Park) .... June 14, 1950
St. Raphael (Crystal) .... June 30, 1951
St. Richard (Richfield) .... January 21, 1952

NEW PARISHES IN RURAL DISTRICTS

St. Mary (Bechyn) .... June 22, 1932
St. Patrick (Kandiyohi) .... January 15, 1933

St. Patrick (Edina)	January 15, 1933
Assumption of the B.V.M. (Assumption)	July 4, 1934
St. John (Hector)	July 10, 1934
Japanese Martyrs (Leavenworth)	January 1, 1935
Sacred Heart (Franklin)	August 2, 1935
St. Mary (Seaforth)	August 10, 1935
Nativity of the B.V.M. (Cleveland)	January 2, 1936
Sacred Heart (Raymond)	January 2, 1936
St. Thomas More (Lake Lillian)	January 25, 1936
St. Gregory (North Branch)	June 19, 1936
St. Andrew (Granite Falls)	June 1, 1938
St. Paul (Zumbrota)	June 11, 1938
Our Lady (Manannah)	January 24, 1939
St. James (Nassau)	October 4, 1939
St. Michael (Milroy)	January 24, 1939
St. Joseph (Rice Lake)	August 30, 1939
St. Joseph (Clements)	September 30, 1939
St. Paul (Walnut Grove)	October 4, 1939
St. Dionysius (Tyler)	June 29, 1940
St. Mary of Czestochowa (Delano)	August 4, 1940
Annuciation of the B.V.M. (Hazelwood)	October 30, 1940
St. Thomas (Sanborn)	July 30, 1941
St. Anthony (Regal)	October 26, 1941
Visitation of the B.V.M. (Brighton)	July 1, 1942
St. Gregory (Lafayette)	August 26, 1942
Holy Name (Vesta)	June 8, 1943
St. Francis de Sales (Winthrop)	September 1, 1943
St. Michael (Gaylord)	September 1, 1943
St. Michael (Kenyon)	January 3, 1944
St. Gertrude (Forest City)	June 20, 1945
St. Bridget of Sweden (Lindstrom)	March 8, 1948
St. George (Long Lake)	August 25, 1948
St. Joseph (Taylor's Falls)	August 25, 1948
St. Joseph (Lexington)	October 14, 1948

LIST OF ABBREVIATIONS

ACA.—Archdiocesan Chancery Archives, St. Paul.

NWC.—The Northwestern Chronicle, St. Paul.

CB.—The Catholic Bulletin, St. Paul.

CBA.—Catholic Bulletin Archives, St. Paul.

CHSA.—Catholic Historical Society Archives, St. Paul Seminary.

AD.—Acta et Dicta (official publication of CHSA), St. Paul Seminary.

CE.—Catholic Encyclopedia (K. of C. edition), New York.

MHSC.—Minnesota Historical Society Collections, St. Paul.

APF.—Annals of the Society for the Propagation of the Faith, Dublin.

BCA.—Baltimore Cathedral Archives, Baltimore, Md.

RDA.—Richmond Diocesan Archives, Richmond, Virginia.

CD.—Catholic Directory (whatever its official title), New York.

Op. Cit.—Book or article already cited.

1:1—Vol. 1, No. 1, and similarly for others.

ff.—the following pages.

Chapter XV

REFERENCES

I

[1] The Kensington Rune Stone: Preliminary Report to the Minnesota Historical Society by Its Museum Committee (St. Paul: 1910), pp. 1 & ff.

This Report tells the story of the finding of the Rune Stone and of the investigation made by the committee, and is incorporated in Volume XV, of MHSC., 1909-1914, pp. 221 & ff.

Schaefer, Rev. F. J., *The Kensington Rune Stone.* AD., 2:2, July, 1910, pp. 206-210.

[2] A slightly different translation is found in the *The Kensington Rune Stone: Is It the Oldest Native Document of American History?* Wisconsin Magazine of History, 3:2, December, 1919, p. 156.

[3] In 1878 the Great Northern Railway reached Alexandria, Douglas County, twenty-five miles from Kensington, and in 1886 it came to Kensington. In 1858 the nearest railroad point to Kensington was La Crosse, Wisconsin.

[4] Minneapolis Sunday Tribune, April 26, 1899, part 3, p. 4.

Minneapolis Journal, February 22, 1899, p. 1.

[5] Hagan, S. N. *The Kensington Runic Inscription.* Speculum, a Journal of Mediaeval Studies, 15:3, July, 1950, p. 349.

[6] MHSC. Vol. XV, 1909-1914, p. 268.

[7] Minnesota History, June, 1936, quoted by H. R. Holand, p. 172.

[8] The Kensington Rune Stone: Preliminary Report. Appendix (Professor Flom's investigation), p. 50.

Anderson, R. B., in Wisconsin Magazine of History, June, 1920, p. 413, called the inscription "a rather clumsy fraud" because the use of runes was "wholly abandoned", as he maintained, "long before 1362"; and the late Professor Larsen of the University of Illinois, in Minnesota History for March, 1936, says that. Dr. M. M. Quaife of the Detroit Public Library condemned the inscription and the legend built round it as "a baseless myth". Professor Larsen believed the "inscription is a forgery".

The writer is indebted to Dr. Emmet J. Mullally of Montreal for two extracts from the Canadian Historical Review, March, 1952, a quarterly publication of the University of Toronto Press, the one referring to Erik Moltke, a Danish scientist, who declares that "a careful analysis of the runic script of the Kensington Stone, found in Minnesota, indicates that the inscription is a forgery" (of the 1890's); the other giving the conclusion of an equally competent scholar, William Thalbitzer, who disagrees completely with the views of his compatriot, and, after a detailed analysis of the runic symbols, "finds that they are not incompatible with the fourteenth-century date of the inscription", and believes that "the stone is genuine and therefore a record of Scandinavian penetration to Minnesota in 1362".

691

[9] Setzler, F. M., Head Curator, Department of Anthropology, Smithsonian Institution, to the writer, Washington, April 8, 1949.

[10] Minneapolis Public Library, Runestone folders containing newspaper clippings and articles from periodicals dealing with the question.

[11] P. 323.

[12] P. 349.

[13] Wisconsin Magazine of History, Vol. III, December, 1919, p. 182, quoted by H. R. Holand in an article on "The Kensington Rune Stone. Is It the Oldest Native Document of American History?"

[14] St. Paul Dispatch, December 4, 1909.

[15] Peterson, C. S. America's Rune Stone of A. D., 1362, Gains Favor. (New York: 1946), Introduction, p. XIX. He gives a long list (pp. 1-25) of prominent scholars who accept the authenticity of the Rune Stone.

[16] Holand, H. R. A Fourteenth Century Columbus. Harper's Weekly, June 26, 1910, p. 25.

Babcock, W. H. Early Norse Visits to North America. Smithsonian Miscellaneous Collections, (Washington: 1913), p. 39.

[17] Speculum, p. 340.

II

[1] CE., Vol. XIV, (New York: 1912), p. 183.

[2] Shea, J. G., The Catholic Church In Colonial Days, 1521-1763. (New York: 1886), p. 112.

[3] Shea, op. cit., p. 224.

[4] Thwaites, R. G. The Jesuit Relations and Allied Documents. (Cleveland: 1896-1907), 1. 7.

[5] Shea, op. cit., p. 228.

[6] Shea, op. cit., p. 266.

[7] Upham, W., Minnesota In Three Centuries, 1655-1908. Vol. I, (St. Paul: 1908), p. 211.

[8] Schaefer. Groseilliers and Radisson. AD., 2:2, July, 1910, pp. 219 & ff. MHSC., Vol. I, 1850-1856, (St. Paul: 1902), p. 241.

[9] Upham, op. cit., pp. 147 and 200.

[10] Hennepin, Rev. L., A Description of Louisiana, edited by John Gilmary Shea. (New York: 1880), pp. 9 & ff.

CE., Vol. VII, (New York: 1910), pp. 215 & ff.

Schaefer, Hennepin, the Discoverer of the Falls of St. Anthony. AD., 6:1, October, 1933, pp. 54 & ff.

Annals of the Minnesota Historical Society, 1856, pp. 22-28; 1872, pp. 302–13. Vol. I, (St. Paul: 1850-56), pp. 247-256.

[11] Hennepin, op. cit., pp. 205 & ff.

[12] Hennepin, op. cit., p. 235.

[13] Hennepin, op. cit., Appendix, p. 367.

[14] Hennepin, op. cit., p. 212.

[15] Dumont, G. H. Louis Hennepin, Explorateur du Mississippi. (Bruxelles-Paris: 1943), pp. 33 & ff.

Hennepin, op. cit., Appendix, p. 343.

[16] Upham, op. cit., p. 248.

[17] CE., Vol. XIII, p. 367. (Schaefer, History of the Diocese of St. Paul).

[18] CE., Vol. IX, p. 46. (CD., 1951, part III, p. 29, says Bishop Laval was consecrated on June 3, 1658).

[19] CE., Vol. XII, p. 593.

[20] McDermott, J. F., Old Cahokia, a Narrative and Documents Illustrating the First Century of Its Existence. (St. Louis: 1949), p. 57.

Ruskowski, Rev. L. F., S.S., French Missions in North America, (New York: 1949), p. 22.

[21] McDermott, *op. cit.*, p. 9.

[22] *A Tableau of the Development of the Dioceses of the Church in the United States from 1789 to 1837.* Typewritten copy, undated and unsigned, written by Reverend William Busch of St. Paul Seminary. CHSA.

III

[1] Schaefer, *Fort Beauharnois.* AD., 2:1, July, 1909, pp. 94-113.

Norton, Sister M. Aquinas, *Catholic Missionary Activities in the Northwest, 1818-1864.* (Washington: 1930), pp. 12 & ff.

[2] Schaefer, *Fort St. Charles.* AD., 3:1, July, 1909, pp. 114-133.

Prud'homme, Judge L. A., *Pierre Gaultier de Varennes, Sieur de la Verendrye.* Bulletin of the Historical Society of St. Boniface, Vol. V, part 2, (St. Boniface: 1916), pp. 38 & ff.

Minnesota History, 7:4, p. 432.

[3] *Out of the Grave, the Discovery of Fort St. Charles in 1908.* Bulletin of the Historical Society of St. Boniface, Vol. V, Fascicle 3, (St. Boniface: 1915),

Extract from the Report on the Discovery of Fort St. Charles. Bulletin of the Historical Society of St. Boniface, Vol. I, appendix 1, of Vol. V, part 2, 1916, pp. 129-152.

Shanahan, Rev. E. A., *Minnesota's Forgotten Martyr.* (Crookston: 1949).

[4] Campbell, Rev. T. J., S. J., *Pioneer Priests of North America.* Vol. III, (New York: 1911), pp. 243 & ff.

[5] Fallon, W. H., to the writer, St. Paul, August 11 and 16, 1950.

[6] "Our Northland Diocese", official paper of the Diocese of Crookston, August, 1951.

[7] Morice, Rev. A. G., O.M.I., *History of the Catholic Church in Western Canada,* Vol. I, (Toronto: 1910), pp. 105 & ff.

Shanley, Rt. Rev. J., *The Founding of the Catholic Church in North Dakota.* Reports of the State Historical Society of North Dakota, Vol. II, (Bismarck: 1908).

[8] Dumoulin, Rev. S.J.N., to Bishop Plessis. Quebec Archiepiscopal Archives.

Morice, *op. cit.*, p. 112.

[9] Norton, *op. cit.*, pp. 101 & ff.

Belcourt, Rev. G. A., *Department of Hudson's Bay.* MHSC. Vol. I, 1850-1856, (St. Paul: 1902), pp. 193 & ff.

[10] Norton, *op. cit.*, pp. 61 & ff.

[11] Norton, *op. cit.*, p. 68.

[12] Memorandum of Rev. Lawrence Schmidt, O.S.B., from the archives of the Church of St. John the Baptist, Grand Marais, of which he is pastor, under date of July 26, 1951. CHSA.

IV

[1] APF., Vol. III, January, 1840, p. 339.

[2] APF., Vol. III, January, 1840, p. 348.

[3] Lovelace, Mrs., *Early Candlelight.* Centennial edition, 1949, p. 265.

[4] Quoted in Minnesota History, December, 1948, p. 319.

Colburn, Mary J., *Minnesota as a Home for Immigrants,* (St. Paul: 1865).

[5] Bishop Loras to Father Furnion, Dubuque, June 6, 1842. APF., Vol. V, p. 392.

[6] Father Galtier to Bishop Grace, Prairie du Chien, January 14, 1864. AD., 1:2, July, 1908, pp. 184-190.

[7] CHSA.

[8] NWC., November 6, 1891.

[9] Ravoux, Rt. Rev. A., *Reminiscences, Memoirs and Lectures.* (St. Paul: 1890), p. 62.

[10] Daggett, P., *Catholic Cemeteries in St. Paul.* AD., 6:1, October, 1933, p. 99.

[11] Ravoux, *Labors Among the Sioux or Dakota Indians, 1841-1844.* (St. Paul: 1897), p. 8.

NWC., January 15, 1876.

[12] Ravoux, *op. cit.*, p. 5.

[13] Father Galtier to Bishop Loras, January 13, 1845.
[14] Hoffmann, Rt. Rev., M. M., *The Church Founders of the Northwest*. (Milwaukee: 1937), p. 189.
[15] Memorandum in Italian in CHSA. Also CD., 1864.
[16] AD., 6:2, October, 1934, p. 268.
[17] Newson, T. W., *Pen Pictures of St. Paul and Biographical Sketches of Old Settlers from the Earliest Settlement to 1857*. (St. Paul: 1884), pp. 24 & 27.
[18] NWC., August 9, 1889.
[19] NWC., November 6, 1891.

V

[1] Facts and information about the life and activities of Monsignor Ravoux are taken largely from *Reminiscences, Memoirs and Lectures*, published in English in 1890 and in French in 1892, copies of which are in CHSA.
Dictionary of American Biography, Vol. XV, (New York: 1935) p. 398.
NWC., April 15, 1879.
His ordination certificates in CHSA, give the dates of his promotion to Minor and Major Orders.
[2] Bishop Loras to Father Furnion, Dubuque, June 8, 1842. AD., 1:1, July, 1907, p. 29, and in APF., Vol. V, 1842, pp. 392 & ff.
[3] Mazzuchelli, Rev. S., O.P., *Memoirs, Historical and Edifying of a Missionary Apostolic.*, translated by Sister Mary Benedicta Kennedy, O.S.D., (Chicago: 1915) pp. 296 & ff.
[4] Ravoux, *op. cit.*, p. 9.
[5] Father Galtier to Bishop Loras, St. Peter's, January 31, 1844, CBA.
[6] AD., 5:1, July, 1907, p. 137.
[7] CBA.
[8] Ravoux, *Reminiscences and Memoirs*, pp. 15 & ff.
[9] Ravoux, *op. cit.*, pp. 19 & ff.
Father Ravoux to Bishop Loras, St. Paul, June 23, 1847, CBA.
[10] Ravoux, *op. cit.*, p. 60.
[11] CD., 1854. NWC., January 4, 1882.
[12] St. Paul Pioneer Press, January 30, 1906, p. 7.
[13] Keller, Rev. G., to Archbishop Ireland, Marine, Minnesota, June 17, 1895. CBA.

VI

[1] *Minnesota Under Four Flags*, edited by Arthur J. Larsen, published by Minnesota Historical Society, Centennial publications, Number 1. Maps and descriptions, 1 to 12.
[2] Cretin, Rt. Rev. J., *Memorialis Tabella*, sed informis, ad serviendum annalibus diocesis Sti. Pauli, Minn., conficiendis. A diary published in Latin and in English in AD., 1:1, July, 1907, pp. 39-42. It tells briefly the story of the erection of the Diocese of St. Paul, his consecration and installation. Also CE., Vol. XIII, p. 367.
[3] Le Duc, W. G., *Minnesota Year Book for 1851*, p. 28, gives the population of St. Paul as 840, of whom 540 were men and 300 women.
[4] Minnesota Pioneer, April 28, 1849.
[5] In 1851 the franc was worth 19.6 cents in American money. (Courtesy of First National Bank, Minneapolis).
Bishop-elect Cretin to Father Bernard, Lyons, January 11, 1851, CBA.
[6] Ireland, Most Rev. J., *Life of Bishop Cretin*, AD., 4:2, July, 1916, p. 187.
Dictionary of American Biography, Vol. 4, p. 542.
Clarke's *Lives of Deceased Bishops*. Vol. II, 1888, p. 420.
[7] CE., Vol. VII, p. 415.
[8] Original in CHSA. Also Oster, Rev. A., in NWC., March 22, 1879.
[9] CD., 1951, p. 79.
[10] Ireland, *op. cit.*, AD., 5:1, July, 1917, p. 24.
[11] La Semaine Religieuse de Bourg, France, quoted in NWC., March 12, 1878.

[12] Father Cretin to l'Abbe Boissonnet, chaplain of the Visitation Convent, Montluel, France, CHSA.

[13] Kettell, Rev. F., to Archbishop Ireland, Loretto, Pa., April 13, 1917. CHSA.

[14] Mazzuchelli, *op. cit.*, p. 259.

[15] Bishop Loras to his sister, Dubuque, July 26, 1839. APF., Vol. III. January 1840, p. 339.

[16] U.S. Catholic Magazine, Vol. I, (Baltimore: 1845) p. 132.

[17] Hoffmann, *The Winnebago Mission: a Cause Celebre.* Mid-America, 2:1, (New Series), July, 1930, pp. 26-52.

[18] Grignon, Mrs. A., to Bishop Cotter of Winona, Trempealeau, Wisconsin, May 2 and 6, 1901. CHSA.

[19] Father Cretin to Bishop Loras, Montluel, France, December 14, 1946.

[20] Cretin, *Memorialis Tabella*, section VIII, CHSA.

[21] Cretin, *op. cit.*, Section IX, CHSA.
Bishop Cretin to Father Bernard, Le Havre, May 22, 1851, CBA.
Boston Pilot, August 9, 1851, CBA.

[22] APF., Vol. XV, p. 368.

[23] Clarke, *op. cit.*, p. 420.

[24] Boston Pilot, August 9, 1851, CBA.

[25] CD., 1856.

[26] Hurley, Sister Helen Angela, *On Good Ground.* (St. Paul: 1951) pp. 30 & ff.

[27] De Vivaldi, Canon F. X., to the Society for the Propagation of the Faith, Long Prairie, Minnesota, June 5, 1852. APF., Vol. XV, p. 368.

[28] Original in CHSA.

[29] Bishop Cretin to Father Trevis, St. Paul, September 28, 1852, CHSA.
Cowles, Rev. Benedict, O.C.S.O., to the writer, Dubuque, October 26, 1951.
Hoffmann, *Church Founders*, p. 332.

[30] Bishop Cretin to Bishop Loras, St. Paul, December 28, 1855.

[31] Boston Pilot, February 16, 1856. CBA.

[32] Interview with Monsignor Guillot, now at the Motherhouse of the Sisters of St. Joseph of Carondelet, St. Paul.

[33] CHSA.

[34] Reardon, Rev. J. M., *The Beginning of the Catholic Total Abstinence Movement in Minnesota.* AD., 1:2, July, 1908, pp. 199-209.

[35] NWC., May 21, 1885, and January 18, 1887.

[36] Father Keller to Archbishop Ireland, Marine, Minnesota, June 17, 1895. CBA.

[37] AD., 7:2, October, 1936, pp. 266-7.

[38] NWC., May 19, 1883.

[39] Copies of this and other budgets from 1851 to 1857, some of them signed by the Bishop himself, together with copies of letters written by him to the Society for the Propagation of the Faith at Lyons and Paris, are in possession of the writer, through the courtesy of the Most Reverend James L. Connolly, Bishop of Fall River. From them are taken the data about the church in the Diocese of St. Paul—the annual receipts, the number of Catholics, of Easter communions, institutions, etc. These reports will ultimately be added to the Cretin collection in CHSA.

[40] Ravoux, *Labors at Mendota, St. Paul, and Other Localities From 1844 to 1851.* Pamphlet, p. 7, CHSA.

[41] Letter to Miss Cretin signed by Father Ravoux and others. CHSA.

[42] AD., 6:2, October, 1934, p. 197.

[43] Copy in CHSA.

[44] AD., 3:2, July, 1914, p. 265.

[45] Minnesota Pioneer, March 24, 1853.

[46] NWC., June 21, 1879.

[47] CD., 1856.

[48] Seliskar, Rev. J., *The Reverend Francis Pirec, Indian Missionary,* AD., 3:1, July, 1911, pp. 66-90.

AD., 7:1, pp. 104-130.

O'Brien, Rt. Rev. F. A. *Two Early Missionaries to the Indians.* Reprinted from Michigan Historical Collections. Vol. 39, pp. 219-32 (Lansing: 1916) pp. 7-15. CHSA.

McDonald, Sister Grace, O.S.B., *Father Francis Pierz, Missionary,* pamphlet (St. Cloud: 1951).

[49] Liber Ordinationum Diocesis Sti. Pauli, September 30, 1851, to April 17, 1898. St. Paul Seminary Archives.

[50] AD., 3:1, July, 1911, p. 80.

[51] AD., 2:2, July, 1910, p. 277.

[52] St. Paul Daily Times, August 16, 1855.

Father Keller to Archbishop Ireland, Marine, Minnesota, March 10, 1895.

[53] Boston Pilot, May 12, 1855. CBA.

[54] Copy in CBA.

[55] Fisher, D. J., to Reverend B. J. McQuaid, St. Paul, February 19, 1853. AD. 1:1, July, 1907, p. 48.

[56] Oster, Rt. Rev. A., *Personal Reminiscences of Bishop Cretin.* AD., 1:1, July, 1907, p. 78.

[57] AD., 4:1, July, 1915, p. 82.

[58] Copy in CHSA.

[59] Letter in CHSA.

[60] Oster, *op. cit.,* p. 83.

[61] St. Paul Pioneer Press, August 9, 1903.

[62] In CHSA.

[63] Oster, *op. cit.,* pp. 84-85.

[64] Autograph Memorandum in CHSA.

[65] NWC., October 16, 1884.

[66] Ravoux, *Reminiscences and Memoirs,* p. 66.

[67] Oster, *op. cit.,* pp. 76 & ff.

[68] CB., January 9, 1932.

VII

[1] Archbishop Kenrick's letter in CHSA.

[2] Rescript in Latin. CHSA.

[3] Boston Pilot, January 14, 1860.

[4] Ravoux, *op. cit.,* p. 68.

[5] Father Pelamourgues to Father Ravoux, Davenport, Iowa, May 22, 1858. CHSA.

[6] AD., 3:2, July, 1914, p. 274.

[7] Typewritten copy in CBA.

[8] Ravoux, *op. cit.,* p. 68.

[9] Boston Pilot, July 10, 1858. CBA.

[10] Boston Pilot, January 8, 1859. CBA.

[11] Ravoux, *op. cit.,* pp. 72 & ff.

[12] AD., 3:2, July, 1914, p. 297.

[13] NWC., February 29, 1868.

[14] Autograph copy in CHSA.

[15] Father Pelamourgues to Father Ravoux, Rome, December 30, 1869. CHSA.

[16] Pontifical Rescript in CHSA.

[17] Quoted in NWC., April 5, 1879, p. 3.

[18] NWC., January 19, 1867.

[19] Father Ravoux to Cardinal Ledochowski, St. Paul, April 6, 1892, signs himself V. G.

[20] St. Paul Pioneer Press, January 21, 1906.

VIII

[1] O'Daniel, Rev. V. F., O. P., *The Father of the Church in Tennessee.* (Washington: 1926), p. 550, note.

[2] Grace, W., to his son, James, in St. Paul, Lindsay, Ontario, January 2, 1887. Also to Bishop Grace, April 3, 1888. CHSA.

Items of Bishop Grace's father, undated and unsigned memo. CHSA.

[3] Memo of William Grace, Lindsay, Ontario, December 3, 1887. CHSA.

"The Tipperary Nationalist", November 26, 1887, (The Grace Family), CHSA. NWC., February 12, 1881, p. 3.

[4] Martin, Rt. Rev. Abbot Eugene J., O.C.S.O., to the writer, Dubuque, October 24, 1949, enclosing memo of Brother Timothy about Brother Barnaby Grace.

[5] NWC., April 12, 1873, and May 19, 1883.

[6] Book of Receptions and Professions of St. Rose Convent, Springfield, Ky., p. 1. Excerpt in CHSA.

[7] Book of Conventual Councils of the Minerva, Rome, 1814-1842, pp. 200 and 208. Excerpt in CHSA.

Archbishop Kenrick of Philadelphia to Dr. Cullen, Rector of the Irish College, Rome, June 13, 1838. CHSA.

[8] A classmate, Father Corcoran, in "New York Catholic Miscellany", August 24, 1850, says Father Grace completed his course of studies at Brescia, Lombardy.

[9] Catholic Telegraph, Cincinnati, January 23, 1845.

[10] O'Daniel, *op. cit.*, p. 417.

[11] O'Daniel, *op. cit.*, p. 507.

[12] Document in Italian in CHSA.

[13] Bishop Miles of Memphis to Archbishop Eccleston of Baltimore, April 8, 1850. Also O'Daniel, *op. cit.*, p. 440.

[14] O'Daniel, *op. cit.*, p. 537.

[15] Document in CHSA.

[16] Father O'Daniel to Archbishop Ireland, Washington, August 24, 1917.

[17] Document in CHSA.

[18] Catholic Telegraph, Cincinnati, September 3, 1859.

[19] Copy in CHSA.

[20] AD., 7:2, October, 1936, pp. 190 & ff.

[21] Boston Pilot, January 14 and February 18, 1860.

[22] AD., 7:2, October, 1936, pp. 196-202.

[23] Correspondence in CHSA.

[24] Boston Pilot, September 22, 1860.

[25] Petition in CHSA.

[26] Correspondence in CHSA. Also Report of the Commissioner for Indian Affairs for 1863.

[27] Original and typewritten copy in CHSA.

[28] Diary of Bishop Grace in CHSA. AD., 1:2, July, 1908, pp. 166-183.

[29] Shanley, *op. cit.*, p. 27.

[30] MacLeod, Margaret A., *The Frozen Priest of Pembina*. Pamphlet, Third Edition, (Winnipeg: 1935).

[31]

THOMAS L. GRACE
DEI ET APOSTOLICAE SEDIS GRATIA
STI. PAULI DE MINNESOTA
EPISCOPUS

Notum facimus universis quod nos, die vigesima secunda Decembris, Dominica quarta Adventus, anno autem millesimo octingesimo sexagesimo primo, Missam pontificaliter in ecclesia nostra cathedrali celebrantes, dilectum nobis in Christo, Joannem Ireland, filium legitimum, Ricardi Ireland et Juliae Naughton conjugum, sufficientem, capacem, idoneum praevio examine repertum ad sacrum presbyteratus ordinem rite et canonice duximus promovendum et intra Missae solemnia promovimus.

Datum Sti. Pauli ex aedibus nostris episcopalibus sub signo nostro et nostri secretarii subscriptione.

† Thomas
Epus Sti. Pauli.
Ex mandato Illmi. et Revmi. D.D. Episcopi.
A. Oster.

Pioneer and Democrat, Sunday, December 22, 1861, p. 1.
St. Paul Daily Press, Sunday, December 22, 1861, Vol. I, p. 1.

[32] CB. December 7, 1918.

[33] St. Paul Pioneer Press, August 12, 1862.

[34] American Ecclesiastical Review, March, 1950, (Washington) p. 223.

[35] AD., 7:1, October, 1935, pp. 62 & ff.

[36] Markoe, W. F., to his mother in Philadelphia, Mrs. John Markoe, St. Paul, November 21, 1862, CHSA.

[37] Wimmer, Abbot Boniface, O.S.B., to Bishop Grace, Rome, June 21, 1866, CHSA.

[38] CD., 1868.

[39] NWC., May 4, 1867.

[40] NWC., May 11 and 25, 1867.

[41] August 2, 1869. BCA.

[42] Bishop Grace to Archbishop Gibbons, St. Paul, September 8, 1878. BCA.

[43] Reilly, Rev. D. F., O. P., The School Controversy, 1891-1893. (Washington: 1943), p. 58. note.

[44] Copy in CHSA.

[45] Reardon, Rev. J. M., The Church of St. Mary, the History of a Pioneer Parish. (St. Paul: 1935), p. 10. CHSA.

[46] Reardon, Rev. J. M., The Basilica of St. Mary of Minneapolis. 1932, p. 27. CHSA.

[47] Gaughan, Rev. J. H., The Catholic Church in Goodhue County. AD., 4:2, July, 1916, p. 246.

[48] Bishop Grace to Archbishop Spalding, St. Paul, April 15, 1866. BCA.

[49] Bishop Grace to Archbishop Spalding, St. Paul, May 4, 1866. BCA.

[50-56] NWC., November 17, 1866; April 27, 1867; August 24, 1867; June 29, 1867; August 10, 1867; February 1, 1868; May 2, 1868.

[57] Decreta Synodi Diocesanae: Primae, (die 10, Julii, A.D., 1861); Secundae, (die 24, Septembris, A.D., 1863); Tertiae, (die 14, Julii, A.D., 1873). CHSA.

[58] Interview with John C. Devereux in 1915. CHSA.

[59] NWC., from 1866 to 1900 in St. Paul Seminary library. Complete file from 1866 to 1935 in Minnesota Historical Society, St. Paul.

Devereux, Miss Teresa, daughter of J.C.D., to the writer, St. Paul, January 5, 1950. CHSA.

[60] Complete file, except from 1878 to 1888, in Minnesota Historical Society, St. Paul. Complete file of The Wanderer since the initial issue in 1931.

[61] Complete file in Minnesota Historical Society, St. Paul.

[62] NWC., November 14, 1868.

[63] Reardon, Rev. J. M., The Catholic Total Abstinence Movement in Minnesota. AD., 2:1, July, 1909, p. 44.

[64] NWC., March 20, 1869.

[65] NWC., January 19, 1869.

[66] St. Paul Pioneer Press, October 31, 1909, in "Forty Years Ago".

[67] AD., 7:1, October, 1936, p. 48. Also NWC., January 25, 1868.

[68] NWC., October 16, 1869.

[69] NWC., December 3 and 24, 1870.

[70] St. Paul Pioneer Press, January 22, 1871. Also NWC., January 28, 1871.

[71] Copy in CHSA.

[72] Mississippi Vista. The Brothers of the Christian Schools in the Midwest, 1849-1949. (Winona: 1948), pp. 180-196. Basilica archives.

[73] In 1874 Archbishop Bayley of Baltimore appointed General Ewing Catholic Commissioner for Indian Missions to represent their interests at Washington. Later, Very Reverend J. B. A. Brouillet, Vicar General of the Diocese of Nesqually (now,

Seattle) was associated with him. The Third Plenary Council of Baltimore instituted the Bureau of Indian Missions as it exists today.

[74] Copy in CHSA.

[75-77] NWC., December 11, 1872; November 22, 1873; December 4, 1875.

[78] Corrigan, Rt. Rev. J. A., *History of St. Mark's and the Midway District*. (St. Paul: 1939), pp. 38 & ff.

[79] CD., 1876.

[80] CD., 1880.

[81] NWC., January 31, 1874.

[82] Apostolic Brief and autograph letter in CHSA.

[83] NWC., December 25, 1875.

[84] CE., Vol. XII, p. 136.

[85] NWC., May 27, 1876.

[86] MHSC., Vol. VI, (St. Paul: 1894). Also St. Paul Daily Globe, July 4, 1880.

[87] MHSC., Vol. VI, (St. Paul: 1894), pp. 65-73.

[88] Ellis, Rev. J. T., *The Formative Years of the Catholic University*. (Washington: 1946), p. 71.

[89] Ellis, *op. cit.*, p. 118.

[90] NWC., November 26, 1881.

[91] The Celtic World, Minneapolis, December 10, 1881. MHSA.

[92-96] NWC., December 2, 1882; June 18, 1881; May 19, 1883; July 31, 1884; July 31, 1884, p. 4.

[97] Copy of letter as well as Apostolic Brief appointing him Titular Bishop of Mennith in CHSA.

[98] Papal Rescript in CHSA.

[99] Archbishop Ireland to Cardinal Gibbons, St. Paul, October 5, 1889. BCA.

[100] NWC., October 4, 1889.

[101] Two note books in CHSA.

[102] CB., November 16, 1918, — extract from last will of Archbishop John J. Keane of Dubuque who died June 22, 1918.

[103] NWC., February 27, 1897.

IX

[1] Baptismal records from the parish of Danesfort, County Kilkenny, Ireland. Basilica archives.

Dictionary of American Biography, Vol. IX, (New York: 1932), pp. 494-497.

[2] Interview with Sister Annetta, C.S.J., a cousin of Archbishop Ireland.

[3] Recorded by a Sister of the Visitation Convent, St. Paul. CHSA.

[4] Guillot, Rt. Rev. J., to the writer, Faribault, November 21, 1918. CHSA.

[5] L'Amie du Clergé, (22nd. year, 3rd. series), September 13, 1900, (Langres: France), pp. 815 & ff. Archives, Notre Dame de Lourdes Church, Minneapolis.

Redwood, Most Rev. F., S.M., to the writer, Wellington, N.Z., January 4, 1933. CHSA.

[6] Hurley, Very Rev. D. H., Assistant Superior General of the Marist Fathers, to the writer, Rome, December 7, 1950, enclosing excerpts in French from "Chroniques et Annales de la Société de Marie", Tome I, pp. 424-425. Also "Extrait des Archives" by Reverend L. Schwehr, S.M., Rome, February 15, 1951.

In another letter from Rome, April 23, 1951, Father Hurley says: "The course at Montbel in the days of Archbishop Ireland consisted of one year of Philosophy and three years of Theology".

In AD., 4:2, July, 1916, Archbishop Ireland says that in the days of Bishop Cretin there was at Meximieux a class in Philosophy in addition to the classics.

[7] See reference 31 in Chapter VIII.

[8] NWC., May 27, 1892.

[9] St. Paul Pioneer Press, May 30, 1906.

[10] NWC., December 15, 1866.

[11] A.D., 4:2, July, 1916, p. 222.

[12-13] NWC., September 19, 1868; April 5 and 12, 1889.

[14] Reardon, op. cit., pp. 44-93.

[15] Original in CHSA.

[16] Papal Brief and autograph letter in Latin to the Pope in CHSA. Also letter to Bishop Grace, St. Paul, April 22, '75.

[17] St. Paul Daily Pioneer Press, December 22, 1875.

NWC., December 25, 1875.

Freeman's Journal, New York, January 1, 1876.

[18] NWC., July 22, 1876.

[19] NWC., January 13, 1877.

[20] Records of the American Catholic Historical Society of Philadelphia, 61:2, June, 1950, p. 97.

[21] Temperance Truths From Many Pens (New York), Vol. I, pp. 7-8. A collection of pamphlets each with its own paging.

[22] Original in Cretin Collection, CHSA.

[23] Moynihan, Rt. Rev. H., Archbishop Ireland's Colonies. AD., 6:2, October, 1934, pp. 212 & ff.

Catholic Colonization in Minnesota, Revised Edition, published by the Catholic Colonization Bureau of Minnesota (St. Paul: 1879), pp. 42 & ff. CHSA.

[24] Catholic Colonization in Minnesota, pp. 45 & ff. CHSA.

[25] Moynihan, op. cit., pp. 220 & ff.

[26] Bishop Ireland to Archbishop Gibbons, St. Paul, February 20, 1881. BCA.

[27] Catholic Colonization in Minnesota: Colony of Avoca, (St. Paul: 1880). CHSA.

[28] Irish-American Colonization Company, Ltd., (John Sweetman, Director), (St. Paul: 1882), pp. 51 & ff. CHSA.

[29] Catholic Colonization in Minnesota: Colony of Minneota, (St. Paul: 1880), CHSA.

[30] ACA.

[31-32] NWC., August 18, 1876; November 16, 1867.

[33] NWC., January 14, 1882.

[34] NWC., June 6, 1882.

[35] NWC., October 28, 1882.

[36] NWC., November 4, 1882.

[37] NWC., July 22, 1882.

[38] NWC., December 30, 1882. Also CD., 1883.

[39] Bishop Ireland to Archbishop Gibbons, St. Paul, February 28, 1884. BCA.

[40] NWC., July 26, 1884.

[41] Newson, op. cit., pp. 361-363.

[42] Ireland, Most Rev. J., The Church and Modern Society. Vol. I, (New York: 1903), pp. 39 and 64.

[43] Cadden, Rev. J. P., The Historiography of the American Catholic Church: 1785-1943, (Washington: 1944), p. 42.

[44-50] NWC., May 27, 1886; June 3, 1886; January 6, 1887; April 7, 1887; March 31, 1887; May 12, 1887; August 24, 1888.

[51] Ellis, op. cit., pp. 201 & ff.

[52] Brown, Rev. H. J., The Catholic Church and the Knights of Labor. Catholic Historical Review, 32:1, April, 1940, pp. 1 & ff.

[52] Scrap book, No. 26, p. 139. CHSA.

[53] Gibbons, Most Rev. J., A Retrospect of Fifty Years. Vol. I, (Baltimore: 1916), pp. 190 & ff.

[54] NWC., November 16, 1888.

[55] Bishop Grace to Archbishop Spalding, St. Paul, August 2, 1869. BCA.

[66] Bishop Grace to Archbishop Gibbons, St. Paul, September 8, 1878. BCA.

[57] Relatio de Quaestione Germanica in Statibus Foederatis a Rev. P. M. Abbelen, Sac. Milw. Conscripta, a Rmo. et Illmo. M. Heiss. Archiep. Milwauk. Approbata,

et Sacrae Congr. de Propaganda Fide, Mense Novembri, 1886, Submissa. CHSA. In the same pamphlet are printed in English the observations of Bishops Ireland and Keane on "The German Question in the Church in the United States".

[58] La Question Allemande Dans l'Eglise Aux Etats-Unis, Rome, le 6, Dec., 1886. A Son Eminence Le Cardinal Simeoni, Prefet de la Congregation de la Propagande, signed by Bishops Ireland and Keane. (A translation into French of the observations above mentioned).

[59] See "Relatio", pp. 39-63, for the reaction of the American hierarchy regarding the demands of the German party.

Gmeiner, Rev. J., *The Church and the Various Nationalities in the United States. Are German Catholics Unfairly Treated?* (Milwaukee: 1887). CHSA.

[60] See "Relatio", Appendix A. p. 64. Decretum S. Congr. de Propaganda Fide. "De Paroeciis pro Fidelibus diversae linguae in eodem territorio degentibus" (8 Jun., 1887).

[61-63] NWC., September 22, 1887; October 26, 1888; May 4, 1888.

[64] Ave Maria, South Bend, Indiana, October 6, 1888, p. 330. NWC., September 28, 1888.

[65] NWC., August 6, 1889.

[66] Quoted in NWC., July 12, 1889.

[67] NWC., January 3, 1890.

[68] Ireland, *op. cit.*, Vol. I, pp. 70 & ff.

[69] Official Report of the Proceedings of the Catholic Congress at Baltimore, November 11-12, 1889, p. VI. CHSA.

[70] Official Report, pp. 187 & ff.

[71] Archbishop Heiss to Archbishop Gibbons, Milwaukee, May 17, 1884. BCA.

[72] Bishop Ireland to Archbishop Gibbons, St. Paul, March 26, 1885. BCA.

[73] Bishops Ireland and Keane to Archbishop Gibbons, American College, Rome, December 14, 1886. BCA.

[74] NWC., September 22, 1887.

[75] Ellis, *op. cit.*, pp. 383 & ff.

Solemnities of the Dedication and Opening of the Catholic University of America, November 13th, 1889, Official Report, (Baltimore: 1889), p. 83.

[76] Official reports, prospectus, pamphlets, etc., in CHSA. References in NWC., from April 18, 1890, to November 30, 1894.

Busch, Rev. W., *The Catholic Truth Society of St. Paul.* Typewritten article of twenty-six pages, undated. CHSA.

[77] History of the Society of Mary in America, written in French, published in San Francisco in 1907. Archives of Notre Dame de Lourdes Church, Minneapolis.

[78] Filed November 14, 1892, in Book 288 of Deeds, p. 199, and conveyed to the Diocese of St. Paul by deed filed December 26, 1893, in Book 281 of Deeds, p. 295.

[79] Omaha Bee, August 7, 1891.

[80] Irish Standard, Minneapolis, October 3, 1891. MHSA.

[81] NWC., February 28, 1896, p. 8.

[82] Third Annual Report for the Year 1890. (St. Paul: 1891), in CHSA.

[83] Interview with Reverend J. Donahoe, pastor of the Church of St. Bridget, Minneapolis.

[84] BCA.

[85] Archbishop Ireland to Cardinal Gibbons, St. Paul, November 19, 1890. BCA.

[86] Archbishop Ireland to Cardinal Gibbons, St. Paul, January 2, 1891. BCA.

[87] Reilly, *op. cit.*, p. 78.

O'Leary, Miss J. M., *Historical Sketch of the Parish of the Immaculate Conception, Faribault, Minnesota.* 1938, pp. 104-106. Basilica archives.

[88] Archbishop Ireland to Cardinal Gibbons, St. Paul, October 17, 1891. BCA.

[89] NWC., August 15, 1890, p. 4.

[90] Archbishop Ireland to Cardinal Gibbons, October 17, 1891. BCA.

[91] Dr. Bouquillon's pamphlet, *"Education: To Whom Does It Belong?"*, Father

Hoiland's brochure, *"The Parent First"*, the former's *"Rejoinder to Critics"* and other pamphlets bearing on the subject in CHSA.

[92] Archbishop Ireland to Cardinal Gibbons, St. Paul, December 28, 1891. BCA.

[93] Archbishop Ireland to Cardinal Gibbons, Rome, February 21, 1892. BCA.

[94] Writer's copy received from Monsignor Moynihan many years ago.

[95] Interview with Monsignor Moynihan.

[96] Interview with Reverend J. C. Byrne, pastor of the Church of St. Luke, St. Paul.

[97] NWC., July 1, 1892.

[98] NWC., May 27, 1892.

[99] Ireland, *op. cit.*, pp. 105 & ff.

[100] Published in Temperance Truths From Many Pens, Vol. I. CHSA.

[101] Register, St. Paul Seminary, 1895.

[102] NWC., September 7, 1895.

[103] Printed copy in CHSA.

[104] NWC., August 17, 1894.

[105] Irish Standard, May 30, 1891.

[106] Irish Standard, October 10, 1891.

[107] G. V. McLaughlin to the writer, Minneapolis, January 12, 1950.

[108] Archbishop Ireland to Cardinal Gibbons, St. Paul, September 13, 1898. BCA.

[109] Hogan, Rev. P. E., S.S.J., *Americanism and the Catholic University of America*. Catholic Historical Review, July, 1947, pp. 158 & ff.

[110] CE., Vol. XIV, p. 538.

[111-113] NWC., March 10, 1889; September 17 and 24; October 1; December 31, 1897.

[114] Archbishop Ireland to Cardinal Gibbons, Washington, April 6, 1898. BCA.

[115-119] Archbishop Ireland to Monsignor O'Connell, Washington, April 8; May 2; May 11; May 28; May 11, 1898. RDA.

[120] Archbishop Ireland to Archbishop Keane, St. Paul, May 28, 1898.

[121] Ireland, Most Rev. J., *The Church and Modern Society*, Vol. I, pp. 365-395.

[122] Archbishop Ireland to Father O'Gorman, St. Paul, February 16, 1894.

[123] Archbishop Ireland to Cardinal Gibbons, St. Paul, December 7, 1894. BCA.

[124] Souvenir of the Catholic Congress, World's Columbian Exposition, Chicago, 1893. CHSA.

[125] The New Catholic Dictionary (Vatican Edition), (New York: 1921), p. 641. CE., Vol. III, p. 750 (article, "Church").

Judge, Rev. T. E., *The Encyclical of Pius X on the Doctrines of the Modernists*. Latin Text and English version with Annotations. (Chicago: 1907). Basilica Archives.

Ireland, Most Rev. J., *The Dogmatic Authority of the Papacy*. North American Review, April, 1908. CHSA.

Modernism: What It Is and Why It Was Condemned, by C.S.B., (London: 1908).

[126] CHSA.

[127-128] Governor Taft to Ben. I. Wheeler, Manila, October 17, 1900; to his brother, Charles, Manila, January 14 and 21, 1901; to Mrs. Bellamy Storer, of Madrid, Manila, January 18, 1901; to Archbishop Ireland, Manila, October 15, 1901, and October 1, 1902, (urging him to secure Catholic teachers); to Bishop O'Gorman, of Sioux Falls, Manila, October 17, 1902; and letter from Archbishop Ireland, St. Paul, August 19, 1901. Taft Papers: Library of Congress; Manuscripts.

[129] Archbishop Ireland to Cardinal Gibbons, St. Paul, September 13, 1898. BCA.

[130] Memorandum of Bishop O'Gorman, May 12, 1902, regarding the Taft Mission to Rome. Taft Papers, manuscript division.

Archbishop Ireland to Monsignor O'Connell, New York, June 7, 1901. RDA.

[131] Memorandum of Bishop O'Gorman, Taft Papers.

Archbishop Ireland to President Roosevelt, Washington, December 12 and 14, 1901. Roosevelt Papers: Library of Congress.

[132] Memorandum of Bishop O'Gorman, p. 4, Taft Papers.

[133] Archbishop Ireland to Monsignor O'Connell, St. Paul, October 31, 1902, RDA.

[134] CB., May 18, 1912.

[135] Kerens, R. C., to Cardinal Gibbons, St. Louis, March 28, 1892. BCA.

[136] Ford, A. E., of the Freeman's Journal to Monsignor O'Connell, New York, April 16, 1892. RDA.

[137-140] Archbishop Ireland to Monsignor O'Connell, St. Paul, August 3, 1892; Washington, July 11, 1892; St. Paul, November 24, 1893; November 16, 1900. RDA.

[141-142] Ireland, op. cit., Vol. II, pp. 69-82, and 31-66.

[143-148] Archbishop Ireland to Monsignor O'Connell, Brussels, May 18; May 22; Paris, June 2; Cork, July 20; on the Atlantic Ocean, July 24; New York, October 21, 1899. RDA.

[149-150] Ireland, op. cit., Vol. II, pp. 103 & ff. and 5 & ff.

[151] Archbishop Ireland to Monsignor O'Connell, St. Paul, October 27, 1900. RDA.

[152-153] Boston Pilot, August 25 and October 6, 1900.

[154] Proceedings of the National Educational Association, 1902, (Lecture reprinted by the University of Chicago Press, 1902). CHSA.

[155] The Diocese of St. Paul. The Golden Jubilee (by Rev. A. McNulty), 1851-1901. CHSA.

[156] CHSA.

[157] The Catholic Mission House of Excelsior, an undated booklet written by Reverend Joseph F. Busch, Superior of the Mission Band (now, Bishop of St. Cloud), giving the story of the project. CHSA.

[158] New Cathedral Bulletin, December, 1905, CHSA.

[159] Kelley, Most Rev. F. C., The Bishop Jots It Down. (New York and London: 1939), p. 138.

[160-162] AD. 1:1, July, 1907, p. 2 & ff.; 3:2, July, 1914, pp. 219 & ff.; 6:1, October, 1933, pp. 5 & ff. CHSA.

[163] NWC., July 21, 1887, and May 25, 1888.

[164] Corrigan, op. cit., pp. 40 & ff.

[165] NWC., May 10, 1889.

[166] New Cathedral Bulletin, August, 1904, (the second number was issued in November, 1905, and it appeared monthly from October, 1906, to October, 1910).

The New Cathedral of St. Paul. Letter of the Most Reverend Archbishop Ireland, August 1, 1905, (translated into several languages). CHSA.

AD., 4:1, July, 1915, p. 126.

[167-168] New Cathedral Bulletin, November, 1905, and March, 1906.

[169] AD., 1:1, July, 1907, pp. 99-151, (description of the cornerstone laying ceremony).

[170] Typewritten statement of contracts and payments to February 10, 1916. CHSA.

[171] AD., 4:1, July, 1915, pp. 77-99. (description of farewell functions in old Cathedral).

[172] History of the New Cathedral Project by the pastor, Reverend L. F. Ryan. (a printed leaflet prepared for the dedication, April 11, 1915). CHSA.

[173] The Pro-Cathedral of Minneapolis. Letter of the Most Reverend Archbishop Ireland, August 1, 1905. (translated into several languages). CHSA.

[174-175] AD., 1:2, July, 1908, pp. 236-269. (description of cornerstone laying ceremony); 3:2, July, 1914, pp. 330 & ff.

CB. May 30, 1914. (Pro-Cathedral of St. Mary Edition).

[176] AD., 3:2, July, 1914, pp. 337 & ff.

[177-178] Records of receipts and disbursements for Pro-Cathedral and Basilica in parochial archives.

[179] AD., 2:2, July, 1910, pp. 283-308 (description of the consecration ceremony).

Twin Cities daily papers of May 19, 1910.

The Living Church (Episcopal) Milwaukee, May 28, 1910.

Catholic Register and Extension, Toronto, May 26, 1910.

[180] AD., 3:1, July, 1910, pp. 157-171 (description of the Cardinal's visit).

New Cathedral Bulletin, October, 1910. CHSA.

[181] AD., 3:1, July, 1911, p. 179.

[182] ACA.

[183] St. Paul Pioneer Press, February 8, 1910.
[184] St. Paul Dispatch, April 4, 1910.
[185] St. Paul Dispatch, April 5, 1910. St. Paul Pioneer Press, April 6, 1910.
[186] ACA.
[187] Lane, Most Rev. R. A., M.M., *Early Days of Maryknoll*, (New York: 1951), p. 167.
[188-189] CB., July 20, 1912; August 15, 1914.
[190] *Criminal Libel Against the Knights of Columbus Exposed.* Undated pamphlet issued by the Knights of Columbus, New Haven, Conn.
Knights of Columbus vs. Criminal Libel and Malicious Bigotry. Issued by Supreme Board of Directors, K. of C., November, 1914. Basilica Archives.
[191] CHSA.
[192] CB., May 11 (Editorial); May 25; June 1; June 8, 1912.
[193] St. Paul, June 8, 1912. BCA.
[194] CB., December 23, 1950. (Society for the Propagation of the Faith column). AD., 4:2, July, 1916, p. 308.
Interview with Reverend J. A. Byrnes of the Church of the Annunciation, Minneapolis.
[195] Pastoral Letter quoted in NWC., January 18, 1889.
[196] NWC., March 13, 1896.
[197] Constitution and By-laws of the St. Paul Clerical Total Abstinence Society (St. Paul: 1900). CHSA.
[198] Priests' Total Abstinence League of America. Report, 1903-4. CHSA.
[199] Letter to the Editor of the Dakota Catholic. NWC., September 22, 1889.
[200] Archbishop Ireland to Cardinal Gibbons, St. Paul, December 7, 1894. BCA.
[201] ACA.
[202] Reardon, Rev. J. M., *Archbishop Ireland: Prelate, Patriot, Publicist, 1838-1918.* A Memoir (St. Paul: 1919), p. 25. CHSA.

X

[1] Interview with Archbishop Dowling.
[2] Dictionary of American Biography, Vol. XXII, Supplement one, p. 262.
[3] Cadden, *op. cit.*, p. 47.
[4] Interview with Archbishop Dowling.
[5] CB., April 27, 1912.
[6] CD., 1913.
[7] CB., May 4, 1912.
[8] Costin, V. Rev. T. J., President of Dowling High School, Des Moines, to the writer, March 20, 1951. Early catalogues of the College from the archives of the school.
[9] Des Moines Diocesan Archives.
[10] CB., June 1, 1912.
[11] Copia Relationis ad S. Sedem Apostolicam Pro Diocesi Des Moinesis in Statu Iowa, U.S.A., Ab Anno Domini, 1912, Usque ad Annum, 1919, ACA.
[12] CB., March 29, 1919.
[13] Several copies in CHSA.
[14] Dowling, Most Reverend A., *The National Catholic Welfare Conference.* Reprint from the Ecclesiastical Review (Washington), October, 1928.
[15] Dowling, *op. cit.*, p. 16.
[16] Dowling, *op. cit.*, pp. 11-12.
[17] Interview with Reverend W. P. Driscoll, pastor of Christ the King Church, Minneapolis.
[18] Meagher, Rev. T. F., Director, Catholic Welfare Association, to the writer, Minneapolis, February 23, 1951.
[19] Doherty, Rev. R. W., Director of Catholic Charities, to the writer, St. Paul, July 6, 1951.
[20] CB., May 13, 1920.

[21] Copies of leaflets in CHSA.

[22] Printed copy of first financial report in CHSA.

[23] CB., January 14, 1922.

[24] Minutes of meetings and records of the School of Social Studies in possession of the Executive Director now residing in Chicago were not available for consultation.

[25] Mimeographed copies of lectures, now in the writer's possession, will ultimately be placed in CHSA.

[26] Printed booklets of these lectures, now in the writer's possession, are destined for the CHSA.

[27-29] CB., November 18; June 24, 1922; February 9, 1924.

[30] ACA.

[31] Report of Professor G. W. C. Ross, May 4, 1950. St. Thomas College Archives.

[32] Flynn, V. Rev. V. J., President of the College of St. Thomas, to the writer, St. Paul, February 20, 1952.

[33] Interview with Reverend J. A. Byrnes, of the Church of the Annunciation, Minneapolis.

[34-36] CB., October 8, 1921; March 17, 1923; June 10, 1922.

[37] Corrigan, op. cit., p. 69.

[38] Relatio Diocesana Archdiocesis Sti. Pauli de Minnesota, 1924. ACA.

[39-42] CB., November 1, 1924; October 31, 1925; November 5, 1927, p. 5; May 16, 1925. Minneapolis Daily Star, November 24, 1925.

[43] The Catholic Universe, London, England, December 18, 1925. Basilica archives.

[44] Letter in CHSA.

[45] CB., June 5, 1926.

[46] Copy in Basilica archives.

[47] Parchment Rescript, framed, in Basilica sacristy. Translation in Minneapolis Daily Star, March 5, 1926.

[48] Nainfa, Rev. J. A., S.S., Minor Basilicas. Ecclesiastical Review, 78:1, January, 1928, (Washington), pp. 1-19. Basilica archives.

[49] Official diplomas, framed, in Basilica sacristy. Also Rescript of monthly plenary indulgence.

[50-54] CB., February 26 and July 17, 1926; April 27, 1929; March 1, 1930; October 16, 1926.

[55] Personal invitation in ACA. Also CB., June 11, 1927.

[56] All documents, agreements, stipulations, letters, etc., connected therewith are in ACA.

[57] CB., December 22, 1928.

[58] Orlando, (former Premier of Italy) in Saturday Evening Post, May 4, 1929.

[59] Through the courtesy of Count Hearn, then residing in Rome, the writer received a copy of L'Illustrazione Italiana, Milano, February 17, 1929, which contains the Official Proclamation issued on February 11, announcing the Concordat, the story of the signing of the Lateran Treaty on February 12, with six official photographs of the event, as well as a history of the Roman Question with photographs of all connected with it—all of which will ultimately be given to CHSA.

[60] Copy in CHSA.

[61] The function was described in the local papers of March 26, 1929.

[62] Duplicate in Basilica archives.

[63-65] CB., August 10; November 16; and August 17, 1929.

[66] Copy of letter in CHSA.

[67-68] CB., October 19, 1929; June 28, 1930, p. 2.

[69] Interview with Reverend E. F. Jennings, one of the founders of the Leaflet Missal.

[70] Harrigan, E. A., The Golden Thread (St. Paul: 1941), (an account of the origin and development of the Catholic Digest).

[71-72] CB.,March 1; August 30, 1930.

[73] The Sixth National Eucharistic Congress. Omaha, Nebraska, September 23-25,

1930, pp. 98 & ff. Basilica Archives.

[74] CB., January 25, 1930.

[75] Copy in Basilica Archives.

[76-79] CB., June 7; November 22; May 31; November 22, 1930.

[80] Minneapolis Daily Star, October 11, 1930. Also CB., October 18, 1930.

[81] Minneapolis Tribune, March 10, 1931.

[82] The Belgian Ambassador to Father Reardon, Washington, June 19, 1939, transmitting an invitation to participate in the function from the President of the Royal Circle Archéologique d'Ath, Belgium, dated May 30, 1939.

Copy of a letter from Orren E. Safford, Belgian Consul in Minneapolis, to Mr. E. Rosier, Belgian Consul General, Chicago, July 19, 1939, forwarding a list of members for the proposed American Committee, selected by Father Reardon and Mr. E. C. Gale.

[83-86] CB., December 1; November 15; December 6; December 6, 1930, p. 4.

[87] Daggett, op. cit., p. 97.

[88-90] CB., December 20, 1930; January 2 and 9, 1932.

XI

N.B. The letters of Archbishop Murray, copies of which are in ACA., are the guideposts and milestones of the material and spiritual progress of the Archdiocese during his administration. They point out the way in which the faithful must walk, proclaim the truths they must hold dearer than self, and allure to the life they must lead if they would reach their destined goal. Around them is built the record of twenty years of progress.

[1] Biographical data furnished by Archbishop Murray. CB., January 9, 1932, p. 3.

[2] Johnson, V. Rev. G. P., V. G., to the writer, Portland, Maine, January, 31, 1949. Souvenir of Diamond Jubilee of Diocese of Portland, May 20-21, 1930.

[3] CB., January 30, 1932.

[4] The account of the installation of Archbishop Murray and subsequent religious and civic events is condensed from the reports in the Catholic weeklies and daily papers of the Twin Cities accessible to readers.

[5] CB., February 13, 1932.

[6] Minneapolis Tribune, February 2, 1932. Minneapolis Journal, January 31, 1932.

[7-10] CB., February 20; February 27; March 12; May 7, 1932.

[11] AD., 6:1, October, 1933, pp. 5 & ff.

[12] Gilligan, Rev. F. J., to the writer, St. Paul, February 29, 1952.

[13] All documents, contracts, correspondence, etc., connected with the transfer of the College of St. Thomas to the Congregation of the Holy Cross, and its restoration to diocesan control are in ACA.

[14] Archbishop's letter, October 1, 1935.

[15] Archbishop's letter, September 17, 1935. Financial statements summarized from subsequent letters, copies of which are in ACA.

[16] The Confraternity Messenger, 3:1, January 1, 1950, pp. 2 & ff.

[17-19] CB., January 13, 1938; October 31, 1936; September 4, 1937.

[20] Minneapolis Tribune, October 4, 1937.

[21] Parish announcement book, Basilica of St. Mary, May 22, 1943.

[22] O'Loughlin, D., Campaign Manager, to the writer, St. Paul, September 26, 1939. C. U. Campaign Bulletin, October 21, 1939. Basilica archives.

[23] Archbishop's letter, May 24, 1937.

[24-26] Parish announcement books, September 11, 1939; June 4, 1939; March 23, 1941.

[27] Complete records of the Ninth National Eucharistic Congress—letters, programs, newspaper articles, financial reports, souvenirs, photographs, display cards, five volumes of phonographic records of Masses, sermons, addresses, etc., in CHSA.

Ninth National Eucharistic Congress, St. Paul and Minneapolis, June 23-26, 1941. Official History and Record. (St. Paul: 1941). A volume of 295 pages giving a complete history of the Congress, with the sermons at the Masses and the addresses at the twenty-six sectional meetings. Copies in St. Paul Seminary Library.

[28] Archbishop's letter of authorization in Latin posted in the Basilica sacristy.

[29] Financial Report, undated, issued by Father Busch. Basilica archives.

[30] Spiritual bouquet for the Pope. Detailed report in ACA.

[31] List of chaplains with dates of service in the Appendix.

[32] Archbishop's letter, December 5, 1945. Also CB., December 5, 1945.

[33] Curtin, Rev. F. W., Director, Diocesan Charity Bureau, to the writer, March 30, 1951.

Archbishop's letter, March 27, 1944.

[34] Connolly, V. Rev. J. L., Rector of St. Paul Seminary, November 20, 1944.

[35] CB., September 29, 1945.

[36] Flynn, V. Rev. V. J., President of the College of St. Thomas, St. Paul, March 24, 1948.

[37] Leaflets published by Archdiocesan Committee on Family Life. CHSA.

[38] Doherty, Rev. R. T., Director of Family Life, to the writer, St. Paul Seminary, September 6, 1950.

Family Digest (Huntington, Ind.), September, 1950, p. 46.

Archbishop's letter, September 8, 1948.

[39] Constitution and By-laws approved September 22, 1949.

[40] Constitution and By-laws approved February 1, 1950.

[41] Cashman, Rev. N. S., Diocesan Director, Society for the Propagation of the Faith, St. Paul, February 5, 1949, letter and summary of the proposed plan and the regulations approved by the Most Reverend Archbishop. ACA.

[42] CB., September 10, 1949.

[43] Archbishop's letter, September 24, 1949.

[44] Special school bulletin issued by Rev. R. J. Connole, Superintendent, September 28, 1950.

[45] Archbishop's letter, October 10, 1950.

[46] CD., 1951.

[47] List of new parishes and dates of organization in Appendix.

INDEX

Abbelen, Rev. P. M., "Relatio," of German-Catholic grievances 261
Academy for Girls, (Winona), 672
Academy of the Holy Angels, (Mpls.), 670
Academy of the Holy Child, (Avoca), 675
Accault, Michael, companion of Father Hennepin, 19
Acta et Dicta, official organ of Catholic Historical Society, 372; Archbishop Ireland writes first four chapters of "Life of Bishop Cretin" for it, 372, 407; final issue in 1936, 372
Ad Limina reports, (Des Moines, 1919), 441; (St. Paul, 1924), 462
Adrian, land offered Catholic settlers, 241
Afro-American League, 267
Aldridge, Rev. J. P., Spiritual Director, Holy Name Diocesan Union, 471
Allouez, Father, extols authority of France in 1671, 16
All Saints Church (Lakeville), 629
All Saints Church (Mpls.), 598-99
American Architect, described St. Paul Cathedral and Minneapolis Pro-Cathedral, 387
American Board of Catholic Missions organized, 465
"Americanism," heresy of nineties, 326-28; Apostolic Letter issued, 328; Archbishop Ireland's reaction, 329; True Americanism reigns, 358-9
Ancient Order of Hibernians keeps vigil at Archbishop's bier, 431
Annunciation Church (Hazelwood), 617
Annunciation Church (Mpls.), 599
Apostolic Briefs lost at sea and recovered, 228
Apostolic Delegation established in United States, 338
Archbishop Ireland Educational Fund, 448-449; goal set at $5,000,000, 449; statistics on diocesan needs, 449-51
Archdiocesan Council of Catholic Men organized, 561-62
Archdiocesan Council of Catholic Women, (St. Paul), 663
Arctander, Rev. George A., convert priest, 290; member of Diocesan Mission Band, 290; pastor of St. Andrews, 290; dies, 290
Ascension Church (Mpls.), 596
Ascension Church (Norwood), 613
Assumption Church (Assumption), 622
Assumption Church (Bear Creek), 626
Assumption Church (Pembina), 603
Assumption Church (St. Paul) organized, 99; placed under Benedictines, 128; Brothers teach in school, 181; corner-stone of present church blessed, 186; second consecrated church in diocese, 186; Archbishop Ireland preaches at golden jubilee, 388; Chronicle, 582
Assumption Church (Richfield), 628
Assumption Seminary (Chaska), 677
Augelle, Anthony, companion of Father Hennepin, 19
Aulneau, Father Jean, S.J. missionary at Fort St. Charles, 29; massacred by Indians, 29; born in La Vendee, France, 30, 31; memorial in Warroad, 31, 569
Avoca, center of new Irish colonization, 242

Baltimore, first Plenary Council, attended by Bishop Cretin, 81, 89; Second Plenary Council, Bishop Grace present, 166; discussed Catholic University project, 275; Seventh Provincial Council, selects St. Paul for see-city, 62
Bandas, Very Rev. R. G., Director, Confraternity of Christian Doctrine, 528
Baraga, Father Frederick, baptized and confirmed in Grand Portage, 37
Bardstown, Diocese of (Louisville), comprised part of Minnesota, 24; links St. Paul to Baltimore, 25
Barrett, Honorable John, of Pan-American Union, lectures at Pro-Cathedral civic dedication, 386
Basilica of St. Mary (Mpls.) (See Pro-Cathedral), honored by Holy See, 474-6; bronze memorial of Archbishop Ireland, dedicated 541, 542; twenty-fifth anniversary of first Mass, 542; consecrated by Cardinal Dougherty, 547; daily Exposition of Blessed Sacrament authorized, 548; Chronicle, 593
Baskfield, Very Rev. Gerald, Director, Friends of Catholic University, 518
Bazille, Judge E. W., speaks for French at Diocesan Golden Jubilee, 367
Beauharnois, Fort, established, 28; second Chapel built in Minnesota 28; first Mass said on its altar, 28; site of Villa Maria Academy, 28; bronze tablet marks site, 29
Beauharnois, Governor of New France, 27
Bedini, Archbishop, Papal Nuncio to Brazil, visits America, 163; warns against division of Church on national lines, 163, 260
Belcourt, Father George Anthony, in Red River Valley, 35; North Dakota's greatest pioneer priest, 35; founded half-breed sisterhood, 35; need of funds, 73; asks for priests, 96

Bench Street, site of first Chapel in St. Paul, 63; principal thoroughfare, 63-4

Benedictine House of Studies, (St. Paul), 664

Benedictines in Minnesota 96, 97; founded Abbey, College and Seminary at Collegeville, 97; helped to found Catholic German Newspaper, 173

"Bennett Law," required English in Wisconsin schools, 295

Benson, Admiral, President of NCCM, lectures in St. Paul, 454

Bethlehem Academy, (Faribault), named by Bishop Grace, 161; Chronicle, 672

Betten, Father, S.J., believes Rune Stone genuine, 8

Birth Control and Sterilization, Catholics forbidden to cooperate with promoting individuals and societies, 532

"Blackrobe," served aborigines, 33

"Blacks," sided with "prisoner" Popes, 352

Blaine, James G., Secretary of State, suggests making Archbishop Ireland Cardinal, 350

Blessed Sacrament Church (St. Paul), 590

Board of Regents of University, greets Archbishop Murray, 518

Boland, Rev. P. J. temporary director of new Cathedral subscription campaign, 375

Bonzano, Archbishop, Apostolic Delegate, notifies Bishop Dowling of his appointmeit as Archbishop, 437

Book of Receptions & Professions, excerpts about Bishop Grace, 138

Bouchard, René, Commandant of Fort Beauharnois, 27

Bouquillon, Dr., of Catholic University, writes controversial pamphlet on Catholic education, 297

Brady, Most Reverend William O., Rector of St. Paul Seminary, made Bishop of Sioux Falls, 540, 680

Brand, Rev. W. A., Spiritual Director, Holy Name Diocesan Union, 472; Executive Secretary of Ninth National Eucharistic Congress, 545

Brothers of the Holy Family, (St. Paul), 645

Brothers of Order of St. Francis had charge of industrial school for boys, 184

Buckley, Dr., Supreme Physician of K. of C., testifies in law suit, 405

Builder of London, England lauds Cathedral and Pro-Cathedral, 388.

Bureau of Catholic Charities in St. Paul, 447

Bureau of Indian Affairs, correspondence with Bishop Grace, 151

Burns, Very Rev. James A., CSC; signs agreement between Holy Cross and Archbishop Dowling, 481; corresponds with Archbishop Murray about plans, 526

Busch, Rt. Rev. Jos. F, student at Catholic University, 280; follows Bishop Trobec in St. Cloud, 332; consecrated Bishop of Lead, 390; superior of Diocesan Mission Band, 368; address at Diocesan Centennial, 575

Butler, Honorable Pierce, speaks at Catholic Educational Association, 413

Butler, Right Reverend Thaddeus, bishop-elect of Concordia, dies on eve of consecration in Rome, 325; Archbishop Ireland preaches at requiem in Chicago, 325

Bussard, Rev. Paul, launches *Leaflet Missal*, 488; joins Father Gales in *Catholic Digest*, 488

Byrne, Reverend James C., secretary to Archbishop Ireland, 250; made irremovable rector, 286; blamed for publicizing famous letter, 301; Administrator of Diocese at Archbishop's death, 430; Vicar General under Archbishop Murray, 514

Byrne, Right Rev. J. J., consecrated Auxiliary Bishop, 519; Diocesan Director of Pontifical Society for Vocations, 558; presides at assignment of two Franciscans, 566; congratulates Archbishop Murray on Jubilee and reads letter from Pope, 571; celebrates Mass at Diocesan Centennial in Minneapolis, 574

Byrnes, Rev. James A., Diocesan Director of Propagation of Faith, 414; Superintendent of Bureau of Education, 458; makes official report on Catholic educational system in Archdiocese, 458; proposes establishment of Normal School, 458; asks for adoption of approved list of text books, 459; convenes education congress 459

Cahensly, Peter P., Priester-Vereins, 260; fosters agitation among German priests, 262; Holy See refuses request for national bishops, 263

Cahokia, first Catholic settlement in Mississippi valley, 23

Caillet, Rev. Louis, founds parish of St. Mary in Lower Town, 165; made irremovable rector, 286; first rector of St. Paul Seminary, 310; Domestic Prelate in 1892, 681

Caldwell, Miss Mary Gwendoline, founds and endows Catholic University 276-277

Calvary Cemetery purchased, 102; bodies transferred, 107; Bishop Cretin buried in vault, 112; reinterred in mortuary chapel, 113; price of lots fixed, 160; mortuary chapel dedicated, 199; third cemetery in St. Paul, 500

Campbell, Scott, Indian interpreter, host to Bishop Loras and Father Galtier at Fort Snelling, 42

Cana days & Pre-Cana days, retreats for married or engaged couples, 559; initiated annual rosary procession to Cathedral, 560; Minneapolis follows suit, 561

Cantwell, Archbishop, of Los Angeles, preaches at National Conference of Catholic Charities in St. Paul, 537

Capel, Monsignor T. J., of England, attends Bishop Grace's jubilee, 193

Carroll, Rt. Rev. John, Bishop of Baltimore, had jurisdiction over Minnesota, 24

Cartier, Jacques, discovers New France, 14

Carty, Rev. C. M., heads Catholic Campaigners for Christ in Minnesota, 540

Cashman, Rev. Neil, director of Propagation of Faith, 414; arranges departure ceremony for Franciscan missionaries, 566

Cathedral of St. Paul: original log chapel, 44; addition built by Father Ravoux, 57; replaced by stone church and residence, 58, 77; dismantled, 270; third Cathedral project, 104; completed and dedicated by Father Ravoux, 124; Cardinal Gibbons presides at Mass, 265; third Cathedral demolished in 1914, 379; plans for new Cathedral, 373-376; Kittson property bought, 374; Board of Counsellors, 374; Masqueray named architect, 374; cornerstone laid, 376-378; receipts and disbursements, 378; funds from business firms, 379; total cost as of Feb. 10, 1916, 379; final services in old Cathedral, 379; first Mass in new Cathedral, 380; formal dedication, 380; Joan of Arc stone, 381; Vannutelli stone, 393; silver anniversary of laying of cornerstone, 522; Chronicle, 581

Cathedral Rectory built, 152; dismantled, 380; temporary rectories, 380; new rectory, 496, 503

Catholic Almanac, for 1844, 46; for 1854, 82, 98; for 1850 with statistics, 116

Catholic Boy Scouts, first church-sponsored troop, 462; vesper service at Basilica 542-543; address by Bishop Kelley, 543; report by Catholic Scouting Committee, 549; Ad Altare Dei award, 549; three Catholic Scoutmasters become executives, 549

Catholic Boys Home, (Mpls.), 665

Catholic Bulletin founded by Archbishop Ireland, 394; Father Reardon Editor-in-Chief, 395-401; Diamond Jubilee edition, 468; reports on Rural Vacation Schools, 478; describes Mission Pageant, 563-565

Catholic Campaigners for Christ, give missions in diocese, 540; Father Carty and David Goldstein, 540

Catholic Colonization Bureau, organized, 240; operates in several counties, 240-3; a tragic incident, 242

Catholic Colonization Land Stock Company, formed to finance purchases, 240

Catholic Colleges put on approved list, 473

Catholic Conference on Industrial problems in St. Paul, 490

Catholic Digest, launched 488; edition in Braille, 489; editions in foreign languages, 489

Catholic Educational Association meets in St. Paul, 413

Catholic Extension Society organized, 369; did not appeal to Archbishop Ireland, 319; converted to the cause later on, 370

Catholic Herald of New York, printed Archbishop Ireland's letter on the silver question, 331

Catholic Historical Association of the United States meets in Minneapolis, 504; Dr. Guilday refers to early church history of the Northwest, 505

Catholic Historical Society of St. Paul has originals of Father Ravoux catechism and hymn book, 54; Bishop Cretin's relics in museum, 120; organized, 370; charter members, 370-371; object, 371; membership, 371; officers, 371; *Acta et Dicta*, official organ, 372; society reorganized, 372, 525, 526; revived under Archbishop Murray, 372; Archbishop Dowling was not interested, 479; ceases to function, 526

Catholic Industrial School of Minnesota incorporated, 183; operated for two years, 184; transferred to Clontarf, 184; Chronicle, 657

Catholic Infants' Home (St. Paul), 662

Catholic Labor School established, 526; aim, 527

Catholic Men's Institute, organizes Archdiocesan Council, 561

Catholic Mutual Benefit Society of St. Paul, 169

Catholic Mutual Insurance Association, 233

Catholic Orphanage (St. Paul), 654

Catholic Rural Life Conference, 472

Catholic Temperance Society, organized by Bishop Cretin, 86, 87, 176; John Ireland a member, 420

Catholic Truth Society 281-283; publications and reports, 282-3; merged with International Catholic Truth Society of Brooklyn, 283

Catholic Union of the Diocese of St. Paul, 182-183

Catholic University of America advocated

by Bishop Grace, 190, 276; Bishops Ireland, Keane and Spalding promote it, 275-6; Washington selected as site, 277; project opposed by Archbishop Corrigan and Bishop McQuaid, 278; approved by Leo XIII, 278; Caldwell Hall, nucleus of University, dedicated, 279; "Friends of Catholic University," 515; efforts to raise $2,000,000, 539-40

Catholic vs Public School Problems, 168

Catholic Welfare Association, 287; Rev. W. P. Driscoll first Director, 447; present Director, Rev. T. F. Meagher, 447

Catholische Volkszeitung, nationality of St. Paul priests, 169

Celtic World, Catholic weekly of Minneapolis, 175

Cemetery, near log chapel, first in St. Paul, 45

Cemetery Sunday established, 388

Centenary of Hierarchy, 273-274

Cerretti, Cardinal, visits St. Paul, 481-482

Champlain, Samuel, founder of Quebec, 14; forced to surrender it, 85; summoned Recollects to convert Indians, 14

Chaplains for Army & Navy in 1890, 290

Chaplains in Armed Forces, 685; in Civil War, Spanish-American War, first and second World Wars, 686; Canadian Army, 687

Chareyre, Father John, Chaplain for Canadian French, 283; professor in St. Paul Seminary, 284, 310

Charlevoix, Father, historian of New France, 27

Chatron, Bishop, of Osaka, classmate of Archbishop Ireland, 218

Chippewa Agency, entitled to Catholic agent, 181

Christ Child Society, dinner and reception for Archbishop Murray, 517; Chronicle, 662

Christian Brothers, arrive in St. Paul, 181; teach in Cretin High, 181; in De LaSalle, 459

Christie, Right Rev. Alexander, Bishop of Victoria, B.C., 354; later transferred to Oregon City (Portland) 354-355; appeals to N.C.W.C. for assistance in defending parochial schools of Oregon, 445

Christ the King Church (Mpls.), 600

Church of Holy Rosary, Grand Portage 37

Church of Immaculate Conception (Mpls.) founded by Father McGolrick, 116; bell blessed by Bishop Ireland, 232; succeeded by Pro-Cathedral of St. Mary, 383, and Basilica of St. Mary, 474

Cicognani, Most Rev. Amleto G., Apostolic Delegate, consecrates Rev. James J. Byrne, Auxiliary Bishop, 519; consecrates Sacred Heart altar in Basilica, 547

City Missionaries, 287-8

Civilta Cattolica, attacks Archbishop Ireland on Catholic education, 298

Cleary, Rev. James M., preaches at Bishop Christie's consecration, 354; speaks at Catholic Educational Association, 413; President, C.T.A.U. of America, 235; represents Archdiocese on Priests Total Abstinence League, 419; golden jubilee, 462; diamond jubilee, 523

Clerical Total Abstinence Society (St. Paul) organized by seminarians, 418-419

Clinton (St. Joseph) Church of St. Joseph, first consecrated church in diocese, 178

Clontarf, center for Irish immigrants, 240; site of second Industrial School, 184

Coffman, Lotus D., President of University, welcomes Archbishop Murray, 518

Cogwin, Rev. R. E., Diocesan Director of scouting for girls, 536

Colbert, Rev. William, Diocesan Mission Band, 369; recalled to Winona Diocese, 369

Coler, Honorable Bird, address at civic dedication of Pro-Cathedral, 386

Colin, Father, Founder of Marists, accepts John Ireland and Thomas O'Gorman into Scholasticate at Montbel, 99

College of St. Catherine, Archbishop Ireland Educational Fund contributes to endowment, 452; Chronicle, 660

College of St. Thomas founded by Bishop Ireland, 309; separated from theological seminary 310; receives $80 000 from clergy on diocesan golden jubilee, 366; given $100,000 for a dormitory for those entering seminary if $150.000 as endowment raised, 427; Archbishop Dowling officiates at dedication of new chapel, 444; Father Cullen resigns presidency, 479; College turned over to Holy Cross Fathers, 480-1; alienates interest of diocesan clergy and friends, 480; dedication of new Arts and Administration building, 515; "Center of Culture," 527; financial statement from Father Schumacher, 528; Holy Cross Fathers asked to withdraw, 529; Rev. James Moynihan appointed President of St. Thomas, 529; campaign to liquidate debt, 529; Navy College program, 551; new buildings, 552; post-war expansion program, 555; has an indebtedness of over one million dollars, 557; Founder's Day instituted, 562; Chronicle, 659

Coller, Honorable Julius, of Shakopee, speaks at Catholic Educational Association, 413

Colorado Catholic, announces abrogation of Bishop Matz ruling about attendance at Catholic schools, 303

Colored Catholics: Archbishop's stand, 265-268

Company of the Sioux, aids in founding Fort Beauharnois, 27

Conaty, Rev. Thomas J., appointed Rector of Catholic University, 343

Conference of Parochial Sodalities of Our Lady, 492-493

Confraternity of Christian Doctrine organized by Archbishop Murray, 530; plans for adults, teachers and vacation schools, 530; establishes Catholic Youth Centers, 531; Bureau of Publicity and Information, 531; vacation schools in all parishes, 531

Congregation of Our Lady of Charity of the B.V.M., establishes girls' high school in St. Paul, 570

"Connemara Patch," colonized from Graceville, 242

Connolly, Most Reverend James L., Rector of St. Paul Seminary, made Coadjutor Bishop of Fall River, Mass., 540; presides at meeting for Archbishop Ireland Memorial Library, 552; preaches at diocesan centennial, 575

Conry, Rev. James J. pastor of Immaculate Conception, Faribault. 291; offers control of parish school to Public School Board, 292

Constitutions of Diocese of St. Paul, 144-146

Consultors, appointed by Archbishop Murray, 514

Convent and Academy of St. Francis Xavier (Pembina), 671

Convent of Our Lady, (Graceville), 676

Convent of Our Lady of the Cenacle, (Mpls.), 670

Convent of the Good Shepherd, (Mpls.), 667

Convent of the Immaculate Conception, (Mendota), 673

Convent of the Visitation, (St. Paul), 656

Corbett, Rt. Rev. T., Bishop of Crookston, 322

Corpus Christi Church (St. Paul), 591

Corrigan, Archbishop, of New York, attacks Cahensly, 263; celebrates Mass at first Lay Catholic Congress, 274; opposes Catholic University, 274; controversies with Archbishop Ireland, 336

Corrigan, Rt. Rev. J. A., made Domestic Prelate, 556; preaches at diocesan centennial, 576

Cotter. Rev. Joseph B., student at St. John's, 160; gives temperance lectures, as National President, C.T.A.U. of A., 235; Bishop of Winona, 272; preaches at Bishop Trobec's consecration, 331; dies, 389

Cowley, Rev. L. P., National Chaplain, Federation of Newman Clubs, 569; preaches at diocesan centennial, 574

Cramsie, Miss Mary T., officer of Sacred Thirst Society, writes poem for diocesan dedication to Sacred Heart, 189

Cretin, Rt. Rev. Joseph, first bishop of St. Paul, 57, 62, 63; received Bulls of appointment, 65; youth and education, 66; ordained priest, 67; writings as seminarian, 67; in Ferney, 68; missionary in Iowa, 69; Vicar General, 69, 70; missionary among Winnebagoes, 70, 71; brings five seminarians from Europe, 72; consecrated bishop in France, 72; installed bishop in log church, 74; lives in log shanty, 76; financial aid for Catholic schools, 78; work among Winnebagoes, 79-81; seeks government aid, 81-89; contracts for teaching Indians, 81; attends First Plenary Council of Baltimore, 81; founds Catholic Temperance Society, 86, 87; builds hospital, 91; becomes U. S. citizen, 91; issues regulations for temporal administration of parishes, 92; interest in immigration, 93, 237; Catholic population doubles, 94; issues Pastoral Letter, 101; diocesan statistics, 101; visits diocese, 103; new Cathedral project, 104-6; last ordination, 106; final letter to Propagation of Faith, 107; last will and testament, 108-109; illness and death. 109-110; funeral, 111; interred in vault 112; reinterred in mortuary chapel, 113; inscription on mural tablet, 113; editorial in Northwestern Chronicle, 114; a saintly prelate. 115; sermon at reinterment by Bishop Ireland, 120; school, avenue and seminary building named after him, 120; also a colony, 242

Cretin High School, 181; forms alumni association, 324; aided by Archbishop Ireland Educational Fund, 452; Chronicle, 650

Crookston Diocese erected, 389; includes Fort St. Charles, 31; Bishop Schenk consecrated, 540; dedicates Father Aulneau memorial altar, 32

Crow Wing, headquarters of Father Pierz, 95; visited by Bishop Grace, 153

Cullen, Rev. Thomas E., pastor of Pro-Cathedral, recites final prayers at graveside of Archbishop Ireland, 434; as President of College of St. Thomas, establishes law school, 456; discontinued in 1933, 457; resigns presidency of St. Thomas, 479

Cullinan, Monsignor J. J., pastor of St. Luke's Church, St. Paul, made Domestic Prelate, 556; builds new school, 570

Culture and Progress, lecture by Archbishop Ireland, published, 247

Curé of Ars, blesses Monsignor Guillot in 1859, 565
Curtin, Rev. Francis W., Director of Diocesan Bureau of Charities, 551

Danehy, Rev. Patrick, student at Catholic University, 280; on faculty of St. Paul Seminary, 310; Spiritual Director of Catholics at University, 320; first priest from Immaculate Conception parish, Minneapolis, 539
Davis, Cushman K., Senator and former Governor, gave principal address at Hennepin celebration, 189
Deaf Mute Institute, (St. Paul), 658
Decree on dancing enforced by Archbishop Dowling, 482; also by Archbishop Murray, 567
De Gonner, Father Nicholas, missionary at Fort Beauharnois, 27; returned to the East, 28
De Graff, center of immigration in Swift County, 240
De La Salle High School receives money from Archbishop Ireland Education Fund, 452; new school built and dedicated, 459; Archbishop Murray attends 25th anniversary banquet of alumni, 517; Chronicle, 667
De La Salle bids Father Hennepin explore the Mississippi, 19; descends Mississippi to the Gulf of Mexico, 20
De Lepidi, Father, gives Imprimatur to French book about Father Hecker, 327
De Marogna, Rev. Demetrius, pastor of Assumption Church, 128; says first Mass in Church of St. Boniface in St. Anthony, 128; made Vicar General for German parishes, 144
Demonstration in St. Paul on behalf of Pope and States of the Church, 180
Demeules, Zephirin, founds French paper in Minneapolis, 174
De Pineda, may have discovered lower Mississippi, 14
Derham, Hugh, settled in Rosemount in 1880, 94; gives fund for hall at St. Catherine's College, 661
Der Wanderer, Catholic German weekly, founded, 173; English edition, 174
"Descent from Cross," painting bought by Bishop Grace, 177
De Smet, Father, in South Dakota, 55; discusses execution of Sioux, 129
De Soto, leads expedition to New World, 13; buried in the Mississippi, 14
De Varennes, Sieur de la Verendrye, built Fort St. Charles, 29
Devereux, John C., founder and editor of Northwestern Chronicle, 172
De Vivaldi, Canon, came to St. Paul with Bishop Cretin, 73-74; in charge of Winnebago mission, 76; runs into debt, 83; follows Winnebagoes to Blue Earth, 83; founds Sisters of the Love of God, 83; final career, 84; meets Archbishop Ireland in Rome, 84; visits St. Paul, 84; dies in France, 84
Devie, Bishop, ordains Father Cretin, 67; sends him to Ferney, 68; consecrates him Bishop of St. Paul, 72; offers to educate students from St. Paul free, 99
De Vos, Rev. Jule E., assists early colonists in Minneota and Ghent, 243
Diocesan Bureau of Charities, 551
Diocesan Centennial, 572-576
Diocesan Mission Band, 367-370; give 75 missions in three years, 368; ceases to exist, 369
Diocesan Priests made Bishops, 679
Diocesan School Board, organized in 1890, 412; report given, 412
Diocesan Statistics for 1849, 116-117; for 1857, 118-119; for 1858, 119; for 1880,

192; for 1884, 252; for 1918 and 1930 compared, 497; second decade of Archbishop Murray's administration, 576-578
Diocesan Teachers' College, 464; Hill residence donated, 464; 10th opening of College 518-519; Department of Elementary Education of College of St. Catherine, 570
Diocesan Theological Society, 180
Diocese of St. Paul, its lineage, 24; erected, 62; arrival of first Bishop, 74; assets, 75; division of diocese, 185; dedicated to Sacred Heart. 188; incorporated, 248; raised to metropolitan rank, 268; 13th ecclesiastical Province, 269; golden jubilee, 468-471; Centennial, 572-576; priests consecrated, 679-80; Vicars General, 681; Domestic Prelates, 681; priests ordained (1851-1894), 682; Churches, chapels, altars consecrated, 684; new parishes (1933-52) 687-89; War Chaplains (1862-1952), 685-87
Doherty, Rev. J. F., city missionary, 288; first director of Bureau of Catholic Charities, 447
Doherty, Rev. R. W., Director of Bureau of Catholic Charities. 446
Doherty, Rev. R. T., Director of Family Guild, 558
Dolphin, Rev. John, designed gift for Mr. Hill, 317
Domestic Prelates of diocese, 681
Donahoe, Rev. James, City Missionary, 287; pastor of St. Bridget's, 287; delegate to National Convention of Catholic Charities, 288; works for Mothers' Pension and other bills, 288
Donahue, Danny, factotum of Archbishop Grace, 203; comforted by Archbishop Ireland, 206
Donaldson, L. S. purchases site for Pro-Cathedral, 383; entertains prelates after laying of cornerstone, 385; Knight of St. Gregory, 427
Doran, Rev. C. F., leads pilgrims to sixth Eucharistic Congress, 491
Dougherty, Dennis, Cardinal Legate, Ninth National Eucharistic Congress, 546; consecrates Basilica, 547
Dougherty, Rev. Michael, ninth priest from Cathedral parish, 355
Dowling, Most Rev. Austin, appointed second Archbishop of St. Paul, 437; early life and education, 438-439; first Bishop of Des Moines, 439; Archbishop Keane preaches at consecration, 439; enthroned, 439; founds college, buys residence, and regulates teaching of Christian doctrine, 440; Archbishop of St. Paul, 441; met at Faribault by clergy, 441; installed 441-444; receptions and functions in his honor, 443; elected national treasurer and chairman of Department of Education of National Catholic Welfare Council, 445; Oregon parochial school case taken to Supreme Court, 445; Oregon law unconstitutional, 446; objectives of Department of Education, 446; Archbishop Ireland Educational Fund, 448-452; lectures for Twin Cities Council of Catholic Men, 453-454; interest in School of Social Studies, 455-457; ; Ad Limina visit to Rome, 456; official report to Holy See, 462-464; six members of Board of Consultors and Chancellor made Domestic Prelates, 457; dedicates new De La Salle High School, 459; asks for educational congress 459-462; inaugurates Pontifical Mass for school children, 460; great love of children, 462; writes article on growth and development of diocese, 468-471; co-ordinates Holy Name Societies,

471-472; Catholic Rural Life Conference, 472-473; Pro-Cathedral made Basilica, 473; preaches at sesquicentennial of San Francisco, 477-478; Rural Religious Vacation Schools, 478; honorary doctorate in Sacred Theology from Louvain, 479; preaches at Mass for signing of Concordat, 482; resigns as treasurer of NCWC, 485; his last address at St. Thomas College, 486; Catholic Conference on Industrial Problems, 490; last ordination ceremony, 491; entertains Cardinal Hayes, 492; his illness, 497; his death and funeral, 498; sermon by Archbishop McNicholas, 499; inscription on tombstone in Calvary Cemetery, 500; Diocese of Providence pays tribute, 500; his sermons, addresses, at home and abroad, 501-504

Driscoll, Rev. W. P., City Missionary of Minneapolis, 288; Director of Catholic Central Bureau of Charities, 447

Dubuque Diocese gave territory to St. Paul Diocese, 24

Duggan, John F. takes notes of Archbishop Ireland's lectures to students and publicizes them, 314

Du Lhut, Sieur, rescues Father Hennepin from Indians, 19

Dumoulin, Father Severe, first pastor of Pembina, 34; offers first Mass in Province of St. Paul 34; records of baptisms, etc., 35

Dunphy, Rt. Rev. John, pastor of Ascension parish, made Domestic Prelate, 556; promotes total abstinence, 419; Spiritual Director of Holy Name Diocesan Union, 471

Du Ranquet, Rev. Dominic, S.J., pastor of Grand Portage for eighteen years, 37

Eberhart, Governor, with staff, present at consecration of six bishops, 391

"Ecclesiastical Preparatory Seminary," opened in 1862 and merged with Cathedral School in 1867, 159

Edge, William, catechist at Pembina and first in Diocese of St. Paul, 34

Egan, Rev. M. J., charter member of Priests T. A. League of America, 419

Egan, Maurice Francis, author of Ten Years Near the German Frontier, 352

Elder, Archbishop, organized Priests T.A. League in Cincinnati, 419

Elliott, Rev. Walter, C.S.P. preaches at triple consecration, 272

Epilogue, 578-580

Erin, Irish settlers, 239

Eucharistic Congress, visitors, 477; sixth at Omaha, 491; ninth in Twin Cities, 545-549; program, 546; broadcast by Pope, 547; receipts and expenses, 547; souvenir volume, 547

Ewing, Charles, Catholic Commissioner for Indian Missions, 181

Fairbanks, Honorable Charles W., former Vice-President of the U. S., refused audience with Pope because of tie-up with Methodists 396-398

Falconio, Archbishop, Apostolic Delegate to the U.S., appointment makes unfavorable impression on Roosevelt and Taft, 348; blesses and lays cornerstone of Pro-Cathedral, 384; at consecration of six bishops, 390; approves Catholic Bulletin, 395; and Priests Total Abstinence League, 419

Family Guild authorized, 558-560; Cana and Pre-Cana days, 559

Faribault, J. B., provides home for Father Galtier, 45

Faribault School Plan, 290-293; attacked by Catholics and non-Catholics, 295,

337; the Poughkeepsie plan, 294; Memorial to Holy See, 300; school returned to parish, 302

Fassbind, Francis, first editor of Der Wanderer, 174

Father Mathew Total Abstinence Society 176-177; 223-227; jubilee celebration, 307; Father Mathew of Northwest, 415; Father Mathew Memorial Chair at Catholic University, 417; history of total abstinence movement in the U.S., 418; Archbishop keeps interest until his death, 420

Federation of Mothers' Clubs, wins health and nursing service, 485; entertains Archbishop Murray, 519

Fenians, opposed by Bishop Grace and Father Ireland, 222

Financial Aid for Catholic schools, 78, 168-9; Faribault School Plan, 290-3

Financial depression of 1857, 124; cathedral building ceases for a time, 125

Finn farm, site of College of St. Thomas, and St. Paul Seminary, 183

Fisher, Father Daniel J., came to St. Paul in 1852, 90; wrote petition for school aid, 78; in charge of Winnebago Indians, 83; returned to East, 90

Foch, Marshal Ferdinand, Generalissimo of Allied Forces in World War 1, honored at Basilica, 483-485; memorial sent to Madame Foch, 485

Foley Brothers, give $40,000 to new Cathedral, 375

Foley, Rev. John P., named Acting President of St. Thomas, 479; pastor of Immaculate Conception Church, Faribault, 480

Foley, Timothy, Knight of St. Gregory, 427; gives $100,000 to College of St. Thomas, 427

Forbes, Governor, of Philippines, approves Friars land sale, 349

Forbin-Janson, Right Rev. Charles Joseph, vists Father Galtier, 42; founds Association of Holy Childhood, 42

Fort Crevecoeur near Peoria whence Father Hennepin set out for Northwest, 19

Fort Pierre, South Dakota, visited by Father Ravoux, 55

Fort Ripley visited by Bishop Cretin who said Mass for soldiers, 103; also by Bishop Grace who confirmed at Crow Wing in the reservation, 153

Fort St. Charles in northern Minnesota, established by La Verendrye, 29; near Massacre Island where Father Aulneau was put to death, 29; site transferred to state, 32; memorial altar erected, 32

Fort Snelling Landing, northernmost point for steamers on the Mississippi, 41; Father Galtier landed there in 1840, 41

Franciscan House of Studies, (St. Paul), 665

Friars' Lands Problem in Philippines, 345-349

Gadd, Monsignor, of Salford, England, presents bust of St. Thomas to Catholic U, 279

Gale, Edward C., made "Officer of the Order of Leopold II," 496

Gales, Rev. Louis A. originates Catholic Digest, 488

Galtier, Rev. Lucien, ordained, 41; missioned to Mendota, 41; builds altar at St. Peter's (Mendota) 42; founds log chapel in St. Paul 42, 43, 44; erects combination church and residence, 46; terminates ministry at St. Peter's, 46; in Keokuk, Iowa, 47; at Prairie du Chien till death, 47; honors offered 47; inscription on tomb, 49

Galvin, Bishop, of Hangyang, China, founds St. Columban Foreign Mission Society, 401

George, Henry, advocates "Single Tax" 339-340; Archbishop Ireland opposes condemnation, 339

Germain, Brother, later Archbishop of Toulouse, classmate of Archbishop Ireland, 218

German Benevolent Catholic Societies, meet in St. Paul, 250; Bishop Ireland preaches, 250

German-speaking Catholic Societies of Minnesota hold convention, 265

German problem in Diocese, 163, 169; Germans buy cemetery, 259; Archbishop Ireland used Slovenian priests who spoke German, 260; Father Abbelen's petition, 260; Bishops Ireland and Keane discuss German "question" before Propaganda, 261; second memorial, 262; convention of German-speaking Catholic societies of Minnesota, 265; attack on Faribault School Plan, 300

German settlers in Minnesota, 94

Gervais, Benjamin, donates ground for log chapel, 43

Ghizoni, George A., Secretary of Archdiocesan Committee on Catholic Scouting, 549

Gibbons, Most Rev. James, of Baltimore created Cardinal 253; sympathetic to Knights of Labor, 257; presents memorial on Knights and receives reply, 258; receives notification from Cardinal Rampolla on German question, 263; visits St. Paul as Cardinal, 264-265; heads commission to present army chaplains' names, 290; sends detailed report to Pope in vindication of Archbishop Ireland, 296; Archbishop Ireland speaks at his episcopal silver jubilee, 306; rumors in American press, about displeasure of Holy See, denied, 335; voiced vigorous protest against ratification of Prohibition Amendment, 421

Gilligan, Rev. Francis, St. Paul Seminary, director of Catholic Labor Schools, 526

Gilmour, Bishop, of Cleveland, preaches at dedication of Catholic University, 279

Girl Scouts rally 536; addressed by Archbishop Murray, 537

Godfert, Rev. Antoine, assists Father Ravoux, 54; attends St. Paul, 116

Goiffon, Rev. Joseph, in Pembina, 36; story of blizzard, amputation, burning of church, 153-6; pastor of Little (now, New) Canada, 156, 193

Golden Jubilee of Pius IX, 189; gifts suggested, 189

Goldsmith, Father, of Chippewa Falls, substitutes for Archbishop Heiss at Bishop Grace's jubilee, 196

Goldstein, David, founder of Catholic Campaigners for Christ, aids work in diocese, 540.

Good Shepherd Church (Mpls.), 602

Good Will Movement, 465-467; clergymen preach on toleration, 466; Star publishes Good Will edition, 466

Gorman, Willis A., Territorial Governor, buried from Cathedral, 189

Gotti, Cardinal, pleased with handling of church affairs in Cuba, 363

Grace family, James, Richard and Patrick, 137-183

Grace, Pierce, father of Bishop Grace, 137-138

Grace, Rt. Rev. Thomas Langdon, Bishop of St. Paul, 127; early life, 137; joins Dominicans and completes studies in Italy, 138; sub-Prior of Dominican house in Kentucky, 139; pastor of St. Peter's, Memphis, Tenn., 139; consecrated Bishop of St. Paul, 141; installed, 142-143; constitution of the diocese, 144; visitation of diocese, 146-147; first Pastoral Letter, 147; correspondence with McMaster, 148; lectures on "Human Rights," 150; on Board of Visitors to Indians, 151, 152; visits missions in Red River Valley, 153; visits south of state, 156; ordains John Ireland and others, 157; attacked for Southern sympathies, 158; first preparatory seminary, 159; lays cornerstone of St. John's, Collegeville, 160; welcomes Sisterhoods, 161; de-Germanizing policy, 163; second Pastoral Letter, 164; new parishes, 165; Ad Limina visit to Rome, 167; school problem, 168; synods, formal and informal, 169-171; Catholic papers founded, 172-5; total abstinence movement, 176-7; dedication of new churches, 177-8; Vatican Council and protest, 179-80; Indian affairs, 151-2; Industrial School, 152-4; division of diocese, 185-6; coadjutor appointed, 187; Father Hennepin celebration, 189; advocates Catholic University, 190-191, 275; urges seminary for diocese, 191; accompanies Archbishop Satolli west, 306; dislikes "ladies' leagues," 192; tragic death of priest, 192; Silver Jubilee, 193; disavows praise, 195; resigns see, 197-199; builds mortuary chapel, 199; appointed Bishop of Mennith, 199; Vicar General, 200; retires to St. Thomas Seminary, 200; Titular Archbishop of Siunia, 201; bookkeeping, 201; will, 202; vists St. Rose's, 203; death and obsequies, 204-207; tributes and comments, 207-211

Grand Army of the Republic, 221; Archbishop Ireland is National Chaplain, 221; becomes a "comrade" in 1897, 330

Grand Portage Mission founded, 36

Grand View (Ghent) site of Belgian colony, 243

Great Bend of the Missouri, scene of Father Ravoux labors, 56

Greely County Nebraska, lands bought for colonists, 244

Gregory, Rev. D. J., Diocesan Chancellor, appointed to promote "Friends of Catholic University," 515

Gros. Father, of St. Louis' Church, classmate of Archbishop Ireland, 218

Groseilliers with Radisson vists Minnesota in 1655, 17; built first chapel and baptized Hurons, 18; first to navigate Lake Superior, 18

Gros Ventres Indians, Father Ravoux suggested a mission among them, 56

Gross, Archbishop, of Oregon City, preached at first lay congress, 274

Guardian Angels Church (Chaska), 612

Guardian Angels Church (Hastings) 178, 606

Guardian Angels Church (Oakdale), 624

Guerin, Vital, donated ground for log chapel, 43; sells Father Ravoux 22 lots for new Cathedral site, 58

Guidi, Archbishop, Apostolic Delegate to Philippines, 348; compliments Taft, 349

Guignas, Father Michael, missionary at Fort Beauharnois, 27; left for Canada 28

Guild of Catholic Women, (St. Paul), 661

Guild of St. Francis for Catholic journalists, 559

Guilday, Rev. Peter, comments on Dr. Bouquillon's brochure, 297; lectures at National Catholic Historical Convention, 503-504

Guillot, Monsignor Joseph, celebrates 70th anniversary of ordination and 65th in diocese, 565-566

Hagan, S. N., makes critical study of Rune Stone, 7 ; inscription not a forgery, 11

Hanna, Archbishop, sends message from hierarchy to Archbishop Dowling, ill, 497

Hardy, Samuel F., pioneer of St. Peter Claver's parish, 266

Harrison, President, present at banquet after dedication of Catholic University, 279 ; suggests Red Hat for Archbishop Ireland, 350

Hart, Rev. William L. organizes first church-sponsored scout troop, 462

Hartigan, J. A., only layman on faculty of St. Paul Seminary (Science), 310

Hayes, Cardinal, visits Archbishop Dowling, 492

Hayes, Professor Carlton, President of Catholic Historical Association, delivers address at Minneapolis convention. 504

Hayes, Reverend Daniel, tragic death of last priest ordained by Bishop Grace, 192

Head covering for women, of obligation, 568

Hearn, Count Edward L., Overseas Commissioner of Knights of Columbus, visits Twin Cities with Cardinal Cerretti, 481 ; attends Christmas Mass at Basilica, 482

Hecker, Rev. Isaac, Founder of Paulists, life written by Father Elliott, 326 ; French translation gives rise to "Americanism" 327

Heffron, Rt. Rev. P. R., Rector, St. Paul Seminary, consecrated Bishop of Winona, 390, 679

Heiss, Archbishop, of Milwaukee, receives Pallium, 248 ; sermon by Bishop Ireland, 248 ; presides at first Provincial Council, 252 ; Bishop Ireland reads address to him, 253

Hennepin, Father Louis, arrives in New France and Minnesota, 19 ; State Memorial Wayside Park 20 ; names the Falls of St. Anthony, 20 ; "New Discovery", 20 ; "Description of Louisiana", 21 ; first white man to visit site of Minneapolis, 21 ; 200th anniversary, 189 ; celebration of 250th anniversary, 493 ; bronze statue erected, 493-494 ; plans made in Belgium for celebration, 496

Hennessy, Bishop, of Dubuque, silver jubilee of consecration, 285 ; invested with Pallium, 305

Henni, Rt. Rev. Martin, Bishop of Milwaukee, has no priest for Grand Portage, 36 ; writes Father Ravoux, 57 ; gives Bishop Cretin title to land, 76

Hill, James J., President of Great Northern Railway, builds and endows St. Paul Seminary, 309 ; with Mrs. Hill present at dedication, 310 ; letter of thanks from Cardinal Rampolla, Papal Secretary of State, 316 ; thanked by clergy of Archdiocese, 316-317 ; faculty and students give reception, 317 ; at laying of cornerstone of Pro-Cathedral, 385

Hill, Louis W., gives $20,000 to new Cathedral, 375

Hodgson, Mayor, orders flag on city hall at half mast at Archbishop's death, 430

Holaind, Father, S.J., challenges Dr. Bouquillon, 297

Holand, Hjalmar R., studies Rune Stone and declares inscription genuine, 5

Holydays of Obligation made uniform, 85 ; Immaculate Conception added, 175

Holy Angels Academy (Mpls.), 665

Holy Childhood Church (St. Paul), 592

Holy Cross Church (Mpls.), 595

Holy Cross Church (St. Paul), 592

Holy Cross Congregation, 479 ; takes over administration of St. Thomas College, 479 ; agreement entered into, 480-1

Holy Family Church (Belle Prairie), 583

Holy Family Church (St. Louis Park), 650

Holy Family Church (St. Paul), large Syrian congregation witnesses confirmation, 518 ; Chronicle, 590

Holy Name Church (Medina, Wayzata P.O.), 629

Holy Name Church (Mpls.), 599

Holy Name Church (Vesta), 648

Holy Name Diocesan Union 470-471 ; holds public rally, at St. Thomas College, at Fort Snelling, 471 ; meetings attended by Archbishop Murray, 516, 520

Holy Redeemer Church, (Marshall), 634

Holy Redeemer Church (Renville), 640

Holy Rosary Church (Graceville), 631

Holy Rosary Church (Mpls.), 594

Holy Rosary Church (North Mankato), 650

Holy Spirit Church (St. Paul), 591

Holy Trinity Church (Goodhue), 647

Holy Trinity Church (New Ulm), 621

Holy Trinity Church (South St. Paul), 651

Holy Trinity Church (Veseli), 627

Holy Trinity Church (Waterville), 630

Holy Trinity Hospital (Graceville), 676

Holy Year, to celebrate fiftieth anniversary of Pius XI ordination, 486

Home of the Sacred Heart, (Iona), 674

House of Good Shepherd, (St. Paul) postulants received by Archbishop Murray, 515 ; Chronicle, 655

Howard, Most Reverend Edward D., Archbishop of Portland, preached at golden jubilee of St. Paul Seminary, 552 ; most distinguished alumnus, 552

Hughes, Archbishop, discouraged organized emigration to the West, 238

Hunt, Father Jerome, O.S.B., donated to Catholic Historical Society three reprints of Father Ravoux Catechism, 54

Immaculate Conception Church (Columbia Hgts.), 599

Immaculate Conception Church (Faribault), 606

Immaculate Conception Church (Lonsdale), 646

Immaculate Conception Church (Marysburg), 610-11

Immaculate Conception Church (St. Peter), 638

Immaculate Conception Church (Trebon), 636

Immaculate Conception Church (Watertown), 617

Immaculate Heart of Mary Church (Glen Lake), 652

Immaculate Heart of Mary Church (St. Paul), 592

Incarnation Church (Mpls.), 598

Industrial School for Boys, (Clontarf), 674

Industrial School for Girls, (Mendota), 674

International Eucharistic Congress in Montreal, attended by Archbishop Ireland, 392 ; Papal Legate asked to St. Paul, 392

International Federation of Catholic Nurses, Archbishop Murray speaks at meeting, 516

Ireland, Archbishop, believed Rune Stone record genuine, 9 ; Fort St. Charles memorial park 31 ; member of Catholic Temperance Society, 87 ; goes to France with Father Ravoux and enters Seminary of Meximieux, 90 ; reminiscences of trip, 215 ; completes education at Montbel, 99 ; sermon on Bishop Cre-

tin, 120; preaches at Monsignor Ravoux' funeral, 134; Chaplain in Civil
War, 157; secretary to Bishop Grace,
157; President of Irish Emigration Society, 160; attends Vatican Council, 179,
227; consecrated coadjutor to Bishop
Grace, 187, 229-31; resigns Vicariate of
Nebraska, 187, 227; speaks at anniversary of Father Hennepin, 189; address
at Bishop Grace's Silver Jubilee, 196;
tribute to Bishop Grace, 208; early life,
213-214; arrives with O'Gormans in St.
Paul, 214; meets Bishop Cretin, 215;
studies in France, 216-18; ordained,
218; chaplain in Army, 218-220; pastor
of Cathedral, 221; organizes Father
Mathew Total Abstinence Society, 223;
T.A. movement, 224-7; raises money for
lectures on total abstinence, 235; Pope
approves the movement, 236; promotes
Catholic colonization, 240-245; toast to
"The Early Pioneers of Minnesota,"
246; publishes Apostolic Church, Culture and Progress, 246-47; Colonel and
Chaplain-General of the Minnesota National Guard, 250; dedicates first church
as bishop, 250; attends with Bishop
Grace Third Plenary Council of Baltimore, 251; in Milwaukee, preaches at
first Provincial Council, 252; commemo-
rates 25th anniversary of ordination,
253; father dies, 253; lectures in Dublin, visits Maynooth, 254; Vice-President of National Conference of Corrections and Charities, 255; against
national divisions in church, 261-264;
speaks at meeting of German Catholic
Societies of Minnesota, 265; interest in
colored Catholics, 265-268; Diocese of
St. Paul raised to metropolitan rank
and Bishop Ireland made first Archbishop, 268-270; consecration of three
bishops, 272-273; centenary of American hierarchy, 274; Catholic Lay Congress, 274-275; on committee for Catholic University, 277; urges Washington
as site, 278; success of establishment
his triumph, 280; member of board of
governors, 280; moves residence to
Portland Ave., 284; laying of cornerstone of Cathedral in Davenport, Iowa,
284;; urges increased donations for
Seminary, 285; credited with preventing
Hall-Fitzsimmons prize fight, 285;
writes Cardinal Gibbons about Minnesota Scandinavians, 288-290; Faribault
School plan, 290-9 ;Germans charge him
with heterodoxy, 296; defends himself
in famous Memorial, 299-303; takes
Cardinal Manning's place at World's
Fair, 306; presides at World's Congress
of Social Purity, 306; speaks at Cardinal Gibbons' episcopal silver jubilee,
306-307; publishes article on temperance in North American Review, 308-
309; Mr. Hill's gift for St. Paul Seminary, 309; dedication of Seminary, 310-
312; draws up Constitution and Rules,
311; founder, father and guide of Seminary for quarter of century 312-316; in
1895 had heavy schedule of sermons and
addresses, 321-323; The Church and
Modern Society, 323-324; "Americanism", 327; Pope's letter on Americanism, 328-9; applauds its teaching, 329;
"comrade" in G.A.R. and member of
Loyal Legion, 330; denies tie-up with
H. H. Kohlsaat in politics, 330; brief
diplomatic career representing Pope Leo
XIII "to obtain from Spain an armistice
for Cuba", 332-334; Vatican not satisfied, 335; controversy with Archbishop
Corrigan of New York, 336-338; against
Henry George's book being placed on

Index, 339; repudiates "Modernism,"
344; article on Dogmatic Authority of the Papacy, 344; negotiates
with government on Friars land question, 345-349; success of settlement
largely due to his efforts, 349; reasons
for his not being made cardinal, 349-
354; speaks at National Jubilee of
Peace, 355; address on Joan of Arc at
Orleans, 355; visits fort won by her,
356; triumphal tour of France, Belgium,
and British Isles, 356-358; Commercial
Club reception in his honor, 359; speaks
at McKinley dinner, 359; address at unveiling of Lafayette statue, 360;
speaks before Pope and twenty-one
cardinals, 360; receives insignia of
Commander of Legion of Honor, 360;
will vote for McKinley and Roosevelt,
361; designates plan for Holy Year
Jubilee, 363; writes introduction for new
translation of Horace, 363; preaches
at diocesan golden jubilee, 365;
receives autograph letter from Pope on
that occasion, 365; presented with jubilee fund and memorial album, 365; organizes Diocesan Mission Band, 367-
370; disapproves at first of Catholic Extension Society, 369; changes his mind,
370; organizes Catholic Historical Society of St. Paul, 370-327; contributes
to Acta et Dicta, 372; plans new Cathedral, 373-376; approves plans and
starts subscription campaign, 376; lays
cornerstone, 376-378; receipts and disbursements for new Cathedral, 378;
blesses cross above facade, 378; celebrates last Mass in old Cathedral, 380;
plans Pro-Cathedral, 381-382; laying of
cornerstone, 384-385; preaches on that
occasion, 384; gives lecture at civic
celebration for Pro-Cathedral, 385;
takes part in formal dedication, 386;
Chaplain-in-Chief of G.A.R., 388;
preachse at golden jubilee of Assumption parish, 388; Cemetery Sunday, 388;
new dioceses of Crookston and Bismarck, 388; consecrates six bishops,
390-392; invites and entertains Cardinal
Vannutelli, 392-394; attends Holy See
in Fairbanks and Roosevelt incidents,
397-401; laying of cornerstone of
Knights of Columbus building, 403;
suggests name for Twin Cities, 406-407;
begins to write life of Bishop Cretin,
407-408; incomplete at his death, 408;
no celebration of golden jubilee of his
ordination, 408; defends Church against
Methodist attacks, 409-12; Diocesan
School Board, 412; "Father Mathew of
Northwest," 415; discussion of Total
Abstinence, 415-418; promotes clerical
total abstinence, 418-419; interest in
Father Mathew Society till death, 420;
prohibition, a last resort, 421; writer,
apologist and preacher, 421-423; place
in national affairs, 423-424; growth
of diocese, 425; old friends die, 426-427;
letter from Roosevelt, 427; procures
honor of Knighthood in Order of St.
Gregory for four, 427; resigns himself
to death, 428, 429; details of funeral
and burial, 429-433; Archbishop Keane
preaches sermon, 433; condolences
from Roosevelt and hierarchy of Ireland, 435; hundredth anniversary of
birth commemorated in Basilica, 541
Ireland, Richard, father of the Archbishop, 213; buried from Cathedral, 253
Irish Catholic Colonization Association
of America, organized, 243
Irish Emigration Society, 160, 239
Irish settlements in Minnesota, 94; 239-
245

Irish Standard, Catholic weekly of Minneapolis, 175
Italian emigration promoted by Archbishop Ireland, 254

Japanese, Martyrs Church (Leavenworth) 622
Jennings, Rev. Edward F., launches *Leaflet Missal*, 488; join Father Gales in *Catholic Digest*, 488-489; Director of Propagation of Faith, 414
Jessenland, Irish settlers as early as 1852, 329
Jesuit Retreat House, (North St. Paul), 676-77
Jesuits in New France, 15, 17, 22-23; come to Mankato, 187
Jogues, Father, and Father Raymbaut, first white men at Sault Ste. Marie, 15
Johnson, Governor, at cornerstone laying of the Cathedral, 385
Joliet, Louis, reaches the Mississippi with Father Marquette, 17
Jubilee Indulgence for the Holy Year of New Century extended, 363

Kain, Bishop John J., of Wheeling, West Va., explains Faribault Plan, 298
Katzer, Archbishop, of Milwaukee, pontificates at German convention, 264; 294
Keane, Bishop, brings Pallium to Archbishop Ireland, 269; chosen rector of Catholic University and confirmed in it by Pope Leo XIII, 278; summarily removed from rectorship, 342; made Titular Archbishop of Damascus and later, Archbishop of Dubuque, 343; resigns See, 427
Keane, Most Rev. James J., consecrated Bishop of Cheyenne in 1902, transferred to Dubuque in 1911 and preached at Archbishop Ireland's funeral, 433-34; died in 1929 and Archbishop Dowling preached funeral sermon, 485
Keefe, Rev. G. W., of Anoka, leads pilgrims to sixth Eucharistic Congress, 491
Kelley, Most Rev. Francis Clement, founds Extension Soceity, 369-370; as Bishop of Oklahoma City-Tulsa, fosters "Scouting Under Catholic Auspices," 462; given doctorate in Sacred Theology, 479; Episcopal Chairman of National Committee on Scouting, 543; preaches on scouting in Basilica, 543
Kelly, William L., gives address at Catholic Lay Congress, 275; speaks for laymen at diocesan golden jubilee, 367
Kensington Rune Stone, see Rune Stone
Kerens, Richard C., would make Archbishop Ireland a cardinal, 350
Kilkenny, Irish settlers, 239
Klapproth, Hugo, second editor of *Der Wanderer*, 174
Klein, Rev. Felix, writes preface for French translation of Father Hecker's life, 326; suppresses book after condemnation, 330
Knauf, Rev. C. J., first pastor of Red Wing, 166; pastor of Adrian, interested in colonization, 24
Knights of Columbus, Fourth Degree, mark site of Fort St. Charles Chapel 32; St. Paul Council, organized Feb. 22, 1899, lays cornerstone of building, 402; National Convention of Order in St. Paul, 403; program 403-405; triumph in bogus oath trial, 406; Fourth Degree form guard of honor for dead Archbishop, 431; reception for Admiral Benson, 455; erects statue of Hennepin, 493; hosts at banquet, 495
Knights of Labor, had Masonic origin, 256; condemned by Canadian Episcopate, 257; ritual changed by Catholic

President, 257; condemnation averted by Cardinal Gibbons and Archbishop Ireland, 258, 337
Knights of Pythias, 340; Catholics allowed nominal membership, 341
Knutson, Paul, sails with expedition for Vinland, 10
Kundig, Father, of Milwaukee, says Germans would be satisfied with non-German bishop, 163

Labissoniere, Isaac, helps erect first Chapel 43
Lacombe, Father Albert, at Pembina, 35; joins Oblates, 104; honored guest at Diocesan Golden Jubilee, 133
Lafleche, Bishop, of Three Rivers, present at Hennepin celebration, 189
Lang, Rev. Francis, member of Diocesan Mission Band, 369; pastor, Church of St. Anthony, 369
Langevin, Archbishop, of St. Boniface discovers Fort St. Charles, 30; visited by Cardinal Vannutelli, 392
Lantscheere, Count, present at anniversary of Father Hennepin, 494; speaks for Belgian Ambassador, 494
Larpenteur, A. L., charter member of St. Vincent de Paul Society, 89; attends its golden jubilee, 89; speaks at golden jubilee of diocese, 367
Laval, Francis de Montmorency, Titular Bishop of Petraea, arrives in Quebec, 22; Minnesota part of his diocese, 22
Lawler, Most Rev. J. J., Auxiliary Bishop of St. Paul, 390; doctorate in Sacred Theology, 479; Bishop of Rapid City, 679
Lay Catholic Congress, 273-275
Lay Retreat Movement, 477
Leaflet Missal, 488
Leary, Peter, commended sobriety of Irish colonists in Minnesota, 244
Le Canadien, Catholic paper in St. Paul, 174
L'Echo de l'Ouest, French weekly in Minneapolis, 174
Ledochowski, Cardinal, Prefect of the Propaganda, interprets "Tolerari Potest", 302
Ledon, Father, pastor of St. Anthony, 76, of Cathedral, 85; dies in France, 85
Legion of Honor, insignia received by Archbishop, 360
Le Sueur, Pierre, erected forts in Minnesota, 22
Little Sisters of the Poor, (St. Paul), 162; Chronicle, 657
Locnikar, Right Reverend Bernard, O.S. B., Abbot of St. John's, 284
Loisy, Father, orthodoxy questioned, 344
Long Prairie, Winnebago Mission, 80, 83
Loras, Right Rev. Mathias, first bishop of Dubuque, offers first Mass in St. Paul Archdiocese, 39; confirms in log chapel, 44; writes about Father Ravoux, 52; with Father Cretin to St. Louis and Dubuque, 69
Loretto Hospital and St. Alexander's Home, (New Ulm), 675
Louisiana named by LaSalle 16; ceded to U. S., 61
Luby, Rev. W., City Missionary for Minneapolis, 288
Luger, Rev. J. J., pastor of St. Peter Claver's, 554; brings Oblate Sisters to St. Paul, 554

Macalester College, gives right of way and funds for electric street railway, 271
Maignen, Rev. Charles, writes "Is Father Hecker a Saint?" and starts Americanism controversy, 237
Malone, Father, of *Colorado Catholic*, announces abrogation of Bishop Matz ruling about Catholic schools, 303

Manning, Cardinal, of Westminster, 226; sympathetic to Knights of Labor, 257; promises paper on T.A. for World's Fair, 306; visited by Bishop Ireland, 416

Mazzuchelli, Father, O.P., pays tribute to Father Cretin, 72

Margaret Barry Settlement House, (Mpls.), 670

Markoe, Lorenzo J., Director, Catholic Central Bureau, 287

Markoe, William, charter member of St. Vincent de Paul Society, 89; attends golden jubilee, 89; headmaster of Preparatory Seminary, 159

Marquette, Father, with Joliet enters the Mississippi at Prairie du Chien, 17

Martinelli, Archbishop, Apostolic Delegate, pontificates at Cathedral on Christmas day 1897, 332-333

Marty, Bishop, Vicar Apostolic of Dakotas, made Bishop of Sioux Falls, 186; Bishop of St. Cloud, 679

Maryknoll, first foreign mission seminary, 401

Masonic Sect, condemned by the church, 340

Masqueray, E. L., architect of new Cathedral 374-375; of Pro-Cathedral, 383; buried from Cathedral, 381

Massacre Island, scene of Father Aulneau's death, 30; site marked by chapel, dedicated to Queen of Martyrs, 30

Maternity of the Blessed Virgin Mary Church (St. Paul), 592

Matt, Joseph, third and present editor of Der Wanderer, 174; Knight of St. Gregory, 174

Matz, Bishop, of Denver, opposes Archbishop Ireland, 303

McCarthy, Rev. Eugene J., ordained in Basilica, 538-539

McDermott, Rev. John, pastor of St. Anthony's church, builds first school in Minneapolis, 165

McDevitt, Miss Annie, Archbishop's housekeeper, 426

McDonald, Morris, made Knight of St. Gregory, 427

McDonnell, Bishop, of New York, National Director of Propagation of Faith, visits St. Paul, 565

McDonnell, Rev. M., builds Sacred Heart Home at Iona for destitute children, 243

McElmeel, Owen J., director of St. Thomas Law School, 457

McGhee, Fred, prominent colored attorney, 317

McGinley, William J., Supreme Secretary of K. of C., testifies in bogus oath trial, 406

McGinnis, Rev. Charles F., Associate Editor of Catholic Bulletin, 396; Archbishop Murray offers first Pontifical Mass of Requiem for him, 514

McGinnity, Rev. Daniel V., originates total abstinence work in diocese, 176, 223

McGlynn, Dr., pastor of St. Stephen's Church, New York, suspended for backing Henry George, 339; excommunicated, 339; absolved and appointed pastor of St. Mary's Church, Newburgh, N. Y., 339; visits Archbishop Ireland, 339

McGolrick, Rev. James, founds Immaculate Conception parish in Minneapolis, 166; reads address from clergy at Bishop Grace's jubilee, 195; consecrated Bishop of Duluth, 272; lays cornerstone of new Cathedral, 377; dies, 426

McMaster, James A., Editor of Freeman's Journal, corresponds with Bishop Grace, 148-150

McNally, Hon. Carlton, Chairman of Archdiocesan Committee on Catholic Scouting, 549

McNicholas, Bishop, of Duluth, promoted to See of Cincinnati, 476; preaches at Archbishop Dowling's funeral, 499

McQuaid, Bishop, of Rochester, opposes Catholic University, 278

McSweeny, Rev. Edward, writes history of total abstinence movement, 418

Meade, Rev. Peter F., pastor of St. Vincent's, St. Paul, had daily Exposition, 548

Meagher, John, Secretary of Executive Committee of new Cathedral, 375

Meagher, Rev. T. F., director of Catholic Welfare Association, 447

Medewakanton Sioux ask Bishop Grace for priests, 150

Membre, Father Zenobius, accompanies La Salle to Gulf of Mexico, 20

Ménard, Father René, lone missionary among Lake Superior Indians, 16

Merry del Val, Cardinal, Papal Secretary of State, defends Holy See's refusal of Roosevelt audience, 399; letter to Archbishop about incident, 400

Mesaiger, Father Charles, S.J., first missionary at Fort St. Charles, 29; first priest to set foot on Grand Portage, 37

Meximieux Seminary, John Ireland prepares for priesthood, 216-17

Michaud, M. D., founded French paper in St. Paul, 174

Miege, Bishop, Vicar Apostolic of Indian Territory, writes to Father Ravoux, 130

Mille Lacs, scene of Father Hennepin's captivity, 19

Milwaukee, first Provincial Council, attended by Bishops Grace and Ireland, 252

Minneapolis Clerical Conference, 308

Minneapolis League of Catholic Women, 668-69

Minneapolis Star, gets out Good Will edition, 466

Minnesota has unique history, 61; northern part of Louisiana territory, 61; Minnesota Territory, definitely established, 62, 237-238; centennial observance asked by bishops, 568

Minnesota Historical Society, receives gifts from Bishop Ireland, 245; elects him President, 246

Minnesota Pioneer, first newspaper in St. Paul, 63

Minor Basilicas in U.S., 476

Missia, Father, has charge of choir at sixfold consecration, 390; at Ninth National Eucharistic Congress, 545

Missionary Cooperative Plan, 566-568

Mission Dolores Church, anniversary sermon by Archbishop Dowling, 477; Minor Basilica, 476

Mission Pageant, in St. Paul, 563-565

"Modernism, synthesis of all the heresies," 343; Papal Encyclical against it, 343-344; Archbishop writes article in North American Review and another (unpublished), on "The New Theology—Modernism," 345

Moniteur de Rome comments on Pope Leo's Brief on T.A. movement, 236-237

Montbel, Marist Scholasticate, attended by John Ireland, 218

Monthly Calendar of Cathedral, 184

Montluel, birthplace of Bishop Cretin, visited by Bishop Ireland, 254

Morrison, A. M. and G. M., charged E. M. Lawless with taking bogus K. of C. oath, 405-406

Most Holy Redeemer Church (Montgomery), 632

Most Holy Redeemer Church (St. Paul), 587

Most Holy Trinity Church (St. Louis Park), 652

Most Holy Trinity Church (Winsted), 629

Mother Clementine, pioneer Visitation nun, dies, 426

Mother Seraphine Ireland, sister of Archbishop, receives the habit, 127; at first Mass in new Cathedral, 380; Archbishop Dowling officiates at obsequies, 487

Moynihan, Reverend Humphrey, helps edit memorial of Archbishop Ireland on school question, 301; on faculty of St. Paul Seminary (Apologetics), 310; lectures to Catholic students at University, 321; presides at a session of educational congress, 460; reads paper at sixth Eucharistic Congress 491; address on *Hennepin and Early Catholic Days in Minnesota*, 495; made Domestic Prelate, 681

Moynihan, Very Rev. James H., President of St. Thomas College, 529; preaches at Founder's Day, 562; address at Diocesan Centennial, 574; made Domestic Prelate, 582

Mundelein, Cardinal, at sixth Eucharistic Congress, 492

Murray County, site of Irish colony, 242

Murray, Most Rev. John Gregory, biography, 507-8; ordained in Louvain, 508; teacher and pastor in Hartford diocese, 508; Auxiliary Bishop, 508; revives Catholic Historical Society, 372; encourages foreign missions, 402; honorary doctorate in Sacred Theology, 479; message to National Catholic Historical Convention, 504; Bishop of Portland, 508; work in that diocese, 508; leader in civic domain, 509; Archbishop of St. Paul, 510; installed, 510-12; civic welcome, 507; coat of arms described, 512; pontificates in Basilica, 513; business men tender reception and dinner, 513; presented check by Knights of Columbus, 514; administers first confirmation, 515; dedicates new Arts and Administration Building at St. Thomas, 515; welcomed by various archdiocesan institutions, 516-518; meeting of Board of Trustees of Catholic University, 517; address for Church of the Air, 519; visitation of diocese interrupted by automobile accident, 520; Auxiliary consecrated, 521; organizes crusades of prayer and of charity, 521; silver jubilee of laying cornerstone of Cathedral, 522; Italians of St. Paul honor him at a dinner, 523; Monsignor Cleary's diamond jubilee, 523; letter on financial status of diocese, 524; establishes reputation for punctuality, 524; warns clergy against meddling in political affairs, 525; Catholic Historical Society reorganized, 525; establishes Catholic Labor Schools, 525; ends Holy Cross regime at St. Thomas, 527; plans to liquidate debt on St. Thomas, 529; Confraternity of Christian Doctrine, 530; vacation schools, 537; confirmation tour of diocese, 532; church music, 532; visit of Cardinal Pacelli, 633-6; girl scouts rally, 536; address at National Conference of Catholic Charities, 537; nationwide radio hookup, 538; novena for vocations, 538; first ordination in Basilica, 538; campaign to eliminate obscene literature, 539; organization of Confraternity of Blessed Sacrament, 539; campaign for Catholic University, 539-540; three bishops consecrated, 540; campaigners for Christ, 540; death of Pope Pius XI, 541; centenary of Archbishop Ireland, 541; silver jubilee of Basilica, 542; convokes synod, 542; bars inter-faith activities, 543-544; consecrates Resurrection Cemetery, 544; ten years' record, 544; Ninth National Eucharistic Congress, 545-7; consecration of Basilica,

547; daily exposition, 548; liturgical week, 548; Catholic scouting report, 549; Catholic scoutmasters turn professional, 549; diocesan charities bureau, 551; buildings at St. Thomas, 551-2; St. Paul Seminary accredited, 553; Spiritual Bouquet for Pope Pius XII, 550; Archbishop Ireland Memorial Library campaign, 553; Silver Jubilee of his own consecration, 554-555; spiritual bouquet, 555; campaign for College, 555-7; two Cardinals visit St. Paul, 556; six Diocesan Consultors elevated to Domestic Prelates, 556; Pontifical Society for Vocations, 558; Family Guild, 558-560; May day celebrations, 560-1; Catholic Men's Institute, 561; Founder's Day at St. Thomas, 562; Mission Pageant, 564; Monsignor Guillot seventy years a priest, 565 (probably last person living who saw the Curé of Ars who died in 1859); 50th anniversary of ordination and 30th of consecration, 571-572; presented with purse, 572

Murray, Honorable William Pitt, speaks at golden jubilee of diocese, 367

National Catholic Welfare Council, 444; Archbishop Dowling elected treasurer of parent body and Chairman of Department of Education, 445; name changed to "Conference" instead of Council, 455

National Conference of Catholic Charities, organized, 287-288; Archbishop Murray host at 23rd Convention, 537-538

National Conference of Corrections and Charities, elects Archbishop Ireland President, 255

National Convention of German-speaking Catholics at Buffalo, 263

National Cyclopedia of American Biography pays tribute to Bishop Grace, 208

National Education Association, in St. Paul hears epochal address from Archbishop Ireland, 295; speaks before it in 1902 on "Devotion to Truth: The Chief Virtue of the Teacher," 364

National Jubilee of Peace, in Chicago hears Archbishop Ireland, 355

National Liturgical Week in St. Paul, 548-549

Nativity Church (Cleveland), 620

Nativity Church (St. Paul), 591

Nativity of the B.V.M. Church (Oxboro), 652

Naughton, Judith (Ireland) Archbishop's mother, 213

Nazareth Conferences, inaugurated, 560

Nazareth Hall, participates in Archbishop Ireland Educational Fund, 452; pet project of Archbishop Dowling, 452; completed and dedicated, 452; financial condition, 489; list of burses, 489; Chronicle, 662-63

Nazareth Hall Convent, 662

New France, eastern portion of French possessions in new world, 15, 61

Newman Club at University of Minnesota, 318-320; purchases Newman Hall, 321; property of diocese, 321; entertains Archbishop Murray, 520; 34th Convention of Newman Clubs in Minneapolis, 569; Father Cowley national chaplain, 569

New Orleans Diocese, second in U.S., 24

Nicollet, Sieur, sought waterway to China, 16

Nienstedt, Herman, speaks for Germans at diocesan golden jubilee, 367

Nolan, Rev. R.E., Chaplain, Archdiocesan Scout Committee, 543; 549

North American Review, articles on "The Catholic Church and the Saloon", 308;

and "The Dogmatic Authority of the Papacy", 344, by Archbishop Ireland
Northwestern Chronicle eulogizes Bishop Cretin 114; quotes Semaine Religieuse, 119; founded, 172; sold to Bishop Ireland, 173; obituary of Bishop Grace, 207; publishes The Apostolic Church, by Archbishop Ireland, 246; reports his toast "The Golden Northwest," 251; quotes Corriere d'Italia about his getting Red Hat, 353; publishes a list of parishes in St. Paul and dates of their organization, 363; ceased publication, 173
Northwestern Immigration Convention, attended by Archbishop Ireland, 245
Norsemen, first white men in Minnesota, 3, 10
Nugent, Monsignor, assists immigration, 242; story about Bishop Ireland, 247; present at dedication of St. Paul Seminary, 311

Obituary notices of priests, 304-305
Oblate Fathers of Manitoba, transfer site of Fort St. Charles to Oblates of Duluth, 32; given pastoral care of missions of Pembina and St. Joseph, 155
Oblate Mission House (White Bear), 676
Oblate Sisters of Providence of Baltimore for colored Catholics, 554
O'Brien, Dillon, secretary of Irish Emigration Society, 160; secretary of meeting to organize Father Mathew T.A. Society, 225
O'Brien, Thomas D., presides at lay meeting at diocesan golden jubilee, 367; first Grand Knight of K. of C. and first State Deputy, 402; dean of St. Thomas College Law School, 457
O'Connell, Monsignor,, postulates Pallium for Archbishop Ireland, 269; gives address on "Americanism According to Father Hecker," 326; correspondent of Archbishop Ireland, passim, 268-425
Odd Fellows, escape condemnation, 340; Catholics allowed nominal membership, 341
O'Gorman, Rev. Thomas, accompanies John Ireland to France, 90, 99; officiated at funeral of Monsignor Ravoux, 132; ordained by Bishop Grace, 157; preaches at Bishop Ireland's consecration, 188, 230; attends first Provincial Council of Milwaukee, 252; professor at Catholic U,. 280; Bishop of Sioux Falls, 322; on Friars' Lands Commission, 347; preaches at golden jubilee of diocese, 365; celebrates final High Mass in old Cathedral, 380; preaches at consecration of six bishops, 391; accompanies Archbishop Ireland to Florida, 246; celebrates Pontifical Mass of Requiem for him, 432
O'Grady, P. W., Executive Secretary, Twin Cities Council of Catholic Men, 453
O'Neil, Mrs. James, President of Minnesota Council of Catholic Women, 537
O'Reilly, Rev. J., irremovable rector, 286; Bishop of Fargo, 390; accompanies Archbishop to Florida, 426; graveside prayers for Archbishop Ireland, 434
Osservatore Romano, deplores attacks on Archbishop Ireland, 304
Oster, Rev. Anatole, accompanies Bishop Cretin on diocesan visits and interprets, 103; writes inscription for cornerstone of Cathedral, 105; ordained, 106; gives details of daily life of Bishop Cretin, 115; teaches in "Preparatory Seminary," 159; Administrator of Diocese and Vicar General, 167; Domestic Prelate, 359; director of Society for the Propagation of the Faith, 414

Our Lady's Church (Manannah), 635
Our Lady of Good Counsel Free Cancer Home, (St. Paul), 664
Our Lady of Grace Church (Edina), 652
Our Lady of Guadalupe Church (St. Paul), 591
Our Lady of the Lake Church (Mound), 648
Our Lady of Lourdes Church (Mpls), 594
Our Lady of Mount Carmel Church (Budejovie), 621
Our Lady of Mount Carmel Church (Mpls.), 597, 600
Our Lady of Peace High School, (St. Paul), 665
Our Lady of Perpetual Help Church (Mpls.), 596
Our Lady of Seven Dolors Church (Long Prairie), 603-04
Our Lady of Victory Church (Lucan), 642
Our Lady of Victory Church (Mpls.), 601
Outlook, Oct. 9, 1918, approves Taft's mission to Rome, 347; comment on Archbishop Ireland's failure to get Red Hat, 354

Pacelli, Cardinal, Papal Secretary of State, sends papal message on Father Hennepin's anniversary, 494; visits St. Paul, 533-535; lunches with President Roosevelt,, receives honorary degrees, impressed by parochial life of Church, 536. (See Pope Pius XII)
Paris Universe, Archbishop Ireland's protest, 302
Parliament of Religions at World's Fair, 341, 342
Paulist Boys' Choir sings at civic dedication of Pro-Cathedral, 386
Pelamourgues, Rev. Anthony, visits St. Peter's (Mendota) with Bishop Loras, 39; in charge of Prairie du Chien, 40; named successor to Bishop Cretin, 125; had appointment revoked, 127; letter from Rome to Father Ravoux, 131
Pembina, rival of St. Paul, 62; visited by Bishop Grace and Father Ravoux, 153-5
Peries, Rev. George, joins in Americanism controversy, 327
Perrot, Nicholas, convoked Council at Sault Ste. Marie, 16; established trading post on Lake Pepin, 22
Peschges, Rev. John H., joins Diocesan Mission Band, 369; Bishop of Crookston, 369
Peyragrosse, Marcellin, came to St. Paul with Bishop Cretin, 73; first Director, Propagation of the Faith, 103; untimely death, 92
Pierz, Rev. Francis, at Grand Portage Mission, 36; invites Germans to Stearns County, 95, 239; establishes mission at Crow Wing, 95; praised by Archbishop Ireland, 97; grave in Austria visited by Bishop Stariha, 409
Pig's Eye, called after Pierre Parrant, never appealed to French colonists, 63
Pilgrimage to Ste. Anne de Beaupre, 456; program enlarged, 455
Piopolis, city visioned by Canon Vivaldi, 84
Plut, Father, attends first Provincial Council of Milwaukee as theologian, 252; celebrates golden jubilee, 413
Pontifical Society for Vocations, 557-558
Pope Alexander VI, ratified Spain's claim to discovery of America, 13, 61
Pope Benedict XV, decided to create Archbishop Ireland Cardinal, 353
Pope Leo XIII, gives official approval to total abstinence movement 235-236; approves Catholic University, 278; sends apostolic letter on Americanism to Cardinal Gibbons and American Hier-

archy, 328; pleased with handling of Church affairs in Cuba and Philippines by American Government, 362

Pope Pius IX spent two years in Chile, South America, 536

Pope Pius X, did not approve of Archbishop Ireland, 352; refused to make him Cardinal, 352

Pope Pius XI, eightieth birthday celebration changed to requiem, 541

Pope Pius XII (Cardinal Pacelli) first Pope to visit North America, 536; Spiritual Bouquet on twenty-fifth anniversary of consecration. 550

Porter, General, on Friars Lands commission, 347

Poughkeepsie arrangement aids Catholic schools, 294

Prairie du Chien visited by Bishop Loras and Father Pelamourgues who was made pastor, 40; Father Cretin, pastor, 70; Father Galtier's pastorate, 47

Prendergast, Jeremiah C., made and placed copper box in cornerstone of third Cathedral, 104; removed it 58 years later, 380

Prendergast, Rev. J. H., Director, Propagation of Faith, 414

Presentation of Blessed Virgin Mary Church (St. Paul), 592

Price, Rev. Thomas F., co-founder of Maryknoll, 401

Priester-Verein. agitation, 260; aided by Cahensly, 262; tactics at convention, 263

Priests' Total Abstinence League of America, 419

Pro-Cathedral of St. Mary, planned by Archbishop Ireland, 382; sites considered, 382; site chosen on Hennepin, 383; laying cornerstone, 384-385; civic celebration, 385; formal dedication, 386; financial statement, 385-387; interior finished, 387; re-named Basilica of St. Mary, 387, 473-475: (See Basilica)

Proclamation of Saint-Lusson, claims America for France, 16

Prohibition Amendment ratified, 421

Propaganda, rules on German situation, 261; establishes five suffragan sees in St. Paul Province, 271; rules on Faribault School Plan, 301

Provencher, Bishop, of St. Boniface, visits Pembina, 34; Father Galtier, 42

Provincial Synod of Milwaukee, requests St. Paul be made archdiocese, 269

Quadrennial Methodist Conference held in Minneapolis, 409-412; attacks President Taft and Catholics, 410; silenced by Archbishop Ireland, 411

Quebec, founded by Champlain, 14; first Bishop consecrated, 22; had jurisdiction over Minnesota, 22, 62; Seminary priests in the West, 23; diocese restricted to Canada, 24

Racine, Bishop, of Sherbrooke, asks for special consideration for French Canadians in U.S., 286

Radisson, accompanies Groseilliers to Prairie Island near Hastings, 17; navigates Lake Superior, 18

Rampolla, Cardinal, opposes Cahenslyism, 263; letter of thanks to J. J. Hill, 316; discusses letter on Americanism, 328; asks Archbishop Ireland to work for peace between U.S. and Spain, 334; Church needs cooperation of American government in Cuba and Philippines, 362

Ramsey, Governor (territorial), Superintendent of Indian Affairs for Minnesota, makes contract with Bishop Cretin, 81; attends Hennepin celebration, 189

Ravoux, Father Augustine, early history, 51; pastor at Prairie du Chien, 52; works with Sioux, 52; builds chapel at Little Prairie (Chaska) 53; publications for Indians, 53, 54; celebrated Mass in South Dakota, 55; attitude toward Indians, 56; alternates between Mendota and St. Paul 57; builds addition to log chapel, 57; buys lots for new cathedral, 58; Vicar General, 58, 76; accompanies John Ireland and Thomas O'Gorman to France, 58, 90, 215; urges Father Cretin to accept bishopric, 65; Administrator of Diocese, 123-124; completes third Cathedral, 124; signs Pastoral Letter, 126; erected Catholic Block, 126; reappointed Vicar General by Bishop Grace, 127, 144; spiritual adviser to condemned Sioux, 128; appointed first Vicar Apostolic of Montana, 129; declines the honor, 129-130; made Domestic Prelate by Pope Leo XIII, 130, 255; description of him, 130-131; Reminiscences, Memoirs and Lectures, 131; last will and testament, 131; death and obsequies, 132-134

Raymbaut, Father, and Father Jogues first white men at Sault Ste. Marie, 15

Reardon, Rev. James M. Superior, Diocesan Mission Band, 369; officiates at first Solemn Benediction in new Cathedral, 380; finishes interior of Pro-Cathedral and builds new residence and sacristy, 387; Editor-in-Chief of the Catholic Bulletin, 394; Irremovable Rector of Church of St. Mary, 396; represents Archdiocese at Priests' Total Abstinence League, 419; representative of Archbishop Dowling on Twin Cities Council of Catholic Men, 453; Officer of the Order of Leopold II, 496; General Chairman of Ninth National Eucharistic Congress, 545; address at Diocesan Centennial celebration, 573

Recollect Fathers, first missionaries in New France, 14; with Jesuits in Mississippi valley, 22

Red River carts between St. Paul and Pembina, 64

Redwood, Archbishop, of Wellington, New Zealand, classmate of Archbishop Ireland, 218; sang Vespers at Cardinal Gibbon's jubilee, 306

References to source material, 691-707

Religious Vacation Schools, 478

Reserve Electric Street Railway, 271

Resurrection Cemetery consecrated, 544

Resurrection Church (Mpls.), 599

Richards, Richard, agent for Northwestern Chronicle, 173

Riordan, Right Reverend Patrick J., Bishop Ireland, co-consecrator, 248

Riss, Rev. Bruno, ordained by Bishop Cretin, 106

Robert, Louis, owned first frame house in St. Paul, 63

Robertson, W. C., editor of Minneapolis Star, 465; comments on Good Will experiment, 466

Roosevelt, Theodore, praises Archbishop Ireland, 307; appoints commission to treat with Holy See about Friars' lands, 347; suggests him for cardinal, 350; asks "Dear Maria" to help but later denies it, 351; refused audience with Pope, 398; letter of sympathy to Archbishop, 427; message of condolence on his death, 435

Rosati, Bishop, of St. Louis, entertains Bishop Loras and Father Cretin, 69

Rouen, Archbishop, claimed jurisdiction over New France, and protested consecration of Bishop Laval, 22, 62

Rune Stone unearthed near Kensington, 3; inscription 4; linguistic difficulties 7; authenticity 8; translation differences 8; invocation 8, 9

Ryan, Rt. Rev. John A., "most distinguished alumnus and professor" of Catholic University, 280

Ryan Hotel, dedicated by Archbishop Ireland, 252; scene of banquet at triple consecration, 273; for Cardinal Gibbons, 264

Ryan, Rev. L. F., city missionary, 288; preaches on Founder's Day at St. Thomas, 562

Sacred College of Cardinals and Archbishop Ireland, 349-354

Sacred Congregation of Rites, solves difficulty for Bishop Grace, 158

Sacred Heart Church (Belle Plaine). 614

Sacred Heart Church (Faribault), 629

Sacred Heart Church (Franklin), 642

Sacred Heart Church (Murdock), 641

Sacred Heart Church (Raymond). 644

Sacred Heart Church (Robbinsdale), 648-49

Sacred Heart Church (Rush City). 624

Sacred Heart Church (St. Paul), 585

Sacred Heart Priests' League started by Archbishop Elder, 419

Safford, Orren E., Belgian Consul for Minnesota. confers honors in name of Belgian King. 495

St. Adalbert's Church (St. Paul), 584

St. Adalbert's Church (Silver Lake), 638

St. Agatha's Church (Coates). 649

St. Agatha's Church (Vermillion), 625

St. Agatha's Conservatory of Music and Art, (St. Paul), 657

St. Agnes Church (Hegbert), 631

St. Agnes Church (St. Paul), 586

St. Albert's Church (Albertville), 644

St. Albert the Great Church (Mpls.), 600

St. Albertus Hall, (St. Paul), 663

St. Aloysius Church (Olivia). 637-38

St. Ambrose Church (St. Paul). 589-90

St. Anastasia's Church (Hutchinson), 634

St. Andrew's Church (Elysian), 640

St. Andrew's Church (Fairfax). 633

St. Andrew's Church (Granite Falls), 636

St. Anne's Church (Hamel), 630

St. Anne's Church (Le Sueur). 608

St. Anne's Church (Mpls.), 599

St. Anne's Church (Wabasso), 643

St. Anthony's Church (Mpls.). 54; Church completed, 85; Chronicle. 593

St. Anthony's Church (Regal), 650

St. Anthony's Church (Watkins), 638

St. Augustine's Church (South St. Paul), 641

St. Austin's Church (Mpls.), 600

St. Barnabas Church (Barry), 645

St. Bartholomew's Church (Wayzata), 649

St. Benedict's Church (St. Benedict), 613

St. Benedict's Convent and Academy (St. Joseph), 671

St. Bernard's Church (Cologne), 613

St. Bernard's Church (St. Paul). 588

St. Boniface Church (Hastings), 623-24

St. Boniface Church (Mpls.), 593

St. Boniface Church (St. Bonifacius), 632

St. Boniface Church (Stewart), 629

St. Brendan's Church (Green Isle), 622

St. Bridget's Church (De Graff), 628

St. Bridget's Church (Mpls.), 598

St. Bridget of Sweden's Church (Lindstrom), 652

St. Canice Church (Kilkenny), 619

St. Casimir's Church (St. Paul), 588

St. Catherine's Church (Redwood Falls), 636

St. Catherine's Church (Spring Lake), 617

St. Cecilia's Church (St. Paul), 590

St. Charles Church (Bayport), 651

St. Charles Church (Chatham), 628

St. Charles Church (Mpls.), 596

St. Charles Borromeo Church (Mpls), 600

St. Clara's Church (Clara City), 639

St. Clement's Church (Mpls.), 596-97

St. Clotilde's Church (Green Valley), 649

St. Clotilde's Church (Mpls.), 595

St. Columba's Church (St. Paul), 590

St. Columban Foreign Mission Society, 401

St. Columbanus Church (Greenleaf), 626

St. Columbkill's Church (Belle Creek), 614

St. Cyril's Church (Mpls.), 596

Sts. Cyril and Methodius Church (Taunton), 641

St. Dionysius Church (Tyler), 642

St. Dominic's Church (Northfield), 623

St. Edward's Church (Minneota), 633

St. Edward's Church (Richland), 627

St. Elizabeth's Church (Mpls.), 594-95

St. Elizabeth's Home for Young Girls, (Mpls.), 667

St. Eloi Church (Ghent), 635

St. Frances Cabrini Church (Mpls.), 601

St. Francis Church (Benson), 632

St. Francis Church (Buffalo). 639

Sz. Francis Church (Crow Wing), 604

St. Francis Church (Franconia), 635

St. Francis de Sales Church (St. Paul) dedicated, 250; Mass said there by Archbishop Martinelli, 332; Chronicle, 585

St. Francis de Sales Church (Winthrop), 651

St. Francis Home and Hospital (Shakopee), 676

St. Francis of Assisi Church (Mpls.), 597

St. Francis of Assisi Church (St. Croix Beach), 650

St. Francis Xavier Church (Little Prairie—Chaska), 602

St. Genevieve's Church (Centerville), 606

St. Genevieve's Church (Lake Benton), 642

St. George's Church (Glencoe), 640

St. George's Church (Long Lake), 649

St. George's Church (West Newton), 612

St. Gertrude's Church (Forest City), 620

St. Gregory's Church (North Branch), 645

St. Gregory the Great Church (Lafayette), 651

St. Gregory the Great Church (St. Paul), 593

St. Gertrude's Convent and Academy, (Shakopee), 672

St. Gertrude's House of Studies (St. Paul), 664

St. Hedwig's Church (Mpls.), 593

St. Helena's Church (Mpls.), 598

St. Henry's Church (Monticello), 648

St. Henry's Church (St. Henry, Le Sueur County), 613

St. Hubert's Church (Chanhassen), 618

St. Ignatius Church (Annandale), 633

St. James Church (Nassau), 645

St. James Church (St. Paul). 586

St. Jeanne de Chantal's Church (Corcoran), 615

St. Jerome's Church (New Canada Township), 651

St. Joan of Arc Church (Mpls.), 601

St. John's Church (Appleton). 639

St. John's Church (Darwin), 629-30

St. John's Church (Hector), 637

St. John's Church (Morton). 638-39

St. John's Church (Ortonville), 645

St. John's Church (St Paul), 586

St. John's Church (Sibley County, Belle Plaine P.O.), 614

St. John's Church (Union Hill), 615

St. John's Church (Vermillion), 633

St. John the Baptist Church (Byrnesville), 605

St. John the Baptist Church (Dayton), 617

St. John the Baptist Church (Excelsior), 645

St. John the Baptist Church (Hugo), 644
St. John the Baptist Church (Interlachen Park), 652
St. John the Baptist Church (Jordon), 611-12
St. John the Baptist Church (New Brighton), 635
St. John the Baptist Church (Rocky Run), 623
St. John the Baptist Church (Savage), 644
St. John the Baptist Church (Searles), 646
St. John Cantius Church (Wilno), 634
St. John the Evangelist Church (Derrynane Township), 616
St. John the Evangelist Church (Little, or New, Canada), 603
St. John's Hospital (Winona), 676
St. John's Seminary (Collegeville), 97; consecration of Abbey Church, 247; Chronicle, 671
St. John Vianney Church (South St. Paul), 652
St. Joseph's Church (Clements), 644
St. Joseph's Church (Delano), 646
St. Joseph's Church (Halloway), 650
St. Joseph's Church (Henderson), 615
St. Joseph's Church (Hopkins), 649-50
St. Joseph's Church (Lamberton), 641
St. Joseph's Church (Lexington), 644
St. Joseph's Church (Medicine Lake), 612
St. Joseph's Church (Miesville), 626
St. Joseph's Church (Mpls.), 594
St. Joseph's Church (Montevideo), 637
St. Joseph's Church (Red Wing), 619
St. Joseph's Church (Rice Lake), 640
St. Joseph's Church (Rosemount), 623
St. Joseph's Church (Rosen), 636
St. Joseph's Church (Scott County, Jordan P.O.), 612
St. Joseph's Church (St. Joseph, Walhalla, N. D.), 604-5
St. Joseph's Church (Russell), 649
St. Joseph's Church (St. Paul), 584
St. Joseph's Church (Silver Lake), 641
St. Joseph's Church (Stillwater), 632-33
St. Joseph's Church (Taylor's Falls), 626
St. Joseph's Church (Waconia), 627
St. Joseph's Church (West St. Paul), 592
St. Joseph's Academy, first school for girls in Minnesota, 91; visited by Cardinal Gibbons, 265; Chronicle, 653
St. Joseph's Home for the Aged Poor, (Mpls.), 667
St. Joseph's Hospital (St. Paul), oldest in Minnesota, 90, 91; Chronicle, 654
St. Joseph's Infant Home (Mpls.), 669-70
St. Joseph's Novitiate (St. Paul), 654
St. Joseph's Orphanage (St. Paul), 657
St. Joseph's Provincialate (St. Paul), 655
St. Jude of the Lake Church (Mahtomedi), 650
St. Kevin's Church (Mpls.), 601
St. Lawrence Church (Faribault), 624
St. Lawrence Church (Mpls.), 595
St. Leo's Church (St. Paul), 592
St. Leo of Burton Church (St. Leo), 634
St. Leonard of Port Maurice Church (Mpls.), 600
St. Louis Church (St. Paul), 583
St. Louis Church (Wheatland), 624
St. Luke's Church (Clearwater), 641
St. Luke's Church (St. Paul), 586
St. Malachy's Church (Clontarf), 630
St. Margaret's Academy, entertain priests after cornerstone laying of Pro-Cathedral, 385; Chronicle, 668
St. Margaret's Church (Hopkins), 630-31
St. Margaret Mary's Church (Mpls.), 601
St. Mark's Church (St. Paul), 588
St. Mark's Church (Shakopee), 608
St. Maron's Church (Mpls.), Maronite Rite, 516; Chronicle, 597
St. Martin's Church (Mpls.), 601
St. Martin's Church (Rogers), 649

St. Mary's Church (Arlington), 631
St. Mary's Church (Bechyn), 631
St. Mary's Church (Bellechester), 619
St. Mary's Church (Beardsley), 646
St. Mary's Church (Bird Island), 631
St. Mary's Church (Crystal, near Robbindale), 638
St. Mary's Church (Hopkins), 641
St. Mary's Church (Le Center), 643
St. Mary's Church (New Trier), 611
St. Mary's Church (New Ulm), 648
St. Mary's Church (Ottawa), 647
St. Mary's Church (St. Paul), 582
St. Mary's Church (Seaforth), 637
St. Mary's Church (Shakopee), 619
St. Mary's Church (Stillwater) consecrated, 249; Chronicle, 618
St. Mary's Church (Tracy), 635
St. Mary's Church (Waverly), 616
St. Mary's Church (White Bear), 632
St. Mary's Church (Willmar), 625
St. Mary, Help of Christians, Church (Sleepy Eye), 628
St. Mary of Czestochowa Church (Franklin Township), 634
St. Mary of the Lake Church (Medicine Lake), 650
St. Mary of the Purification Church (Marystown), 606
St. Mary's (O.P.) Convent (Mpls.), 670
St. Mary's Home (St. Paul), 663
St. Mary's Home for Girls (St. Paul), 658
St. Mary's Hospital (Minneapolis), free clinic for needy children, 490; Chronicle, 666
St. Mary's Mission House (St. Paul), 664
St. Mary's Seminary in Cincinnati suggested for Catholic University, 276
St. Mathias Church (Hampton), 643
St. Mathias Church (Wanda), 634
St. Mathew's Church (St. Paul), 585
St. Michael's Church (Belgrade), 616
St. Michael's Church (Farmington), 647
St. Michael's Church (Gaylord), 636
St. Michael's Church (Kenyon), 651
St. Michael's Church (Madison), 636
St. Michael's Church (Milroy), 646
St. Michael's Church (Montgomery Township), 622
St. Michael's Church (Morgan), 640
St. Michael's Church (Pine Island), 630
St. Michael's Church (Prior Lake), 615
St. Michael's Church (St. Michael), 608
St. Michael's Church (St. Paul), 583
St. Michael's Church (Stillwater), 609
St. Michael's Church (West St. Paul), 178
St. Michael's School, Stillwater, adopts Faribault plan, 293; financial difficulties, 300
St. Nicholas Church (Carver), 622
St. Nicholas Church (Middle Lake), 626
St. Nicholas Church (New Market), 617
St. Olaf's Church (Mpls.), 601
St. Pascal Baylon's Church (St. Paul), 592
St. Patrick's Church (Cedar Lake), 610
St. Patrick's Church (Birch Coulee), 627
St. Patrick's Church (Edina), 610
St. Patrick's Church (Inver Grove), 609
St. Patrick's Church (Kandiyohi), 628
St. Patrick's Church (St. Paul), 585
St. Patrick's Church (Shieldsville), 607
St. Patrick's Day celebration, first on record, 92
St. Paul, territorial capital and episcopal see, 62; named after log chapel, 43, 45; first Bishop installed, 74; first Sisters arrive, 78
St. Paul Catholic Orphan Asylum, 657
St. Paul's Church (Comfrey), 643
St. Paul's Church (Nicollet), 647
St. Paul's Church (Walnut Grove), 647
St. Paul's Church (Zumbrota), 645
St. Paul Dispatch, on Memorial Park at Fort St. Charles, 31; on Bishop Cretin's

apple trees, 75; on Bishop Grace's death, 207

St. Paul Pioneer Press, pays tribute to Monsignor Ravoux, 135; diocesan statistics, 192; value of church property, 232; tribute to Archbishop's efforts in cause of total abstinence, 415

St. Paul Seminary, founded by Mr. J. J. Hill, 309; buildings and faculty, 310; first ordinations, 310; dedication, 310-311; articles of incorporation, 311; Constitution and Rules, 311; reception for Archbishop Martinelli, Apostolic Delegate, 333; consecration of six bishops in its chapel, May 19, 1910, 391; Archbishop Ireland, sponsor, father and guide, 312-5; science course, 313; tribute to founder, 316; Archbishop Murray pay first visit, 513; fiftieth anniversary of dedication, 552; Archbishop Ireland Memorial Library campaign launched, 552; library dedicated, 553; accredited by various agencies, 553-55; scene of final celebration of Diocesan Centennial, 574-575; Memorial Library blessed, 575; Chronicle, 660

St. Paul Tabernacle Society, 659

St. Paul's Priory, 664

St. Peter's Church (Canby), 642

St. Peter's Church (Credit River), 615

St. Peter's Church (Delano), 618

St. Peter's Church (Eden Valley), 646

St. Peter's Church (Forest Lake), 646

St. Peter's Church (Mendota), 602

St. Peter's Church (North St. Paul), 639

St. Peter's Church (Richfield), 651

St. Peter's Church (St. Peter), 608

Sts. Peter and Paul's Church (Belle Plaine), 623

Sts. Peter and Paul's Church (Glencoe), 619

Sts. Peter and Paul's Church (Ivanhoe), 643

Sts. Peter and Paul's Church (Loretto), 622

St. Peter Claver Church, dedication, 268; sodality helps build it, 317; Chronicle, 588

St. Philip's Church (Litchfield), 625

St. Philip's Church (Mpls.), 598

St. Pius V's Church (Canon Falls), 620

St. Raphael's Church (Springfield), 630

St. Raphael's Church (Crystal), 638, 688

St. Raphael Verein and Priester Vereins, 260; International Congress, 262; sends second memorial to Holy See, 262

St. Richard's Church (Richfield), 652

St. Rose of Lima Church (Cherry Grove), 629

St. Rose of Lima Church (St. Paul), 591

St. Scholastica's Church (Heidelberg), 610

St. Stanislaus Church (St. Paul), 583

St. Stephen's Church (Anoka), 627

St. Stephen's Church (Mpls.), 595

St. Therese's Church (Deephaven), 652

St. Therese's Church (St. Paul), 591

St. Thomas Church (Corcoran), 614

St. Thomas Church (Jessenland), 625

St. Thomas Church (Le Sueur P.O.), 621

St. Thomas Church (St. Paul Park), 640

St. Thomas Church (Sanborn), 644

St. Thomas Aquinas Seminary, founded by Bishop Ireland, 271, 309; visited by Cardinal Gibbons, 265; neighboring localities develop, 271; electric railway opened, 271; entertained three new bishops, 273; theological students transferred to St. Paul Seminary, 310; (See College of St. Thomas, St. Paul Seminary)

St. Thomas Military Academy, (St. Paul), 660. (See also College of St. Thomas.)

St. Thomas More Church (Lake Lillian), 650

St. Thomas More Guild, for lawyers, 560

St. Thomas the Apostle's Church (Mpls.), 597

St. Timothy's Church (East Maple Lake) 621

St. Timothy's Church (Maple Lake), 637

St. Timothy's Church (Spring Lake Park), 651

St. Vallier, Bishop, successor to Bishop Laval, sent priests to Mississippi valley, 73

St. Victoria's Church (Victoria), 612

St. Vincent's Church (St. Paul), 587

St. Vincent de Paul's Church (Osseo), 606

St. Vincent de Paul Society founded by Bishop Cretin, 89; fostered by Archbishop Ireland, 287, 325

St. Walburga's Church (Fletcher), 611

St. Wenceslaus Church (New Prague), 611

St. Wilhelmina's Home (St. Paul), 663

St. Willibrord's Church (Gibbon), 639

Satolli, Most Rev. Francis, papal representative, 273; celebrates Mass at dedication of Catholic University, 279; visit to St. Paul, 284; celebrates Pontical Mass at dedication of St. Paul Seminary, 310; Apostolic Delegate (1893), 338

Sault Ste. Marie, scene of historic ceremony in Jesuit Mission, 16

Saux Rapids, first parish of Benedictines in St. Cloud Diocese, 96

Sbaretti, Archbishop, of Havana, appointed Apostolic Delegate Extraordinary to Philippines, 347; persona non grata to President Roosevelt 348; drafts petition to make Pro-Cathedral a Basilica, 473

Scandinavians in Minnesota, Archbishop Ireland plans to convert them, 288-290

Schenk, Most Rev. F. J., Bishop of Crookston, 540; co-consecrator, 519; dedicates granite altar on site of Fort St. Charles, 32; authorized memorial chapel, 569

Schneider, Rev. Cyrinus, O.F.M., unveils statue of Father Hennepin, 494

School of Social Studies, 453-456

Schroeder, Monsignor, Dean of Catholic University Faculty, 280; Latin oration at opening of University, 280

Schumacher, Father, President of St. Thomas College, 526; issues financial statement, 526

Schurman, Jacob Gould, President of Cornell, chairman of first Philippine commission, 346

Secret Societies escape church ban, 340-1

Seidenbusch, Right Rev. Rupert, first Abbot of St. John's, 97; consecrated Vicar Apostolic of Northern Minnesota, 186

Semaine Religieuse de Bourg, praises Father Cretin's work at Ferney, 119

Seton Guild (Mpls.), 669

Seton Hall College, suggested for Catholic University by Bishop Grace, 190

Shanahan, Father, of Warroad, 32; builds memorial church, 33

Shanley, Rt. Rev. John, 35; attends "Preparatory Seminary," 159; studies in Rome for priesthood, 179; Bishop of Jamestown, 271; preaches Bishop Grace's funeral sermon, 204-206; attends first Provincial Council of Milwaukee, 252; writes brief history of the Church in Diocese of Fargo, 35; preaches at blessing of Right Reverend Bernard Locnikar, O.S.B., as Abbot of St. John's, 284; sings Requiem Mass at golden jubilee of diocese, 366; dies, 389

Shea, John Gilmary, discusses Fr. Hennepin's book, 21

Shields, General, invited Irish Catholics to settle in Shieldsville, 239

Sibley, General, house sold to Sisters of St. Joseph for school, 179

Siebenfoercher, Father, organizes total abstinence societies among seminarians, 418-419 ; elected president of Priests Total Abstinence League, 419

Simeoni, Cardinal, opposed Cahenslyism, 263

"Single Tax," explanation, 339

Sinnott, Archbishop, of Winnipeg, blesses statue of Father Hennepin, 494

Sister Antonine, sister of Archbishop Dowling, summoned to death bed, 497

Sister Celestine (Ellen Howard), cousin of Archbishop Ireland, receives habit, 127

Sister Scholastica Vasquez, first teacher of Indians, 80

Sisters of Good Shepherd arrive in St. Paul, 162

Sisters of Propagation of Faith founded by Father Belcourt, 35

Sisters of St. Dominic of Sinsinawa, Wis., establish Bethlehem Academy, 161

Sisters of St. Joseph of Carondelet, arrive in St. Paul, 77 ; establish St. Joseph's· Hospital, 91 ; Academy, 91 ; first reception of postulants, 92 ; first religious professions, 92, 93

Sisters of Visitation, locate in St. Paul, 162

Skolla, Father Otto, O.F.M., visits Grand Portage, 36 ; report on temperance movement among Indians, 88

Slevin, Monsignor John J., appointed Vicar General by Archbishop Dowling, 444

Smith, C. H. F., gives $20,000 to new Cathedral, 375 ; made Knight of St. Gregory, 427

Smith, Judge, of Supreme Court of Manila, on Friars' Lands commission, 347

Smithsonian Institution, and the Rune Stone, 6

Smyth, Bishop, of Dubuque, ordains Fathers Caillet and Tissot, 99

Social security for parish employees, 575

Society for Propagation of the Faith, asked for funds by Bishop-elect Cretin, 65 ; receives appeal from him on behalf of missionaries, 73 ; makes report, 90 ; established in diocese, 99, 413 ; final report from Bishop Cretin, 108 ; diocesan branch established by Archbishop Ireland, 414 ; located in Chancery Building, 414 ; moved to former episcopal residence, 415 ; reorganized, 465 ; sponsors Mission Pageant, 564

Sodalities of Our Lady hold conference, 492 ; form union, 493

Sons of Temperance, escape condemnation, 340 ; Catholics allowed nominal membership, 341

Sorin, Very Reverend Edward, C.S.C., founder of Notre Dame, celebrates golden jubilee with Archbishop Ireland as preacher, 256

Spaeth, Howard, Commissioner of Taxation, rules on status of Fort St. Charles site, 32

Spalding, Rt. Rev. John Lancaster, of Peoria, advocates Catholic University, 190 ; preaches at Bishop Grace's jubilee, 194 ; advocates theological high school for graduates of diocesan seminaries, 275 ; writes appeal for professorial chairs and burses at Catholic University, 278 ; refuses rectorship, 278

Spanish-American War, 333 ; Archbishop Ireland works in cause of peace, 333-336 ; ended by Treaty of Paris, 346

Spellman, Bishop, accompanies Cardinal Pacelli to St. Paul, 533

Stariha, Rt. Rev. J. N., irremovable rector, 286 ; bishop of Lead, but resigns in 1909, 409 ; returns to Austria and visits grave of Father Pierz, 409

Steamer "Schiller" wrecked, with loss of Apostolic Brief, 187

Stephan, Reverend J. A., recommended for Bureau of Catholic Indian Missions, 249

Storer, Maria and Bellamy, urge Archbishop Ireland's promotion to cardinalate, 350

Sweetman, John, colonizes land near Currie with 70 families, 243

Swift County, center for colonization plans, 240

Swift, Father, counsels and directs immigrants, 240

Syllabus of Errors, explained by Bishop Grace in pastoral letter, 164

Synods, formal and informal, 169-171

Taché, Bishop, of St. Boniface, at Hennepin celebration, 189 ; spoke in French at Bishop Grace's jubilee, 196

Taft, William Howard, Governor of Philippines, 346 ; adopts Faribault School Plan, 347 ; goes to Rome to discuss Friars' Lands with Pope, 347 ; questions left to be settled between Gov. Taft and Apostolic Delegate, 348 ; Archbishop Guidi compliments Taft, 349 ; wishes Archbishop Ireland be promoted to Sacred College, 351

Taschereau, Archbishop, of Quebec, created Cardinal, 253 ; condemned Knights of Labor, 257

Temperance Crusaders of St. Paul organized by Father Ireland, 226

Territorial Centennial Celebration, 568-569

Third Plenary Council of Baltimore, advocates total abstinence, 235 ; attended by Bishops Grace and Ireland, 276 ; decides to launch project of Catholic University, 277

Timon, Bishop, of Buffalo, lays cornerstone of third Cathedral, 104

Tisserant, Eugene Cardinal, visits Twin Cities, 556 ; presides at Mass in Maronite Rite in Cathedral, 556

Total Abstinence Movement, originated in Diocese of St. Paul, 223 ; pledged women for first time, 233 ; National Union erects fountain in Philadelphia, 234 ; the Father Mathew of the Northwest, 415-18

Transfiguration Church (St. Paul), 592

Trappists invited to work among Indians by Bishop Cretin, 83

Treaty of the Lateran, settles Roman question between Pope and Italian state, 481

Trobec, Right Rev. James, ordained, 157 ; consecrated third Bishop of St. Cloud, 331, 332 ; lays cornerstone of St. Mary's chapel at Seminary, 366

Twin Cities Council of Catholic Men organized, 453 ; "Twin Cities Plan," 453 ; program, 453-454 ; Admiral Benson's visit, 454

Tyrrell, Father George, S.J., involved in Modernism, 344

University of Minnesota, has largest Catholic student body, 569

United States Catholic Historical Society, 252

Vail, Roger, editor of Irish Standard, 175

Van der Stappen, Bishop, ordains Archbishop Murray, 507

Van Hee, Canon, secures land for Belgian colony, 243

Vannutelli, Cardinal Vincent, visits St. Paul, 392-394 ; says Mass in Cathedral, 392 ; visits institutions, 393 ; banquet in the St. Paul Hotel, 393

Van Scheltema, C. S. Adama, writes Archbishop Ireland about Total Abstinence in Holland, 417
Vatican General Council (1869), attended by Father Ireland, 227
Vicariate Apostolic of the Dakotas, 186
Vicariate of Northern Minnesota, 185
Viel, Father Nicholas, first missionary to die in New France, 14
Villa Marie Academy (Frontenac), site of second fort, 28; dedicated by Archbishop Ireland, 28; Chronicle, 673
Virtue, Bishop, of Portsmouth, England, presents bust of St. Thomas to Catholic University, 279
Visitation Church (Brighton-Swan Lake), 618
Visitation Church (Danvers), 640
Visitation Church (Mpls.), 602
Voltaire owned church in Ferney replaced by Father Cretin, 68
Volz, Rev. John R., second editor of Catholic Bulletin, 396
Von Preysing, Conrad Cardinal, visits St. Paul, expresses gratitude to Catholics, 556

Wabasha, St. Felix parish established by Father Tissot, 127
Walsh, Rt. Rev. J. A., co-founder of Maryknoll, 401; intimate friend of Archbishop Dowling, 497
Walsh, Rev. W. J., interested in foreign mission work, 401; director of Propagation of Faith, 414; dies, 496, 564-565; responsible for Mission Pageant, 563-565
Wang, Rev. Eric, asked for by Archbishop Ireland, 289
Watterson, Bishop, of Columbus, bans liquor dealers from Catholic societies, 308
Welch, Rev. Thomas A., in charge of Archbishop Ireland Educational Fund,

449, 451; Archbishop Dowling's representative on Twin Cities Council of Catholic Men, 453; Vicar General, 449; diocesan chancellor, 449; Bishop of Duluth, 476; officiates at Archbishop Dowling's funeral, 498; co-consecrator of Bishop Byrne, 521; pontificates at Diocesan Centennial, 573
White Earth Agency should have Catholic agent, 182; Father Ireland first priest to visit reservation, 223
White, Rev. Leo, first priest ordained in Basilica, 538
"Whites," favored new Italian regime, 352
Williams, Professor Talcot, of Columbia, lectured at Pro-Cathedral civic dedication, 386
Williamson, Rev. Dr., silenced by Father Ravoux, 56
Willis, Honorable John W., Past Grand Knight of K. of C., gave address at cornerstone laying of K. of C. club house, 402; presides at evening session of educational congress, 460
Winnebagoes, Long Prairie Mission in charge of Canon Vivaldi, 79; transferred to Blue Earth, 83; Government money for education and support, 89
Wittmann, Rev. Cornelius, O.S.B., ordained by Bishop Cretin, 106
Wurtzfeld, Rev. Michael, establishes Church of Assumption, 99, 100; goes to Diocese of Erie, 100

"Young Catholics' Educational Society," aids seminarians, 150

Zardetti, Bishop, of St. Cloud, preaches at German-American convention at Buffalo, 264; blessed Abbot Bernard, 284; Faribault School plan in Diocese, 294
Ziskovsky, Rev. G., master of ceremonies at Diocesan Centennial celebration, 573